PSYCHOLOGICAL PROCESSES THAT AFFECT CRITICAL THINKING

Psychological research has helped to clarify how people think critically—and why, often, they do not. Here are a few of the topics relevant to critical thinking that are discussed in this book, and the chapters in which they appear.

FACTORS THAT ENHANCE CRITICAL THINKING

- Scientific methods and reasoning (chapter 2)
- Conditions promoting independent action and nonconformity (chapter 8)
- Conditions promoting individuation (chapter 8)
- Inductive, deductive, and dialectical reasoning (chapter 9)
- Reflective judgment (chapter 9)
- Creative problem solving (chapter 9)
- Algorithms, heuristics (chapter 9)
- Intelligence (chapter 9)
- Metacognition (chapter 9)
- Improving memory (chapter 10)
- Reducing negative emotions (chapter 11)
- Cognitive development (chapter 14)
- Wisdom derived from life experiences (chapter 14)
- Role of appraisals and rethinking in coping with stress and illness (chapter 15)
- Attributions that affect feelings and behavior (chapters 8, 11, 12)
- Cognitive therapy (chapter 17)

BARRIERS TO CRITICAL THINKING

- Pseudoscientific thinking (chapters 1 and 2)
- Conformity (chapter 8)
- Deindividuation (chapter 8)
- Diffusion of responsibility (chapter 8)
- Entrapment (chapter 8)
- Groupthink (chapter 8)
- Coercive persuasion (chapter 8)
- Prejudice and ethnocentrism (chapter 8)
- Stereotypes (chapter 8)
- Self-serving bias (chapter 8)
- Mindlessness (chapter 9)
- Cognitive biases (e.g., confirmation and hindsight biases) (chapter 9)
- Cognitive dissonance (chapter 9)
- Mental sets (chapter 9)
- Nonreflective judgment (chapter 9)
- Fallibility of memory (chapter 10)
- Emotional reasoning (chapter 11)
- Defense mechanisms (chapter 13)
- Vulnerability to the "Barnum Effect" (chapter 13)
- Cognitive distortions in mood disorders (chapters 11, 16)

Structures and Associated Behavior of the Brain

Two of the brain structures most commonly confused with each other are the hippocampus and the hypothalamus. Both of the structures are located in the limbic system however the two structures are in charge of very different functions in your body. The hippocampus has been found to be important in helping us form memories that last more than just a few seconds and is very important in storing memories of where things are located, called a spatial map. On the other hand, the hypothalamus is important in controlling many of our basic bodily functions, such as sleeping, drinking, eating, and sexual activities. Can you think of any memory device or "trick" to help you keep these two brain structures separate?

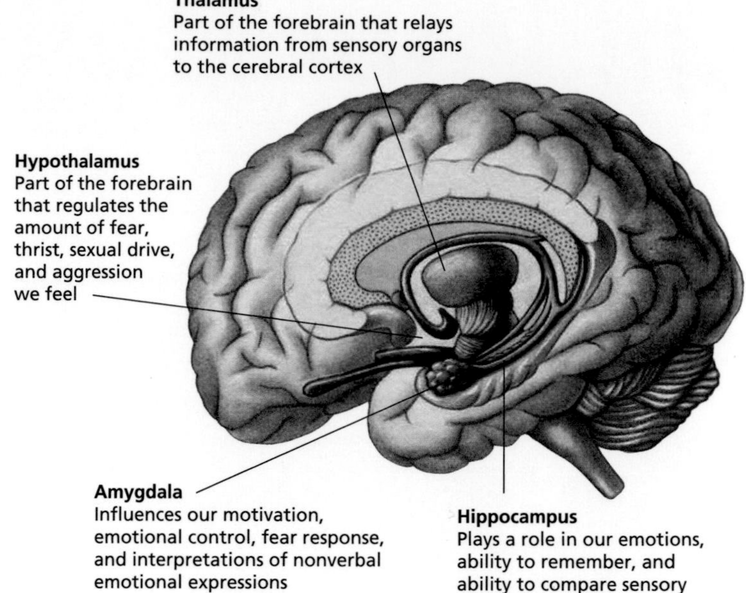

Thalamus
Part of the forebrain that relays information from sensory organs to the cerebral cortex
Hypothalamus
Part of the forebrain that regulates the amount of fear, thrist, sexual drive, and aggression we feel
Amygdala
Influences our motivation, emotional control, fear response, and interpretations of nonverbal emotional expressions
Hippocampus
Plays a role in our emotions, ability to remember, and ability to compare sensory information to expectations

One suggestion might be as follows: If you look at the word hippocampus you can think of the last part of the word – campus. In order to get around on your college campus, you need to keep in mind where certain buildings and areas are located. This is exactly what your hippocampus is involved in. Without your hippocampus, you would have a very hard time finding your way around your college campus.

To remember the hypothalamus, first it might help to understand the name "hypo" means under or below. The hypothalamus is located directly underneath the thalamus. You might also look at the name to try to remember some of the activities the hypothalamus regulates. Recall that we said the hypothalamus plays a role in hunger, sleep, thirst and sex. If you look at the "hypo" of hypothalamus you might memorize "h" – hunger, "y" – yawning, "p" – parched (or very, very thirsty) and "o" – overly excited.

Perspectives of Abnormal Behavior and Types of Therapy

In addition to understanding psychological disorders, it is important to understand the different theories as to the causes of each disorder. Four models of explanation for each disorder are biological, psychoanalytical, behavioral and cognitive. In order to enhance your understanding of these models, study the chart below which describes how each of them would explain the disorders listed. Then, specify the appropriate model in the fill-in-the blank.

Model	Depression	Schizophrenia	Dissociative Identity Disorder
?	anger turned inwards and then repressed	severe breakdown of the ego and regression back to child-like state	motivated forgetting
?	brain chemical imbalance (in neurotransmitters such as serotonin and dopamine)	chemical imbalance and brain structure abnormalities	variation in brain activity between different "personalities"
?	negative and self-defeating thoughts	severe form of illogical thinking	thought avoidance
?	learned helplessness	bizarre behavior that has been shaped through reinforcement	behavior shaped through positive reinforcement such as attention from others

Responses: psychoanalytic, biological, cognitive, behavioral

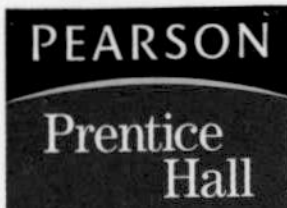

Important Dates in Psychology

Use this timeline to get a better understanding of key dates in the history of psychology. On the other side of this study card you will find study tips for some of the most difficult concepts covered in your introductory psychology text. Be sure to review these tips before your final exam.

B.C.E.

360 Plato write Theaetetus, examining theories of perception, knowledge and truth.

350 Aristotle writes *De Anima* about the relationship of the soul to the body.

350

A.D.

1649 Descartes publishes *The Passion of the Souls,* outlining the pineal gland as the seat of the soul.

1650

1848 Phineas Gage suffers brain damage and provides a famous case study of the effects of brain damage.

1859 Charles Darwin proposes the theory of natural selection, which influences the field of evolutionary psychology.

1860

1860 Gustav Fechner is often credited with performing the first scientific experiments that would form the basis for experimentation in psychology.

1861 Broca's area and its role in speech production is discovered.

1863 Place theory of pitch discovered by Herman von Helmholtz.

1874 Wernicke's area and its role in language comprehension is discovered.

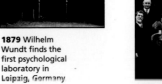

1879 Wilhelm Wundt finds the first psychological laboratory in Leipzig, Germany

1880

1884 James-Lange theory of emotion proposed.

1885 Herman Ebbinghaus introduces the forgetting curve.

1886 Ernest Rutherford discovers the frequency theory of pitch.

1890 William James publishes his book, *Principles of Psychology.*

1892 Structuralism first discovered by Wundt and Titchener.

1894 Margaret Washburn is the first woman to receive a Ph.D. in psychology at Cornell University.

1900

1900 Freud publishes *The Interpretation of Dreams.*

1904 the f Ame Socie

1904 prop facto

Positive vs. Negative Reinforcement and Punishment

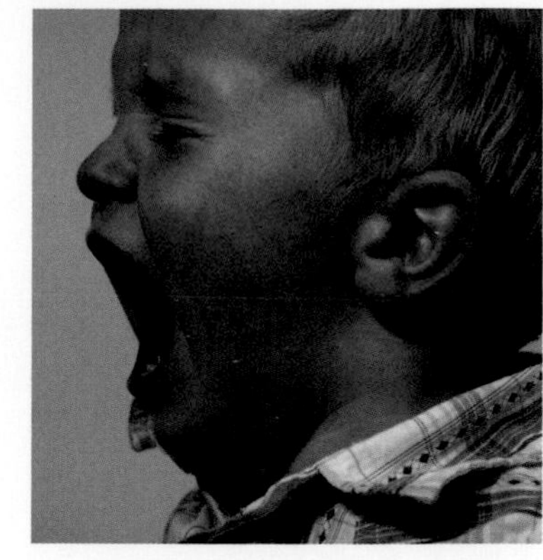

Both positive and negative reinforcement lead to an increase in behavior. In positive reinforcement, something good is given; in negative reinforcement, something bad is taken away. Sometimes it can be confusing because it depends on whose perspective you are using. For example, a child whining in the grocery store line until he gets the candy he wants can be viewed as either positive or negative reinforcement. Keep in mind that from both perspectives the behavior increases. Examine the following chart to see why.

View Point	Behavior	Result/Reinforcer	Type of Reinforcement
Child	Whining	Get candy	Positive (something good is given)
Parent	Give child candy	Whining stops	Negative (something bad – the whining – is taken away)

Negative reinforcement and punishment are often confused. In negative reinforcement, something bad is taken away. In punishment by removal, something good or desirable is taken away. Most people would enjoy being negatively reinforced but would be upset about being punished. Work through the following scenarios to determine whether the person is being negatively reinforced or punished. Check the correct responses below.

Behavior	Consequence	Is something good or bad taken away?	Is this negative reinforcement or punishment?	Will the behavior increase or decrease?
Taking an aspirin for a headache	Headache goes away	bad	?	increase
Running a red light	Driver's license is taken away.	good	?	decrease

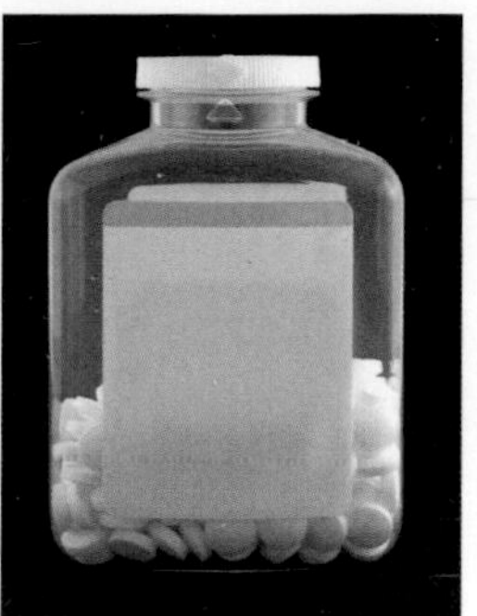

Responses: negative reinforcement, punishment

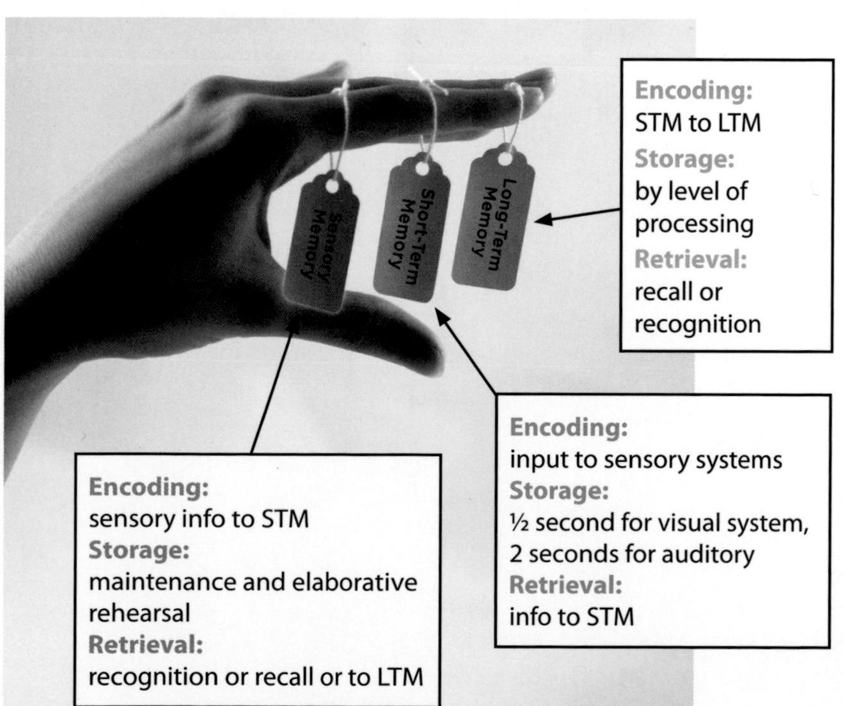

The Three Memory Process and How They Interact to Create a Memory

Two of the most important concepts presented in the memory chapter consist of a three-part model. One concept is the basic processes involved in memory — **encoding, storage, and retrieval.** The other concept is the information processing model of memory, which consists of **sensory, short-term** sometimes referred to as working memory), and **long-term memory.** Students often get these ideas confused. To help you clarify the concepts, review the components of the information processing model in the diagram on the left. Remember that encoding, storage, and retrieval can happen at each of these stages. Review the examples of encoding, storage and retrieval for each stage.

1906 The Journal of Abnormal Psychology is founded.

1906 Ivan Pavlov publishes his findings on classical conditioning.

1906 Ramon y Cajal discovers that the nervous sytem is comprised of individual cells.

1908 Yerkes-Dodson law proposed to explain relationship between performance and arousal.

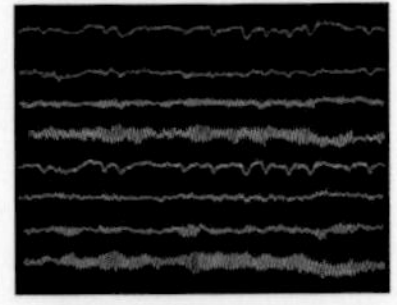

1929 Hans Berger introduces EEG method for studying the human brain.

1929 All traces of cocaine removed from Coca-Cola after addictive nature of the drug was discovered.

1929 Cannon-Bard theory of emotion created.

1938 B.F. Skinner introduces the concept of operant conditioning.

1938 Electroconvulsive shock first used on a human patient.

1939 Clark and Clark classic study on prejudice conducted.

1939 Dollard and Miller propose the frustration-aggression hypothesis.

1948 Alfred Kinsey begins survey research on sexual behavior.

1957 No
Chomsky
es langu
acquisiti
device.

195
Heid
attri
theo

1910 | **1920** | **1930** | **1940** | **1950**

Mary Calkins becomes
rst president of the
ican Psychological
ty.

Spearman
ses a general
r of intelligence.

1905 Freud proposes his psychosexual theory of personality development.

1905 The first IQ test, the Stanford-Binet, was created.

1911 Thorndike discovers the "law of effect."

1912 Gestalt psychology first discovered by Max Wertheimer.

1912 The intelligence quotient is developed by William Stern.

1913 Carl Jung departs from Freud's views and develops his own theory of the conscious.

1915 Freud first proposes the concept of defense mechanisms.

1920 Francis Cecil is the first African American to receive a Ph.D. in psychology at Clark University.

1920 Watson and Rayner publish the "Little Albert" experiment.

1921 The first neurotransmitter, acetylcholine, is discovered.

1921 The Rorschach Inkblot Test is developed.

1921 Allport proposes a trait theory of personality.

1924 Mary Cover Jones publishes "Little Peter" story.

1925 Wolfgang Kohler demonstrates concept of sudden insight in students examining problem-solving with primates.

1925 Terman begins his longitudinal studies on giftedness.

1930 Tolman and Honzik demonstrates latent learning in rats.

1930 Jean Piaget proposes four stages of cognitive development.

1932 Walter Cannon begins research on the "fight or flight" phenomena.

1933 Sigmund Freud proposes the concepts of id, ego, and superego.

1934 Lev Vygotsky proposes concept of zone of proximal development.

1935 Henry Murray creates the Thematic Apperception Test.

1935 Prefrontal lobotomy developed by Dr. Antonio Egas Moniz.

1942 The Minnesota Multiphasic Personality Inventory is created.

1942 Carl Rogers develops client-centered therapy.

1943 Hull proposes drive reduction theory of motivation.

1950 Eric Erikson proposes his psychosocial stages of personality development.

1951 Soloman Asch's classic study on conformity conducted.

1952 The first edition of t
Diagnostic and Statistical
Manual of Mental Disord
is published.

1952 Chlorpromazine firs
drug treatment introduce
for the treatment of
schizophrenia.

1953 REM sleep first discovered.

1953 The American P
Association publishes
edition of Ethical Sta
Psychology.

1954 Abraham M
a hierarchy of ne
human motivatio

Study Tips for the Most Difficult Topics in Introductory Psychology

Independent Variable and Dependant Variable

Be careful not to confuse the independent variable *(i.v.)* with the dependent variable *(d.v.)*. The independent variable is the variable the researcher manipulates her or himself. If you think about it as if you were the researcher conducting the experiment, the independent variable is the one that I control. Another way to make sure you have correctly labeled the variables in an experiment is to insert the variable names into the following phrase and make sure it still makes sense. The test phrase is:

How ______ **affects** ______ .
(i.v.) *(d.v.)*

Here is an example for you to practice using the test phrase: A researcher conducts a study looking at the color of different rooms and aggressiveness. You can see that "How aggressiveness affects room color" does not make sense and is not what the researcher is interested in. However, "How room color affects aggressiveness" does correspond to the researcher's goals. So, in this case, the room color is the independent variable and aggressiveness is the dependent variable.

Piaget's Stages

Perhaps the most influential theory on cognitive development is Jean Piaget's theory. He proposed four stages of cognitive development. To enhance your learning of these stages, study this chart and try to answer the fill-in-the-blanks below.

Stage	Age	Characteristics	How would you test to see if someone is in this stage?
Sensorimotor	0–2 years	➡ Children explore using their ___ and ___ systems. ➡ Develop ___ permanence	Hide a toy under a blanket and see if the child looks under the blanket for the toy.
Preoperational	2–7 years	➡ A lot of ___ thinking. ➡ Children can represent objects ___. ➡ Engage in ___ play. ➡ Do not understand concepts of ___. ➡ Tend to focus on one aspect of an object.	Ask the child if they would rather have two quarters or five pennies (they will probably want the five pennies). See if the child can play a make-believe game.
Concrete Operational	7–12 years	➡ Show an understanding for the principles of ___. ➡ Demonstrate logical thinking and can solve ___. ➡ Focus mostly on ___ objects and ideas.	Divide a string of clay into five pieces and see if the child thinks there is as much clay in the five pieces as there was in the one string.
Formal Operational	12 years and on	➡ Can use ___ reasoning to solve problems. ➡ Able to consider ___ situations.	Ask the child an abstract question and see how they respond. An example of a question could be "What if snow were black?"

Responses:
Sensorimotor: sensory and motor, object
Preoperational: egocentric, mentally, make-believe, conservation
Concrete Operational: conservation, analogies, concrete
Formal operational: abstract, hypothetical

ropos-
e

Fritz
r proposes
ution
y.

959 The first
rug to treat
epression,
ofranil,
pproved by
e FDA.

959 Festinger
nd Carlsmith
ublish their
tudy on cogni-
ve dissonance

959 Harlow
nd Zimmerman
emonstrate the
nportance of
ontact comfort
ith their study
n infant mon-
eys.

1966 Masters and Johnson discover four stages of sexual response cycle.

1967 Seligman demonstrates learned helplessness in dogs.

1967 Holmes and Rahe create the Social Readjustment Rating Scale.

1967 Beck proposes a cognitive theory for explaining depression.

1968 Roger Sperry demonstrates hemispheric specialization with split-brain patients.

1968 Bibb Latané and John Darley identify the five decision points in helping behavior.

1968 The DSM-II is published.

1976 Hans Selye proposes the General Adaptation Syndrome to describe responses to stress.

1977 The stress-vulnerability model of schizophrenia was proposed by Zubin and Spring

1977 Thomas and Chess discover different types of infant temperament.

1977 Hobson and McCarley propose the activation synthesis hypothesis.

1978 Elizabeth Loftus puts into question the validity of eyewitness testimony with discovery of misinformation effect.

1979 Mary Ainsworth uses the Strange Situation to study infant attachment styles.

1986 Robert Sternberg proposes the triangular theory of love.

1987 Gender schema theory of gender role development proposed by Sandra Bem.

1989 Albert Bandura proposes the concept of reciprocal determinism.

1989 Francine Shapiro proposes idea of eye-movement desensitization reprocessing for treating anxiety.

1996 McCrae and Costa propose the Big Five Personality dimensions.

1997 Robert Ellis proposes rational emotive behavioral therapy.

1997 Elisabeth Kubler-Ross outlines the stages of death and dying from studies of terminally ill patients.

1960 **1970** **1980** **1990** **2000**

1960 Visual cliff experiment on depth perception conducted by Eleanor Gibson.

1960 George Sperling performs classic experiments on iconic memory.

1961 Carl Rogers discovers the concepts of ideal self, real self, conditional positive regard, and unconditional positive regard.

1961 Muzafer Sherif conducts the "Robber's Cove" study.

1962 The serial position effect discovered by memory researcher Bennett Murdock.

1962 Cognitive arousal theory of emotion proposed by Schachter and Singer.

e

s

ychological
he first
dards in

1963 Albert Bandura's "Bobo doll" study is conducted.

1963 Stanley Milgram conducts his classic study on obedience.

1963 Lawrence Kohlberg creates his theory of moral development.

aslow proposes
ds to describe
.

1965 Gate control theory proposed by Melzack and Wall.

1971 Phillip Zimbardo and colleagues conduct the "Stanford Prison Study."

1971 American sociologist Adrian Dove creates the "Dove Counterbalance General Intelligence Test" (later known as the Chitling Test).

1973 Flora Rheta Schreiber publishes the book *Sybil,* detailing the life of a woman with multiple personality disorder.

1974 Freidman and Rosenman discover link between heart disease and Type-A personality.

1974 Memory researchers Tulving and Thomson demonstrate encoding specificity.

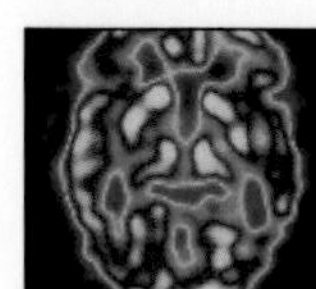

1974 The PET scan is first introduced as a brain imaging technique.

1980 Folkman and Lazarus introduce the concepts of problem-focused and emotion-focused coping.

1980 The DSM-II is published.

1981 David Wechsler begins to devise IQ tests for specific age groups.

1982 Suzanne Kobasa proposes the characteristics of the hardy personality.

1983 Gardner first proposes his theory of multiple intelligences.

1985 Robert Sternberg proposes the Triarchic theory of intelligence.

1991 Stress researcher Richard Lazarus develops his cognitive-mediational theory.

1994 Herrnstein and Murray publish *The Bell Curve.*

1994 Deci and Ryan perform their classic study on intrinsic and extrinsic motivation.

1994 The DSM-IV is published.

1995 Goleman proposes idea of emotional intelligence.

1995 Mischel and Shoda propose the concept of trait-situation interactions in the study of personality.

1995 Raymond Cattell creates the Sixteen Personality Factor Questionnaire.

2002 New Mexico is the first state to allow licensed psychologists to prescribe drug treatments for psychological disorders.

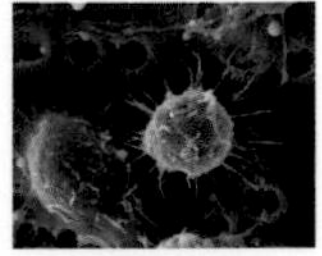

2004 Alexander Storch presents possibility of obtaining stem cells from adults to repair damaged neural tissue.

ninth edition

mypsychlab edition

Carole Wade

Dominican University of California

Carol Tavris

Upper Saddle River, NJ 07458

Library of Congress Cataloging-in-Publication Data

Wade Carole.
Psychology / Carole Wade, Carol Tavris. 9th ed.
p. cm.
Includes bibliographical references and index.
ISBN 0-13-601606-5
1. Psychology Textbooks. I. Tavris, Carol. II. Title.
BF121.W27 2008
150 dc22 2006102411

Editorial Director: Leah Jewell
Executive Editor: Jessica Mosher
Editorial Assistant: Jessica Kupetz
Editor in Chief, Development: Rochelle Diogenes
Media Editor: Bryan Hyland
Director of Marketing: Brandy Dawson
Senior Marketing Manager: Jeanette Moyer
Marketing Assistant: Laura Kennedy
Assistant Managing Editor: Maureen Richardson
Production Liaison: Maureen Richardson/Nicole Girrbach
Manufacturing Manager: Nick Sklitsis
Manufacturing Buyer: Sherry Lewis
Interior Design: Laura Gardner
Cover Design: Laura Gardner
Cover Illustration/Photo: Eric Meola/Image Bank/Getty Images, Inc.
Director, Image Resource Center: Melinda Patelli
Manager, Rights & Permissions: Zina Arabia
Interior Image Specialist: Beth Brenzel
Cover Image Specialist: Karen Sanatar
Image Permission Coordinator: Joanne Dippel
Photo Researcher: Barbara Salz
Composition/Full-Service Project Management: Prepare, Inc.
Printer/Binder: Courier Companies, Inc.

Credits and acknowledgments borrowed from other sources and reproduced, with permission, in this textbook appear on appropriate page within text (or on pages C-1 C-6).

Pearson Education, Ltd., London
Pearson Education Australia PTY, Limited
Pearson Education Singapore, Pte., Ltd.
Pearson Education North Asia Ltd.
Pearson Education, Canada, Ltd.
Pearson Educaci n de Mexico, S.A. de C.V.
Pearson Education Japan
Pearson Education Malaysia, Pte., Ltd.

10 9 8 7 6 5 4 3

ISBN-13: 978-0-13-601606-9

ISBN-10: 0-13-601606-5

Contents at a glance

WHAT IS PSYCHOLOGY?

CHAPTER ONE

The purpose of psychology is to give us a completely different idea of the things we know best.

PAUL VALÉRY

What is psychology? If you were to wander through the psychology section of your local bookstore (perhaps called "self-help" or "personal growth"), you would find books offering the following answers:

- Psychology is all about finding happiness. It will tell you *Why Your Life Sucks and What You Can Do About It*, so long as you also read *I Don't Have to Make Everything All Better*. If you are feeling that nothing will ever get better, you might be cheered up by *The Joy of Stress, The Joy of Failure*, and *Joy No Matter What*. Or you can *Access Your Brain's Joy Center* by using "the free soul method."
- Psychology will make you rich and successful if you read *Baby Steps to Success* or *Giant Steps* or *How to Succeed in Life*. You can learn *How to Make the Impossible Possible* and also how to *Get What You Deserve*.
- Psychology will help you fall in love, stay in love, or get over love. *Love Is the Answer*, but only if you are *Learning to Love Yourself* first and don't develop *Obsessive Love*. You can find out *How to Make Anyone Fall in Love with You* as long as you *Don't Say Yes When You Want to Say No*. Once you're in love, of course, you will need *The Art of Intimacy* and *The Art of Staying Together*, and if your relationship gets into trouble, you may want to resort to *Relationship Rescue*.
- If you love things laid out in easy-to-follow lists, you're really in luck. You can *Live the Life You Love: In Ten Easy Step-by-Step Lessons*, discover the *Ten Secrets for Success and Inner Peace*, try *The Anxiety Cure: An Eight-Step Program for Getting Well*, meditate on *The Six Pillars of Self-Esteem*, and work on *Getting Unstuck: 8 Simple Steps to Solving Any Problem*.

Before you head for the bookstore, however, we want to tell you that the psychology you are about to study—*real* psychology—bears little relation to the popular psychology ("pop psych") found in these and thousands of similar books. It is more complex, more informative, and, we think, far more helpful because it is based on scientific research and **empirical** evidence—evidence gathered by careful observation, experimentation, and measurement.

The psychology you will be studying also addresses a far broader range of issues than does popular psychology. When people think of psychology, they usually think of mental and emotional disorders, personal problems, and psychotherapy. But psychologists take as their subject the entire spectrum of brave and cowardly, intelligent and foolish, beautiful and brutish things that people do. They want to know how ordinary human beings—and other animals, too—learn, remember, solve problems, perceive, feel, and get along (or fail to get along) with others. They are therefore as likely to study commonplace experiences—rearing children, gossiping, remembering a shopping list, daydreaming, making love, and making a living—as exceptional ones.

Psychology can be defined generally as *the discipline concerned with behavior and mental processes and how they are affected by an organism's physical state, mental state, and external environment.* This definition, however, is a little like defining a car as a vehicle for transporting people from one place to another, without explaining how a car differs from a train or a bus, how a Ford differs from a Ferrari, or how a catalytic converter works. To get a

CHAPTER OUTLINE

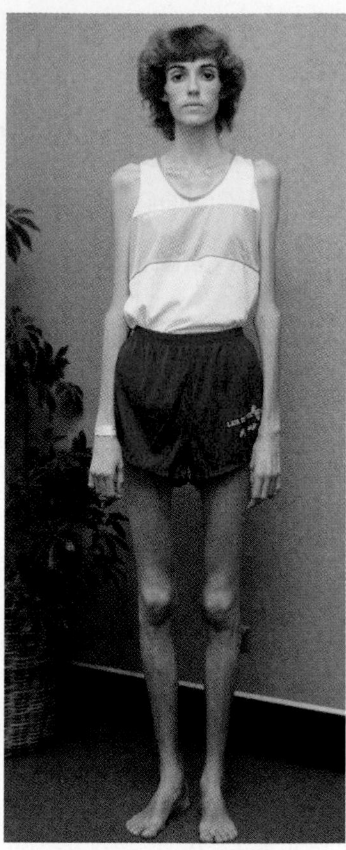

Psychologists use scientific methods to study many puzzles of human behavior. Why do people lose their inhibitions when they dress up in funny outfits? Why do people strive to become champion athletes in spite of physical disabilities? What causes people to become anorexic and even starve themselves to death? And what could motivate terrorists to kill themselves and thousands of innocent people?

clear picture of what psychology is you are going to need to know more about its methods, its findings, and its ways of interpreting information. We will begin by looking more closely at what psychology is *not.*

WHAT'S**AHEAD** 

- How does "psychobabble" differ from serious psychology?
- How accurate are psychologists' nonscientific competitors, such as astrologers and psychics?

 Psychology, Pseudoscience, and Popular Opinion

empirical Relying on or derived from observation, experimentation, or measurement.

psychology The discipline concerned with behavior and mental processes and how they are affected by an organism's physical state, mental state, and external environment; the term is often represented by ψ, the Greek letter psi (usually pronounced "sy").

In recent decades, the public's appetite for psychological information has created a huge market for "psychobabble": pseudoscience and quackery covered by a veneer of psychological and scientific-sounding language. Pseudoscience promises easy fixes to life's problems and challenges, such as resolving your unhappiness as an adult by "reliving" the supposed trauma of your birth, or becoming more creative on the job by "reprogramming" your brain. Some forms of psychobabble play on the modern consumer's love of technology. All sorts of electrical gizmos have been marketed with the promise that they will get both halves of your brain working at their peak: the Graham Potentializer, the Tranquilite, the Floatarium, the Transcutaneous Electro-Neural Stimulator, the Brain SuperCharger, and the Whole Brain Wave Form Synchro-Energizer. (We are not making these up.) And today you can find all sorts of psycho-

babble on the Internet, where promoters promise that a higher IQ or a perfect love life or a better personality is just a click away.

Because so many pop-psych ideas have filtered into public consciousness, the media, education, and even the law, we all need to distinguish between psychobabble and serious psychology, and between unsupported *popular opinion* and findings based on *research evidence.* Are unhappy memories "repressed" and then accurately recalled years later, as if they had been tape-recorded? Do most women suffer from emotional symptoms of "PMS"? Do policies of abstinence from alcohol reduce rates of alcoholism? Do abused children inevitably become abusive parents, caught in a "cycle of abuse"? If you play Baby Beethoven tapes to your infant, will your baby become smarter? At the start of an introductory psychology course, many students hold beliefs such as these—beliefs that have been promoted in popular books and TV shows or that are based on "commonsense" notions in the culture. Empirical evidence, however, has shown that these and many other widely held ideas about human behavior are, in fact, wrong.

The marriage of old-fashioned pseudoscience and modern technology has produced gizmos like the "Synchro-Energizer," which supposedly alters consciousness, boosts intelligence, and enhances sexual functioning, all by bombarding you with lights and sounds of different frequencies and intensities.

CLOSE-UP on Research

MISTAKEN BELIEFS ABOUT HUMAN BEHAVIOR

One purpose of an introductory course like the one you are taking is to correct such misconceptions—by teaching you how psychologists study them and showing you how their research might confirm or dispel ideas that many of us take for granted. Two researchers, Annette Kujawski Taylor and Patricia Kowalski (2004), wondered how many students come into their first psych course with a bunch of mistaken ideas in their heads and whether a semester of learning helps dislodge those ideas.

To answer these questions, they gave 90 introductory students a "Psychological Information" questionnaire on the first day of class. The test consisted of 36 true/false items—for example, "Under hypnosis you can perform feats that are otherwise impossible," "Too much sugar causes hyperactivity in children," "At any point in time, we use only 10 percent of our brains," and "Listening to Mozart will enhance your thinking and creativity." The students also rated their confidence in each of their responses on a scale of 1 (not at all confident) to 10 (very confident). All of the items were on topics that the course was scheduled to cover, and all of them were false. As a group, the students failed the test miserably: Their accuracy was only 38.5 percent, which is actually worse than chance, and they had more confidence in their wrong answers than their correct ones! Moreover, students with high grade-point averages did no better than those with low ones. So much for common sense.

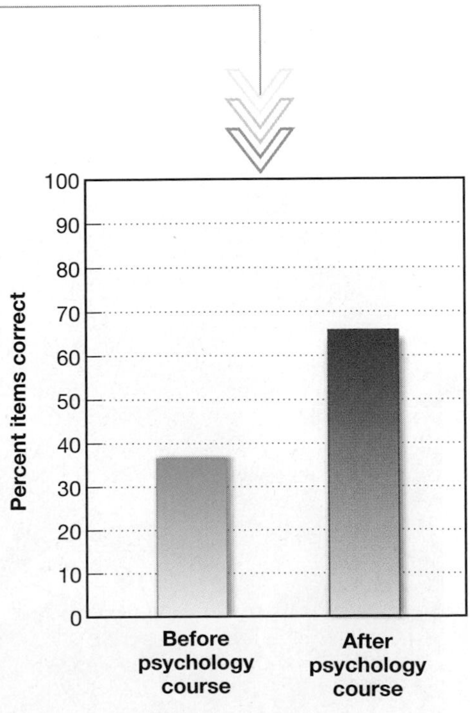

During the last week of class, the same students took another test, one that included all of the earlier items plus 12 new true items that were randomly mixed in but not scored. This time, we're happy to say, the students' overall accuracy was much better: 66.3 percent. The researchers attributed this change in part to the fact that instruction had explicitly focused on the scientific evidence refuting such beliefs. (As you will be seeing, we take the same approach in this book.) Yet even at the end of the course, more than a third of the students' responses were wrong, meaning that there was still plenty of room left for improvement. The researchers then dug deeper into the evidence, analyzing the students' confidence ratings. They found that by the end of the semester, the students had gained confidence in their correct beliefs and lost confidence in those beliefs

that were still incorrect, suggesting that they were beginning to be unsure about their misconceptions, were in the process of questioning them, and perhaps were on the way to giving them up. If so, they were learning one of the most important lessons in science: that uncertainty about untested assumptions and beliefs can be a good thing.

Throughout this book and your introductory course, you, too, will repeatedly find that popular opinion and "common sense" are not always reliable guides to human behavior. The kind of research you will be learning about won't always provide the answers you might have wished for, and sometimes it will be unable to provide final answers. Our goal, however, is to show you why the scientific investigation of even our most cherished beliefs can lead to answers that are far more sensible than "common sense."

Common sense, information in the media, and personal experience are not the only sources of misunderstandings about human behavior. Psychology has many nonscientific competitors: palm reading, graphology, fortune-telling, numerology, and the most popular, astrology. Like psychologists, promoters of these competing systems try to explain people's problems and predict their behavior. If you are having romantic problems, an astrologer may advise you to choose an Aries instead of an Aquarius as your next love, and a "past-lives channeler" may say it's because you were jilted in a former life. Belief in these unscientific approaches is widespread, even in scientifically advanced countries; between one-third and one-half of Americans and Canadians believe in astrology, and 17 percent of Americans have sought out a fortune-teller or psychic for advice (De Robertis & Delaney, 2000; National Science Board, 2000).

Yet whenever the claims of psychics and astrologers are put to the test, those claims turn out to be so vague as to be meaningless ("Spirituality will increase next year")—or just plain wrong (Park, 2000; Radford, 2005; Shermer, 1997). In 2003, in a syndicated column, astrologer Joyce Jillson wrote of actor John Ritter, "Having a Virgo sun sign helps keep his career ticking." Her glowing horoscope was published hours after Ritter died of a ruptured aorta. Sylvia Browne, one of America's most noted psychics, predicted that in 2005, Saddam Hussein would die before his trial, Britney Spears would break up with her husband, Michael Jackson would be convicted of child molestation, and Mount St. Helens would blow up. Obviously, she was mistaken on all counts. Moreover, contrary to what you might think from watching TV shows like *Medium*, no psychic has ever found a missing child, identified a serial killer, or helped police solve any other crime solely by using "psychic powers." The "help" given by psychics merely adds to the heartbreak the victim's family feels. In 2004, when 11-year-old Carlie Brucia was abducted, her family's hopes were raised by a psychic's report that Carlie was alive. In fact, the child had been raped and murdered.

What should have been the fatal blow to astrological and psychic claims occurred on September 11, 2001, when the World Trade Center was destroyed. Not one psychic or astrologer had predicted that devastating event. Yet belief in

Nonscientific approaches to psychological problems, such as astrology and psychic readings, promise easy answers and quick solutions—even for pets! But can they deliver?

the accuracy of psychic claims persists. One reason is that psychobabble confirms our existing beliefs and prejudices (which is why it is so appealing), whereas scientific psychology often challenges them. You do not have to be a psychologist to know that people don't always take kindly to having their beliefs challenged. You rarely hear someone say, cheerfully, "Oh, thank you for explaining to me why my lifelong philosophy of child rearing is wrong! I'm so grateful for your facts!" The person is more likely to say, "Oh, buzz off, and take your stupid ideas with you." (In Chapter 9 you will learn why this is so.)

critical thinking The ability and willingness to assess claims and make judgments on the basis of well-supported reasons and evidence rather than emotion or anecdote.

Psychological findings do not have to be surprising or counterintuitive, however, to be important. Like scientists in other fields, psychological researchers strive not only to discover new phenomena and correct mistaken ideas but also to deepen our understanding of an already familiar world—by identifying the varieties of love, the origins of violence, or the reasons that a great song can lift our hearts.

WHAT'S**AHEAD** 

- Are "critical thinkers" always critical?
- Are all opinions created equal?
- What guidelines can help you evaluate psychological claims?

Thinking Critically and Creatively About Psychology

In this book, you will gain practice in distinguishing scientific psychology from pseudoscience by thinking critically. **Critical thinking** is the ability and willingness to assess claims and make objective judgments on the basis of well-supported reasons and evidence rather than emotion or anecdote. Critical thinkers are able to look for flaws in arguments and to resist claims that have no support. They realize that criticizing an argument is not the same as criticizing the person making it, and they are willing to engage in vigorous debate about the validity of an idea. Critical thinking, however, is not merely negative thinking. It includes the ability to be creative and constructive—the ability to come up with alternative explanations for events, think of implications of research findings, and apply new knowledge to social and personal problems.

Most people know that you have to exercise the body to keep it in shape, but they may not realize that clear thinking also requires effort and practice. All around us we can see examples of flabby thinking. Sometimes people justify their mental laziness by proudly telling you they are open-minded. It's good to be open-minded, many scientists have observed, but not so open that your brains fall out!

One prevalent misreading of what it means to be open-minded is the idea that all opinions are created equal and that everybody's beliefs are as good as everybody else's. On matters of personal preference, that is true; if you prefer the look of a Ford Taurus to the look of a Honda Accord, no one can argue with you. But if you say, "The Ford is a better car than a Honda," you have uttered more than mere opinion. Now you have to support your belief with evidence of the car's reliability, track record, and safety (Ruggiero, 2004).

We often hear that all viewpoints should be taught to students in the name of "fairness" and "open-mindedness," but not all viewpoints, theories, and opinions are equally valid or supported by the evidence.

And if you say, "Fords are the best in the world and Hondas do not exist; they are a conspiracy of the Japanese government," you forfeit the right to have your opinion taken seriously. Your opinion, if it ignores reality, is *not* equal to any other.

Many educators, philosophers, and psychologists believe that contemporary education shortchanges students by not encouraging them to think critically and creatively. Too often, say these critics, teachers and students view the mind as a bin for storing "the right answers" or a sponge for "soaking up knowledge." The mind is neither a bin nor a sponge. Remembering, thinking, and understanding require judgment, choice, and the weighing of evidence. Many high school and college graduates have learned to memorize the "right" answers, but without the ability to think critically, they are unable to formulate a rational argument or see through misleading advertisements that play on their emotions. They may not know how to assess a political proposal or candidate, decide whether or when to have children, evaluate medical remedies, or come up with constructive solutions to their problems.

Critical thinking is not only indispensable in ordinary life; it is also fundamental to all science, including psychological science. By exercising critical thinking, you will be able to distinguish serious psychology from the psychobabble that clutters the airwaves and bookstores. (In the study of introductory students' misconceptions described earlier, students who did well on a critical-thinking test showed the greatest improvement over the semester.) Critical thinking requires logical skills, but other skills and dispositions are also important (Anderson, 2005; Halpern, 2002; Levy, 1997; Paul, 1984; Ruggiero, 2004). Here are eight essential critical-thinking guidelines that we will be emphasizing throughout this book.

Ask Questions; Be Willing to Wonder. What is the one kind of question that most exasperates parents of young children? "Why is the sky blue, Mommy?" "Why doesn't the plane fall?" "Why don't pigs have wings?" Unfortunately, as children grow up, they tend to stop asking "why" questions. (Why do you think this is?)

"The trigger mechanism for creative thinking is the disposition to be curious, to wonder, to inquire," observed Vincent Ruggiero (1988). "Asking 'What's wrong here?' and/or 'Why is this the way it is, and how did it come to be that way?' leads to the identification of problems and challenges." Psychologist Bob Perloff (1992) once reflected on a few questions he would like to have answered. "Why are moths attracted to wool but indifferent to cotton?" he wondered. "Why is a rainbow arched? I used to feel foolish, even dumb, because I didn't know why or how the sun shines until I learned very recently that the astrophysicists themselves are in a quandary about this."

We hope that you will not approach psychology as received wisdom but will ask many questions about the theories and findings presented in this book. Be on the lookout, too, for questions about human behavior that have not yet been asked, or have been asked but not answered—the way a psychological scientist would. In 2005, the editors of *Science*, one of the world's foremost science journals, celebrated the publication's 125th anniversary by identifying 125 scientific puzzles that scientists hope to solve at least partially over the next few decades, and among them were several psychological ones (Kennedy & Norman, 2005). What is the biological basis of consciousness? How are memories stored and retrieved? Why do we sleep and dream? Why are there critical periods for language learning? What causes schizophrenia? What is the biological basis of addiction? Psychological scientists are not discouraged by the fact that questions like these have not yet been answered; they see them as an exciting challenge.

"I still don't have all the answers, but I'm beginning to ask the right questions."

Define Your Terms. Once you have raised a general question, the next step is to frame it in clear and concrete terms. "What makes people happy?" is a fine question for midnight reveries, but it will not lead to answers until you have defined what you mean by "happy." Do you mean being in a state of euphoria most of the time? Do you mean feeling pleasantly contented with life? Do you mean being free of serious problems or pain?

Vague or poorly defined terms in a question can lead to misleading or incomplete answers. For example, have you ever wondered whether animals can use language? The answer depends on how you define language. If you mean "a system of communication," then birds do it, bees do it, and even worms do it. But if you mean "a system of communication that combines sounds or gestures into an infinite number of structured utterances that convey meaning" (which is how linguists define it), then as far as anyone can tell, only people use language, though some animals are able to acquire some aspects of language in special settings (see Chapter 9). Here's another example: How common is it for schoolchildren to be bullied? The answer depends on how you define bullying. If you mean "ever mistreated in any way by another child," then nearly every child has been bullied. If you mean "subjected to repeated verbal harassment and taunting," the numbers are lower. And if you mean "physically attacked and threatened," the numbers are lower still. The definition makes all the difference (Best, 2001).

Examine the Evidence. Have you ever heard someone in the heat of argument exclaim, "I just know it's true, no matter what you say" or "That's my opinion; nothing's going to change it"? Have you ever made such statements yourself? Accepting a conclusion without evidence, or expecting others to do so, is a sure sign of lazy thinking. A critical thinker asks, "What evidence supports or refutes this argument and its opposition? How reliable is the evidence?"

For example, it's common for parents and children to complain that today's students are overburdened with homework. Are they? What does the evidence show? According to one major report that reviewed the existing research, time spent daily on homework increased from an average of 16 minutes in 1981 to slightly more than 19 minutes in 1997, and has not changed much since (Brown Report on Education Policy, 2003). In one study of 8,000 families reviewed in the report, half of all 3- to 12-year-olds said they did no homework at all (Hofferth & Sandberg, 2000). And in a nationwide survey of 282,000 college students, only a third said they had spent more than an hour each weekday on homework during their senior year of high school, the lowest number since statistics were first reported in 1987—and these were seniors who were college-bound (Sax et al., 2002). Some American students may in fact be overburdened by homework, but they are clearly the exception, not the rule.

Sometimes, of course, checking the reliability of the evidence for a claim is not practical. In those cases, critical thinkers consider whether the evidence came from a reliable source (Lipps, 2004). Reliable authorities exercise critical thinking themselves. They have education or experience in the field in which they claim expertise. They don't pressure people to agree with them. They are trusted by other experts in the field. They share their evidence openly. In psychology, they draw on research conducted according to certain rules and procedures, which you will be learning about in the next chapter.

"Are you just pissing and moaning, or can you verify what you're saying with data?"

 **Analyze Assumptions and Biases.** *Assumptions* are beliefs that are taken for granted. Critical thinkers try to identify and evaluate the unspoken assumptions on which claims and arguments may rest—in the books they read, the political speeches they hear, and the advertisements that bombard them every day. The assumption might be "All Democrats (or Republicans) are idiots," or "You need the product we are selling," or "People have free will and are entirely responsible for any crimes they commit" (or, conversely, "People's behavior is a result of their biology or upbringing, so they aren't responsible for anything they do"). Everyone, of course, makes assumptions about how the world works; we could not function otherwise. But if we do not make our own assumptions and those of other people explicit, our ability to judge an argument's merits may be impaired.

When an assumption or belief keeps us from considering the evidence fairly, or causes us to ignore the evidence completely, it becomes a *bias*. Often a bias remains

Thinking Critically and Creatively about Psychological Issues

These eight critical-thinking guidelines will help you evaluate psychological findings, claims in the media, and problems that you encounter in your own life.

Ask Questions; Be Willing to Wonder

When Hurricane Katrina devastated New Orleans and many other areas, volunteers worked tirelessly to save survivors. Why do some people bravely come to the aid of their fellow human beings, even when it's not their official job? And, on the other hand, why do people often behave in ways that are selfish, cruel, or violent? Social psychologists explore ways of explaining both sides of "human nature," as we will see in Chapter 8.

James Nielsen/ZUMA Press

Define Your Terms

People refer to intelligence all the time, but what is it exactly? Does the musical genius of a world-class violinist like Midori count as intelligence? Is intelligence captured by an IQ score, or does it also include wisdom and practical "smarts"? We will consider some answers in Chapter 9.

hidden until someone challenges our belief and we get defensive and angry. For instance, most of us, psychologists included, believe that parents are the most important influence in shaping a child's personality. Could anything be more obvious? Isn't that what parenting books, therapists, and magazine articles have been telling us for years? In 1998, in her book *The Nurture Assumption*, Judith Rich Harris dared to question that assumption. Genes and peers, she argued, are more important influences on a child's personality and behavior than how the parents raise the child. Because this idea challenged a widespread bias, it immediately provoked a storm of disbelief, outrage, and scorn. Some critics focused on Harris's lack of credentials instead of her facts or her logic (although she had authored a successful developmental psychology text, she does not have a Ph.D.), and many attacked the book without even bothering to read it. That is the nature of a bias: It creates

Examine the Evidence
When demonstrating "levitation" and other supposedly magical phenomena, illusionists such as André Kole exploit people's tendency to trust the evidence of their own eyes even when such evidence is misleading, as discussed in Chapter 6.

Analyze Assumptions and Biases
People often assume that drug effects are purely biological, and many Americans also share a cultural bias that all psychoactive drugs are inevitably harmful. The Rastafarian church, however, regards marijuana as a "wisdom weed." Will these young Jamaican members react to the drug in the same way as someone who buys it on the street and smokes it alone or at a party? We will find out in Chapters 5 and 16.

intellectual blinders. (In Chapter 13 we will look more closely at Harris's argument—in as unbiased a manner as possible.)

Avoid Emotional Reasoning. Emotion has a place in critical thinking. Passionate commitment to a view motivates people to think boldly, to defend unpopular ideas, and to seek evidence for creative new theories. But when "gut feelings" replace clear thinking, the results can be dangerous. "Persecutions and wars and lynchings," observed Edward de Bono (1985), "are all a result of gut feeling."

All of us are apt to feel threatened and get defensive whenever our most cherished beliefs are challenged. We value these beliefs highly, in part because they offer explanations for phenomena that might otherwise seem puzzling or frightening—for example, the existence of death and suffering—and because they simplify a complicated world (Preston & Epley, 2005). Because our feelings feel so *right*, so natural, we may not realize that people who hold an opposing viewpoint feel just as strongly as we do. But they usually do, which means that emotional conviction alone cannot settle arguments. You probably hold strong feelings about

Don't Oversimplify

When you're feeling angry, is it better to "let it out" (as Ted Turner certainly is doing here!) or keep it "bottled up"? Either answer oversimplifies. Depending on the circumstances, sometimes it is helpful to express your feelings, but sometimes venting your anger makes everything worse, as we discuss in Chapter 11.

Avoid Emotional Reasoning

Intense feelings about controversial issues can keep us from considering other viewpoints. The resolution of differences requires that we move beyond emotional reasoning and instead weigh point and counterpoint, as discussed in Chapter 9.

many topics of psychological interest, such as drug use, the causes of crime, racism, the origins of intelligence, gender differences, and homosexuality. As you read this book, you may find yourself quarreling with findings that you dislike. Disagreement is fine; it means that you are reading actively and are engaged with the material. All we ask is that you think about why you are disagreeing: Is it because the evidence is unpersuasive or because the results make you feel anxious or annoyed?

Don't Oversimplify. A critical thinker looks beyond the obvious, resists easy generalizations, and rejects either–or thinking. For instance, is it better to feel you have control over everything that happens to you or to accept with tranquility whatever life serves up? Either position oversimplifies. As we will see in Chapter 15, a sense of control has many important benefits, but sometimes it is best to "go with the flow."

One common form of oversimplification is *argument by anecdote*—generalizing from a personal experience or a few examples to everyone: One crime committed by a paroled ex-convict means that parole should be abolished; one friend who hates her school means that everybody who goes there hates it. Anecdotes are often the source of stereotyping as

Consider Other Interpretations
Hypnosis has traditionally been considered a "trance state," in which people involuntarily do things they ordinarily could not or would not do. But might there be another interpretation of the surprising things that hypnotized people often do? We'll look at competing explanations in Chapter 5.

Tolerate Uncertainty
Many questions generate lots of heat and controversy, yet have no firm answers—and until we have answers, we have to live with uncertainty. For example, scientists still have no solid theory to explain why people become gay, straight, or bisexual, as we will see in Chapter 12.

well: One dishonest welfare mother means they are all dishonest; one encounter with an unconventional Californian means they are all flaky. Critical thinkers want more evidence than one or two stories before drawing such sweeping conclusions.

Consider Other Interpretations. A critical thinker creatively generates as many reasonable explanations of the topic at hand as possible before settling on the most likely one. Suppose a news magazine reports that chronically depressed people are more likely than other people to develop cancer. Before concluding that depression causes cancer, you would need to consider some other possibilities. Perhaps depressed people are more likely to smoke and to drink excessively, and it is those unhealthful habits that increase their cancer risk. Or perhaps, in studies of depression and cancer, early, undetected cancers were responsible for patients' feelings of depression. Alternative explanations such as these must be ruled out by further investigation before we can conclude that depression is a direct cause of cancer.

Once several explanations of a phenomenon have been generated, a critical thinker chooses the one that accounts for the most evidence while making the fewest unverified assumptions—a principle known as *Occam's razor*, after the fourteenth-century philosopher who first formulated it. Thus, if a fortune-teller reads your palm and predicts that soon you will fall in love on a blind date, travel to Zanzibar, and have twins, then one of two things must be true (Steiner, 1989):

- The fortune-teller can actually sort out the infinite number of interactions among people, animals, events, objects, and circumstances that could affect your life and can know for sure the outcome. Moreover, this fortune-teller is able to alter all the known laws of physics and defy the hundreds of studies showing that no one, under proper procedures for validating psychic predictions, has been able to predict the future for any given individual.

OR

- The fortune-teller is faking it.

A critical thinker would prefer the second alternative because it requires fewer assumptions and has the most supporting evidence.

Tolerate Uncertainty. Ultimately, learning to think critically teaches us one of the hardest lessons of life: how to live with uncertainty. Sometimes there is little or no evidence available to examine. Sometimes the evidence permits only tentative conclusions. Sometimes the evidence seems strong enough to permit conclusions . . . until, exasperatingly, new evidence throws our beliefs into disarray. Critical thinkers are willing to accept this state of uncertainty. They are not afraid to say, "I don't know" or "I'm not sure." This admission is not an evasion but a spur to further creative inquiry. Critical thinkers know that the more important the question, the less likely it is to have a single simple answer.

The need to accept a certain amount of uncertainty does not mean that we must abandon all beliefs and convictions. That would be impossible, in any case: We all need values and principles to guide our actions. As Vincent Ruggiero (1988) wrote, "It is not the embracing of an idea that causes problems—it is the refusal to relax that embrace when good sense dictates doing so. It is enough to form convictions with care and carry them lightly, being willing to reconsider them whenever new evidence calls them into question."

Critical thinking cannot provide answers to all of life's quandaries. Some questions, such as whether there is a God and what the nature of God might be, are ultimately matters of faith. Moreover, critical thinking is a process, not a once-and-for-all accomplishment. No one ever becomes a perfect critical thinker, entirely unaffected by emotional reasoning and wishful thinking. We are all less open-minded than we

think; it is always easier to poke holes in another person's argument than to critically examine our own position. As philosopher Richard W. Paul (1984) observed, critical thinking is really "fair-mindedness brought into the heart of everyday life."

As you read this book, keep in mind the eight guidelines we have described, which are summarized in Review 1.1. Practice in critical thinking really can help students bulk up their "thinking muscles" and understand psychological concepts better. That is why we have given you many opportunities to apply these guidelines to psychological theories and to the personal and social issues that affect us all. Starting with the next chapter, the "Close-up on Research" feature will highlight some of the guidelines that you should keep in mind when reading about a particular study. From time to time, questions in the margin, accompanied by a light bulb symbol, will draw your attention to a discussion in which one of the guidelines is especially relevant. In Quick Quizzes, the light bulb will identify questions that give you practice in applying the guidelines yourself. The light bulb also appears with photographs and illustrations that raise critical-thinking issues and that provide another chance to practice applying the guidelines. However, critical thinking is important throughout every chapter, not just where the light bulb appears.

REVIEW 1.1

Guidelines to Thinking Critically About Psychological Issues

Guideline	Example
Ask questions; be willing to wonder	"Can I recall events from my childhood accurately?"
Define your terms	"By 'childhood' I mean ages 3 to 12; by 'events' I mean things that happened to me personally, like a trip to the zoo or a stay in the hospital; by 'accurately' I mean the event basically happened the way I think it did."
Examine the evidence	"I *feel* I recall my fifth birthday party perfectly, but studies show that people often reconstruct past events inaccurately."
Analyze assumptions and biases	"I've always assumed that memory is like a tape recorder—perfectly accurate for every moment of my life—but maybe this is just a bias, because it's so reassuring."
Avoid emotional reasoning	"I really *want* to believe this memory is true, but that doesn't mean it *is*."
Don't oversimplify	"Some of my childhood memories could be accurate, others mistaken, and some partly right and partly wrong."
Consider other interpretations	"Some 'memories' could be based on what my parents told me later, not on my own recall."
Tolerate uncertainty	"I may never know for sure whether some of my childhood memories are real or accurate."

NOTE: You will be reading a lot more about the reliability of memory in Chapter 10.

QUICK quiz

Amelia and Harold are arguing about the death penalty. "Look, I just feel strongly that it's barbaric, ineffective, and wrong," says Harold. "You're nuts," says Amelia, "I believe in an eye for an eye, and besides, I'm absolutely sure it's a deterrent to further crime." Which lapses of critical thinking might Amelia and Harold be committing?

Answers:

Here are some problems in their style of argument; feel free to think of others. (1) They are reasoning emotionally ("I feel strongly about this, so I'm right and you're wrong"). (2) They do not cite evidence that supports or contradicts their arguments. What do studies show about the link between the death penalty and crime? Is the death penalty applied fairly to rich and poor, men and women, blacks and whites? How often are innocent people executed? (3) They have not examined the assumptions and biases they bring to the discussion. (4) They may not be clearly defining the problem they are arguing about. What is the purpose of the death penalty, for example? Is it to deter criminals, to satisfy the public desire for revenge, or to keep criminals from being paroled and returned to the streets?

WHAT'S**AHEAD**

- What is the lesson of phrenology for modern psychology?
- How old is the science of psychology?
- Was Sigmund Freud the founder of scientific psychology?

Psychology's Past: From the Armchair to the Laboratory

Now that you know what psychology is and what it isn't, and why studying it requires critical thinking, let us see how psychology developed into a modern science.

Until the nineteenth century, psychology was not a formal discipline. Of course, most of the great thinkers of history, from Aristotle to Zoroaster, raised questions that today would be called psychological. They wanted to know how people take in information through their senses, use information to solve problems, and become motivated to act in brave or villainous ways. They wondered about the elusive nature of emotion, and whether it controls us or is something we can control. Like today's psychologists, they wanted to *describe*, *predict*, *understand*, and *modify* behavior in order to add to human knowledge and increase human happiness. But unlike modern psychologists, scholars of the past did not rely heavily on empirical evidence. Often their observations were based simply on anecdotes or descriptions of individual cases.

This does not mean that the forerunners of modern psychology were always wrong. On the contrary, they often had insights and made observations that were verified by later work. Hippocrates (c. 460 B.C.–c. 377 B.C.), the Greek physician known as the founder of modern medicine, observed patients with head injuries and inferred that the brain must be the ultimate source of "our pleasures, joys, laughter, and jests as well as our sorrows, pains, griefs, and tears." And so it is. In the first century A.D., the Stoic philosophers observed that people do not become angry or sad or anxious because of actual events but because of their explanations of those events. And so they do. In the seventeenth century, the English philosopher John Locke (1643–1704) argued that the mind works by associating ideas arising from experience, and this notion continues to influence many psychologists today.

phrenology The now discredited theory that different brain areas account for specific character and personality traits, which can be "read" from bumps on the skull.

But without empirical methods, the forerunners of psychology also committed terrible blunders. A good example comes from the early 1800s, when the theory of **phrenology** (Greek for "study of the mind") became wildly popular in Europe and America. Inspired by the writings and lectures of Austrian physician Joseph Gall

(1758–1828), phrenologists argued that different brain areas accounted for specific character and personality traits, such as "stinginess" and "religiosity." Moreover, they said, such traits could be "read" from bumps on the skull. Thieves, for example, supposedly had large bumps above the ears. When phrenologists examined people with "stealing bumps" who were *not* thieves, they explained away this counterevidence by saying that other bumps on the skull represented positive traits that must be holding the person's thieving impulses in check.

In the United States, all sorts of people eagerly sought the services of phrenologists. Parents used them to make decisions about child rearing; schools used them to decide which teachers to hire; young people used them when choosing a career or a mate; and businesses used them to find out which employees were likely to be loyal and honest (Benjamin, 1998). Some phrenologists offered classes or self-study programs for people who wanted to overcome their deficiencies—the forerunners of today's many self-improvement programs and seminars. Enthusiasm for phrenology did not disappear until well into the twentieth century, even though phrenology was a classic pseudoscience—sheer nonsense.

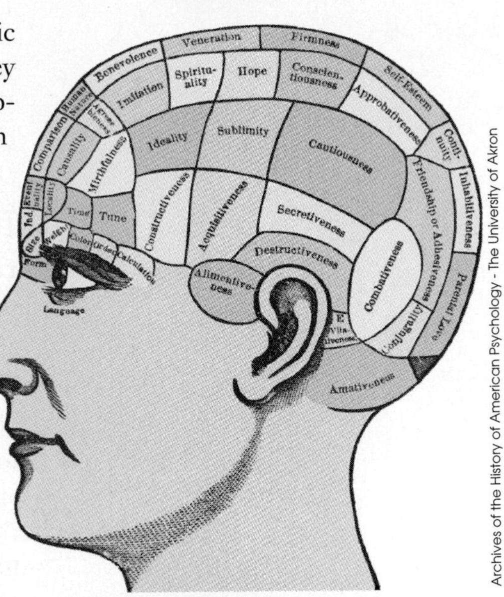

Archives of the History of American Psychology - The University of Akron

On this nineteenth-century phrenology "map," notice the tiny space allocated to self-esteem and the large one devoted to cautiousness!

The Birth of Modern Psychology

At about the time that phrenology was peaking in popularity, several pioneering men and women in Europe and America were starting to study psychological issues using scientific methods. In 1879, the first psychological laboratory was officially established in Leipzig, Germany, by Wilhelm Wundt [VIL-helm Voont]. Wundt (1832–1920), who was trained in medicine and philosophy, wrote many volumes on psychology, physiology, natural history, ethics, and logic. But he is especially revered by psychologists because he was the first person to announce (in 1873) that he intended to make psychology a science and because his laboratory was the first to have its results published in a scholarly journal. Although it started out as just a few rooms in an old building, the Leipzig laboratory soon became the place to go for anyone who wanted to become a psychologist. Many of America's first psychologists got their training there.

Researchers in Wundt's laboratory did not study the entire gamut of topics that modern psychologists do. Most concentrated on sensation, perception, reaction times, imagery, and attention, and avoided learning, personality, and abnormal behavior. One of Wundt's favorite research methods was to train volunteers to carefully observe, analyze, and describe their own sensations, mental images, and emotional reactions. This was not as easy as it sounds. Wundt's volunteers had to make 10,000 practice observations before they were allowed to participate in an actual study. Once trained, they might take as long as 20 minutes to report their inner experiences during a 1.5-second experiment. The goal was to break behavior down into its most basic elements, much as a chemist might break water down into hydrogen plus oxygen.

Wilhelm Wundt (1832–1920), center, with co-workers.

GET INVOLVED!

➤LOOKING INWARD

How reliable is introspection as a method for arriving at generalizations about human experience? Find out for yourself by asking some friends what they experience mentally when they think of a chair. Tell them to be specific about color, shape, size, style, orientation, and so on. Which aspects of the experience do they agree on, and which do they report differently?

Although Wundt hoped that this introspective method would produce reliable, verifiable results, most psychologists eventually rejected it as too subjective. But Wundt is still usually credited with formally initiating the movement to make psychology a science.

Three Early Psychologies

During the early decades of psychology's existence as a formal discipline, three schools of psychological thought became popular. One soon faded, another disappeared as a separate school but continued to influence the field, and the third remains alive today, despite passionate debate about whether it belongs in scientific psychology at all.

Structuralism. In America, Wundt's ideas were popularized in somewhat modified form by one of his students, E. B. Titchener (1867–1927), who gave Wundt's approach the name **structuralism.** Like Wundt, structuralists hoped to analyze sensations, images, and feelings into basic elements. For example, a person might be asked to listen to a metronome clicking and to report exactly what he or she heard. Most people said they perceived a pattern (such as CLICK click click CLICK click click), even though the clicks of a metronome are actually all the same. Or a person might be asked to break down all the different components of taste when biting into an orange (sweet, tart, wet, etc.).

Despite an intensive program of research, however, structuralism soon went the way of the dinosaur. After you have discovered the building blocks of a particular sensation or image and how they link up, then what? Years after structuralism's demise, Wolfgang Köhler (1959) recalled how he and his colleagues had responded to it as students: "What had disturbed us was . . . the implication that human life, apparently so colorful and so intensely dynamic, is actually a frightful bore."

The structuralists' reliance on introspection by volunteers also got them into trouble. Despite their training, introspectors often produced conflicting reports. When asked what image came to mind when they heard the word *triangle*, most respondents said they imagined a visual image of a form with three sides and three corners, but one person might report a flashing red form with equal angles, whereas another reported a revolving colorless form with one angle larger than the other two. Some people even claimed they could think about a triangle without forming any visual image at all (Boring, 1953). It was hard, therefore, to know what mental attributes of a triangle were basic.

William James (1842–1910).

structuralism An early psychological approach that emphasized the analysis of immediate experience into basic elements.

functionalism An early psychological approach that emphasized the function or purpose of behavior and consciousness.

Functionalism. Another early approach to scientific psychology, called **functionalism**, emphasized the function or purpose of behavior, as opposed to its analysis and description. One of functionalism's leaders was William James (1842–1910), an American philosopher, physician, and psychologist who argued that searching for building blocks of experience, as Wundt and Titchener tried to do, was a waste of time. The brain and the mind are constantly changing, he noted. Permanent ideas—of triangles or anything else—do not appear periodically before the "footlights of consciousness." Attempting to grasp the nature of the mind through introspection, wrote James (1890/1950), is "like seizing a spinning top to catch its motion, or trying to turn up the gas quickly enough to see how the darkness looks."

Where the structuralists asked *what* happens when an organism does something, the functionalists asked *how* and *why*. They were inspired in part by the evolutionary theories of British naturalist Charles Darwin (1809–1882). Darwin had argued that a biologist's job is not merely to describe, say, the puffed-out chest of a pigeon or the drab markings of a lizard, but also to figure out how these attributes enhance survival. Do they help the animal attract a mate or hide from its enemies? Similarly, the func-

tionalists wanted to know how specific behaviors and mental processes help a person or animal adapt to the environment, so they looked for underlying causes and practical consequences of these behaviors and processes. Unlike the structuralists, they felt free to pick and choose among many methods, and they broadened the field of psychology to include the study of children, animals, religious experiences, and what James called the "stream of consciousness"—a term still used because it so beautifully describes the way thoughts flow like a river, tumbling over each other in waves, sometimes placid, sometimes turbulent.

As a school of psychology, functionalism, like structuralism, was short-lived. It lacked the kind of precise theory or program of research that wins recruits, and it endorsed the study of consciousness just as that concept was about to fall out of favor. Yet the functionalists' emphasis on the causes and consequences of behavior was to set the course of psychological science.

Psychoanalysis. The nineteenth century also saw the development of various psychological therapies. In the United States, for example, the wildly popular "Mind Cure" movement lasted from 1830 to 1900; "mind cures" were efforts to correct the "false ideas" that were said to make people anxious, depressed, and unhappy (Caplan, 1998). The Mind Cure movement was the forerunner of modern cognitive therapies (see Chapter 17).

However, the form of therapy that would have the greatest impact worldwide for much of the twentieth century had its roots in Vienna, Austria. While researchers in Europe and America were working in their laboratories, struggling to establish psychology as a science, Sigmund Freud (1856–1939), an obscure neurologist, was in his office, listening to his patients' reports of depression, nervousness, and obsessive habits. Freud became convinced that many of his patients' symptoms had mental, not physical, causes. Their distress, he concluded, was due to conflicts and emotional traumas that had occurred in early childhood and that were too threatening to be remembered consciously, such as forbidden sexual feelings for a parent.

Sigmund Freud (1856–1939).

Freud argued that conscious awareness is merely the tip of a mental iceberg. Beneath the visible tip, he said, lies the unconscious part of the mind, containing unrevealed wishes, passions, guilty secrets, unspeakable yearnings, and conflicts between desire and duty. Many of these urges and thoughts are sexual or aggressive in nature. We are not aware of them as we go blithely about our daily business, yet they make themselves known—in dreams, slips of the tongue, apparent accidents, and even jokes. Freud (1905a) wrote, "No mortal can keep a secret. If the lips are silent, he chatters with his fingertips; betrayal oozes out of him at every pore."

Freud's ideas were not an overnight sensation; his first book, *The Interpretation of Dreams* (1900/1953), managed to sell only 600 copies in the eight years following its publication. Eventually, however, his ideas evolved into a broad theory of personality and a method of psychotherapy, both of which became known as **psychoanalysis.** Most Freudian concepts were, and still are, rejected by most empirically oriented psychologists, as we will see. But they had a profound influence on the philosophy, literature, and art of the twentieth century, and Freud's name is now as much a household word as Einstein's.

From these early beginnings in philosophy, natural science, and medicine, psychology has grown into a complex discipline encompassing many specialties, perspectives, and methods. Today the field is like a large, sprawling family. The members of this family share common great-grandparents; many of the cousins have formed alliances, but some are quarreling, and a few are barely speaking to one another.

psychoanalysis A theory of personality and a method of psychotherapy, originally formulated by Sigmund Freud, that emphasizes unconscious motives and conflicts.

QUICK quiz

Make sure psychology's past is still present in your memory by choosing the correct response from each pair of terms in parentheses.

1. Psychology has been a science for more than (2,000/125) years.
2. The forerunners of modern psychology depended heavily on (casual observation/empirical methods).
3. Credit for founding modern psychology is generally given to (William James/Wilhelm Wundt).
4. Early psychologists who emphasized how behavior helps an organism adapt to its environment were known as (structuralists/functionalists).
5. The idea that emotional problems spring from unconscious conflicts originated with (the Mind Cure movement/psychoanalysis).

Answers:

1. 125 **2.** casual observation **3.** Wilhelm Wundt **4.** functionalists **5.** psychoanalysis

WHAT'S**AHEAD**

- What are the five major perspectives in psychology?
- Why is the psychodynamic perspective the "thumb on the hand of psychology"?
- How have humanism and feminism influenced psychology?

Psychology's Present: Behavior, Body, Mind, and Culture

If you had a noisy, rude, surly neighbor, and you asked a group of psychologists to explain why this guy was such a miserable person, they might give you different answers. Depending on their theoretical perspective, they might cite your neighbor's biological makeup, his belligerent attitude toward the world, the way he was brought up, an environment that encourages his nasty temper, or the influence of his unconscious motives. Modern psychologists tend to examine human behavior through several lenses.

The Major Psychological Perspectives

The five lenses that predominate in psychology today are the *biological, learning, cognitive, sociocultural,* and *psychodynamic* perspectives. These approaches reflect different questions about human behavior, different assumptions about how the mind works, and, most important, different ways of explaining why people do what they do.

1 The **biological perspective** focuses on how bodily events affect behavior, feelings, and thoughts. Electrical impulses shoot along the intricate pathways of the nervous system. Hormones course through the bloodstream, telling internal organs to slow down or speed up. Chemical substances flow across the tiny gaps that separate one microscopic brain cell from another. Biological psychologists study how these physical events interact with events in the external environment to produce perceptions, memories, and behavior.

Researchers in this perspective study how biology affects learning and performance, perceptions of reality, the experience of emotion, and vulnerability to emotional disorder. They study how the mind and body interact in illness and health. They investigate the contributions of genes and other biological factors in the devel-

biological perspective A psychological approach that emphasizes bodily events and changes associated with actions, feelings, and thoughts.

opment of abilities and personality traits. And a popular specialty, **evolutionary psychology,** follows in the footsteps of functionalism by focusing on how genetically influenced behavior that was functional or adaptive during our evolutionary past may be reflected in many of our present behaviors, mental processes, and traits (see Chapter 3). The message of the biological approach is that we cannot really know ourselves if we do not know our bodies.

evolutionary psychology A field of psychology emphasizing evolutionary mechanisms that may help explain human commonalities in cognition, development, emotion, social practices, and other areas of behavior.

learning perspective A psychological approach that emphasizes how the environment and experience affect a person's or animal's actions; it includes *behaviorism* and *social-cognitive learning theories.*

cognitive perspective A psychological approach that emphasizes mental processes in perception, memory, language, problem solving, and other areas of behavior.

sociocultural perspective A psychological approach that emphasizes social and cultural influences on behavior.

2 The **learning perspective** is concerned with how the environment and experience affect a person's (or a nonhuman animal's) actions. Within this perspective, *behaviorists* focus on the environmental rewards and punishers that maintain or discourage specific behaviors. Behaviorists do not invoke the mind or mental states to explain behavior. They prefer to stick to what they can observe and measure directly: acts and events taking place in the environment. For example, do you have trouble sticking to a schedule? A behaviorist would analyze the environmental distractions that could help account for this common problem. Behaviorism was the dominant school of scientific psychology in North America for nearly half a century, through the 1960s.

Social-cognitive learning theorists, on the other hand, combine elements of behaviorism with research on thoughts, values, expectations, and intentions. They believe that people learn not only by adapting their behavior to the environment but also by imitating others and by thinking about the events happening around them.

As we will see in other chapters, the learning perspective has many practical applications. Historically, the behaviorists' insistence on precision and objectivity has done much to advance psychology as a science, and learning research in general has given psychology some of its most reliable findings.

3 The **cognitive perspective** emphasizes what goes on in people's heads—how people reason, remember, understand language, solve problems, explain experiences, acquire moral standards, and form beliefs. (The word *cognitive* comes from the Latin for "to know.") A "cognitive revolution" in psychology during the 1970s brought this perspective to the forefront. One of its most important contributions has been to show how people's thoughts and explanations affect their actions, feelings, and choices. Using clever methods to infer mental processes from observable behavior, cognitive researchers have been able to study phenomena that were once only the stuff of speculation, such as emotions, motivations, and insight. They are designing computer programs that model how humans perform complex tasks, discovering what goes on in the mind of an infant, and identifying types of intelligence not measured by conventional IQ tests. The cognitive approach is now one of the strongest forces in psychology, and it has inspired an explosion of research on the intricate workings of the mind.

4 The **sociocultural perspective** focuses on social and cultural forces outside the individual, forces that shape every aspect of behavior, from how we kiss to what and where we eat. Most of us underestimate the impact of other people, the social context, and cultural rules on nearly everything we do. We are like fish that are unaware they live in water, so obvious is water in their lives. Sociocultural psychologists study the water—the social and cultural environment that people "swim" in every day.

Within this perspective, *social psychologists* focus on social rules and roles, how groups affect attitudes and behavior, why people obey authority, and how each of us is affected by other people—spouses, lovers, friends, bosses, parents, and strangers. *Cultural psychologists* examine how cultural rules and values—both explicit and

THINKING CRITICALLY

ASK QUESTIONS: BE WILLING TO WONDER

What makes us who we are? Psychologists often approach this question differently, depending on whether they take a biological, learning, cognitive, sociocultural, or psychodynamic perspective. Today, however, many researchers are asking a better question: How do the many kinds of influences on us combine and interact to make us who we are?

unspoken—affect people's development, behavior, and feelings. They might study how culture influences people's willingness to help a stranger in distress, or how it influences what people do when they are angry. Because human beings are social animals who are profoundly affected by their different cultural worlds, the sociocultural perspective has made psychology a more representative and rigorous discipline.

5 The **psychodynamic perspective** deals with unconscious dynamics within the individual, such as inner forces, conflicts, or instinctual energy. It has its origins in Freud's theory of psychoanalysis, but many other psychodynamic theories now exist. Psychodynamic psychologists try to dig below the surface of a person's behavior to get to its unconscious roots; they think of themselves as archeologists of the mind.

Psychodynamic psychology is the thumb on the hand of psychology—connected to the other fingers, but also set apart from them because it differs radically from the other approaches in its language, methods, and standards of acceptable evidence. Although some psychological scientists are doing empirical studies of psychodynamic concepts, many others believe that psychodynamic approaches belong in philosophy or literature rather than in academic psychology. You are unlikely to find psychoanalysis mentioned much in mainstream journals of psychological science (Robins, Gosling, & Craik, 1999). Outside of empirical psychology, however, many psychotherapists, novelists, and laypeople are attracted to the psychodynamic emphasis on such grand psychological issues as relations between the sexes, the power of sexuality, and the universal fear of death. Later in this book, we will candidly discuss the many controversies surrounding psychodynamic ideas.

Review 1.2 summarizes these five perspectives and shows how they might be applied to a concrete issue, the problem of violence. See if you can apply these perspectives to another issue of your own choosing.

Two Influential Movements in Psychology

Throughout psychology's history, various movements and intellectual trends have emerged that do not fit neatly into any of the major perspectives. In the 1960s, **humanist psychologists** rejected the two dominant psychological approaches of the time, psychoanalysis and behaviorism. Humanists regarded psychoanalysis, with its emphasis on dangerous sexual and aggressive impulses, as too pessimistic a view of human nature, one that overlooked human resilience and the capacity for joy. And humanists regarded behaviorism, with its emphasis on observable acts, as too mechanistic and "mindless" a view of human nature, one that ignored what really matters to most people—their uniquely human hopes and aspirations. In the humanists' view, human behavior is not completely determined by either unconscious conflicts or the environment. People are capable of free will and therefore have the ability to make more of themselves than either psychoanalysts or behaviorists would predict. The goal of humanist psychology was, and still is, to help people express themselves creatively and achieve their full potential.

Although humanism is no longer a dominant movement in psychology, it has had considerable influence both inside and outside the field. Many psychologists across all perspectives embrace some humanist ideas, although most regard humanism as a philosophy of life rather than a systematic approach to psychology. Further, many topics raised by the humanists, such as creativity, joy, humor, and courage, are now being

psychodynamic perspective A psychological approach that emphasizes unconscious dynamics within the individual, such as inner forces, conflicts, or the movement of instinctual energy.

humanist psychology A psychological approach that emphasizes free will, personal growth, resilience, and the achievement of human potential.

REVIEW 1.2
Five Major Psychological Perspectives

Perspective	Major Topics of Study	Sample Finding on Violence
Biological	The nervous system, hormones, brain chemistry, heredity, evolutionary influences	Brain damage caused by birth complications or child abuse might incline some people toward violence.
Learning	Environment and experience	
Behavioral	Environmental determinants of observable behavior	Violence increases when it pays off.
Social-Cognitive	Environmental influences, observation and imitation, beliefs and values	Violent role models can influence some children to behave aggressively.
Cognitive	Thinking, memory, language, problem solving, perceptions	Violent people are often quick to perceive provocation and insult.
Sociocultural	Social and cultural contexts	
Social Psychology	Social rules and roles, groups, relationships	People are often more aggressive in a crowd than they would be on their own.
Cultural Psychology	Cultural norms, values, and expectations	Cultures based on herding rather than agriculture tend to train boys to be aggressive.
Psychodynamic	Unconscious thoughts, desires, and conflicts	A man who murders prostitutes may have unconscious conflicts about his mother and about sexuality.

studied by scientific psychologists from many fields. For example, a contemporary research specialty known as *positive psychology* focuses on the qualities that enable people to be happy, optimistic, and resilient in times of stress (Gable & Haidt, 2005; Seligman & Csikszentmihalyi, 2000). And humanism has had a direct influence on psychotherapy and the human potential and self-help movements.

Another important movement, which emerged in the early 1970s, was **feminist psychology**. As women began to enter psychology in greater numbers, they documented evidence of a pervasive bias in the research methods used and in the very questions that researchers had been asking (Bem, 1993; Crawford & Marecek, 1989). They noted that many studies used only men as subjects—and usually only young, white, middle-class men, at that—and they showed why it was often inappropriate to generalize to everyone else from such a narrow research base. They spurred the growth of research on topics that had long been ignored in psychology, including menstruation, motherhood, the dynamics of power and sexuality in relationships, definitions of masculinity and femininity, gender roles, and sexist attitudes. They critically examined the male bias in psychotherapy, starting with Freud's own case studies. And they analyzed

feminist psychology A psychological approach that analyzes the influence of social inequities on gender relations and on the behavior of the two sexes.

the social consequences of psychological findings, showing how research has often been used to justify the lower status of women and other disadvantaged groups.

Feminist psychology greatly advanced efforts to make psychology the study of all human beings, and other groups have made similar contributions. In 1976, black psychologist Robert Guthrie, in *Even the Rat Was White*, wrote a searing and influential indictment of racism in psychological research. Since the 1970s, African-American, Latino, and Asian psychologists, gay and lesbian psychologists, and disabled psychologists have hugely expanded the theoretical and empirical vistas of psychology, as we will see throughout this book.

QUICK quiz

Anxiety is a common problem. To test your understanding of the major perspectives in psychology, match each possible explanation of anxiety on the left with a perspective on the right.

1. Anxious people often think about the future in distorted ways.
2. Anxiety is due to forbidden, unconscious desires.
3. Anxiety symptoms often bring hidden rewards, such as being excused from exams.
4. Excessive anxiety can be caused by a chemical imbalance.
5. A national emphasis on competition and success promotes anxiety about failure.

a. learning
b. psychodynamic
c. sociocultural
d. biological
e. cognitive

Answers:

1.e 2.b 3.a 4.d 5.c

WHAT'S AHEAD

- If someone is a psychologist, why can't you assume that the person is a therapist?
- If you decided to call yourself a psychotherapist, would you be breaking the law?
- What's the difference between a clinical psychologist and a psychiatrist?

What Psychologists Do

Now you know the main viewpoints that guide psychologists in their work. But what do psychologists actually do with their time between breakfast and dinner?

To most people, the word *psychologist* conjures up an image of a therapist listening intently while a client, perhaps stretched out on a couch, pours forth his or her troubles. Many psychologists do in fact fit this image (though chairs are more common than couches these days). Many others, however, do not. The professional activities of psychologists generally fall into three broad categories: (1) teaching and doing research in colleges and universities; (2) providing health or mental health services, often referred to as *psychological practice*; and (3) conducting research or applying its findings in nonacademic settings, such as business, sports, government, law, and the military (see Review 1.3). Some psychologists move flexibly across these areas. A researcher might also provide counseling services in a mental-health setting, such as a clinic or a hospital; a university professor might teach, do research, and serve as a consultant in legal cases.

REVIEW 1.3

What is a Psychologist?

Not all psychologists do clinical work. Many do research, teach, work in business, or consult. The professional activities of psychologists with doctorates fall into three general categories.

Academic/Research Psychologists	Clinical Psychologists	Psychologists in Industry, Law, or Other Settings
Specialize in areas of pure or applied research, such as:	**Do psychotherapy and sometimes research; may work in any of these settings:**	**Do research or serve as consultants to institutions on, for example:**
Human development	Private practice	Sports
Psychometrics (testing)	Mental-health clinics	Consumer issues
Health	General hospitals	Advertising
Education	Mental hospitals	Organizational problems
Industrial/organizational psychology	Research laboratories	Environmental issues
Physiological psychology	Colleges and universities	Public policy
Sensation and perception		Opinion polls
Design and use of technology		Military training
		Animal behavior
		Legal issues

Psychological Research

Most psychologists who do research have doctoral degrees (Ph.D.s or Ed.D.s, doctorates in education). Some, seeking knowledge for its own sake, work in **basic psychology**, doing "pure" research. Others, concerned with the practical uses of knowledge, work in **applied psychology**. The two approaches are complementary: Applied psychology has direct relevance to human problems, but without basic psychology, there would be little knowledge to apply. A psychologist doing basic research might ask, "How does peer pressure influence people's attitudes and behavior?" An applied psychologist might ask, "How can knowledge about peer pressure be used to reduce binge drinking by college students?"

basic psychology The study of psychological issues in order to seek knowledge for its own sake rather than for its practical application.

applied psychology The study of psychological issues that have direct practical significance; also, the application of psychological findings.

Research psychology is the aspect of psychology least recognized and understood by the public. Ludy Benjamin (2003), bemoaning the fact that psychology has never had a United States postal stamp commemorating the discipline or its founders (unlike dozens of other fields, including poultry farming and truck driving), notes that the public "has minimal understanding of psychology as a science and even less appreciation for what psychological scientists do" or how psychological research contributes to human welfare.

We hope that by the time you finish this book, you will have a greater appreciation for what research psychologists do and for their contributions to human welfare. Here are just a few of the major nonclinical specialties in psychology:

- *Experimental psychologists* conduct laboratory studies of learning, motivation, emotion, sensation and perception, physiology, and cognition. Do not be misled by the term *experimental*, though; other psychologists also do experiments.

"Well, you don't look like an experimental psychologist to me."

- *Educational psychologists* study psychological principles that explain learning and search for ways to improve educational systems. Their interests range from the application of findings on memory and thinking to the use of rewards to encourage achievement.
- *Developmental psychologists* study how people change and grow over time—physically, mentally, and socially. In the past, their focus was mainly on childhood, but many now study adolescence, young adulthood, the middle years, or old age.
- *Industrial/organizational psychologists* study behavior in the workplace. They are concerned with group decision making, employee morale, work motivation, productivity, job stress, personnel selection, marketing strategies, equipment design, and many other issues.
- *Psychometric psychologists* design and evaluate tests of mental abilities, aptitudes, interests, and personality. Nearly all of us have had firsthand experience with one or more of these tests in school, at work, or in the military.

Psychological Practice

Psychological practitioners, whose goal is to understand and improve people's physical and mental health, work in mental hospitals, general hospitals, clinics, schools, counseling centers, and private practice. Since the late 1970s, the proportion of psychologists who are practitioners has steadily increased; practitioners now account for over two-thirds of new psychology doctorates and members of the American Psychological Association (APA), psychology's largest professional organization.

Some practitioners are *counseling psychologists*, who generally help people deal with problems of everyday life, such as test anxiety, family conflicts, or low job motivation. Others are *school psychologists*, who work with parents, teachers, and students to enhance students' performance and resolve emotional difficulties. The majority, however, are *clinical psychologists*, who diagnose, treat, and study mental or emotional problems. Clinical psychologists are trained to do psychotherapy with severely disturbed people, as well as with those who are simply troubled or unhappy or who want to learn to handle their problems better.

Some psychologists are researchers, others are practitioners, and some are both. On the left, psychological scientist Linda Bartoshuk uses technology to study how the anatomy of the tongue influences the way we experience different tastes. On the right, a clinical psychologist helps a couple in therapy.

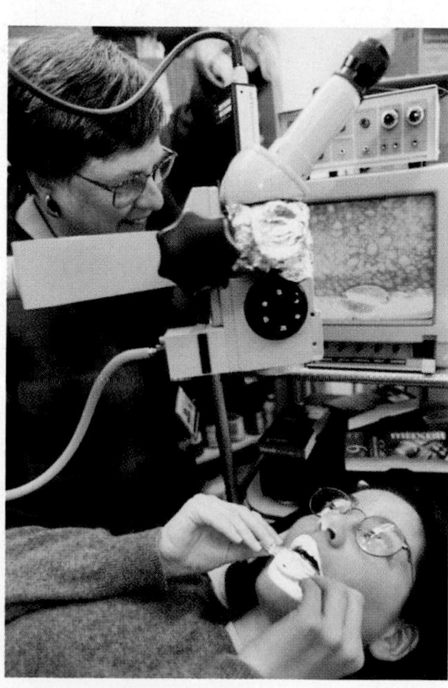

In almost all states, a license to practice clinical psychology requires a doctorate. Most clinical psychologists have a Ph.D., some have an Ed.D., and a smaller number have a Psy.D. (doctorate in psychology, pronounced "sy-dee"), a degree that began to be awarded in the 1970s. Clinical psychologists typically do four or five years of graduate work in psychology, plus at least a year's internship under the direction of a practicing psychologist. Clinical programs leading to a Ph.D. or Ed.D. are usually designed to prepare a person both as a scientist and as a clinical practitioner; they require completion of a *dissertation*, a major scholarly project (usually involving research) that contributes to knowledge in the field. Programs leading to a Psy.D. focus on professional practice and do not usually require a dissertation, although they typically require the student to complete a major study, theoretical paper, or literature review. Psy.D. programs now enroll about a quarter of all doctoral candidates in psychology (Norcross, Kohout, & Wicherski, 2005).

People often confuse *clinical psychologist* with three other terms: *psychotherapist*, *psychoanalyst*, and *psychiatrist*. But these terms mean different things:

- A *psychotherapist* is simply anyone who does any kind of psychotherapy. The term is not legally regulated; in fact, in most states, anyone can say that he or she is a "therapist" of one sort or another without having any training at all.
- A *psychoanalyst* is a person who practices one particular form of therapy, psychoanalysis. To call yourself a psychoanalyst, you must get specialized training at a psychoanalytic institute and undergo extensive psychoanalysis yourself. At one time, admission to a psychoanalytic institute required an M.D. or a Ph.D., but this is no longer true; clinical social workers with master's degrees, and even interested laypeople, are often now admitted.
- A *psychiatrist* is a medical doctor (M.D.) who has done a three-year residency in psychiatry to learn how to diagnose and treat mental disorders under the supervision of more experienced physicians. Like some clinical psychologists, some psychiatrists do research on mental problems instead of, or in addition to, working with patients. In private practice, psychiatrists may treat any kind of emotional disorder; in hospitals, they treat the most severe disorders, such as major depression and schizophrenia. Although psychiatrists and clinical psychologists often do similar work, psychiatrists, because of their medical training, are more likely to focus on possible biological causes of mental disorders and often treat these problems with medication. They can write prescriptions and, at present, most clinical psychologists cannot. (In the United States, New Mexico and Louisiana have given prescription privileges to psychologists who receive special training.) Psychiatrists, however, are often uneducated in current psychological theories and methods and unfamiliar with current research in psychology (Luhrmann, 2000).

Other mental-health professionals include licensed clinical social workers (LCSWs) and marriage, family, and child counselors (MFCCs). These professionals ordinarily treat general problems in adjustment and family conflicts rather than severe mental

GET INVOLVED!

➤THE MANY APPLICATIONS OF PSYCHOLOGY

To get an idea of just how broad a discipline psychology is, take any newspaper and circle the headlines of stories about which psychology might be able to offer insights. Don't skip the sports, business, and "people" sections! How many headlines did you mark?

disturbance, although their work may also bring them into contact with people who have serious problems—violent delinquents, people with drug addictions, sex offenders, individuals involved in domestic violence or child abuse. Licensing requirements vary from state to state but usually include a master's degree in psychology or social work and one or two years of supervised experience. (For a summary of the various types of psychotherapists and the training they receive, see Review 1.4.) As if this weren't complicated enough, there are thousands of counselors who specialize in treating all kinds of problems, from sexual abuse to alcoholism; there is, however, no uniform set of standards regulating their training. Some may have taken nothing more than a brief "certification" course.

Many research psychologists, and some practitioners, are worried about the increase in the number of counselors and psychotherapists who are unschooled in research methods and the empirical findings of psychology, and who use invalid therapy techniques (Beutler, 2000; Lilienfeld, Lynn, & Lohr, 2003). Critics trace this development in part to the rise of freestanding professional schools, which are unaffiliated with any university. Some of these schools offer a quality education, but others do not. Although the verbal Graduate Record Exam scores of applicants have been falling for several decades, acceptance rates in doctoral psychology programs have skyrocketed since the 1970s and 1980s—and the biggest rise has been in clinical programs, from the 4 to 6 percent range in the 1970s to 21 percent in 2003 (Norcross, Kohout, & Wicherski, 2005). In a review of the evidence on graduate training in clinical psychology, Donald Peterson (2003) found that the poorer-quality programs are turning out more and more ill-prepared graduates. "To deny an increased likelihood of incompetent practice by insufficiently talented, poorly trained psychologists," Peterson wrote, "defies all reason."

Because not all therapists are well educated about psychological findings, consumers should ask about a potential therapist's training and credentials.

Many practitioners, on the other hand, argue that psychotherapy is an art and that training in research methods is largely irrelevant to the work they do with clients. In Chapter 17, we will return to the important issue of the widening gap in training and attitudes between scientists and many therapists. In 1987, this gap contributed to the formation of the American Psychological Society (APS) (since renamed the Association for Psychological Science), an organization devoted to the needs and interests of psychology as a science.

REVIEW 1.4

Types of Psychotherapists

Just as not all psychologists are psychotherapists, not all psychotherapists are clinical psychologists. Here are the major terms used to refer to mental-health professionals:

Psychotherapist	A person who does psychotherapy; may have anything from no degree to an advanced professional degree; the term is unregulated.
Clinical psychologist	Diagnoses, treats, and/or studies mental and emotional problems, both mild and severe; has a Ph.D., an Ed.D., or a Psy.D.
Psychoanalyst	Practices psychoanalysis; has specific training in this approach after an advanced degree (usually, but not always, an M.D. or a Ph.D.); may treat any kind of emotional disorder or pathology.
Psychiatrist	Does work similar to that of a clinical psychologist but is likely to take a more biological approach; has a medical degree (M.D.) with a specialty in psychiatry.
Licensed clinical social worker (LCSW); marriage, family, and child counselor (MFCC)	Typically treats common individual and family problems but may also deal with more serious problems such as addiction or abuse. Licensing requirements vary, but generally has at least an M.A. in psychology or social work.

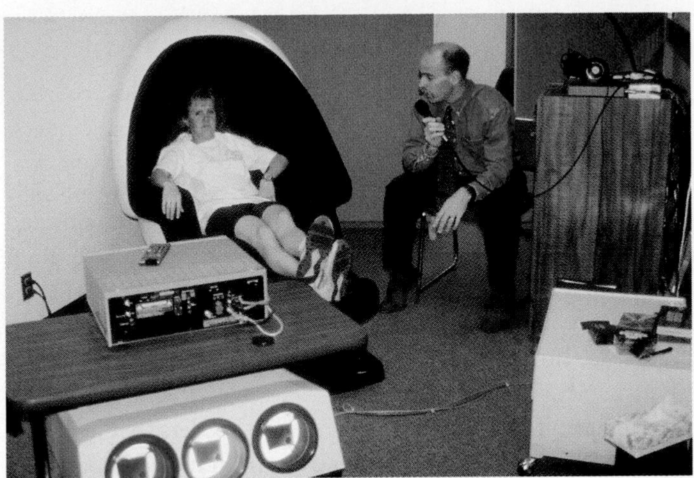

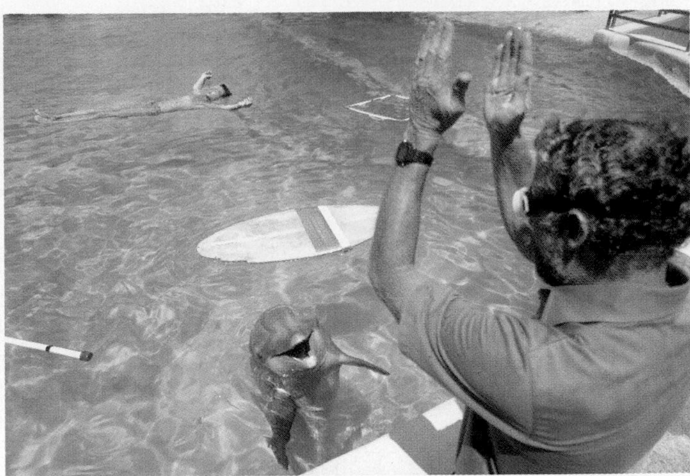

Psychologists work in all sorts of settings, from classrooms to courtrooms. On the left, sports psychologist Sean McCain helps an Olympic athlete relax and rehearse mentally what he would do physically during an actual athletic event. On the right, Louis Herman studies a dolphin's ability to understand an artificial language consisting of hand signals. In response to the gestural sequence "person" and "over," the dolphin will leap over the person in the pool.

Psychology in the Community

During the second half of the twentieth century, psychology expanded rapidly in terms of scholars, publications, and specialties, and today the field is experiencing a "knowledge explosion" (Adair & Vohra, 2003). The American Psychological Association now has 53 divisions. Some represent major fields such as developmental psychology or physiological psychology. Others represent specific research or professional interests, such as the psychology of women, the psychology of men, ethnic minority issues, sports, the arts, environmental concerns, gay and lesbian issues, peace, psychology and the law, and health.

As psychology has grown, psychologists have found ways to contribute to their communities in about as many fields as you can think of. They consult with companies to improve worker satisfaction and productivity. They establish programs to improve race relations and reduce ethnic tensions. They advise commissions on how pollution and noise affect mental health. They do rehabilitation training for people who are physically or mentally disabled. They educate judges and juries about eyewitness testimony. They assist the police in emergencies involving hostages or disturbed persons. They conduct public-opinion surveys. They run suicide-prevention hot lines. They advise zoos on the care and training of animals. They help coaches improve the athletic performance of their teams. And on and on. Is it any wonder that people are a little fuzzy about what a psychologist is?

QUICK quiz

Can you match the specialties on the left with their defining credentials and approaches on the right?

1. psychotherapist
2. psychiatrist
3. clinical psychologist
4. research psychologist
5. psychoanalyst

a. Trained in a therapeutic approach started by Freud.
b. Has a Ph.D., Psy.D., or Ed.D., and does research on, or psychotherapy for, mental-health problems.
c. May have any credential, or none.
d. Has an advanced degree (usually a Ph.D.) and does applied or basic research.
e. Has an M.D.; tends to take a medical approach to mental-health problems.

Answers:

1. c 2. e 3. b 4. d 5. a

BIOLOGY and Psychology

Beyond the Borders

The differences we have described among psychological perspectives and specialties have produced many passionate arguments. These differences are compounded by the fact that psychologists earn their livelihoods in different ways and are often trying to achieve different goals: knowledge for its own sake, practical knowledge, the application of knowledge in real-life settings, or the ability to help people in distress. Not all psychologists, however, feel they must swear allegiance to one approach or another.

Indeed, there is a growing trend in psychology to cross the borders that have traditionally divided one specialty from another. That trend has been fueled in part by a revolution in our understanding of biology's influence on behavior. Although in 1992 few neuroscience programs existed for graduate students being trained in psychology, by 2003 there were 53 such programs (Norcross, Kohout, & Wicherski, 2005). Neuropsychologists are now studying the workings of the brain and its influence on emotions and behavior. Cognitive psychologists are looking at the neurological aspects of thinking, decision making, and problem solving. Social psychologists are taking an interest in the brain and have even developed a new specialty called "social neuroscience." Clinical scientists are examining the separate and combined effects of medication and psychotherapy in the treatment of psychological disorders. Indeed, researchers who study almost any important phenomenon—aggression, anger, love, sexuality, child development, aging, mental illness, prejudice, war—often now do so by combining psychological findings and biological ones. For example, those who are concerned about the growing incidence of obesity throughout the world are looking at how genes, physiology, culture, and social influences such as advertising all contribute to weight and body shape. We will be covering much of the new biological research throughout this book, and, in most chapters, the heading "Biology and . . ." will alert you to discussions of some of the most exciting, cutting-edge findings that have resulted from these efforts.

The modern field of psychology is like a giant mosaic made up of many fragments, yielding a rich, multicolored, psychological portrait. Psychologists who study the human mind, body, and behavior may argue about which part of the portrait is most important, but they also have much in common with one another. Most biological psychologists understand the importance of culture, context, and environment on what people do; most social psychologists understand the contributions of genetics to behavior. All psychological scientists, whatever their specialty, believe in the importance of gathering empirical evidence instead of relying on hunches. Most avoid one-note explanations of behavior and either–or thinking.

And one thing will always unite psychologists: a fascination with the unending mysteries of human behavior and the human mind. If you too have wondered what makes people tick; if you love a mystery and want to know not only who did it but also why they did it; if you are willing to reconsider what you think you think . . . then you are in the right course. We invite you now to step into the world of psychology, the discipline that dares to explore the most complex topic on earth: *you*.

Taking Psychology with You

What Psychology Can Do for You—and What it Can't

If you intend to become a research psychologist or a mental-health professional, you have an obvious reason for taking a course in psychology. But psychology can contribute to your life in many ways, whether you plan to work in the field or not. Here are a few things psychology can do for you:

- **Make you a more informed person.** One purpose of education is to acquaint people with their cultural heritage and with human achievements in literature, the arts, and the sciences. Because psychology plays a large role in contemporary society, being a well-informed person requires knowing something about psychological methods and findings.
- **Satisfy your curiosity about human nature.** When the ancient Greek philosopher Socrates admonished his students to "know thyself," he was only telling them to do what most people want to do anyway. Psychology—along with the other social sciences, literature, history, and philosophy—can help you better understand yourself and others.
- **Help you increase your control over your life.** Psychology cannot solve all your problems, but it does offer techniques that may help you handle your emotions, improve your memory, and eliminate unwanted habits. It can also foster an attitude of objectivity that is useful for analyzing your behavior and your relationships with others.
- **Help you on the job.** Many people who get a bachelor's degree in psychology go on to study other fields. A background in psychology is useful for getting a job in a helping profession, for example, as a welfare caseworker or a rehabilitation counselor. Anyone who works as a nurse, doctor, religious adviser, police officer, or teacher can also put psychology to work on the job. So can waiters, flight attendants, bank tellers, salespeople, receptionists, and others whose jobs involve customer service. Finally, psychology can be useful to those whose jobs require them to predict people's behavior—labor negotiators, politicians, advertising copywriters, managers, product designers, buyers, market researchers, magicians. . . .
- **Give you insights into political and social issues.** Crime, drug abuse, discrimination, and war are not only social issues but also psychological ones. Psychological knowledge alone cannot solve the complex political, social, and ethical problems that plague every society, but it can help citizens make informed judgments about them. If you know how social and cultural practices affect rates of illegal drug use and abuse, this knowledge may affect your views about drug policies; and if you know how punishment affects recidivism rates, this knowledge may affect your views about mandatory sentencing of criminals.

We are optimistic about psychology's role in the world, but we want to caution you that sometimes people expect things from psychology that it cannot deliver. Psychology cannot tell you the meaning of life. A philosophy of life requires not only knowledge but also reflection and a willingness to learn from life's experiences. Nor does psychological understanding relieve people of responsibility for their faults and misdeeds. Knowing that your short temper is a result, in part, of your unhappy childhood does not give you a green light to yell at your family or mistreat your own kids. Finally, as we have repeatedly emphasized, psychology will not provide you with simple answers to complex questions. Instead, it offers findings from many perspectives, which the critical thinker will try to evaluate and integrate. (In the epilogue to this book, we suggest how such an integration might apply to problems in love.)

As you read this book, you will learn that human behavior is extremely complicated—more complicated than practitioners of pseudoscience and psychobabble want you to know. But what you learn will be more helpful and accurate than what pseudoscience offers. Psychologists have made enormous progress in unraveling the secrets of the human brain, mind, and heart. At the end of each chapter, starting with the next one, the "Taking Psychology with You" feature will suggest ways to apply psychological findings to your own life—at school, on the job, or in your relationships.

Summary

Psychology, Pseudoscience, and Popular Opinion

- *Psychology* is the discipline concerned with behavior and mental processes and how they are affected by an organism's external and internal environment. Psychology's methods and reliance on *empirical evidence* distinguish it from pseudoscience and "psychobabble." As we saw in the "Close-up on Research" feature, an introductory psychology course can correct many misconceptions about human behavior.
- Psychologists have many pseudoscientific competitors, such as astrologers and psychics. But when put to the test, the claims and predictions of these competitors turn out to be meaningless or just plain wrong. Psychobabble is appealing because it confirms our beliefs and prejudices; in contrast, psychology often challenges them, although it also seeks to extend our understanding of familiar facts.

Thinking Critically and Creatively About Psychology

- One benefit of studying psychology is the development of *critical-thinking* skills and attitudes. Critical thinking helps people evaluate competing findings on psychological issues that are personally and socially important.
- The critical thinker asks questions, defines terms clearly, examines the evidence, analyzes assumptions and biases, avoids emotional reasoning, avoids oversimplification, considers alternative interpretations, and tolerates uncertainty. Critical thinking is an evolving process rather than a once-and-for-all accomplishment.

Psychology's Past: From the Armchair to the Laboratory

- Psychology's forerunners made some valid observations and had useful insights, but without rigorous empirical methods they also made serious errors in the description and explanation of behavior, as in the case of *phrenology*.
- The official founder of scientific psychology was Wilhelm Wundt, who formally established the first psychological laboratory in 1879, in Leipzig, Germany. His work led to *structuralism*, the first of many approaches to the field. Structuralism emphasized the analysis of immediate experience into basic elements. It was soon abandoned, in part because of its reliance on introspection.
- Another early approach, *functionalism*, was inspired in part by the evolutionary theories of Charles Darwin; it emphasized the purpose of behavior. One of its leading proponents was William James. Functionalism, too, did not last long as a distinct school of psychology, but it greatly affected the course of psychological science.
- Psychology as a method of psychotherapy has roots in Sigmund Freud's theory of *psychoanalysis*, which emphasizes unconscious causes of mental and emotional problems.

Psychology's Present: Behavior, Body, Mind, and Culture

- Several points of view predominate today in psychology. The *biological perspective* emphasizes bodily events associated with actions, thoughts, and feelings, and also genetic contributions to behavior. Within this perspective, a popular specialty, *evolutionary psychology*, is following in the footsteps of functionalism. The *learning perspective* emphasizes how the environment and a person's history affect behavior; within this perspective, *behaviorists* reject mentalistic explanations and *social-cognitive learning theorists* combine elements of behaviorism with the study of thoughts, values, and intentions. The *cognitive perspective* emphasizes mental processes in perception, problem solving, belief formation, and other human activities. The *sociocultural perspective* explores how social contexts and cultural rules affect an individual's beliefs and behavior. And the *psychodynamic perspective*, which originated with Freud's theory of psychoanalysis, emphasizes unconscious motives, conflicts, and desires; it differs greatly from the other approaches in its methods and standards of evidence.
- Not all approaches to psychology fit neatly into one of the five major perspectives. For example, two important movements, *humanist psychology* and *feminist psychology*, have influenced the questions researchers ask, the methods they use, and their awareness of biases in the field. A contemporary research specialty called *positive psychology* follows in the tradition of humanism by focusing on the positive aspects of human behavior.

What Psychologists Do

- Psychologists do research and teach in colleges and universities, provide mental-health services *(psychological practice)*, and conduct research and apply findings in a wide variety of

nonacademic settings. *Applied psychology* is concerned with the practical uses of psychological knowledge. *Basic psychology* is concerned with knowledge for its own sake. Among the many psychological specialties are experimental, educational, developmental, industrial/organizational, psychometric, counseling, school, and clinical psychology.

- *Psychotherapist* is an unregulated term for anyone who does therapy, including persons who have no credentials or training at all. Licensed therapists differ according to their training and approach. *Clinical psychologists* have a Ph.D., an Ed.D., or a Psy.D.; *psychiatrists* have an M.D.; *psychoanalysts* are trained in psychoanalytic institutes; and licensed clinical social workers, counselors with various specialties, and marriage, family, and child counselors may have a variety of postgraduate degrees. Many psychologists are concerned about an increase in poorly trained psychotherapists who lack credentials or a f of research methods and findings.

Biology and Psychology: Beyond the Borders

- Many, if not most, psychologists draw on more than one school of psychology. Indeed, there is a growing trend in psychology to cross the borders that have traditionally divided one specialty from another, especially the border between biology and psychology.
- Although psychologists differ in their perspectives and goals, psychological scientists, whatever their specialty, generally agree on which methods of study are acceptable, and all psychologists are united by their fascination with the mysteries of behavior.

KEY TERMS

Use this list to check your understanding of terms and people in this chapter. If you have trouble with a term, you can find it on the page listed.

Will It Be On the Test?

NOW YOU HAVE READ CHAPTER ONE — ARE YOU PREPARED FOR THE EXAM?

Are you anxious about your next exam? To find out what content you might need help with go to MyPsychLab (MPL) at **www.mypsychlab.com.** Check with your instructor for your course ID number. If your instructor hasn't set up a course, you can use the self-assessment mode of MPL. Registration and log-in are straightforward and there is lots of help to walk you through the site.

Anxiety is a common problem. To test your understanding of the major perspectives in psychology, fill in each possible explanation of anxiety with a perspective:

1) Anxious people often think about the future in distorted ways: the ______ perspective.

2) Anxiety symptoms often bring hidden rewards, such as being excused from exams: the ______ perspective.

3) A national emphasis on competition and success promotes anxiety about failure: the ______ perspective.

1. cognitive 2. learning 3. sociocultural

Click on the help tab, scroll to the "Registration Help for Students" and watch the Registration Tour. Follow the directions for registering and logging in.

PRENTICE HALL
mypsychlab

LEARN ABOUT | BOOKS AVAILABLE | HELP

MyPsychLab is where you save time and improve results.

MyPsychLab is an easy-to-use learning management system that allows instructors to assess student progress and adapt course materials to meet the specific needs of the class.

When students complete an online self-assessment, the results of this test generate a customized study plan, including a variety of tools to help them fully master the material. MyPsychLab then reports these results to the instructor. Based on these reports, the instructor can adapt course material to suit the needs of individual students or the class as a whole.

Learn more...

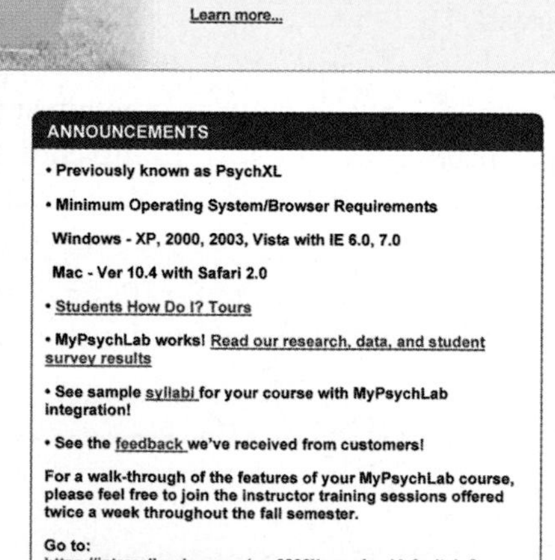
First-time users
Register or buy access here
Students
Instructors
Returning users
Students
Instructors
ANNOUNCEMENTS
• Previously known as PsychXL
• Minimum Operating System/Browser Requirements
Windows - XP, 2000, 2003, Vista with IE 6.0, 7.0
Mac - Ver 10.4 with Safari 2.0
• Students How Do I? Tours
• MyPsychLab works! Read our research, data, and student survey results
• See sample syllabi for your course with MyPsychLab integration!
• See the feedback we've received from customers!
For a walk-through of the features of your MyPsychLab course, please feel free to join the instructor training sessions offered twice a week throughout the fall semester.
Go to:
https://intercall.webex.com/mw0302l/mywebex/default.do?siteurl=intercall
Tuesday at 3PM EST Meeting # 561 249 927
Fridays at 11AM EST Meeting # 563 693 175
Conference line: 1-877-554-0877 code: 2012367171
BOOKS AVAILABLE
Here's a sampling of books available with MyPsychLab. Click GO to see the complete list of books, with ordering information.
GO

TELL ME **MORE** >>

"MyPsychLab is a very user-friendly website. It's even easy for students who don't have a lot of computer skills."

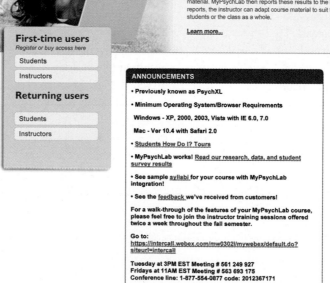

Student
Oklahoma City University

MyPsychLab: Help

http://www.prenhall.com/divisions/hss/app/myLab_hss/MyPsychLab/help.html

PRENTICE HALL mypsychlab

Learn About...

- What is MyPsychLab?
- Take a Tour
- Books Available
- What People Are Saying
- MyPsychLab Works!: Research, Data and Student Surveys
- Try It!

- Home
- Help

Help

- User's Guides
- Your Personal Information
- Instructor Checklist
- Registration help for students
- System Requirements
- Plugins
- Still need help?

User's Guides

View and print instructions for using MyPsychLab by clicking the links below. You will need Adobe Reader (a free program you can install directly from the MyPsychLab installation wizard) in order to view the guide.

MyPsychLab Instructor's Guide (doc, 1mb)

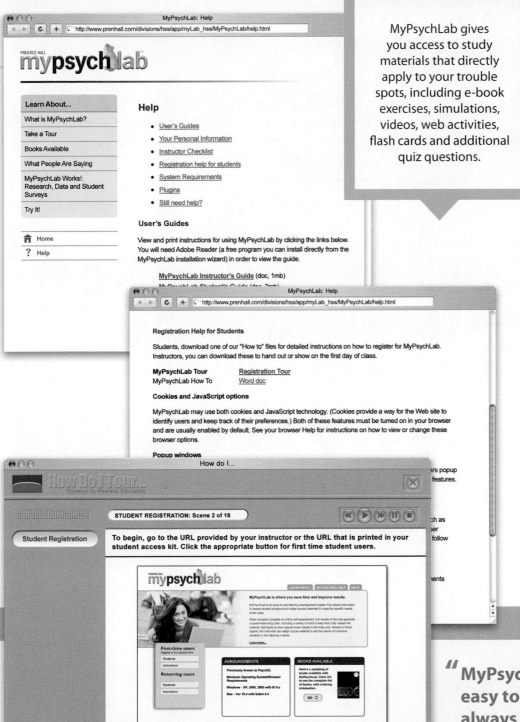

MyPsychLab gives you access to study materials that directly apply to your trouble spots, including e-book exercises, simulations, videos, web activities, flash cards and additional quiz questions.

MyPsychLab: Help

http://www.prenhall.com/divisions/hss/app/myLab_hss/MyPsychLab/help.html

Registration Help for Students

Students, download one of our "How to" files for detailed instructions on how to register for MyPsychLab. Instructors, you can download these to hand out or show on the first day of class.

MyPsychLab Tour Registration Tour
MyPsychLab How To Word doc

Cookies and JavaScript options

MyPsychLab may use both cookies and JavaScript technology. (Cookies provide a way for the Web site to identify users and keep track of their preferences.) Both of these features must be turned on in your browser and are usually enabled by default. See your browser Help for instructions on how to view or change these browser options.

Popup windows

How do I...

How Do I Tour... Powered by Pearson Education

STUDENT REGISTRATION: Scene 2 of 16

Student Registration

To begin, go to the URL provided by your instructor or the URL that is printed in your student access kit. Click the appropriate button for first time student users.

mypsychlab

MyPsychLab is where you save time and improve results.

First-time users

Returning users

ANNOUNCEMENTS

BOOKS AVAILABLE

STUDY TIP

Review the Critical Thinking Guidelines

One of the greatest benefits of studying psychology is that you learn not only about the findings of the field but also how to think critically. Review the Eight Essential Guidelines to Critical Thinking in the inside cover of your book and on pages 7-15 of this chapter.

TELL ME **MORE** >>

"MyPsychLab was easy to sign up, easy to figure out, easy to use, and always available, so I could work on any chapter any time."

Student
Oklahoma City University

What can you find in MyPsychLab?

Self-Directed Tests • Videos • Simulations • eBook • Flash Cards • Web Links . . . and more — organized by chapter, section and learning objective.

HOW PSYCHOLOGISTS DO RESEARCH

CHAPTER TWO

> The negative cautions of science are never popular.
>
> MARGARET MEAD

Suppose that you are the parent of a 9-year-old boy who has been diagnosed as autistic. Your child lives in his own private world, cut off from normal social interaction. He does not speak, and he rarely looks you in the eye. Sometimes he spends hours just rocking back and forth, and occasionally, in frustration, he does self-destructive things, like poking pencils in his ears. He has never been able to function in a public school classroom.

You are ecstatic, then, when you hear about a new technique called "facilitated communication," which promises to release your child from his mental prison. According to proponents of this technique, when autistic or mentally impaired children are placed in front of a keyboard and an adult "facilitator" gently places a hand over the child's hand or forearm, amazing things happen. Children who have never used words are suddenly able to peck out complete sentences, answer questions, and divulge their thoughts. One child reportedly typed, "I amn not a utistivc on thje typ" (I am not autistic on the typewriter). Some children, through their facilitators, have supposedly even mastered high school–level subjects or have written poetry of astonishing beauty. The fee is steep, but it certainly seems worth it.

Or is it?

The situation we have described is not hypothetical; thousands of hopeful parents have been drawn to the promise of facilitated communication. Psychological scientists, however, have been more cautious. Before accepting claims and testimonials about any program or therapy, they put those claims and testimonials to the test. In the case of facilitated communication, they have done experiments involving hundreds of autistic children and their facilitators (see Mostert, 2001; Romanczyk et al., 2003; Twactman-Cullen, 1998). Their techniques have been simple: They show the child a picture to identify but show the facilitator a different picture or no picture at all; or they keep the facilitator from hearing the questions being put to the child. Under these conditions, the child types only what the facilitator sees or hears—not what the child does.

This research shows that what happens in facilitated communication is exactly what happens when a medium guides a person's hand over a Ouija board to help the person receive "messages" from a "spirit": The person doing the "facilitating" unconsciously nudges the other person's hand in the desired direction, remaining unaware of having influenced the responses produced (Wegner, Fuller, & Sparrow, 2003). Facilitated communication, in other words, is really facilitator communication. This finding is vitally important, because if parents waste their time and money on a treatment that doesn't work, they may never get genuine help for their children, and they will suffer when their false hopes are finally shattered by reality. As a recent German review of the literature concluded, "FC has failed to show clinical validity, shows some features of pseudoscience, and bears severe risks of detrimental side effects" (Probst, 2005).

THINKING CRITICALLY

EXAMINE THE EVIDENCE

Using "facilitated communication" (FC), Betsy Wheaton, a child with autism, appeared to type that she had been sexually abused by her family; she was removed from her home. But when researcher Howard Shane tested her by showing pictures of different objects separately to Betsy and her facilitator, Betsy typed only what the facilitator saw. If Betsy saw a cup but the facilitator saw a hat (left), Betsy typed "hat" (right). Because of this evidence, the facilitator stopped using FC and Betsy was reunited with her family.

You can see why research methods matter so much to psychologists: These methods allow researchers to separate reliable information from unfounded beliefs, sort out conflicting views, and correct false ideas that may cause people harm. Some students would rather not study research methods; "Let's just cut straight to the findings," they say. But these methods are the tools of the psychological scientist's trade, and understanding them is crucial for everyone who reads or hears about a new program or an "exciting finding" said to be based on psychological research.

The story of facilitated communication shows how important it is that you consider how psychological results were obtained and interpreted, which you can do by drawing on information in this chapter. Knowing the difference between claims based on good research and those based on sloppy or inadequate research will not only help you pass this course: It also can help you make wiser psychological and medical decisions, it can prevent you from spending money on worthless programs, and sometimes it can even save lives.

WHAT'S AHEAD

- Where do psychological scientists get their hypotheses?
- What's the secret of a good scientific definition?
- In what way are scientists risk takers?
- Why is secrecy a big "no-no" in science?

What Makes Psychological Research Scientific?

When we say that psychologists are scientists, we do not mean they work with complicated gadgets and machines or wear white lab coats (although some do). The scientific enterprise has more to do with attitudes and procedures than with apparatus and apparel. Here are a few key characteristics of the ideal scientist:

1 Precision. Scientists sometimes launch an investigation because they have a hunch about some behavior based on previous findings or casual observations. Often, however, they start out with a general **theory**, an organized system of assumptions and principles that purports to explain certain phenomena and how they are related. Many people misunderstand what scientists mean by a "theory." A scientific theory is not just someone's personal opinion, as in "It's only a theory" or "I have a theory about why he told that lie." It's true that some scientific theories are tentative, pending more research, but others, like the theory of gravity and the theory of evolution, are accepted by nearly all scientists.

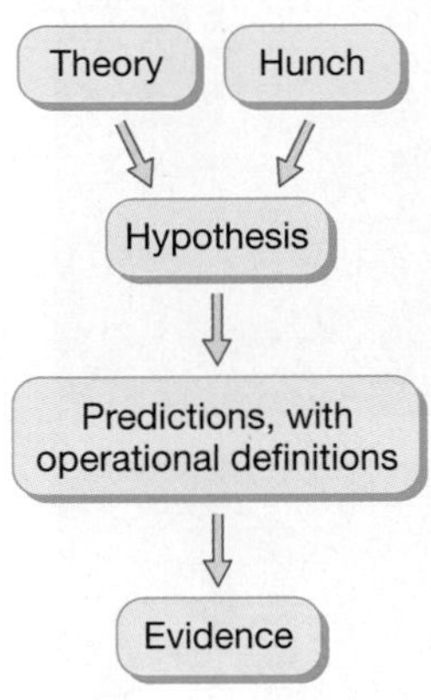

From a hunch or theory, the psychological scientist derives a **hypothesis**, a statement that attempts to describe or explain a given behavior. Initially, this statement may be quite general, as in, say, "Misery loves company." But before any research can be done, the hypothesis must be made more precise. For example, "Misery loves company" might be rephrased as "People who are anxious about a threatening situation tend to seek out others facing the same threat."

A hypothesis, in turn, leads to predictions about what will happen in a particular situation. In a prediction, terms such as *anxiety* or *threatening situation* are given **operational definitions**, which specify how the phenomena in question are to be observed and measured. "Anxiety" might be defined operationally as a score on an anxiety questionnaire; "threatening situation" might be defined as the threat of an electric shock. The prediction might be, "If you raise people's anxiety scores by telling them they are going to receive electric shocks, and then give them the choice of waiting alone or with others in the same situation, they will be more likely to choose to wait with others than they would be if they were not anxious." The prediction can then be tested, using systematic methods.

2 Skepticism. Scientists do not accept ideas on faith or authority; their motto is "Show me!" Some of the greatest scientific advances have been made by those who dared to doubt what everyone else assumed to be true: that the sun revolves around the earth, that illness can be cured by applying leeches to the skin, that madness is a sign of demonic possession. In the world of the researcher, skepticism means treating conclusions, both new and old, with caution. Caution, however, must be balanced by openness to new ideas and evidence. Otherwise, the scientist may wind up as shortsighted as the famous physicist Lord Kelvin, who at the end of the nineteenth century reputedly declared with great confidence that radio had no future, X rays were a hoax, and "heavier-than-air flying machines" were impossible.

3 Reliance on empirical evidence. Unlike plays and poems, scientific theories and hypotheses are not judged by how pleasing or entertaining they are. An idea may initially generate excitement because it is plausible, imaginative, or appealing, but eventually it must be backed by empirical evidence if it is to be taken seriously. A collection of anecdotes or an appeal to authority will not do. Nor will the "intuitive" appeal of the idea or its popularity. As Nobel Prize–winning scientist Peter Medawar (1979) once wrote, "The intensity of the conviction that a hypothesis is true has no bearing on whether it is true or not."

4 Willingness to make "risky predictions." A related principle is that a scientist must state an idea in such a way that it can be *refuted*, or disproved by counterevidence. This principle, known as the **principle of falsifiability**, does not mean that the idea *will* be disproved, only that it *could be* if contrary evidence were to be discovered. Another way of saying this is that a scientist must risk disconfirmation by predicting not only what will happen but also what will *not* happen. In the "misery loves company" study, the

theory An organized system of assumptions and principles that purports to explain a specified set of phenomena and their interrelationships.

hypothesis A statement that attempts to predict or to account for a set of phenomena; scientific hypotheses specify relationships among events or variables and are empirically tested.

operational definition A precise definition of a term in a hypothesis, which specifies the operations for observing and measuring the process or phenomenon being defined.

principle of falsifiability The principle that a scientific theory must make predictions that are specific enough to expose the theory to the possibility of disconfirmation; that is, the theory must predict not only what will happen but also what will not happen.

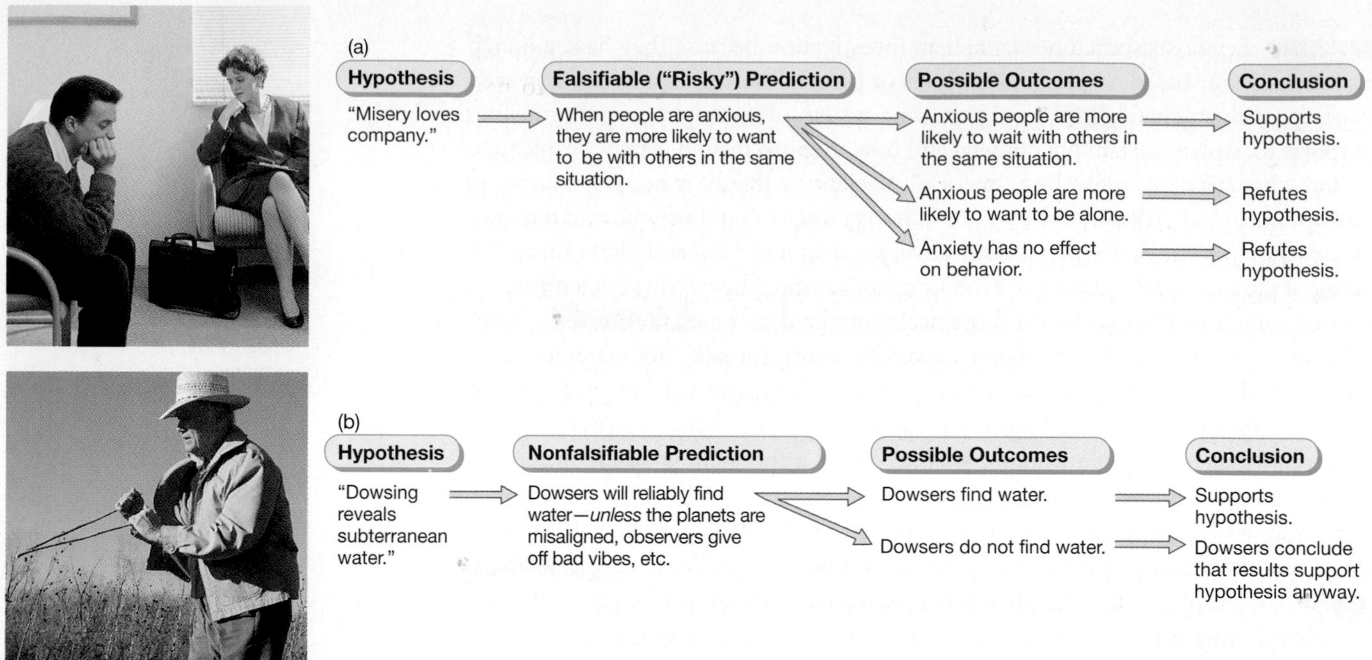

FIGURE 2.1 The Principle of Falsifiability

The scientific method requires researchers to expose their ideas to the possibility of counterevidence, as in row (a). In contrast, people claiming psychic powers, such as dowsers (who say they can find underground water with a "dowsing rod" that bends when water is present), typically interpret all possible outcomes as support for their assertions, as in row (b). Their claims are therefore untestable.

hypothesis would be supported if most anxious people sought each other out, but would be disconfirmed if most anxious people went off alone to sulk and worry, or if anxiety had no effect on their behavior (see Figure 2.1). A willingness to risk disconfirmation forces the scientist to take negative evidence seriously and to abandon mistaken hypotheses. Any researcher who refuses to do this is not a true scientist.

The principle of falsifiability plays a central role in science, because all of us—even scientists—are vulnerable to the **confirmation bias**: the tendency to look for and accept evidence that supports our pet theories and assumptions and to ignore or reject evidence that contradicts our beliefs. The principle of falsifiability compels researchers to resist the confirmation bias and to consider counterevidence.

Many violations of the principle of falsifiability occur in everyday life. For example, when police officers believe a suspect is guilty, they may take even the person's protestations of innocence as evidence of guilt ("the skunk is trying to cover up"). Of course, many guilty people claim to be innocent, but so do innocent people. An interviewer in such situations must therefore be open to evidence that disconfirms his or her beliefs. Similarly, many people who firmly believe in alien abductions violate the principle of falsifiability when they are faced with evidence that "alien spaceships" are merely natural phenomena or weather balloons. True believers will insist that the government must be conspiring to cover up the truth, or that aliens must have clever, sneaky ways of disguising their spacecraft. By explaining away all counterevidence, they avoid ever putting their beliefs to the test.

confirmation bias The tendency to look for or pay attention only to information that confirms one's own belief.

5 **Openness.** Science depends on the free flow of ideas and full disclosure of the procedures used in a study. Secrecy is a big "no-no"; scientists must be willing to tell others where they got their ideas, how they tested them, and what the results were. They must do this clearly and in detail so that other scientists can repeat, or *replicate*, their studies and verify—or challenge—the findings. Replication is an essential part of the scientific process because sometimes what seems to be a fabulous phenomenon turns out to be only a fluke.

If you think about it, you will see that these principles of good science correspond to the critical-thinking guidelines described in Chapter 1. Formulating a prediction with operational definitions corresponds to "define your terms." Openness to new ideas encourages scientists to "ask questions" and to "consider other interpretations." Reliance on empirical evidence is a hallmark of critical thinking and helps scientists avoid the temptation to oversimplify. The principle of falsifiability forces scientists to "analyze assumptions and biases" in a fair-minded fashion. And until their results have been replicated and verified, scientists must "tolerate uncertainty."

Do psychologists and other scientists always live up to the lofty standards expected of them? Of course not. For one thing, when research is sponsored by private, for-profit businesses, such as drug manufacturers, the scientific requirement of full disclosure may come smack up against a company's desire to keep competitors from learning about research on a potentially lucrative product (Angell, 2004). Moreover, scientists, being only human, may not always follow the "rules" the way they should. They may put too much trust in their personal experiences. They may permit ambition to interfere with openness. About 5 percent of scientists even admit (anonymously) to having ignored data that contradicted their previous research or their "gut feelings" (Martinson, Anderson, & de Vries, 2005). It is always easier to be skeptical about someone else's ideas than about your own.

Commitment to one's theories is not in itself a bad thing. Passion is the fuel of progress. It motivates researchers to think boldly, defend unpopular ideas, and do the exhaustive testing that is often required to support an idea. But passion can also cloud perceptions and in a few sad cases has even led to plagiarism, deception, and fraud. That is why science is a communal activity. Scientists are expected to submit their results to professional journals, which send the findings to experts in the field for evaluation and suggest revisions before publishing them. This process, called *peer review*, ensures that the work lives up to accepted scientific standards. Peer review is supposed to precede any announcements to the public through press releases, Internet postings, or popular books. The research community—in our case, the psychological community—acts as a jury, scrutinizing and sifting the evidence, judging its integrity, approving some viewpoints and relegating others to the scientific scrap heap.

The peer review process is not perfect, but it does give science a built-in system of checks and balances. Individuals are not necessarily objective, honest, or rational, but science forces them to subject their findings to scrutiny and to justify their claims.

QUICK quiz

Can you identify which rule of science was violated in each of the following cases?

1. For years, writer Norman Cousins told how he had cured himself of a rare, life-threatening disease through a combination of humor and vitamins. In a best-selling book, he recommended the same approach to others.
2. Benjamin Rush, an eighteenth-century physician, believed that yellow fever should be treated by bloodletting. Many of his patients died, but Rush did not lose faith in his approach; he attributed each recovery to his treatment and each death to the severity of the disease (Stanovich, 1996).

Answers:

1. Cousins offered only a personal account and did not gather or cite empirical evidence from scientific studies or consider cases of sick people who were not helped by humor and vitamins. **2.** Rush violated the principle of falsifiability: He interpreted a patient's survival as support for his treatment and explained away each death by saying that the person had been too ill for the treatment to work. Thus, there was no possible counterevidence that could refute the theory (which, by the way, was dead wrong—the "treatment" was actually as dangerous as the disease).

WHAT'S**AHEAD**

- From what group are participants in psychological studies most often drawn—and why does it matter?
- When are psychological case studies informative, and when are they useless?
- Why do psychologists often observe people in laboratories instead of simply watching them in everyday situations?
- What's the test of a good test?
- Why should you be skeptical about psychological tests in magazines and newspapers or on the Internet?
- What's the difference between a psychological survey and a poll of listeners on talk radio?

Descriptive Studies: Establishing the Facts

Psychologists gather evidence to support their hypotheses by using different methods, depending on the kinds of questions they want to answer. These methods are not mutually exclusive, however. Just as a police detective may rely on DNA samples, fingerprints, and interviews of suspects to figure out "who done it," psychological sleuths often draw on different techniques at different stages of an ongoing investigation.

No matter what technique is used, one of the first major challenges facing any researcher is to select the participants ("subjects") for the study. Ideally, the researcher would prefer to get a **representative sample**, a group of participants that accurately represents the larger population that the researcher is interested in. Suppose you wanted to learn about drug use among college sophomores. Questioning or observing every sophomore in the country would obviously not be practical; instead, you would need to recruit a sample. You could use special selection procedures to ensure that this sample contained the same proportion of women, men, blacks, whites, poor people, rich people, Catholics, Jews, and so on as in the general population of college sophomores. Even then, a sample drawn just from your own school or town might not produce results applicable to the entire country or even your state.

Plenty of studies are based on unrepresentative samples. For example, the American Medical Association reported, based on "a random sample" of 664 women who were polled online, that binge drinking and unprotected sex were rampant among college women during spring break vacations. The media had a field day with this news. Yet the sample, it turned out, was not random. It included only women who volunteered to answer questions, and only a fourth of them had ever taken a spring break trip (Rosenthal, 2006).

Most people do not realize that a sample's size is less critical than its representativeness. A small but representative sample may yield extremely accurate results, whereas a study that fails to use proper sampling methods may yield questionable results, no matter how large the sample. But in practice, psychologists and others who study human behavior must often settle for a sample of people who happen to be available—a "convenience" sample—and more often than not, this means undergraduate college students. Psychologist Peter Killeen notes, with tongue only partly in cheek, that students are "cheaper than white rats, and they're more similar to the population to which we hope to generalize. And they seldom bite" (quoted in Jaffe, 2005).

representative sample A group of subjects, selected from a population for study, which matches the population on important characteristics such as age and sex.

CLOSE-UP on Research

STUDENT "CONVENIENCE" SAMPLES

Oddly enough, psychologists and other social scientists have rarely studied empirically their own reliance on college students as research participants. Robert A. Peterson, a business professor who often publishes in psychology journals, is an exception. Peterson **asked the question**, "Are the differences between students and other people serious enough to limit the results of studies that use only students?" There are, after all, many such differences: College students are younger than the general population, they are more likely to be female, they are more likely to have strong cognitive skills, and they are more homogeneous.

Peterson wanted to analyze social-science studies done in the United States in which student and adult nonstudent samples had been used in the same research. Instead of looking at each individual study, however, he searched for articles that had used a technique called *meta-analysis*, which allows a researcher to do a sort of statistical overview of a whole bunch of studies. (This technique will be described in greater detail later in this chapter.) Peterson spent many years finding such statistical reviews and wound up with reports that cumulatively represented an estimated 350,000 research participants. He then **examined the evidence** by analyzing 64 different behavioral and psychological relationships studied in these reviews—for example, between gender and assertiveness, or television viewing and violence—and the conclusions the researchers had drawn about these relationships.

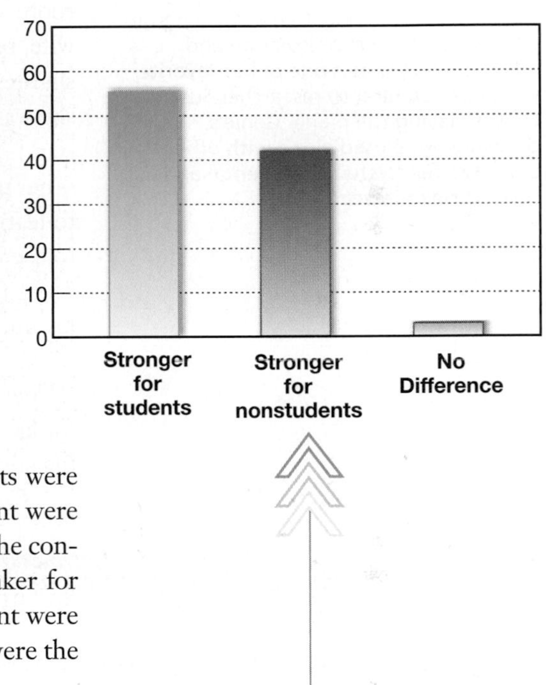

Peterson found that 81 percent of the conclusions based on college students were the same as those based on nonstudents, but of course this means that 19 percent were different; in fact, they went in *opposite* directions. And in many cases, even when the conclusions were the same, the reported relationships were either stronger or weaker for students than for nonstudents. Overall, of the 65 relationships studied, 55 percent were stronger for students, 42 percent were stronger for nonstudents, and 3 percent were the same for the two groups (see the adjacent figure).

These findings do not mean we should throw out results based solely on students—that would be an **oversimplification** of his findings. For one thing, many psychological processes, such as basic perceptual or memory processes, are likely to be the same in students as in anyone else; students are not a separate species, no matter what their professors may sometimes think! In studies of other topics, however, we may need to **tolerate some uncertainty** about conclusions based solely on college students until the research can be replicated with nonstudents.

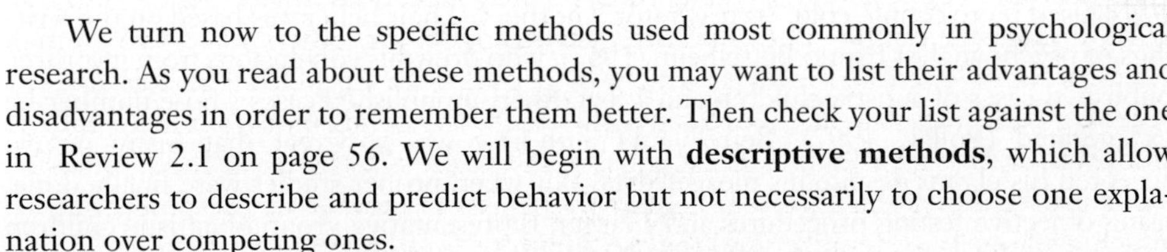

We turn now to the specific methods used most commonly in psychological research. As you read about these methods, you may want to list their advantages and disadvantages in order to remember them better. Then check your list against the one in Review 2.1 on page 56. We will begin with **descriptive methods**, which allow researchers to describe and predict behavior but not necessarily to choose one explanation over competing ones.

descriptive methods Methods that yield descriptions of behavior but not necessarily causal explanations.

Case Studies

This picture, drawn by Genie, a young girl who endured years of isolation and mistreatment, shows one of her favorite pastimes: listening to researcher Susan Curtiss playing the piano. Genie's drawings were used along with other case material to study her mental and social development.

A **case study** (or *case history*) is a detailed description of a particular individual based on careful observation or on formal psychological testing. It may include information about a person's childhood, dreams, fantasies, experiences, relationships, and hopes—anything that will provide insight into the person's behavior. Case studies are most commonly used by clinicians, but sometimes academic researchers use them as well, especially when they are just beginning to study a topic or when practical or ethical considerations prevent them from gathering information in other ways.

For example, suppose you want to know whether the first few years of life are critical for acquiring a first language. Can children who have missed out on hearing speech (or, in the case of deaf children, seeing signs) "catch up" later? Obviously, psychologists cannot answer this question by isolating children and seeing what happens! So instead they have studied unusual cases of language deprivation.

One such case involved a 13-year-old girl who had been cruelly locked up in a small room since the age of 1½, strapped for hours to a potty chair. Her mother, a battered wife, barely cared for her, and no one in the family spoke a word to her. If she made the slightest sound, her severely disturbed father beat her with a large piece of wood. When she was finally rescued, "Genie," as researchers called her, did not know how to chew or stand erect and was not toilet trained. She spat on anything that was handy, including other people, and her only sounds were high-pitched whimpers. Eventually, she was able to learn some rules of social conduct, and she began to understand short sentences and to use words to convey her needs, describe her moods, and even lie. But even after many years, Genie's grammar and pronunciation remained abnormal. She never learned to use pronouns correctly, ask questions, produce proper negative sentences, or use the little word endings that communicate tense, number, and possession (Curtiss, 1977, 1982; Rymer, 1993). This sad case, along with similar ones, suggests that a critical period exists for language development, with the likelihood of fully mastering a first language declining steadily after early childhood and falling off drastically at puberty (Pinker, 1994).

Case studies illustrate psychological principles in a way that abstract generalizations and cold statistics never can, and they produce a more detailed picture of an individual than other methods do. In biological research, cases of patients with brain damage have yielded important clues to how the brain is organized (see Chapter 4). But in most instances, case studies have serious drawbacks. Information is often missing or hard to interpret; for example, no one knows what Genie's language development was like before she was locked up or whether she was born with mental deficits. The observer who writes up the case may have certain biases that influence which facts get noticed and included—or omitted. The person who is the focus of the study may have selective or inaccurate memories, making any conclusions unreliable (see Chapter 10). Most important, that person may be *unrepresentative* of the group the researcher is interested in; therefore, this method has only limited usefulness for deriving general principles of behavior. For all these reasons, case studies are usually only sources, rather than tests, of hypotheses.

THINKING CRITICALLY

DON'T OVERSIMPLIFY

Case studies are often enormously compelling, which is why talk shows love them. But often they are merely anecdotes. What are the dangers in using case studies to draw general conclusions about human nature?

When people do draw conclusions solely on the basis of case studies, the results can be disastrous. For example, at one time, many clinicians believed that childhood autism was caused by rejecting, cold, "refrigerator" mothers. Their belief was based on the writings of psychoanalyst Bruno Bettelheim (1967), who drew his conclusions from just three published cases of autistic children and a few other unpublished cases whose number he exaggerated (Pollak, 1997). Bettelheim's authority was so great that many people accepted his claims despite his meager data. But when proper studies were finally done, using objective testing procedures and a larger, representative group of autistic children

case study A detailed description of a particular individual being studied or treated.

and their parents, scientists learned that parents of autistic children are as psychologically healthy as any other parents. Today we know that autism stems from a neurological problem rather than from any psychological problems of the mothers and that certain genes probably increase susceptibility to the disorder. But because so many people accepted Bettelheim's case studies as reliable evidence for his claims, thousands of women blamed themselves for their children's disorder and suffered needless guilt and remorse.

Be wary, then, of the compelling cases reported in the media by individuals ("I was a multiple personality") or by therapists ("I cured someone who had a multiple personality"). Often these stories are only "arguing by anecdote," and they are not a basis for drawing firm conclusions about anything.

observational study A study in which the researcher carefully and systematically observes and records behavior without interfering with the behavior; it may involve either naturalistic or laboratory observation.

Observational Studies

In **observational studies**, the researcher observes, measures, and records behavior, taking care to avoid intruding on the people (or animals) being observed. Unlike case studies, observational studies usually involve many participants. Often an observational study is the first step in a program of research; it is helpful to have a good description of behavior before you try to explain it.

The primary purpose of *naturalistic observation* is to find out how people or animals act in their normal social environments. Psychologists use naturalistic observation wherever people happen to be—at home, on playgrounds or streets, in schoolrooms, or in offices. In one study, a social psychologist and his students ventured into a common human habitat: bars. They wanted to know whether people in bars drink more when they are in groups than when they are alone. They visited all 32 pubs in a midsized city, ordered beers, and recorded on napkins and pieces of newspaper how much the other patrons imbibed. They found that drinkers in groups consumed more than individuals who were alone. Those in groups did not drink any faster; they just lingered in the bar longer (Sommer, 1977).

Note that the students who did this study did not rely on their impressions or memories of how much people drank. In observational studies, researchers count, rate, or measure behavior in a systematic way. These procedures help to minimize the tendency of observers to notice only what they expect or want to see. Careful record keeping ensures accuracy and allows different observers to cross-check their observations for consistency. Observers must also take pains to avoid being obvious about what they are doing and to disguise their intentions so they can see people as they really are. If the researchers who studied drinking habits had marched in with video cameras and announced that they were psychology students, the bar patrons might not have behaved naturally.

GET INVOLVED!

➤A STUDY OF "PERSONAL SPACE"

Try a little naturalistic observation of your own. Go to a public place where people voluntarily seat themselves near others, such as a movie theater or a cafeteria with large tables. If you choose a setting where many people enter at once, you might recruit some friends to help you; you can divide the area into sections and give each observer one section to observe. As individuals and groups sit down, note how many seats they leave between themselves and the next person. On the average, how far do people tend to sit from strangers? Once you have your results, see how many possible explanations you can come up with.

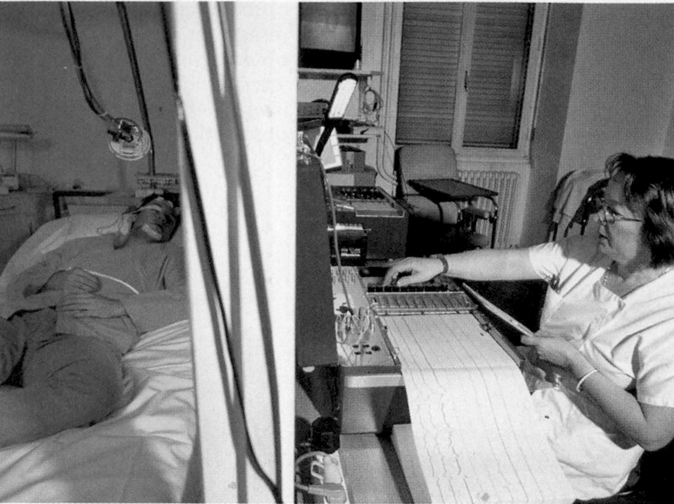

Psychologists using laboratory observation have gathered valuable information about brain and muscle activity during sleep. Psychologists using naturalistic observation have studied how people in crowded places modify their gaze and body position to preserve a sense of privacy.

Sometimes psychologists prefer to make observations in a laboratory setting. In *laboratory observation*, researchers have more control of the situation. They can use sophisticated equipment, determine the number of people who will be observed, maintain a clear line of vision, and so forth. Suppose that you wanted to know how infants of different ages respond when left with a stranger. The most efficient approach might be to have parents and their infants come to your laboratory, observe them playing together for a while through a one-way window, then have a stranger enter the room and, a few minutes later, have the parent leave. You could record signs of distress, interactions with the stranger, and other behavior. If you did this, you would find that very young infants carry on cheerfully with whatever they are doing when the parent leaves. However, by the age of about 8 months, many children will burst into tears or show other signs of what child psychologists call "separation anxiety."

One shortcoming of laboratory observation is that the presence of researchers and special equipment may cause subjects to behave differently than they would in their usual surroundings. Further, observational studies, like other descriptive studies, are more useful for describing behavior than for explaining it. For example, the barroom results we described do not necessarily mean that being in a group makes people drink a lot. People may join a group because they are already interested in drinking and find it more comfortable to hang around the bar if they are with others. Similarly, if we observe infants protesting whenever a parent leaves the room, we cannot be sure *why* they are protesting. Is it because they have become attached to their parents and want them nearby, or have they learned from experience that crying brings an adult with a cookie and a cuddle? Observational studies alone cannot answer such questions.

Tests

psychological tests Procedures used to measure and evaluate personality traits, emotional states, aptitudes, interests, abilities, and values.

Psychological tests, sometimes called *assessment instruments*, are procedures for measuring and evaluating personality traits, emotional states, aptitudes, interests, abilities, and values. Typically, tests require people to answer a series of written or oral questions. The answers may then be totaled to yield a single numerical score, or a set of scores. *Objective tests*, also called *inventories*, measure beliefs, feelings, or behaviors of which an individual is aware; *projective tests* are designed to tap unconscious feelings or motives (see Chapter 16).

At one time or another, you no doubt have taken a personality test, an achievement test, or a vocational-aptitude test. Hundreds of psychological tests are used in industry, education, the military, and the helping professions, and many tests are also used in research studies. Some are given to individuals, others to large groups. These measures help clarify differences among people, as well as differences in the reactions of the same person on different occasions or at different stages of life. Tests may be used to promote self-understanding, to evaluate psychological treatments and programs, or, in scientific research, to draw generalizations about human behavior. Well-constructed psychological tests are a great improvement over simple self-evaluation, because many people have a distorted view of their own abilities and traits. For example, in the workplace, employees tend to overestimate their skills and CEOs are overconfident in their judgments. Both in school and on the job, people are often blissfully unaware of their own lack of competence (Dunning, Heath, & Suls, 2004). Most people think that, like all the children in Garrison Keillor's Lake Woebegon, they are "better than average."

HERE LIES
FREDERICK
JONES
VERBAL - MATH
680 720
R. Chast

One test of a good test is whether it is **standardized**—whether it has uniform procedures exist for giving and scoring the test. It would hardly be fair to give some people detailed instructions and plenty of time and others only vague instructions and limited time. Those who administer the test must know exactly how to explain the tasks involved, how much time to allow, and what materials to use. Scoring is usually done by referring to **norms**, or established standards of performance. The usual procedure for developing norms is to give the test to a large group of people who resemble those for whom the test is intended. Norms determine which scores can be considered high, low, or average.

standardize In test construction, to develop uniform procedures for giving and scoring a test.

norms In test construction, established standards of performance.

reliability In test construction, the consistency of scores derived from a test, from one time and place to another.

validity The ability of a test to measure what it was designed to measure.

Test construction presents many challenges. For one thing, the test must be **reliable**—that is, it must produce the same results from one time and place to the next or from one scorer to another. A vocational-interest test is not reliable if it says that Tom would make a wonderful engineer but a poor journalist, but then gives different results when Tom retakes the test a week later. Psychologists can measure *test-retest reliability* by giving the test twice to the same group of people and then comparing the two sets of scores statistically. If the test is reliable, individuals' scores will be similar from one session to another. This method has a drawback, however: People tend to do better the second time they take a test, after they have become familiar with the strategies required and the actual test items used. A solution is to compute *alternate-forms reliability*, by giving different versions of the same test to the same group on two separate occasions. The items on the two forms are similar in format but are not identical in content. With this method, performance cannot improve because of familiarity with the items, although people may still do somewhat better the second time around because they have learned the procedures expected of them.

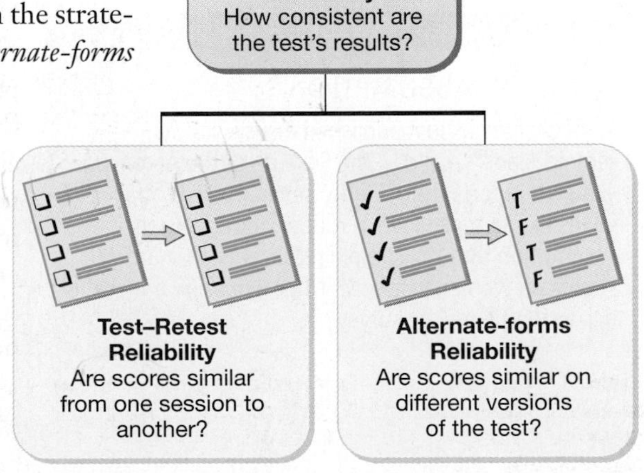
Reliability
How consistent are the test's results?
T
F
T
F
Test–Retest Reliability
Are scores similar from one session to another?
Alternate-forms Reliability
Are scores similar on different versions of the test?

To be useful, a test must also be **valid**, which means that it must measure what it sets out to measure. A creativity test is not valid if what it actually measures is verbal sophistication. If the items broadly represent the trait in question, the test is said to have *content validity*. If you were testing, say, employees' job satisfaction, and your test tapped a

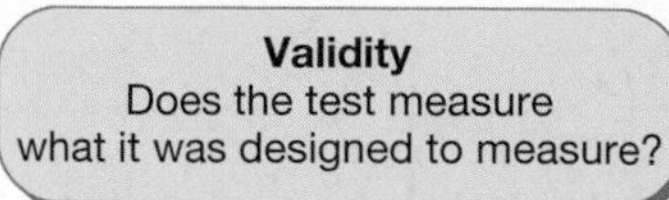
Validity
Does the test measure what it was designed to measure?
Behavior 1
Behavior 2
Behavior 3
Content Validity
Do items broadly represent the trait in question?
Criterion Validity
Do the test results predict other measures of the trait?

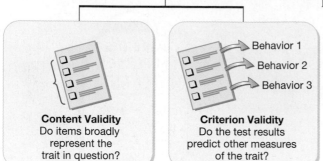

broad array of relevant beliefs and behaviors (e.g., "Do you feel you have reached a dead end at work?" "Are you bored with your assignments?"), it would have content validity. If the test asked only how workers felt about their salary level, it would lack content validity and would be of little use; after all, highly paid people are not always satisfied with their jobs, and people who earn low wages are not always dissatisfied.

Most tests are also judged on *criterion validity*, the ability to predict independent measures, or criteria, of the trait in question. The criterion for a scholastic aptitude test might be college grades; the criterion for a test of shyness might be behavior in social situations. To find out whether your job-satisfaction test had criterion validity, you might return a year later to see whether it correctly predicted absenteeism, resignations, or requests for job transfers.

Unfortunately, teachers, parents, and employers do not always stop to question a test's validity, especially when the results are summarized in a single, precise-sounding number, such as an IQ score of 115 or a job applicant's ranking of 5. But among psychologists and educators, controversy exists about the validity of even some widely used tests. The Scholastic Assessment Test (SAT), which is taken by hundreds of thousands of college applicants every year, has come under fire because people disagree about how well the test predicts college performance and how fair it is to women and minorities. Debate has also raged about the content validity of standardized IQ tests—that is, the extent to which they tap the broad trait known as "intelligence" (see Chapter 9).

Criticisms and reevaluations of psychological tests keep psychological assessment honest and scientifically rigorous. In contrast, the pop-psych tests found in magazines, newspapers, and on the Internet usually have not been evaluated for either validity or reliability. These questionnaires have inviting headlines, such as "Which Breed of Dog Do You Most Resemble?" or "The Seven Types of Lover," but they are merely lists of questions that someone thought sounded good.

surveys Questionnaires and interviews that ask people directly about their experiences, attitudes, or opinions.

volunteer bias A shortcoming of findings derived from a sample of volunteers instead of a representative sample; the volunteers may differ from those who did not volunteer.

Surveys

Psychological tests usually generate information about people indirectly. In contrast, **surveys** are questionnaires and interviews that gather information by asking people *directly* about their experiences, attitudes, or opinions. Most of us are familiar with national opinion surveys, such as the Gallup and Roper polls. Surveys have been done on hundreds of topics, from consumer preferences to sexual preferences.

Surveys produce bushels of data, but they are not easy to do well. Sampling problems are often an issue. For example, when a talk-radio host surveys listeners about a political matter, the results are not likely to generalize to the population as a whole—even if thousands of people respond. Why? As a group, people who listen to Rush Limbaugh are likely to hold different opinions than do those who prefer Al Franken. Popular polls and surveys (like the one about college women on spring break) also frequently suffer from a **volunteer bias**: People who feel strongly enough to volunteer their opinions may differ from those who remain silent. When you read about a survey (or any other kind of study), always ask who participated. A nonrepresentative sample does not necessarily mean that a survey is worthless or uninteresting, but it does mean that the results may not hold true for other groups.

THINKING CRITICALLY

ANALYZE ASSUMPTIONS

A magazine has just published a survey of its female readers, called "The Sex Life of the American Wife." It reports that "Eighty-seven percent of all wives like to make love in rubber boots." Is the assumption that the sample represents all married American women justified? What would be a more accurate title for the survey?

Yet another problem with surveys is that people sometimes lie, especially when the survey is about a touchy topic ("What? Me do that disgusting/illegal/dishonest thing? Never!"). The likelihood of lying is reduced when respondents are guaranteed anonymity. Researchers also have ways to check for lying—for example, by asking the same question several times with different wording and checking for consistency in the answers. But not all surveys use these techniques, and even when respondents are trying to be truthful, they may misinterpret the survey questions or misremember the past.

When you hear about the results of a survey or opinion poll, you also need to consider which questions were (and were not) asked and how the questions were phrased. The questions a researcher asks may reflect his or her assumptions about the topic or may be designed to further a particular agenda (Ericksen & Steffen, 1999). And the phrasing of a question can affect how people respond to it (as political pollsters well know). Many years ago, famed sex researcher Alfred Kinsey, in his pioneering surveys of sexual habits (Kinsey, Pomeroy, & Martin, 1948; Kinsey et al., 1953), made it his practice always to ask, "*How many times have you* (masturbated, had nonmarital sex, etc.)?" rather than "*Have you ever* (masturbated, had nonmarital sex, etc.)?" The first way of phrasing the question tended to elicit more truthful responses than the second because it removed the respondent's potential self-consciousness about having done any of these things. The second way of phrasing the question would have permitted embarrassed respondents to reply with a simple but dishonest "No."

"Are you (a) contented, (b) happy, (c) very happy, (d) wildly happy, (e) deliriously happy?"

Technology can help researchers overcome some of the problems inherent in doing surveys. For example, because many people feel more anonymous when they "talk" to a computer than when they fill out a paper-and-pencil questionnaire, computerized questionnaires can reduce lying (Turner et al., 1998). The Internet also provides researchers with samples that are much larger than traditional ones. Participants are usually volunteers and are not randomly selected, but because Web-based samples are often huge, consisting of hundreds of thousands of respondents, they are more diverse than traditional samples in terms of gender, socioeconomic status, geographic region, and age. In these respects they tend to be more representative of the general population than traditional samples are (Gosling et al., 2004). Even when people from a particular group make up only a small proportion of the respondents, in absolute numbers they may be numerous enough to provide useful information about that group. For example, whereas a typical sample of 1,000 representative Americans might include only a handful of Buddhists, a huge Internet sample might draw hundreds.

Internet surveys also carry certain risks, however (Kraut et al., 2004). Because researchers cannot directly monitor the context in which a survey is answered, it is more difficult to know whether participants understand the instructions and the questions and are taking them seriously. Also, many tests and surveys on the Web have never been validated, which is why drawing conclusions from them about your personality or mental adjustment could be dangerous to your mental health! Always check the credentials of those designing the test or survey and be sure it is not just something someone made up at his or her computer in the middle of the night.

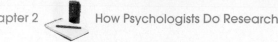

QUICK quiz

How would you describe your understanding of descriptive methods?

A. Which descriptive method would be most appropriate for studying each of the following topics? (All of them, by the way, have been investigated by psychologists.)

1. Ways in which the games of boys differ from those of girls
2. Changes in attitudes toward nuclear disarmament after a television movie about nuclear holocaust
3. The math skills of children in the United States versus Japan
4. Physiological changes that occur when people watch violent movies
5. The development of a male infant who was reared as a female after his penis was accidentally burned off during a routine surgery

a. case study
b. naturalistic observation
c. laboratory observation
d. survey
e. test

B. Professor Flummox gives her new test of aptitude for studying psychology to her psychology students at the start of the year. At the end of the year, she finds that those who did well on the test averaged only a C in the course. The test lacks ____________.

C. Over a period of 55 years, a British woman sniffed large amounts of cocaine, which she obtained legally under British regulations for the treatment of addicts. Yet she appeared to show no negative effects other than drug dependence (Brown & Middlefell, 1989). What does this case tell us about the dangers or safety of cocaine?

Answers:

A. 1. b **2.** d **3.** e **4.** c **5.** a **B.** Validity (more specifically, criterion validity) **C.** Not much. Snorting cocaine may be relatively harmless for some people, such as this woman, but extremely harmful for others. Also, the cocaine she received may have been less potent than cocaine purchased on the street. Critical thinking requires that we resist generalizing from a single case.

WHAT'S**AHEAD** 

- If two things are "negatively" correlated, such as grades and TV watching, what is the relationship between them?
- If attention problems in children and time spent watching TV are "positively" correlated, does that mean watching TV causes attention problems?

Correlational Studies: Looking for Relationships

In descriptive research, psychologists often want to know whether two or more phenomena are related and, if so, how strongly. For example, are students' grade-point averages related to the number of hours they spend watching television? To find out, a psychologist would do a **correlational study**.

correlational study A descriptive study that looks for a consistent relationship between two phenomena.

correlation A measure of how strongly two variables are related to one another.

variables Characteristics of behavior or experience that can be measured or described by a numeric scale.

positive correlation An association between increases in one variable and increases in another—or between decreases in one and in another.

Measuring Correlations

The word **correlation** is often used as a synonym for "relationship." Technically, however, a correlation is a numerical measure of the *strength* of the relationship between two things. The "things" may be events, scores, or anything else that can be recorded and tallied. In psychological studies, such things are called **variables** because they can vary in quantifiable ways. Height, weight, age, income, IQ scores, number of items recalled on a memory test, number of smiles in a given time period—anything that can be measured, rated, or scored can serve as a variable.

A **positive correlation** means that high values of one variable are associated with high values of the other and that low values of one variable are associated with low values

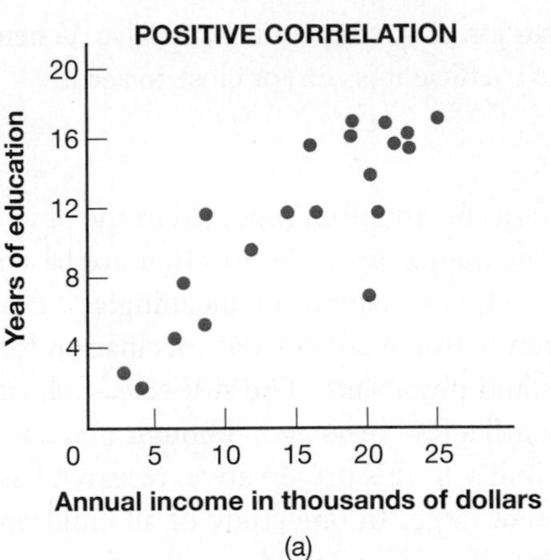

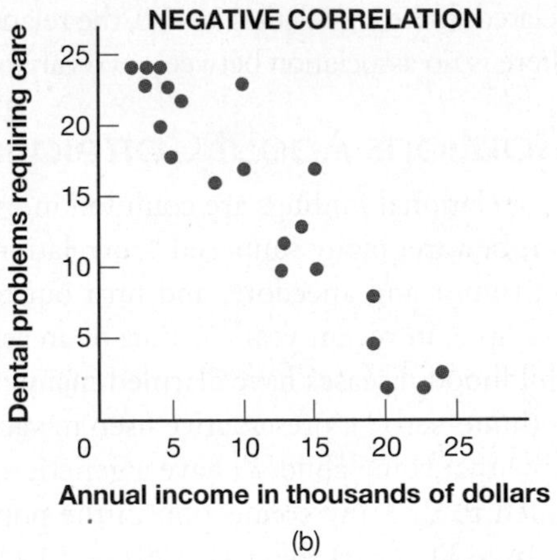

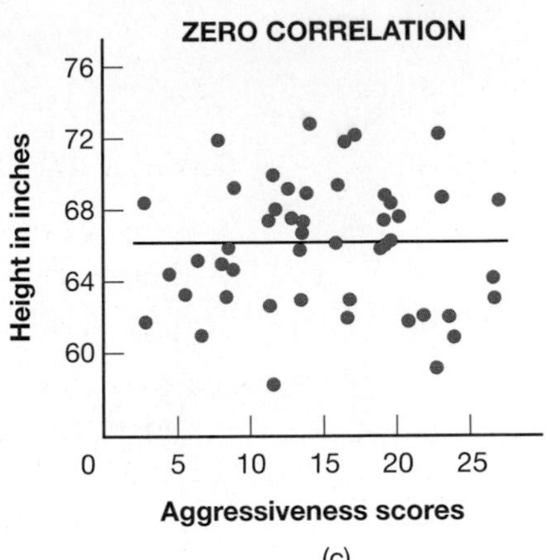

FIGURE 2.2 Correlations

Graph (a) shows a positive correlation: In general, income rises with education. Graph (b) shows a negative correlation: In general, the higher people's incomes, the fewer dental problems they have. Graph (c) shows a zero correlation between height and aggressiveness.

of the other. Height and weight are positively correlated, for example; so are IQ scores and school grades. Rarely is a correlation perfect, however. Some tall people weigh less than some short ones; some people with average IQs are superstars in the classroom and some with high IQs get poor grades. Figure 2.2a shows a positive correlation between men's educational level and their annual income. Each dot represents a man; you can find each man's educational level by drawing a horizontal line from his dot to the vertical axis. You can find his income by drawing a vertical line from his dot to the horizontal axis.

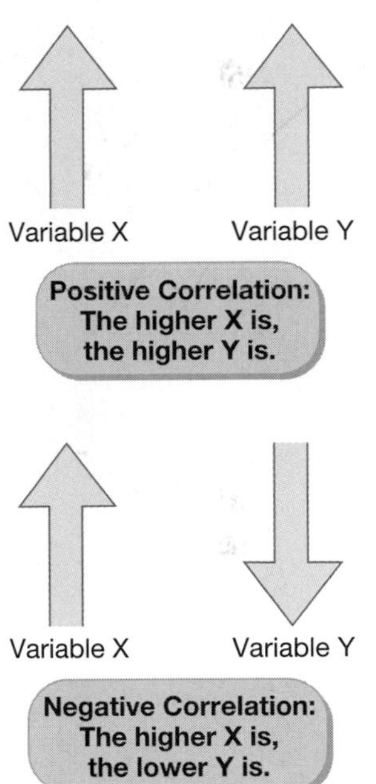

A **negative correlation** means that high values of one variable are associated with *low* values of the other. Figure 2.2b shows a negative correlation between average income and the incidence of dental disease for groups of 100 families. Each dot represents one group. In general, as you can see, the higher the income, the fewer the dental problems. In the automobile business, the older the car, the lower the price, except for antiques and models favored by collectors. As for human beings, in general, the older adults are, the fewer miles they can run, the fewer crimes they are likely to commit, and the fewer hairs they have on their heads. And remember our question about hours spent watching TV and grade-point averages? They're negatively correlated: Spending lots of hours in front of the television is associated with lower grades, possibly because TV watching cuts into studying time (Potter, 1987; Ridley-Johnson, Cooper, & Chance, 1983). That may be why the longer that children spend in front of the television, the less likely they are later on to get through college, even after controlling for IQ, behavioral problems, and socioeconomic status (Hancox, Milne, & Poulton, 2005). See whether you can think of other variables that are negatively correlated. Remember that a negative correlation means that a relationship exists: the *more* of one thing, the *less* of another. If there is no relationship between two variables, we say that they are *uncorrelated* (see Figure 2.2c). For example, shoe size and IQ scores are uncorrelated.

The statistic used to express a correlation is called the **coefficient of correlation**. This number conveys both the size of the correlation and its direction. A perfect positive correlation has a coefficient of +1.00, and a perfect negative correlation has a coefficient of –1.00. Suppose you weighed ten people and listed them from lightest to heaviest, then measured their heights and listed them from shortest to tallest. If the names on the two lists were in exactly the same order, the correlation between weight and height would be +1.00. If the correlation between two variables is +.80, it means that they are strongly

negative correlation An association between increases in one variable and decreases in another.

coefficient of correlation A measure of correlation that ranges in value from –1.00 to +1.00.

related. If the correlation is −.80, the relationship is just as strong, but it is negative. When there is no association between two variables, the coefficient is zero or close to zero.

Cautions About Correlations

Correlational findings are common in psychology and are often reported in the news. But beware; many supposed "correlations" in the media or on the Internet are based on rumor and anecdote, and turn out to be small, nonexistent, or meaningless. For example, in recent years, claims of an association between autism and vaccination for childhood diseases have alarmed many parents and physicians. The suspected culprit is thimerserol, a preservative used in vaccines until a few years ago. Though it is possible that some children have a genetic susceptibility to this preservative, research has failed to find any connection in the population at large. In one study of all children born in Denmark between 1991 and 1998 (over half a million children), the incidence of autism in vaccinated children was actually a bit *lower* than in unvaccinated children (Madsen et al., 2002). Moreover, after vaccines containing thimerserol were removed from the market in Denmark, there was no subsequent decrease in the incidence of autism (Madsen et al., 2003). Symptoms of childhood autism are often first recognized at about the same time that children are vaccinated, but this appears to be a mere coincidence.

Even when correlations are reliable and meaningful, they can be misleading, because *a correlation does not establish causation*. It is often easy to assume that if variable A predicts variable B, A must be causing B—that is, making B happen—but that is not necessarily so. For example, a study recently discovered a positive correlation between the number of hours that children watch television between ages 1 and 3 and their risk of having attention problems (impulsiveness, difficulty concentrating, hyperactivity) by age 7 (Christakis et al., 2004). The news media jumped on this finding and implied that watching TV *causes* later attention problems. Now, that might be true, but it is also possible that attention

CONSIDER OTHER INTERPRETATIONS

The number of hours toddlers spend watching TV is correlated with their risk of having attention problems at age 7. Does that mean TV watching causes attention problems? Are there other possible explanations for this finding?

problems cause TV watching: Perhaps children who have attention problems early on are more attracted to television than calmer children are. Or perhaps the harried parents of distractable children are more likely than other parents to rely on TV as a babysitter. It is also possible that neither variable causes the other directly: Perhaps parents who allow their young kids to watch a lot of TV have attention problems themselves and, therefore, they create a home environment that fosters hyperactivity and inattentiveness. Likewise, the negative correlation between TV watching and grades mentioned earlier might exist for a number of reasons: because heavy TV watchers have less time to study, because they have some personality trait that causes an attraction to TV *and* an aversion to studying, because they use TV as an escape when their grades are low, because TV is especially appealing to people who are not academically inclined . . . you get the idea.

The moral of the story: When two variables are associated, one variable may or may not be causing the other.

QUICK quiz

Are you clear about correlations?

A. Identify each of the following as a positive or negative correlation.

1. The higher a male monkey's level of the hormone testosterone, the more aggressive he is likely to be.
2. The older people are, the less frequently they tend to have sexual intercourse.
3. The hotter the weather, the more crimes against persons (such as muggings) tend to occur.

B. Now see whether you can generate two or three possible explanations for each of the preceding findings.

Answers:

A. 1. positive **2.** negative **3.** positive **B. 1.** The hormone may cause aggressiveness, acting aggressively may stimulate hormone production, or some third factor, such as age or dominance, may influence aggressiveness and hormone production independently. **2.** Older people may have less interest in sex than younger people, have less energy or more physical ailments, or simply have more trouble finding partners. **3.** Hot temperatures may make people edgy and cause them to commit crimes; potential victims may be more plentiful in warm weather because more people go outside; criminals may find it more comfortable to be out committing their crimes in warm weather than in cold. (Our explanations for these correlations are not the only ones possible.)

WHAT'S**AHEAD** 

- Why do psychologists rely so heavily on experiments?
- What, exactly, do control groups control for?
- In a double-blind experiment, who is "blind" and what aren't they supposed to "see"?

Experiments: Hunting for Causes

Researchers gain plenty of illuminating information from descriptive studies, but when they want to actually track down the causes of behavior, they rely heavily on the experimental method. An **experiment** allows the researcher to *control*, or manipulate, the situation being studied. Instead of being a passive recorder of behavior, the researcher actively does something that he or she believes will affect people's behavior and then observes what happens. These procedures allow the experimenter to draw conclusions about cause and effect—about what causes what.

experiment A controlled test of a hypothesis in which the researcher manipulates one variable to discover its effect on another.

independent variable A variable that an experimenter manipulates.

dependent variable A variable that an experimenter predicts will be affected by manipulations of the independent variable.

Experimental Variables

Imagine that you are a psychologist and you come across reports suggesting that cigarette smoking improves reaction time on simple tasks. You have a hunch that nicotine has the opposite effect, however, when the task is as complex and demanding as driving a car. You know that on average, smokers have more car accidents than nonsmokers. But you realize that this relationship does not prove that smoking *causes* accidents. Smokers may simply be greater risk takers than nonsmokers, whether the risk is lung cancer or trying to beat a red light. Or perhaps the distraction of lighting up accounts for the increased accident risk, rather than smoking itself. So you decide to do an experiment to test your hypothesis.

In a laboratory, you ask smokers to "drive" using a computerized driving simulator equipped with a stick shift and a gas pedal. The object, you tell them, is to maximize the distance covered by driving as fast as possible on a winding road while avoiding collisions with other cars. At your request, some of the participants smoke a cigarette immediately before climbing into the driver's seat. Others do not. You are interested in comparing how many collisions the two groups have. The basic design of this experiment is illustrated in Figure 2.3, which you may want to refer to as you read the next few pages.

The aspect of an experimental situation manipulated or varied by the researcher is known as the **independent variable**. The reaction of the subjects—the behavior that the researcher tries to predict—is the **dependent variable**. Every experiment has at

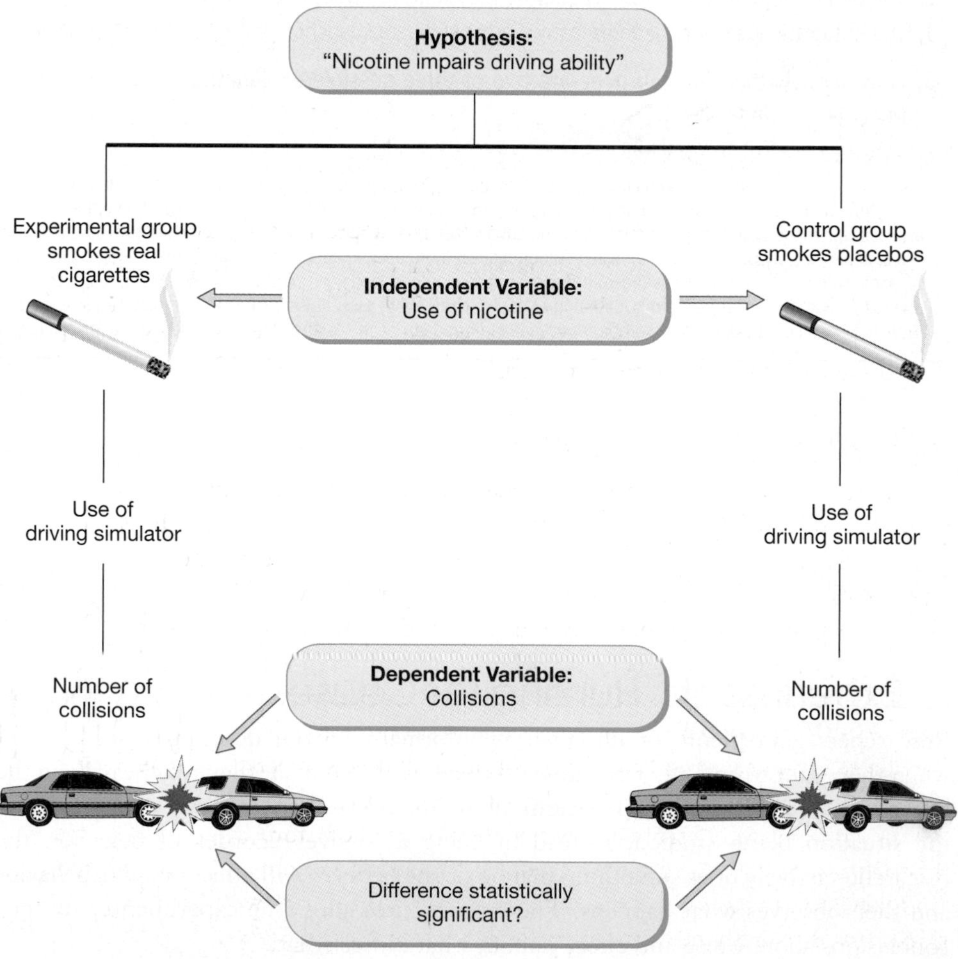

FIGURE 2.3 Do Smoking and Driving Mix?
The text describes this experimental design to test the hypothesis that nicotine in cigarettes impairs driving skills.

least one independent and one dependent variable. In our example, the independent variable is nicotine use: one cigarette versus none. The dependent variable is the number of collisions.

control condition In an experiment, a comparison condition in which subjects are not exposed to the same treatment as in the experimental condition.

Ideally, everything in the experimental situation except the independent variable is held constant—that is, kept the same for all participants. You would not have some people use a stick shift and others an automatic, unless shift type were an independent variable. Similarly, you would not have some people go through the experiment alone and others perform in front of an audience. Holding everything but the independent variable constant ensures that whatever happens is due to the researcher's manipulation and nothing else. It allows you to rule out other interpretations.

Understandably, students often have trouble keeping independent and dependent variables straight. You might think of it this way: The dependent variable—the outcome of the study—*depends* on the independent variable. When psychologists set up an experiment, they think, "If I do X, the people in my study will do Y." The "X" represents the independent variable; the "Y" represents the dependent variable:

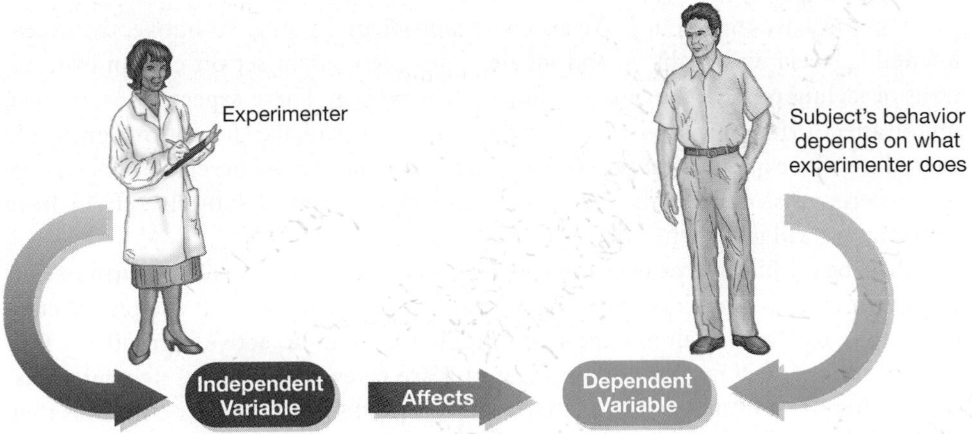

Most variables may be either independent or dependent, depending on what the experimenter wishes to find out. If you want to know whether eating chocolate makes people nervous, then the amount of chocolate eaten is the independent variable. If you want to know whether feeling nervous makes people eat chocolate, then the amount of chocolate eaten is the dependent variable.

Experimental and Control Conditions

Experiments usually require both an experimental condition and a comparison, or **control condition**. In the control condition, subjects are treated exactly as they are in the experimental condition, except that they are not exposed to the same treatment, or manipulation of the independent variable. Without a control condition, you cannot be sure that the behavior you are interested in would not have occurred anyway, even without your manipulation. In some studies, the same subjects can be used in both the control and the experimental conditions; they are said to serve as their own controls. In other studies, subjects are assigned to either an *experimental group* or a *control group*.

In our nicotine experiment, the people who smoke before driving make up the experimental group, and those who refrain from smoking make up the control group. We want these two groups to be roughly the same in terms of average driving skill.

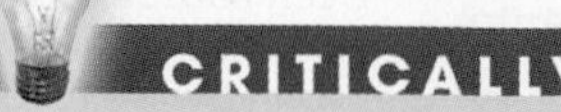

THINKING CRITICALLY

CONSIDER OTHER INTERPRETATIONS

You have developed a new form of therapy that you believe cures anxiety. Sixty-three percent of the people who go through your program improve. What else, besides your therapy, could account for this result? Why shouldn't you rush out to open an anxiety clinic?

It would not do to start out with a bunch of reckless roadrunners in the experimental group and a bunch of tired tortoises in the control group. We probably also want the two groups to be similar in age, education, smoking history, and other characteristics so that none of these variables will affect our results. One way to accomplish this is to use **random assignment** of people to one group or another—for example, by randomly assigning them numbers and putting those with even numbers in one group and those with odd numbers in another. If we have enough participants in our study, individual characteristics that could possibly affect the results are likely to be roughly balanced in the two groups, so we can safely ignore them.

Sometimes researchers use several experimental or control groups. For example, in our nicotine study, we might want to examine the effects of different levels of nicotine by having people smoke one, two, or three cigarettes before "driving," and then comparing each of these experimental groups to each other and to a control group of nonsmokers as well. For now, however, let's focus just on experimental subjects who smoked one cigarette.

We now have two groups. We also have a problem. In order to smoke, the experimental subjects must light up and inhale. These acts might set off certain expectations of feeling relaxed, nervous, confident, or whatever. These expectations, in turn, might affect driving performance. It would be better to have the control group do everything the experimental group does except use nicotine. Therefore, let's change our experimental design a bit. Instead of having the control subjects refrain from smoking, we will give them a **placebo**, a fake treatment.

Placebos, which are critical when testing new drugs, often take the form of pills or injections containing no active ingredients. In our study, we will use phony cigarettes that taste and smell like the real thing but contain no active ingredients. Our control subjects will not know their cigarettes are fakes and will have no way of distinguishing them from real ones. Now if they have substantially fewer collisions than the experimental group, we will feel safe in concluding that nicotine increases the probability of an auto accident.

Control groups, by the way, are also crucial in many nonexperimental studies. For example, in recent years, some psychotherapists have published books arguing that teenage girls develop special problems with self-esteem, confidence, and body image. But unless they have also tested or surveyed a comparable group of teenage boys, there is no way of knowing whether these problems are unique to girls or typical of all adolescents—or none of them. (For the answer, see Chapter 14.)

Experimenter Effects

Because expectations can influence the results of a study, participants should not know whether they are in an experimental or a control group. When this is so (as it usually is), the experiment is said to be a **single-blind study**. But participants are not the only ones who bring expectations to the laboratory; so do researchers. And researchers' expectations, biases, and hopes for a particular result may cause them to inadvertently influence the participants' responses through facial expressions, posture, tone of voice, or some other cue.

Many years ago, Robert Rosenthal (1966) demonstrated how powerful such **experimenter effects** can be. He had students teach rats to run a maze. Half the students were told that their rats had been bred to be "maze bright," and half were told that their rats had been bred to be "maze dull." In reality, there were no genetic

random assignment A procedure for assigning people to experimental and control groups in which each individual has the same probability as any other of being assigned to a given group.

placebo An inactive substance or fake treatment used as a control in an experiment or given by a medical practitioner to a patient.

single-blind study An experiment in which subjects do not know whether they are in an experimental or a control group.

experimenter effects Unintended changes in subjects' behavior due to cues inadvertently given by the experimenter.

GET INVOLVED!

➤THE POWER OF A SMILE

Prove to yourself how easy it is for experimenters to affect the behavior of a study's participants by giving off nonverbal cues. As you walk around campus, quickly glance at individuals approaching you and either smile or maintain a neutral expression; then observe the other person's expression. Try to keep the duration of your glance the same whether you smile or not. You might record the results as you collect them instead of relying on your memory. Chances are that people you smile at will smile back, whereas those you approach with a neutral expression will do the same. What does this tell you about the importance of doing double-blind studies?

differences between the two groups of rats, yet the supposedly brainy rats actually did learn the maze more quickly, apparently because of the way the students treated them. If an experimenter's expectations can affect a rodent's behavior, reasoned Rosenthal, surely they can affect a human being's behavior. He went on to demonstrate this point in many other studies (Rosenthal, 1994). Even an experimenter's friendly smile (or lack of one) can affect people's responses.

One solution to the problem of experimenter effects is to do a **double-blind study**. In such a study, the person running the experiment, the one having actual contact with the subjects, also does not know which subjects are in which groups until the data have been gathered. Double-blind procedures are standard in drug research. Different doses of a drug are coded in some way, and the person administering the drug is kept in the dark about the code's meaning until after the experiment. To run our nicotine study in a double-blind fashion, we would keep the person dispensing the cigarettes from knowing which ones were real and which were placebos.

Single-blind Study
Experimenter knows who is in which group; subjects do not.

Double-blind Study
Neither experimenter nor subjects know who is in which group.

Advantages and Limitations of Experiments

Because experiments allow conclusions about cause and effect, and because they permit researchers to distinguish real effects from placebo effects, they have long been the method of choice in psychology.

However, like all methods, the experiment has its limitations. Just as in other kinds of studies, the participants are typically college students and may not always be representative of the larger population. Moreover, in an experiment, the researcher determines which questions are asked and which behaviors are recorded, and the subjects try to do as they are told. In their desire to cooperate with the experimenter or present themselves in a positive light, they may act in ways that they ordinarily would not (Kihlstrom, 1995).

Thus, research psychologists confront a dilemma: The more control they exercise over the situation, the more artificial the situation—and the results obtained from it—may be. For this reason, many psychologists have called for more **field research**, the careful study of behavior in natural contexts such as schools and the workplace, using

double-blind study An experiment in which neither the subjects nor the individuals running the study know which subjects are in the control group and which are in the experimental group until after the results are tallied.

field research Descriptive or experimental research conducted in a natural setting outside the laboratory.

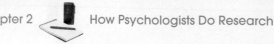

both descriptive and experimental methods. For example, a psychologist interested in ways of reducing prejudice might study that problem not just in the laboratory but also in offices and schools.

Every research method has both its strengths and its weaknesses. Did you make a list of each method's advantages and disadvantages, as we suggested earlier? If so, compare it now with the one in Review 2.1

REVIEW 2.1

Research Methods in Psychology: Their Advantages and Disadvantages

Method	Advantages	Disadvantages
Case study	Good source of hypotheses. Provides in-depth information on individuals. Unusual cases can shed light on situations or problems that are unethical or impractical to study in other ways.	Vital information may be missing, making the case hard to interpret. The person's memories may be selective or inaccurate. The individual may not be representative or typical.
Naturalistic observation	Allows description of behavior as it occurs in the natural environment. Often useful in first stages of a research program.	Allows researcher little or no control of the situation. Observations may be biased. Does not allow firm conclusions about cause and effect.
Laboratory observation	Allows more control than naturalistic observation. Allows use of sophisticated equipment.	Allows researcher only limited control of the situation. Observations may be biased. Does not allow firm conclusions about cause and effect. Behavior may differ from behavior in the natural environment.
Test	Yields information on personality traits, emotional states, aptitudes, and abilities.	Difficult to construct tests that are reliable and valid.
Survey	Provides a large amount of information on large numbers of people.	If sample is nonrepresentative or biased, it may be impossible to generalize from the results. Responses may be inaccurate or untrue.
Correlational study	Shows whether two or more variables are related. Allows qeneral predictions.	Does not permit identification of cause and effect.
Experiment	Allows researcher to control the situation. Permits researcher to identify cause and effect and to distinguish placebo effects from treatment effects.	Situation is artificial, and results may not generalize well to the real world. Sometimes difficult to avoid experimenter effects.

QUICK quiz

Exercise control over your education by taking this quiz.

A. Name the independent and dependent variables in studies designed to answer the following questions:

1. Whether sleeping after learning a poem improves memory for the poem
2. Whether the presence of other people affects a person's willingness to help someone in distress
3. Whether people get agitated from listening to heavy metal music

B. On a talk show, Dr. Blitznik announces a fabulous new program: Chocolate Immersion Therapy (C.I.T.). "People who spend one day a week doing nothing but eating chocolate are soon cured of eating disorders, depression, and poor study habits," claims Dr. Blitznik. What should you find out about C.I.T. before signing up?

Answers:

A. 1. Opportunity to sleep after learning is the independent variable; memory for the poem is the dependent variable. **2.** The presence of other people is the independent variable; willingness to help others is the dependent variable. **3.** Exposure to heavy metal music is the independent variable; agitation is the dependent variable. **B.** Some questions to ask: Is there research showing that people who went through C.I.T. did better than those in a control group who did not have the therapy or who had a different therapy—say, Broccoli Immersion Therapy? If so, how many people were studied? How were they selected, and how were they assigned to the therapy and no-therapy groups? Did the person running the experiment know who was getting C.I.T. and who was not? How long did the "cures" last? Has the research been peer reviewed? Has it been replicated?

WHAT'S**AHEAD** 

- In psychological studies, why are averages sometimes misleading?
- How can psychologists tell whether a finding is impressive or trivial?
- Why are some findings significant statistically yet unimportant in practical terms?

Evaluating the Findings

If you are a psychologist who has just done an observational study, a survey, or an experiment, your work has just begun. Once you have some results in hand, you must do three things with them: (1) describe them, (2) assess how reliable and meaningful they are, and (3) figure out how to explain them.

Descriptive Statistics: Finding Out What's So

Let's say that 30 people in the nicotine experiment smoked real cigarettes and 30 smoked placebos. We have recorded the number of collisions for each person on the driving simulator. Now we have 60 numbers. What can we do with them?

The first step is to summarize the data. The world does not want to hear how many collisions each person had. It wants to know what happened in the nicotine group as a whole, compared to what happened in the control group. To provide this information, we need numbers that sum up our data. Such numbers, known as **descriptive statistics**, are often depicted in graphs and charts.

descriptive statistics Statistical procedures that organize and summarize research data.

A good way to summarize the data is to compute group averages. The most commonly used type of average is the **arithmetic mean**. (For two other types, see the Appendix.) The mean is calculated by adding up all the individual scores and dividing

arithmetic mean An average that is calculated by adding up a set of quantities and dividing the sum by the total number of quantities in the set.

Most people assume that "on average" means "typically"—but sometimes it doesn't! Averages can be misleading if you don't know the extent to which events deviated from the statistical mean and how they were distributed.

standard deviation A commonly used measure of variability that indicates the average difference between scores in a distribution and their mean.

the result by the number of scores. We can compute a mean for the nicotine group by adding up the 30 collision scores and dividing the sum by 30. Then we can do the same for the control group. Now our 60 numbers have been boiled down to 2. For the sake of our example, let's assume that the nicotine group had an average of 10 collisions, whereas the control group's average was only 7.

We must be careful, however, about how we interpret these averages. It is possible that no one in our nicotine group actually had 10 collisions. Perhaps half the people in the group were motoring maniacs and had 15 collisions, whereas the others were more cautious and had only 5. Perhaps almost all the subjects had 9, 10, or 11 collisions. Perhaps the number of accidents ranged from 0 to 15. The mean does not tell us about such variability in the subjects' responses. For that, we need other descriptive statistics. For example, the **standard deviation** tells us how clustered or spread out the individual scores are around the mean; the more spread out they are, the less "typical" the mean is. (See Figure 2.4 and, for more details, the Appendix.) Unfortunately, when research is reported in newspapers or on the nightly news, you usually hear only about the mean.

Inferential Statistics: Asking "So What?"

At this point in our nicotine study, we have one group with an average of 10 collisions and another with an average of 7. Should we break out the champagne? Try to get on TV? Call our mothers?

FIGURE 2.4 Same Mean, Different Meaning

In both distributions of scores, the mean is 5, but in (a) the scores are clustered around the mean, whereas in (b) they are widely dispersed, so the standard deviations for the distributions will be quite different. In which distribution is the mean more "typical" of all scores?

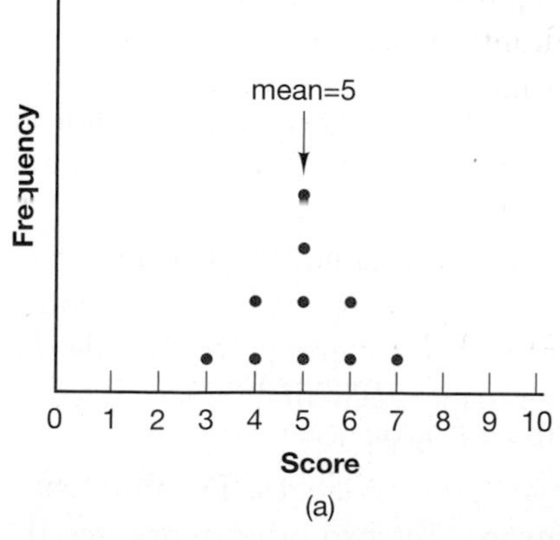

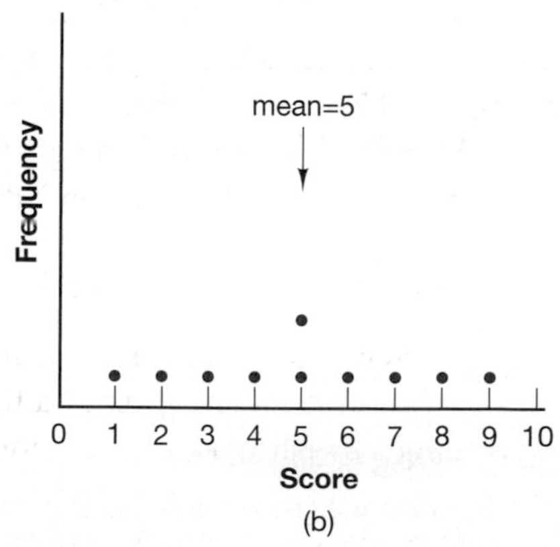

inferential statistics Statistical procedures that allow researchers to draw inferences about how statistically meaningful a study's results are.

significance tests Statistical tests that show how likely it is that a study's results occurred merely by chance.

Better hold off. Perhaps if one group had an average of 15 collisions and the other an average of 1, we could get excited. But rarely does a psychological study hit you between the eyes with a sensationally clear result. In most cases, there is some possibility that the difference between the two groups was due simply to chance. Despite all our precautions, perhaps the people in the nicotine group just happened to be a little more accident-prone, and their collisions had nothing to do with the nicotine.

To find out how impressive the data are, psychologists use **inferential statistics**. These statistics do not merely describe or summarize the data; they permit a researcher to draw *inferences* (conclusions based on evidence) about how meaningful the findings are. Like descriptive statistics, inferential statistics involve the application of mathematical formulas to the data. (Again, see the Appendix for details.)

Historically, the most commonly used inferential statistics have been **significance tests**, which tell researchers how likely a result was to have occurred by chance. In our nicotine study, a significance test will tell us how likely it is that the difference between the nicotine group and the placebo group occurred by chance. It is not possible to rule out chance entirely, but if the likelihood that a result occurred by chance is extremely low, we can say that the result is *statistically significant*. This means that the probability that the difference is "real" is overwhelming—not certain, mind you, but overwhelming.

By convention, psychologists consider a result to be significant if it would be expected to occur by chance 5 or fewer times in 100 repetitions of the study. Another way of saying this is that the result is significant at the .05 ("point oh five") level. If the difference could be expected to occur by chance in 6 out of 100 studies, we would have to say that the results failed to support the hypothesis—that the difference we obtained might well have occurred merely by chance—although we might still want to do further research to be sure. You can see that psychologists refuse to be impressed by just any old result.

Statistically significant results allow psychologists to make general predictions about human behavior. These predictions are usually stated as probabilities ("On average, we can expect 60 percent of all students to do X, Y, or Z"). However, they usually do not tell us with any certainty what a particular individual will do in a particular situation. Probabilistic results are typical in all of the sciences, not just psychology. Medical research, for example, can tell us that the odds are high that someone who smokes will get lung cancer, but because many variables interact to produce any particular case of cancer, research cannot tell us for sure whether Aunt Bessie, who smokes two packs a day, will come down with the disease.

By the way, a nicotine study similar to our hypothetical example was actually done (Spilich, June, & Renner, 1992). Smokers who lit up before driving got a little farther on the simulated road, but they also had significantly more rear-end collisions on average (10.7) than did temporarily abstaining smokers (5.2) or nonsmokers (3.1). After hearing about these findings, the head of Federal Express banned smoking on the job among all of the company's drivers.

Interpreting the Findings

The last step in any study is to figure out what the findings mean. Trying to understand behavior from uninterpreted findings is like trying to become fluent in Swedish by reading a Swedish–English dictionary. Just as you need the grammar of Swedish to tell you how the words fit together, the psychologist needs hypotheses and theories to explain how the facts that emerge from research fit together.

Choosing the Best Explanation. Sometimes it is hard to choose between competing explanations. Does nicotine disrupt driving by impairing coordination, by increasing a driver's vulnerability to distraction, by interfering with the processing of information, by distorting the perception of danger—or by some combination of these factors? In interpreting any study, we must not go too far beyond the facts. Several explanations may fit those facts equally well, which means that more research will be needed to determine the best one.

Sometimes the best interpretation of a finding does not emerge until a hypothesis has been tested in different ways. Although the methods we have described tend to be appropriate for different questions (see Review 2.2), sometimes one method can be used to confirm, disconfirm, or extend the results obtained with another. If the findings of studies using various methods converge, there is greater reason to be confident about them. If they conflict, researchers must modify their hypotheses or do more research.

Here is an example. When psychologists compare the mental-test scores of young people and old people, they usually find that younger people outscore older ones. This type of research, in which groups are compared at a given time, is called **cross-sectional**:

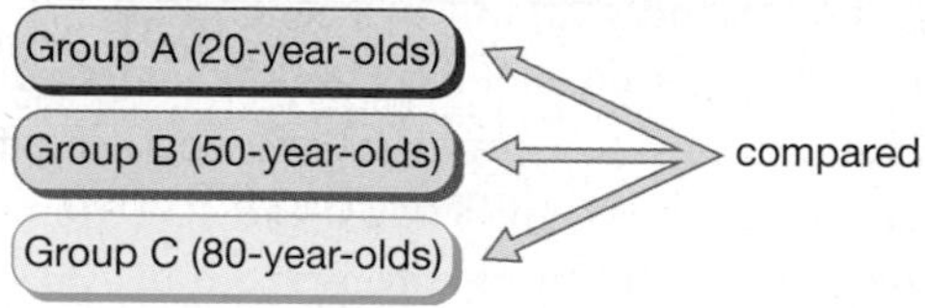

But **longitudinal studies** can also be used to investigate mental abilities across the life span. In a longitudinal study, the same people are followed over a period of time and are reassessed at regular intervals:

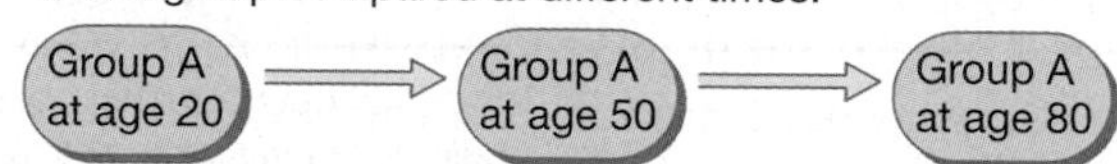

In contrast to cross-sectional studies, longitudinal studies find that as people age, they sometimes perform as well as they ever did on certain mental tests. A *general* decline in ability may not occur until people reach their 70s or 80s (Salthouse, 1998; Schaie, 1993). Why do results from the two types of studies conflict? Probably because cross-sectional studies measure generational differences; younger generations tend to outperform older ones in part because they are better educated or are more familiar with the tests used. Without longitudinal studies, we might falsely conclude that all types of mental ability inevitably decline with advancing age.

Judging the Result's Importance. Sometimes psychologists agree on the reliability and meaning of a finding but not on its ultimate relevance for theory or practice. Statistical significance alone does not provide the answer (Killeen, 2005). A result may be statistically significant yet be small and of little consequence in everyday life because the independent variable does not explain most of the variation in people's behavior. On the other hand, a result may not quite reach statistical significance yet be worth following up on (Falk & Greenbaum, 1995; Hunter, 1997). Because of these and other problems, many psychologists now prefer other statistical procedures that reveal the **effect size**—that is, how powerful the independent variable really is (how much of the variation in the data the variable accounts for). If the independent

cross-sectional study A study in which subjects of different ages are compared at a given time.

longitudinal study A study in which subjects are followed and periodically reassessed over a period of time.

effect size The amount of variance among scores in a study accounted for by the independent variable.

REVIEW 2.2

Psychological Research Methods Contrasted

Psychologists may use different methods to answer different questions about a topic. To illustrate, this table shows some ways in which the methods described in this chapter can be used to study different questions about aggression. The methods listed are not mutually exclusive. That is, sometimes two or more methods can be used to investigate the same question. As discussed in the text, findings based on one method may extend, support, or disconfirm findings based on another.

Method	Purpose	Example
Case study	To understand the development of aggressive behavior in a particular individual; to formulate research hypotheses about the origins of aggressiveness	Developmental history of a serial killer
Naturalistic observation	To describe the nature of aggressive acts in early childhood	Observation, tallying, and description of hitting, kicking, etc. during free-play periods in a preschool
Laboratory observation	To find out whether aggressiveness in pairs of same-sex and different-sex children differs in frequency or intensity	Observation through a one-way window of same-sex and different-sex pairs of preschoolers; pairs must negotiate who gets to play with an attractive toy that has been promised to each child
Test	To compare the personality traits of aggressive and nonaggressive persons	Administration of personality tests to violent and nonviolent prisoners
Survey	To find out how common domestic violence is in the general population	Questionnaire asking anonymous respondents (in a sample representative of the population) about the occurrence of slapping, hitting, etc. in their homes
Correlational study	To examine the relationship between aggressiveness and television viewing	Administration to college students of a paper-and-pencil test of aggressiveness and a questionnaire on number of hours spent watching TV weekly; computation of correlation coefficient
Experiment	To find out whether high air temperatures elicit aggressive behavior	Arrangement for individuals to "shock" a "learner" (actually a confederate of the experimenter) while seated in a room heated to either 72°F or 85°F

meta-analysis A procedure for combining and analyzing data from many studies; it determines how much of the variance in scores across all studies can be explained by a particular variable.

variable explains 5 percent of the variation, it's not very powerful, but if it explains 40 percent, it's pretty impressive.

One popular statistical technique, called **meta-analysis**, combines and analyzes data from many studies instead of assessing each study's results separately. As you may recall, meta-analytic studies provided the data for the comparisons between students and nonstudents described in our "Close-up on Research" feature earlier in this chapter. Meta-analysis tells a researcher how much of the variation in scores across *all* the studies examined can be explained by a particular variable. For example, a meta-analysis of nearly 50 years of research found that gender accounts for a good deal of the variance in performance on certain spatial-visual tasks, with males doing better on average (Voyer, Voyer, & Bryden, 1995). In contrast, other meta-analyses have shown that gender accounts for very little of the variance on tests of verbal and math ability, usually only 1 to 5 percent (Hyde, 2005). Although gender differences on these tests are often reliable, they are small, and scores for males and females greatly overlap.

Techniques such as meta-analysis are useful because rarely does one study prove anything, in psychology or any other field. That is why you should be suspicious of headlines that announce a sudden major scientific breakthrough based on a single study. Such breakthroughs do occur, but they are rare.

QUICK quiz

Major scientific breakthrough! Self–tests help!

A. Check your understanding of the descriptive-inferential distinction by placing a check in the appropriate column for each phrase:

	Descriptive statistics	Inferential statistics
1. Summarize the data	______	______
2. Give likelihood of data occurring by chance	______	______
3. Include the mean	______	______
4. Give measure of statistical significance	______	______
5. Tell you whether to call your mother about your results	______	______

B. If a researcher studies the same group over many years, the study is said to be ______________.

C. On the Internet, you read a posting about a "Fantastic Scientific Breakthrough in Treating Shyness." Why should you be cautious about this announcement?

Answers:

A. 1. descriptive **2.** inferential **3.** descriptive **4.** inferential **5.** inferential **B.** longitudinal **C.** Scientific progress, in psychology or any field, usually proceeds gradually, not all at once. And besides, anyone can post a claim on the Internet, so you will want to ask, "What's the original source of this claim?"

WHAT'S**AHEAD**

- Why do psychologists often lie to their subjects?
- Why do psychologists study nonhuman animals?

Keeping the Enterprise Ethical

Rigorous research methods are the very heart of science, so it is not surprising that psychologists spend considerable time discussing and debating their procedures for collecting and evaluating data. They are also concerned about the ethics of their

activities—the moral principles of conduct governing research. In nearly all colleges and universities, a review committee must approve all studies and be sure they conform to federal regulations. In addition, the American Psychological Association (APA) has a code of ethics that all members must follow.

informed consent The doctrine that human research subjects must participate voluntarily and must know enough about the study to make an intelligent decision about whether to participate.

The Ethics of Studying Human Beings

The APA code calls on psychological scientists to respect the dignity and welfare of human subjects. People must participate voluntarily and must know enough about the study to make an intelligent decision about participating, a doctrine known as **informed consent**. Researchers must also protect participants from physical and mental harm, and if any risk exists, they must warn the subjects in advance and give them an opportunity to withdraw at any time. In the case of our nicotine study, we would have to use only people who were already smokers; exposing nonsmokers to the risks associated with smoking—a risk they would ordinarily not choose to run—would be unethical.

The policy of informed consent sometimes clashes with an experimenter's need to keep subjects in the dark about the true purpose of the study. In such cases, if the purpose were revealed in advance, the results would be ruined because the participants would not behave naturally. In social psychology, especially, a study's design sometimes calls for an elaborate deception, as we will see in Chapter 8. For example, a confederate might pretend to be having a seizure. The researcher can then find out whether bystanders—the uninformed subjects—will respond to a person who needs help. If the subjects knew that the confederate was only acting, obviously they would not bother to intervene or call for assistance.

Sometimes people have been misled about procedures intentionally designed to make them uncomfortable, angry, guilty, ashamed, or anxious so that researchers can learn what people do when they feel this way. In anxiety studies, participants have been led to believe, falsely, that they failed a test or were about to get a painful shock. In studies of embarrassment and anger, people have been made to look clumsy in front of others, or have been called insulting names, or have been told they were incompetent. In studies of dishonesty, participants have been entrapped into cheating and have

"So! How is everybody today?"

then been confronted with evidence of their guilt. The APA's ethical guidelines require researchers to show that any deceptive procedures are justified by a study's potential value, to consider alternative procedures, and to thoroughly debrief participants about the true purpose and methods of the study afterward. When people are debriefed and told why deception was necessary, they are rarely resentful. Most are glad that they participated and say they are willing to take part in further studies. But the issues raised by deception will always be with us, and the APA periodically reevaluates its ethical code to deal with them.

The Ethics of Studying Animals

Another ethical issue concerns the use and treatment of animals in research. Animals have always been used in only a small percentage of psychological studies, and in recent years, the number has declined further. Nonetheless, in certain areas of psychological research, animals still play a crucial role. Usually they are not harmed (as in research on mating in hamsters, which is fun for the hamsters), but sometimes they are (as in research on vision in kittens, when part of the animals' visual systems must be surgically removed). Some studies require an animal's death, as when rats brought up in deprived or enriched environments are sacrificed so that their brains can be examined for any effects.

Psychologists study animals for many reasons:

- ***To conduct basic research on a particular species.*** For example, researchers have learned a great deal about the unusually lusty and cooperative lives of bonobo apes.
- ***To discover practical applications.*** For example, behavioral studies have shown farmers how to reduce crop destruction by birds and deer without resorting to their traditional method—shooting the animals.
- ***To study issues that cannot be studied experimentally with human beings because of practical or ethical considerations.*** For example, research on monkeys has demonstrated the effects of maternal deprivation on emotional development—and the effects of later experience in overcoming early deprivation.
- ***To clarify theoretical questions.*** For example, we might not attribute the longer life spans of women solely to lifestyle factors and health practices if we discover that a male–female difference exists in other mammals as well.

Psychologists sometimes use animals to study learning, memory, emotion, and social behavior. On the left, John Boitano and Kathryn Scavo observe a swimming rat as it learns the location of platforms in a pool of dark water. On the right, Frans de Waal observes a group of chimpanzees socializing in an outdoor play area.

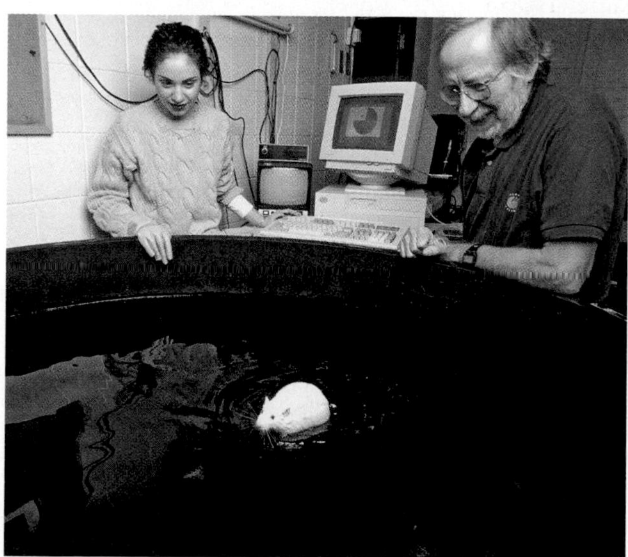

- ***To improve human welfare.*** For example, animal studies have helped researchers develop ways to reduce chronic pain, rehabilitate patients with neurological disorders, and understand the mechanisms underlying memory loss and senility—to name only a few benefits.

Animal research, however, has provoked angry disputes. Many animal-rights proponents want to eliminate all research using animals, and some activists have severely damaged research laboratories (ironically, sometimes causing the deaths of the lab animals they have "freed"). On the other side, some defenders of animal research have refused to acknowledge that confinement in laboratories can be psychologically and physically harmful for some species. This conflict has motivated psychologists to find ways to improve the treatment of research animals. The APA's ethical code covering the humane treatment of animals has been made more comprehensive, and federal laws governing the housing and care of research animals have been strengthened. Many researchers have developed alternative procedures that take advantage of new technology. The difficult task for scientists is to balance the many benefits of animal research with an acknowledgment of past abuses and a compassionate attitude toward species other than our own.

Now that you have finished the first two chapters of this book, you are ready to explore more deeply what psychologists have learned about human psychology. The methods of psychological science, as we will see repeatedly in the remainder of the book, have overturned some deeply entrenched assumptions about the way people think, feel, act, and adapt to the events that have occurred in their lives. Here is just a preview of some of the surprising findings these methods have produced:

- ***Assumption:*** If you are angry and upset, it's a good idea to "let it all out" by expressing your emotions angrily or by displacing them in aggressive activities like violent sports. ***Finding:*** In Chapter 11, you will learn why, on the contrary, ventilating anger only tends to make people angrier.
- ***Assumption:*** If you are under a lot of stress—all that studying! all that work! all that pressure!—you are likely to get sick. ***Finding:*** In Chapter 15, you will learn why the stress–illness link is not so simple, and why many people who are under great stress nonetheless stay healthy.
- ***Assumption:*** Children who have traumatic experiences—for example, who live through war, who have alcoholic parents, or who have been sexually molested—are doomed to have lasting psychological symptoms. ***Finding:*** In Chapter 14, you will learn why most children are remarkably resilient and eventually recover even from terrible experiences.
- ***Assumption:*** If you are the victim of a crime, your ability to identify the perpetrator will, naturally, be extremely accurate. ***Finding:*** In Chapter 10, you will learn why many eyewitnesses to crimes, including crimes in which they themselves were the victims, are wrong in their beliefs about what they saw.
- ***Assumption:*** You don't have to know about research and science to be a therapist; all that matters is empathy, compassion, and training in therapeutic techniques. ***Finding:*** Well, maybe—but as you will learn in Chapter 17, you'd better know about scientific findings if you don't want to be a *bad* therapist.

The methods of science are designed not only to help us learn new things but also to illuminate our errors and biases and enable us to seek knowledge with an open mind. Biologist Thomas Huxley put it well: The essence of science, he said, is "to sit down before the fact as a little child, be prepared to give up every preconceived notion, follow humbly wherever and to whatever abyss nature leads, or you shall learn nothing."

Taking Psychology with You

Lying with Statistics

In this chapter, we have seen that statistical procedures are indispensable tools for assessing research. Without them, scientists would wallow around in numbers, not knowing if they had found anything important. But statistics can also be manipulated, exaggerated, misrepresented, and even made up by people hoping to promote a particular political or social agenda. That is why an essential part of critical and scientific thinking is learning not only how to use statistics correctly but also how to identify their misuse.

A primary reason for the misuse of statistics is "innumeracy" (mathematical illiteracy). In his excellent book *Damned Lies and Statistics,* Joel Best (2001) tells of a graduate student who copied this figure from a professional journal: "Every year since 1950, the number of American children gunned down has doubled." Sounds pretty scary, right? But if the claim were true, then by 1987 the number of children gunned down would have surpassed 137 billion, more than the total human population throughout history; and by 1995, the annual number of victims would have been 35 *trillion!*

Where did this wildly inaccurate number come from? The author of the original article misrepresented a statistic from the Children's Defense Fund (CDF), which claimed in 1994 that "The number of American children killed each year by guns has doubled since 1950." Notice the difference: The CDF was saying that there were twice as many deaths in 1994 as in 1950, not that the number had doubled every year. But even the CDF's claim was misleading, because the U.S. population also nearly doubled during that period, so we would expect child gunshot deaths to have increased considerably just because the population grew.

We don't want you to distrust all statistics. Statistics don't lie; people do—or, more likely, they misinterpret what the numbers mean. When statistics are used correctly, they neither confuse nor mislead. On the contrary, they can expose unwarranted conclusions, promote clarity and precision, and protect us from our biases and blind spots. You need to be careful, though. Here are a few things you can do when you hear that "2 million people do this" or "one out of four people are that":

- **Ask how the number was computed.** Suppose someone on your campus gives a talk about a hot social issue and cites some big number to show how serious and widespread the problem is. You should ask the speaker how the number was calculated. Was it based on government data, such as the census? Did it come from just one small study? Is it from a meta-analysis of many studies? Or is it pure conjecture?
- **Check to see how terms were defined.** For example, if we hear that "one out of every four women" will be raped at some point in her life, we need to ask: How was rape defined? If women are asked if they have ever experienced any act of unwanted sex, the percentages are higher than if they are asked specifically whether they have been forced or coerced into intercourse against their will.
- **Look for the control group.** Everywhere these days there are claims for the success of new therapies, self-improvement methods, or "alternative" medications, based solely on anecdotes, case studies, or self-reports. We read one magazine article in which women claimed that taking Viagra had improved their sex lives dramatically. Are you impressed? In a controlled study of 583 women, 43 percent of women taking a placebo pill said *their* sex lives had also improved—they were no different from the Viagra group (Basson et al., 2002). (In 2004, Pfizer gave up its efforts to show that Viagra is helpful to women with sexual problems.) If a study does not report results from a control group of people with the same problem who did *not* go through the same program or treatment, then, as they say in New York, "fuhgeddaboudit."
- **Separate politics from statistics.** When results challenge conventional wisdom, or offend either conservative or liberal sensibilities, scientific detachment can fly out the window. In studies of politically controversial topics, such as child sexual abuse, homosexuality, the effects of spanking, day care, "recovered" memories, and intellectual differences, most people (including some psychologists) either exaggerate statistically weak findings and accept them

uncritically, or ignore statistically valid findings and reject them out of hand, depending on their personal feelings about the results. The critical thinker, however, will try to analyze the data dispassionately and fairly, regardless of his or her moral, political, or social convictions.

- **Be cautious about correlations.** We said this before, but we'll say it again: Many statistics in the news are correlational, so you can't be sure what's causing what. For example, some research on the effects of day care on young children has found a correlation between time spent in day care and aggressiveness (NICHD, 2001). This news has caused considerable alarm, with many "We told you so's" from people who believe that day care is harmful to children and many outright rejections of the findings from people who believe that day care is neutral or beneficial to kids. Both sides have missed the boat: The correlation was not only quite weak; it also did not establish causation. We can't conclude from such data that day care makes kids aggressive; maybe children who spend more time at home with their mothers simply have fewer playmates around to be aggressive *with!*

In sum, the statistics that most people like best are the ones that support their prejudices. Unfortunately, as Joel Best writes, bad statistics, repeated mindlessly and uncritically, "take on lives of their own"—they infiltrate popular culture and become almost impossible to eradicate. The information in this chapter will get you started on learning to tell the difference between numbers that are helpful and those that mislead or deceive. In future chapters, we will give you other information to help you think critically and scientifically about popular claims and findings that make the news.

Summary

What Makes Psychological Research Scientific?

- Research methods provide a way for psychologists to separate well-supported conclusions from unfounded belief. An understanding of these methods can also help people think critically about psychological issues and become astute consumers of psychological findings and programs.
- The ideal scientist states hypotheses and predictions precisely, is skeptical of claims that rest solely on faith or authority, relies on empirical evidence, resists the *confirmation bias* and complies with the *principle of falsifiability*, and is open about methods and results so that findings can be *replicated*. The public nature of science and the *peer review* process give science a built-in system of checks and balances.

Descriptive Studies: Establishing the Facts

- In any study, the researcher would ideally like to use a representative sample, one that is similar in composition to the larger population that the researcher wishes to describe. But as we saw in the "Close-up on Research" feature, in practice researchers must often use "convenience" samples, which typically means college undergraduates. In the study of many topics, the consequences are probably minimal, but in other cases, conclusions about "people in general" must be taken with caution.
- *Descriptive methods* allow psychologists to describe and predict behavior but not necessarily to choose one explanation over others. Such methods include case studies, observational studies, psychological tests, and surveys, as well as correlational methods.
- *Case studies* are detailed descriptions of individuals. They are often used by clinicians, and they can be valuable in exploring new research topics and addressing questions that would otherwise be difficult to study. But because the person under study may not be representative of people in general, case studies are typically sources rather than tests of hypotheses.
- In *observational studies*, the researcher systematically observes and records behavior without interfering in any way with the behavior. *Naturalistic observation* is used to find out how subjects behave in their natural environments. *Laboratory observation* allows more control and the

use of special equipment; behavior in the laboratory, however, may differ in certain ways from behavior in natural contexts.

- *Psychological tests* are used to measure and evaluate personality traits, emotional states, aptitudes, interests, abilities, and values. A good test is one that has been *standardized*, is scored using established *norms*, and is both *reliable* and *valid*. Critics have questioned the reliability and validity of even some widely used tests.
- *Surveys* are questionnaires or interviews that ask people directly about their experiences, attitudes, and opinions. Unrepresentative samples and *volunteer bias* can influence the generalizability of survey results. Findings can also be affected by the fact that respondents sometimes lie, misremember, or misinterpret the questions. Technology and use of the Internet can help psychologists minimize some of these problems, but they also introduce some new methodological challenges. People should be cautious about tests they take on the Internet because not all of them meet scientific standards.

Correlational Studies: Looking for Relationships

- In descriptive research, studies that look for relationships between phenomena are known as *correlational*. A *correlation* is a measure of the strength of a positive or negative relationship between two variables and is expressed by the *coefficient of correlation*. Many correlations reported in the media or on the Internet are based on rumor and anecdote and are not supported by data. Even when a correlation is real, it does not demonstrate a causal relationship between the variables.

Experiments: Hunting for Causes

- *Experiments* allow researchers to control the situation being studied, manipulate an *independent variable*, and assess the effects of the manipulation on a *dependent variable*. Experimental studies usually require a comparison or *control condition* and often involve *random assignment* of subjects to experimental and control groups. In some studies, people in the control group receive a *placebo*, or fake treatment. *Single-blind* and *double-blind* procedures can be used to prevent the expectations of the subjects or the experimenter from affecting the results.
- Because experiments allow conclusions about cause and effect, they have long been the method of choice in psychology. However, like laboratory observations, experiments create a special situation that may call forth behavior not typical in other environments. Many psychologists, therefore, have called for more *field research*.

Evaluating the Findings

- Psychologists use *descriptive statistics*, such as the *arithmetic mean* and the *standard deviation*, to summarize data. They use *inferential statistics* to find out how impressive the data are. *Significance tests* tell the researchers how likely it is that the results of a study occurred merely by chance. The results are said to be *statistically significant* if this likelihood is very low. Statistically significant results allow psychologists to make predictions about human behavior, but, as in all sciences, probabilistic results do not tell us with any certainty what a particular individual will do in a situation.
- Choosing among competing interpretations of a finding can be difficult, and care must be taken to avoid going beyond the facts. Sometimes the best interpretation does not emerge until a hypothesis has been tested in more than one way—for example, by using both *cross-sectional* and *longitudinal* methods.
- Statistical significance does not always imply real-world importance, because the amount of variation in the data accounted for by the independent variable—the *effect size*—may be small. Conversely, a result that does not quite reach significance may be potentially useful. Therefore, many psychologists are now turning to other inferential measures. The technique of *meta-analysis*, for example, reveals how much of the variation in scores across many different studies can be explained by a particular variable.

Keeping the Enterprise Ethical

- The APA's ethical code requires researchers to obtain the *informed consent* of human subjects, protect them from harm, and warn them in advance of any risks. Many studies require deceptive procedures. Concern about the morality of such procedures has led to guidelines to protect participants.
- Psychologists study animals in order to gain knowledge about particular species, discover practical applications of psychological principles, study issues that cannot be studied with human beings for practical or ethical reasons, clarify theoretical questions, and improve human welfare. Debate over the use of animals in research has led to more comprehensive regulations governing their treatment and care.
- Statistics help scientists to understand the complexities of human behavior, but laypeople need to keep in mind that statistics are often misrepresented or misused to support particular social or political goals.

KEY TERMS

theory 37
hypothesis 37
operational definition 37
principle of falsifiability 37
confirmation bias 38
replicate 38
peer review 39
representative sample 40
descriptive methods 41
case study 42
observational studies 43
naturalistic observation 43
laboratory observation 44
psychological tests 44
standardization 45
norms 45
reliability 45
test-retest reliability 45
alternate-forms reliability 45
validity 45
content validity 45
criterion validity 46
surveys 46
volunteer bias 46
correlational study 48
correlation 48
variables 48
positive correlation 48
negative correlation 49
coefficient of correlation 49
experiment 51
independent variable 52
dependent variable 52
control condition 53
experimental and control groups 53
random assignment 54
placebo 54
single-blind study 54
experimenter effects 54
double-blind study 55
field research 55
descriptive statistics 57
arithmetic mean 57
standard deviation 58
inferential statistics 59
significance tests 59
statistical significance 59
cross-sectional study 60
longitudinal study 60
effect size 60
meta-analysis 62
informed consent 63

What Are the Hardest Concepts?

NOW YOU HAVE READ CHAPTER TWO — ARE YOU PREPARED FOR THE EXAM?

The difference between the dependent and independent variables is one of the key questions you should be able to answer after reading this chapter. It is also one of the topics students most often get wrong on a test.

A researcher is investigating the effects of exercise on weight. Exercise is the ______________ variable in this experiment and weight is the __________ variable.

Section: Experiments: Hunting for Causes (pages 51-57) | How do researchers use dependent and independent variables? (pages 52-53)

independent, dependent

Independent Variable and Dependant Variable

Be careful not to confuse the independent variable *(i.v.)* with the dependent variable *(d.v.)*. The independent variable is the variable the researcher manipulates her or himself. If you think about it as if you were the researcher conducting the experiment, the independent variable is the one that I control. Another way to make sure you have correctly labeled the variables in an experiment is to insert the variable names into the following phrase and make sure it still makes sense. The test phrase is:

How _________ **affects** _________.
(i.v.) *(d.v.)*

Here is an example for you to practice using the test phrase: A researcher conducts a study looking at the color of different rooms and aggressiveness. You can see that "How aggressiveness affects room color" does not make sense and is not what the researcher is interested in. However, "How room color affects aggressiveness" does correspond to the researcher's goals. So, in this case, the room color is the independent variable and aggressiveness is the dependent variable.

TELL ME **MORE** >>

"I would like to see our professor connect MORE to what MyPsychLab offers."

Student
Bowling Green State University

To find out before your next exam what other content you might need help with, go to MyPsychLab (MPL) at **www.mypsychlab.com.**

mypsychlab
Powered by Pegasus

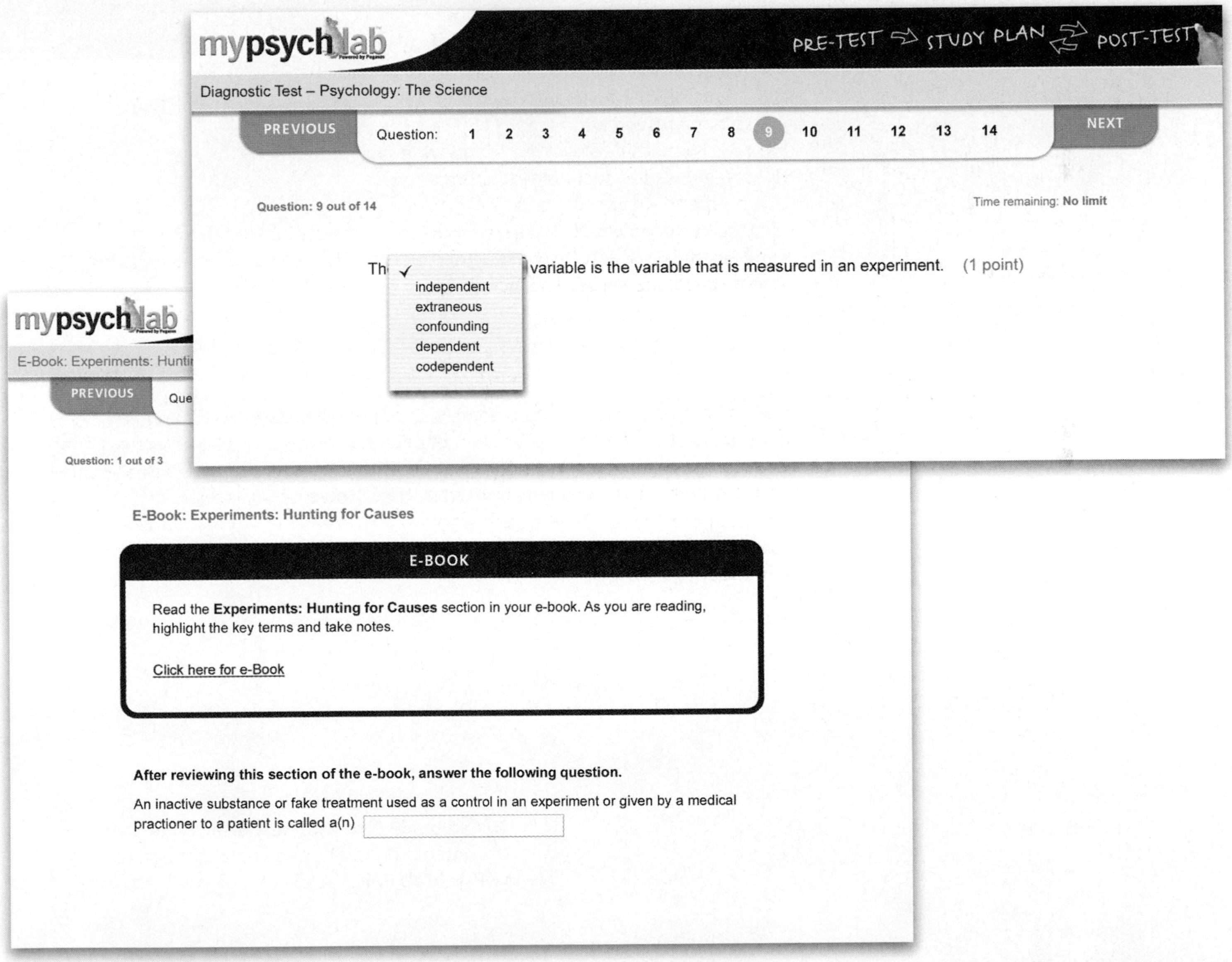

GENES, EVOLUTION, AND ENVIRONMENT

CHAPTER THREE

The tough-minded . . . respect difference. Their goal is a world made safe for differences.

RUTH BENEDICT

Think of all the ways human beings are alike. Everywhere, no matter what their backgrounds or where they live, people love, work, argue, dance, sing, complain, and gossip. They rear families, celebrate marriages, and mourn losses. They reminisce about the past and plan for the future. They help their friends and fight their enemies. They smile with amusement, frown with displeasure, and glare in anger. *Where do all these commonalities come from?*

Think of all the ways human beings differ. Some are extroverts, always ready to make new friends or speak up in a crowd; others are shy and introverted, preferring the safe and familiar. Some are ambitious and enterprising; others are placid, content with the way things are. Some take to book learning like a cat to catnip; others struggle in school but have plenty of street smarts and practical know-how. Some are overwhelmed by even petty problems; others remain calm and resilient in the face of severe difficulties. *Where do all these differences come from?*

For years, psychologists addressing these questions tended to fall into two camps. On one side were the *nativists*, who emphasized genes and inborn characteristics, or *nature*; on the other side were the *empiricists*, who focused on learning and experience, or *nurture*. Edward L. Thorndike (1903), one of the leading psychologists of the early 1900s, staked out the first position when he claimed that "in the actual race of life . . . the chief determining factor is heredity." But in words that became famous, his contemporary, behaviorist John B. Watson (1925), insisted that experience could write virtually any message on the *tabula rasa*, the blank slate, of human nature: "Give me a dozen healthy infants, well-formed, and my own specified world to bring them up in and I'll guarantee to take any one at random and train him to become any type of specialist I might select—doctor, lawyer, artist, merchant-chief and yes, even beggar-man and thief, regardless of his talents, penchants, tendencies, abilities, vocations, and race of his ancestors."

In this chapter, we examine the contributions of both nature and nurture in shaping our human commonalities and our individual differences. We will focus largely on findings from two related areas, evolutionary psychology and behavioral genetics. Researchers in **evolutionary psychology** emphasize the evolutionary mechanisms that might help explain commonalities in language learning, attention, perception, memory, sexual behavior, emotion, reasoning, and many other aspects of human psychology. Researchers in **behavioral genetics** attempt to tease apart the relative contributions of heredity and environment to explain individual differences in personality, mental ability, and other characteristics.

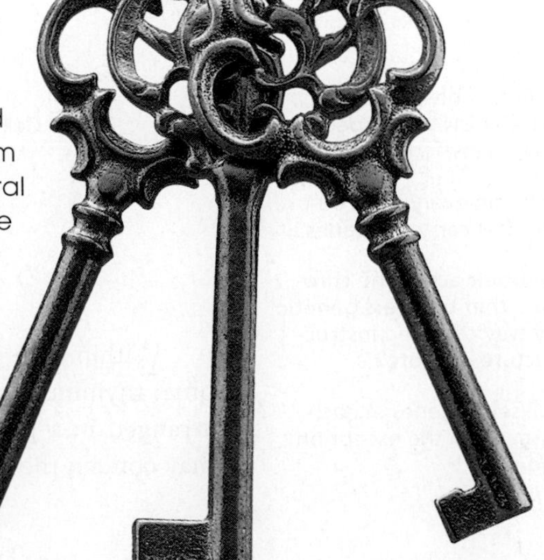

CHAPTER OUTLINE

The long and short of it: Human beings are both similar and different.

Keep in mind, however, that virtually no one argues in terms of nature *versus* nurture anymore. Scientists today understand that heredity and environment constantly interact to produce our psychological traits and even most of our physical ones. This interaction works in two directions. First, genes affect the kinds of experiences we have: A teenager with a genetic aptitude for schoolwork may be more likely than other kids to join a spelling-bee team and get books and science kits as birthday presents. These experiences reward and encourage the development of academic skills. Conversely, although most people don't realize it, experience also affects our genes: Stress, diet, emotional events, and hormonal changes can all influence which genes are active or inactive at any given time over a person's lifetime (Fraga et al., 2005). Try, then, as you read this chapter, to resist the temptation to think of nature and nurture in either–or terms.

WHAT'S**AHEAD** 

- What does the chemical code in our genes encode *for*?
- What can a complete map of the human genes reveal—and not reveal?

Unlocking the Secrets of Genes

Let's begin by looking at what genes are and how they operate. **Genes**, the basic units of heredity, are located on **chromosomes**, rod-shaped structures found in the center (nucleus) of every cell of the body. Each sperm cell and each egg cell (ovum) contains 23 chromosomes, so when a sperm and egg unite at conception, the fertilized egg and all the body cells that eventually develop from it (except for sperm cells and ova) contain 46 chromosomes, arranged in 23 pairs.

Chromosomes consist of threadlike strands of **DNA (deoxyribonucleic acid)** molecules, and genes consist of small segments of this DNA. Each human chromosome contains thousands of genes, each with a fixed location. Collectively, all the genes together—the best estimates put the number around 25,000—are referred to as the human **genome**. Most of these genes are found in other animals as well, but others are uniquely human, setting us apart from chimpanzees, wasps, and mice. Many genes contribute directly to a particular trait, but others work indirectly by switching other genes on or off. Many genes are inherited in the same form by everyone; others vary, contributing to our individuality.

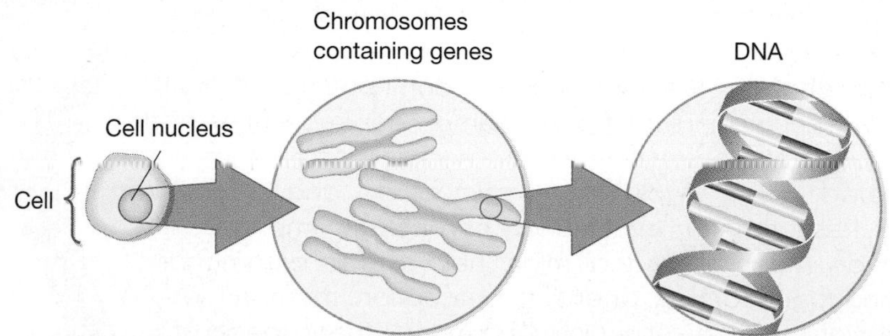

Within each gene, four basic chemical elements of DNA—the amino acids adenine, thymine, cytosine, and guanine, identified by the letters A, T, C, and G—are arranged in a particular order: for example, ACGTCTCTATA. . . . This sequence may contain thousands or even tens of thousands of "letters," which together consti-

evolutionary psychology A field of psychology emphasizing evolutionary mechanisms that may help explain human commonalities in cognition, development, emotion, social practices, and other areas of behavior.

behavioral genetics An interdisciplinary field of study concerned with the genetic bases of individual differences in behavior and personality.

genes The functional units of heredity; they are composed of DNA and specify the structure of proteins.

chromosomes Within every cell, rod-shaped structures that carry the genes.

DNA (deoxyribonucleic acid) The chromosomal molecule that transfers genetic characteristics by way of coded instructions for the structure of proteins.

genome The full set of genes in each cell of an organism (with the exception of sperm and egg cells).

tute a code for the synthesis of one of the many proteins that affect virtually every aspect of the body, from its structure to the chemicals that keep it running. But this is a simplification. Recent work shows that many genes can make more than one protein, depending on when and where different "coding" segments of DNA on the gene are activated. Thus our measly 25,000 or so genes—barely more than a common worm has—are able to produce hundreds of thousands of different proteins (Pennisi, 2005).

Identifying even a single gene is a daunting task; biologist Joseph Levine and geneticist David Suzuki (1993) once compared it to searching for someone when all you know is that the person lives somewhere on Earth. Researchers must usually *clone* (produce copies of) several stretches of DNA on a chromosome, then use indirect methods to locate a given gene.

One method, which has been used to search for the genes associated with many physical and mental conditions, involves doing **linkage studies**. These studies take advantage of the tendency of genes lying close together on a chromosome to be inherited together across generations. The researchers start out by looking for **genetic markers**, DNA segments that vary considerably among individuals and whose locations on the chromosomes are already known. They then look for patterns of inheritance of these markers in large families in which a condition—say, depression or impulsive violence—is common. If a marker tends to exist only in family members who have the condition, then it can be used as a genetic landmark: The gene involved in the condition is apt to be located nearby on the chromosome, so the researchers have some idea where to search for it.

In 2000, after years of heated competition, an international collaboration of researchers called the Human Genome Project and a private company, Celera Genomics, both announced that they had completed a rough draft of a map of the entire human genome, and since then the map has been greatly refined. Using high-tech methods, researchers have identified the sequence of nearly all 3 billion units of DNA (those A's, C's, T's, and G's) and have been able to determine the boundaries between genes and how the genes are arranged on the chromosomes (see Figure 3.1). This project has been costly and time-consuming, but it reflects the view among many scientists that the twenty-first century will be the century of the gene.

Even when researchers locate a gene, however, they do not automatically know its role in physical or psychological functioning. Usually, locating a gene is just the first tiny step in understanding what it does and how it works. Also, be wary of media reports implying that some gene is the *only* one involved in a complex psychological ability or trait, such as intelligence or shyness. It seems that nearly every year brings another report about some gene that supposedly explains a human trait. A few years back, newspapers even announced the discovery of a "worry gene." Don't worry about it!

linkage studies Studies that look for patterns of inheritance of genetic markers in large families in which a particular condition is common.

genetic marker A segment of DNA that varies among individuals, has a known location on a chromosome, and can function as a genetic landmark for a gene involved in a physical or mental condition.

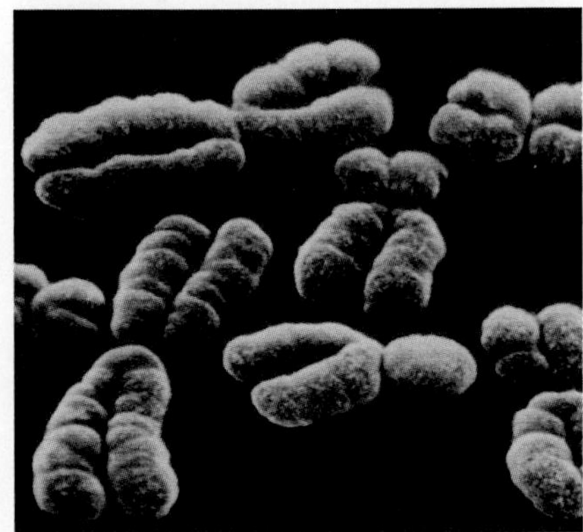

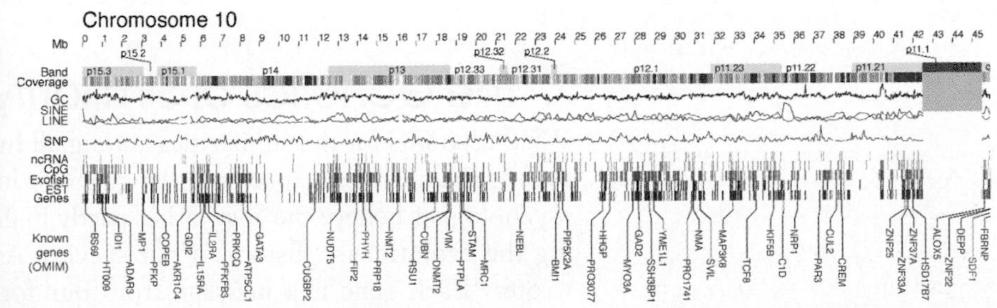

FIGURE 3.1 Mapping Human Genes

Genes are located on chromosomes, some of which are shown on the left, magnified almost 55,000 times. On the right, a small portion of the map for chromosome 10 shows 52 genes identified by the Human Genome Project, including some that have been linked to prostate cancer, leukemia, and obesity.

GET INVOLVED!

➤THUMBS UP!

Ask the members of your family, one person at a time, to clasp their hands together. Include aunts and uncles, grandparents, and as many other biological relatives as possible. Which thumb does each person put on top? About half of all people fold the left thumb over the right and about half fold the right thumb over the left, and these responses tend to run in families. Do your own relatives show one tendency over the other? (If your family is an adoptive one, of course, there is less chance of finding a trend.) Try the same exercise with someone else's family; do you get the same results? Even for behavior as simple as thumb folding, the details of how genes exert their effect remain uncertain (Jones, 1994).

Most human traits, even such seemingly straightforward ones as height and eye color, are influenced by more than one gene pair. Psychological traits are especially likely to depend on multiple genes, with each one accounting for just a small part of the variance among people. Conversely, any single gene is apt to influence many different behaviors. So at this point, all announcements of a "gene for this" or a "gene for that" should be viewed with extreme caution.

QUICK quiz

The Human Genome Project has not discovered any quiz-taking genes.

1. What does it mean to say that the gene–environment interaction works in both directions?
2. The basic unit of heredity is called a (a) gene, (b) chromosome, (c) genome, (d) DNA molecule.
3. What does the code within a gene encode for?
4. *True or false*: Most human genetic traits depend on a single gene.

Answers:

1. Genes affect the environments we experience, and environmental factors affect the activity of genes over a person's lifetime. 2. a 3. the synthesis of a particular protein 4. false

WHAT'S**AHEAD**

- During evolution, why do some traits become more common and others less common?
- In the evolutionary view, why is the capacity to read faces innate but not the capacity to read books?
- Why do so many people ignore signs saying "Don't touch"?

The Genetics of Similarity

What accounts for the similarities among all human beings, everywhere in the world, such as the universal capacity for language or loyalty to a family or clan? Evolutionary psychologists believe the answer lies partly in genetic dispositions that developed during the evolutionary history of our species. As British geneticist Steve Jones (1994) wrote, "Each gene is a message from our forebears and together they contain the whole story of human evolution."

Evolution and Natural Selection

To read the messages from the past that are locked in our genes, we must first understand the nature of evolution itself. **Evolution** is basically a change in gene frequencies within a population, a change that typically takes place over many generations. As particular genes become more common or less common in the population, so do the characteristics they influence. These developments account for changes within a species, and when the changes are large enough, they can result in the formation of new species.

Why do gene frequencies in a population change? Why don't they stay put from one generation to another? One reason is that during the division of the cells that produce sperm and eggs, if an error occurs in the copying of the original DNA sequence, genes can spontaneously change, or *mutate*. In addition, during the formation of a sperm or an egg, small segments of genetic material cross over (exchange places) from one member of a chromosome pair to another, prior to the final cell division. As genes spontaneously mutate and recombine during the production of sperm and eggs, new genetic variations—and therefore potential new traits—keep arising.

Many people at first ridiculed Darwin's notion that humans share a common ancestor with other primates. In this nineteenth-century cartoon, a monkeylike Darwin shows an ape how closely he resembles people. Today, evolutionary principles, which have long guided the biological sciences, are having a growing influence on psychological science as well.

But that is only part of the story. According to the principle of **natural selection**, first formulated in general terms by the British naturalist Charles Darwin in *On the Origin of Species* (1859/1964), the fate of these genetic variations depends on the environment. (Darwin did not actually know about genes, as their discovery had not yet been widely publicized, but he realized that a species' characteristics must somehow be transmitted biologically from one generation to the next.)

The fundamental idea behind natural selection is this: If, in a particular environment, individuals with a genetically influenced trait tend to be more successful than other individuals in finding food, surviving the elements, and fending off enemies—and therefore better at staying alive long enough to produce offspring—their genes will become more and more common in the population. Their genes will have been "selected" by reproductive success, and over many generations, these genes may even spread throughout the species. In contrast, individuals whose traits are not as adaptive in the struggle for survival will not be as "reproductively fit": They will tend to die before reproducing, and therefore their genes, and the traits influenced by those genes, will become less and less common and eventually may even disappear.

Although scientists debate how gradually or abruptly evolutionary changes occur and whether competition for survival is always the primary mechanism of change, they agree on the basic importance of evolution. Over the past century and a half, Darwin's ideas have been resoundingly supported by findings in anthropology, botany, and molecular genetics. Scientists have watched evolutionary developments occurring before their very eyes in organisms that change rapidly, such as microbes, insects, and various plants. And they are now starting to identify specific genes that account for evolutionary changes that have occurred in animals in the wild, such as the transformation of mice and lizards from light colored to dark colored (or vice versa) as the animals have migrated into different environments (Hoekstra et al., 2006; Rosenblum, 2005). Evolutionary principles such as natural selection now guide all of the biological sciences.

evolution A change in gene frequencies within a population over many generations; a mechanism by which genetically influenced characteristics of a population may change.

natural selection The evolutionary process in which individuals with genetically influenced traits that are adaptive in a particular environment tend to survive and to reproduce in greater numbers than do other individuals; as a result, their traits become more common in the population.

Traits and Preferences. Evolutionary biologists often start with an observation about some characteristic and then try to account for it in evolutionary terms. For example, why do male peacocks have such fabulous and flamboyant feathers, whereas females look so drab and dull? The evolutionary answer is that during the history of the species, males who could put on the flashiest display got the attention of females, and such males therefore had a better chance of reproducing. In contrast, all females had to do was hang around and pick the guy with the fanciest feathers; they didn't even have to dress up.

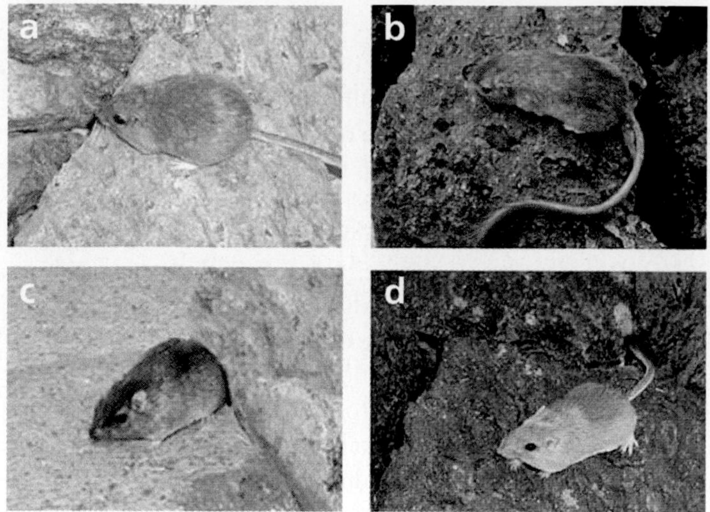

Natural selection allows animals to survive by adapting to the environment. In the deserts of Arizona, most rock pocket mice are sandy-colored and are well camouflaged against the beige rocks they scamper over (a). Their coloring therefore protects them against owls and other predators. But in areas where ancient lava flows have left large deposits of black rock, the same species has evolved to be dark-coated and thus equally well disguised (b). You can see how vulnerable these mice are when their coats do *not* blend with the color of the rocks (c and d). Researchers have identified the gene involved in the evolution of dark coloration in these mice (Nachman, Hoekstra, & D'Agostino, 2003).

Evolutionary psychologists work in the same way as biologists, but some take a slightly different tack: They start by asking what sorts of challenges human beings might have faced in their prehistoric past—say, having to decide which foods were safe to eat, or needing to size up a stranger's intentions quickly. Then they draw inferences about the behavioral tendencies that might have been selected because they helped our forebears solve these survival problems and enhanced their reproductive fitness. (They make no assumption about whether the behavior is adaptive or intelligent in the *present* environment.) Finally, they do research to see if those tendencies actually exist throughout the world.

For example, our ancestors' need to avoid eating poisonous or rancid food might have led eventually to an innate dislike for bitter tastes and rotten smells; those individuals who happened to be born with such dislikes would have stood a better chance of surviving long enough to reproduce. Similarly, it made good survival sense for our ancestors to develop an innate capacity for language and an ability to recognize faces and emotional expressions. But they would not have had much need for an innate ability to read or drive, inasmuch as books and cars had not yet been invented (Pinker, 1994).

Mental Modules. For many evolutionary psychologists, a guiding assumption is that the human mind is not a general-purpose computer waiting to be programmed. Instead, they say, it developed as a collection of specialized and independent "modules" to handle specific survival problems (Buss, 1995, 1999; Cosmides, Tooby, & Barkow, 1992; Marcus, 2004; Mealey, 1996; Pinker, 2002). A particular module may involve several dispersed but interconnected areas of the brain, just as a computer file can be fragmented on a hard drive (Pinker, 1997).

Critics worry that the idea of mental modules is no improvement over instinct theory, the once-popular notion in psychology that virtually every human activity and capacity, from cleanliness to cruelty, is innate. Frans de Waal (2002), an evolutionary theorist who believes that someday all psychology departments will have a picture of Darwin hanging on the wall, has accused some of his colleagues who argue for mental modules of mistakenly assuming that if a trait exists and has a genetic component, then it must be adaptive and must correspond to a module. This assumption, he points out, is incorrect: Male pattern baldness and pimples, for example, are not particularly adaptive! Many evolved and inherited traits are merely by-products of other traits, and

some can even be costly; the problems that many people have with aching backs are no doubt an unfortunate consequence of our evolved ability to walk on two feet. To understand our evolutionary legacy, de Waal argues, we must consider not just individual traits in isolation but also the whole package of traits that characterizes the species. This is as true for psychological traits as for physical ones.

Those who subscribe to the modules approach respond that evidence from psychology and other disciplines can distinguish behavior that has a biological origin from behavior that does not. As Steven Pinker (1994) explains, if a mental module for some behavior exists, then neuroscientists should eventually discover the brain circuits or subsystems associated with it. Further, he adds, "When children solve problems for which they have mental modules, they should look like geniuses, knowing things they have not been taught; when they solve problems that their minds are not equipped for, it should be a long hard slog."

The debate over modules will undoubtedly continue. But whether or not modules are the best way to describe traits that appear to be inherited, you should be careful to avoid the common error of assuming that if some behavior or trait exists, it must be adaptive.

THINKING CRITICALLY

DON'T OVERSIMPLIFY

Many people oversimplify evolutionary theory by concluding that if a trait exists, it must have aided survival by serving some beneficial purpose. Not so! Baldness, for example, may be beautiful, but it is not necessarily adaptive.

Innate Human Characteristics

Because of the way our species evolved, many abilities, tendencies, and characteristics are either present at birth in all human beings or develop rapidly as a child matures. These traits include not just the obvious ones, such as the ability to stand on two legs or to grasp objects with the forefinger and thumb, but also less obvious ones. Here are just a few examples:

1 **Infant reflexes.** Babies are born with a number of reflexes—simple, automatic responses to specific stimuli. For example, all infants will suck something put to their lips; by aiding nursing, this reflex enhances their chances of survival.

2 **An interest in novelty.** Novelty is intriguing to human beings and many other species. If a rat has had its dinner, it will prefer to explore an unfamiliar wing of a maze rather than the familiar wing where food is. Human babies reveal a surprising interest in looking at and listening to unfamiliar things—which, of course, includes most of the world. A baby will even stop nursing momentarily if someone new enters his or her range of vision.

3 **A desire to explore and manipulate objects.** All birds and mammals have this innate inclination. Primates, especially, like to "monkey" with things, taking them apart and scrutinizing the pieces, apparently for the sheer pleasure of it (Harlow, Harlow, & Meyer, 1950). Human babies shake rattles, bang pots, and grasp whatever is put into their tiny hands. For human beings, the natural impulse to handle interesting objects can be overwhelming, which may be one reason why the command "Don't touch" is so often ignored by children, museum-goers, and shoppers.

4 **An impulse to play and fool around.** Think of kittens and lion cubs, puppies and pandas, and all young primates, who will play with and pounce on each other all day until hunger or naptime calls. Play and exploration may be biologically adaptive because they help members of a species find food and other necessities of life and learn to cope with their environments. Indeed, the young of many species enjoy *practice play*,

All primates, including human beings, are innately disposed to explore the environment, manipulate objects, play, and "monkey around."

behavior that will be used for serious purposes when they are adults (Vandenberg, 1985). A kitten, for example, will stalk and attack a ball of yarn. In human beings, play teaches children how to get along with others and gives them a chance to practice their motor and linguistic skills (Pellegrini & Galda, 1993).

5 **Basic cognitive skills.** Many evolutionary psychologists believe that people are born with abilities that make it easy to learn to interpret the expressions and gestures of others, identify faces, figure out what others are thinking or feeling, distinguish plants from animals, distinguish living from nonliving things, and acquire language (Geary & Huffman, 2002). Young infants have even been credited with a rudimentary understanding of number. Of course, tiny infants cannot count. By the age of only 1 week, however, they will spend more time looking at a new set of three items after getting used to a set of two items, or vice versa, which means that they can recognize the difference. By 7 months, most infants prefer to look at videotapes in which the number of adults mouthing a word (two or three adults) matches the number of voices saying the word in synchrony with the images (Jordan & Brannon, 2006). By 18 months, infants know that 4 is more than 3, which is more than 2, which is more than 1—suggesting that the brain is designed to understand "more than" and "less than" relationships for small numbers. Evolutionary psychologists believe that these and other fundamental cognitive skills evolved because they were useful to our ancestors and aided their survival.

Most psychologists accept that certain aspects of human behavior have been naturally selected. In other chapters, we consider the adaptive and evolutionary aspects of sensory and perceptual abilities (Chapter 6), learning (Chapter 7), ethnocentrism (Chapter 8), cognitive biases (Chapter 9), memory (Chapter 10), emotions and emotional expressions (Chapter 11), the tendency to gain weight when food is plentiful (Chapter 12), attachment (Chapter 14), and stress reactions (Chapter 15). For now, let us look more closely at two areas that are of particular interest to evolutionary psychologists and that are also the source of much controversy: the development of language and the nature of mating practices around the world.

QUICK quiz

How evolved is your understanding of evolutionary psychology?

1. What two processes during the formation of sperm and eggs help explain genetic changes within a population?
2. Which is the best statement of the principle of natural selection? (a) Over time, the environment naturally selects some traits over others. (b) Genetic variations become more common over time if they are adaptive in a particular environment. (c) A species constantly improves as parents pass along their best traits to their offspring.
3. Many evolutionary psychologists believe that the human mind evolved as (a) a collection of specialized modules to handle specific survival problems; (b) a general-purpose computer that adapts to any situation; (c) a collection of specific instincts for every human activity or capacity.
4. Which of the following is *not* part of our biological heritage? (a) a sucking reflex at birth; (b) a motive to explore and manipulate objects; (c) a lack of interest in novel objects; (d) a love of play.

Answers:

1. spontaneous genetic mutations and crossover of genetic material between members of a chromosome pair, which occur before the final cell division 2. b 3. a 4. c

WHAT'S AHEAD

- What does language allow us to do that other animals cannot?
- What evidence suggests that evolution has equipped infants' brains with an innate facility for acquiring language?
- How do parents help children acquire language?

Our Human Heritage: Language

Try to read this sentence aloud:

Kamaunawezakusomamanenohayawewenimtuwamaanasana.

Can you tell where one word begins and another ends? Unless you know Swahili, the syllables of this sentence will sound like gibberish.[1]

Well, to a baby learning its native tongue, *every* sentence must, at first, be gibberish. How, then, does an infant pick out discrete syllables and words from the jumble of sounds in the environment, much less figure out what the words mean and how to combine them? Is there something special about the human brain that allows a baby to discover how language works? Darwin thought so: Language, wrote Darwin (1874), is an instinctive ability unique to human beings. Many modern researchers think he was right.

The Nature of Language

To evaluate Darwin's claim, we must first appreciate that a **language** is not just any old communication system; it is a set of rules for combining elements that are inherently meaningless into utterances that convey meaning. The elements are usually sounds,

language A system that combines meaningless elements such as sounds or gestures to form structured utterances that convey meaning.

[1] *Kama unaweza kusoma maneno haya, wewe ni mtu wa maana sana,* in Swahili, means "If you can read these words, you are a remarkable person."

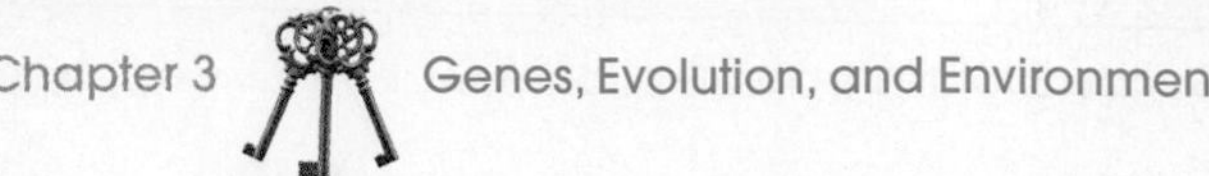

DEFINE YOUR TERMS

People often confuse language with speech. But to a psycholinguist, a language is any communication system that can produce an infinite number of meaningful utterances, whether its elements are gestures or sounds. In North America, many hearing-impaired people use American Sign Language (ASL) and deaf children learn to sign in ASL as easily as hearing children learn to speak.

but they can also be the gestures of American Sign Language (ASL) and other manual languages used by deaf and hearing-impaired people.

Some nonhuman animals are able to acquire aspects of language if they get help from their human friends (see Chapter 9). However, we seem to be the only species that acquires language naturally. Other primates use grunts, screeches, and gestures to warn each other of danger, attract attention, express emotions, and even refer to other individuals, but the sounds are not combined to produce original sentences (at least, as far as anyone can tell). Bongo the chimp may make a sound of delight when he encounters food, but he cannot say, "The bananas in the next grove are a lot riper than the ones we ate last week and sure beat our usual diet of termites."

In contrast, language, whether spoken or signed, allows human beings to express and comprehend an infinite number of novel utterances, created on the spot. This ability is critical; except for a few fixed phrases ("How are you?" "Get a life!"), most of the utterances we produce or hear over a lifetime are new. For example, in this book you will find few, if any, sentences that you have read, heard, or spoken before in exactly the same form. Yet you can understand what you are reading, and you can produce new sentences of your own about the material.

The Innate Capacity for Language

At one time, most psychologists assumed that children acquired language by imitating adults and paying attention when adults corrected their mistakes. Then along came linguist Noam Chomsky (1957, 1980), who argued that language was far too complex to be learned bit by bit, as one might learn a list of world capitals.

Children, said Chomsky, must not only figure out which sounds or gestures form words; they must also take the *surface structure* of a sentence—the way the sentence is actually spoken or signed—and infer an underlying *deep structure*—how the sentence is to be understood. For example, although "Mary kissed John" and "John was kissed by Mary" have different surface structures, any 5-year-old knows that the two sentences have essentially the same underlying meaning, in which Mary is the actor and John gets the kiss:

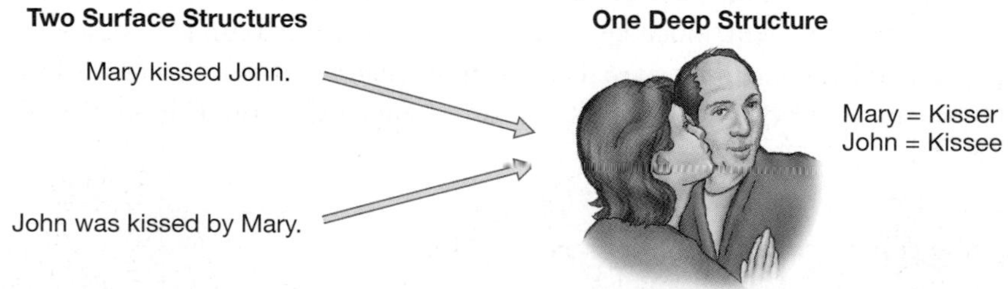

Conversely, "Bill heard the trampling of the hikers," a single surface structure, can have two different underlying structures: one in which the hikers are actors doing the trampling and one in which they are the unfortunate objects of the trampling. Your ability to discern two different deep structures tells you that the sentence's meaning is ambiguous:

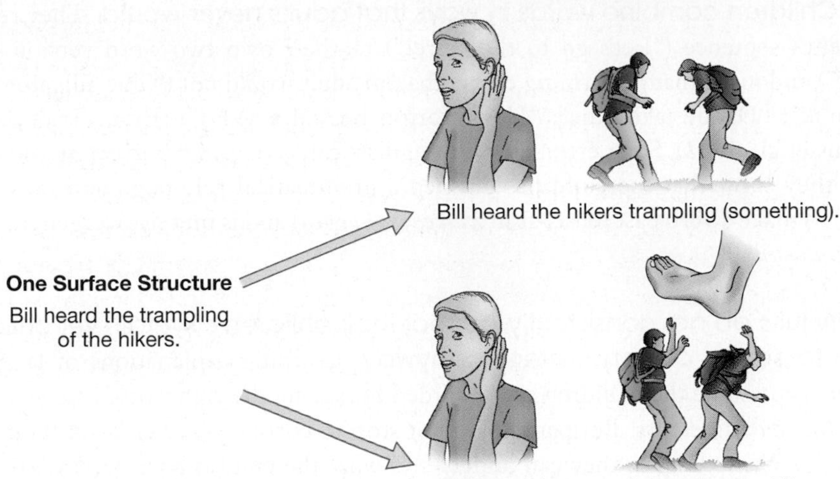
Two Deep Structures
Bill heard the hikers trampling (something).
One Surface Structure
Bill heard the trampling of the hikers.
Bill heard (someone) trampling the hikers.

To transform surface structures into deep ones, said Chomsky, children must apply rules of grammar (*syntax*). These rules govern word order and other linguistic features that determine the role a word plays in a sentence (such as, say, kisser or kissee). Most people, even adults, cannot actually state the grammatical rules of their language (e.g., "In English, adjectives usually precede the noun they describe"), yet they are able to apply thousands of such rules without even thinking about it. No native speaker of English would say, "He threw the ball big."

Because no one actually teaches us grammar when we are toddlers, the human brain, Chomsky argued, must contain a **language acquisition device**, an innate mental module that allows young children to develop language if they are exposed to an adequate sampling of conversation; just as a bird is designed to fly, human beings are designed to use language. Another way of saying this is that children are born with a *universal grammar*—that is, their brains are sensitive to the core features common to all languages, such as nouns and verbs, subjects and objects, and negatives. These common features occur even in languages as seemingly different as Mohawk and English, or Okinawan and Bulgarian (Baker, 2001; Cinque, 1999; Pesetsky, 1999).

Over the years, linguists and *psycholinguists* (researchers who study the psychology of language) have gathered much evidence in support of the Chomskyan position:

1 Children in different cultures go through similar stages of linguistic development. For example, they will often form their first negatives simply by adding "no" or "not" at the beginning or end of a sentence ("No get dirty"); and at a later stage, they will use double negatives ("He don't want no milk"; "Nobody don't like me"), even when their language does not allow such constructions (Klima & Bellugi, 1966; McNeill, 1966).

language acquisition device According to many psycholinguists, an innate mental module that allows young children to develop language if they are exposed to an adequate sampling of conversation.

HEY! I SEEN THAT KID ON THE PLAYGROUND TODAY!
I SAW THAT KID ON THE PLAYGROUND TODAY.
YOU SEEN HIM, TOO?

Even when parents try to correct their children's syntax, it doesn't usually work.

2 **Children combine words in ways that adults never would.** They reduce a parent's sentence ("Let's go to the store!") to their own two-word version ("Go store!") and make many charming errors that an adult would not ("The alligator goed kerplunk"; "Daddy taked me"; "Hey, Horton heared a Who") (Ervin-Tripp, 1964; Marcus et al., 1992). Such errors, which linguists call *overregularizations*, are not random; they show that the child has grasped a grammatical rule (e.g., add the *t* or *d* sound to make a verb past tense, as in *walked* or *hugged*) and is merely overgeneralizing it (*taked*, *goed*).

3 **Adults do not consistently correct their children's syntax, yet children learn to speak or sign correctly anyway.** Learning explanations of language acquisition assume that children are rewarded for saying the right words and are punished for making errors. But parents do not stop to correct every error in their children's speech, so long as they can understand what the child is trying to say (Brown, Cazden, & Bellugi, 1969). Indeed, parents often *reward* children for incorrect statements! The 2-year-old who says "Want milk!" is likely to get it; most parents would not wait for a more grammatical (or polite) request.

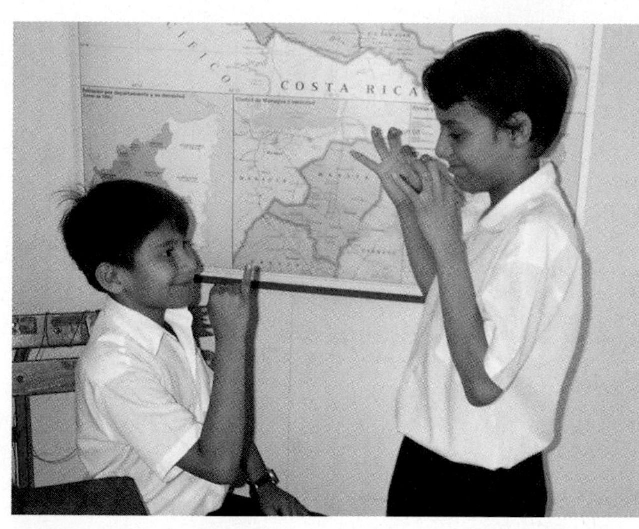

These deaf Nicaraguan children have invented their own grammatically complex sign language, one that is unrelated to Spanish or to any conventional gestural language.

4 **Children not exposed to adult language may invent a language of their own.** Deaf children who have never learned a standard language, either signed or spoken, have made up their *own* sign languages out of thin air. Across cultures, these languages often show similarities in sentence structure; for example, children in America and Taiwan have produced similar languages, as have children in Spain and Turkey (Goldin-Meadow, 2003). The most astounding case comes from Nicaragua, where a group of deaf children of hearing parents, sent to two special schools, created a homegrown but grammatically complex sign language that is unrelated to Spanish (Senghas & Coppola, 2001). Scientists have had a unique opportunity to observe the evolution of this language as it has developed from a few simple signs to a full-blown linguistic system.

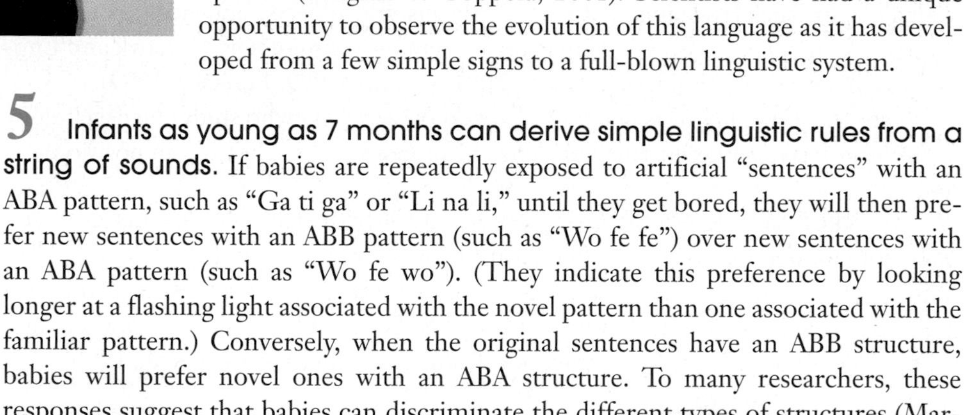

5 **Infants as young as 7 months can derive simple linguistic rules from a string of sounds.** If babies are repeatedly exposed to artificial "sentences" with an ABA pattern, such as "Ga ti ga" or "Li na li," until they get bored, they will then prefer new sentences with an ABB pattern (such as "Wo fe fe") over new sentences with an ABA pattern (such as "Wo fe wo"). (They indicate this preference by looking longer at a flashing light associated with the novel pattern than one associated with the familiar pattern.) Conversely, when the original sentences have an ABB structure, babies will prefer novel ones with an ABA structure. To many researchers, these responses suggest that babies can discriminate the different types of structures (Marcus et al., 1999). Astonishingly, this ability emerges even before they can understand or produce any words.

Chomsky's ideas revolutionized thinking about language and human nature, and even the terms they used (language "acquisition" replaced language "learning"). He himself has had little to say about the evolutionary implications of his argument, but others believe that an innate facility for language evolved in human beings because it was extraordinarily beneficial (Pinker, 1994). In particular, it per-

GET INVOLVED!

➤A GRAMMAR TEST EVERYONE CAN PASS

How would you complete these sentences, spoken aloud?

This morning I saw one *sik*. Later I saw two more __________.
This morning I saw one *wug*. Later I saw two more __________.
This morning I saw one *litch*. Later I saw two more __________.

Think about the sounds you added to these nonsense words; they differed, didn't they? In English, the plural form of most nouns depends on the last sound of the singular form. The precise rules are quite complicated, yet every speaker of English has an implicit knowledge of them and will correctly add an *s* sound to *rat* to make *rats*, a *z* sound to *rag* to make *rags*, and an *iz* sound to *radish* to make *radishes*. (The only exceptions are people with a rare genetic disorder, as described in the text.) When 5- and 6-year-olds are asked for the plural versions of nonsense words, they easily apply the appropriate rules (Berko, 1958). Such evidence has helped to convince many psychologists that human beings have an innate ability to infer the rules of grammar.

mitted our prehistoric ancestors to convey precise information about time, space, and events (as in "Honey, are you going on the mammoth hunt today?") and allowed them to negotiate alliances that were necessary for survival ("If you share your nuts and berries with us, we'll share our mammoth with you"). According to one theorist, language may also have developed because it provides the human equivalent of the mutual grooming that other primates rely on to forge social bonds (Dunbar, 2004). Just as other primates will clean, stroke, and groom each other for hours as a sign of affection and connection, human friends will sit for hours and chat over coffee.

The next logical step might be to identify the specific brain mechanisms and genes that contribute to our ability to acquire language. Scientists have known for a long time which brain parts are generally responsible for processing language (see Chapter 4), and researchers in Israel have shown that the ability to transform surface structures into deep ones is associated with activity in specific brain areas (Ben-Shachar et al., 2003).

Clues also come from a large three-generation British family with a rare genetic disorder that prevents normal language acquisition. Family members with this disorder have pronunciation problems and also have trouble applying grammatical rules for changing tenses or constructing plurals—rules that normal children learn easily and unconsciously. For example, they can learn the distinction between *mice* and *mouse* but they cannot learn the general rule about adding an *s*, *z*, or *iz* sound to make a noun plural, as in *bikes* (*s*), *gloves* (*z*), and *kisses* (*iz*). Instead, they must learn each plural as a separate item, and they make many errors (Gopnik & Goad, 1997; Matthews, 1994). Linkage studies have led British researchers to a mutation in a specific gene that seems to contribute to this syndrome, apparently by orchestrating the activity of other genes during prenatal brain development (Lai et al., 2001). Scientists are still debating whether the gene's ultimate influence is on pronunciation, specific grammar circuits in the brain, or some general intellectual or perceptual process necessary for speech or language. Nonetheless, this research is an important first step in isolating possible genetic influences on language.

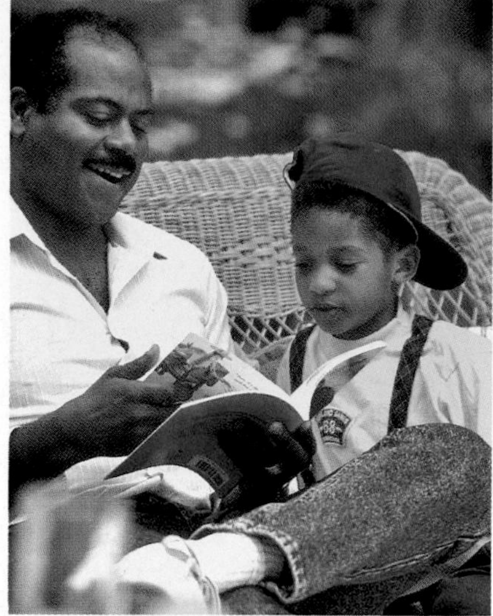

Although the capacity for language may be innate, parents can foster their children's language development by talking and reading with them.

Learning and Language

Despite the evidence for Chomsky's view that language is innate, some theorists still give experience a greater role. They argue that instead of inferring grammatical rules, children learn the probability that any given word or syllable will follow another—something that infants as young as 8 months are able to do (Saffran, Aslin, & Newport, 1996; Seidenberg, 1997; Seidenberg, MacDonald, & Saffran, 2002). In this view, infants are more like statisticians than grammarians.

Using computers, some theorists have been able to design **computer neural networks**, mathematical models of the brain that can "learn" some aspects of language, such as regular and irregular past-tense verbs, without the help of a language acquisition device or preprogrammed rules. Neural networks simply adjust the connections among hypothetical "neurons" in response to incoming data, such as repetitions of a word in its past tense form. The success of these computer models, say their designers, suggests that children, too, may be able to acquire linguistic features without getting a head start from inborn brain modules (Rodriguez, Wiles, & Elman, 1999; Rumelhart & McClelland, 1987).

computer neural networks Mathematical models of the brain that "learn" by adjusting the connections among hypothetical neurons in response to incoming data.

Even theorists who emphasize an inborn grammatical capacity acknowledge that in any behavior as complex as language, nurture must also play a role. Although there are commonalities in language acquisition around the world, there are also some major differences that do not seem explainable by a "universal grammar" (Gopnik, Choi, & Baumberger, 1996; Slobin, 1985, 1991). Further, although most children have the capacity to acquire language from mere exposure to it, parents do help things along. They may not go around correcting their children's speech all day, but they do recast and expand their children's clumsy or ungrammatical sentences ("Monkey climbing!" "Yes, the monkey is climbing the tree") (Bohannon & Stanowicz, 1988). Children, in turn, often imitate those recasts and expansions, suggesting that they are learning from them (Bohannon & Symons, 1988). It is likely, therefore, that language development depends on both biological readiness and social experience.

QUICK quiz

Use your human capacity for language to answer these questions.

1. The central distinction between human language and other communication systems is that language (a) allows for the generation of an infinite number of new utterances, (b) is spoken, (c) is learned only after explicit training, (d) expresses meaning directly through surface structures.
2. What did Chomsky mean by a "language acquisition device"?
3. What five findings support the existence of an innate "universal grammar"?
4. Those who reject Chomsky's ideas believe that instead of figuring out grammatical rules when acquiring language, children learn ____________.

Answers:

1. a 2. an innate mental module that permits young children to develop language if they are exposed to an adequate sampling of conversation 3. Children everywhere go through similar stages of linguistic development; children combine words in ways that adults would not; adults do not consistently correct their children's syntax; groups of children not exposed to adult language may make up their own; and even infants only a few months old appear to distinguish different sentence structures. 4. the probability that any given word or syllable will follow another one

WHAT'S**AHEAD**

- How do evolutionary psychologists explain male–female differences in courtship and sexuality?
- What basic issue divides evolutionary psychologists and their critics?

Our Human Heritage: Courtship and Mating

Most psychologists agree that the evolutionary history of our species has made certain kinds of learning either difficult or easy. Most acknowledge that simple behaviors, such as smiling or preferring sweet tastes, resemble instincts, behaviors that are relatively uninfluenced by learning and that occur in all members of the species. And most agree that human beings inherit some of their cognitive, perceptual, emotional, and linguistic capacities. But social scientists disagree heartily about whether biology and evolution can help account for complex social customs, such as warfare, cooperation, and altruism (the willingness to help others). Nowhere is this disagreement more apparent than in debates over the origins of male–female differences in sexual behavior, so we are going to focus here on that endlessly fascinating topic.

sociobiology An interdisciplinary field that emphasizes evolutionary explanations of social behavior in animals, including human beings.

Evolution and Sexual Strategies

In 1975, one of the world's leading experts on ants, Edward O. Wilson, published a little book that had a big impact. It was titled *Sociobiology: The New Synthesis*, the "synthesis" being the application of biological principles to the social and sexual customs of both nonhuman animals and human beings. **Sociobiology** became a popular topic for researchers and the public, generating great controversy.

Sociobiologists contend that evolution has bred into each of us a tendency to act in ways that maximize our chances of passing on our genes, and to help our close biological relatives, with whom we share many genes, do the same. In this view, just as nature has selected physical characteristics that have proved adaptive, so it has selected psychological traits and social customs that aid individuals in propagating their genes. Customs that enhance the odds of such transmission survive in the form of kinship bonds, dominance arrangements, taboos against female adultery, and many other aspects of social life.

In addition, sociobiologists believe that because the males and females of most species have faced different kinds of survival and mating problems, the sexes have evolved to differ profoundly in aggressiveness, dominance, and sexual strategies (Symons, 1979; Trivers, 1972). In many species, they argue, it is adaptive for males to compete with other males for access to young and fertile females, and to try to win and then inseminate as many females as possible. The more females a male mates with, the more genes he can pass along. (The human record in this regard was achieved by a man who fathered 899 children [Daly & Wilson, 1983]. What else he did with his time is unknown.) But according to sociobiologists, females need to shop for the best genetic deal, as it were, because they can conceive and bear only a limited number of offspring. Having such a large biological investment in each pregnancy, females cannot afford to make mistakes. Besides, mating with a lot of different males would produce no more offspring than staying with just one. So females try to attach themselves to dominant males who have resources and status and are likely to have "superior" genes.

"It's a guy thing."

The result of these two opposite sexual strategies, in this view, is that males generally want sex more often than females do; males are often fickle and promiscuous, whereas females are usually devoted and faithful; males are drawn to sexual novelty and even rape, whereas females want stability and security; males are relatively undiscriminating in their choice of sexual partners, whereas females are cautious and choosy; and males are competitive and concerned about dominance, whereas females are less so.

Evolutionary psychologists generally agree with these conclusions, but whereas sociobiologists often study nonhuman species and argue by analogy, many evolutionary psychologists consider such analogies to be simplistic and misleading. For example, because male scorpion flies force themselves on females, some sociobiologists have drawn an analogy between this behavior and human rape and have concluded that human rape must have the same evolutionary origins and reproductive purposes (Thornhill & Palmer, 2000). But this analogy does not bear scrutiny. Human rape has many motives, including, among others, revenge, sadism, and conformity to peer pressure (see Chapter 12). It is often committed by high-status men who could easily find consenting sexual partners. All too frequently its victims are children or the elderly, who do not reproduce. And sadistic rapists often injure or kill their victims, hardly a way to perpetuate one's genes. In general, therefore, evolutionary psychologists rely less on comparisons with other species than sociobiologists do, focusing instead on commonalities in human mating and dating practices around the world.

Nevertheless, both groups emphasize the evolutionary origins of many human sex differences that appear to be universal, or at least very common. In one massive project, 50 scientists studied 10,000 people in 37 cultures located on six continents and five islands (Buss, 1994; Schmitt, 2003). Around the world, they found, men are more violent than women and more socially dominant. They are more interested in the youth and beauty of their sexual partners, presumably because youth is associated with fertility (see Figure 3.2). According to their responses on questionnaires, they are more sexually jealous and possessive, presumably because if a man's mate had sex with other men, he could never be 100 percent sure that her children were also genetically his. They are quicker than women to have sex with partners they don't know well and more inclined toward polygamy and promiscuity, presumably so that their sperm will be distributed as widely as possible. Women, in contrast, tend to emphasize the financial resources or prospects of a potential mate, his status, and his willingness to com-

FIGURE 3.2 Preferred Age in a Mate

In most societies, men say they prefer to marry women younger than themselves, whereas women prefer men who are older (Buss, 1995). Evolutionary psychologists attribute these preferences to male concern with a partner's fertility and female concern with a partner's material resources and status. When the man is much older than the women, people rarely comment, but when the woman is older, as in the case of actors Demi Moore and Ashton Kutcher, people take notice.

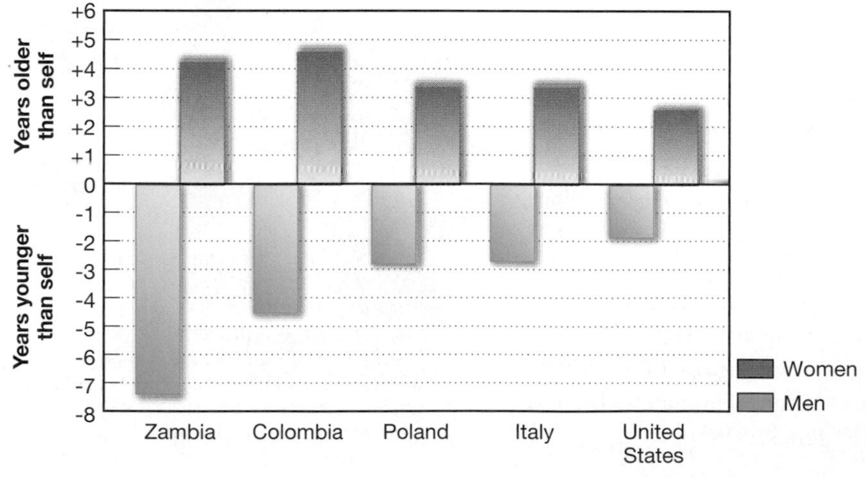

mit to a relationship. On questionnaires, they say they would be more upset by a partner's emotional infidelity than by his sexual infidelity, presumably because abandonment by the partner might leave them without the support and resources needed to raise their offspring. Many studies have reported similar results (e.g., Bailey et al., 1994; Buss, 1996, 2000; Buunk et al., 1996; Daly & Wilson, 1983; Mealey, 2000; Sprecher, Sullivan, & Hatfield, 1994).

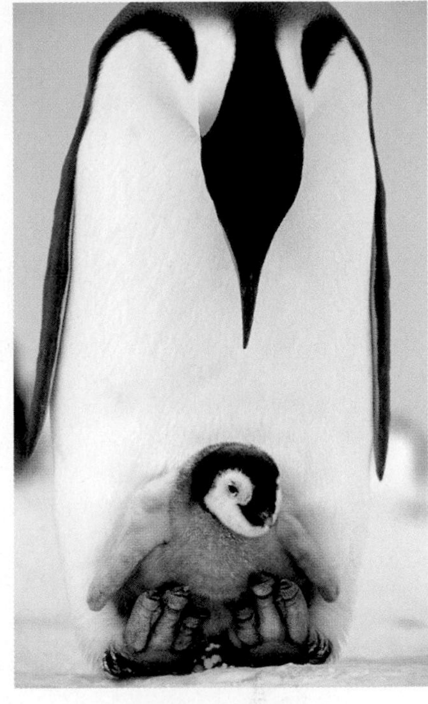

A basic assumption of evolutionary approaches to sexuality is that females across species have a greater involvement in child rearing than males do. But there are many exceptions. Female emperor penguins, for example, take off every winter, leaving behind males like this one to care for the kids.

Culture and the "Genetic Leash"

Evolutionary views of sex differences have become enormously popular. Many academics and laypeople are persuaded that there are indeed evolutionary advantages for males of sowing their seeds far and wide and evolutionary advantages for females of finding a man with a good paycheck.

But critics, including some evolutionary theorists, argue that current evolutionary explanations of infidelity and monogamy are based on simplistic *stereotypes* of gender differences. The actual behavior of humans and other animals often fails to conform to images of sexually promiscuous males and coy, choosy females (Barash & Lipton, 2001; Birkhead, 2001; Fausto-Sterling, 1997; Hrdy, 1994; Roughgarden, 2004). In many species of birds, fish, and mammals, including human beings, females are sexually ardent and often have many male partners. The female's sexual behavior does not seem to depend only on the goal of being fertilized by the male: Females have sex when they are not ovulating and even when they are already pregnant. And in many species, from penguins to primates, males do not just mate and run. They stick around, feeding the infants, carrying them on their backs, and protecting them against predators (Hrdy, 1988; Snowdon, 1997).

Human sexual behavior, especially, is amazingly varied and changeable across time and place. Cultures range from those in which women have many children to those in which they have very few, from those in which men are intimately involved in child rearing to those in which they take no part at all, from those in which women may have many lovers to those in which women may be killed for having sex outside of marriage (Hatfield & Rapson, 1996). In many places, the chastity of a potential mate is much more important to men than to women; but in other places, it is important to both sexes—or to neither one (see Figure 3.3). Sexual attitudes and practices also vary tremendously within a culture, as is immediately apparent to anyone surveying the panorama of sexual attitudes and behaviors within the United States and Canada (Laumann et al., 2004; Levine, 2002).

THINKING CRITICALLY

CONSIDER OTHER INTERPRETATIONS

Sex differences in courtship and mating are common around the world and among nonhuman mammals as well. But human sexual behavior also varies in many ways. Do genes hold culture on a tight leash, a long, flexible one, or none at all?

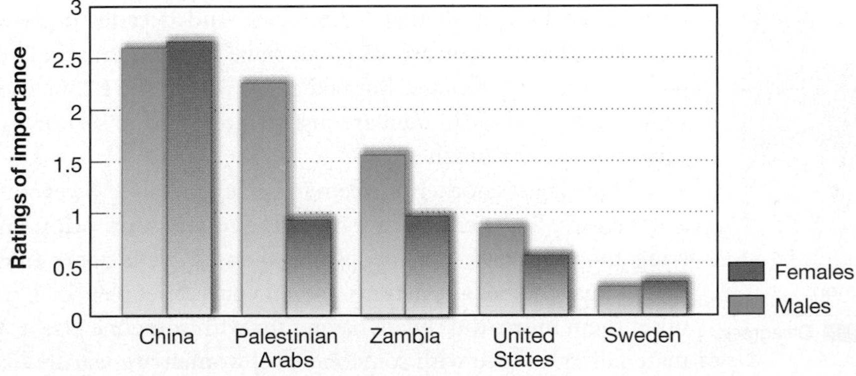

FIGURE 3.3 Attitudes Toward Chastity

In many places, men care more about a partner's chastity than women do, as evolutionary psychologists would predict. But culture has a powerful impact on these attitudes, as this graph shows. Notice that in China, both sexes prefer a partner who has not yet had intercourse, whereas in Sweden, chastity is a nonissue. (From Buss, 1995.)

CLOSE-UP on Research

SURVEYS ON DATING AND MATING

Much of the data cited by evolutionary psychologists have come from questionnaires and interviews. In this research, when people (often undergraduates) are asked to rank the qualities they most value in a potential mate, sex differences appear, just as evolutionary theory would predict (Kenrick et al., 2001). But when we **examine the evidence** more closely, we find problems. For example, despite their differences, *both* sexes usually rank kindness, intelligence, and understanding over physical qualities or financial status.

In Chapter 2 we saw that "convenience samples" of undergraduates sometimes produce research results that do not apply to nonstudents. This may well be the case in much of the evolutionary research on attitudes toward sex and marriage. In a recent national study, researchers at the Centers for Disease Control and Prevention (CDC) interviewed more than 12,000 men and women ages 15 to 44 about sex, living together, marriage, divorce, and parenting (Martinez et al., 2006). The agency had conducted similar surveys since 1973 but only with women. This time, the researchers **asked a question** that in retrospect seems obvious: What about men? Thus they were able to draw conclusions about male and female attitudes based on a sample that was far more representative of the general population than those used by most researchers. What they found throws a different light on evolutionary notions of sex differences.

For example, as we've seen, in the evolutionary view, women on the whole value commitment to a relationship more than men do and are more dedicated to parenting. Yet as you can see in the accompanying figure, 66 percent of the men, compared to only 51 percent of the women, agreed or strongly agreed with the statement "It is better to get married than go through life being single." Further, most women *and* men agreed that "It is more important for a man to spend a lot of time with his family than be successful at his career." Among fathers in their first marriage, 90 percent were living with their kids and spent considerable time feeding and bathing them, helping with homework, and taking them to activities. And 94 percent of both sexes agreed that "The rewards of being a parent are worth it despite the cost and work it takes."

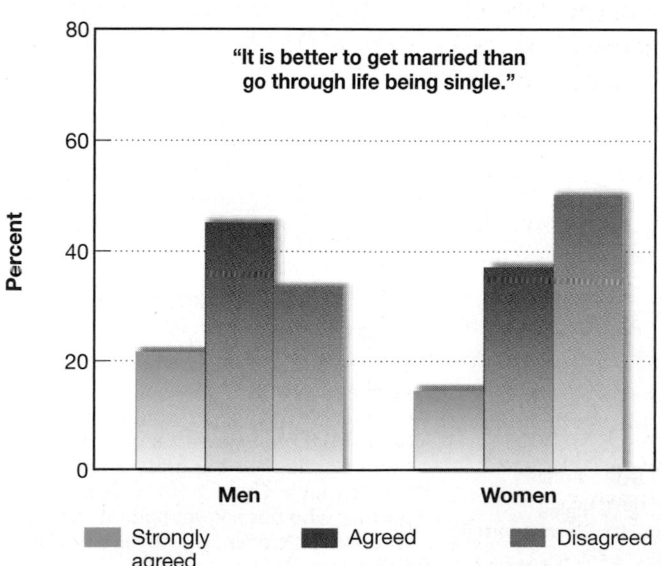

As always, we need to **avoid oversimplification**. Some results did go in the stereotypical direction. More men than women (60 percent versus 51 percent) agreed that it was acceptable for unmarried 18-year-olds to have sexual relations "if they have strong affection for each other." Women were also more likely to be married by age 30 than men were. And decades of research have found that men are likely to have more premarital sexual partners than women are. But taken as a whole, the CDC findings suggest that American men are just as interested in serious family relationships as women are.

There is yet another problem in surveys inspired by evolutionary theories. Some critics have **questioned an assumption** underlying those surveys, that people's responses are a good guide to their actual choices and actions. When you ask people which would upset them more, their mate having sex with someone else or their mate falling in love with someone else, women are usually likelier

than men to say that emotional infidelity would be worse (although there are big variations across cultures). But when one researcher asked people about their *actual* experiences with infidelity, men and women did not differ at all in the degree to which they had focused on the emotional or sexual aspects of their partner's behavior (Harris, 2003). In fact, men, supposedly the more sexually jealous sex, were significantly more likely than women to have tolerated their partner's sexual unfaithfulness, whereas women were more likely to have ended the relationship over it.

In sum, we need to be careful about interpreting surveys that appear to support the evolutionary approach. What undergraduates say about mating and dating is not always typical of everyone, and what people say about mating and dating is not necessarily what they actually do.

Finally, some scientists have questioned evolutionary psychologists' emphasis on the Pleistocene age, which extended from about 2 million years to about 11,000 years ago. Recent analysis of the human genome in Africans, East Asians, and Europeans suggests that during the past ten to fifteen thousand years, natural selection has continued to influence genes associated with taste, smell, digestion, bone structure, skin color, fertility, and even brain function (Voight et al., 2006). Some of these changes may have begun when humans abandoned hunting and gathering in favor of agriculture, a switch that made certain genetic dispositions more adaptive and others less so. David Buller (2005), a philosopher who was captivated by evolutionary psychology until he took a closer look, concludes that "There is no reason to think that contemporary humans are, like Fred and Wilma Flintstone, just Pleistocene hunter-gatherers struggling to survive and reproduce in evolutionarily novel suburban habitats."

How large an influence does our Stone Age past have on our current courtship and mating customs?

Even if the Pleistocene period did strongly influence human mating preferences, those preferences may differ from the ones usually emphasized by evolutionary theory. Our prehistoric ancestors, unlike the undergraduates in many mate-preference studies, did not have 5,000 fellow students to choose from. They lived in small bands, and if they were lucky they might get to choose between Urp and Ork, and that's about it; they could not hold out for some gorgeous babe or handsome millionaire down the road. Because there was a small range of potential partners to choose from, there would have been no need for the kinds of sexual strategies described by evolutionary theorists (Hazan & Diamond, 2000). Instead, evolution might have instilled in us a tendency to select a mate based on similarity (the person's genes, background, and age roughly match our own) and proximity (the person is around a lot). Indeed, similarity and proximity are among the strongest predictors today of the mates people actually choose, whatever they may say on questionnaires (see Chapter 12).

Debate over these matters can become quite heated because of worries that evolutionary arguments will be used to justify social and political inequalities and even violent behavior. In the past, evolutionary ideas have been used to promote *social Darwinism*, the notion that the wealthy and successful are more reproductively fit than other people. Such arguments have also led some people to conclude that men, with less investment in child rearing and more interest in status and dominance, are destined to control business and politics. Edward Wilson (1975) thinks so. "Even with identical education and equal access to all professions [for both sexes]," he wrote,

SHOPPING AT THE EVOLUTIONARY THEORY STORE
Long GENETIC LEASHES
SURE, THEY LACK SOMETHING IN OLD-FASHIONED MASCULINITY, BUT YOU CAN WEAR THEM SO MANY DIFFERENT WAYS!
Short GENETIC LEASHES
BRAIN FLEXIBILITY EXERCISES
THE BUSINESS-WOMAN'S GUIDE

"men are likely to continue to play a disproportionate role in political life, business, and science." This is not a message that people who hope for gender equality welcome!

Ultimately, what evolutionary scientists and their critics are quarreling about is the relative power of biology and culture. In *On Human Nature* (1978), Wilson argued that genes hold culture on a leash. The big question, replied paleontologist Stephen Jay Gould (1987), is how long and tight is that leash? Is it too short and tight to allow much change, or is it long and flexible enough to permit many possible customs? To sociobiologists, the leash is short and tight. To evolutionary psychologists, it is elastic enough to permit culture to modify evolved biological tendencies, although those tendencies can be pretty powerful (Kenrick & Trost, 1993). To critics of both sociobiology and evolutionary psychology, cultural variations mean that no single, genetically determined sexual strategy exists for human beings. What evolution *has* bestowed on us, they say, is an amazingly flexible brain. Therefore, in matters of sex and love, as in all other human behaviors, the leash is long and flexible.

QUICK quiz

Males and females alike have evolved to be able to answer these questions.

1. Which of the following would an evolutionary psychologist expect to be more typical of males than of females? (a) promiscuity, (b) choosiness about sexual partners, (c) concern with dominance, (d) interest in young partners, (e) emphasis on physical attractiveness of partners

2. What major issue divides evolutionary theorists and their critics in debates over courtship and mating?

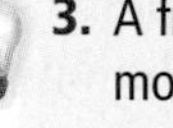

3. A friend of yours, who has read some sociobiology, tells you that men will always be more sexually promiscuous than women because during evolution, the best reproductive strategy for a male primate has been to try to impregnate many females. What kind of evidence would you need in order to evaluate this claim?

Answers:

1. all but b **2.** the relative influence of biology and culture **3.** You would not want to look just for confirming evidence (recall the principle of falsifiability). You would want to look also for evidence of female promiscuity and male monogamy among humans and other species and changes in human sexual customs in response to changing social conditions.

WHAT'S**AHEAD**

- If you have a highly heritable trait, does that mean you are stuck with it forever?
- What kinds of studies allow psychologists to estimate a trait's heritability?

The Genetics of Difference

We have been focusing on the origins of human similarities. We turn now to the second great issue in debates about nature and nurture: the origins of the differences among us. We begin with a critical discussion of what it means to say that a trait is "heritable." Then, to illustrate how behavioral geneticists study differences among

people that might be influenced by genes, we will examine in detail a single, complex issue: the genetic and environmental contributions to intelligence. In other sections of this book, you will be reading about behavioral-genetic findings on many other topics, including biological rhythms (Chapter 5), taste perception (Chapter 6), weight and body shape (Chapter 12), sexual orientation (Chapter 12), personality and temperament (Chapter 13), addiction (Chapter 16), and mental disorders (Chapter 16).

heritability A statistical estimate of the proportion of the total variance in some trait that is attributable to genetic differences among individuals within a group.

The Meaning of Heritability

Suppose you want to measure flute-playing ability in a large group of music students, so you have some independent raters assign each student a score, from 1 to 20. When you plot the scores, you find that some people are what you might call melodically disadvantaged and should forget about a musical career, others are flute geniuses, and the rest fall somewhere in between. What causes the variation in this group of students? Why are some so musically talented and others so inept? Are these differences primarily genetic, or are they the result of experience and motivation?

THINKING CRITICALLY

DEFINE YOUR TERMS

What does it mean to say that some trait is highly heritable? If you want to improve your flute playing and someone tells you that musical ability is heritable, should you stop practicing?

To answer such questions, behavioral geneticists compute a statistic called **heritability**, which gives an estimate of the *proportion of the total variance in a trait that is attributable to genetic variation within a group*. Because the heritability of a trait is expressed as a proportion (such as .60, or 60/100), the maximum value it can have is 1.0 (equivalent to "100 percent of the variance"). Height is highly heritable; that is, within a group of equally well-nourished individuals, most of the variation among them will be accounted for by their genetic differences. In contrast, table manners have low heritability because most variation among individuals is accounted for by differences in upbringing. Our guess is that flute-playing ability—and musical ability in general—falls somewhere in the middle. Differences in the ability to correctly perceive musical pitch and melody appear to be highly heritable; some people, it seems, really are born with a "tin ear" (Drayna et al., 2001). Nonetheless, musical training can enhance normal musical ability, and lack of musical training can keep a person with normal ability from tuning in to the nuances of music.

Many people hold completely mistaken ideas about heritability. But as genetic findings pour in, the public will need to understand this concept more than ever. You cannot understand the nature–nurture issue without understanding the following important facts about heritability:

1 An estimate of heritability applies only to a particular group living in a particular environment.

Heritability may be high in one group and low in another. Suppose that all of the children in Community A are affluent, eat plenty of high-quality food, have kind and attentive parents, and go to the same top-notch schools. Because their environments are similar, any intellectual differences among them will have to be due largely to their genetic differences. In other words, mental ability in this group will be highly heritable. In contrast, suppose the children in Community B are rich, poor, and in between. Some of them have healthy diets; others live on fatty foods and cupcakes. Some attend good schools; others go to inadequate ones. Some have doting parents, and some have unloving and

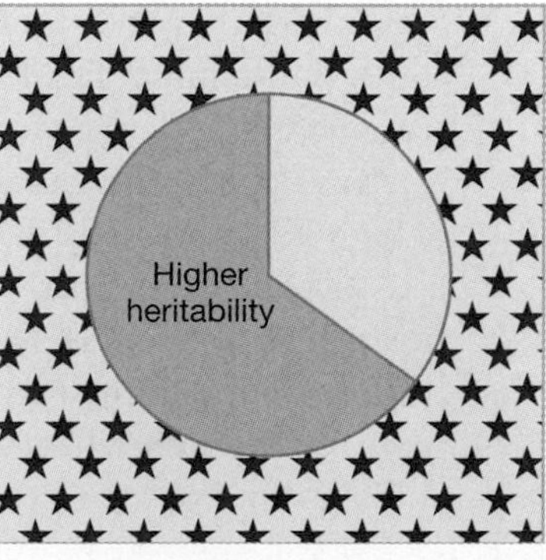

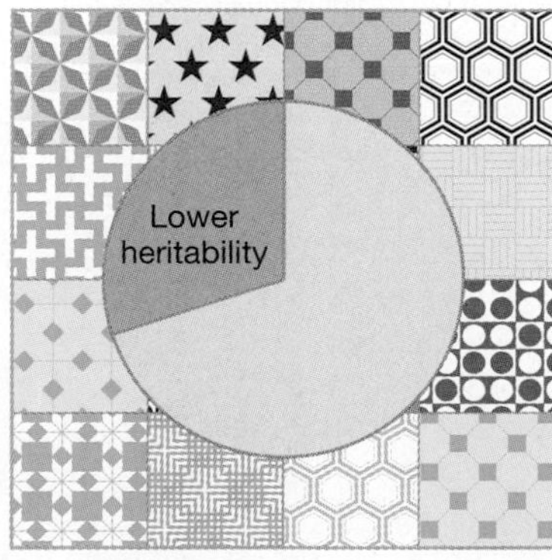

neglectful ones. These children's intellectual differences could be due to their environmental differences, and if that is so, the heritability of intelligence for this group will be low. Indeed, in a study that followed 48,000 American children from birth to age 7, heritability did depend greatly on whether the children were from affluent families or poor ones. In impoverished families, 60 percent of the variance in IQ was accounted for by environmental factors shared by family members, and the contribution of genes was close to zero. In affluent families, the result was nearly exactly the reverse: Heritability was extremely high, and shared environment contributed hardly at all (Turkheimer et al., 2003).

2 Heritability estimates do not apply to individuals, only to variations within a group. You inherited half your genes from your mother and half from your father, but your combination of genes has never been seen before and will never be seen again (unless you have an identical twin). You also have a unique history of family relationships, intellectual training, and life experiences. It is impossible to know just how your genes and your personal history have interacted to produce the person you are today. For example, if you are a great flute player, no one can say whether your ability is mainly a result of inherited musical talent, living all your life in a family of devoted flute players, a private obsession that you acquired at age 6 when you saw the opera *The Magic Flute*—or a combination of all three. For one person, genes may make a tremendous difference in some aptitude or disposition; for another, the environment may be far more important. Scientists can only study the extent to which differences among people in general are explained by their genetic differences.

3 Even highly heritable traits can be modified by the environment. Although height is highly heritable, malnourished children may not grow to be as tall as they would with sufficient food, and children who eat an extremely nutritious diet may grow to be taller than anyone thought they could. The same principle applies to psychological traits, although biological determinists sometimes fail to realize this. They argue, for example, that because IQ is highly heritable, IQ and school achievement cannot be boosted much (Herrnstein & Murray, 1994). But even if the first part of the statement is true, the second part does not necessarily follow, as we will see.

Computing Heritability

Scientists have no way to estimate the heritability of a trait or behavior directly, so they must *infer* it by studying people whose degree of genetic similarity is known. You might think that the simplest approach would be to compare biological relatives within families; everyone knows about families that are famous for some talent or trait. But family traits do not tell us much because close relatives usually share environments as well as genes. If Carlo's parents and siblings all love lasagna, that does not mean a taste for lasagna is heritable! The same applies if everyone in Carlo's family has a high IQ, is mentally ill, or is moody.

A better approach is to study adopted children (e.g., Loehlin, Horn, & Willerman, 1996; Plomin & DeFries, 1985). Such children share half their genes with each birth parent, but they grow up in a different environment, apart from their birth parents. On the other hand, they share an environment with their adoptive parents and siblings but not their genes:

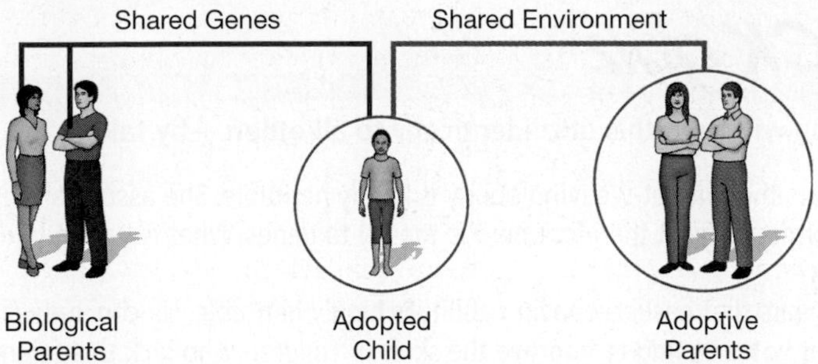

Researchers can compare correlations between the traits of adopted children and those of their biological and adoptive relatives and can use the results to compute an estimate of heritability.

Another approach is to compare identical twins with fraternal twins. **Identical (monozygotic) twins** develop when a fertilized egg (zygote) divides into two parts that then develop as two separate embryos. Because the twins come from the same fertilized egg, they share all their genes. (Identical twins may be slightly different at birth, however, because of differences in the blood supply to the two fetuses or other chance factors.) In contrast, **fraternal (dizygotic) twins** develop when a woman's ovaries release two eggs instead of one and each egg is fertilized by a different sperm. Fraternal twins are wombmates, but they are no more alike genetically than any other two siblings (they share, on average, only half their genes), and they may be of different sexes:

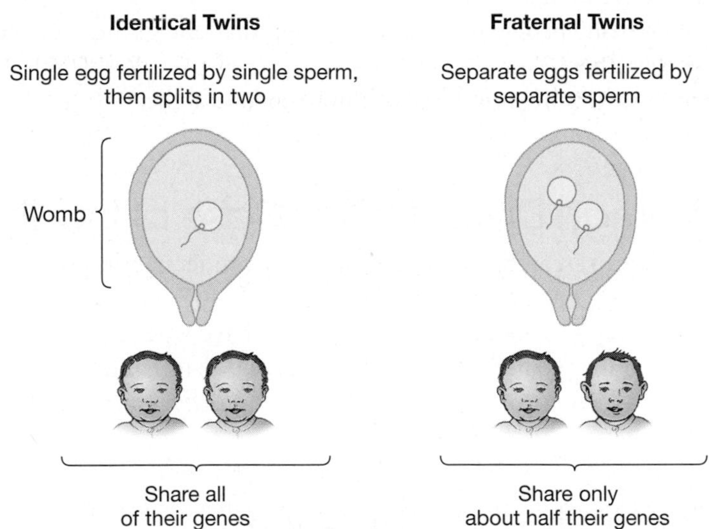

Behavioral geneticists can estimate the heritability of a trait by comparing groups of same-sex fraternal twins with groups of identical twins. The assumption is that if identical twins are more alike than fraternal twins, then the increased similarity must be due to genetic influences. Perhaps, however, identical twins are treated differently than fraternal twins. To avoid this problem, investigators have studied identical twins that were separated early in life and reared apart. (Until recently, adoption policies and attitudes toward births out of wedlock permitted such separations to occur.) In theory, separated identical twins share all their genes but not their environments. Any similarities between them should be primarily genetic and should permit a direct estimate of heritability.

identical (monozygotic) twins Twins that develop when a fertilized egg divides into two parts that develop into separate embryos.

fraternal (dizygotic) twins Twins that develop from two separate eggs fertilized by different sperm; they are no more alike genetically than are any other pair of siblings.

QUICK quiz

We hope you will treat this quiz identically to all others—by taking it.

1. Diane hears that basket-weaving ability is highly heritable. She assumes that her own low performance must therefore be due mostly to genes. What is wrong with her reasoning?
2. Bertram hears that basket-weaving ability is highly heritable. He concludes that schools should not bother trying to improve the skills of children who lack this talent. What is wrong with his reasoning?
3. Basket-weaving skills seem to run in Andy's family. Why shouldn't Andy conclude that his own talent is genetic?
4. Why do behavioral geneticists find it useful to study twins?

Answers:

1. Heritability applies only to differences among individuals within a group, not to particular individuals. **2.** A trait may be highly heritable and still be susceptible to modification. **3.** Family members share not just genes but also environments. **4.** Identical twins growing up together share an environment, and so do fraternal twins. So if identical twins are more alike than fraternal twins, then the increased similarity is assumed to be genetic. Identical twins reared apart share only their genes, not their environment, so similarities between them should also be primarily genetic.

WHAT'S**AHEAD**

- To what extent is intelligence heritable?
- What error do many people make when arguing that one group is genetically smarter than another?
- How does the environment nurture or thwart mental ability?

Our Human Diversity: The Case of Intelligence

Behavioral-genetics research has transformed our understanding of many aspects of behavior that were once explained solely in psychological terms. Some findings, such as the discovery that certain mental illnesses have a genetic component, have been accepted readily. Other findings, however, have inflamed political passions and upset people. No topic has aroused more controversy than the origins of human intelligence.

Genes and Individual Differences

In heritability studies, the usual measure of intellectual functioning is an **intelligence quotient**, or IQ score. Scores on an IQ test reflect how a child has performed compared with other children of the same age, or how an adult has performed compared with other adults. The average score for each age group is arbitrarily set at 100. The distribution of scores in the population approximates a normal (bell-shaped) curve, with scores near the average (mean) most common and very high or very low scores rare. Two-thirds of all test-takers score between 85 and 115.

intelligence quotient (IQ) A measure of intelligence originally computed by dividing a person's mental age by his or her chronological age and multiplying the result by 100; it is now derived from norms provided for standardized intelligence tests.

Most psychologists believe that IQ tests measure a general quality that affects most aspects of mental ability, but the tests also have many critics. Some argue that intelligence comes in many varieties, more than are captured by a sin-

gle score. Others argue that IQ tests are culturally biased, tapping mostly those abilities that depend on experiences in a middle-class environment and favoring white people over people of other ethnicities. We discuss the measurement of intelligence and debates surrounding this concept more fully in Chapter 9. For now, keep in mind that most heritability estimates apply only to those mental skills that affect IQ test scores and that these estimates are likely to be more valid for some groups than for others.

Separated at birth, the Mallifert twins meet accidentally.

Despite these important qualifications, it is clear that the kind of intelligence that produces high IQ scores is highly heritable, at least in the middle-class samples usually studied. For children and adolescents, heritability estimates average around .40 or .50; that is, about half of the variance in IQ scores is explainable by genetic differences (Chipuer, Rovine, & Plomin, 1990; Devlin, Daniels, & Roeder, 1997; Plomin, 1989). For adults, the estimates until late middle age are even higher—in the .60 to .80 range (Bouchard, 1995; McClearn et al., 1997; McGue et al., 1993). That is, the genetic contribution becomes relatively larger and the environmental one relatively smaller with age.

In studies of twins, the scores of identical twins are always much more highly correlated than those of fraternal twins, a difference that reflects the influence of genes. In fact, the scores of identical twins reared *apart* are more highly correlated than those of fraternal twins reared *together*, as you can see in Figure 3.4. In adoption studies, the scores of adopted children are more highly correlated with those of their birth parents than with those of their biologically unrelated adoptive parents; the higher the birth parents' scores, the higher the child's score is likely to be. As adopted children grow into adolescence, the correlation between their IQ scores and those of their biologically unrelated family members diminishes, and in adulthood, the correlation falls to *zero* (Bouchard, 1997b; Scarr, 1993; Scarr & Weinberg, 1994). (This does not mean that adoption has no positive effects; adopted children score higher on IQ tests than do birth siblings who were not adopted, probably because adoptees grow up in a more enriched environment [van IJzendoorn et al., 2005].)

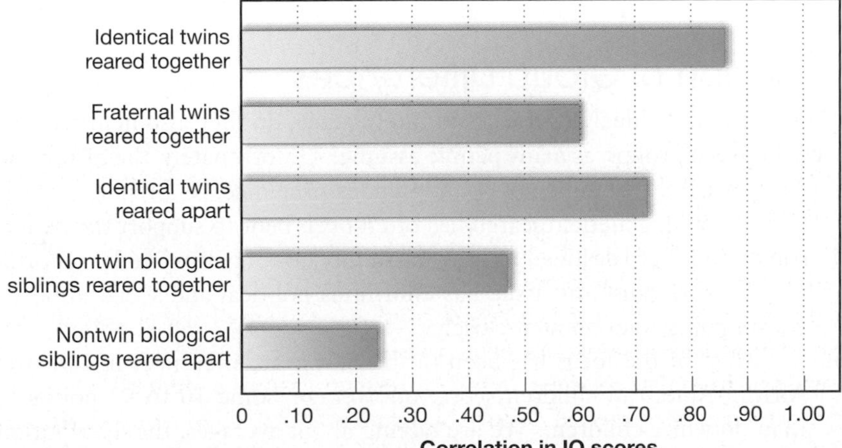

FIGURE 3.4 Correlations in Siblings' IQ Scores

The IQ scores of identical twins are highly correlated, even when they are reared apart. The figures represented in this graph are based on average correlations across many studies (Bouchard & McGue, 1981).

BIOLOGY and Intellect

Genes and Brainy Brains

How might genes affect intelligence? One possibility is by influencing the number of nerve cells in the brain or the number of connections among them, as reflected by the total volume of gray matter. Two brain-scan studies, in Holland and Finland, have reported moderately high correlations between general intelligence and gray-matter volume. This research also found that gray-matter volume was highly correlated in identical twins—the correlations were over 80 percent, compared to only about 50 percent in fraternal twins. The remarkably high correlation in the identical twins indicates that gray-matter volume is indeed highly heritable (Posthuma et al., 2002; Thompson et al., 2001).

The timetable for the brain's development may also play a role. A recent longitudinal study used MRI scans to study the brains of 307 children from early childhood to the late teens. In the brightest children (as measured by IQ tests), the brain's outer covering, the cerebral cortex, which is involved in higher mental processes, started out thinner than in other kids, with *less* gray matter. But the cortex in the brightest children developed more rapidly and for a longer time, reaching its maximum thickness several years later than in other children (Shaw et al., 2006). In kids with average IQs, the peak occurred at age 7 or 8, but in those with the highest IQs, the peak did not occur until age 11 or 12. Children whose IQs were not quite as high fell in between. Genes may be responsible for these different developmental trajectories. But the results must be interpreted with caution, because experience, intellectual stimulation, and even diet can also affect the number of connections among nerve cells in the brain and, thus, development of the brain's gray matter. As always with correlational studies, it is hard to know what is causing what.

Researchers are now looking for genes that might influence performance on IQ and other mental tests. They have identified some possible candidates, but progress has been much slower than anticipated. Far more genes are likely to be involved than was originally thought, and each of these genes is likely to contribute just a tiny piece to the puzzle of genetic variation in intelligence (Plomin et al., 2003; Posthuma & de Geus, 2006).

The Question of Group Differences

If genes influence individual differences in intelligence, do they also help account for differences between groups, as many people assume? Unfortunately, the history of this issue has been marred by ethnic, class, and gender prejudice. As Stephen Jay Gould (1996) noted, genetic research has often been bent to support the belief that some groups are destined by "the harsh dictates of nature" to be subordinate to others. Because this issue has enormous political and social importance, we are going to examine it closely.

THINKING CRITICALLY

ANALYZE ASSUMPTIONS AND BIASES

Most behavioral-genetics studies show the heritability of intelligence to be high. A popular book argues that heredity must play a similarly large role in average IQ differences between ethnic groups. What's wrong with the assumption behind that reasoning?

Most of the focus has been on black–white differences in IQ, because African-American children score, on average, some 10 to 12 points lower than do white children. (We are talking about averages; the distributions of scores for black children and white children overlap considerably.) A few psychologists have proposed a genetic explanation of this difference (Jensen,

1969, 1981; Rushton, 1988). As you can imagine, this topic is not merely academic. Racists have used theories of genetic differences between groups to justify their own hatreds, and politicians have used them to argue for cuts in programs that would benefit blacks, other minorities, and poor children. Some researchers themselves have concluded that there is little point in spending money on programs that try to raise the IQs of low-scoring children, of whatever race (Herrnstein & Murray, 1994).

Genetic explanations, however, have a fatal flaw: They use heritability estimates based mainly on white samples to estimate the role of heredity in *group* differences, a procedure that is not valid. This problem sounds pretty technical, but it is really not too difficult to understand, so stay with us.

Consider, first, not people but tomatoes. (Figure 3.5 will help you visualize the following "thought experiment.") Suppose you have a bag of tomato seeds that vary genetically; all things being equal, some will produce tomatoes that are puny and tasteless, and some will produce tomatoes that are plump and delicious. Now you take a bunch of these seeds in your left hand and another bunch from the same bag in your right hand. Though one seed differs genetically from another, there is no *average* difference between the seeds in your left hand and those in your right. You plant the left hand's seeds in pot A, with some enriched soil that you have doctored with nitrogen and other nutrients, and you plant the right hand's seeds in pot B, with soil from which you have extracted nutrients. You sing to pot A and put it in the sun; you ignore pot B and leave it in a dark corner.

FIGURE 3.5 The Tomato Plant Experiment

In the hypothetical experiment described in the text, even if the differences among plants within each pot were due entirely to genetics, the average differences between pots could be environmental. The same general principle applies to individual and group differences among human beings.

When the tomato plants grow, they will vary *within* each pot in terms of height, the number of tomatoes produced, and the size of the tomatoes, purely because of genetic differences. But there will also be an average difference between the plants in pot A and those in pot B: The plants in pot A will be healthier and bear more tomatoes. This difference *between* pots is due entirely to the different soils and the care that has been given to them—even though the heritability of the *within*-pot differences is 100 percent (Lewontin, 1970). The same is true for real plants, by the way; if you take identical, cloned plants and grow them at different elevations, they will develop differently (Lewontin, 2001).

The principle is the same for people as it is for tomatoes. Although intellectual differences *within* groups are at least partly genetic in origin, that does not mean differences *between* groups are genetic. Blacks and whites do not grow up, on the average, in the same "pots" (environments). Because of a long legacy of racial discrimination and de facto segregation, black children, as well as Latino and other minority children,

often receive far fewer nutrients—literally, in terms of food, and figuratively, in terms of education, encouragement by society, and intellectual opportunities. Ethnic groups also differ in countless cultural ways that affect their performance on IQ tests. And negative stereotypes about ethnic groups may cause members of these groups to doubt their own abilities, become anxious and self-conscious, and perform more poorly than they otherwise would on tests (see Chapter 9).

Doing good research on the origins of group differences in IQ is extremely difficult in the United States, where racism affects the lives of even affluent, successful African-Americans. However, the few studies that have overcome past methodological problems fail to reveal any genetic differences between blacks and whites in whatever it is that IQ tests measure. One study found that children fathered by black and white American soldiers in Germany after World War II and reared in similar German communities by similar families did not differ significantly in IQ (Eyferth, 1961). Another showed that contrary to what a genetic theory would predict, degree of African ancestry (which can be roughly estimated from skin color, blood analysis, and genealogy) is not related to measured intelligence (Scarr et al., 1977). And white and black infants do equally well on a test that measures their preference for novel stimuli, a predictor of later IQ scores (Fagan, 1992).

An intelligent reading of the research on intelligence, therefore, does not direct us to conclude that differences among cultural, ethnic, or national groups are permanent, genetically determined, or signs of any group's innate superiority. On the contrary, the research suggests that we should make sure that all children grow up in the best possible soil, with room for the smartest and the slowest to find a place in the sun.

The Environment and Intelligence

By now you may be wondering what kinds of experiences hinder intellectual development and what kinds of environmental "nutrients" promote it. Here are some of the influences associated with reduced mental ability:

- ***Poor prenatal care.*** If a pregnant woman is malnourished, contracts infections, takes certain drugs, smokes, is exposed to secondhand smoke, or drinks alcohol regularly, her child is at risk of having learning disabilities and a lower IQ.
- ***Malnutrition.*** The average IQ gap between severely malnourished and well-nourished children can be as high as 20 points (Stoch & Smythe, 1963; Winick, Meyer, & Harris, 1975).
- ***Exposure to toxins.*** Lead, especially, can damage the nervous system, even at fairly low levels, producing attention problems, lower IQ scores, and poorer school achievement (Lanphear et al., 2005; Needleman et al., 1996). Many children in the United States are exposed to dangerous levels of lead from dust, contaminated soil, lead paint, and old lead pipes, and the concentration of lead in black children's blood is 50 percent higher than in white children's (Lanphear et al., 2002). Air pollution, which people cannot directly control, also appears to be a serious risk factor. A recent longitudinal study of nonsmoking inner-city women found a link between delayed cognitive development in the women's children and the level of pollutants from fossil fuels that the mothers were exposed to during pregnancy. The culprit appears to be a chemical spewed from vehicles and power plants. Even after controlling for other factors, such as lead exposure, the researchers found that by age 3, children of highly exposed mothers were more than twice as likely as other children to be developmentally delayed (Perera et al., 2006).

- ***Stressful family circumstances.*** Factors that predict reduced intellectual competence include, among others, having a father who does not live with the family, a mother with a history of mental illness, parents with limited work skills, and a history of stressful events, such as domestic violence, early in life (Sameroff et al., 1987). On average, each risk factor reduces a child's IQ score by 4 points. Children with seven risk factors score more than *30 points lower* than those with no risk factors.

In contrast, a healthy and stimulating environment can raise mental performance (Guralnick, 1997; Nelson, Westhues, & MacLeod, 2003; Ramey & Ramey, 1998). In one longitudinal study called the Abecedarian Project, inner-city children who got lots of mental enrichment at home and in child care or school, starting in infancy, had much better school achievement than did children in a control group (Campbell & Ramey, 1995).

Although no single activity is going to turn anyone into a genius, certain experiences do appear to contribute to overall intelligence. In general, children's mental abilities improve when their parents talk to them about many topics and describe things accurately and fully, encourage them to think things through, read to them, and expect them to do well. Some kinds of enrichment classes may also help. When Canadian researchers randomly assigned first graders to get weekly piano, singing, or drama lessons during the school year, or to be in a control group that received no extracurricular lessons, those children who learned to play the piano or sing showed an average IQ increase of 7 points by the end of the school year—compared to 4.3 points in the other groups. This difference was not large, but it was statistically significant (Schellenberg, 2004). The music lessons may have helped the children pay attention, use their memories, and hone their fine-motor skills, thus contributing to development of brain areas involved in intelligence.

Perhaps the best evidence for the importance of environmental influences on intelligence is the fact that IQ scores in developed countries have been climbing

The children of migrant workers (left) often spend long hours in backbreaking field work and may miss out on the educational opportunities and intellectual advantages available to middle-class children (right).

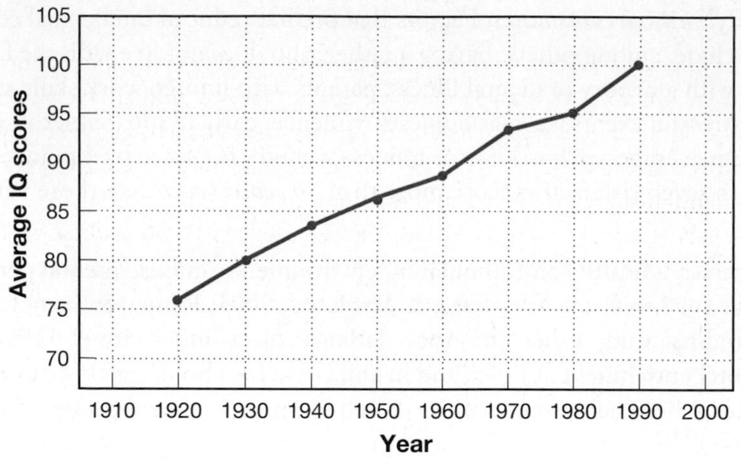

FIGURE 3.6 Climbing IQ Scores

Raw scores on IQ tests have been rising in developed countries for many decades at a rate much too steep to be accounted for by genetic changes. Because test norms are periodically readjusted to set the average score at 100, most people are unaware of the increase. On this graph, average scores are calibrated according to 1989 norms. As you can see, performance was much lower in 1918 than in 1989. (Adapted from Horgan, 1995.)

steadily for at least three generations (Flynn, 1987, 1999) (see Figure 3.6). A similar increase has been documented in Kenya, a developing country: Rural children ages 6 to 8 scored about 11 points higher in 1998 than their peers did in 1984—the fastest rise in a group's average IQ scores ever reported (Daley et al., 2003). Genes cannot possibly have changed enough to account for these findings. Most psychologists attribute the increases to improvements in education, the growth in jobs requiring abstract thought, and better nutrition and health (Neisser, 1998).

We see, then, that although heredity may provide the range of a child's intellectual potential—a Homer Simpson can never become an Einstein—many other factors affect where in that range the child will fall.

Are you thinking intelligently about intelligence?

1. On average, behavioral-genetic studies estimate the heritability of intelligence to be (a) about .90, (b) about .20, (c) low at all ages, (d) higher for adults than for children.
2. *True or false:* If a trait such as intelligence is highly heritable within a group, then differences between groups must also be due mainly to heredity.
3. The available evidence (does/does not) show that ethnic differences in average IQ scores are due to genetic differences.
4. Name four environmental factors associated with reduced mental ability.

Answers:

1. d 2. false 3. does not 4. poor prenatal care, malnutrition, exposure to toxins, and stressful family circumstances

Beyond Nature Versus Nurture

This chapter opened with two questions: What makes us alike as human beings, and why do we differ? Today, a prevalent but greatly oversimplified answer is: It's all genetic. Genes, it's claimed, make men sexually adventurous and women sexually choosy. You either have a gene for smartness, musical ability, math genius, or friendliness, or you don't. In this climate, many people who believe in the importance of learning, opportunities, and experience feel that they must take an equally oversimplified position: Genes, they say, don't matter at all.

THINKING CRITICALLY

TOLERATE UNCERTAINTY

Many people would like to specify precisely how much genes and the environment independently contribute to human qualities. But is this goal achievable? Is a human being like a jigsaw puzzle made up of separate components, or more like a cake with blended ingredients that interact to produce its unique taste?

As we have seen, however, heredity and environment always interact to produce the unique mixture of qualities that make up a human being. At the start of this chapter, we mentioned that genes switch on or off depending on the experiences a person has and on the activity of other genes. Gene "expression" (activity) also varies because of random biochemical processes within bodily cells, which geneticists call "noise." Because of such "noise," identical twins and even cloned, genetically identical animals living in exactly the same environment can differ considerably in appearance and behavior (Raser & O'Shea, 2005). The timing and pattern of genetic activity are critical not just before birth but also throughout life, which means that the genome is not a static blueprint for development but more like a constantly changing network of interlinked influences.

Thus we can no more speak of genes, or of the environment, "causing" personality or intelligence in a straightforward way than we can speak of butter, sugar, or flour individually causing the taste of a cake (Lewontin, Rose, & Kamin, 1984). Many people do speak that way, however, out of a desire to make things clearer than they actually are, and sometimes to justify prejudices about ethnicity, gender, or class.

An unstated assumption in many debates about nature and nurture is that the world would be a better place if certain kinds of genes prevailed. This assumption overlooks the fact that nature loves genetic diversity, not similarity. The ability of any species to survive depends on such diversity. If every penguin, porpoise, or person had exactly the same genetic strengths and weaknesses, these species could not survive changes in the environment; a new virus or a change in climate would wipe out the entire group. With diversity, at least some penguins, porpoises, or people have a chance of making it.

Psychological diversity is adaptive, too. Each of us has something valuable to contribute, whether it is artistic talent, academic ability, creativity, social skill, athletic prowess, a sense of humor, mechanical aptitude, practical wisdom, a social conscience, or the energy to get things done. In our complicated, fast-moving world, all of these qualities are needed. The challenge, for any society, is to promote the potential of each of its members.

Genes are not destiny. In fact, because of "noise" and other influences on gene expression, even identical twins and cloned animals are not exactly alike. The first cat ever cloned (left) was named cc, for "carbon copy," but she's not really a carbon copy of her genetically identical mother. The two have different coat patterns and different personalities.

Taking Psychology with You

Genetic Testing and You

Imagine that you have been feeling depressed and you go to a clinical psychologist for help. The psychologist interviews you, gives you a battery of psychological tests, lets you talk about your problems—and then has your blood drawn to check your DNA, to find out if you have a genetic predisposition for depression.

Has your blood drawn? Right now, this scenario is purely hypothetical, but perhaps not for long. Two leading experts in behavioral genetics, Robert Plomin and John Crabbe (2000), have predicted that in the not-so-distant future, therapists will routinely have their clients' DNA tested to gather information for use in diagnosis and treatment. This is already possible, they note, for Alzheimer's disease: Having a DNA marker for a gene that codes for a particular protein heightens an individual's risk of developing the disease.

Would you want to be tested for a gene that increases the risk of developing Alzheimer's? How would you feel about being tested for a gene that increases the risk of an early death? Would you want to know so that you could plan accordingly, or would you rather let matters fall where they may?

Pregnant women and their partners are often tested to determine whether they are carrying genes that are likely to condemn their child to a fatal or painful disease. When the test results are positive, many choose to abort the pregnancy. But what if you could be tested for a gene that increases your future child's risk of developing a mental or emotional disorder, such as schizophrenia or autism? Would you want to have that sort of test, and what would you do with the results? What if the test were for a more common condition, such as a reading disability or obesity? And what if the condition was homosexuality, which is not a disorder at all but which some people fear; or being very short, which in some quarters is a social disadvantage but is hardly a disability? If prenatal genetic testing revealed that your child had a somewhat increased chance of being gay or short, what would you do with that information? Would you consider aborting the fetus then?

In coming years, as noninvasive methods of genetic testing such as blood tests are introduced and become widespread, all of us are going to have to think long and hard about such questions. You can use information from this chapter to evaluate the pros and cons of such testing for yourself or a family member. Here are some things to keep in mind:

"I've been looking over your genetic code, Stockard, and I like what I see!"

- **Genes are not destiny.** It is true that some diseases, such as Huntington's, are caused by a single gene. However, as we have seen, most traits are influenced by many genes, by environmental factors, and by biochemical and other events within cells. That is why knowing that you have markers for one or two genes that *may* contribute to a trait or disorder does not necessarily tell you much in practical terms.
- **Genetic information could be used to discriminate against individuals.** Critics of genetic testing worry that insurance companies will refuse coverage to adults and children who are currently healthy but who, their DNA reveals, have some genetic predisposition for developing a physical or psychological disorder later in life. Employers who pay insurance premiums for their workers may be reluctant to hire such individuals. So far, such cases of genetic discrimination have been rare. But some bioethicists and scholars are concerned that current laws may not adequately protect people's right to keep genetic information private.
- **Knowing your genetic risk does not necessarily tell you what to do about it.** If your child has a physical disorder called phenylke-

tonuria (PKU), which prevents the body from assimilating protein and causes mental retardation, the solution is obvious: Limit the intake of protein. (All children in the United States are screened for PKU at birth.) But in the case of behavioral, cognitive, or emotional problems, the answer is usually not so straightforward. Often we simply don't yet know how to treat problems that have a genetic component, or many possible approaches exist and we don't know which one is best.

- **Genetic testing can be liberating or stigmatizing.** Knowing that a condition or trait is "not your fault" may help you live with it or accept the limitations it imposes. For example, knowing that your child's autism is genetic and not caused by bad parenting will keep you from feeling unnecessary guilt. On the other hand, genetic testing can activate prejudices against anyone with less than ideal looks or abilities.

  In the past, such prejudices led to the discredited social movement called *eugenics,* which aimed to "improve" the species through forced sterilization of low-IQ people. As a result, from the beginning of the twentieth century until the mid-1960s, thousands of mentally ill and developmentally delayed Americans were sterilized against their will (Bruinius, 2006). Today, say some social critics, the desire to improve children reflects a view of children as products to be perfected instead of individuals to be appreciated for their own unique strengths and qualities.

- **Knowing about a genetic disposition can create a premature diagnosis or a self-fulfilling prophecy.** If parents and school officials know that a child is at risk of developing a learning disorder, they may treat the child as cognitively impaired even though the child has not shown any signs of a problem. If a person is aware of having a genetic predisposition toward depression, he or she may not develop the skills to cope with setbacks, deciding incorrectly that "there's nothing I can do."

- **Genes do not absolve you of responsibility.** Some judges are allowing or even compelling defendants in criminal cases to be genetically tested for mental conditions or behavioral tendencies in order to help determine the extent of their responsibility for the crime or likelihood of repeating it (Hoffmann & Rothenberg, 2005). But "my genes made me do it" is not necessarily a good excuse for bad behavior. Not only does the environment play a large role in behavior, but also the flexible human brain allows us to do an end run around many of our genetic tendencies by modifying them, ignoring them, or controlling them. As David Barash (2001), an evolutionary psychologist, put it, a strong case can be made that "we are never so human as when we behave contrary to our natural inclinations, those most in tune with our biological impulses."

We hope we have given you some things to think about. Would you be tested if some of your relatives had a disease that was influenced by heredity? How would you cope if the results were unfavorable? If abortion would be an option for you, how serious and how likely would an inherited condition have to be before you would consider aborting a fetus: Would a 10 percent likelihood be enough, or 50 percent, or would you require near certainty? Would you want to know, while you are still young, that you carry genes associated with some disorder that usually doesn't strike until middle or old age? And how might this information change your life?

Summary

Unlocking the Secrets of Genes

- In general, *evolutionary psychologists* study our commonalities and *behavioral geneticists* study our differences. Historically, *nativists* have emphasized "nature" and *empiricists* "nurture," but scientists today understand that heredity and environment interact to produce our psychological traits and even most of our physical ones. This interaction works in both directions: Genes affect the environments we choose, and the environment affects the activity of genes over our lifetimes.
- *Genes,* the basic units of heredity, are located on *chromosomes,* which consist of strands of *DNA.* Within each gene, a sequence of four elements of DNA constitutes a chemical code that helps determine the synthesis of a particular protein. In turn, proteins affect virtually all the structural and biochemical characteristics of the organism.
- Most human traits depend on more than one gene pair, which makes tracking down the genetic contributions to a trait extremely difficult. One method for doing so involves the use of *linkage studies,* which look for patterns of inheri-

tance of *genetic markers* whose locations on the genes are already known.

- Researchers have completed a map of the entire human *genome*. However, this map does not automatically tell us what a particular gene does or how it does it, or how multiple genes interact and influence behavior.

The Genetics of Similarity

- Evolutionary psychologists argue that many fundamental human similarities can be traced to the processes of *evolution*, especially *natural selection*. They draw inferences about the behavioral tendencies that might have been selected because they helped our forebears solve survival problems and enhanced reproductive fitness; they then do research to see if such tendencies actually exist throughout the world.
- Many evolutionary psychologists believe that the mind is not a general-purpose computer, but instead evolved as a collection of specialized *mental modules* to handle specific survival problems. Among the candidates for such modules are inborn reflexes, an attraction to novelty, a motive to explore and manipulate objects, an impulse to play, and the capacity for certain basic cognitive skills, including a rudimentary understanding of number. However, because some behavior or trait exists does not necessarily mean that it is adaptive or the product of natural selection.

Our Human Heritage: Language

- Human beings are the only species that uses language to express and comprehend an infinite number of novel utterances. Noam Chomsky argued that the ability to take the *surface structure* of any utterance and apply rules of syntax to infer its underlying *deep structure* must depend on an innate faculty for language, a *language acquisition device* sensitive to a *universal grammar* (features common to all languages). Many findings support this view: Children from different cultures go through similar stages of language development; children's language is full of *overregularizations* reflecting grammatical rules; adults do not consistently correct their children's syntax; groups of children who have never been exposed to adult language often invent their own; and young infants can derive linguistic rules from strings of sounds. An innate capacity for language may have evolved in humans because it enhanced the chances of survival.
- Some scientists, on the other hand, have devised models of language acquisition that do not assume an innate capacity (*computer neural networks*). Some argue that instead of inferring grammatical rules, children learn the statistical probability that any given word or syllable will follow another. Moreover, it seems clear that parental practices, such as recasting a child's incorrect sentence, aid in language acquisition. Biological readiness and experience thus interact in the development of language.

Our Human Heritage: Courtship and Mating

- *Sociobiologists* and evolutionary psychologists argue that males and females have evolved different sexual and courtship strategies in response to survival problems faced in the distant past. In this view, it has been adaptive for males to be promiscuous, to be attracted to young partners, and to want sexual novelty; and for females to be monogamous, to be choosy about partners, and to prefer security to novelty.
- Cross-cultural studies and animal studies support some evolutionary predictions about courtship and mating, but critics argue that human sexual behavior is too varied and changeable to fit a single evolutionary explanation. As we saw in "Close-up on Research," what people actually do often conflicts with what they have told evolutionary researchers on questionnaires. Moreover, our ancestors probably did not have a wide range of partners to choose from; what may have evolved is mate selection based on similarity and proximity. Many critics take exception to the entire line of evolutionary reasoning. The central issue dividing evolutionary theorists and their critics is the length of the "genetic leash."

The Genetics of Difference

- Behavioral geneticists often study differences among individuals by using data from studies of adopted children and of *identical* and *fraternal twins*. These data yield an estimate of the *heritability* of traits and abilities—the extent to which differences in a trait or ability within a group of individuals are accounted for by genetic differences.
- Heritability estimates do not apply to specific individuals or to differences between groups. They apply only to differences within a particular group living in a particular environment; for example, heritability is higher for children in affluent families than in impoverished ones. Moreover, even highly heritable traits can often be modified by the environment.

Our Human Diversity: The Case of Intelligence

- Heritability estimates for intelligence (as measured by IQ tests) average about .40 to .50 for children and adolescents and .60 to .80 for adults. Identical twins are more similar in IQ-test performance than fraternal twins, and adopted children's scores correlate more highly with those of their biological parents than with those of their nonbiological relatives. These results do not mean that genes determine intelligence; the remaining variance in IQ scores must be due largely to environmental influences.
- As we saw in "Biology and Intellect," researchers have recently found that the total volume of gray matter in the brain (which is highly heritable) is correlated with general intelligence. And in bright children, the cerebral cortex starts out thinner than in other children but develops more rapidly and for a longer time. Several studies have reported markers for genes that may influence IQ performance. But each of these genes, if confirmed, is likely to contribute just a tiny piece to the puzzle of genetic variation in intelligence.
- It is a mistake to draw conclusions about *group* differences from heritability estimates based on differences *within* a group. The available evidence fails to support genetic explanations of black–white differences in performance on IQ tests.
- Environmental factors such as poor prenatal care, malnutrition, exposure to toxins, and stressful family circumstances are associated with lower performance on intelligence tests. Conversely, a healthy and stimulating environment, and certain kinds of enrichment activities, can improve performance. IQ scores have been rising in many countries for several generations, most likely because of improved diet and education and the increase in jobs requiring abstract thought.

Beyond Nature Versus Nurture

- Neither nature nor nurture can entirely explain people's similarities or differences. Genetic and environmental influences blend and become indistinguishable in the development of any individual.

KEY TERMS

nativists 71
empiricists 71
evolutionary psychology 71
behavioral genetics 71
genes 72
chromosomes 72
DNA (deoxyribonucleic acid) 72
genome 72
linkage studies 73
genetic markers 73
evolution 75
mutate 75
natural selection 75
Charles Darwin 75
mental modules 76
language 79
surface structure 80
deep structure 80
syntax 81
language acquisition device 81
universal grammar 81
psycholinguists 81
overregularizations 82
computer neural networks 84
sociobiology 85
social Darwinism 89
heritability 91
identical (monozygotic) twins 93
fraternal (dizygotic) twins 93
intelligence quotient (IQ) 94
eugenics 103

How Have We Evolved?

NOW YOU HAVE READ CHAPTER THREE — ARE YOU PREPARED FOR THE EXAM?

1) Identifying a single gene has been compared to searching for someone when all you know is:

a) that the person lives in New York City.

b) that the person lives in the United States.

c) that the person lives in the Westsern Hemisphere.

d) that the person lives somewhere on Earth.

What can a complete map of the human genes reveal — and not reveal? (pages 71-74)

d) Identifying single genes is like searching for a "needle in a haystack" or one person living somewhere on earth.

2) Which of the following is NOT an innate human characteristic?

a) An interest in novelty

b) An impulse to play

c) A preference for constancy

d) A desire to explore and manipulate objects

Why do so many people ignore signs saying "Don't Touch" (pages 75-76)

c) A preference for novelty, not constancy, is innate.

3) An aspect of language that is unique to humans is:

a) the ability to communicate using sounds.

b) the ability to communicate using gestures.

c) the ability to create unlimited, unique sentences.

d) the ability to understand the meaning of sounds produced by others.

What does language allow us to do that other animals cannot? (pages 79-84)

c) Human language allows for an infinite number of new utterances, unlike communication in other animals.

These are the types of questions you will be asked on your test. For more practice exams, go to **www. mypsychlab.com.**

What are the different elements of a language and its structure?

One issue that can get confusing is the various components of language analysis. Use the activities in the Language section of this chapter of MyPsychLab to make sure you have a clear understanding of these components.

Kanzi looks at the keyboard used in teaching language to chimpanzees. Kanzi's language abilities were learned through watching the researchers train his mother rather than directly—much as a human infant learns through listening to the speech of adults.

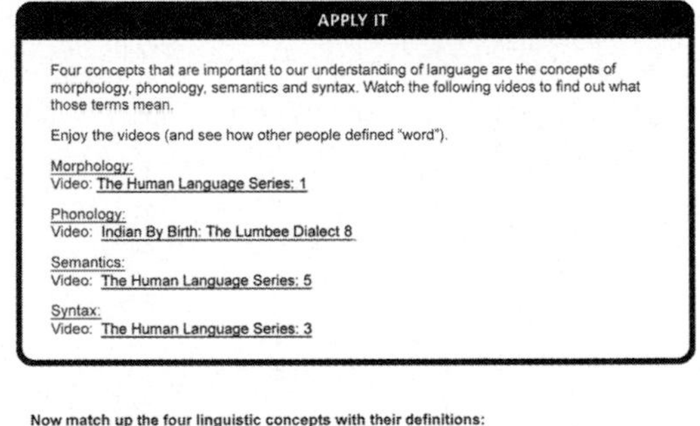

APPLY IT

Four concepts that are important to our understanding of language are the concepts of morphology, phonology, semantics and syntax. Watch the following videos to find out what those terms mean.

Enjoy the videos (and see how other people defined "word").

Morphology:
Video: The Human Language Series: 1

Phonology:
Video: Indian By Birth: The Lumbee Dialect 8

Semantics:
Video: The Human Language Series: 5

Syntax:
Video: The Human Language Series: 3

Now match up the four linguistic concepts with their definitions:

Syntax
Semantics
Morphology
Phonology

the study of the structure of words and their forms
the study of meaning of words, phrases, sentences, and text
the study of the rules that govern the way the words in a sentence come together
the study of the sounds of a particular language

Key Term

language

a system for combining symbols (such as words) so that unlimited number of meaningful statements can be made purpose of communicating with others.

Close

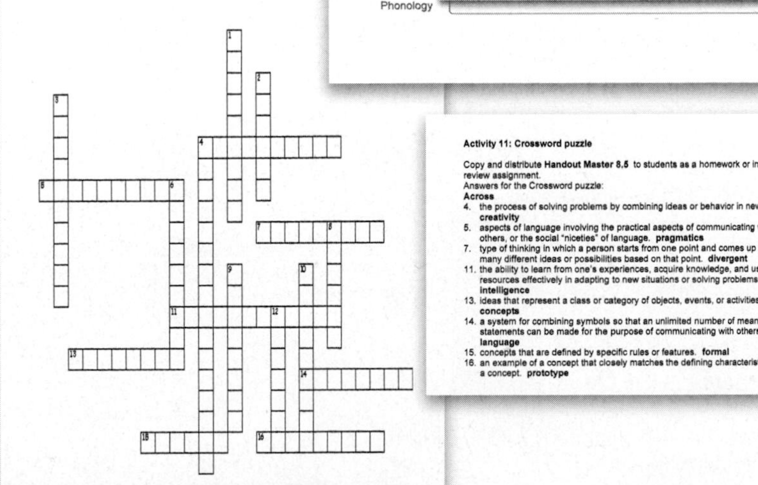

Activity 11: Crossword puzzle

Copy and distribute **Handout Master 8.5** to students as a homework or in-class review assignment.
Answers for the Crossword puzzle:
Across
4. the process of solving problems by combining ideas or behavior in new ways. **creativity**
5. aspects of language involving the practical aspects of communicating with others, or the social "niceties" of language. **pragmatics**
7. type of thinking in which a person starts from one point and comes up with many different ideas or possibilities based on that point. **divergent**
11. the ability to learn from one's experiences, acquire knowledge, and use resources effectively in adapting to new situations or solving problems. **intelligence**
13. ideas that represent a class or category of objects, events, or activities. **concepts**
14. a system for combining symbols so that an unlimited number of meaningful statements can be made for the purpose of communicating with others. **language**
15. concepts that are defined by specific rules or features. **formal**
16. an example of a concept that closely matches the defining characteristics of a concept. **prototype**

TELL ME **MORE** >>

"MPL gave me principles to focus on when I was studying."

Student
Georgia College and State University

What can you find in MyPsychLab?

Self-Directed Tests • Videos • Simulations • eBook • Flash Cards • Web Links . . . and more — organized by chapter, section and learning objective.

CHAPTER FOUR

It's amazing to think that the body feeds the brain sugar and amino acids, and what comes out is poetry and pirouettes.

ROBERT COLLINS

CHAPTER 4

After suffering damage to the right side of the brain, a Swiss stroke patient developed a puzzling symptom. Although the left side of his body was weak and he had trouble seeing objects in his left field of vision, what concerned him most was the blandness of the hospital food. The man had become obsessed with fine dining—a phenomenon his neuropsychologist later dubbed "gourmand syndrome." In his diary, the patient wrote "It is time for . . . a good sausage with hash browns or some spaghetti Bolognese, or risotto and a breaded cutlet, nicely decorated, or a scallop of game in cream sauce with spaetzle." After recovering, he quit his job as a political journalist and became a food columnist (Regard & Landis, 1997).

A former English teacher and poet had a tumor in a part of the brain that processes the expressive qualities of speech, such as rhythm and intonation. Although she could understand words and sentences perfectly well, she could not tell whether a speaker was indignant, cheerful, or dejected unless she carefully analyzed the person's facial expressions and gestures. She was deaf to the emotional nuances of speech, the variations of tone and cadence that can move a listener to laughter, tears, or outrage. But she had one skill that many people lack. Because she could not be swayed by verbal theatrics or tone of voice, she could easily spot a lie (Sacks, 1985).

These two fascinating cases, and thousands like them, teach us that the 3-pound organ inside our skulls provides the bedrock for everything we do and think. When injury or disease affects the brain's functioning, life is inevitably changed, either physically or mentally. Sometimes the changes are subtle and even benign, as in the case of "gourmand syndrome." All too often they are not.

Neuropsychologists, along with neuroscientists from other disciplines, study the brain and the rest of the nervous system in hopes of gaining a better understanding of behavior. Among their many interests are the biological foundations of consciousness (Chapter 5), perception (Chapter 6), memory (Chapter 10), emotion (Chapter 11), stress (Chapter 15), and mental disorders (Chapter 16). In this chapter, we will examine the structure of the brain and the rest of the nervous system as background for our later discussions of these and other topics.

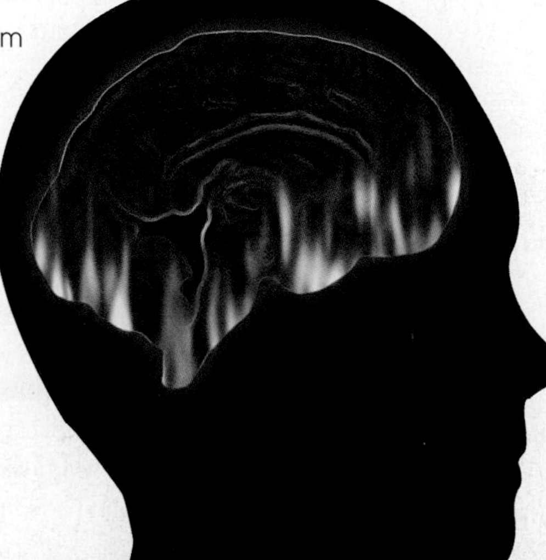

OUTLINE

THINKING CRITICALLY
ASK QUESTIONS

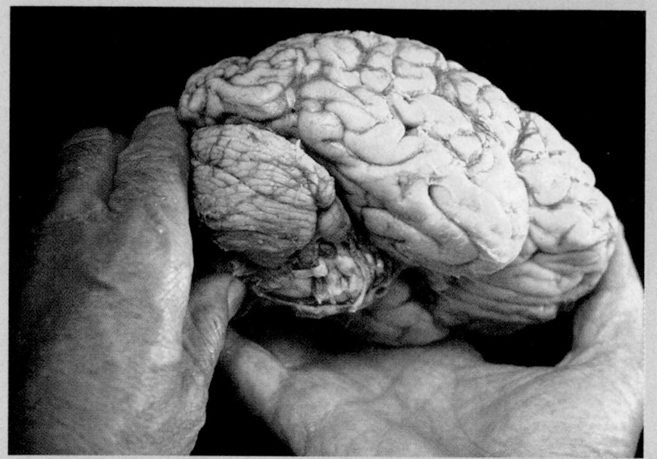

The study of this mysterious 3-pound organ raises many challenging scientific and philosophical questions. Why can a small glitch in the brain's circuits be devastating to some people, whereas others can function with major damage? How do experiences in life alter our brains? And where in this collection of cells and circuits are the mind and our sense of self to be found?

At this very moment, your own brain, assisted by other parts of your nervous system, is busily taking in these words. Whether you are excited, curious, or bored, your brain is registering some sort of emotional reaction. As you continue reading, your brain will (we hope) store away much of the information in this chapter. Later on, your brain may enable you to smell a flower, climb the stairs, greet a friend, solve a personal problem, or chuckle at a joke. But the brain's most startling accomplishment is its knowledge that it is doing all these things. This self-awareness makes brain research different from the study of anything else in the universe. Scientists must use the cells, biochemistry, and circuitry of their own brains to understand the cells, biochemistry, and circuitry of brains in general.

William Shakespeare called the brain "the soul's frail dwelling house." Actually, this miraculous organ is more like the main room in a house filled with many alcoves and passageways—the "house" being the nervous system as a whole. Before we can understand the windows, walls, and furniture of this house, we need to become acquainted with the overall floor plan. It's a pretty technical plan, which means that you will be learning many new terms, but you will need to know these terms in order to understand how biological psychologists go about studying psychological topics.

WHAT'S**AHEAD** 

- Why do you automatically pull your hand away from something hot "without thinking"?
- In an emergency, which part of your nervous system whirls into action?

The Nervous System: A Basic Blueprint

The function of a nervous system is to gather and process information, produce responses to stimuli, and coordinate the workings of different cells. Even the lowly jellyfish and the humble earthworm have the beginnings of such a system. In very simple organisms that do little more than move, eat, and eliminate wastes, the "system" may be no more than one or two nerve cells. In human beings, who do such complex things as dance, cook, and take psychology courses, the nervous system contains billions of cells. Scientists divide this intricate network into two main parts: the central nervous system and the peripheral (outlying) nervous system (see Figure 4.1).

central nervous system (CNS) The portion of the nervous system consisting of the brain and spinal cord.

spinal cord A collection of neurons and supportive tissue running from the base of the brain down the center of the back, protected by a column of bones (the spinal column).

peripheral nervous system (PNS) All portions of the nervous system outside the brain and spinal cord; it includes sensory and motor nerves.

The Central Nervous System

The **central nervous system (CNS)** receives, processes, interprets, and stores incoming sensory information—information about tastes, sounds, smells, color, pressure on the skin, the state of internal organs, and so forth. It also sends out messages destined for muscles, glands, and internal organs. The CNS is usually conceptualized as having two components: the brain, which we will consider in detail later, and the **spinal cord**. The spinal cord is actually an extension of the brain. It runs from the base of the brain down the center of the back, protected by a column of bones (the spinal column), and it acts as a bridge between the brain and the parts of the body below the neck.

The spinal cord produces some behaviors on its own without any help from the brain. These *spinal reflexes* are automatic, requiring no conscious effort. For example, if you accidentally touch a hot iron, you will immediately pull your hand away, even before your brain has had a chance to register what has happened. Nerve impulses bring a message to the spinal cord (hot!), and the spinal cord immediately sends out a command via other nerve impulses, telling muscles in your arm to contract and to pull your hand away from the iron. (Reflexes above the neck, such as sneezing and blinking, involve the lower part of the brain rather than the spinal cord.)

The neural circuits underlying many spinal reflexes are linked to neural pathways that run up and down the spinal cord, to and from the brain. Because of these connections, reflexes can sometimes be influenced by thoughts and emotions. An example is erection in men, a spinal reflex that can be inhibited by anxiety or distracting thoughts and initiated by erotic thoughts. Some reflexes can be brought under conscious control. If you concentrate, you may be able to keep your knee from jerking when it is tapped, as it normally would. Similarly, most men can learn to voluntarily delay ejaculation, another spinal reflex. (Yes, they can.)

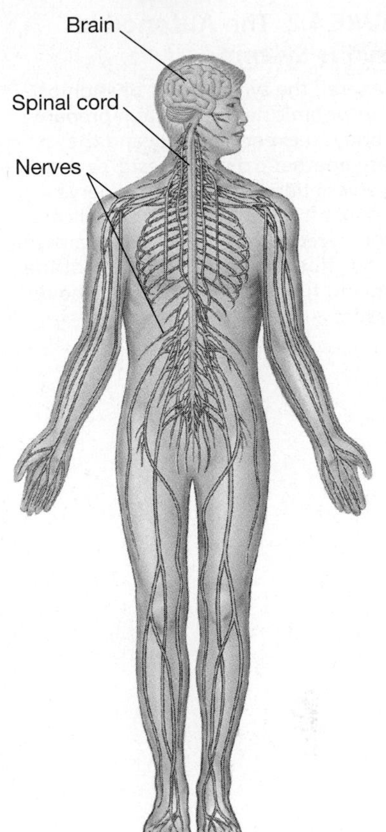

FIGURE 4.1 The Central and Peripheral Nervous Systems

The central nervous system includes the brain and the spinal cord. The peripheral nervous system consists of 43 pairs of nerves that transmit information to and from the central nervous system. Twelve pairs of cranial nerves in the head enter the brain directly; 31 pairs of spinal nerves enter the spinal cord at the spaces between the vertebrae.

The Peripheral Nervous System

The **peripheral nervous system (PNS)** handles the central nervous system's input and output. It contains all portions of the nervous system outside the brain and spinal cord, right down to the nerves in the tips of the fingers and toes. If your brain could not collect information about the world by means of a peripheral nervous system, it would be like a radio without a receiver. In the peripheral nervous system, *sensory nerves* carry messages from special receptors in the skin, muscles, and other internal and external sense organs to the spinal cord, which sends them along to the brain. These nerves put us in touch with both the outside world and the activities of our own bodies. *Motor nerves* carry orders from the central nervous system to muscles, glands, and internal organs. They enable us to move, and they cause glands to contract and to secrete substances, including chemical messengers called *hormones*.

Scientists further divide the peripheral nervous system into two parts: the somatic (bodily) nervous system and the autonomic (self-governing) nervous system. The **somatic nervous system**, sometimes called the *skeletal nervous system*, consists of nerves that are connected to sensory receptors—cells that enable you to sense the world—and also to the skeletal muscles that permit voluntary action. When you feel a bug on your arm, or when you turn off a light or write your name, your somatic system is active. The **autonomic nervous system** regulates the functioning of blood vessels, glands, and internal (visceral) organs such as the bladder, stomach, and heart. When you see someone you have a crush on and your heart pounds, your hands get sweaty, and your cheeks feel hot, you can blame your autonomic nervous system.

The autonomic nervous system is itself divided into two parts: the **sympathetic nervous system** and the **parasympathetic nervous system**. These two parts work together, but in opposing ways, to adjust the body to changing circumstances (see Figure 4.2 on the next page). The sympathetic system acts like the accelerator of a car, mobilizing the body for action and an output of energy. It makes you blush, sweat, and breathe more deeply, and it pushes up your heart rate and blood pressure. As we will see in Chapter 15, when you are in a situation that requires you to fight, flee, or cope, the sympathetic nervous system whirls into action. The parasympathetic system is more like a brake: It does not stop the body, but it does tend to slow things down or keep them running smoothly. It enables the body to conserve and store energy. If you have to jump out of the way of a speeding motorcyclist, sympathetic nerves increase your heart rate. Afterward, parasympathetic nerves slow it down again and keep its rhythm regular.

somatic nervous system The subdivision of the peripheral nervous system that connects to sensory receptors and to skeletal muscles; sometimes called the *skeletal nervous system*.

autonomic nervous system The subdivision of the peripheral nervous system that regulates the internal organs and glands.

sympathetic nervous system The subdivision of the autonomic nervous system that mobilizes bodily resources and increases the output of energy during emotion and stress.

parasympathetic nervous system The subdivision of the autonomic nervous system that operates during relaxed states and that conserves energy.

FIGURE 4.2 The Autonomic Nervous System

In general, the sympathetic division of the autonomic nervous system prepares the body to expend energy and the parasympathetic division restores and conserves energy. Sympathetic nerve fibers exit from areas of the spinal cord shown in red in this illustration; parasympathetic fibers exit from the base of the brain and from spinal cord areas shown in green.

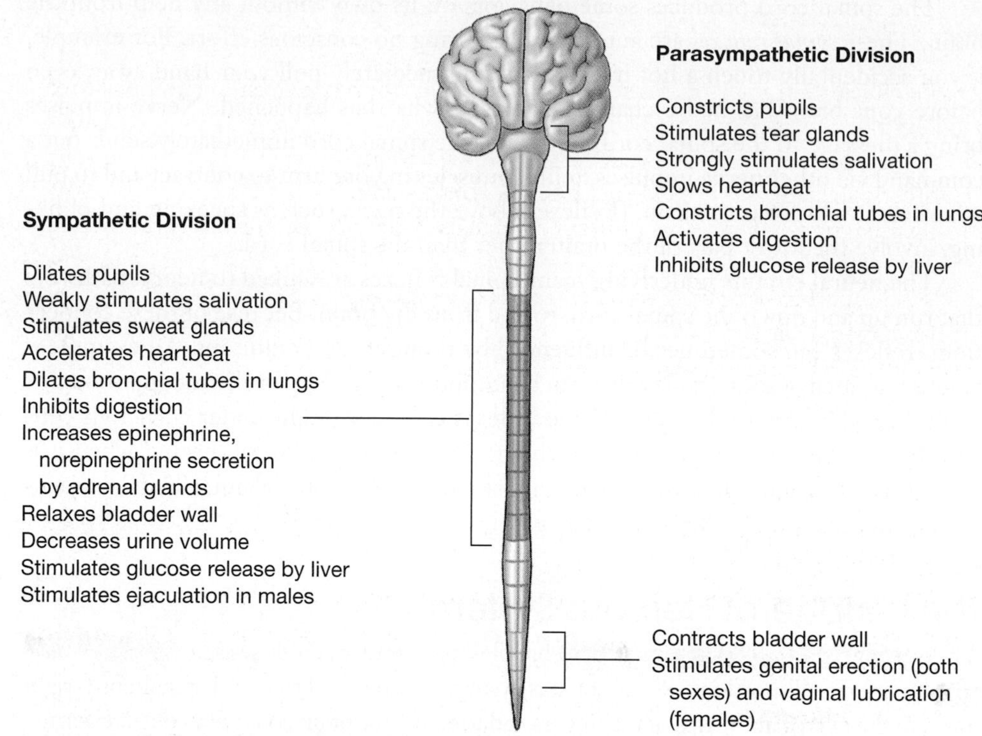

QUICK quiz

Pause now to test your memory by mentally filling in the missing parts of the nervous system "house." Then see whether you can briefly describe what each part of the system does.

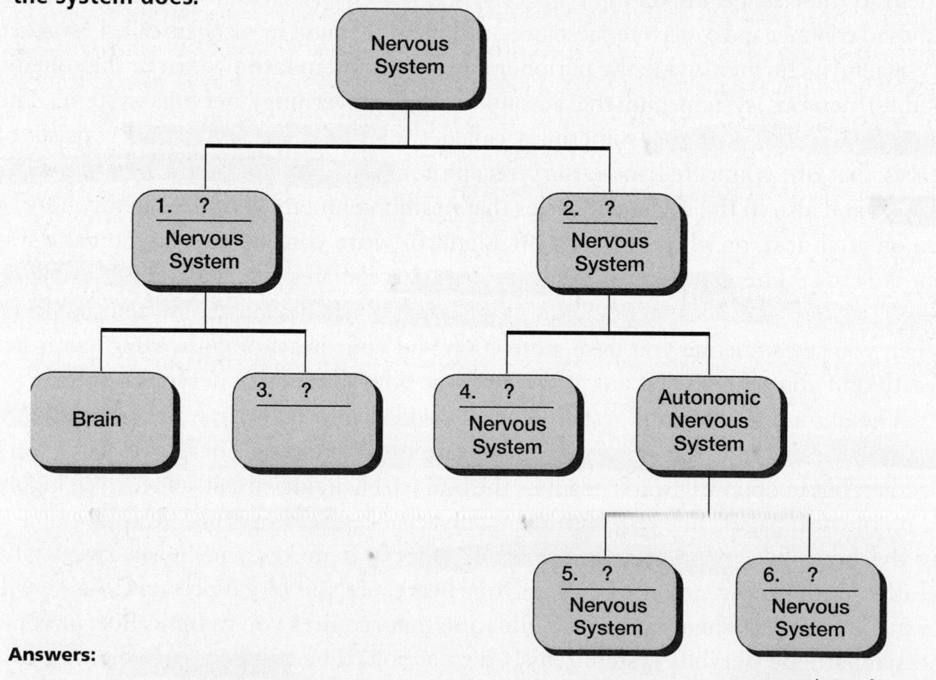

Answers:

1. central: processes, interprets, and stores information and issues orders to muscles, glands, and organs 2. peripheral: transmits information to and from the CNS 3. spinal cord: serves as a bridge between the brain and the peripheral nervous system, produces reflexes 4. somatic: controls the skeletal muscles 5. sympathetic: mobilizes the body for action, energy output 6. parasympathetic: conserves energy, maintains the body in a quiet state

WHAT'S**AHEAD**

- Which cells are the nervous system's "communication specialists," and how do they "talk" to each other?
- Are you born with all the brain cells you'll ever have?
- How do learning and experience alter the brain's circuits?
- What happens when levels of brain chemicals called neurotransmitters are too low or too high?
- Which brain chemicals mimic the effects of morphine by dulling pain and promoting pleasure?
- Do men and women have different "sex hormones"?

neuron A cell that conducts electrochemical signals; the basic unit of the nervous system; also called a *nerve cell.*

glia [GLY-uh or GLEE-uh] Cells that support, nurture, and insulate neurons, remove debris when neurons die, enhance the formation and maintenance of neural connections, and modify neuronal functioning.

Communication in the Nervous System

The blueprint we just described provides only a general idea of the nervous system's structure. Now let's turn to the details.

The nervous system is made up in part of **neurons**, or *nerve cells.* Neurons are the brain's communication specialists, transmitting information to, from, and within the central nervous system. They are held in place by **glia**, or *glial cells* (from the Greek for "glue"), which make up 90 percent of the brain's cells.

For a long time, people thought that glial cells merely provided scaffolding for the more important and exciting neurons. We now know, however, that glial cells have many vital functions: They provide the neurons with nutrients, insulate them, protect the brain from toxic agents, and remove cellular debris when neurons die. Glial cells also communicate chemically with each other and with neurons, and without them, neurons probably could not function effectively. One kind of glial cell appears to give neurons the go-ahead to form connections and to start "talking" to each other (Ullian, Christopherson, & Barres, 2004). And over time, glia help determine which neural connections get stronger or weaker, suggesting that they play a vital role in learning and memory (Fields, 2004).

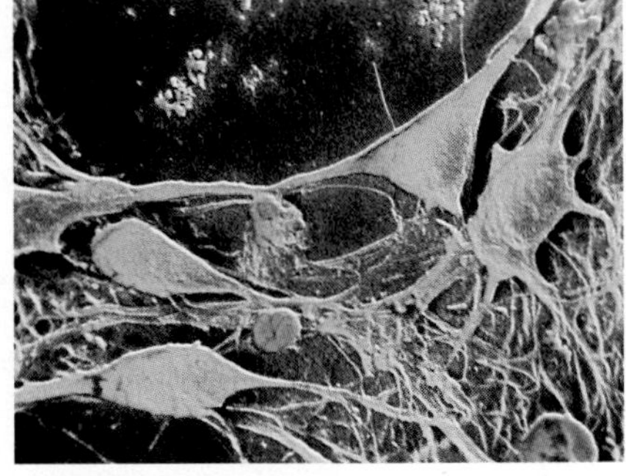

Neurons in the outer layers of the brain.

It's neurons, though, that are considered the building blocks of the nervous system, though in structure they are more like snowflakes than blocks, exquisitely delicate and differing from one another greatly in size and shape (see Figure 4.3). In the giraffe, a neuron that runs from the spinal cord down the animal's hind leg may be 9 feet long! In the human brain, neurons are microscopic. No one is sure how many neurons the human brain contains, but a typical estimate is 100 billion, about the same number as there are stars in our galaxy—and some estimates go much higher.

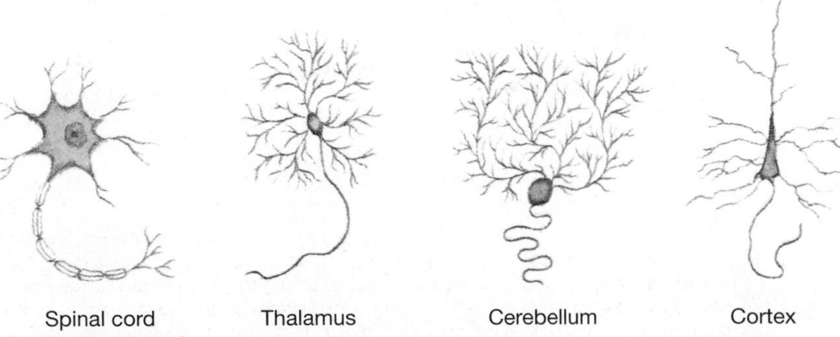

FIGURE 4.3 Different Kinds of Neurons

Neurons vary in size and shape, depending on their location and function. More than 200 types of neurons have been identified in mammals.

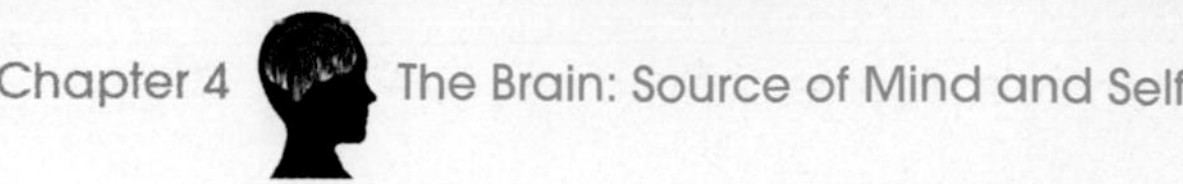

The Structure of the Neuron

dendrites A neuron's branches that receive information from other neurons and transmit it toward the cell body.

cell body The part of the neuron that keeps it alive and determines whether it will fire.

axon A neuron's extending fiber that conducts impulses away from the cell body and transmits them to other neurons.

myelin sheath A fatty insulation that may surround the axon of a neuron.

nerve A bundle of nerve fibers (axons and sometimes dendrites) in the peripheral nervous system.

As you can see in Figure 4.4, a neuron has three main parts: *dendrites*, a *cell body*, and an *axon*. The **dendrites** look like the branches of a tree; indeed, the word *dendrite* means "little tree" in Greek. Dendrites act like antennas, receiving messages from as many as 10,000 other nerve cells and transmitting these messages toward the cell body. They also do some preliminary processing of those messages. The **cell body**, which is shaped roughly like a sphere or a pyramid, contains the biochemical machinery for keeping the neuron alive. It also plays the key role in determining whether the neuron should "fire"—transmit a message to other neurons—depending on inputs from other neurons. The **axon** (from the Greek for "axle") transmits messages away from the cell body to other neurons or to muscle or gland cells. Axons commonly divide at the end into branches called *axon terminals*. In adult human beings, axons vary from only 4 thousandths of an inch to a few feet in length. Dendrites and axons give each neuron a double role: As one researcher put it, a neuron is first a catcher, then a batter (Gazzaniga, 1988).

Many axons, especially the larger ones, are insulated by a surrounding layer of fatty material called the **myelin sheath**, which in the central nervous system is made up of glial cells. Constrictions in this covering, called *nodes*, divide it into segments, which make it look a little like a string of link sausages (see Figure 4.4 again). One purpose of the myelin sheath is to prevent signals in adjacent cells from interfering with each other. Another, as we will see shortly, is to speed up the conduction of neural impulses. In individuals with multiple sclerosis, loss of myelin causes erratic nerve signals, leading to loss of sensation, weakness or paralysis, lack of coordination, or vision problems.

In the peripheral nervous system, the fibers of individual neurons (axons and sometimes dendrites) are collected together in bundles called **nerves**, rather like the lines in a telephone cable. The human body has 43 pairs of peripheral nerves; one nerve from each pair is on the left side of the body, and the other is on the right. Most of these nerves enter or leave the spinal cord, but 12 pairs in the head, the *cranial nerves*, connect directly to the brain. In Chapter 6, we will discuss the cranial nerves involved in smell, hearing, and vision.

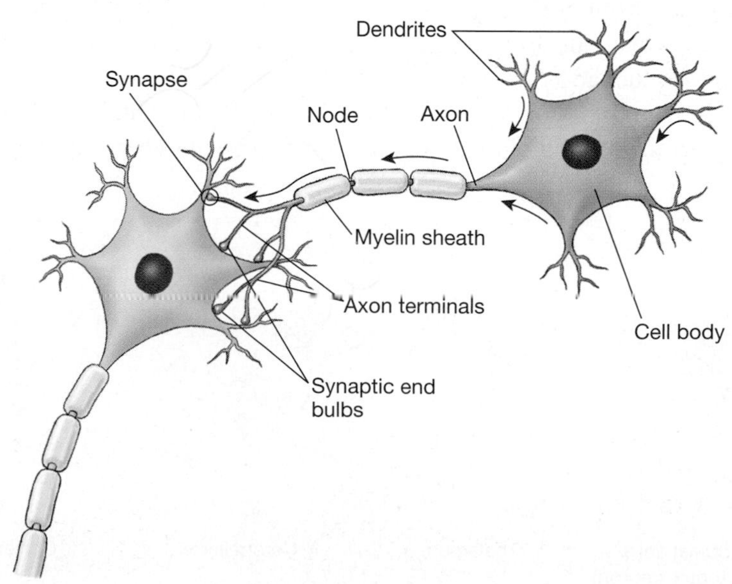

FIGURE 4.4 The Structure of a Neuron

Incoming neural impulses are received by the dendrites of a neuron and are transmitted to the cell body. Outgoing signals pass along the axon to terminal branches.

Neurons in the News

Until recently, neuroscientists assumed that if neurons in the central nervous system were injured or damaged, they could never regenerate (grow back). But then the conventional wisdom got turned upside down. Animal studies showed that severed axons in the spinal cord *can* regrow if you treat them with certain nervous system chemicals (Schnell & Schwab, 1990). Researchers are now working to fine-tune this process and are exploring other approaches as well; many are hopeful that regenerated axons will eventually enable people with spinal cord injuries to use their limbs again (Kraft, 2005).

neurogenesis The production of new neurons from immature stem cells.

stem cells Immature cells that renew themselves and have the potential to develop into mature cells; given encouraging environments, stem cells from early embryos can develop into any cell type.

Scientists have also had to rethink another entrenched assumption, which they had accepted for most of the twentieth century despite some contradictory evidence: that mammals produce no new CNS cells after infancy. In the early 1990s, Canadian neuroscientists, working with mice, immersed immature cells from the animals' brains in a growth-promoting protein and showed that these cells could give birth to new neurons in a process called **neurogenesis**. Even more astonishing, the new neurons then continued to divide and multiply (Reynolds & Weiss, 1992). One of the researchers, Samuel Weiss, said that this result "challenged everything I had read; everything I had learned when I was a student" (quoted in Barinaga, 1992).

Since then, scientists have discovered that the human brain and other body organs also contain such cells, which are now referred to as **stem cells**. These, too, give rise to new neurons when treated in the laboratory. Stem cells involved in learning and memory seem to divide and mature throughout adulthood—a discovery that holds tremendous promise for human well-being (Eriksson et al., 1998; Gage et al., 1998; Gould et al., 1998; Gould, Reeves, et al., 1999). We may even have some control over that process: In animal studies, physical exercise and mental activity promote the production and survival of new cells (Gould, Beylin, et al., 1999; van Praag, Kempermann, & Gage, 1999). On the other hand, stress can inhibit the production of new cells and nicotine can kill them (Berger, Gage, & Vijayaraghavan, 1998; Gould et al., 1998).

Stem-cell research is one of the hottest areas in biology and neuroscience and also one of the most hotly debated. In the United States, federal funding for basic stem-cell research has faced strong resistance by antiabortion activists. The reason: Scientists prefer working with cells from aborted fetuses and from embryos that are a few

In an area associated with learning and memory, immature stem cells give rise to new neurons, and physical and mental stimulation promotes the production and survival of these neurons. These mice, who have toys to play with, tunnels to explore, wheels to run on, and other mice to share their cage with, will grow more cells than mice living alone in standard cages.

days old, which consist of just a few cells. (Fertility clinics store many such embryos because several "test tube" fertilizations are created for every patient who hopes to become pregnant; eventually, the extra embryos are destroyed.) Embryonic stem (ES) cells are especially useful because they can differentiate into any type of cell, from neurons to kidney cells, whereas those from adults are far more limited and are also harder to keep alive.

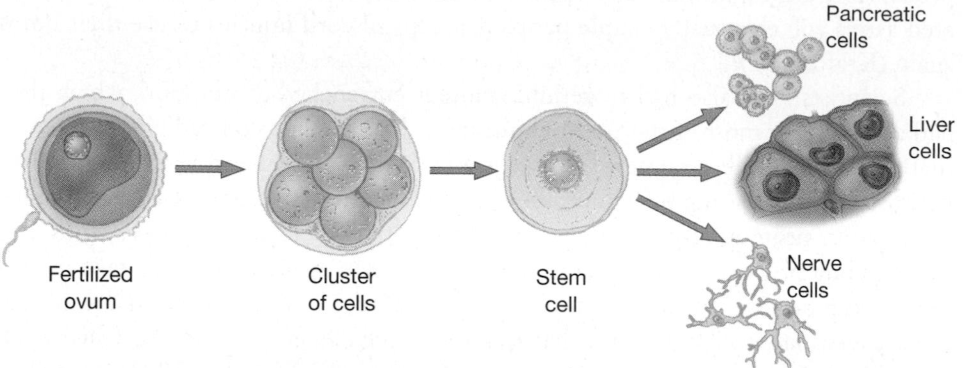

One new technique, developed in mice, may overcome some objections to the use of ES cells by avoiding destruction of the embryo. Researchers removed a single cell from an 8-cell embryo and then coaxed it to form cells with the properties of embryonic stem cells. Then they implanted the 7-cell embryo into a mouse's uterus, where it grew, normally, to term (Chung et al., 2005). (This technique is similar to one that is routinely used during human in vitro fertilization to test for genetic defects.) Work is proceeding on applying this method to human cells (Klimanskaya et al., 2006). Some scientists have also reported success in coaxing stem cells from adult organs, such as bone marrow and skin, to transform themselves into brain cells (e.g., Brazelton et al., 2000; Toma et al., 2001). And a team in Germany, working with mice, recently reported success in turning cells that produce sperm into cells with many characteristics of ES cells (Guan et al., 2006). However, other attempts at finding alternatives to ES cells have been unsuccessful, and we still do not know whether adult stem cells can develop reliably into more than one kind of tissue in human beings.

In 2001, an executive order by President George W. Bush required American researchers who rely on federal funding (which is most of them) to get their cells from only a few, already established sources; new cell lines cannot be developed. Unfortunately, for technical reasons, cells from the existing cell lines can never be transplanted into human beings. Scientists and patient-advocacy groups, however, have been pressing for the ban to be lifted because transplanted stem cells may eventually help people recover from diseases of the brain (such as Alzheimer's) and from damage to the spinal cord and other parts of the body. Scientists have already had some success in animals. For example, in one study, mice with recent spinal cord injuries regained much of their ability to walk normally after being injected with stem cells derived from human fetal brain tissue; microscopic analysis showed that most of the cells had turned into either neurons or a particular type of glial cell (Cummings et al., 2005).

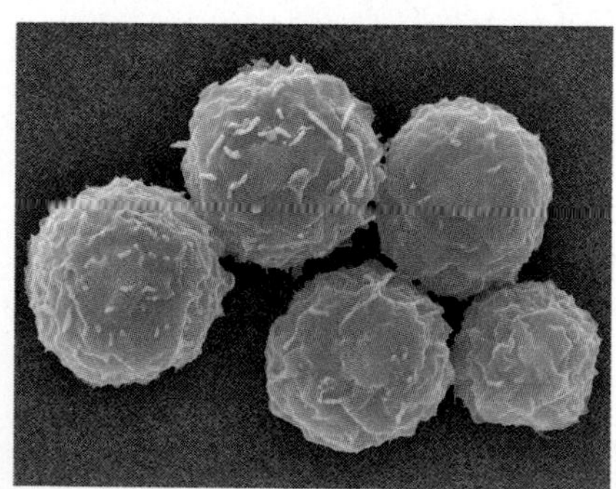
Tiny stem cells like these (magnified 1,200 times in this photo) have provoked both excitement and controversy.

Each year brings more incredible findings about neurons, findings that only a short time ago would have seemed like science fiction. A long road lies ahead, and many daunting technical hurdles remain to be overcome before these findings yield practical benefits for human patients. Eventually, however, new treatments for medical and psychological disorders may be among the most stunning contributions of this line of basic biological research.

How Neurons Communicate

Neurons do not directly touch each other, end to end. Instead, they are separated by a minuscule space called the *synaptic cleft*, where the axon terminal of one neuron nearly touches a dendrite or the cell body of another. The entire site—the axon terminal, the cleft, and the covering membrane of the receiving dendrite or cell body—is called a **synapse**. Because a neuron's axon may have hundreds or even thousands of terminals, a single neuron may have synaptic connections with a great many others. As a result, the number of communication links in the nervous system runs into the trillions or perhaps even the quadrillions.

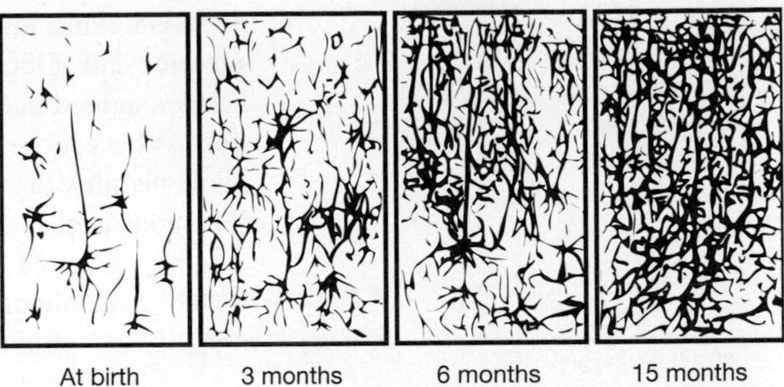

FIGURE 4.5 Getting Connected

Neurons in a newborn's brain are widely spaced, but they immediately begin to form new connections. These drawings show the marked increase in the number of connections from birth to age 15 months.

When we are born, most of these synapses have not yet formed, but during infancy new synapses proliferate at a great rate (see Figure 4.5). Axons and dendrites continue to grow, and tiny projections on dendrites, called *spines*, increase in size and number, producing more complex connections among the brain's nerve cells. Just as new learning and stimulating environments promote the production of new neurons, they also produce the greatest increases in synaptic complexity (Diamond, 1993; Greenough & Anderson, 1991; Greenough & Black, 1992; Rosenzweig, 1984). During childhood, unused synaptic connections are also "pruned away" as cells or their branches die and are not replaced, leaving behind a more efficient neural network. Such pruning may be as important as synaptic growth (Kolb, Gibb, & Robinson, 2003). But these changes—pruning and increases in synaptic density—are not confined to the early years; they continue all through life.

CLOSE-UP on Research

THE PLASTIC BRAIN

The brain's remarkable **plasticity**, its flexibility in adapting to new experiences, may help explain why people with brain damage sometimes have amazing recoveries—why individuals who cannot recall simple words after a stroke may be speaking normally within a matter of months, and why patients who cannot move an arm after a head injury may regain full use of it after physical therapy. Their brains have rewired themselves to adapt to the damage (Liepert et al., 2000).

It has long been documented that some blind people are superior to sighted people at identifying things by touch and at tasks requiring an acute sense of hearing. One research team with an interest in brain plasticity **raised an intriguing question**: When people who have been blind from birth or early childhood try to determine where a sound is coming from, what happens in the part of the brain that in sighted people processes visual information? The researchers reasoned that brain regions normally devoted primarily to vision might "switch gears" in some blind individuals and begin to process input from other senses instead. To **gather evidence** for this hypothesis, they used brain-scan technology called positron-emission tomography (PET, to be described later in this chapter) to examine the brains of people who were localizing sounds heard through speakers. Some of the participants were sighted; others had been blind from early in life. When the participants heard sounds through both ears, activity in the occipital lobe, an area associated with vision, decreased in the sighted

synapse The site where transmission of a nerve impulse from one nerve cell to another occurs; it includes the axon terminal, the synaptic cleft, and receptor sites in the membrane of the receiving cell.

plasticity The brain's ability to change and adapt in response to experience—for example, by reorganizing or growing new neural connections.

persons but not in the blind ones. When one ear was plugged, blind participants with superior skill at localizing sound showed activation in two areas of the occipital cortex; neither sighted people nor blind people without superior ability showed such activation. What's more, the degree of activation in these regions was correlated with the blind people's accuracy on the task, as you can see in the accompanying figure. (Gougoux et al., 2005). The brains of those with the best performance had apparently adapted to blindness by recruiting visual areas to take part in activities involving hearing—a dramatic example of plasticity.

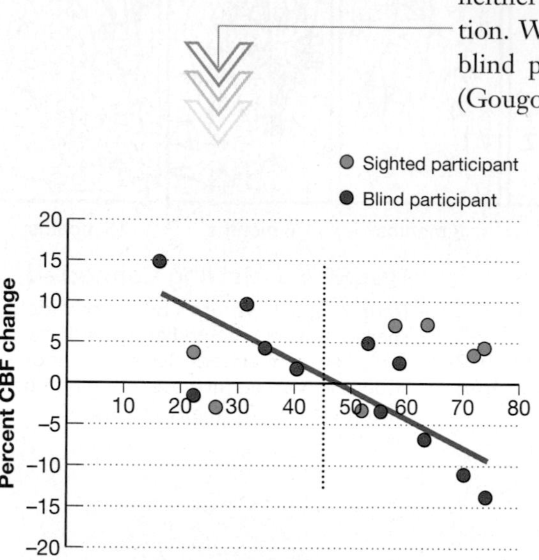

The purple circles to the left of the dotted line represent blind individuals with low error rates in a sound-localization task; those to the right represent blind individuals with high error rates. The graph shows that error rates for blind people—but not sighted ones—were correlated with changes in cerebral blood flow (CBF), and thus neural activity, in a *visual* area of the brain. The more accurate blind people were, the greater the activity in this region.

Building on this research, the researchers **asked a different question**: What would happen if sighted persons were blindfolded, so that they, too, were "blind"? In a series of studies, sighted people wore blindfolds for five days. Before they donned the blindfolds, brain scans showed that the visual areas in their brains were quiet during tasks requiring hearing or touch (for example, touching Braille letters). By day 5, however, these areas were lighting up during the tasks. Then, after the blindfolds were removed, the visual centers once again quieted down (Pascual-Leone et al., 2005).

The researchers have **considered different interpretations** of brain plasticity in blind individuals. One is that the brains of blind people have formed new connections in the visual centers to handle sound or touch. But in the blindfold studies, the changes in activity in the visual areas of sighted people's brains happened extremely quickly, probably too quickly for new connections to be established. The researchers therefore suggest that the visual areas of the brain possess the "computational machinery" necessary for processing nonvisual information, machinery that remains dormant until circumstances require its activation (Amedi et al., 2005). These explanations are not mutually exclusive: In sighted people, existing "machinery" may be able to take over new tasks in a pinch; in those who have been blind for most of their lives, new connections may have time to form, permitting more lasting structural changes in the brain's wiring.

Whatever the explanation, this research teaches us that the brain is a dynamic organ: Its circuits are continually being modified in response to information, challenges, and changes in the environment. As scientists come to understand this process better, they may be able to apply their knowledge by designing improved rehabilitation programs for people with sensory impairments, developmental disabilities, and brain injuries.

Neurons speak to one another, or in some cases to muscles or glands, in an electrical and chemical language. When a nerve cell is stimulated, a change in electrical potential occurs between the inside and the outside of the cell. The physics of this process involves the sudden, momentary inflow of positively charged sodium ions across the cell's membrane, followed by the outflow of positively charged potassium ions. The result is a brief change in electrical voltage, called an **action potential**, which produces an electrical current, or impulse.

action potential A brief change in electrical voltage that occurs between the inside and the outside of an axon when a neuron is stimulated; it serves to produce an electrical impulse.

If an axon is unmyelinated, the action potential at each point in the axon gives rise to a new action potential at the next point; thus, the impulse travels down the axon somewhat as fire travels along the fuse of a firecracker. But in myelinated axons, the process is a little different. Conduction of a neural impulse beneath the sheath is impossible, in part because sodium and potassium ions cannot cross the cell's membrane except at the breaks (nodes) between the myelin's "sausages." Instead, the action potential "hops" from one node to the next. (More precisely, positively charged ions flow down the axon at a fast rate, causing regeneration of the action

potential at each node.) This arrangement allows the impulse to travel faster than it could if the action potential had to be regenerated at every point along the axon. Nerve impulses travel more slowly in babies than in older children and adults, because when babies are born, the myelin sheaths on their axons are not yet fully developed.

When a neural impulse reaches the axon terminal's buttonlike tip, it must get its message across the synaptic cleft to another cell. At this point, *synaptic vesicles*, tiny sacs in the tip of the axon terminal, open and release a few thousand molecules of a chemical substance called a **neurotransmitter**. Like sailors carrying a message from one island to another, these molecules then diffuse across the synaptic cleft (see Figure 4.6).

When they reach the other side, the neurotransmitter molecules bind briefly with *receptor sites*, special molecules in the membrane of the receiving neuron's dendrites (or sometimes cell body), fitting these sites much as a key fits a lock. Changes occur in the receiving neuron's membrane, and the ultimate effect is either *excitatory* (a voltage shift in a positive direction) or *inhibitory* (a voltage shift in a negative direction), depending on which receptor sites have been activated. If the effect is excitatory, the probability that the receiving neuron will fire increases; if it is inhibitory, the probability decreases. Inhibition in the nervous system is extremely important. Without it, we could not sleep or coordinate our movements. Excitation of the nervous system would be overwhelming, producing convulsions.

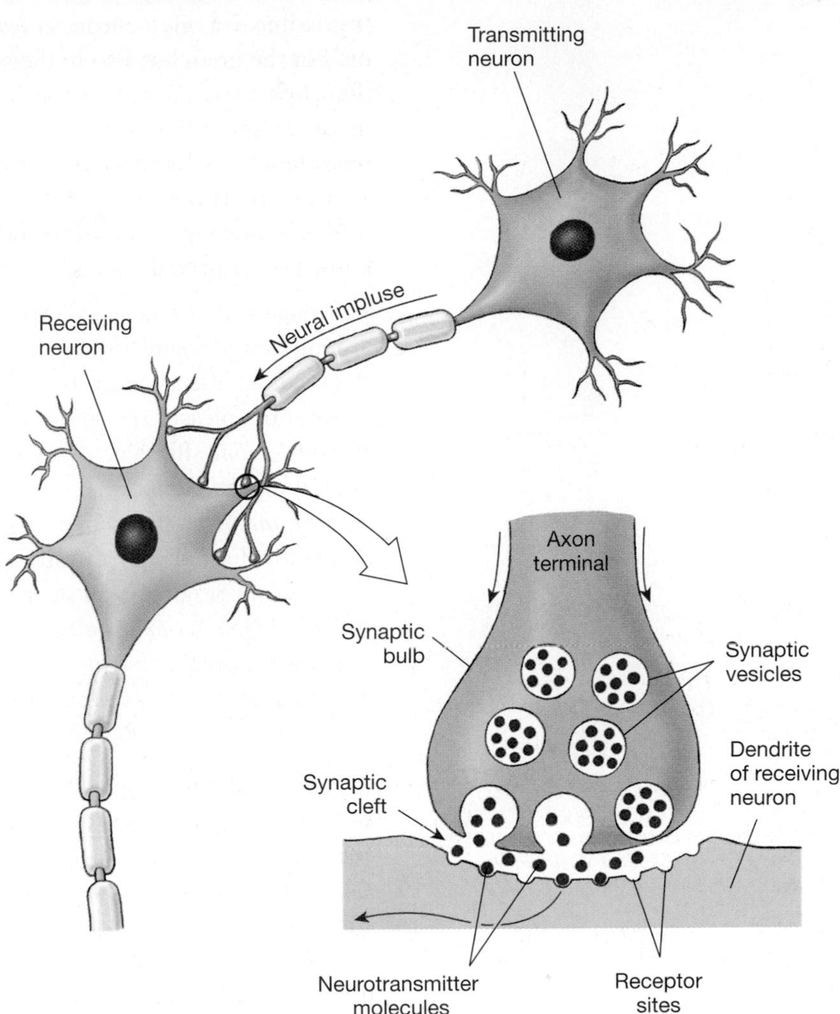

FIGURE 4.6 Neurotransmitter Crossing a Synapse
Neurotransmitter molecules are released into the synaptic cleft between two neurons from vesicles (chambers) in the transmitting neuron's axon terminal. The molecules then bind to receptor sites on the receiving neuron. As a result, the electrical state of the receiving neuron changes and the neuron becomes either more likely to fire an impulse or less so, depending on the type of neurotransmitter.

What any given neuron does at any given moment depends on the net effect of all the messages being received from other neurons. Only when the cell's voltage reaches a certain threshold will it fire. Thousands of messages, both excitatory and inhibitory, may be coming into the cell, and the receiving neuron must essentially average them. The message that reaches a final destination depends on the rate at which individual neurons are firing, how many are firing, what types of neurons are firing, where the neurons are located, and the degree of synchrony among different neurons. It does *not* depend on how strongly the individual neurons are firing, however, because a neuron always either fires or it doesn't. Like the turning on of a light switch, the firing of a neuron is an all-or-none event.

Chemical Messengers in the Nervous System

The nervous system "house" would remain forever dark and lifeless without chemical couriers such as the neurotransmitters. Let's look more closely now at these substances and at two other types of chemical messengers: endorphins and hormones.

neurotransmitter A chemical substance that is released by a transmitting neuron at the synapse and that alters the activity of a receiving neuron.

Neurotransmitters: Versatile Couriers. As we have seen, neurotransmitters make it possible for one neuron to excite or inhibit another. Neurotransmitters exist not only in the brain but also in the spinal cord, the peripheral nerves, and certain glands. Through their effects on specific nerve circuits, these substances can affect mood, memory, and well-being. The nature of the effect depends on the level of the neurotransmitter, its location, and the type of receptor it binds with. Hundreds of substances are known or suspected to be neurotransmitters, and the number keeps growing. Here are a few of the better-understood neurotransmitters and some of their known or suspected effects:

- *Serotonin* affects neurons involved in sleep, appetite, sensory perception, temperature regulation, pain suppression, and mood.
- *Dopamine* affects neurons involved in voluntary movement, learning, memory, emotion, pleasure or reward, and, possibly, response to novelty.
- *Acetylcholine* affects neurons involved in muscle action, cognitive functioning, memory, and emotion.
- *Norepinephrine* affects neurons involved in increased heart rate and the slowing of intestinal activity during stress, and neurons involved in learning, memory, dreaming, waking from sleep, and emotion.
- *GABA (gamma-aminobutyric acid)* functions as the major inhibitory neurotransmitter in the brain.
- *Glutamate* functions as the major excitatory neurotransmitter in the brain; it is released by about 90 percent of the brain's neurons.

Harmful effects can occur when neurotransmitter levels are too high or too low. Low levels of serotonin and dopamine have been associated with severe depression and other mental disorders. Abnormal GABA levels have been implicated in sleep and eating disorders and in convulsive disorders, including epilepsy. People with Alzheimer's disease lose brain cells responsible for producing acetylcholine and other neurotransmitters, and these deficits helps account for their devastating memory problems. A loss of cells that produce dopamine is responsible for the tremors and rigidity of Parkinson's disease. In multiple sclerosis, immune cells overproduce glutamate, which damages or kills the glial cells that normally make myelin.

We want to warn you, however, that pinning down the relationship between neurotransmitter abnormalities and behavioral or physical abnormalities is extremely tricky. Each neurotransmitter plays multiple roles, and the functions of different substances often overlap. Further, it is always possible that something about a disorder leads to abnormal neurotransmitter levels instead of the other way around. Although drugs that boost or decrease levels of particular neurotransmitters are sometimes effective in treating disorders, this fact does not necessarily mean that abnormal neurotransmitter levels are *causing* the disorders. After all, aspirin can relieve a headache, but headaches are not caused by a lack of aspirin!

Muhammad Ali and Michael J. Fox both have Parkinson's disease, which involves a loss of dopamine-producing cells. They have used their fame to draw public attention to the disorder.

Many of us regularly ingest things that affect our own neurotransmitters. For example, most recreational drugs produce their effects by blocking or enhancing the actions of neurotransmitters. So do some herbal remedies. St. John's wort, which is often taken for depression, prevents the cells that release serotonin from reabsorbing excess molecules

that have remained in the synaptic cleft; as a result, serotonin levels rise. Many people do not realize that such remedies, because they affect the nervous system's biochemistry, can interact with other medications and can be harmful in high doses. Even ordinary foods can influence the availability of neurotransmitters in the brain, as we discuss in "Taking Psychology with You."

"PSST—ENDORPHINS. AND THEY'RE PERFECTLY LEGAL."

Endorphins: The Brain's Natural Opiates. Another intriguing group of chemical messengers is known collectively as *endogenous opioid peptides*, or more popularly as **endorphins**. Endorphins have effects similar to those of natural opiates; that is, they reduce pain and promote pleasure. They are also thought to play a role in appetite, sexual activity, blood pressure, mood, learning, and memory. Some endorphins function as neurotransmitters, but most act primarily by altering the effects of neurotransmitters—for example, by limiting or prolonging those effects.

Endorphins were first identified in the early 1970s. Candace Pert and Solomon Snyder (1973) were doing research on morphine, a pain-relieving and mood-elevating substance derived from opium, which is made from poppies. They found that morphine works by binding to receptor sites in the brain. This seemed odd. As Snyder later recalled, "We doubted that animals had evolved opiate receptors just to deal with certain properties of the poppy plant" (quoted in Radetsky, 1991). Pert and Snyder reasoned that if opiate receptors exist, then the body must produce its own internally generated, or *endogenous*, morphinelike substances, which they named "endorphins." Soon they and other researchers confirmed this hypothesis.

Endorphin levels seem to shoot up when an animal or a person is afraid or under stress. This is no accident; by making pain bearable in such situations, endorphins give a species an evolutionary advantage. When an organism is threatened, it needs to do something fast. Pain, however, can interfere with action: A mouse that pauses to lick a wounded paw may become a cat's dinner; a soldier who is overcome by an injury may never get off the battlefield. But, of course, the body's built-in system of counteracting pain is only partly successful, especially when painful stimulation is prolonged.

In Chapter 12, we will see that a link also exists between endorphins and the pleasures of social contact. Research with animals suggests that in infancy, contact with the mother stimulates the flow of endorphins, which strengthens the infant's bond with her. Some researchers now think that this "endorphin rush" also occurs in the early stages of passionate love between adults, accounting for the feeling of euphoria that "falling" for someone creates (Diamond, 2004).

Hormones: Long-Distance Messengers. **Hormones**, which make up the third class of chemical messengers, are produced primarily in **endocrine glands**. They are released directly into the bloodstream, which carries them to organs and cells that may be far from their point of origin. Hormones have dozens of jobs, from promoting bodily growth to aiding digestion to regulating metabolism.

Neurotransmitters and hormones are not always chemically distinct; the two classifications are like social clubs that admit some of the same members. A particular chemical, such as norepinephrine, may belong to more than one classification, depending on where it is located and what function it is performing. Nature has been efficient, giving some substances more than one task to perform.

endorphins [en-DOR-fins] Chemical substances in the nervous system that are similar in structure and action to opiates; they are involved in pain reduction, pleasure, and memory and are known technically as *endogenous opioid peptides*.

hormones Chemical substances, secreted by organs called *glands*, that affect the functioning of other organs.

endocrine glands Internal organs that produce hormones and release them into the bloodstream.

The following hormones, among others, are of particular interest to psychologists:

1 **Melatonin**, which is secreted by the *pineal gland* deep within the brain, helps to regulate daily biological rhythms and promotes sleep, as we will discuss further in Chapter 5.

2 **Oxytocin**, which is secreted by another small gland in the brain, the *pituitary gland*, enhances uterine contractions during childbirth and facilitates the ejection of milk during nursing. Psychologists are interested in this hormone because recent research suggests that it also contributes to relationships in both sexes by promoting attachment and trust (see Chapter 12).

3 **Adrenal hormones**, which are produced by the *adrenal glands* (organs that are perched right above the kidneys), are involved in emotion and stress (see Chapters 11 and 15). These hormones also rise in response to other conditions, such as heat, cold, pain, injury, burns, and physical exercise, and in response to some drugs, such as caffeine and nicotine. The outer part of each adrenal gland produces *cortisol*, which increases blood-sugar levels and boosts energy. The inner part produces *epinephrine* (popularly known as adrenaline) and *norepinephrine*. When adrenal hormones are released in your body, activated by the sympathetic nervous system, they increase your arousal level and prepare you for action. Adrenal hormones also enhance memory, as we will see in Chapter 10.

4 **Sex hormones**, which are secreted by tissue in the gonads (testes in men, ovaries in women) and also by the adrenal glands, include three main types, all occurring in both sexes but in differing amounts and proportions in males and females after puberty. *Androgens* (the most important of which is *testosterone*) are masculinizing hormones produced mainly in the testes but also in the ovaries and the adrenal glands. Androgens set in motion the physical changes males experience at puberty—for example, a deepened voice and facial and chest hair—and cause pubic and underarm hair to develop in both sexes. Testosterone also influences sexual arousal in both sexes. *Estrogens* are feminizing hormones that bring on physical changes in females at puberty, such as breast development and the onset of menstruation, and that influence the course of the menstrual cycle. *Progesterone* contributes to the growth and maintenance of the uterine lining in preparation for a fertilized egg, among other functions. Estrogens and progesterone are produced mainly in the ovaries but also in the testes and the adrenal glands.

Researchers are studying the possible involvement of sex hormones in behavior not linked to sex or reproduction. For example, some researchers believe that the body's natural estrogen may contribute to learning and memory in both sexes by promoting the formation of synapses in certain areas of the brain (Maki & Resnick, 2000; Sherwin, 1998a; Wickelgren, 1997). But the most common belief about the nonsexual effects of sex hormones—that fluctuating levels of estrogen and progesterone make most women "emotional" before menstruation—has not been borne out by research, as we will see in Chapter 5.

Review 4.1 summarizes the three types of brain chemicals we have discussed and their effects.

melatonin A hormone, secreted by the pineal gland, that is involved in the regulation of daily biological rhythms.

oxytocin A hormone, secreted by the pituitary gland, that stimulates uterine contractions during childbirth, facilitates the ejection of milk during nursing, and seems to promote, in both sexes, attachment and trust in relationships.

adrenal hormones Hormones that are produced by the adrenal glands and that are involved in emotion and stress.

sex hormones Hormones that regulate the development and functioning of reproductive organs and that stimulate the development of male and female sexual characteristics; they include androgens, estrogens, and progesterone.

REVIEW 4.1
Nervous-System Chemicals and their Effects

Type	Function	Effects	Where Produced	Examples
Neurotransmitters	Enable neurons to excite or inhibit each other	Diverse, depending on which circuits are activated or suppressed	Brain, spinal cord, peripheral nerves, certain glands	Serotonin, dopamine, norepinephrine
Endorphins	Usually modulate the effects of neurotransmitters	Reduce pain, promote pleasure; also linked to learning, memory, and other functions	Brain, spinal cord	(Several varieties, not discussed in this text)
Hormones	Affect functioning of target organs and tissues	Dozens, ranging from promotion of digestion to regulation of metabolism	Primarily in endocrine glands	Epinephrine, norepine-phrine, estrogens, androgens

QUICK quiz

Get your glutamate going by taking this quiz.

A. Which word in parentheses better fits each of the following definitions?

1. Basic building blocks of the nervous system (*nerves, neurons*)
2. Cell parts that receive nerve impulses (*axons, dendrites*)
3. Site of communication between neurons (*synapse, myelin sheath*)
4. Opiatelike substance in the brain (*dopamine, endorphin*)
5. Chemicals that make it possible for neurons to communicate (*neurotransmitters, hormones*)
6. Hormone closely associated with emotional excitement (*epinephrine, estrogen*)

B. Imagine that you are depressed, and you hear about a treatment for depression that affects the levels of several neurotransmitters thought to be involved in the disorder. Based on what you have learned, what questions would you want to ask before deciding whether to try the treatment?

Answers:

A. 1. neurons **2.** dendrites **3.** synapse **4.** endorphin **5.** neurotransmitters **6.** epinephrine **B.** You might want to ask, among other things, about side effects (each neurotransmitter has several functions, all of which might be affected by the treatment); about evidence that the treatment works; about whether there is any reason to believe that your own neurotransmitter levels are abnormal; and about whether there may be other reasons for your depression.

WHAT'S**AHEAD**

- Why are patterns of electrical activity in the brain called "brain waves"?
- What scanning techniques reveal changes in brain activity while people listen to music or solve math problems?
- Is there a "gum-chewing center" in the brain?

Mapping the Brain

We come now to the main room of the nervous system "house": the brain. A disembodied brain stored in a formaldehyde-filled container is a putty-colored, wrinkled glob of tissue that looks a little like an oversized walnut. It takes an act of imagination to envision this modest-looking organ writing *Hamlet*, discovering radium, or inventing the paper clip.

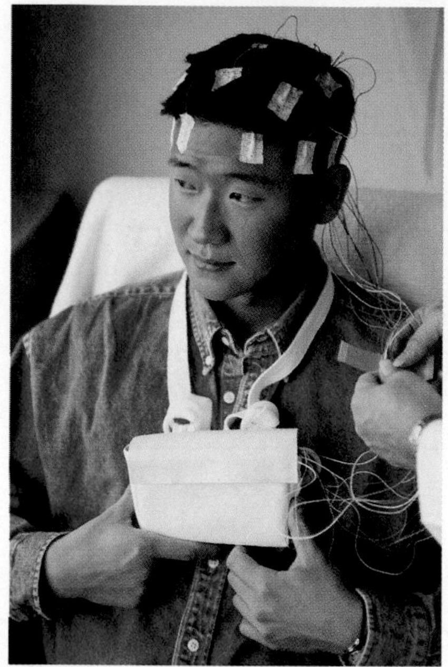

Electrodes are used to produce an overall picture of electrical activity in different areas of the brain.

In a living person, of course, the brain is encased in a thick protective vault of bone. How, then, can scientists study it? One approach is to study patients who have had a part of the brain damaged or removed because of disease or injury. Another, the *lesion method*, involves damaging or removing sections of brain in animals and then observing the effects.

Electrical and Magnetic Detection. The brain can also be probed with devices called *electrodes*. Some electrodes are coin-shaped and are simply pasted or taped onto the scalp. They detect the electrical activity of millions of neurons in particular regions of the brain and are widely used in research and medical diagnosis. The electrodes are connected by wires to a machine that translates the electrical energy from the brain into wavy lines on a moving piece of paper or visual patterns on a screen. That is why electrical patterns in the brain are known as "brain waves." Different wave patterns are associated with sleep, relaxation, and mental concentration (see Chapter 5).

A brain-wave recording is called an **electroencephalogram (EEG)**. A standard EEG is useful but not very precise because it reflects the activities of many cells at once. "Listening" to the brain with an EEG machine is like standing outside a sports stadium: You know when something is happening, but you can't be sure what it is or who is doing it. Fortunately, computer technology can be combined with EEG technology to get a clearer picture of brain activity patterns associated with specific events and mental processes. The computer suppresses all the background "noise," leaving only the pattern of electrical response to the event being studied.

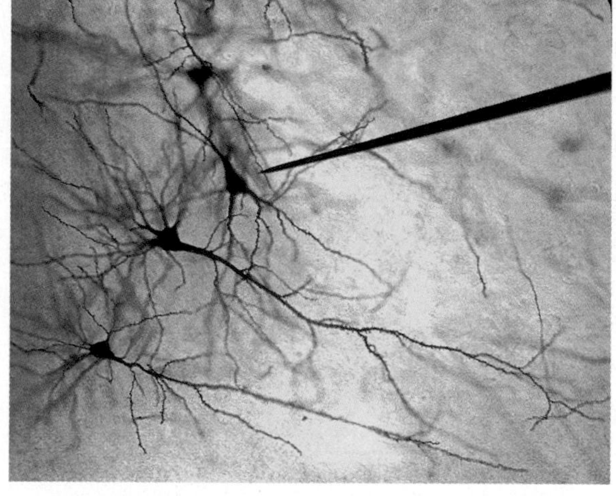

This microelectrode is being used to record the electrical impulses generated by a single cell in the brain of a monkey.

For even more precise information, researchers use *needle electrodes*, very thin wires or hollow glass tubes that can be inserted into the brain, either directly in an exposed brain or through tiny holes in the skull. Only the skull and the membranes covering the brain need to be anesthetized; the brain itself, which processes all sensation and feeling, paradoxically feels nothing when touched. Therefore, a human patient or an animal can be awake and not feel pain during the procedure. Needle electrodes can be used both to record electrical activity from the brain and to stimulate the brain with weak electrical currents. Stimulating a given area often results in a specific sensation or movement. *Microelectrodes* are so fine that they can be inserted into single cells.

A more recently devised method of stimulating the brain, **transcranial magnetic stimulation (TMS)**, delivers a large current through a wire coil placed on a person's head. The current produces a magnetic field about 40,000 times greater than the earth's natural magnetic field (Travis, 2000). This procedure causes neurons under the coil to fire. It can be used to produce motor responses (say, a twitch in the thumb or a knee jerk) and can also be used by researchers to temporarily inactivate an area and observe the effects on behavior—functioning, in effect, as a "virtual" (and temporary) lesion method. The drawback is that when neurons fire, they cause many other neurons to become active too, so it is often hard to tell which neurons are critical for a particular task. Still, TMS has produced some important findings—for example, that a brain area involved in processing visual patterns is also active when a person merely imagines the stimulus (Kosslyn et al., 1999). TMS has also been used to treat depression, as we will see in Chapter 17.

electroencephalogram (EEG) A recording of neural activity detected by electrodes.

transcranial magnetic stimulation (TMS) A method of stimulating brain cells, using a powerful magnetic field produced by a wire coil placed on a person's head; it can be used by researchers to temporarily inactivate neural circuits and is also being used therapeutically.

Scanning the Brain. Since the mid-1970s, many other amazing doors to the brain have opened. The **PET scan (positron-emission tomography)** goes beyond anatomy to record biochemical changes in the brain as they are happening. One type

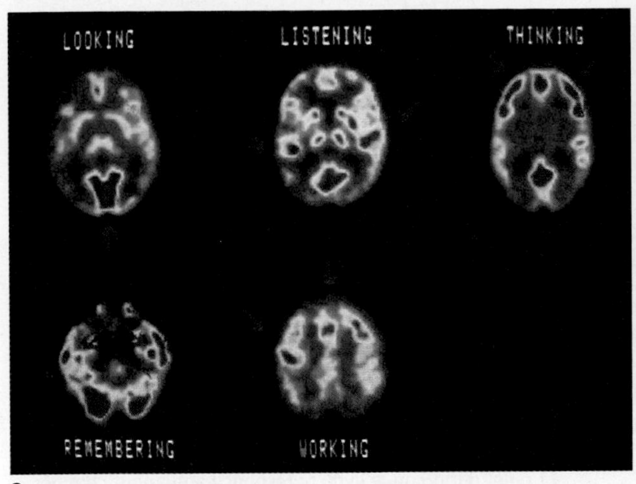

a

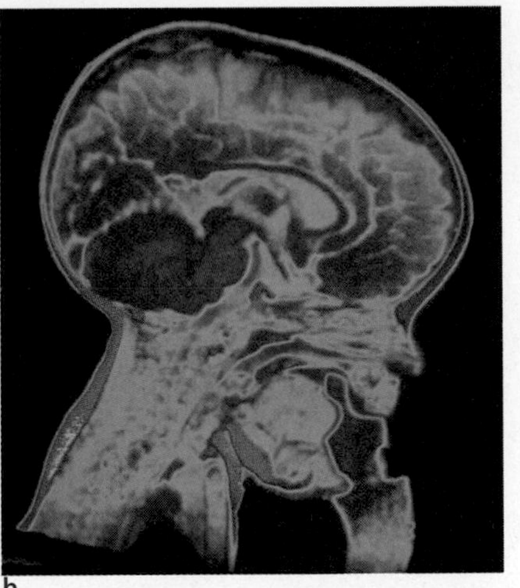
b

FIGURE 4.7 Scanning the Brain
In the PET scans on the left, arrows and the color red indicate areas of highest activity and violet indicates areas of lowest activity as a person does different things. On the right, an MRI shows a child's brain—and the bottle he was drinking from while the image was obtained.

of PET scan takes advantage of the fact that nerve cells convert glucose, the body's main fuel, into energy. A researcher can inject a person with a glucoselike substance that contains a harmless radioactive element. This substance accumulates in brain areas that are particularly active and are consuming glucose rapidly. The substance emits radiation, which is detected by a scanning device, and the result is a computer-processed picture of biochemical activity on a display screen, with different colors indicating different activity levels. Other kinds of PET scans measure blood flow or oxygen consumption, which also reflect brain activity.

PET scans, which were originally designed to diagnose abnormalities, have produced evidence that certain brain areas in people with emotional disorders are either unusually quiet or unusually active. But PET technology can also show which parts of the brain are active during ordinary activities and emotions. It lets researchers see which areas are busiest when a person hears a song, recalls a sad memory, works on a math problem, or shifts attention from one task to another. The PET scans in Figure 4.7a show what an average brain looks like when a person is doing various tasks.

Another technique, **MRI (magnetic resonance imaging)**, allows the exploration of "inner space" without injecting chemicals. Powerful magnetic fields and radio frequencies are used to produce vibrations in the nuclei of atoms making up body organs, and the vibrations are then picked up as signals by special receivers. A computer analyzes the signals, taking into account their strength and duration, and converts them into a high-contrast picture of the organ (see Figure 4.7b). An ultrafast version of MRI, called *functional MRI*, can capture brain changes many times a second as a person performs a task, such as reading a sentence or solving a puzzle. The number of published studies using functional MRI jumped from just 10 in 1991 to 864 in 2001 (Illes, Kirschen, & Gabrieli, 2003), and today, thousands of facilities across the United States are using MRIs for research and assessment.

Review 4.2 on page 124 summarizes the methods we have discussed, and others are becoming available with each passing year. Researchers are using brain scans, in particular, to correlate activity in specific brain areas with everything from racial attitudes to moral reasoning to spiritual meditation. Researchers in an applied field called "neuromarketing" are even using them to study which parts of the brain are activated while people watch TV commercials or political ads.

PET scan (positron-emission tomography) A method for analyzing biochemical activity in the brain, using injections of a glucoselike substance containing a radioactive element.

MRI (magnetic resonance imaging) A method for studying body and brain tissue, using magnetic fields and special radio receivers.

Controversies and Cautions. Exciting though these developments and technologies are, however, we need to understand that technology cannot replace critical thinking (Wade, 2006). As one team of psychologists who are using MRIs to

REVIEW 4.2
Windows on the Brain

Method	What Is Learned
Case studies of persons with brain damage	How damage to or loss of neural circuits affects behavior and cognition
Lesion studies with animals	How damage to or loss of neural circuits affects behavior
EEGs	Patterns of electrical activity in the brain
Needle electrodes and microelectrodes	More precise information about electrical activity in small groups of neurons or single neurons
Transcranial magnetic stimulation (TMS)	What happens behaviorally when a brain area is temporarily inactivated
PET scans	Visually displayed information about areas that are active or quiet during an activity or response and about changes associated with disorders
MRI	Visually displayed information about brain structures
Functional MRI	Visually displayed information about areas that are active or quiet during an activity or response and about changes associated with disorders

THINKING CRITICALLY

DON'T OVERSIMPLIFY

Brain scans provide us with fabulous windows on the brain. But if a scan shows that a brain area is active when you're doodling, does that mean the area is a "doodling center"?

study cognition and emotion wrote, "Just because you're imaging the brain doesn't mean you can stop using your head" (Cacioppo et al., 2003). Because brain-scan images seem so "real" and scientific, many people fail to realize that these images can convey oversimplified and sometimes misleading impressions. For example, by manipulating the color scales used in PET scans, researchers can either accentuate or minimize contrasts between two brains. Small contrasts can be made to look dramatic, larger ones to look insignificant. An individual's brain can even be made to appear completely different depending on the colors used, as the photographs in Figure 4.8 show (Dumit, 2004).

There's another reason for caution about these methods: As of yet, brain scans do not tell us precisely what is happening inside a person's head, either mentally or physiologically. They tell us *where* things happen, but not *why* or *how* they happen—for example, how different circuits connect to produce behavior. Enthusiasm for new technology has produced a mountain of findings, but it has also resulted in some unwarranted conclusions about "brain centers" or "critical circuits" for this or that behavior. If you know that one part of the brain is activated when you are thinking hot thoughts of your beloved, what, exactly, do you know about love? Does that part also light up when you are watching a hot love scene in a movie, looking at a luscious hot-fudge sundae, or thinking about happily riding your horse, Horace, through the hills?

For these reasons, one neuroscientist has called the search for brain centers and circuits "the new phrenology" (Uttal, 2001). Another drew this analogy (cited in Wheeler, 1998): A researcher scans the brains of gum-chewing volunteers, finds out which parts of their brains are active, and concludes that he or she has found the brain's "gum-chewing center"!

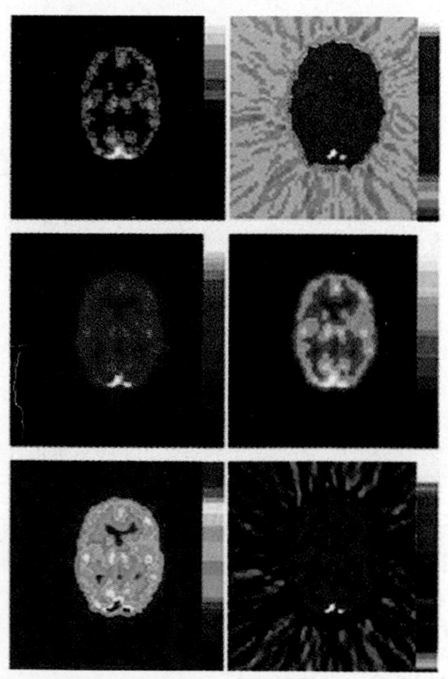

FIGURE 4.8 Coloring the Brain
By altering the colors used in a PET scan, researchers can create the appearance of dramatic brain differences. These scans are actually images of the same brain.

Even if there were a gum-chewing center, yours might not be in the same place as someone else's. Each brain is unique, not only because a unique genetic package is present in each of us at birth but also because a lifetime of experiences and sensations is constantly altering the brain's biochemistry and neural networks. Thus, if you are a string musician, the area in your brain associated with music production is likely to be

larger than that of nonmusicians; and the earlier in life you started to play, the larger it becomes (Jancke, Schlaug, & Steinmetz, 1997). And if you are a cab driver, the area in your hippocampus responsible for visual representations of the environment is likely to be larger than average (Maguire et al., 2000). Variability among brains is one reason that efforts to diagnose mental disorders like depression and attention deficit disorder by examining brain scans have so far been disappointing. Roger Sperry (1982), a brain researcher whom we will meet again in this chapter, said it well: "The individuality inherent in our brain networks makes that of fingerprints or facial features gross and simple by comparison."

Descriptive studies using brain scans, then, are just a first step in understanding brain processes and must be interpreted with great caution. Nonetheless, they provide an exciting look at the brain at work and play, and we will be reporting many findings from PET scan and MRI research throughout this book. The brain can no longer hide from researchers behind the fortress of the skull. It is now possible to get a clear visual image of our most enigmatic organ without so much as lifting a scalpel.

WHAT'S**AHEAD**

- Which brain part acts as a "traffic officer" for incoming sensations?
- Which brain part functions as the "gateway to memory"?
- Why is it a good thing that the outer covering of the human brain is so wrinkled?
- How did a bizarre nineteenth-century accident illuminate the role of the frontal lobes?

A Tour Through the Brain

Most modern brain theories assume that different brain parts perform different (though greatly overlapping) tasks. This concept, known as **localization of function**, goes back at least to Joseph Gall (1758–1828), the Austrian anatomist who thought that personality traits were reflected in the development of specific areas of the brain (see Chapter 1). Gall's theory of phrenology was completely wrong-headed (so to speak), but his general notion of specialization in the brain had merit.

To learn about what the major brain structures do, let's take an imaginary stroll through the brain. Pretend, now, that you have shrunk to a microscopic size and that you are wending your way through the "soul's frail dwelling house," starting at the lower part, just above the spine. Figure 4.9 shows the major structures we will encounter along our tour; you may want to refer to it as we proceed. Keep in mind, though, that in any activity—feeling an emotion, having a thought, performing a task—many different structures are involved. Our description, therefore, is a simplification.

localization of function Specialization of particular brain areas for particular functions.

The Brain Stem

We begin at the base of the skull with the **brain stem**, which began to evolve some 500 million years ago in segmented worms. The brain stem looks like a stalk rising out of the spinal cord. Pathways to and from upper areas of the brain pass through its two main structures: the medulla and the pons. The **pons** is involved in (among other things) sleeping, waking, and dreaming. The **medulla** is responsible for bodily functions that do not have to be consciously willed, such as breathing and heart rate. Hanging has long been used as a method of execution because when it breaks the neck, nerve pathways from the medulla are severed, stopping respiration.

brain stem The part of the brain at the top of the spinal cord, consisting of the medulla and the pons.

pons A structure in the brain stem involved in, among other things, sleeping, waking, and dreaming.

medulla [muh-DUL-uh] A structure in the brain stem responsible for certain automatic functions, such as breathing and heart rate.

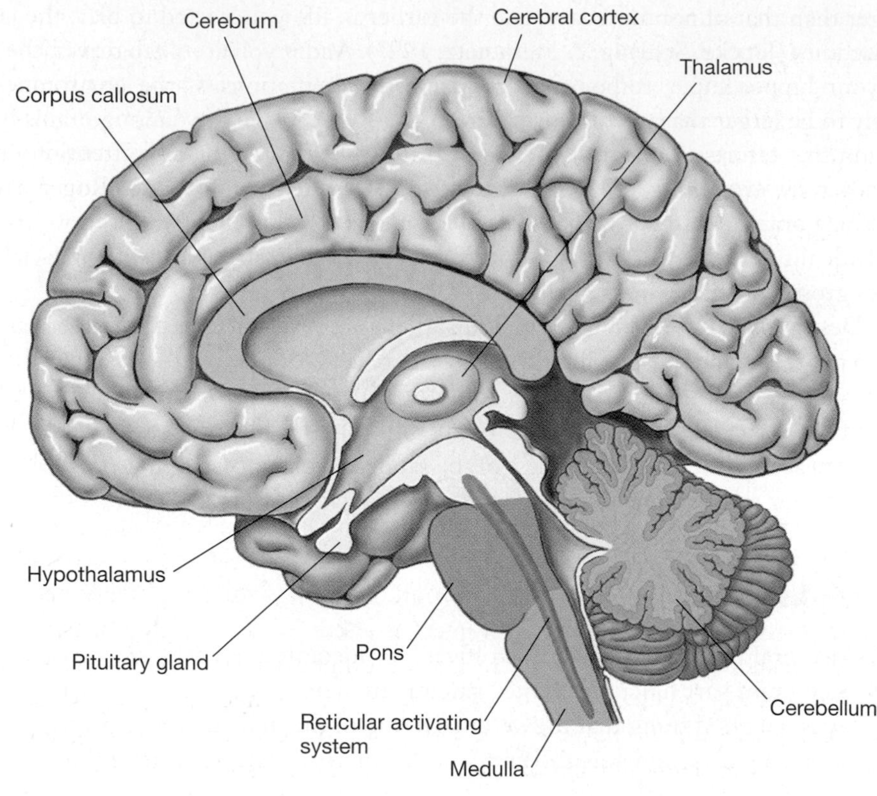

FIGURE 4.9 The Human Brain
This cross section depicts the brain as if it were split in half. The view is of the inside surface of the right half, and it shows the structures described in the text.

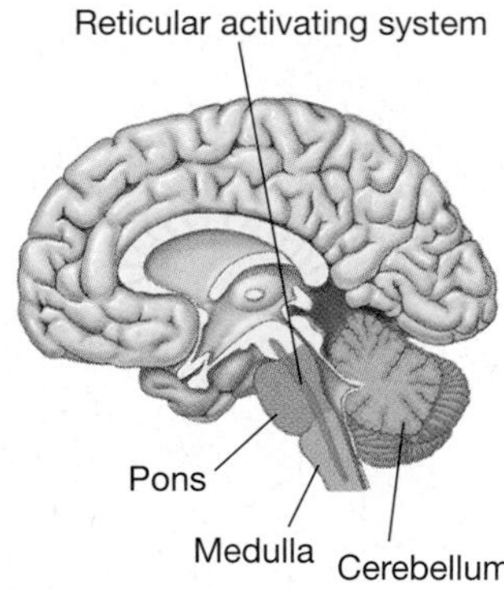

Extending upward from the core of the brain stem is the **reticular activating system (RAS)**. This dense network of neurons, which extends above the brain stem into the center of the brain and has connections with areas that are higher up, screens incoming information and arouses the higher centers when something happens that demands their attention. Without the RAS, we could not be alert or perhaps even conscious.

The Cerebellum

Standing atop the brain stem and looking toward the back part of the brain, we see a structure about the size of a small fist. It is the **cerebellum**, or "lesser brain," which contributes to a sense of balance and coordinates the muscles so that movement is smooth and precise. If your cerebellum were damaged, you would probably become exceedingly clumsy and uncoordinated. You might have trouble using a pencil, threading a needle, or even walking. In addition, this structure is involved in remembering certain simple skills and acquired reflexes (Daum & Schugens, 1996; Krupa, Thompson, & Thompson, 1993). Evidence has also accumulated that the cerebellum, which was once considered just a motor center, is not as "lesser" as its name implies: It appears to play a part in such complex cognitive tasks as analyzing sensory information, solving problems, and understanding words (Fiez, 1996; Gao et al., 1996; Müller, Courchesne, & Allen, 1998).

The Thalamus

Deep in the brain's interior, roughly at its center, we can see the **thalamus**, the busy traffic officer of the brain. As sensory messages come into the brain, the thalamus directs them to higher areas. For example, the sight of a sunset sends

reticular activating system (RAS) A dense network of neurons found in the core of the brain stem; it arouses the cortex and screens incoming information.

cerebellum A brain structure that regulates movement and balance and is involved in the learning of certain kinds of simple responses.

thalamus A brain structure that relays sensory messages to the cerebral cortex.

signals that the thalamus directs to a vision area, and the sound of an oboe sends signals that the thalamus sends on to an auditory area. The only sense that completely bypasses the thalamus is the sense of smell, which has its own private switching station, the *olfactory bulb*. The olfactory bulb lies near areas involved in emotion. Perhaps that is why particular odors—the smell of fresh laundry, gardenias, a steak sizzling on the grill—often rekindle memories of important personal experiences.

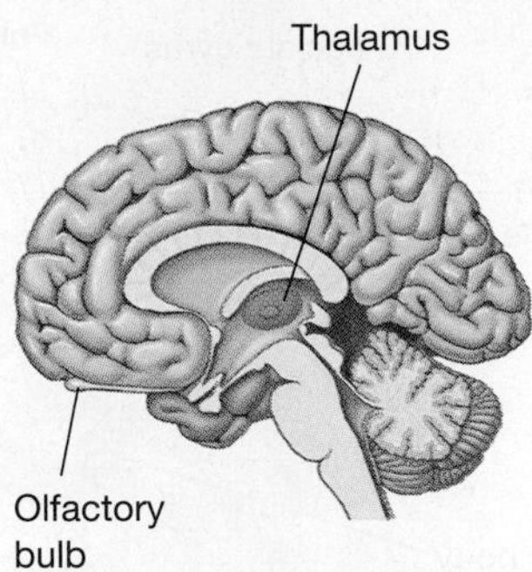

The Hypothalamus and the Pituitary Gland

Beneath the thalamus sits a structure called the **hypothalamus** (*hypo* means "under"). It is involved in drives associated with the survival of both the individual and the species—hunger, thirst, emotion, sex, and reproduction. It regulates body temperature by triggering sweating or shivering, and it controls the complex operations of the autonomic nervous system. It also contains the biological clock that controls the body's daily rhythms (see Chapter 5).

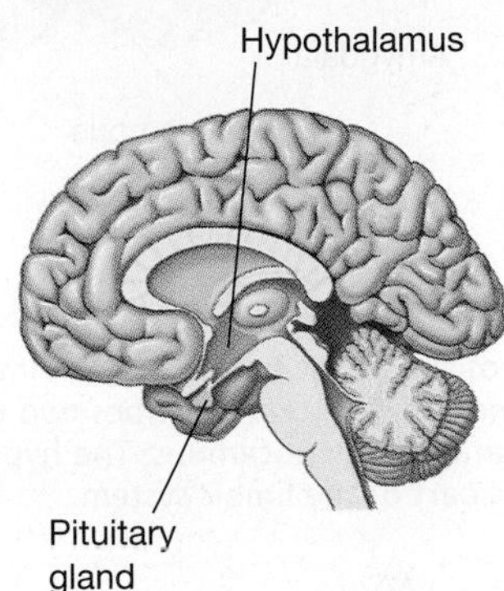

Hanging down from the hypothalamus, connected to it by a short stalk, is a cherry-sized endocrine gland called the **pituitary gland**, which we mentioned earlier in our discussion of hormones. The pituitary is often called the body's "master gland" because the hormones it secretes affect many other endocrine glands. The master, however, is really only a supervisor. The true boss is the hypothalamus, which sends chemicals to the pituitary that tell it when to "talk" to the other endocrine glands. The pituitary, in turn, sends hormonal messages out to these glands.

Many years ago, in a study that became famous, James Olds and Peter Milner reported finding "pleasure centers" in the hypothalamus (Olds, 1975; Olds & Milner, 1954). Olds and Milner trained rats to press a lever in order to get a buzz of electricity delivered through tiny electrodes to parts of the hypothalamus. Some rats would press the bar thousands of times an hour, for 15 or 20 hours at a time, until they collapsed from exhaustion. When they revived, they went right back to the bar. When forced to make a choice, the pleasure-loving little rodents opted for electrical stimulation over such temptations as water, food, and even an attractive rat of the other sex making provocative gestures (provocative to another rat, anyway).

It certainly did seem as though the brain had "pleasure centers." However, controversy has existed ever since about just how to interpret the rats' responses. Were Olds and Milner's rats really feeling pleasure or merely some kind of craving or compulsion? (When people's brains are stimulated in the same way, they do not report feelings of pleasure or behave like those rats did.) Moreover, today researchers believe that brain stimulation activates complex neural pathways rather than discrete "centers."

The hypothalamus, along with the two structures we will come to next, has often been considered part of a loosely interconnected set of structures called the **limbic system**, shown in Figure 4.10 on the next page. (*Limbic* comes from the Latin for "border": These structures form a sort of border between the higher and lower parts of the brain.) Some anatomists also include parts of the thalamus in this system. Structures in this region are heavily involved in emotions that we share with other animals, such as rage and fear (MacLean, 1993). The usefulness of speaking of the limbic system as an integrated set of structures is now in dispute, because these structures also have other functions, and because parts of the brain outside of the limbic system are involved in emotion. However, the term *limbic system* is still in wide use among researchers, so we thought you should know it.

hypothalamus A brain structure involved in emotions and drives vital to survival, such as fear, hunger, thirst, and reproduction; it regulates the autonomic nervous system.

pituitary gland A small endocrine gland at the base of the brain, which releases many hormones and regulates other endocrine glands.

limbic system A group of brain areas involved in emotional reactions and motivated behavior.

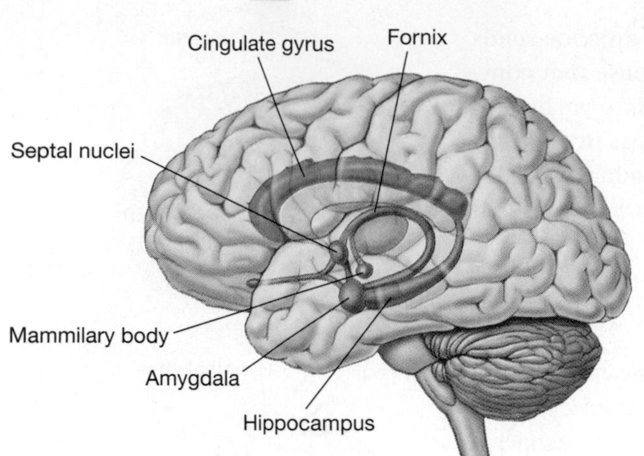

FIGURE 4.10 The Limbic System
Structures of the limbic system play an important role in memory and emotion. The text describes two of these structures, the amygdala and the hippocampus. The hypothalamus is also often included as part of the limbic system.

The Amygdala

The **amygdala** (from the ancient Greek word for "almond") is responsible for evaluating sensory information, quickly determining its emotional importance, and contributing to the initial decision to approach or withdraw from a person or situation (see Chapter 11). For example, it instantly assesses danger or threat. The amygdala also plays an important role in mediating anxiety and depression; PET scans find that depressed and anxious patients show increased neural activity in this structure (Davidson et al., 1999; Drevets, 2000). This structure also plays a role in emotional memory (see Chapter 10).

The Hippocampus

Another important area traditionally classified as "limbic" is the **hippocampus**, which has a shape that must have reminded someone of a sea horse, for in Latin that is what its name means. This structure compares sensory information with what the brain has learned to expect about the world. When expectations are met, it tells the reticular activating system to "cool it." There's no need for neural alarm bells to go off every time a car goes by, a bird chirps, or you feel your saliva trickling down the back of your throat!

The hippocampus has also been called the "gateway to memory." It enables us to form spatial memories so that we can accurately navigate through our environment (Maguire et al., 2000). And, along with adjacent brain areas, it enables us to form new memories about facts and events—the kind of information you need to identify a flower, tell a story, or recall a vacation trip. The information is then stored in the cerebral cortex, which we will be discussing shortly. For example, when you recall meeting someone yesterday, various aspects of the memory—information about the person's greeting, tone of voice, appearance, and location—are probably stored in different locations in the cortex (Damasio et al., 1996; Squire, 1987). But without the hippocampus, the information would never get to these destinations (Mishkin et al., 1997; Squire & Zola-Morgan, 1991). We know about the "gateway" function of the hippocampus in part from research on brain-damaged patients with severe memory problems, as we will see in Chapter 10.

amygdala [uh-MIG-dul-uh] A brain structure involved in the arousal and regulation of emotion and the initial emotional response to sensory information.

hippocampus A brain structure involved in the storage of new information in memory.

The Cerebrum

At this point in our tour, the largest part of the brain still looms above us. It is the cauliflower-like **cerebrum**, where the higher forms of thinking take place. The complexity of the human brain's circuitry far exceeds that of any computer in existence, and much of its most complicated wiring is packed into this structure. Compared with many other creatures, we humans may be ungainly, feeble, and thin-skinned, but our well-developed cerebrum enables us to overcome these limitations and creatively control our environment (and, some would say, to mess it up).

The cerebrum is divided into two separate halves, or **cerebral hemispheres**, connected by a large band of fibers called the **corpus callosum**. In general, the right hemisphere is in charge of the left side of the body and the left hemisphere is in charge of the right side of the body. As we will see shortly, the two hemispheres also have somewhat different tasks and talents, a phenomenon known as **lateralization**.

cerebrum [suh-REE-brum] The largest brain structure, consisting of the upper part of the brain; divided into two hemispheres, it is in charge of most sensory, motor, and cognitive processes. From the Latin for "brain."

cerebral hemispheres The two halves of the cerebrum.

corpus callosum [CORE-puhs cah-LOW-suhm] The bundle of nerve fibers connecting the two cerebral hemispheres.

lateralization Specialization of the two cerebral hemispheres for particular operations.

The Cerebral Cortex. Working our way right up through the top of the brain, we find that the cerebrum is covered by several thin layers of densely packed cells known collectively as the **cerebral cortex**. Cell bodies in the cortex, as in many other parts of the brain, produce a grayish tissue; hence the term *gray matter*. In other parts of the brain (and in the rest of the nervous system), long, myelin-covered axons prevail, providing the brain's *white matter*. Although the cortex is only about 3 millimeters (1/8 inch) thick, it contains almost three-fourths of all the cells in the human brain. The cortex has many deep crevasses and wrinkles, which enable it to contain its billions of neurons without requiring us to have the heads of giants—heads that would be too big to permit us to be born. In other mammals, which have fewer neurons, the cortex is less crumpled; in rats, it is quite smooth.

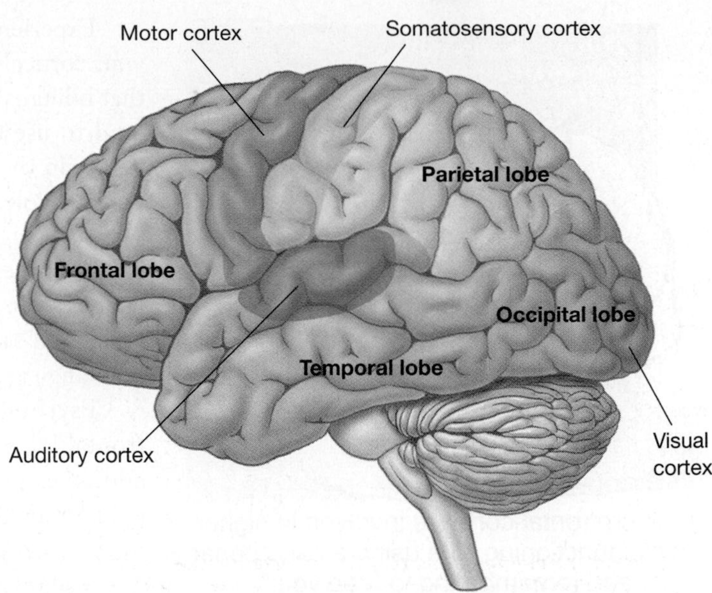

FIGURE 4.11 Lobes of the Cerebrum

Deep fissures divide the cortex of each cerebral hemisphere into four regions.

Lobes of the Cortex. In each cerebral hemisphere, deep fissures divide the cortex into four distinct regions, or lobes (see Figure 4.11):

- The **occipital lobes** (from the Latin for "in back of the head") are at the lower back part of the brain. Among other things, they contain the *visual cortex*, where visual signals are processed. Damage to the visual cortex can cause impaired visual recognition or blindness.
- The **parietal lobes** (from the Latin for "pertaining to walls") are at the top of the brain. They contain the *somatosensory cortex*, which receives information about pressure, pain, touch, and temperature from all over the body. The areas of the somatosensory cortex that receive signals from the hands and the face are disproportionately large because these body parts are particularly sensitive. Parts of the parietal lobes are also involved in attention and various mental operations.
- The **temporal lobes** (from the Latin for "pertaining to the temples") are at the sides of the brain, just above the ears and behind the temples. They are involved in memory, perception, and emotion, and they contain the *auditory cortex*, which processes sounds. An area of the left temporal lobe known as *Wernicke's area* is involved in language comprehension.
- The **frontal lobes**, as their name indicates, are located toward the front of the brain, just under the skull in the area of the forehead. They contain the *motor cortex*, which issues orders to the 600 muscles of the body that produce voluntary movement. In the left frontal lobe, a region known as *Broca's area* handles speech production. During short-term memory tasks, areas in the frontal lobes are especially active (Goldman-Rakic, 1996). The frontal lobes are also involved in emotion and in the ability to make plans, think creatively, and take initiative.

Because of their different functions, the lobes of the cerebral cortex tend to respond differently when stimulated. If a surgeon applied electrical current to your somatosensory cortex in the parietal lobes, you would probably feel a tingling in the skin or a sense of being gently touched. If your visual cortex in the occipital lobes were electrically stimulated, you might report a flash of light or swirls of color. And, eerily, many areas of your cortex, when stimulated, would produce no obvious response or sensation; these "silent" areas are sometimes called the *association cortex* because they are involved in higher mental processes.

cerebral cortex A collection of several thin layers of cells covering the cerebrum; it is largely responsible for higher mental functions. *Cortex* is Latin for "bark" or "rind."

occipital [ahk-SIP-uh-tuhl] lobes Lobes at the lower back part of the brain's cerebral cortex; they contain areas that receive visual information.

parietal [puh-RYE-uh-tuhl] lobes Lobes at the top of the brain's cerebral cortex; they contain areas that receive information on pressure, pain, touch, and temperature.

temporal lobes Lobes at the sides of the brain's cerebral cortex; they contain areas involved in hearing, memory, perception, emotion, and (in the left lobe, typically) language comprehension.

frontal lobes Lobes at the front of the brain's cerebral cortex; they contain areas involved in short-term memory, higher-order thinking, initiative, social judgment, and (in the left lobe, typically) speech production.

Mike Baldwin/CartoonStock Ltd. CSL

"The prefrontal cortex is involved in higher mental functioning, like using a can opener and remembering to feed you."

Experiences at different times of your life can affect how specific areas in your cortical lobes are organized. For example, functional MRI studies show that bilingual people who learned both of their languages in early childhood tend to use a single, uniform Broca's area when generating complex sentences in the two languages. But in people who learned a second language during adolescence, Broca's area is divided into two distinct regions, one for each language (Kim et al., 1997). The explanation may be that the brain's wiring process for language production occurs differently in childhood than it does later on. This may be why people who learn a second language in childhood can usually speak it more fluently than can those who learn a second language in adulthood.

Psychologists are especially interested in the most forward part of the frontal lobes, the *prefrontal cortex*. This area barely exists in mice and rats and takes up only 3.5 percent of the cerebral cortex in cats and about 7 percent in dogs, but it accounts for fully 29 percent of the cortex in human beings.

Scientists have long known that the frontal lobes, and the prefrontal cortex in particular, must have something to do with personality. The first clue appeared in 1848, when a bizarre accident drove an inch-thick, 3½-foot-long iron rod clear through the head of a young railroad worker named Phineas Gage. As you can see in Figure 4.12, the rod (which is still on display at Harvard University, along with Gage's skull) entered beneath the left eye and exited through the top of the head, destroying much of the prefrontal cortex (H. Damasio et al., 1994). Miraculously, Gage survived this trauma and, by most accounts, he retained the ability to speak, think, and remember. But his friends complained that he was "no longer Gage." In a sort of Jekyll-and-Hyde transformation, he had changed from a mild-mannered, friendly, efficient worker into a foul-mouthed, ill-tempered, undependable lout who could not hold a steady job or stick to a plan. His employers had to let him go, and he was reduced to exhibiting himself as a circus attraction.

Today, there is some controversy about the details of this sad incident. For example, no one is really sure what Gage was like before his accident; perhaps the doctors

FIGURE 4.12 A Famous Skull

On the left is Phineas Gage's skull and a cast of his head. You can see where an iron rod penetrated his skull, altering his behavior and personality dramatically. The exact location of the brain damage remained controversial for almost a century and a half, until Hanna and Antonio Damasio and their colleagues (1994) used measurements of Gage's skull and MRIs of normal brains to plot possible trajectories of the rod. The reconstruction on the right shows that the damage occurred in an area of the prefrontal cortex associated with emotional processing and rational decision making.

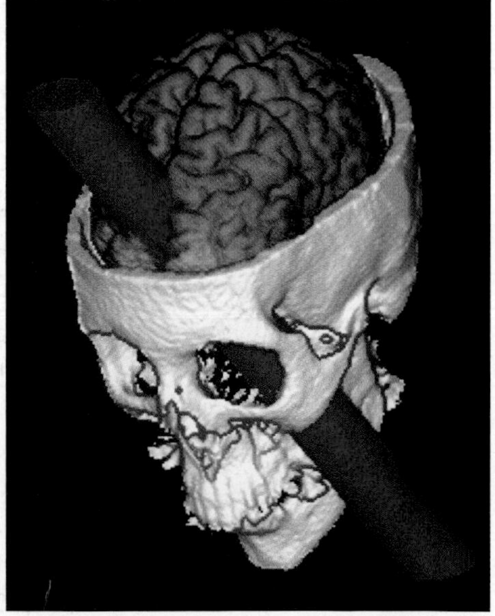

exaggerated the extent of his personality transformation (Macmillan, 2000). But many other cases of brain injury, whether from stroke or trauma, support the conclusion that most scientists draw from the Gage case: that parts of the frontal lobes are involved in social judgment, rational decision making, and the ability to set goals and to make and carry through plans. Like Gage, people with damage in these areas sometimes mismanage their finances, lose their jobs, and abandon their friends. Interestingly, the mental deficits that characterize damage to these areas are accompanied by a flattening out of emotion and feeling, which suggests that normal emotions are necessary for everyday reasoning and the ability to learn from mistakes (Damasio, 1994, 2003).

The frontal lobes also govern the ability to do a series of tasks in the proper sequence and to stop doing them at the proper time. The pioneering Soviet psychologist Alexander Luria (1980) studied many cases in which damage to the frontal lobes disrupted these abilities. One man observed by Luria kept trying to light a match after it was already lit. Another planed a piece of wood in the hospital carpentry shop until it was gone and then went on to plane the workbench!

Review 4.3 summarizes the major parts of the brain that we have discussed and their primary functions.

REVIEW 4.3

Functions Associated with the Major Brain Structures

The functions listed here are just some of those that have been linked with these structures.

Structure	Functions
Brain stem	
Pons	Sleeping, waking, dreaming
Medulla	Automatic functions such as breathing, heart rate
Reticular activating system (RAS) (extends into center of the brain)	Screening of incoming information, arousal of higher centers, consciousness
Cerebellum	Balance, muscular coordination, memory for simple skills and learned reflexes, possible involvement in more complex mental tasks
Thalamus	Relay of impulses from higher centers to the spinal cord and of incoming sensory information (except for olfactory sensations) to other brain centers
Hypothalamus	Behaviors necessary for survival, such as hunger, thirst, emotion, reproduction; regulation of body temperature; control of autonomic nervous system
Pituitary gland	Under direction of the hypothalamus, secretion of hormones that affect other glands
Amygdala	Initial evaluation of sensory information to determine its importance; mediation of anxiety and depression
Hippocampus	Comparison of sensory information with expectations, modulation of the RAS; formation of new memories about facts and events
Cerebrum (including cerebral cortex)	Higher forms of thinking
Occipital lobes	Visual processing
Parietal lobes	Processing of pressure, pain, touch, temperature
Temporal lobes	Memory, perception, emotion, hearing, language comprehension
Frontal lobes	Movement, short-term memory, planning, setting goals, creative thinking, initiative, social judgment, rational decision making, speech production

QUICK quiz

Pause to see how your own brain is working by taking this quiz.

Match each description on the left with a term on the right.

1. Filters out irrelevant information
2. Known as the "gateway to memory"
3. Controls the autonomic nervous system; involved in drives associated with survival
4. Consists of two hemispheres
5. Wrinkled outer covering of the brain
6. Site of the motor cortex; associated with planning and taking initiative

a. reticular activating system
b. cerebrum
c. hippocampus
d. cerebral cortex
e. frontal lobes
f. hypothalamus

Answers:

1. a 2. c 3. f 4. b 5. d 6. e

WHAT'S**AHEAD** 

- If the two cerebral hemispheres were out of touch, would they feel different emotions and think different thoughts?
- Why do researchers often refer to the left hemisphere as "dominant"?
- Should you sign up for a program that promises to perk up the right side of your brain?

The Two Hemispheres of the Brain

We have seen that the cerebrum is divided into two hemispheres that control opposite sides of the body. Although similar in structure, these hemispheres have somewhat separate talents, or areas of specialization.

Split Brains: A House Divided

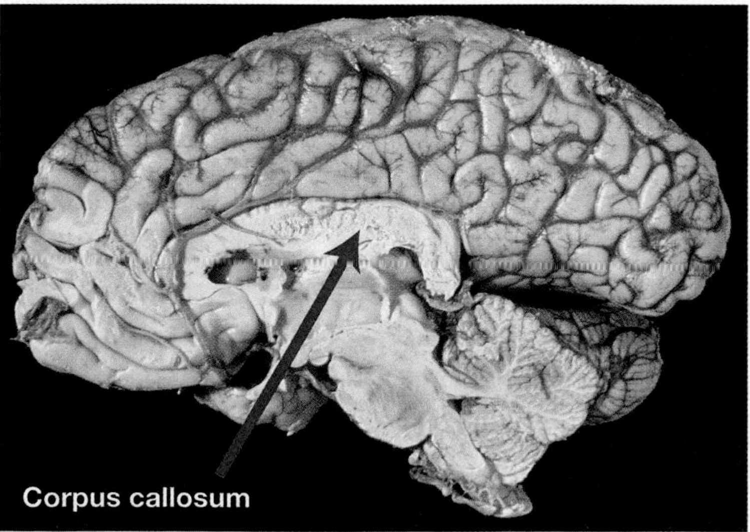

A cross section of a human brain, showing the corpus callosum.

In a normal brain, the two hemispheres communicate with one another across the corpus callosum, the bundle of fibers that connects them. Whatever happens in one side of the brain is instantly flashed to the other side. What would happen, though, if the two sides were cut off from one another?

In 1953, Ronald E. Myers and Roger W. Sperry took the first step toward answering this question by severing the corpus callosum in cats. They also cut parts of the nerves leading from the eyes to the brain. Normally, each eye transmits messages to both sides of the brain. After this procedure, a cat's left eye sent information only to the left hemisphere and its right eye sent information only to the right hemisphere.

At first, the cats did not seem to be affected much by this drastic operation. But Myers and Sperry showed that

something profound had happened. They trained the cats to perform tasks with one eye blindfolded; for example, a cat might have to push a panel with a square on it to get food but ignore a panel with a circle. Then the researchers switched the blindfold to the cat's other eye and tested the animal again. Now the cats behaved as if they had never learned the trick. Apparently, one side of the brain did not know what the other side was doing; it was as if the animals had two minds in one body. Later studies confirmed this result with other species, including monkeys (Sperry, 1964).

In all the animal studies, ordinary behavior, such as eating and walking, remained normal. In the early 1960s, a team of surgeons decided to try cutting the corpus callosum in patients with debilitating, uncontrollable epilepsy. In severe forms of this disease, disorganized electrical activity spreads from an injured area to other parts of the brain. The surgeons reasoned that cutting the connection between the two halves of the brain might stop the spread of electrical activity from one side to the other. The surgery was done, of course, for the sake of the patients, who were desperate. But there was a bonus for scientists, who would be able to find out what each cerebral hemisphere can do when it is quite literally cut off from the other.

The results of this *split-brain surgery* generally proved successful. Seizures were reduced and sometimes disappeared completely. In their daily lives, split-brain patients did not seem much affected by the fact that the two hemispheres were incommunicado. Their personalities and intelligence remained intact; they could walk, talk, and in general lead normal lives. Apparently, connections in the undivided deeper parts of the brain kept body movements and other functions normal. But in a series of ingenious studies, Sperry and his colleagues (and later other researchers) showed that perception and memory had been affected, just as they had been in the earlier animal research. In 1981, Sperry won a Nobel Prize for his work.

It was already known that the two hemispheres are not mirror images of each other. In most people, language is largely handled by the left hemisphere; thus, a person who suffers brain damage because of a stroke—a blockage in or rupture of a blood vessel in the brain—is much more likely to have language problems if the damage is in the left side than if it is in the right. Sperry and his colleagues wanted to know how splitting the brain would affect language and other abilities.

To understand this research, you must know how nerves connect the eyes to the brain. (The human patients, unlike Myers and Sperry's cats, did not have these nerves cut.) If you look straight ahead, everything in the left side of the scene before you—the "visual field"—goes to the right half of your brain, and everything in the right side of the scene goes to the left half of your brain. This is true for both eyes (see Figure 4.13).

The procedure was to present information only to one or the other side of the patients' brains. In one early study, the researchers took photographs of different faces, cut them in two, and pasted different halves together (Levy,

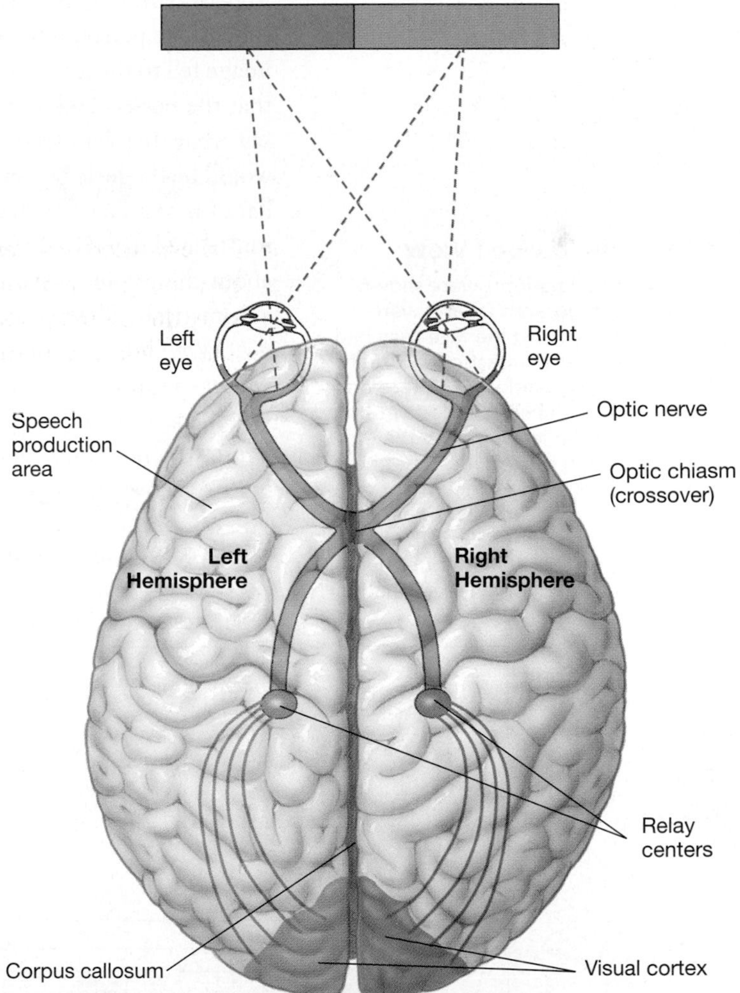

FIGURE 4.13 Visual Pathways

Each cerebral hemisphere receives information from the eyes about the opposite side of the visual field. Thus, if you stare directly at the corner of a room, everything to the left of the juncture is represented in your right hemisphere and vice versa. This is so because half the axons in each optic nerve cross over (at the optic chiasm) to the opposite side of the brain. Normally, each hemisphere immediately shares its information with the other one, but in split-brain patients, severing the corpus callosum prevents such communication.

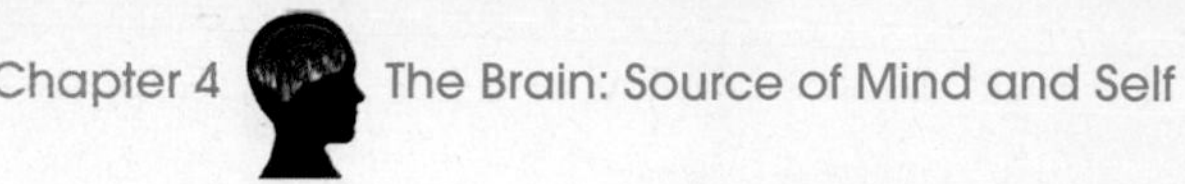

GET INVOLVED!

➤TAP, TAP, TAP

Have a right-handed friend tap on a paper with a pencil held in the right hand for one minute. Then have the person do the same with the left hand, using a fresh sheet of paper. Finally, repeat the procedure, having the person talk at the same time as tapping. For most people, talking will decrease the rate of tapping—but more for the right hand than for the left, probably because both activities involve the same hemisphere (the left one), and there is "competition" between them. (Left-handed people vary more in terms of which hemisphere is dominant for language, so the results for them will be more variable.)

Trevarthen, & Sperry, 1972). The reconstructed photographs were then presented on slides. The person was told to stare at a dot on the middle of the screen, so that half the image fell to the left of this point and half to the right. Each image was flashed so quickly that the person had no time to move his or her eyes. When the patients were asked to say what they had seen, they named the person in the right part of the image (which would be the little boy in Figure 4.14). But when they were asked to point with their left hands to the face they had seen, they chose the person in the left side of the image (the mustached man in the figure). Further, they claimed they had noticed nothing unusual about the original photographs! Each side of the brain saw a different half-image and automatically filled in the missing part. Neither side knew what the other side had seen.

Why did the patients name one side of the picture but point to the other? Speech centers are usually in the left hemisphere. When the person responded with speech, it was the left side of the brain doing the talking. When the person pointed with the left hand, which is controlled by the right side of the brain, the right hemisphere was giving its version of what the person had seen.

In another study, the researchers presented slides of ordinary objects and then suddenly flashed a slide of a nude woman. Both sides of the brain were amused, but

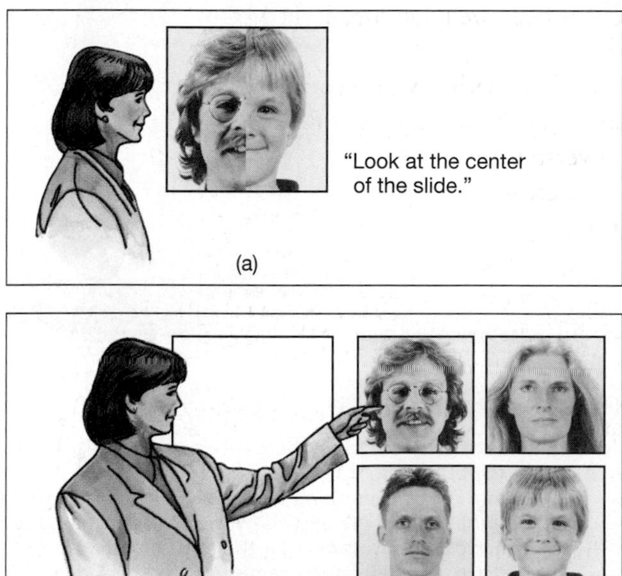

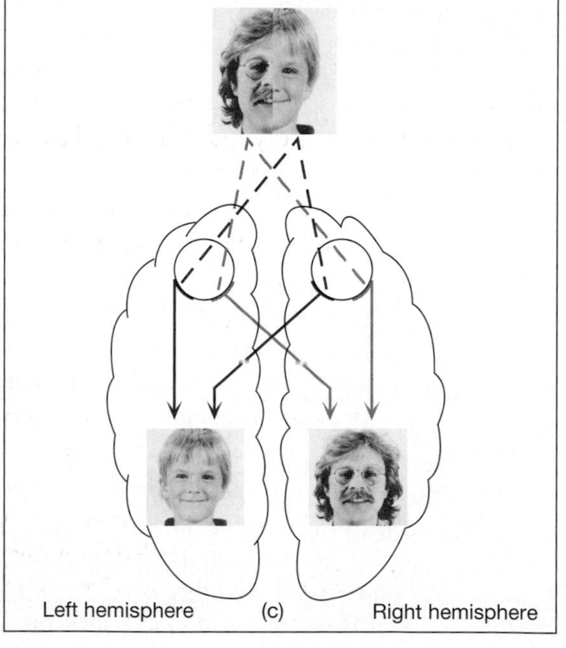

FIGURE 4.14 Divided View

When split-brain patients were shown composite photographs (a) and were then asked to pick out the face they had seen from a series of intact photographs (b), they said they had seen the face on the right side of the composite—yet they pointed with their left hands to the face that had been on the left. Because the two cerebral hemispheres could not communicate, the verbal left hemisphere was aware of only the right half of the picture, and the relatively mute right hemisphere was aware of only the left half (c).

because only the left side has speech, the two sides responded differently. When the picture was flashed to one woman's left hemisphere, she laughed and identified it as a nude. When it was flashed to her right hemisphere, she said nothing but began to chuckle. Asked what she was laughing at, she said, "I don't know . . . nothing . . . oh—that funny machine." The right hemisphere could not describe what it had seen, but it reacted emotionally just the same (Gazzaniga, 1967).

The Two Hemispheres: Allies or Opposites?

The split-brain operation is still being performed, and split-brain patients continue to be studied. Research on left–right differences is also being done with people whose brains are intact (Springer & Deutsch, 1998). Electrodes and brain scans are used to measure activity in the left and right hemispheres while people perform different tasks. The results confirm that nearly all right-handed people and a majority of left-handers process language mainly in the left hemisphere. The left side is also more active during some logical, symbolic, and sequential tasks, such as solving math problems and understanding technical material.

Because of its cognitive talents, many researchers refer to left hemisphere *dominance*. They believe that the left hemisphere usually exerts control over the right hemisphere. Split-brain researcher Michael Gazzaniga (1983) once argued that without help from the left side, the right side's mental skills would probably be "vastly inferior to the cognitive skills of a chimpanzee." He and others also believe that a mental "module" in the left hemisphere is constantly trying to explain actions and emotions generated by brain parts whose workings are nonverbal and outside of awareness. As one neuropsychologist put it, the left hemisphere is the brain's spin doctor (Broks, 2004).

Other researchers, including Sperry (1982), have rushed to the right hemisphere's defense. The right side, they point out, is no dummy. It is superior in problems requiring spatial–visual ability, the ability you use to read a map or follow a dress pattern, and it excels in facial recognition and the ability to read facial expressions. It is active during the creation and appreciation of art and music. It recognizes nonverbal sounds, such as a dog's barking. The right brain also has some language ability. Typically, it can read a word briefly flashed to it and can understand an experimenter's instructions. In a few split-brain patients, right-brain language ability has been well developed, showing that individual variation exists in brain lateralization.

Some researchers have also credited the right hemisphere with having a cognitive style that is intuitive and holistic, in contrast to the left hemisphere's more rational and analytic mode. Over the years, this idea has been oversold by books and programs that promise to make people more creative by making them more "right-brained." But the right hemisphere is not always a "hero": For example, it contains regions that process fear and sadness, emotions that often cause us to withdraw from others (see Chapter 11). Further, the differences between the two hemispheres are relative, not absolute—a matter of degree. In most real-life activities, the two sides cooperate naturally, with each making a valuable contribution. For example, mathematical ability involves not only areas in the left frontal lobe but also areas in both the left and the right parietal lobes. The former are needed to compute exact sums using language ("2 times 5 is 10"), and the latter are needed for using visual or spatial imagery, such as a mental "number line," to estimate quantity or magnitude ("6 is closer to 9 than to 2") (Dehaene et al., 1999).

Harley Schwadron/CartoonStock Ltd. CSL

Be cautious, then, about thinking of the two sides as two "minds." As Sperry (1982) himself noted long ago, "The left–right dichotomy . . . is an idea with which it is very easy to run wild."

QUICK quiz

Use as many parts of your brain as necessary to answer these questions.

1. Keeping in mind that both sides of the brain are involved in most activities, see whether you can identify which of the following is (are) more closely associated with the left hemisphere: (a) enjoying a musical recording, (b) wiggling the left big toe, (c) giving a speech in class, (d) balancing a checkbook, (e) recognizing a long-lost friend
2. Thousands of people have taken courses and bought tapes that promise to develop the "creativity" and "intuition" of their right hemispheres. What characteristics of human thought might explain the eagerness of some people to glorify "right-brainedness" and disparage "left-brainedness" (or vice versa)?

Answers:

1. c, d **2.** One possible answer: Human beings like to make sense of the world, and one easy way to do that is to divide humanity into opposing categories. This kind of either–or thinking can lead to the conclusion that fixing up one brain hemisphere (e.g., making "left-brained" types more "right-brained") will make individuals happier and the world a better place. If only it were that simple!

WHAT'S AHEAD

- Why do some brain researchers think a unified "self" is only an illusion?
- Do men talk about sports and women about feelings because their brains are different?

Two Stubborn Issues in Brain Research

If you have mastered the definitions and descriptions in this chapter, you are prepared to read popular accounts of advances in neuropsychology. But many questions remain about how the brain works, and we will end this chapter with two of them.

Where Is the Self?

When we think about the remarkable blob of tissue in our heads that allows us to remember, to dream, and to think—the blob that can make our existence a hideous nightmare when it is damaged or diseased—we are led, inevitably, to a question that has been pondered for thousands of years: Where, exactly, is the self?

When you say, "I am feeling unhappy," your amygdala, your serotonin receptors, your endorphins, and all sorts of other brain parts and processes are active, but who, exactly, is the "I" doing the feeling? When you say, "My mind is playing tricks on me," who is the "me" watching your mind play those tricks, and who is it that's being tricked? Isn't the self observing itself a little like a finger pointing at its own tip? Because the brain is the site of self-awareness, people even disagree about what language to use when referring to it. If we say that your brain stores events or registers emotions, we imply a

THINKING CRITICALLY

TOLERATE UNCERTAINTY

We all have a sense of being a conscious "self," and brain research shows that consciousness arises from our brains. But if that is the case, where in the brain is this self located? Can this age-old question be answered?

separate "you" that is "using" that brain. But if we leave "you" out of the picture and just say the brain does these things, we risk ignoring the motives, personality traits, and social conditions that also powerfully affect what people do.

Most religions resolve the problem by teaching that an immortal self or soul exists entirely apart from the mortal brain. But modern brain scientists usually consider mind to be a matter of matter. They may have personal religious convictions about a soul or a spiritual response to the awesome complexity and interconnectedness of nature, but most assume that what we call "mind," "consciousness," "self-awareness," or "subjective experience" can be explained in physical terms as a product of the cerebral cortex.

"THEN IT'S AGREED—YOU CAN'T HAVE A MIND WITHOUT A BRAIN, BUT YOU CAN HAVE A BRAIN WITHOUT A MIND."

Our conscious sense of a unified self may even be an illusion. Neurologist Richard Restak (1983, 1994) has noted that many of our actions and choices occur without any direction by a conscious self. He concludes that "the brains of all creatures are probably organized along the lines of multiple centers and various levels." Cognitive scientist Daniel Dennett (1991) suggests that the brain or mind consists of independent brain parts that deal with different aspects of thought and perception, constantly conferring with each other and revising their "drafts" of reality. Likewise, Michael Gazzaniga proposes that the brain is organized as a loose confederation of independent modules, or mental systems, all working in parallel, with most of these modules operating outside of conscious awareness. As we saw, Gazzaniga believes that one verbal module, an "interpreter" (usually in the left hemisphere), is constantly explaining the actions, moods, and thoughts produced by the other modules (Gazzaniga, 1998; Roser & Gazzaniga, 2004). The result is the sense of a unified self.

Interestingly, the idea that the self is an illusion is consistent with the teachings of many Eastern spiritual traditions. Buddhism, for example, teaches that the self is not a unified "thing" but rather a collection of thoughts, perceptions, concepts, and feelings that shift and change from moment to moment. To Buddhists, the unity and the permanence of the self are a mirage. Such notions are contrary, of course, to what most people in the West, including psychologists, have always believed about their "selves."

Over a century ago, William James (1890/1950) described the "self-as-knower," the inner sense we all have of being a distinct person who thinks, feels, and acts. But the age-old mind–brain puzzle continues to plague philosophers and scientists. Even in these days of modern technology, the neural circuits responsible for our sense of self remain hazy. One possibility is that an area in the prefrontal cortex, directly behind the eyes in the cleft between the two hemispheres, binds together perceptions and memories throughout the brain to produce a sense of oneself (Macrae, Kelley, & Heatherton, 2004). But no one yet has a clear picture of how the inner life of the mind, our sense of subjective experience, is linked to the physical processes of the brain. Some brain-injured patients who are unable to store new memories about their experiences can nonetheless describe what kind of person they have been since the injury occurred—say, shy or outgoing, calm or worried, cautious or brave. Others, who have lost the ability to remember anything that happened to them prior to the injury, nonetheless retain the ability to describe what their personality traits were before the injury occurred (Klein et al., 2002). How are their brains able to know themselves? Equally mysterious, some patients with severe degeneration of the frontal lobes have unimpaired memories and language yet undergo a change in "self" comparable to Phineas Gage's transformation. One woman, a lifelong conservative, began to declare that "Republicans should be taken off the earth" (Miller et al., 2001).

Psychologists, neuroscientists, cognitive scientists, and philosophers all hope to learn more about how our brains and nervous systems give rise to the self-as-knower. In the meantime, what do you think about the existence and location of your own "self" . . . and who, by the way, is doing the thinking?

Are There "His" and "Hers" Brains?

THINKING CRITICALLY

AVOID EMOTIONAL REASONING

Perhaps no topic in brain research generates as much passion and emotional thinking as that of sex differences in the brain. To think clearly about this issue, we need to distinguish what the empirical evidence shows from what it means for people's everyday lives.

A second stubborn issue for brain scientists concerns the existence of sex differences in the brain. On this issue, either–or thinking is a great temptation for many people. Because of the centuries of prejudice against women and a legacy of biased research on gender differences, some scientists and laypeople do not even want to consider the possibility that the brains of women and men might differ, on average, in some ways. Others go overboard in the opposite direction, convinced that most, if not all, differences between the sexes are in fact "all in the brain." To evaluate this issue intelligently, we need to ask two separate questions: *Do* the brains of males and females differ anatomically? And if so, what, if anything, do the differences have to do with men's and women's behavior, abilities, or ways of solving problems?

Let's consider the first question. Many anatomical and biochemical sex differences have been found in animal brains, especially in areas related to reproduction, such as the hypothalamus, but also in other areas. Advances in technology have revealed some intriguing differences in human brains as well. For example, in a study of nine autopsied brains, researchers found that the women's brains had an average of 11 percent more cells in areas of the cortex associated with the processing of auditory information; in fact, all of the women had more of these cells than did any of the men (Witelson, Glazer, & Kigar, 1994). Brain scans show that parts of the frontal lobes and the limbic system are larger in women, relative to the overall size of their brains, whereas parts of the parietal cortex and the amygdala are larger in men (Goldstein et al., 2001; Gur et al., 2002). Women also have more cortical folds in the frontal and parietal lobes (Luders et al., 2004).

Researchers are also using brain scans to search for average sex differences in brain activity when people work on particular tasks. In one study (Shaywitz et al., 1995), 19 men and 19 women were asked to say whether pairs of nonsense words rhymed, a task that required them to process and compare sounds. MRI scans showed

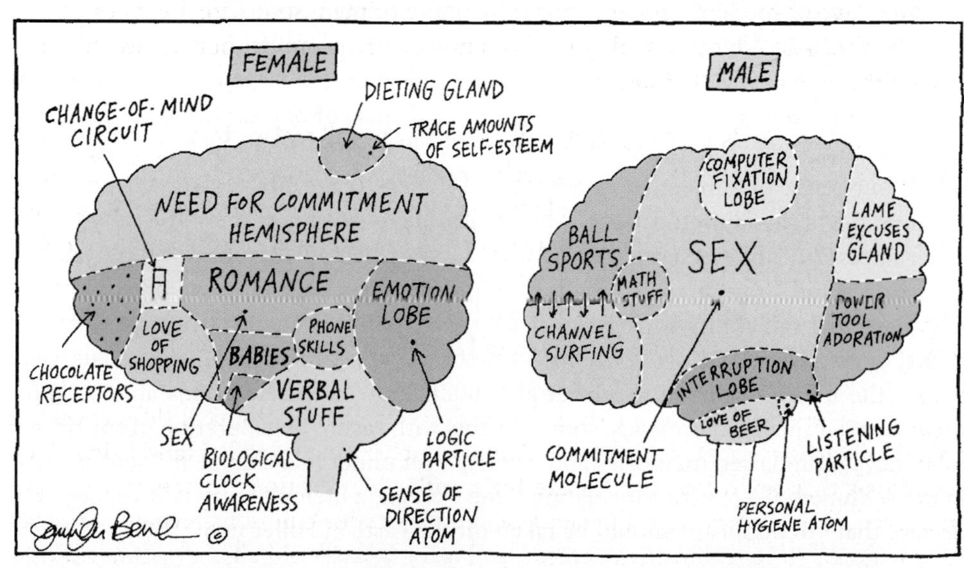

Cartoons like this one make most people laugh because men and women do differ, on average, in things like "love of shopping" and "power-tool adoration." But what does the research show about sex differences in the brain—and what they mean in real life?

that in both sexes an area at the front of the left hemisphere was activated. But in 11 of the women and none of the men, the corresponding area in the right hemisphere was also active. In another MRI study, 10 men and 10 women listened to a John Grisham thriller being read aloud. Men and women alike showed activity in the left temporal lobe, but women also showed some activity in the right temporal lobe, as you can see in Figure 4.15 (Phillips et al., 2001). These findings, along with many others, provide evidence for a sex difference in lateralization: For some types of tasks, especially those involving language, men seem to rely more heavily on one side of the brain whereas women tend to use both sides.

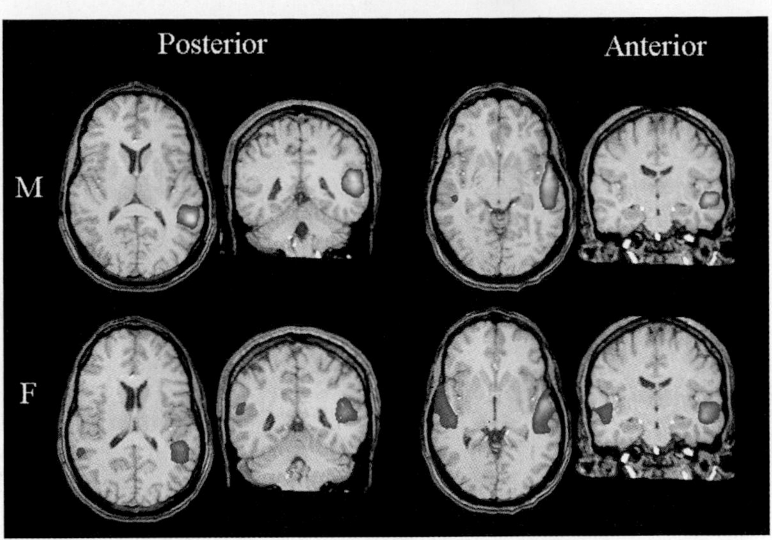

FIGURE 4.15 Gender and the Brain

When women and men listened to a John Grisham thriller read aloud, they showed activity in the left temporal lobe, but women also showed some activity in the right temporal lobe (Philips et al., 2001). (Because of the orientation of these MRI images, the left hemisphere is seen on the right and vice versa.) Along with other evidence, these results suggest a sex difference in lateralization on tasks involving language.

Thus, the answer to our first question is that yes, average sex differences in the brain do exist. But we are still left with our second question: *What do the differences mean for the behavior or personality traits of men and women in ordinary life?* Some popular writers have been quick to assume that brain differences explain, among other things, women's allegedly superior intuition, women's love of talking about feelings and men's love of talking about sports, women's greater verbal ability, men's edge in math ability, and why men won't ask for directions when they're lost. There are at least three problems with such conclusions:

1 **These supposed gender differences (in intuition, abilities, and so forth) are stereotypes.** In each case, the overlap between the sexes is greater than the difference between them. As we saw in Chapter 2, even when differences are statistically significant, they are often quite small in practical terms (Hyde, 2000).

2 **A brain difference does not necessarily explain behavior or performance.** In the rhyme-judgment study, for example, both sexes did equally well, despite the differences in their MRIs. The same has been true in other studies: Males and females may show different patterns of brain activity during a particular task, but they do not differ in their ability to do it. As for how brain differences might be related to more general mental abilities, or how men and women make judgments or behave socially, speculations are as plentiful as swallows in summer, but at present they remain just that—speculations.

3 **Sex differences in the brain could be the result rather than the cause of behavioral differences.** As we saw earlier in this chapter, experiences in life are constantly sculpting the circuitry of the brain, affecting the way brains are organized and how they function—and males and females often have different experiences. Thus, in commenting on the study that had people listen to a John Grisham novel, one of the researchers noted: "We don't know if the difference is because of the way we're raised, or if it's hard-wired in the brain" (quoted in Hotz, 2000).

In sum, the answer to our second question, whether anatomical differences are linked to behavior, is: "It's uncertain." Animal studies have provided tantalizing clues, suggesting that sex differences in the brain influence reactions to acute or chronic stress, the likelihood of suffering depression, memory for emotional events, strategies for navigating around the environment, and other aspects of behavior (Cahill, 2005).

But we simply do not yet know which, if any, of these findings are important for how human males and females manage their everyday lives—their work, their relationships, their families. It is important to keep an open mind about new findings on sex differences in the brain, but because the practical significance of these findings (if any) is not yet clear, it is also important not to oversimplify. The topic of sex differences in the brain is a sexy one, and research in this area can easily be exaggerated and misused.

QUICK quiz

Men and women alike have brains that can answer these questions.

1. Many brain researchers and cognitive scientists believe that the self is not a unified "thing" but a collection of ___________.
2. A new study reports that in a sample of 11 brains, 4 of the 6 women's brains but only 2 of the 5 men's brains had multiple chocolate receptors. (*Note:* We made this up; there's no such thing as a chocolate receptor!) The researchers conclude that their findings explain why so many women are addicted to chocolate. What concerns should a critical thinker have about this study?

Answers:

1. independent modules or mental systems **2.** The sample size was very small; have the results been replicated? Were the sex difference more impressive than the similarities? Might eating chocolate affect chocolate receptors rather than the other way around? Most important, was the number of receptors actually related to the amount of chocolate eaten by the brains' owners in real life?

Using Our Brains About Brain Research

The study of the brain illuminates the capacities we all share as human beings—thought, language, memory, emotion. But it also raises many questions for individuals and society to consider. A new interdisciplinary specialty, *neuroethics*, has recently arisen to address the legal, ethical, and scientific implications of this research (Gazzaniga, 2005).

Betsy Streeter/CartoonStock Ltd. CSL

Scholars in this area are exploring the implications of using drugs to enhance brain function in healthy people as well as in cognitively impaired ones. What are the ethics and dangers involved when drugs that were designed to treat disorders are instead used to improve test performance in school or increase alertness on the job? Of course, millions of people pep up their brains every day by drinking coffee, and functional MRI shows that just one or two cups produces increased activity in the frontal lobes, where working memory occurs, and also in another part of the brain that controls attention (Koppelstaetter et al., 2005). But new drugs may offer far more lasting effects. Some bioethicists and neuroscientists say such cognitive enhancement is perfectly fine, that it is human nature for people to try to improve themselves, and that society will benefit when people learn faster and remember more. Others consider it to be a form of cheating that will give those who can afford the drugs an unfair advantage. As Steven Hyman, a former director of the National Institute of Mental Health, says, "Society has to decide whether it's going to disapprove of such drugs the way we disapprove of the use of performance-enhancing steroids in sports" (quoted in Guterman, 2004).

Neuroethicists are also raising questions about the future possibility of using brain scans to try to determine what an individual is privately thinking or feeling—and especially whether the person is lying. That is not presently possible, but if the technology does become available to permit such uses, neuroethicists argue, some people will misuse it, and society had better be prepared. In the legal area, defense lawyers are already using brain scans to argue that their clients should get lighter sentences; is this use of technology a proper one, given the variability in brains that we discussed earlier and the brain's inherent complexity?

Some critics worry that the current emphasis on brain findings, exciting though they are, will deflect attention from all the other things in the world around us that make us who we are, for better or worse: our relationships, our experiences, our standing in society, our culture. Analyzing a human being in terms of physiology alone is like analyzing the Taj Mahal solely in terms of the materials that were used to build it. Even if we could monitor every cell and circuit of the brain, we would still need to understand the circumstances, thoughts, and cultural rules that affect whether we are gripped by hatred, consumed by grief, lifted by love, or transported by joy.

Taking Psychology with You

Food for Thought: Diet and the Brain

"Vitamin improves sex!" "Sugar makes kids wild!" "Chocolate chases the blues!" Claims like these have given nutritional theories of behavior a bad reputation. In the late 1960s, when Nobel laureate Linus Pauling proposed treating some mental disorders with massive doses of vitamins, few researchers listened. Mainstream medical authorities classified Pauling's vitamin therapy with such infamous cure-alls as snake oil and leeches.

Today, most mental-health professionals remain skeptical of nutritional cures for mental illness. But the underlying premise of nutritional treatments, that diet affects the brain and therefore behavior, is no longer considered a loony idea. Diet may indeed make a difference in cognitive function and in some types of disorders. In one double-blind study, researchers asked depressed patients to abstain from refined sugar and caffeine. Over a three-month period, these patients showed significantly more improvement in their symptoms than did patients who refrained from eating red meat and from using artificial sweeteners (Christensen & Burrows, 1990).

Diet can also affect how well the brain functions. Studies with rats have found that a week after a mild knock on the head, animals on a diet supplemented with omega-3 fish oil learned more quickly than control rats, and their brains had higher levels of a protein that encourages nerve cells to grow and form new connections (Wu, Ying, & Gómez-Pinilla, 2004). On the other hand, rats fed a high-fat, high-sugar diet—one comparable to diets popular in the Western world—learned more slowly than did rats on a standard diet and produced lower levels of proteins associated with learning and memory (Molteni et al., 2002).

There is also some evidence that older people may be able to benefit mentally by taking supplements containing modest amounts of vitamins, minerals, and trace elements. The B vitamin niacin in particular—a vitamin found in lean meats, legumes, milk, coffee, tea, and fortified cereals—may protect against Alzheimer's disease and mental decline in the elderly (Morris et al., 2004). And the

same may be true for the B vitamin folate, which is found in dark green leafy vegetables, in some beans, and in fruits such as oranges and strawberries (Durga et al., 2006). Other research suggests that a diet approximating a "Mediterranean diet," which contains fruits, vegetables, some fish, unsaturated fat, and moderate amounts of alcohol and is low in meat and whole-fat dairy products, is associated with a low risk of Alzheimer's (Scarmeas et al., 2006).

Researchers have been arguing for decades about whether food additives affect children's behavior, especially their activity level. British researchers recently studied this issue by having 3-year-olds drink either regular juice or juice laced with food colorings and a common preservative on alternate weeks. The toddlers' parents—who were blind to the study's design and did not know which kind of juice their children were drinking—reported significant increases in their children's twitching, restlessness, and difficulties concentrating during the weeks when the juice contained the additives (Bateman et al., 2004). Other studies have found no effects of additives, so this research needs to be replicated, but the fact that it was done in a double-blind fashion gives us, well, food for thought.

Some of the most fascinating work on diet and behavior has looked at the role played by nutrients in the synthesis of neurotransmitters, the brain's chemical messengers. *Tryptophan*, an amino acid found in protein-rich foods (dairy products, meat, fish, and poultry), is a precursor (building block) of serotonin. *Tyrosine*, another amino acid found in proteins, is a precursor of norepinephrine, epinephrine, and dopamine. *Choline*, a component of the lecithin found in egg yolks, soy products, and liver, is a precursor of acetylcholine.

In the case of tryptophan, the path between the dinner plate and the brain is indirect. Tryptophan leads to the production of serotonin, which reduces alertness, promotes relaxation, and hastens sleep. Because tryptophan is found in protein, you might think that a high-protein meal would make you drowsy and that carbohydrates (sweets, bread, pasta, potatoes) would make you relatively alert. Actually, the opposite is true. High-protein foods contain several amino acids, not just tryptophan, and they all compete for a ride on carrier molecules headed for brain cells. Because tryptophan occurs in foods in small quantities, it doesn't stand much of a chance if all you eat is protein. It is in the position of a tiny child trying to push aside a crowd of adults for a seat on the subway.

Carbohydrates, however, stimulate the production of the hormone insulin, and insulin causes all the other amino acids to be drawn out of the bloodstream while having little effect on tryptophan. So carbohydrates increase the odds that tryptophan will make it to the brain. Paradoxically, then, a high-carbohydrate, no-protein meal is likely to make you relatively calm or lethargic and a high-protein one is likely to promote alertness, all else being equal (Spring, Chiodo, & Bowen, 1987). Research with people who tend to become frustrated, angry, or depressed in stressful situations suggests that high-carbohydrate food can reduce these responses and help them cope (Markus et al., 2000).

Keep in mind, though, that many other factors influence mood and behavior, that nutritional effects are subtle, and that some of these effects depend on a person's age, the circumstances, and even the time of day. Further, nutrients interact with each other in complex ways. If you don't eat protein, you won't get enough tryptophan, but if you go without carbohydrates, the tryptophan found in protein will be useless.

In sum, if you're looking for brain food, you are most likely to find it in a well-balanced diet.

Summary

- The brain is the bedrock of consciousness, perception, memory, and emotion.

The Nervous System: A Basic Blueprint

- The function of the nervous system is to gather and process information, produce responses to stimuli, and coordinate the workings of different cells. Scientists divide it into the *central nervous system (CNS)* and the *peripheral nervous system (PNS)*. The CNS, which includes the brain and *spinal cord*, receives, processes, interprets, and stores information and sends out messages destined for muscles, glands, and organs. The PNS transmits information to and from the CNS by way of *sensory* and *motor nerves*.

- The peripheral nervous system consists of the *somatic nervous system*, which permits sensation and voluntary actions, and the *autonomic nervous system*, which regulates blood vessels, glands, and internal (visceral) organs. The autonomic system usually functions without conscious control. The autonomic nervous system is further divided into the *sympathetic nervous system*, which mobilizes the body for action, and the *parasympathetic nervous system*, which conserves energy.

Communication in the Nervous System

- Neurons are the basic units of the nervous system. They are held in place by *glial cells*, which nourish, insulate, and protect them, and enable them to function properly. Each neuron consists of *dendrites*, a *cell body*, and an *axon*. In the peripheral nervous system, axons (and sometimes dendrites) are collected together in bundles called *nerves*. Many axons are insulated by a *myelin sheath* that speeds up the conduction of neural impulses and prevents signals in adjacent cells from interfering with one another.
- Recent research has undermined two old assumptions: that neurons in the human central nervous system cannot be induced to regenerate and that no new neurons form after early infancy. In the laboratory, neurons have been induced to regenerate. And scientists have learned that *stem cells* in brain areas associated with learning and memory continue to divide and mature throughout adulthood, giving rise to new neurons. A stimulating environment seems to enhance this process of *neurogenesis*.
- Communication between two neurons occurs at the *synapse*. Many synapses have not yet formed at birth. During development, axons and dendrites continue to grow as a result of both physical maturation and experience with the world, and throughout life, new learning results in new synaptic connections in the brain. Thus, the brain's circuits are not fixed and immutable but are continually changing in response to information, challenges, and changes in the environment, a phenomenon known as *plasticity*. As we saw in the "Close-up on Research," in some people who have been blind from an early age, brain regions usually devoted to vision are activated by sound and touch—a dramatic example of plasticity. Such people show superior performance in tasks involving these senses.
- When a wave of electrical voltage *(action potential)* reaches the end of a transmitting axon, *neurotransmitter* molecules are released into the *synaptic cleft*. When these molecules bind to *receptor sites* on the receiving neuron, that neuron becomes either more likely to fire or less so. The message that reaches a final destination depends on how frequently particular neurons are firing, how many are firing, what types are firing, their degree of synchrony, and where they are located.
- Through their effects on neural circuits, neurotransmitters play a critical role in mood, memory, and psychological well-being. Abnormal levels of neurotransmitters have been implicated in several disorders, including depression, Alzheimer's disease, and Parkinson's disease.
- *Endorphins*, which act primarily by modifying the action of neurotransmitters, reduce pain and promote pleasure. Endorphin levels seem to shoot up when an animal or person is afraid or is under stress. Endorphins have also been linked to the pleasures of social contact.
- *Hormones*, produced mainly by the *endocrine glands*, affect and are affected by the nervous system. Psychologists are especially interested in *melatonin*, which promotes sleep and helps regulate bodily rhythms; *oxytocin*, which plays a role in attachment and trust; *adrenal hormones* such as *epinephrine* and *norepinephrine*, which are involved in emotions and stress; and the *sex hormones*, which are involved in the physical changes of puberty, the menstrual cycle (*estrogens and progesterone*), sexual arousal (*testosterone*), and some nonreproductive functions—including, some researchers believe, mental functioning.

Mapping the Brain

- Researchers study the brain by observing patients with brain damage; by using the *lesion method* with animals; and by using such techniques as *electroencephalograms (EEGs)*, *transcranial magnetic stimulation (TMS)*, *positron emission tomography (PET scans)*, and *magnetic resonance imaging (MRI)*.
- Brain scans reveal which parts of the brain are active during different tasks but do not tell us precisely what is happening, either physically or mentally, during the task. They do not reveal discrete "centers" for a particular function, and they must be interpreted cautiously.

A Tour Through the Brain

- All modern brain theories assume *localization of function*, although a particular area may have several functions and many areas are likely to be involved in any particular activity.
- In the lower part of the brain, in the *brain stem*, the *medulla* controls automatic functions such as heartbeat and breathing, and the *pons* is involved in sleeping, waking, and dreaming. The *reticular activating system (RAS)* screens incoming information and is responsible for

alertness. The *cerebellum* contributes to balance and muscle coordination and may also play a role in some higher mental operations.

- The *thalamus* directs sensory messages to appropriate higher centers. The *hypothalamus* is involved in emotion and in drives associated with survival. It also controls the operations of the autonomic nervous system, and sends out chemicals that tell the *pituitary gland* when to "talk" to other endocrine glands. Along with other structures, the hypothalamus has traditionally been considered part of the *limbic system*, which is involved in emotions that we share with other animals. However, the usefulness of speaking of the limbic system as an integrated set of structures is now in dispute.
- The *amygdala* is responsible for evaluating sensory information and quickly determining its emotional importance, and for the initial decision to approach or withdraw from a person or situation. The *hippocampus* has been called the "gateway to memory" because it plays a critical role in the formation of long-term memories for facts and events. (Like the hypothalamus, these two structures have traditionally been classified as "limbic.")
- Much of the brain's circuitry is packed into the *cerebrum*, which is divided into two *hemispheres* and is covered by thin layers of cells known collectively as the *cerebral cortex*. The *occipital*, *parietal*, *temporal*, and *frontal lobes* of the cortex have specialized (but partially overlapping) functions. The *association cortex* appears to be responsible for higher mental processes. The *frontal lobes*, particularly areas in the *prefrontal cortex*, are involved in social judgment, the making and carrying out of plans, and decision making.

The Two Hemispheres of the Brain

- Studies of *split-brain* patients, who have had the *corpus callosum* cut, show that the two cerebral hemispheres have somewhat different talents. In most people, language is processed mainly in the left hemisphere, which generally is specialized for logical, symbolic, and sequential tasks. The right hemisphere is associated with spatial–visual tasks, facial recognition, and the creation and appreciation of art and music. In most mental activities, however, the two hemispheres cooperate as partners, with each making a valuable contribution.

Two Stubborn Issues in Brain Research

- One of the oldest questions in the study of the brain is where the "self" resides. Many brain researchers and cognitive scientists believe that a unified self may be something of an illusion. Some argue that the brain operates as a collection of independent modules or mental systems, perhaps with one of them functioning as an "interpreter." An area in the prefrontal cortex may be critical for a unified sense of self. But much remains to be learned about the relationship between the brain and the mind.
- Brain scans and other techniques have revealed some differences in the brains of males and females in various anatomical structures, and in lateralization during tasks involving language (with females more likely to use both hemispheres). Controversy exists, however, about what these differences mean in real life. Speculation has often focused on behavioral or cognitive differences that are small and insignificant. Biological differences do not necessarily explain behavioral ones, and sex differences in experience could affect brain organization rather than the other way around.

Using Our Brains About Brain Research

- Scholars in the new field of *neuroethics* are raising questions about the implications of "cognitive enhancement" and the potential misuse of brain scanning techniques. In evaluating research on the brain and behavior, it is important to remember that findings about the brain are most illuminating when they are integrated with psychological and cultural ones.

KEY TERMS

central nervous system 108
spinal cord 108
spinal reflexes 109
peripheral nervous system 109
sensory nerves 109
motor nerves 109
somatic nervous system 109
autonomic nervous system 109
sympathetic nervous system 109
parasympathetic nervous system 109
neuron 111
glia 111
dendrites 112
cell body 112
axon 112
axon terminals 112
myelin sheath 112
nodes 112
nerve 112
neurogenesis 113
stem cells 113
synaptic cleft 115
synapse 115
plasticity 115
action potential 116
synaptic vesicles 117
neurotransmitter 117
receptor sites 117
endorphins 119
hormones 119
endocrine glands 119
melatonin 120
oxytocin 120
adrenal hormones 120
cortisol 120
epinephrine and norepinephrine 120
sex hormones (androgens, estrogens, progesterone) 120
lesion method 122
electrode 122
electroencephalogram (EEG) 122
transcranial magnetic stimulation (TMS) 122
PET scan (positron-emission tomography) 122
MRI (magnetic resonance imaging) 123
localization of function 125
brain stem 125
pons 125
medulla 125
reticular activating system (RAS) 126
cerebellum 126
thalamus 126
olfactory bulb 127
hypothalamus 127
pituitary gland 127
limbic system 127
amygdala 128
hippocampus 128
cerebrum 128
cerebral hemispheres 128
corpus callosum 128
lateralization 128
cerebral cortex 129
occipital lobes 129
visual cortex 129
parietal lobes 129
somatosensory cortex 129
temporal lobes 129
auditory cortex 129
Wernicke's area 129
frontal lobes 129
motor cortex 129
Broca's area 129
association cortex 129
prefrontal cortex 130
split-brain surgery 133
(hemispheric) dominance 135
neuroethics 140

Will It Be On the Test?

NOW YOU HAVE READ CHAPTER FOUR — ARE YOU PREPARED FOR THE EXAM?

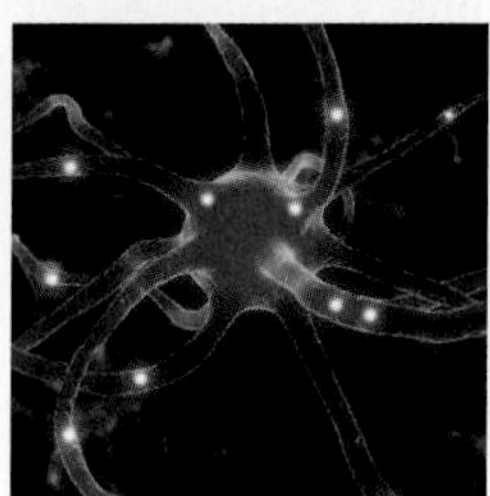

During action potential, is the electrical charge inside the neuron positive or negative compared to the electrical charge outside the neuron?

What are neurons and nerves and how do they work? (pages 113–117)

positive

Neurotransmitters bind briefly with _________ _________, like a key fitting a lock.

How do neurons communicate with each other and with the body? (pages 115–117)

receptor sites

If you are having difficulty staying awake during the day and sleeping through the night, your difficulties are MOST likely due to problems in the _________.

What are the different structures of the base of the brain and what do they do? (pages 125–126)

pons

These questions could be on your next exam. Before you face your grade, make sure you understand the key content of Chapter 4 by taking the practice tests in MyPsychLab at **www.mypsychlab.com.**

How does the autonomic nervous system control the body's reaction to stress?

Work through the simulations on MyPsychLab at your own pace to get a better understanding.

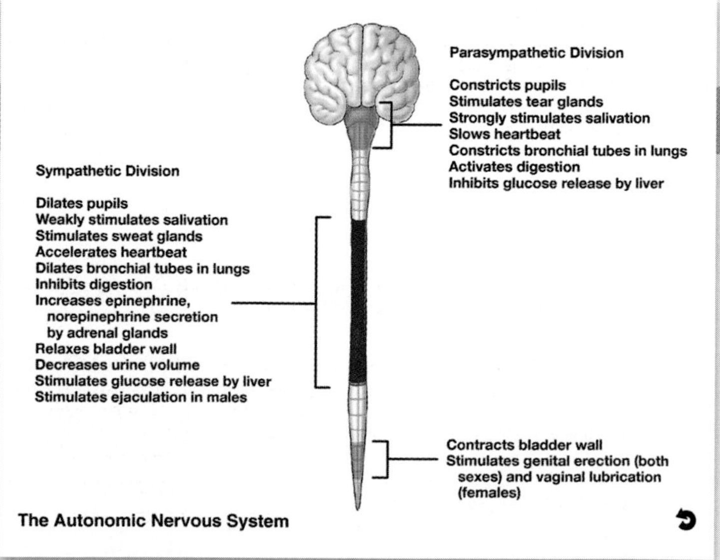

How does the somatic nervous system allow people to interact with their surroundings?

Look at the photo of the girls playing soccer and answer the questions to see if you really do know the answer.

Read through this section in your eBook and test your understanding of the key terms needed to understand the peripheral nervous system.

The Nervous System: A Basic Blueprint

How does the somatic nervous system allow people and animals to interact with their surroundings?

How does the autonomic system control the body's automatic functions and its reactions to stress?

APPLY IT

Look at the following image and answer the question below.

The young soccer players are using their senses and voluntary muscles controlled by the [ ] division of the peripheral system of the [ ] nervous system.

The Nervous System: A Basic Blueprint

How does the somatic nervous system allow people and animals to interact with their surroundings?

How does the autonomic system control the body's automatic functions and its reactions to stress?

E-BOOK

For the Wade e-book, go to the link below and click on the **Nervous System: A Basic Blueprint** in the outline for Chapter 4. As you are reading this section, highlight the key terms—to highlight and take notes, click on the "+" symbol beside the relevant paragraph. Also as you are reading, keep in mind the key learning objectives for this section, listed at the top of the page.

E-Book

After reviewing this section of the e-book, match the following key terms with the correct definition using the pull down menu in the boxes:

autonomic nervous system
somatic nervous system
parasympathetic division
sympathetic division
peripheral nervous system (PNS)

✓
Nerves and neurons not contained in the spinal cord but run through the body
Consisting of nerves that carry information to the CNS and to voluntary muscles
Consisting of nerves that control all of the involuntary muscles
Also known as the fight-or-flight system
Sometimes referred to as the rest-and-digest system

CHAPTER FIVE

Like a bird's life, (consciousness) seems to be made of an alternation of flights and perchings.

WILLIAM JAMES

CHAPTER 5

OUTLINE

In Lewis Carroll's immortal story *Alice's Adventures in Wonderland,* the ordinary rules of everyday life keep dissolving in a sea of logical contradictions. First Alice shrinks to within only a few inches of the ground; then she shoots up taller than the treetops. The strange antics of Wonderland's inhabitants make her smile one moment and shed a pool of tears the next. "Dear dear!" muses the harried heroine. "How queer everything is today! . . . I wonder if I've been changed in the night? Let me think: *was* I the same when I got up this morning? I almost think I can remember feeling a little different. But if I'm not the same, the *next* question is, 'Who in the world am I?' Ah, *that's* the great puzzle!"

In a way, we all live in a sort of Wonderland. For a third of our lives, we reside in a realm where the ordinary rules of logic and experience are suspended: the dream world of sleep. Throughout the day, mood, alertness, efficiency, and *consciousness* itself—our awareness of ourselves and the environment—are in perpetual flux, sometimes shifting as dramatically as Alice's height. Sometimes we are hyperalert and attentive to our own feelings and everything around us; at other times we daydream, "space out," or go on "automatic pilot."

Starting from the assumption that mental and physical states are as intertwined as sunshine and shadow, psychologists, along with other scientists, are exploring the links between fluctuations in subjective experience and changes in brain activity and hormone levels. They have come to view changing states of consciousness as part of the rhythmic ebb and flow of experience over time. For example, dreaming, traditionally classified as a state of consciousness, is also part of a 90-minute cycle of brain activity.

Examining a person's ongoing rhythmic cycles is like watching a motion picture of consciousness. Studying the person's distinct states of consciousness is more like looking at separate snapshots. In this chapter, we will first run the motion picture, to see how functioning and consciousness vary predictably over time. Then we will zoom in on one specific snapshot—the world of dreams—and examine it in some detail. Finally, we will turn to two techniques that have been used to "retouch" or alter the film: hypnosis and the use of recreational drugs.

WHAT'S**AHEAD**

- Do popular biorhythm charts tell you anything about what scientists call biological rhythms?
- Why do you feel out of sync when you fly across time zones or change shifts at work?
- If you feel sad in the winter, do you have SAD?
- Does PMS cause most women to feel depressed or irritable before their periods?

Biological Rhythms: The Tides of Experience

Pseudoscientific ideas about biological rhythms have been around for more than a century. At some point, you may have come across an ad on the Internet for "biorhythm charts," which supposedly foretell fluctuations in mood, alertness, and physical performance over your entire lifetime—solely on the basis of when you were born. Those who sell these charts claim they can foresee your good days and tell when you will be susceptible to accidents, errors, and illness. Well, save your money. Whenever researchers have taken the trouble to test such claims scientifically—for example, by examining occupational accidents in light of the charts' predictions—they have found the charts to be utterly useless (Hines, 1998).

It *is* true, however, that the human body changes over the course of a day, a week, a year. We all experience dozens of periodic, fairly regular ups and downs in physiological functioning, which is what scientists mean when they speak of **biological rhythms**. A biological clock in our brains governs the waxing and waning of hormone levels, urine volume, blood pressure, and even the responsiveness of brain cells to stimulation. Biological rhythms are typically synchronized with external events, such as changes in clock time, temperature, and daylight—a process called **entrainment**. But many of these rhythms continue to occur even in the absence of external time cues; they are **endogenous**, or generated from within.

Many biological rhythms, called **circadian rhythms**, occur approximately every 24 hours. The best-known circadian rhythm is the sleep–wake cycle, but there are hundreds of others that affect physiology and performance. For example, body temperature fluctuates about 1 degree centigrade each day, peaking, on average, in the late afternoon and hitting a low point, or trough, in the wee hours of the morning.

Other rhythms occur less frequently than once a day—say, once a month, or once a season. In the animal world, seasonal rhythms are common. Birds migrate south in the fall, bears hibernate in the winter, and marine animals become active or inactive, depending on bimonthly changes in the tides. In human beings, the female menstrual cycle occurs every 28 days on average. And some rhythms occur more frequently than once a day, many of them on about a 90-minute cycle. These include physiological changes during sleep and (unless social customs intervene) stomach contractions, hormone levels, susceptibility to visual illusions, verbal and spatial performance, brainwave responses during cognitive tasks, alertness, and daydreaming (Escera, Cilveti, & Grau, 1992; Klein & Armitage, 1979; Kripke, 1974; Lavie, 1976).

Biological rhythms influence everything from the effectiveness of medicines taken at different times of the day to alertness and performance on the job. With a better understanding of these internal tempos, we may be able to design our days to take better advantage of our bodies' natural tempos. Let's look more closely at how these cycles operate.

biological rhythm A periodic, more or less regular fluctuation in a biological system; it may or may not have psychological implications.

entrainment The synchronization of biological rhythms with external cues, such as fluctuations in daylight.

endogenous Generated from within rather than by external cues.

circadian [sur-CAY-dee-un] rhythm A biological rhythm with a period (from peak to peak or trough to trough) of about 24 hours; from the Latin *circa,* "about," and *dies,* "a day."

Stefania Follini (left) spent four months in a New Mexico cave (above), 30 feet underground, as part of an Italian study on biological rhythms. Her only companions were a computer and two friendly mice. In the absence of clocks, natural light, or changes in temperature, she tended to stay awake for 20 to 25 hours and then sleep for 10. Because her days were longer than usual, when she emerged she thought she had been in the cave for only two months.

Circadian Rhythms

Circadian rhythms exist in plants, animals, insects, and human beings. They reflect the adaptation of organisms to the many changes associated with the rotation of the earth on its axis, such as changes in light, air pressure, and temperature.

In most societies, external time cues abound, and people's circadian rhythms become entrained to them, following a strict 24-hour schedule. To identify endogenous rhythms, therefore, scientists must isolate volunteers from sunlight, clocks, environmental sounds, and all other cues to time. Some hardy souls have spent weeks or even months alone in caves and salt mines, linked to the outside world only by a one-way phone line and a cable transmitting physiological measurements to the surface. Nowadays, however, volunteers usually live in specially designed rooms equipped with audio systems, comfortable furniture, and temperature controls.

When participants in these studies have been allowed to sleep, eat, and work whenever they wished, free of the tyranny of the timepiece, a few have lived a "day" that is much shorter or longer than 24 hours. If allowed to take daytime naps, however, most people soon settle into a day that averages about 24.3 hours (Moore, 1997). And when people are put on an artificial 28-hour day, in an environment free of all time cues, their body temperature and certain hormone levels follow a cycle that is very close to 24 hours—24.18 hours, to be precise (Czeisler et al., 1999). These rhythms are remarkably similar in length from one person to the next.

The Body's Clock. Circadian rhythms are controlled by a biological clock, or overall coordinator, located in a tiny teardrop-shaped cluster of cells in the hypothalamus called the **suprachiasmatic nucleus (SCN)**. Neural pathways from special receptors in the back of the eye transmit information to the SCN and allow it to respond to

suprachiasmatic [soo-pruh-kye-az-MAT-ick] nucleus (SCN) An area of the brain containing a biological clock that governs circadian rhythms.

melatonin A hormone secreted by the pineal gland; it is involved in the regulation of circadian rhythms.

internal desynchronization A state in which biological rhythms are not in phase (synchronized) with one another.

changes in light and dark. The SCN then sends out messages that cause the brain and body to adapt to these changes. Other clocks also exist, scattered around the body, and some may operate independently of the SCN, but for most circadian rhythms, the SCN is regarded as the master pacemaker.

The SCN regulates fluctuating levels of hormones and neurotransmitters, and they in turn provide feedback that affects the SCN's functioning. For example, during the dark hours, one hormone regulated by the SCN, **melatonin**, is secreted by the pineal gland, deep within the brain. When you go to sleep in a darkened room, your melatonin level rises; when you wake up in the morning to a lightened room, it falls. Melatonin, in turn, appears to help keep the biological clock in phase with the light–dark cycle (Haimov & Lavie, 1996; Lewy et al., 1992).

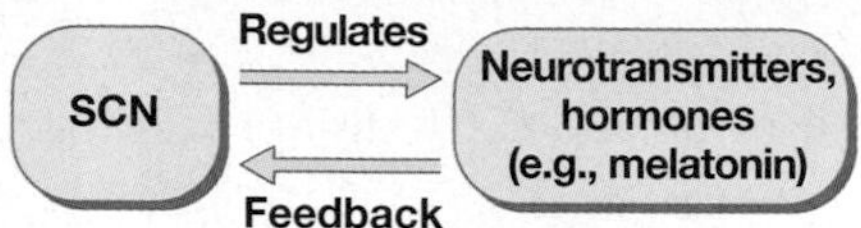

Melatonin treatments have been used to treat insomnia and synchronize the disturbed sleep–wake cycles of blind people who lack light perception and whose melatonin production does not cycle normally (Sack & Lewy, 1997). But efforts to treat the insomnia of *sighted* people by giving them melatonin have had mixed results. Lots of people are taking over-the-counter melatonin supplements to help them sleep or to reduce jet lag, but it's unlikely that these supplements are very helpful. There are no federal standards to assure their quality, and no one has yet identified which dosages are effective (if any) or studied their long-term safety.

When the Clock Is Out of Sync. Under normal conditions, the rhythms governed by the SCN are synchronized, just as wristwatches can be synchronized. Their peaks may occur at different times, but they occur in phase with one another; thus, if you know when one rhythm peaks, you can predict fairly well when another will. But when your normal routine changes, your circadian rhythms may be thrown out of phase with one another. Such **internal desynchronization** often occurs when people take airplane flights across several time zones. Sleep and wake patterns usually adjust quickly, but temperature and hormone cycles can take several days to return to normal. The resulting jet lag affects energy level, mental skills, and motor coordination.

Internal desynchronization also occurs when workers must adjust to a new shift. Efficiency drops, the person feels tired and irritable, accidents become more likely, and sleep disturbances and digestive disorders may occur. For police officers, emergency-room personnel, airline pilots, truck drivers, and operators of nuclear power plants, the consequences can be a matter of life and death. A National Commission on Sleep Disorders concluded that lack of alertness in night-shift equipment operators may have contributed, along with other factors, to the 1989 Exxon *Valdez* oil spill off the coast of Alaska and to disastrous accidents during the 1980s at two nuclear power plants, the Three Mile Island plant in the United States and the Chernobyl plant in Russia.

Travel can be exhausting, and jet lag makes it worse.

Night work itself is not necessarily a problem: With a schedule that always stays the same, even on weekends, people often adapt and do fine. However, many swing- and night-shift assignments are made on a rotating basis, so a worker's circadian rhythms never have a chance to resynchronize. Some scientists hope eventually to help rotating-shift workers resynchronize their rhythms by using melatonin or other techniques to

"reset the clock" (Revell & Eastman, 2005), but so far these techniques are not ready for prime time. The best approach at present is to follow circadian principles by switching workers from one shift to another as infrequently as possible.

One reason that a simple cure for desynchronization has so far eluded scientists is that circadian rhythms are not perfectly regular in daily life. They can be affected by illness, stress, fatigue, excitement, exercise, drugs, mealtimes, and ordinary daily experiences. Further, circadian rhythms differ greatly from individual to individual because of genetic differences (Hur, Bouchard, & Lykken, 1998). For example, a variation in a single gene seems to be the reason that some people are early birds, bouncing out of bed at the crack of dawn, whereas others are night owls who do their best work late at night and can't be pried out of bed until noon (Archer et al., 2003). (Schools are not designed to accommodate night owls.) You may be able to learn about your own personal pulses through careful self-observation, and you may want to try putting that information to use when planning your daily schedule.

"IF WE EVER INTEND TO TAKE OVER THE WORLD, ONE THING WE'LL HAVE TO DO IS SYNCHRONIZE OUR BIOLOGICAL CLOCKS."

Moods and Long-Term Rhythms

According to Ecclesiastes, "To every thing there is a season, and a time for every purpose under heaven." Modern science agrees: Long-term cycles have been observed in everything from the threshold for tooth pain to conception rates. Folklore holds that our moods follow similar rhythms, particularly in response to seasonal changes and, in women, to menstrual changes. But do they?

Does the Season Affect Moods? Clinicians report that some people become depressed during particular seasons, typically winter, when periods of daylight are short—a pattern that has come to be known as **seasonal affective disorder (SAD)** (Rosenthal, 1998). During the winter months, SAD patients report feelings of sadness, lethargy, drowsiness, and a craving for carbohydrates. To counteract the presumed effects of sunless days, some physicians and therapists have been treating SAD patients with phototherapy, having them sit in front of bright fluorescent lights at specific times of the day, usually early in the morning.

seasonal affective disorder (SAD) A controversial disorder in which a person experiences depression during the winter and an improvement of mood in the spring.

Evaluating the actual prevalence of SAD is difficult, however. Information comes mainly from clinical case reports rather than controlled studies, and, as we saw in

GET INVOLVED!

➤MEASURING YOUR ALERTNESS CYCLES

For at least three days, except when you are sleeping, keep an hourly record of your mental alertness level, using this five-point scale: 1 = extremely drowsy or mentally lethargic, 2 = somewhat drowsy or mentally lethargic, 3 = moderately alert, 4 = alert and efficient, 5 = extremely alert and efficient. Does your alertness level appear to follow a circadian rhythm, reaching a high point and a low point once every 24 hours? Or does it follow a shorter rhythm, rising and falling several times during the day? Are your cycles the same on weekends as during the week? Most important, how well does your schedule mesh with your natural fluctuations in alertness?

These young Norwegian women are receiving light therapy for seasonal affective disorder (SAD). This type of treatment has become popular and appears to be effective, but fewer people actually have SAD than is commonly thought, and the causes remain uncertain.

Chapter 2, case studies have serious drawbacks. Many clinicians, extrapolating from patients who believe they suffer from SAD, think the disorder may affect as much as 20 percent of the population. But a national survey estimated the lifetime prevalence of major seasonal depression in the United States at only 0.4 percent, and the prevalence of major or minor seasonal depression at only 1 percent (Blazer, Kessler, & Swartz, 1998).

As for the effectiveness of light treatments, research on this question too has been flawed. A review of 173 light-treatment studies published between 1975 and 2003 found that only 20 had used an acceptable design and suitable controls (Golden et al., 2005). However, a meta-analysis of the data from those 20 studies did throw some light on the subject, so to speak. When people with SAD were exposed to either a brief period (e.g., 30 minutes) of bright light after waking or to light that slowly became brighter, simulating the dawn, their symptoms were in fact reduced. Light therapy even helped people with mild to moderate non-seasonal depression (see also Wirz-Justice et al., 2005).

Some researchers have concluded that SAD patients must have some abnormality in the way they produce or respond to melatonin. For example, in one study, SAD patients produced melatonin for about half an hour longer at night in the winter than in the summer, whereas control subjects showed no such seasonal pattern (Wehr et al., 2001). However, why would light therapy also help some people with *non*-seasonal cases of depression? True cases of SAD may in fact have a biological basis, but the evidence to date remains inconclusive. When people get the winter blues, the reason could also be that they hate cold weather, are physically inactive, do not get outside much, or feel lonely during the winter holidays.

Does the Menstrual Cycle Affect Moods? Controversy has also raged about another long-term rhythm, the female menstrual cycle, which occurs, on average, every 28 days. During the first half of this cycle, an increase in the hormone estrogen causes the lining of the uterus to thicken in preparation for a possible pregnancy. At midcycle, the ovaries release a mature egg, or ovum. Afterward, the ovarian sac that contained the egg begins to produce progesterone, which helps pre-

pare the uterine lining to receive the egg. Then, if conception does not occur, estrogen and progesterone levels fall, the uterine lining sloughs off as the menstrual flow, and the cycle begins again.

"PMS" remedies line the shelves of drugstores, and most people assume that the syndrome is common—but is it?

The interesting question for psychologists is whether these physical changes are correlated with emotional or intellectual changes, as folklore and tradition would have us believe. Most people seem to think so. In the 1970s, a vague cluster of physical and emotional symptoms associated with the days preceding menstruation—including fatigue, headache, irritability, and depression—came to be thought of as an illness and was given a label: *premenstrual syndrome ("PMS")*. Since then, several popular books and countless magazine articles have asserted that most women suffer from it. The medical literature, too, assumes a high incidence; when we scanned the abstracts of articles on "PMS" spanning three recent years, we found estimates ranging from 13 percent to "most women."

What does the evidence actually show? Many women do have *physical* symptoms associated with menstruation, including cramps, breast tenderness, and water retention, although women vary tremendously in this regard. And, of course, these physical symptoms can make some women feel grumpy or unhappy, just as pain can make men feel grumpy or unhappy. But *emotional* symptoms associated with menstruation—notably, irritability and depression—are pretty rare, which is why we put "PMS" in quotation marks. Just as with SAD, more people claim to have symptoms than actually do. In reality, fewer than 5 percent of all women have such symptoms predictably over their cycles (Brooks-Gunn, 1986; Reid, 1991; Walker, 1994).

If true PMS is relatively uncommon, then why do so many women think they have it? One possibility is that they tend to notice feelings of depression or irritability when these moods happen to occur premenstrually but overlook times when such moods are *absent* premenstrually. Or they may label symptoms that occur before a period as "PMS" ("I am irritable and cranky; I must be getting my period") and attribute the same symptoms at other times of the month to a stressful day or a low grade on an English paper ("No wonder I'm irritable and cranky; I worked really hard on that paper and only got a C"). A woman's perceptions of her own emotional ups and downs can also be influenced by cultural attitudes and myths about menstruation. Some studies have encouraged biases in the reporting of premenstrual and menstrual symptoms by using questionnaires with gloomy, negative titles such as "Menstrual Distress Questionnaire."

THINKING CRITICALLY

EXAMINE THE EVIDENCE

Many women say they become more irritable or depressed premenstrually. Does the evidence support their self-reports? How might attitudes and expectations be affecting these accounts? What happens when women report their daily moods and feelings without knowing that menstruation is being studied?

To get around these problems, psychologists have polled women about their psychological and physical well-being without revealing the true purpose of the study (e.g., AuBuchon & Calhoun, 1985; Chrisler, 2000; Englander-Golden, Whitmore, & Dienstbier, 1978; Gallant et al., 1991; Hardie, 1997; Parlee, 1982; Rapkin, Chang, & Reading, 1988; Slade, 1984; Vila & Beech, 1980; Walker, 1994). Using double-blind procedures, they have had women report symptoms for a single day and have then gone back to see what phase of the menstrual cycle the women were in; or they have had women keep daily records over an extended period of time. Some studies have included a control group that is usually excluded from research on hormones and moods: men!

CLOSE-UP on Research

MOOD AND "PMS"

Because so many people now take it for granted that most women have "PMS" and that it is a serious emotional problem for some, the two of us have sometimes been accused of bias for simply reporting the data disputing these assumptions. But stay with us as we describe more closely what the research has found.

In one typical study (McFarlane, Martin, & Williams, 1988), the researchers began by **asking the question**, do women's moods differ from men's in a predictable way because of women's menstrual cycles? To find out, they examined changes in the pleasantness, arousal level, and stability of moods over time, by having 15 women on birth-control pills, 12 normally cycling women, and 15 men rate their moods every day for 70 days. During this time, none of the participants knew that the study had anything to do with menstruation; they thought it was a straightforward study of mood and health. After the 70 days were up, the women then recalled their average moods for each week and phase of their menstrual cycle.

When the researchers **examined the evidence**, they found that in their daily reports, normally cycling women reported more pleasant moods than the other participants during the menstrual phase and the follicular phase (when an egg is forming). But there were no differences at all during the premenstrual phase. In fact, women's moods fluctuated less over the menstrual cycle than over days of the week! (Mondays, it seems, are tough for most people.) Moreover, women and men did not differ significantly in their emotional symptoms or the number of mood swings they reported at any time of the month, as you can see in the adjacent figure. By comparing the women's daily reports with their retrospective reports, the researchers were also able to **question the cultural assumptions** about "PMS." The women *recalled* feeling more angry, irritable, and depressed in the premenstrual and menstrual phases than they had reported in their daily journals, showing that their retrospective reports had been influenced by their expectations and their belief that "PMS" is a reliable, recurring event.

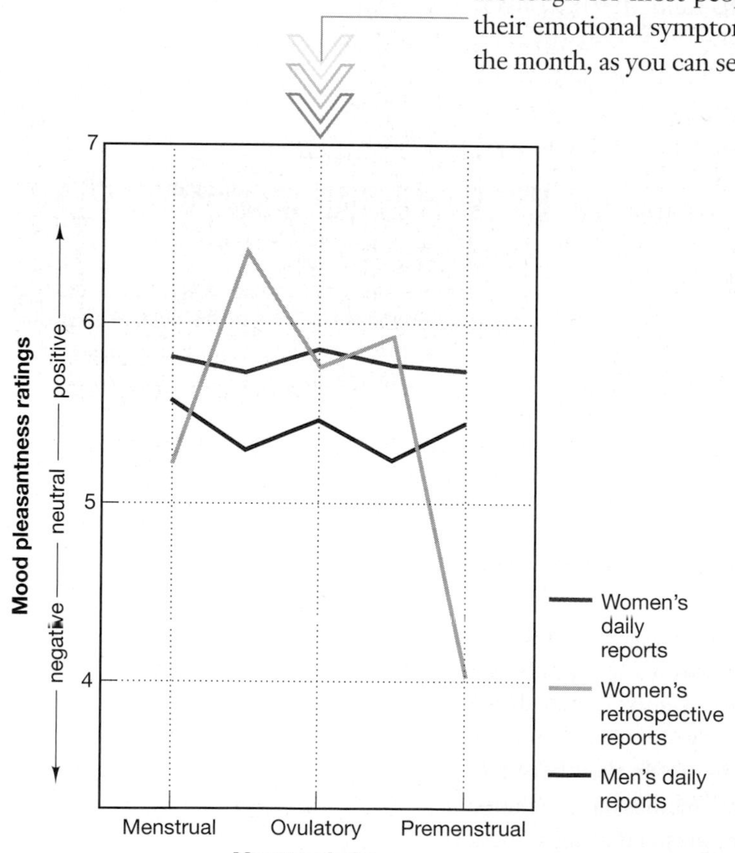

All findings, of course, require replication before we can be confident of the results. In this case, other investigations have confirmed that most women do not have typical "PMS" symptoms even when they firmly believe that they do (Hardie, 1997; McFarlane & Williams, 1994). For example, although women have often reported that they cry more premenstrually than at other times, an interesting Dutch study that had women keep "crying and mood diaries" found no association between crying and phase of the menstrual cycle (van Tilburg & Becht, 2003). Even when women know that they are in a study of menstruation, most do not consistently report negative (or positive) psychological changes from one cycle to the next.

Like all good psychologists, researchers who do such studies are careful to **avoid oversimplification**. They do not conclude that "PMS" is nonexistent. They do not deny that

some women, in *some* months, have unpleasant moods before or during their periods. However, the accumulated research shows clearly that more women think they have "PMS" symptoms than actually do and that fewer women need to be treated for it than is commonly assumed.

The really important question, of course, is whether "PMS" affects women's ability to work, think, study, do brain surgery, or run a business. In the laboratory, some researchers have found that women tend be faster on tasks such as reciting words quickly or sorting objects manually before and after ovulation, when their estrogen is high (e.g., Saucier & Kimura, 1998). But empirical research has failed to establish any connection between phase of the menstrual cycle and real-world behavior in the vast majority of women. There is *no* relationship between phase of the menstrual cycle and work efficiency, problem solving, college exam scores, creativity, or any other behavior that matters in real life (Golub, 1992; Richardson, 1992). In a recent British study, female college students *said* that "PMS" interfered with their academic work, but the researchers could find no association between the number of symptoms reported by the students and their actual grades and test scores (Earl-Novell & Jessop, 2005). In the workplace, men and women report similar levels of stress, well-being, and ability to do the work required of them—and it doesn't matter whether the women are premenstrual, menstrual, postmenstrual, or nonmenstrual (Hardie, 1997).

These results are unknown to most people and have usually been ignored by doctors, therapists, and the media. During the 1970s, psychologists emphasized the psychological and cultural influences on women's experience of menstruation, but since the 1980s, premenstrual symptoms have come to be defined almost solely in medical and psychiatric terms (Parlee, 1994). In 1994, over the objections of many psychologists, the American Psychiatric Association included "premenstrual dysphoric disorder" (PMDD) in an appendix of the *Diagnostic and Statistical Manual of Mental Disorders*, the official guide to psychiatric diagnosis. The label is supposed to describe a rare and debilitating disorder, but its description includes the same hodgepodge of physical and emotional symptoms as "PMS" does. A few years ago, the antidepressant Prozac was repackaged and marketed as Sarafem, a medication supposedly just for PMDD.

"You've been charged with driving under the influence of testosterone."

For both sexes, the hormonal excuse rarely applies.

As we have seen, for many people it isn't easy to avoid emotional reasoning when thinking about the menstrual cycle. Hormones do influence all of us, of course, as do many other internal processes. In a minority of cases, hormonal abnormalities or sudden hormonal changes can make women *and* men feel depressed, listless, irritable, or "not

GET INVOLVED!

➤A CLOSER LOOK AT "PMS" REMEDIES

Go to your local drugstore and find the over-the-counter medications for menstrual symptoms. Do the containers mention only physical symptoms, such as water retention and cramps, or do they also mention emotional symptoms, such as mood swings? Do they refer to "PMS" or "premenstrual tension" as an illness? Are the active ingredients in these products unique to them, or are they generic painkillers such as ibuprofen? What kinds of claims are made for these remedies, and how would you evaluate those claims on the basis of the information in this chapter?

themselves." Yet decades of research show that few women are likely to undergo personality shifts solely because of their hormones, and the same holds true for men. (In Chapter 13, we will see that testosterone doesn't "make" men violent.) In most instances, the body only provides the clay for people's symptoms and feelings; learning and culture mold that clay by teaching us which symptoms are important or worrisome and which are not. The impact of any bodily change depends on how we interpret it and how we respond to it.

QUICK quiz

There are no hormonal excuses for avoiding this quiz.

1. The functioning of the biological clock governing circadian rhythms is affected by the hormone __________.

2. Jet lag occurs because of __________.

3. For most women, the days before menstruation are reliably associated with (a) depression, (b) irritability, (c) elation, (d) creativity, (e) none of these, (f) a and b.

4. A researcher tells male subjects that testosterone usually peaks in the morning and that it probably causes hostility. She then asks them to fill out a "HyperTestosterone Syndrome Hostility Survey" in the morning and again at night. Based on your knowledge of menstrual-cycle findings, what do you think her study will reveal? How could she improve her study?

Answers:

1. melatonin **2** internal desynchronization **3.** e **4** Because of the expectations that the men now have about testosterone, they may be biased to report more hostility in the morning. It would be better to keep them in the dark about the hypothesis and to measure their actual hormone levels at different points in the day, because individuals vary in their biological rhythms. Also, a control group of women could be added to see whether their hostility levels vary in the same way that men's do. Finally, the title on that questionnaire is pretty biased. A more neutral title, such as "Health and Mood Checklist," would be better.

WHAT'S**AHEAD**

- How do brain waves change during the night?
- Why do we sleep?
- What happens when we go too long without enough sleep?

The Rhythms of Sleep

Perhaps the most perplexing of all our biological rhythms is the one governing sleep and wakefulness. Sleep, after all, puts us at risk: Muscles that are usually ready to respond to danger relax, and senses grow dull. As the late British psychologist Christopher Evans (1984) once noted, "The behavior patterns involved in sleep are glaringly, almost insanely, at odds with common sense." Then why is sleep such a profound necessity?

The Realms of Sleep

Let's start with some of the changes that occur in the brain during sleep. Until the early 1950s, little was known about these changes. Then a breakthrough occurred in the laboratory of physiologist Nathaniel Kleitman, who at the time was the only person in the world who had spent his entire career studying sleep. Kleitman had given one of his

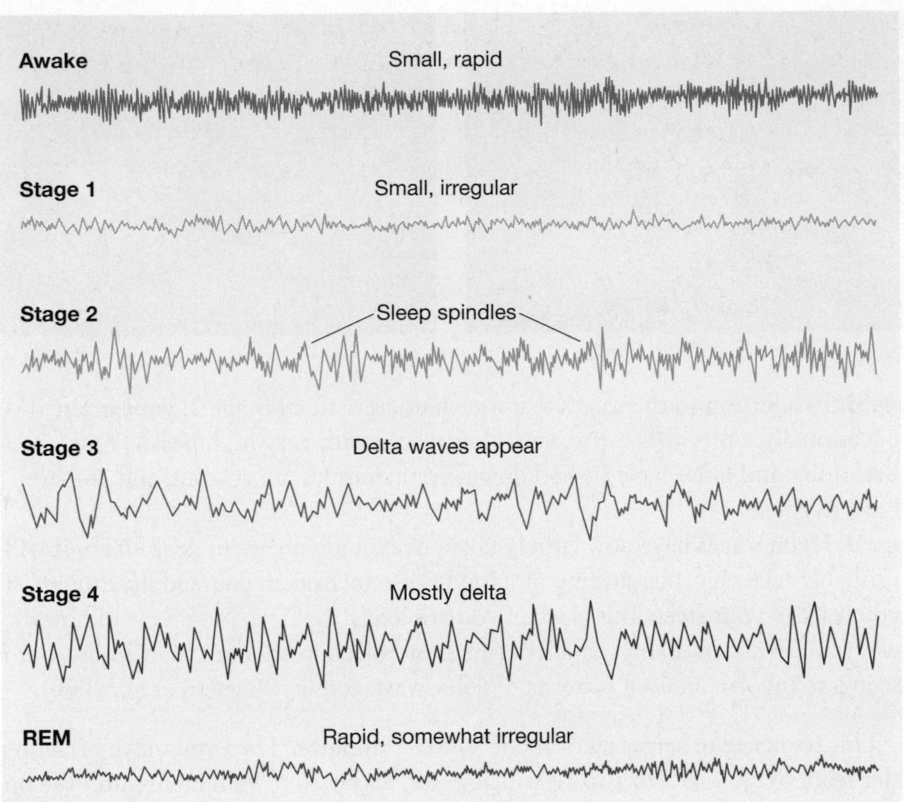

FIGURE 5.1 Brain-Wave Patterns During Wakefulness and Sleep
Most types of brain waves are present throughout sleep, but different ones predominate at different stages.

graduate students, Eugene Aserinsky, the tedious task of finding out whether the slow, rolling eye movements that characterize the onset of sleep continue throughout the night. To both men's surprise, eye movements did occur but they were rapid, not slow (Aserinsky & Kleitman, 1955). Using the electroencephalograph (EEG) to measure the brain's electrical activity (see Chapter 4), these researchers, along with another of Kleitman's students, William Dement, were able to correlate the rapid eye movements with changes in sleepers' brain-wave patterns (Dement, 1992). Adult volunteers were soon spending their nights sleeping in laboratories while scientists measured changes in their brain activity, muscle tension, breathing, and other physiological responses.

As a result of this research, today we know that during sleep, periods of **rapid eye movement (REM)** alternate with periods of fewer eye movements, or *non-REM (NREM) sleep*, in a cycle that recurs every 90 minutes or so. The REM periods last from a few minutes to as long as an hour, averaging about 20 minutes in length. Whenever they begin, the pattern of electrical activity from the sleeper's brain changes to resemble that of alert wakefulness. Non-REM periods are themselves divided into distinct stages, each associated with a particular brain-wave pattern (see Figure 5.1).

When you first climb into bed, close your eyes, and relax, your brain emits bursts of *alpha waves*. On an EEG recording, alpha waves have a regular, slow rhythm and high amplitude (height). Gradually, these waves slow down even further, and you drift into the Land of Nod, passing through four stages, each deeper than the previous one:

Stage 1. Your brain waves become small and irregular, and you feel yourself drifting on the edge of consciousness, in a state of light sleep. If awakened, you may recall fantasies or a few visual images.

Stage 2. Your brain emits occasional short bursts of rapid, high-peaking waves called *sleep spindles*. Minor noises probably won't disturb you.

rapid eye movement (REM) sleep Sleep periods characterized by eye movement, loss of muscle tone, and vivid dreams.

Because cats sleep up to 80 percent of the time, it is easy to catch them in the various stages of slumber. A cat in non-REM sleep (left) remains upright, but during the REM phase (right), its muscles go limp and it flops onto its side.

Stage 3. In addition to the waves that are characteristic of Stage 2, your brain occasionally emits *delta waves*, very slow waves with very high peaks. Your breathing and pulse have slowed down, your muscles are relaxed, and you are hard to rouse.

Stage 4. Delta waves have now largely taken over, and you are in deep sleep. It will probably take vigorous shaking or a loud noise to awaken you. Oddly, though, if you walk in your sleep, this is when you are likely to do so. No one yet knows what causes sleepwalking, which occurs more often in children than adults, but it seems to involve unusual patterns of delta-wave activity (Bassetti et al., 2000).

This sequence of stages takes about 30 to 45 minutes. Then you move back up the ladder from Stage 4 to 3 to 2 to 1. At that point, about 70 to 90 minutes after the onset of sleep, something peculiar happens. Stage 1 does not turn into drowsy wakefulness, as one might expect. Instead, your brain begins to emit long bursts of very rapid, somewhat irregular waves. Your heart rate increases, your blood pressure rises, and your breathing gets faster and more irregular. Small twitches in your face and fingers may occur. In men, the penis becomes somewhat erect as vascular tissue relaxes and blood fills the genital area faster than it exits. In women, the clitoris enlarges and vaginal lubrication increases. At the same time, most skeletal muscles go limp, preventing your aroused brain from producing physical movement. You have entered the realm of REM.

Because the brain is extremely active while the body is entirely inactive, REM sleep has also been called "paradoxical sleep." It is during these periods that vivid dreams are most likely to occur. People report dreams when they are awakened from non-REM sleep, too; in one study, dream reports occurred 82 percent of the time when sleepers were awakened during REM sleep, but they also occurred 51 percent of the time when people were awakened during non-REM sleep (Foulkes, 1962). Non-REM dreams, however, tend to be shorter, less vivid, and more realistic than REM dreams, except in the hour or so before a person wakes up in the morning.

Occasionally, as the sleeper wakes up, a curious phenomenon occurs. The person emerges from REM sleep before the muscle paralysis characteristic of that stage has entirely disappeared, and becomes aware of an inability to move. About 30 percent of the general population has experienced at least one such episode, and about 5 percent have had a "waking dream" in this state. Their eyes are open, but what they "see" are dreamlike hallucinations, most often shadowy figures. They may even "see" a ghost or space alien sitting on their bed or hovering in a hallway, a scary image that they would regard as perfectly normal it if were part of a midnight nightmare. Instead of saying, "Ah! How interesting! I am having a waking dream!" some people interpret this experience literally and come to believe they have been visited by aliens or are being haunted by ghosts (Clancy, 2005; McNally, 2003).

THINKING CRITICALLY

CONSIDER OTHER INTERPRETATIONS

In a state between sleeping and waking, some people have thought they've seen a ghost or a visitor from space in their bedroom—a pretty scary experience. What other explanation is possible?

REM and non-REM sleep continue to alternate throughout the night. As the hours pass, Stages 3 and 4 tend to become shorter or even disappear and REM periods tend to get longer and closer together (see Figure 5.2). This pattern may explain why you are likely to be dreaming when the alarm clock goes off in the morning. But the cycles are far from regular. An individual may bounce directly from Stage 4 back to Stage 2 or go from REM to Stage 2 and then back to REM. Also, the time between REM and non-REM is highly variable, differing from person to person and also within any given individual.

The reasons for REM sleep are still a matter of controversy. If you wake people up every time they lapse into REM sleep, nothing dramatic will happen. When finally allowed to sleep normally, however, they will spend a longer time than usual in the REM phase, and it will be hard to rouse them. Electrical brain activity associated with REM may burst through into non-REM sleep and even into wakefulness, as if the person is making up for something he or she had been deprived of. Some researchers have proposed that this "something" is connected with dreaming, but that idea has problems. For one thing, in rare cases, brain-damaged patients have lost the capacity to dream, yet they continue to show the normal sleep stages, including REM (Bischof & Bassetti, 2004). Moreover, although all mammals experience REM sleep—the only known exceptions are the bottlenose dolphin and the porpoise—it seems unlikely that rats and anteaters have the cognitive abilities required to construct dreams. Moles, which can hardly move their eyes at all, nonetheless show EEG patterns associated with REM sleep. According to one well-known dream researcher, "no one, but no one, has been able to come up with a convincing explanation for REM sleep" (G. William Domhoff, personal communication).

Awake
Stage 1
Stage 2
Stage 3
Stage 4
1 2 3 4 5 6 7
Hours of sleep
REM sleep

FIGURE 5.2 A Typical Night's Sleep for a Young Adult
In this graph, the thin horizontal red bars represent time spent in REM sleep. REM periods tend to lengthen as the night wears on; but Stages 3 and 4, which dominate during non-REM sleep early in the night, may disappear as morning approaches.

Why We Sleep

Generally speaking, sleep appears to provide a time-out period, so that the body can eliminate waste products from muscles, repair cells, conserve or replenish energy stores, strengthen the immune system, or recover abilities lost during the day. When we do not get enough sleep, our bodies operate abnormally. For example, levels of hormones necessary for normal muscle development and proper immune-system functioning decline (Leproult, Van Reeth, et al., 1997).

Whatever your age, sometimes the urge to sleep is irresistible, especially because in fast-paced modern societies, many people—even young children—do not get as much sleep as they need.

sleep apnea A disorder in which breathing briefly stops during sleep, causing the person to choke and gasp and momentarily awaken.

narcolepsy A sleep disorder involving sudden and unpredictable daytime attacks of sleepiness or lapses into REM sleep.

Although most people can still get along reasonably well after a day or two of sleeplessness, sleep deprivation that lasts for four days or longer becomes uncomfortable and soon becomes unbearable. In animals, forced sleeplessness leads to infections and eventually death, and the same seems to be true for people. In one tragic case, a 51-year-old man abruptly began to lose sleep. After sinking deeper and deeper into an exhausted stupor, he developed a lung infection and died. An autopsy showed that he had lost almost all the large neurons in two areas of the thalamus that have been linked to sleep and hormonal circadian rhythms (Lugaresi et al., 1986).

The Mental Consequences of Sleeplessness. Sleep is also necessary for normal mental functioning. Chronic sleep deprivation increases levels of the stress hormone cortisol, which may damage or impair brain cells that are necessary for learning and memory (Leproult et al., 1997). Also, new brain cells may either fail to develop or may mature abnormally (Guzman-Marin, et al., 2005). Perhaps in part because of such damage, after the loss of even a single night's sleep, mental flexibility, attention, and creativity all suffer. After several days of staying awake, people may even begin to have hallucinations and delusions (Dement, 1978).

Of course, sleep deprivation rarely reaches that point, but people frequently suffer from milder sleep problems. According to the National Sleep Foundation, about 10 percent of adults are plagued by chronic insomnia—difficulty in falling or staying asleep. Insomnia can result from worry and anxiety, psychological problems, physical problems such as arthritis, and irregular or overly demanding work and study schedules. The result can be grogginess the next day. (For advice on how to get a better night's sleep, see "Taking Psychology with You.")

Another cause of daytime sleepiness is **sleep apnea**, a disorder in which breathing periodically stops for a few moments, causing the person to choke and gasp. Breathing may cease hundreds of times a night, often without the person's knowing it. Sleep apnea has several causes, from blockage of air passages to failure of the brain to control respiration correctly, and over time it can cause high blood pressure and irregular heartbeat. In **narcolepsy**, another serious disorder, an individual is subject to irresistible and unpredictable daytime attacks of sleepiness lasting from 5 to 30 minutes. When the person lapses into sleep, he or she is likely to fall immediately into the REM stage. A quarter of a million people in the United States suffer from this condition, many without knowing it. Narcolepsy seems to be caused by the degeneration of certain neurons in the hypothalamus, possibly due to an autoimmune malfunction or genetic abnormalities (Lin, Hungs, & Mignot, 2001; Mieda et al., 2004).

The driver of this truck crashed when he apparently fell asleep at the wheel. Thousands of serious and fatal car and truck accidents occur each year because of driver fatigue. In the late 1990s, the U.S. Congress recommended lowering the number of hours that truck drivers are permitted to drive at one stretch. But in 2003, the government instead *increased* the number of allowable hours from 10 to 11, a move that truck companies applauded but many drivers denounced.

Other disorders also disrupt sleep, including some that involve odd or dangerous behavior. For example, in *REM behavior disorder*, the muscle paralysis associated with REM sleep does not occur, and the sleeper (usually a male) becomes physically active, often acting out a dream. If dreaming about football, he may try to "tackle" a piece of furniture; if dreaming about a kitten, he may try to pet it. A person with this disorder is unaware of what he is doing, but his partner is likely to be all too aware!

However, the most common cause of daytime sleepiness is probably the most obvious one—staying up late and, therefore, not getting enough sleep. Two-thirds of all Americans get fewer than the recommended seven or eight hours of sleep and American students get only about six hours a night, on average. Some people do fine on relatively few hours of sleep, but most need more than six hours for optimal performance and many adolescents need ten. When people don't get enough sleep, they are more likely to get into traffic and work accidents. The National Transportation Safety Board estimates that drowsiness is involved in 100,000 vehicle accidents a year, causing 1,500 road deaths and 71,000 injuries.

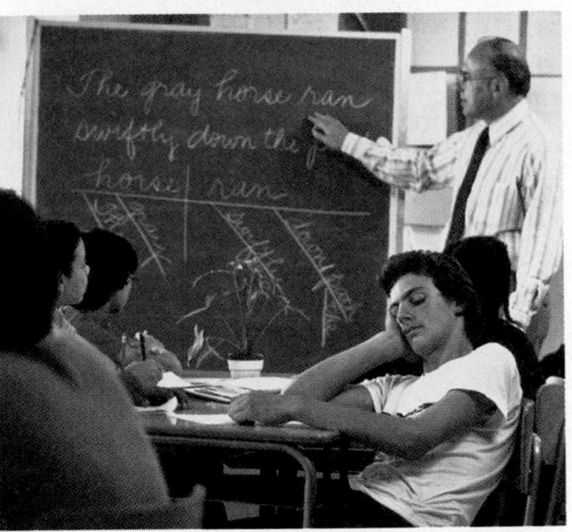

Late hours or inadequate sleep won't do anything for your grade-point average. Daytime drowsiness can interfere with reaction time, concentration, and the ability to learn.

Don't doze off as we tell you this, but lack of sleep has also been linked to lower grades (Wolfson & Carskadon, 1998). In one real-world experiment, researchers had elementary and middle school students go to sleep at their normal time for a week, earlier than usual for a week, and much later than usual for a week. Their teachers, who were blind to which condition a child was in during any given week, reported more academic and attention problems when a child stayed up late (Fallone et al., 2005). And it is not just young kids who need their sleep. As sleep researcher James Maas (1998) has noted, many high school and college students drag themselves through the day "like walking zombies . . . moody, lethargic, and unprepared or unable to learn."

The Mental Benefits of Sleep. Just as sleepiness can interfere with good mental functioning, a good night's sleep can promote it—and not just because you are well rested. Some researchers believe that sleep contributes to memory *consolidation*, a process by which the synaptic changes associated with recently stored memories become durable and stable, causing memory to become more reliable (Stickgold, 2005). Improvements in memory have been associated most closely with REM sleep and slow-wave sleep, and with memory for specific motor and perceptual skills. For example, when people or animals learn a perceptual task and are allowed to get normal REM sleep, their memory for the task is better the next day, even when they have been awakened during non-REM periods. But when they are deprived of REM sleep, their memories are impaired (Karni et al., 1994). And when people learn a computerized task—hitting keys when they see a dot in different places on a screen—some of the same brain areas that are active during the task are active later during REM sleep (Maquet et al., 2000).

GET INVOLVED!

➤A SURVEY OF SLEEP PATTERNS

Get an idea of the variation in people's sleep patterns by asking some friends and relatives what time they typically go to sleep, what time they get up, and whether they routinely take daytime naps. Ask them, too, whether this pattern is their natural one or is simply required by their schedule (for instance, having to be at school or the office by 9:00 A.M.). Do people sleep longer on weekends, and if so, what does this fact suggest about the adequacy of their sleep during the week?

If sleep enhances memory, perhaps it also enhances problem solving, which relies on information stored in memory. At least one study suggests that it does. German researchers gave volunteers a math test that required them to use two mathematical rules to generate one string of numbers from another and to deduce the final digit in the new sequence as quickly as possible. The volunteers were not told about a hidden shortcut that would enable them to calculate the final digit almost immediately. One group was trained in the evening and then got to snooze for eight hours before returning to the problem. Another group also got trained in the evening but then stayed awake for eight hours before coming back to the problem. A third group was trained in the morning and stayed awake all day, as they normally would, before taking the test. Those people who got the nighttime sleep were nearly three times likelier to discover the hidden shortcut as those in the other two groups (Wagner et al., 2004). On the basis of other research, the scientist who led this study attributed the insight-enhancing effects of sleep to the long-term storage of memories during deep (slow-wave) sleep, which occurs primarily during the first four hours of the night.

Remember this research the next time you are tempted to pull an all-nighter or shortchange yourself on your 40 winks. Even a quick nap can help your mental functioning (Mednick et al., 2002). Sleep is not a waste of time; it's an excellent use of it.

QUICK quiz

Wake up and take this quiz.

A. Match each term with the appropriate phrase.

1. REM periods   **a.** delta waves and talking in one's sleep
2. alpha   **b.** irregular brain waves and light sleep
3. Stage 4 sleep   **c.** relaxed but awake
4. Stage 1 sleep   **d.** active brain but inactive muscles

B. Sleep is necessary for normal (a) physical and mental functioning, (b) mental functioning but not physical functioning, (c) physical functioning but not mental functioning.

C. *True or false:* Most people need more than six hours of sleep a night.

D. *True or false:* Only REM sleep has been associated with dreaming and memory consolidation.

Answers:

A. 1. d 2. c 3. a 4. b B. a C. true D. false

WHAT'S**AHEAD** 

- Why did Freud call dreams the "royal road to the unconscious"?
- How might dreams be related to your current problems and concerns?
- How might dreams be related to ordinary daytime thoughts?
- Could dreams be caused by meaningless brain-stem signals?

Exploring the Dream World

Every culture has its theories about dreams. In some cultures, dreams are believed to occur when the spirit leaves the body to wander the world or speak to the gods. In others, dreams are thought to reveal the future. A Chinese Taoist of the third century B.C.

lucid dream A dream in which the dreamer is aware of dreaming.

pondered the possible reality of the dream world. He told of dreaming that he was a butterfly flitting about. "Suddenly I woke up and I was indeed Chuang Tzu. Did Chuang Tzu dream he was a butterfly, or did the butterfly dream he was Chuang Tzu?"

For years, researchers believed that everyone dreams, and, indeed, most people who claim they never have dreams will in fact report them if they are awakened during REM sleep. However, as we noted earlier, there are rare cases of people who apparently do not dream at all. Most of these individuals have suffered some brain injury (Pagel, 2003).

In dreaming, the focus of attention is inward, though occasionally an external event, such as a wailing siren, can influence the dream's content. While a dream is in progress, it may be vivid or vague, terrifying or peaceful. It may also seem to make perfect sense—until you wake up and recall it as illogical, bizarre, and disjointed. Although most of us are unaware of our bodies or where we are while we are dreaming, some people say that they occasionally have **lucid dreams**, in which they know they are dreaming and feel as though they are conscious (LaBerge & Levitan, 1995). A few even claim that they can control the action in these dreams, much as a scriptwriter decides what will happen in a movie, although this ability is probably rare.

One issue that has bothered sleep researchers for years is whether the eye movements of REM sleep correspond to events and actions in a dream. Are the eyes tracking these images? Some researchers believe that in adult dreamers, eye movements do resemble those of waking life, when the eyes and head move in synchrony as the person moves about and shifts his or her gaze (Herman, 1992). But others think that eye movements are no more related to dream content than are inner-ear muscle contractions, which also occur during REM sleep.

Why do the images in dreams arise at all? Why doesn't the brain just rest, switching off all thoughts and images and launching us into a coma? Why, instead, do we spend our nights taking a chemistry exam, reliving an old love affair, flying through the air, or fleeing from monsters in the fantasy world of our dreams? We will consider four of the leading explanations and then evaluate them.

Dreams as Unconscious Wishes

One of the first psychological theorists to take dreams seriously was Sigmund Freud, the founder of psychoanalysis. After analyzing many of his patients' dreams and some of his own, Freud concluded that our nighttime fantasies provide insight into desires, motives, and conflicts of which we are unaware—a "royal road to the unconscious." In dreams, said Freud (1900/1953), we are able to express our unconscious wishes and desires, which are often sexual or violent in nature.

According to Freud, every dream is meaningful, no matter how absurd the images might seem. But if a dream's message arouses anxiety, the rational part of the mind must disguise and distort it. Otherwise, the dream would intrude into consciousness and waken the dreamer. In dreams, therefore, one person may be represented by another—for example, a father by a brother—or even by several different characters. Similarly, thoughts and objects are translated into symbolic images. A penis may be disguised as a snake, umbrella, or dagger; a vagina as a tunnel or cave; and the human body as a house. Because reality is distorted in such ways, a dream resembles a psychosis, a severe mental disturbance; each night, we must become temporarily delusional so that our anxiety will be kept at bay and our sleep will not be disrupted.

To understand a dream, said Freud, we must distinguish its *manifest content*, the aspects of it that we consciously experience during sleep and may remember upon wakening, from its *latent* (hidden) *content*, the unconscious wishes and thoughts being expressed symbolically. Freud warned against the simpleminded translation of symbols, however—the kind of interpretation that often turns up in magazines and popular books promising to tell you exactly what your dreams mean. Each dream, said Freud, had to be analyzed in the context of the dreamer's waking life, as well as the person's associations to the dream's contents. Not everything in a dream is symbolic. Sometimes, Freud cautioned, "A cigar is only a cigar."

Dreams as Efforts to Deal with Problems

Another explanation holds that dreams reflect the ongoing *conscious* preoccupations of waking life, such as concerns over relationships, work, sex, or health (Cartwright, 1977; Hall, 1953a, b). In this *problem-focused approach* to dreaming, the symbols and metaphors in a dream do not disguise its true meaning; they convey it. For example, psychologist Gayle Delaney told of a woman who dreamed she was swimming underwater. The woman's 8-year-old son was on her back, his head above the water. Her husband was supposed to take a picture of them, but for some reason he wasn't doing it, and she was starting to feel as if she were going to drown. To Delaney, the message was obvious: The woman was "drowning" under the responsibilities of child care, and her husband wasn't "getting the picture" (in Dolnick, 1990).

The problem-focused explanation of dreaming is supported by findings that dreams are more likely to contain material related to a person's current concerns than chance would predict (Domhoff, 1996). For example, among college students, who are often worried about grades and tests, test-anxiety dreams are common: The dreamer is unprepared for or unable to finish an exam, or shows up for the wrong exam, or can't find the room where the exam is being given (Halliday, 1993; Van de Castle, 1994). (Sound familiar?) For their part, instructors sometimes dream that they have forgotten their lecture notes at home, or that their notes contain only blank pages and they have nothing to say! Traumatic experiences can also affect people's dreams. In a cross-cultural study in which children kept dream diaries for a week, Palestinian children living in neighborhoods under threat of violence reported more themes of persecution and violence than did Finnish or Palestinian children living in peaceful environments (Punamaeki & Joustie, 1998).

Some psychologists believe that dreams not only reflect our waking concerns but also provide us with an opportunity to resolve them (Barrett, 2001; Cartwright, 1996). Rosalind Cartwright has been investigating this hypothesis for many years. Among people suffering from the grief of divorce, she has found, recovery is related to a particular pattern of dreaming: The first dream of the night often comes sooner than it ordinarily would, lasts longer, and is more emotional and storylike. Depressed people's dreams tend to become less negative and more positive as the night wears on, and this pattern, too, predicts recovery (Cartwright et al., 1998). Cartwright concludes that getting through a crisis or a rough period in life takes "time, good friends, good genes, good luck, and a good dream system."

Dreams as Thinking

Like the problem-focused approach, the *cognitive approach* to dreaming emphasizes current concerns, but it makes no claims about problem solving during sleep. In this view, dreaming is simply a modification of the cognitive activity that goes on when we are awake. In

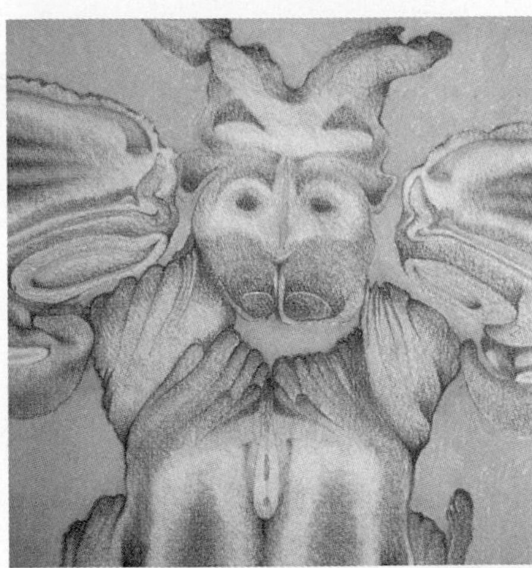

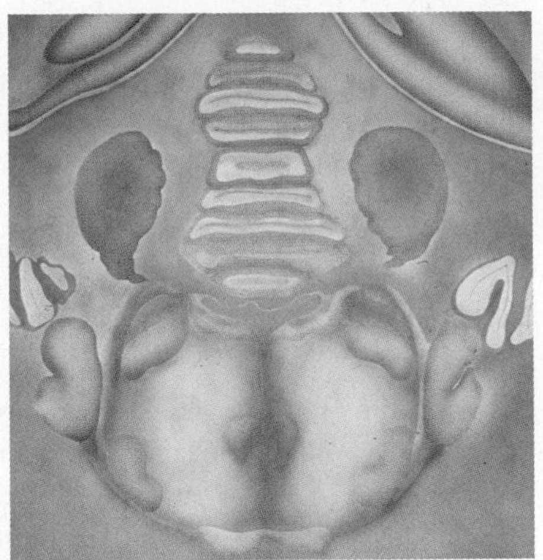

These drawings from dream journals show that the images in dreams can be either abstract or literal. In either case, the dream may reflect a person's concerns, problems, and interests. The two fanciful paintings at the top represent the dreams of a person who worked all day long with brain tissue, which the drawings rather resemble. The desk was sketched in 1939 by a scientist to illustrate his dream about a mechanical device for instantly retrieving quotations—a sort of early desktop computer!

dreams, we construct reasonable simulations of the real world, drawing on the same kinds of memories, knowledge, metaphors, and assumptions about the world that we do when we are not sleeping (Antrobus, 1991, 2000; Domhoff, 2003; Foulkes, 1999). Thus the content of our dreams may include thoughts, concepts, and scenarios that may or may not be related to our daily problems. We are most likely to dream about our families, friends, studies, jobs, or recreational interests—topics that also occupy our waking thoughts.

In the cognitive view, the brain is doing the same kind of work during dreams as it does when we are awake, which is why parts of the cerebral cortex involved in perceptual and cognitive processing are highly activated during dreaming. The difference is that when we are asleep we are cut off from sensory input and feedback from the world and our bodily movements; the only input to the brain is its own output. Our dreaming thoughts, therefore, tend to be more unfocused and diffuse than our waking ones—unless, of course, we're daydreaming!

This view predicts that if a person could be totally cut off from all external stimulation while awake, mental activity would be much like that during dreaming, with the same hallucinatory quality. In Chapter 6, we will see that this is, in fact, the case. The cognitive approach also predicts that as cognitive abilities and brain connections mature during childhood, dreams should change in nature, and they do. Toddlers may not dream at all, in the sense that adults do. And although young children may experience visual images during sleep, their cognitive limitations keep them from creating true narratives until age 7 or 8 (Foulkes, 1999). Their dreams are infrequent and tend to be bland and static, about everyday things ("I saw a dog; I was sitting"). But as they grow up, their dreams gradually become more and more intricate, dynamic, and storylike.

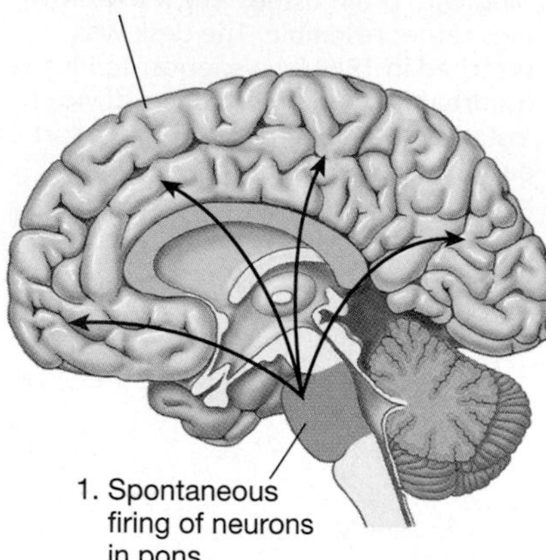
ACTIVATION–SYNTHESIS THEORY OF DREAMS
2. Cerebral cortex synthesizes signals, tries to interpret them ("I'm running through the woods")
1. Spontaneous firing of neurons in pons

Dreams as Interpreted Brain Activity

A fourth approach to dreaming, the **activation–synthesis theory**, draws heavily on physiological research. According to this explanation, first proposed by psychiatrist J. Allan Hobson (1988, 1990), dreams are not "children of an idle brain," as Shakespeare called them. Rather, they are largely the result of neurons firing spontaneously in the lower part of the brain, in the pons, during REM sleep. These neurons control eye movement, gaze, balance, and posture, and they send messages to sensory and motor areas of the cortex responsible during wakefulness for visual processing and voluntary action.

According to the activation–synthesis theory, the signals originating in the pons have no psychological meaning in themselves. But the cortex tries to make sense of them by *synthesizing*, or integrating, them with existing knowledge and memories to produce some sort of coherent interpretation. This is just what the cortex does when signals come from sense organs during ordinary wakefulness. The idea that one part of the brain interprets what has gone on in other parts—whether you are awake or asleep—is consistent with many modern theories of how the brain works (see Chapter 4).

When neurons fire in the part of the brain that handles balance, for instance, the cortex may generate a dream about falling. When signals occur that would ordinarily produce running, the cortex may manufacture a dream about being chased. Because the signals from the pons occur randomly, the cortex's interpretation—the dream—is likely to be incoherent and confusing. And because the cortical neurons that control the initial storage of new memories are turned off during sleep, we typically forget our dreams upon waking unless we write them down or immediately recount them to someone else.

Since Hobson's original formulation, he and his colleagues have added further details and modifications (Hobson, Pace-Schott, & Stickgold, 2000). The brain stem, they say, sets off responses in emotional and visual parts of the brain. At the same time, brain regions that handle logical thought and sensations from the external world shut down. These changes would account for the fact that dreams tend to be emotionally charged, hallucinatory, and illogical.

activation–synthesis theory The theory that dreaming results from the cortical synthesis and interpretation of neural signals triggered by activity in the lower part of the brain.

Wishes, in this view, do not cause dreams; brain mechanisms do. Dream content, says Hobson (2002), may be "as much dross as gold, as much cognitive trash as treasure, and as much informational noise as a signal of something." But that does not mean dreams are *always* meaningless. Hobson (1988) has argued that the brain "is so inexorably bent upon the quest for meaning that it attributes and even creates meaning when there is little or none to be found in the data it is asked to process." By studying these attributed meanings, you can learn about your unique perceptions, conflicts,

GET INVOLVED!

➤KEEP A DREAM DIARY

It can be fun to record your dreams. Keep a notebook or a tape recorder by your bedside. As soon as you wake up in the morning (or if you awaken during the night while dreaming), record everything you can about your dreams—even short fragments. After you have collected several dreams, see which theory or theories discussed in this chapter seem to best explain them. Do your dreams contain any recurring themes? Do they provide any clues to your current problems, activities, or concerns? (By the way, if you are curious about other people's dreams, you can find lots of them online at www.dreambank.net.)

and concerns—not by trying to dig below the surface of the dream, as Freud would, but by examining the surface itself. Or you can relax and enjoy the nightly entertainment that dreams provide.

Evaluating Dream Theories

How are we to evaluate these attempts to explain dreaming? All four approaches account for some of the evidence, but each one also has its drawbacks (see Review 5.1).

THINKING CRITICALLY

TOLERATE UNCERTAINTY

Researchers dream of explaining dreams, and some popular writers say they can tell you what yours mean. But at present, we can't be sure about the function and meaning of dreams. Do all dreams have hidden meanings? Are all dreams due to random firing of brain cells? Is dreaming all that different from our waking thoughts?

Most psychologists today accept Freud's notion that dreams are more than incoherent ramblings of the mind and that they can have psychological meaning. But most consider the traditional psychoanalytic interpretations of dreams to be far-fetched. No reliable rules exist for interpreting the supposedly latent content of dreams, and there is no objective way to know whether a particular interpretation is correct. Nor is there any convincing empirical support for most of Freud's claims. Freudian interpretations are common in popular books and newspaper columns, and, of course, on the Internet, but they are only the writers' personal hunches.

As for dreaming as a way of solving problems, it seems pretty clear that some dreams are related to current worries and concerns. But skeptics doubt that people can actually solve problems or resolve conflicts while sound asleep (Blagrove, 1996; Squier & Domhoff, 1998). Dreams, they say, merely give expression to our problems. The insights into those problems that people attribute to dreaming could be occurring after they wake up and have a chance to think about what is troubling them.

The activation–synthesis theory has also come in for criticism (Domhoff, 2003). Not all dreams are as disjointed or as bizarre as the theory predicts; in fact, many tell a coherent, if fanciful, story. Moreover, the activation–synthesis approach does not account well for dreaming that goes on outside of REM sleep. Some neuropsychologists emphasize different brain mechanisms involved in dreams, and many believe that dreams do reflect a person's goals and desires.

Finally, the cognitive approach to dreams is a fairly new one, so some of its specific claims remain to be tested against neurological and cognitive evidence. At present, however, it is a leading contender because it incorporates many elements of other theories and fits what we currently know about waking cognition and cognitive development.

REVIEW 5.1

Four Dream Theories Compared

Theory	Purpose of Dreaming	Weaknesses
Psychoanalytic	To express unconscious wishes, thoughts, and conflicts	Interpretations are often far-fetched; there is no reliable way to interpret "latent" meanings
Problem-focused	To express ongoing concerns of waking life and/or resolve current concerns and problems	Some theorists are skeptical about the ability to resolve problems during sleep
Cognitive	Same as in waking life—to express concerns and interests	Some specific claims remain to be tested
Activation–synthesis	None; dreams occur because of random brain-stem signals, though cortical interpretations of those signals may reflect concerns and conflicts	Does not explain coherent, storylike dreams or non-REM dreams

Perhaps it will turn out that different kinds of dreams have different purposes and origins. We all know from experience that some of our dreams seem to be related to daily problems, some are vague and incoherent, and some are anxiety dreams that occur when we are worried or depressed. For the time being, we are going to have to live with uncertainty about what those fascinating stories and images in our sleeping brains really mean.

QUICK quiz

See if you can dream up an answer to this question.

In his dreams, Andy is an infant crawling through a dark tunnel looking for something he has lost. Which theory of dreams would be most receptive to each of the following explanations?

1. Andy recently found a valuable watch he had misplaced.
2. While Andy was sleeping, neurons in his pons that would ordinarily stimulate parts of the brain involved in leg-muscle movements were active.
3. Andy has repressed an early sexual attraction to his mother; the tunnel symbolizes her vagina.
4. Andy has broken up with his lover and is working through the emotional loss.

Answers:

1. the cognitive approach (the dreamer is thinking about a recent experience) **2.** the activation–synthesis theory **3.** psychoanalytic theory **4.** the problem-focused approach

WHAT'S**AHEAD**

- Can a hypnotist force you to do things against your will?
- Can hypnosis help you remember the past more accurately?
- What are the legitimate uses of hypnosis in psychology and medicine?
- Are hypnotized persons merely faking or playacting?

The Riddle of Hypnosis

For many years, stage hypnotists, "past-lives channelers," and some psychotherapists have been reporting that they can "age regress" hypnotized people to earlier years or even earlier centuries. Some therapists claim that hypnosis helps their patients accurately retrieve long-buried memories, and a few even claim that hypnosis has helped their patients recall alleged abductions by extraterrestrials. What are we to make of all this?

Hypnosis is a procedure in which a practitioner suggests changes in the sensations, perceptions, thoughts, feelings, or behavior of the subject (Kirsch & Lynn, 1995). The hypnotized person, in turn, tries to alter his or her cognitive processes in accordance with the hypnotist's suggestions (Nash & Nadon, 1997). Hypnotic suggestions typically involve performance of an action ("Your arm will slowly rise"), an inability to perform an act ("You will be unable to bend your arm"), or a distortion of normal perception or memory ("You will feel no pain," "You will forget being hypnotized until I give you a signal"). People usually report that their response to a suggestion feels involuntary, as if it happened without their willing it.

hypnosis A procedure in which the practitioner suggests changes in a subject's sensations, perceptions, thoughts, feelings, or behavior.

To induce hypnosis, the hypnotist typically suggests that the person being hypnotized feels relaxed, is getting sleepy, and feels the eyelids getting heavier and heavier. In

a singsong or monotonous voice, the hypnotist assures the subject that he or she is sinking "deeper and deeper." Sometimes the hypnotist has the person concentrate on a color or a small object, or on certain bodily sensations. People who have been hypnotized report that the focus of attention turns outward, toward the hypnotist's voice. They sometimes compare the experience to being totally absorbed in a good movie or favorite piece of music. The hypnotized person almost always remains fully aware of what is happening and remembers the experience later unless explicitly instructed to forget it—and even then, the memory can be restored by a prearranged signal.

Because hypnosis has been used for everything from parlor tricks and stage shows to medical and psychological treatments, it is important to understand just what this procedure can and cannot achieve. We will begin with a general look at the major findings on hypnosis; then we will consider two leading explanations of hypnotic effects.

The Nature of Hypnosis

Since the late 1960s, thousands of articles on hypnosis have appeared. Based on controlled laboratory and clinical studies, most researchers agree on the following points (Kirsch & Lynn, 1995; Nash, 2001; Nash & Nadon, 1997):

1 **Hypnotic responsiveness depends more on the efforts and qualities of the person being hypnotized than on the skill of the hypnotist.** Some people are more responsive to hypnosis than others, but why they are is unknown. Surprisingly, hypnotic susceptibility is unrelated to general personality traits such as gullibility, trust, submissiveness, or conformity (Nash & Nadon, 1997). And it is only weakly related to the ability to become easily absorbed in activities and the world of imagination (Council, Kirsch, & Grant, 1996; Nash & Nadon, 1997).

2 **Hypnotized people cannot be forced to do things against their will.** Like drunkenness, hypnosis can be used to justify letting go of inhibitions ("I know this looks silly, but after all, I'm hypnotized"). Hypnotized individuals may even comply with a suggestion to do something that looks embarrassing or dangerous. But the individual is choosing to turn responsibility over to the hypnotist and to cooperate with the hypnotist's suggestions (Lynn, Rhue, & Weekes, 1990). There is no evidence that hypnotized people will do anything that actually violates their morals or constitutes a real danger to themselves or others (Laurence & Perry, 1988).

3 **Feats performed under hypnosis can be performed by motivated people without hypnosis.** Hypnotized subjects sometimes perform what seem like extraordinary mental or physical feats, but most research finds that hypnosis does not actually enable people to do things that would otherwise be impossible. With proper motivation, support, and encouragement, the same people could do the same things even without being hypnotized (Chaves, 1989; Spanos, Stenstrom, & Johnson, 1988).

THINKING CRITICALLY

ANALYZE ASSUMPTIONS AND BIASES

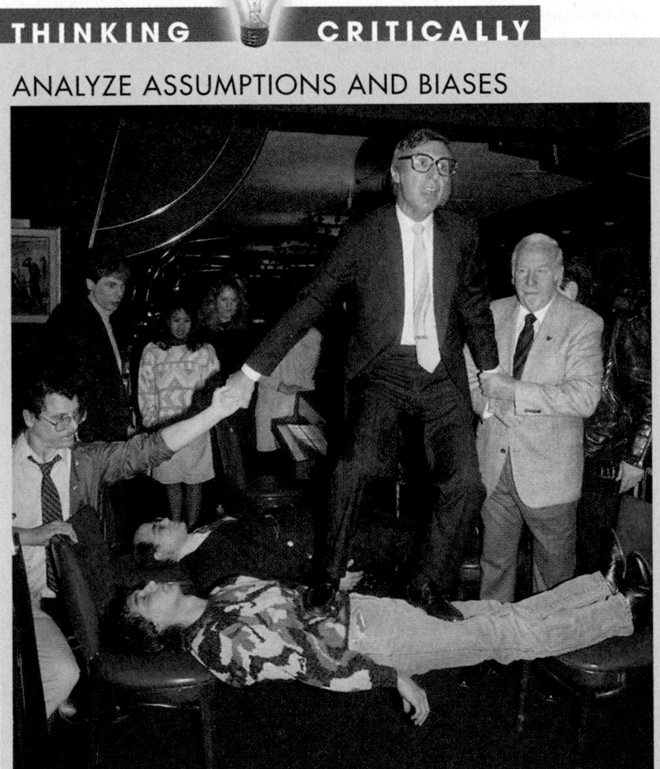

Is it hypnosis that enables the man stretched out between two chairs to hold the weight of the man standing on him, without flinching? This audience assumes so, but the only way to find out whether hypnosis produces unique abilities is to do research with control groups. It turns out that people can do the same thing even when they are not hypnotized.

"THE WITNESS HAS BARKED, MEOWED AND GIVEN US FIVE MINUTES OF BABY TALK. I'D SAY HYPNOSIS IS NOT THE ANSWER."

4 Hypnosis does not increase the accuracy of memory. Many people assume that hypnosis can enhance the recall of forgotten experiences, but this is not true. In rare cases, hypnosis has been used successfully to jog the memories of crime victims, but usually the memories of hypnotized witnesses have been completely mistaken. Although hypnosis does sometimes boost the amount of information recalled, it also increases *errors*, perhaps because hypnotized people are more willing than others to guess, or because they mistake vividly imagined possibilities for actual memories (Dinges et al., 1992; Kihlstrom, 1994). The hypnotized person is often completely convinced that his or her memories are real, but they are not. Because pseudomemories and errors are so common in hypnotically induced recall, the American Psychological Association and the American Medical Association oppose the use of "hypnotically refreshed" testimony in courts of law.

5 Hypnosis does not produce a literal reexperiencing of long-ago events. When clinical psychologist Michael Yapko (1994) surveyed 869 members of the American Association of Marriage and Family Therapists, he was alarmed to discover that more than half believed that "hypnosis can be used to recover memories from as far back as birth." This belief is just plain wrong. When people are regressed to an earlier age, their mental and moral performance remains adultlike (Nash, 1987). Their brain-wave patterns and reflexes do not become childish; they do not reason as children do or show child-sized IQs. They may use baby talk or report that they feel 4 years old again, but the reason is not that they are actually reliving the experience of being 4; they are just willing to play the role.

A person whose arm is immersed in ice water ordinarily feels intense pain. But Ernest Hilgard, a pioneer in hypnosis research, found that when hypnotized people are told the pain will be minimal, they report little or no discomfort and seem unperturbed.

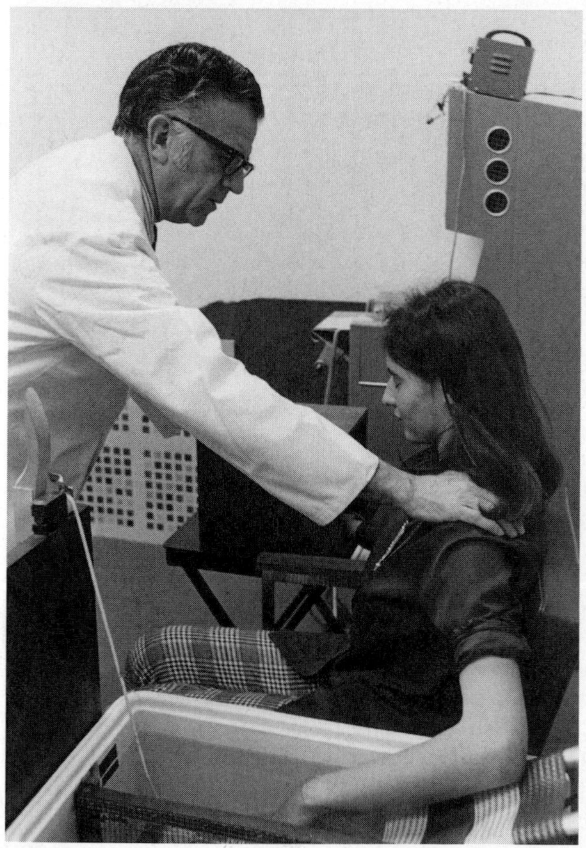

6 Hypnotic suggestions have been used effectively for many medical and psychological purposes. Although hypnosis is not of much use for finding out what happened in the past, it can be useful in the treatment of psychological and medical problems. Its greatest success is in pain management; some people experience dramatic relief of pain resulting from conditions as diverse as burns, cancer, and childbirth; others have learned to cope better emotionally with chronic pain. Hypnotic suggestions have also been used in the treatment of stress, anxiety, obesity, asthma, irritable bowel syndrome, chemotherapy-induced nausea, and even skin disorders (Nash & Barnier, 2007; Patterson & Jensen, 2003).

Theories of Hypnosis

Over the years, people have proposed many explanations of what hypnosis is and how it produces its effects. One early notion, that hypnosis is a "trance state," was eventually rejected by most researchers. Today, two competing theories predominate, with many scientists taking a position somewhere in the middle.

Dissociation Theories. One leading approach was originally proposed by the late Ernest Hilgard (1977, 1986), who argued that hypnosis, like lucid dreaming and even simple distraction, involves **dissociation**, a split in consciousness in which one part of the mind operates independently of the rest of consciousness. In many hypnotized persons, said Hilgard, while most of the mind is subject to hypnotic suggestion, one part is a *hidden observer*, watching but not participating. Unless given special instructions, the hypnotized part remains unaware of the observer.

dissociation A split in consciousness in which one part of the mind operates independently of others.

In his research, Hilgard attempted to question the hidden observer directly. In one procedure, hypnotized volunteers had to submerge an arm in ice water for several seconds, an experience that is normally excruciating. They were told that they would feel no pain, but that the nonsubmerged hand would be able to signal the level of any hidden pain by pressing a key. In this situation, many people said they felt little or no pain—yet at the same time, their free hand was busily pressing the key. After the session, these people continued to insist that they had been pain-free, unless the hypnotist asked the hidden observer to issue a separate report.

A related theory holds that during hypnosis, dissociation occurs between an "executive" system in the brain (probably in the frontal lobes) and other brain systems involved in thinking and acting (Woody & Bowers, 1994). The result is an altered state of consciousness similar to that found in patients with frontal lobe disorders. Because the dissociated systems are freed from control by the executive, they are more easily influenced by suggestions from the hypnotist. Like the activation–synthesis theory of dreaming, dissociation theories of hypnosis are consistent with modern brain theories, which hold that one part of the brain operates as a reporter and interpreter of activities carried out unconsciously by other brain parts (see Chapter 4).

DISSOCIATION THEORIES OF HYPNOSIS

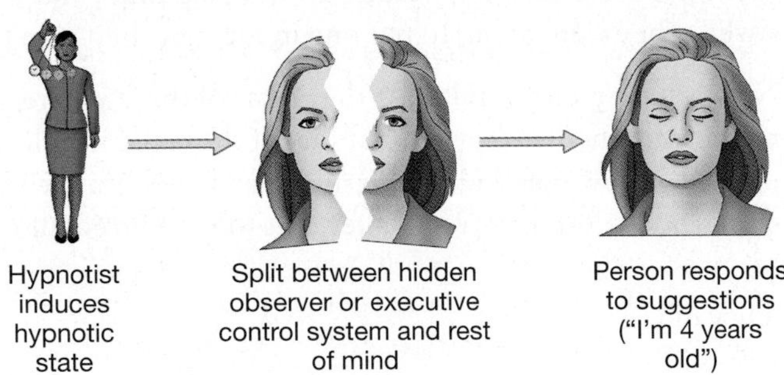
Hypnotist induces hypnotic state
Split between hidden observer or executive control system and rest of mind
Person responds to suggestions ("I'm 4 years old")

The Sociocognitive Approach. The second major approach to hypnosis, the *sociocognitive explanation*, holds that the effects of hypnosis result from an interaction between the social influence of the hypnotist (the "socio" part) and the abilities, beliefs, and expectations of the subject (the "cognitive" part) (Kirsch, 1997; Sarbin, 1991; Spanos, 1991). The hypnotized person is basically playing a role, one that has analogies in ordinary life, where we willingly submit to the suggestions of parents, teachers, doctors, therapists, and television commercials. In this view, even the "hidden observer" is simply a reaction to the social demands of the situation and the suggestions of the hypnotist (Kirsch & Lynn, 1998).

The hypnotized person is not merely faking or play-acting, however. A person who has been instructed to fool an observer by faking a hypnotic state will tend to overplay the role and will stop playing it as soon as the other person leaves the room. In contrast, hypnotized subjects continue to follow the hypnotic suggestions even when they think they are not being watched (Kirsch et al., 1989; Spanos et al., 1993). Like many social roles,

SOCIOCOGNITIVE THEORIES OF HYPNOSIS

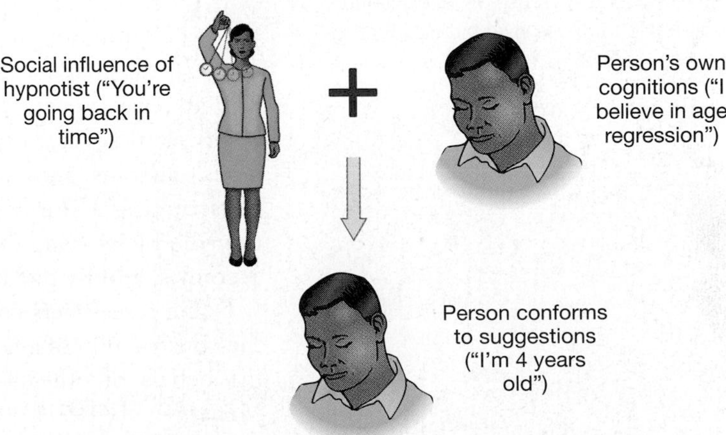
Social influence of hypnotist ("You're going back in time")
Person's own cognitions ("I believe in age regression")
Person conforms to suggestions ("I'm 4 years old")

the role of hypnotized person is so engrossing and involving that actions required by the role may occur without the person's conscious intent.

Sociocognitive views explain why some people under hypnosis report spirit possession or "memories" of alien abductions (Clancy, 2005; Spanos, 1996). The individual goes to a therapist looking for an explanation of his or her loneliness, unhappiness, nightmares, puzzling symptoms (such as waking up in the middle of the night in a cold sweat), or the waking dreams we described earlier. If the therapist already believes in alien abduction, he or she may hypnotize the person and then shape the client's story by giving subtle and not-so-subtle hints about what the person should say. Here is an exchange between one therapist who believes in UFO abductions and a supposed abductee who has been hypnotized (quoted in Newman & Baumeister, 1996):

Dr. Fiore: Now I'm going to ask you a few questions at this point. You will remember everything because you want to remember. When you were being poked everywhere, did they do any kind of vaginal examination?

Sandi: I don't think they did.

Dr. Fiore: Now you're going to let yourself know if they put a needle in any part of your body, other than the rectum.

Sandi: No. They were carrying needles around, big ones, and I was scared for a while they were going to put one in me, but they didn't. [*Body tenses.*]

Dr. Fiore: Now just let yourself relax. At the count of three you're going to remember whether they did put one of those big needles in you. If they did, know that you're safe, and it's all over, isn't it? And if they didn't, you're going to remember that too, at the count of three. One . . . two . . . three.

Sandi: They did.

THINKING CRITICALLY

CONSIDER OTHER INTERPRETATIONS

Under hypnosis, Jim describes the chocolate cake at his fourth birthday and Joan remembers a former life as a twelfth-century French peasant. But lemon cake was served at Jim's party and Joan can't speak twelfth-century French. What explanation best accounts for these vivid but incorrect memories?

The sociocognitive view can also explain apparent cases of past-life regression. In a fascinating program of research, Nicholas Spanos and his colleagues directed hypnotized Canadian university students to regress past their own births to previous lives. About a third of the students (who already believed in reincarnation) reported being able to do so. But when they were asked, while supposedly reliving a past life, to name the leader of their country, say whether the country was at peace or at war, or describe the money used in their community, the students could not do it. (One young man, who thought he was Julius Caesar, said the year was 50 A.D. and he was emperor of Rome. But Caesar died in 44 B.C. and was never crowned emperor, and dating years as A.D. or B.C. did not begin until several centuries later.) Not knowing anything about the language, dates, customs, and events of their "previous life" did not deter the students from constructing a story about it, however. They tried to fulfill the requirements of the role by weaving events, places, and persons from their *present* lives into their accounts, and by picking up cues from the experimenter.

The researchers concluded that the act of "remembering" another self involves the construction of a fantasy that accords with the rememberer's own beliefs and also the beliefs of others—in this case, those of the authoritative hypnotist (Spanos, Menary et al., 1991).

BIOLOGY and Hypnosis

Now You See It . . .

Debates over what hypnosis really is and how it works have intensified as scientists have begun to use technology in hopes of better understanding this mysterious phenomenon. We have known for some time from EEG studies that alpha waves are common when a person is in a relaxed hypnotic state. This is not surprising, because alpha waves are associated with relaxed wakefulness. The invention of brain scans, however, permits a far more detailed and useful picture of what is going on in the brain of a hypnotized person.

One recent brain-scan study showed that hypnosis can reduce conflict between two mental tasks (Raz, Fan, & Posner, 2005). The researchers gave participants the Stroop test, which is often used to study what happens when color perception conflicts with reading. You look at words denoting colors (*blue, red, green, yellow*. . .), with some letters printed in the corresponding color (e.g., *red* printed in red) and others in a different color (e.g., *red* printed in blue). It is a lot harder to identify the color of the ink a word is printed in when the word's meaning and its color are different. To see what we mean, try identifying as quickly as you can the color of the words in the adjacent illustration. It's pretty hard, right?

red
yellow
green
blue
red
blue
yellow
green
blue
red

In the study, hypnotized subjects were told that later, after they were no longer hypnotized, they would see words from the Stroop test on a computer screen, but the words would seem like strings of meaningless symbols—like "characters in a foreign language that you do not know." During the test, easily hypnotized people were faster and better at identifying the clashing colors the words were printed in than people who were less easily hypnotized; in fact, the "Stroop effect" virtually disappeared. Apparently, the easily hypnotized people were literally not seeing the color words; they were seeing gibberish. Moreover, during the task, these people had reduced activity in a brain area that decodes written words and in another area toward the front of the brain that monitors conflicting thoughts. Because of the suggestions made while they had been hypnotized, these individuals apparently were able to pay less attention to the words themselves during the task and thus were able to avoid reading them. They could focus solely on the color of the ink.

Other research has found changes in various regions of the brain when people are hypnotized and lying in a PET scanner. In one study, highly hypnotizable people, under hypnosis, were able to visually drain color from a drawing of red, blue, green, and yellow rectangles, or to see color when the same drawing was presented in gray tones. When they were told to see color in the gray drawing, their brains showed activation in areas associated with color perception; when they were told to see gray in the colored drawing, the same areas had decreased activation (Kosslyn et al., 2000).

But what do findings like these mean for theories of hypnosis? The fact that hypnosis can affect patterns of activity in the brain has encouraged those who believe that hypnosis is a special state, different from elaborate role playing or extreme concentration. Others feel that it is far too soon to draw any conclusions from this research about the mechanisms or nature of hypnosis. *Every* experience alters the brain in some way; there is no reason to think that hypnosis is any exception, however it may work. Moreover, recent research finds that suggestion can reduce the Stroop effect in highly suggestible people even *without* hypnosis (Raz et al., 2006).

Further research may tell us whether there is something special about hypnosis or not. But whatever the outcome of this debate, all hypnosis researchers agree on certain things—for example, that hypnosis does not cause memories to become sharper or allow early experiences to be replayed with perfect accuracy. The study of hypnosis is teaching us much about human suggestibility, the power of imagination, and the way we perceive the present and remember the past.

QUICK quiz

We'd like to plant a suggestion in your mind—that you'd be wise to take this quiz.

A. True or false:

1. A hypnotized person is usually aware of what is going on and remembers the experience later.
2. Hypnosis gives us special powers that we do not ordinarily have.
3. Hypnosis reduces errors in memory.
4. Hypnotized people play no active part in controlling their behavior and thoughts.
5. According to Hilgard, hypnosis is a state of consciousness involving a "hidden observer."
6. Sociocognitive theorists view hypnosis as mere faking or conscious playacting.

B. Some people believe that hypnotic suggestions can bolster the immune system and help a person fight disease. However, support for this belief has so far been modest, and many studies have had methodological flaws (Miller & Cohen, 2001). One therapist dismissed these concerns by saying that a negative result just means that the hypnotist lacks skill or the right personality. As a critical thinker, can you spot what is wrong with his reasoning? (Think back to Chapter 2 and the way a scientific hypothesis must be stated.)

Answers:

A. 1. true 2. false 3. false 4. false 5. true 6. false B. The therapist's argument violates the principle of falsifiability. If a result is positive, he counts it as evidence. But if a result is negative, he refuses to count it as counterevidence ("Maybe the hypnotist just wasn't good enough"). With this kind of reasoning, there is no way to tell whether the hypothesis is right or wrong.

WHAT'S AHEAD

- In its physiological effects, is alcohol a "downer" or an "upper"?
- How do recreational drugs affect the brain?
- Why can a glass of wine make you feel tired at one time but sociable and pepped up at another?
- In debates over legalizing recreational drugs, what errors in thinking do both sides make?

Consciousness-Altering Drugs

In Jerusalem, hundreds of Hasidic men celebrate the completion of the annual reading of the holy Torah by dancing for hours in the streets. For them, dancing is not a diversion; it is a path to religious ecstasy. In South Dakota, several Lakota (Sioux) adults sit naked in the darkness and crushing heat of the sweat lodge; their goal is euphoria, the transcendence of pain, and connection with the Great Spirit of the Universe. In the Amazon jungle, a young man training to be a shaman, a religious leader, takes a whiff of hallucinogenic snuff made from the bark of the virola tree; his goal is to enter a trance and communicate with animals, spirits, and supernatural forces.

These three rituals, although seemingly quite different, are all aimed at release from the confines of ordinary consciousness. Cultures around the world have devised such practices, often as part of their religions. Because attempts to alter mood and consciousness appear to be universal, some writers believe they reflect a human need, one as basic as the need for food and water (Siegel, 1989).

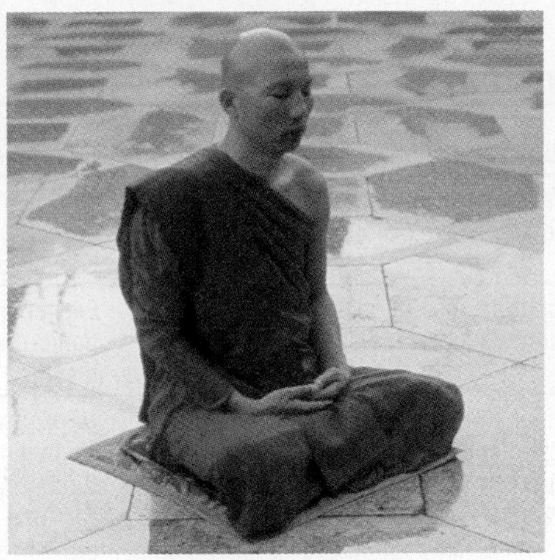

All cultures have found ways to alter consciousness. The Maulavis of Turkey (left), the famous whirling dervishes, spin in an energetic but controlled manner in order to achieve religious rapture. People in many cultures meditate (center) as a way to quiet the mind and achieve spiritual enlightenment. And in some cultures, psychoactive drugs are used for religious or artistic inspiration, as in the case of the Huichol Indians of western Mexico (right), shown here harvesting hallucinogenic mushrooms.

William James (1902/1936), who was fascinated by alterations in consciousness, would have agreed. After inhaling nitrous oxide ("laughing gas"), he wrote, "Our normal waking consciousness, rational consciousness as we call it, is but one special type of consciousness, whilst all about it, parted from it by the filmiest of screens, there lie potential forms of consciousness entirely different." James hoped that psychologists would study these other forms of consciousness, but for half a century, few did. Then, in the 1960s, attitudes changed. During that decade of social upheaval, millions of people began to seek ways of deliberately producing *altered states of consciousness*, especially through the use of psychoactive drugs. Researchers became interested in the psychology, as well as the physiology, of such drugs. The filmy screen described by James finally began to lift.

Classifying Drugs

A **psychoactive drug** is a substance that alters perception, mood, thinking, memory, or behavior by changing the body's biochemistry. Around the world and throughout history, people have used psychoactive drugs: tobacco, alcohol, marijuana, mescaline, opium, cocaine, peyote—and, of course, tea and coffee. The reasons for taking psychoactive drugs have varied: to alter consciousness, as part of a religious ritual, for recreation, to decrease physical pain or discomfort, and for psychological escape. But human beings are not the only species that likes to get high on occasion; so do many other animals. Baboons ingest tobacco, elephants love the alcohol in fermented fruit, and reindeer and rabbits seek out intoxicating mushrooms (Siegel, 1989).

In Western societies, a whole pharmacopeia of recreational drugs exists, and each year seems to see the introduction of new ones, both natural and synthetic. Most of these drugs can be classified as *stimulants*, *depressants*, *opiates*, or *psychedelics*, depending on their effects on the central nervous system and their impact on behavior and mood (see Review 5.2). Here we describe only their physiological and psychological effects; Chapter 16 covers addiction and Chapter 17 covers drugs that are used in the treatment of mental and emotional disorders.

1 **Stimulants speed up activity in the central nervous system.** They include, among other drugs, nicotine, caffeine, cocaine, amphetamines ("uppers"), and methamphetamine ("meth"). In moderate amounts, stimulants produce feelings of excitement, confidence, and well-being or euphoria. In large amounts, they make a person anxious, jittery, and hyperalert. In very large doses, they may cause convulsions, heart failure, and death.

psychoactive drug A drug capable of influencing perception, mood, cognition, or behavior.

stimulants Drugs that speed up activity in the central nervous system.

REVIEW 5.2

Some Psychoactive Drugs and their Effects

Class of Drug	Type	Common Effects	Results of Abuse/Addiction
Ampahetamines Methamphetamine	Stimulants	Wakefulness, alertness, raised metabolism, elevated mood	Nervousness, headaches, loss of appetite, high blood pressure, delusions, psychosis, heart damage, convulsions, death
Cocaine	Stimulant	Euphoria, excitation, feelings of energy, suppressed appetite	Excitability, sleeplessness, sweating, paranoia, anxiety, panic, depression, heart damage, heart failure, injury to nose if sniffed
Tobacco (nicotine)	Stimulant	Varies from alertness to calmness, depending on mental set, setting, and prior arousal; decreases appetite for carbohydrates	*Nicotine:* heart disease, high blood pressure, impaired circulation, erectile problems in men, damage throughout the body due to lowering of a key enzyme *Tar:* lung cancer, emphysema, mouth and throat cancer, many other health risks
Caffeine	Stimulant	Wakefulness, alertness, shortened reaction time	Restlessness, insomnia, muscle tension, heartbeat irregularities, high blood pressure
Alcohol (1–2 drinks)	Depressant	Depends on setting and mental set; tends to act like a stimulant because it reduces inhibitions and anxiety	
Alcohol (several/ many drinks)	Depressant	Slowed reaction time, tension, depression, reduced ability to store new memories or to retrieve old ones, poor coordination	Blackouts, cirrhosis of the liver, other organ damage, mental and neurological impairment, psychosis, death with very large amounts
Tranquilizers (e.g., Valium); barbiturates (e.g., phenobarbital)	Depressant	Reduced anxiety and tension, sedation	Increased dosage needed for effects; impaired motor and sensory functions, impaired permanent storage of new information, withdrawal symptoms; possibly convulsions, coma, death (especially when taken with other drugs)
Opium, heroin, morphine	Opiate	Euphoria, relief of pain	Loss of appetite, nausea, constipation, withdrawal symptoms, convulsions, coma, possibly death
LSD, psilocybin, mescaline	Psychedelic	Exhilaration, visions and hallucinations, insightful experiences	Psychosis, paranoia, panic reactions
Marijuana	Mild psychedelic (classification controversial)	Relaxation, euphoria, increased appetite, reduced ability to store new memories, other effects depending on mental set and setting	Throat and lung irritation, possible lung damage if smoked heavily

Amphetamines are synthetic drugs taken in pill form, injected, smoked, or inhaled. Methamphetamine is structurally similar to amphetamines and is used in the same ways; it comes in two forms, as a powder ("crank," "speed") or in a purer form, a crystalline solid ("glass," "ice"). Cocaine ("coke") is a natural drug, derived from the leaves of the coca plant. Rural workers in Bolivia and Peru chew coca leaf every day without apparent ill effects. In North America, the drug is usually inhaled, injected, or smoked in the highly refined form known as crack. These methods give the drug a more immediate, powerful, and dangerous effect than when coca leaf is chewed. Amphetamines, methamphetamine, and cocaine make users feel charged up but do not actually increase energy reserves. Fatigue, irritability, and depression may occur when the effects of these drugs wear off.

depressants Drugs that slow activity in the central nervous system.

2 **Depressants slow down activity in the central nervous system.** They include alcohol, tranquilizers, barbiturates, and most of the common chemicals that

some people inhale ("huffing"). Depressants usually make a person feel calm or drowsy, and they may reduce anxiety, guilt, tension, and inhibitions. In large amounts, they may produce insensitivity to pain and other sensations. Like stimulants, in very large doses they can cause irregular heartbeats, convulsions, and death.

People are often surprised to learn that alcohol is a central nervous system depressant. In small amounts, alcohol has some of the effects of a stimulant because it suppresses activity in parts of the brain that normally inhibit impulsive behavior, such as loud laughter and clowning around. In the long run, however, it slows down nervous system activity. Like barbiturates and opiates, alcohol can be used as an anesthetic; if you drink enough, you will eventually pass out. Over time, alcohol damages the liver, heart, and brain. Extremely large amounts of alcohol can kill by inhibiting the nerve cells in brain areas that control breathing and heartbeat. Every so often the news reports the death of a college student who had large amounts of alcohol "funneled" into him as part of an initiation or drinking competition. On the other hand, *moderate* drinking—a drink or two of wine or liquor a day—is associated with a variety of health benefits, especially for adults over 40. These benefits include a reduced risk of heart attack and stroke, and antidiabetic effects (Davies et al., 2002; Mukamal et al., 2003; Reynolds et al., 2003).

opiates Drugs, derived from the opium poppy, that relieve pain and commonly produce euphoria.

psychedelic drugs Consciousness-altering drugs that produce hallucinations, change thought processes, or disrupt the normal perception of time and space.

3 **Opiates relieve pain.** They include opium, derived from the opium poppy; morphine, a derivative of opium; heroin, a derivative of morphine; and synthetic drugs such as methadone. All of these drugs mimic the action of endorphins, and most have a powerful effect on the emotions. When injected, they may produce a rush—a sudden feeling of euphoria. They may also decrease anxiety and motivation, although the effects vary.

4 **Psychedelic drugs disrupt normal thought processes,** such as the perception of time and space. Sometimes psychedelics produce hallucinations, especially visual ones. Some psychedelics, such as lysergic acid diethylamide (LSD), are made in the laboratory. Others, such as mescaline (from the peyote cactus), *Salvia divinorum* (a plant native to Mexico), and psilocybin (from certain species of mushrooms), are natural substances. Emotional reactions to psychedelics vary from person to person and from one time to another for any individual. A "trip" may be mildly pleasant or unpleasant, a mystical revelation or a nightmare.

An LSD trip can be a ticket to agony or ecstasy. These drawings were done under the influence of the drug as part of a test conducted by the U.S. government in the late 1950s. Twenty minutes after the first dose, before the drug had taken effect, the artist drew the charcoal self-portrait on the left. After 2 hours and 45 minutes, he had become agitated and inarticulate and drew the "portrait" in the center. Three hours later, as the drug was wearing off ("I can feel my knees again"), he made the crayon drawing on the right, complaining that the "pencil" in his hand was hard to hold.

Some commonly used drugs fall outside these four classifications, combine elements of more than one category, or have uncertain effects. One is *marijuana* ("pot," "grass," "weed"), which is smoked or, less commonly, eaten in foods such as brownies, and is the most widely used illicit drug in North America and Europe. Some researchers classify it as a psychedelic, but others feel that its chemical makeup and its psychological effects place it outside the major classifications. The main active ingredient in marijuana is tetrahydrocannabinol (THC), derived from the hemp plant, *Cannabis sativa*. In some respects, THC appears to be a mild stimulant, increasing heart rate and making tastes, sounds, and colors seem more intense. But users often report reactions ranging from mild euphoria to relaxation or even sleepiness. Although THC has not been shown to be carcinogenic, some researchers believe that very heavy smoking of the drug (which is high in tar) may increase the risk of lung damage (Barsky et al., 1998; Zhu et al., 2000). In moderate doses, it can interfere with the transfer of information to long-term memory, a characteristic it shares with alcohol, and in large doses, it can cause hallucinations and a sense of unreality. Sometimes the drug impairs coordination, concentration, and reaction times, though it is not clear how long these effects last. On the other hand, marijuana has some medical benefits, as we will see later when we discuss the debate over legalizing drugs.

The Physiology of Drug Effects

Psychoactive drugs produce their effects primarily by acting on brain neurotransmitters, the chemical substances that carry messages from one nerve cell to another. A drug may increase or decrease the release of neurotransmitters at the synapse, prevent the reabsorption of excess neurotransmitter molecules by the cells that have released them, block the effects of a neurotransmitter on a receiving nerve cell, or bind to receptors that would ordinarily be triggered by a neurotransmitter (see Chapter 4). Figure 5.3 shows how one drug, cocaine, increases the amount of norepinephrine and dopamine in the brain by blocking the reabsorption of these substances. Cocaine also seems to increase the transmission of serotonin (Rocha et al., 1998).

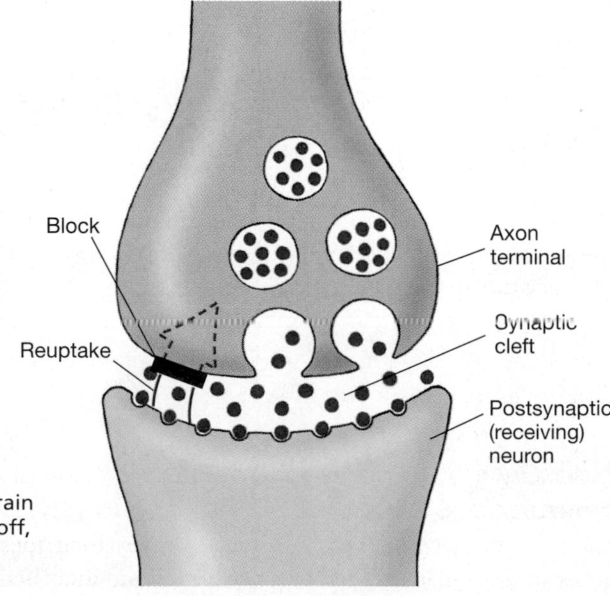

FIGURE 5.3 Cocaine's Effect on the Brain

Cocaine blocks the brain's reabsorption ("reuptake") of the neurotransmitters dopamine and norepinephrine, so levels of these substances rise. The result is overstimulation of certain brain circuits and a brief euphoric high. Then, when the drug wears off, a depletion of dopamine may cause the user to "crash" and become sleepy and depressed.

These biochemical changes affect cognitive and emotional functioning. For example, because of alcohol's effect on parts of the brain involved in judgment, drinkers often are unable to gauge their own competence. Just a couple of drinks can affect perception, response time, coordination, and balance, despite the drinker's own impression of unchanged or even improved performance. Liquor also affects memory, possibly by interfering with the work of serotonin. Information stored before a drinking session remains intact during the session but is retrieved more slowly (Haut et al., 1989). The ability to store new memories for later use also suffers after the consumption of only two or three drinks (Parker, Birnbaum, & Noble, 1976). Consuming small amounts does not seem to affect *sober* mental performance, but even occasional heavy drinking impairs later abstract thought. In other words, a Saturday night binge is potentially more dangerous than a daily drink.

As for other recreational drugs, there is little evidence that *light* or *moderate* use can damage the human brain enough to affect cognitive functioning, but nearly all researchers agree that heavy or very frequent use is another matter (see Chapter 16). For example, one study found that heavy users of methamphetamine had damage to dopamine cells and performed more poorly than other people on tests of memory, attention, and movement, even though they had not used the drug for at least 11 months (Volkow et al., 2001).

Not all drugs are equally dangerous, however. Controversy exists especially about Ecstasy (MDMA), a synthetic drug that has properties of both a hallucinogen and a stimulant and that is said to increase empathy, insight, and energy. Ecstasy has provoked a great deal of hysteria; claims have been made, mostly on the basis of research with animals receiving huge doses, that the drug permanently damages serotonin cells, wipes out memory, and causes tremors like those of Parkinson's disease. But some of the best-known reports of these presumed dangers were based on research having major methodological problems; one influential report even had to be retracted in 2003 by the prestigious journal *Science* after irregularities and errors came to light. An impartial review of Ecstasy research concluded that there was no evidence that Ecstasy causes lasting damage "with the possible (but as yet unproven) exception of mild memory loss" (Kish, 2003). Heavy use may cause a reduction in serotonin levels, but this change has not been shown to be permanent, and it could be caused by other drugs that most heavy users take (Buchert et al., 2003).

The use of some psychoactive drugs, such as heroin and tranquilizers, can lead to **tolerance**: Over time, more and more of the drug is needed to get the same effect. When habitual heavy users stop taking a drug, they may suffer severe **withdrawal** symptoms, which, depending on the drug, may include nausea, abdominal cramps, sweating, muscle spasms, depression, and sleep problems.

tolerance Increased resistance to a drug's effects accompanying continued use.

withdrawal Physical and psychological symptoms that occur when someone addicted to a drug stops taking it.

The Psychology of Drug Effects

People often assume that the effects of a drug are automatic, the inevitable result of the drug's chemistry ("I couldn't help what I said—the booze made me do it"). But reactions to a psychoactive drug involve more than the drug's chemical properties. They also depend on a person's individual characteristics, experience with the drug, environmental setting, and mental set.

CONSIDER OTHER INTERPRETATIONS

One person takes a drink and flies into a rage. Another has a drink and "mellows out." What qualities of the user rather than the drug might account for this difference?

1 Individual factors include body weight, metabolism, initial state of emotional arousal, personality characteristics, and physical tolerance for the drug. For example, women generally get drunker than men on the same amount of alcohol because women are smaller, on average, and their bodies metabolize

The motives for using a drug, expectations about its effects, and the setting in which it is used all contribute to a person's reactions to the drug. For example, drinking alone to drown your sorrows is likely to produce a different reaction than binging during a competitive drinking game, like "beer pong."

alcohol differently (Fuchs et al., 1995). Similarly, many Asians have a genetically determined adverse reaction to even small amounts of alcohol, which can cause severe headaches, facial flushing, and diarrhea (Cloninger, 1990). For individuals, a drug may have one effect after a tiring day and a different one after a rousing quarrel, or the effect may vary with the time of day because of the body's circadian rhythms. And some differences among individuals in their responses to a drug may be due to their personality traits. PET scans show that when people who are prone to anger and irritability wear nicotine patches, dramatic bursts of activity occur in the brain while they are working on competitive or aggressive tasks. These changes do not occur, however, in more relaxed and cheerful people, or in control subjects wearing fake patches (Fallon et al., 2004).

2 **Experience with the drug refers to the number of times a person has taken it.** Trying a drug—a cigarette, an alcoholic drink, a stimulant—for the first time is often a neutral or unpleasant experience. But reactions typically change once a person has become familiar with the drug's effects.

3 **"Environmental setting" refers to the context in which a person takes the drug.** A person might have one glass of wine at home alone and feel sleepy but have three glasses of wine at a party and feel full of energy. Someone might feel happy and high drinking with good friends but fearful and nervous drinking with strangers. In one early study of reactions to alcohol, most of the drinkers became depressed, angry, confused, and unfriendly. Then it dawned on the researchers that anyone might become depressed, angry, confused, and unfriendly if asked to drink bourbon at 9:00 A.M. in a bleak hospital room, which was the setting for the experiment (Warren & Raynes, 1972).

4 **"Mental set" refers to a person's expectations about the drug's effects and reasons for taking it.** Some people drink to become more sociable, friendly, or seductive; some drink to try to reduce feelings of anxiety or depression; and some drink in order to have an excuse for abusiveness or violence. Addicts use drugs to escape from the real world; people living with chronic pain use the same drugs in order to function in the real world (Portenoy, 1994). As we will see again in Chapter 16, the motives for taking a drug greatly influence its effects.

Expectations can sometimes have a more powerful effect than the chemical properties of the drug itself. In several imaginative studies, researchers compared people who were drinking liquor (vodka and tonic) with those who *thought* they were drinking liquor but were actually getting only tonic and lime juice. (Vodka has a subtle taste, and most people could not tell the real and phony drinks apart.) The experimenters found a *"think–drink" effect:* Men behaved more belligerently when they thought they were drinking vodka than when they thought they were drinking plain tonic water, *regardless of the actual content of the drinks.* And both sexes reported feeling sexually aroused when they thought they were drinking vodka, whether they actually got vodka or not (Abrams & Wilson, 1983; Marlatt & Rohsenow, 1980).

"Oh, that wasn't me talking. It was the alcohol talking."

Expectations and beliefs about drugs are, in turn, shaped by the culture in which you live. Many people start their day with a cup of coffee because it increases alertness, but when coffee was first introduced in Europe, people protested against it. Women said it suppressed their husbands' sexual performance and made men inconsiderate—and maybe it did! In the nineteenth century, Americans regarded marijuana as a mild sedative with no mind-altering properties. They did not expect it to give them a high, and it didn't; it merely put them to sleep (Weil, 1972/1986). Today, most people who smoke do it to get high, and that expectation has no doubt affected how people respond to the drug.

None of this means that alcohol and other drugs are merely placebos. Psychoactive drugs, as we have seen, do have physiological effects, many of them extremely potent. But an understanding of the psychological factors involved in drug use can help us think critically about the ongoing national debate about which drugs, if any, should be legal.

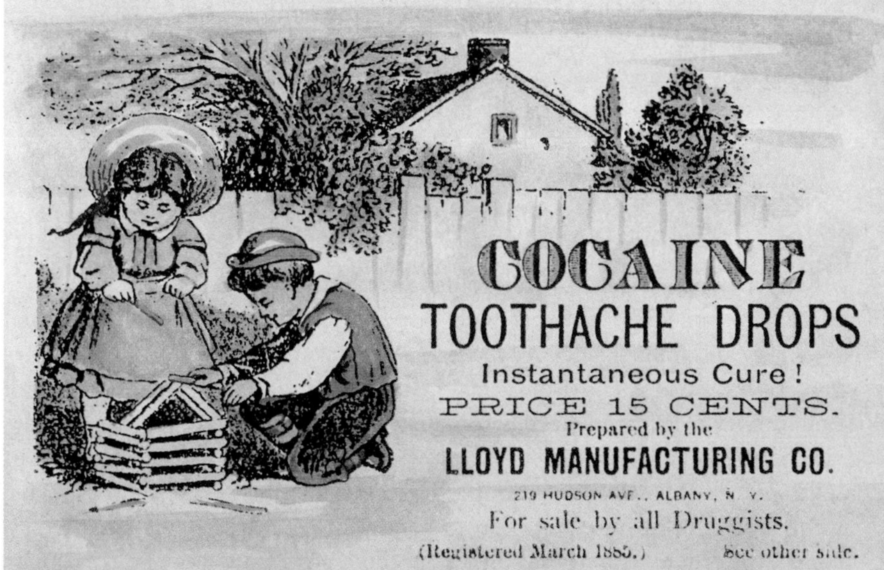

Cultural attitudes toward drugs vary with the times. Until recent decades, cigarette smoking was promoted as healthy and glamorous. And before it was banned in the United States in the 1920s, cocaine was widely touted as a cure for everything from toothaches to timidity. It was used in teas, tonics, throat lozenges, and even soft drinks (including, briefly, Coca-Cola, which derived its name from the coca plant).

The Drug Debate

When a drug interferes with a person's functioning or disrupts the person's relationships with others, *use* turns into *abuse* (see Chapter 16). Because the consequences of drug abuse are so devastating to individuals and to society, people often have trouble thinking critically about drug laws and policies; the debate usually becomes highly emotional. At one extreme, some people cannot accept evidence that their favorite drug—be it coffee, tobacco, alcohol, or marijuana—might have harmful effects. At the other extreme, some cannot accept the evidence that their most hated drug—be it alcohol, morphine, marijuana, or the coca leaf—might not be dangerous in all forms or amounts and might even have some beneficial effects. Both sides often confuse potent drugs with others that have only subtle effects and confuse light or moderate use with heavy or excessive use.

Once a drug is declared illegal, many people assume it is deadly, even though some legal drugs are more dangerous than illegal ones. Addiction to prescription painkillers and sedatives used for recreational rather than medical purposes ("pharming") has risen dramatically in the past decade among teenagers and adults, yet these drugs are legal. Nicotine, which of course is legal, is as addictive as heroin and cocaine, which are illegal. Tobacco use contributes to more than 435,000 deaths in the United States every year, 24 times the number of deaths from all illegal forms of drug use combined (Fellows et al., 2002). Yet most people have a far more negative view of heroin and cocaine than of nicotine and prescription painkillers.

Emotions have run especially high in debates over marijuana. As we saw, heavy use has some physical risks, just as heavy use of any drug does. For most people, however, both the physical risks and the psychological ones are much lower than for other common drugs. A review of studies done between 1975 and 2003 failed to find any compelling evidence that marijuana causes chronic mental or behavioral problems in teenagers or young adults, and the researchers observed that cause and effect could just as well work the other way. That is, people with problems are more likely to abuse the drug (Macleod et al., 2004). Another review found only a small impairment in memory and learning among long-term users versus nonusers, less than that typically found in users of alcohol and other drugs (Grant et al., 2003).

Moreover, marijuana has certain medical benefits: It reduces the nausea and vomiting that often accompany chemotherapy treatment for cancer and treatments for AIDS; it reduces the physical tremors, loss of appetite, and other symptoms caused by multiple sclerosis; it helps reduce the frequency of seizures in some patients with epilepsy; and it alleviates the retinal swelling caused by glaucoma (Grinspoon & Bakalar, 1993; Zimmer & Morgan, 1997). For these reasons, Spain, Italy, Portugal, the Netherlands, and Belgium have decriminalized marijuana, and Canada's National Health Service has begun a pilot project that allows pharmacies in British Columbia to sell medicinal marijuana without a prescription. But in the United States, where voters in 11 states (as of 2006) have approved the medical use of marijuana, the federal government has nonetheless continued its staunch opposition to such use. Possession of any amount of pot remains illegal, and punishment for first offenses ranges from a few years in prison to life imprisonment without parole (Schlosser, 2003). Nearly half of all drug

THINKING CRITICALLY

AVOID EMOTIONAL REASONING

In debates over drug policy, emotional images and arguments often take precedence over reasoning and research. Marijuana was once regarded as a mild and harmless sedative, but its image changed in the 1930s, when books and movies began to warn about the dire consequences of "reefer madness." Scare tactics are still often used to try to dissuade people from using drugs.

arrests nationwide are now for marijuana use, up sharply in recent years. In many states, a person who has been convicted of marijuana possession cannot later get food stamps or welfare, which even convicted rapists and murderers are entitled to.

In spite of the U.S. government's "war on drugs," no end to the battle is in sight. Nonetheless, many people remain committed to the eradication of all currently illegal drugs. Other people think that all recreational drugs should be decriminalized. Some people would legalize narcotics for people who are in chronic pain and marijuana for recreational and medicinal use, but they would ban tobacco and most hard drugs. And some people think that instead of punishing or incarcerating people who use drugs, society would be better off regulating where drugs are used (never at work or when driving, for example), providing treatment for addicts, and educating people about the benefits and hazards of using particular drugs.

Where, given the research findings, do you stand in the drug debate? Which illegal psychoactive drugs, if any, do you think should be legalized? Can we create mental sets and environmental settings that promote safe recreational use of some drugs, minimize the likelihood of drug abuse, and permit the medicinal use of beneficial drugs? What do you think?

THINKING CRITICALLY

DON'T OVERSIMPLIFY

In the debate over drugs, many people think that legal drugs are relatively harmless and illegal drugs are always bad. What might be a more useful way to think about the legalization or prohibition of drugs?

QUICK quiz

There is no debate about whether you should take this quiz.

A. Name the following:

1. Three stimulants used illegally
2. Two drugs that interfere with the formation of new long-term memories
3. Three types of depressant drugs
4. A legal recreational drug that acts as a depressant on the central nervous system
5. Four factors that influence a person's psychological reactions to a drug

B. A bodybuilder who has been taking anabolic steroids says the drugs make him more aggressive. What are some other possible interpretations?

Answers:

A. 1. cocaine, amphetamines, and methamphetamine **2.** marijuana and alcohol **3.** barbiturates, tranquilizers, and alcohol **4.** alcohol **5.** the person's physical condition, prior experience with the drug, mental set, and the environmental setting **B.** The bodybuilder's increased aggressiveness could be due to his expectations (a placebo effect); bodybuilding itself may increase aggressiveness; the culture of the bodybuilding gym may encourage aggressiveness; other influences in his life or other drugs he is taking may be making him more aggressive; or he may only think he is more aggressive, and his behavior may contradict his self-perceptions.

As we have seen in this chapter, fluctuations and changes in consciousness, though interesting in themselves, also show us how expectations and explanations of our own mental and physical states affect what we do and how we feel. Research on SAD and "PMS," the purposes of sleep, the meaning of dreams, the nature of hypnosis, and the dangers and benefits of drugs have done much to dispel many popular but mistaken ideas about these topics. In this way, the scientific scrutiny of biological rhythms, dreaming, hypnotic suggestion, and drug-induced states has deepened our understanding of the intimate relationship between body and mind.

Taking Psychology with You

How to Get a Good Night's Sleep

You hop into bed, turn out the lights, close your eyes, and wait for slumber. An hour later, you're still waiting. Finally you drop off, but at 3:00 A.M., to your chagrin, you're awake again. By the time the rooster crows, you have put in a hard day's night.

Insomnia affects most people at one time or another and many people most of the time. No wonder over-the-counter and prescription sleeping pills are a multimillion-dollar business. But many of these pills have side effects, such as making you feel a little foggy-headed the next day. Many hasten sleep only slightly and lose their effectiveness over time. Some can actually make matters worse; barbiturates, for example, greatly suppress REM sleep, a result that eventually causes wakefulness, and they also suppress Stages 3 and 4, the deeper stages of sleep. Although pills can be helpful on a temporary basis, they do not get at stress and anxiety that may be at the root of your insomnia, and once you stop taking the pills, your insomnia is likely to return. Sleep research suggests some alternatives:

- **Be sure you actually have a sleep problem.** Many people only *think* they don't sleep well. They overestimate how long it takes them to doze off and underestimate how much sleep they are getting. When they are observed in the laboratory, they usually fall asleep in less than 30 minutes and are awake for only very short periods during the night (Bonnet, 1990; Carskadon, Mitler, & Dement, 1974). The real test for diagnosing a sleep deficit is not how many hours you sleep—as we saw, people vary in how much they need—but how you feel during the day. Do you doze off without intending to? Do you feel drowsy in class or at meetings?
- **Get a correct diagnosis of the sleep problem.** Do you suffer from sleep apnea (see p. 160)? Do you have a physical disorder that is interfering with sleep? Do you live in a noisy place? (Try earplugs!) Are you fighting your personal biological rhythms by going to bed too early or too late? Do you go to bed early one night and late another? It's better to go to bed at about the same time every night and get up at the same time every morning.
- **Avoid excessive use of alcohol or other drugs.** Many drugs interfere with sleep. For instance, coffee, tea, cola, energy drinks, and chocolate all contain caffeine, which is a stimulant; alcohol suppresses REM sleep; and some tranquilizers reduce Stage 4 sleep.
- **Use relaxation techniques.** For example, listening to soft music at bedtime, which slows down your heartbeat and breathing, can help older people sleep better and longer (Lai & Good, 2005), and it may help younger people as well.
- **Avoid lying awake for hours waiting for sleep.** Your frustration will cause arousal that will keep you awake. If you can't sleep, get up and do something else, preferably something dull and relaxing, in another room. When you feel drowsy, try sleeping again.

Finally, when insomnia is related to anxiety and worry, it makes sense to get to the source of your problems, and that may mean a brief round of cognitive-behavior therapy (CBT), which teaches you how to change the negative thoughts that are keeping you awake. A placebo-controlled study that compared the effectiveness of a leading sleep pill and a six-week course of CBT found that both approaches helped alleviate chronic insomnia, but CBT worked better both in the short run and the long run (Jacobs at al., 2004). Other research, too, finds that CBT helps people fall asleep sooner and stay asleep longer than pills do (Morin, 2004). (We discuss cognitive-behavior therapy in Chapter 17.)

Woody Allen once said, "The lamb and the lion shall lie down together, but the lamb will not be very sleepy." Like a lamb trying to sleep with a lion, you cannot expect to sleep well with stress hormones pouring through your bloodstream and worries crowding your mind. In an evolutionary sense, sleeplessness is an adaptive response to danger and threat. When your anxieties decrease so may your sleepless nights.

Summary

Biological Rhythms: The Tides of Experience

- *Consciousness* is the awareness of oneself and the environment. Changing states of consciousness are often associated with *biological rhythms*—periodic fluctuations in physiological functioning. These rhythms are typically *entrained* (synchronized) to external cues, but many are also *endogenous*, generated from within even in the absence of time cues. *Circadian* fluctuations occur about once a day; other rhythms occur less frequently or more frequently than that.
- When people live in isolation from all time cues, they tend to live a day that is slightly longer than 24 hours. Circadian rhythms are governed by a biological "clock" in the *suprachiasmatic nucleus (SCN)* of the hypothalamus. The SCN regulates and, in turn, is affected by the hormone *melatonin*, which is responsive to changes in light and dark and which increases during the dark hours. When a person's normal routine changes, the person may experience *internal desynchronization*, in which the usual circadian rhythms are thrown out of phase with one another. The result may be fatigue, mental inefficiency, and an increased risk of accidents.
- Folklore holds that moods follow long-term biological rhythms. Some people do show a recurrence of depression every winter in a pattern that has been labeled *seasonal affective disorder (SAD)*, but serious seasonal depression is rare. The causes of SAD are not yet clear but may involve an abnormality in the secretion of melatonin. Light treatments can be effective.
- Another long-term rhythm is the menstrual cycle, during which various hormones rise and fall. Well-controlled, double-blind studies on "PMS," such as the one described in "Close-up on Research," do not support claims that emotional symptoms are reliably and universally tied to the menstrual cycle. Overall, women and men do not differ in the emotional symptoms they report or in the number of mood swings they experience over the course of a month.
- Expectations and learning affect how both sexes interpret bodily and emotional changes. Few people of either sex are likely to undergo dramatic monthly mood swings or personality changes because of hormones.

The Rhythms of Sleep

- During sleep, periods of *rapid eye movement (REM)* alternate with *non-REM sleep* in approximately a 90-minute rhythm. Non-REM sleep is divided into four stages on the basis of characteristic brain-wave patterns. During REM sleep, the brain is active, and there are other signs of arousal, yet most of the skeletal muscles are limp; vivid dreams are reported most often during REM sleep. Some people have had "waking dreams" when they emerge from REM sleep before the paralysis of that stage has subsided, and occasionally, people have interpreted the resulting hallucinations as real. The purposes of REM are still a matter of controversy.
- Sleep is necessary not only for bodily restoration but also for normal mental functioning. Many people get less than the optimal amount of sleep. Some suffer from insomnia, *sleep apnea*, *narcolepsy*, or *REM behavior disorder.* Researchers are concerned about the growing number of sleep-deprived people in modern societies.
- Sleep may be necessary for the consolidation of memories. Improvements in memory due to sleep have been associated most closely with REM sleep and slow-wave sleep and with memory for specific skills. Sleep also seems to improve insight and problem solving.

Exploring the Dream World

- Dreams are sometimes recalled as illogical and disjointed. Some people say they have *lucid dreams* in which they know they are dreaming. Researchers disagree about whether the eye movements of REM sleep are related to events and actions in dreams.
- The *psychoanalytic theory of dreams* holds that they allow us to gratify forbidden or unrealistic wishes and desires that have been forced into the unconscious part of the mind. In dreams, according to Freud, thoughts and objects are disguised as symbolic images.
- The *problem-solving approach to dreams* holds that they express current concerns. They may even help us solve current problems and work through emotional issues, especially during times of crisis. Findings on the dreams of divorced people support this view.

- The *cognitive approach to dreams* holds that they are simply a modification of the cognitive activity that goes on when we are awake. The difference is that during sleep we are cut off from sensory input from the world and our bodily movements, so our thoughts tend to be more diffuse and unfocused. This explanation is supported by research on the content of dreams and changes in children's dreams as they mature cognitively.
- The *activation–synthesis theory of dreaming* holds that dreams occur when the cortex tries to make sense of, or interpret, spontaneous neural firing initiated in the pons. The resulting synthesis of these signals with existing knowledge and memories results in a dream. In this view, dreams do not disguise unconscious wishes, but they can reveal a person's perceptions, conflicts, and concerns.
- All of the current theories of dreams have some support, and all have weaknesses. Most psychologists today accept the notion that dreams are more than incoherent ramblings of the mind, but many psychologists quarrel with psychoanalytic interpretations. Some psychologists doubt that people can solve problems during sleep. The activation–synthesis theory does not seem to explain coherent, storylike dreams or non-REM dreams. The cognitive approach is now a leading contender, but some of its specific claims remain to be tested.

The Riddle of Hypnosis

- *Hypnosis* is a procedure in which the practitioner suggests changes in a subject's sensations, perceptions, thoughts, feelings, or behavior, and the subject tries to comply. Although hypnosis has been used successfully for many medical and psychological purposes, it does not produce special abilities. Hypnosis can sometimes improve memory for facts about real events, but it also results in confusion between facts and vividly imagined possibilities. Therefore, "hypnotically refreshed" accounts are often full of errors and pseudomemories.
- A leading explanation of hypnosis and its effects is that hypnosis involves *dissociation*, a split in consciousness. In one version of this approach, the split is between a part of consciousness that is hypnotized and a *hidden observer* that watches but does not participate. In another version, the split is between an executive-control system in the brain and other brain systems responsible for thinking and acting. Dissociation theories are consistent with modern models of the brain.
- Another leading approach, the *sociocognitive explanation*, regards hypnosis as a product of normal social and cognitive processes. In this view, hypnosis is a form of role-playing in which the hypnotized person uses active cognitive strategies, including imagination, to comply with the hypnotist's suggestions. The role is so engrossing that the person interprets it as real. Sociocognitive processes can account for the apparent age and past-life "regressions" of people under hypnosis and their reports of alien abductions: These individuals are simply playing a role based on fantasy, imagination, and suggestion.
- As we saw in "Biology and Hypnosis," brain-scan studies are increasing our understanding of what happens in the brain during hypnosis. But it is too soon to draw any conclusions from this research about what hypnosis really is and how it works.

Consciousness-Altering Drugs

- In all cultures, people have found ways to produce *altered states of consciousness*. For example, *psychoactive drugs* alter cognition and emotion by acting on neurotransmitters in the brain. Most psychoactive drugs are classified as *stimulants*, *depressants*, *opiates*, or *psychedelics*, depending on their central nervous system effects and their impact on behavior and mood. However, some common drugs, such as marijuana, straddle or fall outside these categories.
- When used frequently and in large amounts, some psychoactive drugs can damage neurons in the brain and impair learning and memory. Their use may lead to *tolerance*, in which increasing dosages are needed for the same effect, and *withdrawal* symptoms if a person tries to quit. But certain drugs, such as alcohol and marijuana, are also associated with some health benefits when used in moderation. And the effects of Ecstasy are controversial; much of the research has been flawed, and permanent negative effects so far are unproven.
- Reactions to a psychoactive drug are influenced not only by its chemical properties but also by the user's individual characteristics, prior experience with the drug, environmental setting, and *mental set*—the person's expectations and motives for taking the drug. Expectations can be even more powerful than the drug itself, as shown by the *"think–drink" effect.* Expectations and beliefs about drugs are in turn affected by a person's culture.
- People often find it difficult to distinguish drug use from drug abuse, to differentiate between heavy use and light or moderate use, and to separate issues of a drug's legality or illegality from the drug's potential dangers and benefits.

KEY TERMS

consciousness 147
biological rhythm 148
entrainment 148
endogenous 148
circadian rhythm 148
suprachiasmatic nucleus (SCN) 149
melatonin 150
internal desynchronization 150
seasonal affective disorder (SAD) 151
"premenstrual syndrome" ("PMS") 153
rapid eye movement (REM) sleep 157
non-REM (NREM) sleep 157
alpha waves 157
sleep spindles 157
delta waves 158
sleep apnea 160
narcolepsy 160
REM behavior disorder 161
consolidation 161
lucid dream 163
psychoanalytic theory of dreams 163
manifest versus latent content of dreams 164
problem-focused approach to dreams 164
cognitive approach to dreams 164
activation–synthesis theory of dreams 166
hypnosis 168
dissociation 170
hidden observer 170
sociocognitive explanation of hypnosis 171
altered states of consciousness 175
psychoactive drug 175
stimulants 175
depressants 176
opiates 177
psychedelic drugs 177
marijuana 178
tolerance 179
withdrawal 179
"think–drink" effect 181

Who Has Time to Study?

NOW YOU HAVE READ CHAPTER FIVE — ARE YOU PREPARED FOR THE EXAM?

Sleep deprivation can result in all of the following EXCEPT:

a) decline of hormones necessary for a proper immune system.

b) decline in mental flexibility, attention, and creativity.

c) occurrence of hallucinations and delusions.

d) increased muscle pain and lack of coordination.

The Rhythms of Sleep (pages 151-152)

d) Sleep deprivation can cause changes in hormones as well as changes in cognitive functions, but does not cause muscle pain or lack of coordination.

Do you feel sleep deprived? Many students are juggling a heavy school schedule, jobs, friends and family priorities while trying to study and get a good grade. For tools that help you study more effectively and save you time, use your resources on MPL at **www.mypsychlab.com.**

TELL ME **MORE** >>

"MyPsychLab is a great study tool, mainly because it saves so much time."

Student
Montana State University

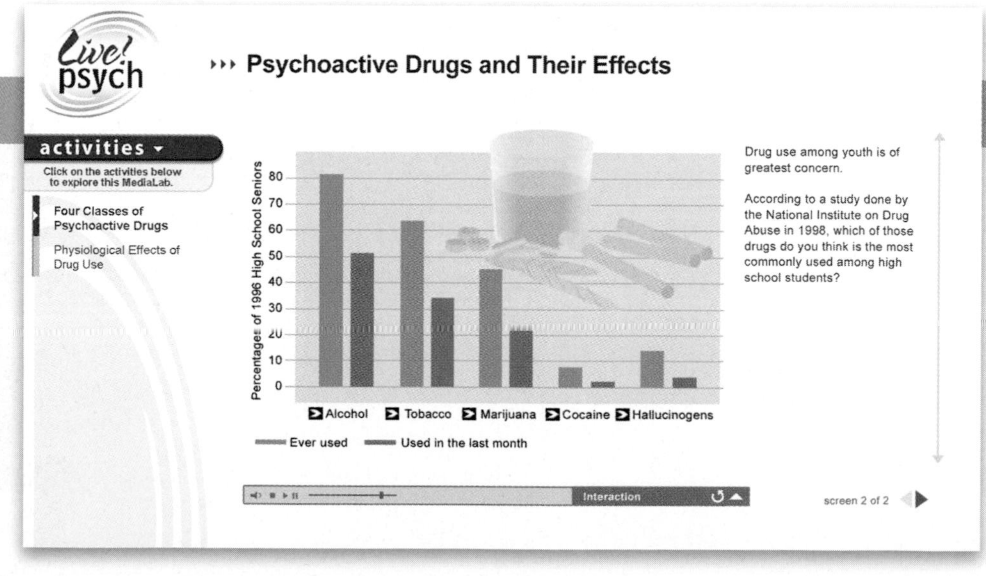

What is the difference between a physical dependence and a psychological dependence on a drug?

One piece of information that students often find confusing in this chapter is the drug types and actions on the nervous system. Fill in the blanks and use the chart to organize the information for yourself.

Drug Category	Examples	Action of Nervous System
Stimulants	Caffeine, cocaine, nicotine and amphetamines	Increase activity, speed up heart rate and breathing, raise blood pressure and suppress appetite: can produce feelings of power, happiness, energy, and increased alertness
?	Barbiturates, alcohol	?
?	?	Reduce pain, activate endorphin receptor sites, cause feelings of wellbeing and is highly addictive
?	LSD, PCP, MDMA, mescaline and marijuana	?

Go to the Consciousness-Altering Drugs section of MPL, take the quiz and try the Apply It exercises to make sure you can fill out this chart correctly and do well on your next exam.

Live! psych

››› **Psychoactive Drugs and Their Effects**

activities

Click on the activities below to explore this MediaLab.

Four Classes of Psychoactive Drugs

Physiological Effects of Drug Use

Neurotransmitter

Synaptic vesicle

Synaptic cleft

Receptor

Physiological effects of drug use

Psychoactive drugs produce their effects by acting on brain neurotransmitters, the substances that carry messages from one nerve cell to another. Drugs can either facilitate or inhibit neural transmission.

Drugs that enhance the activity of a neurotransmitter are called agonists. Drugs can enhance synaptic transmission in six different ways.

Interaction

screen 1 of 4

Step through simulations to get another angle on the material.

TELL ME **MORE** >>

"I wish all classes had a site like MyPsychLab because it just makes everything a lot easier."

Student
Patrick Henry Community College

What can you find in MyPsychLab?

Self-Directed Tests • Videos • Simulations • eBook • Flash Cards • Web Links . . . and more — organized by chapter, section and learning objective.

SENSATION AND PERCEPTION

CHAPTER SIX

Nothing we use or hear or touch can be expressed in words that equal what is given by the senses.

HANNAH ARENDT

What do you think might be going on here?

- A college student in Missouri reports spotting three triangular "UFOs" hovering over the highway during rush hour. Although she never put much stock in UFO stories before, she says she is now intrigued by the possibility that UFOs might be real.
- An image of Jesus on a garage door draws huge crowds of people who regard the likeness with reverence. A similar image makes the news when a woman claims she sees the face of Jesus in, of all places, a tortilla.
- A photograph published shortly after the events of September 11, 2001, is widely circulated on the Internet. It appears to show a sinister face, which some people interpret as Satan's and others as Osama bin Laden's, in smoke billowing from the doomed World Trade Center.

We have all heard reports like these. Some of us scoff at them; others take them seriously. Are UFOs, visions of faces in everyday objects, and other strange sightings reported only by people who are gullible, or do smart, savvy people see them too? If such experiences are illusions, then why are they so frequent and so detailed, and why are those who have them so confident that what they saw was real?

In this chapter, we will try to answer these questions by exploring how our senses take in information from the environment and how our brains use this information to construct a model of the world. We will focus on two closely connected sets of processes that enable us to know what is happening both inside our bodies and in the world beyond our own skins. The first, **sensation**, is the detection of physical energy emitted or reflected by physical objects. The cells that do the detecting are located in the *sense organs*—the eyes, ears, tongue, nose, skin, and internal body tissues. Sensory processes produce an immediate awareness of sound, color, form, and other building blocks of consciousness. Without sensation, we would lose touch—literally—with reality. But to make sense of the world impinging on our senses, we also need **perception**, a set of mental operations that organizes sensory impulses into meaningful patterns. Our sense of vision produces a two-dimensional image on the back of the

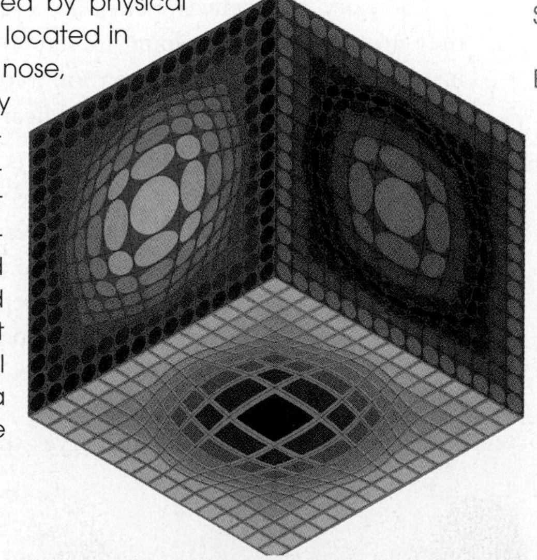

CHAPTER OUTLINE

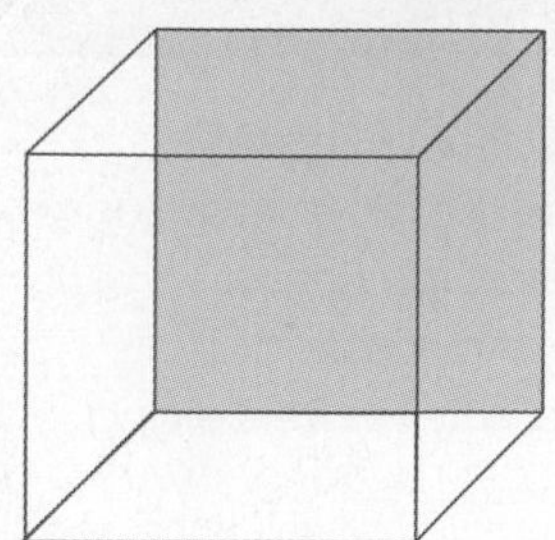

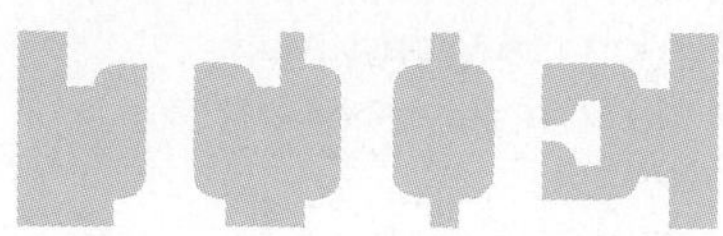

If you stare at the cube, the surface on the outside and front will suddenly be on the inside and back or vice versa, because your brain can interpret the sensory image in two different ways. The other blue-and-white drawing can also be perceived in two ways. Do you see them?

eye, but we *perceive* the world in three dimensions. Our sense of hearing brings us the sound of a C, an E, and a G played simultaneously on the piano, but we *perceive* a C-major chord. Sometimes, a single sensory image produces two alternating perceptions, as illustrated by the examples in the margin.

Sensation and perception are the foundation of learning, thinking, and acting, and findings on these processes can often be put to practical use—for example, in the design of hearing aids and industrial robots and in the training of flight controllers, astronauts, and others who must make crucial decisions based on what they sense and perceive. An understanding of sensation and perception can also help us think more critically about our own experiences, because although these processes are usually accurate, sometimes they are not.

WHAT'S **AHEAD**

- What kind of code in the nervous system helps explain why a pinprick and a kiss feel different?
- Why does your dog hear a "silent" doggie whistle when you can't?
- What bias can influence whether you think you hear the phone ringing when you are in the shower?
- What happens when people are deprived of all external sensory stimulation?
- Why do we sometimes fail to see an object that we're looking straight at?

Our Sensational Senses

At some point you probably learned that there are five senses, corresponding to five sense organs: vision (eyes), hearing (ears), taste (tongue), touch (skin), and smell (nose). Actually, there are more than five senses, though scientists disagree about the exact number. The skin, which is the organ of touch or pressure, also senses heat, cold, and pain, not to mention itching and tickling. The ear, which is the organ of hearing, also contains receptors that account for a sense of balance. The skeletal muscles contain receptors responsible for a sense of bodily movement.

All of our senses evolved to help us survive. Even pain, which causes so much human misery, is an indispensable part of our evolutionary heritage, for it alerts us to illness and injury. People who are born with a rare condition that prevents them from feeling the usual hurts and aches of life are susceptible to burns, bruises, and broken bones, and they often die at an early age because they can't take advantage of pain's warning signals.

Sensory experiences contribute immeasurably to our quality of life, even when they are not directly helping us stay alive. They entertain us, amuse us, soothe us, inspire us. If we really pay attention to our senses, said poet William Wordsworth, we can "see into the life of things" and hear "the still, sad music of humanity."

sensation The detection of physical energy emitted or reflected by physical objects; it occurs when energy in the external environment or the body stimulates receptors in the sense organs.

perception The process by which the brain organizes and interprets sensory information.

sense receptors Specialized cells that convert physical energy in the environment or the body to electrical energy that can be transmitted as nerve impulses to the brain.

The Riddle of Separate Sensations

Sensation begins with the **sense receptors**, cells located in the sense organs. The receptors for smell, pressure, pain, and temperature are extensions (dendrites) of sensory neurons (see Chapter 4). The receptors for vision, hearing, and taste are specialized cells separated from sensory neurons by synapses.

When the sense receptors detect an appropriate stimulus—light, mechanical pressure, or chemical molecules—they convert the energy of the stimulus into electrical impulses that travel along nerves to the brain. Sense receptors are like military

scouts who scan the terrain for signs of activity. These scouts cannot make many decisions on their own. They must transmit what they learn to field officers—sensory neurons in the peripheral nervous system. The field officers in turn must report to generals at a command center—the cells of the brain. The generals are responsible for analyzing the reports, combining information brought in by different scouts, and deciding what it all means.

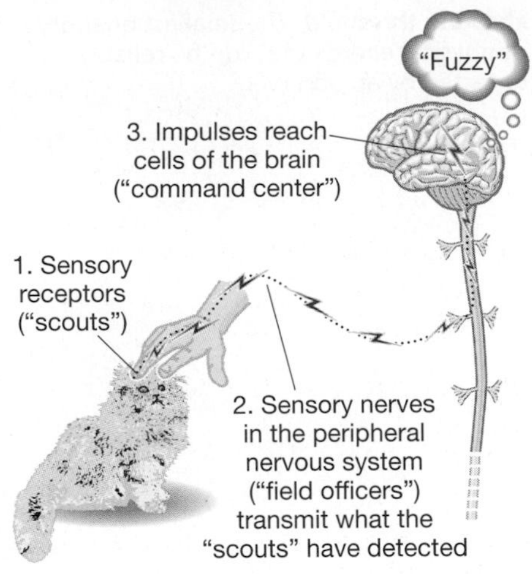
"Fuzzy"
3. Impulses reach cells of the brain ("command center")
1. Sensory receptors ("scouts")
2. Sensory nerves in the peripheral nervous system ("field officers") transmit what the "scouts" have detected

The "field officers" in the sensory system—the sensory nerves—all use exactly the same form of communication, a neural impulse. It is as if they must all send their messages on a bongo drum and can only go "boom." How, then, are we able to experience so many different kinds of sensations? The answer is that the nervous system *encodes* the messages. One kind of code, which is *anatomical*, was first described in 1826 by the German physiologist Johannes Müller in his **doctrine of specific nerve energies**. According to this doctrine, different sensory modalities (such as vision and hearing) exist because signals received by the sense organs stimulate different nerve pathways leading to different areas of the brain. Signals from the eye cause impulses to travel along the optic nerve to the visual cortex. Signals from the ear cause impulses to travel along the auditory nerve to the auditory cortex. Light and sound waves produce different sensations because of these anatomical differences.

The doctrine of specific nerve energies implies that what we know about the world ultimately reduces to what we know about the state of our own nervous system: We see with the brain, not the eyes, and hear with the brain, not the ears. It follows that if sound waves could stimulate nerves that end in the visual part of the brain, we would "see" sound. In fact, a similar sort of crossover does occur if you close your right eye and press lightly on the right side of the lid: You will see a flash of light seemingly coming from the left. The pressure produces an impulse that travels up the optic nerve to the visual area in the right side of the brain, where it is interpreted as coming from the left side of the visual field. By taking advantage of such *sensory substitution*, researchers hope one day to enable blind people to see by teaching them to interpret impulses from other senses that are then routed to the visual areas of the brain. Canadian neuroscientist Maurice Ptito, for example, is studying the effectiveness of a device that translates images from a camera into a pattern of electronic pulses that is sent to electrodes on the tongue, which in turn sends information about the pattern to areas of the brain that process images (Ptito et al., 2005). Using this device, congenitally blind people have learned to make out shapes, and their visual areas, long quiet, have suddenly become active!

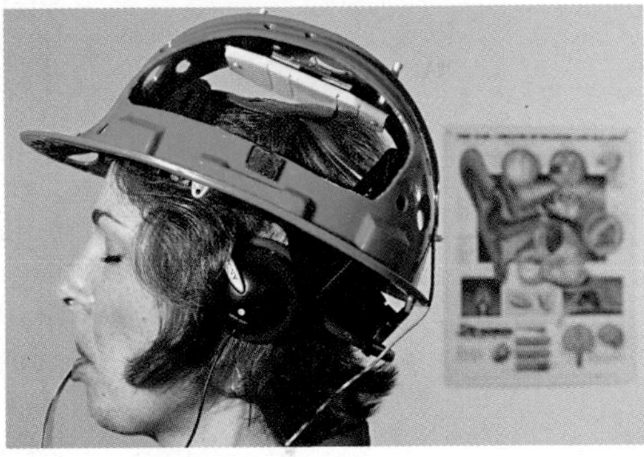
This experimental device, which sends signals from the tongue to visual brain areas, has reportedly enabled blind persons to make out some shapes—sensory substitution applied to a real-life problem.

Sensory crossover also occurs in a rare condition called **synesthesia**, in which the stimulation of one sense also consistently evokes a sensation in another. A person with synesthesia may say that the color purple smells like a rose, the aroma of cinnamon feels like velvet, or the sound of a note on a clarinet tastes like cherries. To a synesthete, these are not mere metaphors; the person actually experiences the second sensation. Novelist Vladimir Nabokov said that the letter *b* made him see burnt sienna and *t* made him see pistachio green; physicist Richard Feynman saw the *n* in an equation as "mildly violet-bluish." People who see digits or letters in different colors (e.g., the number "2" in red) may have trouble naming the color of a digit or letter when it is printed in a competing color (e.g., the number "2" printed in blue) (Smilek et al., 2002). No one knows yet why this fascinating phenomenon occurs, but many theories have been offered (Baron-Cohen & Harrison, 1997; Cytowic, 2002; Martino & Marks, 2001). For example, it could be that synesthetes have an unusual number of neural connections among different sensory areas of the brain.

doctrine of specific nerve energies The principle that different sensory modalities exist because signals received by the sense organs stimulate different nerve pathways leading to different areas of the brain.

synesthesia A condition in which stimulation of one sense also evokes another.

absolute threshold The smallest quantity of physical energy that can be reliably detected by an observer.

Synesthesia, however, is an anomaly; for most of us, the senses remain separate. Anatomical encoding does not completely solve the riddle of why this is so. For one thing, linking the different skin senses to distinct nerve pathways has proved difficult. The doctrine of specific nerve energies also fails to explain variations of experience *within* a particular sense—the sight of pink versus red, the sound of a piccolo versus the sound of a tuba, or the feel of a pinprick versus the feel of a kiss. An additional kind of code is therefore necessary. This second kind of code has been called *functional*.

Functional codes rely on the fact that sensory receptors and neurons fire, or are inhibited from firing, only in the presence of specific sorts of stimuli. At any particular time, then, some cells in the nervous system are firing and some are not. Information about *which* cells are firing, *how many* cells are firing, the *rate* at which cells are firing, and the *patterning* of each cell's firing forms a functional code. You might think of such a code as the neurological equivalent of Morse code but much more complicated. Functional encoding may occur all along a sensory route, starting in the sense organs and ending in the brain.

Measuring the Senses

Just how sensitive are our senses? The answer comes from the field of *psychophysics*, which is concerned with how the physical properties of stimuli are related to our psychological experience of them. Drawing on principles from both physics and psychology, psychophysicists have studied how the strength or intensity of a stimulus affects the strength of sensation in an observer.

Absolute Thresholds. One way to find out how sensitive the senses are is to show people a series of signals that vary in intensity and ask them to say which signals they can detect. The smallest amount of energy that a person can detect reliably is known as the **absolute threshold**. The word *absolute* is a bit misleading because people detect borderline signals on some occasions and miss them on others. Reliable detection is said to occur when a person can detect a signal 50 percent of the time.

If you were having your absolute threshold for brightness measured, you might be asked to sit in a dark room and look at a wall or screen. You would then be shown flashes of light varying in brightness, one flash at a time. Your task would be to say whether you noticed a flash. Some flashes you would never see. Some you would always see. And sometimes you would miss seeing a flash, even though you had noticed one of equal brightness on other trials. Such errors seem to occur in part because of random firing of cells in the nervous system, which produces fluctuating background noise, something like the background noise in a radio transmission.

Different species sense the world differently. The flower on the left was photographed under normal light. The one on the right, photographed under ultraviolet light, is what a butterfly might see, because butterflies have ultraviolet receptors. The hundreds of tiny bright spots are nectar sources.

By studying absolute thresholds, psychologists have found that our senses are very sharp indeed. If you have normal sensory abilities, you can see a candle flame on a clear, dark night from 30 miles away. You can hear a ticking watch in a perfectly quiet room from 20 feet away. You can taste a teaspoon of sugar diluted in two gallons of water, smell a drop of perfume diffused through a three-room apartment, and feel the wing of a bee falling on your cheek from a height of only one centimeter (Galanter, 1962).

difference threshold The smallest difference in stimulation that can be reliably detected by an observer when two stimuli are compared; also called *just noticeable difference* (*jnd*).

Yet despite these impressive sensory skills, our senses are tuned in to only a narrow band of physical energies. For example, we are visually sensitive to only a tiny fraction of the electromagnetic energy that surrounds us; we do not see radio waves, infrared waves, or microwaves (see Figure 6.1). Other species can pick up signals that we cannot. Dogs can detect high-frequency sound waves that are beyond our range, as you know if you have ever called your pooch with a "silent" doggie whistle. Bats and porpoises can hear sounds two octaves beyond our range, and bees can see ultraviolet light, which merely gives human beings a sunburn.

"And only you can hear this whistle?"

Difference Thresholds. Psychologists also study sensory sensitivity by having people compare two stimuli and judge whether they are the same or different. For example, a person might be asked to compare the weight of two blocks, the brightness of two lights, or the saltiness of two liquids. The smallest difference in stimulation that a person can detect reliably (again, half of the time) is called the **difference threshold** or *just noticeable difference* (*jnd*). When you compare two stimuli, A and B, the difference threshold will depend on the intensity or size of A. The larger or more intense A is, the greater the change must be before you can detect a difference. If you are comparing the weights of two pebbles, you might be able to detect a difference of only a fraction of an ounce, but you would not be able to detect such a subtle difference if you were comparing two massive boulders.

Signal-Detection Theory. Despite their usefulness, the procedures we have described have a serious limitation. Measurements for any given individual may be affected by the person's general tendency, when uncertain, to respond, "Yes, I noticed a signal (or a difference)" or "No, I didn't notice anything." Some people are habitual yea-sayers, willing to gamble that the signal was really there. Others are habitual

FIGURE 6.1 The Visible Spectrum of Electromagnetic Energy
Our visual system detects only a small fraction of the electromagnetic energy around us.

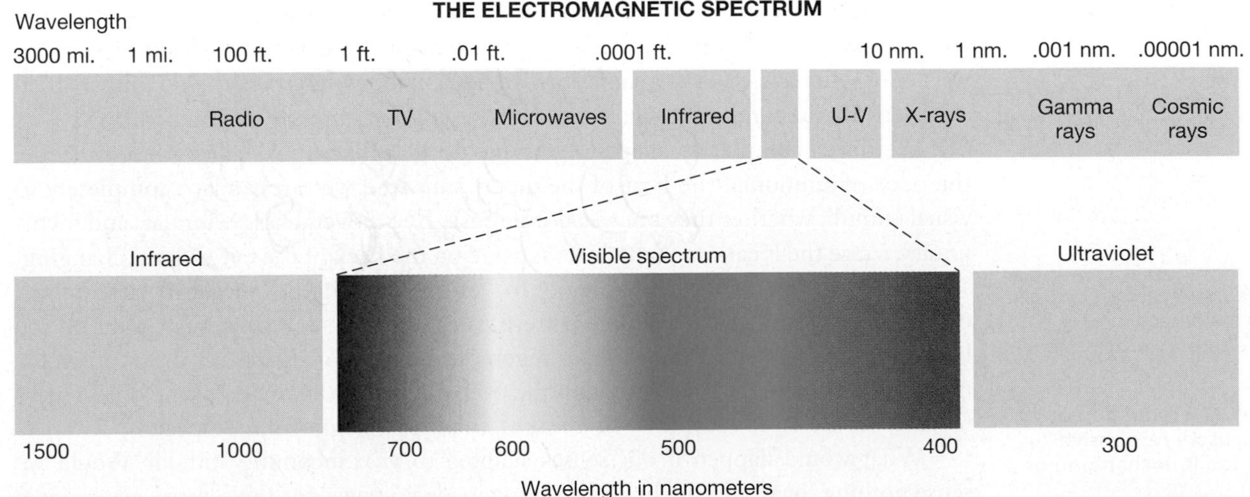

naysayers, cautious and conservative. In addition, alertness, motives, and expectations can influence how a person responds on any given occasion. If you are in the shower and you are expecting an important call, you may think you heard the telephone ring when it did not. In laboratory studies, when observers want to impress the experimenter, they may lean toward a positive response.

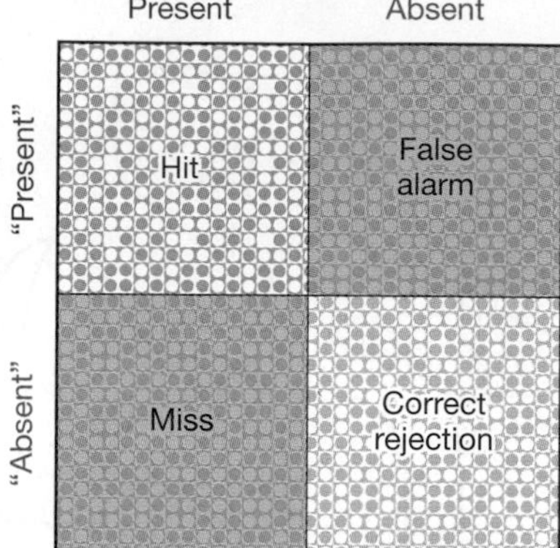

RESPONSES IN SIGNAL DETECTION
Stimulus Is...
Present
Absent
Person's Response
"Present"
"Absent"
Hit
False alarm
Miss
Correct rejection

Fortunately, these problems of *response bias* are not insurmountable. According to **signal-detection theory**, an observer's response in a detection task can be divided into a *sensory process*, which depends on the intensity of the stimulus, and a *decision process*, which is influenced by the observer's response bias. Methods are available for separating these two components. For example, the researcher can include some trials in which no stimulus is present and others in which a weak stimulus is present. Under these conditions, four kinds of responses are possible: The person (1) detects a signal that was present (a "hit"), (2) says the signal was there when it wasn't (a "false alarm"), (3) fails to detect the signal when it was present (a "miss"), or (4) correctly says that the signal was absent when it was absent (a "correct rejection").

Yea-sayers will have more hits than naysayers, but they will also have more false alarms because they are too quick to say, "Yup, it was there." Naysayers will have more correct rejections than yea-sayers, but they will also have more misses because they are too quick to say, "Nope, nothing was there." This information can be fed into a mathematical formula that yields separate estimates of a person's response bias and sensory capacity. The individual's true sensitivity to a signal of any particular intensity can then be predicted.

The old method of measuring thresholds assumed that a person's ability to detect a stimulus depended solely on the stimulus. Signal-detection theory assumes that there is no single threshold because at any given moment a person's sensitivity to a stimulus depends on a decision that he or she actively makes. Signal-detection methods have many real-world applications, from screening applicants for jobs requiring keen hearing to training air-traffic controllers, whose decisions about the presence or absence of a blip on a radar screen may mean the difference between life and death.

Sensory Adaptation

Variety, they say, is the spice of life. It is also the essence of sensation, for our senses are designed to respond to change and contrast in the environment. When a stimulus is unchanging or repetitious, sensation often fades or disappears. Receptors or nerve cells higher up in the sensory system get "tired" and fire less frequently. The resulting decline in sensory responsiveness is called **sensory adaptation**. Such adaptation is usually useful because it spares us from having to respond to unimportant information; for example, most of the time you have no need to feel your watch sitting on your wrist. Sometimes, however, adaptation can be hazardous, as when you no longer smell a gas leak that you thought you noticed when you first entered the kitchen.

We never completely adapt to extremely intense stimuli—a terrible toothache, the odor of ammonia, the heat of the desert sun. And we rarely adapt completely to visual stimuli, whether they are weak or intense. Eye movements, voluntary and involuntary, cause the location of an object's image on the back of the eye to keep changing, so visual receptors do not have a chance to "fatigue." But in the laboratory, researchers can stabilize the image of a simple pattern, such as a line, at a particular point on the back of a person's eye. They use an ingenious device consisting of a tiny projector mounted on a contact lens. Although the eyeball moves, the image of the object stays focused on the same receptors. In minutes, the image begins to disappear.

What would happen if our senses adapted to *most* incoming stimuli? Would we sense nothing, or would the brain substitute its own images for the sensory experiences

signal-detection theory A psychophysical theory that divides the detection of a sensory signal into a sensory process and a decision process.

sensory adaptation The reduction or disappearance of sensory responsiveness when stimulation is unchanging or repetitious.

sensory deprivation The absence of normal levels of sensory stimulation.

GET INVOLVED!

➤NOW YOU SEE IT, NOW YOU DON'T

Sensation depends on change and contrast in the environment. Hold your hand over one eye and stare at the dot in the middle of the circle on the right. You should have no trouble maintaining an image of the circle. However, if you do the same with the circle on the left, the image will fade. The gradual change from light to dark does not provide enough contrast to keep your visual receptors firing at a steady rate. The circle reappears only if you close and reopen your eye or shift your gaze to the *X*.

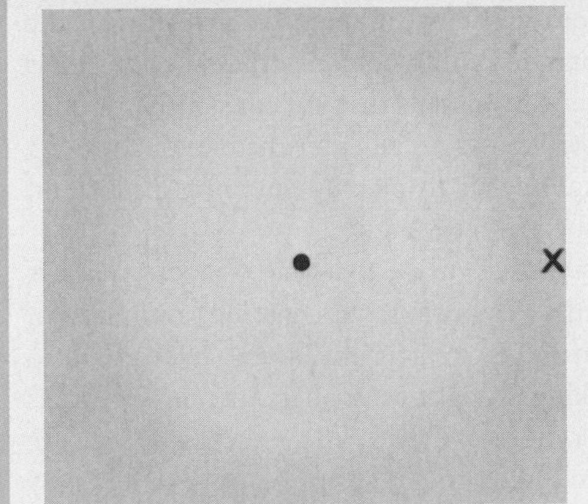

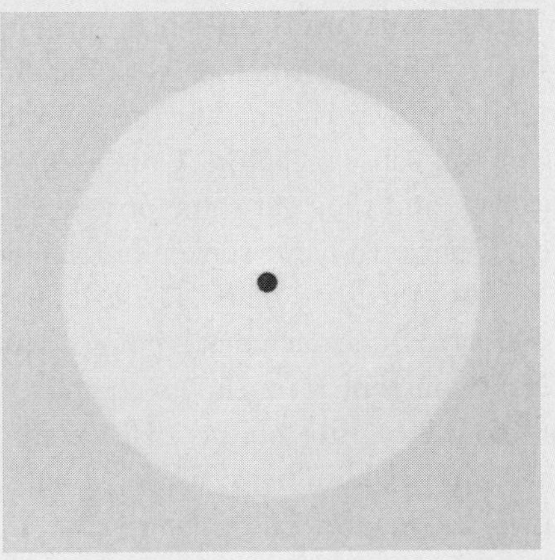

no longer available by way of the sense organs? In early studies of **sensory deprivation**, researchers studied this question by isolating male volunteers from all patterned sight and sound. Vision was restricted by a translucent visor, hearing by a U-shaped pillow and noise from an air conditioner and fan, and touch by cotton gloves and cardboard cuffs. The volunteers took brief breaks to eat and use the bathroom, but otherwise they lay in bed, doing nothing. The results were dramatic. Within a few hours, many of the men felt edgy. Some were so disoriented that they quit the study the first day. Those who stayed longer became confused, restless, and grouchy. Many reported bizarre visions, such as a squadron of squirrels or a procession of marching eyeglasses. It was as though they were having the kind of "waking dreams" described in Chapter 5. Few people were willing to remain in the study for more than two or three days (Heron, 1957).

But the notion that sensory deprivation is unpleasant or even dangerous turned out to be an oversimplification (Suedfeld, 1975). Later research, using better methods, showed that hallucinations are less frequent and less disorienting than had first been thought. Many people enjoy limited periods of deprivation, and some perceptual and intellectual abilities actually improve. Your response to sensory deprivation depends on your expectations and interpretations of what is happening. Reduced sensation can be scary if you are locked in a room for an indefinite period, but relaxing if you have retreated to that room voluntarily for a little time-out—at, say, a luxury spa or a monastery.

Still, it is clear that the human brain requires a minimum amount of sensory stimulation in order to function normally. This need may help explain why people who live alone often keep the radio or television set running continuously and why prolonged solitary confinement is used as a form of punishment or even torture.

DON'T OVERSIMPLIFY

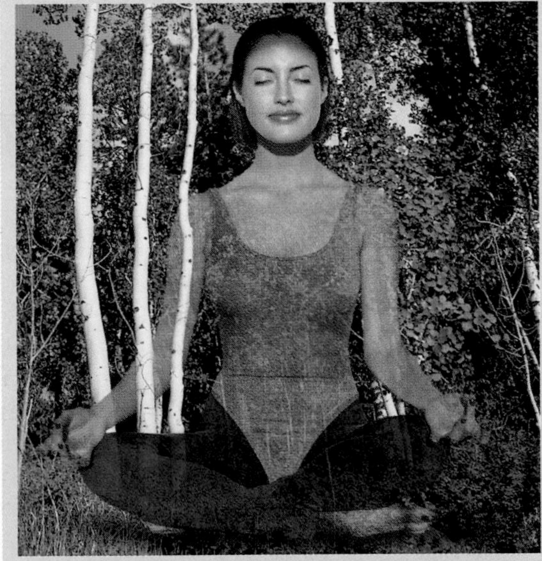

Is sensory deprivation pleasant or unpleasant? The answer isn't "either–or"; it depends on the circumstances and how you interpret your situation. Being isolated against your will can be terrifying, but many people have found meditating alone, away from all sights and sounds, to be calming and pleasant.

selective attention The focusing of attention on selected aspects of the environment and the blocking out of others.

inattentional blindness Failure to consciously perceive something you are looking at because you are not attending to it.

In his films, famed director Alfred Hitchcock always appeared briefly in one of the scenes, but few noticed him even when they were aware he would appear—an instance of inattentional blindness.

Sensing Without Perceiving

If too little stimulation can be bad for you, so can too much, because it can lead to fatigue and mental confusion. If you have ever felt exhausted, nervous, and headachy after a day crammed with activities, you know firsthand about sensory overload. When people find themselves in a state of overload, they often cope by blocking out unimportant sights and sounds and focusing only on those they find interesting or useful. Psychologists have called this the "cocktail party phenomenon" because at a noisy cocktail party a person typically focuses on just one conversation, ignoring other voices, the clink of ice cubes, and bursts of laughter across the room.

Even when overload is not a problem, our capacity for **selective attention**—the ability to focus on some parts of the environment and block out others—protects us from being overwhelmed by the countless sensory signals that are constantly impinging on our sense receptors. Competing sensory messages all enter the nervous system, however, and they get some processing, enabling us to pick up anything important, such as our own name spoken by someone several yards away.

That's the good news. The bad news is that selective attention, by its very nature, causes us to miss much that is going on around us; as a result, our conscious awareness of the environment is much less complete than most people think. We may even fail to consciously register objects that we are looking straight at, a phenomenon known as **inattentional blindness**: We look, but we do not see (Mack, 2003). When people are shown a video of a ball-passing game and are asked to count up the passes, they may even miss something as seemingly obvious as a man in a gorilla suit walking slowly through the ball court and thumping his chest (Simons & Chabris, 1999).

Selective attention, then, is a mixed blessing. It protects us from overload and allows us to focus on what's important, but it also deprives us of sensory information that we may need. That could be disastrous if you are so focused on listening to a voice on your cell phone while you are driving that you fail to see a pedestrian crossing the street in front of you.

QUICK quiz

If you are not on overload, try answering these questions.

1. Even on the clearest night, some stars cannot be seen by the naked eye because they are below the viewer's __________ threshold.
2. If you jump into a cold lake but moments later the water no longer seems so cold, sensory __________ has occurred.
3. If you are immobilized in a hospital bed, with no roommate and no TV or radio, and you feel edgy and disoriented, you may be suffering the effects of __________.
4. During a break from your job in a restaurant, you are so engrossed in a book that you fail to notice the clattering of dishes or orders being called out to the cook. This is an example of __________.
5. In real-life detection tasks, is it better to be a "naysayer" or a "yea-sayer"?

Answers:

1. absolute **2.** adaptation **3.** sensory deprivation **4.** selective attention **5.** Neither; it depends on the consequences of a "miss" or a "false alarm" and the probability of an event occurring. You might want to be a yea-sayer if you are just out the door, you think you hear the phone ringing, and you are expecting a call about a job interview. You might want to be a naysayer if you are just out the door, you think you hear the phone ringing, and you are on your way to a job interview and don't want to be late.

WHAT'S AHEAD

- How does the eye differ from a camera?
- Why can we describe a color as bluish green but not as reddish green?
- If you were blind in one eye, why might you misjudge your distance from a painting on the wall but not the distance to buildings a block away?
- As a friend approaches, her image on your retina grows larger; why do you continue to see her as the same size?
- Why are perceptual illusions valuable to psychologists?

Vision

Vision is the most frequently studied of all the senses, and with good reason. More information about the external world comes to us through our eyes than through any other sense organ. (Perhaps that is why people say "I see what you mean" instead of "I hear what you mean.") Because we evolved to be most active in the daytime, we are equipped to take advantage of the sun's illumination. Animals that are active at night tend to rely more heavily on hearing.

hue The dimension of visual experience specified by color names and related to the wavelength of light.

brightness Lightness or luminance; the dimension of visual experience related to the amount (intensity) of light emitted from or reflected by an object.

saturation Vividness or purity of color; the dimension of visual experience related to the complexity of light waves.

What We See

The stimulus for vision is light; even cats, raccoons, and other creatures famous for their ability to get around in the dark need some light to see. Visible light comes from the sun and other stars and from light bulbs, and it is also reflected off objects. Light travels in the form of waves, and the *physical* characteristics of these waves affect three *psychological* dimensions of our visual world: hue, brightness, and saturation.

1 **Hue**, the dimension of visual experience specified by color names, is related to the *wavelength* of light—that is, to the distance between the crests of a light wave. Shorter waves tend to be seen as violet and blue, longer ones as orange and red. (We say "tend to" because other factors also affect color perception, as we will see later.) The sun produces white light, a mixture of all the visible wavelengths. Sometimes, drops of moisture in the air act like a prism: They separate the sun's white light into the colors of the visible spectrum, and we are treated to a rainbow.

2 **Brightness** is the dimension of visual experience related to the amount, or *intensity*, of the light an object emits or reflects. Intensity corresponds to the amplitude (maximum height) of the wave. Generally speaking, the more light an object reflects, the brighter it appears. However, brightness is also affected by wavelength: Yellows appear brighter than reds and blues when physical intensities are actually equal.

3 **Saturation** (colorfulness) is the dimension of visual experience related to the *complexity* of light—that is, to how wide or narrow the range of wavelengths is. When light contains only a single wavelength, it is said to be pure, and the resulting color is said to be completely saturated. At the other extreme is white light, which lacks any color and is completely unsaturated. In nature, pure light is extremely rare. Usually, we sense a mixture of wavelengths, and we see colors that are duller and paler than completely saturated ones.

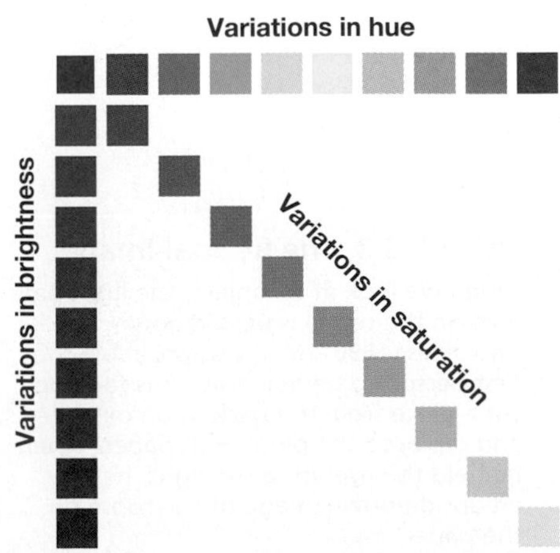

retina Neural tissue lining the back of the eyeball's interior, which contains the receptors for vision.

rods Visual receptors that respond to dim light.

cones Visual receptors involved in color vision.

An Eye on the World

Light enters the visual system through the eye, a wonderfully complex and delicate structure. As you read this section, examine Figure 6.2. Notice that the front part of the eye is covered by the transparent *cornea*. The cornea protects the eye and bends incoming light rays toward a *lens* located behind it. A camera lens focuses incoming light by moving closer to or farther from the shutter opening. However, the lens of the eye works by subtly changing its shape, becoming more or less curved to focus light from objects that are close by or far away. The amount of light that gets into the eye is controlled by muscles in the *iris*, the part of the eye that gives it color. The iris surrounds the round opening, or *pupil*, of the eye. When you enter a dim room, the pupil widens, or dilates, to let more light in. When you emerge into bright sunlight, the pupil gets smaller, contracting to allow in less light. You can see these changes by watching your eyes in a mirror as you change the lighting.

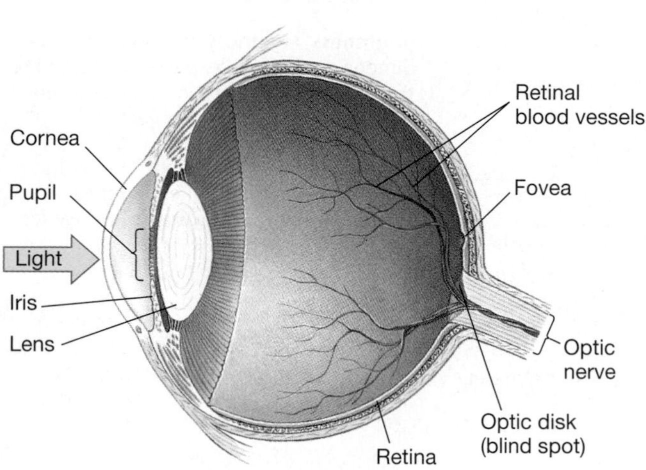

FIGURE 6.2 Major Structures of the Eye

Light passes through the pupil and lens and is focused on the retina at the back of the eye. The point of sharpest vision is at the fovea.

The visual receptors are located in the back of the eye, or **retina**. (The retina also contains special cells that communicate information about light and dark to the brain area that regulates biological rhythms, as discussed in Chapter 5.) In a developing embryo, the retina forms from tissue that projects out from the brain, not from tissue destined to form other parts of the eye; thus, the retina is actually an extension of the brain. As Figure 6.3 shows, when the lens of the eye focuses light on the retina, the result is an upside-down image (which can actually be seen with an instrument used by eye specialists). Light from the top of the visual field stimulates light-sensitive receptor cells in the bottom part of the retina, and vice versa. The brain interprets this upside-down pattern of stimulation as something that is right side up.

About 120 to 125 million receptors in the retina are long and narrow and are called **rods**. Another 7 or 8 million receptors are cone shaped and are called, appropriately enough, **cones**. The center of the retina, or *fovea*, where vision is sharpest, contains only cones, clustered densely together. From the center to the periphery, the ratio of rods to cones increases, and the outer edges contain virtually no cones.

Rods are more sensitive to light than cones are. They enable us to see in dim light and at night. (Cats see well in dim light in part because they have a high proportion of rods.) Because rods occupy the outer edges of the retina, they also handle peripheral (side) vision. But rods cannot distinguish different wavelengths of light so they are not sensitive to color, which is why it is often hard to distinguish colors clearly in dim

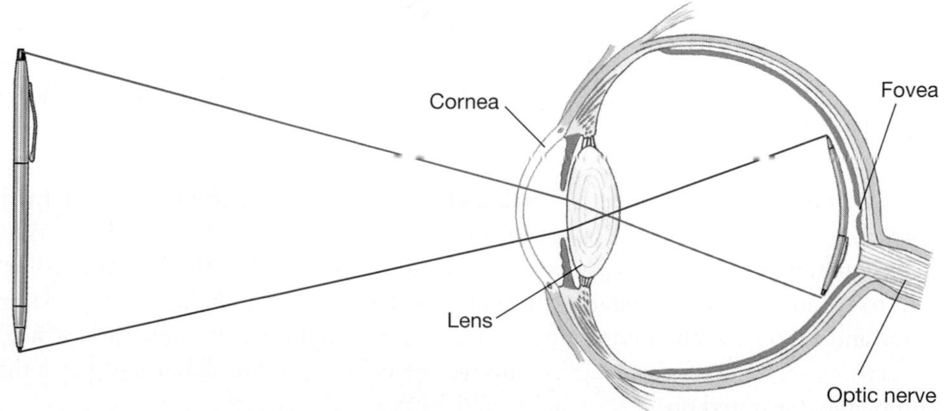

FIGURE 6.3 The Retinal Image

When we look at an object, the light pattern on the retina is upside down. René Descartes (1596–1650) was probably the first person to demonstrate this fact. He cut a piece from the back of an ox's eye and replaced the piece with paper. When he held the eye up to the light, he saw an upside-down image of the room on the paper!

REVIEW 6.1
Differences Between Rods and Cones

	Rods	Cones
How many?	120–125 million	7–8 million
Where most concentrated?	Periphery of retina	Center (fovea) of retina
How sensitive?	High sensitivity	Low sensitivity
Sensitive to color?	No	Yes

light. The cones, on the other hand, are differentially sensitive to specific wavelengths of light and allow us to see colors. But they need much more light than rods do to respond, so they don't help us much when we are trying to find a seat in a darkened movie theater. (These differences are summarized in Review 6.1.)

We have all noticed that it takes some time for our eyes to adjust fully to dim illumination. This process of **dark adaptation** involves chemical changes in the rods and cones. The cones adapt quickly, within 10 minutes or so, but they never become very sensitive to the dim illumination. The rods adapt more slowly, taking 20 minutes or longer, but are ultimately much more sensitive. After the first phase of adaptation, you can see better but not well; after the second phase, your vision is as good as it ever will get.

Rods and cones are connected by synapses to *bipolar cells*, which in turn communicate with neurons called **ganglion cells** (see Figure 6.4). The axons of the ganglion cells converge to form the *optic nerve*, which carries information out through the back of the eye and on to the brain. Where the optic nerve leaves the eye, at the *optic disk*, there are no rods or cones. The absence of receptors produces a blind spot in the field of vision. Normally, we are unaware of the blind spot because (1) the image projected

dark adaptation A process by which visual receptors become maximally sensitive to dim light.

ganglion cells Neurons in the retina of the eye, which gather information from receptor cells (by way of intermediate bipolar cells); their axons make up the optic nerve.

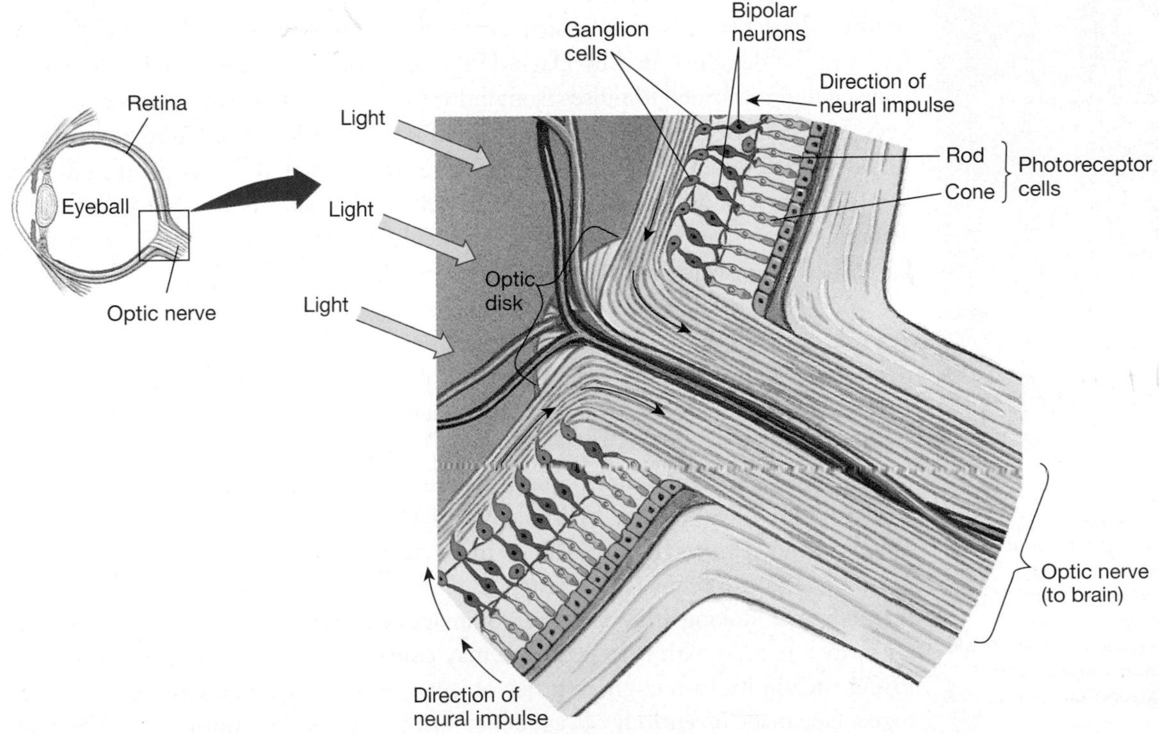

FIGURE 6.4 The Structures of the Retina
For clarity, all cells in this drawing are greatly exaggerated in size. In order to reach the receptors for vision (the rods and cones), light must pass through the ganglion and bipolar cells as well as the blood vessels that nourish them (not shown). Normally, we do not see the shadow cast by this network of cells and blood vessels because the shadow always falls on the same place on the retina, and such stabilized images are not sensed. But when an eye doctor shines a moving light into your eye, the treelike shadow of the blood vessels falls on different regions of the retina and you may see it—a rather eerie experience.

GET INVOLVED!

➤FIND YOUR BLIND SPOT

A blind spot exists where the optic nerve leaves the back of your eye. Find the blind spot in your left eye by closing your right eye and looking at the magician. Then slowly move the book toward and away from yourself. The rabbit should disappear when the book is between 9 and 12 inches from your eye.

feature detectors Cells in the visual cortex that are sensitive to specific features of the environment.

on the spot is hitting a different, "nonblind" spot in the other eye; (2) our eyes move so fast that we can pick up the complete image; and (3) the brain fills in the gap. You can find your blind spot by doing the Get Involved exercise on this page.

Cases of brain damage support the idea that particular systems of brain cells are highly specialized. One man's injury left him unable to identify ordinary objects, which, he said, often looked like "blobs." Yet he had no trouble with faces, even when they were upside down or incomplete. When shown this painting, he could easily see the face, but he could not see the vegetables comprising it (Moscovitch, Winocur, & Behrmann, 1997).

Why the Visual System Is Not a Camera

Although the eye is often compared with a camera, the visual system, unlike a camera, is not a passive recorder of the external world. Neurons in the visual system actively build up a picture of the world by detecting its meaningful features.

Ganglion cells and neurons in the thalamus of the brain respond to simple features in the environment, such as spots of light and dark. But in mammals, special **feature-detector** cells in the visual cortex respond to more complex features. This fact was first demonstrated by David Hubel and Torsten Wiesel (1962, 1968), who painstakingly recorded impulses from individual cells in the brains of cats and monkeys. In 1981, they were awarded a Nobel Prize for their work. Hubel and Wiesel found that different neurons were sensitive to different patterns projected on a screen in front of an animal's eyes. Most cells responded maximally to moving or stationary lines that were oriented in a particular direction and located in a particular part of the visual field. One type of cell might fire most rapidly in response to a horizontal line in the lower right part of the visual field, another to a diagonal line at a specific angle in the upper left part of the visual field. In the real world, such features make up the boundaries and edges of objects.

Since this pioneering work was done, scientists have found that other cells in the visual system have more complex specialties, such as bull's eyes and spirals. Some cells in the right temporal lobe even appear to respond maximally to *faces* (Kanwisher, 2000; Ó Scalaidhe, Wilson, & Goldman-Rakic, 1997; Young & Yamane, 1992). Some scientists have concluded that evolution has equipped us with an innate *face module* in the brain. The existence of such a module could help explain why infants prefer looking at faces instead of images that scramble the features of a face, and why a person with brain damage may continue to recognize faces even after losing the ability to recognize other objects. In one case, a patient could recognize a face made up entirely of vegetables, like the one in the painting in the margin,

but he could not recognize the vegetables (Moscovitch, Winocur, & Behrmann, 1997).

A facility for deciphering faces makes evolutionary sense because it would have ensured our ancestors' ability to quickly distinguish friend from foe or, in the case of infants, mothers from strangers. However, the existence of face modules remains controversial among neuroscientists. Some think that infants' apparent preference for faces is really a preference for curved lines, or eye contact, or patterns that have more elements in the upper part (e.g., two eyes) than in the lower part (e.g., just a mouth) (Turati, 2004). Moreover, some of the brain cells that supposedly make up the face module respond to other things, too, depending on a person's experiences and interests. In one fascinating study, cells in the presumed face module fired when car buffs examined pictures of classic cars but not when they looked at pictures of exotic birds, whereas the exact opposite was true for birdwatchers (Gauthier et al., 2000). Cars, of course, do not have faces! In another study by the same researchers, cells in the "face module" fired after people were trained to distinguish among cute—but faceless—imaginary creatures called greebles (Gauthier et al., 1999) (see Figure 6.5).

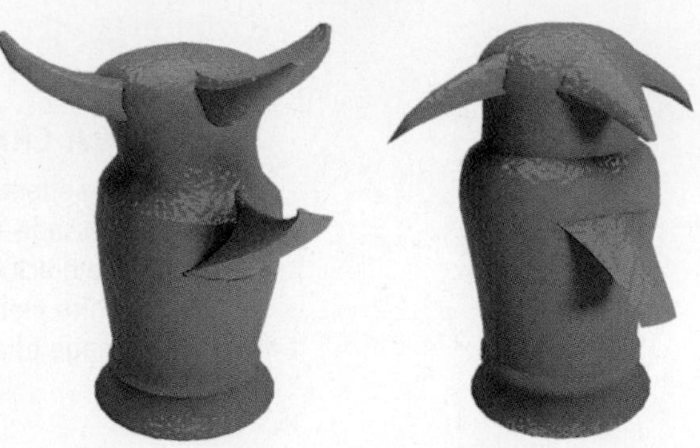

FIGURE 6.5 Greebles

Researchers trained people to identify the "family" and "sex" of these hypothetical creatures according to subtle differences in their features. During the task, presumed face modules in the participants' brains were active—yet greebles have no faces (Gauthier et al., 1999).

Even if face and other specialized modules do exist, the brain cannot possibly contain a special area for every conceivable object. In general, the brain's job is to take fragmentary information about edges, angles, shapes, motion, brightness, texture, and patterns and figure out that a chair is a chair and that it is next to the dining room table. The perception of any given object probably depends on the activation of many cells in far-flung parts of the brain and on the overall pattern and rhythm of their activity (Bower, 1998).

How We See Colors

For 300 years, scientists have been trying to figure out why we see the world in living color. We now know that different processes explain different stages of color vision.

The Trichromatic Theory. The **trichromatic theory** (also known as the *Young-Helmholtz theory*) applies to the first level of processing, which occurs in the retina of the eye. The retina contains three basic types of cones. One type responds maximally to blue, another to green, and a third to red. The thousands of colors we see result from the combined activity of these three types of cones.

Total color blindness is usually due to a genetic variation that causes cones of the retina to be absent or malfunctional. The visual world then consists of black, white, and shades of gray. Many species of animals are totally color-blind, but the condition is extremely rare in human beings. Most "color-blind" people are actually *color deficient*. Usually, the person is unable to distinguish red and green; the world is painted in shades of blue, yellow, brown, and gray. In rarer instances, a person may be blind to blue and yellow and may see only reds, greens, and grays. Color deficiency is found in about 8 percent of white men, 5 percent of Asian men, and 3 percent of black men and Native American men (Sekuler & Blake, 1994). Because of the way the condition is inherited, it is rare in women.

trichromatic theory A theory of color perception that proposes three mechanisms in the visual system, each sensitive to a certain range of wavelengths; their interaction is assumed to produce all the different experiences of hue.

The Opponent-Process Theory. The **opponent-process theory** applies to the second stage of color processing, which occurs in ganglion cells in the retina and in neurons in the thalamus and visual cortex of the brain. These cells, known as *opponent-process cells*, either respond to short wavelengths but are inhibited from firing by long wavelengths, or vice versa (DeValois & DeValois, 1975). Some opponent-process cells respond in opposite fashion to red and green; that is, they fire in response to one and turn off in response to the

opponent-process theory A theory of color perception that assumes that the visual system treats pairs of colors as opposing or antagonistic.

GET INVOLVED!

➤A CHANGE OF HEART

Opponent-process cells that switch on or off in response to green send an opposite message—"red"—when the green is removed, producing a negative afterimage. Stare at the black dot in the middle of this heart for at least 20 seconds. Then shift your gaze to a white piece of paper or a white wall. Do you get a "change of heart"? You may see an image of a red or pinkish heart with a blue border.

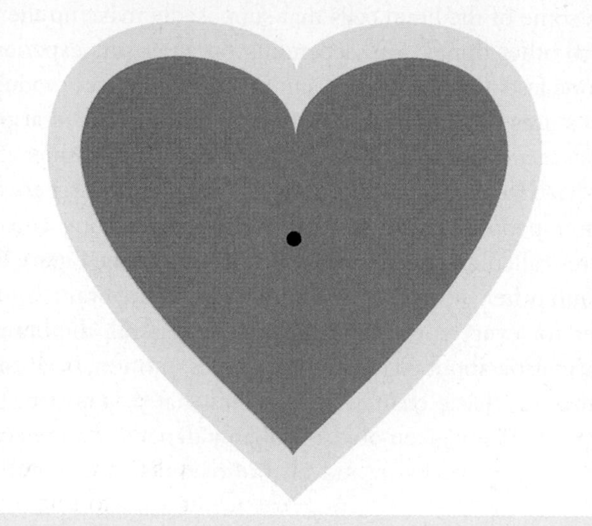

other. Others respond in opposite fashion to blue and yellow. (A third system responds in opposite fashion to white and black and thus yields information about brightness.) The net result is a color code that is passed along to the higher visual centers. Because this code treats red and green, and also blue and yellow, as antagonistic, we can describe a color as bluish green or yellowish green but not as reddish green or yellowish blue.

Opponent-process cells that are *inhibited* by a particular color produce a burst of firing when the color is removed, just as they would if the opposing color were present. Similarly, cells that *fire* in response to a color stop firing when the color is removed, just as they would if the opposing color were present. These facts explain why we are susceptible to *negative afterimages* when we stare at a particular hue—why we see, for instance, red after staring at green (see the Get Involved exercise above). A sort of neural rebound effect occurs: The cells that switch on or off to signal the presence of "green" send the opposite signal ("red") when the green is removed and vice versa.

Constructing the Visual World

We do not see a retinal image; that image is merely grist for the mill of the mind, which actively interprets the image and constructs the world from the often fragmentary data of the senses. In the brain, sensory signals that give rise to vision, hearing, taste, smell, and touch are combined from moment to moment to produce a unified model of the world. This is the process of *perception*.

Form Perception. To make sense of the world, we must know where one thing ends and another begins. In vision, we must separate the teacher from the lectern; in hearing, we must separate the piano solo from the orchestral accompaniment; in taste, we

must separate the marshmallow from the hot chocolate. This process of dividing up the world occurs so rapidly and effortlessly that we take it completely for granted, until we must make out objects in a heavy fog or words in the rapid-fire conversation of someone speaking a foreign language.

Gestalt principles Principles that describe the brain's organization of sensory information into meaningful units and patterns.

The *Gestalt psychologists*, who belonged to a movement that began in Germany and was influential in the 1920s and 1930s, were among the first to study how people organize the world visually into meaningful units and patterns. In German, *Gestalt* means "form" or "configuration." The Gestalt psychologists' motto was "The whole is more than the sum of its parts." They observed that when we perceive something, properties emerge from the configuration as a whole that are not found in any particular component. When you watch a movie, for example, the motion you see is nowhere in the film, which consists of separate static frames projected at 24 frames per second.

One thing the Gestalt psychologists noted was that people always organize the visual field into *figure* and *ground*. The figure stands out from the rest of the environment (see Figure 6.6). Some things stand out as figure by virtue of their intensity or size; it is hard to ignore the blinding flash of a camera or a tidal wave approaching your piece of beach. The lower part of a scene tends to be seen as figure, the upper part as background (Vecera, Vogel, & Woodman, 2002). Unique objects also stand out, such as a banana in a bowl of oranges. Moving objects in an otherwise still environment, such as a shooting star, will usually be seen as figure. Indeed, it is hard to ignore a sudden change of any kind in the environment because our brains are geared to respond to change and contrast. However, selective attention—the ability to concentrate on some stimuli and to filter out others—gives us some control over what we perceive as figure and ground, and sometimes it blinds us to things we would otherwise interpret as figure, as we saw earlier.

Other **Gestalt principles** describe strategies used by the visual system to group sensory building blocks into perceptual units (Kohler, 1929; Wertheimer, 1923/1958). The Gestalt psychologists believed that these strategies were present from birth or

FIGURE 6.6 Figure and Ground

Which do you notice first in this drawing by M. C. Escher—the fish, geese, or salamanders? It will depend on whether you see the blue, red, or gold sections as figure or ground.

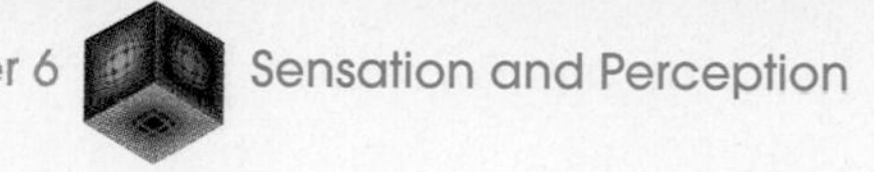

developed automatically early in infancy as a result of maturation. Modern research, however, suggests that at least some of them depend on experience (Quinn & Bhatt, 2005). Here are a few well-known Gestalt principles:

1 **Proximity.** Things that are near each other tend to be grouped together. Thus you perceive the dots on the left as three groups of dots, not as twelve separate, unrelated ones. Similarly, you perceive the pattern on the right as vertical columns of dots, not as horizontal rows:

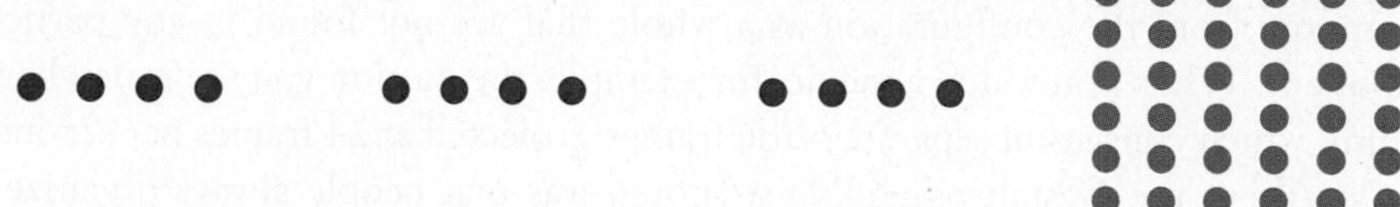

2 **Closure.** The brain tends to fill in gaps in order to perceive complete forms. This is fortunate because we often need to decipher less-than-perfect images. The following figures are easily perceived as a triangle, a face, and the letter *e*, even though none of the figures is complete:

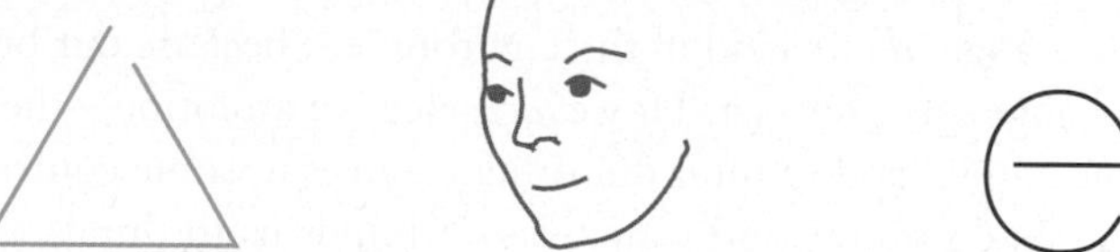

3 **Similarity.** Things that are alike in some way (for example, in color, shape, or size) tend to be perceived as belonging together. In the figure on the left, you see the circles as forming an *X*. In the one on the right, you see horizontal bars rather than vertical columns because the horizontally aligned stars are either all red or all outlined in red:

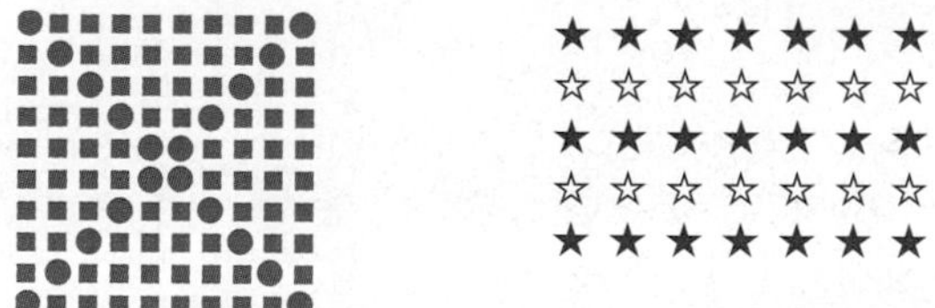

4 **Continuity.** Lines and patterns tend to be perceived as continuing in time or space. You perceive the figure on the left as a single line partially covered by an oval rather than as two separate lines touching an oval. In the figure on the right, you see two lines, one curved and one straight, instead of two curved and two straight lines, touching at one focal point:

Since the Gestalt principles were discovered, researchers have identified other cues that help us identify which parts of what we see form objects or scenes. But consumer products are sometimes designed with little thought for these cues, which is why it can be a major challenge to find the pause button on your DVD player's remote control or change from AM to FM on your car radio (Bjork, 2000; Norman, 1988). Good design requires, among other things, that crucial distinctions be visually obvi-

ous. For instance, knobs and switches with different functions should differ in color, texture, or shape, and they should stand out as figure. How would you use this information to redesign some of the products that you use?

Depth and Distance Perception. Ordinarily we need to know not only what something is but also where it is. Touch gives us this information directly, but vision does not, so we must infer an object's location by estimating its distance or depth.

To perform this remarkable feat, we rely in part on **binocular cues**—cues that require the use of two eyes. One such cue is **convergence**, the turning of the eyes inward, which occurs when they focus on a nearby object. The closer the object, the greater the convergence, as you know if you have ever tried to cross your eyes by looking at your own nose. As the angle of convergence changes, the corresponding muscular changes provide information to the brain about distance.

The two eyes also receive slightly different retinal images of the same object. You can prove this by holding a finger about 12 inches in front of your face and looking at it with only one eye at a time. Its position will appear to shift when you change eyes. Now hold up two fingers, one closer to your nose than the other. Notice that the amount of space between the two fingers appears to change when you switch eyes. The slight difference in lateral (sideways) separation between two objects as seen by the left eye and the right eye is called **retinal disparity**. Because retinal disparity increases as the distance between two objects increases, the brain can use it to infer depth and calculate distance.

Binocular cues help us estimate distances up to about 50 feet. For objects farther away, we use only **monocular cues**, cues that do not depend on using both eyes. One such cue is *interposition*: When an object is interposed between the viewer and a second object, partly blocking the view of the second object, the first object is perceived as being closer. Another monocular cue is *linear perspective*: When two lines known to be parallel appear to be coming together or converging, they imply the existence of depth. For example, if you are standing between railroad tracks, they appear to converge in the distance. These and other monocular cues are illustrated on the next pages.

Visual Constancies: When Seeing Is Believing. Your perceptual world would be a confusing place without still another important perceptual skill. Lighting conditions, viewing angles, and the distances of stationary objects are all continually changing as we move about, yet we rarely confuse these changes with changes in the objects themselves. This ability to perceive objects as stable or unchanging even though the sensory patterns they produce are constantly shifting is called **perceptual constancy**. The best-studied constancies are visual, and they include the following:

1 **Shape constancy.** We continue to perceive an object as having a constant shape even though the shape of the retinal image produced by the object changes when our point of view changes. If you hold a Frisbee directly in front of your face, its image on the retina will be round. When you set the Frisbee on a table, its image becomes elliptical, yet you continue to identify the Frisbee as round.

2 **Location constancy.** We perceive stationary objects as remaining in the same place even though the retinal image moves about as we move our eyes, heads, and bodies. As you drive along the highway, telephone poles and trees fly by—on your retina. But you know that these objects do not move on their own, and you also know that your body is moving, so you perceive the poles and trees as staying put.

binocular cues Visual cues to depth or distance requiring two eyes.

convergence The turning inward of the eyes, which occurs when they focus on a nearby object.

retinal disparity The slight difference in lateral separation between two objects as seen by the left eye and the right eye.

monocular cues Visual cues to depth or distance, which can be used by one eye alone.

perceptual constancy The accurate perception of objects as stable or unchanged despite changes in the sensory patterns they produce.

Size constancy in action.

3 **Size constancy.** We see an object as having a constant size even when its retinal image becomes smaller or larger. A friend approaching on the street does not seem to be growing; a car pulling away from the curb does not seem to be shrinking. Size constancy depends in part on familiarity with objects; you know people and cars do not change size from moment to moment. It also depends on the apparent distance of an object. An object that is close produces a larger retinal image than the same object farther away, and the brain takes this into account. For example, when you move your hand toward your face, your brain registers the fact that the hand is getting closer, and you correctly perceive its unchanging size despite the growing size of its retinal image. There is, then, an intimate relationship between perceived size and perceived distance.

4 **Brightness constancy.** We see objects as having a relatively constant brightness even though the amount of light they reflect changes as the overall level of illumination changes. Snow remains white even on a cloudy day. We are not fooled because

Monocular Cues To Depth

Most cues to depth do not depend on having two eyes. Some monocular (one-eyed) cues are shown here.

Light and shadow
Both of these attributes give objects the appearance of three dimensions.

Interposition
An object that partly blocks or obscures another one must be in front of the other one and is, therefore, seen as closer.

Motion parallax
When an observer is moving, objects appear to move at different speeds and in different directions. The closer an object, the faster it seems to move; and close objects appear to move backward, whereas distant ones seem to move forward.

the brain registers the total illumination in the scene and we automatically take this information into account.

5 Color constancy. We see an object as maintaining its hue despite the fact that the wavelength of light reaching our eyes from the object may change as the illumination changes. For example, outdoor light is "bluer" than indoor light, and objects outdoors therefore reflect more "blue" light than those indoors. Conversely, indoor light from incandescent lamps is rich in long wavelengths and is therefore "yellower." Yet an apple looks red whether you look at it in your kitchen or outside on the patio. Part of the explanation involves sensory adaptation, which we discussed earlier. Outdoors, we quickly adapt to short-wavelength (bluish) light, and indoors, we adapt to long-wavelength light. As a result, our visual responses are similar in the two situations. Also, when computing the color of a particular object, the brain takes into account *all* the wavelengths in the visual field immediately around the object. If an apple is bathed in bluish light, so, usually, is everything else around it. The increase in blue light

Relative size
The smaller an object's image on the retina, the farther away the object appears.

Texture gradients
Distant parts of a uniform surface appear denser; that is, its elements seem spaced more closely together.

Relative clarity
Because of particles in the air from dust, fog, or smog, distant objects tend to look hazier, duller, or less detailed.

Linear perspective
Parallel lines will appear to be converging in the distance; the greater the apparent convergence, the greater the perceived distance. This cue is often exaggerated by artists to convey an impression of depth.

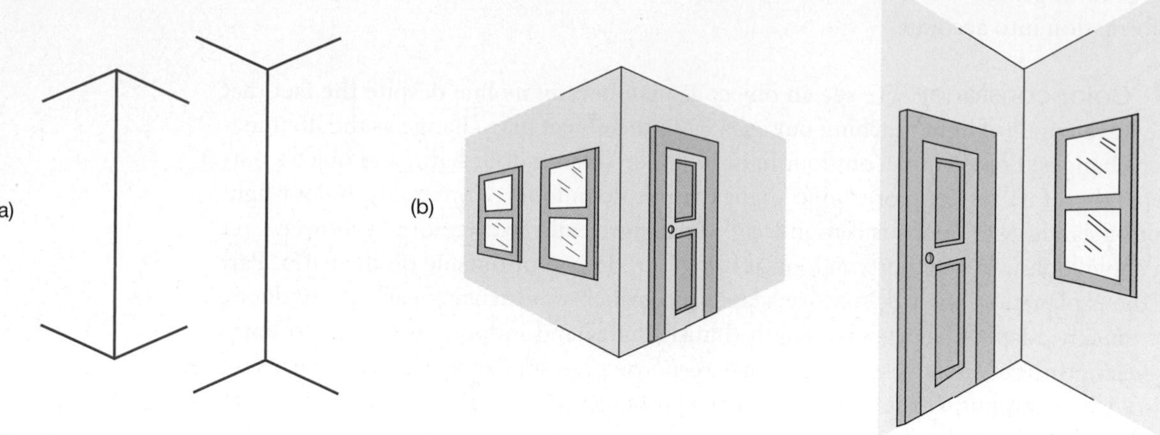

FIGURE 6.7 The Müller-Lyer Illusion

The two lines in (a) are exactly the same length. We are probably fooled into perceiving them as different because the brain interprets the one with the outward-facing branches as farther away, as if it were the far corner of a room, and the one with the inward-facing branches as closer, as if it were the near edge of a building (b).

reflected by the apple is canceled in the visual cortex by the increase in blue light reflected by the apple's surroundings, and so the apple continues to look red.

Visual Illusions: When Seeing Is Misleading. Perceptual constancies allow us to make sense of the world. Occasionally, however, we can be fooled, and the result is a *perceptual illusion*. For psychologists, illusions are valuable because they are systematic errors that provide us with hints about the perceptual strategies of the mind.

Although illusions can occur in any sensory modality, visual illusions have been the best studied. Visual illusions sometimes occur when the strategies that normally lead to accurate perception are overextended to situations where they do not apply. Compare the lengths of the two vertical lines in Figure 6.7. If you are like most people, you perceive the line on the right as slightly longer than the one on the left. Yet they are exactly the same length. (Go ahead, measure them; everyone does.) This is the Müller-Lyer illusion, named after the German sociologist who first described it in 1889.

One explanation for the Müller-Lyer illusion is that the branches on the lines serve as perspective cues that normally suggest depth (Gregory, 1963). The line on the left is like the near edge of a building; the one on the right is like the far corner of a room (see part b of the figure). Although the two lines produce retinal images of the same size, the one with the outward-facing branches suggests greater distance. We are fooled into perceiving it as longer because we automatically apply a rule about the relationship between size and distance that is normally useful: When two objects produce the same-sized retinal image and one is farther away, the farther one is larger. The problem, in this case, is that there is no actual difference in the distance of the two lines, so the rule is inappropriate.

Just as there are size, shape, location, brightness, and color constancies, so there are size, shape, location, brightness, and color *in*constancies, resulting in illusions. For example, the perceived color of an object depends on the wavelengths reflected by its immediate surroundings, a fact well-known to artists and interior designers. Thus, you never see a good, strong red unless other objects in the surroundings reflect the blue and green part of the spectrum. When two objects that are the same color have different surroundings, you may mistakenly perceive them as different (see Figure 6.8).

FIGURE 6.8 Color in Context

The way you perceive a color depends on the color surrounding it. In this work by Joseph Albers, the adjacent *X*s are actually the same color, but against different backgrounds they look different.

Some illusions are simply a matter of physics. Thus, a chopstick in a half-filled glass of water looks bent because water and air refract light differently. Other illusions occur due to misleading messages from the sense organs, as in sensory adaptation. Still

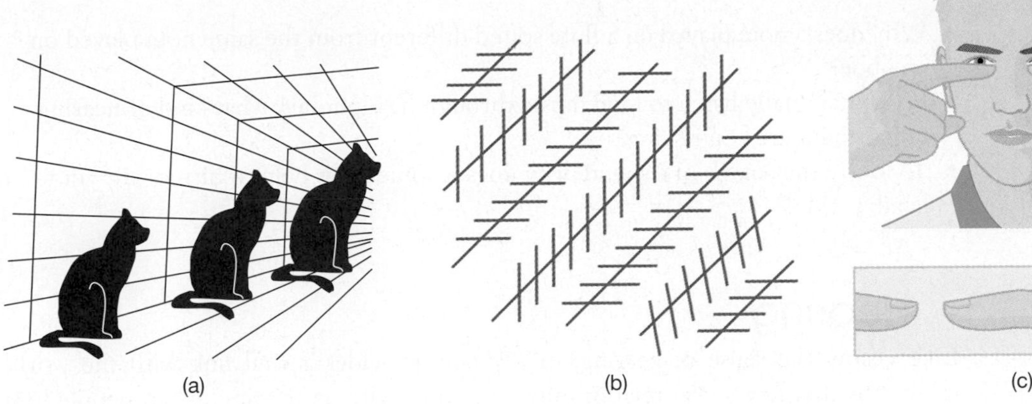

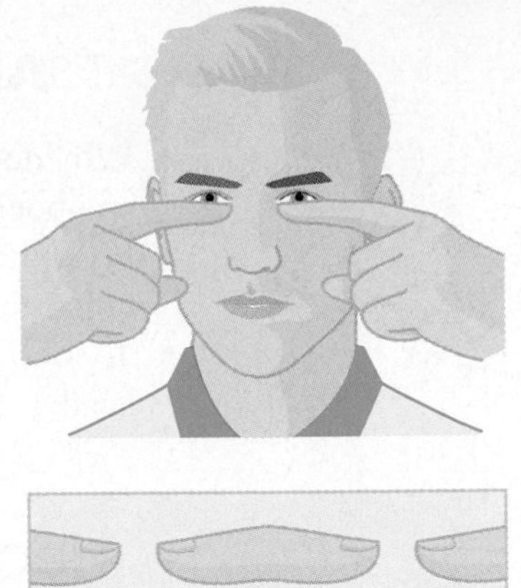

FIGURE 6.9 Fooling the Eye

Although perception is usually accurate, we can be fooled. In (a) the cats as drawn are exactly the same size; in (b) the diagonal lines are all parallel. To see the illusion depicted in (c), hold your index fingers 5 to 10 inches in front of your eyes as shown and then focus straight ahead. Do you see a floating "fingertip frankfurter"? Can you make it shrink or expand?

others, like the Müller-Lyer illusion, seem to occur because the brain misinterprets sensory information. Figure 6.9 shows some other startling illusions.

In everyday life, most illusions are harmless and entertaining. Occasionally, however, an illusion interferes with the performance of some task or skill. For example, in baseball, two types of pitches that drive batters batty are the rising fastball, in which the ball seems to jump a few inches when it reaches home plate, and the breaking curveball, in which the ball seems to loop toward the batter and then appears to fall at the last moment. Both of these pitches are physical impossibilities. According to one explanation, such illusions occur when batters wrongly estimate a ball's speed and momentarily shift their gaze to where they think it will cross home plate (Bahill & Karnavas, 1993).

Some illusions can also contribute to industrial and automobile accidents. For example, because large objects often appear to move more slowly than small ones, drivers sometimes underestimate the speed of onrushing trains at railroad crossings and think they can beat the train, with tragic results.

QUICK quiz

This quiz is no illusion.

1. How can two Gestalt principles help explain why you can make out the Big Dipper on a starry night?
2. *True or false*: Binocular cues help us locate objects that are very far away.
3. Hold one hand about 12 inches from your face and the other one about 6 inches away. (a) Which hand will cast the smaller retinal image? (b) Why don't you perceive that hand as smaller?
4. From an evolutionary point of view, people are most likely to have a mental module for recognition of (a) flowers, (b) bugs, (c) faces, (d) chocolate, (e) cars.

Answers:

1. *Proximity* of certain stars encourages you to see them as clustered together to form a pattern; *closure* allows you to "fill in the gaps" and see the contours of a "dipper." **2.** false **3a.** The hand that is 12 inches away will cast a smaller retinal image. **3b.** Your brain takes the differences in distance into account in estimating size; also, you know how large your hands are. The result is size constancy. **4.** c

WHAT'S**AHEAD**

- Why does a note played on a flute sound different from the same note played on an oboe?
- If you habitually listen to loud music through headphones, what kind of hearing impairment are you risking?
- To locate the source of a sound, why does it sometimes help to turn or tilt your head?

Hearing

Like vision, the sense of hearing, or *audition*, provides a vital link with the world around us. Because social relationships rely so heavily on hearing, when people lose their hearing they sometimes come to feel socially isolated. That is why many hearing-impaired people feel strongly about teaching deaf children American Sign Language (ASL) or other gestural systems, which allow them to communicate and forge close relationships with other signers.

What We Hear

The stimulus for sound is a wave of pressure created when an object vibrates (or, sometimes, when compressed air is released, as in a pipe organ). The vibration (or release of air) causes molecules in a transmitting substance to move together and apart. This movement produces variations in pressure that radiate in all directions. The transmitting substance is usually air, but sound waves can also travel through water and solids, as you know if you have ever put your ear to the wall to hear voices in the next room.

As with vision, *physical* characteristics of the stimulus—in this case, a sound wave—are related in a predictable way to *psychological* aspects of our experience:

1 **Loudness** is the psychological dimension of auditory experience related to the *intensity* of a wave's pressure. Intensity corresponds to the amplitude, or maximum height, of the wave. The more energy contained in the wave, the higher it is at its peak. Perceived loudness is also affected by how high or low a sound is. If low and high sounds produce waves with equal amplitudes, the low sound may seem quieter.

Sound intensity is measured in units called *decibels* (dB). A decibel is one-tenth of a *bel*, a unit named for Alexander Graham Bell, the inventor of the telephone. The average absolute threshold of hearing in human beings is zero decibels. Decibels are not equally distant, as inches on a ruler are. A 60-decibel sound (such as that of a sewing machine) is not 50 percent louder than a 40-decibel sound (such as that of a whisper)—it is 100 times louder.

loudness The dimension of auditory experience related to the intensity of a pressure wave.

2 **Pitch** is the dimension of auditory experience related to the frequency of the sound wave and, to some extent, its intensity. *Frequency* refers to how rapidly the air (or other medium) vibrates—that is, the number of times per second the wave cycles through a peak and a low point. One cycle per second is known as 1 *hertz* (Hz). The healthy ear of a young person normally detects frequencies in the range of 16 Hz (the lowest note on a pipe organ) to 20,000 Hz (the scraping of a grasshopper's legs).

pitch The dimension of auditory experience related to the frequency of a pressure wave; the height or depth of a tone.

3 **Timbre** is the distinguishing quality of a sound. It is the dimension of auditory experience related to the *complexity* of the sound wave—to the relative breadth of the range of frequencies that make up the wave. A pure tone consists of only one fre-

timbre The distinguishing quality of a sound; the dimension of auditory experience related to the complexity of the pressure wave.

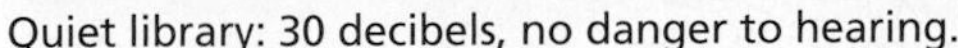
Quiet library: 30 decibels, no danger to hearing.

Rock concert near speakers: 120 decibels, immediate danger.

quency, but in nature, pure tones are extremely rare. Usually what we hear is a complex wave consisting of several subwaves with different frequencies. A particular combination of frequencies results in a particular timbre. Timbre is what makes a note played on a flute, which produces relatively pure tones, sound different from the same note played on an oboe, which produces very complex sounds.

When many sound-wave frequencies are present but are not in harmony, we hear noise. When all the frequencies of the sound spectrum occur, they produce a hissing sound called *white noise*. Just as white light includes all wavelengths of the visible light spectrum, so white noise includes all frequencies of the audible sound spectrum. People sometimes use white-noise machines to mask other sounds when they are trying to sleep.

An Ear on the World

As Figure 6.10 on the next page shows, the ear has an outer, a middle, and an inner section. The soft, funnel-shaped outer ear is well designed to collect sound waves, but hearing would still be quite good without it. The essential parts of the ear are hidden from view, inside the head.

A sound wave passes into the outer ear and through an inch-long canal to strike an oval-shaped membrane called the *eardrum*. The eardrum is so sensitive that it can respond to the movement of a single molecule! A sound wave causes it to vibrate with the same frequency and amplitude as the wave itself. This vibration is passed along to three tiny bones in the middle ear, the smallest bones in the human body. These bones, known informally as the hammer, the anvil, and the stirrup, move one after the other, which has the effect of intensifying the force of the vibration. The innermost bone, the stirrup, pushes on a membrane that opens into the inner ear.

The actual organ of hearing, the **organ of Corti**, is a chamber inside the **cochlea**, a snail-shaped structure within the inner ear. The organ of Corti plays the same role in hearing that the retina plays in vision. It contains the all-important receptor cells, which in this case look like bristles and are called *hair cells*, or *cilia*. Brief exposure to extremely loud noises, like those from a gunshot or a jet airplane (140 dB), or sustained exposure to more moderate noises, like those from shop tools or truck traffic (90 dB), can damage these fragile cells. They flop over, like broken blades of grass, and if the damage reaches a critical point, hearing loss occurs. In modern societies, with their rock concerts, deafening bars, and millions of automobiles, snowmobiles, power

organ of Corti [core-tee] A structure in the cochlea containing hair cells that serve as the receptors for hearing.

cochlea [KOCK-lee-uh] A snail-shaped, fluid-filled organ in the inner ear, containing the organ of Corti, where the receptors for hearing are located.

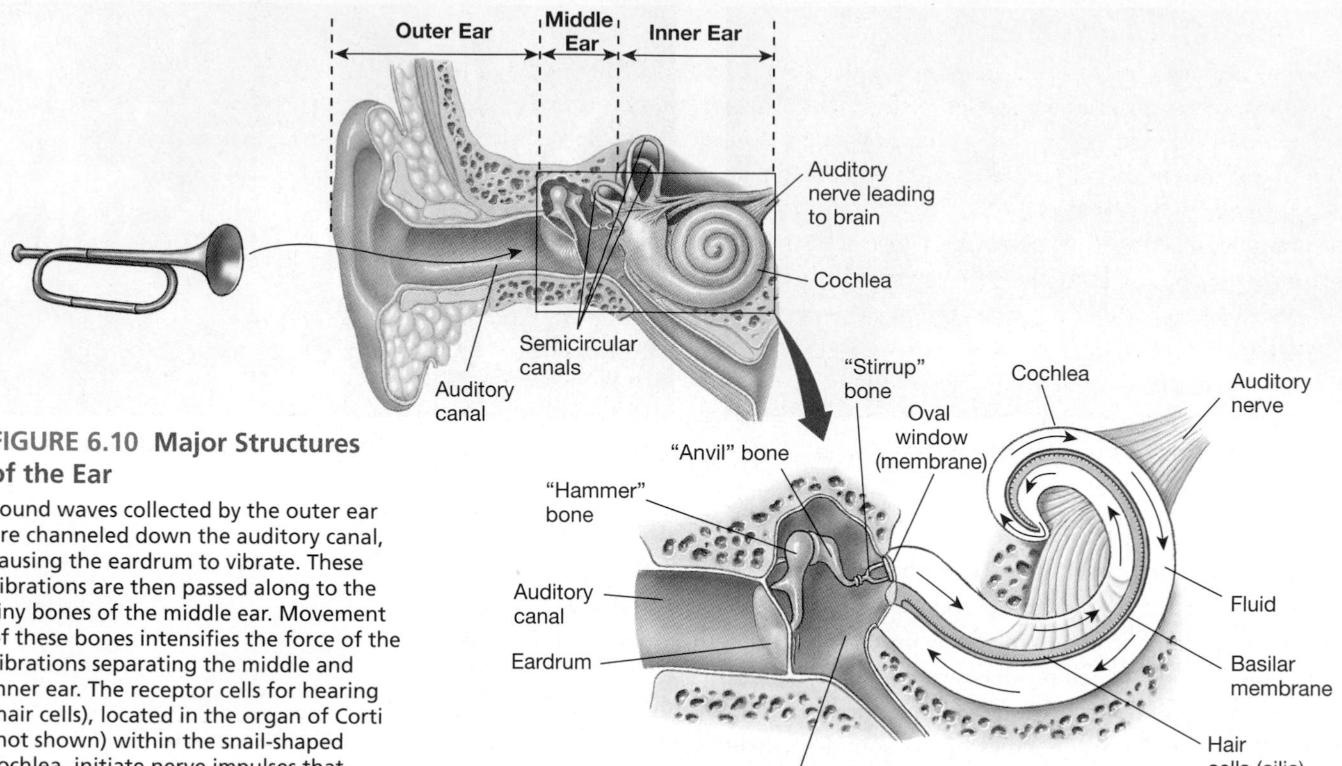

FIGURE 6.10 Major Structures of the Ear

Sound waves collected by the outer ear are channeled down the auditory canal, causing the eardrum to vibrate. These vibrations are then passed along to the tiny bones of the middle ear. Movement of these bones intensifies the force of the vibrations separating the middle and inner ear. The receptor cells for hearing (hair cells), located in the organ of Corti (not shown) within the snail-shaped cochlea, initiate nerve impulses that travel along the auditory nerve to the brain.

saws, leaf blowers, jackhammers, and MP3 players (often played at full blast), such damage is common, even among teenagers and young adults. Unfortunately, damaged hair cells do not regenerate. Scientists are now doing basic research on possible ways to grow new hair cells (Izumikawa et al., 2005; Sage et al., 2005), but these approaches have not yet led to therapies for hearing loss, and damage to these cells in human beings is currently irreversible.

The hair cells of the cochlea are embedded in the rubbery *basilar membrane*, which stretches across the interior of the cochlea. When pressure reaches the cochlea, it causes wavelike motions in fluid within the cochlea's interior. These waves of fluid push on the basilar membrane, causing it to move in a wavelike fashion, too. Just above the hair cells is yet another membrane. As the hair cells rise and fall, their tips brush against it, and they bend. This causes the hair cells to initiate a signal that is passed along to the *auditory nerve*, which then carries the message to the brain. The particular pattern of hair-cell movement is affected by the manner in which the basilar membrane moves. This pattern determines which neurons fire and how rapidly they fire, and the resulting code in turn helps determine the sort of sound we hear. For example, we discriminate high-pitched sounds largely on the basis of where activity occurs along the basilar membrane; activity at different sites leads to different neural codes. We discriminate low-pitched sounds largely on the basis of the frequency of the basilar membrane's vibration; again, different frequencies lead to different neural codes.

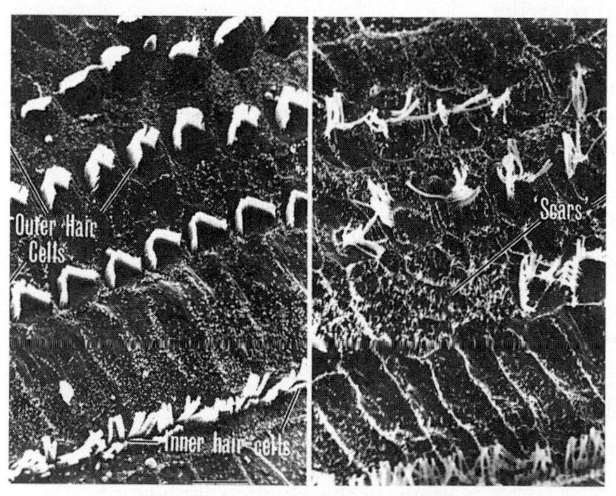

After prolonged intense sound, similar in level to that of loud rock music, normal hair cells in a guinea pig's cochlea (left) are damaged or destroyed (right). In humans and other mammals, these cells do not regenerate and the resultant hearing loss is permanent.

Could anyone ever imagine such a complex and odd arrangement of bristles, fluids, and snail shells if it did not already exist?

Constructing the Auditory World

Just as we do not see a retinal image, so we do not hear a chorus of brushlike tufts bending and swaying in the dark recesses of the cochlea. Just as we do not see a jumbled collection of lines and colors, so we do not hear a chaotic collection of disconnected pitches and timbres. Instead, we use our perceptual powers to organize patterns of sound and to construct a meaningful auditory world.

For example, in class, your psychology instructor hopes you will perceive his or her voice as *figure* and the hum of a passing airplane, cheers from the athletic field, or distant sounds of a construction crew as *ground*. Whether these hopes are realized will depend, of course, on where you choose to direct your attention. Other Gestalt principles also seem to apply to hearing. The *proximity* of notes in a melody tells you which notes go together to form phrases; *continuity* helps you follow a melody on one violin when another violin is playing a different melody; *similarity* in timbre and pitch helps you pick out the soprano voices in a chorus and hear them as a unit; *closure* helps you understand a cell phone caller's words even when interference makes some of the individual sounds unintelligible.

Besides needing to organize sounds, we also need to know where they are coming from. We can estimate the *distance* of a sound's source by using loudness as a cue. For example, we know that a train sounds louder when it is 20 yards away than when it is a mile off. To locate the *direction* a sound is coming from, we depend in part on the fact that we have two ears. A sound arriving from the right reaches the right ear a fraction of a second sooner than it reaches the left ear, and vice versa. The sound may also provide a bit more energy to the right ear (depending on its frequency) because it has to get around the head to reach the left ear. It is hard to localize sounds that are coming from directly in back of you or from directly above your head because such sounds reach both ears at the same time. When you turn or cock your head, you are actively trying to overcome this problem. Many animals do not have to do this because the lucky creatures can move their ears independently of their heads.

QUICK quiz

How well can you localize the answers to these questions?

1. Which psychological dimensions of hearing correspond to the intensity, frequency, and complexity of the sound wave?
2. Fred has a nasal voice and Ted has a gravelly voice. Which psychological dimension of hearing describes the difference?
3. An extremely loud or sustained noise can permanently damage the _______ of the ear.
4. During a lecture, a classmate draws your attention to a buzzing fluorescent light that you had not previously noticed. What will happen to your perception of figure and ground?

Answers:

1. loudness, pitch, timbre **2.** timbre **3.** hair cells (cilia) **4.** The buzzing sound will become figure and the lecturer's voice will become ground, at least momentarily.

WHAT'S**AHEAD**

- Why do saccharin and caffeine taste bitter to some people but not to others?
- Why do you have trouble tasting your food when you have a cold?
- Why is pain such a puzzle?

Other Senses

Psychologists have been particularly interested in vision and audition because of the importance of these senses to human survival. However, research on other senses is growing rapidly as awareness of how they contribute to our lives increases and new ways are found to study them.

Taste: Savory Sensations

Taste, or *gustation*, occurs because chemicals stimulate thousands of receptors in the mouth. These receptors are located primarily on the tongue, but some are also found in the throat, inside the cheeks, and on the roof of the mouth. If you look at your tongue in a mirror, you will notice many tiny bumps; they are called **papillae** (from the Latin for "pimples"), and they come in several forms. In all but one of these forms, the sides of each papilla are lined with **taste buds**, which up close look a little like segmented oranges (see Figure 6.11). Because of genetic differences, human tongues can have as few as 500 or as many as 10,000 taste buds (Miller & Reedy, 1990).

The taste buds are commonly referred to, mistakenly, as the receptors for taste. The actual receptor cells are *inside* the buds, 15 to 50 to a bud. These cells send tiny fibers out through an opening in the bud; the receptor sites are on these fibers. The receptor cells are replaced by new cells about every ten days. However, after age 40 or so, the total number of taste buds (and therefore receptors) declines.

Traditionally, researchers have considered four tastes to be basic: *salty*, *sour*, *bitter*, and *sweet*, each produced by a different type of chemical. Today, most researchers also include a fifth taste, *umami* (from the Japanese for "delicious"), which is the taste of monosodium glutamate (MSG); it is found in many protein-rich foods, including meat, shellfish, and seaweed. The basic tastes are part of our evolutionary heritage: Bitterness and sourness help us identify foods that are rancid or poisonous; sweetness helps us identify foods that are healthful or rich in calories; salt is necessary for all bodily functions; and umami may help us identify protein-rich foods.

The basic tastes can be perceived at any spot on the tongue that has receptors, and differences among the areas are small. Interestingly, the center of the tongue contains no taste buds, and so it cannot produce any sort of taste sensation. But, as in the case of the eye's blind spot, you will not usually notice the lack of sensation because the brain fills in the gap.

When you bite into an egg or a piece of bread or an orange, its unique flavor is composed of some combination of the four or five basic tastes, but the physiological

papillae [pa-PILL-ee] Knoblike elevations on the tongue, containing the taste buds. (Singular: *papilla*.)

taste buds Nests of taste-receptor cells.

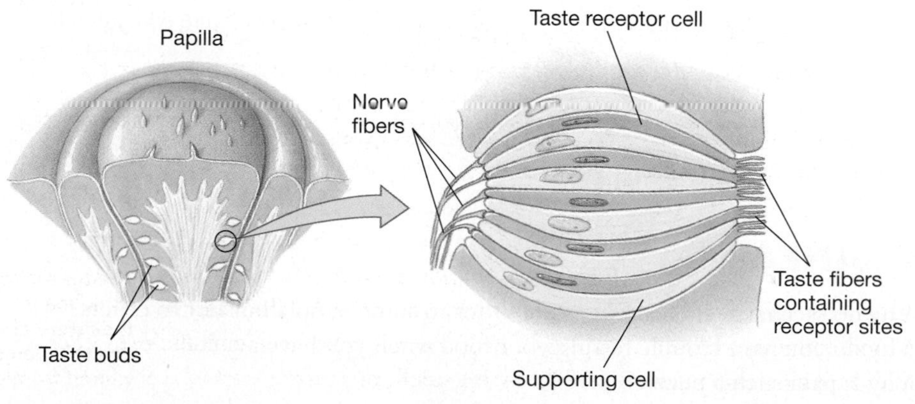

FIGURE 6.11 Taste Receptors

The illustration on the left shows taste buds lining the sides of a papilla on the tongue's surface. The illustration on the right shows an enlarged view of a single taste bud.

GET INVOLVED!

➤THE SMELL OF TASTE

Demonstrate for yourself that smell enhances the sense of taste. Take a bite of a slice of apple, holding your nose, and then do the same with a slice of raw potato. You may find that you can't taste much difference! If you think you do taste a difference, maybe your expectations are influencing your response. Try the same thing, but close your eyes and have someone else feed you the slices. Can you still tell them apart?

details are still hazy. It has even been difficult to identify the receptors for the basic tastes, although researchers have proposed candidates for the receptors that process bitter, sweet, and umami (Chaudhari, Landin, & Roper, 2000; Damak et al., 2003; Huang et al., 1999; Max et al., 2001; Montmayeur et al., 2001; Zhang et al., 2003).

Everyone knows that people live in different "taste worlds" (Bartoshuk, 1998). Some people love broccoli and others hate it. Some people can eat chili peppers that are burning hot and others cannot tolerate the mildest jalepeño. One reason for these differences is genetic. In the United States, about 25 percent of people are *supertasters* who find saccharin, caffeine, broccoli, and many other substances to be unpleasantly bitter. (Women, especially Asian women, are overrepresented in this group.) "Tasters," in contrast, detect less bitterness, and "nontasters" detect none at all. Supertasters also perceive sweet tastes as sweeter and salty tastes as saltier than other people do, and they feel more "burn" from substances such as ginger, pepper, and hot chilies (Bartoshuk et al., 1998; Lucchina et al., 1998). Supertasters have more taste buds than other people, and certain papillae on their tongues are smaller, are more densely packed, and look different from those of nontasters (Reedy et al., 1993).

Other taste preferences are a matter of culture and learning. Many North Americans who enjoy raw oysters, raw smoked salmon, and raw herring are nevertheless put off by other forms of raw seafood that are popular in Japan, such as sea urchin and octopus. And within a given culture, some people will greedily gobble up a dish that makes others turn green. Some of these learned taste preferences seem to begin in the womb or during breast-feeding. A baby whose mother drank carrot juice while pregnant or nursing is likely to be more enthusiastic about eating porridge mixed with carrot juice than porridge mixed with water, whereas babies without this exposure show no such preference (Mennella, Jagnow, & Beauchamp, 2001).

The attractiveness of a food can be affected by its color, temperature, and texture. As Goldilocks found out, a bowl of cold porridge is not nearly as delicious as one that is properly heated. And any peanut butter fan will tell you that chunky and smooth peanut butters just don't taste the same. Even more important for taste is a food's odor. Much of what we call "flavor" is really the smell of gases released by the foods we put in our mouths. Indeed, subtle flavors such as chocolate and vanilla would have little taste if we could not smell them (see Figure 6.12). Smell's influence on flavor explains why you have trouble tasting your food when you have a stuffy nose. Most people who have chronic trouble detecting tastes have a problem with smell, not taste.

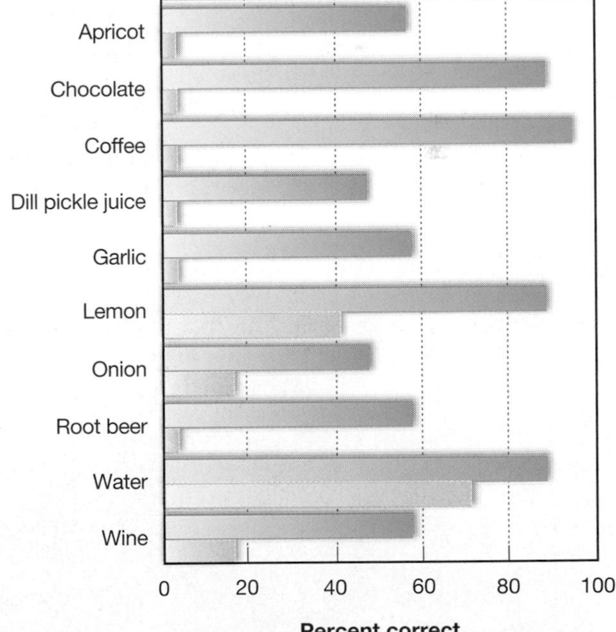

FIGURE 6.12 Taste Test
The turquoise bars show the percentages of people who could identify a substance dropped on the tongue when they were able to smell it. The gold bars show the percentage that could identify the substance when they were prevented from smelling it (Mozell et al., 1969).

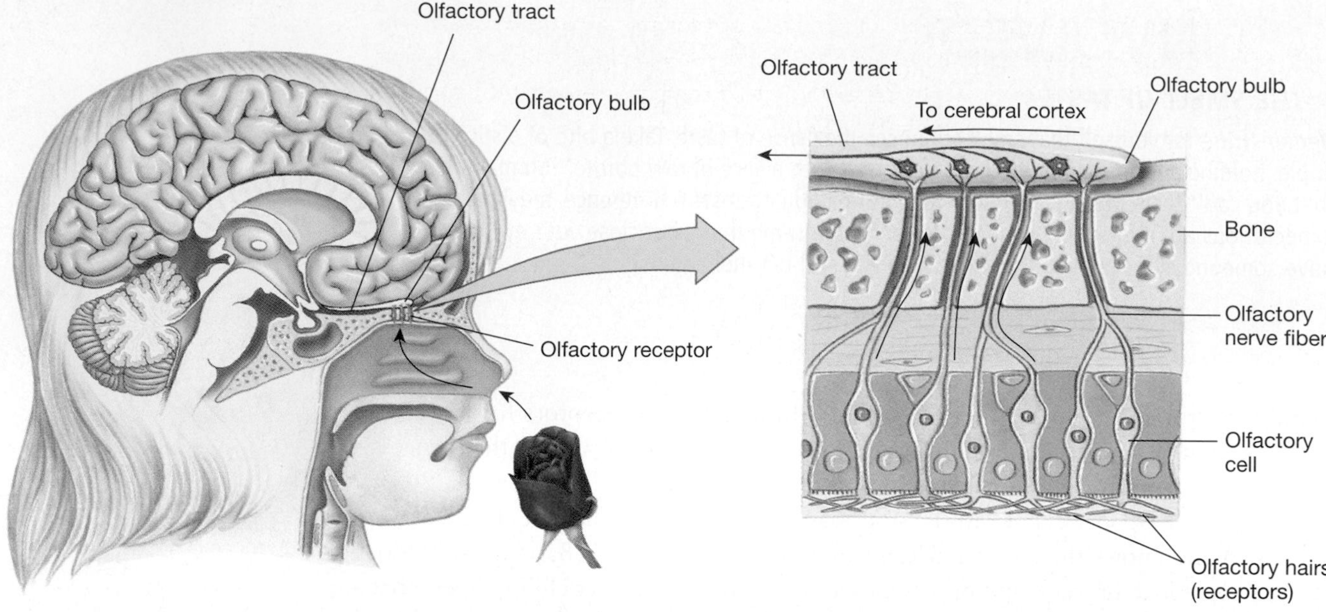

FIGURE 6.13 Receptors for Smell
Airborne chemical molecules (vapors) enter the nose and circulate through the nasal cavity, where the smell receptors are located. The receptors' axons make up the olfactory nerve, which carries signals to the brain. When you sniff, you draw more vapors into the nose and speed their circulation. Vapors can also reach the nasal cavity through the mouth by way of a passageway from the throat.

Smell: The Sense of Scents

The great author and educator Helen Keller, who became blind and deaf as a toddler, once called smell "the fallen angel of the senses." Yet our sense of smell, or *olfaction*, although seemingly crude when compared to a bloodhound's, is actually quite good; the human nose can detect aromas that the most sophisticated machines fail to detect. And this sense is also far more useful than most people realize.

The receptors for smell are specialized neurons embedded in a tiny patch of mucous membrane in the upper part of the nasal passage, just beneath the eyes (see Figure 6.13). Millions of receptors in each nasal cavity respond to chemical molecules in the air. When you inhale, you pull these molecules into the nasal cavity, but they can also enter from the mouth, wafting up the throat like smoke up a chimney. These molecules trigger responses in the receptors that combine to yield the yeasty smell of freshly baked bread or the spicy smell of a eucalyptus tree. Signals from the receptors are carried to the brain's olfactory bulb by the *olfactory nerve*, which is made up of the receptors' axons. From the olfactory bulb, they travel to a higher region of the brain.

Smell has not only evolutionary but also cultural significance. These pilgrims in Japan are purifying themselves with holy incense for good luck and health.

Figuring out the neural code for smell has been a real challenge. Of the 10,000 or so smells we detect (rotten, burned, musky, fruity, spicy, flowery, resinous, putrid . . .), none seems to be more basic than any other. Moreover, as many as a thousand kinds of receptors exist, each kind responding to a part of an odor molecule's structure (Axel, 1995; Buck & Axel, 1991). (In 2004, Richard Axel and Linda Buck won a Nobel Prize for this discovery.) Distinct odors activate unique combinations of receptors, and signals from different types of receptors are combined in individual neurons in the brain. Some neurons seem to respond only to particular mixtures of odors rather than the individual odors in a mixture, which may explain why a mixture of clove and rose may be perceived as carnation rather than as two separate smells (Zou & Buck, 2006).

Although smell is less vital for human survival than for the survival of other animals, it is still important. We sniff out danger by smelling smoke, food spoilage, and gas leaks; thus, a deficit in the sense of smell is nothing to turn up your nose at. Such a loss can result from infection, disease, injury to the olfactory nerve, or smoking. A person who has smoked two packs a day for ten years must abstain from cigarettes for ten more years before the sense of smell returns to normal (Frye, Schwartz, & Doty, 1990).

CLOSE-UP on Research

NOSY BEHAVIOR

Odors, of course, have psychological effects on us, which is why we buy perfumes and sniff flowers. Perhaps because olfactory centers in the brain are linked to areas that process memories and emotions, specific smells often evoke vivid, emotionally colored memories (Herz & Cupchik, 1995; Vroon, 1997). The smell of hot chocolate may trigger fond memories of cozy winter mornings from your childhood; the smell of rubbing alcohol may remind you of an unpleasant trip to the hospital. Odors can also influence people's everyday behavior, which is why shopping malls and hotels often install aroma diffusers in hopes of putting you in a good mood.

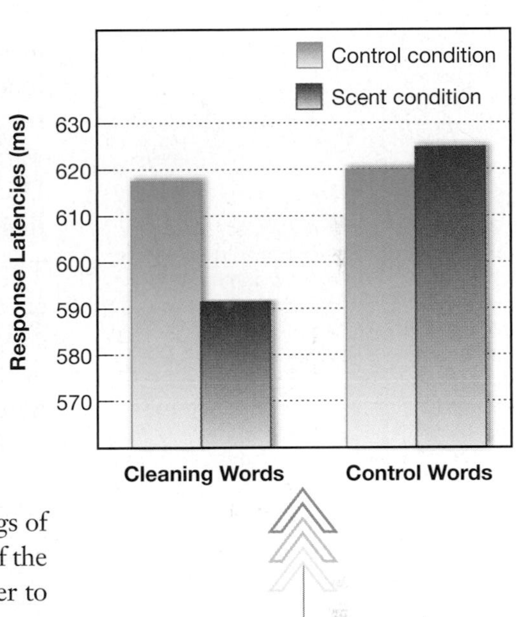

Many claims have been made for aroma's effects on behavior without much science to back up such claims. Now, however, some good science is starting to be done. For example, in three Dutch studies (Holland, Hendriks, & Aarts, 2005), researchers **asked an interesting question**: Can the citrus scent of an all-purpose cleaner (unobtrusively left in a hidden bucket) activate the mental concept *cleaning* and even affect people's "cleaning behavior"? In the first study, they presented strings of letters to participants and asked them to say whether each string formed a word. Half the strings were words and half were not. Participants exposed to the scent were quicker to identify cleaning-related words than control subjects were, as you can see in the adjacent figure. They were also quicker at identifying cleaning-related words than other words. These results suggest that the scent made the concept *cleaning* more mentally accessible. In the second study, the researchers asked the participants to write down five activities they were planning to do during the rest of the day. Those exposed to the scent listed a cleaning activity more often than the other subjects did, again suggesting that the scent had activated the concept *cleaning*.

In the third study, the researchers first had participants fill out a questionnaire (one not related to the study) and then moved them to another room where there was no scent and asked them to sit at a table and eat a crumbly biscuit. A hidden video camera recorded the participants' hand movements. People who had been previously exposed to the scent were much more likely than control subjects to wipe away the crumbs from the table! Apparently, activation of the concept *cleaning* made them more likely to clean up after themselves.

Can you think of an **alternative interpretation** of these results? One possibility is that the participants guessed the hypothesis. But the researchers had thought of that. After each study, they questioned the participants and found that none had been aware of the scent's influence. In fact, most were not even aware of having smelled the scent at all. "Together," write the researchers, "these observations provide compelling evidence that scent can have a nonconscious influence on thinking."

Senses of the Skin

The skin's usefulness is more than just skin deep. Besides protecting our innards, our two square yards of skin help us identify objects and establish intimacy with others. By providing a boundary between ourselves and everything else, the skin also gives us a sense of ourselves as distinct from the environment.

The basic skin senses include *touch* (or pressure), *warmth*, *cold*, and *pain*. Within these four types are variations such as itch, tickle, and painful burning. Although certain spots on the skin are especially sensitive to the four basic skin sensations, for many years scientists had difficulty finding distinct receptors for these sensations, except in the case of pressure. But then Swedish researchers found a new kind of nerve fiber that seems responsible for some types of itching (Schmelz et al., 1997). And scientists have also identified a possible cold receptor (McKemy, Neuhausser, & Julius, 2002; Peier et al., 2002).

Perhaps specialized fibers will also be discovered for other skin sensations. In the meantime, many aspects of touch continue to baffle science—for example, why gently touching adjacent pressure spots in rapid succession produces tickle, why scratching relieves (or sometimes worsens!) an itch, and why the simultaneous stimulation of warm and cold spots produces not a lukewarm sensation but the sensation of heat. Decoding the messages of the skin senses will eventually tell us how we are able to distinguish sandpaper from velvet and glue from grease.

The Mystery of Pain

Pain, which is not only a skin sense but also an internal sense, has come under special scrutiny. Pain differs from other senses in an important way: When the stimulus producing it is removed, the sensation may continue—sometimes for years. Chronic pain disrupts lives, puts stress on the body, and causes depression and despair. (For ways of coping with chronic pain, see "Taking Psychology with You.")

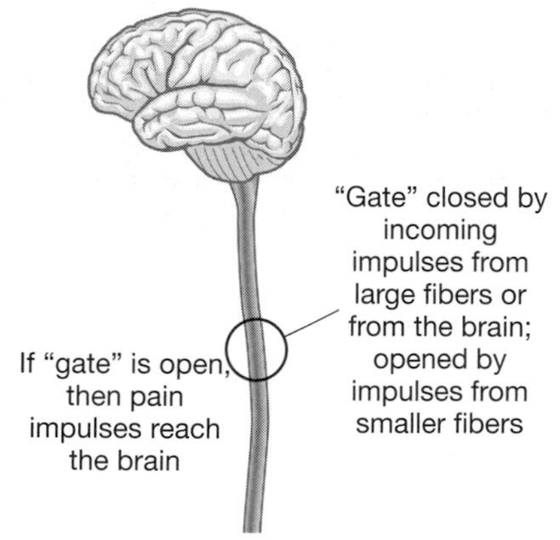
"Gate" closed by incoming impulses from large fibers or from the brain; opened by impulses from smaller fibers
If "gate" is open, then pain impulses reach the brain

The Gate-Control Theory of Pain. For many years, a leading explanation of pain has been the **gate-control theory**, which was first proposed by Canadian psychologist Ronald Melzack and British physiologist Patrick Wall (1965). According to this theory, pain impulses must get past a "gate" in the spinal cord. The gate is not an actual structure, but rather a pattern of neural activity that either blocks pain messages coming from the skin, muscles, and internal organs or lets those signals through. Normally, the gate is kept shut, either by impulses coming into the spinal cord from large fibers that respond to pressure and other kinds of stimulation or by signals coming down from the brain itself. But when body tissue is injured, the large fibers are damaged and smaller fibers open the gate, allowing pain messages to reach the brain unchecked.

Because the gate-control theory emphasizes the role of the brain in controlling the gate, it correctly predicts that thoughts and feelings can influence our reactions to pain. When we dwell on our pain, focusing on it and talking about it constantly instead of acting in spite of it, we often intensify our experience of it (Sullivan et al., 1998). Conversely, when we are distracted from our pain, we may not feel it as we usually would, which is why we hear, from time to time, of athletes who are able to finish a performance despite sprained ankles or even broken bones. The gate-control theory also correctly predicts that mild pressure, or other kinds of stimulation, can interfere with severe or protracted pain by closing the spinal gate. When we vigorously rub a banged elbow or apply ice packs, heat, or stimulating ointments to injuries, we are applying this principle.

gate-control theory The theory that the experience of pain depends in part on whether pain impulses get past a neurological "gate" in the spinal cord and thus reach the brain.

Updating the Gate-Control Theory. The gate-control theory has been highly useful, but it does not fully explain the many instances of severe, chronic pain that occur without any sign of injury or disease whatsoever. In the strange phenomenon of **phantom pain**, for instance, a person continues to feel pain that seemingly comes from an amputated limb or from an organ that has been surgically removed. An amputee may feel the same aching, burning, or sharp pain from sores, calf cramps, throbbing toes, or even ingrown toenails that he or she endured before the surgery. Even when the spinal cord has been completely severed, amputees often continue to report phantom pain from areas below the break. There are no nerve impulses for the spinal-cord gate to block or let through. So why is there pain?

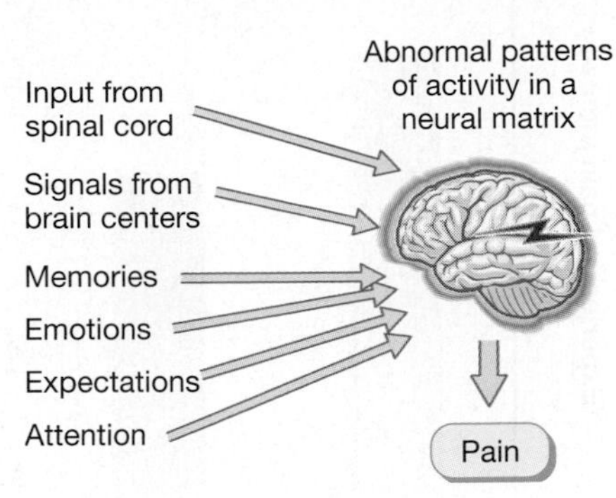

These puzzles led Ronald Melzack (1992, 1993) to revise the gate-control theory. The brain, he says, not only responds to incoming signals from sensory nerves but is also capable of generating pain (and other sensations) entirely on its own. An extensive *matrix* (network) of neurons in the brain gives us a sense of our own bodies and body parts. When this matrix produces abnormal patterns of activity, the result is pain. Such abnormal patterns can occur not only because of input from peripheral nerves but also as a result of memories, emotions, expectations, or signals from various brain centers. In the case of phantom pain, the abnormal patterns may arise because of a lack of sensory stimulation or because of the the brain's efforts to move a nonexistent limb. Evidence that brain areas associated with a missing limb continue to function in its absence is consistent with this view (K. Davis et al., 1998).

At present, however, no general theory completely explains phantom pain, or for that matter normal pain, which has turned out to be extremely complicated, both physiologically and psychologically. Different types of pain (from, say, a thorn, a bruise, or a hot iron) involve different chemical changes and different changes in nerve-cell activity at the site of injury or disease, as well as in the spinal cord and brain. These changes may suppress the pain or may amplify it by making neurons hyperexcitable. Further, recent evidence suggests that chronic, pathological pain involves *glia*, the cells that support nerve cells (see Chapter 4). Challenges to the immune system during viral and bacterial infections, and substances released by neurons along the pain pathway after an injury, activate glial cells in the spinal cord. The glia then release inflammatory substances that may worsen the pain and keep it going (Watkins & Maier, 2003). These chemicals can spread to spinal cord areas far from the site where they were released, which may help explain why injured people sometimes report pain in body areas that were not hurt.

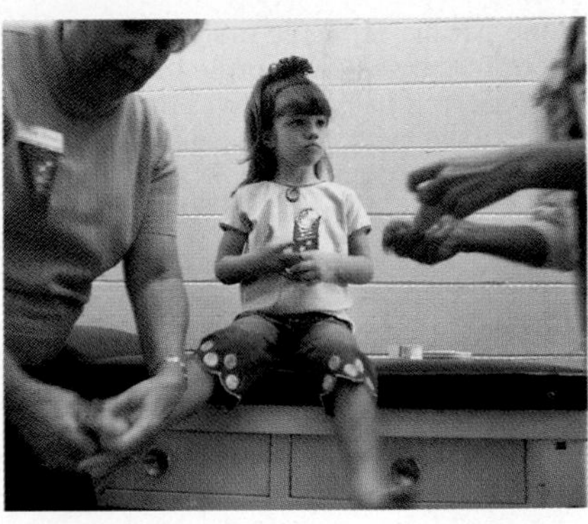
A nurse examines Ashlyn Blocker's feet for injuries. Because of a rare condition, Ashlyn cannot feel pain from scrapes and scratches. Despite the suffering that pain causes, it is also useful because it alerts us to injury.

BIOLOGY and Expectations of Pain

Positive Thinking and the Power of the Placebo

Another mystery of pain is the enormous variation among individuals: The same spinal condition that causes some people to live with agonizing back pain can be untroubling to others. One reason for this variation may be genetic differences in the production of pain-reducing endorphins (Zubieta et al., 2003). Another explanation, however, has to do with differences in people's expectations: If you expect to feel pain, you may focus on it, producing a self-fulfilling prophecy. And if you expect *not* to feel pain, that expectation, too, can become self-fulfilling.

Recently, researchers have been using brain scans to pinpoint the effects of positive thoughts on a person's pain. In one study, ten healthy volunteers had heat

phantom pain The experience of pain in a missing limb or other body part.

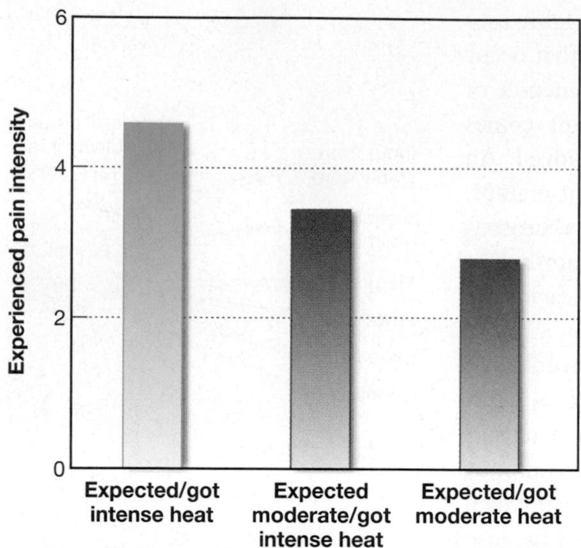

FIGURE 6.14 Expectations and Pain

When people expected moderate heat but got intense heat (purple bar), their self-reported pain was lower than it would have been had they expected the intense heat (green bar).

applied to their lower legs (Koyama et al., 2005). The volunteers had been trained to expect jolts of heat of varying intensity depending on the delay between a tone and application of the heat. (The longer the delay, the stronger the heat.) Functional MRI showed that the stronger the pain expected by the volunteers, the greater the activity in certain brain regions, and most of these regions were the same ones that responded to the actual pain. But when the researchers gave the signal for moderately painful heat and then instead delivered the most painful heat, the subjects' self-reported pain fell by 28 percent, compared with when they expected the most painful heat and actually got it (see Figure 6.14). This decrease was equal to what they would have experienced had they received a shot of morphine!

Findings like these suggest a mechanism for how placebos reduce pain: When placebos affect expectations ("I'm going to get relief"), they also affect the brain mechanisms underlying pain. Indeed, in another study, when volunteers had an "analgesic cream" (actually a placebo) rubbed on their skin before getting a painful shock to the wrist, MRI scans showed decreased activity in the pain matrix, the pain-sensitive areas of their brains (Wager et al., 2004).

Placebos also promote the production of endorphins, the body's natural pain-relieving opiates. Researchers in another study gave volunteers a slow, harmless injection of a pain-inducing solution in the jaw and had them rate their level of pain (Zubieta et al., 2005). As the injection continued, the researchers told some of the subjects (falsely) that a pain-reliving serum had been added and again asked all of the subjects to rank their discomfort. Throughout the procedure, PET scans tracked the activity of endorphins in the subjects' brains. Those who got the placebo produced endorphins in particular brain areas, which is just what would have happened had they taken various pain-relieving medications. By inducing chemical changes in the brain, expectations of relief produced a self-fullfilling prophecy.

Expectations about pain are affected not only by placebos but also by your environment (for example, does it make you feel safe or apprehensive?), what your doctor tells you, psychological factors such as a focus on yourself, and cultural beliefs governing how appropriate it is to notice symptoms and express distress. These nonmedical influences on pain contribute to the rise and fall of pain epidemics, as in sudden, apparently mysterious outbreaks of back pain, whiplash, and repetitive-motion injuries (Gawande, 1998). The individuals who suffer during such epidemics are not faking it, and their pain is not "just in their heads." But it may be in their brains.

The Environment Within

kinesthesia [KIN-es-THEE-sis] The sense of body position and movement of body parts; also called *kinesthesia*.

We usually think of our senses as pipelines to the world around us, but two senses keep us informed about the movements of our own bodies. **Kinesthesis** tells us where our bodily parts are located and lets us know when they move. This information is provided by pain and pressure receptors located in the muscles, joints, and tendons (tissues that connect muscles to bones). Without kinesthesis, you could not touch your finger to your nose with your eyes shut. In fact, you would have trouble with any vol-

untary movement. Think of how hard walking is when your leg has fallen asleep or how clumsy chewing is when a dentist has numbed your jaw.

Equilibrium, or the sense of balance, gives us information about our bodies as a whole. Along with vision and touch, it lets us know whether we are standing upright or on our heads and tells us when we are falling or rotating. Equilibrium relies primarily on three **semicircular canals** in the inner ear (see Figure 6.10 on page 212). These thin tubes are filled with fluid that moves and presses on hairlike receptors whenever the head rotates. The receptors initiate messages that travel through a part of the auditory nerve that is not involved in hearing.

Normally, kinesthesis and equilibrium work together to give us a sense of our own physical reality, something we take utterly for granted but should not. Oliver Sacks (1985) told the heartbreaking story of Christina, a young British woman who suffered irreversible damage to her kinesthetic nerve fibers because of a mysterious inflammation. At first, Christina was as floppy as a rag doll; she could not sit up, walk, or stand. Then, slowly, she learned to do these things, relying on visual cues and sheer willpower. But her movements remained unnatural; she had to grasp a fork with painful force or she would drop it. More important, despite her remaining sensitivity to light touch on the skin, she said she could no longer experience herself as physically embodied: "It's like something's been scooped right out of me," she told Sacks, "right at the center."

This break dancer obviously has exceptional kinesthetic talents and equilibrium.

With equilibrium, we come, as it were, to the end of our senses. Every second, millions of sensory signals reach the brain, which combines and integrates them to produce a model of reality from moment to moment. How does it know how to do this? Are our perceptual abilities inborn, or must we learn them? We turn next to this issue.

equilibrium The sense of balance.

semicircular canals Sense organs in the inner ear that contribute to equilibrium by responding to rotation of the head.

QUICK quiz

See if you can make sense of the following quiz items.

A. What explanation of each problem is most likely?

1. April always has trouble tasting foods, especially those with subtle flavors.
2. May, a rock musician, does not hear as well as she used to.
3. June has chronic shoulder pain, though the injury that initially caused it seems to have healed. [Hint: Think about the gate-control theory and its revision.]

B. After reading about the scent studies in "Close-up on Research," what further questions might you want to ask?

C. After seeing a new pain-relief ointment advertised on TV, you try it and find that it seems to work. What other explanation is possible for the decrease in your pain?

Answers:

A. 1. April may have an impaired sense of smell, possibly due to disease, illness, or cigarette smoking. **2.** Hearing impairment has many causes, but in May's case, we might suspect that prolonged exposure to loud music has damaged the hair cells of her cochlea. **3.** Nerve fibers that normally close the pain "gate" may have been damaged, or a matrix of cells in the brain may be producing abnormal activity. **B.** Some questions to ask: Do other scents also affect behavior, and if so, which ones? (We do not want to oversimplify by assuming that similar results would occur for all scents.) Are pleasant and unpleasant scents equally likely to affect behavior? Would the effects be even stronger if the participants were aware of the scent? Most important, will other research replicate these initial findings? **C.** The relief you feel may be due at least in part to a placebo effect, which has decreased activity in the pain matrix of your brain or has led to increased production of endorphins.

WHAT'S**AHEAD**

- Do babies see the world the way adults do?
- Why do blind children whose sight has been restored see better than adults in the same situation?
- What psychological motives could cause people to see the face of a religious figure on a cinnamon bun?

Perceptual Powers: Origins and Influences

What happens when babies first open their eyes? Do they see the same sights, hear the same sounds, smell the same smells, taste the same tastes as an adult does? Are their strategies for organizing the world wired into their brains from the beginning? Or is an infant's world, as William James once suggested, only a "blooming, buzzing confusion," waiting to be organized by experience and learning? The truth lies somewhere between these two extremes.

Inborn Abilities

In human beings, most basic sensory abilities and many perceptual skills are inborn or develop very early. Infants can distinguish salty from sweet and can discriminate among odors. They can distinguish a human voice from other sounds. They will startle to a loud noise and turn their heads toward its source, showing that they perceive sound as being localized in space. Many visual skills, too, are present at birth or develop shortly afterward. Human infants can discriminate sizes and colors very early, possibly even right away. They can distinguish contrasts, shadows, and complex patterns after only a few weeks. And depth perception develops during the first few months.

Testing an infant's perception of depth requires considerable ingenuity. One clever procedure that was used for decades was to place infants on a device called a *visual cliff* (Gibson & Walk, 1960). The "cliff" is a pane of glass covering a shallow surface and a deep one (see Figure 6.15). Both surfaces are covered by a checkerboard pattern. The infant is placed on a board in the middle, and the child's mother tries to lure the baby across either the shallow side or the deep side. Babies only 6 months of age will crawl across the shallow side but will refuse to crawl out over the "cliff." Their hesitation shows that they have depth perception.

FIGURE 6.15 A Cliff-Hanger
Infants as young as 6 months usually hesitate to crawl past the apparent edge of a visual cliff, which suggests that they are able to perceive depth.

Of course, by 6 months of age, a baby has had quite a bit of experience with the world. But infants younger than 6 months can also be tested on the visual cliff, even though they cannot yet crawl. At only 2 months of age, babies show a drop in heart rate when placed on the deep side of the cliff but no change when they are placed on the shallow side. A slowed heart rate is usually a sign of increased attention. Thus, although these infants may not be frightened the way an older infant would be, it seems they can perceive the difference between the shallow and deep sides of the cliff (Banks & Salapatek, 1984).

Critical Periods

Although many perceptual abilities are inborn, experience also plays a vital role. If an infant misses out on certain experiences during a crucial window of time—a *critical period*—perception will be impaired. Innate abilities will not survive because cells in the nervous system deteriorate, change, or fail to form appropriate neural pathways.

One way to study critical periods is to see what happens when the usual perceptual experiences of early life fail to take place. To do this, researchers usually study animals whose sensory and perceptual systems are similar to our own. For example, like human infants, kittens are born with the visual ability to detect horizontal and vertical lines and other spatial orientations as well; at birth, kittens' brains are equipped with the same kinds of feature-detector cells that adult cats have. But if they are deprived of normal visual experience, these cells deteriorate or change and perception suffers (Crair, Gillespie, & Stryker, 1998; Hirsch & Spinelli, 1970).

FIGURE 6.16 Vision and Early Experience

Cats were reared in darkness for five months after birth, but for several hours each day they were put into a special cylinder that permitted them to see only vertical or horizontal lines and nothing else. Later, cats that were exposed only to vertical lines had trouble perceiving horizontal ones, and those exposed only to horizontal lines had trouble perceiving vertical ones (Blakemore & Cooper, 1970).

In one famous study, kittens were exposed to either vertical or horizontal black and white stripes. Special collars kept them from seeing anything else, even their own bodies (see Figure 6.16). After several months, the kittens exposed only to vertical stripes seemed blind to all horizontal contours; they bumped into horizontal obstacles, and they ran to play with a bar that an experimenter held vertically but not to a bar held horizontally. In contrast, those exposed only to horizontal stripes bumped into vertical obstacles and ran to play with horizontal bars but not vertical ones (Blakemore & Cooper, 1970).

Critical periods for sensory development also exist in human beings. When adults who have been blind from infancy have their vision restored, they may see, but often they do not see well. Areas in the brain normally devoted to vision may have taken on different functions when these individuals were blind. As a result, their depth perception may be poor, causing them to trip constantly. They cannot always make sense of what they see; to identify objects, they may have to touch or smell them. They may have trouble recognizing faces and emotional expressions. They may even lack size constancy and may need to remind themselves that people walking away from them are not shrinking in size (Fine et al., 2003)! But if an infant's congenital blindness is corrected early, during a critical period occurring during the first nine months or so, the prognosis is much better (though visual discriminations may never become entirely normal). In one study of infants who underwent corrective surgery when they were from 1 week to 9 months of age, improvement started to occur after as little as one hour of visual experience (Maurer et al., 1999).

Similar findings apply to hearing. When adults who were born deaf, or who lost their hearing before learning to speak, receive cochlear implants (devices that stimulate the auditory nerve and allow auditory signals to travel to the brain), they tend to find sounds confusing. They are unable to learn to speak normally, and sometimes they ask to have the implants removed. But cochlear implants are more successful in children and in adults who became deaf late in life (Rauschecker, 1999). Young children presumably have not yet passed through the critical period for processing sounds, and adults have already had years of auditory experience.

In sum, our perceptual powers are both inborn and dependent on experience. Because neurological connections in infants' brains and sensory systems are not completely formed, their senses are far less acute than an adult's. It takes time and experience for their sensory abilities to fully develop. But an infant's world is clearly not the blooming, buzzing confusion that William James took it to be.

People often see what they want to see. A man in Nashville bought a cinnamon bun at a coffee shop and thought he saw a likeness of Mother Teresa in it. The bun was then shellacked and enshrined at the coffee shop, and hundreds traveled to see it. Later it was stolen, perhaps by someone who was very devout or very hungry.

Psychological and Cultural Influences

The fact that some perceptual processes appear to be innate does not mean that all people perceive the world in the same way. A camera doesn't care what it "sees." A tape recorder doesn't ponder what it "hears." A robot arm on a factory assembly line holds no opinion about what it "touches." But because we human beings care about what we see, hear, taste, smell, and feel, psychological factors can influence what we perceive and how we perceive it. Here are a few of these factors:

1 **Needs.** When we need something, have an interest in it, or want it, we are especially likely to perceive it. For example, hungry individuals are faster than others at seeing words related to hunger when the words are flashed briefly on a screen (Wispé & Drambarean, 1953).

2 **Beliefs.** What we hold to be true about the world can affect our interpretation of ambiguous sensory signals. For example, if you believe that extraterrestrials occasionally visit the earth, and you see a round object in the sky (where there are few points of reference to help you judge distance), you may think you see a spaceship. (Impartial investigations of UFO sightings show that they are really weather balloons, rocket launchings, swamp gas, military aircraft, or ordinary celestial bodies, such as planets and meteors.) Images that remind people of a crucified Jesus have been reported on walls, dishes, and plates of spaghetti, causing great excitement among those who believe that divine messages can be found on everyday objects—until other explanations emerge. Do you remember that image of Jesus on the garage door in California, in our opening story? It turned out to be caused by two streetlights that merged the shadows of a bush and a "For Sale" sign in the yard.

3 **Emotions.** Emotions can also influence our interpretation of sensory information. A small child afraid of the dark may see a ghost instead of a robe hanging on the door or a monster instead of a beloved doll. Pain, in particular, is affected by emotion. Soldiers who are seriously wounded often deny being in much pain, even though they are alert and are not in shock. Their relief at being alive may offset the anxiety and fear that contribute so much to pain (although distraction and the body's own pain-fighting mechanisms may also be involved). Conversely, negative emotions such as anger, fear, sadness, or depression can prolong and intensify a person's pain (Fernandez & Turk, 1992; Fields, 1991).

4 **Expectations.** Previous experiences often affect how we perceive the world (Lachman, 1996). The tendency to perceive what you expect is called a **perceptual set**. Perceptual sets can come in handy; they help us fill in words in sentences, for example, when we haven't really heard every one. But perceptaul sets can also cause misperceptions. In Center Harbor, Maine, local legend has it that veteran newscaster Walter Cronkite was sailing into port one day when he heard a small crowd on shore shouting "Hello, Walter . . . Hello, Walter." Pleased, he waved and took a bow. Only when he ran aground did he realize what they had really been shouting: "Shallow water . . . shallow water."

By the way, the previous paragraph has a misspelled word. Did you notice it? If not, probably it was because you expected all the words in this book to be spelled correctly.

Our needs, beliefs, emotions, and expectations are all affected, in turn, by the culture we live in. Different cultures give people practice with different environments. In a classic study done in the 1960s, researchers found that members of some African tribes were much less likely to be fooled by the Müller-Lyer illusion and other geometric illusions than were

perceptual set A habitual way of perceiving, based on expectations.

Westerners. In the West, the researchers observed, people live in a "carpentered" world, full of rectangular structures built with the aid of straightedges and carpenter's squares. Westerners are also used to interpreting two-dimensional photographs and perspective drawings as representations of a three-dimensional world. Therefore, they interpret the kinds of angles used in the Müller-Lyer illusion as right angles extended in space, a habit that would increase susceptibility to the illusion. The rural Africans in the study, living in a less carpentered environment and in round huts, seemed more likely to take the lines in the figures literally, as two-dimensional, which could explain why they were less susceptible to the illusion (Segall, Campbell, & Herskovits, 1966; Segall et al., 1999).

Culture also affects perception by shaping our stereotypes, directing our attention, and telling us what to notice or ignore. Westerners, for example, tend to focus mostly on the figure when viewing a scene and much less on the ground. East Asians, in contrast, tend to pay attention to the overall context and the relationship between figure and ground. When Japanese and Americans were shown underwater scenes containing brightly colored fish that were larger and moving faster than other objects in the scene, they reported the same numbers of details about the fish, but the Japanese reported more details about everything else in the background (Masuda & Nisbett, 2001). One of the researchers, Richard Nisbett, commented, "If it ain't moving, it doesn't exist for an American" (quoted in Shea, 2001).

Why should the Japanese pay more attention to context than Americans? One possibility is that a greater concern with the social world directs the attention of the Japanese to contexts of all types. Another possibility is that in Japanese environments, specific objects really do stand out less than in comparable American environments, so living in Japan tends to direct a person's attention to the whole visual field. Indeed, when researchers randomly sampled pictures of hotels, elementary schools, and post offices from small, medium, and large cities in Japan and the United States, they found that the Japanese scenes were more ambiguous and contained more elements than comparable American scenes—just the kind of scenes that encourage attention to context (Miyamoto, Nisbett, & Masuda, 2006).

THINKING CRITICALLY

CONSIDER OTHER INTERPRETATIONS

These photos of a U.S. school (left) and a Japanese school (right) were among a large number of randomly selected photos of schools, hotels, and post offices taken in the two countries. Japanese scenes tend to be more ambiguous and complex than American scenes, which may help explain why the Japanese attend more closely to context than Americans do (Miyamoto, Nisbett, & Masuda, 2006).

QUICK quiz

Direct your perceptual attention now to this quiz.

1. On the visual cliff, most 6-month-old babies (a) go right across because they cannot detect depth, (b) cross even though they are afraid, (c) will not cross because they can detect depth, (d) cry or get bored.
2. Newborns and infants (a) have few perceptual abilities, (b) need visual experiences during a critical period for vision to develop normally, (c) see as well as adults.
3. "Have a nice . . . " says Dewey, but then he gets distracted and doesn't finish the thought. Yet Clarence is sure he heard Dewey wish him a nice *day*. Why?

Answers:

1. c 2. b 3. perceptual set due to expectations

WHAT'S**AHEAD**

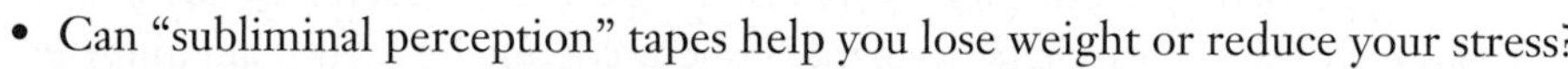

- Can "subliminal perception" tapes help you lose weight or reduce your stress?

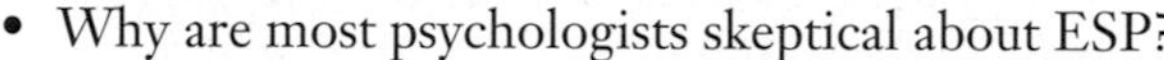

- Why are most psychologists skeptical about ESP?

Puzzles of Perception

We come, finally, to two intriguing questions about perception that have captured the public's imagination for years. First, can we ever perceive what is happening in the world when it is below our usual sensory threshold? Second, can we pick up signals from the world or from other people without using our usual sensory channels at all?

Subliminal Perception: How Persuasive?

As we saw earlier in our discussion of selective attention, even when people are oblivious to speech sounds, they are processing and recognizing those sounds at some level. But such sounds and sights are above people's absolute thresholds. Is it also possible to perceive and respond to messages that are *below* the absolute threshold—too quiet to be consciously heard or too brief or dim to be consciously seen? Perhaps you have seen ads for products that will supposedly help you learn another language or raise your self-esteem (or, our favorite, learn to love housework) by taking advantage of "subliminal perception." What are the facts?

Perceiving Without Awareness. First, a simple visual stimulus can indeed affect your behavior even when you are unaware that you saw it. For example, people sometimes correctly sense a change in a scene (say, in the color or location of an object) even though the change was shown too quickly to be consciously recognized and identified (Rensink, 2004). And people subliminally exposed to a face will tend to prefer that face over one they did not "see" in this way (Bornstein, Leone, & Galley, 1987). In many studies, researchers have used a method called **priming**, in which a person is exposed to information (subliminally or explicitly) and is later tested to see whether the information affects performance on another task (see Chapter 10). Researchers have found that when words flashed subliminally are related to some personality trait, such as honesty, people are more likely later to judge someone they read about as having that trait. They have been "primed" to evaluate the person that way (Bargh, 1999).

priming A method used to measure unconscious cognitive processes, in which a person is exposed to information and is later tested to see whether the information affects behavior or performance on another task or in another situation.

Thus, people often know more than they know they know. In fact, nonconscious processing appears to occur not only in perception but also in memory, thinking, and decision making, as we will see in Chapter 9 and Chapter 10. However, even in the laboratory, where researchers have considerable control, subliminal perception can be hard to demonstrate and replicate. The strongest evidence comes from studies using simple stimuli (faces or single words such as *bread*) rather than complex stimuli such as sentences ("Eat whole-wheat bread, not white bread").

Perception Versus Persuasion. If subliminal priming can affect judgments and preferences, can it be used to manipulate people's attitudes and behavior? Subliminal persuasion techniques were a hot topic back in the 1950s, when an advertising executive claimed to have increased popcorn and Coke sales at a theater by secretly flashing the words EAT POPCORN and DRINK COKE on the movie screen. The claim turned out to be a hoax, devised to save the man's struggling advertising company. Ever since, scientists have been skeptical, and most attempts to demonstrate subliminal persuasion have been disappointing.

EXAMINE THE EVIDENCE

For just $29.95, a "subliminal tape" promises to tune up your sluggish motivation. Many perceptual processes do occur outside of awareness, but does that mean that these tapes can change your behavior or improve your life?

That has not deterred people who market subliminal tapes that promise to help you lose weight, stop smoking, relieve stress, read faster, boost your motivation, lower your cholesterol, stop biting your nails, overcome jet lag, or stop taking drugs, all without any effort on your part. If only those claims were true! But in study after study, placebo tapes—tapes that do not contain the messages that participants think they do—are just as "effective" as subliminal tapes (Eich & Hyman, 1992; Merikle & Skanes, 1992; Moore, 1992, 1995). In one typical experiment, people listened to tapes labeled "memory" or "self-esteem," but some heard tapes that were incorrectly labeled. About half showed improvement in the area specified by the label *whether it was correct or not*; the improvement was due to expectations alone (Greenwald et al., 1991).

Three psychologists in Canada have suggested that previous efforts at subliminal persuasion left out an important ingredient: the person's motivation. Instead of trying to influence people directly by using a subliminal message such as "Drink Coke," these researchers used subliminal messages—the words *thirst* and *dry*—to make subjects feel thirsty and prime them to drink. Later, when given a chance to drink, the primed participants did in fact drink more than control subjects did, but only if they had been moderately thirsty to begin with (Strahan, Spencer, & Zanna, 2002).

Does this mean that advertisers can seduce us into buying soft drinks or voting for political candidates by slipping subliminal slogans and images into television and magazine ads? The priming research has renewed the debate. However, given the many studies that have found no evidence of subliminal persuasion and the subtlety of the effects that do occur (e.g., you have to be somewhat thirsty already to be primed to want to drink), we think there's little cause for worry about subliminal manipulation. If advertisers want you to buy something, they would probably do better to spend

their money on *above*-threshold messages. And if you want to improve yourself or your life, you'll have to do it the old-fashioned way: by working at it consciously.

Extrasensory Perception: Reality or Illusion?

Eyes, ears, mouth, nose, skin—we rely on these organs for our experience of the external world. Some people, however, claim they can send and receive messages about the world without relying on the usual sensory channels, by using *extrasensory perception (ESP)*. Reported ESP experiences involve things like telepathy, the direct communication of messages from one mind to another without the usual sensory signals, and precognition, the perception of an event that has not yet happened.

Most ESP claims challenge everything we currently know to be true about the way the world and the universe operate. A lot of people are ready to accept these claims. Should they?

Evidence or Coincidence? Much of the supposed evidence for extrasensory perception comes from anecdotal accounts. But people are not always reliable reporters of their own experiences. They often embellish and exaggerate, or they recall only part of what happened. They also tend to forget incidents that do not fit their beliefs, such as "premonitions" of events that fail to occur. Many ESP experiences could merely be unusual coincidences that are memorable because they are dramatic. What passes for telepathy or precognition could also be based on what a person knows or deduces through ordinary means. If Joanne's father has had two heart attacks, her premonition that her father will die shortly (followed, in fact, by her father's death) may not be so impressive.

> **THINKING CRITICALLY**
>
> **EXAMINE THE EVIDENCE**
>
> ESP would certainly be useful before a tough exam or a blind date. But it's one thing to wish ESP existed and another to conclude that it does. What kind of evidence would convince you that ESP is real, and what kind is only wishful thinking?

The scientific way to establish a phenomenon is to produce it under controlled conditions. Extrasensory perception has been studied extensively by researchers in the field of *parapsychology*. But ESP studies have often been poorly designed, with inadequate precautions against fraud and improper statistical analysis. After an exhaustive review, the National Research Council concluded that there was "no scientific justification . . . for the existence of parapsychological phenomena" (Druckman & Swets, 1988).

The issue has not gone away, however. Many people *really, really* want to believe that ESP exists. James Randi, a famous magician who is dedicated to educating the public about psychic deception, has for years offered a million dollars to anyone who can demonstrate ESP or other paranormal powers under close observation. Many have taken up the challenge; no one has succeeded. We think Randi's money is safe.

The history of research on psychic phenomena has been one of initial enthusiasm because of apparently positive results (Bem & Honorton, 1994; Dalton et al., 1996), followed by disappointment when the results cannot be replicated (Milton & Wiseman, 1999, 2001). The thousands of studies done since the 1940s have failed to make a convincing case for ESP. One researcher who tried for 30 years to establish the reality of psychic phenomena finally gave up in defeat. "I found no psychic phenomena," she wrote, "only wishful thinking, self-deception, experimental error, and even an occasional fraud. I became a skeptic" (Blackmore, 2001).

"What do you mean you didn't know that we were having a pop quiz today?"

Lessons from a Magician. Despite the lack of evidence for ESP, about half of all Americans say they believe in it. Even many college students believe in it—in one recent study, 28 percent said they did, with another 39 percent "not sure" (Farha &

THINKING CRITICALLY

CONSIDER OTHER INTERPRETATIONS

"Seeing is believing," they say, but is it? The engraving on the left shows a "living half-woman," seemingly swinging in midair. The sketch on the right shows how the illusion is produced. The woman reclines on an artificial bust, her body supported by another swing and hidden by black curtains. Due to a trick of lighting, the viewer sees only the swing, the face, the necklace, and the sword beneath the swing. The moral: Be skeptical about paranormal claims, even if you "saw it with your own eyes."

Steward, 2006). Perhaps you yourself have had an experience that seemed to involve ESP, or perhaps you have seen a convincing demonstration by someone else. Surely you can trust the evidence of your own eyes. Or can you? We will answer this question with a true story, one that contains an important lesson not only about ESP but about ordinary perception as well.

During the 1970s, Andrew Weil (who is now known for his efforts to promote alternative medicine) set out to investigate the claims of a self-proclaimed psychic named Uri Geller (Weil, 1974a, b). Weil, who believed in telepathy, felt that ESP might be explained by principles of modern physics, and he was receptive to Geller's claims. When he met Geller at a private gathering, he was not disappointed. Geller correctly identified a cross and a Star of David sealed inside separate envelopes. He made a stopped watch start running and a ring sag into an oval shape, apparently without touching them. He made keys change shape in front of Weil's very eyes. Weil came away a convert. What he had seen with his own eyes seemed impossible to deny . . . until he went to visit the Amazing Randi.

To Weil's astonishment, Randi was able to duplicate much of what Geller had done. He, too, could bend keys and guess the contents of sealed envelopes. But Randi's feats were tricks, and he was willing to show Weil exactly how they were done. Weil suddenly experienced "a sense of how strongly the mind can impose its own interpretations on perceptions; how it can see what it expects to see, but not see the unexpected."

Weil was dis-illusioned—literally. He was forced to admit that the evidence of one's own eyes is not always reliable. Even when he knew what to look for in a trick, he could not catch the Amazing Randi doing it. Weil learned that our sense impressions of reality are not the same as reality. Our eyes, our ears, and especially our brains can play tricks on us.

QUICK quiz

ESP won't help you answer these questions.

1. A study appears to find evidence of "sleep learning"—the ability to perceive and retain material played on an audiotape while a person sleeps. What would you want to know about this research before deciding to tape this chapter and play it by your bedside all night instead of studying it in the usual way?

2. What factors in human perception might explain why so many people interpret unexplained sensations as evidence of ESP, telepathy, and other "psychic" phenomena?

Answers:

1. Was there a control group that listened to, say, a musical selection or white noise? How complicated was the material that was allegedly learned—a few key words, whole sentences, a whole lecture by Professor Arbuckle? Were the results large enough to have any practical applications? How did the researchers determine that the participants really were asleep? (When brain-wave measures are used to verify that volunteers are actually sleeping, no "sleep learning" takes place. So if you want to learn the material in this chapter, you'll have to stay awake!) **2.** psychological and cultural factors, such as perceptual sets, needs, emotions, wishes, and beliefs

Throughout this chapter, we have seen that we do not passively register the world "out there"; we mentally construct it. All of us, even those of us who are not usually gullible, have needs and beliefs that can fool us into seeing things that we *want* to see. All of us occasionally read meanings into sensory experiences that are not inherent in the experience itself; who has not seen nonexistent water on a hot highway or felt a nonexistent insect on the skin after merely thinking about bugs?

The ancient Greek philosopher Plato once said that "knowledge is nothing but perception," but he was wrong. Simple perception is *not* always the best path to knowledge. Because our sense organs evolved for particular purposes, our sensory windows on the world are partly shuttered. But we can use reason, ingenuity, and scientific inquiry to pry those shutters open. Ordinary perception tells us that the sun circles the earth, but the great astronomer Copernicus was able to figure out nearly five centuries ago that the opposite is true. Ordinary perception will never let us see ultraviolet and infrared rays directly, but we know they are there, and we can measure them. If research can enable us to overturn the everyday evidence of our senses, who knows what surprises science has in store for us?

Taking Psychology with You

Living with Pain

Temporary pain is an unpleasant but necessary part of life, a warning of disease or injury. Chronic pain is another matter, a serious problem in itself. Back injuries, arthritis, migraine headaches, and serious illnesses can cause unrelieved misery to pain sufferers and their families. Chronic pain can also impair the immune system, putting patients at risk of further complications from their illnesses (Page et al., 1993).

At one time, the only way to combat pain was with drugs and surgery, which often were ineffective. Today, these

approaches have improved somewhat, but surgery carries its own risks and drugs often have side effects. Moreover, it has become clear that pain is affected by attitudes, actions, emotions, and circumstances and that treatment must take these influences into account. Even social roles can influence a person's response to pain. For example, although women tend to report greater pain than men do, a real-world study of people who were in pain for more than six months found that men suffered more psychological distress than women did, possibly because the male role made it hard for them to admit their pain (Snow et al., 1986).

Many pain-treatment programs encourage patients to manage their pain themselves instead of relying entirely on medication and health-care professionals. Usually, these programs combine several strategies:

- **Involvement by family and friends.** When a person is in pain, friends and relatives understandably tend to sympathize and to excuse the sufferer from regular responsibilities. The sufferer takes to bed, avoids physical activity, and focuses on the pain. As we discuss in Chapter 7, attention from others is a powerful reinforcer of whatever behavior produces the attention. Also, focusing on pain tends to increase it, and inactivity can lead to shortened muscles, muscle spasms, and fatigue. So sympathy and attention can sometimes backfire and may actually prolong the agony (Flor, Kerns, & Turk, 1987). Many pain experts now encourage family members to reward activity, distraction, and wellness instead of simply offering sympathy. This approach, however, must be used carefully, preferably under the direction of a medical or mental-health professional, because a patient's complaints about pain are an important diagnostic tool for the physician.
- **Self-management.** Patients can learn to identify how, when, and where their pain occurs. This knowledge helps them determine whether the pain is being maintained by external events or is most intense at a certain time of day, and tells them what they might need to do to reduce their pain. Just having a sense of control over pain can have a powerful pain-reducing effect (Cioffi & Holloway, 1993).
- **Relaxation, hypnosis, and acupuncture.** A blue-ribbon panel of experts concluded that relaxation techniques, such as deep breathing, meditating, or focusing on reducing tension in specific muscle groups, can help reduce chronic pain from a variety of medical conditions (NIH Technology Assessment Panel, 1996). Hypnosis can be useful too, especially when it is combined with behavior modification, physical therapy, and, if the person is anxious or depressed, psychotherapy (Patterson, 2004). Some studies find that acupuncture also helps in reducing some kinds of pain, possibly by stimulating the release of endorphins (Holden, 1997).
- **Cognitive-behavior therapy.** When pain is chronic, people may begin to define themselves in terms of their pain ("I am an ill, suffering person"), which can add to their distress and make management of the pain more difficult (Pincus & Morley, 2001). Cognitive-behavior therapy teaches people how to recognize the connections among thoughts, feelings, and pain; substitute adaptive thoughts for negative ones; and use coping strategies such as distraction, relabeling of sensations, and imagery to alleviate suffering (see Chapter 17).

For further information, go to the Internet, where there are many pain-management sites run by reputable institutions such as universities, medical associations, and the federal government. For example, New York's Beth Israel Medical Center runs www.stoppain.org. You can also contact a pain clinic in a teaching hospital or in a medical school; there are many reputable clinics around the country, some specializing in specific disorders, such as migraines or back injuries. But take care: There are also many untested therapies and quack practitioners who only prey on people's pain.

Summary

- *Sensation* is the detection and direct experience of physical energy as a result of environmental or internal events. *Perception* is the process by which sensory impulses are organized and interpreted.

Our Sensational Senses

- Sensation begins with the *sense receptors*, which convert the energy of a stimulus into electrical impulses that travel along nerves to the brain. Separate sensations can be accounted for by *anatomical codes* (as set forth by the *doctrine of specific nerve energies*) and *functional codes* in the nervous system. In *sensory substitution*, sensory crossover from one modality to another occurs, and in *synesthesia*, sensation in one modality consistently evokes a sensation in another, but these experiences are rare.
- Psychologists specializing in *psychophysics* have studied sensory sensitivity by measuring *absolute* and *difference thresholds*. *Signal-detection theory*, however, holds that responses in a detection task consist of both a sensory process and a decision process and will vary with the person's motivation, alertness, and expectations.

- Our senses are designed to respond to change and contrast in the environment. When stimulation is unchanging, *sensory adaptation* occurs. Too little stimulation can cause *sensory deprivation*. Too much stimulation can cause *sensory overload*. *Selective attention* prevents overload and allows us to focus on what is important, but it also deprives us of sensory information we may need, as in *inattentional blindness*.

Vision

- Vision is affected by the wavelength, intensity, and complexity of light, which produce the psychological dimensions of visual experience—*hue*, *brightness*, and *saturation*. The visual receptors, *rods* and *cones*, are located in the *retina* of the eye. They send signals (via other cells) to the *ganglion cells* and ultimately to the *optic nerve*, which carries visual information to the brain. Rods are responsible for vision in dim light; cones are responsible for color vision. *Dark adaptation* occurs in two stages.
- Specific aspects of the visual world, such as lines at various orientations, are detected by *feature-detector cells* in the visual areas of the brain. Some of these cells respond maximally to complex patterns. A debate is going on about the possible existence of specialized "face modules" in the brain. In general, however, the brain takes in fragmentary information about lines, angles, shapes, motion, brightness, texture, and other features of what we see and comes up with a unified view of the world.
- The *trichromatic* and *opponent-process* theories of color vision apply to different stages of processing. In the first stage, three types of cones in the retina respond selectively to different wavelengths of light. In the second, *opponent-process cells* in the retina and the thalamus respond in opposite fashion to short and long wavelengths of light.
- Perception involves the active construction of a model of the world from moment to moment. The *Gestalt principles* (e.g., *figure and ground*, *proximity*, *closure*, *similarity*, and *continuity*) describe visual strategies used by the brain to perceive forms.
- We localize objects in visual space by using both *binocular* and *monocular* cues to depth. Binocular cues include *convergence* and *retinal disparity*. Monocular cues include, among others, *interposition* and *linear perspective*. *Perceptual constancies* allow us to perceive objects as stable despite changes in the sensory patterns they produce. *Perceptual illusions* occur when sensory cues are misleading or when we misinterpret cues.

Hearing

- Hearing (*audition*) is affected by the intensity, frequency, and complexity of pressure waves in the air or other transmitting substance, corresponding to the experience of *loudness*, *pitch*, and *timbre* of the sound. The receptors for hearing are *hair cells (cilia)* embedded in the *basilar membrane*, located in the *organ of Corti* in the interior of the *cochlea*. These receptors pass signals along to the *auditory nerve*. The sounds we hear are determined by patterns of hair-cell movement, which produce different neural codes. When we localize sounds, we use as cues subtle differences in how pressure waves reach each of our ears.

Other Senses

- Taste (*gustation*) is a chemical sense. Elevations on the tongue, called *papillae*, contain many *taste buds*, which in turn contain the taste receptors. The basic tastes include salty, sour, bitter, sweet, and probably umami. Responses to a particular taste depend in part on genetic differences among individuals; for example, some people are "supertasters." Taste preferences are also affected by culture and learning and by the texture, temperature, and smell of food.
- Smell (*olfaction*) is also a chemical sense. No basic odors have been identified, and up to a thousand different receptor types exist. But researchers have discovered that distinct odors activate unique combinations of receptor types, and they have identified some of those combinations. Odors also have psychological effects and, as we saw in "Close-up on Research," can affect behavior even when people are unaware of their influence. Cultural and individual differences affect people's responses to particular odors.
- The skin senses include touch (pressure), warmth, cold, pain, and variations such as itch and tickle. Except in the case of pressure, it has been difficult to identify specialized receptors for these senses, but researchers have reported a receptor for some types of itching and a possible receptor for cold.
- Pain is both a skin sense and an internal sense. According to the *gate-control theory*, the experience of pain depends on whether neural impulses get past a "gate" in the spinal cord and reach the brain. According to a revised version of this theory, a matrix of neurons in the brain can generate pain even in the absence of signals from sensory neurons, which may help explain the puzzling phenomenon of *phantom pain*. No one theory, however, completely explains perception of pain, which involves the release of many chemicals all along the pain pathways, and also the involvement of *glial cells*. Pain comes in many varieties, both physiologically and psychologically, and is affected by genetics, expectations, and culture. The "Biology and Expectations of Pain" feature described recent research on how expectations and placebos affect the subjective experience of pain through their effects on brain activity and endorphin production.

- *Kinesthesis* tells us where our body parts are located and *equilibrium* tells us the orientation of the body as a whole. Together, these two senses provide us with a feeling of physical embodiment.

Perceptual Powers: Origins and Influences

- Many fundamental perceptual skills are inborn or are acquired shortly after birth. By using the *visual cliff*, for example, psychologists have learned that babies have depth perception by the age of 6 months and probably even earlier. However, without certain experiences during *critical periods* early in life, cells in the nervous system deteriorate, change, or fail to form appropriate neural pathways, and perception is impaired. This is why efforts to correct congenital blindness or deafness are most successful when they take place early in life.
- Psychological influences on perception include needs, beliefs, emotions, and expectations (which produce *perceptual sets*). These influences are affected by culture, which gives people practice with certain kinds of experiences and influences what they attend to.

Puzzles of Perception

- In the laboratory, studies using *priming* show that simple visual subliminal messages can influence certain behaviors, judgments, and motivational states, such as thirst. However, there is no evidence that complex behaviors can be altered by "subliminal-perception" tapes or similar subliminal techniques.
- *Extrasensory perception* (*ESP*) refers to paranormal abilities such as telepathy and precognition. Years of research have failed to produce convincing evidence for ESP. Many so-called psychics take advantage of people's desire to believe in ESP, but what they do is no different from the tricks of any good magician. The story of ESP illustrates a central fact about human perception: It does not merely capture objective reality but also reflects our needs, biases, and beliefs.

KEY TERMS

How Do You Like to Study?

NOW YOU HAVE READ CHAPTER SIX — ARE YOU PREPARED FOR THE EXAM?

If you get into a hot bath, but moments later the water no longer seems so hot, sensory ______ has occurred.

How are our senses designed to respond to change in our environment? (pages 194–196)

adaptation

If you stare at red and then look at white, you will see green. This phenomenon BEST supports the ______ ______ theory of color vision.

How do we see colors? (pages 201–202)

opponent-process

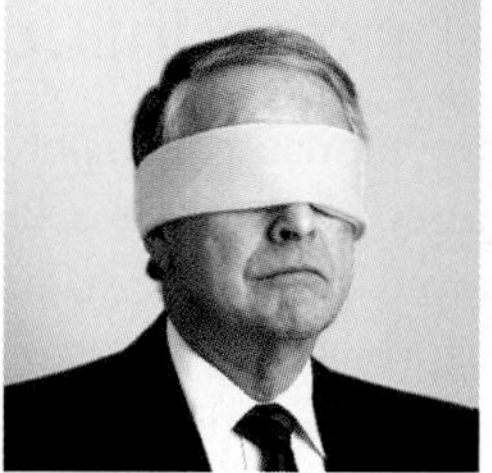

People's tendency to perceive a thing a certain way because their previous experiences or expectations influence them is called ________ _______.

What factors can influence perception? (pages 224–226)

perceptual set

STUDY
TIP

These are questions you might find on your next exam. How can you get better prepared? Everyone has a different learning style. If you want to assess your own learning style, look up some of the self-assessment links on **http://en.wikipedia.org/wiki/Learning_styles.** Many different activities for visual, auditory and kinesthetic learners can be found in MyPsychLab (MPL) at **www.mypsychlab.com.**

Use the MPL Flashcards to help you recall key concepts. You can build your own deck of cards and quiz yourself.

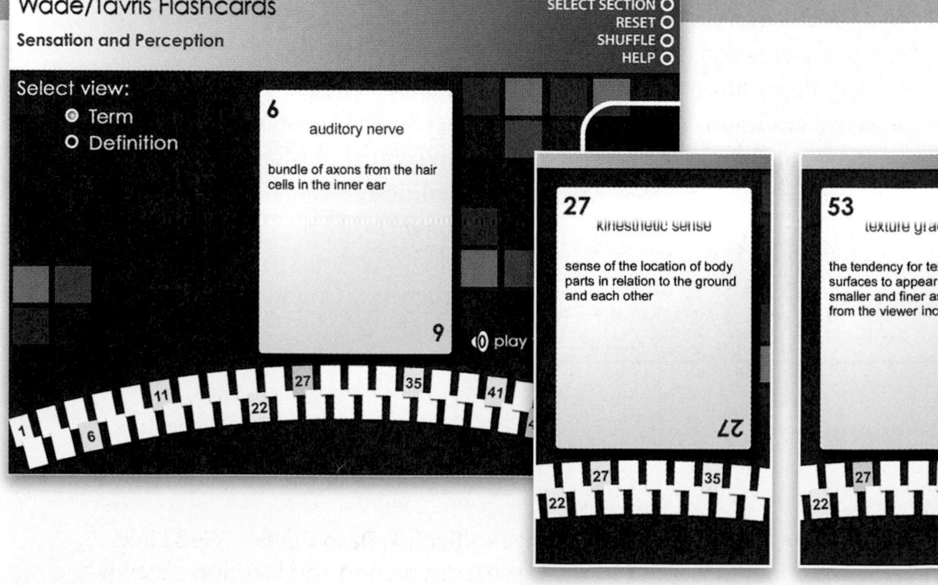
Wade/Tavris Flashcards
Sensation and Perception
SELECT SECTION
RESET
SHUFFLE
HELP
Select view:
Term
Definition
6
auditory nerve
bundle of axons from the hair cells in the inner ear
9
play
27
kinesthetic sense
sense of the location of body parts in relation to the ground and each other
53
texture gradient
the tendency for textured surfaces to appear to become smaller and finer as distance from the viewer increases

What is light? How do the parts of the eye work together? How do the eyes see, and how do the eyes see different colors?

Participate at your own pace — trying out the simulations and listening to the overview of key points will help you better remember content.

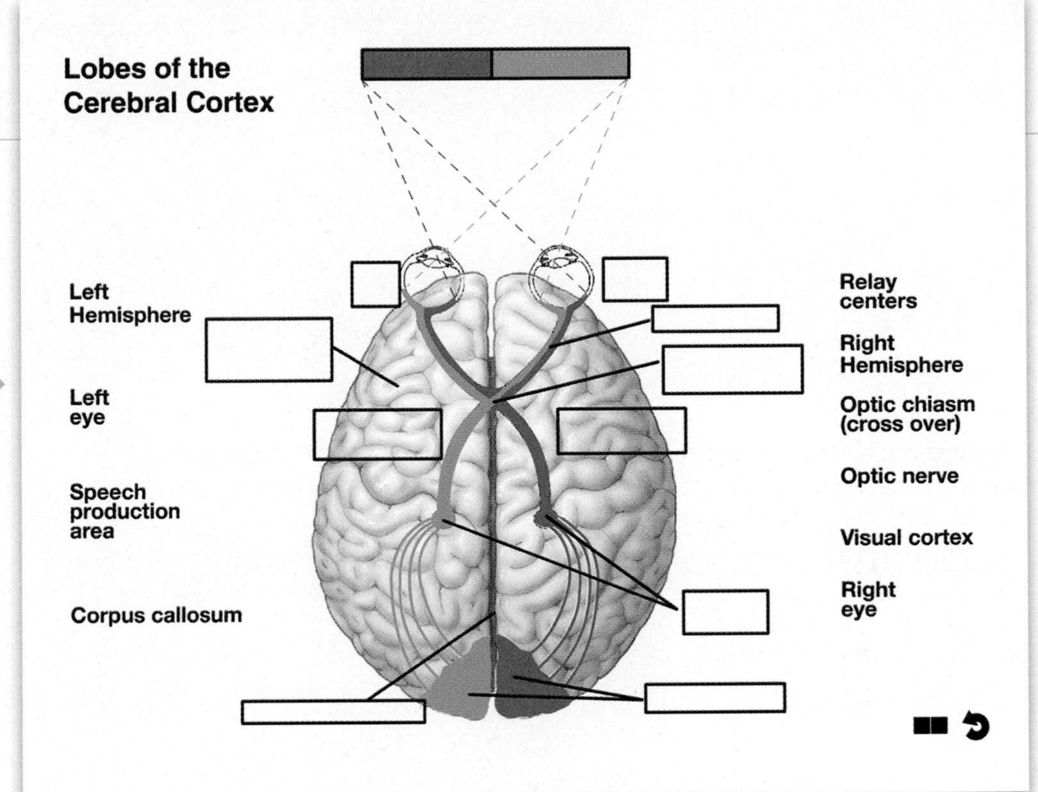

Apply It exercises give you activities and lead you to different sites to help you gain more information.

Our Sensational Senses

What is sensation and how does it enter the central nervous system?

APPLY IT

Look at the following image and answer the question below.

The office workers in this photograph are able to concentrate because they have been ______ to all the noise around them.

TELL ME **MORE** >>

"MyPsychLab is a fun way to learn. It's a good way to get your head out of the book and apply the concepts."

Student
Oklahoma City University

What can you find in MyPsychLab?

Self-Directed Tests • Videos • Simulations • eBook • Flash Cards • Web Links . . . and more — organized by chapter, section and learning objective.

LEARNING AND CONDITIONING

Reward and punishment . . . are the spur and reins whereby all mankind are set on work, and guided.

JOHN LOCKE

It's January 1, a brand-new year. The sins and lapses of the old year are behind you; the slate is clean and you're ready for a fresh start. Optimistically, you sit down to record your New Year's resolutions: to eat less fatty foods, study harder, control your temper, get more exercise, manage your spending, . . . (you can fill in the rest). How likely are you to achieve these goals? Within weeks, days, or even hours, many people find themselves reverting to their old habits ("Well, maybe just one *small* dish of double chocolate ice cream"). They may decide that trying to mend their ways is pointless because they lack the willpower, brains, or courage to do it. In this chapter, however, we will see that willpower, brains, and courage often have little to do with a person's ability to alter bad habits.

People do not just want to fix their own behavior, of course; they are forever trying to fix the bad behavior of other people as well. We imprison criminals, spank children, shout at rude strangers, give the finger to a driver who cuts us off, and impose zero tolerance policies for the slightest infraction of a rule. On the other hand, we also give children gold stars for good work, give their parents bumper stickers that praise their children's successes, give bonuses to employees, and give out trophies for top performance. Do any of these efforts get the results we hope for? Well, yes and no. Once you understand the laws of **learning**, you will realize that behavior, whether it's your own or other people's, *can* change for the better—and you will also understand why often it does not.

Research on learning has been heavily influenced by **behaviorism**, the school of psychology that accounts for behavior in terms of observable acts and events, without reference to mental entities such as "mind" or "will" (see Chapter 1). Behaviorists focus on a basic kind of learning called **conditioning**, which involves associations between environmental stimuli and responses. In fact, behaviorism is sometimes referred to informally as stimulus–response ("S–R") psychology. Behaviorists have shown that two types of conditioning, *classical conditioning* and *operant conditioning*, can explain much of human behavior.

But other approaches, including *social-cognitive learning theories*, hold that omitting mental processes from explanations of human learning is like omitting passion from descriptions of sex: You may explain the form, but you miss its essence. To social-cognitive theorists, learning includes not only changes in behavior but also changes in our thoughts, expectations, and knowledge.

WHAT'S**AHEAD**

- Why would a dog salivate when it sees a light bulb or hears a buzzer?
- How can classical conditioning help explain prejudice?
- If you have learned to fear collies, why might you also be scared of sheepdogs?

Classical Conditioning

learning A relatively permanent change in behavior (or behavioral potential) due to experience.

behaviorism An approach to psychology that emphasizes the study of observable behavior and the role of the environment as a determinant of behavior.

conditioning A basic kind of learning that involves associations between environmental stimuli and the organism's responses.

At the turn of the century, the great Russian physiologist Ivan Pavlov (1849–1936) was studying salivation in dogs as part of a research program on digestion. His work would shortly win him the Nobel Prize. One of Pavlov's procedures was to make a surgical opening in a dog's cheek and insert a tube that conducted saliva away from the animal's salivary gland so that the saliva could be measured. To stimulate the reflexive flow of saliva, Pavlov placed meat powder or other food in the dog's mouth. This procedure was later refined by others (see Figure 7.1).

Pavlov was a truly dedicated scientific observer. Many years later, as he lay dying, he even dictated his sensations for posterity! And he instilled in his students the same passion for detail. During his salivation studies, one of these students noticed something that most people would have overlooked or dismissed as trivial. After a dog had been brought to the laboratory a number of times, it would start to salivate *before* the food was placed in its mouth. The sight or smell of the food, the dish in which the food was kept, and even the sight of the person who delivered the food each day or the sound of the person's footsteps were enough to start the dog's mouth watering. These new salivary responses clearly were not inborn, so they must have been acquired through experience.

At first, Pavlov treated the dog's drooling as just an annoying secretion. But he quickly realized that his student had stumbled onto an important phenomenon, one that Pavlov came to believe was the basis of most learning in human beings and other animals (Pavlov, 1927). He called that phenomenon a "conditional" reflex—conditional because it depended on environmental conditions. Later, an error in the translation of his writings transformed "conditional" into "conditioned," the word most commonly used today.

Pavlov soon dropped what he had been doing and turned to the study of conditioned reflexes, to which he devoted the last three decades of his life. Why were his dogs salivating to things other than food?

FIGURE 7.1 A Modification of Pavlov's Method

In the apparatus on the right, which was based on Pavlov's techniques, saliva from a dog's cheek flowed down a tube and was measured by the movement of a needle on a revolving drum. In the photo, you can see Ivan Pavlov himself (in the white beard), flanked by his students and a canine subject.

New Reflexes from Old

Pavlov initially speculated about what his dogs might be thinking and feeling to make them drool before getting their food. Was the doggy equivalent of "Oh boy, this means chow time" going through their minds? Eventually, however, he decided that speculating about his dogs' mental abilities was pointless. Instead, he focused on analyzing the environment in which the conditioned reflex arose.

The original salivary reflex, according to Pavlov, consisted of an **unconditioned stimulus (US)**, food, and an **unconditioned response (UR)**, salivation. By an unconditioned stimulus, Pavlov meant an event or thing that elicits a response automatically or reflexively. By an unconditioned response, he meant the response that is automatically produced:

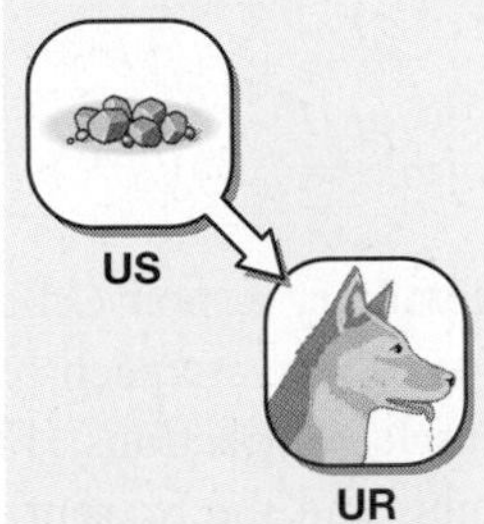

Learning occurs, said Pavlov, when a neutral stimulus (one that does not yet produce a particular response, such as salivation) is regularly paired with an unconditioned stimulus:

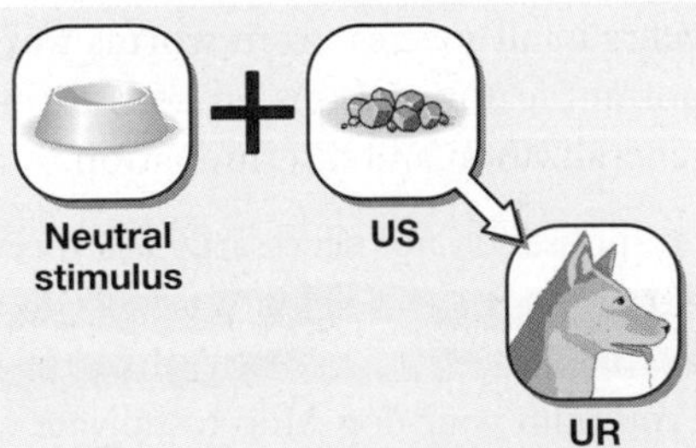

The neutral stimulus then becomes a **conditioned stimulus (CS)**, which elicits a learned or **conditioned response (CR)** that is usually similar to the original, unlearned one. In Pavlov's laboratory, the sight of the food dish, which had not previously elicited salivation, became a CS for salivation:

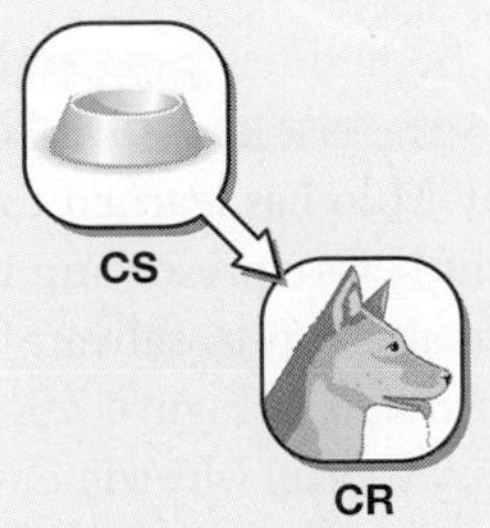

The procedure by which a neutral stimulus becomes a conditioned stimulus became known as **classical conditioning**, also called *Pavlovian* or *respondent* conditioning. Pavlov and his students went on to show that all sorts of things can become conditioned stimuli for salivation if they are paired with food: the ticking of a metronome, the musical tone of a bell or tuning fork, the vibrating sound of a buzzer, a touch on the leg, a triangle drawn on a large card, even a pinprick or an electric shock. And since

unconditioned stimulus (US) The classical-conditioning term for a stimulus that elicits a reflexive response in the absence of learning.

unconditioned response (UR) The classical-conditioning term for a reflexive response elicited by a stimulus in the absence of learning.

conditioned stimulus (CS) The classical-conditioning term for an initially neutral stimulus that comes to elicit a conditioned response after being associated with an unconditioned stimulus.

conditioned response (CR) The classical-conditioning term for a response that is elicited by a conditioned stimulus; it occurs after the conditioned stimulus is associated with an unconditioned stimulus.

classical conditioning The process by which a previously neutral stimulus acquires the capacity to elicit a response through association with a stimulus that already elicits a similar or related response.

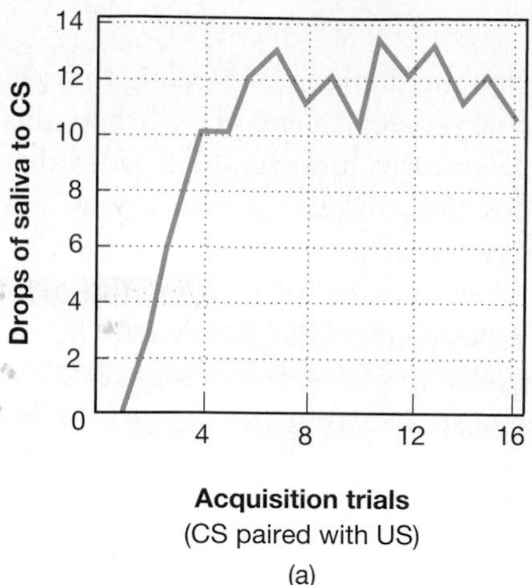

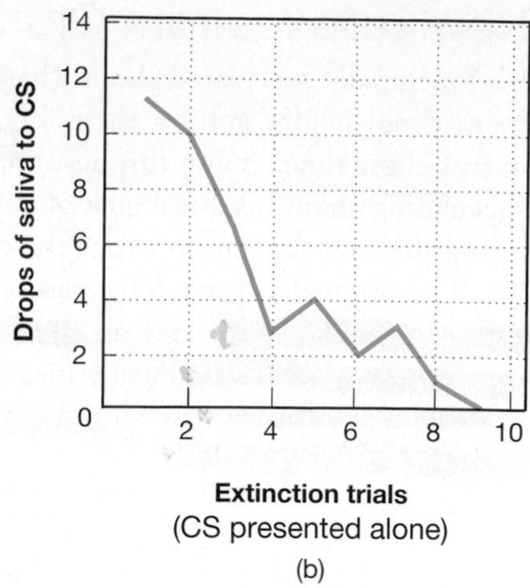

FIGURE 7.2 Acquisition and Extinction of a Salivary Response
A neutral stimulus that is consistently followed by an unconditioned stimulus for salivation will become a conditioned stimulus for salivation (left). But when this conditioned stimulus is then repeatedly presented without the unconditioned stimulus, the conditioned salivary response will weaken and eventually disappear (right); it has been extinguished.

Pavlov's day, many automatic, involuntary responses besides salivation have been classically conditioned—for example, heartbeat, stomach secretions, blood pressure, reflexive movements, blinking, and muscle contractions. The optimal interval between the presentation of the neutral stimulus and the presentation of the US depends on the kind of response involved; in the laboratory, the interval is often less than a second.

Principles of Classical Conditioning

Classical conditioning occurs in all species, from worms to *Homo sapiens*. Let us look more closely at some important features of this process: extinction, higher-order conditioning, and stimulus generalization and discrimination.

Extinction. Conditioned responses do not necessarily last forever. If, after conditioning, the conditioned stimulus is repeatedly presented without the unconditioned stimulus, the conditioned response eventually disappears, and **extinction** is said to have occurred (see Figure 7.2). Suppose that you train your dog Milo to salivate to the sound of a bell, but then you ring the bell every five minutes and do *not* follow it with food. Milo will salivate less and less to the bell and will soon stop salivating altogether; salivation will have been extinguished. Extinction is not the same as unlearning or forgetting, however. If you come back the next day and ring the bell, Milo may salivate again for a few trials. The reappearance of the response, called **spontaneous recovery**, explains why completely eliminating a conditioned response usually requires more than one extinction session.

Higher-Order Conditioning. Sometimes a neutral stimulus can become a conditioned stimulus by being paired with an already established CS, a procedure known as **higher-order conditioning**. Say Milo has learned to salivate to the sight of his food dish. Now you flash a bright light before presenting the dish. With repeated pairings of the light and the dish, Milo may learn to salivate to the light. The procedure for higher-order conditioning is illustrated in Figure 7.3.

Higher-order conditioning may explain why some words trigger emotional responses in us—why they can inflame us to anger or evoke warm, sentimental feelings. When words are paired with objects or other words that already elicit some emotional response, they, too, may come to elicit that response (Chance, 1999; Staats & Staats, 1957). For example, a child may learn a positive response to the word *birthday* because of its association with gifts and attention. Conversely, the child may learn a negative response to ethnic or national labels, such as *Swede*, *Turk*, or *Jew*, if those words are paired with words that the child has already learned are disagreeable, such as *dumb* or *dirty*. Higher-order conditioning, in other words, may contribute to the formation of prejudices.

extinction The weakening and eventual disappearance of a learned response; in classical conditioning, it occurs when the conditioned stimulus is no longer paired with the unconditioned stimulus.

spontaneous recovery The reappearance of a learned response after its apparent extinction.

higher-order conditioning In classical conditioning, a procedure in which a neutral stimulus becomes a conditioned stimulus through association with an already established conditioned stimulus.

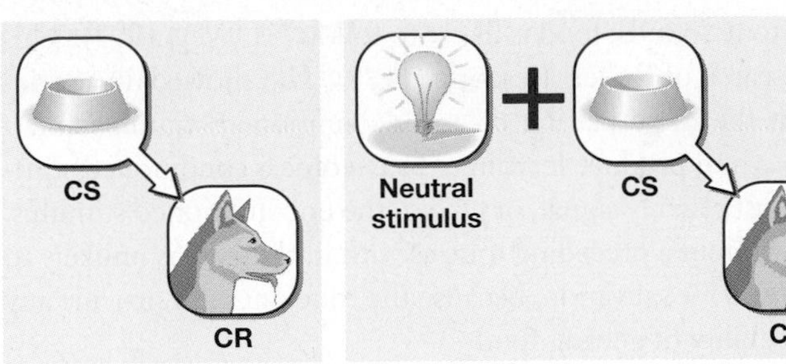

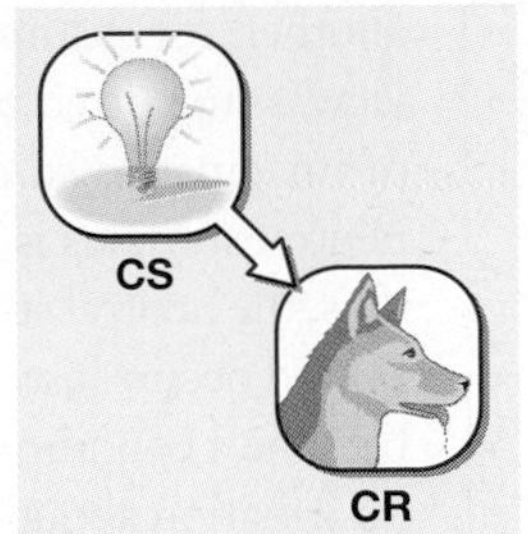

FIGURE 7.3 Higher-Order Conditioning

In this illustration of higher-order conditioning, the food dish is a previously conditioned stimulus for salivation (left). When the light, a neutral stimulus, is paired with the dish (center), the light also becomes a conditioned stimulus for salivation (right).

Stimulus Generalization and Discrimination. After a stimulus becomes a conditioned stimulus for some response, other, similar stimuli may produce a similar reaction—a phenomenon known as **stimulus generalization**. For example, if you condition your patient pooch Milo to salivate to middle C on the piano, Milo may also salivate to D, which is one tone above C, even though you did not pair D with food. Stimulus generalization is described nicely by an old English proverb: "He who hath been bitten by a snake fears a rope."

The mirror image of stimulus generalization is **stimulus discrimination**, in which *different* responses are made to stimuli that resemble the conditioned stimulus in some way. Suppose that you have conditioned Milo to salivate to middle C on the piano by repeatedly pairing the sound with food. Now you play middle C on a guitar, *without* following it by food (but you continue to follow C on the piano by food). Eventually, Milo will learn to salivate to a C on the piano and not to salivate to the same note on the guitar; that is, he will discriminate between the two sounds. If you keep at this long enough, you could train Milo to be a pretty discriminating drooler!

What Is Actually Learned in Classical Conditioning?

For classical conditioning to be most effective, the stimulus to be conditioned should *precede* the unconditioned stimulus rather than follow it or occur simultaneously with it. This makes sense because in classical conditioning, the conditioned stimulus becomes a signal for the unconditioned stimulus. Classical conditioning is in fact an evolutionary adaptation, one that enables the organism to anticipate and prepare for a biologically important event that is about to happen. In Pavlov's studies, for instance, a bell, buzzer, or other stimulus was a signal that meat was coming, and the dog's salivation was preparation for digesting food.

Today, therefore, many psychologists contend that what an animal or person actually learns in classical conditioning is not merely an association between two paired stimuli that occur close together in time, but rather *information* conveyed by one stimulus about

stimulus generalization After conditioning, the tendency to respond to a stimulus that resembles one involved in the original conditioning; in classical conditioning, it occurs when a stimulus that resembles the CS elicits the CR.

stimulus discrimination The tendency to respond differently to two or more similar stimuli; in classical conditioning, it occurs when a stimulus similar to the CS fails to evoke the CR.

GET INVOLVED!

➤CONDITIONING AN EYE-BLINK RESPONSE

Try out your behavioral skills by conditioning an eye-blink response in a willing friend, using classical conditioning procedures. You will need a drinking straw and something to make a ringing sound; a spoon tapped on a water glass works well. Tell your friend that you are going to use the straw to blow air in his or her eye, but do not say why. Immediately before each puff of air, make the ringing sound. Repeat this procedure ten times. Then make the ringing sound but *don't* puff. Your friend will probably blink anyway, and may continue to do so for one or two more repetitions of the sound before the response extinguishes. Can you identify the US, the UR, the CS, and the CR in this exercise?

"To hell with the call of the wild, all
I want to hear is the call of the can opener."

another: for example, "If a tone sounds, food is likely to follow" (Davey, 1992). This view is supported by the research of Robert Rescorla (1988), who showed, in a series of imaginative studies, that the mere pairing of an unconditioned stimulus and a neutral stimulus is not enough to produce learning. To become a conditioned stimulus, the neutral stimulus must reliably signal, or *predict*, the unconditioned stimulus. If food occurs just as often without a preceding tone as with it, the tone is unlikely to become a conditioned stimulus for salivation, because the tone does not provide any information about the probability of getting food.

In everyday life, too, a potential CS may sometimes predict an unconditioned stimulus and sometimes not, so conditioning is less certain than when the CS and US always occur together in the laboratory. A friend of ours, behaviorist Paul Chance, gave us this example: Suppose you work in an office where you are allowed to receive routine phone calls only from other employees; you may take outside calls only in emergencies. One day, there are three emergencies: Your lover calls to jilt you, the police call to report that your new car was stolen, and your landlord calls to tell you that a broken water pipe has flooded your apartment. If these were the only calls you got, the next time you heard the phone ring (the CS) you might freak out (the CR). But if they occurred randomly among 50 routine business calls, the phone's ringing would probably not upset you (any more than it already has!) because it would not necessarily signal another disaster.

Rescorla (1988) concluded that "Pavlovian conditioning is not a stupid process by which the organism willy-nilly forms associations between any two stimuli that happen to co-occur. Rather, the organism is better seen as an information seeker using logical and perceptual relations among events, along with its own preconceptions, to form a sophisticated representation of its world." Not all learning theorists agree with this conclusion; an orthodox behaviorist would say that it is silly to talk about the preconceptions of a rat. The important point, however, is that concepts such as "information seeking," "preconceptions," and "representations of the world" open the door to a more cognitive view of classical conditioning.

QUICK quiz

Classical-conditioning terms can be hard to learn, so be sure to take this quiz before going on.

A. Name the unconditioned stimulus, unconditioned response, conditioned stimulus, and conditioned response in these two situations.

1. Five-year-old Samantha is watching a storm from her window. A huge bolt of lightning is followed by a tremendous thunderclap, and Samantha jumps at the noise. This happens several more times. There is a brief lull and then another lightning bolt. Samantha jumps in response to the bolt.

2. Gregory's mouth waters whenever he eats anything with lemon in it. One day, while reading an ad that shows a big glass of lemonade, Gregory finds that his mouth has started to water.

B. In the view of many learning theorists, pairing a neutral and unconditioned stimulus is not enough to produce classical conditioning; the neutral stimulus must __________ the unconditioned stimulus.

Answers:

A. 1. US = the thunderclap; UR = jumping elicited by the noise; CS = the sight of the lightning; CR = jumping elicited by the lightning. **2.** US = the taste of lemon; UR = salivation elicited by the taste of lemon; CS = the picture of a glass of lemonade; CR = salivation elicited by the picture **B.** signal or predict

- Why do advertisers often include pleasant music and gorgeous scenery in ads for their products?
- How would a classical-conditioning theorist explain your irrational fear of heights or mice?
- If you eat licorice and then happen to get the flu, how might your taste for licorice change?
- How can sitting in a doctor's office make you feel sick?

Classical Conditioning in Real Life

If a dog can learn to salivate to the ringing of a bell, so can you. In fact, you probably have learned to salivate to the sound of a lunch bell, not to mention the phrase *hot fudge sundae*, "mouth-watering" pictures of food, and a voice calling out "Dinner's ready!" But the role of classical conditioning goes far beyond the learning of simple reflexive responses; conditioning affects us every day in many ways.

One of the first psychologists to recognize the real-life implications of Pavlovian theory was John B. Watson, who founded American behaviorism and enthusiastically promoted Pavlov's ideas. Watson believed that the whole rich array of human emotion and behavior could be accounted for by conditioning principles. For example, he thought that you learned to love another person when that person was paired with stroking and cuddling. Watson turned out to be wrong about love, which is a lot more complicated than he thought (see Chapter 12). But he was right about the power of classical conditioning to affect our emotions, preferences, and tastes.

John B. Watson (1878–1958).

Learning to Like

Classical conditioning plays a big role in our emotional responses to objects, people, symbols, events, and places. It can explain why sentimental feelings sweep over us when we see a school mascot, a national flag, or the logo of the Olympic games: These objects have been associated in the past with positive feelings:

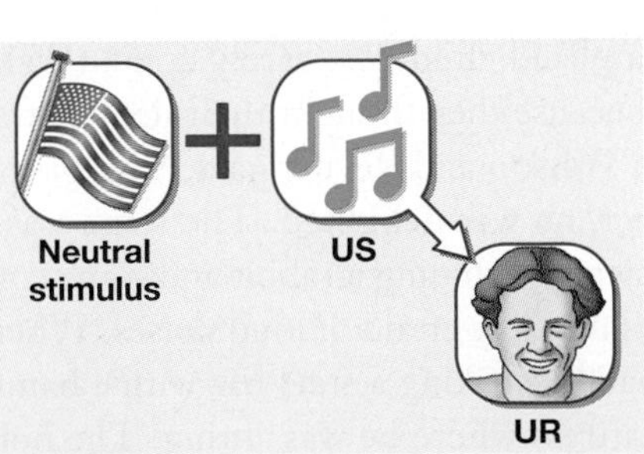

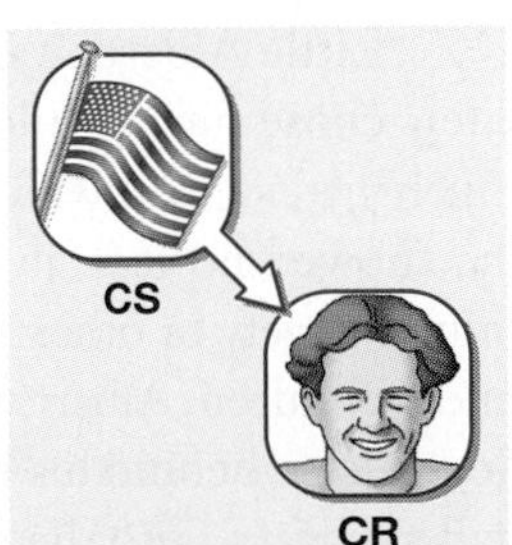

Many advertising techniques for getting us to like certain products are also based on the principles first demonstrated by Pavlov, whether advertising executives realize it or not. In one study, college students looked at slides of either a beige pen or a blue pen. During the presentation, half of the students heard a song from a recent American musical film, and half heard a selection of traditional music from India. (The experimenter made the reasonable assumption that the American music would be more appealing to the young Americans in the study.) Later the students were allowed

to choose one of the pens. Almost three-fourths of those who heard the popular music chose a pen that was the same color as the one they had seen in the slides. An equal number of those who heard the Indian music chose a pen that *differed* in color from the one they had seen (Gorn, 1982).

In classical-conditioning terms, the music in this study was an unconditioned stimulus for internal responses associated with pleasure or displeasure, and the pens became conditioned stimuli for similar responses. You can see why television commercials often pair their products with music, attractive people, or other appealing sounds and images.

Learning to Fear

On the TV show *Monk*, the lead character has a phobic fear of germs. How did he get to be that way?
Brian Lowe/ZUMA Press

Positive emotions are not the only ones that can be classically conditioned; so can dislikes and negative emotions such as fear. A person can learn to fear just about anything if it is paired with something that elicits pain, surprise, or embarrassment. Human beings, however, are biologically primed or "prepared" to learn some kinds of fears more readily than others. It is far easier to establish a conditioned fear of spiders, snakes, and heights than of butterflies, flowers, and toasters. The former can be dangerous to your health, so in the process of evolution, human beings acquired a tendency to learn quickly to be wary of them (Öhman & Mineka, 2001). Some theorists believe that evolution has also instilled in humans a readiness to learn to fear unfamiliar members of ethnic groups other than their own, and that this tendency may contribute to the emotional underpinnings of prejudice (Olsson et al., 2005; see Chapter 8).

When fear of an object or situation becomes irrational and interferes with normal activities, it qualifies as a *phobia*. To demonstrate how a phobia might be learned, John Watson and Rosalie Rayner (1920/2000) deliberately established a rat phobia in an 11-month-old boy named Albert. Their goal was to demonstrate how an inborn reaction of fear could transfer to a wide range of stimuli; today we call this stimulus generalization. They also wanted to demonstrate that adult emotional responses, such as specific fears, could originate in early childhood. The research procedures used by Watson and Rayner have been criticized over the years, and for ethical reasons, no psychologist today would attempt to do such a thing to a child. Nevertheless, the study remains a classic, and its main conclusion, that fears can be conditioned, is still well accepted.

"Little Albert" was a placid child who rarely cried. (Watson and Rayner deliberately chose such a child because they thought their demonstration would do him relatively little harm.) When Watson and Rayner gave Albert a live, furry rat to play with, he showed no fear; in fact, he was delighted. The same was true when they showed him a variety of other objects, including a rabbit and some cotton wool. However, like most children, Albert was innately afraid of loud noises. When the researchers made a loud noise behind his head by striking a steel bar with a hammer, he would jump and fall sideways onto the mattress where he was sitting. The noise made by the hammer was an unconditioned stimulus for the unconditioned response of fear.

Having established that Albert liked rats, Watson and Rayner set about teaching him to fear them. Again they offered him a rat, but this time, as Albert reached for it, one of the researchers struck the steel bar. Startled, Albert fell onto the mattress. A week later, the researchers repeated this procedure several times. Albert began to whimper and tremble. Finally, they held out the rat to him without making the noise. Albert fell over, cried, and crawled away so quickly that he almost reached the edge of the table he was sitting on before an adult caught him; the rat had become a conditioned stimulus for fear:

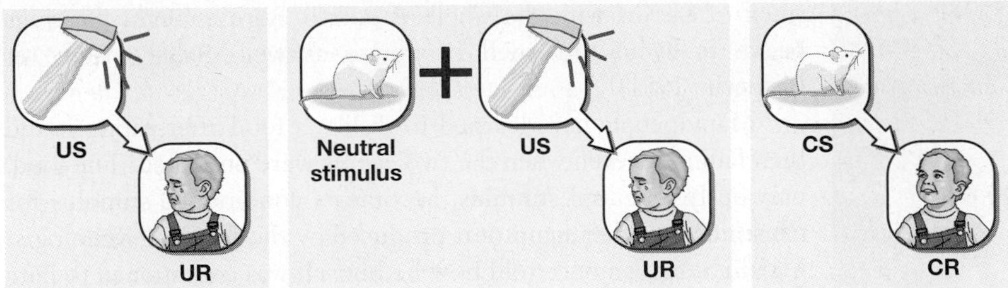

Tests done a few days later showed that Albert's fear had generalized to other hairy or furry objects, including a white rabbit, cotton wool, a Santa Claus mask, and even John Watson's hair.

Unfortunately, Watson and Rayner lost access to Little Albert, so we do not know how long the child's fears lasted. (We do know, however, that at a final session his fears had already diminished somewhat and had to be "freshened" by repeating the pairing of the conditioned stimuli with the loud noise.) Further, because the study ended early, Watson and Rayner had no opportunity to reverse the conditioning. However, Watson and Mary Cover Jones did reverse another child's conditioned fear—one that was, as Watson put it, "home-grown" rather than psychologist-induced (Jones, 1924). A 3-year-old named Peter was deathly afraid of rabbits. Watson and Jones eliminated his fear with a method called **counterconditioning**, in which a conditioned stimulus is paired with some other stimulus that elicits a response incompatible with the unwanted response. In this case, the rabbit (the CS) was paired with a snack of milk and crackers, and the snack produced pleasant feelings that were incompatible with the conditioned response of fear. At first, the researchers kept the rabbit some distance from Peter, so that his fear would remain at a low level. Otherwise, Peter might have learned to fear milk and crackers! But gradually, over several days, they brought the rabbit closer and closer. Eventually Peter learned to like rabbits:

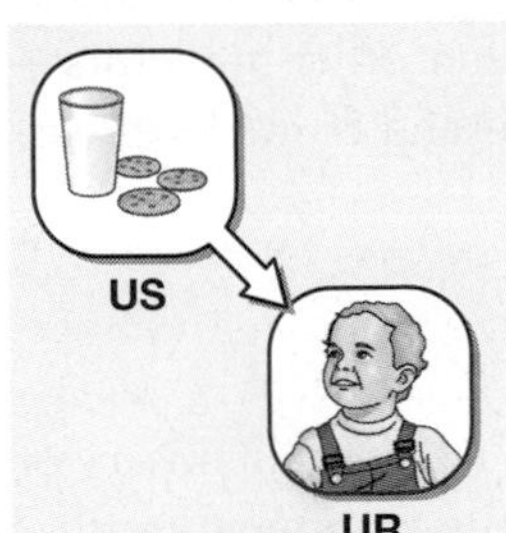

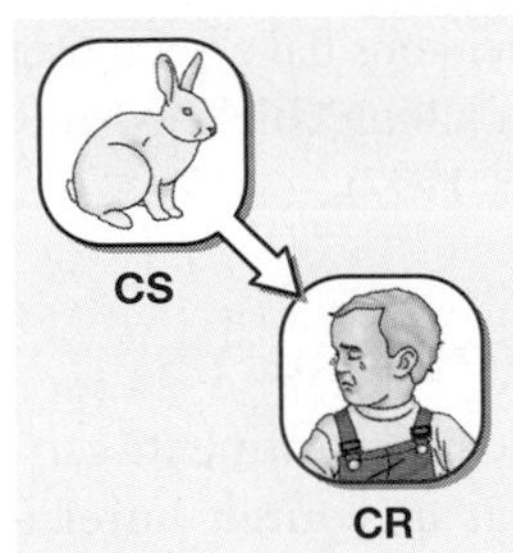

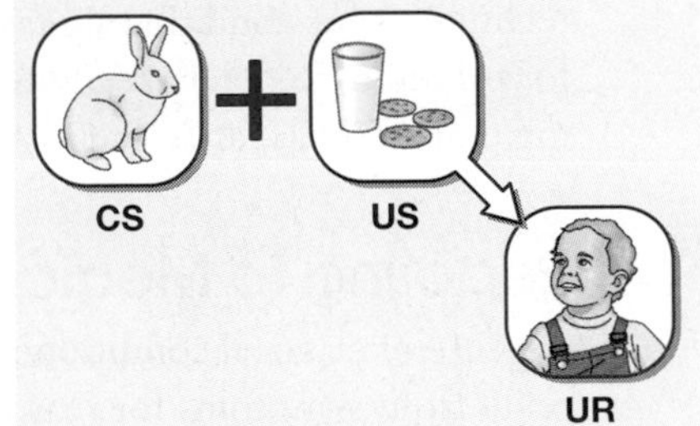

Peter was even able to sit with the rabbit in his lap, playing with it with one hand while he ate with the other. A variation of this procedure, called *systematic desensitization*, was later devised for treating phobias in adults (see Chapter 17).

Accounting for Taste

Classical conditioning can also explain how we learn to like and dislike many foods and odors. In the laboratory, researchers have taught animals to dislike foods or odors by pairing them with drugs that cause nausea or other unpleasant symptoms. One research team trained slugs to associate the smell of carrots, which slugs normally like, with a bitter-tasting chemical they detest. Soon the slugs were avoiding the smell of carrots. The researchers then demonstrated higher-order conditioning by pairing the

counterconditioning In classical conditioning, the process of pairing a conditioned stimulus with a stimulus that elicits a response that is incompatible with an unwanted conditioned response.

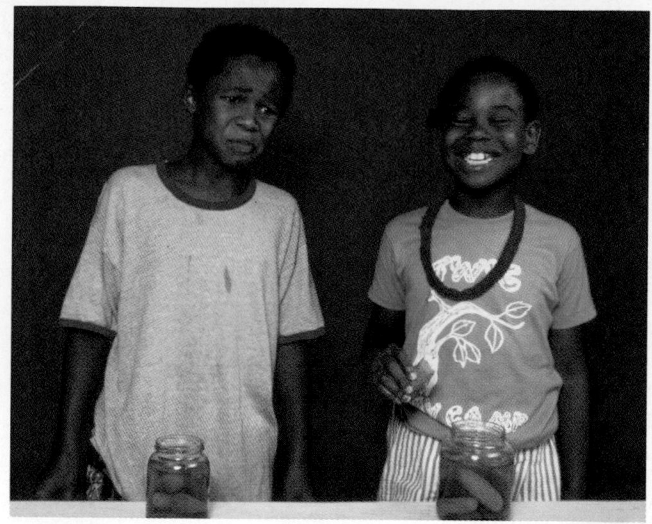

Whether we say "yuck" or "yum" to a food may depend on a past experience involving classical conditioning.

smell of carrots with the smell of potato. Sure enough, the slugs began to avoid the smell of potato as well (Sahley, Rudy, & Gelperin, 1981).

Many people have learned to dislike a food after eating it and then falling ill, even when the two events were unrelated. The food, previously a neutral stimulus, becomes a conditioned stimulus for nausea or for other symptoms produced by the illness. Psychologist Martin Seligman once told how he himself was conditioned to hate béarnaise sauce. One night, shortly after he and his wife ate a delicious filet mignon with béarnaise sauce, he came down with the flu. Naturally, he felt wretched. His misery had nothing to do with the béarnaise sauce, of course, yet the next time he tried it, he found to his annoyance that he disliked the taste (Seligman & Hager, 1972).

Notice that unlike conditioning in the laboratory, Seligman's aversion to the sauce occurred after only one pairing of the sauce with illness and with a considerable delay between the conditioned and unconditioned stimuli. Moreover, Seligman's wife did not become a conditioned stimulus for nausea, and neither did his dinner plate or the waiter, even though they also had been paired with illness. Why? In earlier work with rats, John Garcia and Robert Koelling (1966) had provided the answer: the existence of a greater biological readiness to associate sickness with taste than with sights or sounds. Later work established the same principle (the "Garcia effect") for many species, including human beings. Like the tendency to acquire certain fears, this biological tendency probably evolved through natural selection because it enhanced survival: Eating bad food is more likely to be followed by illness and death than are particular sights or sounds.

Psychologists have taken advantage of this phenomenon to develop humane ways of discouraging predators from preying on livestock, using conditioned taste aversions instead of traps and poisons. In one classic study, researchers laced sheep meat with a nausea-inducing chemical; coyotes and wolves fell for the bait, and as a result they developed a conditioned aversion to sheep (Gustavson et al., 1974, 1976). Similar techniques for conditioning taste aversions have been used to deter other predators—for example, to deter raccoons from killing chickens, and ravens and crows from eating crane eggs (Garcia & Gustavson, 1997).

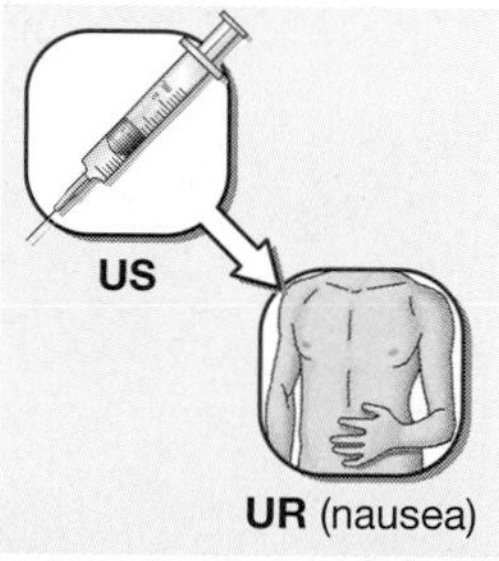

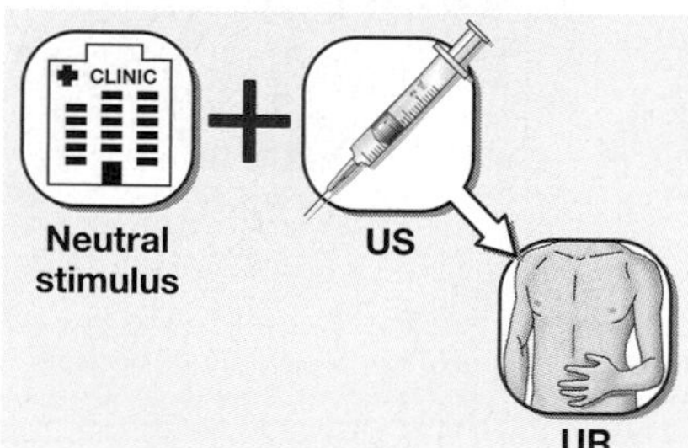

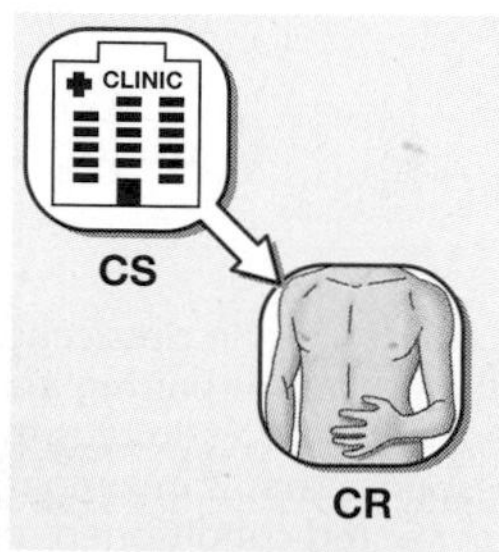

Reacting to Medical Treatments

Because of classical conditioning, medical treatments can create unexpected misery or relief from symptoms for reasons that are entirely unrelated to the treatment itself.

For example, unpleasant reactions to a treatment can generalize to a wide range of other stimuli. This is a particular problem for cancer patients. The nausea and vomiting resulting from chemotherapy often generalize to the place where the therapy takes place, the waiting room, the sound of a nurse's voice, or the smell of rubbing alcohol. The drug treatment is an unconditioned stimulus for nausea and vomiting, and through association, the other previously neutral stimuli become conditioned stimuli for these responses. Even *mental images* of the sights and smells of the clinic can become conditioned stimuli for nausea (Dadds et al., 1997; Redd et al., 1993).

Some cancer patients also acquire a classically conditioned anxiety response to anything associated with their chemotherapy. In one study, patients who drank lemon-lime Kool-Aid before their therapy sessions developed an anxiety response to the drink—an example of higher-order conditioning. They continued to feel anxious even when the drink was offered in their homes rather than at the clinic (Jacobsen et al., 1995).

On the other hand, patients may have *reduced* pain and anxiety when they receive *placebos*, pills and injections that have no active ingredients or treatments that have no direct physical effect on the problem (see Chapters 2 and 6). Placebos can be amazingly powerful, especially when they take the form of an injection, a large pill, or a pill with a brand name (Benedetti & Levi-Montalcini, 2001). Why do they work? Biological psychologists have shown that placebos can actually affect the brain in much the same way as real treatments do (see Chapter 6). Cognitive psychologists emphasize the role of expectations (at least in humans); expectations of getting better may reduce anxiety and thus boost the immune system, or perhaps they encourage us to cope better with our symptoms. Behaviorists, in contrast, argue that the doctor's white coat, the doctor's office, and pills or injections all become conditioned stimuli for relief from symptons because these stimuli have been associated in the past with *real* drugs (Ader, 2000). The real drugs are the unconditioned stimuli, the relief they bring is the unconditioned response, and the placebos acquire the ability to elicit similar reactions, thereby becoming conditioned stimuli.

The expectancy explanation of placebo effects and the classical conditioning explanation are not mutually exclusive (Kirsch, 2004; Stewart-Williams & Podd, 2004). As we saw earlier, many researchers now accept the view that classical conditioning itself involves expectancies—namely, the expectation that the conditioned stimulus will be followed by the unconditioned stimulus. Thus, at least some classically conditioned placebo effects may involve the patient's expectations. In fact, the patient's previous conditioning history may be what created those expectations to begin with.

BIOLOGY and Classical Conditioning

Pavlov and Peanut Butter

A century ago, when Ivan Pavlov taught dogs to salivate to the sound of a bell, he was limited to studying the observable associations between unconditioned and conditioned stimuli and responses. Today, technology has enabled researchers to go an important step further by exploring what happens deep within the brain during classical conditioning. Their research crosses the borders that have traditionally divided psychologists who study conditioning, motivation, and the brain.

In one imaginative study, British researchers trained 13 hungry volunteers to associate abstract computer images with the pleasant smell of peanut butter or vanilla (Gottfried, O'Doherty, & Dolan, 2003). The volunteers had to say which side of the screen an image appeared on, and soon they were reacting faster to the images associated with the pleasant food odors than to other images. Using functional MRI, the researchers discovered that when the participants saw the images—which presumably had now become conditioned stimuli for pleasure or appetite—the volunteers' brains showed surges of activity in two areas known to be involved in motivation and emotion, the amygdala (see Chapter 4) and an area of the cortex called the *orbitofrontal cortex*.

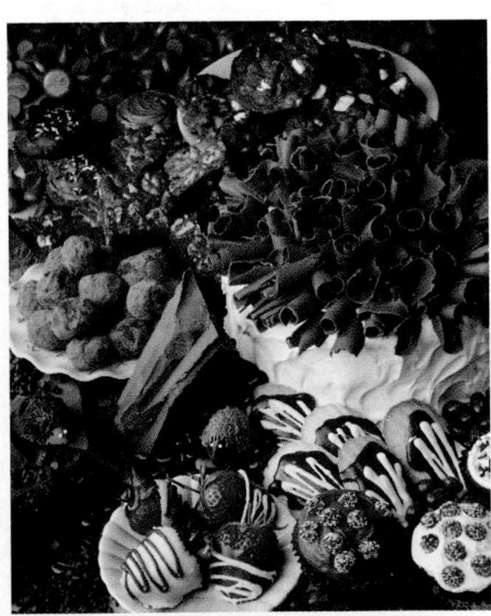

You're stuffed after a good meal, yet you suddenly find room for dessert. Why?

Then the participants got to eat either vanilla ice cream or peanut-butter sandwiches until they no longer wanted any more. Afterward, the images associated with the food a person had just eaten no longer produced such quick reactions and no longer evoked the same brain activity as before. The images associated with the other food, however, continued to produce the same reaction times and brain responses. These results may explain why feeling full isn't an all-or-none phenomenon—why we

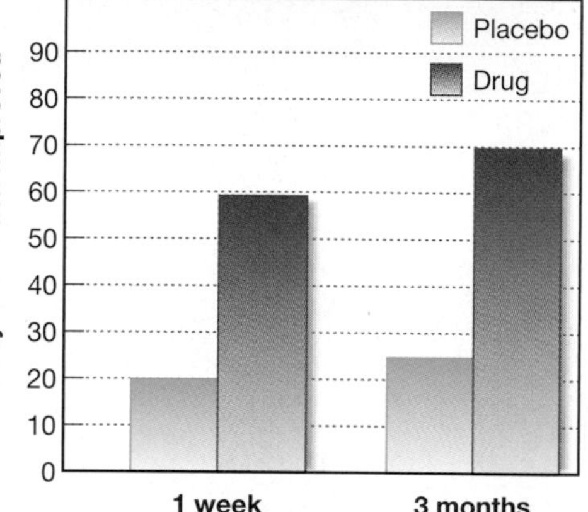

FIGURE 7.4 A Drug for Extinction

The photo shows one of the virtual-reality images used in therapy with people with a phobia for heights. Participants had to "look down" to the bottom of a building while peering over a catwalk. Those who received a drug that facilitates extinction improved significantly more than did those who got a placebo.

can have our fill of one food, yet still be tempted by another: The stimuli associated with the second food continue to fire up our motivational brain centers. This helps to ensure that we eat a variety of foods and get a variety of nutrients. But Jay Gottfried, who led the British study, noted that the results can also explain the "restaurant phenomenon" (cited in Goode, 2003). At a restaurant, just when you think you are full and can't eat another bite, the server brings the dessert cart and suddenly you have room for that luscious-looking piece of cheesecake after all. So if you're trying to avoid sweets, you probably shouldn't look at the desserts—or even the cart.

Researchers are also exploring the biological basis of fear conditioning and fear extinction. The acquisition of a conditioned fear appears to involve a receptor for the neurotransmitter glutamate in the amygdala of the brain. Giving rats a drug that blocks this receptor prevents extinction of a conditioned fear, whereas giving a drug that enhances the receptor's activity speeds up extinction (Walker et al., 2002). Inspired by these results, researchers recently set out to learn whether the receptor-enhancing drug (which is safe in humans) could help people with a phobic fear of heights (Davis et al., 2005). Using a double-blind procedure, they gave the drug to 15 such people and a placebo to 15 others. The participants then underwent two sessions of a therapy in which they donned "virtual reality" goggles and "rode" a virtual glass elevator to progressively higher floors in a hotel—an incredibly scary thing to do if you're terrified of heights! They could also "walk" out on a bridge and look down on a fountain in the hotel lobby. During each session, and again at one-week and three-month follow-up sessions, the participants rated their discomfort at each "floor." Combining the therapy with the drug reduced symptoms far more than combining it with the placebo, as you can see in Figure 7.4. Further, in their everyday lives, people who got the drug were less likely than the control subjects to avoid actual heights. If these results are replicated, they may lead to improved treatment of phobias and possibly of more complex disorders, such as posttraumatic stress disorder and panic disorder.

QUICK quiz

We hope you have not acquired a classically conditioned fear of quizzes. See whether you can supply the correct term to describe the outcome in each of these situations.

1. After a child learns to fear spiders, he also responds with fear to ants, beetles, and other crawling bugs.
2. A toddler is afraid of the bath, so her father puts just a little water in the tub and gives the child a lollipop to suck on while she is being washed. Soon the little girl loses her fear of the bath.
3. A factory worker notices that his mouth waters whenever a noontime bell signals the beginning of his lunch break. One day, the bell goes haywire and rings every half hour. By the end of the day, the worker has stopped salivating to the bell.
4. Work on how certain brain areas respond to conditioned stimuli associated with food shows that (a) brain activity decreases after a person fills up on the food but remains high for other foods; (b) the brain responds equally to desired and disliked foods; (c) brain mechanisms ensure that we eat the same basic set of foods all the time; (d) taste preferences cannot be classically conditioned.

Answers:

1. stimulus generalization 2. counterconditioning 3. extinction 4. a

WHAT'S AHEAD

- What do praising a child and quitting your nagging have in common?
- How can operant principles account for superstitious rituals?
- What is the best way to discourage a friend from interrupting you while you are studying?
- How do trainers teach guide dogs to perform the amazing services they do for their owners?

Operant Conditioning

At the end of the nineteenth century, in the first known scientific study of anger, G. Stanley Hall (1899) asked people to describe angry episodes they had experienced or observed. One person told of a 3-year-old girl who broke out in seemingly uncontrollable sobs when she was punished by being kept home from a ride. In the middle of her tantrum, the child suddenly stopped crying and asked her nanny in a perfectly calm voice if her father was in. Told no, she immediately resumed her sobbing.

Children, of course, cry for many valid reasons—pain, discomfort, fear, illness, fatigue—and these cries deserve an adult's sympathy and attention. The child in Hall's study, however, was crying because she had learned from prior experience that an outburst of sobbing would pay off by bringing her attention and possibly the ride she wanted. Her tantrum illustrates one of the most basic laws of learning: *Behavior becomes more likely or less likely depending on its consequences.*

This principle is at the heart of **operant conditioning** (also called *instrumental conditioning*), the second type of conditioning studied by behaviorists. In classical conditioning, it does not matter whether an animal's or person's behavior has consequences. In Pavlov's procedure, for example, the dog learned an association between two events that were not under its control (e.g., a tone and the delivery of food) and the animal got food whether it salivated or not. But in operant conditioning, the organism's response (the little girl's sobbing, for example) *operates* or produces effects on the environment. These effects, in turn, influence whether the response will occur again.

Classical conditioning and operant conditioning also tend to differ in the types of responses they involve. In classical conditioning, the response is typically reflexive, an automatic reaction to something happening in the environment, such as the sight of food or the sound of a bell. Generally, responses in operant conditioning are complex and are not reflexive—for instance, riding a bicycle, writing a letter, climbing a mountain, . . . or throwing a tantrum.

the neighborhood Jerry Van Amerongen

An instantaneous learning experience.

The Birth of Radical Behaviorism

Operant conditioning has been studied since the start of the twentieth century, although it was not called that until later. Edward Thorndike (1898), then a young doctoral candidate, set the stage by observing cats as they tried to escape from a complex "puzzle box" to reach a scrap of fish located just outside the box. At first, the cat would scratch, bite, or swat at parts of the box in an unorganized way. Then, after a few minutes, it would chance on the successful response (loosening a bolt, pulling a string, or hitting a button) and rush out to get the reward. Placed in the box again, the cat now took a little less time to escape, and after several trials, the animal immediately made the correct response. According to Thorndike, this response had been "stamped in" by the satisfying result of getting the food. In contrast, annoying or unsatisfying results "stamped out" behavior. Behavior, said Thorndike, is controlled by its consequences.

operant conditioning The process by which a response becomes more likely to occur or less so, depending on its consequences.

This general principle was elaborated and extended to more complex forms of behavior by B. F. (Burrhus Frederic) Skinner (1904–1990). Skinner called his approach "radical behaviorism" to distinguish it from the behaviorism of John Watson, who emphasized classical conditioning. Skinner argued that to understand behavior we should focus on the external causes of an action and the action's consequences. He avoided terms that Thorndike used, such as "satisfying" and "annoying," which reflect assumptions about what an organism feels and wants. To explain behavior, he said, we should look outside the individual, not inside.

The Consequences of Behavior

In Skinner's analysis, which has inspired an immense body of research, a response ("operant") can lead to three types of consequences:

1 **A neutral consequence neither increases nor decreases the probability that the response will recur.** If a door handle squeaks each time you turn it, but you ignore the sound and it has no effect on your likelihood of opening the door in the future, the squeak is considered a neutral consequence. We will not be concerned further with neutral consequences.

2 **Reinforcement strengthens the response or makes it more likely to recur.** When your dog begs for food at the table, and you give her the lamb chop off your plate, her begging is likely to increase:

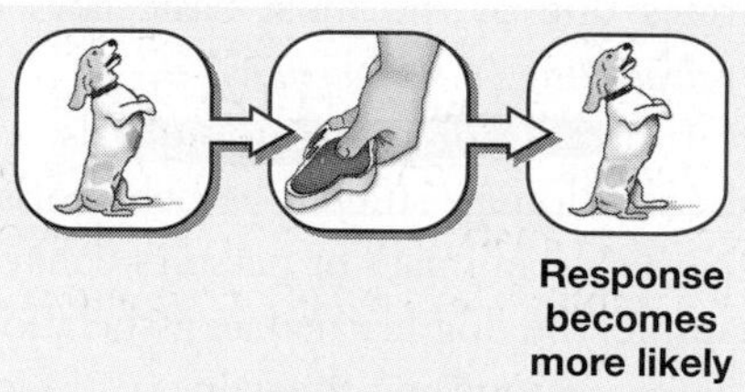

Reinforcers are roughly equivalent to rewards, and many psychologists use *reward* and *reinforcer* as approximate synonyms. However, strict behaviorists avoid the word *reward* because it implies that something has been earned that results in happiness or satisfaction. To a behaviorist, a stimulus is a reinforcer if it strengthens the preceding behavior, whether or not the organism experiences pleasure or a positive emotion. Conversely, no matter how pleasurable a stimulus is, it is not a reinforcer if it does not increase the likelihood of a response. It's great to get a paycheck, but if you get paid regardless of the effort you put into your work, the money will not reinforce "hard-work behavior."

3 **Punishment weakens the response or makes it less likely to recur.** Any aversive (unpleasant) stimulus or event may be a *punisher*. If your dog begs for a lamb chop off your plate, and you lightly swat her nose and shout "No," her begging is likely to decrease—as long as you don't feel guilty and then give her the lamb chop anyway:

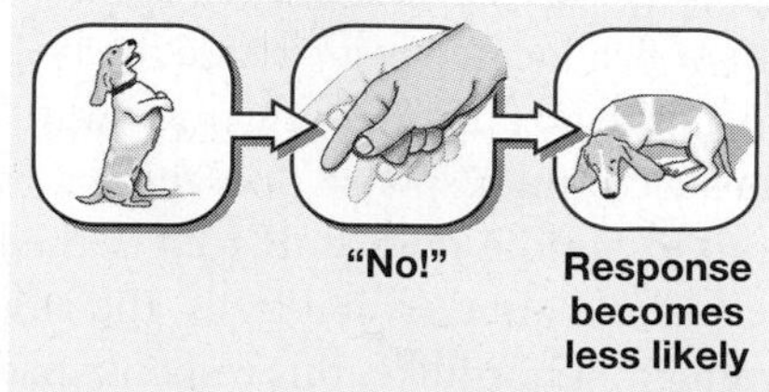

reinforcement The process by which a stimulus or event strengthens or increases the probability of the response that it follows.

punishment The process by which a stimulus or event weakens or reduces the probability of the response that it follows.

Parents, employers, and governments resort to reinforcers and punishers all the time—to get kids to behave well, employees to work hard, and constituents to pay taxes—

but they do not always use them effectively. For example, they may wait too long to deliver the reinforcer or punisher. In general, the sooner a consequence follows a response, the greater its effect; you are likely to respond more reliably when you do not have to wait ages for a paycheck, a smile, or a grade. When there is a delay, other responses occur in the interval, and the connection between the desired or undesired response and the consequence may not be made.

"Oh, not bad. The light comes on, I press the bar, they write me a check. How about you?"

Primary and Secondary Reinforcers and Punishers. Food, water, light stroking of the skin, and a comfortable air temperature are naturally reinforcing because they satisfy biological needs. They are therefore known as **primary reinforcers.** Similarly, pain and extreme heat or cold are inherently punishing and are therefore known as **primary punishers.** Primary reinforcers and punishers can be very powerful, but they have some drawbacks, both in real life and in research. For one thing, a primary reinforcer may be ineffective if an animal or person is not in a deprived state; a glass of water is not much of a reward if you just drank three glasses. Also, for obvious ethical reasons, psychologists cannot go around using primary punishers (say, by hitting their subjects) or taking away primary reinforcers (say, by starving their subjects).

Fortunately, behavior can be controlled just as effectively by **secondary reinforcers** and **secondary punishers,** which are learned. Money, praise, applause, good grades, awards, and gold stars are common secondary reinforcers. Criticism, demerits, catcalls, scoldings, fines, and bad grades are common secondary punishers. Most behaviorists believe that secondary reinforcers and punishers acquire their ability to influence behavior by being paired with primary reinforcers and punishers. (If that reminds you of classical conditioning, reinforce your excellent thinking with a pat on the head! Indeed, secondary reinforcers and punishers are often called *conditioned* reinforcers and punishers.) As a secondary reinforcer, money has considerable power over most people's behavior because it can be exchanged for primary reinforcers such as food and shelter. It is also associated with other secondary reinforcers, such as praise and respect.

Positive and Negative Reinforcers and Punishers. In our example of the begging dog, something pleasant (getting the lamb chop) followed the dog's begging response, so the response increased. Similarly, if you get a good grade after studying, your efforts to study are likely to continue or increase. This kind of process, in which a pleasant consequence makes a response more likely, is known as **positive reinforcement.** But there is another type of reinforcement, **negative reinforcement**, which involves the *removal* of something *unpleasant*. For example, if someone nags you all the time to study but stops nagging when you comply, your studying is likely to increase—because you will then avoid the nagging:

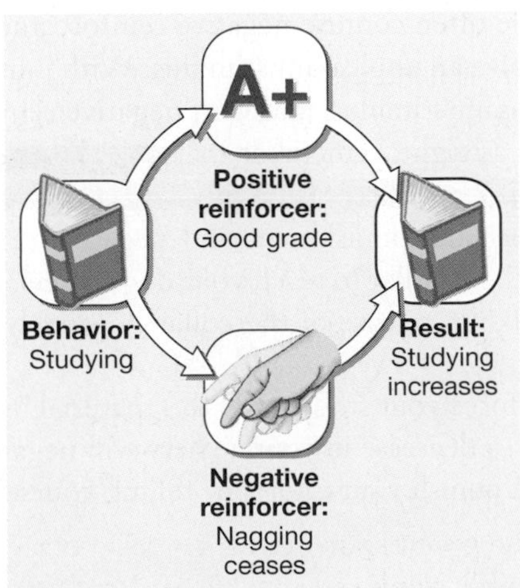

primary reinforcer A stimulus that is inherently reinforcing, typically satisfying a physiological need; an example is food.

primary punisher A stimulus that is inherently punishing; an example is electric shock.

secondary reinforcer A stimulus that has acquired reinforcing properties through association with other reinforcers.

secondary punisher A stimulus that has acquired punishing properties through association with other punishers.

positive reinforcement A reinforcement procedure in which a response is followed by the presentation of, or increase in intensity of, a reinforcing stimulus; as a result, the response becomes stronger or more likely to occur.

negative reinforcement A reinforcement procedure in which a response is followed by the removal, delay, or decrease in intensity of an unpleasant stimulus; as a result, the response becomes stronger or more likely to occur.

The positive–negative distinction can also be applied to punishment: Something unpleasant may occur following some behavior (positive punishment), or something *pleasant* may be *removed* (negative punishment). For example, if your friends tease you for being an egghead (positive punishment) or if studying makes you lose time with your friends (negative punishment), you may stop studying:

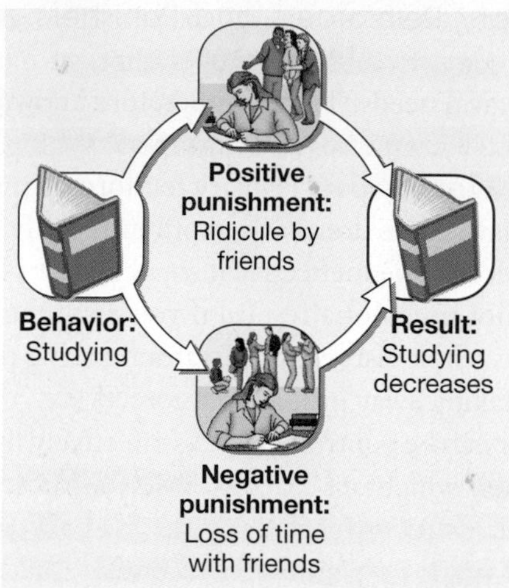

The distinction between positive and negative reinforcement and punishment has been a source of confusion for generations of students, turning many strong minds to mush. You will master these terms more quickly if you understand that "positive" and "negative" have nothing to do with "good" or "bad." They refer to procedures—giving something or taking something away.

In the case of reinforcement, think of a positive reinforcer as something that is added or obtained (you might picture a plus sign) and a negative reinforcer as avoidance of, or escape from, something unpleasant (you might picture a minus sign). *In either case, a response becomes more likely.* Do you recall what happened when Little Albert learned to fear rats through a process of classical conditioning? After he acquired this fear, crawling away was negatively reinforced by escape from the now-fearsome rodent. The negative reinforcement that results from escaping or avoiding something unpleasant explains why so many fears are long-lasting. When you avoid a feared object or situation, you also cut off all opportunities for extinguishing your fear.

Understandably, people often confuse negative reinforcement with positive punishment, because both involve an unpleasant stimulus. With punishment, though, you are subjected to the unpleasant stimulus, and with negative reinforcement, it is taken away. To keep these terms straight, remember that punishment, whether positive or negative, *decreases* the likelihood of a response; and reinforcement, whether positive or negative, *increases* it. In real life, punishment and negative reinforcement often go hand in hand. If you use a chain collar to teach your dog to heel, a brief tug on the collar punishes the act of walking; release of the collar negatively reinforces the act of standing by your side.

You can positively reinforce your studying of this material by taking a snack break. As you master the material, a decrease in your anxiety will negatively reinforce studying. But we hope you won't punish your efforts by telling yourself "I'll never get it" or "It's too hard"!

QUICK quiz

What kind of consequence will follow if you can't answer these questions?

1. A child nags her father for a cookie; he keeps refusing. Finally, unable to stand the nagging any longer, he hands over the cookie. For him, the ending of the child's pleading is a __________. For the child, the cookie is a __________.
2. An able-bodied driver is careful not to park in a handicapped space anymore after paying a large fine for doing so. The loss of money is a __________.
3. Identify which of the following are commonly used as secondary reinforcers: quarters spilling from a slot machine, a winner's blue ribbon, a piece of candy, an A on an exam, frequent-flyer miles.
4. During late afternoon "happy hours," bars and restaurants sell drinks at a reduced price and appetizers are often free. What undesirable behavior may be rewarded by this practice?

Answers:

1. negative reinforcer; positive reinforcer **2.** punisher—or more precisely, a negative punisher (because something desirable was taken away) **3.** All but the candy are secondary reinforcers. **4.** One possible answer: The reduced prices, free appetizers, and cheerful atmosphere all reinforce heavy alcohol consumption just before rush hour, thus possibly contributing to binge drinking and drunk driving.

Principles of Operant Conditioning

Thousands of operant conditioning studies have been done, many using animals. A favorite experimental tool is the *Skinner box*, a cage equipped with a device that delivers food into a dish when an animal makes a desired response (see Figure 7.5). In the original version, a machine connected to the cage automatically recorded each response and produced a graph on a piece of paper, showing the cumulative number of responses across time; today, computers are used.

Early in his career, Skinner (1938) used the Skinner box for a classic demonstration of operant conditioning. A rat that had previously learned to eat from the pellet-releasing device was placed in the box. Because no food was present, the animal proceeded to do typical ratlike things, scurrying about the box, sniffing here and there, and randomly

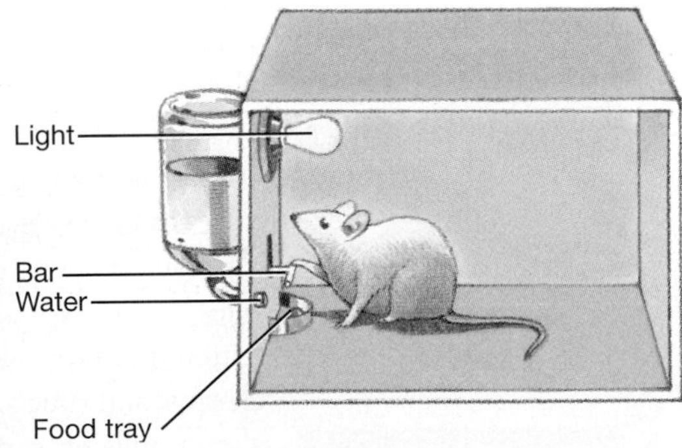

FIGURE 7.5 The Skinner Box
When a rat in a Skinner box presses a bar, a food pellet or drop of water is automatically released. The photo shows Skinner at work on one of the boxes.

extinction The weakening and eventual disappearance of a learned response; in operant conditioning, it occurs when a response is no longer followed by a reinforcer.

stimulus generalization In operant conditioning, the tendency for a response that has been reinforced (or punished) in the presence of one stimulus to occur (or be suppressed) in the presence of other similar stimuli.

stimulus discrimination In operant conditioning, the tendency of a response to occur in the presence of one stimulus but not in the presence of other, similar stimuli that differ from it on some dimension.

discriminative stimulus A stimulus that signals when a particular response is likely to be followed by a certain type of consequence.

continuous reinforcement A reinforcement schedule in which a particular response is always reinforced.

intermittent (partial) schedule of reinforcement A reinforcement schedule in which a particular response is sometimes but not always reinforced.

touching parts of the floor and walls. Quite by accident, it happened to press a lever mounted on one wall, and immediately a pellet of tasty rat food fell into the food dish. The rat continued its movements and again happened to press the bar, causing another pellet to fall into the dish. With additional repetitions of bar pressing followed by food, the animal began to behave less randomly and to press the bar more consistently. Eventually, Skinner had the rat pressing the bar as fast as it could. Since then, behavioral researchers have used the Skinner box and similar devices to discover many important techniques and applications of operant conditioning.

Extinction. In operant conditioning, as in classical, **extinction** is a procedure that causes a previously learned response to stop. In operant conditioning, extinction takes place when the reinforcer that maintained the response is removed or is no longer available. At first, there may be a spurt of responding, but then the responses gradually taper off and eventually cease. Suppose you put a coin in a vending machine and get nothing back. You may throw in another coin, or perhaps even two, but then you will probably stop trying. The next day, you may put in yet another coin, an example of *spontaneous recovery*. Eventually, however, you will give up on that machine. Your response will have been extinguished.

Stimulus Generalization and Discrimination. In operant conditioning, as in classical, **stimulus generalization** may occur. That is, responses may generalize to stimuli that were not present during the original learning situation but that resemble the original stimuli. For example, a pigeon that has been trained to peck at a picture of a circle may also peck at a slightly oval figure. But if you wanted to train the bird to discriminate between the two shapes, you would present both the circle and the oval, giving reinforcers whenever the bird pecked at the circle and withholding reinforcers when it pecked at the oval. Eventually, **stimulus discrimination** would occur.

Sometimes an animal or human being learns to respond to a stimulus only when some other stimulus, called a **discriminative stimulus**, is present. The discriminative stimulus signals whether a response, if made, will pay off. In a Skinner box containing a pigeon, a light may serve as a discriminative stimulus for pecking at a circle. When the light is on, pecking brings a reward; when it is off, pecking is futile. Human behavior is controlled by many discriminative stimuli, both verbal ("Store hours are 9 to 5") and nonverbal (traffic lights, doorbells, the ring of a telephone, other people's facial expressions). We all learn to respond correctly when such stimuli are present in order to get through the day efficiently and get along with others.

Learning on Schedule. When a response is first acquired, learning is usually most rapid if the response is reinforced each time it occurs; this procedure is called **continuous reinforcement**. However, once a response has become reliable, it will be more resistant to extinction if it is rewarded on an **intermittent (partial) schedule of reinforcement**, which involves reinforcing only some responses, not all of them. Skinner (1956) happened on this fact when he ran short of food pellets for his rats and was forced to deliver reinforcers less often. Not all scientific discoveries are planned!

Intermittent reinforcement helps explain why people often get attached to "lucky" hats, charms, and rituals. A batter pulls his earlobe, gets a home run, and from then on always pulls his earlobe before each pitch. A student takes an exam with a purple pen and gets an A, and from then on will not take an exam without a purple pen. Such rituals persist because sometimes they are followed, purely coincidentally, by a reinforcer—a hit, a good grade—and so they become resistant to extinction.

THINKING CRITICALLY

CONSIDER OTHER INTERPRETATIONS

People cling to superstitious rituals because they think they work. Could this "effectiveness" be an illusion, explainable in terms of operant principles?

Skinner (1948) once demonstrated this phenomenon by creating eight "superstitious" pigeons in his laboratory. He rigged the pigeons' cages so that

food was delivered every 15 seconds, even if the birds didn't lift a feather. Pigeons are often in motion, so when the food came, each animal was likely to be doing something. That something was then reinforced by delivery of the food. The behavior, of course, was reinforced entirely by chance, but it still became more likely to occur and thus to be reinforced again. Within a short time, six of the pigeons were practicing some sort of consistent ritual—turning in counterclockwise circles, bobbing their heads up and down, or swinging their heads to and fro. None of these activities had the least effect on the delivery of the reinforcer; the birds were behaving "superstitiously," as if they thought their movements were responsible for bringing the food.

"Maybe you're right, maybe it won't ward off evil spirits, but maybe it will, and these days who wants to take a chance?"

Many kinds of intermittent schedules have been studied. Some deliver a reinforcer only after a certain number of responses have occurred; others do so only if a response is made after a certain amount of time has passed since the last reinforcer. The number of responses that must occur or the amount of time that must pass may be fixed (e.g., three responses or five seconds) or may vary around some average. These patterns of reinforcement affect the rate, form, and timing of behavior. The details are beyond the scope of this book, but here is an example. Suppose your sweetheart sends you ten e-mails a day, playfully spacing them at unpredictable intervals, although they come on average every hour or so. You will probably check your e-mail regularly at a low but steady rate. But if your sweetheart sends you just one romantic e-mail every day, around dinnertime, you will probably start checking around 5:00 P.M., keep doing so until the message arrives (your reward), and then stop looking at all until the next evening.

Now listen up, because here comes one of the most useful things to know about operant conditioning: If you want a response to persist after it has been learned, you should reinforce it *intermittently*, not continuously. If you are giving Harry, your hamster, a treat every time he pushes a ball with his nose, and then you suddenly stop the reinforcement, Harry will soon stop pushing that ball. Because the change in reinforcement is large, from continuous to none at all, Harry will easily discern the change. But if you have been reinforcing Harry's behavior only every so often, the change will not be so dramatic, and your hungry hamster will keep responding for quite a while. Pigeons, rats, and people on intermittent schedules of reinforcement have responded in the laboratory thousands of times without reinforcement before throwing in the towel, especially when the timing of the reinforcer varies. Animals will sometimes work so hard for an unpredictable, infrequent bit of food that the energy they expend is greater than that gained from the reward; theoretically, they could actually work themselves to death!

GET INVOLVED!

➤THE WELL-BEHAVED PET

If you have a pet, you can use operant conditioning to teach your animal something you'd like it to do. Choose something simple. One student we know taught her cat to willingly enter the garage for the night by feeding the animal a special treat there each evening at the same time. Soon the cat was "asking" to get into the garage at bedtime. Another student taught her pastured horse to come to her for haltering by rewarding the animal's occasional approach with a carrot. Soon the horse was approaching regularly and could be put on an intermittent schedule of reinforcement. Be creative, and see whether you can make your pet better behaved or more cooperative in some way.

shaping An operant-conditioning procedure in which successive approximations of a desired response are reinforced.

successive approximations In the operant-conditioning procedure of shaping, behaviors that are ordered in terms of increasing similarity or closeness to the desired response.

It follows that if you want to get rid of a response, whether your own or someone else's, you should be careful *not* to reinforce it intermittently. If you are going to extinguish undesirable behavior by ignoring it—a child's tantrums, a friend's midnight phone calls, a parent's unwanted advice—you must be absolutely consistent in withholding reinforcement (your attention). Otherwise, the other person will learn that if he or she keeps up the screaming, calling, or advice giving long enough, it will eventually be rewarded. One of the most common errors people make, from a behavioral point of view, is to reward intermittently the very responses that they would like to eliminate.

Shaping. For a response to be reinforced, it must first occur. But suppose you want to train Harry the hamster to pick up a marble, a child to use a knife and fork properly, or a friend to play terrific tennis. Such behaviors, and most others in everyday life, have almost no probability of appearing spontaneously. You could grow old and gray waiting for them to occur so that you could reinforce them. The operant solution to this dilemma is a procedure called **shaping**.

In shaping, you start by reinforcing a tendency in the right direction, and then you gradually require responses that are more and more similar to the final desired response. The responses that you reinforce on the way to the final one are called **successive approximations**. In the case of Harry and the marble, you might deliver a food pellet if the hamster merely turned toward the marble. Once this response was well established, you might then reward the hamster for taking a step toward the marble. After that, you could reward him for approaching the marble, then for touching the marble, then for putting both paws on the marble, and finally for holding it. With the achievement of each approximation, the next one would become more likely, making it available for reinforcement.

Using shaping and other techniques, Skinner was able to train pigeons to play Ping-Pong with their beaks and to "bowl" in a miniature alley, complete with a wooden ball and tiny bowling pins. (Skinner had a great sense of humor.) Animal trainers routinely use shaping to teach animals to act as the "eyes" of the blind and to act as the "limbs" of people with spinal cord injuries; these talented companions learn to turn on light switches, open refrigerator doors, and reach for boxes on shelves.

Biological Limits on Learning. All principles of operant conditioning, like those of classical conditioning, are limited by an animal's genetic dispositions and physical

Behavioral techniques such as shaping have many useful applications. Monkeys have been trained to assist their paralyzed owners by opening doors, helping with feeding, and turning the pages of books. Miniature "guide horses" help blind people navigate city streets. Note the horse's cool protective sneakers!

characteristics; if you try to use shaping to teach a fish to dance the samba, you're going to get pretty frustrated (and wear out the fish). Operant conditioning procedures always work best when they capitalize on inborn tendencies.

"Why? You cross the road because it's in the script—that's why!"

Years ago, two psychologists who became animal trainers, Keller and Marian Breland (1961), learned what happens when you ignore biological constraints on learning. They found that their animals were having trouble learning tasks that should have been easy. One animal, a pig, was supposed to drop large wooden coins in a box. Instead, the animal would drop the coin, push at it with its snout, throw it in the air, and push at it some more. This odd behavior actually delayed delivery of the reinforcer (food, which is *very* reinforcing to a pig), so it was hard to explain in terms of operant principles. The Brelands finally realized that the pig's rooting instinct—using its snout to uncover and dig up edible roots—was keeping it from learning the task. They called such a reversion to instinctive behavior **instinctive drift**.

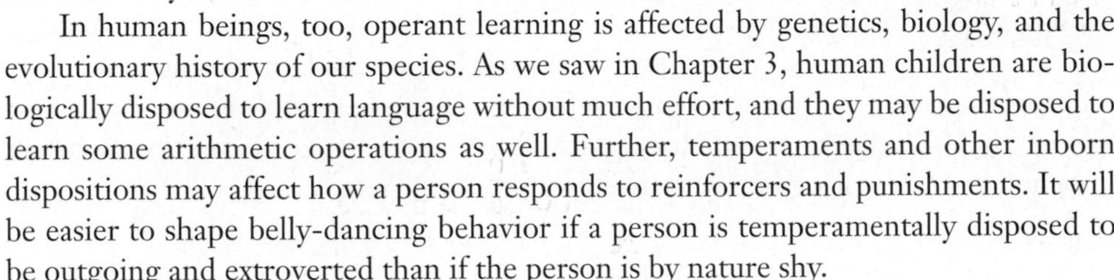

In human beings, too, operant learning is affected by genetics, biology, and the evolutionary history of our species. As we saw in Chapter 3, human children are biologically disposed to learn language without much effort, and they may be disposed to learn some arithmetic operations as well. Further, temperaments and other inborn dispositions may affect how a person responds to reinforcers and punishments. It will be easier to shape belly-dancing behavior if a person is temperamentally disposed to be outgoing and extroverted than if the person is by nature shy.

Skinner: The Man and the Myth

Because of his groundbreaking work on operant conditioning, B. F. Skinner is one of the best known of American psychologists. He is also one of the most misunderstood. For example, many people (even some psychologists) think that Skinner denied the existence of human consciousness and the value of studying it. In reality, Skinner (1972, 1990) maintained that private internal events—what we call perceptions, emotions, and thoughts—are as real as any others, and we can study them by examining our own sensory responses, the verbal reports of others, and the conditions under which such events occur. But he insisted that thoughts and feelings cannot *explain* behavior. These components of consciousness, he said, are themselves simply behaviors that occur because of reinforcement and punishment.

Skinner aroused strong passions in both his supporters and his detractors. Perhaps the issue that most provoked and angered people was his insistence that free will is an illusion. In contrast to humanist and some religious doctrines that human beings have the power to shape their own destinies, his philosophy promoted the *determinist view* that we are shaped by our environments and our genetic heritage. Skinner refused to credit personal traits (such as curiosity and perseverance) or mental events (such as intentions and motives) for anyone's accomplishments, including his own. He regarded himself not as a "self" but as a "repertoire of behaviors" resulting from an environment that encouraged looking, searching, and investigating (Bjork, 1993).

Because Skinner thought the environment should be manipulated to alter behavior, some critics have portrayed him as cold-blooded. One famous controversy regarding Skinner occurred when he invented an enclosed "living space," the Air Crib, for his younger daughter Deborah when she was an infant. This "baby box," as it came to be known, had temperature and humidity controls to eliminate the usual discomforts suffered by babies: heat, cold, wetness, and confinement by blankets and clothing. Skinner

instinctive drift During operant learning, the tendency for an organism to revert to instinctive behavior.

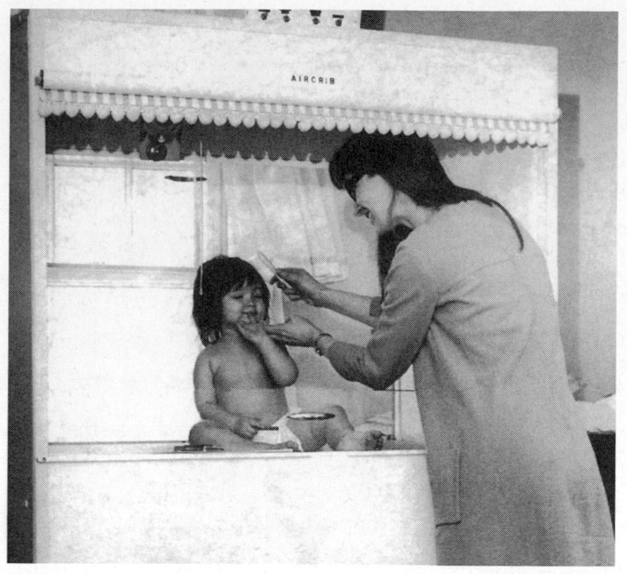

B. F. Skinner invented the Air Crib to provide a more comfortable, less restrictive infant bed than the traditional crib with its bars and blankets. The baby in this Air Crib is Skinner's granddaughter Lisa, with her mother, Julie.

believed that to reduce a baby's cries of discomfort and make infant care easier for the parents, you should fix the environment. But people imagined, incorrectly, that the Skinners were leaving their child in the baby box all the time without cuddling and holding her, and rumors circulated for years that she had sued her father, gone insane, or killed herself. Actually, both of Skinner's daughters were cuddled and doted on, loved their parents deeply, and turned out to be perfectly well-adjusted and very successful. Yet as recently as 2004, in a popular book about famous psychologists, a writer named Lauren Slater repeated some of these rumors, once again, as if they were true. In a British newspaper, Deborah, who lives in England, accused Slater of doing a disservice to her and the Skinner family and of debasing the intellectual history of psychology. "I'm not crazy or dead," she wrote, "but I'm very angry."

Skinner, a kind and mild-mannered man, felt that it would be unethical *not* to try to improve human behavior by applying behavioral principles. And he practiced what he preached, proposing many ways to improve society and reduce human suffering. At the height of public criticism of Skinner, in 1972, the American Humanist Association recognized his efforts on behalf of humanity by honoring him with its Humanist of the Year Award.

QUICK quiz

Can you apply the principles of operant conditioning? In each of the following situations, choose the best alternative, and give your reason for choosing it.

1. You want your 2-year-old to ask for water with a word instead of a grunt. Should you give him water when he says "wa-wa" or wait until his pronunciation improves?
2. Your roommate keeps interrupting your studying even though you have asked her to stop. Should you ignore her completely or occasionally respond for the sake of good manners?
3. Your father, who rarely calls you, has finally left a voice-mail message. Should you reply quickly, or wait a while so he will know how it feels to be ignored?

Answers:

1. You should reinforce "wa-wa," an approximation of *water*, because complex behaviors need to be shaped. 2. From a behavioral view, you should ignore her completely because intermittent reinforcement (attention) could cause her interruptions to persist. 3. If you want to encourage communication, you should reply quickly because immediate reinforcement is more effective than delayed reinforcement.

WHAT'S**AHEAD** 

- Why do efforts to crack down on wrongdoers often go awry?
- What's the best way to discourage a child from throwing tantrums?
- Why does paying children for good grades sometimes backfire?

Operant Conditioning in Real Life

Operant principles can clear up many mysteries about why people behave as they do. They can also explain why people have trouble changing when they want to, in spite of all the motivational seminars they attend or resolutions they make. If life at work and at home remains full of the same old reinforcers, punishers, and discriminative

You don't have to be a psychologist to apply behavioral principles. On the left, a police officer in Palo Alto, California, reinforces law-abiding behavior by giving a gift certificate to a pedestrian. On the right, a mother reinforces her autistic son's learning by applauding.
Chris Maynard/The New York Times

stimuli (a grumpy boss, an unresponsive spouse, a refrigerator stocked with high-fat goodies), any new responses that have been acquired may fail to generalize.

To help people change unwanted, dangerous, or self-defeating habits, behaviorists have carried operant principles out of the laboratory and into the wider world of the classroom, athletic field, prison, mental hospital, nursing home, rehabilitation ward, child-care center, factory, and office. The use of operant techniques in such real-world settings is called **behavior modification** (also known as *applied behavior analysis*).

behavior modification The application of operant conditioning techniques to teach new responses or to reduce or eliminate maladaptive or problematic behavior; also called *applied behavior analysis*.

Behavior modification has had some enormous successes (Kazdin, 2001). Behaviorists have taught parents how to toilet train their children in only a few sessions (Azrin & Foxx, 1974). They have trained disturbed and mentally retarded adults to communicate, dress themselves, mingle socially with others, and earn a living (Lent, 1968; McLeod, 1985). They have taught brain-damaged patients to control inappropriate behavior, focus their attention, and improve their language abilities (McGlynn, 1990). They have developed programs for helping autistic children improve their social and language skills (Green, 1996 a, b). And they have helped ordinary folk get rid of unwanted habits, such as smoking and nail biting, or acquire desired ones, such as practicing the piano or studying.

Yet when nonpsychologists try to apply the principles of conditioning to commonplace problems, their efforts sometimes miss the mark. They may not have a good grasp of behavioral principles; for example, they may delay the reward too long or reinforce unwanted behavior intermittently. And both punishment and reinforcement have their pitfalls, as we are about to see.

The Pros and Cons of Punishment

In a novel called *Walden Two* (1948/1976), Skinner imagined a utopia in which reinforcers were used so wisely that undesirable behavior was rare. Unfortunately, we do not live in a utopia; bad habits and antisocial acts abound.

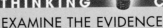

THINKING  CRITICALLY

EXAMINE THE EVIDENCE

The response to wrongdoing is often punishment. People assume that fines, long prison terms, yelling, and spanking are good ways to get rid of undesirable behavior. What does the evidence show?

Punishment might seem to be an obvious solution. Nearly all Western countries have banned the physical punishment of schoolchildren by principals and teachers, but many American states still permit it for disruptiveness, vandalism, and other misbehavior. The United States is also far more likely than any other developed country to jail its citizens for nonviolent crimes such as drug use and to enact the ultimate punishment—the death penalty—for violent crimes. And, of course, in their relationships people punish one another frequently by yelling, scolding, and sulking. Does all this punishment work?

When Punishment Works. Sometimes punishment is unquestionably effective. For example, punishment can deter some young criminals from repeating their

offenses. A study of the criminal records of all Danish men born between 1944 and 1947 (nearly 29,000 men) examined repeat arrests (recidivism) through age 26 (Brennan & Mednick, 1994). After any given arrest, punishment reduced rates of subsequent arrests for both minor and serious crimes, though recidivism still remained fairly high. Contrary to the researchers' expectations, however, the severity of punishment made no difference: Fines and probation were about as effective as jail time. What mattered most was the *consistency* of the punishment. This is understandable in behavioral terms: When lawbreakers sometimes get away with their crimes, their behavior is intermittently reinforced and therefore becomes resistant to extinction.

Unfortunately, that is exactly the situation in the United States. Young offenders are punished far less consistently than they are in Denmark, in part because prosecutors, juries, and judges do not want to condemn them to mandatory prison terms. This fact helps to explain why harsh sentencing laws and simplistic efforts to "crack down" on wrongdoers often fail or even backfire. Further, when harsh punishment is imposed, it does not teach young offenders to want to go straight. Indeed, despite its high incarceration rates, the United States has a far higher rate of violent crime than other developed countries do. And within the United States, crime rates are not consistently correlated with rates of incarceration or the imposition of the death penalty (Currie, 1998).

When Punishment Fails. What about punishment that occurs every day in families, schools, and workplaces? Laboratory and field studies find that it, too, often fails, for several reasons:

1 People often administer punishment inappropriately or mindlessly. They swing in a blind rage or shout things they don't mean, applying punishment so broadly that it covers all sorts of irrelevant behaviors. And even when people are not carried away by anger, they often misunderstand the proper application of punishment. One student told us his parents used to punish their children before leaving them alone for the evening because of all the naughty things they were *going* to do. Naturally, the children did not bother to behave like angels.

THINKING CRITICALLY

ASK QUESTIONS

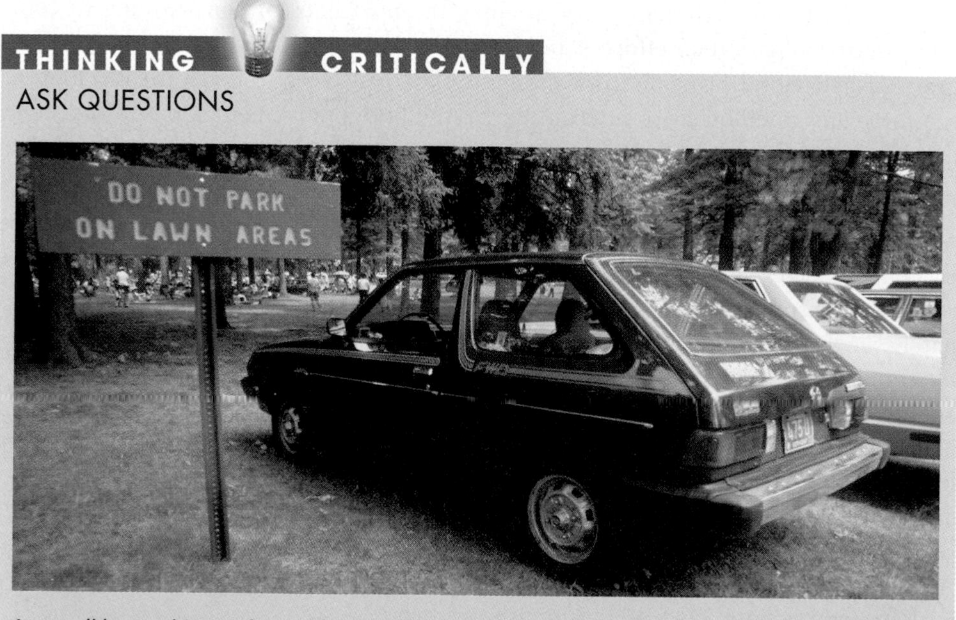

As we all know, drivers often park where they're not supposed to. Have you ever wondered why so many people ignore warnings and threats of punishment?

2 The recipient of punishment often responds with anxiety, fear, or rage. Through a process of classical conditioning, these emotional side effects may then generalize to the entire situation in which the punishment occurs—the place, the person delivering the punishment, and the circumstances. These negative emotional reactions can create more problems than the punishment solves. A teenager who has been severely punished may strike back or run away. A spouse who is constantly abused will feel bitter and resentful and is likely to retaliate with small acts of hostility. Being physically punished in childhood is a risk factor for depression, low self-esteem, violent behavior, and many other problems (Barrish, 1996; Gershoff, 2002; Straus & Kantor, 1994).

3 The effectiveness of punishment is often temporary, depending heavily on the presence of the punishing person or circumstances. All of us can probably remember some transgressions of childhood that we never dared commit when our parents were around but that we promptly resumed as soon as they were gone. All we learned was not to get caught.

4 Most misbehavior is hard to punish immediately. Punishment, like reward, works best if it quickly follows a response. But outside the laboratory, rapid punishment is often hard to achieve, and during the delay, the behavior may be reinforced many times. For example, if you punish your dog when you get home for getting into the doggie biscuits and eating them all up, the punishment will not do any good because you are too late: Your pet's misbehavior has already been reinforced by all those delicious treats.

5 Punishment conveys little information. If it immediately follows the misbehavior, punishment may tell the recipient what *not* to do, but it does not communicate what the person (or animal) *should* do. Spanking a toddler for messing in her pants will not teach her to use the potty chair, and scolding a student for learning slowly will not teach him to learn more quickly.

6 An action intended to punish may instead be reinforcing because it brings attention. Indeed, in some cases, angry attention may be just what the offender is after. If a mother yells at a child who is throwing a tantrum, the very act of yelling may give him what he wants—a reaction from her. In the schoolroom, teachers who scold children in front of other students, thus putting them in the limelight, often unwittingly reward the very misbehavior they are trying to eliminate.

Because of these drawbacks, most psychologists believe that punishment, especially severe punishment, is a poor way to eliminate unwanted behavior. In special cases, for example when mentally disabled children are in immediate danger of seriously injuring themselves, temporary physical restraint may be necessary. But even in these cases, alternatives to punishment are now preferred. Unfortunately, many residential schools for youngsters with disabilities still use harsh punishment. So do programs variously called "attachment therapy," "holding" therapy, or "restraint" therapy, which supposedly

CONSIDER OTHER INTERPRETATIONS

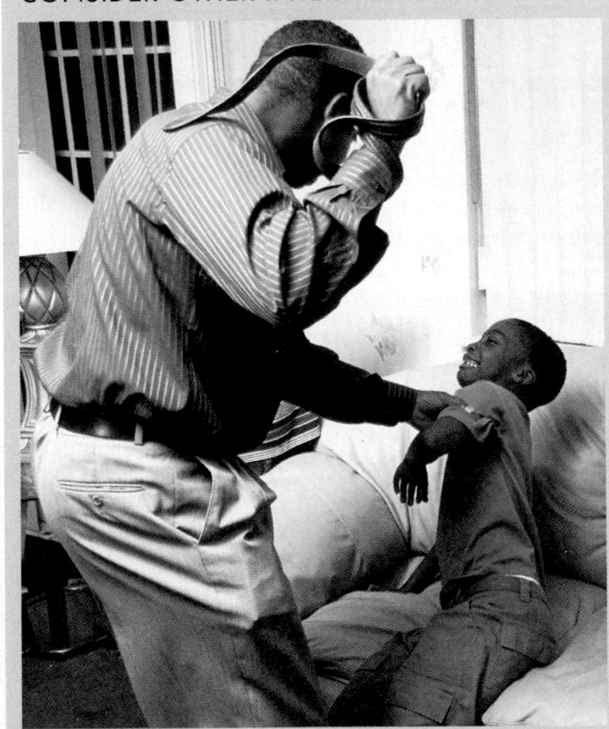

Many harried parents habitually resort to physical punishment without being aware of its many negative consequences for themselves and their children. Based on your reading of this chapter, what alternatives does this father have?

help troubled children bond with their parents; their practitioners have punished children for disobedience by using abusive practices such as physical coercion and restraint, humiliation, social isolation, and withholding of food, water, or access to a toilet (see Chapter 17).

When punishment must be applied, these guidelines should be kept in mind: (1) It should not involve physical abuse; instead, parents can use time-outs and loss of privileges (negative punishers); (2) it should be accompanied by information about what kind of behavior would be appropriate; and (3) it should be followed, whenever possible, by the reinforcement of desirable behavior.

Fortunately, a good alternative to punishment exists: extinction of the responses you want to discourage. Of course, the simplest form of extinction—ignoring the behavior—is often hard to carry out. It is not easy to ignore a child nagging for a cookie before dinner, a roommate interrupting your concentration, or a dog barking its lungs out. A teacher cannot ignore a child who is hitting a playmate. The dog owner who ignores Fido's backyard barking may soon hear "barking" of another sort from the neighbors. A parent whose child is a video-game addict cannot ignore the behavior because playing video games is rewarding to the child. One solution: Combine extinction of undesirable acts with reinforcement of alternative ones. For example, the parent of a video-game addict might ignore the child's pleas for "just one more game" and at the same time praise the child for doing something else that is incompatible with video-game playing, such as reading or playing basketball.

The Problems with Reward

So far, we have been praising the virtues of reinforcement. But like punishers, rewards do not always work as expected. Let's look at two complications that arise when people try to use them.

THINKING CRITICALLY

DON'T OVERSIMPLIFY

Because reinforcers increase desirable behavior, some teachers give out high grades whether students deserve them or not. Does this practice improve the students' performance or self-esteem? What do these rewards actually reinforce?

Misuse of Rewards. Suppose you are a fourth-grade teacher, and a student has just turned in a paper full of grammatical and punctuation errors. This child has little self-confidence and is easily discouraged. What should you do? Many people think you should give the paper a high mark anyway, in order to bolster the child's self-esteem. Teachers everywhere are handing out lavish praise, happy-face stickers, and high grades in hopes that students' performance will improve as they learn to "feel good about themselves," even though study after study has found that high self-esteem does not improve academic performance (Baumeister et al., 2003). One obvious result has been grade inflation at all levels of education. In many colleges and universities, Cs, which once meant average or satisfactory, are nearly extinct.

The problem, from a behavioral point of view, is that to be effective, rewards must be tied to the behavior you are trying to increase. When rewards are dispensed indiscriminately, without being earned, they become meaningless because they no longer reinforce desired behavior; all that teachers get is minimal effort and mediocre work. Real self-esteem emerges from effort, persistence, and the gradual acquisition of skills, and is nurtured by a teacher's genuine appreciation of the content of a child's work (Damon, 1995). In the case of the child who turned in a poorly written paper, the teacher could praise its strengths but also give feedback on the paper's weaknesses and show the child how to correct them.

extrinsic reinforcers Reinforcers that are not inherently related to the activity being reinforced.

Why Rewards Can Backfire. Most of our examples of operant conditioning have involved **extrinsic reinforcers**, which come from an outside source and are not inherently related to the activity being reinforced. Money, praise, gold stars,

applause, hugs, and thumbs-up signs are all extrinsic reinforcers. But people (and probably some other animals, too) also work for **intrinsic reinforcers**, such as enjoyment of the task and the satisfaction of accomplishment. As psychologists have applied operant conditioning in real-world settings, they have found that extrinsic reinforcement sometimes becomes too much of a good thing: If you focus on it exclusively, it can kill the pleasure of doing something for its own sake.

intrinsic reinforcers Reinforcers that are inherently related to the activity being reinforced.

CLOSE-UP on Research

HOW TO KILL INTRINSIC MOTIVATION

Consider what happened in a classic study of how praise affects children's intrinsic motivation (Lepper, Greene, & Disbett, 1973). The researchers **asked an interesting question**: Is it possible to reduce children's interest in an activity by making it a means to an end rather than the end itself? When that happens, does play turn into work? To find out, they first gave nursery-school children the chance to draw with felt-tipped pens during free play and recorded how long each child spontaneously played with the pens. The children clearly enjoyed this activity. Then the researchers told some of the children that if they would draw with felt-tipped pens for a man who had come "to see what kinds of pictures boys and girls like to draw with Magic Markers," they would get a prize—a "Good Player Award" complete with gold seal and red ribbon. After drawing for six minutes, each child got the award as promised. Other children did not expect an award and were not given one. And in a third condition, children were not told there would be an award but got one anyway.

A week later, the researchers again observed the children's free play. Those children who had expected and received an award spent much less time with the pens than they had before the start of the experiment. In contrast, children who had neither expected nor received an award continued to show as much interest in playing with the pens as they had initially, as you can see in the adjacent figure. Children in the third condition also continued to show a high level of interest in the pens. Similar results have occurred in many other studies when children have been offered a reward for playing with a toy or doing something they already enjoy.

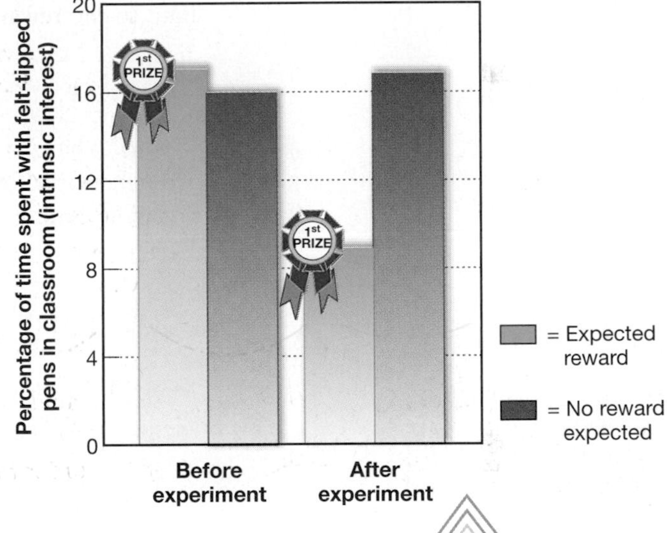

Why should extrinsic rewards undermine the pleasure of doing something for its own sake? Psychologists have **considered alternative interpretations** for this finding. One possibility is that when we are paid for an activity, we interpret it as work. We see our actions as the result of external factors instead of our own interests, skills, and efforts. It is as if we say to ourselves, "I'm doing this because I'm being paid for it. Since I'm being paid, it must be something I wouldn't do if I didn't have to." When the reward is withdrawn, we refuse to "work" any longer. This is the explanation that was favored by the researchers in the felt-tipped pen study. Another possibility is that we tend to regard extrinsic rewards as controlling, so they make us feel pressured and reduce our sense of autonomy and choice ("I guess I have to do what I'm told to do—but *only* what I'm told to do") (Deci et al., 1999). A third, more behavioral explanation is that extrinsic reinforcement sometimes raises the rate of responding above some

optimal, enjoyable level—for example, by causing the children in the felt-tipped pen study to play with the pens longer than they would have on their own. Then the activity really does become work.

We must be careful, however, to **avoid oversimplification**. Extrinsic rewards do not always weaken the impact of intrinsic ones; their effects depend on many factors, including a person's initial motivation, the context in which rewards are achieved, and, when praise is given, the sincerity of the person giving it (Henderlong & Lepper, 2002). If you get praise, money, a high grade, or a trophy for doing a task *well* or for achieving a certain level of performance, rather than for just doing the task, your intrinsic motivation is not likely to decline; in fact, it may increase (Cameron, Banko, & Pierce, 2001; Dickinson, 1989). Such rewards are apt to make you feel competent rather than controlled. If rewards are tied to increasingly demanding standards for performance, as opposed to an unchanging standard, your intrinsic motivation is especially likely to remain high (Pierce et al., 2003). And if you have always been crazy about reading or playing the banjo, you will probably keep reading or playing even when you do not happen to be getting a grade or applause for doing so. In such cases, you will probably attribute your continued involvement in the activity to your own intrinsic interests and motivation rather than to the reward.

So, what is the take-home message about extrinsic rewards? First, often they are necessary: Few people would trudge off to work every morning if they never got paid; and in the classroom, teachers may need to offer incentives to unmoti-

GET INVOLVED!

➤WHAT'S REINFORCING YOUR BEHAVIOR?

For each activity that you do, indicate whether the reinforcers controlling your behavior are primarily extrinsic or intrinsic.

Activity	Reinforcers mostly extrinsic	Reinforcers mostly intrinsic	Reinforcers about equally extrinsic and intrinsic
Studying	_____	_____	_____
Housework	_____	_____	_____
Worship	_____	_____	_____
Grooming	_____	_____	_____
Job	_____	_____	_____
Dating	_____	_____	_____
Attending class	_____	_____	_____
Reading unrelated to school	_____	_____	_____
Sports	_____	_____	_____
Cooking	_____	_____	_____

Is there an area of your life in which you would like intrinsic reinforcement to play a larger role? What can you do to make that happen?

vated students. Second, extrinsic rewards should be used sparingly, so that intrinsic pleasure in an activity can blossom. As one mother wrote in *Newsweek*, children need to discover for themselves "the joy of music from songs, the power of mathematics from counting and all of human wisdom from reading" (Skreslet, 1987). Finally, educators and employers can avoid the trap of either–or thinking by recognizing that most people do their best when they get tangible rewards for real achievement *and* when they have interesting, challenging, and varied kinds of work to do (see Chapter 12).

Effective behavior modification, as you can see, is not only a science but also an art. In "Taking Psychology with You," we offer additional guidelines for mastering that art.

"That is the correct answer, Billy," but I'm afraid you don't win anything for it.

QUICK quiz

Is the art of mastering quizzes intrinsically reinforcing yet?

A. According to behavioral principles, what is happening here?

1. An adolescent whose parents have hit him for minor transgressions since he was small runs away from home.
2. A young woman whose parents paid her to clean her room while she was growing up is a slob when she moves to her own apartment.
3. Two parents scold their young daughter every time they catch her sucking her thumb. The thumb sucking continues anyway.

B. In cities across America, public school systems are now rewarding students for perfect attendance by giving them money, shopping sprees, laptops, video games—even the chance to win a car in a raffle (*The New York Times*, February 5, 2006). What are the pros and cons of such practices?

C. In a fee-for-service health-care system, doctors are paid for each visit by a patient or for each service performed; the more services performed the higher the fee. In contrast, some health maintenance organizations (HMOs) pay their doctors a fixed amount per patient for an entire year. If the amount spent is less, the physician gets a bonus, and in some systems, if the amount spent is more, the physician must pay a penalty. Given what you know about operant conditioning, what are the advantages and disadvantages of each system?

Answers:

A. 1. The physical punishment was painful, and through a process of classical conditioning, the situation in which it occurred also became unpleasant. Because escape from an unpleasant stimulus is negatively reinforcing, the boy ran away. **2.** Extrinsic reinforcers are no longer available, and room-cleaning behavior has been extinguished. Also, extrinsic rewards may have displaced the intrinsic satisfaction of having a tidy room. **3.** Punishment has failed, possibly because it rewards thumb sucking with attention or because thumb sucking still brings the child pleasure whenever the parents are not around. **B.** The rewards may improve attendance (they have in some schools), and students who attend more regularly may wind up more interested in their studies and do better in school. But extrinsic rewards can also decrease intrinsic motivation, and when they are withdrawn (e.g., when the student goes to another school or to college), attendance may plummet ("If there's no reward, why should I attend?"). Further, students may come to expect bigger and bigger rewards, upping the ante. In some schools, especially those that have de-emphasized penalties for *poor* attendance, the rewards have backfired and attendance has actually fallen. **C.** In a fee-for-service system, the doctor is likely to provide the attention and tests that patients need. However, this system also rewards doctors for unnecessary tests and patient visits, contributing to the explosion in health-care costs. The policies of the HMOs help contain these costs, but because doctors are rewarded for reducing costs and in some cases penalized for running up charges, some patients may not get the attention or services they need.

WHAT'S**AHEAD**

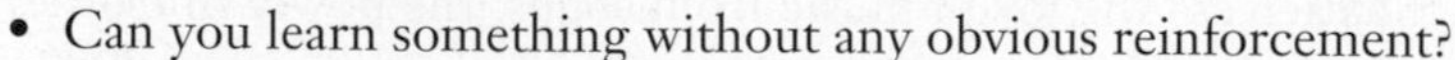

- Can you learn something without any obvious reinforcement?
- Why do two people often learn different lessons from exactly the same experience?
- Does watching violence on TV make people more aggressive?

Learning and the Mind

For half a century, most American learning theories held that learning could be explained by specifying the behavioral "ABCs"—*antecedents* (events preceding behavior), *behaviors*, and *consequences*. Behaviorists liked to compare the mind to an engineer's hypothetical "black box," a device whose workings must be inferred because they cannot be observed directly. To them, the box contained irrelevant wiring; it was enough to know that pushing a button on the box would produce a predictable response. But even as early as the 1930s, a few behaviorists could not resist peeking into that black box.

Latent Learning

Behaviorist Edward Tolman (1938) committed virtual heresy at the time by noting that his rats, when pausing at turning points in a maze, seemed to be *deciding* which way to go. Moreover, the animals sometimes seemed to be learning even without any reinforcement. What, he wondered, was going on in their little rat brains that might account for this puzzle?

In a classic experiment, Tolman and C. H. Honzik (1930) placed three groups of rats in mazes and observed their behavior daily for more than two weeks. The rats in Group 1 always found food at the end of the maze and quickly learned to find it without going down blind alleys. The rats in Group 2 never found food and, as you would expect, they followed no particular route. Group 3 was the interesting group. These rats found no food for ten days, and seemed to wander aimlessly, but on the eleventh they received food, and then they quickly learned to run to the end of the maze. By the next day, they were doing as well as Group 1, which had been rewarded from the beginning (see Figure 7.6)

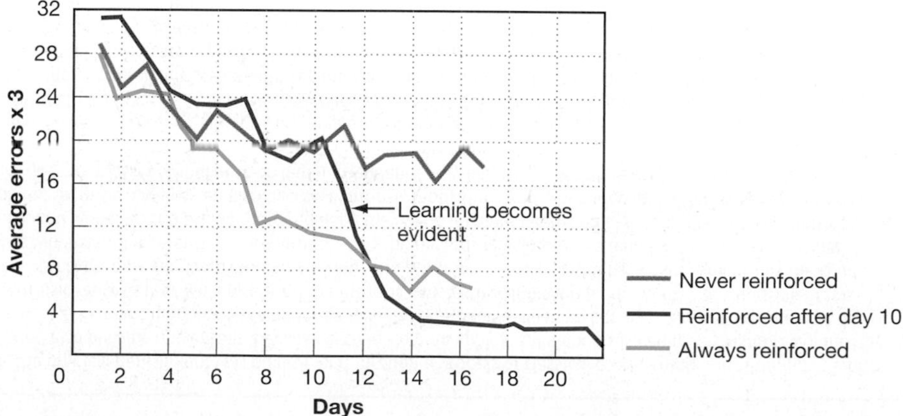

FIGURE 7.6 Latent Learning

In a classic experiment, rats that always found food in a maze made fewer and fewer errors in reaching the food (green curve). In contrast, rats that received no food showed little improvement (blue curve). But rats that got no food for ten days and they did on the eleventh day showed rapid improvement from then on (red curve). This result suggests that learning involves cognitive changes that can occur in the absence of reinforcement and that may not be acted on until a reinforcer becomes available (Tolman & Honzik, 1930).

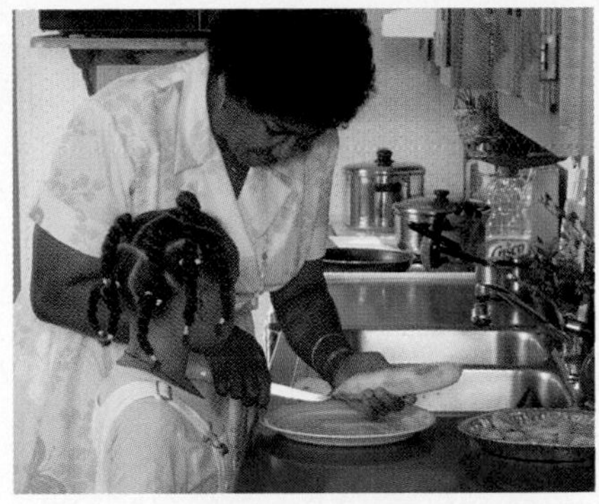
Because of latent learning, when this little girl is older and ready to make her own meals, she will already have some knowledge about how to do it.

Group 3 had demonstrated **latent learning**, learning that is not immediately expressed in performance. A great deal of human learning also remains latent until circumstances allow or require it to be expressed. A driver finds her way to Fourth and Kumquat Streets using a new route she has never used before. A little boy observes a parent setting the table or tightening a screw but does not act on this learning for years; then he finds he knows how to do these things, even though he has never done them before.

Latent learning not only occurs without any obvious reinforcer; it also raises questions about what, exactly, is learned during learning. In the Tolman and Honzik study, the rats that did not get any food until the eleventh day seemed to have acquired a mental representation of the maze. They had been learning the whole time; they simply had no reason to act on that learning until they began to find food. Similarly, the driver taking a new route can do so because she already knows how the city is laid out.

What seems to be acquired in latent learning, therefore, is not a specific response, but *knowledge* about responses and their consequences. We learn how the world is organized, which paths lead to which places, and which actions can produce which payoffs. This knowledge permits us to be creative and flexible in reaching our goals.

Social-Cognitive Learning Theories

The black box was opened further in the 1940s, when two social scientists proposed a major modification of radical behaviorism, which they called *social-learning theory* (Dollard & Miller, 1950). Most human learning, they argued, is acquired by observing other people in a social context, rather than through standard conditioning procedures. By the 1960s and 1970s, social-learning theory was in full bloom, and a new element had been added: the human capacity for higher-level cognitive processes. Its proponents agreed with behaviorists that human beings, along with the rat and the rabbit, are subject to the laws of operant and classical conditioning. But they added that human beings, unlike the rat or the rabbit, are full of attitudes, beliefs, and expectations that affect the way they acquire information, make decisions, reason, and solve problems.

These mental processes affect what individuals will do at any given moment and also, more generally, the personality traits they develop (see Chapter 13). That is why two people can live through the same event and come away with entirely different

latent learning A form of learning that is not immediately expressed in an overt response; it occurs without obvious reinforcement.

lessons from it (Bandura, 2001). All siblings know this. One may regard being grounded by their father as evidence of his all-around meanness, and another may see the same behavior as evidence of his care and concern for his children.

Because of this focus on mental processes, one leading theorist, Walter Mischel, has called his approach *cognitive social-learning theory* (Mischel, 1973; Mischel & Shoda, 1995); and another, Albert Bandura, calls his *social-cognitive theory* (Bandura, 1986). We will use the general term **social-cognitive theory** to include all modern social-learning approaches (Barone, Maddux, & Snyder, 1997). They share an emphasis on the importance of beliefs, perceptions, and observations of other peoples' behavior in determining what we learn and how we behave.

Learning by Observing. Late one night, a friend who lives in a rural area was awakened by a loud clattering and banging. Her whole family raced outside to find the source of the commotion. A raccoon had knocked over a "raccoon-proof" garbage can and seemed to be demonstrating to an assembly of other raccoons how to open it: If you jump up and down on the can's side, the lid will pop off. According to our friend, the observing raccoons learned from this episode how to open stubborn garbage cans, and the observing humans learned how smart raccoons can be. In short, they all benefited from **observational learning**: learning by watching what others do and what happens to them for doing it.

The behavior the raccoons learned through observation was an operant one, but observational learning also plays an important role in the acquisition of automatic, reflexive responses, such as fears and phobias (Mineka & Zinbarg, 2006; Olsson & Phelps, 2004). Thus, in addition to learning to be frightened of rats directly through classical conditioning, as Little Albert did, you might also learn to fear rats by observing the emotional expressions of other people when they see or touch one. The perception of someone else's reaction serves as an unconditioned stimulus for your own fear, and the learning that results may be as strong as it would be if you had had a direct encounter with the rat yourself. Children often learn to fear things in this way, for example, after observing a parent's fearful reaction whenever a dog approaches. Adults can acquire fears even by watching suspenseful movies. After seeing the classic horror film *Psycho*, in which a character is knifed to death in a shower, some people became nervous about taking a shower. Similarly, after seeing the movie *Jaws*, with its horrific scenes of shark attacks and its gripping music, some people became afraid to swim in the ocean.

Behaviorists have always acknowledged the importance of observational learning, which they call *vicarious conditioning*, and have tried to explain it in stimulus–response terms. But social-cognitive theorists believe that in human beings observational learning cannot be fully understood without taking into account the thought processes of the learner (Meltzoff & Gopnik, 1993). They emphasize the knowledge that results when a person sees a *model*—another person—behaving in certain ways and experiencing the consequences (Bandura, 1977).

None of us would last long without observational learning. We would have to learn to avoid oncoming cars by walking into traffic and suffering the consequences or learn to swim by jumping into a deep pool and flailing around. Learning would be not only inefficient but also dangerous. Parents and teachers would be busy 24 hours a day shaping children's behavior. Bosses would have to stand over their employees' desks, rewarding every little link in the complex behavioral chains we call typing, report writing, and accounting.

Many years ago, Albert Bandura and his colleagues showed just how important observational learning is, especially for children who are learning the rules of social

social-cognitive theories Theories that emphasize how behavior is learned and maintained through observation and imitation of others, positive consequences, and cognitive processes such as plans, expectations, and beliefs.

observational learning A process in which an individual learns new responses by observing the behavior of another (a model) rather than through direct experience; sometimes called *vicarious conditioning*.

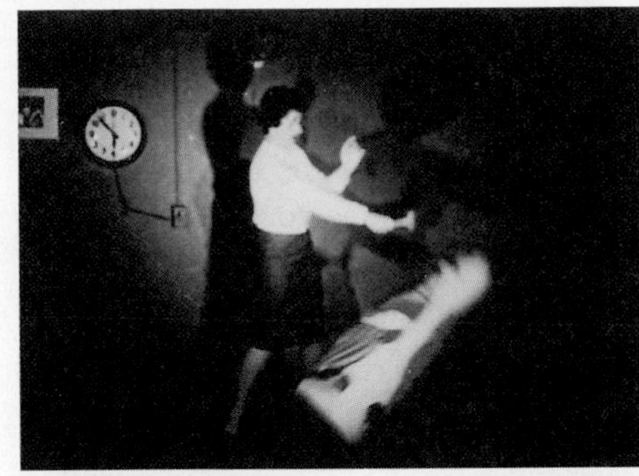

Adults and children alike learn through observation. In studies by Albert Bandura and his colleagues, children watched films of an adult kicking, punching, and hammering on a big rubber doll (top). Later, the children imitated the adult's behavior, some of them almost exactly.

behavior (Bandura, Ross, & Ross, 1963). The researchers had nursery school children watch a short film of two men, Rocky and Johnny, playing with toys. (Apparently the children did not think this behavior was the least bit odd.) In the film, Johnny refuses to share his toys, and Rocky responds by clobbering him. Rocky's aggressive actions are rewarded because he winds up with all the toys. Poor Johnny sits dejectedly in the corner, while Rocky marches off with a sack full of loot and a hobbyhorse under his arm.

After viewing the film, each child was left alone for 20 minutes in a playroom full of toys, including some of the items shown in the film. Watching through a one-way mirror, the researchers found that the children were much more aggressive in their play than a control group that had not seen the film. Some children imitated Rocky almost exactly. At the end of the session, one little girl even asked the experimenter for a sack!

Of course, people imitate positive activities that they observe, too. Matt Groening, the creator of the cartoon show *The Simpsons*, decided it would be funny if the Simpsons' 8-year-old daughter Lisa played the baritone sax. Sure enough, across the country little girls began imitating her. Cynthia Sikes, a saxophone teacher in New York, told *The New York Times* that "When the show started, I got an influx of girls coming up to me saying, 'I want to play the saxophone because Lisa Simpson plays the saxophone.'"

The Case of Media Violence. These findings on latent learning, the role of perceptions in learning, and observational learning are relevant to an ongoing emotional debate: Does media violence make people behave more aggressively? Every time an American child or teenager commits a shocking murder or assault, a public outcry occurs about the countless acts of violence that children see on

television, in films, and in video games. Politicians and parents blame the media, and the media claim to be blameless. What does the evidence show?

THINKING CRITICALLY

DON'T OVERSIMPLIFY

Does playing violent video games make children more aggressive? The answer is more complicated than "yes" or "no."

First, since Bandura's early research, hundreds of experimental studies of children, teenagers, and adults have corroborated his findings, convincing many psychologists that observing aggression does increase aggression (APA Commission on Violence and Youth, 1993; Bushman & Anderson, 2001; Eron, 1995). Meta-analysis shows that the greater the exposure to violence in movies and on television, the stronger the likelihood of a person's behaving aggressively, even after researchers control for social class, intelligence, and other factors (e.g., Anderson & Bushman, 2001). Moreover, when grade-school children cut back on time spent watching TV or playing video games, which are often violent in nature, their aggressiveness declines (Robinson et al., 2001). A review by a group of eminent scientists concluded that "research on violent television and films, video games, and music reveals unequivocal evidence that media violence increases the likelihood of aggressive and violent behavior," both in the short term and long term (Anderson et al., 2003).

But some psychologists and social critics believe that the relationship is not strong enough to worry about (Freedman, 2002). Media violence does not cause all viewers, or even most viewers, to become aggressive. Children watch many different programs and movies and have many models to observe besides those they see in the media, including parents and peers. For every teenager who is obsessed with playing *Mortal Kombat* and who entertains violent fantasies of blowing up the world, dozens more think the game is just plain fun and then go off to do their homework. Interestingly, although the number of violent video games increased throughout the 1990s, overall rates of teenage violence actually declined.

Further, cause and effect work in the opposite direction as well: Children and adults who are already habitually aggressive are more drawn to violent shows and are more affected by them than unaggressive people are. After watching violent films, they feel angrier than unaggressive people do and are more likely to behave aggressively toward others (Bushman, 1995).

In the social-cognitive view, both conclusions about the correlation between media violence and violent behavior have merit. Repeated acts of aggression in the media *do* model behavior and responses to conflict that some people will imitate, just as media ads influence what many people buy and what many people think the ideal male or female body should look like. Violent media images provide people with "scripts" for behaving aggressively, promote permissive beliefs about aggression as a way to solve problems, and desensitize people to the effects of violence (Anderson et al., 2003). Video games that directly reward violence—for example, by awarding points or moving the player to the next level after a "kill"—increase feelings of hostility, aggressive thinking, and aggressive behavior (Carnagey & Anderson, 2005). But perceptions and interpretations, along with personality dispositions such as aggressiveness and sociability, intervene between what we see, what we learn, and how we respond. One person may learn from seeing people being blown away in a film that violence is cool and masculine; another may conclude that violent images are ugly and stupid, or that they don't mean anything at all—that they are just part of the story.

What should individuals or society do, if anything, about media violence? Even if only a small percentage of viewers learn to be aggressive from observing all that violence, the social consequences can be huge, because the total audiences for TV, movies, and video games are immense and the cumulative effects over many years may be long-lasting (Bushman & Anderson, 2001). But censorship, which some people think is the answer, brings its own set of problems: Should we ban *Hamlet*? Cartoons? Batman? Funny Jackie Chan martial-arts films? Fancy special-effects films like *Matrix Reloaded*? All the *Star Wars* movies except the first one? In the United States, censorship would violate the constitutional guarantee of free speech. As for voluntary censorship, parents already have the opportunity to install "V-chips" on their TVs to block violent programs, yet only a tiny number of parents actually use them. As you can see, determining a fair and equitable policy regarding media violence will not be easy.

QUICK quiz

Does your perception of quizzes make you feel violent or motivated?

1. A friend asks you to meet her at a new restaurant across town. You have never been to this specific address, but you find your way there anyway because you have experienced __________ learning.
2. To a social-cognitive theorist, the fact that we can learn without being reinforced for any obvious responses shows that we do not learn specific responses but rather __________.
3. After watching her teenage sister put on lipstick, a little girl takes a lipstick and applies it to her own lips. She has acquired this behavior through a process of __________.
4. The families of victims shot at a high school by two fellow students claimed in a $5 billion lawsuit against several video-game manufacturers that the tragedy would not have happened had the killers not had access to violent games. How would you evaluate this claim?

Answers:

1. latent 2. knowledge about responses and their consequences 3. observational learning 4. Although a link has been established between media violence and aggressiveness, it is impossible to prove cause and effect in any given case. Violence has many different causes; for example, some teenagers kill because they have been taunted and rejected by their classmates. Further, a person's response to media violence is influenced by his or her perceptions and attitudes.

Although the behavioral and social-cognitive approaches to learning differ in emphasis, they share a fundamental optimism about the possibilities of change for individuals and societies. In the learning view, we do not have to sit around hoping that people will magically have a change of heart and stop harming themselves or others. Instead, we can focus on changing the reinforcers, role models, and media images that affect people's attitudes and actions.

Skinner himself never wavered in his determination to apply learning principles to fashion better, healthier environments for everyone. In 1990, just a week before his death, ailing and frail, he addressed an overflow crowd at the annual meeting of the American Psychological Association, making the case one last time for the approach he was convinced could create a better society.

When you see the world as the learning theorist views it, Skinner was saying, you see the folly of human behavior, but you also see the possibility of improving it.

Taking Psychology with You

Shape Up!

Operant conditioning can seem deceptively simple—a few rewards here, a bit of shaping there, and you're done. In practice, though, behavior modification can be full of unwanted surprises, even in the hands of experts. You can find information on using behavioral techniques in books such as *Don't Shoot the Dog: The New Art of Teaching and Training*, by Karen Pryor (1999), and *Behavior Modification: What It Is and How to Do It*, by Garry Martin and Joseph Pear (1999). In addition, here are a few things to keep in mind if you want to modify someone's behavior.

- **Accentuate the positive.** Most people notice bad behavior more than good and therefore miss opportunities to use reinforcers. Parents, for example, often scold a child for bed-wetting but fail to give praise for dry sheets in the morning, or they punish a child for poor grades but fail to reward studying.
- **Reinforce small improvements.** A common error is to withhold reinforcement until behavior is perfect (which may be never). Has your child's grade in math improved from a D to a C? Has your favorite date, who is usually an awful cook, managed to serve up a half-decent omelette? Has your messy roommate left some dirty dishes in the sink but vacuumed the rug? It's probably time for a reinforcer. On the other hand, you do not want to overdo praise or give it insincerely. Gushing about every tiny step in the right direction will cause your praise to lose its value, and soon nothing less than a standing ovation will do.
- **Find the right reinforcers.** You may have to experiment a bit to find which reinforcers a person (or animal) actually wants. Try varying the reinforcers; the same ones used again and again can get boring. Reinforcers, by the way, do not have to be *things*. You can also use valued activities, such as going out to dinner, to reinforce other behavior.
- **Always examine what you are reinforcing.** It is easy to reinforce undesirable behavior just by responding to it. Suppose someone is always yelling at you at the slightest provocation, and you want it to stop. If you respond to it at all, whether by crying, apologizing, or yelling back, you are likely to reinforce it. An alternative might be to explain in a calm voice that you will henceforth not respond to complaints unless they are communicated without yelling—and then, if the yelling continues, walk away. When the person does speak civilly, you can reward this behavior with your attention and goodwill.
- **Analyze the reasons for a person's undesirable behavior before responding to it.** A child screaming in a supermarket may be saying, "I'm going out of my head with boredom. Help!" A lover who sulks may be saying, "I'm not sure you really care about me; I'm frightened." Once you understand the purpose of someone's behavior, you may be more effective in dealing with it.

These guidelines apply to your own behavior as well. Assume, for example, that you want to get yourself to study more. Here are some behavioral strategies for increasing the time you spend with your books:

- **Analyze the situation.** Are there circumstances that keep you from studying, such as a friend who is always pressuring you to go out or a rock band that practices next door? If so, you need to change your environment during study periods. Try to find a comfortable, cheerful, quiet place. Not only will you concentrate better, but you may also have positive emotional responses to the environment, which may generalize to the activity of studying.
- **Set realistic goals.** Goals should be demanding but achievable. If a goal is too vague, as in "I'm going to work harder," you don't know what behavioral changes are necessary to reach it or how to know when you have done so (what does "harder" mean?). If your goal is focused, as in "I am going to study two hours every evening instead of one" or "I will read 25 pages instead of 15," you have specified both a course of action and a goal you can achieve (and reward).
- **Keep records.** Chart your progress in some way, perhaps by making a

graph or keeping a diary. This will keep you honest, and the progress you see on the graph or in your diary will serve as a secondary reinforcer.

- **Don't punish yourself.** If you did not study enough last week, don't brood about it or berate yourself with self-defeating thoughts, such as "I'll never be a good student" or "I'm a failure." Think about the coming week instead.

Above all, be patient. Shaping behavior is a creative skill that takes time to learn. Like Rome, new habits cannot be built in a day.

Summary

- Research on *learning* has been heavily influenced by *behaviorism*, which accounts for behavior in terms of observable events without reference to mental entities such as "mind" or "will." Behaviorists have focused on two types of *conditioning:* classical and operant.

Classical Conditioning

- *Classical conditioning* was first studied by Russian physiologist Ivan Pavlov. In this type of learning, when a neutral stimulus is paired with an *unconditioned stimulus* (*US*) that elicits some reflexive *unconditioned response* (*UR*), the neutral stimulus comes to elicit a similar or related response. The neutral stimulus then becomes a *conditioned stimulus* (*CS*), and the response it elicits is a *conditioned response* (*CR*). Nearly any kind of involuntary response can become a CR.
- In *extinction*, the conditioned stimulus is repeatedly presented without the unconditioned stimulus, and the conditioned response eventually disappears—although later it may reappear (*spontaneous recovery*). In *higher-order conditioning*, a neutral stimulus becomes a conditioned stimulus by being paired with an already established conditioned stimulus. In *stimulus generalization*, after a stimulus becomes a conditioned stimulus for some response, other similar stimuli may produce the same reaction. In *stimulus discrimination*, different responses are made to stimuli that resemble the conditioned stimulus in some way.
- Many theorists believe that what an animal or person learns in classical conditioning is not just an association between the unconditioned and conditioned stimulus but also information conveyed by one stimulus about another. Indeed, classical conditioning appears to be an evolutionary adaptation that allows an organism to prepare for a biologically important event. Considerable evidence exists to show that a neutral stimulus does not become a CS unless it reliably signals or predicts the US.

Classical Conditioning in Real Life

- Classical conditioning helps account for positive emotional responses to particular objects and events, fears and phobias, the acquisition of likes and dislikes, and reactions to medical treatments and placebos. John Watson showed how fears may be learned and then may be unlearned through a process of *counterconditioning*. Because of evolutionary adaptations, human beings (and many other species) are biologically primed to acquire some adaptive responses easily, such as conditioned taste aversions and certain fears.
- As we saw in "Biology and Classical Conditioning," work on classical conditioning is now integrating findings on motivation, learning, and biology. One recent study explored brain changes in the amygdala and *orbitofrontal cortex* that occur in response to conditioned stimuli for appetite or pleasure, and how those responses may affect people's motivation to eat. These results can explain, for example, the "restaurant phenomenon." Another study found that using a drug to enhance the activity of a certain receptor in the amygdala speeds up the extinction of a phobia (fear of heights) during virtual-reality treatments.

Operant Conditioning

- In *operant conditioning*, behavior becomes more likely to occur or less so depending on its consequences. Responses in operant conditioning are generally not reflexive and are more complex than in classical conditioning. Research in this area is closely associated with B. F. Skinner, who called his approach "radical behaviorism."

- In the Skinnerian analysis, *reinforcement* strengthens or increases the probability of a response and *punishment* weakens or decreases the probability of a response. Immediate consequences usually have a greater effect on a response than do delayed consequences.
- Reinforcers are called *primary* when they are naturally reinforcing (because they satisfy a biological need). They are called *secondary* when they have acquired their ability to strengthen a response through association with other reinforcers. A similar distinction is made for punishers.
- Reinforcement and punishment may be either positive or negative, depending on whether the consequence involves a stimulus that is presented or one that is removed or avoided. In *positive reinforcement*, something pleasant follows a response; in *negative reinforcement*, something unpleasant is removed. In *positive punishment*, something unpleasant follows the response; in *negative punishment*, something pleasant is removed.
- Using the Skinner box and similar devices, behaviorists have shown that *extinction*, *stimulus generalization*, and *stimulus discrimination* occur in operant conditioning as well as in classical conditioning. A *discriminative stimulus* signals that a response is likely to be followed by a certain type of consequence.
- The pattern of responding in operant conditioning depends in part on the *schedule of reinforcement. Continuous reinforcement* leads to the most rapid learning. However, *intermittent* (*partial*) *reinforcement* makes a response resistant to extinction (and, therefore, helps account for the persistence of superstitious rituals). Different intermittent patterns of reinforcement produce different patterns of responding. One of the most common errors people make is to reward intermittently the responses they would like to eliminate.
- *Shaping* is used to train behaviors with a low probability of occurring spontaneously. Reinforcers are given for *successive approximations* to the desired response until the desired response is achieved.
- Biology places limits on what an animal or person can learn through operant conditioning. For example, animals sometimes have trouble learning a task because of *instinctive drift*.

Operant Conditioning in Real Life

- *Behavior modification*, the application of operant conditioning principles, has been used successfully in many settings, but reinforcement and punishment both have their pitfalls.
- Punishment, when used properly, can discourage undesirable behavior, including criminal behavior. But it is frequently misused and can have unintended consequences. It is often administered inappropriately because of the emotion of the moment; it may produce rage and fear; its effects are often only temporary; it is hard to administer immediately; it conveys little information about the kind of behavior that is desired; and it may provide attention that is rewarding. Extinction of undesirable behavior, combined with reinforcement of desired behavior, is generally preferable to the use of punishment.
- Reinforcers can also be misused. Rewards that are given out indiscriminately, as in efforts to raise children's self-esteem, do not reinforce desirable behavior. And, as we saw in "Close-up on Research," an exclusive reliance on *extrinsic reinforcement* can sometimes undermine the power of *intrinsic reinforcement*. But money and praise do not usually interfere with intrinsic pleasure when a person is rewarded for succeeding or making progress rather than for merely participating in an activity, or when a person is already highly interested in the activity.

Learning and the Mind

- Even during behaviorism's heyday, some researchers were probing the "black box" of the mind. In the 1930s, Edward Tolman studied *latent learning*, in which no obvious reinforcer is present during learning and a response is not expressed until later on, when reinforcement does become available. What seems to be acquired in latent learning is not a specific response but rather knowledge about responses and their consequences.
- The 1960s and 1970s saw the increased influence of *social-cognitive theories* of learning, which focus on *observational learning* and the role played by beliefs, interpretations of events, and other cognitions. Social-cognitive theorists argue that in observational learning, as in latent learning, what is acquired is knowledge rather than a specific response.
- Because people differ in their perceptions and beliefs, they may learn different lessons from the same event or situation. For example, some people become more aggressive after exposure to violent images in the media, but most people do not. Moreover, cause and effect also work in the opposite direction: Aggressive individuals tend to be drawn to violent images and are more affected by them than other people are.

KEY TERMS

learning 235
behaviorism 235
conditioning 235
unconditioned stimulus (US) 237
unconditioned response (UR) 237
conditioned stimulus (CS) 237
conditioned response (CR) 237
classical conditioning 237
extinction (in classical conditioning) 238
spontaneous recovery 238
higher-order conditioning 238
stimulus generalization (in classical conditioning) 239
stimulus discrimination (in classical conditioning) 239
phobia 242
counterconditioning 243
orbitofrontal cortex 245
operant conditioning 247
reinforcement/reinforcers 248
punishment/punishers 248
primary reinforcers and punishers 249
secondary reinforcers and punishers 249
positive and negative reinforcement and punishment 249
Skinner box 251
extinction (in operant conditioning) 252
stimulus generalization (in operant conditioning) 252
stimulus discrimination (in operant conditioning) 252
discriminative stimulus 252
continuous reinforcement 252
intermittent (partial) reinforcement 252
shaping 254
successive approximations 254
instinctive drift 255
determinist view 255
behavior modification (applied behavior analysis) 257
extrinsic reinforcers 260
intrinsic reinforcers 261
behavioral "ABCs" 264
latent learning 265
social-cognitive theories 266
observational (vicarious) learning 266

Will It Be On the Test?

NOW YOU HAVE READ CHAPTER SEVEN — ARE YOU PREPARED FOR THE EXAM?

Many students get confused with the terms of classical conditioning. There are four major components to this type of learning: unconditioned stimulus (US), conditioned stimulus (CS), unconditioned response (UR) and conditioned response (CR). The best way to keep these terms straight is to ask yourself two questions:

1. Is the event I am interested in a stimulus or a response?
If an event is a stimulus, it will cause something else to happen. For example: a bright light, a loud siren, a touch on your arm. Examples of some possible responses are blinking your eyes, jumping up, and/or an increase in heart rate.

2. Is the stimulus/response something that was learned or something that occurs naturally, by instinct?
If the stimulus/response is something the subject had to learn, it would be a learned or conditioned stimulus. If the stimulus/response is something that causes the response automatically, then it is an unlearned or unconditioned stimulus.

Your heart speeds up as you see a police car pull up behind you. Your increased heart rate is a ________.

(Select the correct term from the table below.)

	Stimulus	Response
Learned	CS	CR
Unlearned	US	UR

What are the important concepts in classical conditioning? (pages 237–260)

CR

Another difficult concept in this chapter is the question: How does punishment affect behavior? (pages 257-260)

Negative reinforcement and punishment are often confused. Make sure you are clear on the difference by taking the quizzes on Operant Conditioning in MyPsychLab at **www.mypsychlab.com.** Also, check out the study card packaged with your book "Study Tips for the Most Difficult Topics in Introductory Psychology."

TELL ME **MORE** >>

"The quiz and homework sections covered information that helped me prepare for my exams."

Student
Bowling Green State University

How do operant stimuli control behavior?

The simulation in the study plan discusses key concepts in operant conditioning and shaping. Work through the content, listening to and watching the audio-visual portion, and reading the script. Then, answer the questions and take the post test to help prepare you for your next exam.

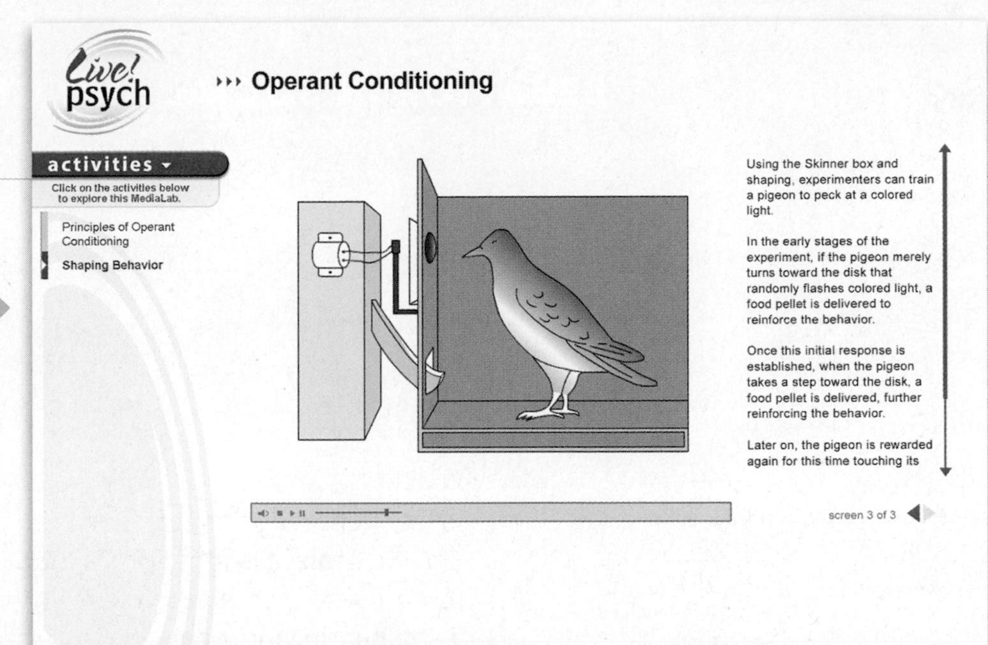

Live! psych
Operant Conditioning
activities
Click on the activities below to explore this MediaLab.
Principles of Operant Conditioning
Shaping Behavior
Using the Skinner box and shaping, experimenters can train a pigeon to peck at a colored light.
In the early stages of the experiment, if the pigeon merely turns toward the disk that randomly flashes colored light, a food pellet is delivered to reinforce the behavior.
Once this initial response is established, when the pigeon takes a step toward the disk, a food pellet is delivered, further reinforcing the behavior.
Later on, the pigeon is rewarded again for this time touching its
screen 3 of 3

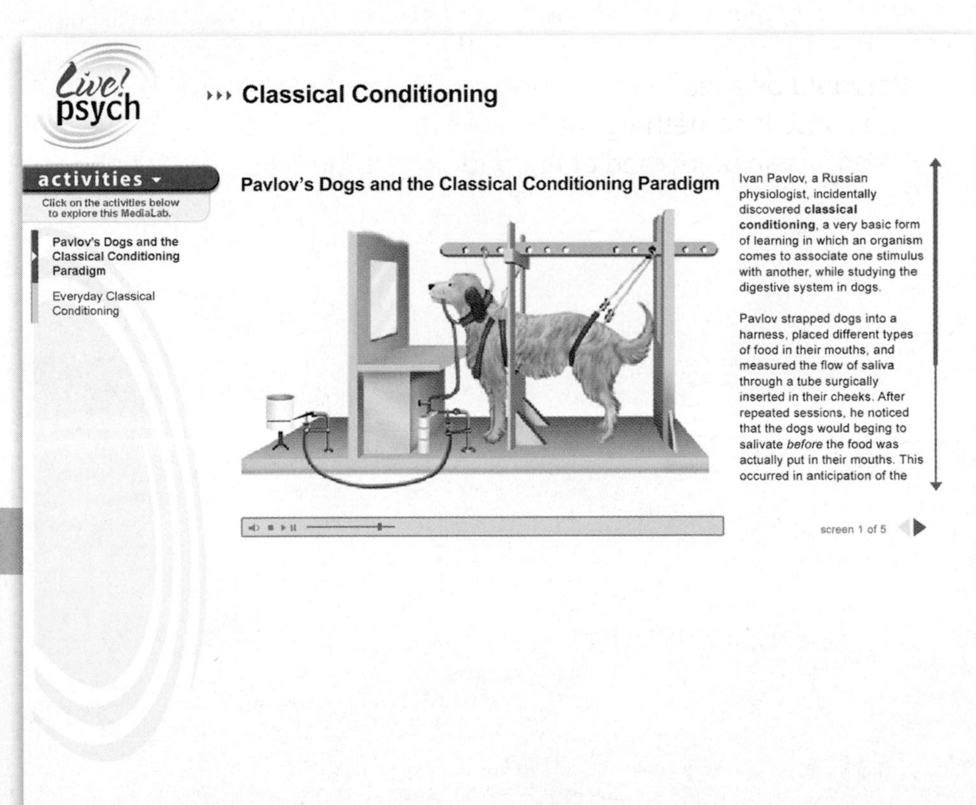

Live! psych
Classical Conditioning
activities
Click on the activities below to explore this MediaLab.
Pavlov's Dogs and the Classical Conditioning Paradigm
Everyday Classical Conditioning
Pavlov's Dogs and the Classical Conditioning Paradigm
Ivan Pavlov, a Russian physiologist, incidentally discovered classical conditioning, a very basic form of learning in which an organism comes to associate one stimulus with another, while studying the digestive system in dogs.
Pavlov strapped dogs into a harness, placed different types of food in their mouths, and measured the flow of saliva through a tube surgically inserted in their cheeks. After repeated sessions, he noticed that the dogs would beging to salivate before the food was actually put in their mouths. This occurred in anticipation of the
screen 1 of 5

TELL ME **MORE** >>

"The content and features [of MPL] were very useful in preparing for the exams."

Student
Clayton College and State University

What can you find in MyPsychLab?

Self-Directed Tests • Videos • Simulations • eBook • Flash Cards • Web Links . . . and more — organized by chapter, section and learning objective.

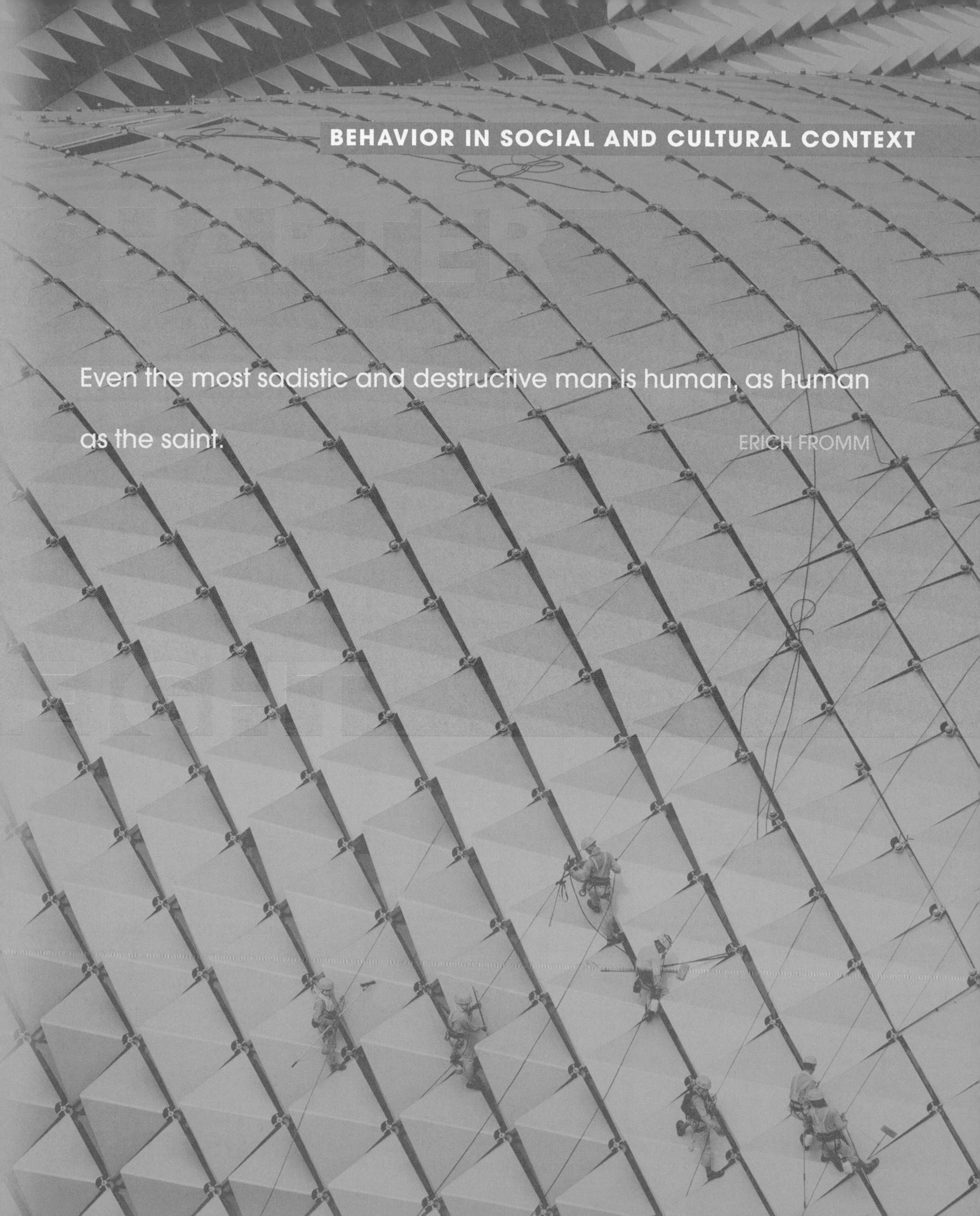

BEHAVIOR IN SOCIAL AND CULTURAL CONTEXT

Even the most sadistic and destructive man is human, as human as the saint.

ERICH FROMM

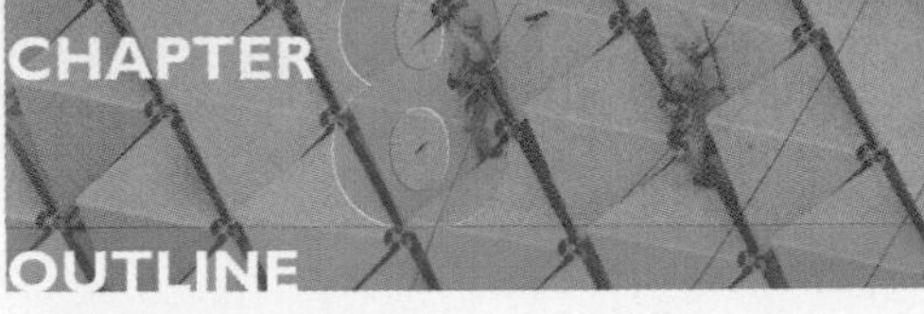

CHAPTER

OUTLINE

When Mohamed Atta was in graduate school in Germany, studying urban planning, his friends saw him as a good man who, like many students, was troubled by the social injustice he observed in the world. Atta was especially disturbed by the gap between rich and poor, although he himself came from a well-to-do family; his father was a lawyer and two sisters became university professors. "I knew Mohamed as a guy searching for justice," his German friend Volker Hauth told *The Los Angeles Times* (September 27, 2001). "Atta was very religious," said another friend. "He was very full of idealism and he was a humanist." In 2000, Atta left Germany for good. On September 11, 2001, he led the 19 hijackers who attacked the World Trade Center and the Pentagon, killing almost 3,000 people.

In Rwanda in 1994, members of the Hutu tribe shot or hacked to death hundreds of thousands of Tutsi, a rival tribe. At one point, thousands of Tutsi took refuge in a Benedictine convent, believing the nuns there would shelter them. Instead, the mother superior, Sister Gertrude, and another nun, Sister Maria Kisito—both of them Hutu—reported the Tutsi refugees to the Hutu militia. More than 7,000 Tutsi were killed in the ensuing massacre. When the two nuns were brought to trial in Belgium, where they had fled after the war, Sister Gertrude told the court she did it because "we were all going to perish." But observers testified that when 500 Tutsi fled to the convent's garage, the two nuns brought the militiamen gasoline. The garage was set afire, and anyone trying to escape the flames was hacked to death. The two women were sentenced to 15- and 12-year terms for crimes against humanity.

In 2004, seven American soldiers were arrested for acts of assault and indecency and for maltreating Iraqi prisoners in the Abu Ghraib prison in Baghdad. Naked, hooded prisoners were stacked on top of one another, some were threatened with attack dogs or electrocution, and others were sexually abused and humiliated. Photos of these abuses, including one of Pfc. Lynndie England dragging a prisoner on a leash, shocked the world. "Certain people in the Army told her to do what she did. She follows orders," said England's sister. "She's a caring person."

In 1961, Adolf Eichmann, who had been a high-ranking officer of the Nazi elite, was sentenced to death for his part in the deportation and killing of millions of Jews during World War II. He was proud of his efficiency at his work and his ability to resist feeling pity for his victims.

THINKING CRITICALLY

ASK QUESTIONS

Mohamed Atta, Rwandan Hutu nuns Sister Gertrude and Sister Maria Kisito at their trial in Brussels, Pfc. Lynndie England at her trial in the United States, and Adolf Eichmann at his trial in Israel. All of these people committed crimes that horrified the world. Were they "monsters"?

But when the Israelis captured him, he insisted that he was not anti-Semitic: He had had a Jewish mistress and he personally arranged for the protection of his Jewish half-cousin, two dangerous crimes for an SS officer. Shortly before his execution, Eichmann said, "I am not the monster I am made out to be. I am the victim of a fallacy" (R. Brown, 1986).

The fallacy to which Eichmann referred was the widespread belief that a person who does monstrous deeds must be a monster. Mohamed Atta, Sisters Gertrude and Maria Kisito, the young soldiers at Abu Ghraib prison, and Adolf Eichmann all committed terrible deeds. Were they all deranged? Or evil? There does seem to be so much evil and cruelty in the world, and yet so much kindness, sacrifice, and heroism, too. How can we even begin to explain either side of human nature?

The fields of *social psychology* and *cultural psychology* approach this question by examining the powerful influence of the social and cultural environment on the actions of individuals and groups. In this chapter, we will focus on the foundations of social psychology, basic principles that can help us understand why some people who are not "crazy" or "monstrous" nonetheless do unspeakably evil things—and why some otherwise ordinary people reach heights of heroism when the occasion demands. In particular, we will look at the influence of roles, attitudes, and groups and at the conditions under which people conform or dissent. Then we will consider some of the social and cultural reasons for prejudice and conflict between groups.

WHAT'S**AHEAD**

- How do social rules regulate behavior, and what is likely to happen when you violate them?
- Do you have to be mean or disturbed to inflict pain on someone just because an authority tells you to?
- Can ordinary college students be transformed into heartless prison guards?
- How can people be entrapped into violating their moral principles?

Many roles in modern life require us to give up our individuality. If one of these members of the British Coldstream Guards suddenly broke into a dance, his career would be brief—and the dazzling effect of the parade would be ruined. But when does adherence to a role go too far?

Roles and Rules

"We are all fragile creatures entwined in a cobweb of social constraints," social psychologist Stanley Milgram once said. The constraints he referred to are social **norms**, rules about how we are supposed to act, enforced by threats of punishment if we violate them and promises of reward if we follow them. Norms are the conventions of everyday life that make interactions with other people predictable and orderly; like a cobweb, they are often as invisible as they are strong. Every society has norms for just about everything in human experience: for conducting courtships, for raising children, for making decisions, for behavior in public places. Some norms are enshrined in law, such as "A person may not beat up another person, except in self-defense." Some are unspoken cultural understandings, such as "A man may beat up another man who insults his masculinity." And some are tiny, unspoken regulations that people learn to follow unconsciously, such as "You may not sing at the top of your lungs on a public bus."

In every society, people also fill a variety of social **roles**, positions that are regulated by norms about how people in those positions should behave. Gender roles define the proper behavior for a man and a woman. Occupational roles determine the correct behavior for a manager and an employee, a professor and a student. Family roles set tasks for parent and child, husband and wife. Certain aspects of every role must be carried out or there will be penalties—emotional, financial, or professional. As a student, for instance, you know just what you have to do to pass your psychology course (or you should by now!). How do you know what a role requirement is? You know when you violate it, intentionally or unintentionally, because you will probably feel awfully uncomfortable, or other people will try to make you feel that way.

The requirements of a social role are in turn shaped by the culture you live in. **Culture** can be defined as a program of shared rules that govern the behavior of people in a community or society, and a set of values, beliefs, and customs shared by most members of that community and passed from one generation to another (Lonner,

GET INVOLVED!

DARE TO BE DIFFERENT

Either alone or with a friend, try a mild form of "norm violation" (nothing alarming, obscene, dangerous, or offensive). For example, stand backward in line at the grocery store or cafeteria; sit right next to a stranger in the library or at a movie, even when other seats are available; sing or hum loudly for a couple of minutes in a public place; or stand "too close" to a friend in conversation. Notice the reactions of onlookers, as well as your own feelings, while you violate this norm. If you do this exercise with someone else, one of you can be the "violator" and the other can write down the responses of others; then switch places. Was it easy to do this exercise? Why or why not?

norms (social) Rules that regulate social life, including explicit laws and implicit cultural conventions.

role A given social position that is governed by a set of norms for proper behavior.

culture A program of shared rules that govern the behavior of people in a community or society, and a set of values, beliefs, and customs shared by most members of that community.

Arabs stand much closer in conversation than Westerners do, close enough to feel one another's breath and "read" one another's eyes. Most Westerners would feel "crowded" standing so close, even when talking to a friend.

1995). You learn most of your culture's rules and values the way you learn your culture's language: without thinking about it.

For example, cultures differ in their rules for *conversational distance*: how close people normally stand to one another when they are speaking (Hall, 1959, 1976). Arabs like to stand close enough to feel your breath, touch your arm, and see your eyes—a distance that makes white Americans, Canadians, and northern Europeans uneasy, unless they are talking intimately with a lover. The English and the Swedes stand farthest apart when they converse; southern Europeans stand closer; and Latin Americans and Arabs stand the closest (Keating, 1994; Sommer, 1969). If you are talking to someone who has different cultural rules for distance from yours, you are likely to feel very uncomfortable without knowing why. You may feel that the person is either "crowding" you or being strangely cool and "distant." A student of ours from Lebanon told us how relieved he was to understand how cultures differ in their rules for conversational distance. "When Anglo students moved away from me, I thought they were prejudiced," he said. "Now I see why I was more comfortable talking with Latino students. They like to stand close, too."

Naturally, people bring their own personalities and interests to the roles they play. Just as two actors will play the same part differently although they are reading from the same script, you will have your own reading of how to play the role of student, friend, parent, or employer. Nonetheless, the requirements of a social role are strong, so strong that they may even cause you to behave in ways that shatter your fundamental sense of the kind of person you are. We turn now to two classic studies that illuminate the power of social roles in our lives.

The Obedience Study

In the early 1960s, Stanley Milgram (1963, 1974) designed a study that would become world-famous. Milgram wanted to know how many people would obey an authority figure when directly ordered to violate their ethical standards. Participants in the study, however, thought they were part of an experiment on the effects of punishment on learning. Each was assigned, apparently at random, to the role of "teacher." Another person, introduced as a fellow volunteer, was the "learner." Whenever the learner, seated in an adjoining room, made an error in reciting a list of word pairs he was supposed to have memorized, the teacher had to give him an electric shock by depressing a lever on a machine (see Figure 8.1). With each error, the voltage (marked from 0 to 450) was to be increased by another 15 volts. The shock levels on the machine were labeled from SLIGHT SHOCK to DANGER—SEVERE SHOCK and, finally, ominously, XXX. In reality, the learners were confederates of Milgram and did not receive any shocks, but none of the teachers ever realized this during the study. The actor-victims played their parts convincingly: As the study continued, they shouted in pain and pleaded to be released, all according to a prearranged script.

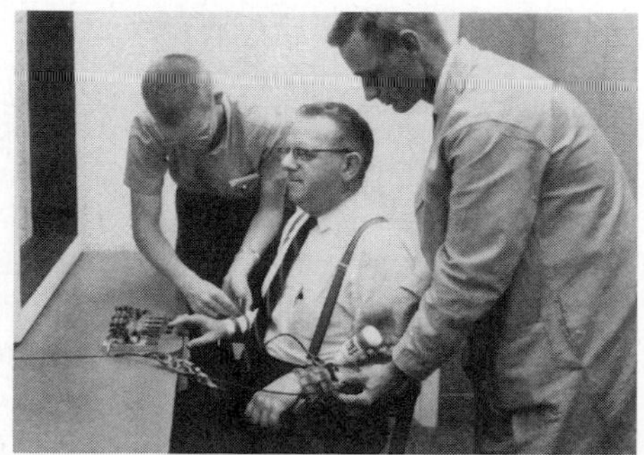

FIGURE 8.1 The Milgram Obedience Experiment

On the left is Milgram's original shock machine; in 1963, it looked pretty ominous. On the right, the "learner" is being strapped into his chair by the experimenter and the "teacher."

(left) Archives of the History of American Psychology - The University of Akron; (right) Copyright 1965 by Stanley Milgram. From the film OBEDIENCE, distributed by Penn State Media Sales.

Before doing this study, Milgram asked a number of psychiatrists, students, and middle-class adults how many people they thought would "go all the way" to XXX on orders from the researcher. The psychiatrists predicted that most people would refuse to go beyond 150 volts, when the learner first demanded to be freed, and that only one person in a thousand, someone who was disturbed and sadistic, would administer the highest voltage. The nonprofessionals agreed with this prediction, and all of them said that they personally would disobey early in the procedure.

THINKING CRITICALLY

ASK QUESTIONS

Jot down your best guess in answering these three questions: (1) What percentage of people are sadistic? (2) If told by an authority to harm an innocent person, what percentage of people would do it? (3) If *you* were instructed to harm an innocent person, would you do it or would you refuse?

That is not, however, the way the results turned out. Every single person administered some shock to the learner, and about two-thirds of the participants, of all ages and from all walks of life, obeyed to the fullest extent. Many protested to the experimenter, but they backed down when he calmly asserted, "The experiment requires that you continue." They obeyed no matter how much the victim shouted for them to stop and no matter how painful the shocks seemed to be. They obeyed even when they themselves were anguished about the pain they believed they were causing. As Milgram (1974) noted, participants would "sweat, tremble, stutter, bite their lips, groan, and dig their fingernails into their flesh"—but still they obeyed.

Over the decades, more than 3,000 people have gone through replications of the Milgram study. Most of them, men and women equally, inflicted what they thought were dangerous amounts of shock to another person. Researchers in other countries have also found high percentages of obedience, ranging to more than 90 percent in Spain and the Netherlands (Meeus & Raaijmakers, 1995; Smith & Bond, 1994).

Milgram and his team subsequently set up several variations of the study to determine the circumstances under which people might disobey the experimenter. They found that virtually nothing the victim did or said changed the likelihood of compliance, even when the victim said he had a heart condition, screamed in agony, or stopped responding entirely, as if he had collapsed. However, people *were* more likely to disobey under the following conditions:

In Milgram's study, when the "teacher" had to administer shock directly to the learner, most subjects refused, but this one continued to obey.

- ***When the experimenter left the room***, many people subverted authority by giving low levels of shock but reporting that they had followed orders.
- ***When the victim was right there in the room***, and the teacher had to administer the shock directly to the victim's body, many people refused to go on.
- ***When two experimenters issued conflicting demands***, with one telling participants to continue and another saying to stop at once, no one kept inflicting shock.
- ***When the person ordering them to continue was an ordinary man***, apparently another volunteer instead of the authoritative experimenter, many participants disobeyed.
- ***When the subject worked with peers who refused to go further***, he or she often gained the courage to disobey.

Obedience, Milgram concluded, was more a function of the *situation* than of the personalities of the participants. "The key to [their] behavior," Milgram (1974) summarized, "lies not in pent-up anger or aggression but in the nature of their relationship to authority. They have given themselves to the authority; they see themselves as instruments for the execution of his wishes; once so defined, they are unable to break free."

The Milgram study has had its critics. Some consider it unethical because people were kept in the dark about what was really happening until the session was over (of course, telling them in advance would have invalidated the study) and because many suffered emotional pain (Milgram countered that they would not have felt pain if they had simply disobeyed instructions). Others question the conclusion that personality traits always have less influence on behavior than the demands of the situation; certain traits, such as hostility and rigidity, do increase obedience to authority in real life (Blass, 2000).

Some psychologists also object to the parallel Milgram drew between the behavior of the study's participants and the brutality of the Nazis and others who have committed acts of barbarism in the name of duty (Darley, 1995). The people in Milgram's study obeyed only when the experimenter was hovering right there, and many of them felt enormous discomfort and conflict. In contrast, most Nazis acted without direct supervision by authorities, without external pressure, and without feelings of anguish. Nevertheless, this compelling study has had a tremendous influence on public awareness of the dangers of uncritical obedience. As John Darley (1995) observed, "Milgram shows us the beginning of a path by means of which ordinary people, in the grip of social forces, become the origins of atrocities in the real world."

The Prison Study

Another famous demonstration of the power of roles is known as the Stanford Prison Study. Its designers, Philip Zimbardo and Craig Haney, wanted to know what would happen if ordinary college students were randomly assigned to the roles of prisoners and guards (Haney, Banks, & Zimbardo, 1973). And so they set up a serious-looking "prison" in the basement of a Stanford building, complete with individual cells and different uniforms for prisoners and guards (including nightsticks for the guards). The students agreed to live there for two weeks.

The results were dramatic. Within a short time, most of the prisoners became distressed and helpless. They developed emotional symptoms and physical ailments. Some became apathetic; others became rebellious. One panicked and broke down. Within an equally short time, the guards began to enjoy their new power. Some tried to be nice, helping the prisoners and doing little favors for them. Some were "tough but fair," holding strictly to "the rules." But about a third became punitive and harsh, even when the prisoners were not resisting in any way. One guard became unusually sadistic, smacking his nightstick into his palm as he vowed to "get" the prisoners and instructing two of them to simulate sexual acts (they refused). The researchers, who had not expected such a speedy and alarming transformation of ordinary students, ended this study after only six days.

CONSIDER OTHER INTERPRETATIONS

Why did the guards at Abu Ghraib abuse and humiliate their prisoners? Were those guards just "bad apples"? Social psychologists think the answer lies in the roles they were assigned; the implicit permission, if not direct orders, given by their leaders; and the group norms of their peers. The fact that the guards willingly posed for pictures—in many, they are smiling proudly—indicates that they were showing off for their friends and that they believed their behavior was normal and appropriate.

Generations of students and the general public have seen emotionally charged clips from videos of the study made at the time. To the researchers, the results demonstrated how roles affect behavior: The guards' aggression, they said, was entirely a result of wearing a guard's uniform and having the power conferred by a guard's authority (Haney & Zimbardo, 1998). Some social psychologists, however, have argued that the prison study is really another example of obedience to authority and of how willingly some people obey instructions—in this case, from Zimbardo himself (Haslam & Reicher, 2003). Consider the briefing that Zimbardo provided to the guards at the beginning of the study.

> You can create in the prisoners feelings of boredom, a sense of fear to some degree, you can create a notion of arbitrariness that their life is totally controlled by us, by the system, you, me, and they'll have no privacy. . . . We're going to take away their individuality in various ways. In general what all this leads to is a sense of powerlessness. That is, in this situation we'll have all the power and they'll have none (The Stanford Prison Study video, quoted in Haslam & Reicher, 2003).

These are pretty powerful suggestions to the guards about how they would be permitted to behave, and they convey Zimbardo's personal encouragement ("*we'll* have all the power"), so perhaps it is not surprising that some took Zimbardo at his word and behaved quite brutally. The one sadistic guard now says he was just trying to play the role of the "worst S.O.B. guard" he'd seen in the movies. On the other hand, in real prisons guards do have the kind of power that was given to these students, and they too may be given instructions that encourage them to treat prisoners harshly. Thus the prison study remains a powerful demonstration of how the *social situation*—whether the role itself or obedience to authority—affects behavior, causing some people to behave in ways that seem out of character.

Prisoners and guards quickly learn their respective roles, which often have more influence on their behavior than their personalities do.

Many people see parallels between the prison study and the brutality committed by the American soldiers at Abu Ghraib prison. As Zimbardo himself told *The New York Times* (May 6, 2004): "Prisons, where the balance of power is so unequal, tend to be brutal and abusive places . . . At Stanford and in Iraq, it's not that we put bad apples in a good barrel. We put good apples in a bad barrel. The barrel corrupts anything that it touches."

Why People Obey

Of course, obedience to authority or to the norms of a situation is not always harmful or bad. A certain amount of routine compliance with rules is necessary in any group, and obedience to authority has many benefits for individuals and society. A nation could not operate if all its citizens ignored traffic signals, cheated on their taxes, dumped garbage wherever they chose, or assaulted each other. An organization could not function if its members came to work only when they felt like it. But obedience also has a darker aspect. Throughout history, the plea "I was only following orders" has been offered to excuse actions carried out on behalf of orders that were foolish, destructive, or illegal. The writer C. P. Snow once observed that "more hideous crimes have been committed in the name of obedience than in the name of rebellion."

Most people follow orders because of the obvious consequences of disobedience: They can be suspended from school, fired from their jobs, or arrested. They may also obey because of what they hope to gain: being liked, getting certain advantages or promotions from the authority, or learning from the authority's greater knowledge or experience. Primarily, though, people obey because they are deeply convinced of the authority's legitimacy. They obey not only in hopes of gaining some tangible benefit, but also because they like and respect the authority and value the relationship.

But what about all those obedient people in Milgram's study who felt they were doing wrong and who wished they were free, but who could not untangle themselves from the "cobweb of social constraints"? Why do people obey when it is not in their interests, or when obedience requires them to ignore their own values or even commit a crime? How do they become morally disengaged from the consequences of their actions, as the guards did at Abu Ghraib? Researchers looking at the social context of behavior draw our attention to several factors that cause people to obey when they would rather not (Bandura, 1999; Gourevich, 1998; Kelman & Hamilton, 1989; Staub, 1999):

1 **Allocating responsibility to the authority.** One common way that people justify their behavior is to hand over responsibility to the authority, thereby absolving

The routinization of torture allows people to commit or collaborate in atrocities. More than 16,000 political prisoners were tortured and killed at Tuol Sleng prison by Cambodia's Khmer Rouge during the genocidal regime of Pol Pot. Prison authorities kept meticulous records and photos of each victim in order to make their barbarous activities seem mundane and normal. This man, Ing Pech, one of only seven survivors, was spared because he had skills useful to his captors. He now runs a museum at the prison.

themselves of accountability for their own actions. In Milgram's study, individuals who refused to give high levels of shock took responsibility for their own actions. "One of the things I think is very cowardly," said a 32-year-old engineer, "is to try to shove the responsibility onto someone else. See, if I now turned around and said, 'It's your fault . . . it's not mine,' I would call that cowardly" (Milgram, 1974). In contrast, many who administered the highest levels of shock adopted the attitude "It's his problem; I'm just following orders." Similarly, the seven soldiers who were charged with brutality at Abu Ghraib said they were only following orders from intelligence officers to "soften up" the prisoners, and the brigadier general who was in charge of all prisons in Iraq said she was only following orders given by her own superiors.

2 **Routinizing the task.** When people define their actions in terms of routine duties and roles, their behavior starts to feel normal, just a job to be done. Becoming absorbed in busywork distracts them from raising doubts or ethical questions, and it fosters an uncritical, mindless attention to detail that obscures the larger picture. In the Milgram study, some people became so fixated on the "learning task" that they shut out any moral concerns about the learner's demands to be let out. Routinization is typically the mechanism by which governments enlist citizens to aid and abet programs of genocide. Nazi bureaucrats kept meticulous records of every victim, and in Cambodia in the 1970s, the Khmer Rouge recorded the names and histories of the millions of victims they tortured and killed.

3 **Wanting to be polite.** Good manners protect people's feelings and make relationships and civilization possible. But once people are caught in what they perceive to be legitimate roles and are obeying a legitimate authority, good manners ensnare them into further obedience. They do not want to rock the boat, appear to doubt the experts, or be rude because they know they will be disliked or shunned for doing so (Collins & Brief, 1995).

Most people literally lack the words to justify disobedience and rudeness toward an authority they respect. In the Milgram study, many people could not find the words to justify walking out, so they stayed. One woman kept apologizing to the experimenter, trying not to offend him with her worries for the victim: "Do I go right to the end, sir? I hope there's nothing wrong with him there." (She did go right to the end.) A man repeatedly protested and questioned the experimenter, but he too obeyed, even when the victim had apparently collapsed in pain. "He thinks he is killing someone," Milgram (1974) commented, "yet he uses the language of the tea table."

4 **Becoming entrapped.** **Entrapment** is a process in which individuals escalate their commitment to a course of action in order to justify their investment in it (Brockner & Rubin, 1985). The first steps of entrapment pose no difficult choices, but one step leads to another, and before you realize it, you have become committed to a course of action that poses problems. In Milgram's study, once subjects had given a 15-volt shock, they had committed themselves to the experiment. The next level was "only" 30 volts. Because each increment was small, before they knew it most people were administering what they believed were dangerously strong shocks. At that point,

entrapment A gradual process in which individuals escalate their commitment to a course of action to justify their investment of time, money, or effort.

it was difficult to explain a sudden decision to quit. Participants who questioned the procedure early were less likely to become entrapped and more likely to eventually disobey (Modigliani & Rochat, 1995).

Slot machines rely on the principle of entrapment, which is why casinos win millions and most players don't. A person vows to spend only a few dollars but, after losing them, says, "Well, maybe another couple of tries" or "I've spent so much, now I really have to win something to get back what I've lost."

Individuals and nations alike are vulnerable to the sneaky process of entrapment. You start dating someone you like moderately; before you know it, you have been together so long that you can't break up, although you don't want to become committed, either. Government leaders start a war they think will end quickly. Years later, the nation has lost so many soldiers and so much money that the leaders believe they cannot retreat without losing face.

A chilling study of entrapment was conducted with 25 men who had served in the Greek military police during the authoritarian regime that ended in 1974 (Haritos-Fatouros, 1988). A psychologist interviewed the men, identifying the steps used in training them to use torture in questioning prisoners. First the men were ordered to stand guard outside the interrogation and torture cells. Then they stood guard inside the detention rooms, where they observed the torture of prisoners. Then they "helped" beat up prisoners. Once they had obediently followed these orders and became actively involved, the torturers found their actions easier to carry out. The same procedures have been used to train police interrogators to use torture on political opponents and terrorist suspects in places as diverse as Chicago, England, Israel, and Brazil (Conroy, 2000; Huggins, Haritos-Fatouros, & Zimbardo, 2003).

As Milgram would have predicted, even torturers see themselves as otherwise "good guys" who are just "doing their jobs." This is a difficult concept for people who divide the world into "good guys" versus "bad guys" and cannot imagine that good guys might do cruel things. Yet in everyday life, as in the Milgram study, people often set out on a path that is morally ambiguous, only to find that they have traveled a long way toward violating their own principles. From Greece's torturers to the Khmer Rouge's dutiful clerks, from the African nuns to the American military guards, from Milgram's well-meaning volunteers to all of us in our everyday lives, people face the difficult task of drawing a line beyond which they will not go. For many, the demands of the role and the social pressures of the situation defeat the inner voice of conscience.

QUICK quiz

Step into your role of student to answer these questions.

1. About what proportion of the people in Milgram's obedience study administered the highest level of shock? (a) two-thirds, (b) one-half, (c) one-third, (d) one-tenth
2. Which of the following actions by the "learner" reduced the likelihood of being shocked by the "teacher" in Milgram's study? (a) protesting noisily, (b) screaming in pain, (c) complaining of having a heart ailment, (d) nothing he did made a difference
3. A friend of yours, who is moving, asks you to bring over a few boxes. Since you are there anyway, he asks you to fill them with books. Before you know it, you have packed up his kitchen, living room, and bedroom. What social-psychological process is at work here?

Answers:

1. a 2. d 3. entrapment

WHAT'S AHEAD

- What is one of the most common mistakes people make when explaining the behavior of others?
- Why do so many people blame victims of tragedy or crime for having brought their misfortunes on themselves?
- What is the "Big Lie," and why does it work so well?
- When do ordinary techniques of persuasion become coercive and controlling?

Social Influences on Beliefs

social cognition An area in social psychology concerned with social influences on thought, memory, perception, and beliefs.

attribution theory The theory that people are motivated to explain their own and other people's behavior by attributing causes of that behavior to a situation or a disposition.

Social psychologists are interested not only in what people do in social situations, but also in what goes on in their heads while they're doing it. Researchers in the area of **social cognition** examine how people's perceptions of themselves and others affect their relationships and how the social environment influences thoughts, beliefs, and values. Some have joined forces with neuroscientists and cognitive psychologists to develop a new specialty called *social-cognitive neuroscience*, which draws upon technologies from neuroscience to study the emotional and social processes underlying beliefs, prejudices, and social behavior (Harris, Todorov, & Fiske, 2005). We will consider two important topics in social cognition: explanations about behavior and the formation of attitudes.

Attributions

People read detective stories to find out *who* did the dirty deed, but in real life we also want to know *why* people do things. Was it because of a terrible childhood, a mental illness, possession by a demon, or what? According to **attribution theory**, the explanations we make of our behavior and the behavior of others generally fall into two categories. When we make a *situational attribution*, we are identifying the cause of an action as something in the situation or environment: "Joe stole the money because his family is starving." When we make a *dispositional attribution*, we are identifying the cause of an action as something in the person, such as a trait or a motive: "Joe stole the money because he is a born thief."

In the classic musical *West Side Story*, a member of the Jets gang tells Officer Krupke, "I'm depraved on account of I'm deprived." What kind of attribution is he making to explain his delinquency?

The attributions you make about your own and other people's behavior can have huge consequences. For example, happy couples usually attribute their partners' occasional thoughtless lapses to something in the situation ("Poor guy is under a lot of stress") and their partners' loving actions to a stable, internal disposition ("He has the sweetest nature"). But unhappy couples do just the reverse. They attribute lapses to their partners' personalities ("He is a hopeless mama's boy") and good behavior to the situation ("Yeah, he gave me a present, but only because his mother told him to") (Karney & Bradbury, 2000). You can see why the attributions you make about your partner, your parents, and your friends will make a big difference in how you get along with them—and how long you will put up with their failings!

When people are trying to find reasons for someone else's behavior, they reveal a common bias: They tend to overestimate personality traits and underestimate the

influence of the situation (Forgas, 1998; Nisbett & Ross, 1980). In terms of attribution theory, they tend to ignore situational attributions in favor of dispositional ones. This tendency has been called the **fundamental attribution error** (Jones, 1990; Van Boven, Kamada, & Gilovich, 1999). Were the hundreds of people who obeyed Milgram's experimenters sadistic by nature? Were the student guards in the prison study cruel and the prisoners cowardly by temperament? Those who think so are committing the fundamental attribution error. The impulse to explain other people's behavior in terms of their personalities is so strong that we do it even when we know that the other person was *required* to behave in a certain way (Yzerbyt et al., 2001).

People are especially likely to overlook situational attributions when they are in a good mood and are not inclined to think about other people's motives critically, or when they are distracted and preoccupied and don't have time to stop and ask themselves, "Why, exactly, *is* Aurelia in such a mean and crabby mood today?" Instead, they leap to the easiest attribution, which is dispositional: It's all because of her mean and crabby personality (Forgas, 1998). They are less likely to wonder whether Aurelia has recently joined a group of friends who are encouraging meanness or whether she is under unusual pressure that is making her temporarily crabby.

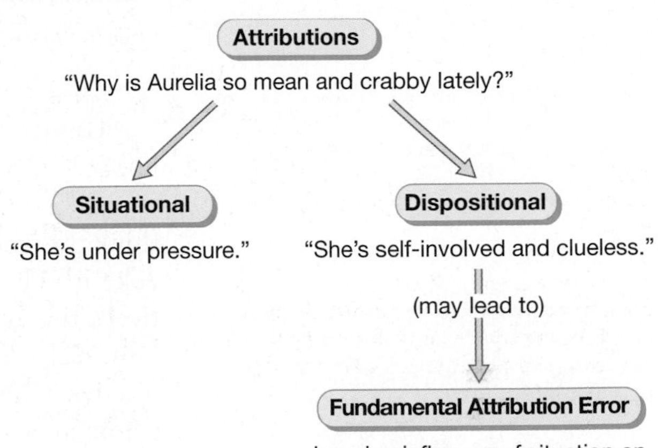

The fundamental attribution error is especially prevalent in Western nations, where middle-class people tend to believe that individuals are responsible for their own actions. In countries such as India, where everyone is embedded in caste and family networks, and in Japan, China, Korea, and Hong Kong, where people are more group oriented than in the West, people are more likely to be aware of situational constraints on behavior (Choi et al., 2003; Miyamoto & Kitayama, 2002). Thus, if someone is behaving oddly, makes a mistake, or plays badly in a soccer match, a person from India or China, unlike a Westerner, is more likely to make a situational attribution of the person's behavior ("He's under pressure") than a dispositional one ("He's incompetent") (Menon et al., 1999).

Westerners do not always prefer dispositional attributions, however. When it comes to explaining their *own* behavior, they often reveal a **self-serving bias**: They tend to choose attributions that are favorable to them, taking credit for their good actions (a dispositional attribution) but letting the situation account for their failures, embarrassing mistakes, or harmful actions (Mezulis et al., 2004). For instance, most North Americans, when angry, will say, "I am furious for good reason—this situation is intolerable." They are less likely to say, "I am furious because I am an ill-tempered grinch." On the other hand, if they do something admirable, such as donating to charity, they are likely to attribute their motives to a personal disposition ("I'm so generous") instead of the situation ("That guy on the phone pressured me into it").

According to the **just-world hypothesis**, attributions are also affected by the need to believe that the world is fair and that justice prevails and, particularly, that good people are rewarded and bad guys punished. This belief helps people make sense out of senseless events and feel safe in the presence of threatening events (Lerner, 1980). When the belief is thrown into doubt, people are motivated to restore it. For example, students who felt most strongly that the world is fair, as measured in their replies to a questionnaire before the events of 9/11, later were the most distressed about the attacks and had the strongest desire for revenge (Kaiser, Vick, & Major, 2004).

fundamental attribution error The tendency, in explaining other people's behavior, to overestimate personality factors and underestimate the influence of the situation.

self-serving bias The tendency, in explaining one's own behavior, to take credit for one's good actions and rationalize one's mistakes.

just-world hypothesis The notion that many people need to believe that the world is fair and that justice is served, that bad people are punished and good people rewarded.

Children learn the value of self-serving attributions at an early age.

Unfortunately, one common way of restoring the belief in a just world is to call upon a dispositional attribution called *blaming the victim*. If a friend is fired, a woman is raped, or an innocent bystander is shot by the police, it is reassuring to think that they all must have done something to deserve what happened or to provoke it: The friend wasn't doing his work, the woman was dressed too provocatively, the bystander shouldn't have been in the way. Blaming the victim is virtually universal when people are ordered to harm others or find themselves entrapped into harming others (Bandura, 1999). In the Milgram study, some "teachers" made comments such as "[The learner] was so stupid and stubborn he deserved to get shocked" (Milgram, 1974).

Of course, sometimes dispositional (personality) attributions *do* explain a person's behavior. The point to remember is that attributions, whether they are accurate or not, have tremendously important consequences for how we feel about ourselves, others, and the world.

QUICK quiz

To what do you attribute your success in answering these questions?

1. What kind of attribution is being made in each case, situational or dispositional? (a) A man says, "My wife has sure become a grouchy person." (b) The same man says, "I'm grouchy because I've had a bad day at the office." (c) A woman reads about high unemployment in poor communities and says, "Well, if those people weren't so lazy, they would find work."
2. What principles of attribution theory are suggested by the items in the preceding question?

Answers:

1. a. dispositional b. situational c. dispositional 2. Item a illustrates the fundamental attribution error; *b*, the self-serving bias; and *c*, blaming the victim, possibly because of the just-world hypothesis.

Attitudes

People hold attitudes about all sorts of things—politics, food, children, movies, sports heroes, you name it. An *attitude* is a belief about people, groups, ideas, or activities. Some attitudes are *explicit*: We are aware of them, they shape our conscious decisions and actions, and they can be measured on self-report questionnaires. Others are *implicit*: We are unaware of them, they may influence our behavior in ways we do not

recognize, and they are measured in various indirect ways, as we will see later in discussing prejudice (Rudman, 2004; Wilson, Lindsey, & Schooler, 2000).

Some of your attitudes change when you have new experiences, and on occasion they change because you rationally decide you were wrong about something. But attitudes also change because of the psychological need for consistency and the mind's normal biases in processing information. In Chapter 9, we discuss **cognitive dissonance**, the uncomfortable feeling that occurs when two attitudes, or an attitude and behavior, are in conflict (are dissonant). To resolve this dissonance, most people will change one of their attitudes. For example, if a politician or celebrity you admire does something stupid, immoral, or illegal, you can restore consistency either by lowering your opinion of the person or by deciding that the person's behavior wasn't so stupid or immoral after all. Usually, people restore cognitive consistency by dismissing evidence that might otherwise throw their fundamental beliefs into question (Aronson, 2004).

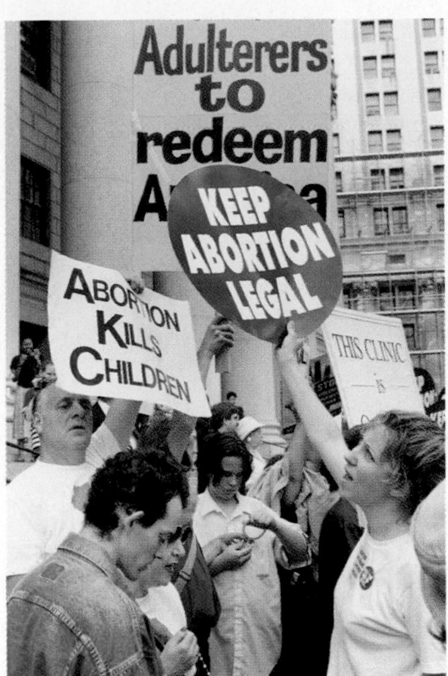

When people hold attitudes that are central to their religious and political philosophies, they often fail to realize that the other side feels just as strongly.

Shifting Opinions and Bedrock Beliefs. On most everyday topics, such as movies and sports, people's attitudes range from casual to committed. If your best friend is neutral about baseball whereas you are an insanely devoted fan, your friendship will probably survive. But when the subject is one involving beliefs that give meaning and purpose to a person's life—most notably, politics and religion—it's another ball game, so to speak.

Wars have been fought, and are being fought as you read this, over people's most passionate convictions. Perhaps the attitude that causes the most controversy and bitterness around the world is the one toward religious diversity: accepting or intolerant. Some people of all religions accept a world of differing religious views and practices; they believe that church and state should be separate. But for many fundamentalists (in any religion), religion and politics are inseparable; they believe that one religion should prevail (Jost et al., 2003). You can see, then, why these irreconcilable attitudes cause continuing conflict, and sometimes are used to justify terrorism and war.

BIOLOGY and Beliefs

Do Genes Influence Our Attitudes?

Where do attitudes come from? For decades, social psychologists have assumed that all attitudes are learned, acquired from the groups people belong to, the lessons their parents teach them, the experiences they have, their economic circumstances, and other social and environmental influences. Certainly, many attitudes are acquired in these ways, and they may change when a person has new experiences or moves into a different social group that has different values and views.

Now, however, psychological scientists are discovering that some attitudes are not solely a result of learning. They have been drawing on research from *behavioral genetics*, which has found that some core attitudes stem from personality traits that are highly heritable. That is, the variation among people in these attitudes is due in part to their genetic differences (see Chapters 3 and 13). One such trait is "openness to experience." We would expect people who are open to new experiences to hold positive attitudes toward novelty and change in general—say, in religion, art, music, and social and political events in the larger culture. We would expect people who prefer the familiar and conventional to be drawn to conservative politics, religious denominations, and philosophies. And that is what the research is finding.

Religious *affiliation*—whether a person is a Methodist, Muslim, Catholic, Jew, Hindu, and so on—is not heritable; most people choose a religious group because

cognitive dissonance A state of tension that occurs when a person simultaneously holds two cognitions that are psychologically inconsistent or when a person's belief is incongruent with his or her behavior.

of their parents, ethnicity, culture, and social class. But, as studies of twins reared apart have found, *religiosity*—a person's depth of religious feeling and adherence to a religion's rules—does have a genetic component. In a study of liberal and fundamentalist Protestant Christians, the fundamentalists scored much lower than the liberals on the dimension of openness to experience (Streyffeler & McNally, 1998). When religiosity combines with conservatism and authoritarianism (an unquestioning trust in authority), the result is a deeply ingrained acceptance of tradition and dislike of those who question it (Olson et al., 2001; Saucier, 2000).

Likewise, political affiliation is not heritable; it is largely related to your upbringing and to the friends you make in early adulthood, the key years for deciding which party you want to join. Nor do the casual political opinions held by many "swing voters" or people who are politically disengaged have a genetic component. But political conservatism has high heritability: .65 in men and .45 in women (Bouchard, 2004; Bouchard & McGue, 2003). Various political positions on emotionally hot topics that are associated with conservative or liberal views are also partly heritable. A team of researchers investigated this possibility by drawing on two large samples of more than 8,000 sets of twins who had been surveyed about their personality traits, religious beliefs, and political attitudes (Alford, Funk, & Hibbing, 2005). The researchers compared the opinions of fraternal twins (who share, on average, 50 percent of their genes) with those of identical twins (who share 100 percent of their genes). They calculated how often the identical twins agreed on each issue, subtracted the rate at which fraternal twins agreed, and ended up with a rough measure of heritability. As you can see in Figure 8.2, the attitudes showing the highest heritability were those about school prayer and property taxes; attitudes showing the lowest influence of genes included those about segregation, divorce, and abortion.

These findings are provocative, but it is important not to oversimplify them—say, by incorrectly assuming that everyone's political opinions are hardwired and unaffected by events that happen to them. In fact, the factor that accounted for

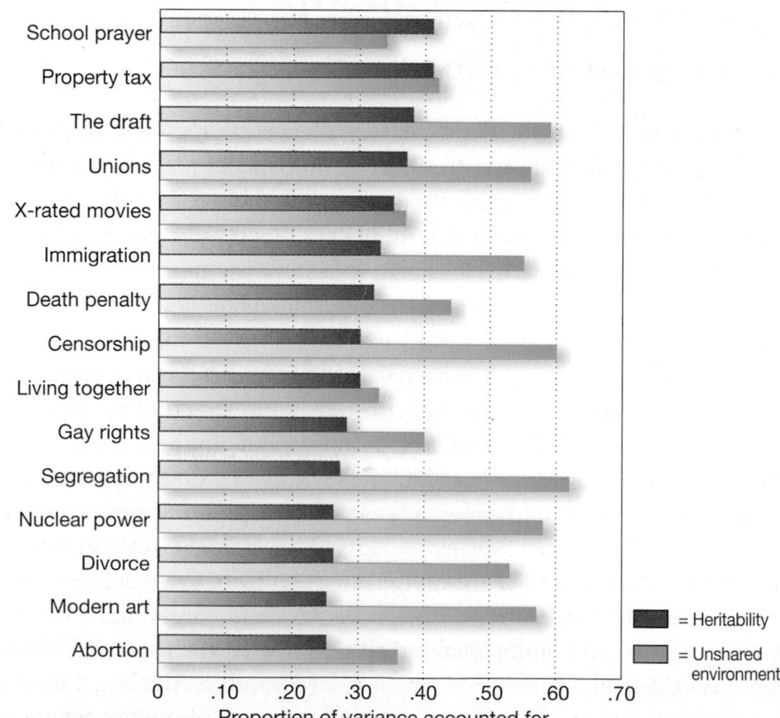

FIGURE 8.2 The Genetics of Belief

Thousands of identical and fraternal twins indicated whether they were for, against, or uncertain about various topics. This bar graph illustrates the approximate genetic contribution to the variation in each attitude. Heritability was greatest for school prayer and property tax, and lowest for divorce and abortion. But in many cases, a person's unique life experiences, the "nonshared environment," were far more influential than genes, especially on attitudes toward topics as unrelated as segregation and modern art (Alford, Funk, & Hibbing, 2005).

even *more* of the variation in political attitudes than heritability was individual life experiences, or what behavioral geneticists call the *nonshared environment* (see Chapter 13). The researchers observed that many people originally join a political party out of family or regional loyalty, yet later find themselves temperamentally opposed to some of that party's positions on emotional issues—in which case, they may change parties. But given the fact that during most of human evolution there were no schools, military drafts, property taxes, or X-rated movies, what genes might have evolved to shape our opinions about them today? What do you think might be the personality dispositions underlying our ideological commitments? And what might be the individual life experiences that shape or change our opinions and passions?

Friendly Persuasion. Core beliefs are obviously going to be resistant to change, especially those that stem from personality traits or from a carefully reasoned philosophy. But many of our everyday attitudes and beliefs are vulnerable to social influence—efforts by others to get us to believe one thing or another, or to persuade us to change our minds.

The more familiar things are, the more we tend to like them. The Oreo name on this cereal takes advantage of the familiarity effect; Oreos have been advertised since 1912.

All around you, every day, advertisers, politicians, and friends are trying to influence your attitudes. One weapon they use is the drip, drip, drip of a repeated idea. Repeated exposure even to a nonsense syllable such as *zug* is enough to make a person feel more positive toward it (Zajonc, 1968). The **familiarity effect**, the tendency to hold positive attitudes toward familiar people or things, is a robust phenomenon. It has been demonstrated across cultures, across species, and across states of awareness, from alert to preoccupied. It works even for stimuli you aren't aware of seeing (Monahan, Murphy, & Zajonc, 2000).

A related phenomenon is the **validity effect**, the tendency of people to believe that something is true simply because it has been repeated many times. Repeat something often enough, even the basest lie, and eventually the public will believe it. Hitler's propaganda minister, Joseph Goebbels, called this technique the "Big Lie."

In a series of experiments, Hal Arkes and his associates demonstrated how the validity effect operates (Arkes, 1993; Arkes, Boehm, & Xu, 1991). In a typical study, people read a list of statements, such as "Mercury has a higher boiling point than copper" or "Over 400 Hollywood films were produced in 1948." They had to rate each statement for its validity, on a scale of 1 (definitely false) to 7 (definitely true). A week or two later, they again rated the validity of some of these statements and also rated others that they had not seen previously. The result: Mere repetition increased the perception that the familiar statements were true. The same effect also occurred for other kinds of statements, including unverifiable opinions (e.g., "At least 75 percent of all politicians are basically dishonest"), opinions that subjects initially felt were true, and even opinions they initially felt were false. "Note that no attempt has been made to persuade," said Arkes (1993). "No supporting arguments are offered. We just have subjects rate the statements. Mere repetition seems to increase rated validity. This is scary."

Another effective technique for influencing people's attitudes is to have arguments presented by someone who is considered admirable, knowledgeable, or beautiful; this is why advertisements are full of sports heroes, experts, and models (Pratkanis & Aronson, 2001). Persuaders may also try to link their message with a nice, warm, fuzzy feeling. In one early study, students who were given peanuts and Pepsi while listening to a speaker's point of view were more likely to be convinced by it than were students who listened to the same words without the pleasant munchies and soft

familiarity effect The tendency of people to feel more positive toward a person, item, product, or other stimulus the more familiar they are with it.

validity effect The tendency of people to believe that a statement is true or valid simply because it has been repeated many times.

Fear tactics to get people to quit doing risky things usually backfire. But perhaps this campaign to persuade men to quit smoking will be the exception!

drinks (Janis, Kaye, & Kirschner, 1965). This finding has been replicated many times, perhaps explaining why so much business is conducted over lunch and so many courtships over dinner!

In sum, here are three good ways to influence attitudes:

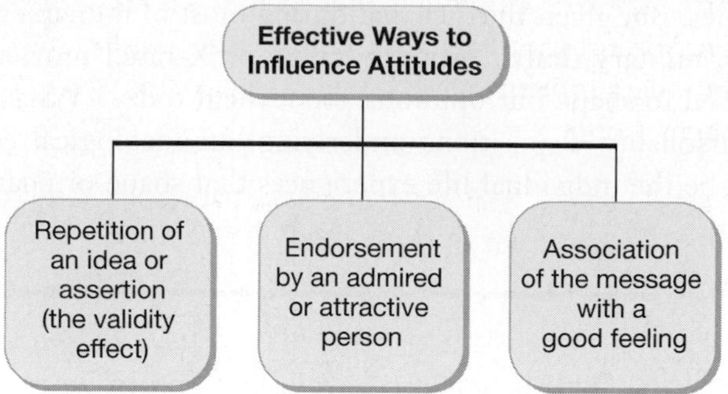

On the other hand, one of the most common ways of trying to get people to change their attitudes and behavior, by scaring them to death, is actually one of the least effective. Fear tactics are often used to try to persuade people to quit smoking, drive only when sober, use condoms, check for signs of cancer, and, nowadays, prepare for terrorist attacks. But the use of fear can backfire. It often scares people so much that they become defensive or feel hopeless and hence ignore the message ("That will never happen to me, and if it does, there isn't anything I can do about it"). Fear tactics tend to be successful only when the message also provides specific information about how to avoid the danger and when people feel able to take advantage of this information (Cialdini, 2001).

Coercive Persuasion. Every time there is news of a suicide bombing, observers are horrified and deeply puzzled. How could someone strap on a bomb and blow up innocent adults and children at random, sacrificing his or her own life in the process? Why would anyone commit suicide simply because a religious leader instructed them to?

In the 1970s, Jim Jones told members of his "People's Temple" that the time had come to die, and 913 people dutifully lined up to drink Kool-Aid mixed with cyanide, after giving it to their infants and children. In the 1990s, David Koresh, leader of the Branch Davidian cult in Waco, Texas, led his followers to a fiery death in a shoot-out with the FBI. A few years later, Marshall Applewhite, leader of the Heaven's Gate cult in San Diego, persuaded his 38 followers that if they committed suicide, they would travel to heaven in a spaceship in the tail of a comet. (When they bought a telescope in order to see the spaceship more clearly, and found no evidence of any such object anywhere near the comet, they returned the telescope to the store. It was, they said, obviously defective.)

Were all of these people mentally ill? Had they all been "brainwashed"? "Brainwashing" implies that a person has had a sudden change of mind without being aware of what is happening; it sounds mysterious and strange. In fact, the methods of persuasion involved are neither mysterious nor unusual, but they are *coercive*—that is, designed to suppress an individual's ability to reason, think critically, and make choices in his or her own best interests. Studies of religious, political, and psychological sects and of terrorist cells have identified some of the key processes of coercive persuasion (Bloom, 2005; Moghaddam, 2005; Ofshe & Watters, 1994; Singer, 2003; Zimbardo & Leippe, 1991):

1 **The person is put under physical or emotional stress.** The individual may not be allowed to eat, sleep, or exercise; may be isolated in a dark room with no stimulation or food; or may be induced into a trancelike state through repetitive chanting or fatigue.

These members of the Aum Shinrikyo ("Supreme Truth") sect in Japan, wearing masks of their leader's face, take the uniformity of cult identity to an extreme. The group's founder instructed his devotees to place nerve gas in a Japanese subway, which killed 10 and sickened thousands of other passengers. One former member said of the sect, "Their strategy is to wear you down and take control of your mind. They promise you heaven, but they make you live in hell."

2 The person's problems are reduced to one simple explanation, which is repeatedly emphasized. There are as many simplistic explanations as there are groups that offer them. Are you afraid or unhappy? It all stems from the pain of being born. Are you struggling financially? It's your fault for not fervently wanting to be rich. Members may also be taught to simplify their problems by blaming a single enemy: Jews, the government, nonbelievers. . . .

3 The leader offers unconditional love, acceptance, and attention. The new recruit may be given a "love bath" from the group—constant praise and affection. Euphoria and well-being are intense because they typically follow exhaustion and fatigue. In exchange, the leader demands everyone's adoration and obedience.

4 A new identity based on the group is created. The recruit is told that he or she is part of the chosen, the elite, or the saved. To foster this new identity, members are required to wear special clothes, eat special diets, or assume a new name.

5 The person is subjected to entrapment. At first, the new member agrees only to do small things, but gradually the demands increase: for example, to spend a weekend with the group, then another weekend, then take weekly seminars, then advanced courses, then to contribute money, and so on. No leader ever says to a new recruit at the outset, "If you follow me, you will eventually give up your marriage, home, children, and perhaps your life"; but by the end, that is just what many do.

6 The person's access to information is severely controlled. As soon as a person is a committed believer or follower, the group limits the person's choices, denigrates critical thinking, makes fun of doubts, and insists that any private distress is due to lack of belief in the group. Total conformity is demanded. The person may be physically isolated from the outside world and thus from antidotes to the leader's ideas. In many groups, members are required to break all ties with their parents, who are the strongest link to the members' former world and thus the greatest threat to the leader's control.

Some people may be more vulnerable than others to coercive influence, but these techniques are powerful enough to overwhelm even mentally healthy and well-educated individuals. For example, research on contemporary suicide bombers in the Middle East—including Mohamed Atta, who led the attack on the World Trade Center—shows that they usually have no psychopathology and are often quite educated and affluent (Silke, 2003). Like other revolutionaries, people who become suicide bombers are idealistic and angry about perceived injustices. But they take extreme measures because, over time, they have become entrapped in closed groups led by charismatic leaders. They are separated from their families, are indoctrinated and trained for 18 months or more, and eventually become emotionally bonded to the group and the leader (Atran, 2003; Bloom, 2005). Future suicide bombers are also given "love baths"; they are celebrated and honored by their families and communities. In Sri Lanka, where a civil war has been waging for years, pictures of young Tamil suicide bombers are framed with garlands and displayed in training camps, so that other children will come to revere them and learn their names— "the way," one social scientist

observed, "young American kids know the names of sports stars. They look up to them, and want to emulate what they have done" (Bloom, 2005).

A key step in increasing resistance to coercive persuasion, therefore, is to dispel people's illusion of invulnerability to these tactics. Another is to teach people how to articulate and defend their own positions and think critically. These skills prepare people to resist propaganda and make them less vulnerable to manipulation by others (Tormala & Petty, 2002).

QUICK quiz

Now, how can we persuade you to take this quiz without using coercion?

1. Candidate Carson spends $3 million to make sure his name is seen and heard frequently and to repeat unverified charges that his opponent is a thief. What psychological processes is he relying on to win?
2. A friend urges you to join a "life-renewal" group called "The Feeling Life." Your friend has been spending increasing amounts of time with her fellow Feelies, and you have some doubts about them. What questions would you want to have answered before joining up?

Answers:

1. The familiarity effect and the validity effect 2. A few things to consider: Is there an autocratic leader who suppresses all dissent and criticism, while rationalizing this practice as a benefit for members? ("Doubt and disbelief are signs that your feeling side is being repressed.") Have long-standing members given up their friends, families, interests, and ambitions for this group? Does the leader offer simple but unrealistic promises to repair your life and all your troubles? Are members required to make sacrifices by donating large amounts of time and money?

WHAT'S**AHEAD** 

- Why do people in groups often go along with the majority even when the majority is dead wrong?
- How can "groupthink" lead to bad, even catastrophic, decisions?
- In an emergency, are you more likely to get help when there are lots of strangers in the area or only a few?
- What enables some people to be nonconformists, take risks to help others, or blow the whistle on wrongdoers?

Individuals in Groups

Even when a group is not at all coercive, something happens to us when we join a bunch of other people. We act differently than we would on our own, regardless of whether the group has convened to solve problems and make decisions, has gathered to have fun, consists of anonymous bystanders or members of an Internet chat room, or is just a loose collection of individuals hanging out in a bar. The decisions we make and the actions we take in groups may depend less on our personal desires than on the structure and dynamics of the group itself.

Conformity

One thing that people in groups do is conform, taking action or adopting attitudes as a result of real or imagined group pressure.

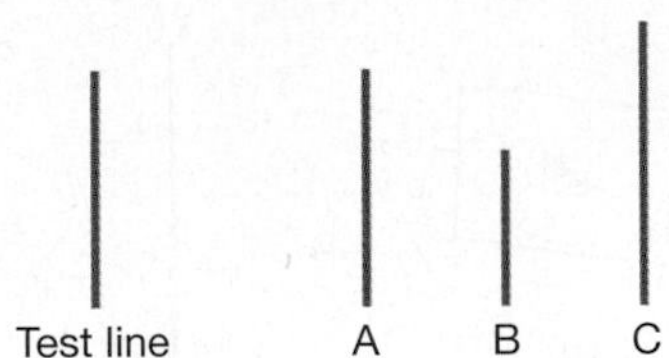

Suppose that you are required to appear at a psychology laboratory for an experiment on perception. You join seven other students seated in a room. You are shown a 10-inch line and asked which of three other lines is identical to it. The correct answer, line A, is obvious, so you are amused when the first person in the group chooses line B. "Bad eyesight," you say to yourself. "He's off by 2 whole inches!" The second person also chooses line B. "What a dope," you think. But by the time the fifth person has chosen line B, you are beginning to doubt yourself. The sixth and seventh students also choose line B, and now you are worried about *your* eyesight. The experimenter looks at you. "Your turn," he says. Do you follow the evidence of your own eyes or the collective judgment of the group?

This was the design for a series of famous studies of conformity conducted by Solomon Asch (1952, 1965). The seven "nearsighted" students were actually Asch's confederates. Asch wanted to know what people would do when a group unanimously contradicted an obvious fact. He found that when people made the line comparisons on their own, they were almost always accurate. But in the group, only 20 percent of the students remained completely independent on every trial, and often they apologized for not agreeing with the others. One-third conformed to the group's incorrect decision more than half the time, and the rest conformed at least some of the time. Whether they conformed or not, the students often felt uncertain of their decision. As one participant later said, "I felt disturbed, puzzled, separated, like an outcast from the rest."

Asch's experiment has been replicated many times and in many countries over the years. In America, conformity has declined since the 1950s, when Asch first did his work, suggesting that conformity reflects social norms, which can change over time (Bond & Smith, 1996). Conformity varies with cultural norms, too. People in cultures that value individual rights and place the "self" above duty to others, as in the United States, are somewhat less conformist than people in cultures that consider social harmony to be more important than individual rights, as in Korea (Kim & Markus, 1999). (In Chapter 13, we discuss this important difference between cultures in detail.)

Regardless of culture, however, everyone conforms under some circumstances and for similar reasons. Some do so because they identify with group members and want to be like them. Some want to be liked. Some believe the group has knowledge that is superior to their own. And some conform out of pure self-interest, to keep their

Sometimes people like to conform in order to feel part of the group . . . and sometimes they like to assert their individuality.

"I don't know how it started, either. All I know is that it's part of our corporate culture."

jobs, get promoted, or win votes. Also, it is not so easy to be a nonconformist, as we will see shortly. Group members are often uncomfortable with dissenters and will try to persuade them to conform. If pleasant persuasion fails, the group may punish, isolate, or reject the nonconformist.

Like obedience, conformity has both positive and negative sides. Society runs more smoothly when people know how to behave in a given situation and when they share the same attitudes and manners. Conformity in dress, preferences, and ideas confers a sense of being in sync with friends and colleagues. But conformity can also suppress critical thinking and creativity. In a group, many people will deny their private beliefs, agree with silly notions, and even repudiate their own values.

Groupthink

Close, friendly groups usually work well together. But they face the problem of getting the best ideas and efforts from their members while avoiding an extreme form of conformity called **groupthink**, the tendency to think alike and suppress dissent. According to Irving Janis (1982, 1989), groupthink occurs when a group's need for total agreement overwhelms its need to make the wisest decision. The symptoms of groupthink include the following:

- ***An illusion of invulnerability***. The group believes it can do no wrong and is 100 percent correct in its decisions.
- ***Self-censorship***. Dissenters decide to keep quiet rather than make trouble, offend their friends, or risk being ridiculed.
- ***Pressure on dissenters to conform***. The leader teases or humiliates dissenters or otherwise pressures them to go along.
- ***An illusion of unanimity***. By discouraging dissent and failing to consider alternative courses of action, leaders and group members create an illusion of consensus; they may even explicitly order suspected dissenters to keep quiet.

Throughout history, groupthink has led to disastrous decisions in military and civilian life. In 1961, President John F. Kennedy and his advisers approved a CIA plan to invade Cuba at the Bay of Pigs and try to overthrow the government of Fidel Castro; the invasion was a humiliating defeat. In the mid-1960s, President Lyndon Johnson and his cabinet escalated the war in Vietnam in spite of obvious signs that further bombing and increased troops were not bringing the war to an end. In 1986, NASA officials insulated themselves from the dissenting objections of engineers who warned them that the space shuttle *Challenger* was unsafe; NASA launched it anyway, and it exploded shortly after takeoff. Tragically, NASA appears not to have learned from this disaster. When an expert panel warned in 2002 that the space shuttles still had many safety problems, NASA removed five of the panel's nine members and two of its consultants. Early in 2003, the *Columbia* exploded upon reentry, killing its entire crew.

groupthink The tendency for all members of a group to think alike for the sake of harmony and to suppress disagreement.

Janis (1982) examined the records of historical military decisions, such as the Bay of Pigs fiasco, and identified key features of groups that are vulnerable to groupthink: Their members feel that they are part of a tightly connected team; they are isolated from other viewpoints; they feel under pressure from outside forces; and they have a

directive leader. Do you notice the similarities between these features and those of coercive groups?

Groupthink can be counteracted by explicitly rewarding the expression of doubt and dissent, protecting and encouraging minority views, generating as many alternative solutions to a problem as group members can think of, and fostering a group identity that encourages members to think of themselves as open-minded problem solvers rather than invulnerable know-it-alls (Turner, Pratkanis, & Samuels, 2003).

"All those in favor say 'Aye.'" "Aye." "Aye." "Aye." "Aye." "Aye."

The nature of the group is often determined by the leader, of course. For many people in positions of power, from presidents to company executives to movie moguls, the temptation is great to surround themselves with others who agree with what they want to do, and to demote or fire those who disagree on the grounds that they are being "disloyal." Sometimes, though, a great leader rises above this temptation. According to historian Doris Kearns Goodwin (2005), Abraham Lincoln understood the importance of surrounding himself with dissenters. Lincoln invited four of his strongest political competitors to join his cabinet and gave them important posts. As a result of the ensuing debates with his critics, Lincoln was able to avoid the illusion that he had group consensus on every decision, consider alternatives, and eventually enlist the respect and support of his team.

The Anonymous Crowd

Suppose you were in trouble on a city street or in another public place—say, being mugged or having a sudden appendicitis attack. Do you think you would be more likely to get help if (a) one other person was passing by, (b) several other people were in the area, or (c) dozens of people were in the area? Most people would choose the third answer, but that is not how human beings operate. On the contrary, the more people there are around you, the *less* likely it is that one of them will come to your aid. Why?

Diffusion of Responsibility. The answer has to do with a group process called the **diffusion of responsibility**, in which responsibility for an outcome is diffused, or spread, among many people, reducing each individual's personal sense of accountability. One result is *bystander apathy*: In crowds, when someone is in trouble, individuals often fail to take action or call for help because they assume that someone else will do so (Darley & Latané, 1968). For example, in a case that became famous many years ago, a woman named Kitty Genovese was repeatedly stabbed to death on the street as dozens of her neighbors listened and watched, without ever calling for help. Similar tragedies still happen all too frequently. People are most likely to come to a stranger's aid if they are the only ones around to help, because responsibility cannot be diffused.

In work groups, the diffusion of responsibility sometimes takes the form of *social loafing*: Each member of a team slows down, letting others work harder (Karau & Williams, 1993; Latané, Williams, & Harkins, 1979). Social loafing increases when individual group members are not accountable for the work they do, when people feel that working harder would only duplicate their colleagues' efforts, when workers feel that others are getting a free ride, or when the work itself is uninteresting (Shepperd, 1995). If people feel that no one else is able and willing to do the job, though, they are more inclined to pitch in and work harder to compensate (Hart, Bridgett, & Karau, 2001).

diffusion of responsibility In groups, the tendency of members to avoid taking action because they assume that others will.

People in crowds, feeling anonymous, may do destructive things they would never do on their own. These soccer hooligans are kicking a fan of the opposition team during a night of violence.

Deindividuation. The most extreme instances of the diffusion of responsibility occur in large, anonymous mobs or crowds. The crowds may consist of cheerful sports spectators or angry rioters. Either way, people often lose awareness of their individuality and seem to hand themselves over to the mood and actions of the crowd, a state called **deindividuation** (Festinger, Pepitone, & Newcomb, 1952). You are more likely to feel deindividuated in a large city, where no one recognizes you, than in a small town, where it is hard to hide. (You are also more likely to feel deindividuated in large classes, where you might—mistakenly!—think you are invisible to the teacher, than in small ones.) Sometimes organizations actively promote the deindividuation of their members in order to enhance conformity and allegiance to the group. This is an important function of uniforms or masks, which eliminate each member's distinctive identity.

Deindividuation has long been considered a prime reason for mob violence. According to this explanation, because deindividuated people in crowds "forget themselves" and do not feel accountable for their actions, they are more likely to violate social norms and laws than they would be on their own: breaking store windows, looting, getting into fights, or rioting at a sports event. But deindividuation does not always make people more combative. Sometimes it makes them more friendly; think of all the chatty, anonymous people on buses and planes who reveal things to their seatmates they would never tell anyone they knew.

deindividuation In groups or crowds, the loss of awareness of one's own individuality.

What really seems to be happening when people are in large crowds or anonymous situations is not that they become mindless or uninhibited. Rather, they become more likely to conform to the norms of the *specific situation* (Postmes & Spears, 1998). College students who go on wild sprees during spring break may be violating the local laws and norms of Palm Springs or Key West not because their aggressiveness has been released but because they are conforming to the "let's party!" norms of their fellow students. Crowd norms can also foster helpfulness, as they often do in the aftermath of disasters, when strangers come out to help victims and rescue workers, leaving food, clothes, and tributes.

Two classic experiments illustrate the power of the situation to influence what deindividuated people will do. In one, women who wore Ku Klux Klan–like disguises that completely covered their faces and bodies (see photo) delivered twice as much apparent electric shock to another woman as did women who not only were undisguised but also wore large name tags (Zimbardo, 1970). In a second experiment, women who wore nurses' uniforms gave *less* shock than did women in regular dress (Johnson & Downing, 1979). Evidently, the KKK disguises were a signal to behave aggressively; the nurses' uniforms were a signal to behave nurturantly.

Wearing a uniform or disguise increases deindividuation and provides a cue for behavior.

Anonymity and Responsibility. Deindividuation has important legal as well as psychological implications. Should individuals in a crowd be held accountable for their harmful "deindividuated" behavior? In South Africa, years ago, six black residents of an impoverished township were accused of murdering an 18-year-old black woman who was having an affair with a hated black police officer. The woman was "necklaced" (a tire was placed around her neck

and set afire) during a community protest against the police. The crowd danced and sang as she burned to ashes.

The six men were convicted of murder, but their sentence was commuted to 20 months of prison when a British social psychologist, Andrew Colman (1991), testified that deindividuation should reduce the moral blameworthiness of their behavior. The young men were swept up in the mindless behavior of the crowd, he argued, and hence were not fully responsible for their actions. Do you agree? An African social scientist, Pumla Gobodo-Madikizela (1994), did not. She interviewed some of the men accused of the necklacing and found they had not been mindless after all. Some were tremendously upset, were well aware of their actions, had debated the woman's guilt, thought about running away, and consciously tried to rationalize their behavior. Moreover, she argued, we must remember that in every crowd, some people do not go along; they remain mindful of their own values.

And so, should the deindividuation excuse, like the "I was only following orders" excuse, exonerate a person of responsibility for looting, rape, or murder? If so, to what degree? What do you think?

THINKING CRITICALLY

EXAMINE THE EVIDENCE

How mindless are "mindless" crowds? Should deindividuation be a legitimate excuse for people who loot, rape, or commit murder because the mob is doing it?

QUICK quiz

On your own, take responsibility for identifying which phenomenon is illustrated in each of the following situations.

1. The president's closest advisers are afraid to disagree with his views on energy policy.
2. You are at a costume party wearing a silly gorilla suit. When you see a chance to play a practical joke on the host, you do it.
3. Walking down a busy street, you see that fire has broken out in a store window. "Someone must already have called the fire department," you say.

Answers:

1. groupthink 2. deindividuation 3. diffusion of responsibility (causing bystander apathy)

Altruism and Dissent

We have seen how roles, norms, and pressures to obey authority and conform to one's group can cause people to behave in ways they might not otherwise. Yet throughout history men and women have disobeyed orders they believed to be wrong and have gone against prevailing cultural beliefs; their actions have changed the course of history. In 1955, in Montgomery, Alabama, a shy, quiet woman named Rosa Parks refused to give up her bus seat to a white passenger, and she was arrested for breaking the law. Her protest sparked a 381-day bus boycott and helped launch the modern civil-rights movement.

When we think of heroes, we tend to think of men like the firefighters who worked so hard to rescue others on 9/11. But heroism comes in many forms.

When people think of heroes, they usually think of men rescuing a child, risking gunfire to bring a fellow soldier to safety, or standing up to a bully. This is the kind of heroism traditionally expected of men, who in general have greater physical strength than women. Indeed, a study of Canadian awards that have been given since 1904 to individuals who risked or lost their lives to save others found that only 9 percent have gone to women. But there are other kinds of heroism that do not require physical strength. During the Holocaust, women in France, Poland, and the Netherlands were as likely as men to risk their lives to save Jews. Women are more likely than men to donate an organ such as a kidney to save another person's life, and women are more

likely to volunteer to serve in dangerous postings around the world in the Peace Corps (Becker & Eagly, 2004).

Dissent and *altruism*, the willingness to take selfless or dangerous action on behalf of others, are in part a matter of personal convictions and conscience. However, just as there are situational reasons for obedience and conformity, so there are external influences on a person's decision to state an unpopular opinion, choose conscience over conformity, or help a stranger in trouble. Here are some of the situational factors involved in deciding to behave courageously:

1 **You perceive the need for intervention or help.** It may seem obvious, but before you can take independent action, you must realize that such action is necessary. Sometimes people willfully blind themselves to wrongdoing to justify their own inaction ("I'm just minding my business"; "I have no idea what they're doing over there at that concentration camp"). But blindness to the need for action also occurs when a situation imposes too many demands on people's attention, as it often does for residents of densely populated cities.

2 **The situation increases the likelihood that you will take responsibility.** When you are in a large crowd of observers or in a large organization, it is easy to avoid action because of the diffusion of responsibility. Conversely, when you are in an environment or situation that rewards independent thinking and dissent, you may behave accordingly.

3 **Cultural norms encourage you to take action.** Some cultures place a higher value on helping strangers than other cultures do. Community-oriented Hindus in India, for example, believe that people are obligated to help anyone who needs it—parent, friend, or stranger—even if the need is minor. In contrast, individualistic Americans do not feel as obligated to help friends and strangers, or even parents who merely have minor needs (Miller, Bersoff, & Harwood, 1990). In studies of strangers' helpfulness to one another across 23 U.S. cities and 22 cities in other countries, cultural norms were more important than population density in predicting levels of helpfulness. Pedestrians in busy Copenhagen and Vienna, for example, were kinder to strangers than were passersby in slow-paced Kuala Lumpur or busy New York City (Levine, 2003).

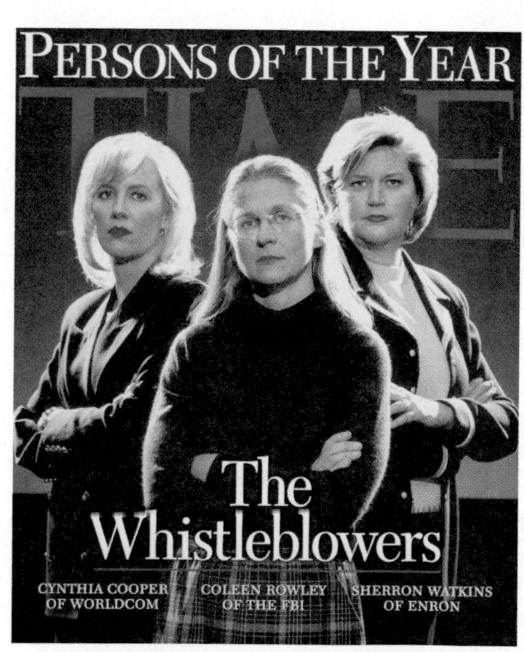

Cynthia Cooper of WorldCom, Coleen Rowley of the FBI, and Sherron Watkins of Enron were *Time*'s persons of the year for their courage in exposing wrongdoing in their organizations.

4 **The cost-benefit ratio supports your decision to get involved.** It is easier to be a whistle-blower or to protest a company policy when you know you can find another job, but what if jobs in your field are scarce and you have a family to support? People are less likely to take an independent action if the personal, physical, or financial costs to them are high. On the other hand, the cost of *not* helping or remaining silent might be guilt, blame from others, loss of honor, or the injury or death of others.

Sadly, the costs of dissent and honesty are often high. Most whistle-blowers, far from being rewarded for their bravery, are punished for it. Three women were named *Time* magazine's Persons of the Year for their courage in exposing wrongdoing in their organizations—Enron, WorldCom, and the FBI—yet all paid a steep professional price for doing so. The two soldiers who first exposed the abuses going on at Abu Ghraib, Samuel J. Provance and James Darby, were shunned by many of their peers and received death threats; one was threatened with a court-martial. Studies of whistle-blowers find that half to two-thirds lose their jobs and have to leave their professions entirely. Many lose their homes and families (Alford, 2001).

5 You have an ally. In Asch's conformity experiment, the presence of one other person who gave the correct answer was enough to overcome agreement with the majority. In Milgram's experiment, the presence of someone who disobeyed the experimenter's instruction to shock the learner sharply increased the number of people who also disobeyed. One dissenting member of a group may be viewed as a troublemaker, but two or three are a coalition. An ally reassures a person of the rightness of the protest, and their combined efforts may eventually persuade the majority (Wood et al., 1994).

6 You become entrapped. Once having taken the initial step of getting involved, most people will increase their commitment. In one study, nearly 9,000 federal employees were asked whether they had observed wrongdoing at work, whether they had told anyone about it, and what happened if they had told. Nearly half of the sample had observed some serious cases of wrongdoing, such as stealing federal funds, accepting bribes, or creating a situation that was dangerous to public safety. Of that half, 72 percent had done nothing at all, but the other 28 percent reported the problem to their immediate supervisors. Once they had taken that step, a majority of the whistle-blowers eventually took the matter to higher authorities (Graham, 1986).

As you can see, certain social and cultural factors make altruism, disobedience, and dissent more likely to occur, just as other factors suppress them.

QUICK quiz

If you weigh the costs and benefits, you'll surely decide to take action and answer this question.

Imagine that you are chief executive officer of a new electric-car company. You want your employees to feel free to offer their suggestions and criticisms to improve productivity and satisfaction. You also want them to inform managers if they find any evidence that the cars are unsafe, even if that means delaying production. What concepts from this chapter could you use in setting company policy?

Answers:

Some possibilities: You could encourage, or even require, dissenting views; avoid deindividuation by rewarding innovative suggestions and implementing the best ones; stimulate employees' commitment to the task (building a car that will solve the world's pollution problem); and establish a written policy to protect whistle-blowers. What else can you think of?

WHAT'S AHEAD

- In what different ways do people balance their ethnic identity and their membership in the larger culture?
- What is an effective antidote to "us–them" thinking?
- How do stereotypes benefit us, and how do they distort reality?

Us Versus Them: Group Identity

Each of us develops a personal identity that is based on our particular traits and unique life history. But we also develop **social identities** based on the groups we belong to, including our national, religious, political, and occupational groups (Brewer & Gardner, 1996; Tajfel & Turner, 1986). Social identities are important because they give us

social identity The part of a person's self-concept that is based on his or her identification with a nation, religious or political group, occupation, or other social affiliation.

"It's not enough that we succeed. Cats must also fail."

a sense of place and position in the world. Without them, most of us would feel like loose marbles rolling around in an unconnected universe. It feels good to be part of an "us." But does that mean that we must automatically feel superior to "them"?

Ethnic Identity

In multicultural societies such as the United States and Canada, different social identities sometimes collide. In particular, people often face the dilemma of balancing an **ethnic identity**, a close identification with a religious or ethnic group, and **acculturation**, identification with the dominant culture (Phinney, 1996; Spencer & Dornbusch, 1990). The hallmarks of having an ethnic identity are that you identify with the group, feel proud to be a member, feel emotionally attached to the group, and behave in ways that conform to the group's rules, values, and norms—for example, in what you wear, what you eat, and what customs you observe (Ashmore, Deaux, & McLaughlin-Volpe, 2004).

There are four ways of balancing ethnic identity and acculturation, depending on whether ethnic identity is strong or weak and whether identification with the larger culture is strong or weak (Berry, 1994; Phinney, 1990). People who are *bicultural* have strong ties both to their ethnicity and to the larger culture: They say, "I am proud of my ethnic heritage, but I identify just as much with my country." They can alternate easily between their culture of origin and the majority culture, slipping into the customs and language of each as circumstances dictate. People who choose *assimilation* have weak feelings of ethnicity but a strong sense of acculturation: Their attitude, for example, might be "I'm an American, period." *Ethnic separatists* have a strong sense of ethnic identity but weak feelings of acculturation: They may say, "My ethnicity comes first; if I join the mainstream, I'm betraying my origins and selling out." And some people feel *marginal*, connected to neither their ethnicity nor the dominant culture: They do not want to identify with any ethnic or national group, or they feel that they don't belong anywhere.

ethnic identity A person's identification with a racial or ethnic group.

acculturation The process by which members of minority groups come to identify with and feel part of the mainstream culture.

GET INVOLVED!

➤HOW ACCULTURATED ARE YOU?

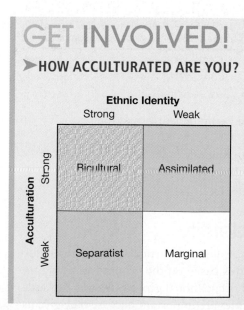

Acculturation \ Ethnic Identity	Strong	Weak
Strong	Bicultural	Assimilated
Weak	Separatist	Marginal

Take a look at the illustration here, with its categories of bicultural, assimilated, separatist, or marginal. Can you locate yourself in one of those categories or don't you fit? Are you bicultural about some things and separatist about others? Ask five friends, relatives, or acquaintances, ideally from different ethnic groups, where they would place themselves, and why. If you feel that you do not have an ethnic heritage other than a national identity, why is that? Would your parents and grandparents feel the same as you do?

Monica Almeida/The New York Times

Ethnic identities are changing these days, as bicultural (and increasingly multiethnic) North Americans blend aspects of mainstream culture with their own traditions. But many people like to celebrate the traditions of their ethnic heritage, as illustrated in these photos of Japanese-American college students reviving *taiko*, traditional Japanese drumming, Ukrainian-American teens wearing national dress, and African-American children lighting Kwaanza candles.

A person's degree of acculturation may change throughout life in response to experiences and societal events. For example, many immigrants arrive in North America with every intention of becoming "true" Canadians or Americans. If they encounter discrimination or setbacks, however, they may decide that acculturation is harder than they anticipated or that ethnic separatism offers greater solace. In any case, acculturation is rarely a complete accommodation to mainstream culture. Many individuals pick and choose among the values, food, traditions, and customs of the mainstream culture, while also keeping aspects of their heritage that are important to their self-identity (Chun, Organista, & Marin, 2002).

On the other hand, it is a sign of our multiethnic times that many people are now refusing to be pigeonholed into any single ethnic category. In the 2000 U.S. census, nearly 7 million people listed themselves as having various combinations of identities. New "combo" ethnic identities are emerging out of the familiar ones such as Latino or Native American: Blaxican (African-American and Mexican), Negripino (African-American and Filipino), Hafu (half Japanese, half something else), Chino-Latino (Chinese and Hispanic). Some observers think that young people are becoming less likely to define themselves by their ethnic identity than by their youth identity—a hip-hopper, a *roquero* (rocker), a pop-culture fan, and so forth. Do you agree? In your world, are traditional ethnic identities breaking down, or are they as strong as ever?

Ethnocentrism

For most people, having a national, religious, or cultural identity is still important. Unfortunately, it often leads to **ethnocentrism**, the belief that your own culture, nation, or religion is superior to all others. Ethnocentrism is universal, probably

ethnocentrism The belief that one's own ethnic group, nation, or religion is superior to all others.

It's Hard To Be Humble
When You Are Swedish

As bumper stickers and lapel pins show, everyone, but everyone, is ethnocentric!

because it aids survival by increasing people's attachment to their own group and their willingness to work on its behalf. Ethnocentrism is even embedded in some languages: The Chinese word for China means "the center of the world" and the Navajo, the Kiowa, and the Inuit call themselves simply "The People."

Ethnocentrism rests on a fundamental social identity: us. As soon as people have created a category called "us," however, they invariably perceive everybody else as "not-us." This in-group solidarity can be manufactured in a minute in the laboratory, as Henri Tajfel and his colleagues (1971) demonstrated in an experiment with British schoolboys. Tajfel showed the boys slides with varying numbers of dots on them and asked the boys to guess how many dots there were. The boys were arbitrarily told that they were "overestimators" or "underestimators" and were then asked to work on another task. In this phase, they had a chance to give points to other boys identified as overestimators or underestimators. Although each boy worked alone in his cubicle, almost every single one assigned far more points to boys he thought were like him, an overestimator or an underestimator. As the boys emerged from their rooms, they were asked, "Which were you?" The answers received a mix of cheers and boos from the others.

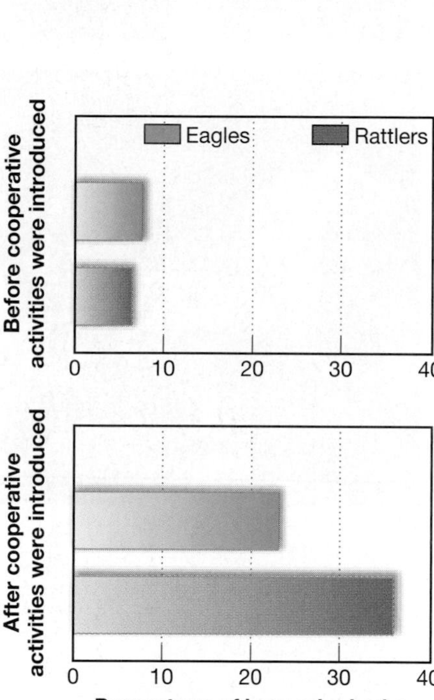

FIGURE 8.3 The Experiment at Robbers Cave

In this study, competitive games fostered hostility between the Rattlers and the Eagles. Few boys had a best friend from the other group (upper graph). But after the teams had to cooperate to solve various problems, the percentage who made friends across "enemy lines" shot up (lower graph) (Sherif et al., 1961).

Us–them social identities are strengthened when two groups compete with each other. Years ago, Muzafer Sherif and his colleagues used a natural setting, a Boy Scout camp called Robbers Cave, to demonstrate the effects of competition on hostility and conflict between groups (Sherif, 1958; Sherif et al., 1961). Sherif randomly assigned 11- and 12-year-old boys to two groups, the Eagles and the Rattlers. To build a sense of in-group identity and team spirit, he had each group work together on projects such as making a rope bridge and building a diving board. Sherif then put the Eagles and Rattlers in competition for prizes. During fierce games of football, baseball, and tug-of-war, the boys whipped up a competitive fever that soon spilled off the playing fields. They began to raid each other's cabins, call each other names, and start fist-fights. No one dared to have a friend from the rival group. Before long, the Rattlers and the Eagles were as hostile toward each other as any two gangs fighting for turf or any two nations fighting for dominance. Their hostility continued even when they were just sitting around together watching movies.

Then Sherif decided to try to undo the hostility he had created and make peace between the Eagles and Rattlers. He and his associates set up a series of predicaments in which both groups needed to work together to reach a desired goal—for example, pooling their resources to get a movie they all wanted to see or pulling a staff truck up a hill on a camping trip. This policy of *interdependence in reaching mutual goals* was highly successful in reducing the boys' "ethnocentrism," competitiveness, and hostility; the boys eventually made friends with their former enemies (see Figure 8.3). Interdependence has a similar effect in adult groups (Gaertner et al., 1990). The reason, it seems, is that cooperation causes people to think of themselves as members of one big group instead of two opposed groups, "us" and "them."

Stereotypes

stereotype A summary impression of a group, in which a person believes that all members of the group share a common trait or traits (positive, negative, or neutral).

You can probably think of a million ways that your friends and family members differ: Jeff is stodgy, Ruth is bossy, Farah is outgoing. But if you have never met a person from Turkey or Tibet, you are likely to stereotype Turks and Tibetans. A **stereotype** is a summary impression of a group of people in which all members of the group are viewed as sharing a common trait or traits. Stereotypes may be negative, positive, or neutral. There are stereotypes of people who drive Hummers or Hondas, of men who wear ear-

rings and women who wear business suits, of engineering students and art students, of feminists and fraternity men.

Stereotypes aren't necessarily bad. They are, as some psychologists have called them, useful tools in the mental toolbox—energy-saving devices that allow us to make efficient decisions (Macrae & Bodenhausen, 2000). They help us quickly process new information and retrieve memories. They allow us to organize experience, make sense of differences among individuals and groups, and predict how people will behave. In fact, the brain automatically registers and encodes the basic categories of gender, ethnicity, and age, suggesting that there is a neurological basis for the cognitive efficiency of stereotyping (Ito & Urland, 2003).

However, although stereotypes reflect real differences among people, they also distort that reality in three ways (Judd et al., 1995). First, *they exaggerate differences between groups*, making the stereotyped group seem odd, unfamiliar, or dangerous, not like "us." Second, *they produce selective perception*; people tend to see only the evidence that fits the stereotype and reject any perceptions that do not fit. Third, *they underestimate differences within other groups*. Stereotypes create the impression that all members of other groups are the same.

Cultural values affect how people evaluate the actions of another group. Chinese students in Hong Kong, where communalism and respect for elders are valued, think that a student who comes late to class or argues with a parent about grades is being selfish and disrespectful of adults. But Australian students, who value individualism, think that the same behavior is perfectly appropriate (Forgas & Bond, 1985). You can see how the Chinese might form negative stereotypes of "disrespectful" Australians, and how the Australians might form negative stereotypes of the "spineless" Chinese. And it is a small step from negative stereotypes to prejudice.

THINKING CRITICALLY

ANALYZE ASSUMPTIONS AND BIASES

Which woman is the chemical engineer and which is the assistant? The Western stereotype holds that (a) women are not engineers in the first place, but (b) if they are, they are Western. Actually, the engineer at this refinery is the Kuwaiti woman on the left.

QUICK quiz

Do you have a positive or a negative stereotype of quizzes?

1. Frank, an African-American college student, finds himself caught between two philosophies on his campus. One holds that blacks should move toward full integration into mainstream culture. The other holds that blacks should immerse themselves in the history, values, and contributions of African culture. The first group values __________ whereas the second emphasizes __________.
2. John knows and likes the Chicano minority in his town, but he privately believes that Anglo culture is superior to all others. His belief is evidence of his __________.
3. What strategy does the Robbers Cave study suggest for reducing "us–them" thinking and hostility between groups?

Answers:

1. acculturation, ethnic idenity 2. ethnocentrism 3. interdependence in reaching mutual goals

WHAT'S AHEAD

- Is prejudice more likely to be a cause of war or a result of it?
- If you believe that women are naturally better than men, are you sexist?
- Can you be unconsciously prejudiced even though you think you aren't?
- Why isn't mere contact between cultural groups enough to reduce prejudice between them? What does work?

Group Conflict and Prejudice

A **prejudice** consists of a negative stereotype and a strong, unreasonable dislike or hatred of a group. A central feature of a prejudice is that it remains immune to evidence. In his classic book *The Nature of Prejudice*, Gordon Allport (1954/1979) described the responses characteristic of a prejudiced person when confronted with evidence contradicting his or her beliefs:

Mr. X: The trouble with Jews is that they only take care of their own group.

Mr. Y: But the record of the Community Chest campaign shows that they give more generously, in proportion to their numbers, to the general charities of the community, than do non-Jews.

Mr. X: That shows they are always trying to buy favor and intrude into Christian affairs. They think of nothing but money; that is why there are so many Jewish bankers.

Mr. Y: But a recent study shows that the percentage of Jews in the banking business is negligible, far smaller than the percentage of non-Jews.

Mr. X: That's just it; they don't go in for respectable business; they are only in the movie business or run night clubs.

Notice that Mr. X doesn't even try to respond to Mr. Y's evidence; he just moves along to another reason for his dislike of Jews. That is the slippery nature of prejudice.

The Origins of Prejudice

When social psychologists began to study prejudice in earnest after World War II, they regarded it as a form of mental illness: Only mentally unhealthy people, they thought, could be prejudiced. (They were thinking of Hitler.) Since then, they have learned that, on the contrary, prejudice is a universal human experience that affects just about every human being (Dovidio, 2001). Prejudice is universal because it has so many sources and functions: psychological, social, cultural, and economic.

1 Psychological functions. Prejudice often serves to ward off feelings of doubt, fear, and insecurity. As research from many nations has confirmed, it is a tonic for low self-esteem: People puff up their own feelings of low self-worth by disliking or hating groups they see as inferior (Islam & Hewstone, 1993; Stephan et al., 1994). Prejudice also allows people to use the target group as a scapegoat ("Those people are the source of all my troubles"). Scapegoating allows people to displace feelings of anger and cope with feelings of powerlessness. Immediately after 9/11, some white Americans took

prejudice A strong, unreasonable dislike or hatred of a group, based on a negative stereotype.

AVOID EMOTIONAL REASONING

In times of war, most people fall victim to emotional reasoning about the enemy. They start thinking of "them" as aggressors who are less than human—often as "vermin," dogs, or pigs. After 9/11, anti-American demonstrators in Jakarta portrayed George Bush as a rabid dog, and an American cartoonist lumped all Arab Muslims and nations into a "barrel of vermin."

out their anger on fellow Americans who happened to be Arab, Sikh, Pakistani, Hindu, or Afghan. Two men in Chicago beat up an Arab-American taxi driver, yelling, "This is what you get, you mass murderer!"

2 Social and cultural functions. Not all prejudices have deep-seated psychological roots. Some are acquired through social pressure to conform to the views of friends, relatives, or associates. Some are passed along mindlessly from one generation to another, as when parents communicate to their children, "We don't associate with people like that." And some unconscious (implicit) prejudices are acquired from advertising, TV shows, and news reports that contain derogatory images and negative stereotypes of certain groups.

Prejudice also serves cultural purposes, bonding people to their own ethnic or national group and its ways; this may be a major evolutionary reason for its universality and persistence (Fishbein, 1996). In this respect, prejudice is the flip side of ethnocentrism; it is not only that *we* are good and kind, but also that *they* are bad or evil. By disliking "them," we feel closer to others who are like "us."

3 Economic functions. Prejudice makes official forms of discrimination seem legitimate, by justifying the majority group's dominance, status, or greater wealth (Sidanius, Pratto, & Bobo, 1996). Historically, for example, white men in positions of power have justified their exclusion of women and minorities from the workplace and politics by claiming those groups were inferior, irrational, or incompetent (Gould, 1996). But any majority group—of any ethnicity, gender, or nationality—that discriminates against a minority will call upon prejudice to legitimize its actions (Islam & Hewstone, 1993).

Although it is widely believed that prejudice is a primary cause of conflict between groups, prejudice is actually more often a *result* of conflict. When any two groups are in direct competition for jobs, or when people are worried about their incomes and the stability of their communities, prejudice between them increases (Doty, Peterson, & Winter, 1991). Consider the rise and fall of attitudes toward Chinese immigrants in the United States in the nineteenth century, as reported in newspapers of the time (Aronson, 2004). When the Chinese were working in the gold mines and potentially taking jobs from white laborers, the white-run newspapers described them as depraved, vicious, and bloodthirsty. Just a decade later, when the Chinese began working on the transcontinental railroad—doing difficult and dangerous jobs that few white men wanted—prejudice against them declined. Whites described them as hardworking, industrious, and law-abiding. Then, after the railroad was finished and the Chinese had to compete with Civil War veterans for scarce jobs, white attitudes changed again. Whites now thought the Chinese were "criminal," "crafty," "conniving," and "stupid." (The newspapers did not report the attitudes of the Chinese.)

The Many Targets of Prejudice

Prejudice has a long and universal history. Why do new prejudices keep emerging, others fade away, and some old ones persist?

Some prejudices rise and fall with events. When France refused to support America's decision to go to war with Iraq in 2003, anti-French anger erupted, as the scrawled sign (below center) indicates. Anti-Japanese feelings in the United States ran high in the 1920s (below left) and again in the 1990s, but this prejudice has faded. In contrast, some hatreds, notably homophobia and anti-Semitism, reflect people's deeper anxieties and are therefore more persistent.

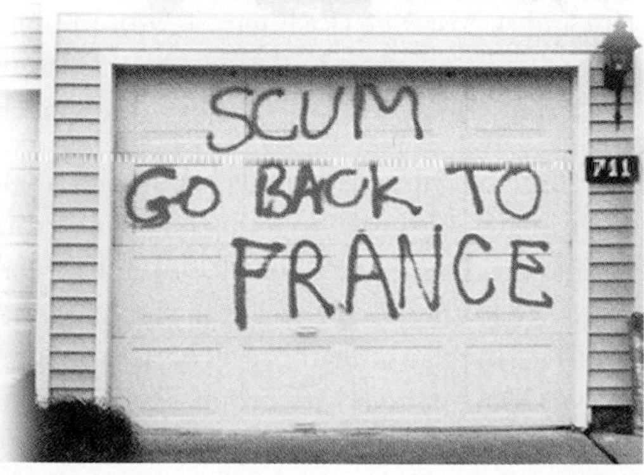

GET INVOLVED!

➤PROBING YOUR PREJUDICES

Are you prejudiced? No? Is there any group of people you tend to regard in a negative light because of their gender, ethnicity, sexual orientation, nationality, religion, physical appearance, or political views? Write down your deepest thoughts and feelings about this group. Take as long as you want, and do not censor yourself or say what you think you ought to say. Now reread what you have written. Which of the sources of prejudice discussed in the text might be contributing to your views? Do you feel that your attitudes toward the group are legitimate, or are you uncomfortable about having them?

The ultimate competition between groups, of course, is war. When two nations are at war, prejudice against the enemy allows each side to continue feeling righteous about its cause. Drawing on the principles of persuasion and influence described earlier (such as the validity effect), along with propaganda images that demonize and dehumanize the enemy, each side tries to convince its citizens that the enemy is less than human and thus deserves to be killed (Keen, 1986). Fomenting prejudice against the perceived enemy—calling them vermin, rats, mad dogs, heathens, baby killers, or monsters—legitimizes the attackers' motives for war. (Review 8.1 summarizes the sources of prejudice.)

Prejudices toward Native Americans, women, and African-Americans have long been part of American history. Women have been excluded from men's clubs, and segregation of blacks was legal in America until the 1950s. Other prejudices emerge with changing historical events. In the aftermath of 9/11, hostility mounted toward Middle Easterners and Muslims.

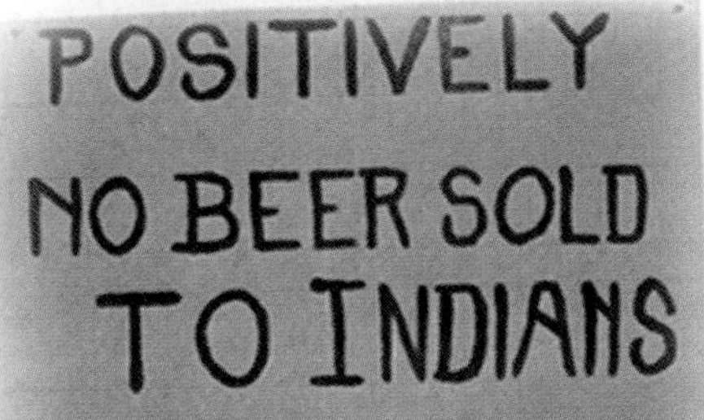

REVIEW 8.1
Sources of Prejudice

Psychological	Social	Economic	Cultural
Low self-esteem Anxiety Insecurity	Groupthink Conformity Parental messages Societal messages (ads, etc.)	Majority's desire to preserve its status Competition for jobs, power, resources	Ethnocentrism Desire for group identity The justification of war
Examples of resulting prejudice			
"Those people are not as moral and decent as we are."	"My parents taught me that those people are just no good."	"Those people aren't smart enough to do this work."	"We have to protect our religion/country/government from those people."

THINKING CRITICALLY

DEFINE YOUR TERMS

What does it mean to be "prejudiced"? Is prejudice blatant hostility, vague discomfort with another group, a patronizing attitude of superiority, or unconscious feelings of dislike? Does ignorance about an unfamiliar culture count as prejudice?

Defining and Measuring Prejudice

Prejudice is like a weasel—hard to grasp and hold on to. One problem is that not all prejudiced people are prejudiced in the same way or to the same extent. Suppose that Raymond wishes to be tolerant and open-minded, but he grew up in a small homogeneous community and feels uncomfortable with members of other cultural and religious groups. Should we put Raymond in the same category as Rupert, an outspoken bigot who actively discriminates against others? Do good intentions count? What if Raymond knows nothing about Muslims and mindlessly blurts out a remark that reveals his ignorance? Is that prejudice or thoughtlessness? These questions complicate the measurement of prejudice.

Similar complexities occur in defining "sexism." In research with 15,000 men and women in 19 nations, psychologists found that *hostile sexism*, which reflects active dislike of women, is different from *benevolent sexism*, in which superficially positive attitudes put women on a pedestal but nonetheless reinforce women's subordination. The latter type of sexism is affectionate but patronizing, conveying the attitude that women are so wonderful, good, kind, and moral that they should stay at home, away from the rough-and-tumble (and power and income) of public life (Glick et al., 2000). In all 19 countries studied, men had significantly higher hostile sexism scores than women did, but in about half the countries, women endorsed benevolent sexism as much as men did.

Because benevolent sexism lacks a tone of hostility to women, it doesn't seem like a prejudice to many people, and many women find it alluring to think they are better than men. But both forms of sexism—whether you think women are too good for equality or not good enough—legitimize gender discrimination and, in some cultures, wife abuse. Studies in Turkey and Brazil found that men who abuse their wives score high not only on hostile sexism but also on benevolent sexism—

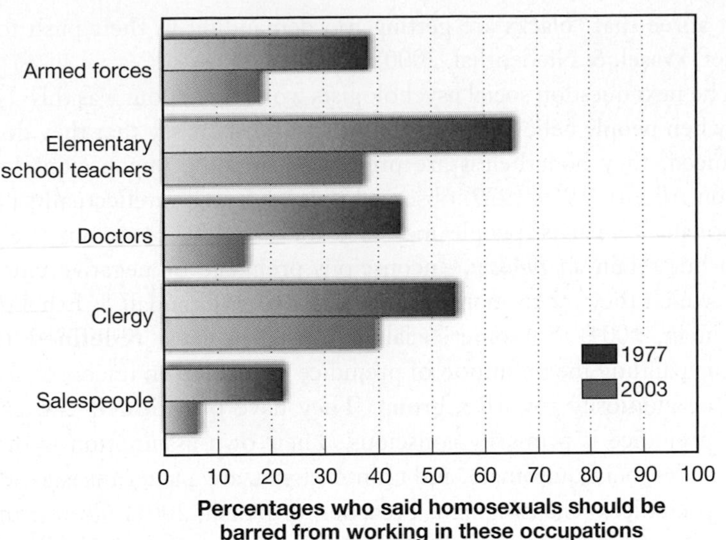

FIGURE 8.4 Changing Attitudes Toward Gays

American attitudes toward the employment of gay men and lesbians have changed dramatically over the years. In 1977, large numbers of straight people thought that gays should not be permitted to serve in the military or work as teachers, doctors, and clergy. By 2003, the percentages were much lower (American Enterprise Institute, 2004).

because if the wife dares to step down from her pedestal, she deserves to be beaten (Glick et al., 2002).

Perhaps you are thinking: "Hey, what about men? There are plenty of prejudices against men, too—that they are sexual predators, emotionally heartless, domineering and arrogant." In fact, when the same group of researchers completed a 16-nation study of attitudes toward men, they found that many people do believe that men are aggressive and predatory, and overall just not as warm and wonderful as women (Glick et al., 2004). This attitude seems hostile to men, the researchers found, but it also reflects and supports gender inequality by characterizing men as being designed for leadership and dominance.

The good news is that on surveys in the United States and Canada, prejudice of all kinds has been dropping sharply. The numbers of people who admit to believing that blacks are inferior to whites, women inferior to men, and gays inferior to straights have plummeted in the last 20 years (Dovidio, 2001; Plant & Devine, 1998). (See Figure 8.4.)

CLOSE-UP on Research

PINNING DOWN UNCONSCIOUS PREJUDICES

Some social psychologists, while welcoming the evidence that prejudices have declined, have **asked questions** about how to interpret these surveys. First, do the changing numbers simply reflect a growing awareness that it isn't cool to admit prejudice rather than a real decline in prejudiced feelings? **There is considerable evidence** for that view: In studies of job-hiring practices, most whites do not discriminate against black candidates who have strong qualifications, but they are far more likely to choose *average* white candidates over *average* black ones (Dovidio & Gaertner, 2000). This finding suggests that although old-fashioned discrimination ("We would never hire a black person") may be gone, it lives on in a subtler form ("We would hire Colin Powell and Tiger Woods in a heartbeat, but they are the exceptions . . ."). Moreover, the same whites who will not admit to disliking African-Americans

might agree that "blacks are getting too demanding in their push for equal rights" (Brauer, Wasel, & Niedenthal, 2000).

The next question social psychologists wondered about was this: Is it possible that even when people believe they are not prejudiced, or say that they do not want to be prejudiced, they nonetheless are prejudiced at some unconscious level? Years ago, Gordon Allport (1954/1979) observed that "defeated intellectually, prejudice lingers emotionally." That is, people may lose their *explicit*, conscious prejudice toward a group but retain an *implicit*, unconscious prejudice or negative emotional feelings, which they try to suppress in everyday life (Crandall & Eshelman, 2003; Rudman, 2004). So some social psychologists have **redefined their terms** by expanding the definition of prejudice to include an unconscious level of dislike or animosity toward a group. They have **questioned the assumption** that prejudice is primarily conscious. Their own assumption is that implicit attitudes, being automatic and unintentional, are a truer measure of a person's real prejudices (Cunningham, Preacher, & Banaji, 2001). To test their assumption empirically, they have developed several ways of measuring implicit prejudices.

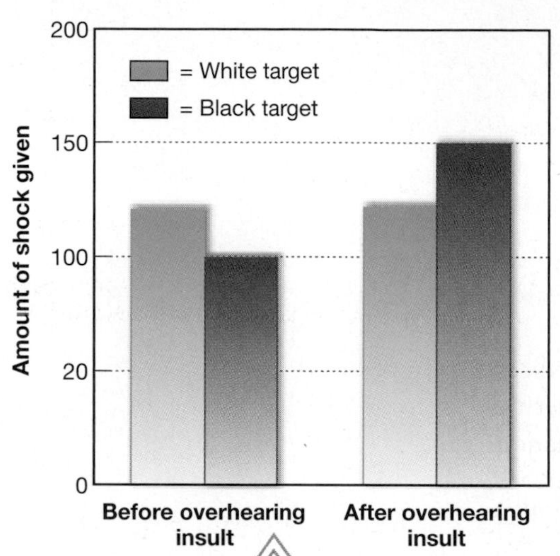

The first method is to pay attention to what people do, not what they say, when they are with a possible object of prejudice, especially when they are angered or stressed (Jones, 1991; Sinclair & Kunda, 1999). In one of the first experiments to do this, white students were asked to administer shock to black or white confederates of the experimenter in what the students believed was a study of biofeedback. In the experimental condition, participants overheard the biofeedback "victim" (who actually received no shock) saying derogatory things about them. In the control condition, participants overheard no such nasty remarks. Then all the participants had another opportunity to shock the victims, and their degree of "aggression" was defined as the amount of shock they administered. As you can see in the accompanying figure, white students actually showed *less* aggression toward blacks than toward whites. But as soon as the white students were angered by overhearing derogatory remarks about themselves, they showed *more* aggression toward blacks than toward whites (Rogers & Prentice-Dunn, 1981).

This research has been replicated many times. The same pattern appears in studies of how English-speaking Canadians behave toward French-speaking Canadians (Meindl & Lerner, 1985), straights toward homosexuals, non-Jewish students toward Jews (Fein & Spencer, 1997), and men toward women (Maass et al., 2003). So it seems that many people are willing to control their negative feelings under normal conditions, but as soon as they are angry or frustrated, or get a jolt to their self-esteem, their unconscious prejudice reveals itself.

A second method relies on fMRI and PET scans to determine which parts of the brain are involved in forming stereotypes, holding prejudiced beliefs, and feeling disgust, anger, and other negative feelings about a group (Amodio, Harmon-Jones, & Devine, 2003; Cacioppo et al., 2003; Harris & Fiske, 2006). In one study, when African-Americans and whites saw pictures of each other, activity in the amygdala (the brain structure associated with fear and other negative emotions) was elevated. But it was not elevated when people saw pictures of members of their own group (Hart et al., 2000).

The researchers **did not oversimplify**, for example by concluding that prejudice is hardwired and thus inevitable. Instead, they **asked the next crucial question**: Under what conditions does this brain activation occur in response to pictures of people from other ethnicities? To find out, Mary Wheeler and Susan Fiske (2005)

recorded brain activity in the amygdalas of white participants as they looked at photographs of white and black faces. Areas of brain activation depended on what the subjects had been asked to do with the photos. When participants were registering the faces as individuals or as part of a simple visual test rather than as members of the category "blacks," there was no increased activation in the amygdala. The brain may be designed to register differences, it appears, but any negative associations with those differences depend on context and learning.

A third, more controversial method is the *Implicit Association Test (IAT)*, which measures the speed of people's positive and negative associations to a target group (Greenwald, McGhee, & Schwartz, 1998). Its proponents have argued that if, for example, white students take longer to respond to black faces associated with positive words (e.g., *triumph, honest*) than to black faces associated with negative words (e.g., *devil, failure*), it must mean that white students have an unconscious prejudice toward blacks. The test has also been used to identify alleged prejudices toward Asians, women, old people, and other groups (Cunningham, Preacher, & Banaji, 2001; Dovidio, 2001).

We say "alleged" prejudices because other social psychologists have **considered other interpretations** of findings based on the IAT, maintaining that whatever the test measures, it is not a stable prejudice. Two researchers got an IAT effect by matching target faces with nonsense words and neutral words that had no evaluative connotations at all. They concluded that the IAT does not measure emotional evaluations of the target but rather the *salience* of the word associated with it—how much it stands out. (Negative words attract more attention in general.) When the researchers corrected for these factors, the presumed unconscious prejudice faded away (Rothermund & Wentura, 2004).

Moreover, as we saw earlier, people find familiar names, products, and even nonsense syllables to be more pleasant than unfamiliar ones. Indeed, some investigators argue that the IAT may simply be measuring, say, white subjects' unfamiliarity with African-Americans and the greater salience of white faces to them, rather than a true prejudice (Kinoshita & Peek-O'Leary, 2005).

As you can see, defining and measuring prejudice are not easy tasks. The research clearly cautions us **not to oversimplify**. To understand prejudice, we must distinguish explicit attitudes from unconscious ones, active hostility from simple discomfort, what people say from what they feel, and what people feel from how they actually behave.

BLACK FACES | WHITE FACES

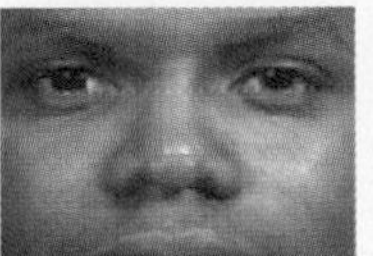
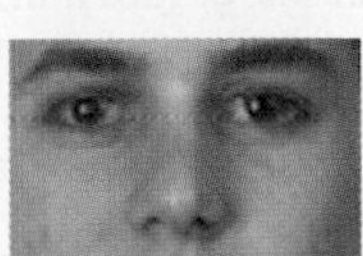
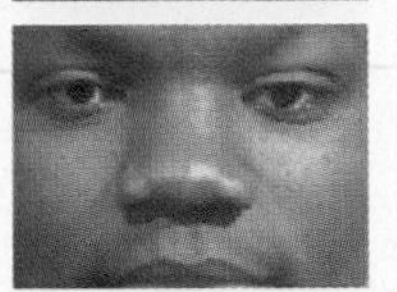

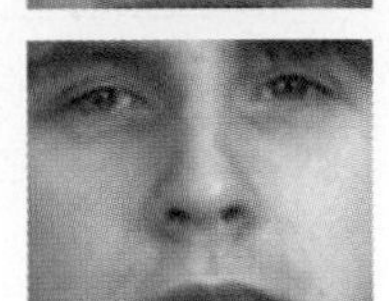

GOOD WORDS
love joy triumph
terrific peace
champion honest

BAD WORDS
maggot poison
hatred agony devil
failure detest filth

Typical stimuli used in the IAT.

Reducing Conflict and Prejudice

The findings that emerge from the study of prejudice show us that efforts to reduce prejudice by appealing to moral or intellectual arguments are not enough. They must also touch people's deeper insecurities, fears, or negative associations with a group. One study of white students who took a diversity course found that the students' explicit prejudices toward African-Americans declined by the end of the term, a result of their greater understanding of racial issues and their wish to overcome their own biases. But their implicit prejudices were reduced only when they lost their negative emotional associations with African-Americans, by making black friends in the course and developing respect and affection for the black professor who taught it (Rudman, 2004).

When classrooms are structured so that students of different ethnic groups must cooperate in order to do well on a lesson, prejudice decreases.

Just as social psychologists investigate the situations that increase prejudice and animosity toward other groups, they have also examined the situations that might reduce them. Of course, given the many sources and functions of prejudice, no one method will work in all circumstances or for all prejudices. But social psychologists have identified four of the conditions that must be met before prejudice and conflict between groups can be lessened (Dovidio, Gaertner, & Validzic, 1998; Pettigrew, 1998; Slavin & Cooper, 1999; Staub, 1999; Stephan, 1999):

1 **Both sides must have equal legal status, economic opportunities, and power.** This requirement is the spur behind efforts to change laws that permit discrimination. Integration of public facilities in the American South would never have occurred if civil rights advocates had waited for segregationists to have a change of heart. Women would never have gotten the right to vote, attend college, or do "men's work" without persistent challenges to the laws that permitted gender discrimination. But changing the law is not enough if two groups remain in competition for jobs or if one group retains power and dominance over the other.

2 **Authorities and community institutions must provide moral, legal, and economic support for both sides.** Society must establish norms of equality and support them in the actions of its officials—teachers, employers, the judicial system, government officials, and the police. Where segregation is official government policy or an unofficial but established practice, conflict and prejudice not only will continue but also will seem normal and justified.

3 **Both sides must have opportunities to work and socialize together, formally and informally.** According to the *contact hypothesis*, prejudice declines when people have the chance to get used to one another's rules, food, music, customs, and attitudes, thereby discovering their shared interests and shared humanity. Stereotypes are shattered once people realize that "those people" aren't, in fact, "all alike." The contact hypothesis has been supported by many studies in the laboratory and in the real world: studies of newly integrated housing projects in the American South during the 1950s and 1960s; relationships between German and immigrant Turkish children in German schools; young people's attitudes toward the elderly; healthy people's attitudes toward the mentally ill; nondisabled children's attitudes toward the disabled; and straight people's prejudices toward gay men and lesbians (Fishbein, 1996; Herek & Capitanio, 1996; Tropp & Pettigrew, 2005; Wilner, Walkley, & Cook, 1955).

Tensions between groups often subside when people work together on a common goal. Here volunteers from Habitat for Humanity build a new home for low-income people in Los Angeles.

4 Both sides must cooperate, working together for a common goal. Clearly, contact between two groups is not enough; at many multiethnic high schools, ethnic groups form cliques and gangs, fighting one another and defending their own ways. To reduce the intergroup tension and competition that exist in many schools, Elliot Aronson and his colleagues have developed the "jigsaw" method of building cooperation. Students from different ethnic groups work together on a task that is broken up like a jigsaw puzzle; each person needs to cooperate with the others to put the assignment together. Students in such classes, from elementary school through college, tend to do better, like their classmates better, and become less stereotyped and prejudiced in their thinking than students in traditional classrooms (Aronson, 2000; Aronson & Patnoe, 1997; Slavin & Cooper, 1999). As we saw, cooperation often reduces us–them thinking and prejudice by creating an encompassing social identity—the Eagles and Rattlers solution.

Each of these four approaches to creating greater harmony between groups is important, but none is sufficient on its own. Perhaps one reason that group conflicts and prejudice are so persistent is that all four conditions for reducing them are rarely met at the same time.

QUICK quiz

Try to overcome your prejudice against quizzes by taking this one.

1. What are three ways of measuring implicit or unconscious prejudice?
2. What are four important conditions required for reducing prejudice and conflict between groups?
3. Surveys find that large percentages of African-Americans, Asian-Americans, and Latinos hold negative stereotypes of one another and resent other minorities almost as much as they resent whites. What are some reasons that people who have themselves been victims of stereotyping and prejudice would hold the same attitudes toward others?

Answers:

1. Studying how aggressively people behave toward a target person when they are angry or stressed, observing physiological changes in the brain, and measuring unconscious negative associations with a target group. 2. Both sides must have equal status and power; have the moral, legal, and economic support of authorities; have opportunities to socialize formally and informally; and cooperate for a common goal. 3. ethnocentrism; low self-esteem; conformity with relatives and friends who share these prejudices; parental lessons and messages conveyed by the media; and economic competition for jobs and resources.

WHAT'S**AHEAD**

- Are "age-old tribal hatreds" the best explanation for war and genocide?
- What is the "banality of evil," and what does it tell us about human nature?

The Question of Human Nature

Throughout this chapter, we have seen that human nature contains the potential for unspeakable acts of cruelty and inspiring acts of goodness. Most people believe that some cultures and individuals are inherently good or evil; if we can just get rid of those few evil ones—those Nazis, those Hutu, those bad guards at Abu Ghraib prison—everything will be fine. But from the standpoint of social and cultural psychology, all human beings, like all cultures, contain the potential for both: "Evil" resides in the demands of roles and governments.

THINKING CRITICALLY

DON'T OVERSIMPLIFY

Many people like to divide individuals and nations into those that are good and those that are evil. What is wrong with thinking this way?

That is why, although people everywhere love their families and are loyal to their friends and country, virtually no country or group has bloodless hands. Yes, the Nazis systematically exterminated millions of Jews, Gypsies, homosexuals, disabled people, and anyone not of the "pure" Aryan "race." But Americans and Canadians slaughtered native peoples in North America, Turks slaughtered Armenians, the Khmer Rouge slaughtered millions of fellow Cambodians, the Spanish conquistadors slaughtered native peoples in Mexico and South America, Idi Amin waged a reign of terror against his own people in Uganda, the Japanese slaughtered Koreans and Chinese, despotic political regimes in Argentina and Chile killed thousands of dissidents and rebels, and in the former Yugoslavia, Bosnian Serbs massacred Bosnian Muslims in the name of "ethnic cleansing."

It's easy to conclude that these outbreaks of violence are a result of inner aggressive drives, the sheer evilness of the perpetrators, or age-old tribal hatreds. But in the social-psychological view, they result from the all-too-normal processes we have discussed in this chapter, including ethnocentrism, obedience to authority, conformity,

These paintings done during wartime poignantly illustrate one child's effort to portray the horror of war and another's dream of peace. Can we learn to design a world in which conflicts and group differences, though inevitable, need not lead to violence?

groupthink, deindividuation, stereotyping, and prejudice. These processes are especially likely to be activated when a government feels weakened and vulnerable. By generating an outside enemy, rulers create "us–them" thinking to impose order and cohesion among their citizens and to create a scapegoat for the country's economic problems (Smith, 1998; Staub, 1996). The good news is that when circumstances within a nation change, societies can also change from being warlike to being peaceful. Sweden was once one of the most warlike nations on earth, but today it is among the most pacifistic and egalitarian.

The philosopher Hannah Arendt (1963), who covered the trial of Adolf Eichmann, used the phrase *the banality of evil* to describe how it was possible for Eichmann and other ordinary people in Nazi Germany to commit the monstrous acts they did. (*Banal* means "commonplace" or "unoriginal.") The compelling evidence for the banality of evil is, perhaps, the hardest lesson in psychology. Of course, some people do stand out as being unusually heroic or unusually sadistic. But as we have seen, good people can do terribly disturbing things when their roles encourage or require them to do so, when the situation takes over and they do not stop to think critically.

The research discussed in this chapter suggests that ethnocentrism and prejudice will always be with us, as long as differences exist among groups. But it can also help us formulate ways of living in a diverse world. By identifying the conditions that create the banality of evil, perhaps we can create others that foster the "banality of virtue"—everyday acts of kindness, selflessness, and generosity.

Taking Psychology with You

Travels Across the Cultural Divide

A French salesman worked for a company that was bought by Americans. When the new American manager ordered him to step up his sales within the next three months, the employee quit in a huff, taking his customers with him. Why? In France, it takes years to develop customers; in family-owned businesses, relationships with customers may span generations. The American wanted instant results, as Americans often do, but the French salesman knew this was impossible and quit. The American view was "He wasn't up to the job; he's lazy and disloyal, so he stole my customers." The French view was "There is no point in explaining anything to a person who is so stupid as to think you can acquire loyal customers in three months" (Hall & Hall, 1987).

Both men were committing the fundamental attribution error: assuming that the other person's behavior was due to personality rather than the situation, in this case a situation governed by cultural rules. Many corporations now realize that such rules are not trivial and that success in a global economy depends on understanding them. You, too, can benefit from the psychological research on cultures, whether you plan to do business abroad, intend to visit as a tourist, or just want to get along better in your own society.

- **Be sure you understand the other culture's rules, manners, and customs.** If you find yourself getting angry over something a person from another culture is doing, try to find out whether your expectations and perceptions of that person's behavior are appropriate. For example, Koreans typically do not shake hands when greeting strangers, whereas most North Americans and Europeans do. People who shake hands as a

gesture of friendship and courtesy are likely to feel insulted if another person refuses to do the same, unless they understand this cultural difference.

Or suppose that you are shopping in the Middle East or Latin America, where bargaining on a price is the usual practice. If you are not used to bargaining, the experience is likely to be exasperating because you will not know whether you got taken or got a great deal. On the other hand, if you are from a bargaining culture, you will feel just as exasperated if a seller offers you a flat price. "Where's the fun in this?" you'll say. "The whole human transaction of shopping is gone!"

Whichever kind of culture you come from, you may need a "translator" to help you navigate the unfamiliar system. In Los Angeles, a physician we know could not persuade his Iranian patients that office fees are fixed, not negotiable. They kept offering him half, then 60 percent . . . and each time he said "no" they thought he was just taking a hard negotiating position. It took a bicultural relative of the patients to explain the odd American custom of fixed prices for services.

- **When in Rome, do as the Romans do.** Most of the things you really need to know about a culture are not to be found in guidebooks. To learn the unspoken rules of a culture, look, listen, and observe. What is the pace of life like? Do people regard brash individuality and loud speech as admirable or embarrassing? When customers enter a shop, do they greet and chat with the shopkeeper or ignore the person as they browse?

  Remember, though, that even when you know the rules, you may find it difficult to carry them out. In the Middle East, two men will look directly at one another as they talk, but such direct gazes would be deeply uncomfortable to most Japanese and a sign of insult or confrontation to some African-Americans (Keating, 1994). Knowing this fact about gaze rules can help people accept the reality of different customs, but most of us will still feel uncomfortable trying to change our own ways.
- **Avoid stereotyping.** Try not to let your awareness of general cultural differences cause you to overlook individual variations within cultures. During a dreary Boston winter, Roger Brown (1986) went to the Bahamas for a vacation. To his surprise, he found the people he met unfriendly, rude, and sullen. As a social psychologist, he came up with a situational attribution for their behavior: He decided that the reason was that Bahamians had to deal with spoiled, demanding foreigners. He tried out this hypothesis on a cab driver. The cab driver looked at Brown in amazement, smiled cheerfully, and told him that Bahamians don't mind tourists—just *unsmiling* tourists.

  And then Brown realized what had been going on. "Not tourists generally, but this tourist, myself, was the cause," he wrote. "Confronted with my unrelaxed wintry Boston face, they had assumed I had no interest in them and had responded noncommittally, inexpressively. I had created the Bahamian national character. Everywhere I took my face it sprang into being. So I began smiling a lot, and the Bahamians changed their national character. In fact, they lost any national character and differentiated into individuals."

Wise travelers can use their knowledge of cultural differences while avoiding the trap of stereotyping. Sociocultural research teaches us to appreciate the many cultural rules that govern people's behavior, values, and attitudes. Yet we should not forget Roger Brown's lesson that every human being is an individual: one who not only reflects his or her culture but also shares the common concerns of all humanity.

Summary

- Social and cultural psychologists emphasize environmental influences on behavior. *Social psychologists* study how social roles, attitudes, relationships, and groups influence individuals; *cultural psychologists* study the influence of culture on human behavior.

Roles and Rules

- Two classic studies illustrate the power of *norms* and *roles* to affect individual actions. In Milgram's obedience study, most people in the role of "teacher" inflicted what they thought was extreme shock on another person because of the authority of the experimenter. In Zimbardo's prison study, college students quickly fell into the role of "prisoner" or "guard."
- Obedience to authority contributes to the smooth running of society, but obedience can also lead to actions that are deadly, foolish, or illegal. People obey orders because they can be punished if they do not, out of respect for the authority, and to gain advantages. Even when they would

rather not obey, they may do so because they hand over responsibility for their actions to the authority; because their role is routinized into duties that are performed mindlessly; because they are embarrassed to violate the rules of good manners and lack the words to protest; or because they have been *entrapped.*

Social Influences on Beliefs

- Researchers in the area of *social cognition* study how people's relationships and social environment affect their beliefs and perceptions. A specialty called *social-cognitive neuroscience* draws on the technologies of neuroscience to study social processes in the brain.
- According to *attribution theory*, people are motivated to search for causes to which they can attribute their own and other people's behavior. Their attributions may be *situational* or *dispositional*. The *fundamental attribution error* occurs when people overestimate personality traits as a cause of behavior and underestimate the influence of the situation. A *self-serving bias* allows people to excuse their mistakes by blaming the situation yet taking credit for their good deeds. According to the *just-world hypothesis*, most people need to believe that the world is fair and that people get what they deserve. To preserve this belief, they may blame victims of abuse or injustice for provoking or deserving it.
- People hold many *attitudes* about people, things, and ideas. Attitudes may be *explicit* (conscious) or *implicit* (unconscious). Attitudes may change through experience, conscious decision, or as an effort to reduce *cognitive dissonance*.
- As discussed in "Biology and Beliefs," many attitudes are acquired through learning and social influence, but some are associated with personality traits that have a genetic component and are deeply ingrained. Religious and political affiliations are not heritable, but religiosity and certain political attitudes do have relatively high heritability. Attitudes are also profoundly affected by the *nonshared environment*, an individual's unique life experiences.
- One powerful way to influence attitudes is by taking advantage of the *familiarity effect* and the *validity effect:* Simply exposing people repeatedly to a name or product makes them like it more, and repeating a statement over and over again makes it seem more believable. Other techniques of attitude change include associating a product or message with someone who is famous, attractive, or expert, and linking the product with good feelings. Fear tactics tend to backfire.
- Tactics of *coercive persuasion* include putting a person under extreme physical and emotional stress; defining problems simplistically; offering the appearance of unconditional love and acceptance in exchange for unquestioning loyalty; creating a new identity for the person; using entrapment; and controlling access to outside information. Even ordinary people without any psychopathology can be vulnerable to these techniques.

Individuals in Groups

- In groups, individuals often behave differently than they would on their own. Conformity has many benefits; it permits the smooth running of society and allows people to feel in harmony with others like them. But as the famous Asch experiment showed, most people will conform to the judgments of others even when the others are plain wrong. People in group-oriented cultures value conformity and the sense of group harmony it creates more than do people in individualist cultures, but everyone conforms under some conditions.
- Most people conform to social pressure because they identify with a group, trust the group's judgment or knowledge, hope for personal gain, or wish to be liked. But they also may conform mindlessly and self-destructively, violating their own preferences and values because "everyone else is doing it."
- Groups that are isolated from other views, are under outside pressure, and have strong leaders are vulnerable to *groupthink*, the tendency of group members to think alike, censor themselves, actively suppress disagreement, and feel that their decisions are invulnerable. Groupthink often produces faulty decisions because group members fail to seek disconfirming evidence for their ideas. However, groups can be structured to counteract groupthink.
- *Diffusion of responsibility* in a group can lead to inaction on the part of individuals, such as *bystander apathy* and *social loafing*. The diffusion of responsibility is likely to occur under conditions that promote *deindividuation*, the loss of awareness of one's individuality. Deindividuation increases when people feel anonymous, as in a large group or crowd, or when they are wearing masks or uniforms. In some situations, crowd norms lead deindividuated people to behave aggressively, but in others, crowd norms foster helpfulness.

- The willingness to speak up for an unpopular opinion, blow the whistle on illegal practices, or help a stranger in trouble and perform other acts of *altruism* is partly a matter of personal belief and conscience. But several situational factors are also important: The person perceives that help is needed; cultural norms support taking action; the situation increases the likelihood that the person will take responsibility; the costs of not doing anything are greater than the costs of getting involved; the person has an ally; and the person becomes entrapped in a commitment to help or dissent.

Us Versus Them: Group Identity

- People develop *social identities* based on their group affiliations, including nationality, religion, occupation, and other social memberships. Social identities provide a feeling of place and connection in the world.
- In culturally diverse societies, many people face the problem of balancing their *ethnic identity* with *acculturation* into the larger society. Depending on whether ethnic identity and acculturation are strong or weak, a person may become *bicultural*, choose *assimilation*, become an *ethnic separatist*, or feel *marginal*.
- *Ethnocentrism*, the belief that one's own ethnic group or religion is superior to all others, promotes "us–them" thinking. One effective strategy for reducing us–them thinking and hostility between groups is having both sides work together to reach a common goal.
- *Stereotypes* help people rapidly process new information, organize experience, and predict how others will behave. But they distort reality by exaggerating differences between groups, underestimating the differences within groups, and producing selective perception.

Group Conflict and Prejudice

- A *prejudice* is an unreasonable negative feeling toward a category of people. Psychologically, prejudice wards off feelings of anxiety and doubt, provides a simple explanation of complex problems, and bolsters self-esteem when a person feels threatened. Other causes of prejudice are social: People acquire prejudices because of conformity and groupthink, parental lessons, and media images. Prejudice has the cultural purpose of bonding people to their social groups and nations. And prejudice also serves to justify a majority group's economic interests and dominance and even to legitimize war. During times of economic insecurity and competition for jobs, prejudice rises significantly.
- Prejudice is a challenge to define and measure. For example, *hostile sexism* is different from *benevolent sexism*, though both legitimize gender discrimination. As discussed in "Close-up on Research," psychologists disagree on whether racism and other prejudices are declining or have merely taken new forms. Because many people are unwilling to admit their prejudices openly, some researchers are trying to measure prejudice indirectly: by seeing whether people are more likely to behave aggressively toward a target when they are stressed or insulted; by observing changes in the brain; or by assessing unconscious positive or negative associations with a group, as with the *Implicit Association Test* (IAT). However, the IAT has many critics who claim it is not capturing true prejudice.
- Efforts to reduce prejudice need to target both the explicit and implicit attitudes that people have. Four external conditions are required for reducing prejudice and conflict between groups: Both sides must have equal legal status, economic standing, and power; both sides must have the legal, moral, and economic support of authorities and cultural institutions; both sides must have opportunities to work and socialize together (the *contact hypothesis*); and both sides must work together for a common goal.

The Question of Human Nature

- Although many people believe that only bad or evil people do bad deeds, the principles of social and cultural psychology show that under certain conditions, good people often can be induced to do bad things too. All individuals are affected by the rules and norms of their cultures. And everyone is influenced to one degree or another by the social processes of obedience, conformity, persuasion, bystander apathy, groupthink, deindividuation, ethnocentrism, stereotyping, and prejudice.

KEY TERMS

social psychology 276
cultural psychology 276
norms (social) 277
role 277
culture 277
conversational distance 278
entrapment 282
social cognition 284
social-cognitive neuroscience 284
attribution theory 284
situational attributions 284
dispositional attributions 284
fundamental attribution error 285
self-serving bias 285
just-world hypothesis 285
blaming the victim 286
attitude 286
implicit and explicit attitudes 286
cognitive dissonance 287
nonshared environment 289
familiarity effect 289
validity effect 289
coercive persuasion 290
groupthink 294
diffusion of responsibility 295
bystander apathy 295
social loafing 295
deindividuation 296
altruism 298
social identity 299
ethnic identity 300
acculturation 300
bicultural, assimilated, ethnic separatist, and marginal identities 300
ethnocentrism 301
stereotype 302
prejudice 304
hostile and benevolent sexism 308
Implicit Association Test (IAT) 311
contact hypothesis 312

Did You Get It?

NOW YOU HAVE READ CHAPTER EIGHT — ARE YOU PREPARED FOR THE EXAM?

Selena is trying to get her boyfriend to wash the dishes for her. She starts by asking her boyfriend to cook dinner for her. When her boyfriend refuses she asks "Will you at least wash the dishes then?" to which he readily agrees. Selena has just used the _____.

What are common ways to gain the compliance of another? (pages 286–292)

door-in-the-face technique

When opposites attract it is said that they have _____ characteristics.

What factors cause people to be attracted to each other? (pages 284–288)

complimentary

In a crowded mall parking lot, dozens of people hear a female voice yell, "He's killing me!" Yet, no one calls the police. What is the reason for the lack of action, according to Darley and Latane?

What is the bystander effect? (page 316–317)

diffusion of responsibility

Attitudes can be broken down into different components. Check out the activities in the Social Influences on Belief section to get a better understanding of these components.

Social Influences on Belief

What are the three components of an attitude?

What are the ways that people form their attitudes?

How can attitudes be changed?

E-BOOK

For the Wade e-book, go to the link below and click on the **Social Influences on Belief.**

Read the **Social Influences on Belief** section in your e-book. As you are reading, highlight the key terms—to highlight and take notes, click on the "+" symbol beside the relevant paragraph. Also as you are reading, keep in mind the key learning objectives, listed at the top of the page.

E-Book

After reviewing this section of the e-book, match the following key terms using the pull down menu in each box to choose the correct definition:

cognitive dissonance

attitude

central-route processing

impression formation

peripheral-route processing

✓

Tendency to respond positively or negatively toward a certain person, object, idea, or situation

Attending to the content of the message itself

Attending to factors not involved in the message, such as the length of the message

Sense of discomfort that occurs when a person's behavior does not correspond to their attitudes

The forming of the first knowledge that a person has concerning another person

APPLY IT

The website below provides an instrument that demonstrates how the affective and cognitive components of attitudes are measured. Complete the questionnaire, and then calculate your results (by clicking on the "Calculate" button at the bottom of the screen).

Web Link

Once you have completed the activity, fill in the blanks in the following statements using the pull down menu:

The ____________ component of an attitude is the way a person feels toward the object, person, or situation.

The ____________ component of an attitude is the way a person thinks about the object, person, or situation.

The ____________ component of an attitude is the action a person takes in regard to the object, person, or situation.

✓

affective

behavior

cognitive

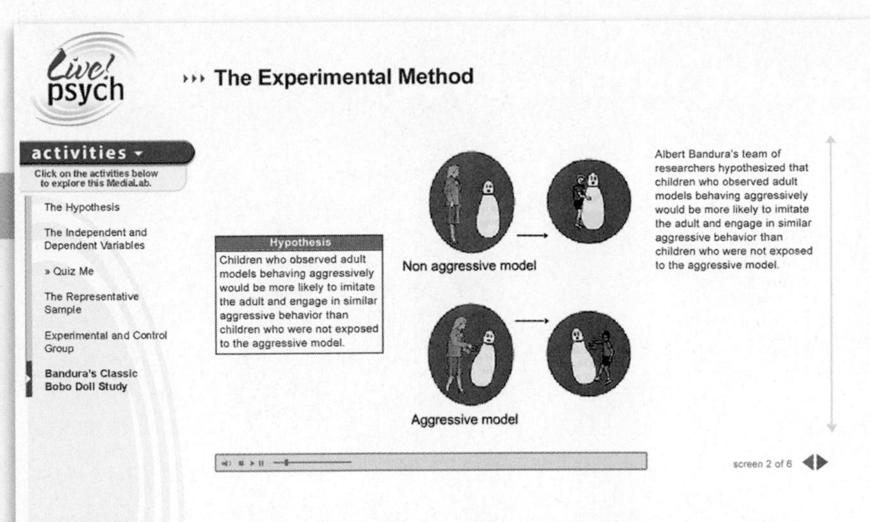

TELL ME **MORE** >>

"It's much easier to remember when you can do several different study activities besides reading the text."

Student
Patrick Henry Community College

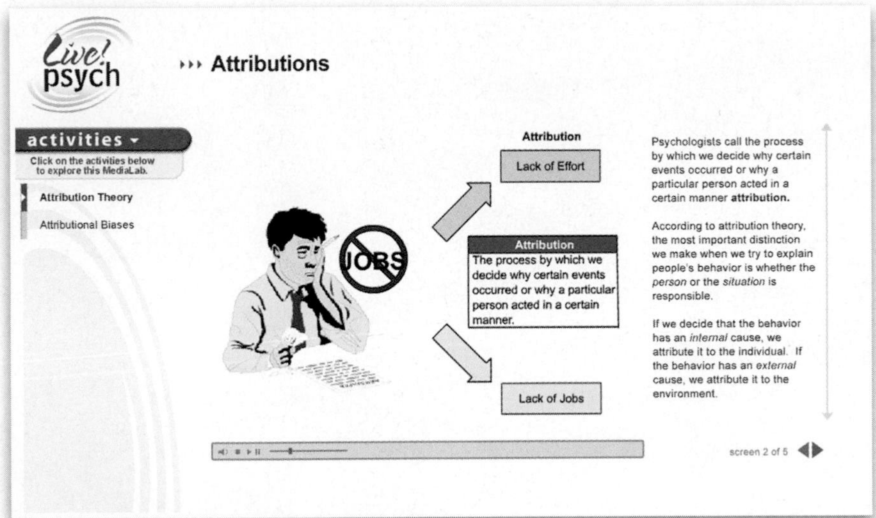

Social psychology contains a large number of well-known researchers along with the famous studies they carried out. It is important to be able to remember which researcher goes with which study.

To get a better understanding of this research, try out the experiments and simulations in the Social Influence, Groups and Prejudice sections. Trying out the experiments will give you a better understanding of the findings of these key researchers.

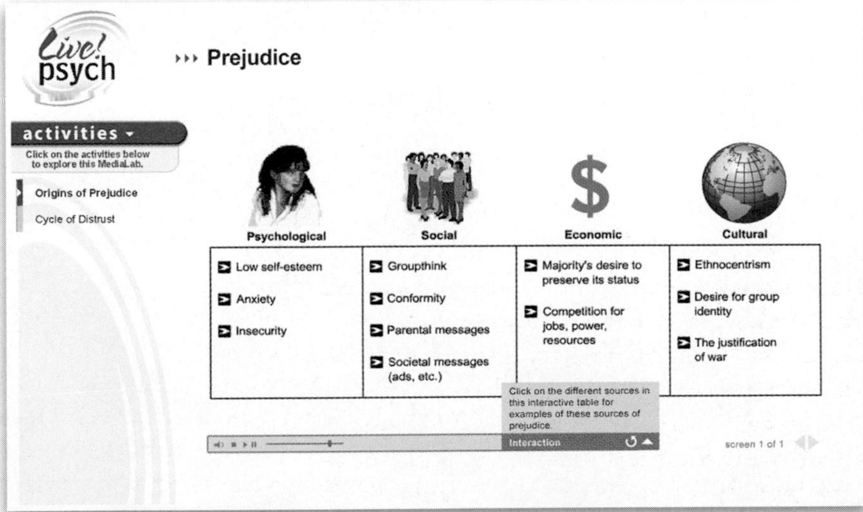

THINKING AND INTELLIGENCE

CHAPTER NINE

A great many people think they are thinking when they are merely rearranging their prejudices.

WILLIAM JAMES

CHAPTER 

OUTLINE

Each day, in the course of ordinary living, we all make decisions, draw up plans, draw inferences, construct explanations, and organize and reorganize the contents of our mental world. Descartes' famous declaration "I think, therefore I am" could just as well have been reversed: "I am, therefore I think." Our powers of thought and intelligence have inspired us to immodestly call ourselves *Homo sapiens*, Latin for wise or rational man. But just how "sapiens" are we, really? Consider:

- As children, we all learn how clocks arbitrarily divide time into hours, minutes, and seconds. Yet each spring, when daylight savings time begins, some people fret about tampering with "normal time." One woman in Colorado complained to her local newspaper that the "extra hour of sunlight" was burning up her front lawn!
- In Seal Beach, California, a visitor to a library asked whether the library had a newspaper clipping announcing the birth of Jesus.
- Many people confuse fictional characters in novels, films, and TV programs with real people. The town of Nottingham, England, distributed flyers to visitors telling them that Robin Hood and his pals never actually lived in nearby Sherwood Forest inasmuch as they were not real persons. Tourism plummeted and the flyers were discontinued.
- At a fast-food restaurant in Kentucky, a customer paid for a $2 order with a phony $200 bill depicting former President George H. W. Bush and a drawing of the White House with a lawn sign reading "We like broccoli" (Bush hates broccoli). The cashier accepted the bill and gave the customer $198 in change.

The human mind, which has managed to come up with poetry, penicillin, and pantyhose, is a miraculous thing; but the human mind has also managed to come up with traffic jams, junk mail, and war. To better understand why the same species that figured out how to get to the moon is also capable of breathtaking bumbling here on Earth, we will examine in this chapter how people reason, solve problems, and grow in intelligence, as well as some sources of their mental shortcomings.

WHAT'S AHEAD

- When you think of a bird, why are you more likely to recall a robin than a penguin?
- Does the language you speak affect the way you think?
- How are visual images like images on a computer screen?
- What is happening mentally when you mistakenly take your geography notes to your psychology class?

Thought: Using What We Know

Think for a moment about what thinking does for you. It frees you from the confines of the immediate present: You can think about a trip taken three years ago, a party next Saturday, or the War of 1812. It carries you beyond the boundaries of reality: You can imagine unicorns and utopias, Martians and magic. Because you think, you do not need to grope your way blindly through your problems but can apply knowledge to solve them intelligently and creatively.

To explain such abilities, many cognitive psychologists liken the human mind to an information processor, analogous to a computer but far more complex. Information-processing approaches capture the fact that the brain does not passively record information but actively alters and organizes it. When we take action, we physically manipulate the environment; when we think, we *mentally* manipulate internal representations of objects, activities, and situations.

What is this?

The Elements of Cognition

One type of mental representation is the **concept**, a mental category that groups objects, relations, activities, abstractions, or qualities having common properties. The instances of a concept are seen as roughly similar. For example, *golden retriever*, *cocker spaniel*, and *border collie* are instances of the concept *dog*; and *anger*, *joy*, and *sadness* are instances of the concept *emotion*. Concepts simplify and summarize information about the world so that it is manageable and so that we can make decisions quickly and efficiently. You may never have seen a *basenji* or eaten *escargots*, but if you know that the first is an instance of *dog* and the second an instance of *food*, you will know, roughly, how to respond (unless you do not like to eat snails, which is what escargots are).

Basic concepts have a moderate number of instances and are easier to acquire than those having either few or many instances (Rosch, 1973). What is the object pictured in the margin? You will probably call it an apple. The concept *apple* is more basic than *fruit*, which includes many more instances and is more abstract. It is also more basic than *McIntosh apple*, which is quite specific. Similarly, *book* is more basic than either *printed matter* or *novel*. Children seem to learn basic-level concepts earlier than others, and adults use them more often than others, because basic concepts convey an optimal amount of information in most situations.

concept A mental category that groups objects, relations, activities, abstractions, or qualities having common properties.

basic concepts Concepts that have a moderate number of instances and that are easier to acquire than those having few or many instances.

prototype An especially representative example of a concept.

The qualities associated with a concept do not necessarily all apply to every instance: Some apples are not red; some dogs do not bark; some birds do not fly or perch on trees. But all the instances of a concept do share a family resemblance. When we need to decide whether something belongs to a concept, we are likely to compare it to a **prototype**, a representative example of the concept (Rosch, 1973). For instance, which dog is doggier, a golden retriever or a chihuahua? Which fruit is more fruitlike, an apple or a pineapple? Which activity is more representative of sports, football or

Some instances of a concept are more representative or prototypical than others. For example, Hollywood heartthrob George Clooney clearly qualifies as a "bachelor," an unmarried man—he is resolutely single! But is the Pope a bachelor? What about Elton John, who celebrated a civil union ceremony in England with his longtime male partner?

weight lifting? Most people within a culture can easily tell you which instances of a concept are most representative, or *prototypical*.

The words used to express concepts may influence or shape how we think about them. Many decades ago, Benjamin Lee Whorf, an insurance inspector by profession and a linguist and anthropologist by inclination, proposed that language molds cognition and perception. For example, said Whorf (1956), because English has only one word for snow and Eskimos (the Inuit) have many (for powdered snow, slushy snow, falling snow . . .), the Inuit notice differences in snow that English speakers do not. He also argued that grammar—the way words are formed and arranged to convey tense and other concepts—affects how we think about the world.

Whorf's theory became popular and then fell from favor; English speakers can see all those Inuit kinds of snow, after all, and they have plenty of adjectives to describe the different varieties. But today Whorf's ideas are once again getting attention. Some researchers are finding that vocabulary and grammar do affect how we perceive the location of objects, think about time, attend to shapes and colors, and remember events (Boroditsky, 2003; Gentner & Goldin-Meadow, 2003). For example, a language spoken by a group in Papua, New Guinea, refers to blue and green with one word, but distinct shades of green with two separate words. On perceptual discrimination tasks, New Guineans who speak this language handle green contrasts better than blue–green ones, whereas the reverse holds true for English speakers (Roberson, Davies, & Davidoff, 2000). Similar results on the way language affects color perception have been obtained in studies comparing English with certain African languages (Özgen, 2004).

Language may influence our concepts and perceptions of the world. How do you divide up these hues? People who speak a language that has only one word for blue and green, but separate words for shades of green, handle green contrasts better than the blue–green distinction. English speakers do just the opposite.

Consider another example. In many languages, speakers must specify whether an object is linguistically masculine or feminine (in Spanish, for example, *la cuenta*, the bill, is feminine but *el cuento*, the story, is masculine). It seems that labeling a concept as masculine or feminine affects the attributes that native speakers ascribe to it. Thus,

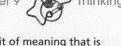

proposition A unit of meaning that is made up of concepts and expresses a single idea.

cognitive schema An integrated mental network of knowledge, beliefs, and expectations concerning a particular topic or aspect of the world.

mental image A mental representation that mirrors or resembles the thing it represents; mental images occur in many and perhaps all sensory modalities.

subconscious processes Mental processes occurring outside of conscious awareness but accessible to consciousness when necessary.

a German speaker will describe a key (masculine in German) as hard, heavy, jagged, metal, serrated, and useful, whereas a Spanish speaker is more likely to describe a key (feminine in Spanish) as golden, intricate, little, lovely, shiny, and tiny. German speakers will describe a bridge (feminine in German) as beautiful, elegant, fragile, peaceful, pretty, and slender, whereas Spanish speakers are more likely to describe a bridge (masculine in Spanish) as big, dangerous, long, strong, sturdy, and towering (Boroditsky, Schmidt, & Phillips, 2003).

Concepts are the building blocks of thought, but they would be of limited use if we merely stacked them up mentally. We must also represent their relationships to one another. One way we accomplish this may be by storing and using **propositions**, units of meaning that are made up of concepts and that express a unitary idea. A proposition can express nearly any sort of knowledge ("Hortense raises border collies") or belief ("Border collies are smart"). Propositions, in turn, are linked together in complicated networks of knowledge, associations, beliefs, and expectations. These networks, which psychologists call **cognitive schemas**, serve as mental models of aspects of the world. For example, gender schemas represent a person's beliefs and expectations about what it means to be male or female (see Chapter 14). People also have schemas about cultures, occupations, animals, geographical locations, and many other features of the social and natural environment.

Mental images—especially visual images, pictures in the mind's eye—are also important in thinking and in the construction of cognitive schemas. Although no one can directly see another person's visual images, psychologists are able to study them indirectly. One method is to measure how long it takes people to rotate an image in their imaginations, scan from one point to another in an image, or read off some detail from an image. The results suggest that visual images are much like images on a computer screen: We can manipulate them, they occur in a mental "space" of a fixed size, and small ones contain less detail than larger ones (Kosslyn, 1980; Shepard & Metzler, 1971). Most people also report auditory images (for instance, a song, slogan, or poem you can hear in your "mind's ear"), and many report images in other sensory modalities as well—touch, taste, smell, or pain. Some even report kinesthetic images, imagined feelings in the muscles and joints.

Here, then, is a visual summary of the elements of cognition:

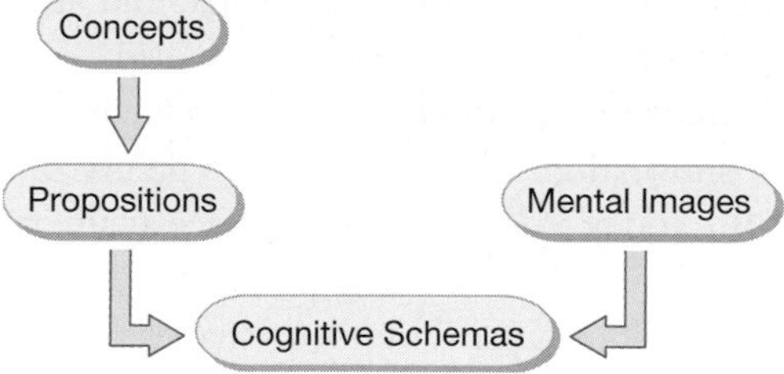

How Conscious Is Thought?

When we think about thinking, we usually have in mind those mental activities that are carried out in a deliberate way with a conscious goal in mind, such as solving a problem, drawing up plans, or making decisions. However, not all mental processing is conscious.

Subconscious Thinking. Some cognitive processes lie outside of awareness but can be brought into consciousness with a little effort when necessary. These **subconscious processes** allow us to handle more information and to perform more complex tasks than if we depended entirely on conscious, deliberate thought. Consider all the automatic routines performed "without thinking," though they might once have required careful, conscious attention: knitting, typing, driving a car, decoding the letters in a word in order to read it.

Some well-learned skills do not require much conscious thought and can be performed while doing other things. But multitasking can also get you into trouble. It's not a good idea to talk on your cell phone, eat, and try to drive all at the same time.

Because of the capacity for automatic processing, people can eat lunch while reading a book or drive a car while listening to music. In such cases, one of the tasks has become automatic and does not require much executive control from the brain's prefrontal cortex. In the laboratory, with lots of practice, some people can learn to do two challenging things at once—even read and take dictation—without much loss in accuracy (Hirst, Neisser, & Spelke, 1978). But in ordinary life, "multitasking" is inefficient, even with easy tasks. In fact, far from saving time, toggling between two or more tasks increases the time required to complete them; stress goes up, errors increase, reaction times lengthen, and memory suffers (Lien, Ruthruff, & Johnston, 2006; Rubinstein, Meyer, & Evans, 2001). Multitasking can even be hazardous to your health. A government study found that dialing a cell phone while driving increases the likelihood of an accident almost threefold, and other distractions are just as dangerous (Klauer et al., 2006). Participants in the study were caught on camera checking their stocks, fussing with MP3 players, drinking beer, reading e-mails, applying makeup, flossing their teeth, and putting in contact lenses—all while hurtling down the highway at high speeds.

Even when multitasking doesn't put you at risk of crashing your car, it is often a bad idea. When you do two things at once, brain activity devoted to each task decreases; and while you are switching between tasks, your prefrontal cortex, which prioritizes tasks and enables higher-order thinking, becomes relatively inactive (Jiang, Saxe, & Kanwisher, 2004; Just et al., 2001). So we hope you are not trying to learn these facts while you're also watching TV and messaging your friends!

Nonconscious Thinking. Other kinds of thought processes, **nonconscious processes**, remain outside of awareness. For example, you have no doubt had the odd experience of having a solution to a problem pop into mind after you have given up trying to find one. With sudden insight, you see how to solve an equation, assemble a cabinet, or finish a puzzle without quite knowing how you managed to find the solution. Similarly, people will often say they rely on intuition—hunches and gut feelings—rather than conscious reasoning to make judgments and decisions.

Insight and intuition probably involve two stages of mental processing (Bowers et al., 1990). In the first stage, clues in the problem automatically activate certain memories or knowledge, and you begin to see a pattern or structure in the problem, although you cannot yet say what it is. This nonconscious process guides you toward a hunch or a hypothesis. Then, in the second stage, your thinking becomes conscious, and you become aware of a possible solution. This stage may feel like a sudden revelation ("Aha, now I see!"), but considerable nonconscious mental work has already occurred.

Sometimes people solve problems or learn new skills without experiencing the second stage at all. For example, some people discover the best strategy for winning a card game without ever being able to consciously identify what they are doing (Bechara et al., 1997). Psychologists call this phenomenon **implicit learning**: You learn a rule or an adaptive behavior, either with or without a conscious intention to do so; but you don't know how you learned it, and you can't state, either to yourself or to others, exactly what it is you have learned (Frensch & Rünger, 2003; Lieberman, 2000). Many of our abilities, from speaking our native language properly to walking up a flight of stairs, are the result of implicit learning.

nonconscious processes Mental processes occurring outside of and not available to conscious awareness.

implicit learning Learning that occurs when you acquire knowledge about something without being aware of how you did so and without being able to state exactly what it is you have learned.

Mindlessness. Even when our thinking is conscious, often we are not thinking very *hard*. Like the cashier who cheerfully cashed the phony $200 bill, we may act, speak, and make decisions out of habit, without stopping to analyze what we are doing or

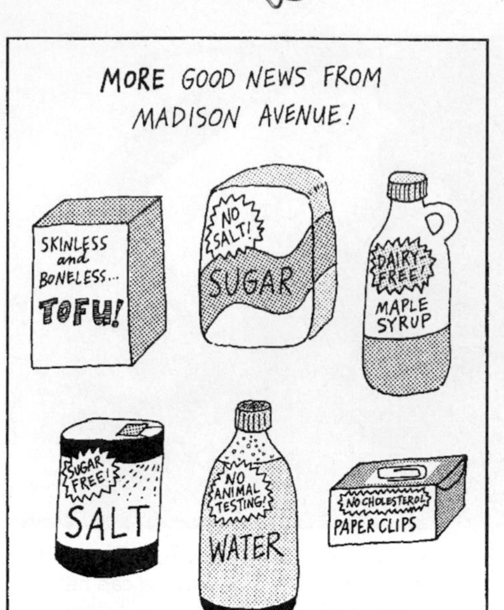

Advertisers sometimes count on mindlessness in consumers.

why we are doing it. This sort of *mindlessness*—mental inflexibility, inertia, and obliviousness to the present context—keeps people from recognizing when a change in a situation requires a change in behavior (Langer, 1989, 1997).

In a classic study of mindlessness, a researcher approached people as they were about to use a photocopier and made one of three requests: "Excuse me, may I use the Xerox machine?" "Excuse me, may I use the Xerox machine, because I have to make copies?" or "Excuse me, may I use the Xerox machine, because I'm in a rush?" Normally, people will let someone go before them only if the person has a legitimate reason, as in the third request. In this study, however, people also complied when the reason sounded like an authentic explanation but was actually meaningless ("because I have to make copies"). They heard the form of the request but they did not hear its content, and they mindlessly stepped aside (Langer, Blank, & Chanowitz, 1978).

Jerome Kagan (1989) has argued that fully conscious awareness is needed only when we must make a deliberate choice, when events happen that cannot be handled automatically, and when unexpected moods and feelings arise. "Consciousness," he wrote, "can be likened to the staff of a fire department. Most of the time, it is quietly playing pinochle in the back room; it performs [only] when the alarm sounds." Some researchers go further, arguing that for certain kinds of complex decisions, such as choosing which car or house to buy, "gut feelings" sometimes lead to better choices and more satisfaction than conscious deliberation does (Dijksterhuis et al., 2006). That may be so, but most of us would probably benefit if our mental "firefighters" paid a little more attention to their jobs. Multitasking, mindlessness, and operating on automatic pilot have their benefits, but they can also lead to errors and mishaps, ranging from the trivial (putting the butter in the dishwasher or locking yourself out of your apartment) to the serious (driving carelessly while daydreaming). Cognitive psychologists have, therefore, devoted a great deal of study to mindful, conscious thought and the capacity to reason.

QUICK quiz

Stay fully conscious while taking this quiz.

1. Which concept is most basic: *furniture, chair*, or *high chair*?
2. Which example of the concept *chair* is prototypical: *high chair, rocking chair*, or *dining room chair*?
3. What two findings in the previous section support Whorf's theory that language affects perception and cognition?
4. In addition to concepts and images, ___________, which express a unitary idea, have been suggested as a basic form of mental representation.
5. Peter's mental representation of *Thanksgiving* includes associations (e.g., to turkeys), attitudes ("It's a time to be with relatives"), and expectations ("I'm going to gain weight from all that food"). They are all part of his ___________ for the holiday.
6. Zelda discovers that she has called her boyfriend's phone number instead of her mother's, as she intended. Her error can be attributed to ___________.

Answers:

1. chair **2.** A plain, straight-backed dining room chair will be prototypical for most people. **3.** Color terms can affect how people respond to colors on visual discrimination tasks, and the linguistic gender of a word can affect people's descriptions of the concept it represents. **4.** propositions **5.** cognitive schema **6.** mindlessness

WHAT'S**AHEAD**

- Mentally speaking, why is making a cake, well, a piece of cake?
- Why can't logic solve all of our problems?
- What kind of reasoning do juries need to be good at?
- When people say that all opinions and claims are equally valid, what error are they making?

Reasoning Rationally

Reasoning is purposeful mental activity that involves operating on information in order to reach conclusions. Unlike impulsive or nonconscious responding, reasoning requires us to draw specific inferences from observations, facts, or assumptions.

Formal Reasoning: Algorithms and Logic

In *formal reasoning problems*—the kind you might find, say, on an intelligence test or a college entrance exam—the information needed for drawing a conclusion or reaching a solution is specified clearly, and there is a single right (or best) answer. Established methods usually exist for solving the problem, and you usually know when it has been solved (Galotti, 1989).

In some formal problems and well-defined tasks, all you have to do is apply an **algorithm**, a set of procedures guaranteed to produce a solution even if you do not really know how it works. To solve a problem in long division, you apply a series of operations that you learned in elementary school. To make a cake, you apply an algorithm called a recipe.

For other formal problems, the rules of formal logic are crucial tools to have in your mental toolbox. One such tool is **deductive reasoning**, in which a conclusion *necessarily* follows from a set of observations or propositions (*premises*):

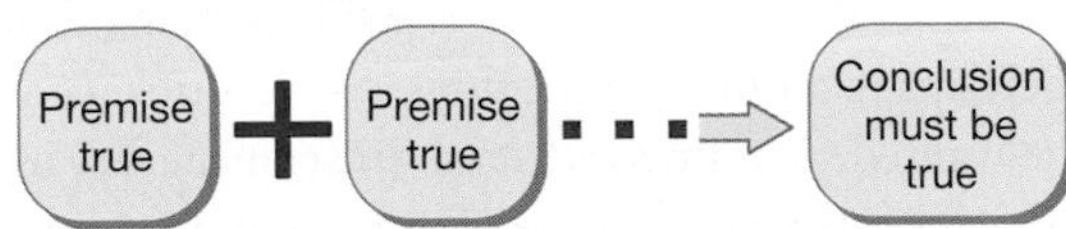

For example, if the premises "All human beings are mortal" and "I am a human being" are true, then the conclusion "I am mortal" must also be true.

We all use deductive reasoning all the time, although many of our premises are implicit rather than explicitly spelled out: "I never have to work on Saturday. Today is Saturday. Therefore, I don't have to work today." But the ability to apply deductive reasoning to abstract problems that are divorced from everyday life does not come as naturally; it depends to some degree on experience, culture, and schooling (Segall et al., 1999). And even in everyday life, almost everyone has trouble thinking deductively in some situations, especially when reasoning about an emotional topic (Blanchette & Richards, 2004). For example, many people mentally reverse a premise, and this error can have serious consequences, as one of our students recognized when he worried about the effects of confusing "All rapists are men" with "All men are rapists."

reasoning The drawing of conclusions or inferences from observations, facts, or assumptions.

algorithm A problem-solving strategy guaranteed to produce a solution even if the user does not know how it works.

deductive reasoning A form of reasoning in which a conclusion follows necessarily from certain premises; if the premises are true, the conclusion must be true.

Another important form of logical thinking is **inductive reasoning**, in which a conclusion *probably* follows from certain premises but could conceivably be false:

INDUCTIVE REASONING

Premise true + Premise true + Possibility of discrepant information · · · ⇒ Conclusion probably true

People often think of inductive reasoning as the drawing of general conclusions from specific observations, as when you generalize from past experience: "I had three good meals at Joe's restaurant; they sure have great food." But an inductive argument can also have premises that are general statements (Copi & Burgess-Jackson, 1992). If your premises are that all cows are mammals and have lungs, all whales are mammals and have lungs, and all humans are mammals and have lungs, you might reasonably conclude that probably all mammals have lungs. Inductive arguments can also have specific conclusions: If your premises are that most people with season tickets to the concert love music, and that Jeannine has season tickets to the concert, you might conclude that Jeannine probably loves music.

Science depends heavily on inductive reasoning because scientists make careful observations and then draw conclusions that they think are probably true. But in inductive reasoning, no matter how much supporting evidence you gather, it is always possible that new information will turn up to show you are wrong. For example, the three meals you ate at Joe's Restaurant may not be typical; perhaps everything else on the menu is awful. And perhaps Jeannine bought those concert tickets not because she loves music but because she wanted to impress a friend. In science, too, new information may show that previous conclusions were faulty and must therefore be revised or modified.

Informal Reasoning: Heuristics and Dialectical Thinking

Useful as they are, algorithms and logical reasoning cannot solve all, or even most, of life's problems. In *informal reasoning problems*, there is often no clearly correct solution. Many approaches, viewpoints, or possible solutions may compete, and you may have to decide which one is most reasonable. Further, the information at your disposal may be incomplete, or people may disagree on what the premises should be. Your position on the controversial issue of abortion, for example, will depend on your premises about when meaningful human life begins, what rights an embryo has, and what rights a woman has to control her own body. People on opposing sides of this issue even disagree on how the premises should be phrased, because they have different emotional reactions to terms such as "rights," "meaningful life," and "control over one's body."

inductive reasoning A form of reasoning in which the premises provide support for a conclusion, but it is still possible for the conclusion to be false.

Formal and informal problems usually call for different approaches. Whereas formal problems can often be solved with an algorithm, informal problems often call for a **heuristic**, a rule of thumb that suggests a course of action without guaranteeing an optimal solution. Anyone who has ever played chess or a card game such as hearts is familiar with heuristics (e.g., "Get rid of high cards first"). In these games, working out all the possible sequences of moves would be impossible. Heuristics are also useful to an investor trying to predict the stock market, a renter trying to decide whether to lease an apartment, a doctor trying to determine the best treatment for a patient, and a factory owner trying to boost production: All are faced with incomplete information on which to base a decision and may therefore resort to rules of thumb that have proved effective in the past.

Whether you are a chess grand master, pondering your next move in a match against a computer, or just an ordinary person solving ordinary problems, you need to use heuristics, rules of thumb that help you decide on a strategy.

In thinking about real-life problems, a person must also be able to use **dialectical reasoning**, the process of comparing and evaluating opposing points of view in order to resolve differences. Philosopher Richard Paul (1984) has described dialectical reasoning as movement "up and back between contradictory lines of reasoning, using each to critically cross-examine the other":

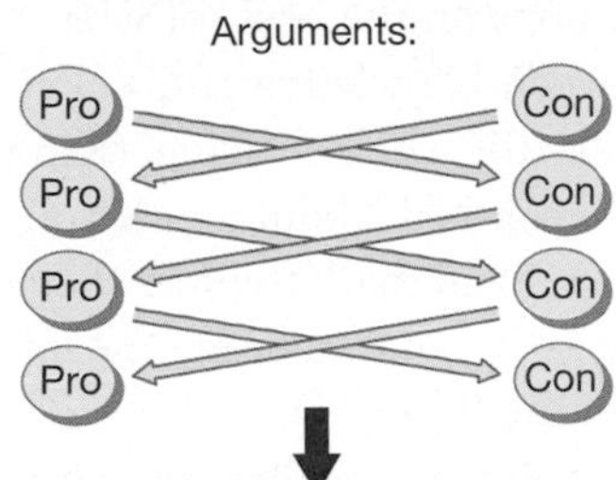

Dialectical reasoning is what juries are supposed to do to arrive at a verdict: consider arguments for and against the defendant's guilt, point and counterpoint. It is also what voters are supposed to do when thinking about whether the government should raise taxes or lower them, or about the best way to improve public education.

Reflective Judgment

Many adults clearly have trouble thinking dialectically; they take one position, and that's that. When do people develop the ability to think critically—to question assumptions, evaluate and integrate evidence, consider alternative interpretations, and reach conclusions that can be defended as most reasonable?

To find out, Karen Kitchener and Patricia King interviewed adolescents and adults of all ages and occupations (King & Kitchener, 1994). They began by providing their interviewees with statements that described opposing viewpoints on various topics. Then the interviewer asked: What do you think about these statements? How did you come to hold that point of view? On what do you base your position? Can you ever know for sure that your position is correct? Why do you suppose disagreement exists about this issue? Based on the responses, King and Kitchener identified seven cognitive stages on the road to what they call *reflective judgment* (and we have called critical thinking). At each stage, people make different assumptions about how things are known and use different ways of justifying or defending their beliefs.

heuristic A rule of thumb that suggests a course of action or guides problem solving but does not guarantee an optimal solution.

dialectical reasoning A process in which opposing facts or ideas are weighed and compared, with a view to determining the best solution or resolving differences.

GET INVOLVED!

➤PRACTICE YOUR DIALECTICAL REASONING

Choose a controversial topic, such as whether marijuana should be legalized or the death penalty should be revoked. First list all the arguments you can to support your own position. Then list all the arguments you can on the other side of the issue. You do not have to agree with these arguments; just list them. Do you feel a mental block or emotional discomfort while doing this? Can you imagine how opponents of your position would answer your arguments? Having strong opinions is fine; you should have an informed opinion on matters of public interest. But does that opinion get in the way of even imagining a contrary point of view or of altering your view if the evidence warrants a change?

In general, people in two early *prereflective stages* assume that a correct answer always exists and that it can be obtained directly through the senses ("I know what I've seen") or from authorities ("They said so on the news"; "That's what I was brought up to believe"). If authorities do not yet have the truth, prereflective thinkers tend to reach conclusions on the basis of what "feels right" at the moment. They do not distinguish between knowledge and belief or between belief and evidence, and they see no reason to justify a belief (King & Kitchener, 1994). One respondent at this stage, when asked about evolution, said: "Well, some people believe that we evolved from apes and that's the way they want to believe. But I would never believe that way and nobody could talk me out of the way I believe because I believe the way that it's told in the Bible."

During three *quasi-reflective stages*, people recognize that some things cannot be known with absolute certainty, and they realize that judgments should be supported by reasons, yet they pay attention only to evidence that fits what they already believe. They seem to think that because knowledge is uncertain, any judgment about the evidence is purely subjective. Quasi-reflective thinkers will defend a position by saying that "we all have a right to our own opinion," as if all opinions are created equal. One college student at this stage, when asked whether one opinion on the safety of food additives was right and others were wrong, answered: "No. I think it just depends on how you feel personally because people make their decisions based upon how they feel and what research they've seen. So what one person thinks is right, another person might think is wrong. . . . If I feel that chemicals cause cancer and you feel that food is unsafe without it, your opinion might be right to you and my opinion is right to me."

Talk-radio shows do not exactly encourage reflective judgment!

In the last two stages, a person becomes capable of reflective judgment. He or she understands that although some things can never be known with certainty, some judgments are more valid than others because of their coherence, their fit with the available evidence, their usefulness, and so on. People at these *reflective stages* are willing to consider evidence from a variety of sources and to reason dialectically. This interview with a graduate student illustrates reflective thinking:

Interviewer: Can you ever say you know for sure that your point of view on chemical additives is correct?

Student:	No, I don't think so. . . . [but] I think that we can usually be reasonably certain, given the information we have now, and considering our methodologies. . . . it might be that the research wasn't conducted rigorously enough. In other words, we might have flaws in our data or sample, things like that.
Interviewer:	How then would you identify the "better opinion"?
Student:	One that takes as many factors as possible into consideration. I mean one that uses the higher percentage of the data that we have, and perhaps that uses the methodology that has been most reliable.
Interviewer:	And how do you come to a conclusion about what the evidence suggests?
Student:	I think you have to take a look at the different opinions and studies that are offered by different groups. Maybe some studies offered by the chemical industry, some studies by the government, some private studies. . . . You have to try to interpret people's motives and that makes it a more complex soup to try to strain out.

One reason that Auguste Rodin's *The Thinker* became world famous and has been much imitated is that it captures so perfectly the experience of thinking reflectively.

Most people do not show evidence of reflective judgment until their middle or late twenties, if at all. However, when college students get support for thinking reflectively and have opportunities to practice it in their courses, their thinking tends to become more complex, sophisticated, and well-grounded (Kitchener et al., 1993). As one writer noted, the gradual development of thinking skills among college students represents an abandonment of "ignorant certainty" in favor of "intelligent confusion" (Kroll, 1992). It may not seem so, but this is a big step forward! You can see why, in this book, we emphasize thinking about and evaluating psychological findings, and not just memorizing them.

QUICK quiz

Reflect on the answers to these questions.

1. Most of the holiday gifts Mervin bought this year cost more than they did last year, so he concludes that inflation is increasing. Is he using inductive, deductive, or dialectical reasoning?
2. Yvonne is arguing with Henrietta about whether real estate is a better investment than stocks. "You can't convince me," says Yvonne. "I just know I'm right." Yvonne needs training in ___________ reasoning.
3. Seymour thinks the media have a liberal political bias, and Sophie thinks they are too conservative. "Well," says Seymour, "I have my truth and you have yours. It's purely subjective." Which of King and Kitchener's levels of thinking describes Seymour's statement?
4. What kind of evidence might resolve the issue that Seymour and Sophie are arguing about?

Answers:

1. inductive **2.** dialectical **3.** quasi-reflective **4.** Researchers might have raters watch a random sample of TV news shows and measure the time devoted to conservative and liberal viewpoints. Or raters could read a random sample of newspaper editorials from across the country and evaluate them as liberal or conservative in outlook. Perhaps you can think of other strategies. Be careful, though: Ratings can be affected by what people want or expect to perceive.

WHAT'S**AHEAD**

- Why do people worry about dying in an airplane crash but ignore dangers that are far more likely?
- How might your physician's choice of words about alternative treatments for your illness affect which one you choose?
- When deciding how to divide up some money, will people always try to maximize their gain?
- When Monday-morning quarterbacks say they knew all along who would win Sunday's big game, what bias might they be showing?
- Why will a terrible hazing make you more loyal to the group that hazed you?

Barriers to Reasoning Rationally

Although most people have the capacity to think logically, reason dialectically, and make judgments reflectively, it is abundantly clear that they do not always do so. One obstacle is the need to be right; if your self-esteem depends on winning arguments, you will find it hard to listen with an open mind to competing views. But human thought processes are also tripped up by many predictable biases and errors. Psychologists have studied dozens of these cognitive pitfalls (Kahneman, 2003). Here we describe just a few.

Exaggerating the Improbable (and Minimizing the Probable)

One common bias is the inclination to exaggerate the probability of rare events—a bias that helps to explain why so many people enter lotteries and buy disaster insurance. There are many reasons for this bias. For example, as we discuss in Chapter 7, evolution has equipped us to fear certain things, such as snakes, but the fear has outlasted the actual threat, so we overestimate the danger. The risk of a rattler sinking its fangs into you in Chicago or New York is pretty low! Evolution has also given us brains that are terrific at responding to an immediate danger (say, a threatening animal) or to acts that provoke moral outrage even though they pose no threat to the survival of the species (for instance, flag burning). But unfortunately, our brains were not designed to become alarmed by serious *future* threats that do not seem to pose much danger right now, such as global warming (Gilbert, 2006).

When judging probabilities, people are strongly influenced by the **affect heuristic**: the tendency to consult their emotions (affect) instead of judging probabilities objectively (Slovic et al., 2002). Emotions can often help us make decisions by narrowing our options, but emotions can also mislead us by preventing us from accurately assessing risk. One unusual field study looked at how people in France responded to the "mad cow" crisis that occurred a few years ago. (Mad cow disease affects the brain and can be contracted by eating meat from contaminated cows.) Whenever many newspaper articles reported the dangers of "mad cow disease," beef consumption fell during the following month. But when news articles, reporting the same dangers, used the technical names of the disease—Creutzfeldt-Jakob disease or bovine spongiform encephalopathy—beef consumption stayed the same (Sinaceur, Heath, & Cole, 2005). The more alarming label caused people to reason emotionally and to overestimate the

affect heuristic The tendency to consult one's emotions instead of estimating probabilities objectively.

danger. During the entire period of the supposed crisis, only six people in France were diagnosed with the disease.

Our judgments about risks are also influenced by the **availability heuristic**, the tendency to judge the probability of an event by how easy it is to think of examples or instances of it (Tversky & Kahneman, 1973). The availability heuristic often works hand in hand with the affect heuristic. For example, catastrophes and shocking accidents evoke a strong emotional reaction in us, and thus stand out in our minds. They are more "available" mentally than other kinds of negative events. This is why people overestimate the frequency of deaths from tornadoes and underestimate the frequency of deaths from asthma, which occur more than 20 times as often but do not make headlines (Lichtenstein et al., 1978). It is why a scary film about sharks or news accounts of a shark attack make people fear shark-attack "epidemics," even though such attacks on humans are extremely rare. And it is why, after 9/11, people were afraid to fly in airplanes, even though they took a much greater risk (65 times as great) by driving to their destinations (Sivak & Flannagan, 2003).

Because of the affect and availability heuristics, many of us overestimate the chances of suffering a shark attack. Shark attacks are extremely rare, but they are terrifying and easy to visualize.

Of course, the affect and availability heuristics are not all bad. They can also cause you to overestimate the probability of happy, joyous events—at least, if you're an optimist.

Avoiding Loss

In general, people try to avoid or minimize risks and losses when they make decisions. So when a choice is framed in terms of the risk of losing something, they will respond more cautiously than when the same choice is framed in terms of gain. They will choose a ticket that has a 1 percent chance of winning a raffle to one that has a 99 percent chance of losing. Or they will rate a condom as effective when they are told it has a 95 percent success rate in protecting against the AIDS virus, but not when they are told it has a 5 percent failure rate—which is exactly the same thing (Linville, Fischer, & Fischhoff, 1992).

Suppose you had to choose between two health programs to combat a disease expected to kill 600 people. Which would you prefer: a program that will definitely save 200 people, or one with a one-third probability of saving all 600 people and a two-thirds probability of saving none? (Problem 1 in Figure 9.1 on the next page illustrates this choice.) When asked this question, most people, including physicians, say they would prefer the first program. In other words, they reject the riskier though potentially more rewarding solution in favor of a sure gain. However, people will take a risk if they see it as a way to *avoid loss*. Suppose now that you have to choose between a program in which 400 people will definitely die and a program in which there is a one-third probability of nobody dying and a two-thirds probability that all 600 will die. If you think about it, you will see that the alternatives are exactly the same as in the first problem; they are merely worded differently (see Problem 2 in Figure 9.1). Yet this time most people choose the second solution. They reject risk when they think of the outcome in terms of lives saved, but they accept risk when they think of the outcome in terms of lives lost (Tversky & Kahneman, 1981).

Few of us will have to face a decision involving hundreds of lives, but we may have to choose between different medical treatments for ourselves or a relative. Our decision may be affected by whether the doctor frames the choice in terms of chances of surviving or chances of dying.

availability heuristic The tendency to judge the probability of a type of event by how easy it is to think of examples or instances.

FIGURE 9.1 A Matter of Wording
The decisions we make depend on how the alternatives are framed. When asked to choose between the two programs in Problem 1, which are described in terms of lives saved, most people choose the first program. When asked to choose between the programs in Problem 2, which are described in terms of lives lost, most people choose the second program. Yet the alternatives in the two problems are actually identical.

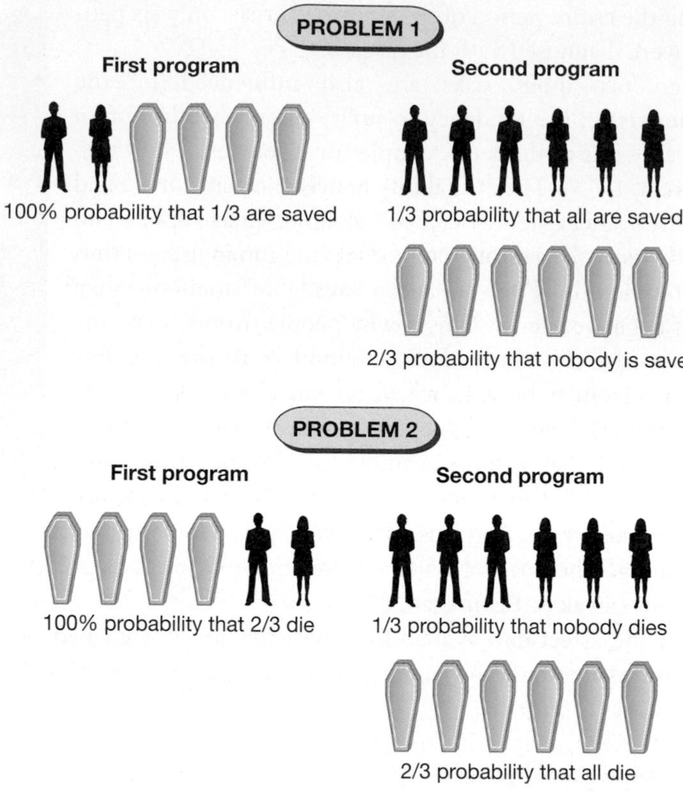

The Fairness Bias

Interestingly, in certain circumstances we do not try to avoid loss altogether, because we are subject to a *fairness bias*. Imagine that you are playing a two-person game called the *Ultimatum Game*, in which your partner gets $10 and must decide how much to share with you. You can choose to accept your partner's offer, in which case you both get to keep your respective portions, or you can reject the offer, in which case neither of you gets a penny. How low an offer would you accept?

If you think about it, you'll see that it makes sense to accept any amount at all, no matter how paltry, because then at least you will get *something*. But that is not how people respond when playing the Ultimatum Game. If the offer is too low, they are likely to reject it. In industrial societies, offers of 50 percent are typical and offers below 20 or 30 percent are commonly rejected, even when the absolute sums are large. In other societies, the amounts offered and accepted may be higher or lower, but there is always some amount that people consider unfair and refuse to accept (Henrich et al., 2001). People may be competitive and love to win, but they are also powerfully motivated to cooperate and to see fairness prevail.

This finding has intrigued scientists from many disciplines, including psychology, philosophy, economics, anthropology, evolutionary biology, and neuroscience. Using the Ultimatum Game and other laboratory games, they are exploring how a sense of fairness often takes precedence over rational self-interest when people make economic choices. Their work, which belongs to a field called *behavioral economics*, verifies and extends the pioneering work of Nobel Prize winner Herbert Simon (1955), who first showed that economic decisions are not always strictly rational.

Unlike this hockey player, most people have a sense of fair play.

BIOLOGY and Economic Choice

Rejecting Unfair Offers

Why does a desire for fair play sometimes outweigh the desire for economic gain? Evolutionary theorists believe that cooperative tendencies and a desire for fairness and reciprocity evolved because they were beneficial to our forbears (Fehr & Fischbacher, 2003; Trivers, 2004). Of course, cultures also play a role, by establishing rules of cooperation and fairness to ensure peace and harmony among their members, and they enforce these rules by rewarding those who abide by them and punishing cheaters. But the idea that the Golden Rule has a basis in biology has gained support from research with nonhuman primates.

In one study, capuchin monkeys received a token that they could then exchange for a slice of cucumber. The monkeys regarded this exchange as a pretty good deal—until they saw a neighboring monkey exchanging tokens for an even better reward, a grape. At that point, they began to refuse to exchange their tokens, even though they were then left with no reward at all (Brosnan & de Waal, 2003). Sometimes they even threw the cucumber slice on the ground in apparent disgust!

Some behavioral economists have drawn on the methods of neuroscience, using MRI scans to examine brain activity when people play variations of the Ultimatum Game (Camerer, 2003; Sanfey et al., 2003). While a person is deciding whether to accept a low offer, two brain areas are active: a part of the prefrontal cortex linked to rational problem solving and an area called the anterior insula, which is associated with pain, disgust, and other unpleasant feelings. According to economist Colin Camerer (quoted in D'Antonio, 2004), "Basically the brain toggles between 'Yes, money is good' and 'Ugh, this guy is treating me like crap.'" People with greater activation of the prefrontal cortex are likely to accept low offers; those with greater activation of the anterior insula are likely to refuse. In fact, Camerer estimates that researchers can predict the outcome 70 percent of the time simply by looking at participants' brain scans.

Now, if only the apparently innate desire for fairness didn't lead human beings to inflict suffering so often on those whom they perceive as unfair, and if only their ability to cooperate didn't lead so often to cooperation in waging war.

The Hindsight Bias

Would you have predicted the results of the last election? Would you have predicted the most recent Oscar winner for best picture? When people learn the outcome of an event or the answer to a question, they are often sure that they "knew it all along." Armed with the wisdom of hindsight, they see the outcome that actually occurred as inevitable, and they overestimate their ability to have predicted what happened beforehand (Fischhoff, 1975; Hawkins & Hastie, 1990). This **hindsight bias** shows up all the time in evaluating relationships ("I always knew their marriage wouldn't last"), medical judgments ("I could have told you that mole was cancerous"), and military opinions ("The generals should have known that the enemy would attempt a surprise attack").

The hindsight bias can be adaptive. When we try to make sense of the past, we focus on explaining just one outcome, the one that actually occurred, because explaining outcomes that did not take place can be a waste of time. Then, in light of current knowledge, we reconstruct and misremember our previous judgment (Hoffrage,

hindsight bias The tendency to overestimate one's ability to have predicted an event once the outcome is known; the "I knew it all along" phenomenon.

confirmation bias The tendency to look for or pay attention only to information that confirms one's own belief.

Hertwig, & Gigerenzer, 2000). But as Scott Hawkins and Reid Hastie (1990) wrote, "Hindsight biases represent the dark side of successful learning and judgment." They are the dark side because when we are sure that we knew something all along, we are also less willing to find out what we need to know in order to make accurate predictions in the future. In medical conferences, for example, when doctors are told what the postmortem findings were for a patient who died, they tend to think the case was easier to diagnose than it actually was ("I would have known it was a brain tumor"), and so they learn less from the case than they should (Dawson et al., 1988).

Perhaps you feel that we are not telling you anything new because you have always known about the hindsight bias. But then, you may just have a hindsight bias about the hindsight bias!

The Confirmation Bias

When people want to make the most accurate judgment possible, they usually try to consider all of the relevant information. But as we saw in Chapter 2, when they are thinking about an issue they already feel strongly about, they often succumb to the **confirmation bias**, paying attention only to evidence that confirms their belief and finding fault with evidence or arguments that point in a different direction (Edwards & Smith, 1996; Kunda, 1990; Nickerson, 1998). You rarely hear someone say, "Oh, thank you for explaining to me why my lifelong philosophy of child rearing (or politics, or investing) is wrong. I'm so grateful for the facts!" The person usually says, "Oh, buzz off, and take your cockamamie ideas with you."

Once you start looking for it, you will see the confirmation bias everywhere. Politicians brag about economic reports that confirm their party's position and dismiss

GET INVOLVED!

➤CONFIRMING THE CONFIRMATION BIAS

Suppose someone deals out four cards, each with a letter on one side and a number on the other. You can see only one side of each card:

Your task is to find out whether the following rule is true: "If a card has a vowel on one side, then it has an even number on the other side." Which two cards do you need to turn over to find out?

The vast majority of people say they would turn over the E and the 6, but they are wrong. You do need to turn over the E (a vowel), because if the number on the other side is even, it confirms the rule, and if it is odd, the rule is false. However, the card with the 6 tells you nothing. The rule does *not* say that a card with an even number must always have a vowel on the other side. Therefore, it doesn't matter whether the 6 has a vowel or a consonant on the other side. The card you do need to turn over is the 7, because if it has a vowel on the other side, that fact disconfirms the rule.

People do poorly on this problem because they are biased to look for confirming evidence and to ignore the possibility of disconfirming evidence. Don't feel too bad if you missed it. Most judges, lawyers, and people with Ph. D.s do, too.

counterevidence as biased or unimportant. Police officers who are convinced of a suspect's guilt take anything the suspect says or does as evidence that confirms it, including the suspect's claims of innocence. The confirmation bias also affects jury members. Instead of considering and weighing possible verdicts against the evidence, many people quickly construct a story about what happened and then consider only the evidence that supports their version of events. These same people are the most confident in their decisions and most likely to vote for an extreme verdict (Kuhn, Weinstock, & Flaton, 1994).

The confirmation bias can affect how you react to what you are learning in school. When students read about scientific findings that dispute one of their own cherished beliefs or that challenge the wisdom of their own actions, they tend to acknowledge but minimize the strengths of the research. In contrast, when a study supports their view, they will acknowledge any flaws (such as a small sample or a reliance on self-reports) but will give these flaws less weight than they otherwise would (Sherman & Kunda, 1989). In thinking critically, people apply a double standard: They think most critically about results they dislike.

mental set A tendency to solve problems using procedures that worked before on similar problems.

Mental Sets

Another barrier to rational thinking is the development of a **mental set**, a tendency to try to solve new problems by using the same heuristics, strategies, and rules that worked in the past on similar problems. Mental sets make human learning and problem solving efficient; because of them, we do not have to keep reinventing the wheel. But mental sets are not helpful when a problem calls for fresh insights and methods. They cause us to cling rigidly to the same old assumptions and approaches, blinding us to better or more rapid solutions. (For an illustration of this point, try the Get Involved exercise on this page.)

One general mental set is the tendency to find patterns in events. This tendency is adaptive because it helps us understand and exert some control over what happens in our lives. But it also leads us to see meaningful patterns even when they do not exist. For example, many people with arthritis think that their symptoms follow a pattern dictated by the weather. They suffer more, they say, when the barometric pressure changes or when the weather is damp or humid. Yet when researchers followed 18 arthritis patients for 15 months, no association whatsoever emerged between weather conditions and the patients' self-reported pain levels, their ability to function in daily

GET INVOLVED!

➤CONNECT THE DOTS

Copy this figure, and try to connect the dots by using no more than four straight lines without lifting your pencil or pen. A line must pass through each point. Can you do it?

Most people have difficulty with this problem because they have a mental set to interpret the arrangement of dots as a square. They then assume that they can't extend a line beyond the apparent boundaries of the square. Now that you know this, you might try again if you haven't yet solved the puzzle. Some solutions are given after the Appendix, on page A-10.

life, or a doctor's evaluation of their joint tenderness (Redelmeier & Tversky, 1996). Of course, because of the confirmation bias, the patients refused to believe the results.

The Need for Cognitive Consistency

THINKING CRITICALLY

ASK QUESTIONS

Time and again, doomsday predictions fail. Why don't people who wrongly predict a devastating earthquake or the end of the world feel embarrassed when their forecasts flop?

Mental sets and the confirmation bias cause us to avoid evidence that contradicts our beliefs. But what happens when disconfirming evidence finally smacks us in the face, and we cannot ignore or discount it any longer? For example, as the twentieth century rolled to an end, predictions of the end of the world escalated. Similar doomsday predictions have been made throughout history and continue to be made today (Kirsch, 2006). When these predictions fail, how come we never hear believers say, "Boy, what a fool I was"?

According to the theory of **cognitive dissonance**, people will resolve such conflicts in predictable, though not always obvious, ways (Festinger, 1957). *Dissonance*, the opposite of consistency (*consonance*), is a state of tension that occurs when you hold either two cognitions (beliefs, thoughts, attitudes) that are psychologically inconsistent with one another or a belief that is incongruent with your behavior. This tension is uncomfortable, so you will be motivated to reduce it. You may do this by rejecting or modifying one of those inconsistent beliefs, changing your behavior, denying the evidence, or rationalizing:

cognitive dissonance A state of tension that occurs when a person holds two cognitions that are psychologically inconsistent, or when a person's belief is incongruent with his or her behavior.

COGNITIVE DISSONANCE

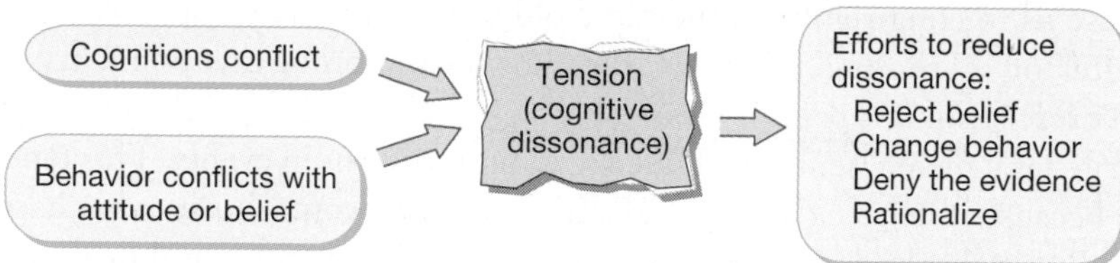
Cognitions conflict
Behavior conflicts with attitude or belief
Tension (cognitive dissonance)
Efforts to reduce dissonance:
Reject belief
Change behavior
Deny the evidence
Rationalize

YESTERDAY IN THIS SPACE I PREDICTED THAT THE WORLD WOULD COME TO AN END. IT DID NOT, HOWEVER. I REGRET ANY INCONVENIENCE THIS MAY HAVE CAUSED.

Many years ago, in a famous field study, Leon Festinger and two associates explored people's reactions to failed prophecies by infiltrating a group of people who thought the world would end on December 21 (Festinger, Riecken, & Schachter, 1956). The group's leader, whom the researchers called Marian Keech, promised that the faithful would be picked up by a flying saucer and whisked to safety at midnight on December 20. Many of her followers quit their jobs and spent all their savings, waiting for the end to come. What would they do or say, Festinger and his colleagues wondered, to reduce the dissonance between "The world is still muddling along on the 21st" and "I predicted the end of the world and sold off all my worldly possessions"?

The researchers predicted that believers who had made no public commitment to the prophecy, who awaited the end of the world by themselves at home, would simply lose their faith. But those who had acted on their conviction by selling their property and waiting with Keech for the spaceship would be in a state of dissonance. They would have to *increase* their religious belief to avoid the intolerable realization that they had behaved foolishly and others knew it. That is just what happened. At 4:45 a.m., long past the

appointed hour of the saucer's arrival, the leader had a new vision. The world had been spared, she said, because of the impressive faith of her little band.

Cognitive-dissonance theory predicts that in more ordinary situations, too, people will resist or rationalize information that conflicts with their existing ideas, just as the people in the arthritis study did. For example, cigarette smokers are often in a state of dissonance, because smoking is dissonant with the fact that smoking causes illness. Smokers may try to reduce the dissonance by trying to quit, by rejecting evidence that smoking is bad, by persuading themselves that they will quit later on, by emphasizing the benefits of smoking ("A cigarette helps me relax"), or by deciding that they don't want a long life, anyhow ("It will be shorter but sweeter").

You are particularly likely to try to reduce dissonance under three conditions (Aronson, 2004):

1 **When you need to justify a choice or decision that you freely made.** All car dealers know about buyer's remorse: The second that people buy a car, they worry that they made the wrong decision or spent too much, a phenomenon called **postdecision dissonance**. You may try to resolve this dissonance by deciding that the car you chose (or the toaster, or house, or spouse) is really, truly the best in the world. However, if someone else made your decision for you, you will not feel much dissonance if it proves misguided. There is no dissonance between "The Army drafted me; I had no choice about being here" and "I hate basic training."

2 **When you need to justify behavior that conflicts with your view of yourself.** If you consider yourself to be honest, cheating will put you in a state of dissonance. To avoid feeling like a hypocrite, you will try to reduce the dissonance by justifying your behavior ("Everyone else does it"; "It's just this once"; "I had to do it to get into med school and learn to save lives"). Or if you see yourself as a kind person and you harm someone, you may reduce your dissonance by blaming the person you have victimized or by finding other self-justifying excuses.

3 **When you need to justify the effort put into a decision or choice.** The harder you work to reach a goal, or the more you suffer for it, the more you will try to convince yourself that you value the goal, even if the goal itself is not so great after all (Aronson & Mills, 1959). This explains why hazing, whether in social clubs, on athletic teams, or in the military, turns new recruits into loyal members (see Figure 9.2). You might think that people would hate the group that caused them pain and embarrassment. But the cognition "I went through a lot of awful stuff to join this group" is dissonant with the cognition "only to find I hate the group." Therefore, people must decide either that the hazing was not so bad or that they really like the group. This mental reevaluation is called the **justification of effort**, and it is one of the most popular methods of reducing dissonance.

Some people are secure enough to own up to their mistakes instead of rationalizing them, or do not have a great need for consistency and so do not experience much cognitive dissonance (Cialdini, Trost, & Newsom, 1995). Moreover, in certain cultures, such as those of East Asia, contradictions and inconsistencies are seen as inevitable in human life, so people are generally less motivated to resolve dissonance than Westerners are (Choi & Nisbett, 2000; Peng & Nisbett, 1999). Still, in many people a need for cognitive consistency can lead to irrational, self-defeating decisions and actions.

postdecision dissonance In the theory of cognitive dissonance, tension that occurs when you believe you may have made a bad decision.

justification of effort The tendency of individuals to increase their liking for something that they have worked hard or suffered to attain; a common form of dissonance reduction.

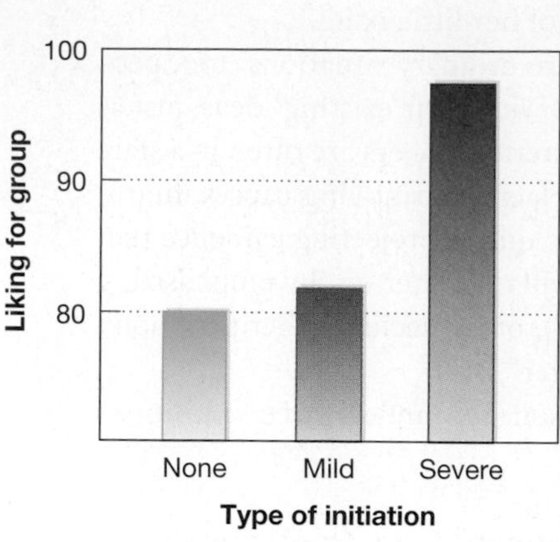

FIGURE 9.2 The Justification of Effort

The more effort you put into reaching a goal, the more highly you are likely to value it. As you can see in the graph on the left, after people listened to a boring group discussion, those who went through a severe initiation to join the group rated it most highly (Aronson & Mills, 1959). In the photo on the right, new cadets at the Virginia Military Institute are forced to crawl through mud until they are covered from head to toe. They will probably become devoted to the military.

Overcoming Our Cognitive Biases

The fact that our decisions and judgments, and the feelings of regret or pleasure that follow, are not always logical or rational has enormous implications for the legal system, business, medicine, government—in fact, for all areas of life. Sometimes these biases are a good thing. For example, cognitive dissonance reduction helps us preserve our self-confidence, and a sense of fairness keeps us from behaving like self-centered louts. From this point of view, such biases are not really so "irrational" after all. Mental biases, however, can also cause us to make poor decisions.

Most people have a "bias blind spot": They acknowledge that *other* people have biases that distort reality, but they think that they themselves are free of bias and see the world as it really is (Pronin, Gilovich, & Ross, 2004). This blind spot is itself a bias! And it is a dangerous one, because it can prevent individuals, nations, ethnic groups, and religious groups from resolving conflicts with others. Each side thinks that its own proposals for ending a conflict are reasonable and fair but the other side's proposals are "biased."

The situation is not entirely hopeless, however. For one thing, people are not equally irrational in all situations. When they are doing things they have some expertise in or are making personal decisions that have serious consequences, their cognitive biases often diminish (Smith & Kida, 1991). Further, once we understand a bias, we may, with some effort, be able to reduce or eliminate it, especially if we make an active, mindful effort to do so and take time to think carefully (Kida, 2006).

Some people, of course, seem to think more rationally than others a great deal of the time; we call them "intelligent." But just what is intelligence, and how can we measure and improve it? We take up these questions next.

QUICK quiz

In hindsight, will you say this quiz was easy?

1. In 2001, an unknown person sent anthrax through the United States post office. Many people became afraid to open their mail, although the risk for any given individual was extremely small (five people died during the attacks). What heuristics help to explain this reaction?
2. *True or false:* Research on the Ultimatum Game shows that people usually act out of rational self-interest.
3. Stu meets a young woman at the student cafeteria. They hit it off and eventually get married. Says Stu, "I knew that day that something special was about to happen." What cognitive bias is affecting his thinking, charmingly romantic though it is?

4. In a classic experiment on cognitive dissonance, students did some boring, repetitive tasks and then had to tell another student, who was waiting to participate in the study, that the work was interesting and fun (Festinger & Carlsmith, 1959). Half the students were offered $20 for telling this lie and the others only $1. Based on what you have learned about cognitive dissonance reduction, which students do you think decided later that the tasks had been fun after all? Why?

Answers:

1. the affect and availability heuristics **2** false **3.** the hindsight bias **4.** The students who got only $1 were more likely to say that the task had been fun. They were in a state of dissonance because "The task was as dull as dishwater" is dissonant with "I said I enjoyed it—and for a mere dollar, at that." Those who got $20 could rationalize that the large sum (which really was large in the 1950s) justified the lie.

WHAT'S AHEAD

- Why do psychologists debate whether a single thing called "intelligence" actually exists?
- How did the original purpose of intelligence testing change when IQ tests came to America?
- Why hasn't it been possible to design intelligence tests that are free of cultural influence?

Measuring Intelligence: The Psychometric Approach

Intelligent people disagree on just what intelligence is. Some equate it with the ability to reason abstractly, others with the ability to learn and profit from experience in daily life. Some emphasize the ability to think rationally, others the ability to act purposefully. These qualities are all probably part of what most people mean by **intelligence**, but theorists weigh them differently.

intelligence An inferred characteristic of an individual, usually defined as the ability to profit from experience, acquire knowledge, think abstractly, act purposefully, or adapt to changes in the environment.

One of the longest-running debates in psychology is whether a global quality called "intelligence" even exists. A typical intelligence test asks you to do several things: provide a specific bit of information, notice similarities between objects, solve arithmetic problems, define words, fill in the missing parts of incomplete pictures, arrange

A psychologist gives a student an intelligence test.

pictures in a logical order, arrange blocks to resemble a design, assemble puzzles, use a coding scheme, or judge what behavior would be appropriate in a particular situation. Researchers use a statistical method called **factor analysis** to try to identify which basic abilities underlie performance on the various items. This procedure identifies clusters of correlated items that seem to be measuring some common ability, or factor. Most scientists believe that a general ability, or **g factor**, underlies the specific abilities and talents measured by intelligence tests (Gottfredson, 2002; Jensen, 1998; Lubinski, 2004; Spearman, 1927; Wechsler, 1955). But others dispute the existence of a g factor, maintaining that a person can excel in some tasks yet do poorly in others (Gould, 1994; Guilford, 1988). Disagreements over how to define intelligence have led some writers to argue, only half jokingly, that intelligence is "whatever intelligence tests measure."

The traditional approach to intelligence, the **psychometric** approach, focuses on how well people perform on standardized aptitude tests, which are designed to measure the ability to acquire skills and knowledge.

The Invention of IQ Tests

The first widely used intelligence test was devised in 1904, when the French Ministry of Education asked psychologist Alfred Binet (1857–1911) to find a way to identify children who were slow learners so they could be given remedial work. The ministry was reluctant to let teachers identify such children because the teachers might have prejudices about poor children or might assume that shy or disruptive children were mentally impaired. The government wanted a more objective approach.

Binet's Brainstorm. Wrestling with the problem, Binet had a great insight: In the classroom, the responses of "dull" children resembled those of ordinary children of younger ages. Bright children, on the other hand, responded like children of older ages. The thing to measure, then, was a child's **mental age (MA)**, or level of intellectual development relative to that of other children. Then instruction could be tailored to the child's capabilities.

The test devised by Binet and his colleague, Théodore Simon, measured memory, vocabulary, and perceptual discrimination. Items ranged from those that most young children could do easily to those that only older children could handle, as determined by the testing of large numbers of children. A scoring system developed later by others used a formula in which the child's mental age was divided by the child's chronological age to yield an **intelligence quotient**, or **IQ** (a quotient is the result of division). Thus a child of 8 who performed like the average 10-year-old would have a mental age of 10 and an IQ of 125 (10 divided by 8, times 100). All average children, regardless of age, would have an IQ of 100 because mental age and chronological age would be the same.

This method of figuring IQ had serious flaws, however. At one age, scores might cluster tightly around the average, whereas at another age they might be more dispersed. As a result, the score necessary to be in the top 10 or 20 or 30 percent of your age group varied, depending on your age. Also, the IQ formula did not make sense for adults; a 50-year-old who scores like a 30-year-old does not have low intelligence! Today, therefore, intelligence tests are scored differently. The average is usually set arbitrarily at 100, and tests are constructed so that about two-thirds of all people score

factor analysis A statistical method for analyzing the intercorrelations among various measures or test scores; clusters of measures or scores that are highly correlated are assumed to measure the same underlying trait, ability, or aptitude (factor).

g factor A general intellectual ability assumed by many theorists to underlie specific mental abilities and talents.

psychometrics The measurement of mental abilities, traits, and processes.

mental age (MA) A measure of mental development expressed in terms of the average mental ability at a given age.

intelligence quotient (IQ) A measure of intelligence originally computed by dividing a person's mental age by his or her chronological age and multiplying by 100; it is now derived from norms provided for standardized intelligence tests.

between 85 and 115. Individual scores are computed from tables based on established norms. These scores are still informally referred to as IQs, and they still reflect how a person compares with other people, either children of a particular age or adults in general. At all ages, the distribution of scores approximates a normal (bell-shaped) curve, with scores near the average (mean) more common than high or low scores (see Figure 9.3).

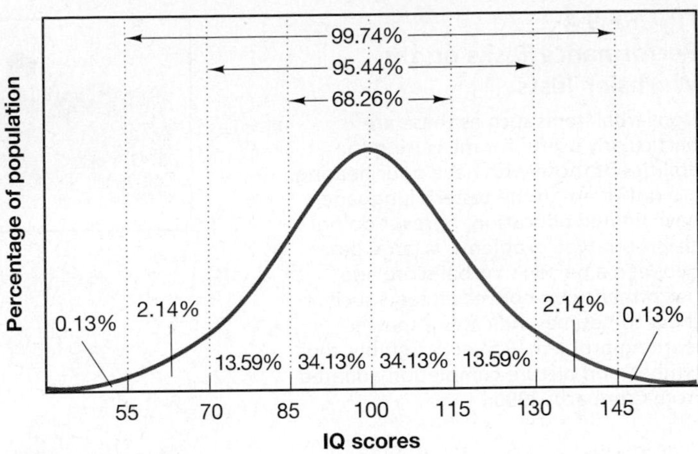

FIGURE 9.3 Expected Distribution of IQ Scores
In a large population, IQ scores tend to be distributed on a normal (bell-shaped) curve. On most tests, about 68 percent of, all people will score between 85 and 115; about 95 percent will score between 70 and 130, and about 99.7 percent will score between 55 and 145. In any actual sample, however, the distribution will depart somewhat from the theoretical ideal.

The IQ Test Comes to America. In the United States, Stanford psychologist Lewis Terman revised Binet's test and established norms for American children. His version, the *Stanford–Binet Intelligence Scale*, was first published in 1916 and has been updated several times since. The test asks a person to perform a variety of tasks—for example, to fill in missing words in sentences, answer questions requiring general knowledge, predict how a folded paper will look when unfolded, measure a quantity of water using two containers of different sizes, and distinguish between concepts that are similar but not exactly the same (such as, say, vigor and energy). The older the test taker is, the more the test requires in the way of verbal comprehension and fluency, spatial ability, and reasoning.

Two decades later, David Wechsler designed another test expressly for adults, which became the *Wechsler Adult Intelligence Scale (WAIS)*; it was followed by the *Wechsler Intelligence Scale for Children (WISC)*. Although the Wechsler tests produced a general IQ score, they also provided specific scores for different kinds of ability. Verbal items tested vocabulary, arithmetic abilities, immediate memory span, ability to recognize similarities (e.g., "How are books and movies alike?"), and general knowledge and comprehension (e.g., "Who was Thomas Jefferson?" "Why do people who want a divorce have to go to court?"). Performance items tested nonverbal skills, such as the ability to re-create a block design within a specified time limit and to identify a part missing from a picture. The current versions of the Wechsler tests have more subtests and, in addition to an overall IQ score, yield four separate scores: for verbal comprehension, perceptual reasoning, working memory (the ability to hold information in mind so it can be used), and processing speed. (See Figure 9.4 for some sample items.)

Binet had emphasized that his test merely *sampled* intelligence and did not measure everything covered by that term. A test score, he said, could be useful, along with other information, for predicting school performance, but it should not be confused with intelligence itself. The tests were designed to be given individually, so that the test-giver could tell when a child was ill or nervous, had poor vision, or was unmotivated. The purpose was to identify children with learning problems, not to rank all children. But when intelligence testing was brought from France to the United States, its original purpose got lost at sea. In America, IQ tests became widely used not to bring slow learners up to the average, but to categorize people in school and in the armed services according to their presumed "natural ability." The testers overlooked the fact that in America, with its many ethnic groups, people did not all share the same background and experience (Gould, 1996).

FIGURE 9.4
Performance Tasks on the Wechsler Tests

Nonverbal items such as these are particularly useful for measuring the abilities of those who have poor hearing, are not fluent in the tester's language, have limited education, or resist doing classroom-type problems. A large gap between a person's verbal score and performance on nonverbal tasks such as these sometimes indicates a specific learning problem. (Object assembly, digit symbol, and picture completion adapted from Cronbach, 1990.)

Picture arrangement
(Arrange the panels to make a meaningful story)

Object assembly
(Put together a jigsaw puzzle)

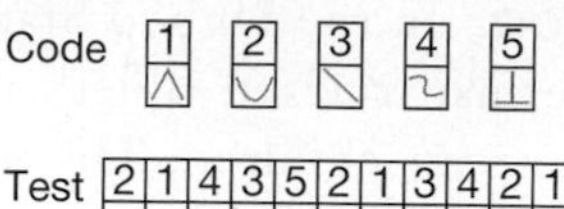

Digit symbol
(Using the key at the top, fill in the appropriate symbol beneath each number)

Picture completion
(Supply the missing feature)

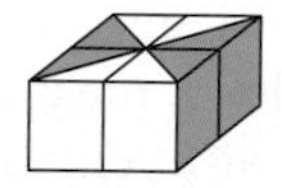

Block design
(Copy the design shown, using another set of blocks)

Culture and Testing

THINKING CRITICALLY

CONSIDER OTHER INTERPRETATIONS

When tests find IQ differences between groups of children from different cultures, many people assume that the children who score lower are inherently less intelligent. What other explanations are possible?

Intelligence tests developed between World War I and the 1960s for use in schools favored city children over rural ones, middle-class children over poor ones, and white children over nonwhite children. One item, for example, asked whether the Emperor Concerto was written by Beethoven, Mozart, Bach, Brahms, or Mahler. (The answer is Beethoven.) Critics complained that the tests did not measure the kinds of knowledge and skills that indicate intelligent behavior in a minority neighborhood or in the hills of Appalachia. They feared that because teachers thought IQ scores revealed the limits of a child's potential, low-scoring children would not get the educational attention or encouragement they needed.

Test-makers responded by trying to construct tests that were unaffected by culture or that incorporated knowledge and skills common to many different cultures. But these efforts were disappointing. One reason was that cultures differ in the problem-solving strategies they emphasize (Serpell, 1994). In the West, white, middle-class children typically learn to classify things by category—to say that an apple and a peach are similar because they are both fruits, and that a saw and a rake are similar because they are both tools. But children who are not trained in middle-class ways of sorting things may classify objects according to their sensory qualities or functions. For example, they may say that an apple and a peach are similar because they taste good. We think that's a charming and innovative answer, but it is one that test-givers interpret as less intelligent (Miller-Jones, 1989).

Testing experts also discovered that cultural values and experiences affect many things besides responses to specific test items. These include a person's general attitude toward exams, comfort in the settings required for testing, motivation, rapport with the test-giver, competitiveness, comfort in solving problems independently rather than with others, and familiarity with the conventions for taking tests (Anastasi & Urbina, 1997; López, 1995; Sternberg, 2004).

stereotype threat A burden of doubt a person feels about his or her performance, due to negative stereotypes about his or her group's abilities.

Moreover, people's performance on IQ and other mental-ability tests depends on their own expectations about how they will do, and those expectations are shaped in part by cultural stereotypes. Stereotypes that portray women or members of certain ethnic, age, or socioeconomic groups as unintelligent can actually depress the performance of people in these groups. You might think that a woman would say, "So sexists think women are dumb at math? I'll show them!" or that an African-American would say, "So racists believe that blacks aren't as smart as whites? Just give me that exam." But often that is not what happens.

On the contrary, such individuals commonly feel a burden of doubt about their abilities that Claude Steele (1992, 1997) has labeled **stereotype threat**. The threat occurs when people believe that if they do not do well, they will confirm the stereotypes about their group. Their anxiety may then worsen their performance. Negative thoughts may intrude and disrupt their concentration ("I hate this test," "I'm no good at math") (Cadinu et al., 2005). Or they may cope by "disidentifying" with the test, telling themselves, in effect, "The outcome of this test has no bearing on how I feel about myself" (Major et al., 1998). As a result, they may not be motivated to do well:

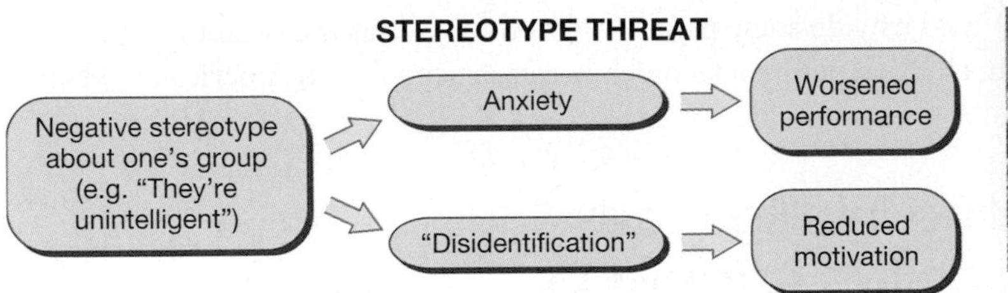

More than 100 studies have shown that stereotype threat can affect the test performance of many African-Americans, Latinos, low-income people, women, and elderly people, all of whom perform better when they are not feeling self-conscious about themselves as members of negatively stereotyped groups (Aronson & Salinas, 1997; Brown & Josephs, 1999; Croizen & Claire, 1998; Inzlicht & Ben-Zeev, 2000; Levy, 1996; Quinn & Spencer, 2001; Steele & Aronson, 1995). Anything that increases the salience of group stereotypes can increase stereotype threat and affect performance, including taking the test in a setting where you are the only member from your group, or being asked to state your race before taking the test. The media and even some scholars have sometimes misinterpreted these results to mean that stereotype threat is the sole reason for group differences in test performance, which it is not (Sackett, Harison, & Cullen, 2004). It is, however, an important contributing factor.

What can be done to reduce stereotype threat? One possibility is simply to tell people about it. When students taking introductory statistics were given a difficult test, with no mention of stereotype threat, women did worse than men. But when students were informed about stereotype threat, the sex difference disappeared (Johns, Schmader, & Martens, 2005). (See how psychology can help people?)

This simple approach is unlikely to eliminate all group differences in test scores, however. And that fact points to a dilemma at the heart of intelligence and mental-ability testing. Intelligence and other mental-ability tests put some groups of people at a disadvantage, yet they also measure skills and knowledge useful in the classroom. How can psychologists and educators recognize and accept cultural differences and, at the same time, promote the mastery of the skills, knowledge, and attitudes that can help people succeed in school and in the larger society?

QUICK quiz

What's your Quiz Quotient (QQ)?

1. What was Binet's great insight?
2. *True or false:* IQ tests designed to avoid cultural bias have failed to eliminate average group differences in IQ scores.
3. Hilda, who is 66, is about to take an IQ test, but she is worried because she knows that older people are often assumed to have diminished mental abilities. Hilda is being affected by ___________.

Answers:

1. Mental age does not necessarily correspond to chronological age. 2. true 3. stereotype threat

WHAT'S AHEAD

- What kind of intelligence allows you to master the unspoken rules for academic success?
- What is "EQ" and why do some psychologists think it is as important as IQ?
- Why do Asian children perform so much better in school than American students do?

Dissecting Intelligence: The Cognitive Approach

Critics of standard intelligence tests point out that such tests tell us little about *how* a person goes about answering questions and solving problems. Nor do the tests explain why people with low scores often behave intelligently in real life—making smart consumer decisions, winning at the racetrack, and making wise choices in their relationships instead of repeating the same dumb patterns. Some researchers, therefore, have rejected the psychometric approach to the study and measurement of intelligence and mental abilities in favor of a cognitive approach. Thinking critically, cognitive psychologists have questioned prevailing assumptions about the very meaning of intelligence and the best way to measure it. In contrast to the psychometric approach, which is concerned with how many answers a person gets right on a test, the *cognitive approach* assumes there are many kinds of intelligence and emphasizes the strategies people use when thinking about a problem and arriving at a solution.

Psychologists who take this approach reject the emphasis on a g factor in research on intelligence. The g factor, in their view, may simply reflect the fact that a variety of different abilities are taught in Western schools and emphasized in Western societies. In countries like Kenya, where children are taught how to succeed in a trade but often not much else, a g factor is less likely to emerge from the children's test scores (Sternberg, 2004).

The Triarchic Theory

triarchic [try-ARE-kick] theory of intelligence A theory of intelligence that emphasizes information-processing strategies, the ability to creatively transfer skills to new situations, and the practical application of intelligence.

One well-known cognitive theory is Robert Sternberg's **triarchic theory of intelligence** (1988) (*triarchic* means "three-part"). Sternberg (2004) defines intelligence as "the skills and knowledge needed for success in life, according to one's own definition of success, within one's sociocultural context." He distinguishes three aspects of intelligence:

1 **Componential intelligence** refers to the information-processing strategies you draw on when you are thinking intelligently about a problem. These mental "components" include recognizing and defining the problem, selecting a strategy for solving it, mastering and carrying out the strategy, and evaluating the result. Such components are required in every culture but are applied to different kinds of problems. One culture may emphasize the use of these components to solve abstract problems, whereas another may emphasize using the same components to maintain smooth relationships.

metacognition The knowledge or awareness of one's own cognitive processes.

Some of the operations in componential intelligence require not only analytic skills but also **metacognition**, the knowledge or awareness of your own cognitive processes and the ability to monitor and control those processes. Metacognitive skills help you learn. Students who are weak in metacognition fail to notice when a passage in a textbook is difficult, and they do not always realize that they haven't understood what they've been reading. As a result, they spend too little time on difficult material and too much time on material they already know (Nelson & Leonesio, 1988). In contrast, students who are strong in metacognition check their comprehension by restating what they have read, backtracking when necessary, and questioning what they are reading, so they learn better (Bereiter & Bird, 1985).

It works in the other direction, too: The kind of intelligence that enhances academic performance can also help you develop metacognitive skills. Students with poor academic skills typically fail to realize how little they know; they think they're doing fine (Dunning, 2005). The very weaknesses that keep them from doing well on tests or in their courses also keep them from realizing their weaknesses. In one study, students in a psychology course estimated how well they had just done on an exam relative to other students. As you can see in Figure 9.5, those who had performed in the bottom quartile greatly overestimated their own performance (Dunning et al., 2003). In contrast, people with strong academic skills tend to be more realistic. Often they even underestimate slightly how their performance compares with the performance of others.

2 **Experiential or creative intelligence** refers to your creativity in transferring skills to new situations. People with experiential intelligence cope well with novelty and learn quickly to make new tasks automatic. Those who are lacking in this area perform well only under a narrow set of circumstances. For example, a student may do well in school, where assignments have specific due dates and feedback is immediate, but be less successful after graduation if her job requires her to set her own deadlines and her employer doesn't tell her how she is doing.

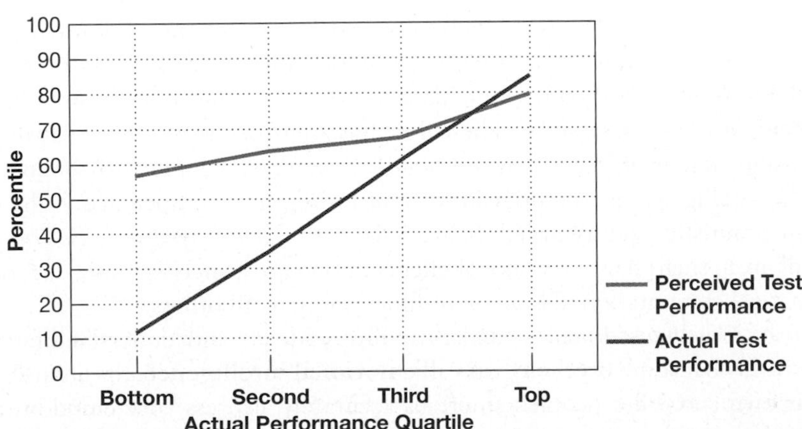

FIGURE 9.5 Ignorance Is Bliss

In school and in other settings as well, people who perform poorly often have poor metacognitive skills and therefore fail to recognize their own lack of competence. As you can see, the lower students' scores were on an exam, the greater the gap between how they thought they had done and how they actually had done (Dunning et al., 2003).

GET INVOLVED!

➤ARE YOU A SAVVY STUDENT?

How good is your tacit knowledge about how to be a student? List as many strategies for success as you can. Consider what the successful student does when listening to lectures, participating in class discussions, communicating with instructors, preparing for exams, writing term papers, and dealing with an unexpectedly low grade. Many of these strategies are never explicitly taught. You may want to do this exercise with a friend and compare lists. Are there some strategies that one of you thought of and the other did not?

"You're wise, but you lack tree smarts."

3 **Contextual or practical intelligence** refers to the practical application of intelligence, which requires you to take into account the different contexts in which you find yourself. If you are strong in contextual intelligence, you know when to adapt to the environment (you are in a dangerous neighborhood, so you become more vigilant). You know when to change environments (you had planned to be a teacher but discover that you dislike working with kids, so you switch to accounting). And you know when to fix the situation (your marriage is rocky, so you and your spouse go for counseling).

Contextual knowledge allows you to acquire **tacit knowledge**—practical, action-oriented strategies for achieving your goals that usually are not formally taught or even verbalized but must instead be inferred by observing others (Sternberg et al., 1995). In studies of college professors, business managers, and salespeople, tacit knowledge and practical intelligence are strong predictors of effectiveness on the job (Sternberg et al., 2000). In college students, tacit knowledge about how to be a good student actually predicts academic success as well as entrance exams do (Sternberg & Wagner, 1989).

Domains of Intelligence

Other psychologists, too, are expanding our understanding of what it means to be intelligent. They point out that someone who is intelligent in one area, or domain, is not necessarily intelligent in all others. A Nobel Prize winner in medicine may be helpless when it comes to making up a budget or resolving personal dilemmas; a physicist who is cautious in his own field may uncritically accept pop-psych claims.

Howard Gardner (1983, 1995) has proposed that the domains of intelligence be expanded to include musical aptitude, kinesthetic intelligence (the bodily grace and physical self-awareness of athletes and dancers), and the capacity for insight into oneself, others, or the natural world. These domains, Gardner argues, are relatively independent and may even have separate neural structures. People with brain damage often lose intelligence in one domain without losing their competence in the others. And some autistic and retarded individuals with *savant syndrome* (*savant* means "learned" in French) have exceptional talents in one area, such as music, art, or rapid mathematical computation, despite poor functioning in all others.

Two of Gardner's domains, understanding yourself and understanding others, overlap with what some psychologists call **emotional intelligence**, the ability to identify your own and other people's emotions accurately, express your emotions clearly, and manage emotions in yourself and others (Mayer & Salovey, 1997; Salovey & Gre-

tacit knowledge Strategies for success that are not explicitly taught but that instead must be inferred.

emotional intelligence The ability to identify your own and other people's emotions accurately, express your emotions clearly, and regulate emotions in yourself and others.

wal, 2005). People with high emotional intelligence, popularly known as "EQ," use their emotions to motivate themselves, to spur creative thinking, and to deal empathically with others. People who are lacking in emotional intelligence are often unable to identify their own emotions; they may insist that they are not depressed when a relationship ends, for example, but meanwhile they start drinking too much, become extremely irritable, and stop going out with friends. They may express emotions inappropriately, say by acting violently or impulsively when they are angry or worried. And often they misread nonverbal signals from others; they will give a long-winded account of all their problems even when the listener is obviously bored.

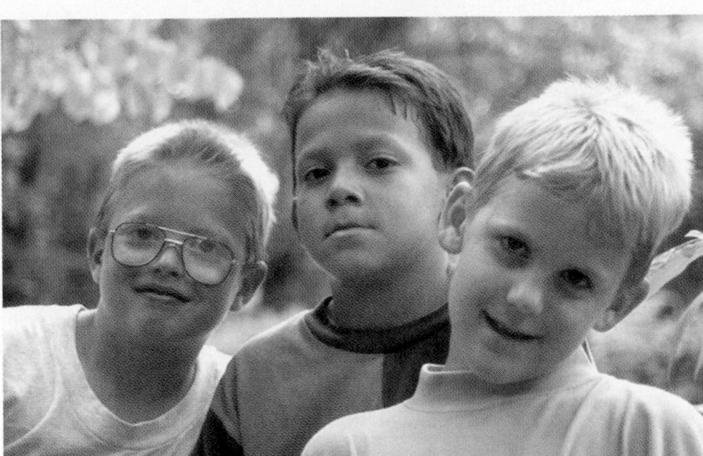

People with emotional intelligence are skilled at reading nonverbal emotional cues. Which of these boys do you think feels the most confident and relaxed, which one is shyest, and which feels most anxious? What cues are you using to answer?

Studies of brain-damaged adults suggest a biological basis for emotional intelligence. Neuroscientist Antonio Damasio (1994) has studied patients with prefrontal-lobe damage that makes them incapable of experiencing strong feelings. Although they score in the normal range on conventional mental tests, these patients persistently make "dumb," irrational decisions in their lives because they cannot assign values to different options based on their own emotional reactions and cannot read emotional cues from others. As we will see again in Chapter 11, feeling and thinking are not always incompatible, as many people assume; in fact, one requires the other.

Thinking Critically About Intelligence(s)

Not everyone is enthusiastic about the proliferation of new "intelligences." Some argue that emotional intelligence is not a special cognitive ability but a collection of personality traits, such as empathy and extroversion, and that nothing is gained by giving it a trendy name (Davies, Stankov, & Roberts, 1998; Matthews, Zeidner, & Roberts, 2003). Others maintain that abilities such as Gardner's musical and kinesthetic intelligences are better thought of as talents, or else the very concept of intelligence

THINKING CRITICALLY

DEFINE YOUR TERMS

Some theorists who argue for an expanded definition of intelligence would say that the Dixie Chicks have musical intelligence, a surveyor has spatial intelligence, and a compassionate friend has emotional intelligence. Should the definition be broadened in this way? Or are these abilities better defined as talents?

REVIEW 9.1

The Psychometric and Cognitive Approaches to Intelligence, Compared

	Psychometric	Cognitive
Main focus	How well people perform on standardized tests	Strategies people use when solving problems
What intelligence is	A general intellectual ability captured by IQ scores; or a range of specific verbal and nonverbal abilities	Many different skills and talents in addition to intellectual ones
Deals with emotional intelligence?	No	Yes
Deals with practical intelligence?	No	Yes
Uses well-validated standardized tests?	Yes	Tests currently being developed

loses all meaning. What is to prevent someone from adding "handicraft intelligence" or "financial intelligence" or "farming intelligence"?

Those who believe that there is a general factor in intelligence can marshal a century of research to support their view (Lubinski, 2004). Tests of *g* do a better job than measures of personality or specific aptitudes at predicting not only academic achievement but also the cognitive complexity of people's jobs and their occupational success (Kuncel, Hezlett, & Ones, 2004; Schmidt & Hunter, 2004). One longitudinal study followed pairs of brothers who had been reared in the same household but differed in their scores on tests of general intelligence. One brother in each pair had an IQ in the average range (90 to 110) and the other had scored above or below that range. In this sample, in which socioeconomic background was the same for each pair of siblings, IQ strongly predicted which brother finished college, which one earned more money, and which one wound up in a more prestigious occupation (Murray, 1998).

Nonetheless, broadening the notion of intelligence has been extremely useful for several reasons. It has forced us to think more critically about what we mean by intelligence and to consider how different kinds of "smarts" help us function in our everyday lives. It has generated research on tests that provide ongoing feedback to the test-taker so that the person can learn from the experience and improve his or her performance (Sternberg, 2004). The cognitive approach has also led to a focus on teaching children strategies for improving their abilities in reading, writing, doing homework, and taking tests. For example, children have been taught to manage their time so they don't procrastinate and to study differently for multiple-choice exams than for essay exams (Sternberg et al., 1995). Most important, new approaches to intelligence encourage us to overcome the mental set of assuming that the only kind of intelligence necessary for a successful life is the kind captured by IQ tests.

For a summary of the differences between the psychometric and cognitive approaches, see Review 9.1.

Motivation, Hard Work, and Intellectual Success

Even with a high IQ, emotional intelligence, and practical know-how, you still might get nowhere at all. Talent, unlike cream, does not inevitably rise to the top; success also depends on drive and determination.

Consider a finding from one of the longest-running psychological studies ever conducted. In 1921, researchers began following more than 1,500 children with IQ scores in the top 1 percent of the distribution. These boys and girls were nicknamed

Termites after Lewis Terman, who originally directed the research. The Termites started out bright, physically healthy, sociable, and well adjusted. As they entered adulthood, most became successful in the traditional ways of the times: men in careers and women as homemakers (Sears & Barbee, 1977; Terman & Oden, 1959). However, some gifted men failed to live up to their early promise, dropping out of school or drifting into low-level work. When the researchers compared the 100 most successful men in the Terman study with the 100 least successful, they found that motivation made the difference. The successful men were ambitious, were socially active, had many interests, and were encouraged by their parents. The least successful drifted casually through life. There was no average difference in IQ between the two groups.

CLOSE-UP on Research

GRADES, IQ, AND SELF-DISCIPLINE

Once you are motivated to succeed intellectually, you need self-discipline to reach your goals. Yet there has been remarkably little research on this important trait. For every ten scholarly psychological articles on academic achievement and intelligence, there is only one article on academic achievement and self-discipline.

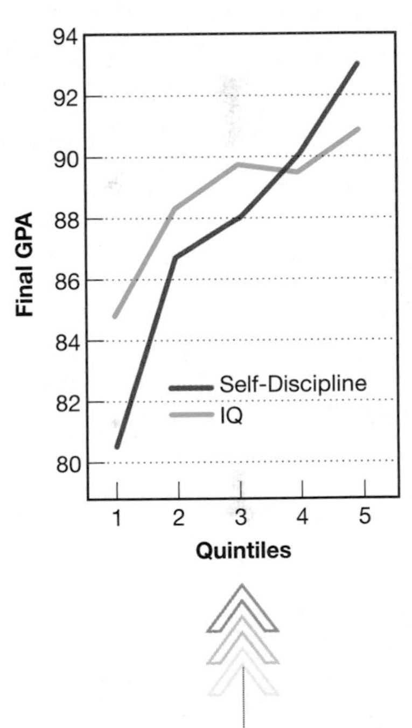

This fact prompted Angela Duckworth and Martin Seligman (2005) to **ask an intriguing question**: Which is a better predictor of academic performance among adolescents, IQ or self-discipline? To answer it, they conducted a longitudinal study of ethnically diverse eighth graders attending a magnet school. At the beginning of the semester, they assigned each student a self-discipline score based on a broad range of measures, including self-reports, parents' reports, teachers' reports, and questionnaires. They added a behavioral measure of self-discipline, too: the teenagers' ability to delay gratification. The teens had to choose between taking an envelope containing a dollar or returning it in exchange for getting two dollars a week later. To measure IQ, the researchers used a standard intelligence test. To measure academic performance, they used grades, achievement-test scores, attendance, and selection into a competitive high-school program in the spring semester.

Examining the evidence, the researchers found that self-discipline accounted for more than twice as much of the variance in final grades as IQ did. Compared with their more impulsive classmates, students with strong self-discipline earned higher final grades and achievement-test scores and were more likely to gain admission to the competitive high-school program. As the accompanying graph shows, when the researchers divided the students into five groups (quintiles) based on their IQ scores, final grade point average varied much more steeply as a function of self-discipline than of IQ. That is, overall, correlations between self-discipline and academic performance were much stronger than those between IQ and academic performance. The researchers concluded that "self-discipline has a bigger effect on academic performance than does intellectual talents."

The researchers went on to **consider other interpretations** of the findings, interpretations based on statistical arguments. One was that because the participants attended a school that based admission on their past academic success, and because academic success and self-discipline are highly correlated, the results might not apply to the general population of students, which is more diverse. The researchers therefore plan to continue their research with more representative

samples. They believe, however, that underachievement among American students occurs not because the kids lack academic ability but because they don't use it. A failure to exercise self-discipline, the researchers suggest, may be due to American society's emphasis on instant gratification. They therefore argue that "programs that build self-discipline may be the royal road to building academic achievement."

Self-discipline and motivation to work hard at intellectual tasks depend in turn on your attitudes about intelligence and achievement, which are strongly influenced by cultural values. For many years, Harold Stevenson and his colleagues studied attitudes toward achievement in Asia and the United States, comparing large samples of grade-school children, parents, and teachers in Minneapolis, Chicago, Sendai (Japan), Taipei (Taiwan), and Beijing (Stevenson, Chen, & Lee, 1993; Stevenson & Stigler, 1992). Their results have much to teach us about the cultivation of intellect.

In 1980, the Asian children far outperformed the American children on a broad battery of mathematical and reading tests. On computations and word problems, there was virtually no overlap between schools, with the lowest-scoring Beijing schools doing better than the highest-scoring Chicago schools. (A similar gap occurred in reading scores.) By 1990, the gulf between the Asian and American children had grown even greater. Only 4 percent of the Chinese children and 10 percent of the Japanese children had math scores as low as those of the *average* American child. These differences could not be accounted for by educational resources: The Chinese had worse facilities and larger classes than the Americans, and on average, the Chinese parents were poorer and less educated than the American parents. Nor did it have anything to do with intellectual abilities in general; the American children were just as knowledgeable and capable as the Asian children on tests of general information.

But this research found that Asians and Americans are worlds apart in their attitudes, expectations, and efforts:

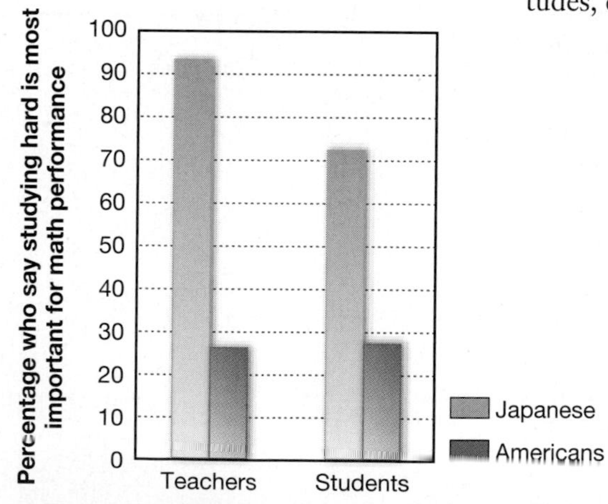

FIGURE 9.6 What's the Secret of Math Success?

Japanese schoolteachers and students are much more likely than their American counterparts to believe that the secret to doing well in math is working hard. Americans tend to think that you either have mathematical intelligence or you don't.

- ***Beliefs about intelligence.*** American parents, teachers, and children are far more likely than Asians to believe that mathematical ability is innate (see Figure 9.6). Americans tend to think that if you have this ability you don't have to work hard, and if you don't have it, there's no point in trying.
- ***Standards.*** American parents have far lower standards for their children's performance; they are satisfied with scores barely above average on a 100-point test. In contrast, Chinese and Japanese parents are happy only with very high scores.
- ***Values.*** American students do not value education as much as Asian students do, and they are more complacent about mediocre work. When asked what they would wish for if a wizard could give them anything they wanted, more than 60 percent of the Chinese fifth graders named something related to their education. Can you guess what the American children wanted? A majority said money or possessions.

When it comes to intellect, then, it's not just what you've got that counts, but what you do with it. Complacency, fatalism, low standards, and a desire for immediate gratification can prevent people from recognizing what they don't know and reduce their efforts to learn.

QUICK quiz

We hope you're not feeling complacent about your quiz performance.

1. What goals do cognitive theories of intelligence have that psychometric theories do not?
2. Logan understands the material in his statistics class, but on tests he spends the entire period on the most difficult problems and never even gets to the problems he can solve easily. According to the triarchic theory of intelligence, which aspect of intelligence does he need to improve?
3. Tracy does not have an unusually high IQ, but at work she is quickly promoted because she knows how to set priorities, communicate with management, and make others feel valued. Tracy has ___________ knowledge about how to succeed on the job.
4. According to a recent study of eighth graders, ___________ is more strongly correlated with school performance than ___________ is.

5. What is wrong with defining intelligence as "whatever intelligence tests measure"?

Answers:

1. to understand people's strategies for solving problems and use this information to improve mental performance **2.** componential intelligence (which includes metacognition) **3.** tacit **4.** self-discipline, IQ **5.** This definition implies that a low score must be entirely the scorer's fault rather than the fault of the test. But the test-taker may be intelligent in ways that the test fails to measure, and the test may be measuring traits other than intelligence.

WHAT'S AHEAD

- Why do some researchers think that animals can think?
- People love to talk to their pets; can their pets learn to talk back?

Animal Minds

A green heron swipes some bread from a picnicker's table and scatters the crumbs on a nearby stream. When a minnow rises to the bait, the heron strikes, swallowing its prey before you can say "dinner time." A sea otter, floating calmly on its back, bangs a mussel shell against a stone that is resting on its stomach. When the shell cracks apart, the otter devours the tasty morsel inside, tucks the stone under its flipper, and dives for another shell, which it will open in the same way. Incidents such as these have convinced some biologists, psychologists, and ethologists that we are not the only animals with cognitive abilities—that "dumb beasts" are not so dumb after all. But how smart are they?

How smart is this otter?

Animal Intelligence

In the 1920s, Wolfgang Köhler (1925) put chimpanzees in situations in which some tempting bananas were just out of reach and watched to see what the apes would do. Most did nothing, but a few turned out to be quite clever. If the bananas were outside the cage, the animal might pull them in with a stick. If they were hanging overhead, and there were boxes in the cage, the chimpanzee might pile up the boxes and climb on top of them to reach the fruit. Often the solution came after the animal had been sitting quietly for a while. It appeared as though the chimp had been thinking about the problem and was struck by a sudden insight.

Learning theorists felt that this seemingly impressive behavior could be accounted for perfectly well by the standard principles of operant learning, without

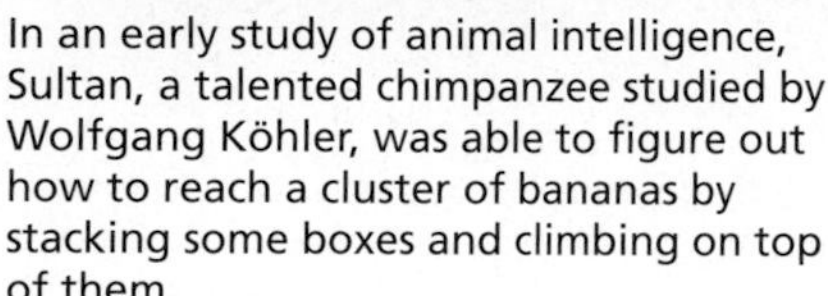

In an early study of animal intelligence, Sultan, a talented chimpanzee studied by Wolfgang Köhler, was able to figure out how to reach a cluster of bananas by stacking some boxes and climbing on top of them.

resorting to mental explanations (see Chapter 7). Because of their influence, for years any scientist who claimed that animals could think was likely to be ignored or laughed at. Today, however, the study of animal intelligence is enjoying a resurgence, especially in the interdisciplinary field of **cognitive ethology**. (Ethology is the study of animal behavior, especially in natural environments.) Cognitive ethologists argue that some animals can anticipate future events, make plans, and coordinate their activities with those of their comrades (Griffin, 2001).

When we think about animal cognition, we must be careful, because even complex behavior that appears to be purposeful can be genetically prewired and automatic (Wynne, 2004). The assassin bug of South America catches termites by gluing nest material on its back as camouflage, but it is hard to imagine how the bug's tiny dab of brain tissue could enable it to plan this strategy consciously. Moreover, an animal could be aware of its environment and know some things without knowing that it knows and without being able to think about its own thoughts as human beings do. In short, an animal might have cognition but not metacognition (Budiansky, 1998; Hauser, 2000).

Yet explanations of animal behavior that leave out any sort of consciousness at all and that attribute animals' actions entirely to instinct do not seem to account for some of the amazing things that animals can do. Like the otter that uses a stone to crack mussel shells, many animals use objects in the natural environment as rudimentary tools, and in some nonhuman primates the behavior is learned. For example, chimpanzee mothers occasionally show their young how to use stones to open hard nuts (Boesch, 1991). Orangutans in one particular Sumatran swamp have learned to use sticks as tools, held in their mouths, to pry insects from holes in tree trunks and to get seeds out of cracks in a bulblike fruit, whereas nearby groups of orangutans use only brute force to get to the delicacies (van Schaik, 2006). Even some nonprimates may have the capacity to learn to use tools, although the evidence remains controversial among ethologists. Female bottlenose dolphins off the coast of Australia attach sea sponges to their beaks while hunting for food, which protects them from sharp coral and stinging stonefish, and they seem to have acquired this unusual skill from their mothers (Krützen et al., 2005). Is this yet another case of mothers telling their daughters what to wear?

cognitive ethology The study of cognitive processes in nonhuman animals.

In the laboratory, nonhuman primates have accomplished even more surprising things. For example, dozens of studies have found that chimpanzees have a rudimentary sense of number. In one study, chimpanzees compared two pairs of food wells containing chocolate chips. One pair might contain, say, 5 chips and 3 chips, the other 4 chips and 3 chips. Allowed to choose which pair they wanted, the chimps almost always chose the one with the higher combined total, showing some sort of summing ability (Rumbaugh, Savage-Rumbaugh, & Pate, 1988). Chimpanzees can even remember over a period of 20 minutes which of two containers holds more bananas (e.g., 5 versus 8, or 6 versus 10), after watching the bananas being placed one at a time into the containers. In fact, they do as well as young children on this task (Beran & Beran, 2004).

Dodger, a 2-year-old dolphin In Shark Bay, Australia, carries a sea sponge on her sensitive beak, apparently as protection against stinging creatures and sharp coral. Recent evidence suggests that dolphin "sponge moms" teach the behavior to their daughters.

One of the most controversial questions about animal cognition is whether any animals besides human beings have a **theory of mind**: a system of beliefs about the way one's own mind and the minds of others work, and an understanding of how thoughts and feelings affect behavior. A theory of mind enables you to draw conclusions about the intentions, feelings, and beliefs of others; empathize with others ("What would I experience if I were in the other person's position?"); deceive others; recognize when someone else is lying; recognize yourself in a mirror; and know when others can or cannot see you. In human beings, a theory of mind starts to develop in the second year and is clearly present by about age 3 or 4 (see Chapter 14).

Some researchers believe that the great apes—chimpanzees, gorillas, and orangutans—and possibly dolphins and elephants, as well, have at least some abilities that depend on a theory of mind (de Waal, 2001a; Plotnik, de Waal, & Reiss, 2006; Suddendorf & Whiten, 2001). When looking in a mirror, these animals may try to find marks on their bodies that are not directly visible, suggesting self-recognition (or at least bodily awareness). In addition, chimpanzees console other chimps who are in distress, use deceptive tactics when competing for food, and point to draw attention to objects, suggesting that they are able to grasp what is going on in another chimp's mind. In the wild, when one male African chimp makes an exaggerated scratching movement on part of its body during social grooming—say, on the forehead—a comrade will then groom the indicated spot, even if he was already grooming some other spot (Pika & Mitani, 2006).

theory of mind A system of beliefs about the way one's own mind and the minds of others work, and of how individuals are affected by their beliefs and feelings.

Animals and Language

A primary ingredient of human cognition is *language*, the ability to combine elements that are themselves meaningless into an infinite number of utterances that convey meaning. Language is often regarded as the last bastion of human uniqueness, a result of evolutionary forces that produced our species (see Chapter 3). Do animals have anything comparable? Many people have wished they could ask their pet what it's like to be a dog, or a cat, or a horse. If only animals could speak!

To qualify as a language, a communication system must meet certain criteria. It must use combinations of sounds, gestures, or symbols that are *meaningful*, not random. It must permit *displacement*, communication about objects and events that are not present here and now but rather are displaced in time or space; merely pointing to things is not language. And it must have a grammar (syntax) that permits *productivity*, the ability to produce and comprehend an infinite number of new utterances. By these criteria, no nonhuman species has its own language. Animals do communicate, of course, using gestures, body postures, facial expressions, vocalizations, and odors. And some of these signals have highly specific meanings. For example, vervet monkeys seem to have separate calls to warn about leopards versus eagles versus snakes (Cheney & Seyfarth, 1985). But

"It's always 'Sit,' 'Stay,' 'Heel'—never 'Think,' 'Innovate,' 'Be yourself.'"

vervets cannot combine these sounds to produce entirely novel utterances, as in "Look out, Harry, that eagle-eyed leopard is a real snake-in-the-grass."

Perhaps, however, some animals could acquire language if they got a little help from their human friends. Since the 1960s, many researchers have provided such help. Because the vocal tract of an ape does not permit speech, most researchers have used innovative approaches that rely on gestures or visual symbols. In one project, chimpanzees learned to use as words geometric plastic shapes arranged on a magnetic board (Premack & Premack, 1983). In another, they learned to punch symbols on a computer-monitored keyboard (Rumbaugh, 1977). In yet another, they learned hundreds of signs in American Sign Language (ASL) (Fouts & Rigby, 1977; Gardner & Gardner, 1969).

Animals in these studies learned to follow instructions, answer questions, and make requests. They even seemed to use their newfound skills to apologize for being disobedient, scold their trainers, and talk to themselves. Koko, a lowland gorilla, reportedly used signs to say that she felt happy or sad, to refer to past and future events, to mourn for her dead pet kitten, and even to lie when she did something naughty, (Patterson & Linden, 1981). Most important, the animals combined individual signs or symbols into longer utterances that they had never seen before.

Because the apes were lovable and the findings appealing, in early studies it was easy for emotional reasoning to prevail over critical thinking. In their desire to talk to the animals and their affection for their primate friends, some researchers overinterpreted the animals' utterances, reading all sorts of meanings and intentions into a single sign or symbol, and unwittingly giving nonverbal cues that might enable the apes to respond correctly. Further, to some observers, the animals appeared to be stringing signs and symbols together in no particular order instead of using grammatical rules to produce novel utterances. "Me eat banana" seemed to be no different for them than "Banana eat me."

THINKING CRITICALLY

AVOID EMOTIONAL REASONING

It's easy to love apes who use symbols to apologize or lie. But emotion can sometimes get in the way of objectivity. What does research show about the ability of animals to use language?

Over the past few decades, however, most researchers have greatly improved their procedures. They have shown that with careful training, chimps can indeed acquire the ability to use symbols to refer to objects. Some animals have also used signs spontaneously to converse with each other, suggesting that they are not merely imitating or trying to get a reward (Van Cantfort & Rimpau, 1982). Bonobos (a type of ape) are especially adept at language. One bonobo named Kanzi has learned to understand English words, short sentences, and keyboard symbols without formal training (Savage-Rumbaugh & Lewin, 1994; Savage-Rumbaugh, Shanker, & Taylor, 1998). Kanzi responds correctly to commands such as "Put the key in the refrigerator" and "Go get the ball that is outdoors," even when he has never heard the words combined in that particular way before. He picked up language as children do—by observing others using it and through normal social interaction. He has also learned, with training, to manipulate keyboard symbols to request favorite foods or activities (games, TV, visits to friends) and to announce his intentions.

Kanzi, a bonobo who answers questions and makes requests by punching symbols on a specially designed computer keyboard, also understands short English sentences. Kanzi is shown here with researcher Sue Savage-Rumbaugh.

You do not even have to be a primate to acquire some aspects of language. During the 1990s, Louis Herman and his colleagues taught dolphins to respond to requests made in two artificial languages,

one consisting of computer-generated whistles and another of hand and arm gestures (Herman, Kuczaj, & Holder, 1993; Herman & Morrel-Samuels, 1996). To interpret a request correctly, the dolphins had to take into account both the meaning of the individual symbols in a string of whistles or gestures and the order of the symbols (syntax). For example, they had to understand the difference between "To left Frisbee, right surfboard take" and "To right surfboard, left Frisbee take."

A few years ago, a 9-year-old border collie named Rico made the news when researchers in Germany reported that the dog appeared to have a vocabulary of more than 200 words (Kaminski, Call, & Fisher, 2004). When Rico's owner asked him to retrieve an object from another room, Rico could pick the correct object from a group of 10 items. Even more impressive, Rico, like a human child, could learn a new word in just one trial, something chimpanzees cannot do. If given the name of a new object, he could usually infer that his owner wanted him to select that object from among more familiar ones and would often remember the new label weeks later. But as far as we know (we've found no subsequent reports), Rico knows words only for fetchable things, like toys, balls, and socks, and has learned words only by playing the fetching game. And it's uncertain whether he understands that words refer to objects, rather than something you do with them ("Bring-the-sock") (Bloom, 2004). (One commentator observed that his dog knows 200 words too, but all of them mean "ball.")

In another fascinating project, Irene Pepperberg (2000, 2002) has been working since the late 1970s with an African gray parrot named Alex, teaching him to count, classify, and compare objects by vocalizing English words. Alex is no birdbrain, even though his brain is the size of a walnut; he shows evidence of both linguistic and cognitive ability. When he is shown up to six items and is asked how many there are, he responds with spoken (squawked?) English phrases, such as "two cork(s)" or "four key(s)." He can even respond correctly to questions about items specified on two or three dimensions, as in "How many blue key(s)?" or "What matter [material] is orange and three-cornered?" Alex also makes requests ("Want pasta") and answers simple questions about objects ("What color [is this]?" "Which is bigger?"). When presented with a blue cork and a blue key and asked "What's the same?" he will correctly respond "Color." He actually scores slightly better with new objects than with familiar ones, suggesting that he is not merely "parroting" a set of stock phrases. In recent work, he shows evidence of being able to sum two small sets of objects, such as nuts or jelly beans, for sums up to six (Pepperberg, 2006). In informal interactions, Alex tells Pepperberg, "I love you," "I'm sorry," and "Calm down." Work in Pepperberg's laboratory with other parrots shows that social interaction and modeling of appropriate responses during training are critical elements in the education of these very social (and smart!) animals.

Alex is one clever bird. His abilities raise intriguing questions about the intelligence of animals and their capacity for specific aspects of language.

Thinking About the Thinking of Animals

These results on animal language and cognition are impressive, but scientists are still divided over just what the animals in these studies are doing. Do they have true language? Are they thinking, in human terms? How intelligent are they? Are Rico and Alex unusual, or are they typical of their species?

On one side are those who worry about *anthropomorphism*, the tendency to falsely attribute human qualities to nonhuman beings (Wynne, 2004). They like to tell the story of Clever Hans, a "wonder horse" at the turn of the century who was said to possess mathematical and other abilities (Spitz, 1997). For example, Clever Hans would answer math problems by stamping his hoof the appropriate number of times. But a little careful experimentation by psychologist Oskar Pfungst (1911/1965) revealed that

CONSIDER OTHER INTERPRETATIONS

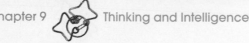

This old photo shows Clever Hans in action. His story has taught researchers to beware of anthropomorphism when they interpret findings on animal cognition.

when Hans was prevented from seeing his questioners, his powers left him. It seems that questioners were staring at the horse's feet and leaning forward expectantly after stating the problem, then lifting their eyes and relaxing as soon as he completed the right number of taps. Clever Hans was indeed clever, but not at math or other human skills. He was merely responding to nonverbal signals that people were inadvertently providing. (Perhaps he had a high EQ.)

On the other side are those who warn against *anthropodenial*—the tendency to think, mistakenly, that human beings have nothing in common with other animals, who are, after all, our evolutionary cousins (de Waal, 1997, 2001a; Fouts, 1997). The need to see our own species as unique, they say, may keep us from recognizing that other species, too, have cognitive abilities, even if not as intricate as our own. Those who take this position point out that most modern researchers have gone to great lengths to avoid the Clever Hans problem.

The outcome of this debate is bound to have an effect on how we view ourselves and our place among other species. Perhaps, as cognitive ethologist Marc Hauser (2000) has suggested, we can find a way to study and respect animal minds and emotions without assuming sentimentally that they are just like ours.

QUICK quiz

Regrettably, your pet beagle can't help you answer these questions.

1. Which of the following abilities have primates demonstrated, either in the natural environment or the laboratory? (a) the use of objects as simple tools; (b) the summing of quantities; (c) the use of symbols to make requests; (d) an understanding of short English sentences
2. A honeybee performs a little dance that communicates to other bees the direction and distance of food. Because the bee can "talk" about something that is located elsewhere, its communication system shows ____________. But because the bee can create only utterances that are genetically wired into its repertoire, its communication system lacks ____________.
3. Barnaby thinks his pet snake Curly is harboring angry thoughts about him because Curly has been standoffish and won't curl around his neck anymore. What error is Barnaby making?

Answers:

1. all of them 2. displacement, productivity 3. anthropomorphism

We human beings are used to thinking of ourselves as the smartest species around because of our astounding ability to adapt to change, find novel solutions to problems, invent endless new gizmos, and use language to create everything from puns to poetry. Yet, as this chapter has shown, we are not always as wise in our thinking as we might think. We can, however, boast of one crowning accomplishment: We are the only species that tries to understand its own misunderstandings. We want to know what we don't know; we are motivated to overcome our mental shortcomings. Our uniquely human capacity for self-examination is probably the best reason to remain optimistic about our cognitive abilities.

Taking Psychology with You

Becoming More Creative

Take a few moments to answer these items based on the Remote Associates Test. Your task is to come up with a fourth word that is associated with each item in a set of three words (Mednick, 1962). For example, an appropriate answer for the set *news-clip-wall* is *paper*. Got the idea? Now try these (the answers are given after the Appendix, page A-10):

1. piggy—green—lash
2. surprise—political—favor
3. mark—shelf—telephone
4. stick—maker—tennis
5. cream—cottage—cloth

Associating elements in new ways by finding a common connection among them is an important component of creativity. People who are uncreative rely on *convergent thinking*, following a particular set of steps that they think will converge on one correct solution. Once they have solved a problem, they tend to develop a mental set and approach future problems the same way.

Creative people, in contrast, exercise *divergent thinking*; instead of stubbornly sticking to one tried-and-true path, they explore side alleys and generate several possible solutions. They come up with new hypotheses, imagine other interpretations, and look for connections that are not immediately obvious. They can think of many uses for familiar objects, such as, say, unneeded CD-ROM disks (which can be used as mobiles, Christmas tree decorations, coasters, . . .). Creative thinking can be found in the auto mechanic who invents a new tool, the mother who designs and makes her children's clothes, or the office manager who devises a clever way to streamline work flow (Richards, 1991).

A high IQ does not guarantee creativity. Personality characteristics seem more important, especially these three (Helson, Roberts, & Agronick, 1995; MacKinnon, 1968; McCrae, 1987; Schank, 1988):

- **Nonconformity.** Creative individuals are not overly concerned about what others think of them. They are willing to risk ridicule by proposing ideas that may initially appear foolish or off the mark. Geneticist Barbara McClintock's research was ignored or belittled by many for nearly 30 years. But she was sure she could show how genes move around and produce sudden changes in heredity. In 1983, when McClintock won the Nobel Prize, the judges called her work the second greatest genetic discovery of our time, after the discovery of the structure of DNA.
- **Curiosity.** Creative people are open to new experiences; they notice when reality contradicts expectations, and they are curious about the reason. For example, Wilhelm Roentgen, a German physicist, was studying cathode rays when he noticed a strange glow on one of his screens. Other people had seen the glow, but they ignored it because it didn't jibe with their understanding of cathode rays. Roentgen studied the glow, found it to be a new kind of radiation, and thus discovered X-rays (Briggs, 1984).
- **Persistence.** After that imaginary light bulb goes on over your head, you still have to work hard to make the illumination last. Or, as Thomas Edison, who invented the real light bulb, reportedly put it, "Genius is one-tenth inspiration and nine-tenths perspiration." No invention or work of art springs forth full-blown from a person's head. There are many false starts and painful revisions along the way.

In addition to traits that foster creativity, there are *circumstances* that do. Creativity flourishes when schools and employers encourage intrinsic motivation and not just extrinsic rewards such as gold stars and money (see Chapter 7 and Chapter 12). Intrinsic motives include a sense of accomplishment, intellectual fulfillment, the satisfaction of curiosity, and the sheer love of the activity. Creativity also increases when people have control over how to perform a task or solve a problem, are evaluated unobtrusively instead of being constantly observed and judged, and work independently (Amabile, 1983). Organizations encourage creativity when they let people take risks, give them plenty of time to think about problems, and welcome innovation.

In sum, if you hope to become more creative, there are two things you can do. One is to cultivate qualities in yourself: your skills, creativity, intrinsic motivation, and self-discipline. The other is to seek out the kinds of situations that will permit you to express your abilities and experiment with new ideas.

Summary

Thought: Using What We Know

- Thinking is the mental manipulation of information. Our mental representations simplify and summarize information from the environment.
- A *concept* is a mental category that groups objects, relations, activities, abstractions, or qualities that share certain properties. *Basic concepts* have a moderate number of instances and are easier to acquire than concepts with few or many instances. *Prototypical* instances of a concept are more representative than others. The language we use to express concepts may influence how we perceive and think about the world—a notion first proposed years ago by Benjamin Lee Whorf that is now getting renewed attention.
- *Propositions* are made up of concepts and express a unitary idea. They may be linked together to form *cognitive schemas*, which serve as mental models of aspects of the world. *Mental images* also play a role in thinking.
- Not all mental processing is conscious. *Subconscious processes* lie outside of awareness but can be brought into consciousness when necessary. They allow us to perform two or more actions at once when one action is highly automatic. But multitasking is usually inefficient, introduces errors, and can even be dangerous, for example if done while driving. *Nonconscious processes* remain outside of awareness but nonetheless affect behavior; they are involved in what we call "intuition" and "insight," and in *implicit learning*. Conscious processing may be carried out in a *mindless* fashion if we overlook changes in context that call for a change in behavior.

Reasoning Rationally

- *Reasoning* is purposeful mental activity that involves drawing inferences and conclusions from observations, facts, or assumptions (premises). *Formal reasoning problems* can often be solved by applying an *algorithm*, a set of procedures guaranteed to produce a solution, or by using logical processes, such as *deductive* and *inductive reasoning*. *Informal reasoning problems* often have no clearly correct solution. Disagreement may exist about basic premises, information may be incomplete, and many viewpoints may compete. Such problems often call for the application of *heuristics*, rules of thumb that suggest a course of action without guaranteeing an optimal solution. They may also require *dialectical thinking* about opposing points of view.
- Studies of *reflective judgment* show that many people have trouble thinking dialectically. People in the *prereflective* stages do not distinguish between knowledge and belief or between belief and evidence. Those in the *quasi-reflective* stages think that because knowledge is sometimes uncertain, any judgment about the evidence is purely subjective. Those who think *reflectively* understand that although some things cannot be known with certainty, some judgments are more valid than others, depending on their coherence, fit with the evidence, and so on. Higher education moves people gradually closer to reflective judgment.

Barriers to Reasoning Rationally

- The ability to reason clearly and rationally is affected by many cognitive biases. People tend to exaggerate the likelihood of improbable events in part because of the *affect and availability heuristics*. They are swayed in their choices by the desire to *avoid loss*. They forgo economic gain because of a *fairness bias*, which, as we saw in "Biology and Economic Choice," appears to have evolutionary roots and is being studied using brain scans. They often overestimate their ability to have made accurate predictions (the *hindsight bias*), attend mostly to evidence that confirms what they want to believe (the *confirmation bias*), and can be mentally rigid, forming *mental sets* and seeing patterns where none exists.
- The theory of *cognitive dissonance* holds that people are motivated to reduce the tension that exists when two cognitions, or a cognition and a behavior, conflict—by rejecting or changing a belief, changing their behavior, or rationalizing. People are especially likely to do so when they need to reduce *postdecision dissonance*, when their actions violate their concept of themselves as honest and kind, and when they have put hard work into an activity (the *justification of effort*).

Measuring Intelligence: The Psychometric Approach

- *Intelligence* is hard to define. Most theorists believe that a general ability (a *g factor*) underlies the many specific abilities tapped by intelligence tests, whereas others do not.
- The traditional approach to intelligence, the *psychometric approach*, focuses on how well people perform on standardized aptitude tests. The *intelligence quotient*, or *IQ*, represents how a person has done on an intelligence test compared to other people. Alfred Binet designed the first widely used intelligence test, to identify children who could benefit from remedial work. But in the United States, people assumed that intelligence tests revealed

"natural ability" and used the tests to categorize people in school and in the armed services.

- IQ tests have been criticized for being biased in favor of white, middle-class people. However, efforts to construct tests that are free of cultural influence have been disappointing. Culture affects nearly everything to do with taking a test, from attitudes to problem-solving strategies. Negative stereotypes about a person's ethnicity, gender, or age may cause the person to suffer *stereotype threat*, which can lead to anxiety or "disidentification" with the test.

Dissecting Intelligence: The Cognitive Approach

- In contrast to the psychometric approach, *cognitive approaches* to intelligence emphasize several kinds of intelligence and the strategies people use to solve problems.
- Sternberg's *triarchic theory of intelligence* proposes three aspects of intelligence: *componential* (including *metacognition*), *experiential* or *creative*, and *contextual* or *practical*. Contextual intelligence allows you to acquire *tacit knowledge*, practical strategies that are important for success but are not explicitly taught.
- Howard Gardner proposes that there are actually several "intelligences" besides those usually considered, including musical and kinesthetic intelligence, and the capacity to understand the natural world, yourself, or others. The latter two overlap with what some psychologists call *emotional intelligence*.
- Intellectual achievement also depends on motivation, hard work, and attitudes. As we saw in "Close-up on Research," in teenagers self-discipline predicts grades better than IQ does. Cross-cultural work shows that beliefs about the origins of mental abilities, parental standards, and attitudes toward education can also help account for differences in academic performance.

Animal Minds

- Some researchers, especially those in *cognitive ethology*, argue that nonhuman animals have greater cognitive abilities than is usually thought. Some animals can use objects as simple tools. Chimpanzees have shown evidence of a single understanding of number. Some researchers believe that the great apes, and possibly other animals, have some aspects of a *theory of mind*, an understanding of how their own minds and the minds of others work.
- In several projects using visual symbol systems or American Sign Language (ASL), primates have acquired linguistic skills. Some animals (even some nonprimates) seem able to use simple grammatical ordering rules to convey or comprehend meaning. However, scientists are still divided about how to interpret these findings and the research on animal cognition, with some worrying about *anthropomorphism* and others worrying about *anthropodenial*.

KEY TERMS

concept 322
basic concept 322
prototype 322
Benjamin Lee Whorf 323
proposition 324
cognitive schema 324
mental image 324
subconscious processes 324
nonconscious processes 325
implicit learning 325
mindlessness 326
reasoning 327
formal reasoning 327
algorithm 327
deductive reasoning 327
premise 327
inductive reasoning 328
informal reasoning 328
heuristic 329
dialectical reasoning 329
reflective judgment 329
prereflective stages 330
quasi-reflective stages 330
reflective stages 330
affect heuristic 332
availability heuristic 333
avoidance of loss 333
fairness bias 334
Ultimatum Game 334
behavioral economics 334
hindsight bias 335
confirmation bias 336
mental set 337
cognitive dissonance 338
postdecision dissonance 339
justification of effort 339
intelligence 341
factor analysis 342
g factor 342
psychometric approach to intelligence 342
mental age (MA) 342
intelligence quotient (IQ) 342
Stanford–Binet Intelligence Scale 343
Wechsler Adult Intelligence Scale (WAIS) 343
Wechsler Intelligence Scale for Children (WISC) 343
stereotype threat 345
cognitive approach to intelligence 346
triarchic theory of intelligence 346
componential intelligence 347
metacognition 347
experiential (creative) intelligence 347
contextual (practical) intelligence 348
tacit knowledge 348
emotional intelligence 348
cognitive ethology 354
theory of mind 355
anthropomorphism 357
anthropodenial 358
convergent versus divergent thinking 359

Can You Think of the Answers?

NOW YOU HAVE READ CHAPTER NINE — ARE YOU PREPARED FOR THE EXAM?

Zach could not remember the four-digit combination needed to open the lock on his bicycle. After struggling to figure it out, he turned to start the long walk home. All of a sudden he remembered the combination to the lock. The problem-solving strategy Zach used would be best described as ______.

What methods do people use to solve problems and make decisions?
(pages 324–326)

insight

The ability to understand the world, think rationally or logically, and use resources effectively when faced with challenges or problems, or the characteristics needed to succeed in one's culture is the psychologist's working definition of ______.

How do intelligence tests measure intelligence?
(page 341–342)

intelligence

If a test consistently produces the same score when administered to the same person under identical conditions, that test can be said to be high in ______.

Why hasn't it been possible to design intelligence tests that are free from cultural influence?
(pages 341–346)

reliability

STUDY
TIP

The two most commonly used methods to assess any psychological test is to determine the validity and reliability of the test. **Reliability** indicates a test consistency, while **validity** indicates accuracy, or how well the test measures what it says it measures.

Examine the following test descriptions and determine whether the test has a potential problem with its reliability or validity:

A personality test gives a very different score for the same person when they retake it six months later.

reliability issue — the scores are not consistent

An individual takes an online IQ test that measures how long she can hold her breath.

validity issue — does holding your breath give a very accurate assessment of your IQ?

35
reliability
the tendency of a test to produce the same scores again and again each time it is given to the same people
35
44
validity
the degree to which a test actually measures what it's supposed to measure
44

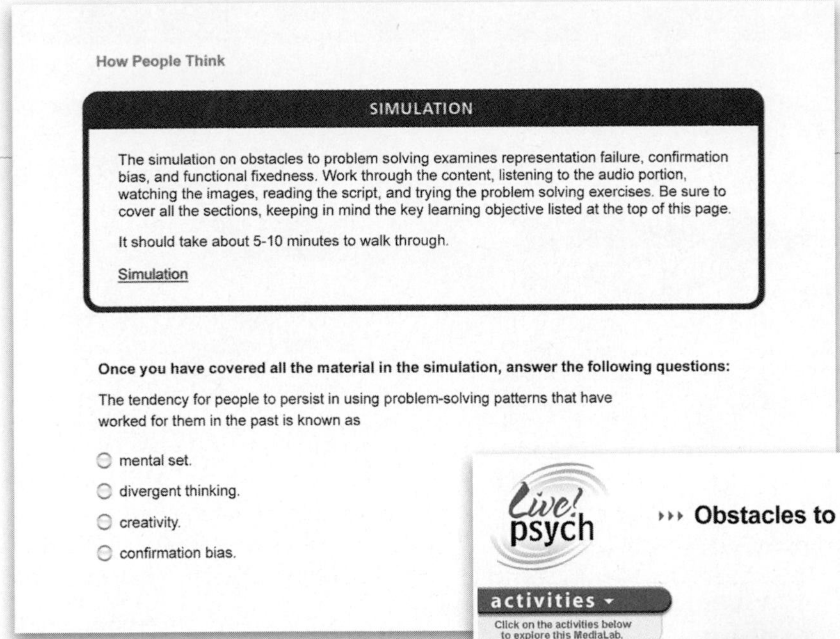

How People Think

SIMULATION

The simulation on obstacles to problem solving examines representation failure, confirmation bias, and functional fixedness. Work through the content, listening to the audio portion, watching the images, reading the script, and trying the problem solving exercises. Be sure to cover all the sections, keeping in mind the key learning objective listed at the top of this page.

It should take about 5-10 minutes to walk through.

Simulation

Once you have covered all the material in the simulation, answer the following questions:

The tendency for people to persist in using problem-solving patterns that have worked for them in the past is known as

- mental set.
- divergent thinking.
- creativity.
- confirmation bias.

One of the key areas in this chapter is the discussion of problem solving. Do the quizzes and try the simulations on **MyPsychLab** to better understand this key area.

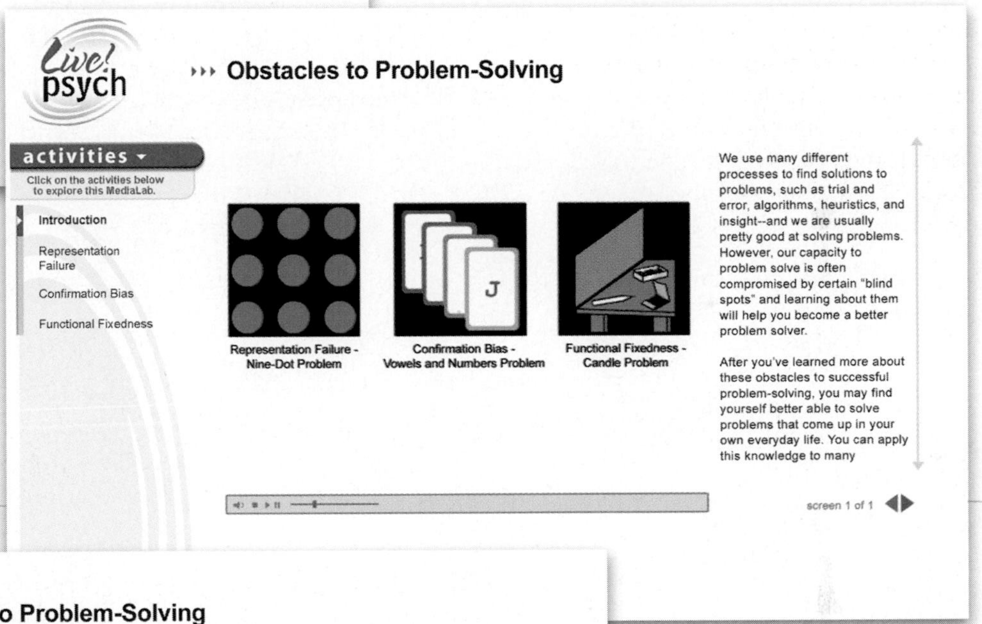

Live! psych

››› **Obstacles to Problem-Solving**

activities

Click on the activities below to explore this MediaLab.

- Introduction
- Representation Failure
- Confirmation Bias
- Functional Fixedness

Representation Failure - Nine-Dot Problem

Confirmation Bias - Vowels and Numbers Problem

Functional Fixedness - Candle Problem

We use many different processes to find solutions to problems, such as trial and error, algorithms, heuristics, and insight--and we are usually pretty good at solving problems. However, our capacity to problem solve is often compromised by certain "blind spots" and learning about them will help you become a better problem solver.

After you've learned more about these obstacles to successful problem-solving, you may find yourself better able to solve problems that come up in your own everyday life. You can apply this knowledge to many

screen 1 of 1

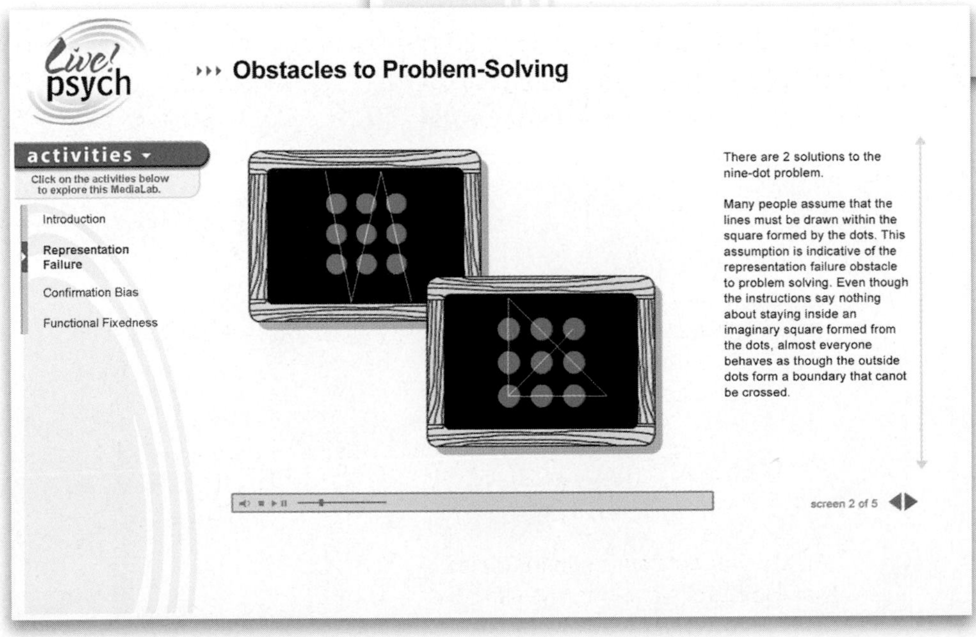

Live! psych

››› **Obstacles to Problem-Solving**

activities

Click on the activities below to explore this MediaLab.

- Introduction
- Representation Failure
- Confirmation Bias
- Functional Fixedness

There are 2 solutions to the nine-dot problem.

Many people assume that the lines must be drawn within the square formed by the dots. This assumption is indicative of the representation failure obstacle to problem solving. Even though the instructions say nothing about staying inside an imaginary square formed from the dots, almost everyone behaves as though the outside dots form a boundary that canot be crossed.

screen 2 of 5

What can you find in MyPsychLab?

Self-Directed Tests • Videos • Simulations • eBook • Flash Cards • Web Links . . . and more — organized by chapter, section and learning objective.

CHAPTER TEN

Better by far that you should forget and smile than that you should remember and be sad.

CHRISTINA ROSSETTI

CHAPTER 10

In 1985, a young man named Alan Newton was convicted of brutally raping a 25-year-old woman in an abandoned Bronx building. His accuser had picked him out of a lineup. Newton was sentenced to up to 40 years in prison, and there he remained for over two decades, steadfastly maintaining his innocence. Because he was determined to clear his name, he refused to improve his chances for parole by joining a sex offenders' rehab group.

In 1994, Newton filed a motion requesting a DNA test, which he was sure would exonerate him, but his request was denied because the evidence was said to be unavailable. Then, in 2005, at the request of the nonprofit Innocence Project, the Bronx district attorney's office asked the New York Police Department to search once again for the rape kit in the case at an evidence warehouse in Queens. The kit turned up this time, exactly where it had originally been stored and had remained all those years, and the results of testing showed conclusively that Newton could not have been the assailant. In 2006, after spending more than two decades of his life in prison, Alan Newton, now 44, finally became a free man. He thanked his attorneys and said he felt no bitterness toward the woman whose testimony had led to his confinement at the state's toughest penitentiaries. "My unjust conviction denied both of us justice," he said. "It opens up old wounds and denies her closure. . . . Being angry will not allow you to grow."

At one time, most prosecutors and juries would have immediately dismissed the testimony of rape victims, because public opinion tended to blame them for having "provoked" the attack or for failing to fight back strongly enough. As people became more aware of the horrific nature of rape and the unfairness of blaming victims, however, their acceptance of women's testimony increased. Today, some defendants, like Alan Newton, are being sent to prison or even sentenced to death almost solely on the strength of the victim's testimony.

But is an eyewitness's account always reliable? In the absence of corroborating evidence, should a witness's confidence in her memory be sufficient for establishing guilt? Much is at stake in our efforts to answer these questions: getting justice for rape victims and also avoiding the false conviction of men who are innocent.

As you read this chapter, ask yourself: When should we trust our memories, and when should we be cautious about doing so? We all forget a great deal, of course. Do we also "remember" things that never happened? Are memory malfunctions the exception to the rule or are they commonplace? And if memory is not always reliable, how can any of us hope to know the story of our own lives? How can we hope to understand the past?

OUTLINE

THINKING CRITICALLY

ASK QUESTIONS

Alan Newton in court after his release from prison. DNA evidence established that he could not have committed the rape for which he was convicted even though the victim had identified him by picking him out of a lineup. In thinking about this case, a critical thinker would ask: How accurate is eyewitness testimony, even when the witness is the victim? How trustworthy are our memories, even of traumatic events? Psychologists have learned some startling answers, as this chapter will show.

Ozier Muhammad/The New York Times

WHAT'S**AHEAD** 

- What's wrong with thinking of memory as a mental movie camera?
- Why do "flashbulb" memories of surprising or shocking events sometimes have less wattage than we think?
- If you have a strong emotional reaction to a remembered event, does that mean your memory is accurate?

Reconstructing the Past

Memory refers to the capacity to retain and retrieve information, and also to the structures that account for this capacity. Human beings are capable of astonishing feats of memory. Most of us can easily remember the tune of our national anthem, how to use an automated teller machine, the most embarrassing experience we ever had, zillions of details about our favorite sports or films, and hundreds of thousands of other bits of information. Memory confers competence; without it we would be as helpless as newborns, unable to carry out even the most trivial of our daily tasks. Memory also endows us with a sense of personal identity; each of us is the sum of our recollections, which is why we feel so threatened when others challenge our memories. Individuals and cultures alike rely on a remembered history for a sense of coherence and meaning; memory gives us our past and guides our future.

Imagine what life would be like if you could never form any new memories. That does in fact happen in older people who are suffering from dementia, and sometimes it also occurs in younger people who have brain injuries or diseases. The case of one man, known to researchers as H. M., is probably the most intensely studied in the annals of medicine (Corkin, 1984; Corkin et al., 1997; Hilts, 1995; Milner, 1970; Ogden & Corkin, 1991). In 1953, when H. M. was 27, surgeons removed most of his hippocampus, along with part of the amygdala. The operation was a last-ditch effort to relieve H. M.'s severe and life-threatening epilepsy, which was causing unrelenting, uncontrollable seizures. The operation did achieve its goal: Afterward, the young man's seizures were milder and could be managed with medication. His memory, however, had been affected profoundly. Although H. M. continued to recall most events that had occurred before the operation, he could no longer remember new experiences for much longer than 15 minutes; facts, songs, stories, and faces all vanished like water down the drain. He would read the same magazine over and over without realizing it. He could not recall the day of the week, the year, or even his last meal.

In the movie *50 First Dates,* Adam Sandler woos Drew Barrymore over and over again because she has lost her ability, in a car crash, to retain any new memories, so she doesn't recognize him from one day to the next. The movie is a comedy, but what would it really be like to retain all new memories for only a short time?

Today, H. M., now elderly, will occasionally recall an unusually emotional event, such as the assassination of someone named Kennedy. He sometimes remembers that both his parents are dead, and he knows he has memory problems. But according to Suzanne Corkin, who has studied H. M. extensively, these "islands of remembering" are the exceptions in a vast sea of forgetfulness. This good-natured man still does not know the scientists who have studied him for decades. He thinks he is much younger than he is, and he can no longer recognize a photograph of his own face; he is stuck in a time warp from the past. We will meet H. M. again at several points in this chapter.

The Manufacture of Memory

In ancient times, philosophers compared memory to a soft wax tablet that would preserve anything that chanced to make an imprint on it. Then, with the advent of the printing press, they began to think of memory as a gigantic library, storing specific events and facts for later retrieval. Today, in the audiovisual age, many people compare memory to a tape recorder or movie camera, automatically recording every moment of their lives.

Popular and appealing though this belief about memory is, however, it is utterly wrong. Not everything that happens to us or impinges on our senses is tucked away for later use. Memory is selective. If it were not, our minds would be cluttered with mental junk—the temperature at noon on Thursday, the price of turnips two years ago, a phone number needed only once. Moreover, recovering a memory is not at all like replaying a tape of an event; it is more like watching a few unconnected frames and then figuring out what the rest of the scene must have been like.

If these children remember this birthday party later in life, their constructions may include information picked up from family photographs, videos, and stories. And they will probably be unable to distinguish their actual memories from information they got elsewhere.

One of the first scientists to make this point was the British psychologist Sir Frederic Bartlett (1932). Bartlett asked people to read lengthy, unfamiliar stories from other cultures and then tell the stories back to him. As the volunteers tried to recall the stories, they made interesting errors: They often eliminated or changed details that did not make sense to them, and they added other details to make the story coherent, sometimes even adding a moral. Memory, Bartlett concluded, must therefore be largely a *reconstructive* process. We may reproduce some kinds of simple information by rote, said Bartlett, but when we remember complex information, we

source misattribution The inability to distinguish an actual memory of an event from information you learned about the event elsewhere.

typically alter it in ways that help us make sense of the material, based on what we already know or think we know. Since Bartlett's time, hundreds of studies have found this to be true for everything from stories to conversations to personal experiences.

In reconstructing their memories, people often draw on many sources. Suppose, for example, that someone asks you to describe one of your early birthday parties. You may have some direct recollection of the event, but you may also incorporate information from family stories, photographs, or home videos, and even from accounts of other people's birthdays and reenactments of birthdays on television. You take all these bits and pieces and build one integrated account. Later, you may not be able to distinguish your actual memory from information you got elsewhere—a phenomenon known as **source misattribution**, or sometimes *source confusion* (Johnson, Hashtroudi, & Lindsay, 1993).

A dramatic instance of reconstruction once occurred with H. M. (Ogden & Corkin, 1991). After eating a chocolate Valentine's Day heart, H. M. stuck the shiny red wrapping in his shirt pocket. Two hours later, while searching for his handkerchief, he pulled out the paper and looked at it in puzzlement. When a researcher asked why he had the paper in his pocket, he replied, "Well, it could have been wrapped around a big chocolate heart. It must be Valentine's Day!" But a short time later, when she asked him to take out the paper again and say why he had it in his pocket, he replied, "Well, it might have been wrapped around a big chocolate rabbit. It must be Easter!"

Sadly, H. M. *had* to reconstruct the past; his damaged brain could not recall it in any other way. But those of us with normal memory abilities also reconstruct, far more often than we realize.

The Fading Flashbulb

Of course, some unusual, shocking, or tragic events, such as earthquakes or accidents, do hold a special place in memory, especially when we have experienced them personally. Such events seem frozen in time, with all the details intact. Years ago, Roger Brown and James Kulik (1977) labeled these vivid recollections of emotional events *flashbulb memories* because that term captures the surprise, illumination, and seemingly photographic detail that characterize them. They speculated that the capacity for flashbulb memories may have evolved because such memories had survival value: Remembering the details of a surprising or dangerous experience could have helped our ancestors avoid similar situations.

Many people have vivid "flashbulb" memories of the attack on the World Trade Center on September 11, 2001. But even flashbulb memories are not always complete or accurate, and they often change over time. For example, some people are convinced they saw the first attack on television as it was occurring. But that is impossible, as no film crews knew in advance that it would happen!

In some cases, flashbulb memories have lasted for years, even decades. For example, in a Danish study, older people who had lived through the Nazi occupation of their country in World War II often had an accurate memory of verifiable wartime events, such as the time of day that the radio had announced liberation and what the weather had been like at the time (Berntsen & Thomsen, 2005). Despite their intensity, however, even flashbulb memories are not always complete or accurate records of the past. Usually people remember the *gist* of a startling, emotional event they experienced or witnessed, such as a violent shoot-out, the assassination of an admired politician, or the explosion of a space shuttle. But when researchers question them about their memories over time, errors creep into the details, and after a few years, some people even forget the gist (Neisser & Harsch, 1992).

On September 12, 2001, just one day after the attacks on the World Trade Center and the Pentagon, researchers asked 54 college students when they had first heard the news of the attacks, who had told them the news, and what they had been doing at the time. The students were also asked to report details about a mundane event from the days immediately before the attacks, so that the researchers could compare ordinary memories with flashbulb ones. One group was then retested a week later, a second group 6 weeks later, and a third group 32 weeks later. The students also completed a questionnaire that measured the vividness and emotional intensity of their memories and their confidence in their accuracy. Over time, the vividness of the flashbulb memories and the students' confidence in these memories remained higher than for the everyday memories. Their confidence, however, was misplaced. The details reported by the students became less and less consistent for *both* types of memories; in fact, the flashbulb memories contained just as many inconsistent details as the everyday ones (Talarico & Rubin, 2003).

Even with flashbulb memories, then, facts tend to get mixed with a little fiction. Remembering is an active process, one that involves not only dredging up stored information but also putting two and two together to reconstruct the past. Sometimes, unfortunately, we put two and two together and get five.

confabulation Confusion of an event that happened to someone else with one that happened to you, or a belief that you remember something when it never actually happened.

The Conditions of Confabulation

Because memory is reconstructive, it is subject to **confabulation**—confusing an event that happened to someone else with one that happened to you, or coming to believe that you remember something that never really happened. Such confabulations are especially likely under certain circumstances (Garry et al., 1996; Hyman & Pentland, 1996; Johnson, 1995):

1 You have thought, heard, or told others about the imagined event many times. Suppose that at family gatherings you keep hearing about the time that Uncle Sam scared everyone at a New Year's party by pounding a hammer into the wall with such force that the wall collapsed. The story is so colorful that you can practically see Uncle Sam in your mind's eye. The more you think about this event, the more likely you are to believe that you were actually there, even if you were sound asleep in another house. This process has been called *imagination inflation*, because your own active imagination inflates your belief that the event really occurred (Garry & Polaschek, 2000). Even merely explaining how a hypothetical childhood experience *could* have happened inflates people's confidence that it really did. Explaining an event makes it seem more familiar and thus real (Sharman, Manning, & Garry, 2005).

2 The image of the event contains lots of details that make it feel real. Ordinarily, we can distinguish an imagined event from a real one by the amount of detail we recall; real events tend to produce more details. However, the longer you think about an imagined event, the more details you are likely to add—what Sam was wearing, the fact that he'd had too much to drink, the crumbling plaster, people standing around in party hats—and these details may in turn persuade you that the event really happened and that you have a direct memory of it.

3 The event is easy to imagine. If imagining an event takes little effort (as does visualizing a man pounding a wall with a hammer), then we tend to think that our

In the 1980s, Whitley Strieber published the best-seller *Communion*, in which he claimed to have had encounters with some sort of nonhuman beings, possibly aliens from outer space. An art director designed this striking cover. Since then, many people have assumed that this is what an extraterrestrial must look like, and some have imported the image into their own confabulated memories of alien abduction.

memory is real. In contrast, when we must make an effort to form an image of an experience—for example, of being in a place we have never seen or doing something that is utterly foreign to us—our cognitive efforts apparently serve as a cue that the event did not really take place, or that we were not there when it did.

As a result of imagination inflation, you can end up with a memory that feels emotionally, vividly real to you, yet it can be completely false. This means that your feelings about an event, no matter how strong they are, do not guarantee that the event really happened. Consider again our Sam story, which happens to be true. A woman we know believed for years that she had been present in the room as an 11-year-old child when her uncle destroyed the wall. Because the story was so vivid and upsetting to her, she felt angry at him for what she thought was his mean and violent behavior, and she assumed that she must have been angry at the time as well. Then, as an adult, she learned that she was not at the party at all but had merely heard about it repeatedly over the years. Moreover, Sam had not pounded the wall in anger, but as a joke, to inform the assembled guests that he and his wife were about to remodel their home. Nevertheless, our friend's family has had a hard time convincing her that her "memory" of this event is entirely wrong, and they are not sure she believes them yet.

As the Sam story illustrates, and as laboratory research verifies, false memories can be as stable over time as true ones (Brainerd, Reyna, & Brandse, 1995; Poole, 1995; Roediger & McDermott, 1995). There's just no getting around it: Memory is reconstructive.

QUICK quiz

Can you reconstruct what you have read so far in order to answer these questions?

1. Memory is like (a) a wax tablet, (b) a giant file cabinet, (c) a video camera, (d) none of these.
2. *True or false:* Because they are so vivid, flashbulb memories remain perfectly accurate over time.
3. Which of the following confabulated "memories" might a person be most inclined to accept as having really happened to them, and why? (a) getting lost in a shopping center at the age of 5, (b) taking a class in astrophysics, (c) visiting a monastery in Tibet as a child, (d) being bullied by another kid in the fourth grade.

Answers:

1. d **2** false **3.** a and d, because they are common events that are easy to imagine and that contain a lot of vivid details. It would be harder to induce someone to believe that he or she had studied astrophysics or visited Tibet because these are rare events that take an effort to imagine.

WHAT'S AHEAD

- Can your memories of an event be affected by the way someone questions you about it?
- Can children's testimony about sexual abuse always be trusted?

Memory and the Power of Suggestion

The reconstructive nature of memory helps the mind work efficiently. Instead of cramming our brains with infinite details, we can store the essentials of an experience and then use our knowledge of the world to figure out the specifics when we need

them. But precisely because memory is reconstructive, it is also vulnerable to suggestion—to ideas implanted in our minds after the event, which then become associated with it. This fact raises thorny problems in legal cases that involve eyewitness testimony or people's memories of what happened, when, and to whom.

THINKING CRITICALLY

ANALYZE ASSUMPTIONS AND BIASES

If you watch TV shows such as *Law & Order*, you might assume that lineups help witnesses identify criminals. But, in fact, lineups can mislead witnesses, who may wrongly identify a person simply because he or she resembles the actual culprit more closely than the other people standing there do. Psychologists are now studying other methods, such as having witnesses look at photos of suspects one at a time without being able to go back to an earlier photo.

The Eyewitness on Trial

Without the accounts of eyewitnesses, many guilty people would go free. But eyewitness testimony is not always reliable, even when the witness is dead certain about the accuracy of his or her report. Lineups—a staple of TV shows like *Law and Order*—don't necessarily help, because witnesses may simply identify the person in the line who looks most like the perpetrator of the crime (Wells & Olson, 2003). As a result, some convictions based on eyewitness testimony, like that of Alan Newton, turn out to be tragic mistakes.

Eyewitnesses are especially likely to make mistaken identifications when the suspect's ethnicity differs from their own. When people say of another group, "They all look alike to me," often, unfortunately, they are telling the truth. Because of unfamiliarity with other ethnic groups, the eyewitness may focus solely on the ethnicity of the person they see committing a crime ("He's black"; "She's white"; "He's an Arab") and ignore the distinctive features that would later make identification more accurate (Levin, 2000; Meissner & Brigham, 2001).

In a program of research spanning over three decades, Elizabeth Loftus and her colleagues have shown that memories are also influenced by the way in which questions are put to the eyewitness and by suggestive comments made during an interrogation or interview. In one classic study, the researchers showed how even subtle changes in the wording of questions can lead a witness to give different answers. Participants first viewed short films depicting car collisions. Afterward, the researchers asked some of them, "About how fast were the cars going when they hit each other?" Other viewers were asked the same question, but with the verb changed to *smashed*, *collided*, *bumped*, or *contacted*. Estimates of how fast the cars were going varied, depending on which word was used. *Smashed* produced the highest average speed estimates (40.8 mph), followed by *collided* (39.3 mph), *bumped* (38.1 mph), *hit* (34.0 mph), and *contacted* (31.8 mph) (Loftus & Palmer, 1974).

In a similar study, the researchers asked some participants, "Did you see a broken headlight?" but asked others "Did you see the broken headlight?" (Loftus & Zanni, 1975). The question with *the* presupposes a broken headlight and merely asks whether the witness saw it, whereas the question with *a* makes no such presupposition. People who received questions with *the* were far more likely to report having seen something that had not really appeared in the film than were those who received questions with *a*. If a tiny word like *the* can lead people to "remember" what they never saw, you can imagine how the leading questions of police detectives and lawyers might influence a witness's recall.

Misleading information from other sources, too, can profoundly alter what witnesses report. Consider what happened when students were shown the face of a young man who had straight hair, then heard a description of the face supposedly written by another witness—a description that wrongly said the man had light, curly hair (see

FIGURE 10.1 The Influence of Misleading Information

In a study described in the text, students saw the face of a young man with straight hair and then had to reconstruct it from memory. On the left is one student's reconstruction in the absence of misleading information about the man's hair. On the right is another person's reconstruction of the same face after exposure to misleading information that mentioned curly hair (Loftus & Greene, 1980).

Figure 10.1). When the students reconstructed the face using a kit of facial features, a third of their reconstructions contained the misleading detail, whereas only 5 percent contained it when curly hair was not mentioned (Loftus & Greene, 1980).

Leading questions, suggestive comments, and misleading information affect people's memories not only for events they have witnessed but also for their own experiences. Researchers have successfully used these techniques to induce people to "recall" complicated events from early in life that never actually happened, such as getting lost in a shopping mall, being hospitalized for a high fever, being harassed by a bully, getting in trouble for playing a prank on a first-grade teacher, or spilling punch all over the mother of the bride at a wedding (Hyman & Pentland, 1996; Lindsay et al., 2004; Loftus & Pickrell, 1995; Mazzoni et al., 1999). In one such study, when people were shown a phony Disneyland ad featuring Bugs Bunny, about 16 percent later recalled having met a Bugs character at Disneyland (Braun, Ellis, & Loftus, 2002). In later studies, using several versions of the ad, the percentages were even higher. Some people even claimed to remember shaking hands with the character, hugging him, or seeing him in a parade. But these "memories" were impossible, because Bugs Bunny is a Warner Bros. creation and would definitely be rabbit non grata at Disneyland!

Children's Testimony

The power of suggestion can affect anyone, but many people are especially concerned about its impact on children who are being questioned regarding possible sexual or physical abuse. How can adults find out whether a young child has been sexually molested without influencing or tainting what the child says? The answer is crucial. Throughout the 1980s and 1990s, accusations of child abuse in day-care centers across the United States skyrocketed. After being interviewed by therapists and police investigators, children were claiming that their teachers had molested them in the most terrible ways: hanging them in trees, putting handcuffs on them, raping them, and even forcing them to eat feces. Although in no case had parents actually seen the day-care teachers treating the children badly, although none of the children had complained to their parents, and although none of the parents had noticed any symptoms or problems in their children, most of the accused teachers were sentenced to many years in prison.

THINKING  **CRITICALLY**

DON'T OVERSIMPLIFY

Some people claim that children's memories of sexual abuse are always accurate; others claim that children can't distinguish fantasy from reality. How can we avoid either–or thinking on this emotional issue? Is the question "Are children's memories accurate?" even the right one to ask?

Thanks largely to important research by psychological scientists, the hysteria eventually subsided and people were able to assess more clearly what had gone wrong in the interviewing of the children in these cases. Today we know that although most children *do* recollect accurately much of what they have observed or experienced, many children will say that something happened when it did not. Like adults, they can be influenced by leading questions and suggestions from the person interviewing them (Ceci & Bruck, 1995). Yet many wrongfully convicted teachers remain in prison, and others, though released, must live out their lives as registered sex offenders.

Children's testimony is often crucial in child sexual abuse cases. Under what conditions do children make reliable or unreliable witnesses?

CLOSE-UP on Research

HOW NOT TO INTERVIEW CHILDREN

Many of the people who interviewed children in the 1980s and 1990s did not **analyze their assumptions and biases**. Some assumed that young children are suggestible and that their testimony is therefore almost always unreliable. Others assumed that children never lie about sexual abuse or other distressing experiences. When psychological scientists began to investigate this topic, they realized that both points of view oversimplified. They knew from research that people of any age can be influenced to report things that never happened, so instead of asking whether children ever lie, they **asked a better question**: "Under what conditions are children apt to be suggestible, to report that something happened to them when in fact it did not?"

The clear answer, after many years of investigation, is that a child is more likely to give a false report when the interviewer strongly believes that the child has been molested and then uses suggestive techniques to get the child to "reveal" molestation (Bruck, 2003). Interviewers who are biased in this way do not think critically. They seek only confirming evidence and ignore discrepant evidence and other explanations for a child's behavior. They reject a child's denial of having been molested and assume the child is merely "in denial." They use techniques that encourage imagination inflation ("Let's pretend it happened") and that blur reality and fantasy in the child's mind. They praise the child for saying what the interviewer wants to hear—namely, that abuse occurred. They pressure or encourage the child to say that terrible things happened, badger the child with repeated questions, tell the child that "everyone else" said it happened, or use bribes and threats (Poole & Lamb, 1998).

In an important field study with real-world relevance, a team of researchers analyzed the actual transcripts of interrogations of children in the first highly publicized sexual abuse case, the McMartin preschool case (which ended in a hung jury). Then they applied the same suggestive techniques in an experiment with preschool children (Garven et al., 1998). A young man visited children at their preschool, read them a story, and handed out treats. The man did nothing aggressive, inappropriate, or surprising. A week later an experimenter questioned the children individually about the

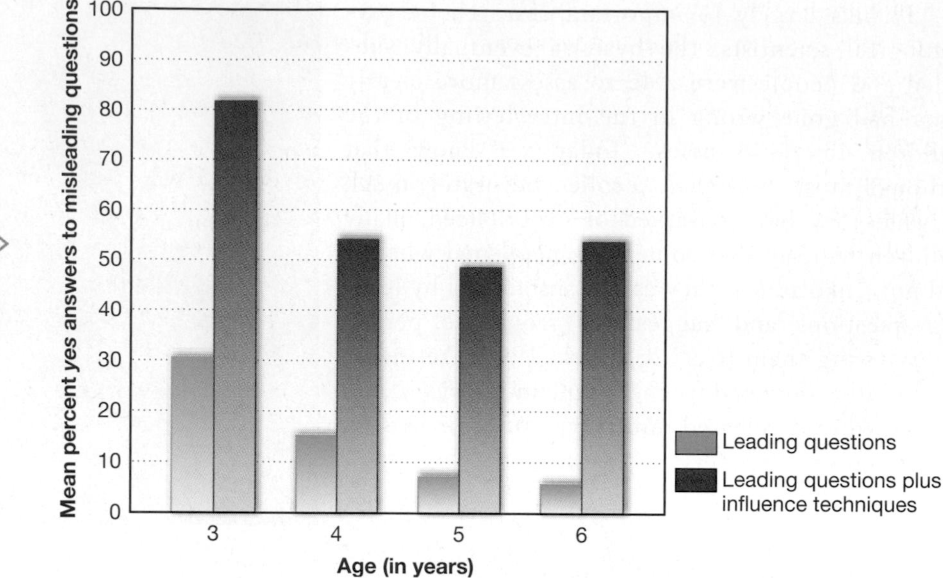

man's visit. She asked children in one group leading questions ("Did he bump the teacher? Did he throw a crayon at a kid who was talking?" "Did he tell you a secret and tell you not to tell?"). She asked a second group the same questions but also used influence techniques used by interrogators in the McMartin and other day-care cases: for example, telling the children what "other kids" had supposedly said, expressing disappointment if answers were negative, and praising the children for making allegations.

When the researchers **examined the resulting evidence**, they found that in the first group, children said "yes, it happened" to about 17 percent of the false allegations about the man's visit. This finding alone refutes the notion that children never lie, misremember, or make things up. And in the second group, they said "yes" to the false allegations suggested to them a whopping 58 percent of the time. As you can see in the figure above, the 3-year-olds in this group, on average, said "yes" to over 80 percent of the false allegations, and the 4- to 6-year-olds said "yes" to over half of the allegations Note that the interviews in this study lasted only 5 to 10 minutes, whereas in actual investigations, interviewers often question children repeatedly over many weeks or months.

Once again, however, we must be careful **not to oversimplify**: Even in the group exposed to the full package of influence techniques, some children remained unswayed. Other researchers have asked why that might be, investigating characteristics of the child that might reduce or increase the chances that the child will be vulnerable to leading questions and other influence techniques (Clarke-Stewart, Allhusen, & Malloy, 2004). Children who have relatively poor language skills, who are impatient and lack self-control in real-life situations, and who have unsupportive or distant parents are the most susceptible. Conversely, children who have good verbal comprehension and expression, who have a high degree of self-control, and who enjoy a secure relationship with psychologically healthy parents are best able to resist an interviewer's efforts to influence them.

Finally, researchers have **examined the widely held assumption** that children cannot be induced to make up experiences that are truly traumatic. They have found that this assumption, too, is unsupported. In a study in which schoolchildren were asked for their recollections of an actual sniper incident at their school, many children who had been absent from school that day reported memories of hearing shots, seeing someone lying on the ground, and other details they could not possibly have experienced directly. Apparently, they had been influenced by the accounts of the children who had been there (Pynoos & Nader, 1989). Rumor and hearsay play a big role in promoting false beliefs and memories in children, just as they do in adults. Young chil-

dren often think they have experienced an event when in fact they have merely overheard adults or other children talking about it (Principe et al., 2006).

By examining assumptions and avoiding emotional reasoning, researchers have been able to develop better ways of interviewing children that reduce the chances of false reporting. For example, if the interviewer says, "Tell me the reason you came to talk to me today," and nothing more, most actual victims will disclose what happened to them (Bruck, 2003). The interviewer must be unbiased and must not assume that the child was molested, must avoid leading or suggestive questions, and must understand that children do not speak the way adults do. Young children often drift from topic to topic, for example, and their words may not be the words adults use (Poole & Lamb, 1998). One little girl thought her "private parts" were her elbows!

In sum, children, like adults, can be accurate in what they report and, also like adults, they can distort, forget, fantasize, and be misled. As research shows, their memory processes are only human.

QUICK quiz

Now see how accurate your own memory processes are.

1. *True or false*: Mistaken identifications are more likely when a suspect's ethnicity differs from that of the eyewitness, even when the witness feels certain about being accurate.
2. Research suggests that the best way to encourage truthful testimony by children is to (a) reassure them that their friends have had the same experience, (b) reward them for saying that something happened, (c) scold them if you believe they are lying, (d) avoid leading questions.
3. In psychotherapy, hundreds of people have claimed to recall long-buried memories of having taken part in satanic rituals involving animal and human torture and sacrifice. Yet investigators and the FBI have been unable to confirm any of these reports. Based on what you have learned so far, how might you explain such "memories"?

Answers:

1. true 2. d 3. Therapists who uncritically assume that satanic cults are widespread may ask leading questions and otherwise influence their patients. Patients who are susceptible to their therapists' interpretations may then confabulate and "remember" experiences that did not happen, borrowing details from fictionalized accounts or from other troubling experiences in their lives. The result may be source misattribution and the patient's mistaken conviction that the memory is real.

WHAT'S**AHEAD** 

- In general, which is easier, a multiple-choice item or a short-answer essay item?
- Can you know something without knowing that you know it?
- Why is the computer often used as a metaphor for the mind?

In Pursuit of Memory

Now that we have seen how memory *doesn't* work—namely, like a tape recorder, an infallible filing system, or a journal written in indelible ink—we turn to studies of how it *does* work. The ability to remember is not an absolute talent; it depends on the type of performance being called for. If you have a preference for multiple-choice, essay, or true–false exams, you already know this.

Measuring Memory

Conscious, intentional recollection of an event or an item of information is called **explicit memory**. It is usually measured using one of two methods. The first method tests for **recall**, the ability to retrieve and reproduce information encountered earlier. Essay and fill-in-the-blank exams and memory games such as Trivial Pursuit or Jeopardy require recall. The second method tests for **recognition**, the ability to identify information you have previously observed, read, or heard about. The information is given to you, and all you have to do is say whether it is old or new, or perhaps correct or incorrect, or pick it out of a set of alternatives. The task, in other words, is to compare the information you are given with the information stored in your memory. True–false and multiple-choice tests call for recognition.

Recognition tests can be tricky, especially when false items closely resemble correct ones. Under most circumstances, however, recognition is easier than recall. Recognition for visual images is particularly impressive. If you show people 2,500 slides of faces and places, and later you ask them to identify which ones they saw out of a larger set, they will be able to identify more than 90 percent of the original slides accurately (Haber, 1970).

The superiority of recognition over recall was once demonstrated in a study of people's memories of their high school classmates (Bahrick, Bahrick, & Wittlinger, 1975). The participants, ages 17 to 74, first wrote down the names of as many classmates as they could remember. Recall was poor; even when prompted with yearbook pictures, the youngest people failed to name almost a third of their classmates, and the oldest failed to name most of them. Recognition, however, was far better. When asked to look at a series of cards, each of which contained a set of five photographs, and to say which picture in each set showed a former classmate, recent graduates were right 90 percent of the time—and so were people who had graduated 35 years earlier. The ability to recognize names was nearly as impressive.

Sometimes, information encountered in the past affects our thoughts and actions even though we do not consciously or intentionally remember it, a phenomenon known as **implicit memory** (Graf & Schacter, 1985; Schacter, Chiu, & Ochsner, 1993). To get at this subtle sort of memory, researchers must rely on indirect methods instead of the direct ones used to measure explicit memory. One common method, **priming**, which we introduced in Chapter 6 in our discussion of subliminal perception, asks you to read or listen to some information and then tests you later to see whether the information affects your performance on another type of task.

Suppose that you had to read a list of words, some of which began with the letters *def* (such as *define*, *defend*, or *deform*). Later you might be asked to complete word stems (such as *def-*) with the first word that came to mind. Even if you could not recognize or

explicit memory Conscious, intentional recollection of an event or of an item of information.

recall The ability to retrieve and reproduce from memory previously encountered material.

recognition The ability to identify previously encountered material.

implicit memory Unconscious retention in memory, as evidenced by the effect of a previous experience or previously encountered information on current thoughts or actions.

priming A method for measuring implicit memory in which a person reads or listens to information and is later tested to see whether the information affects performance on another type of task.

GET INVOLVED!

➤RECALLING RUDOLPH'S FRIENDS

You can try this test of recall if you are familiar with the poem that begins "'Twas the Night Before Christmas" or the song "Rudolph the Red-Nosed Reindeer." Rudolph had eight reindeer friends; name as many of them as you can. After you have done your best, turn to the Get Involved exercise on page 376 for a recognition test on the same information.

recall the original words very well, you would be more likely to complete the word fragments with words from the list than you would be if you had not seen the list. In this procedure, the original words "prime" certain responses on the word-completion task (that is, make them more available), showing that people can retain more knowledge about the past than they realize. They know more than they know that they know (Richardson-Klavehn & Bjork, 1988; Roediger, 1990).

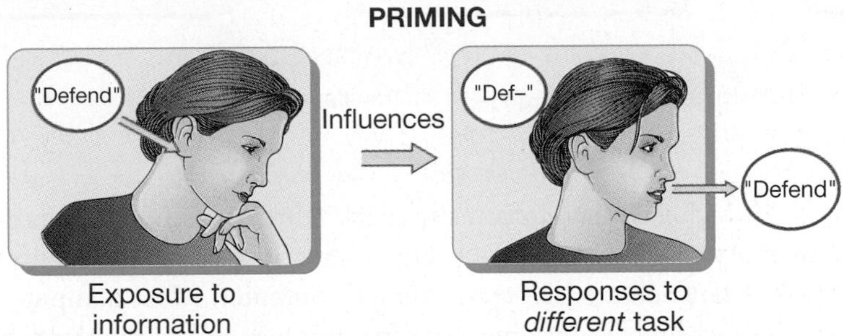

Another method of measuring implicit memory, the **relearning method**, or *savings method*, was devised by Hermann Ebbinghaus (1885/1913) in the nineteenth century. The relearning method requires you to relearn information or a task that you already learned earlier. If you master it more quickly the second time around, you must be remembering something from the first experience.

relearning method A method for measuring retention that compares the time required to relearn material with the time used in the initial learning of the material.

Models of Memory

Although people usually refer to memory as a single faculty, as in "I must be losing my memory" or "He has a memory like an elephant's," the term *memory* actually covers a complex collection of abilities and processes. If video or movie cameras are not accurate metaphors for capturing these diverse components of memory, then what metaphor would be better?

Many cognitive psychologists liken the mind to an information processor, along the lines of a computer, though more complex. They have constructed *information-processing models* of cognitive processes, liberally borrowing computer programming terms such as *input*, *output*, *accessing*, and *information retrieval*. When you type something on your computer's keyboard, the machine encodes the information into an electronic language, stores it on a disk, and retrieves it when you need to use it. Similarly, in information-processing models of memory, we *encode* information (convert it to a form that the brain can process and use), *store* the information (retain it over time), and *retrieve* the information (recover it for use). In storage, the information may be represented as concepts, propositions, images, or *cognitive schemas*, mental networks of knowledge, beliefs, and expectations concerning particular topics or aspects of the world. (If you can't retrieve these terms, see Chapter 9.)

In most information-processing models, storage takes place in three interacting memory systems. A *sensory register* retains incoming sensory information for a second or two, until it can be processed further. *Short-term memory (STM)* holds a limited amount of information for a brief period of time, perhaps up to 30 seconds or so, unless a conscious effort is made to keep it there longer. *Long-term memory (LTM)* accounts for longer storage—from a few minutes to decades (Atkinson & Shiffrin, 1968, 1971). Information can pass from the sensory register to short-term memory and in either direction between short-term and long-term memory, as illustrated in Figure 10.2.

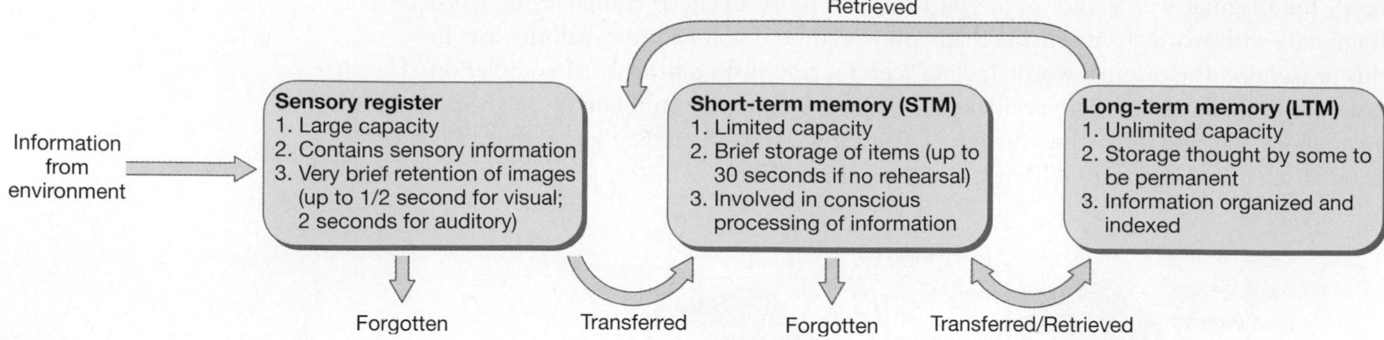

FIGURE 10.2 Three Memory Systems

In the "three-box model" of memory, information that does not transfer out of the sensory register or short-term memory is assumed to be forgotten forever. Once in long-term memory, information can be retrieved for use in analyzing incoming sensory information or performing mental operations in short-term memory.

This model, which is known informally as the "three-box model," has dominated research on memory since the late 1960s. However, critics of the model note that the human brain does not operate like your average computer. Most computers process instructions and data sequentially, one item after another, and so the three-box model has emphasized sequential operations. However, the human brain performs many operations simultaneously, in parallel. It recognizes patterns all at once rather than as a sequence of information bits, and it perceives new information, produces speech, and searches memory all at the same time. It can do these things because millions of neurons are active at once, and each neuron communicates with thousands of others, which in turn communicate with millions more.

Because of these differences between human beings and machines, some cognitive scientists prefer a **parallel distributed processing (PDP)** or *connectionist* model. Instead of representing information as flowing from one system to another, a PDP model represents the contents of memory as connections among a huge number of interacting processing units, distributed in a vast network and all operating in parallel—just like the neurons of the brain (McClelland, 1994; Rumelhart, McClelland, & the PDP Research Group, 1986). As information enters the system, the ability of these units to excite or inhibit each other is constantly adjusted to reflect new knowledge.

parallel distributed processing (PDP) model A model of memory in which knowledge is represented as connections among thousands of interacting processing units, distributed in a vast network, and all operating in parallel.

Memory researchers are still arguing about which model of memory is most useful. In this chapter, we emphasize the three-box model, but keep in mind that the computer metaphor that inspired it could one day be as outdated as the metaphor of memory as a camera.

GET INVOLVED!

➤RECOGNIZING RUDOLPH'S FRIENDS

If you took the recall test in the Get Involved exercise on page 374, now try a recognition test. From the following list, see whether you can identify the correct names of Rudolph the Red-Nosed Reindeer's eight reindeer friends. The answers are at the end of the Appendix, on page A-10—but no fair peeking!

Blitzen	Dander	Dancer	Masher
Cupid	Dasher	Prancer	Comet
Kumquat	Donder	Flasher	Pixie
Bouncer	Blintzes	Trixie	Vixen

Which was easier, recall or recognition? Can you speculate on the reason?

QUICK quiz

How well have you encoded and stored what you just learned?

1. Alberta solved a crossword puzzle a few days ago. She no longer recalls the words in the puzzle, but while playing a game of Scrabble, she unconsciously tends to form words that were in the puzzle, showing that she has __________ memories of some of the words.
2. The three basic memory processes are __________, storage, and __________.
3. Do the preceding two questions ask for recall, recognition, or relearning? (And what about *this* question?)
4. One objection to traditional information-processing theories of memory is that, unlike most computers, the brain performs many independent operations __________.

Answers:

1. implicit 2. encoding, retrieval 3. The first two questions both measure recall; the third question measures recognition. 4. simultaneously, or in parallel

- Why is short-term memory like a leaky bucket?
- When a word is on the tip of your tongue, what errors are you likely to make in recalling it?
- What's the difference between "knowing how" and "knowing that"?

The Three-Box Model of Memory

The information model of three separate memory systems—sensory, short-term, and long-term—remains a leading approach because it offers a convenient way to organize the major findings on memory, does a good job of accounting for these findings, and is consistent with the biological facts about memory, some of which we will describe later. Let us now peer into each of the "boxes."

The Sensory Register: Fleeting Impressions

In the three-box model, all incoming sensory information must make a brief stop in the **sensory register**, the entryway of memory. The sensory register includes a number of separate memory subsystems, as many as there are senses. Visual images remain in a visual subsystem for a maximum of half a second. Auditory images remain in an auditory subsystem for a slightly longer time, by most estimates up to two seconds or so.

The sensory register acts as a holding bin, retaining information in a highly accurate form until we can select items for attention from the stream of stimuli bombarding our senses. It gives us a brief time to decide whether information is extraneous or important; not everything detected by our senses warrants our attention. And the identification of a stimulus on the basis of information already contained in long-term memory occurs during the transfer of information from the sensory register to short-term memory.

If the visual sensory register did not clear quickly, multiple images might interfere with the accurate perception and encoding of memory.

Information that does not quickly go on to short-term memory vanishes forever, like a message written in disappearing ink. That is why people who see an array of twelve letters for just a fraction of a second can only report four or five of them; by the time they answer, their sensory memories are already fading (Sperling, 1960). The fleeting nature of incoming sensations is actually beneficial; it prevents multiple sensory

GET INVOLVED!

➤YOUR SENSORY REGISTER AT WORK

In a dark room or closet, swing a flashlight rapidly in a circle. You will see an unbroken circle of light instead of a series of separate points. The reason: The successive images remain briefly in the sensory register.

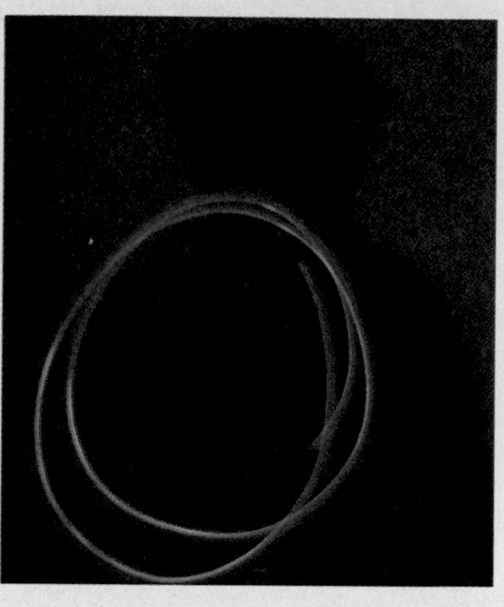

images—"double exposures"—that might interfere with the accurate perception and encoding of information.

Short-Term Memory: Memory's Scratch Pad

Like the sensory register, **short-term memory (STM)** retains information only temporarily—for up to about 30 seconds by many estimates, although some researchers think that the maximum interval may extend to a few minutes for certain tasks. In short-term memory, the material is no longer an exact sensory image but is an encoding of one, such as a word or a phrase. This material either transfers into long-term memory or decays and is lost forever.

Individuals with brain injury, such as H. M., demonstrate the importance of transferring new information from short-term memory into long-term memory. H. M. can store information on a short-term basis; he can hold a conversation and his behavior appears normal when you first meet him. However, for the most part, H. M., and other patients like him, cannot retain explicit information about new facts and events for longer than a few minutes. Their terrible memory deficits involve a problem in transferring explicit memories from short-term storage into long-term storage. With a great deal of repetition and drill, they can learn some new visual information, retain it in long-term memory, and recall it normally (McKee & Squire, 1992). But usually information does not get into long-term memory in the first place.

sensory register A memory system that momentarily preserves extremely accurate images of sensory information.

short-term memory (STM) In the three-box model of memory, a limited-capacity memory system involved in the retention of information for brief periods; it is also used to hold information retrieved from long-term memory for temporary use.

working memory In many models of memory, a memory system comprising short-term memory plus the mental processes that control retrieval of information from long-term memory and interpret that information appropriately for a given task.

Working Memory. Besides retaining new information for brief periods while we are learning it, short-term memory holds information that has been retrieved from long-term memory for temporary use, providing the mental equivalent of a scratch pad while we solve particular problems and carry out particular tasks. Many psychologists now use the term **working memory** to refer to (a) short-term memory plus (b) the mental processes that control the rehearsal and retrieval of information from long-term memory and interpret that information appropriately depending on the task you are doing (Baddeley, 1992). When you do an arithmetic problem, your working memory contains the numbers and the instructions for doing the necessary operations, and it also carries out those operations and retains the intermediate results from each step. Working memory may also involve the ability to control attention and avoid distraction in order to maintain information in an accessible or active state and retrieve it easily (Engle, 2002). People who do well on tests of working memory tend to do well in reading comprehen-

sion, ability to follow directions, note taking, bridge playing, vocabulary learning, and many other real-life tasks.

These card players are having a great time giving their working memories a workout.

The ability to bring information from long-term memory into short-term memory or to use working memory is not disrupted in patients like H. M. They can not only converse but can also do arithmetic, relate events that predate their injury, and do anything else that requires retrieval of information from long-term into short-term memory. Their problem is with the flow of information in the other direction, from short-term to long-term memory.

People such as H. M. fall at the extreme end on a continuum of forgetfulness, but even those of us with normal memories know from personal experience how frustratingly brief short-term retention can be. We look up a telephone number, are distracted for a moment, and find that the number has vanished from our minds. We meet someone at a meeting and two minutes later find ourselves groping unsuccessfully for the person's name. Is it any wonder that short-term memory has been called a "leaky bucket"?

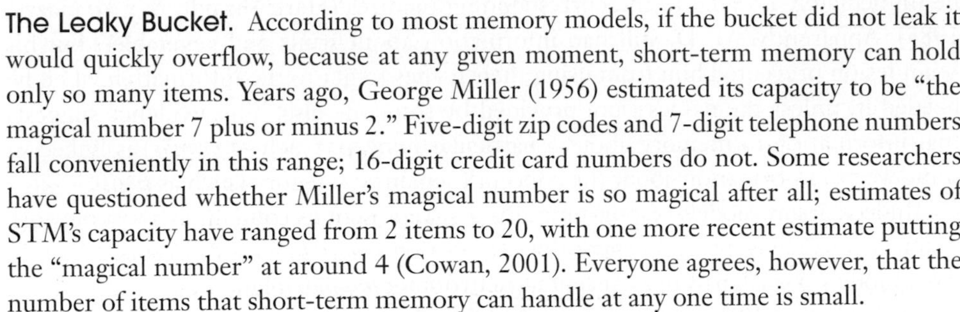

The Leaky Bucket. According to most memory models, if the bucket did not leak it would quickly overflow, because at any given moment, short-term memory can hold only so many items. Years ago, George Miller (1956) estimated its capacity to be "the magical number 7 plus or minus 2." Five-digit zip codes and 7-digit telephone numbers fall conveniently in this range; 16-digit credit card numbers do not. Some researchers have questioned whether Miller's magical number is so magical after all; estimates of STM's capacity have ranged from 2 items to 20, with one more recent estimate putting the "magical number" at around 4 (Cowan, 2001). Everyone agrees, however, that the number of items that short-term memory can handle at any one time is small.

If this is so, then how do we remember the beginning of a spoken sentence until the speaker reaches the end? After all, most sentences are longer than just a few words. According to most information-processing models of memory, we overcome this problem by grouping small bits of information into larger units, or **chunks**. The real capacity of STM, it turns out, is not a few bits of information but a few chunks. A chunk may be a word, a phrase, a sentence, or even a visual image, and it depends on previous experience. For most Americans, the acronym *FBI* is one chunk, not three, and the date *1492* is one chunk, not four. In contrast, the number *9214* is four chunks and *IBF* is three—unless your address is 9214 or your initials are IBF. To take a visual example: If you are unfamiliar with football and look at a field full of players, you probably won't be able to remember their positions when you look away. But if you are a fan of the game, you may see a single chunk of information—say, a wishbone formation—and be able to retain it.

Even chunking, however, cannot keep short-term memory from eventually filling up. Information that is needed for longer periods must therefore be transferred to long-term memory. Items that are particularly meaningful or that have an emotional impact may transfer quickly. But items that require more processing will be displaced with new information, and will thus be lost, unless we do something to keep it in STM for a while, as we will discuss shortly.

Long-Term Memory: Final Destination

The third box in the three-box model of memory is **long-term memory (LTM)**. The capacity of long-term memory seems to have no practical limits. The vast amount of information stored there enables us to learn, get around in the environment, and build a sense of identity and a personal history.

chunk A meaningful unit of information; it may be composed of smaller units.

long-term memory (LTM) In the three-box model of memory, the memory system involved in the long-term storage of information.

Organization in Long-Term Memory. Because long-term memory contains so much information, it must be organized in some way, so that we can find the particular items we are looking for. One way to organize words (or the concepts they represent) is by the *semantic categories* to which they belong. *Chair*, for example, belongs to the category *furniture*. In a study done many years ago, people had to memorize 60 words that came from four semantic categories: animals, vegetables, names, and professions. The words were presented in random order, but when people were allowed to recall the items in any order they wished, they tended to recall them in clusters corresponding to the four categories (Bousfield, 1953). This finding has been replicated many times.

Evidence on the storage of information by semantic category also comes from cases of people with brain damage. In one such case, a patient called M. D. appeared to have made a complete recovery after suffering several strokes, with one odd exception: He had trouble remembering the names of fruits and vegetables. M. D. could easily name a picture of an abacus or a sphinx, but he drew a blank when he saw a picture of an orange or a carrot. He could sort pictures of animals, vehicles, and other objects into their appropriate categories but did poorly with pictures of fruits and vegetables. On the other hand, when M. D. was *given* the names of fruits and vegetables, he immediately pointed to the corresponding pictures (Hart, Berndt, & Caramazza, 1985). Apparently, M. D. still had information about fruits and vegetables, but his brain lesion prevented him from using their names to get to the information when he needed it, unless the names were provided by someone else. This evidence suggests that information in memory about a particular concept (such as *orange*) is linked in some way to information about the concept's semantic category (such as *fruit*).

Indeed, many models of long-term memory represent its contents as a vast network of interrelated concepts and propositions (Anderson, 1990; Collins & Loftus, 1975). In these models, a small part of a conceptual network for *animals* might look something like the one in Figure 10.3. The way people use these networks, however, depends on expe-

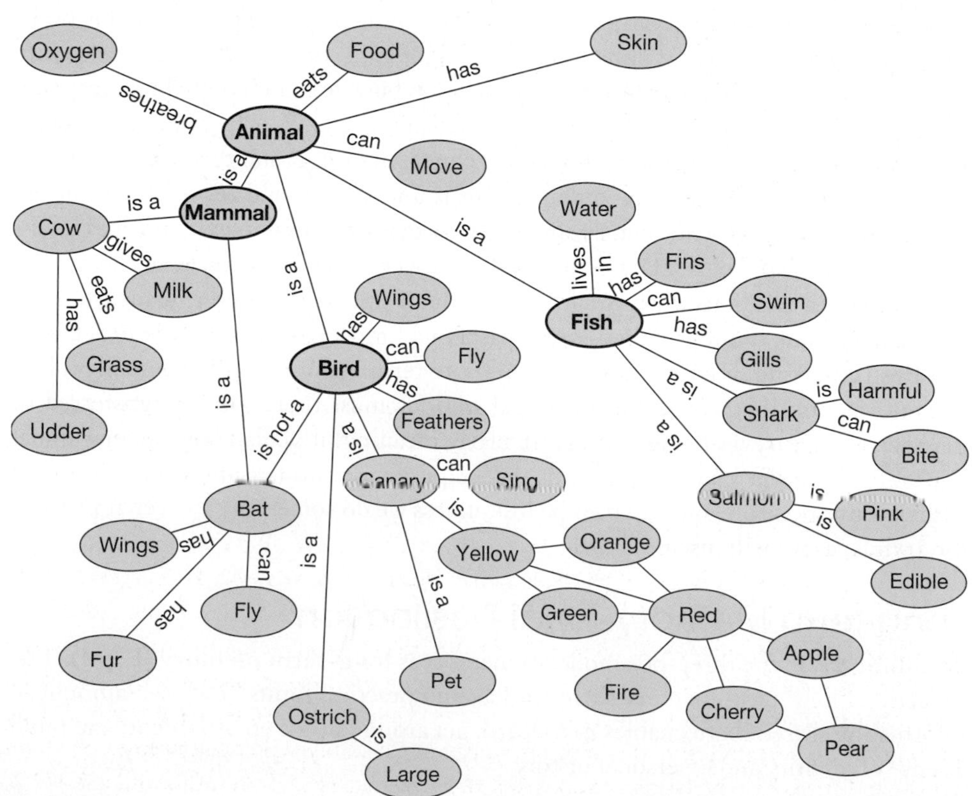

FIGURE 10.3 Part of a Conceptual Grid in Long-Term Memory

Many models of memory represent the contents of long-term semantic memory as an immense network or grid of concepts and the relationships among them. This illustration shows part of a hypothetical grid for *animals*.

rience and education. For example, in rural Liberia, the more schooling children have, the more likely they are to use semantic categories in recalling lists of objects (Cole & Scribner, 1974). This makes sense, because in school, children must memorize a lot of information in a short time, and semantic grouping can help. Unschooled children, having less need to memorize lists, do not cluster items and do not remember them as well. But this does not mean that unschooled children have poor memories. When the task is one that is meaningful to them, such as recalling objects that were in a story or a village scene, they remember extremely well (Mistry & Rogoff, 1994).

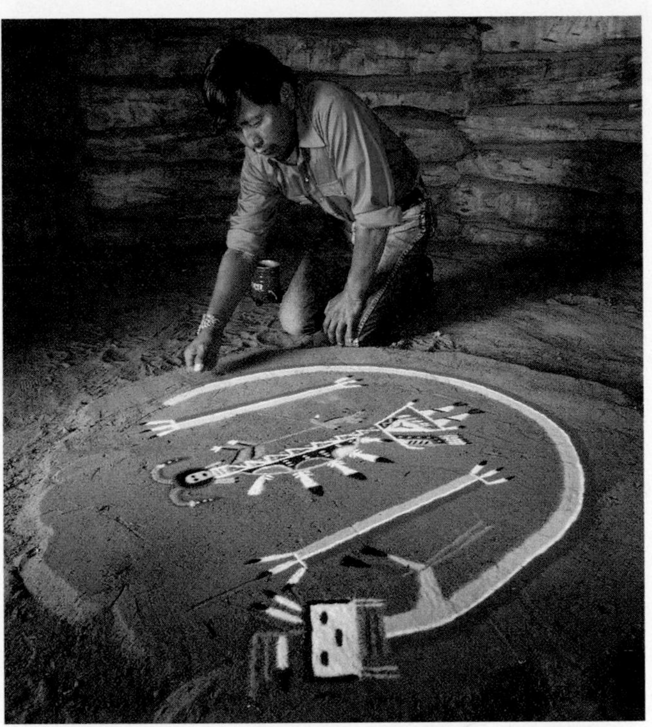

Culture affects the encoding, storage, and retrieval of information in long-term memory. Navajo healers, who use stylized, symbolic sand paintings in their rituals, must commit to memory dozens of intricate visual designs because no exact copies are made and the painting is destroyed after each ceremony.

We organize information in long-term memory not only by semantic groupings but also in terms of the way words sound or look. Have you ever tried to recall some word that was on the "tip of your tongue"? Nearly everyone experiences such *tip-of-the-tongue (TOT) states*, especially when trying to recall the names of acquaintances or famous persons, the names of objects and places, or the titles of movies or books (Burke et al., 1991). TOT states are reported even by users of sign language, who call them tip-of-the-finger states (Thompson, Emmorey, & Gollan, 2005).

When a word is on the tip of the tongue, people tend to come up with words that are similar in meaning to the right one before they finally recall it. But verbal information in long-term memory also seems to be indexed by sound and form, and it is retrievable on that basis. Incorrect guesses often have the correct number of syllables, the correct stress pattern, the correct first letter, or the correct prefix or suffix (R. Brown & McNeill, 1966). For example, for the target word *sampan* (an Asian boat), a person might say "Siam" or "sarong."

Information in long-term memory may also be organized by its familiarity, relevance, or association with other information. The method used in any given instance probably depends on the nature of the memory; you would no doubt store information about the major cities of Europe differently from information about your first date. To understand the organization of long-term memory, then, we must know what kinds of information can be stored there.

The Contents of Long-Term Memory. Most theories of memory distinguish skills or habits ("knowing how") from abstract or representational knowledge ("knowing that"). **Procedural memories** are memories of knowing how to do something—for example, knowing how to comb your hair, use a pencil, solve a jigsaw puzzle, knit a sweater, or swim. Many researchers consider procedural memories to be implicit, because once skills and habits are learned well, they do not require much conscious processing. **Declarative memories**, on the other hand, involve knowing that something is true, as in knowing that Ottawa is the capital of Canada; they are usually assumed to be explicit.

Declarative memories, in turn, come in two varieties, semantic memories and episodic memories (Tulving, 1985). **Semantic memories** are internal representations of the world, independent of any particular context. They include facts, rules, and concepts—items of general knowledge. On the basis of your semantic memory of the concept *cat*, you can describe a cat as a small, furry mammal that typically spends its time eating, sleeping, prowling, and staring into space, even though a cat may not be present when you give this description, and you probably won't know how or when you first learned it. **Episodic memories** are internal representations of personally

procedural memories Memories for the performance of actions or skills ("knowing how").

declarative memories Memories of facts, rules, concepts, and events ("knowing that"); they include semantic and episodic memories.

semantic memories Memories of general knowledge, including facts, rules, concepts, and propositions.

episodic memories Memories of personally experienced events and the contexts in which they occurred.

FIGURE 10.4 Types of Long-Term Memories

This diagram summarizes the distinctions among long-term memories. Can you come up with other examples of each memory type?

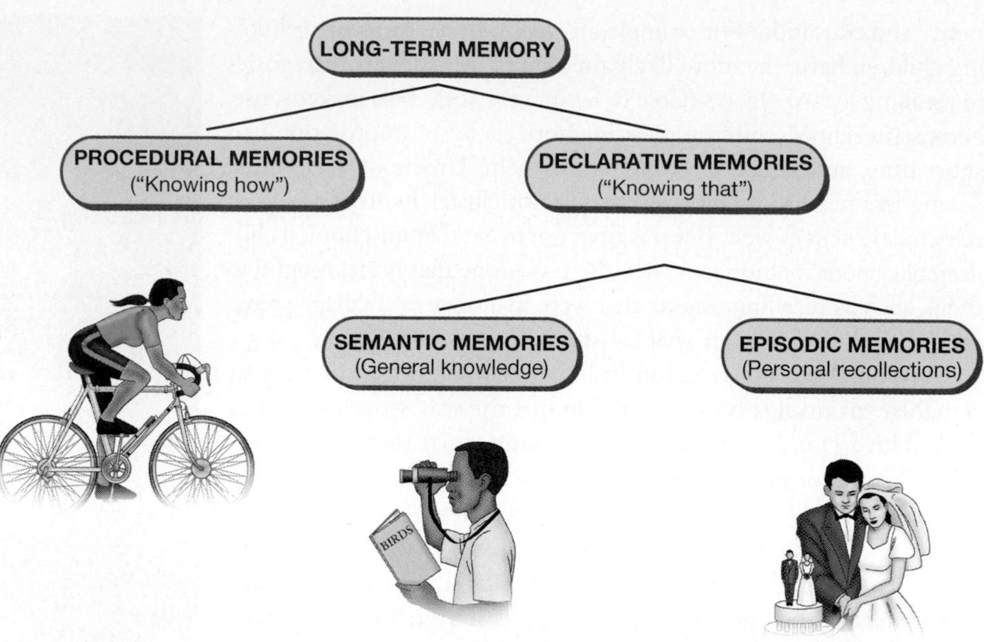

serial-position effect The tendency for recall of the first and last items on a list to surpass recall of items in the middle of the list.

experienced events. When you remember how your cat once surprised you in the middle of the night by pouncing on your face as you slept, you are retrieving an episodic memory. Figure 10.4 summarizes these kinds of memories.

From Short-Term to Long-Term Memory: A Puzzle. The three-box model of memory is often invoked to explain an interesting phenomenon called the **serial-position effect**. If you are shown a list of items and are then asked immediately to recall them, your retention of any particular item will depend on its position in the list (Glanzer & Cunitz, 1966). Recall will be best for items at the beginning of the list (the *primacy effect*) and at the end of the list (the *recency effect*). When retention of all the items is plotted, the result will be a U-shaped curve, as shown in Figure 10.5. A serial-position effect occurs when you are introduced to a lot of people at a party and find you can recall the names of the first few people you met and the last few, but almost no one in between.

FIGURE 10.5 The Serial-Position Effect

When people try to recall a list of similar items immediately after learning it they tend to remember the first and last items best and the ones in the middle worst.

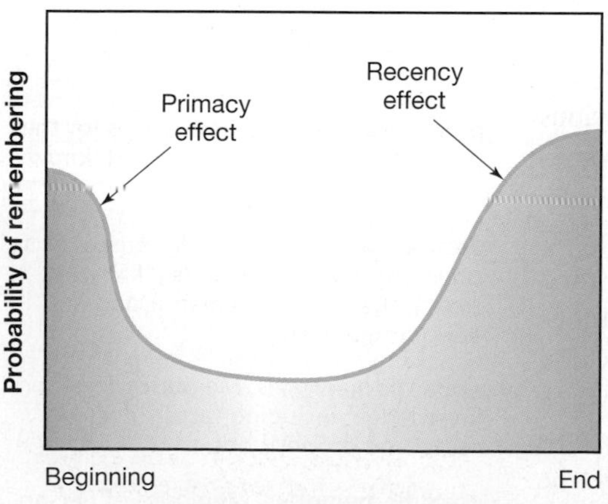

According to the three-box model, the first few items on a list are remembered well because short-term memory was relatively empty when they entered, so these items did not have to compete with others to make it into long-term memory. They were thoroughly processed, so they remain memorable. The last few items are remembered for a different reason: At the time of recall, they are still sitting in short-term memory. The items in the middle of a list, however, are not so well retained because by the time they get into short-term memory, it is already crowded. As a result, many of these items drop out of short-term memory before they can be stored in long-term memory. This explanation is supported by a functional MRI study in which recognition memory for words early in a list activated areas in the hippocampus associated with retrieval from long-term memory, but recognition for words that came near the end of the list did not (Talmi et al., 2005). The problem with this explanation is that the recency effect sometimes occurs even after a considerable delay, when the items at the end of a list can no longer be in short-term memory (Davelaar et al., 2004). The serial-position curve, therefore, remains something of a puzzle.

QUICK quiz

Find out whether the findings just discussed have transferred from your short-term memory to your long-term memory.

1. The __________ holds images for a fraction of a second.
2. For most people, the abbreviation *USA* consists of __________ informational chunk(s).
3. Suppose you must memorize a long list of words that includes the following: *desk, pig, gold, dog, chair, silver, table, rooster, bed, copper,* and *horse*. If you can recall the words in any order you wish, how are you likely to group them in recall? Why?
4. When you roller-blade, are you relying on procedural, semantic, or episodic memory? How about when you recall the months of the year? Or when you remember falling while roller-blading on an icy January day?
5. If a child is trying to memorize the alphabet, which sequence should present the greatest difficulty: *abcdefg, klmnopq,* or *tuvwxyz?* Why?

Answers:

1. sensory register **2.** one **3.** *Desk, chair, table,* and *bed* would probably form one cluster; *pig, dog, rooster,* and *horse* a second; and *gold, silver,* and *copper* a third. Concepts tend to be organized in long-term memory in terms of semantic categories, such as *furniture, animals,* and *metals.* **4.** procedural; semantic; episodic **5.** *klmnopq,* because of the serial-position effect.

WHAT'S AHEAD

- What changes occur in your neurons when you store a long-term memory?
- Where in the brain are memories for facts and events stored?
- Which hormones can improve your memory?

The Biology of Memory

We have been discussing memory solely in terms of information processing, but what is happening in the brain while all that processing is going on?

Changes in Neurons and Synapses

Forming a memory involves chemical and structural changes at the level of neurons, and these changes differ for short-term memory and long-term memory.

In short-term memory, changes within neurons temporarily alter the neurons' ability to release neurotransmitters, the chemicals that carry messages from one cell to another (see Chapter 4). Evidence comes from studies with sea snails, sea slugs, and other organisms that have small numbers of easily identifiable neurons (Alkon, 1989; Kandel & Schwartz, 1982). These primitive animals can be taught simple conditioned responses, such as withdrawing or not withdrawing parts of their bodies in response to a light touch. When the animal retains the skill for only the short term, the neuron or neurons involved temporarily show an increase or decrease in readiness to release neurotransmitter molecules.

In contrast, long-term memory involves lasting structural changes in the brain. To mimic what they think may happen during the formation of a long-term memory, researchers apply brief, high-frequency electrical stimulation to groups of neurons in the brains of animals or to brain cells in a laboratory culture. In various areas, especially the hippocampus, this stimulation increases the strength of synaptic responsiveness, a phenomenon known as **long-term potentiation** (Bliss & Collingridge, 1993;

long-term potentiation A long-lasting increase in the strength of synaptic responsiveness, thought to be a biological mechanism of long-term memory.

McNaughton & Morris, 1987). In other words, certain receiving neurons become more responsive to transmitting neurons, so those synaptic pathways become more excitable.

Most researchers believe that long-term potentiation underlies many and perhaps all forms of learning and memory. The neurotransmitter glutamate seems to play a key role in this process, though the exact biochemical and molecular changes involved are still being debated. Whatever the mechanism, the ultimate result is that the receiving neurons become more receptive to the next signal that comes along. It is a little like increasing the diameter of a funnel's neck to permit more flow through the funnel. In addition, during long-term potentiation, dendrites grow and branch out, and certain types of synapses increase in number (Greenough, 1984). At the same time, in another process, some neurons become *less* responsive than they were previously (Bolshakov & Siegelbaum, 1994).

Most of these changes take time, which probably explains why long-term memories remain vulnerable to disruption for a while after they are stored—why, for example, a blow to the head may disrupt new memories even though old ones are unaffected. Just as concrete takes time to set, the neural and synaptic changes in the brain that underlie long-term memory take a while to develop fully. Memories therefore undergo a gradual period of **consolidation**, or stabilization, before they "solidify." Consolidation can continue for weeks in animals and for several years in human beings.

Locating Memories

Scientists have used microelectrodes, brain-scan technology, and other techniques to identify the brain structures responsible for the formation and storage of specific types of memories. During short-term memory tasks, areas in the frontal lobes of the brain are especially active (Goldman-Rakic, 1996). In the formation of long-term declarative memories (memories for facts and events, or "knowing that"), the hippocampus plays a critical role: As we have seen in the case of H. M., damage to this structure can cause amnesia for new facts and events. The prefrontal cortex and areas adjacent to the hippocampus in the temporal lobe are also important for the efficient encoding of pictures and words (Brewer et al., 1998; Schacter, 1999; Wagner et al., 1998).

The formation and retention of procedural memories (memory for skills and habits) seem to involve other brain structures and pathways. For example, in work with rabbits, Richard Thompson (1983, 1986) showed that one kind of procedural memory—a simple, classically-conditioned response to an unpleasant stimulus, such as an eye blink in response to a tone—depends on activity in the cerebellum. Human patients with damage in the cerebellum are incapable of this type of conditioning (Daum & Schugens, 1996).

The formation of declarative and procedural memories in different brain areas could explain a curious finding about patients like H. M. Despite their inability to form new declarative memories, with sufficient practice such patients can acquire new procedural memories that enable them to solve a puzzle, read mirror-reversed words, or play tennis—even though they do not recall the training sessions in which they learned these skills. Apparently, the parts of the brain involved in acquiring new procedural memories have remained intact. Patients such as H. M. also retain some implicit memory for verbal material, as measured by priming tasks. Some psychologists conclude that there must therefore be separate systems in the brain for implicit and explicit tasks. As Figure 10.6 shows, this view has been bolstered by brain scans,

consolidation The process by which a long-term memory becomes durable and stable.

which reveal differences in the location of brain activity when normal subjects perform explicit versus implicit memory tasks (Reber, Stark, & Squire, 1998; Squire et al., 1992).

The brain circuits that take part in the *formation* of long-term memories, however, are not the same as those involved in long-term *storage* of those memories. The role of the hippocampus, for example, appears to be only temporary, and the ultimate destinations of declarative memories seem to lie in parts of the cerebral cortex (Maviel et al., 2004). Some scientists suspect that memories are stored in the same cortical areas that were involved in the original perception of the information (Mishkin & Appenzeller, 1987). Brain-scan studies support this view. When people remember pictures, visual parts of the brain become active. And when people remember sounds, auditory areas become active, just as they did when the information was first perceived (Nyberg et al., 2000; Thompson & Kosslyn, 2000; Wheeler, Petersen, & Buckner, 2000).

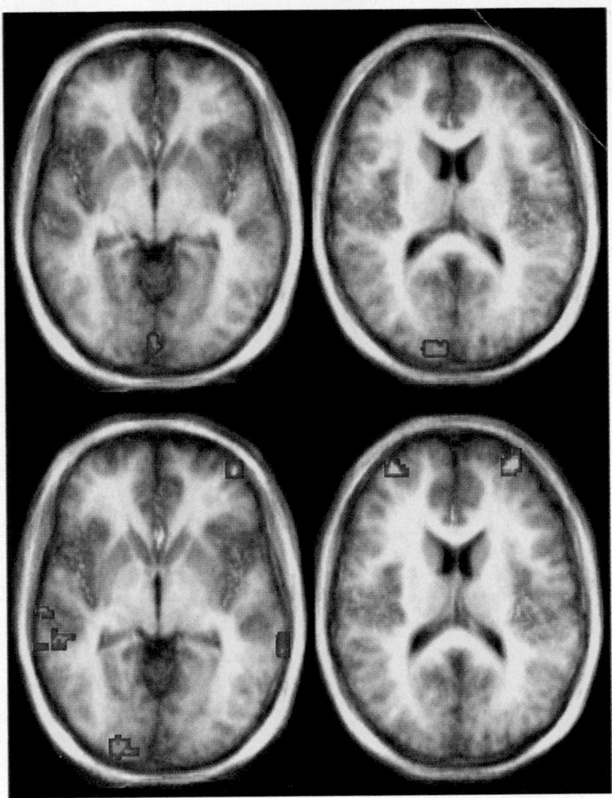

FIGURE 10.6 Brain Activity in Explicit and Implicit Memory

As these composite functional MRI scans show, patterns of brain activity differ depending on the type of memory task involved. When people had an explicit memory for dot patterns they had seen earlier, areas in the visual cortex, temporal lobes, and frontal lobes (indicated by orange in the lower photos) were more active. When people's implicit memories were activated, areas in the visual cortex (blue in the upper photos) were relatively inactive (Reber, Stark, & Squire, 1998).

The typical "memory" is a complex cluster of information. When you recall meeting a man yesterday, you remember his greeting, his tone of voice, how he looked, and where he was. Even a single concept, such as *shovel*, includes a lot of information (about its length, what it's made of, what it's used for . . .). These different pieces of information are probably processed separately and stored at different locations that are distributed across wide areas of the brain, with all the sites participating in the representation of the event or concept as a whole (Damasio et al., 1996; Squire, 1987). The role of the hippocampus may be to somehow bind together the diverse aspects of a memory at the time it is formed, so that even though these aspects are stored in different cortical sites, the memory can be retrieved as one coherent entity (Squire & Zola-Morgan, 1991).

Review 10.1 on the next page shows the structures that we have discussed and summarizes some of the memory-related functions associated with them. But we have given you just a few small nibbles from the smorgasbord of findings now available. Neuroscientists hope that someday they will be able to describe the entire stream of events in the brain that occur from the moment you say to yourself "I must remember this" to the moment you actually do remember . . . or find that you can't.

Hormones and Memory

Have you ever smelled fresh cookies and recalled a tender scene from your childhood? Do you have a vivid memory of seeing a particularly horrifying horror movie? Emotional memories such as these are often especially intense, and the explanation resides partly in our hormones.

Hormones released by the adrenal glands during stress and emotional arousal, including epinephrine (adrenaline) and certain steroids, enhance memory. If you give people a drug that prevents their adrenal glands from producing these hormones, they will remember less about emotional stories they heard than a control group will (Cahill et al., 1994). Conversely, if you give animals epinephrine right after learning, their memories will improve (McGaugh, 1990). The link between emotional arousal and memory makes evolutionary sense: Arousal tells the brain that an event or piece of information is important enough to encode and store for future use. Extreme arousal is not necessarily a good thing, however. When animals or people are given very high

REVIEW 10.1
Some Brain Areas Involved in Memory

No simple summary of brain areas associated with memory can do this complex topic justice. Here are just a few of the areas and functions that have been studied.

Brain Area	Associated Memory Function
Frontal lobes	Short-term memory tasks
Prefrontal cortex, parts of temporal lobes	Efficient encoding of words, pictures
Hippocampus	Formation of long-term declarative memories; may "bind together" diverse elements of a memory so it can be retrieved later as a coherent entity
Cerebellum	Formation and retention of simple classically conditioned responses
Cerebral cortex	Storage of long-term memories, possibly in areas involved in the original perception of the information

Frontal lobe
Cerebral cortex
Prefrontal cortex
Hippocampus
Cerebellum

doses of stress hormones, their memories for learned tasks sometimes suffer instead of improving; a moderate dose may be optimal. So if you want to remember material for a test, you should probably aim for an arousal level while studying that is somewhere between "hyper" and "laid back."

How might hormones produced in the adrenal glands affect storage of information in the brain? One possibility is that epinephrine causes the level of glucose (a sugar) to rise in the bloodstream. Although epinephrine does not readily enter the brain from the bloodstream, glucose does. Once in the brain, glucose may enhance memory either directly or by altering the effects of neurotransmitters (Gold, 1987). In any case, glucose seems to act as fuel for the brain; when brain areas are active, those areas consume more glucose.

It follows that increasing the amount of glucose available to the brain could enhance memory. Indeed, this "sweet memories" effect does occur both in aged rats and mice and in human beings. In one encouraging study, healthy older people fasted overnight, drank a glass of lemonade sweetened with either glucose or saccharin, and then took two memory tests. The saccharine-laced drink had no effect on their performance, but lemonade with glucose greatly boosted their ability to recall a taped passage 5 or 40 minutes after hearing it (Manning, Hall, & Gold, 1990). And this effect is not confined to older people. If the memory task is challenging, college students' memories also benefit from a shot of glucose (Korol & Gold, 1998). Research with rats suggests that a challenging task drains glucose specifically from the hippocampus, the "gateway to memory" (McNay et al., 2006).

Fuel for your memory?

Before you reach for a candy bar, you should know that the fat in most sugary treats blunts the positive effects of glucose. Moreover, the effective dose of glucose is narrow; too much can impair cognitive functioning instead of helping it. The "sweet memories" effect also depends on your metabolism, what you have eaten that day, and the level of glucose in your brain before you ingest it. In this area, as in others in the biology of memory, many findings are still provisional, and we have much to learn. No one knows yet exactly how the brain actually stores information, how different memory circuits link up with one another, or how a student is able to locate and retrieve information at the drop of a multiple-choice item.

QUICK quiz

We hope your memory circuits will link up to help you answer this quiz.

1. Is long-term potentiation associated with (a) increased responsiveness of certain receiving neurons to transmitting neurons, (b) a decrease in receptors on certain receiving neurons, or (c) reaching your true potential?
2. The cerebellum has been associated with __________ memories; the hippocampus has been associated with __________ memories.
3. *True or false:* Hormone research suggests that if you want to remember well, you should be as relaxed as possible while learning.
4. After reading about glucose and memory, should you immediately start gulping down lemonade? Why or why not?

Answers:

1. a 2. procedural, declarative 3. false 4. You should not pig out on sugar yet. You do not know what amount might be effective for you, given your metabolism, brain levels of glucose, and dietary habits. And you need to consider the health risks of consuming sugary foods with lots of calories and little nutritional value.

WHAT'S AHEAD

- What's wrong with trying to memorize in a rote fashion when you are studying, and what's a better strategy?
- Memory tricks are fun, but are they always useful?

How We Remember

Once we understand how memory works, we can use that understanding to encode and store information so that it sticks in our minds and will be there when we need it. What are the best strategies to use?

Effective Encoding

Our memories, as we have seen, are not exact replicas of experience. Sensory information is summarized and encoded—for example, as words or images—almost as soon as it is detected. When you hear a lecture you may hang on every word (we hope you do), but you do not memorize those words verbatim. You extract the main points and encode them.

To remember information well, you have to encode it accurately in the first place. With some kinds of information, accurate encoding takes place automatically, without effort. Think about where you usually sit in your psychology class. When were you last there? You can probably provide this information easily, even though you never made a deliberate effort to encode it. But many kinds of information require *effortful encoding*—the plot of a novel, the procedures for assembling a cabinet, the arguments for and against a proposed law. To retain such information, you might have to select the main points, label concepts, or associate the information with personal experiences or with material you already know. Experienced students know that most of the information in a college course requires effortful encoding (otherwise known as studying).

Encoding classroom material for later recall usually requires a deliberate effort. Which of these students do you think will remember best?

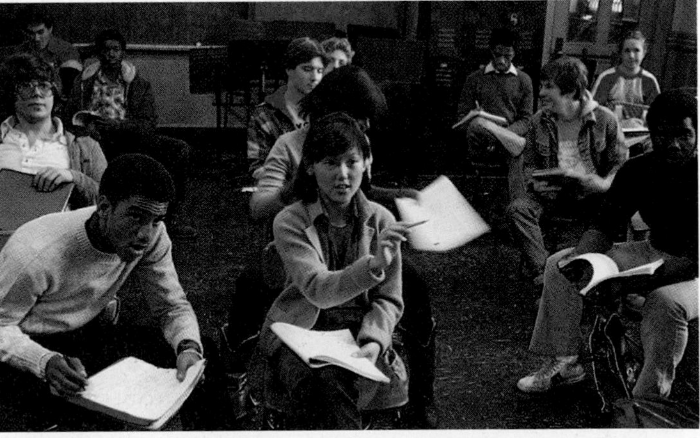

Rehearsal

maintenance rehearsal Rote repetition of material in order to maintain its availability in memory.

elaborative rehearsal Association of new information with already stored knowledge and analysis of the new information to make it memorable.

deep processing In the encoding of information, the processing of meaning rather than simply the physical or sensory features of a stimulus.

An important technique for keeping information in short-term memory and increasing the chances of long-term retention is *rehearsal*, the review or practice of material while you are learning it. When people are prevented from rehearsing, the contents of their short-term memories quickly fade (Peterson & Peterson, 1959). You are taking advantage of rehearsal when you look up a phone number and then repeat it over and over in order to keep it in short-term memory until you no longer need it. And, when you can't remember a phone number because you have always used speed dial to call it, you are learning what happens when you *don't* rehearse!

A poignant demonstration of the power of rehearsal once occurred during a session with H. M. (Ogden & Corkin, 1991). The experimenter gave H. M. five digits to repeat and remember, but then she was unexpectedly called away. When she returned after more than an hour, H. M. was able to repeat the five digits correctly. He had been rehearsing them the entire time.

Short-term memory holds many kinds of information, including visual information and abstract meanings. But most people, or at least most hearing people, seem to favor speech for encoding and rehearsing the contents of short-term memory. The speech may be spoken aloud or to oneself. When people make errors on short-term memory tests that use letters or words, they often confuse items that sound the same or similar, such as *d* and *t*, or *bear* and *bare*. These errors suggest that they have been rehearsing verbally.

Some strategies for rehearsing are more effective than others. **Maintenance rehearsal** involves merely the rote repetition of the material. This kind of rehearsal is fine for keeping information in STM, but it will not always lead to long-term retention. A better strategy if you want to remember for the long haul is **elaborative rehearsal**, also called *elaboration of encoding* (Cermak & Craik, 1979; Craik & Tulving, 1975). Elaboration involves associating new items of information with material that has already been stored or with other new facts. It can also involve analyzing the physical, sensory, or semantic features of an item.

Suppose, for example, that you are studying the hypothalamus, discussed in Chapter 4. Simply memorizing the definition of the hypothalamus in a rote manner is unlikely to help much. But if you can elaborate the concept of the hypothalamus, you are more likely to remember it. For example, knowing that *hypo* means "under" tells you its location—under the thalamus. Knowing that it is part of the limbic system should clue you that it is probably involved in survival drives and emotion. Many students try to pare down what they are learning to the bare essentials, but in fact, knowing more details about something makes it more memorable; that is what elaboration means

When actors learn a script, they do not rely on maintenance rehearsal alone. They also use elaborative rehearsal and deep processing—by analyzing the meaning of their lines and by associating their lines with imagined information about the character they are playing.

A related strategy for prolonging retention is **deep processing**, or the processing of meaning (Craik & Lockhart, 1972). If you process only the physical or sensory features of a stimulus, such as how the word *hypothalamus* is spelled and how it sounds, your processing will be shallow even if it is

elaborated. If you recognize patterns and assign labels to objects or events ("The *hypo*thalamus is *below* the thalamus"), your processing will be somewhat deeper. If you fully analyze the meaning of what you are trying to remember (for example, by encoding the functions and importance of the hypothalamus), your processing will be deeper yet.

Shallow processing is sometimes useful; when you memorize a poem, for instance, you will want to pay attention to (and elaborately encode) the sounds of the words and the patterns of rhythm in the poem and not just the poem's meaning. Usually, however, deep processing is more effective. That is why, if you try to memorize information that has little or no meaning for you, the information may not stick.

mnemonics Strategies and tricks for improving memory, such as the use of a verse or a formula.

Mnemonics

In addition to using elaborative rehearsal and deep processing, people who want to give their powers of memory a boost sometimes use **mnemonics** [neh-MON-iks], formal strategies and tricks for encoding, storing, and retaining information. (Mnemosyne, pronounced neh-MOZ-eh-nee, was the ancient Greek goddess of memory. Can you remember her?) Some mnemonics take the form of easily memorized rhymes (e.g., "Thirty days hath September/April, June, and November . . ."). Others use formulas (e.g., "**E**very **g**ood **b**oy **d**oes **f**ine" for remembering which notes are on the lines of the treble clef in musical notation). Still others use visual images or word associations. The best mnemonics force you to encode material actively and thoroughly. They may also reduce the amount of information by chunking it, which is why, in ads, many companies use words for their phone numbers instead of unmemorable numbers ("Dial GET RICH").

Some stage performers with amazing recall rely on far more complicated mnemonics. We are not going to spend time on them here, because for ordinary memory tasks, such tricks are often no more effective than rote rehearsal, and sometimes they are actually worse (Wang, Thomas, & Ouellette, 1992). Most memory researchers do not use such mnemonics themselves (Hébert, 2001). After all, why bother to memorize a grocery list using a fancy mnemonic when you can write down what you need to buy? The fastest route to a good memory is to follow the principles suggested by the findings in this section and by research reviewed in "Taking Psychology with You."

- How might new information "erase" old memories?

"YOU SIMPLY ASSOCIATE EACH NUMBER WITH A WORD, SUCH AS 'TABLE' AND 3,476,029."

QUICK quiz

Perhaps Mnemosyne will help you answer this question.

Camille is furious with her history professor. "I read the chapter three times, but I still failed the exam," she fumes. "The test must have been unfair." What's wrong with Camille's reasoning, and what are some other possible explanations for her poor performance, based on principles of critical thinking and what you have learned so far about memory?

Answer:

Camille is reasoning emotionally and is not examining the assumptions underlying her explanation. Perhaps she relied on automatic rather than effortful encoding, used maintenance instead of elaborative rehearsal, and used shallow instead of deep processing when she studied. She may also have tried to encode everything instead of being selective.

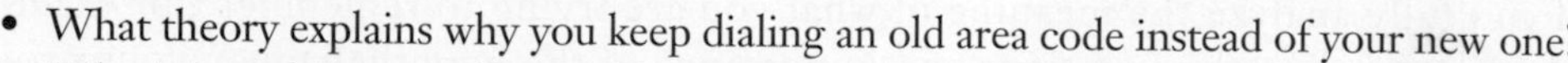

- What theory explains why you keep dialing an old area code instead of your new one?
- Why is it easier to recall experiences from elementary school if you see pictures of your classmates?
- Why are many researchers skeptical about claims of "repressed" and "recovered" memories?

Why We Forget

Have you ever, in the heat of some deliriously happy moment, said to yourself, "I'll never forget this, never, *never*, NEVER"? Do you find that you can more clearly remember saying those words than the deliriously happy moment itself? Sometimes you encode an event, you rehearse it, you analyze its meaning, you tuck it away in long-term storage—and still you forget it. Is it any wonder that most of us have wished, at one time or another, for a "photographic memory"?

Actually, having a perfect memory is not the blessing that you might suppose. The Russian psychologist Alexander Luria (1968) once told of a journalist, S., who could reproduce giant grids of numbers both forward and backward, even after the passage of 15 years. To accomplish his astonishing feats, he used mnemonics, especially the formation of visual images. But you should not envy him, for he had a serious problem: He could not forget even when he wanted to. Along with the diamonds of experience, he kept dredging up the pebbles. Images he had formed in order to remember kept creeping into consciousness, distracting him and interfering with his ability to concentrate. At times he even had trouble holding a conversation because the other person's words would set off a jumble of associations. Eventually, S. took to supporting himself by traveling from place to place, demonstrating his mnemonic abilities for audiences.

WELL, FOR CRYING OUT LOUD! AL TOWBRIDGE! WHAT IS IT, NINE YEARS, SEVEN MONTHS, AND TWELVE DAYS SINCE I LAST RAN INTO YOU? TEN-THIRTY-TWO A.M., A SATURDAY, FELCHER'S HARDWARE STORE. YOU WERE BUYING SEALER FOR YOUR BLACKTOP DRIVEWAY. TELL ME, AL, HOW DID THAT SEALER WORK? DID IT HOLD UP?

MR. TOTAL RECALL

Or consider a modern case, of a woman called A. J. (Parker, Cahill, & McGaugh, 2006). A. J., who is in her early forties and has average intelligence, possesses an extraordinary memory for her own past. When given any date back to 1980, A. J. is able to say instantly what she was doing, what day of the week it was, and whether anything of great importance happened on that date. A. J. does not have any special talent for memorizing meaningless material such as numbers or letters. Nor does she use mnemonics; rather, she describes her recollections as nonstop and uncontrollable. Like other people who have unusually accurate memories, she finds her abilities to be a mixed blessing. Although she enjoys recalling events from her past, especially happy occasions, she finds it "totally exhausting." "Some call it a gift," she says, "but I call it a burden. I run my entire life through my head every day and it drives me crazy!!!"

Paradoxically, then, forgetting is adaptive: We need to forget some things if we wish to remember efficiently (Bjork, Bjork, & Anderson, 1998). Nonetheless, most of us forget more than we would like to, and we would like to know why. In the early days of psychology, in an effort to measure pure memory loss independent of personal experience, Hermann Ebbinghaus (1885/1913) memorized long lists of nonsense syllables, such as *bok*, *waf*, or *ged*, and then tested his retention over a period of several weeks. Most of his forgetting occurred soon after the initial learning and then leveled off (see Figure 10.7a). Ebbinghaus's method of studying memory was adopted by generations of psychologists, even though it did not tell them much about the kinds of memories that people care about most.

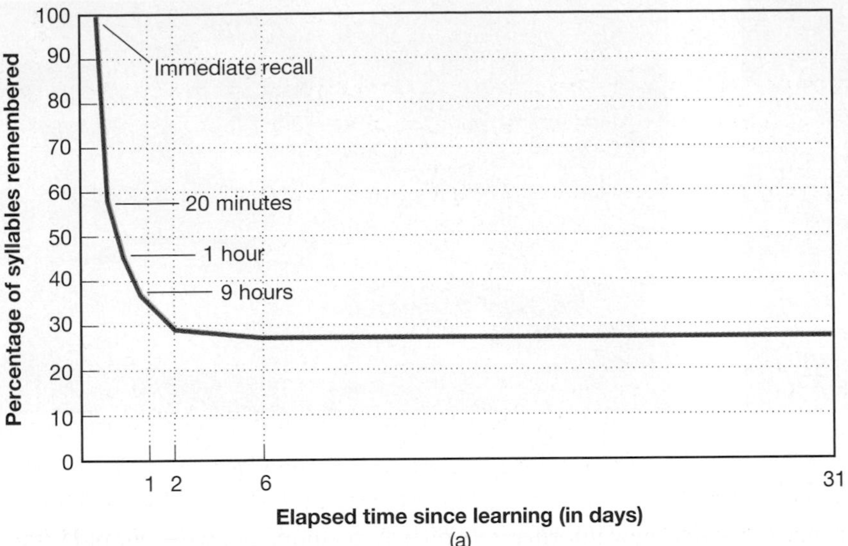

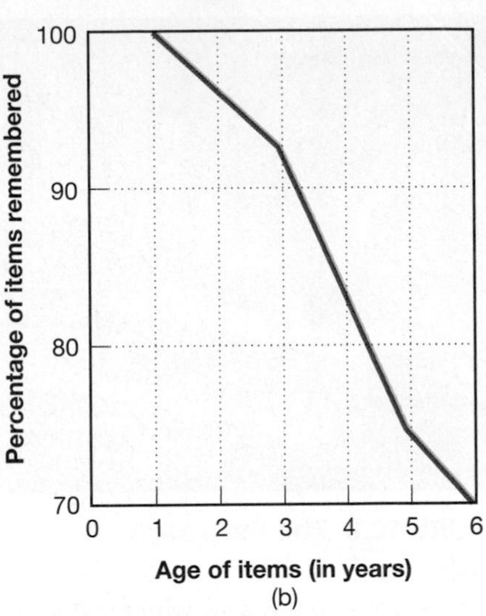

FIGURE 10.7 Two Kinds of Forgetting Curves

When Hermann Ebbinghaus tested his own memory for nonsense syllables, forgetting was rapid at first and then tapered off (a). In contrast, when Marigold Linton tested her own memory for personal events over a period of several years, her retention was excellent at first, but then it fell off at a gradual but steady rate (b).

A century later, Marigold Linton decided to find out how people forget real events rather than nonsense syllables. Like Ebbinghaus, she used herself as a subject, but she charted the curve of forgetting over years rather than days. Every day for 12 years she recorded on a 4- × 6-inch card two or more things that had happened to her that day. Eventually, she accumulated a catalogue of thousands of discrete events, both trivial ("I have dinner at the Canton Kitchen: delicious lobster dish") and significant ("I land at Orly Airport in Paris"). Once a month, she took a random sampling of all the cards accumulated to that point, noted whether she could remember the events on them, and tried to date the events. Linton (1978) expected the kind of rapid forgetting reported by Ebbinghaus. Instead, as you can see in Figure 10.7b, she found that long-term forgetting was slower and proceeded at a much more constant pace, as details gradually dropped out of her memories.

Of course, some memories, especially those that mark important transitions, are more memorable than others. But why did Marigold Linton, like the rest of us, forget so many details? Psychologists have proposed five mechanisms to account for forgetting: decay, replacement of old memories by new ones, interference, cue-dependent forgetting, and psychological amnesia brought on by repression.

decay theory The theory that information in memory eventually disappears if it is not accessed; it applies better to short-term than to long-term memory.

Decay

One commonsense view, the **decay theory**, holds that memory traces fade with time if they are not accessed now and then. We have already seen that decay occurs in sensory memory and that it occurs in short-term memory as well unless we keep rehearsing the material. However, the mere passage of time does not account so well for forgetting in long-term memory. People commonly forget things that happened only yesterday while remembering events from many years ago. Indeed, some memories, both procedural and declarative, can last a lifetime. If you learned to swim as a child, you will still know how to swim at age 30, even if you have not been in a pool or lake for 22 years. We are also happy to report that some school lessons have great staying power. In one study, people did well on a Spanish test some 50 years after taking Spanish in high school, even though most had hardly used Spanish at all in the intervening years (Bahrick, 1984). Decay alone, although it may play some role, cannot entirely explain lapses in long-term memory.

Motor skills, which are stored as procedural memories, can last a lifetime; they never decay.

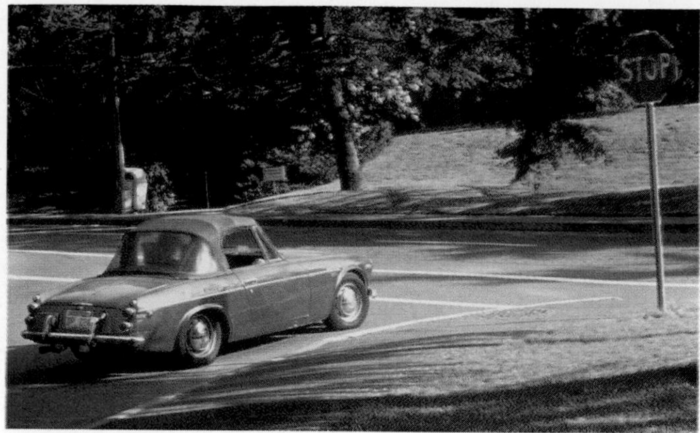

FIGURE 10.8 The Stop Sign Study
When people who saw a car with a yield sign (left) were later asked if they had seen "the stop sign" (a misleading question), many said they had. Similarly, when those shown a stop sign were asked if they had seen "the yield sign," many said yes. These false memories persisted even after the participants were told about the misleading questions, suggesting that misleading information had erased their original mental representations of the signs (Loftus, Miller, & Burns, 1978).

Replacement

Another theory holds that new information entering memory can wipe out old information, just as rerecording on an audiotape or videotape will obliterate the original material. In a study supporting this view, researchers showed people slides of a traffic accident and used leading questions to get them to think that they had seen a stop sign when they had really seen a yield sign, or vice versa (see Figure 10.8). People in a control group who were not misled in this way were able to identify the sign they had actually seen. Later, all the participants were told the purpose of the study and were asked to guess whether they had been misled. Almost all of those who had been misled continued to insist that they had *really, truly* seen the sign whose existence had been planted in their minds (Loftus, Miller, & Burns, 1978). The researchers interpreted this finding to mean that the subjects had not just been trying to please them and that people's original perceptions had in fact been erased by the misleading information.

Interference

A third theory holds that forgetting occurs because similar items of information interfere with one another in either storage or retrieval; the information may get into memory and stay there, but it becomes confused with other information. Such interference, which occurs in both short- and long-term memory, is especially common when you have to recall isolated facts—names, addresses, personal identification numbers, area codes, and the like.

Suppose you are at a party and you meet someone named Julie. A little later you meet someone named Judy. You go on to talk to other people, and after an hour, you again bump into Julie, but by mistake you call her Judy. The second name has interfered with the first. This type of interference, in which new information interferes with the ability to remember old information, is called **retroactive interference**:

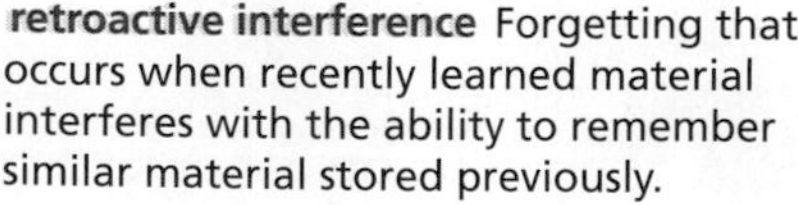
retroactive interference Forgetting that occurs when recently learned material interferes with the ability to remember similar material stored previously.

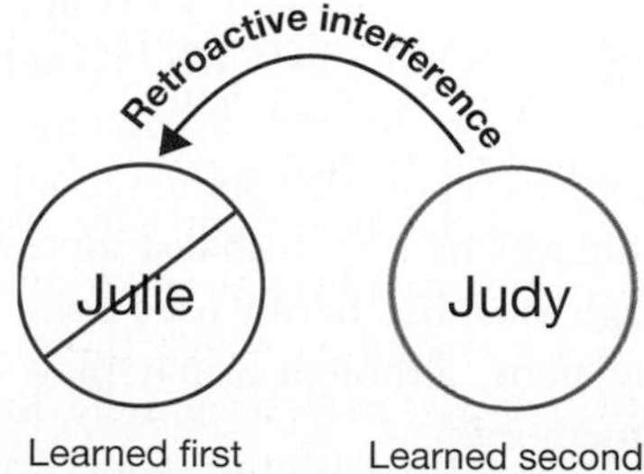

Retroactive interference is illustrated by the story of an absentminded professor of ichthyology (the study of fish) who complained that whenever he learned the name of a new student, he forgot the name of a fish. But whereas with replacement, the new memory erases the old and makes it irretrievable, in retroactive interference the loss of the old memory is sometimes just temporary. With a little concentration, that professor could probably recall his new students and his old fish.

Because new information is constantly entering memory, we are all vulnerable to the effects of retroactive interference, or at least most of us are. H. M. is an exception; his memories of childhood and adolescence are unusually detailed, clear, and unchanging. H. M. can remember actors who were famous when he was a child, the films they were in, and who their costars were. He also knows the names of friends from the second grade. Presumably, these early declarative memories were not subject to interference from memories acquired since the operation, for the simple reason that H. M. has not acquired any new memories.

Interference also works in the opposite direction. Old information (such as the Spanish you learned in high school) may interfere with the ability to remember new information (such as the French you are trying to learn now). This type of interference is called **proactive interference**:

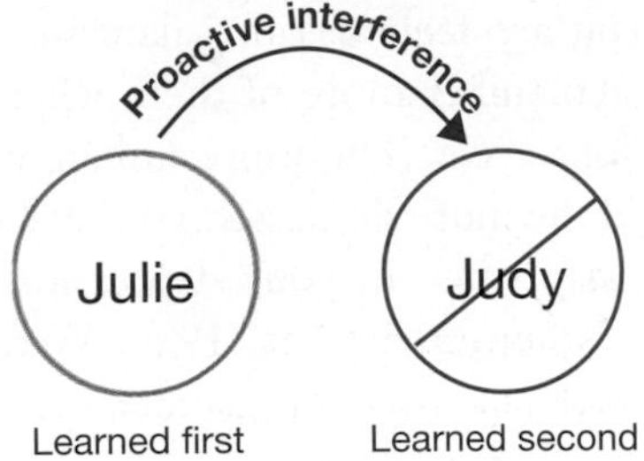

Over a period of weeks, months, and years, proactive interference may cause more forgetting than retroactive interference does, because we have stored up so much information that can potentially interfere with anything new.

Cue-Dependent Forgetting

Often, when we need to remember, we rely on *retrieval cues*, items of information that can help us find the specific information we're looking for. For example, if you are trying to remember the last name of an actor, it might help to know the person's first name or the name of a recent movie the actor starred in.

When we lack retrieval cues, we may feel as if we are lost in the mind's library. In long-term memory, this type of memory failure, called **cue-dependent forgetting**, may be the most common type of all. Willem Wagenaar (1986), who, like Marigold Linton, recorded critical details about events in his life, found that within a year, he had forgotten 20 percent of those details, and after five years, he had forgotten 60 percent. However, when he gathered cues from witnesses about ten events that he thought he had forgotten, he was able to recall something about all ten, which suggests that some of his forgetting was cue dependent.

Cues that were present when you learned a new fact or had an experience are apt to be especially useful later as retrieval aids. That may explain why remembering is often easier when you are in the same physical environment as you were when an event occurred: Cues in the present context match those from the past. Ordinarily, this overlap helps us remember the past more accurately. But it may also help account for the eerie phenomenon of *déjà vu*, the fleeting sense of having been in *exactly* the

proactive interference Forgetting that occurs when previously stored material interferes with the ability to remember similar, more recently learned material.

cue-dependent forgetting The inability to retrieve information stored in memory because of insufficient cues for recall.

Charlie Chaplin's film *City Lights* provides a classic illustration of state-dependent memory. After Charlie saves a drunken millionaire's life, the two spend the rest of the evening carousing. But the next day, after sobering up, the millionaire fails to recognize Charlie and gives him the cold shoulder. Then, once again, the millionaire gets drunk—and once again greets Charlie as a pal. (Note: This is not an endorsement of drunkenness! Your memory will be best if you are sober during both encoding and recall.)

same situation that you are in now (*déjà vu* means "already seen" in French). Some element in the present situation, familiar from some other context that you cannot identify—even a dream, a novel, or a movie—may make the entire situation seem so familiar that it feels like it happened before (Brown, 2004).

Your mental or physical state may also act as a retrieval cue, evoking a **state-dependent memory**. For example, if you are fearful or relaxed at the time of an event, you may remember that event best when you are once again in the same emotional state (Lang et al., 2001). When victims of violent crimes have trouble recalling details of the experience, it may be in part because they are feeling different emotions than they felt at the time of the crime (Clark, Milberg, & Erber, 1987).

Your memories can also be biased by whether or not your current mood is consistent with the emotional nature of the material you are trying to remember, a phenomenon known as **mood-congruent memory** (Fiedler et al., 2001; Mayer, McCormick, & Strong, 1995). You are more likely to remember happy events, and forget or ignore unhappy ones, when you are feeling happy than when you are feeling sad. Likewise, you are apt to remember unhappy events better and remember more of them when you are feeling unhappy, which in turn creates a vicious cycle. The more unhappy memories you recall, the more depressed you feel, and the more depressed you feel, the more unhappy memories you recall . . . so you stay stuck in your depression and make it even worse (Lyubomirsky, Caldwell, & Nolen-Hoeksema, 1998; Wenzel, 2005). You can break out of this trap by deliberately focusing on memories of happy events instead of unpleasant ones.

The Repression Controversy

A final theory of forgetting is concerned with **amnesia**, the loss of memory for important personal information. Amnesia most commonly results from organic conditions such as brain disease or head injury, and is usually temporary. In *psychogenic amnesia*, however, the causes of forgetting are psychological, such as a need to escape feelings of embarrassment, guilt, shame, disappointment, or emotional shock. Psychogenic amnesia begins immediately after the precipitating event, involves massive memory loss including loss of personal identity, and usually ends suddenly, after just a few weeks. Despite its frequent portrayal in films and novels, in real life it is quite rare (McNally, 2003).

Psychologists generally accept the notion of psychogenic amnesia. *Traumatic amnesia*, however, is far more controversial. Traumatic amnesia allegedly involves the burying of specific traumatic events for a long period of time, often for many years. When the memory returns, it is supposedly immune to the usual processes of distortion and confabulation, and is recalled with perfect accuracy. The notion of traumatic amnesia originated with the psychoanalytic theory of Sigmund Freud, who argued that the mind defends itself from unwelcome and upsetting memories through the mechanism of **repression**—the involuntary pushing of threatening or upsetting information into the unconscious (see Chapter 13).

Most memory researchers reject the argument that a special unconscious mechanism called "repression" is necessary to explain either psychogenic or traumatic amnesia. Richard McNally (2003) reviewed the experimental and clinical evidence carefully

state-dependent memory The tendency to remember something when the rememberer is in the same physical or mental state as during the original learning or experience.

mood-congruent memory The tendency to remember experiences that are consistent with one's current mood and overlook or forget experiences that are not.

amnesia The partial or complete loss of memory for important personal information.

repression In psychoanalytic theory, the selective, involuntary pushing of threatening or upsetting information into the unconscious.

and concluded, "The notion that the mind protects itself by repressing or dissociating memories of trauma, rendering them inaccessible to awareness, is a piece of psychiatric folklore devoid of convincing empirical support." The problem for most people who have suffered disturbing experiences is not that they cannot remember, but rather that they cannot forget: The memories keep intruding. There is no case on record of anyone who has "repressed" the memory of being in a concentration camp, being in combat, or being the victim of an earthquake or a terrorist attack, although details of even these horrible experiences are subject to distortion and fading over time, as are all memories.

THINKING CRITICALLY

CONSIDER OTHER INTERPRETATIONS

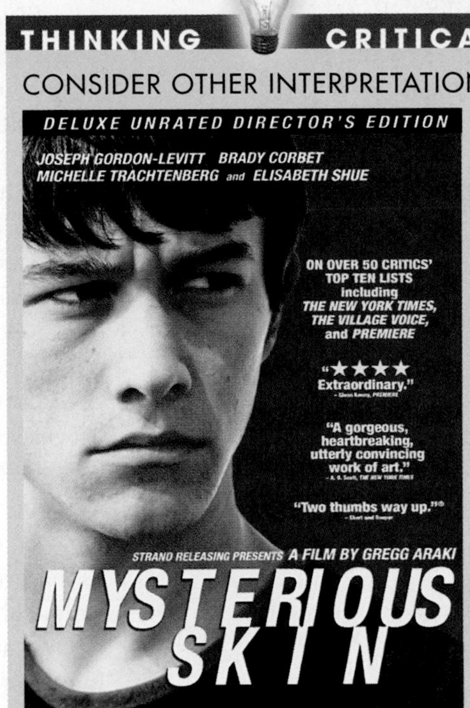

In the movie *Mysterious Skin*, a young man comes to believe that he has repressed a memory of being abducted by aliens when he was a child. In real life, how can critical thinkers evaluate claims of "repressed" and "recovered" memories? What other possible explanations should we consider when hearing stories about memories that are said to have been repressed until surfacing after the passage of many years?

Further, "repression" is hard to distinguish from normal forgetting. People who seem to forget disturbing experiences could be intentionally keeping themselves from retrieving their painful memories by distracting themselves whenever a memory is reactivated. Or they may be focusing consciously on positive memories instead. Perhaps, understandably, they are not rehearsing unhappy memories, so the memories fade with time. Perhaps they are simply avoiding the retrieval cues that would evoke the memories. But a reluctance to think about an upsetting experience is not the same as an *inability* to remember it (McNally, 2003).

The debate over traumatic amnesia and repression erupted into the public arena in the 1990s, when claims of recovered memories of sexual abuse began to occur. Many women and some men came to believe, during psychotherapy, that they could recall long-buried—repressed—memories of having been sexually victimized, usually by a father. For therapists who accepted the notion of repression, such claims were entirely believable (Brown, Scheflin, & Whitfield, 1999; Herman, 1992). But most researchers argue that although real abuse certainly occurs, many false memories of victimization have been encouraged by therapists who are unaware of the research we described earlier on the power of suggestion and the dangers of confabulation (Lindsay & Read, 1994; Loftus & Ketchem, 1994; McNally, 2003; Schacter, 2001). By asking leading questions, and by encouraging clients to construct vivid images of abuse, revisit those images frequently, and focus on emotional aspects of the images, such therapists unwittingly set up the very conditions that encourage confabulation and false memories—just as researchers have done purposely in the laboratory.

Since the 1990s, accusations have steadily declined and many accusers have reconciled with their families, some after realizing that their memories were false (Gardner, 2006; McHugh et al., 2004). The concept of repression, however, refuses to die. One team of researchers has even claimed to have discovered where in the brain repression occurs (Anderson et al., 2004). They had volunteers learn pairs of words consisting of a cue word and a target word (e.g., *ordeal–roach*), and then tested them for the target word by presenting just the cue word. During testing, the participants were told to either remember the target word or avoid thinking about it, while functional MRI scans monitored their brain activity. The "remember" instructions produced somewhat more accurate recall than the "don't remember" instructions. That is hardly evidence of repression, though, because the "don't remember" instructions would have discouraged rehearsal of the target word. Besides, participants remembered most of the target words that they were supposed to "repress"! The brain scans did show elevated activity in the prefrontal cortex and reduced activity in the hippocampus when the volunteers were trying not to think about the target words. But that is not necessarily evidence for repression either, because the volunteers might simply have been distract-

I recently recovered a crucial repressed memory. But then I forgot it.

ing themselves to comply with the instructions. Most important, what does the forgetting of mundane words have to do with the "repression" of painful experiences (Garry & Loftus, 2004)? The uncritical response to this research did prove one thing, though: Many people are unwilling to repress the concept of repression, despite the lack of evidence supporting it.

On the other hand, it is obviously possible for someone to forget a single unhappy or deeply unpleasant experience and remember it years later, just as going back to your elementary school might trigger a memory of the time you were embarrassed in front of your whole class. How then should we respond to an individual's claim to have repressed and later recovered memories of an early trauma? Some people think that recovered memories of sexual abuse or other traumas should always be trusted, and some think that such memories are almost always likely to be inaccurate. How can we resist either–or thinking and draw on the findings of psychological science when evaluating someone's claim to have recovered a long-buried memory?

First, a person's recollections are likely to be trustworthy if there is some kind of corroborating evidence available (for example, from medical records, police or school reports, or the accounts of family members). In the absence of supporting evidence, it is important to consider the content of the recovered memory and how it was recovered. The plausibility of the memory increases when it concerns specific possible events, and when the person spontaneously recalled those events without being pressured or influenced by other people.

But given what we know about memory, we should be skeptical if the person says that he or she has memories from the first year or two of life. (As we will see in the next section, this is not possible.) We should also be skeptical if a person suddenly recovers a traumatic memory as a result of therapy or after hearing about supposed cases of recovered memory in the news or reading about them in autobiographies. We should be skeptical if, over time, the person's memories become more and more implausible—for instance, the person says that sexual abuse continued day and night for 15 years without ever being remembered and without anyone else in the household ever noticing anything amiss. And we should hear alarm bells go off if a therapist used suggestive techniques, such as hypnosis, dream analysis, "age regression," guided imagery, and leading questions, to "help" a patient recall the alleged abuse, because these techniques increase confabulation (see Chapter 17).

QUICK quiz

If you have not repressed what you just read, try these questions.

1. When reading the novel *Even Cowgirls Get the Blues* years ago, Wilma became a fan of the author, Tom Robbins. Later, she developed a crush on actor/director Tim Robbins, but every time she tried to recall his name, she called him "Tom." Why?
2. When a man at his twentieth high-school reunion sees his old friends, he recalls incidents he thought were long forgotten. Why?
3. What mechanisms other than repression could account for a person's psychogenic amnesia?

Answers:

1. proactive interference 2. The sight of his friends provides retrieval cues for the incidents. 3. The person could be intentionally avoiding the memory by using distraction or focusing on positive experiences; failure to rehearse the memory may be causing it to fade; or the person may be avoiding retrieval cues that would evoke the memory.

WHAT'S**AHEAD**

- Why are the first few years of life a mental blank?
- Why have human beings been called the "storytelling animal"?

Autobiographical Memories

For most of us, our memories about our own experiences are by far the most fascinating. We use them to entertain ("Did I ever tell you about the time . . . ?"); we modify them—some people even publish them—in order to create an image of ourselves; we analyze them to learn more about who we are.

Childhood Amnesia: The Missing Years

A curious aspect of autobiographical memory is that most adults cannot recall any events from earlier than the third or fourth year of life. A few people apparently can recall momentous experiences that occurred when they were as young as 2 years old, such as the birth of a sibling, but not earlier ones (Newcombe et al., 2000; Usher & Neisser, 1993). As adults, we cannot remember being fed in infancy by our parents, taking our first steps, or uttering our first halting sentences. We are victims of **childhood amnesia** (sometimes called *infantile amnesia*).

THINKING CRITICALLY

AVOID EMOTIONAL REASONING

Many people get upset at the idea that their earliest experiences are lost to memory and angrily insist that memories from the first two years must be accurate. How can research help us think clearly about this issue?

There is something disturbing about childhood amnesia—so disturbing that some people adamantly deny it, claiming to remember events from the second or even the first year of life. But like other false memories, these are merely reconstructions based on photographs, family stories, and imagination. The "remembered" event may not even have taken place. Swiss psychologist Jean Piaget (1952b) once reported a memory of nearly being kidnapped at the age of 2. Piaget remembered sitting in his pram, watching his nurse as she bravely defended him from the kidnapper. He remembered the scratches she received on her face. He remembered a police officer with a short cloak and white baton who finally chased the kidnapper away. But when Piaget was 15, his nurse wrote to his parents confessing that she had made up the entire story. Piaget noted, "I therefore must have heard, as a child, the account of this story . . . and projected it into the past in the form of a visual memory, which was a memory of a memory, but false."

Of course, we all retain procedural memories from the toddler stage, when we first learned to use a fork, drink from a cup, and pull a wagon. We also retain semantic memories acquired early in life: the rules of counting, the names of people and things, knowledge about objects in the world, words and meanings. Toddlers who are only 1 to 2 years old often reveal nonverbally that they remember past experiences (for example, by imitating something they saw earlier); and some 4-year-olds can remember experiences that occurred before age $2^1/_2$ (Bauer, 2002; McDonough & Mandler, 1994; Tustin & Hayne, 2006). What young children do not do well is encode and retain their early episodic memories—memories of particular events—and carry them into later childhood or adulthood.

Freud thought that childhood amnesia was a special case of repression, but memory researchers today think that repression has nothing to do with it. Biological psychologists believe that childhood amnesia occurs because brain areas involved in the formation or storage of events, and other areas involved in working memory and decision making (such as the prefrontal cortex), are not well developed until a few years after birth (McKee & Squire, 1993; Newcombe et al., 2000).

childhood (infantile) amnesia The inability to remember events and experiences that occurred during the first two or three years of life.

Psychologists have devised ingenious methods to measure memory in infants. This infant, whose leg is attached by a string to a colorful mobile, will learn within minutes to kick in order to make the mobile move. She may remember the trick a week later—an example of procedural memory (Rovee-Collier, 1993). However, when she is older she will not remember the experience itself. Like the rest of us, she will fall victim to childhood amnesia.

Cognitive psychologists have proposed other explanations, which include the following:

1 **Lack of a sense of self.** In one view, we cannot have an autobiographical memory of our*selves* until we have a self to remember. Indeed, autobiographical memories do not begin until the emergence of a self-concept, an event that occurs at somewhat different ages for different children, but usually not before the age of 2 (Howe, Courage, & Peterson, 1994).

2 **Impoverished encoding.** Young children's limited vocabularies and language skills prevent them from narrating some aspects of an experience to themselves or others. Later, after their linguistic abilities have matured, they still cannot use them to recall earlier, preverbal memories (Simcock & Hayne, 2002). It is as if children's ability to talk about a memory is frozen in time; to recall it, they can use only the words they knew when the experience happened. Moreover, even with increasing verbal ability, preschoolers encode their experiences far less elaborately than adults do because they have not yet mastered the social conventions for reporting events; they do not know what is important and interesting to others. Instead, they tend to rely on adults' questions to provide retrieval cues ("Where did we go for breakfast?" "Who did you go trick-or-treating with?"). This dependency on adults may prevent them from building up a stable core of remembered material that will be available when they are older (Fivush & Hamond, 1991).

3 **A focus on the routine.** Preschoolers tend to focus on the routine, familiar aspects of an experience, such as eating lunch or playing with toys, rather than the distinctive aspects that will provide retrieval cues and make an event memorable in the long run (Fivush & Hamond, 1991).

4 **Children's ways of thinking about the world.** The cognitive schemas used by preschoolers are very different from those used by older children and adults. Only after acquiring language and starting school do children learn to think like adults. Their new, adultlike schemas do not contain the information and cues necessary for recalling earlier experiences, so memories of those experiences are lost (Howe & Courage, 1993).

Whatever the explanation for childhood amnesia, our first memories, even when they are not accurate, may provide useful insights into our personalities, current concerns, ambitions, and attitudes toward life. What are *your* first memories—or at least, what do you think they are?

GET INVOLVED!

➤ANALYZE A CHILDHOOD MEMORY

Write down as much as you can about an incident in your childhood that stands out in your memory. Now ask a friend or family member who was present at the time to write a description of the same event. Do your accounts differ? If so, why? What does this exercise tell you about the nature of memory and about your own personality or present concerns?

Memory and Narrative: The Stories of Our Lives

The communications researcher George Gerbner once observed that human beings are unique because they are the only animals that tell stories and live by the stories they tell. This view of human beings as the "storytelling animal" has had a huge impact in cognitive psychology. The *narratives* we compose to simplify and make sense of our lives have a profound influence on our plans, memories, love affairs, hatreds, ambitions, and dreams.

"And here I am at two years of age. Remember? Mom? Pop? No? Or how about this one. My first day of school. Anyone?"

Thus we say, "I am this way because, as a small child, this happened to me, and then my parents. . . ." We say, "Let me tell you the story of how we fell in love." We say, "When you hear what happened, you'll understand why I felt entitled to take such cold-hearted revenge." These stories are not necessarily fictions, as in the child's meaning of "tell me a story." Rather, they are attempts to provide a unifying theme that organizes and gives meaning to the events of our lives. But because these narratives rely heavily on memory, and because memories are reconstructed and are constantly shifting in response to present needs, beliefs, and experiences, our stories are also, to some degree, works of interpretation and imagination. Adult memories thus reveal as much about the present as they do about the past.

The nature of our autobiographical narratives depends on many of the processes discussed in this chapter. For example, elaborative encoding and deep processing help us retain memories about our own lives. This fact may help explain why girls and women tend to remember more childhood events than boys and men do, especially when the memories are emotional (Davis, 1999; Seidlitz & Diener, 1998). The two sexes are equally motivated to remember past events, equally likely to rehearse details about these events, and equally adept at describing the events, but females may encode more details in the first place, and these details may provide them with retrieval cues that enhance their recall.

When you construct a narrative about an incident in your life, you have many choices about how to do it. The "spin" you put on a story depends on who the audience is; you are apt to put in, leave out, understate, and embellish different things depending on whether you are telling about an event in your life to a therapist, your boss, or a new acquaintance on MySpace.com. Your story is also influenced by your purpose in relating it: for example, to convey facts, entertain, or elicit sympathy. As a result of these influences, distortions are apt to creep in, even when you think you're being accurate. And once those distortions are part of the story, they are likely to become part of your memory of the events themselves (Marsh & B. Tversky, 2004).

Your culture may also affect how you encode and tell your story. American college students live in a culture that emphasizes individuality, personal feelings, and self-expression, and their earliest childhood memories reflect that fact: They tend to report lengthy, emotionally elaborate memories of events, memories that focus on—who else?—themselves. In contrast, Chinese students, who live in a culture that emphasizes group solidarity, social roles, and personal humility, tend to report early memories of family or neighborhood activities, general routines, and emotionally neutral events (Wang, 2001).

Once we have formulated a story's central theme ("My parents opposed my plans," "My lover was domineering"), that theme may then serve as a cognitive schema that guides what we remember and what we forget (Mather, Shafir, & Johnson, 2000). For example, teenagers who have strong and secure attachments to their

mothers remember previous quarrels with their moms as being less intense and conflicted than they reported at the time. And teenagers who have more ambivalent and insecure attachments remember such quarrels as being worse than they were (Feeney & Cassidy, 2003). A story's theme may also influence our judgments of events and people in the present. If you have a fight with your lover, the central theme in your story about the fight might be negative ("He was a jerk") or neutral ("It was a mutual misunderstanding"). This theme may bias you to blame or forgive your partner long after you have forgotten what the conflict was all about or who said what (McGregor & Holmes, 1999). You can see that the spin you give a story is critical, so be careful about the stories you tell!

Important transitions in our lives tend to stand out in memory: going off to college, getting a first job, falling in love. But as we have seen throughout this chapter, many details about events, even those landmarks in our lives that we think we recall clearly, are distorted, forgotten, or added after the fact. Think of all the factors you have learned about that can trip you up when you are constructing your life story: confabulation, source misattribution, poor encoding and rehearsal strategies, interference, inadequate retrieval cues, suggestibility, and biases. By now, you should not be surprised that memory can be as fickle as it can be accurate. As cognitive psychologists have shown repeatedly, we are not merely actors in our personal life dramas; we also write the scripts.

QUICK quiz

You can't blame childhood amnesia if you have forgotten the answers to these questions.

1. Name four possible cognitive explanations of childhood amnesia.

2. Why are the themes in our life "stories" so important?

Answers:

1. lack of a sense of self in early childhood; impoverished encoding in early childhood; the tendency of preschoolers to focus on routine rather than distinctive aspects of an experience; the differences between earlier and later cognitive schemas **2.** They serve as cognitive schemas that guide what we remember and forget about the past, and they influence our judgments of events and people in the present.

Memory and Myth

The information you have read about in this chapter is having a significant impact on the criminal justice system. In part because of the work of psychological scientists, awareness about the fallibility of memory is growing among police, interrogators, prosecutors, and judges.

The case of Alan Newton, described at the start of this chapter, is far from unique. When psychological scientists examined 40 cases in which wrongful conviction had been established beyond a doubt, they found that 90 percent of those cases had involved a false identification by one or more eyewitnesses (Wells et al., 1998). Of course, not all eyewitness testimony is erroneous, and such testimony certainly needs to be heard and taken into account. But the potential for errors in identification makes it obvious how important it is to gather evidence carefully, ensure adequate legal representation for defendants, conduct police interviews using proper procedures, reduce pressure on witnesses, and obtain a DNA analysis whenever possible.

After Ronald Cotton was exonerated of the rape of Jennifer Thompson, the two became friends. Thompson says she has lived with constant anguish because of her mistaken identification.

Inspired by the Innocence Project at the Cardozo School of Law in New York City, grassroots organizations of lawyers and students have been successfully challenging questionable convictions. Since the early 1990s, these efforts have led to the exoneration of hundreds of innocent people, some of whom had been condemned to death. One man in Illinois, who had been on death row for 16 years, was just hours from execution when a group of Northwestern University journalism students produced evidence that another man had committed the crime. In 2006, a documentary film, "After Innocence," chronicled seven cases of wrongful imprisonment; the men involved are still struggling to get their convictions expunged from their records.

How would you feel if your testimony resulted in the conviction of an innocent person? Would you be able to admit your mistake, or would you, as some have, cling more stubbornly than ever to the accuracy of your memory?

In one such case, Jennifer Thompson, a rape victim whose testimony had led to the clearance of the actual perpetrator and conviction of the wrong man, later wrote in a *New York Times* editorial (June 18, 2000), "The man I was so sure I had never seen in my life was the man who was inches from my throat, who raped me, who hurt me, who took my spirit away, who robbed me of my soul. And the man I had identified so emphatically on so many occasions was absolutely innocent." Thompson believes she initially picked out the photo of the innocent man, Ronald Cotton, because, of those presented to her, it most closely resembled the composite sketch she had already provided. Then, when she looked at an actual physical lineup, "I picked out Ronald because, subconsciously, in my mind, he resembled the photo, which resembled the composite, which resembled the attacker. All the images became enmeshed in one image that became Ron, and Ron became my attacker" (quoted in Simon, 2003).

Jennifer Thompson decided to meet Cotton and apologize to him personally. Amazingly, they were both able to put this tragedy behind them, overcome the racial barrier that divided them, and become friends. Nevertheless, she wrote, she still lives "with constant anguish that my profound mistake cost him so dearly. I cannot begin to imagine what would have happened had my mistaken identification occurred in a capital case." Thompson learned from personal experience what you have learned from this chapter: that eyewitnesses can and do make mistakes, that ethnic differences can increase these mistakes, that even memories for shocking or traumatic experiences are vulnerable to distortion and influence by others, and that our confidence in our memories is not a reliable guide to their accuracy.

The most important lesson to be learned from the research in this chapter, the lesson Jennifer Thompson learned to her despair and to her credit, is that human memory has both tremendous strengths and tremendous weaknesses. Because our deepest sense of ourselves relies on our memories, this is a difficult truth to accept. If we can do so, we will be able to respect the great power of memory and at the same time retain humility about our capacity for error, confabulation, and self-deception.

Taking Psychology with You

How to . . . Uh . . . Remember

Someday in the near future, a "memory pill" may be available to perk up our memories. For the time being, however, those of us who hope to improve our memories must rely on mental strategies. Some simple mnemonics can be useful, but as we have seen, complicated ones are often more bother than they're worth. A better approach is to follow some general guidelines based on the principles in this chapter:

- **Pay attention!** It seems obvious, but often we fail to remember because we never encoded the information in the first place. For example, which of the Lincoln pennies below is the real one? Most Americans have trouble recognizing the real penny because they have never attended to the details of a penny's design (Nickerson & Adams, 1979). We are not advising you to do so, unless you happen to be a coin collector or a counterfeiting expert. Just keep in mind that when you do have something to remember, such as the material in this book, you will do better if you encode it well. (The real penny, by the way, is the left one in the bottom row.)
- **Encode information in more than one way.** The more elaborate the encoding of information, the more memorable it will be. Use your imagination! For instance, in addition to remembering a telephone number by the sound of the individual digits, you might note the spatial pattern they make as you punch them in on the telephone.
- **Add meaning.** The more meaningful the material, the more likely it is to link up with information already in long-term memory. Meaningfulness also reduces the number of chunks of information you have to learn. Common ways of adding meaning include making up a story about the material (fitting the material into a cognitive schema), thinking of examples, and forming visual images. (Some people find that the odder the image, the better.) If your license plate happens to be 236MPL, you might think of 236 maples. If you are trying to remember the concept of procedural memory from this chapter, you might make the concept meaningful by thinking of an example from your own life, such as your ability to ride a mountain bike, and then imagine a "P" superimposed on an image of yourself on your bike.
- **Take your time.** Leisurely learning, spread out over several sessions, usually produces better results than harried cramming (although *reviewing* material just before a test can be helpful). In terms of hours spent, "distributed" (spaced) learning sessions are more efficient than "massed" ones. In other words, three separate one-hour study sessions may result in more retention than one session of three hours.
- **Take time out.** If possible, minimize interference by using study breaks for rest or recreation. Sleep is the ultimate way to reduce interference. In a classic study, students who slept for eight hours after learning lists of nonsense syllables retained them better than students who went about their usual business (Jenkins & Dallenbach, 1924). Sleep is not always possible, of course, but periodic mental relaxation usually is.
- **Overlearn.** You can't remember something you never learned well in the first place. Overlearning—studying information even after you think you know it—is one of the best ways to ensure that you'll remember it.
- **Monitor your learning.** Test yourself frequently, rehearse thoroughly, and review periodically to see how you are doing. Don't just evaluate your learning immediately after reading the material, though; because the information is still in short-term memory, you are likely to feel a false sense of confidence about your ability to recall it later. If you delay making a judgment for

at least a few minutes, your evaluation will probably be more accurate (Nelson & Dunlosky, 1991).

Whatever strategies you use, you will find that active learning produces more comprehension and better retention than does passive reading or listening. The mind does not gobble up information automatically; you must make the material digestible. Even then, you should not expect to remember everything you read or hear. Nor should you want to. Piling up facts without distinguishing the important from the trivial is just confusing. Popular books and tapes that promise a "perfect," "photographic" memory, or "instant recall" of everything you learn, fly in the face of what psychologists know about how the mind operates. Our advice: Forget them.

Summary

Reconstructing the Past

- Unlike a tape recorder or video camera, human memory is highly selective and is *reconstructive*: People add, delete, and change elements in ways that help them make sense of information and events. They often experience *source misattribution*, the inability to distinguish information stored during an event from information added later. Even vivid *flashbulb memories* tend to become less accurate or complete over time.
- Because memory is reconstructive, it is subject to *confabulation*, the confusion of imagined events with actual ones. Confabulation is especially likely when people have thought, heard, or told others about the imagined event many times and thus experience *imagination inflation*, the image of the event contains many details, or the event is easy to imagine. Confabulated memories can feel emotionally, vividly real yet be false.

Memory and the Power of Suggestion

- The reconstructive nature of memory makes memory vulnerable to suggestion. Eyewitness testimony is especially vulnerable to error when the suspect's ethnicity differs from that of the witness, when leading questions are put to witnesses, or when the witnesses are given misleading information.
- As we saw in "Close-up on Research," findings on memory help clarify the issues in the debate about children's testimony. Like adults, children often remember the essential aspects of an event accurately. However, like adults, they can also be suggestible, especially when responding to biased interviewing by adults—for example, when they are asked questions that blur the line between fantasy and reality or are asked leading questions. Children who have strong language skills, have self-control in real-life situations, and have supportive, psychologically healthy parents are best able to resist biased interview techniques.

In Pursuit of Memory

- The ability to remember depends in part on the type of performance called for. In tests of *explicit memory* (conscious recollection), *recognition* is usually better than *recall*. In tests of *implicit memory*, which is measured by indirect methods such as *priming* and the *relearning method*, past experiences may affect current thoughts or actions even when these experiences are not consciously remembered.
- In *information-processing models*, memory involves the *encoding*, *storage*, and *retrieval* of information. In the *three-box model*, there are three interacting systems: the sensory register, short-term memory, and long-term memory. Some cognitive scientists prefer a *parallel distributed processing (PDP)* or *connectionist* model, which represents knowledge as connections among numerous interacting processing units, distributed in a vast network and all operating in parallel. But the three-box model continues to offer a convenient way to organize the major findings on memory.

The Three-Box Model of Memory

- In the three-box model, incoming sensory information makes a brief stop in the *sensory register*, which momentarily retains it in the form of sensory images.
- *Short-term memory (STM)* retains new information for up to 30 seconds by most estimates (unless rehearsal takes place). *Working memory* consists of STM and the mental processes that control the retrieval of information from long-term memory and interpret that information appropriately depending on the task you are doing. Or, alternatively, it may involve the ability to control attention and maintain information in an active, accessible state. The capacity of STM is extremely limited but can be extended if information is organized into larger units by *chunking*.

- *Long-term memory (LTM)* contains an enormous amount of information that must be organized to make it manageable. Words (or the concepts they represent) are often organized by semantic categories. Many models of LTM represent its contents as a network of interrelated concepts. The way people use these networks depends on experience and education. Research on *tip-of-the-tongue (TOT) states* shows that words are also indexed in terms of sound and form.
- *Procedural memories* ("knowing how") are memories for how to perform specific actions; *declarative memories* ("knowing that") are memories for abstract or representational knowledge. Declarative memories include *semantic memories* (general knowledge) and *episodic memories* (memories for personally experienced events).
- The three-box model is often invoked to explain the *serial-position effect* in memory, but although it can explain the *primacy effect*, it cannot explain why a *recency effect* sometimes occurs after a considerable delay.

The Biology of Memory

- Short-term memory involves temporary changes within neurons that alter their ability to release neurotransmitters, whereas long-term memory involves lasting structural changes in neurons and synapses. *Long-term potentiation*, an increase in the strength of synaptic responsiveness, seems to be an important mechanism of long-term memory. Neural changes associated with long-term potentiation take time to develop, which helps explain why long-term memories require a period of *consolidation*.
- Areas of the frontal lobes are especially active during short-term memory tasks. The prefrontal cortex and parts of the temporal lobes are involved in the efficient encoding of words and pictures. The hippocampus plays a critical role in the formation of long-term declarative memories. Other areas, such as the cerebellum, are crucial for the formation of procedural memories. Studies of patients with amnesia suggest that different brain systems are active during explicit and implicit memory tasks. The long-term storage of declarative memories possibly takes place in cortical areas that were active during the original perception of the information or event. The various components of a memory are probably stored at different sites, with all of these sites participating in the representation of the event as a whole.
- Hormones released by the adrenal glands during stress or emotional arousal, including epinephrine and some steroids, enhance memory. Epinephrine causes the level of glucose to rise in the bloodstream, and glucose may enhance memory directly or by altering the effects of neurotransmitters. But very high hormone levels can interfere with the retention of information; a moderate level is optimal for learning new tasks.

How We Remember

- In order to remember material well, we must encode it accurately in the first place. Some kinds of information, such as material in a college course, require *effortful*, as opposed to *automatic*, encoding. Rehearsal of information keeps it in short-term memory and increases the chances of long-term retention. *Elaborative rehearsal* is more likely to result in transfer to long-term memory than is *maintenance rehearsal*, and *deep processing* is usually a more effective retention strategy than *shallow processing*.
- *Mnemonics* can also enhance retention by promoting elaborative encoding and making material meaningful, but for ordinary memory tasks, complex memory tricks are often ineffective or even counterproductive.

Why We Forget

- Forgetting can occur for several reasons. Information in sensory and short-term memory appears to *decay* if it does not receive further processing. New information may "erase" and replace old information in long-term memory. *Proactive* and *retroactive interference* may take place. *Cue-dependent forgetting* may occur when *retrieval cues* are inadequate. The most effective retrieval cues are those that were present at the time of the initial experience. A person's mental or physical state may also act as a retrieval cue, evoking a *state-dependent memory*. We tend to remember best those events that are congruent with our current mood (*mood-congruent memory*).
- *Amnesia*, the forgetting of personal information, usually occurs because of disease or injury to the brain. *Psychogenic amnesia*, which involves a loss of personal identity and has psychological causes, is rare. *Traumatic amnesia*, which allegedly involves the forgetting of specific traumatic events for long periods of time, is highly controversial, as is *repression*, the psychodynamic explanation of traumatic amnesia. Because these concepts lack good empirical support, psychological scientists are skeptical about their validity and about the accuracy of "recovered memories." Critics argue that many therapists, unaware of the power of suggestion and the dangers of confabulation, have encouraged false memories of victimization.

Autobiographical Memories

- Most people cannot recall any events from earlier than the third or fourth year of life. The reason for such *childhood amnesia* may be partly biological. Cognitive explanations include the lack of a sense of self until the age of 2 or 3, young children's impoverished and nonverbal encoding of their experiences, their focus on routine rather than distinctive aspects of an experience, and their immature cognitive schemas.
- A person's *narrative* "life story" organizes the events of his or her life and gives them meaning. Narratives change as people build up a store of episodic memories, and life stories are, to some degree, works of interpretation and imagination. The stories we tell people are affected by our purpose in telling them and who the audience is. The central themes of our stories, which are affected by gender and culture, can guide recall and influence our judgments of people and events.

Memory and Myth

- As DNA evidence has exonerated people falsely conficted of rape, murder, and other crimes, people are becoming more aware of the limitations of eyewitness testimony and the fallibility of memory.

KEY TERMS

memory 364
reconstructive memory 365
source misattribution 366
"flashbulb memories" 366
confabulation 367
imagination inflation 367
leading questions 370
explicit memory 374
recall 374
recognition 374
implicit memory 374
priming 374
relearning method 375
information-processing models 375
encoding, storage, and retrieval 375
cognitive schemas 375
"three-box model" 376
parallel distributed processing (PDP) model 376
sensory register 377
short-term memory (STM) 378
working memory 378
chunks 379
long-term memory (LTM) 379
semantic categories 380
tip-of-the-tongue (TOT) state 381
procedural memories 381
declarative memories 381
semantic memories 381
episodic memories 381
serial-position effect 382
primacy and recency effects 382
long-term potentiation 383
consolidation 384
effortful versus automatic encoding 387
maintenance rehearsal 388
elaborative rehearsal 388
deep processing 388
shallow processing 389
mnemonics 389
decay theory 391
retroactive interference 392
proactive interference 393
retrieval cues 393
cue-dependent forgetting 393
state-dependent memory 394
mood-congruent memory 394
amnesia 394
psychogenic amnesia 394
traumatic amnesia 394
repression 394
childhood (infantile) amnesia 397
narratives 399

How Much Do You Remember?

NOW YOU HAVE READ CHAPTER TEN — ARE YOU PREPARED FOR THE EXAM?

Joe finished the essay question on his exam. As he left, he realized that there were a few more things he should have included. Joe's problem is the ______ component of memory?

What are some of the different models of how memory works? (pages 375–377)

retrieval

A filing cabinet is a good analogy for the way _______ memory is conceptualized.

What is long-term memory? (pages 376)

long-term

Flashbulb memories usually concern events that are emotionally charged. True or False?

What is a flashbulb memory? (pages 366–367)

true

Will you be like Joe and have trouble retrieving information on your next exam? To help you prepare, take the practice tests on www.mypsychlab.com and try out the activities, simulations and e-book exercises.

It is important to understand the difference between retroactive and proactive interference. In retroactive interference, newly learned information interferes with information learned in the past. In proactive interference, information learned in the past interferes with newly learned information.

Example 1: Luc studied for his biology exam and then studied for his psychology exam. Now he keeps writing down psychology terms on his biology test.

Info Learned in Past	Info Learned in Present	Type of Interference
Biology	Psychology	Retroactive — because the present is interfering with the old information

Example 2: Abby keeps getting herself in trouble by calling her new boyfriend "Stan" (the name of her old boyfriend) instead of Matt.

Info Learned in Past	Info Learned in Present	Type of Interference
Old boyfriend's name was "Stan"	New boyfriend's name is "Matt"	Proactive — because the past is interfering with the new information

Two important concepts presented in this chapter consist of a three-part model. One concept is the basic processes involved in memory – encoding, storage, and retrieval. The other concept is the information processing model of memory, which consists of sensory, short-term and long-term memory. Students often get these ideas confused.

To help you clarify the concepts, take the MPL quizzes for the chapter, use the Flashcards on the site and try out the information processing model simulation.

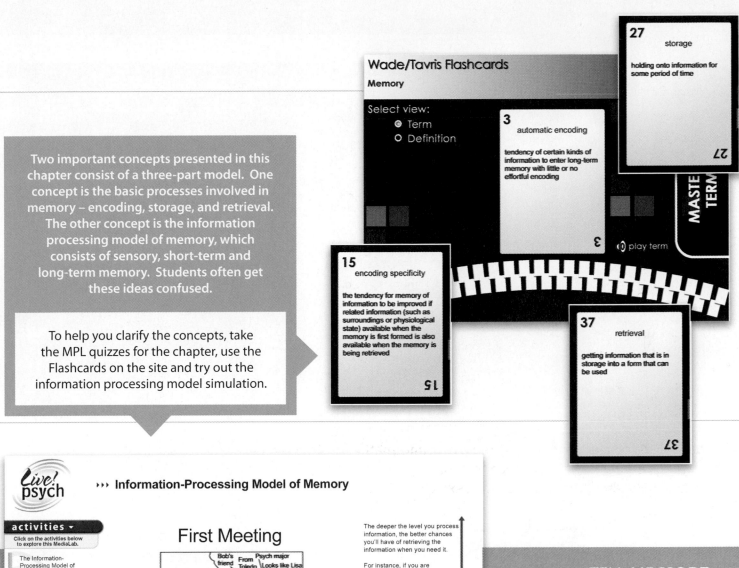

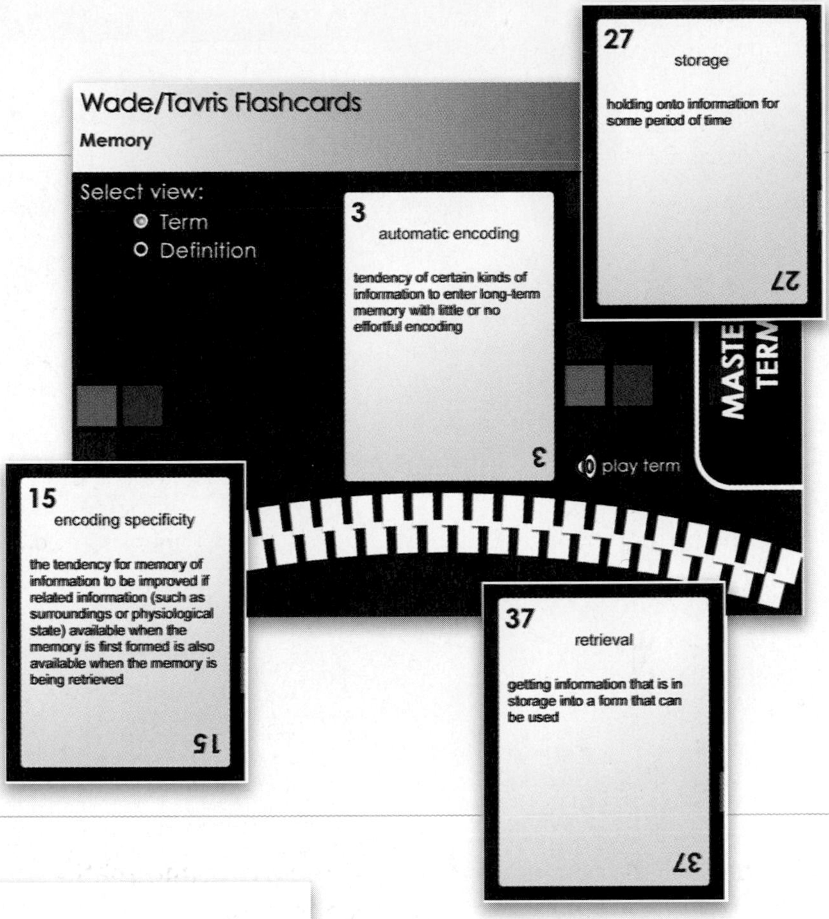

Wade/Tavris Flashcards

Memory

Select view:

Term

Definition

27 storage

holding onto information for some period of time

3 automatic encoding

tendency of certain kinds of information to enter long-term memory with little or no effortful encoding

play term

15 encoding specificity

the tendency for memory of information to be improved if related information (such as surroundings or physiological state) available when the memory is first formed is also available when the memory is being retrieved

37 retrieval

getting information that is in storage into a form that can be used

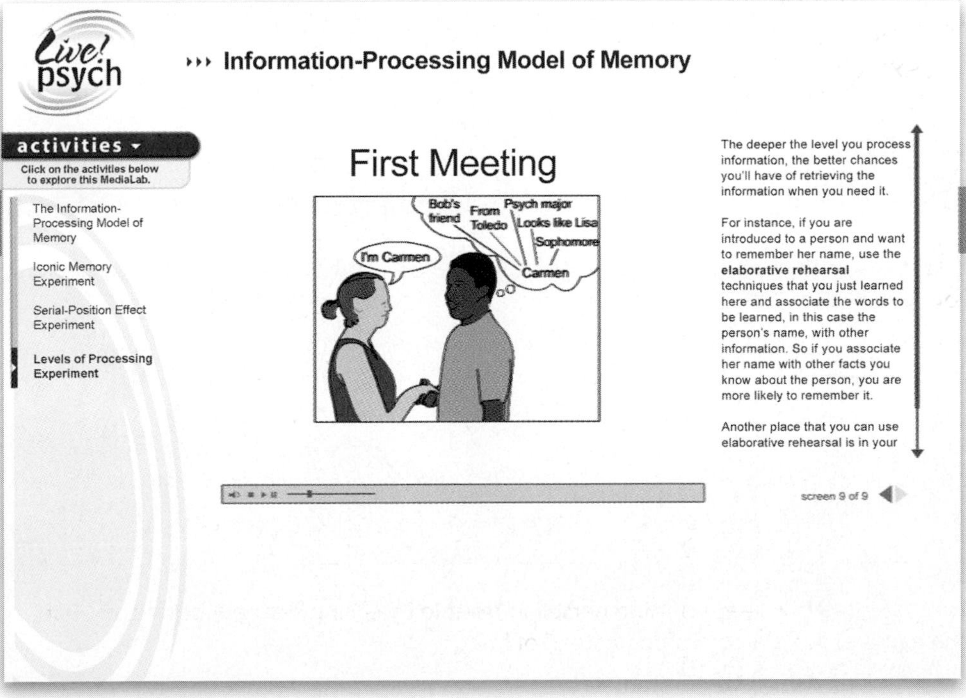

Live! psych

››› Information-Processing Model of Memory

activities

Click on the activities below to explore this MediaLab.

The Information-Processing Model of Memory

Iconic Memory Experiment

Serial-Position Effect Experiment

Levels of Processing Experiment

First Meeting

I'm Carmen

Bob's friend

From Toledo

Psych major

Looks like Lisa

Sophomore

Carmen

The deeper the level you process information, the better chances you'll have of retrieving the information when you need it.

For instance, if you are introduced to a person and want to remember her name, use the **elaborative rehearsal** techniques that you just learned here and associate the words to be learned, in this case the person's name, with other information. So if you associate her name with other facts you know about the person, you are more likely to remember it.

Another place that you can use elaborative rehearsal is in your

screen 9 of 9

TELL ME **MORE** >>

"When the actual test was given, some terms seemed to jump out because of the MPL review."

Student
Montana State University

What can you find in MyPsychLab?

Self-Directed Tests • Videos • Simulations • eBook • Flash Cards • Web Links . . . and more — organized by chapter, section and learning objective.

CHAPTER ELEVEN

The beauty of the world has two edges, one of laughter, one of anguish, cutting the heart asunder.

VIRGINIA WOOLF

CHAPTER 11

OUTLINE

For the first seven years of her life, Chelsea Thomas was a happy, cheerful child with an unusual problem. Chelsea had been born with Möbius syndrome, in which a nerve that transmits commands from the brain to the facial muscles is missing. As a result, she had a perpetually grumpy look. She could not convey delight at being given a present, amusement at watching a favorite TV show, or happiness at meeting a friend. Then surgeons transplanted nerves from Chelsea's leg to both sides of her mouth, and today Chelsea can do what most people in the world take for granted: smile.

Temple Grandin is a successful scientist and writer who also has an unusual condition. Because she has a neurological disorder, a form of autism, Grandin's emotions differ in quality and kind from those of most other people. She can feel the anguish of animals but not of human beings. She has never known romantic love or been moved by the beauty of a sunset. Unable to feel the array of normal emotions, she is unable to read the emotions of others; she is out of tune with the rest of humanity.

Cases like these are poignant reminders of how important it is to be able to feel and express emotions and to recognize emotions in others. Emotions are the heart and soul of human experience. If you lacked emotion, your life would be easier in some ways: You would never again worry about a test result, a job interview, or a first date, and you would never be riled by injustice. But you would also be unmoved by the magic of music. You would never feel the grief of losing someone you love, not only because you wouldn't know sadness but also because you wouldn't know love. You would never laugh because nothing would strike you as funny.

People often curse their emotions, wishing to be freed from the pain of anger, jealousy, shame, guilt, grief, and unrequited love. The belief that we are at the mercy of our irrational emotions has been part of Western culture for centuries. Emotions and cognitions have been regarded as two separate, indeed warring processes, with the clash between them causing eternal muddles and miseries. Modern psychological research, however, shows that the historical distinction between our "rational" human abilities of thought and our supposedly irrational mammalian heritage of emotion is a false one. As we saw in our discussions of thinking (Chapter 9) and memory (Chapter 10), human cognition is not always rational; it involves many biases in what we perceive and remember. Conversely, emotions are not always irrational. They bind people together, regulate relationships, and motivate people to achieve their goals. Without the capacity to feel emotion, people have difficulty making decisions and planning for the future. When you are faced with a decision between two appealing and justifiable career alternatives, for example, your sense of which one "feels right" emotionally may help you make the best choice (Damasio, 1994).

DON'T OVERSIMPLIFY

Many people wish they could be free of the "irrational" emotions that make them miserable. But what would our lives be like without emotions? Are they really so irrational?

As psychologists have moved away from regarding emotions solely as disorganizing and disruptive influences on human behavior, they have identified some of the evolutionarily adaptive and beneficial functions of emotions and their expression. Disgust, which is pretty disgusting, probably evolved as a mechanism that protects infants and adults from eating tainted or poisonous food. Even embarrassment, so painful to the individual, serves important functions: It appeases others when you feel you have made a fool of yourself, broken a moral rule, or violated a social norm. Signs of embarrassment—acting nervous and awkward, blushing, biting your tongue, withdrawing, apologizing—make other people feel sympathetic toward you, more willing to forgive your blunder (Keltner & Anderson, 2000).

In defining **emotion**, psychologists focus on three major components: *physiological* changes in the face, brain, and body, *cognitive* processes such as interpretations of events, and *cultural* influences that shape the experience and expression of emotion. If we compare human emotions to a tree, the biological capacity for emotion is the trunk and root system; thoughts and explanations create the many branches; and culture is the gardener that shapes the tree and prunes it, cutting off some limbs and cultivating others. We will begin with the trunk.

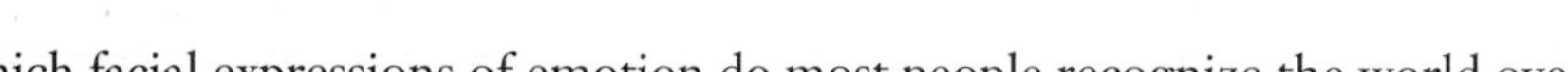

WHAT'S**AHEAD**

- Which facial expressions of emotion do most people recognize the world over?
- Why might hanging around with a depressed friend make you gloomy, too?
- Which little structure in the brain sees to it that you cross the street fast when a truck is headed toward you?
- Which two hormones can make you "too excited to eat"?
- What do "lie detectors" actually detect?

Elements of Emotion 1: The Body

Research on the physiological aspects of emotion suggests that people everywhere are born with certain basic or **primary emotions**. Although psychologists differ somewhat in the emotions they consider to be primary, the list typically includes fear, anger, sadness, joy, surprise, disgust, and contempt. These emotions have distinctive physiological patterns and corresponding facial expressions, and the situations that evoke them are generally the same all over the world: Everywhere, sadness follows perception of loss, fear follows perception of threat and bodily harm, anger follows perception of insult or injustice, and so forth (Scherer, 1997). In contrast, **secondary emotions** include all the variations and blends of emotion that vary from one culture to another and develop gradually with increasing cognitive maturity.

emotion A state of arousal involving facial and bodily changes, brain activation, cognitive appraisals, subjective feelings, and tendencies toward action, all shaped by cultural rules.

primary emotions Emotions considered to be universal and biologically based; they generally include fear, anger, sadness, joy, surprise, disgust, and contempt.

secondary emotions Emotions that develop with cognitive maturity and vary across individuals and cultures.

Neuroscientists and other researchers study three major biological aspects of emotion: facial expressions, brain regions and circuits, and the autonomic nervous system.

The Face of Emotion

"There are characteristic facial expressions that are observed to accompany anger, fear, erotic excitement, and all the other passions," wrote Aristotle (384–322 B.C.). Two thousand years later, Charles Darwin (1872/1965) added an evolutionary expla-

nation for Aristotle's observation. Human facial expressions—the smile, the frown, the grimace, the glare—are, he said, as wired in as the wing flutter of a frightened bird, the purr of a contented cat, or the snarl of a threatened wolf. Such expressions evolved because they allowed our forebears to tell at a glance the difference between a friendly stranger and a hostile one. They make it possible for us to signal our feelings and intentions to others, and they "serve as the first means of communication between the mother and her infant." Darwin was right on all counts.

Universal Expressions of Emotion. Modern psychologists have supported Darwin's ideas by showing that some emotional displays are recognized the world over (see Figure 11.1). Paul Ekman and his colleagues have gathered evidence for the universality of seven facial expressions of emotion—expressions that correspond to the list of emotions usually identified as primary: anger, happiness, fear, surprise, disgust, sadness, and contempt (Ekman, 1997; Ekman et al., 1987). In every culture they have studied—in Brazil, Chile, Estonia, Germany, Greece, Hong Kong, Italy, Japan, New Guinea, Scotland, Sumatra, Turkey, and the United States—a large majority of people recognize the basic emotional expressions portrayed by those in other cultures. Even most members of isolated groups who have never watched a movie or read *People* magazine, such as the Foré of New Guinea or the Minangkabau of West Sumatra, can recognize the basic emotions in pictures of people who are entirely foreign to them, and we can recognize theirs. Some researchers have argued that pride is also a basic human emotion. Children as young as age 4 and people from an isolated culture in Africa can reliably identify facial and bodily expressions of pride (Tracy & Robins, 2004; Tracy, Robins, & Lagattuta, 2005).

FIGURE 11.1 Some Universal Expressions

Can you tell which feelings are being conveyed here? Most people around the world can readily identify expressions of surprise, disgust, happiness, sadness, anger, fear, and contempt—no matter what the age, culture, sex, or historical epoch of the person conveying the emotion. Some researchers think that pride might also be a universal emotion. Can you find the face of pride in this group?

Jessica Tracy, University of British Columbia, Tracy, J.L., & Robins, R.W. (2004). Show your pride: Evidence for a discrete emotion expression. Psychological Science, 15, 194-197.

GREAT MOMS IN HISTORY.
IT WON'T KILL YOU TO SMILE A LITTLE, MONA!
MRS. LISA

Great moms have always understood the importance of facial feedback.

Ekman and his associates developed a special coding system to analyze and identify each of the nearly 80 muscles of the face, as well as the combinations of muscles associated with various emotions (Ekman, 2003). Make an expression of disgust and notice what you are doing: You are probably wrinkling your nose, dropping the corners of your mouth, and retracting your upper lip. When people try to hide their feelings and put on an emotion, they use different groups of muscles than they do for authentic ones. For example, when people try to pretend that they feel sad, only 15 percent manage to get the eyebrows, eyelids, and forehead wrinkle exactly right, mimicking the way true grief is expressed spontaneously. Authentic smiles last only 2 seconds; false smiles may last 10 seconds or more (Ekman, Friesen, & O'Sullivan, 1988).

The Functions of Facial Expressions. Interestingly, facial expressions not only can reflect our internal feelings; they also may *influence* them. In the process of **facial feedback**, the facial muscles send messages to the brain about the basic emotion being expressed: A smile tells us that we're happy, a frown that we're angry or perplexed (Izard, 1990). When people are told to smile and look pleased or happy, their positive feelings increase; when they are told to look angry, displeased, or disgusted, positive feelings decrease (Kleinke, Peterson, & Rutledge, 1998).

Facial feedback affects emotional states even when people are not specifically asked to imitate an emotion, but just to alter their facial muscles. For example, when people are told to contract the facial muscles involved in smiling (though not actually instructed to smile) and are then shown cartoons, they find the cartoons funnier than if they are contracting their muscles in a way that is incompatible with smiling (Strack, Martin, & Stepper, 1988). And when they are asked to contort their facial muscles into patterns associated with anger, that is often the emotion they feel. As one young man put it, "When my jaw was clenched and my brows down, I tried not to be angry but it just fit the position" (Laird, 1974). If you put on an angry face, your heart rate will even rise faster than if you put on a happy face (Levenson, Ekman, & Friesen, 1990).

As Darwin suggested, facial expressions also probably evolved to help us communicate our emotional states to others and provoke a response from them—"Come help me!" "Get away!" (Fridlund, 1994). This signaling function begins in infancy. A baby's expressions of misery, angry frustration, or disgust are apparent to most parents, who respond by soothing an uncomfortable baby, feeding a grumpy one, or removing unappealing food from a disgusted one (Izard, 1994b; Stenberg & Campos, 1990). And an infant's smile of joy usually melts the heart of the weariest parent, provoking a happy cuddle. Obviously a baby's facial expressions have survival value!

Babies, in turn, react to the facial expressions and emotional tones of their parents and other adults. American, German, Greek, Japanese, Trobriand Island, and Yanomamo mothers all infect their babies with happy moods by displaying happy expressions (Keating, 1994). Babies also seem primed to respond in other ways to happy facial expressions. Tiny newborns will suck longer on a pacifier if it produces a happy face than if it produces a face with a neutral or negative expression (Walker-Andrews, 1997). If you become a parent, remember this.

Starting at the end of their first year, babies begin to alter their own behavior in reaction to adults' facial expressions of emotion. When year-old infants watched a videotape of an adult actress reacting to a toy either with enthusiastic pleasure or with fear and alarm, the babies later imitated her when they were given the toy: They played with it if she had been enthusiastic and avoided the toy, cried, or frowned if the actress had responded to it with fear (Mumme & Fernald, 2003). (An inadvertent finding of this study was the power of television over the emotional responses of even 1-year-olds.)

facial feedback The process by which the facial muscles send messages to the brain about the basic emotion being expressed.

GET INVOLVED!

➤PUT ON A HAPPY FACE

See whether facial feedback works for you. The next time you are feeling sad or afraid, try purposely smiling, even if no one is around. Keep smiling. Does your facial expression affect your mood?

This ability to learn quickly from an adult's facial expressions definitely has survival value. The visual-cliff studies described in Chapter 6 were originally designed to test for depth perception, which emerges early in infancy. But in one experiment, 1-year-old babies were put on a more ambiguous visual cliff that did not drop off sharply and thus did not automatically evoke fear, as the original cliff did. In this case, the babies' behavior depended on the mother's expression: 74 percent crossed the cliff when their mothers put on a happy, reassuring expression, but not a single infant crossed when the mother showed an expression of fear (Sorce et al., 1985). If you have ever watched a toddler take a tumble and then look at his or her parent before deciding whether to cry or to forget it, you will understand the influence of parental facial expressions, and why they have such importance for babies. An infant needs to be able to read the parent's facial signals of alarm or safety because young children do not yet have the experience necessary for judging danger.

Finally, facial expressions of emotion can actually generate emotions in others. This is why moods can often literally be contagious, spreading from one person to another. Have you ever been in a cheerful mood, then had lunch with a depressed friend and come away feeling vaguely depressed yourself? Have you ever stopped to have a chat with a friend who was nervous about an upcoming exam and ended up feeling panicked yourself? That's *mood contagion* at work. In the laboratory, when people see pictures of facial expressions of emotion or other nonverbal emotional signals, their own facial muscles mimic the ones they are observing, activating a similar emotional state in themselves (Dimberg, Thunberg, & Elmehed, 2000). In daily life, if you are intentionally trying to create rapport with another person, you are, without realizing it, likely to start mimicking that person's facial expressions and other nonverbal cues. If someone mimics *your* expressions and body language, you are more likely to be helpful toward that person (Lakin & Chartrand, 2003; van Baaren et al., 2004). When two people are talking, the greater their synchrony, the higher the rapport and emotional harmony they will feel toward one another (see Figure 11.2).

FIGURE 11.2 The Contagion of Emotion

These volunteers, videotaped in a study of conversational synchrony, are obviously in sync with one another, even though they have just met. The degree to which two people's gestures and expressions are synchronized affects the rapport they feel with one another. Such synchrony can also create a contagion of moods (Grahe & Bernieri, 1999).

Facial expressions do not always convey the emotion being felt. A posed, social smile like Gloria Vanderbilt's (left) may have nothing to do with true feelings of happiness. And true feelings of happiness may not be obvious at all. Russian pole vaulter Yelena Isinbayeva (right) looks angry or in pain, but she is actually feeling joyful after winning a gold medal at the 2004 Olympics.

As you might expect, people who live or work together are especially vulnerable to mood contagion, which may be why, over time, dating couples and college roommates become more similar in their emotional responses (Anderson, Keltner, & John, 2003). In one three-week study, roommates of depressed students became more depressed themselves, even when the researchers statistically controlled for upsetting life events that might have been affecting them (Joiner, 1994). If you are starting to feel gloomy at school or work, perhaps you should check out your friends' or co-workers' moods and facial expressions before you decide that *you* are the one who is depressed!

Facial Expressions in Social and Cultural Context. Despite the apparent universality of certain facial expressions, there are important social and cultural influences on how well people recognize them (Elfenbein & Ambady, 2002). While most people in most cultures do recognize basic emotions as portrayed in photographs, sometimes a large minority does not. Across 20 studies of Western cultures, for example, fully 95 percent of the participants agreed in their judgments of happy faces, but only 78 percent agreed on expressions of sadness and anger. And across 11 non-Western societies, 88 percent recognized happiness, but only 74 percent agreed on sadness and 59 percent on anger (Ekman, 1994). When people are not forced to select a particular emotion label in a multiple-choice item ("Is it anger or fear?") and are simply asked what facial expression a photo is conveying, agreement drops even further (Frank & Stennett, 2001).

If emotional expression is hardwired by evolution, why don't people across and within cultures always agree?

1 Familiarity affects the ability to read facial expressions. People are better at identifying emotions expressed by others in their own ethnic, national, or regional group than they are at recognizing the emotions of foreigners. As people become more familiar with members of other cultures, they become better able to correctly identify their facial expressions. In one study, only 21 percent of Chinese respondents living in China recognized non-Asian Americans' expression of fear, but 62 percent of the Chinese living in the United States did. Likewise, Tibetans and Africans living in the United States can identify the facial expressions of white Americans more accurately than do their counterparts in their native countries (Elfenbein & Ambady, 2003).

2 Facial expressions can mean different things at different times, depending on the social context and the expresser's intentions. Within a

culture, facial expressions can have many different meanings. A frown might mean "Look out, I am really angry at you" or "I'm being *serious* about this, so listen up!" A smile might not mean "I'm happy," but rather "I'm trying to be pleasant," "Don't be mad at me," or even "Nyahhh, I was right and you were wrong."

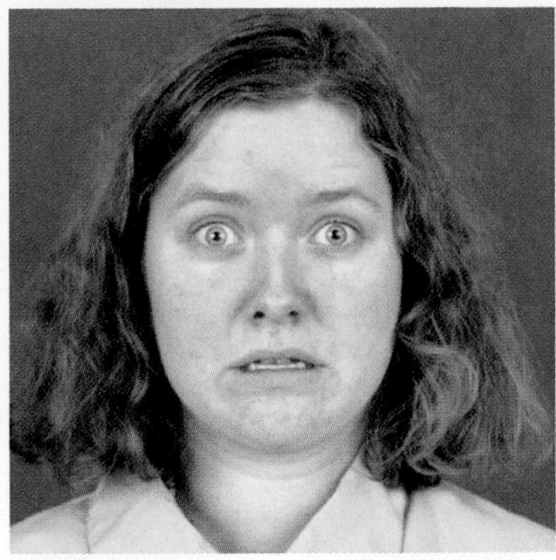

Can you guess her emotion? Most people say it's fear. But if they have been told that she has good reason to be irritated (having been kept waiting in a restaurant for an hour), they will say she is angry. In this way, the context affects the expressions we "see" in others (Carroll & Russell, 1996).

3 Cultures differ in the attention they pay to the context of emotional expression. Is a facial expression a sign of what a person actually feels, or is it a reflection of what is going on in the situation? Individualistically oriented Americans tend to see a person's facial expression as a direct reflection of his or her internal emotional state. When Americans are asked to look at a photo of people's faces, they will say that a happy face is a happy face even if other people in the same photo are expressing sadness or fear. But because the Japanese regard each individual as being embedded in a network of relationships that require constant adjustment for the sake of harmony, they regard a facial expression by itself as inconclusive. To evaluate what it means, they consider the context in which it occurs. Therefore, if asked what emotion that happy face is expressing, Japanese respondents will consider the expressions of other people in the background (Mesquita et al., 2004). This may be why they have more difficulty than Westerners in reading a photo of a particular facial expression on its own.

4 People often use facial expressions to lie about their feelings as well as to express them. In Shakespeare's play *Henry VI*, the villain who will become the evil King Richard III says,

> *Why, I can smile, and murder while I smile;*
> *And cry content to that which grieves my heart;*
> *And wet my cheeks with artificial tears,*
> *And frame my face to all occasions.*

In short, facial expressions not only reveal and communicate our true feelings, but also disguise and deceive. Even Paul Ekman, who has been studying them for years, concludes, "There is obviously emotion without facial expression and facial expression without emotion." Most people do not go around scowling and clenching their jaws whenever they are angry. Many people grieve and feel enormously sad without weeping. When you are at home by yourself, you are unlikely to sit there smiling even if you are feeling happy; you will save your smiles until you have an audience (or are watching a funny TV show). Facial expressions are only the first chapter in the emotion story, not the whole book.

QUICK quiz

Smile now, and see whether that makes you feel better about taking this quiz.

1. Which of the following emotions is (are) not generally considered to be among the most universal ones? (a) anger, (b) pride, (c) fear, (d) disgust, (e) regret, (f) happiness, (g) sadness, (h) embarrassment
2. What are the functions of facial expressions? (Use the whole preceding section to answer this question.)
3. Why doesn't everyone agree on what emotion a given facial expression is revealing?

Answers:

1. e, h Pride is the most recent emotion to be added to the list of "universals." **2.** They signal our intentions, reflect our feelings, permit nonverbal communication between parents and infants, provide cues to ourselves about what we are feeling (facial feedback), affect other people's emotions and behavior (as in mood contagion), and enable us to lie and deceive. **3.** Cultures differ in how much attention people pay to the social context in which the expression occurs; familiarity affects the ability to accurately read another person's expression; facial expressions mean different things in different situations; and people use facial expressions to disguise or lie about their real feelings.

The Brain and Emotion

Another line of physiological research seeks to identify parts of the brain responsible for different emotions and for specific components of emotional experience: recognizing another person's emotion, feeling an emotion, expressing an emotion, acting on an emotion, and controlling or regulating an emotion.

The capacity to feel or recognize particular emotions is associated with specific parts of the brain. For example, people who have a disease or a stroke that affects two areas involved in disgust are often unable to feel disgusted. One young man with stroke damage in these regions could recognize all of the basic facial expressions except for disgust, and he had little or no emotional response to images and ideas that would be disgusting to most people, such as feces-shaped chocolate (Calder et al., 2000). (Are you making a disgusted expression as you read that? He couldn't.) And people with damage in another part have trouble understanding jokes or getting the emotions portrayed in films and stories (Heller, Nitschke, & Miller, 1998).

The two cerebral hemispheres are also associated with somewhat different emotional jobs. The right side of the brain is important for recognizing emotional expressions and processing emotional *feeling* ("Uh oh, Adam is really angry at himself today"), whereas the left is active in processing emotional *meaning* ("No wonder; he just misplaced a $100 bill") (Vingerhoets, Berckmoes, & Stroobant, 2003).

Researchers are rapidly identifying the areas, circuits, and even specific neurons in the brain that are involved in every aspect of emotional experience. Here we consider a few more of their major discoveries.

The Role of the Amygdala. A small structure in the brain, the *amygdala*, plays a key role in emotion, especially fear. The amygdala is responsible for evaluating incoming sensory information, quickly determining its emotional importance, and making the initial decision to approach or withdraw from a person or situation (Adolphs, 2001; LeDoux, 1996). The amygdala quickly assesses danger or threat, which is a good thing, because otherwise you could be standing in the street asking, "Is it wise to cross now,

GET INVOLVED!

➤TURN ON YOUR RIGHT HEMISPHERE

These faces have expressions of happiness on one side and sadness on the other. Look at the nose of each face: Which face looks happier? Which face looks sadder?

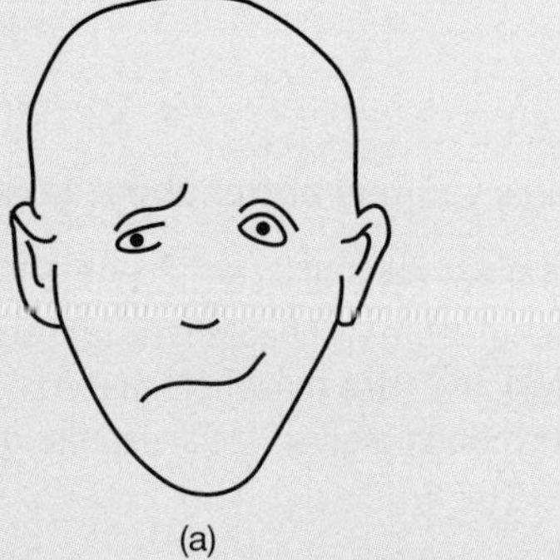

(a)

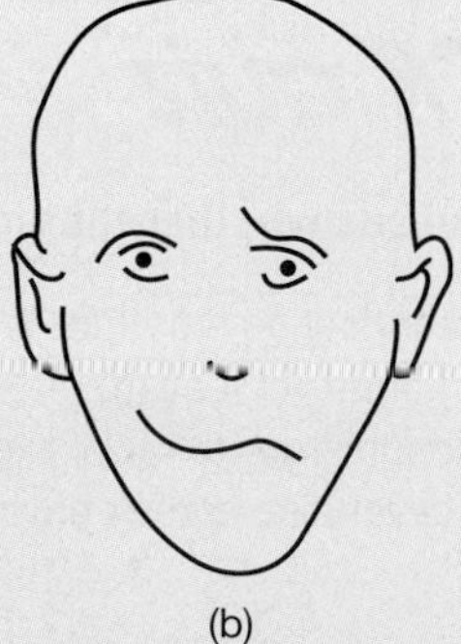

(b)

You are likely to see face (b) as the happier one and face (a) as the sadder one. The likely reason is that in most people the left side of a picture is processed by the right side of the brain, where recognition of emotional expression primarily occurs (Oatley & Jenkins, 1996).

while that very large truck is coming toward me?" The amygdala's initial response may then be overridden by a more accurate appraisal from the cortex. This is why you jump with fear when you suddenly feel a hand on your back in a dark alley. And it is why your fear evaporates when the cortex registers that the hand belongs to a friend whose lousy idea of humor is to scare you in a dark alley.

If either the amygdala or critical areas of the cortex are damaged, abnormalities result in the ability to process fear. A rat with a damaged amygdala "forgets" to be afraid when it should be and may not be able to acquire conditioned fears. People with damage in the amygdala often have difficulty recognizing fear in others (Adolphs, 2001). One such woman could accurately display fear and other emotions herself, but she could not perceive or recognize other people's expressions of fear (Anderson & Phelps, 2000).

2. The cerebral cortex generates a more complete picture; it can override signals sent by the amygdala ("It's only Mike in a down coat").

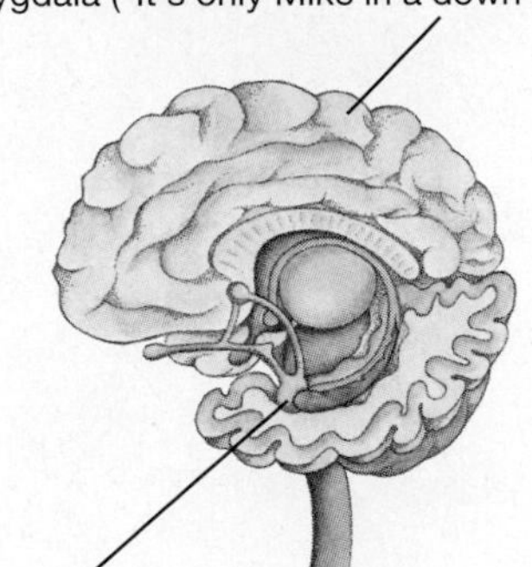

1. The amygdala scrutinizes information for its emotional importance ("It's a bear! Be afraid! Run!").

The Role of the Prefrontal Cortex. Most emotions motivate a response of some sort: to embrace or approach the person who instills joy in you, attack a person who makes you angry, withdraw from a scene that disgusts you, or flee from a person or situation that frightens you. The prefrontal regions of the brain are involved in these impulses to approach or withdraw. Regions of the *right* prefrontal cortex are specialized for withdrawal or escape (as in disgust and fear) (Harmon-Jones & Sigelman, 2001). Regions of the *left* prefrontal cortex are specialized for the motivation to approach others (as with happiness, a positive emotion, and anger, a negative one) (Pizzagalli et al., 2005). People who have greater-than-average activation in this left area, compared with the right, have more positive feelings, higher well-being, a quicker ability to recover from negative emotions, and a greater ability to suppress negative emotions (Urry et al., 2004). People with damage to this area often lose the capacity for joy. Even in people without brain damage, those who are clinically depressed have less activation in the left frontal regions and greater right-sided activation than nondepressed people do. However, no one yet knows whether this difference is learned or inborn, or is a result of depression rather than a cause (Davidson et al., 2002).

Differences in prefrontal activation that reflect approach or avoidance tendencies occur even in infants. In one study, 10-month-old babies were briefly separated from their mothers and then monitored during the happy reunion. The babies smiled, their happy left prefrontal regions were active, and they reached out to their moms. But when the babies were only smiling socially at strangers, these areas showed no increased activation, and the babies did not reach out (Fox & Davidson, 1988). Even a baby brain reveals a difference between the warm happiness of a loving smile directed toward someone worthy of approaching (mom) and the cooler pleasure of a social smile directed toward mom's friends.

Parts of the prefrontal cortex are also involved in the *regulation* of emotion, keeping us on an even keel (Jackson et al., 2003). Feeling an emotion is important for communication and connection, as we noted, but social life also depends on the ability to modify and control what we feel. Some people seem unable to manage inappropriate feelings, or they have roller-coaster emotional swings without provocation, or they feel constantly worried or angry. People with abnormalities in a key part of the frontal lobes, an area connected to the amygdala and other circuits involved in emotional processing, often lose the capacity to put aside their fear when the emotion is no longer necessary. The result can be constant, irrational feelings of doom and anxiety or obsessive thoughts of danger, as occur in obsessive-compulsive disorder (see Chapter 16). Remarkably, injury to this area does not impair language or memory, but it does disrupt people's ability to regulate their emotions in their dealings with others. As in the tragic case of Phineas Gage, described in Chapter 4, their emotions often seem jarring or inappropriate (Beer et al., 2003).

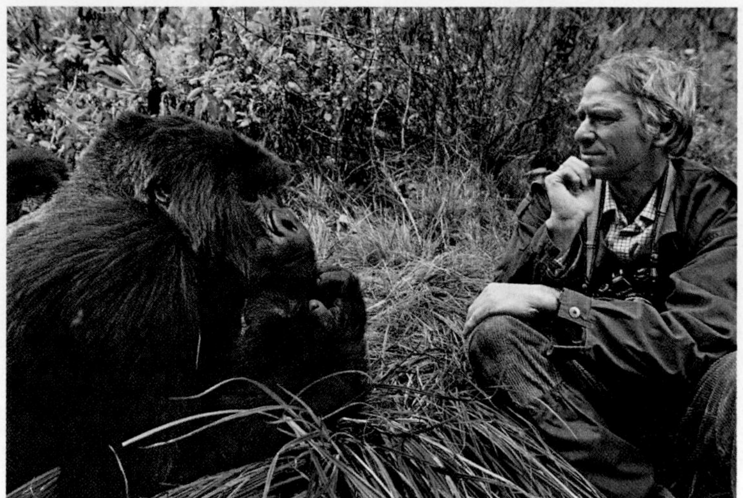

Mirror neurons are clearly at work in this conversation.

Mirror, Mirror, in the Brain: Neurons for Imitation and Empathy. Some years ago, a team of Italian neuroscientists made an accidental and astonishing discovery. They had implanted wires in the brains of macaque monkeys, in regions involved in planning and carrying out movement. Every time a monkey moved and grasped an object, the cells fired and the monitor registered a sound. One day, a graduate student heard the monitor go off when the monkey was simply observing him eating an ice-cream cone. Over the next few years, the neuroscientists found that certain neurons in the monkeys' brains were firing not only when the monkeys were picking up peanuts and eating them but also when the monkeys were merely observing their human caretakers doing exactly the same thing. Other cells fired when the animals picked up different objects—bananas, toys, pliers—and when they watched someone else pick up these items (Ferrari, Rozzi, & Fogassi, 2005). Incredibly, these neurons responded only to very specific actions: A neuron that fired when a monkey grasped a peanut would also fire when the scientist grasped a peanut but not when the scientist grasped something else. The scientists called these cells **mirror neurons**.

Since that original discovery, research with fMRIs and other brain-imaging technologies has suggested that human beings have mirror neurons that are even more complex and evolved than those found in monkeys (Arbib, 2005; Buxbaum, Kyle, & Menon, 2005; Molnar-Szakacs et al., 2005). They are found in several key areas of the brain and specialize in helping us identify with what others are feeling, understand other people's intentions, imitate their actions, and read their emotions. For example, when you see another person in pain, one reason you feel a jolt of empathy is that mirror neurons involved in pain are firing. When you watch a spider crawl up someone's leg, one reason you have a creepy sensation is that your mirror neurons are firing—the same ones that would fire if the spider were crawling up your own leg.

Incredibly, when people observe a hand grasping a cup, the mirror neurons in parts of the brain associated with motor activity become more active when the hand is intentionally doing something with the cup—picking it up to drink from it or to clean off the table—than when it is simply holding it or when the observer has no context for interpreting what the hand is doing. In other words, human mirror neurons do not simply recognize another person's action; they actually provide a neural basis for helping us encode the intentions of that person's action (Iacoboni et al., 2005).

Mirror neurons appear to be the underlying mechanism for human empathy, nonverbal rapport, and the contagion of moods we mentioned earlier. If this is so, it may be that abnormalities in the mirror-neuron system are part of the reason for the emotional deficits that occur in autism, which involves a lack of empathy, and in schizophrenia, which involves an inability to process sounds and language accurately and connect with other people (Arbib & Mundhenk, 2005; Williams et al., 2006). Because of these findings, scientists are enormously excited about the possible links between mirror neurons and many aspects of psychology—not only emotion but also motivation, evolution, child development, language, learning, and mental disorders. Stay tuned.

mirror neurons A class of cells, distributed throughout various parts of the brain, that fire when an animal sees or hears an action *and* carries out the same action on its own; these cells are far more evolved and varied in human beings than in other animals.

Hormones and Emotion

When the amygdala and prefrontal cortex signal "Danger! Get outta here!" you need to be able to move fast. The next stage of the emotional relay is the release of hormones,

CartoonStock Ltd. CSL

Intense but short-lived "road rage" results in part from physiological arousal caused by the stress of driving. That's why passengers rarely get as furious as the driver does, especially when the driver is in a rat race!

which produces the energy of emotion. When you are under stress or feeling an intense emotion, the sympathetic division of the autonomic nervous system spurs the adrenal glands to send out two hormones, *epinephrine* and *norepinephrine* (see Chapter 15). These chemical messengers produce a state of arousal and alertness. The pupils dilate, widening to allow in more light; the heart beats faster; breathing speeds up; and blood sugar rises, providing the body with more energy to act. Digestion slows down, so that blood flow can be diverted from the stomach and intestines to the muscles and surface of the skin. (This is why, when you are excited, scared, furious, or wildly in love, you may not want to eat.) The ultimate purpose of all these changes is to prepare the body to respond quickly to danger or threat, excitement or opportunity.

The adrenal glands produce epinephrine and norepinephrine in response to many challenges in the environment. These hormones will surge if you are laughing at a funny movie, playing a video game, worrying about an exam, cheering at a sports event, or driving on a hot day in terrible traffic. Epinephrine in particular provides the energy of an emotion—that familiar tingle of excitement. At high levels, it can create the sensation of being seized or flooded by an emotion that is out of your control. In a sense, you *are* out of control, because people cannot consciously alter their heart rate, blood pressure, and digestive tract. However, you can learn to control your actions when you are under the sway of an emotion, even one that feels as intense as anger (see "Taking Psychology with You"). And no emotion, no matter how urgent or compelling, lasts forever. As arousal subsides, anger may pale into annoyance, ecstasy into contentment, fear into suspicion, past emotional whirlwinds into calm breezes.

Although epinephrine and norepinephrine are released during many emotional states, emotions also differ from one another physiologically. Fear, disgust, anger, sadness, surprise, and happiness are associated with different patterns of brain activity and autonomic nervous system activity, as measured by heart rate, electrical conductivity of the skin, and finger temperature (Damasio et al., 2000; Levenson, 1992). These distinctive patterns may explain why people all over the world use similar terms to describe basic (primary) emotions, saying they feel hot and bothered when they are angry, feel cold and clammy when they are afraid, and have a lump in the throat when they are sad. These metaphors capture what is going on in their bodies (Mesquita & Frijda, 1992).

In sum, the physiology of emotion involves characteristic facial expressions; activity in specific parts of the brain, notably the amygdala, specialized parts of the prefrontal cortex, and mirror neurons; and sympathetic nervous system activity that prepares the body for action (see Review 11.1).

REVIEW 11.1

Emotion and the Body

Facial Expressions	Reflect internal feelings, influence internal feelings (facial feedback), communicate feelings, signal intentions, affect behavior and feelings of others (mood contagion), conceal or pretend an emotion (lie).
The Brain	Specific areas are involved in specific emotions (e.g., disgust) and in different aspects of emotion (e.g., recognizing facial expressions in others, expressing an emotion oneself).
Amygdala	Determines emotional importance of incoming sensory information; is responsible for initial decision to approach or withdraw; is involved in learning, recognizing, and expressing fear.
Cortex	Appraises the significance of emotional information from the amygdala. The left prefrontal cortex is associated with "approach" emotions (e.g., happiness, anger), the right prefrontal cortex with "withdrawal" emotions (e.g., fear, sadness).
Mirror neurons	Found in various parts of the brain, these cells fire in imitation of the actions or emotions of another person, creating empathy for another's feelings of pain or emotion.
Cerebral Hemispheres	Have different specialties; the right hemisphere is involved in recognizing emotional expression and processing emotional tone, the left, in processing emotional meaning.
Autonomic Nervous System	Activates the hormones epinephrine and norepinephrine, which produce energy and alertness. Certain emotions are associated with distinctive patterns of autonomic nervous system activity (e.g., making people feel "hot" when they are angry, "cold" when they are afraid).

BIOLOGY and Deception

Can Lies Be Detected in the Brain and Body?

Lots of people want to be able to nab a liar: governments, employers, police, and partners. The desire to detect a deceiver is especially urgent when the deceiver is hiding important information: who committed a crime, who is a spy, who stole the secrets, who is planning a terrorist strike. The problem is that justice depends not only on finding out "who done it" but also on protecting those who didn't do anything at all. The challenge for social scientists and for law enforcement is to better identify liars without falsely accusing truth-tellers.

THINKING CRITICALLY

ANALYZE ASSUMPTIONS AND BIASES

Many people assume that because physiological changes, such as an elevated heart rate, are involved in emotional states, physiological measurements can tell us whether someone is afraid, guilty or lying. Is this assumption valid? What evidence does it overlook?

For centuries, people have tried to determine when a person is lying by detecting physiological responses that cannot be controlled consciously. This is the idea behind the *polygraph machine*, commonly called the "lie detector," which was invented in 1915 by a Harvard professor named William Marston. (Marston went on to become famous for a *really* important creation—Wonder Woman.) The polygraph is based on the assumption that a lie generates emotional arousal. Thus, a person who is guilty and fearful of being found out will have increased activity in the autonomic nervous system while responding to incriminating questions: a faster heart rate, increased respiration rate, and increased electrical conductance of the skin.

Law-enforcement officers are still enthusiastic about the polygraph, but most psychological scientists are not. In fact, most researchers regard polygraph tests as invalid because no physiological patterns of autonomic arousal are specific to lying (Furedy, 1996; Lilienfeld, 1993; Lykken, 1998; Saxe, 1994; Zelicoff, 2001). Machines cannot tell whether you are feeling guilty, angry, nervous, amused, or revved up from an exciting

day. Innocent people may be tense and nervous about the whole procedure. They may react to the word *bank* not because they robbed a bank, but because they recently bounced a check; in either case, the machine will record a lie. The reverse mistake is also common: People who are motivated to escape detection can often beat the machine by tensing muscles or thinking about an exciting experience during neutral questions.

The main problem with the polygraph is that it has high rates of falsely labeling the innocent as having lied (Saxe, 1994). When large numbers of people are given screening polygraph tests by employers, the government, or police (in an effort to identify cheats, spies, or criminals), the polygraph will correctly catch many liars and guilty people but will also misidentify a very high number of innocent people (see Figure 11.3). Because of such findings, about half of the states in the United States have ruled that polygraph results are inadmissible in court. In 2002, a panel of the National Academy of Sciences advised Congress that lie detectors are not reliable enough to be used in screening. But some government agencies and most police departments continue to use them, not for their accuracy but because they hope to scare people into telling the truth and induce suspects to confess—by telling them that they failed the test. Many accused people use them too, hoping the polygraph will prove that they are innocent.

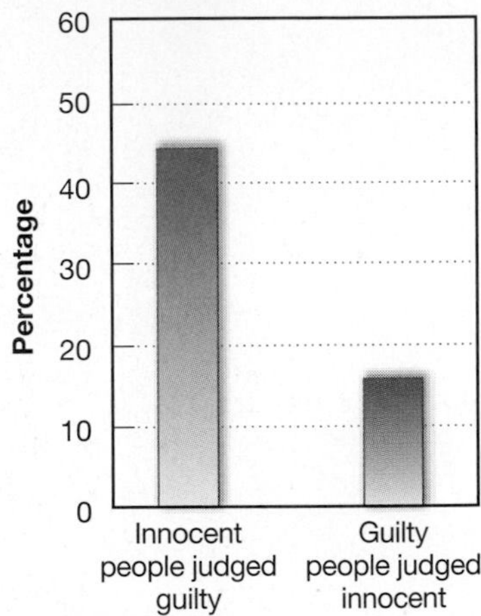

FIGURE 11.3 Misjudging the Innocent

This graph shows the average percentages across three studies of incorrect classifications by lie detectors. Nearly half of the innocent people were classified as guilty, and a significant number of guilty people were classified as innocent. The investigators independently confirmed a suspect's guilt or innocence by other means, such as confessions of other suspects (Iacono & Lykken, 1997).

Because of the unreliability of the polygraph, researchers are trying to find other ways of measuring physiological signs of lying. A popular one is the Computer Voice Stress Analyzer, a technology based on the assumption that the human voice contains telltale signals that betray a speaker's emotional state and intent to deceive. Its promoters claim high degrees of accuracy, but research has yielded negative or inconclusive findings (Air Force Research Laboratory, 2000). Like the polygraph, the voice analyzer detects physiological changes that may indicate fear, anger, or other signs of stress rather than lying.

A better method is the *Guilty Knowledge Test*, which uses a series of multiple-choice questions, each offering one relevant answer about the crime under investigation and several neutral answers, chosen so that an innocent suspect will not be able to discriminate them from the relevant one (Lykken, 1998). If a suspect's physiological responses to the relevant answer are consistently larger than to the neutral alternatives, the investigator infers that the suspect is guilty (Ben-Shakhar & Elaad, 2003). This method has a much better track record of identifying the guilty without falsely accusing the innocent; it is widely used in by law enforcement in Japan. But it, too, has limitations because the investigator must have enough information about the crime to be able to ask questions that only the guilty person knows and remembers.

Other researchers are using thermal imaging to monitor brain waves and fluctuations in blood flow, designing computer programs to read authentic versus faked facial expressions, recording nonverbal gestures and eye gazes, and taking MRIs of brain activity to see whether they can infer whether a person possesses guilty knowledge of a crime and is lying about it. They are trying to find "brain fingerprints." But if the basic assumption in all this work is faulty—that there are inevitable, universally identifiable signs in the brain or face that reveal when a person is lying—these methods will also be unreliable. People may speak hesitantly in telling a story, using lots of ums and ers, or seem stressed in their speech, or avoid looking you in the eye, or have racing hearts, not because they are lying but because they are ambivalent, conflicted, or uncertain about what happened (DePaulo et al., 2003). People from different cultures often have different nonverbal gestures, as we will see; a man being interviewed by an officer may avert his eyes not because he is guilty but because he finds it rude to gaze

directly at a stranger. And because of the normal variability among people in their autonomic and brain reactivity, innocent but highly reactive people are still likely to be mislabeled guilty by these tests (Zelicoff, 2001).

In this section, we have seen that physiological indicators alone are not a sure guide to what a person is feeling. We cannot know just from measuring someone's hormones or heart rate whether he or she is lying or telling the truth, feeling thrilled or frightened, is sick or just in love. Nor can biology alone explain why, of two students about to take an exam, one feels psyched up and the other feels overwhelmed by anxiety. To understand emotions, you must also know what is going on in a person's mind.

QUICK quiz

Aren't you longing to take this quiz? Don't lie—we can tell.

1. A 3-year-old sees her dad dressed as a gorilla and screams in fear. What brain structure is probably involved in her reaction?
2. Luisa is watching an old Laurel and Hardy film, which makes her laugh and want to see more of them. Which side of her prefrontal cortex is likely to be activated?
3. Luis is watching *Horrible Hatchet Homicides in the Dorm.* Which cells in his brain are making him wince in sympathy when the hero is attacked by the villain?
4. Luis is watching *Horrible Hatchet Homicides in the Dorm II.* Which hormones cause his heart to pound and his palms to sweat when the murderer stalks an unsuspecting victim?
5. Some years ago, a congressman was questioned about the mysterious disappearance of a young woman who had been his intern and lover. He agreed to take a lie detector test given by an expert of his choice. He passed, but the police were unimpressed and wanted him to take another polygraph administered by *their* expert. In either case, what would the results tell us?

Answers:
1. the amygdala **2.** the left **3.** mirror neurons **4.** epinephrine, norepinephrine **5.** Not much. The polygraph is not very reliable, regardless of who administers it, because so many factors can affect a person's physiological responses to it.

WHAT'S**AHEAD**

- When people say, "The more I thought about it, the madder I got," what does that tell us about emotion?
- In a competition, who is likely to be happier, the third-place winner or the second-place winner—and why?
- Why can't an infant feel shame or guilt?

Elements of Emotion 2: The Mind

Two friends of ours returned from a mountain-climbing trip to Nepal. One said, "I was ecstatic! The crystal-clear skies, the millions of stars, the friendly people, the majestic mountains, the harmony of the universe!" The other said, "I was miserable! The bedbugs and fleas, the lack of toilets, the yak-butter tea, the awful food, the unforgiving mountains!"

Same trip, two different reactions to it. Why? As we saw in Chapter 1, in the first century A.D., the Stoic philosophers suggested an answer: People do not become

angry or sad or anxious because of actual events but because of their explanations of those events. Modern psychologists have verified the Stoics' ideas experimentally and are identifying the cognitive processes involved in emotions.

Does this woman's touch signify affection, dominance, harassment, sexual interest, or simple friendliness? Depending on how the man interprets her action, he may respond with happiness, annoyance, anger, or discomfort.

How Thoughts Create Emotions

Imagine that you have had a crush for weeks on a fellow student. Finally, you get up the nerve to start a conversation. Heart pounding, palms sweating, you manage to say, "Hi, there!" Before you can continue, the object of your passion has walked right past you without even a nod. Do you feel angry? Sad? Embarrassed? Your answer will depend on how you explain the other student's behavior:

Angry: "What a rude thing to do, to ignore me like that!"

Sad: "I knew it; I'm no good. Plus it means I'm ugly."

Embarrassed: "Oh, no! Everyone saw how I was humiliated!"

Notice that it is not the student's behavior, but your *interpretation* of it, that generates your emotional response. Perceptions are involved in every emotion, even those widely considered to be primary, such as happiness and anger (Schacter & Singer, 1962). Emotions can be generated and influenced by beliefs, perceptions of the situation, expectations, and *attributions*—the explanations that people make of their own and other people's behavior (see Chapter 8). Human beings, after all, are the only species that says, "The more I thought about it, the madder I got."

Consider this example: Imagine that you get an A on your psychology midterm; how will you feel? Or perhaps you get a D on that exam; how will you feel then? Most people assume that success brings happiness and failure brings unhappiness, but the emotions you feel will depend more on how you *explain* your grade than on what you actually get. Do you attribute your grade to your own efforts (or lack of them) or to the teacher, fate, or luck? In a series of experiments, students who believed they did well because of their own efforts tended to feel proud, happy, and satisfied. Those who believed they did well because of a lucky fluke tended to feel gratitude, surprise, or guilt ("I don't deserve this"). Those who believed their failures were their own fault tended to feel guilty. And those who blamed others tended to feel angry (Weiner, 1986).

Here is a more surprising example of how thoughts affect emotions. Of two Olympic finalists, one who wins a second-place silver medal and one who wins a third-place bronze medal, which will feel happier? Won't it be the silver medalist? Nope. In a study of athletes' reactions to placing second and third in the 1992 Olympics and the 1994 Empire State games, the bronze medalists were happier than the silver medalists (Medvec, Madey, & Gilovich, 1995). Apparently, the athletes were comparing their performance to what might have been. The second-place winners, comparing themselves to the gold medalists, were unhappy that they didn't get the gold. But the third-place

GET INVOLVED

➤EXAMINING YOUR EMOTIONS AFTER AN EXAM

After your next psychology test, write down the reasons you think you got the grade you did. Do you attribute the reasons to your own efforts (or lack of effort)? If you did not do as well as you hoped, do you blame yourself or the teacher? If you did do well, do you take credit, or do you think your success was a lucky fluke? How are these explanations related to your feelings about your grade?

THINKING CRITICALLY
ANALYZE ASSUMPTIONS AND BIASES

Most people assume that second-place winners feel happier about their performance than third-place winners do. But when psychologists questioned this assumption, they found that the opposite is true. Certainly, Olympic fencing bronze medalist Jean-Michel Henry of France (left) is happier than silver medalist Pavel Kolobkov of the Unified Team (right). (Eric Strecki, center, won the gold for France.)

winners, comparing themselves to those who did worse than they, were happy that they had earned a medal at all. Over a century ago, William James commented on the paradox of an athlete who is "shamed to death" because he is merely the second best in the whole world: "That he is able to beat the whole population of the globe minus one is nothing; he has 'pitted' himself to beat that one; and as long as he doesn't do that nothing else counts."

The complicated mix of emotions that people feel when they have "disappointing wins" (outcomes that were not as good as they had expected) or "relieving losses" (bad outcomes that could have been worse) shows how powerfully thoughts affect emotional responses—and why we can even feel two emotions, such as pleasure and regret, simultaneously (Larsen et al., 2004). Our thoughts are constantly affecting our reactions to events. If you decide that being stuck in a traffic jam is trivial and you can't do anything about it anyway, you may take it calmly. If you are on the way to your best friend's wedding, you see that the traffic is getting worse, and being late is *really* going to be bad for you because your friend will personally kill you, you are likely to feel hopping mad at those stupid cars that are blocking your way.

The cognitions involved in emotion range from your immediate perceptions of a specific event to your general philosophy of life (Lazarus, 2000a). If your guiding philosophy is that winning is everything and trying your best counts for nothing, you may feel depressed rather than happy if you "only" come in second, just like those silver medalists. If you think a friend's criticism is intentionally mean rather than well-meaning, you may respond with anger rather than gratitude. If you are a perfectionist about your work, brooding and obsessing about your occasional mistakes, you will become more anxious and depressed than if you are able to put your errors behind you (Flett et al., 1998). Cognitive appraisals are thus an essential part of the experience of emotion.

CLOSE-UP on Research

MISPREDICTING FUTURE FEELINGS

If you won a lottery for $20 million, how long do you think your initial happiness would last? If a tornado destroyed your house and most of your town, how long do you think you would feel frightened and miserable? People make many decisions based on how they imagine they will feel in the future and on how long they predict their feelings will continue. For example, you might turn down an offer of a trip with friends three months from now because you predict that you will still be feeling miserable about a recent breakup with the love of your life. Or you might spend more money than you can afford on a car or sound system because you think that *this* is what will make you truly happy.

In a series of studies, Timothy Wilson and Daniel Gilbert (2005) **analyzed the common assumption** that people know themselves well enough to predict how they will feel about what happens to them in the future. They began by **asking these questions**: Given that memory plays tricks on us when we look backward in time, is there

any reason to think our imaginations won't play tricks on us when we look *forward* in time? Are we really any good at knowing what will make us happiest and what will make us miserable? Are we good at predicting how long those feelings will last?

When they **examined the evidence**, they found, surprisingly, that people routinely mispredict how much pleasure or unhappiness future events will bring, and they are even worse at predicting whether those feelings will last a few hours or a few months. For example, in one real-life longitudinal study, college students who were about to be randomly assigned to a dorm had to predict how happy or unhappy they would feel (on a scale from 1 = unhappy to 7 = happy) after being assigned to a "desirable" or "undesirable" house, which they also rated on a scale of desirability (Dunn, Wilson, & Gilbert, 2003). The students predicted that their dorm assignments would have a huge impact on their overall level of happiness and that being assigned to an "undesirable" dorm would essentially wreck their satisfaction for the whole year. In fact, as you can see from the figure, one year later, when the researchers asked them to rate their happiness, those who were living in desirable and undesirable dorms had nearly identical levels.

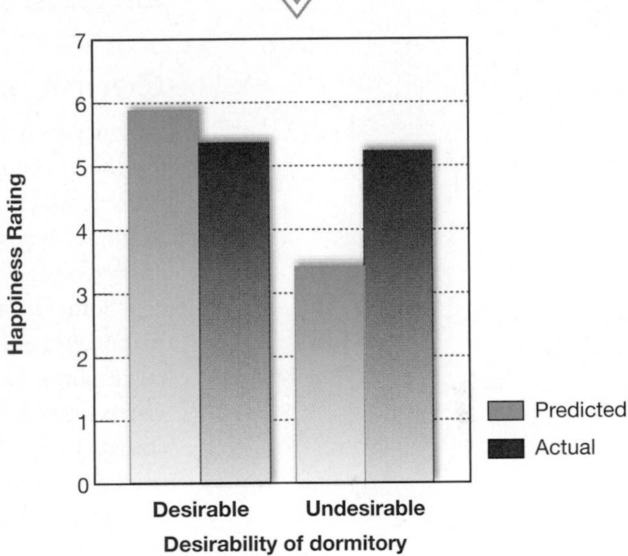

The researchers **considered other interpretations** of their findings. Perhaps the undesirable dorms turned out to be unexpectedly pleasant, with cool people living in them? No. The students had focused on the wrong factors when imagining their future feelings of happiness in the houses; they had placed far more importance on what the house looked like and on its location than on its inhabitants, but in fact it's people who make a place fun or unpleasant to live in—and all of the houses had likable people in them. Because the students could not foresee this, or how much they would like their new roommates, they mispredicted their future happiness.

In another study, 57 male and 41 female students completed a questionnaire that asked them to imagine a series of events involving someone who committed a transgression against them (Gilbert et al., 2004). For example, they asked someone out and were politely turned down, their roommate borrowed their boots without permission, they were told they couldn't use a restaurant's restroom because they were not a customer, they caught someone trying to break into their gym locker, their best friend had a romantic encounter with their former girlfriend or boyfriend, or a careless driver dented their car in a parking lot and then sped away. The students estimated the intensity of their initial reactions to each transgression by indicating how they thought they would feel about the transgressor at the moment it happened, using a scale whose endpoints were labeled *dislike very much* (–4) and *like very much* (+4). They also estimated how long these feelings would last by indicating on the same scale how they thought they would feel about the transgressor one week later. Participants believed that the *intensity* of their current feelings would predict *how long* those feelings would last: The correlations were strong and significant. But in a series of subsequent studies, the researchers found that when people have intense negative reactions to someone who is important to them, they are motivated to reduce those feelings. So they often reinterpret the offender's behavior in a more forgiving light, excusing the seriousness of the transgression. As a result, contrary to their own predictions, they often end up being *least* angry at the people who hurt them *most!*

The researchers called the tendency to overestimate the intensity and duration of one's own emotional reactions to events (whether good or bad) the "impact bias." They have replicated the basic findings in many different contexts and the impact bias remains: The good is rarely as good as we imagine it will be, and the bad is rarely as terrible. The reason seems to be that people adjust quickly to happy changes—new relationships, a promotion, a raise—and fail to anticipate that they will cope psychologically

just as quickly with bad experiences. The human need to make sense of unexpected events, even tragedies, and to make excuses for our blunders—or the blunders of those who hurt us—smoothes the bumps in the road of life.

Ironically, overestimating the impact of negative events may create unnecessary fear and anxiety in the present; some people may even put off lifesaving procedures because they anticipate that they will suffer too much. By not taking into account their own resilience when forecasting their future emotions, people may reduce their chances of true happiness and better health.

Cognitions and Emotional Complexity

Cognitions and physiology are inextricably linked in the experience of emotion. They are the yin and yang of human passion. Each affects the other in an endless loop: Cognitions affect emotions, and emotional states influence cognitions (Gray, 2004). For example, blaming others for your woes can make you feel angry, but once you are angry you may be more inclined to think the worst of other people's motives.

Some emotions require only minimal, simple cognitions or are primitive feelings that occur beneath awareness (Winkielman & Berridge, 2004). A conditioned sentimental response to a patriotic symbol, a conditioned disgust response to an ugly bug, and a warm fuzzy feeling toward a familiar object all involve simple, nonconscious reactions (Izard, 1994a; Murphy, Monahan, & Zajonc, 1995). An infant's primitive emotions do not have much mental sophistication: "Hey, I'm mad because no one is feeding me!"

As a child's cerebral cortex matures, however, cognitions and, therefore, emotions become more cognitively complex: "Hey, I'm mad because this situation is entirely unfair!" Some emotions depend entirely on the maturation of higher cognitive capacities. Shame and guilt, for example, do not occur until after infancy because these self-conscious emotions require the emergence of a sense of self and the perception that you have behaved badly or let another person down (Baumeister, Stillwell, & Heatherton, 1994; Tangney et al., 1996).

Because our cognitions constantly shift as we interact with others, so do our emotions, which is another reason for emotional complexity in real-life situations. Richard Lazarus (2000a) once described a quarrel between a husband and wife at breakfast. She had not given him freshly squeezed juice as usual, and when he asked why, the wife, who was feeling annoyed that he had come home the night before in a sullen mood, told him he could make his own %&*$! juice. Annoyed and hurt by her harsh tone, he withdrew and sulked, making her angrier. Before long the quarrel had escalated into mutual accusations about other matters. Then, as the husband was about to storm out of the house, he mentioned that he had learned the day before that he would have to take a pay cut at work and that many employees were being fired. He admitted how anxious he was feeling about his job, and the wife realized why he had been so remote the previous night. She apologized for her outburst and felt guilty for having yelled at him.

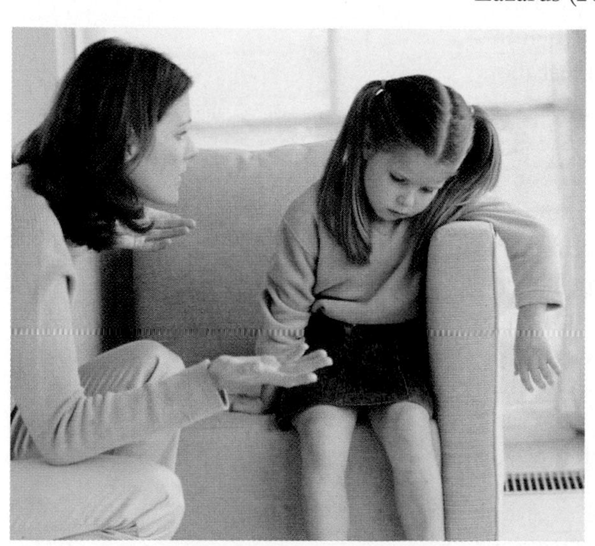

Children need to be old enough to have a sense of self before they can feel the moral emotions of shame, guilt, or remorse.

Notice how many emotions flared up and subsided during this brief interaction, depending on what each spouse was thinking: anger, guilt, anxiety, hurt, empathy. When both spouses were feeling misunderstood and mistreated, they felt angry; when each saw another explanation for the partner's behavior, the anger dissipated.

The evidence that thinking affects emotions suggests that when people are in the throes of an unpleasant emotion, they may be able to

change their feelings by reappraising the situation and their perceptions of it (Gross & John, 2003). (As we will see in Chapter 17, cognitive therapy is based on this assumption.) They can ask themselves what the evidence is for their belief that the world will collapse if they get a C in biology, that no one loves them, or that they will be lonely forever. In such cases, it is not emotional reasoning that prevents critical thinking; it is the failure to think critically that creates the emotion!

An individual's experience of emotion, then, combines mind and body. Yet there is still one part of the emotion tree missing. Thoughts may influence emotion, but where do these thoughts come from? When people feel that it is shameful for a man to dance on a table with a lampshade on his head, or for a woman to walk down a street with her arms and legs uncovered, where do their ideas about shame originate? If you punch the walls when you are angry, where did you learn how to express your feelings in that way? To answer these questions, we turn to the third major aspect of emotional experience: the role of culture.

QUICK quiz

Are your thoughts about quizzes affecting your feelings about taking this one?

1. Dara and Dinah get Bs on their psychology midterm, but Dara is ecstatic and proud and Dinah is furious. What thoughts are probably affecting their emotional reactions?
2. *True or false:* People are pretty good at knowing what will make them happy.
3. At a party, a stranger is flirting with your date. You are flooded with jealousy. What cognitions might be causing this emotion? *Be specific.* What alternative thoughts might reduce your jealousy?

Answers:

1. Dara was probably expecting a lower grade and is attributing her B to her own efforts; Dinah was probably expecting a higher grade and is attributing her B to the instructor's unfairness, bad luck, or other external causes. 2. false 3. Possible thoughts causing jealousy are "My date finds other people more attractive," "That person is trying to steal my date," or "My date's behavior is humiliating me." But you could be saying, "It's a compliment to me that other people find my date attractive" or "It pleases me that my date is getting such deserved attention."

WHAT'S AHEAD

- Why does one person find bugs disgusting and another consider them a culinary treat?
- Do Germans, Japanese, and Americans always mean the same thing when they smile at others?
- Why do people show sadness at funerals even when they are not feeling sad?

Elements of Emotion 3: The Culture

A young wife leaves her house one morning to draw water from the local well as her husband watches from the porch. On her way back from the well, a male stranger stops her and asks for some water. She gives him a cupful and then invites him home to dinner. He accepts. The husband, wife, and guest have a pleasant meal together. The husband, in a gesture of hospitality, invites the guest to spend the night—with his wife. The guest accepts. In the morning, the husband leaves early to bring home breakfast. When he returns, he finds his wife again in bed with the visitor.

At what point in this story does the husband feel angry? The answer depends on his culture (Hupka, 1981, 1991). A North American husband would feel rather angry at a wife who had an extramarital affair, and a wife would feel rather angry at being offered to a guest as if she were a lamb chop. But these reactions are not universal. A Pawnee husband of the nineteenth century would be enraged at any man who dared ask his wife for water. An Ammassalik Inuit husband finds it perfectly honorable to offer his wife to a stranger, but only once. He would be angry to find his wife and the guest having a second encounter. And a Toda husband at the turn of the century in India would not be angry at all because the Todas allowed both husband and wife to take lovers. Both spouses might feel angry, though, if one of them had a *sneaky* affair without announcing it publicly.

People in most cultures feel angry in response to insult and the violation of social rules. But as this story shows, they often disagree about what an insult is or what the correct rule should be. In this section, we will explore how culture influences the emotions we feel and the ways in which we express them.

How Culture Shapes Emotions

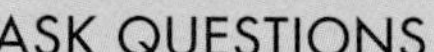

THINKING CRITICALLY

ASK QUESTIONS

What does it mean if one language has a term for an emotion that another language lacks, like *litost* or *hagaii*? Are people whose languages include these words actually more likely to feel the emotion—or just to have a term that describes it?

Are some emotions specific to particular cultures and not found elsewhere? What does it mean, for example, that some languages have words for subtle emotional states that other languages lack? The Germans have *schadenfreude*, a feeling of malicious joy at another's misfortune. The Japanese speak of *hagaii*, helpless anguish tinged with frustration. *Litost* is a Czech word that combines grief, sympathy, remorse, and longing; the Czech writer Milan Kundera used it to describe "a state of torment caused by a sudden insight into one's own miserable self."

Conversely, some languages lack words for emotions that seem universal. For example, Tahitians lack the Western concept of and word for sadness. If you ask a Tahitian who is grieving over the loss of a lover what is wrong, he will say, "A spirit has made me ill." In contrast, Tahitians have a word for an emotion that most Westerners do not experience: *Mehameha* refers to "a sense of the uncanny," a trembling sensation that Tahitians feel when ordinary categories of perception are suspended—at twilight, in the brush, watching fires glow without heat. To Westerners, an event that cannot be identified is usually greeted with fear. Yet *mehameha* does not describe what Westerners call fear or terror (Levy, 1984).

Do these interesting linguistic differences mean that Germans are more likely than others actually to feel *schadenfreude*, the Japanese to feel *hagaii*, the Czechs to feel *litost*, and the Tahitians to feel *mehameha?* Or are they just more willing to give these subtle, multifaceted emotions a single name? Certainly many non-German Westerners feel something like *schadenfreude* at the downfall or humiliation of their political opponents or ex-lovers, or, as one study confirmed, the ultimate defeat of a rival who has beaten them in a sporting event (Leach et al., 2003). Do Tahitians experience sadness the way Westerners do even though they identify it as illness?

Many psychologists, especially those studying the biology of emotion, believe that all human beings are capable of feeling the primary, hardwired emotions—the ones that have distinctive physiological hallmarks in the brain, face, and nervous system. Yet, they say, individuals might indeed differ in their likelihood of feeling secondary emotions, including variations such as *schadenfreude*, *hagaii*, or *mehameha*.

The difference between primary emotions and more complex adult variations is reflected in language all over the world. In Chapter 9, we noted that a *prototype* is a

typical representative of a class of things. Most people consider the primary emotions to be core examples of the concept *emotion:* For example, they will say that anger and sadness are more representative of an emotion than irritability and nostalgia are. Prototypical emotions are reflected in the emotion words that young children learn first: *happy, sad, mad,* and *scared.* As children develop, they begin to draw emotional distinctions that are less prototypical and more specific to their language and culture, such as *ecstatic, depressed, hostile,* or *anxious* (Hupka, Lenton, & Hutchison, 1999; Russell & Fehr, 1994; Shaver, Wu, & Schwartz, 1992). In this way, they come to experience the gradations and nuances of emotional feeling that their cultures emphasize.

Some psychologists, however, don't think much of the primary–secondary distinction because, for them, there is *no* aspect of any emotion that is not influenced by culture or context, and there is no pure emotion with clear-cut boundaries that separate it from other emotions (Barrett, 2006; Elfenbein & Ambady, 2003). Anger may be universal, they say, but the way it is experienced and expressed will vary from culture to culture—whether it feels good or bad, horrible or exhilarating, useful or destructive. Culture even affects which emotions are defined as basic or primary. Anger is regarded as a primary emotion by individualistic Western psychologists, but in group-oriented cultures, shame and loss of face are more central emotions (Kitayama & Markus, 1994). And on the tiny Micronesian atoll of Ifaluk, everyone would say that *fago* is the most fundamental emotion. *Fago,* translated as "compassion/love/sadness," reflects the sad feeling one has when a loved one is absent or in need, and the pleasurable sense of compassion in being able to care and help (Lutz, 1988).

THINKING CRITICALLY

ASK QUESTIONS

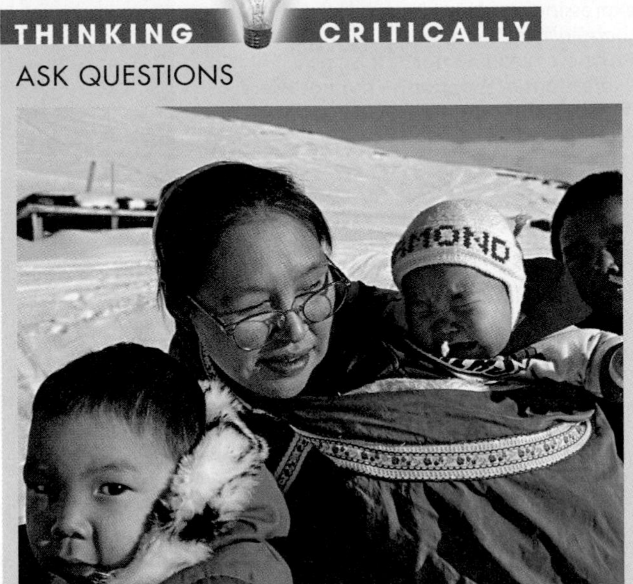

Anger is considered a primary emotion in Western societies. But in some cultures, such as the Inuit, anger is not tolerated because it threatens the community's need for closeness. Inuit mothers like this one often calmly ignore an angry baby, conveying the message that complaining is not welcome. What emotions would be "primary" among the Inuit? Does culture shape the basic experience of emotion or only the forms it takes?

What, then, would theories of primary emotions look like from a non-Western perspective? They might start with shame and *fago,* which are just blips on the radar screen of Western emotion research. And they might also include empathy, gratitude, regret, envy, greed, and love, which are felt by human beings everywhere yet are omitted from most lists of "universals" because they don't seem to have corresponding facial expressions (Bartlett & DeSteno, 2006; Zajonc, 2003).

Everyone agrees, however, that cultures determine much of what people feel emotional *about.* As we saw, the ability to feel disgust is universal, but the content of what produces disgust changes as an infant matures, and it varies across cultures. People in some cultures learn to become disgusted by bugs (which other people find beautiful or tasty), unfamiliar sexual practices, dirt, death, contamination by a handshake with a stranger, particular foods (e.g., meat if they are vegetarian, or pork if they are Muslims or Orthodox Jews), or violation of their religious taboos (Rozin, Lowery, & Ebert, 1994).

What some of us do for love: Ulrich von Lichtenstein disguised as Venus.

Culture and Emotional Expression

On Sunday, April 25, in the year 1227, a knight named Ulrich von Lichtenstein disguised himself as the goddess Venus. Wearing an ornate white gown, waist-length braids, and heavy veils, Ulrich traveled from Venice to Bohemia, challenging all local

Around the world, the cultural rules for expressing emotions (or suppressing them) differ. The display rule for a formal Japanese wedding portrait is "no expressions of emotion"—but not every member of this family has learned that rule yet.

display rules Social and cultural rules that regulate when, how, and where a person may express (or must suppress) emotions.

warriors to a duel. By his own count (which may have been exaggerated), Ulrich broke 307 lances, unhorsed four opponents, and completed his five-week journey with an undefeated record. The reason for Ulrich's knightly performance was his passion for a princess, nameless to history, who barely gave poor Ulrich the time of day. Ulrich trembled in her presence, suffered in her absence, and constantly endured feelings of longing, misery, and melancholy—a state of love that apparently made him very happy (Hunt, 1959/1967).

We will have a lot more to say about love in the next chapter, but for the moment consider only Ulrich's expression of his passion. If someone tried to win your heart by performing a modern version of such acts of bravery, would you be charmed, irritated, or alarmed?

Display Rules. In some cultures, people would find Ulrich's extravagant demonstration of love exciting and touching. In others, they would find it weird; they would be suspicious of Ulrich's real motives. Likewise, in some cultures grief is expressed by noisy wailing and weeping; in others, by tearless resignation; and in still others, by merry dance, drink, and song. Cultures everywhere have **display rules** that specify when, where, and how emotions are to be expressed or when they should be squelched (Ekman et al., 1987; Gross, 1998). Once you feel an emotion, how you express it is rarely a matter of "I say what I feel." You may be obliged to disguise what you feel. You may wish you could feel what you say.

Even the smile, which seems a straightforward signal of friendliness, has many meanings and uses that are not universal. Americans smile more frequently than Germans, not because Americans are friendlier but because they differ in their notions of when a smile is appropriate. After a German–American business meeting, the Americans often complain that Germans are cold and aloof, and the Germans often complain that Americans are excessively cheerful, hiding their real feelings under the mask of a smile (Hall & Hall, 1990). The Japanese smile even more than Americans, to disguise embarrassment, anger, or other negative emotions whose public display is considered rude and incorrect.

THINKING CRITICALLY

CONSIDER OTHER INTERPRETATIONS

A European who behaves in a way that conveys good manners and dignified restraint may seem cold to the average American. An American who smiles effusively may seem superficial and childish to the average European. How might each of them interpret the other's behavior more constructively?

CHAPTER TWELVE

Just don't give up trying to do what you really want to do. Where there is love and inspiration, I don't think you can go wrong.

ELLA FITZGERALD

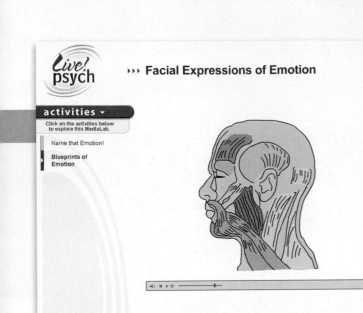

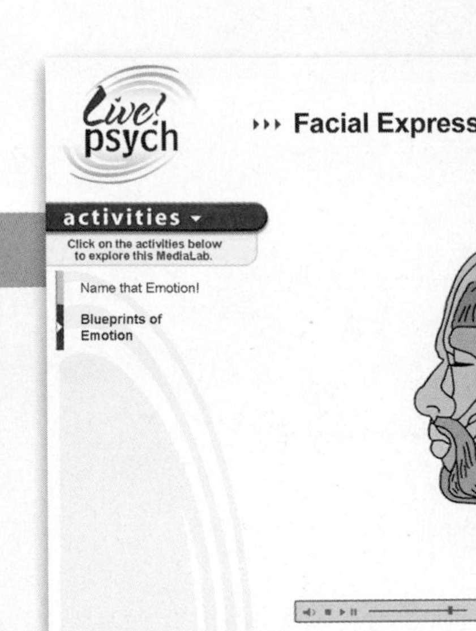

››› Facial Expressions of Emotion

Emotion is accompanied by changes in facial expression. There are 80 muscles in the human face that can create more than 7,000 different expressions!

Researchers use a physiological device called the facial electromyograph (EMG) to measure the activity of facial muscles and their associations with emotion.

Participants in facial EMG studies are shown images that evoke positive or negative emotions, while electrodes attached to the face record the activity of various muscles.

screen 1 of 3

TELL ME **MORE** >>

"The content and features were very useful in preparing for the exams."

Student
Clayton State University

Snarling dog

ANS arousal

Conscious fear

Emotion

9.13 What are the three elements of emotion?

SIMULATION

The simulation on facial expressions of emotion examines nonverbal communication through facial expressions and how expressions are formed. Work through the content, listening to the audio portion, watching the images, reading the script and trying the drag and drop exercise. Be sure to cover both sections.

It should take about 5-10 minutes to walk through.

Simulation

Once you have covered all the material in the simulation, answer the following questions:

According to Ekman, which of the following is NOT one of the universal facial expressions?

- disgust
- contempt
- fear
- shame

What can you find in MyPsychLab?

Self-Directed Tests • Videos • Simulations • eBook • Flash Cards • Web Links . . . and more — organized by chapter, section and learning objective.

How Do You Feel?

NOW YOU HAVE READ CHAPTER ELEVEN — ARE YOU PREPARED FOR THE EXAM?

Which of the following emotions is (are) not generally considered to be among the most universal ones?

a) pride

b) happiness

c) sadness

d) embarrassment

e) regret

f) anger

g) disgust

h) fear

regret and embarrassment

How do you feel about how you are doing in this class? If you are at all concerned about you next exam, check out the resources available to you at **www.mypsychlab.com.**

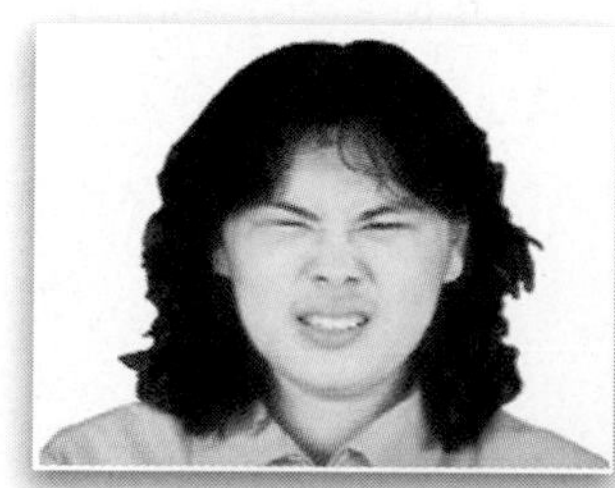

What are the three elements of emotion?

What constitutes an emotion? Review the three elements of emotion: physiology, behavior, and subjective experience.

What are the major theories of emotion?

By far, the most confusing concept of this chapter is keeping track of the theories of emotion. Check out the simulations in the Emotion section of MyPsychLab to help you clarify these concepts.

KEY TERMS

emotion 408
primary emotions 408
secondary emotions 408
facial feedback 410
mood contagion 411
amygdala 414
prefrontal cortex 415
emotion regulation 415
mirror neurons 416
epinephrine 417
norepinephrine 417
polygraph ("lie detector") 418
Guilty Knowledge Test 419
attributions 421
emotion prototypes 427
display rules 428
emotion work 429
body language 429

especially involved in fear. The *prefrontal cortex* provides the cognitive ability to override this initial appraisal. Emotions generally involve the motivation to approach or withdraw: Regions of the *left* prefrontal cortex appear to be specialized for the motivation to approach others (as with happiness and anger), whereas regions of the *right* prefrontal cortex are specialized for withdrawal or escape (as with disgust and fear). Parts of the prefrontal cortex are also involved in regulating emotions and keeping them on an even keel. *Mirror neurons* throughout the brain are activated when people observe others. These neurons are involved in empathy, imitation, learning, language, synchrony, and many other aspects of human psychology.

- During the experience of any emotion, *epinephrine* and *norepinephrine* produce a state of physiological arousal to prepare the body for an output of energy. But different emotions are also associated with different biochemical responses and different patterns of autonomic nervous system activity.
- As discussed in "Biology and Deception," many people have tried to find ways of reliably determining, through the use of physiological measurements, when someone is lying. The most popular method is the *polygraph machine*, or "lie detector," but it has low reliability and validity because there are no patterns of autonomic nervous system activity specific to lying. Other methods, such as measures of "voice stress" and changes in the brain, are being tried, but they have similar drawbacks. The *Guilty Knowledge Test* has been more successful. The challenge for social scientists and for law enforcement is to identify liars without falsely accusing truth-tellers.

Elements of Emotion 2: The Mind

- Some psychologists study the cognitive processes involved in emotion, such as the *attributions* people make about others' behavior and the way people interpret and evaluate events. The cognitions involved in emotion range from immediate perceptions of a specific event to one's philosophy of life.
- As discussed in the "Close-up on Research," people are often poor at predicting how a future event will make them feel, whether it is a happy event or a sad one, and at predicting how long their future feelings will last.
- Thoughts and emotions operate reciprocally, each influencing the other. Some emotions, such as those that appear in infancy or that reflect conditioned responses to emotional symbols, involve simple, nonconscious reactions. Others, such as shame and guilt, require complex cognitive abilities and the emergence of a sense of self. In any emotional encounter, cognitions and appraisals are constantly changing, affecting the emotions the participants feel.

Elements of Emotion 3: The Culture

- Many psychologists believe that all human beings share the ability to experience primary emotions, whereas secondary emotions may be culture specific—a view supported by research on emotion *prototypes*. But cultural psychologists believe that culture affects every aspect of emotional experience, including which emotions are considered basic. All researchers agree that culture affects what people feel emotional about.
- Culture strongly influences the *display rules* that regulate how and whether people express their emotions. *Emotion work* is the effort a person makes to display an emotion he or she does not feel but feels obliged to convey. People also convey emotions through the gestures and nonverbal expressions of *body language*.

Putting the Elements Together: Emotion and Gender

- Women and men are equally likely to feel all emotions, from love to grief to anger. Many men seem to be more physiologically reactive to conflict than women are, however, and the sexes sometimes differ in the perceptions and attributions that generate emotion and emotional intensity.
- Men and women differ primarily in expressiveness—in the display rules they follow for expressing emotions, which vary across cultures. In North America, women are more likely than men to cry and to reveal feelings of fear, sadness, guilt, and loneliness; men are more likely to deny or mask such feelings, which many consider to be signs of weakness. North American men express one emotion more freely than women: anger toward strangers. But gender differences in expressiveness depend on gender roles, cultural norms, and the specific situation. Both sexes are less expressive to a person with higher status or power, both sexes will do the emotion work their job requires, and some situations foster expressiveness in everybody.
- The example of gender and emotion shows that to understand the full experience and expression of emotion, we must understand biology, cognitive attributions and perceptions, and cultural rules. Examining just one component gives an incomplete picture.

- **Beware of road rage—yours and the other person's.** Driving increases everyone's level of physiological arousal, but not everyone becomes a hotheaded driver. Some drivers make themselves angry by having vengeful and retaliatory thoughts about other drivers (who have the nerve to change lanes or want to park, or who dare to drive at the speed limit in a school zone!). Hotheaded drivers take more risks while driving (rapidly switching lanes in their impatience), behave more aggressively (swearing, giving other drivers the finger or cursing them), and have more accidents (Deffenbacher et al., 2003).
- **If you decide that expressing anger is appropriate, be sure you use the right verbal and nonverbal language to make yourself understood.** Because cultures (and families) have different display rules, be sure the recipient of your anger understands what you are feeling and what complaint you are trying to convey. If your way of expressing anger is to sulk, expecting everyone else to read your mind and apologize to you, you are not communicating clearly.
- **Think carefully about how to express anger so that you will get the results you want.** What do you want your anger to accomplish? Do you just want to make the other person feel bad, or do you want the other person to understand your concerns and take steps to respond to them? Shouting "You moron! How *could* you be so stupid!" might accomplish the former goal, but it's not likely to get the person to apologize, let alone to change his or her behavior.

If your goal is to improve a bad situation or achieve justice, then learning how to express anger so the other person will listen is essential. People who have been the targets of injustice have learned that outbursts of anger may draw society's attention to a problem, but real change requires sustained political effort, challenges to unfair laws, and the use of tactics that persuade rather than alienate the opposition.

Of course, if you just want to blow off steam, go right ahead, but you risk becoming a hothead.

Summary

- Emotion and cognition are not opposites, with one being irrational and the other rational. Emotions bind people together, regulate relationships, motivate people to achieve their goals, and help them make plans and decisions. The experience of *emotion* involves physiological changes in the brain, face, and autonomic nervous system; cognitive processes; and cultural norms and regulations.

Elements of Emotion 1: The Body

- *Primary emotions* are those that appear to be inborn and universal; they have corresponding physiological patterns and facial expressions. *Secondary emotions* include all the variations and blends of emotion that may vary across cultures.
- Some basic facial expressions—anger, fear, sadness, happiness, disgust, surprise, contempt—are widely recognized across cultures. Pride also seems to be a universal emotion. These emotions probably evolved to foster communication with others, enhance infant survival, and signal our intentions to others. As studies of *facial feedback* show, they also help us to identify our own emotional states. Facial expressions can also generate emotions in others and produce unconscious mimickry, which is why one person can often catch another's mood (*mood contagion*). The ability to synchronize moods through facial expressions and other nonverbal cues is important for establishing rapport and interacting smoothly.
- Certain facial expressions may be universal, but all of them take place in a social context, which is why people don't always agree, across and within cultures, on what a given expression conveys. Familiarity affects the ability to read facial expressions accurately, cultures differ in the attention they pay to the social context of emotion, facial expressions may have different meanings in different contexts, and people often use facial expressions to lie about their real emotions.
- Many aspects of emotion are associated with specific parts of the brain. Damage to certain areas, for example, may affect a person's ability to feel disgust. The right side of the brain is important for processing emotional feeling whereas the left is active in processing emotional meaning. The *amygdala* is responsible for initially evaluating the emotional importance of incoming sensory information and is

Taking Psychology with You

"Let It Out" or "Bottle It Up"? The Dilemma of Anger

What do you do when you feel angry? Do you tend to brood and sulk, collecting your righteous complaints like acorns for the winter, or do you erupt, hurling your wrath upon anyone or anything at hand? Do you discuss your feelings when you have calmed down? Does "letting anger out" get rid of it for you, or does it only make it more intense? The answer is crucial for how you get along with your family, neighbors, employers, and strangers.

Chronic feelings of anger and an inability to control anger can be as emotionally devastating and unhealthy as chronic problems with depression or anxiety. In contrast to much pop-psych advice, research shows that expressing anger does not always get it "out of your system"; often people feel worse after an angry confrontation, both physically and mentally. When people brood and ruminate about their anger, talk to others incessantly about how angry they are, or ventilate their feelings in hostile acts, their blood pressure shoots up, they often feel angrier, and they behave even *more* aggressively later than if they had just let their feelings of anger subside (Bushman et al., 2005; Tavris, 1989). Conversely, when people learn to control their tempers and express anger constructively, they usually feel better, not worse; calmer, not angrier. Charles Darwin (1872/1965) was right again when he observed: "The free expression by outward signs of an emotion intensifies it . . . He who gives way to violent gestures will increase his rage."

BiZarRO by Dan Piraro
Would anyone in the group like to respond to the way Frank is dealing with his anger?
©DAN PIRARO
Dist. by Universal Press Synd. WWW.UEXPRESS.COM

When people are feeling angry, they have a choice of doing any number of things. First, they can try to rethink the situation to reduce its emotional impact; this approach nips anger in the bud and is often more effective than trying to suppress the feeling completely—or just venting it (Gross, 2001). Second, they can choose how to behave: They can write about their feelings in a diary or to a friend (or to the person they are angry with), play the piano, jog, bake bread, try to solve the problem that is causing their anger, abuse their friends or family, hit a punching bag, or yell. If a given action soothes their feelings or gets the desired response from others, they are likely to acquire a habit that feels "natural," as if it could never be changed. Some habits are better than others, though. Baking bread is fine, whereas many people justify their violent tempers by saying, "I couldn't help myself." But they can. If you have acquired an abusive or aggressive habit, the research in this chapter offers practical suggestions for learning constructive ways of managing anger:

- **Don't sound off in the heat of anger; let bodily arousal cool down.** Whether your arousal comes from background stresses such as heat, crowds, or loud noise, or from conflict with another person, take time to relax. Time allows you to decide whether you are really angry or just tired and tense. This is the reason for that sage old advice to count to 10, count to 100, or sleep on it. Other cooling-off strategies include taking a time-out in the middle of an argument, meditating or relaxing, and calming yourself with a distracting activity.
- **Don't take it personally.** If you feel that you have been insulted, check your perception for its accuracy. Could there be another reason for the behavior you find offensive? People who are quick to feel anger tend to interpret other people's actions as intentional offenses. People who are slow to anger tend to give others the benefit of the doubt, and they are not as focused on their own injured pride. Empathy ("Poor guy, he's feeling rotten") is usually incompatible with anger, so practice seeing the situation from the other person's perspective.

(LaFrance, Hecht, & Paluck, 2003). Men are as likely as women to control their tempers when the target of anger is someone with higher status or power; few people, no matter how angry, will readily sound off at a professor, police officer, or employer. The sexes do not differ much in smiling and cooing with their children. And you won't find many gender differences in emotional expressiveness at a football game.

Emotion Work. Both sexes know the experience of having to hide emotions they feel and show emotions they do not feel. There are no sex differences in expressiveness in jobs that require it: For example, women and men who work in "cabin services," the branch of the airline industry that deals directly with passengers, are expected to express warm and positive emotions to customers (Rutherford, 2001).

On the whole, however, women tend to be involved in the flight-attendant side of emotion work, persuading others that they are friendly and warm, and making sure others are happy (DePaulo, 1992; Shields, 2005). Thus, many North American women smile more often than men do as part of their emotion work—to pacify others, smooth over conflicts, or convey deference (Hess, Abrams, & Hecht, 2005; LaFrance, Hecht, & Paluck, 2003). If women do *not* smile when others expect them to, they are often disliked, even if they are actually smiling as often as men would. Girls learn this lesson early; between ages 6 and 10, they become knowledgeable about when they should disguise their true feelings and put on a polite smile—for instance, when they are given a gift they don't like. Boys are much less likely to mask their negative feelings in this way (Davis, 1995; Saarni, 1989).

And so the answer to "Which sex is more emotional?" is: sometimes men, sometimes women, and sometimes neither. The answer depends on how you define "emotional," the situations people are in, the nature of their relationships, their culture's roles and requirements, and the work they do.

QUICK quiz

Both sexes have the emotional stamina to take this quiz.

Indicate whether each of these descriptions applies (a) more to men than to women, (b) more to women than to men, or (c) to both sexes equally.

1. Does "emotion work" to make other people feel good.
2. Finds it difficult to express anger to a superior.
3. Expresses anger to a stranger.
4. Feels grief when a relationship ends.
5. Admits feeling scared to death.

Answers:

1. b 2. c 3. a 4. c 5. b

As we have seen in this chapter, the emotion tree can take many shapes, depending on physiology, cognitive processes, and cultural rules. The case of gender and emotion shows that if we look at just one part of the tree, we come up with an incomplete or misleading picture. And it shows, too, that emotions have many purposes: They allow us to establish close bonds, threaten and warn, get help from others, reveal or deceive. The many varieties and expressions of emotion suggest that although we feel emotions physically, we use them socially. Emotions always involve thinking and feeling, perception and action—head and heart.

Israeli parents (left) and an Iraqi father (right) react to the deaths of their children. Notice that the men are following different display rules for the expression of grief: Let it out versus keep it in. Your own culture's rules may affect your reactions to these scenes: Do you think the Israeli father is being cold and uptight or mature and manly? Is the Iraqi father being unmasculine or humanly expressive?

far more likely than men to cry and to acknowledge emotions that reveal vulnerability and weakness, such as "hurt feelings," fear, sadness, loneliness, shame, and guilt (Grossman & Wood, 1993; Timmers, Fischer, & Manstead, 1998).

In contrast, most North American men express only one emotion more freely than women: anger toward strangers, especially other men, when they believe they have been challenged or insulted. Otherwise, men are expected to control and mask negative feelings. When they are worried or afraid, they are more likely than women to say they feel moody, irritable, frustrated, or on edge (Fehr et al., 1999; Smith & Reise, 1998).

An unfortunate consequence of the taboo on male expressiveness may be difficulty in recognizing when men are seriously unhappy. Many boys and men fail to be diagnosed correctly because the tests for depression are based on typically female reactions—crying and talking (Riessman, 1990; Stapley & Haviland, 1989). But most North American men do not express grief this way. Instead, they try to distract themselves, work harder or quit working altogether, bury their feelings in alcohol or other drugs, or, in extreme cases, become violent. Because the sexes tend to have different ways of coping with depression, some people wrongly infer that men suffer less than women when relationships end or that men are incapable of deep feeling.

Gender differences in emotional expressiveness, however, are strongly affected by a person's culture and the situation he or she is in. Expressive people, male or female, tend to come from cultures in which expressiveness is the rule (Kring & Gordon, 1998). Italian, French, Spanish, and Middle Eastern men can have entire conversations using highly expressive hand gestures and facial expressions; there aren't many sex differences in nonverbal expressiveness in their cultures. In contrast, in Asian cultures, both sexes are taught to control emotional expression (Matsumoto, 1996). Cultures also determine which particular emotions men and women may express most freely. Israeli and Italian men are more likely than women to mask feelings of sadness, but British, Spanish, Swiss, and German men are *less* likely than their female counterparts to inhibit this emotion (Wallbott, Ricci-Bitti, & Bänninger-Huber, 1986).

Likewise, a particular situation or role requirement often determines whether you will express your feelings or inhibit them, regardless of your gender or culture

Emotional Reactivity. If we define emotionality in terms of how quickly and intensely people react to provocation, men are often more emotional than women. Conflict with intimate partners is often physiologically more upsetting for men than for women, which may be why many men try to avoid arguments entirely. During actual quarrels between married couples, men's heart rates, unlike women's, often soar as soon as signs of conflict begin and stay high longer (Levenson, Carstensen, & Gottman, 1994).

"It's truly remarkable, Louis, thirty-seven years next Tuesday and never a cross word between us."

One possible explanation for these differences is that the male's autonomic nervous system is generally more sensitive and reactive than the female's. When men are under stress or in a competitive situation, many show a more pronounced elevation in blood pressure, heart rate, and epinephrine than women do (T. Smith et al., 1996). But another explanation is that men are more likely than women to rehearse angry thoughts, such as "I don't have to take this" or "It's all her fault." These thoughts prolong and intensify the physiological reactions involved in anger (Rusting & Nolen-Hoeksema, 1998). Women, in contrast, are more likely than men to ruminate about, and thus prolong, feelings of depression and sadness (see Chapter 16).

Cognitions. If a woman touches a man on his arm, is she signaling affection or sexual interest? How about if he touches her? Men and women often differ in their perceptions of the same event (Lakoff, 1990; Stapley & Haviland, 1989). Their different interpretations, in turn, can create different emotional responses. For example, although men and women often feel angry in response to betrayal and injustice, they sometimes differ in the kinds of everyday events that provoke their anger. Women are more likely than men to become angry over things they perceive as signs of a partner's disregard, such as forgetting a birthday; men are more likely than women to become angry about damage to their property or affronts by a stranger (Fehr et al., 1999). When your partner blows up over something you think is trivial, it is easy to conclude that he or she is being too emotional.

Expressiveness. The one gender difference that undoubtedly contributes most to the stereotype that women are more emotional than men is women's greater willingness to express their feelings. In North America, women on average smile more than men do, gaze at their listeners more, have more emotionally expressive faces, use more expressive hand and body movements, and touch others more (DePaulo, 1992; Kring & Gordon, 1998). Women also talk about their emotions more than men do. They are

Both sexes feel emotionally attached to friends, but often they express their affections differently. From childhood on, girls in many cultures tend to prefer "face-to-face" friendships based on shared feelings; boys tend to prefer "side-by-side" friendships based on shared activities—such as catching frogs.

QUICK quiz

Please use verbal communication rather than body language to answer these questions.

1. In Western theories of emotion, anger would be called a ______ emotion, whereas *fago* would be called a ______ emotion.
2. In a class discussion, a student says something that embarrasses a student from another culture. The second student smiles to disguise his discomfort; the first student, thinking he is not being taken seriously, gets angry. These students' misunderstanding reflects their different ______ for the expression of embarrassment and anger.
3. Maureen works in a fast-food restaurant and is becoming irritated with a customer who isn't ordering fast enough. "Hey, whaddaya want to order, slowpoke?" she snaps at him. To keep her job, and her temper, Maureen needs practice in ______.

Answers:

1. primary, secondary 2. display rules 3. emotion work

WHAT'S**AHEAD**

- Are women really more emotional than men?
- What factors other than your sex predict how well you can tell what someone is feeling?
- What factors other than your sex predict how emotionally expressive you are?

Putting the Elements Together: Emotion and Gender

THINKING CRITICALLY

DEFINE YOUR TERMS

People say that women are the emotional sex, but they often fail to define their terms. What, for example, does *emotional* mean? Does it refer to how quickly or intensely people react, the kinds of thoughts that provoke them, or how emotions are expressed?

"Women are too emotional," men often complain. "Men are too uptight," women often reply. But what does "too emotional" mean? We need to define our terms and examine our assumptions. There is little evidence that one sex *feels* any of the everyday emotions more often than the other, whether the emotion is anger, worry, happiness, embarrassment, anxiety, jealousy, love, or grief (Archer, 2004; Deffenbacher et al., 2003; Fischer et al., 1993; Harris, 2003; Kring & Gordon, 1998; Shields, 2005).

However, people see what they expect to see, and stereotypes may guide their expectations. For example, most North Americans think it is appropriate for men to express anger and women to express sadness, but not the other way around. Therefore, they often have trouble recognizing male sadness or female anger. Even unambiguous expressions of anger by women are commonly rated as a mixture of anger and sadness (Plant et al., 2000). When women do unmistakably express anger, many people perceive their expressions as being more intense—angrier—than when men do the same thing. In one study, participants rated identical drawings of gender-neutral expressions of emotion. Each face was framed by a male or female hairstyle. When an apparent man expressed anger, participants rated him as being less angry than when an apparent woman did exactly the same thing (Hess, Adams, & Kleck, 2004). So the study of gender differences in emotionality is complicated because researchers have to separate *whether* the sexes differ from whether people *perceive* differences inaccurately.

Emotion Work. Display rules tell us not only what to do when we *are* feeling an emotion but also how and when to show an emotion we do *not* feel. Most people are expected to demonstrate sadness at funerals, happiness at weddings, and affection toward relatives. What if we don't actually feel sad, happy, or affectionate? Acting out an emotion we do not really feel because we believe it is socially appropriate is called **emotion work**. It is part of our normal efforts to regulate our emotions when we are with others (Gross, 1998). Sometimes emotion work is a job requirement: Flight attendants, waiters, and customer-service representatives must put on a happy face to convey cheerfulness, even if they are privately angry about a rude or drunken customer. And bill collectors must put on a stern face to convey threat, even if they feel sorry for the person they are collecting money from (Hochschild, 1983).

Smiling to convey friendliness is part of the job description for flight attendants, whether they are male or female—but not necessarily for the passengers they serve.

Body Language. Culture affects our verbal expressions of emotion and also our *body language*, nonverbal signals of body movement, posture, gesture, and gaze. Fiorello LaGuardia, who was mayor of New York from 1933 to 1945, was fluent in three languages: English, Italian, and Yiddish. LaGuardia knew more than the words of those languages; he also knew the gestures that went along with each one. Researchers who studied films of his speeches could tell which language he was speaking with the sound turned off! They could do so by reading his body language (Birdwhistell, 1970). Italians and Jews often embellish their speech with circular movements of their arms and hands, and by measuring the radius of those movements you can actually predict whether a speaker is of Italian or Jewish descent: The larger the radius, the more likely the speaker is Italian (Keating, 1994).

emotion work Expression of an emotion that the person does not really feel, often because of a role requirement.

Some signals of body language, like some facial expressions, seem to be spoken universally. Across cultures, people generally recognize body movements that reveal pleasure or displeasure, liking or dislike, tension or relaxation, high status or low status, grief and anger (Matsumoto, 1996). When people are depressed, it shows in their walk, stance, and head position. When people feel proud, they tend to tilt their heads back, put their hands on their hips, and stand erect (Tracy & Robins, 2004). However, many aspects of body language are specific to particular spoken languages and cultures, which makes even the simplest gesture subject to misunderstanding and offense. The sign of the University of Texas football team, the Longhorns, is to extend the index finger and the pinkie. But be careful where you make this gesture: In Italy and other parts of Europe, it means a man's wife has been unfaithful to him—a serious insult.

When people are talking to each other, mismatched body language will make a conversation feel out of sync; they may feel as confused and emotionally upset as if they had had a verbal misunderstanding. When people feel uncomfortable with someone from another culture, the reason may simply be that they are not speaking the same body language.

Arms and hands communicate interest, emphasis, and emotion, just as words do.

OUTLINE

A young woman named Jennifer Rosenthal, age 28, decided to take usnic acid, a chemical found in certain lichen plants, because the label on the bottle said the chemical would make the body burn calories at an accelerated rate. So Rosenthal, who was not overweight but wanted to "stay in shape," took the pills for 17 days. A month later she suffered liver failure and fell into a coma; if she had not quickly received a liver transplant, she would have died. She later learned that usnic acid had been implicated in liver disease or death in a significant number of cases. The FDA subsequently banned usnic acid and also the sale of ephedra, which had been linked to deaths, strokes, seizures, and heart disorders, but hundreds of untested products that promise quick and safe weight loss remain on the market.

Andrew Luster, 39, the wealthy great-grandson of cosmetics magnate Max Factor, was convicted of raping three women after drugging them with the date-rape drug Liquid X (GHB), a powerful sedative that can induce coma. After the women passed out, he then videotaped himself having sex with them. He escaped to Mexico, but was convicted in absentia and sentenced to 124 years in prison. Luster eluded capture for five months but was finally nabbed by a bounty hunter.

In 1875, a teenager named Annie Oakley defeated Frank Butler, the star of the Buffalo Bill Wild West Show, in a sharpshooting competition. "It was her first big match—my first defeat," wrote Butler. "The next day I came back to see the little girl who had beaten me, and it was not long until we married." He became her manager, and for the next 50 years, they traveled together across Europe and America, where her skills with a gun made her the toast of both continents. Throughout his life, Frank published love poems to Annie, and they remained devoted until their deaths, within 18 days of one another, in 1926 (Kreps, 1990).

In 2005, Lance Armstrong won the grueling, 2,125-mile-long Tour de France for the seventh time, the first man ever to have done so in the history of this arduous biking race over the mountains of France. Armstrong's victories and motivation to keep racing astonished and delighted the world because of his 1996 recovery from testicular cancer, which had spread to his abdomen, lungs, and brain. Armstrong had decided at the time to retire from the sport, but eventually he came back to win this most difficult of bicycle races, not just once but repeatedly.

What motivated Lance Armstrong to fight not only his cancer, but also his impulse to give up racing, and triumph so dramatically over his illness?

motivation An inferred process within a person or animal that causes movement either toward a goal or away from an unpleasant situation.

intrinsic motivation The pursuit of an activity for its own sake.

extrinsic motivation The pursuit of an activity for external rewards, such as money or fame.

What motivated a slim young woman to take an unproven drug to stay in shape? Why would an attractive, wealthy man like Andrew Luster resort to sexual coercion and rape? What kept Annie Oakley and Frank Butler in love for 50 years, when so many other romantic passions die in five years—or five weeks?

The word *motivation*, like the word *emotion*, comes from the Latin root meaning "to move," and the psychology of motivation is indeed the study of what moves us, why we do what we do. To psychologists, **motivation** refers to a process within a person or animal that causes that organism to move toward a goal or away from an unpleasant situation. The motive may be to satisfy a psychological goal, say, by getting married or avoiding marriage; it may be to satisfy a biological need, say, by eating a sandwich to reduce hunger; or it may be to fulfill a psychological ambition, say, by being the first to row across the Atlantic in a dinghy (it's been done).

For many decades, the study of motivation was dominated by a focus on biological *drives*, such as those to acquire food and water, to have sex, to seek novelty, and to avoid cold and pain. Some psychologists still think that people are motivated by certain drives, especially sex and hunger. But drive theories cannot account for the full complexity of human motivation, because people are conscious creatures who think and plan ahead, set goals for themselves, and plot strategies to reach those goals. People are motivated to eat, for instance, but that information doesn't tell us why some individuals with strong political commitments will go on hunger strikes to protest injustice.

In this chapter, we will examine four central areas of human motivation: food, love, sex, and achievement. We will see how happiness and well-being are affected by the kinds of goals we set for ourselves, and by whether we are spurred to reach them because of **intrinsic motivation**, the desire to do something for its own sake and the pleasure it brings, or **extrinsic motivation**, the desire to pursue a goal for external rewards.

WHAT'S AHEAD

- Is being overweight usually a result of psychological problems?
- What theory explains why it's so hard for heavy people to lose weight, and just as hard for thin people to gain it?
- Why are people all over the world getting fatter?
- Why are eating disorders increasing among young men?

The Hungry Animal: Motives to Eat

Some people are skinny; others are plump. Some are shaped like string beans; others look more like pears. Some can eat anything they want without gaining an ounce; others struggle unsuccessfully their whole lives to shed pounds. Some hate being fat, and others think that fat is just fine. How much do genes, psychology, and environment affect our motivation to eat or not to eat?

THINKING  CRITICALLY

ANALYZE ASSUMPTIONS AND BIASES

Obesity is caused mainly by psychological problems and lack of willpower, isn't it? When researchers questioned this common assumption, they were in for a surprise.

The Biology of Weight

At one time, most psychologists thought that being overweight was a sign of emotional disturbance. If you were fat, it was because you hated your mother, feared intimacy, or were trying to fill an emotional hole in your psyche by loading up on rich desserts. The evidence for psychological theories of overweight, however, came mainly from self-reports and from flawed studies that lacked control groups or objective measures of how much people

were actually eating. When researchers did controlled experiments, they learned that fat people, on average, are no more and no less emotionally disturbed than average-weight people. Even more surprising, they found that heaviness is not always caused by overeating (Stunkard, 1980). Many heavy people do eat large quantities of food, but so do some thin people. In one study, in which volunteers gorged themselves for months, it was as hard for slender people to gain weight as it is for most heavy people to lose weight. The minute the study was over, the slender people lost weight as fast as dieters gained it back (Sims, 1974).

set point The genetically influenced weight range for an individual; it is maintained by biological mechanisms that regulate food intake, fat reserves, and metabolism.

Genetic Influences on Weight and Body Shape. The explanation that emerged from such findings was that a biological mechanism keeps your body weight at a genetically influenced **set point**, the weight you stay at when you are not trying to gain or lose (Lissner et al., 1991). The set point can vary about 10 percent in either direction. For example, a woman with a set point of 150 pounds might weigh anywhere from 135 to 165. But if her weight dips below 135 or goes above 165, her body will produce either an insatiable urge to eat or a loss of appetite to bring its fat levels back into line.

Set-point research has focused on how the body regulates appetite, eating, and weight gain and loss. Everyone has a genetically programmed *basal metabolism rate*, the rate at which the body burns calories for energy, and a fixed number of fat cells, which store fat for energy and can change in size. A complex interaction of metabolism, fat cells, and hormones keeps people at the weight their bodies are designed to be, much in the way that a thermostat keeps a house at a constant temperature. When a heavy person diets, the body's metabolism slows down to conserve energy and fat reserves (Ravussin et al., 1988). When a thin person overeats, metabolism speeds up, burning energy. In one study, in which 16 slender volunteers ate 1,000 extra calories every day for eight weeks, their metabolisms sped up to burn the excess calories. They were like hummingbirds, in constant movement: fidgeting, pacing, changing their positions frequently while seated, and so on (Levine, Eberhardt, & Jensen, 1999).

Set-point theory predicts that the heritability of weight and body fat should be high, and indeed it is: In twin and adoption studies, heritability estimates fall between .40 and .70 (Comuzzie & Allison, 1998). Pairs of adult identical twins who grew up in different families are just as similar in body weight and shape as twins raised together. And when identical twins gain weight, they gain it in the same place: Some pairs store extra pounds around their waists, others on their hips and thighs (C. Bouchard et al., 1990).

Body weight and shape are strongly affected by genetic factors. Set-point theory helps explain why the Pimas of the American Southwest gain weight easily but lose it slowly, whereas the Bororo nomads of Nigeria can eat a lot of food yet remain slender.

Both of these mice have a mutation in the *ob* gene, which usually makes mice chubby, like the one on the left. But when leptin is injected daily, the mice eat less and burn more calories, becoming slim, like his friendly pal. Unfortunately, leptin injections have not had the same results in most human beings.

When there is a mutation in the genes that regulate normal eating and weight control, the result may be obesity. For example, one gene, called *obese*, or *ob* for short, causes fat cells to secrete a protein, which researchers have named *leptin* (from the Greek *leptos*, "slender"). Leptin travels through the blood to the brain's hypothalamus, which is involved in the regulation of appetite. When leptin levels are normal, people eat just enough to maintain their weight. When a mutation of the *ob* gene causes leptin levels to be too low, however, the hypothalamus thinks the body lacks fat reserves and signals the individual to overeat (Zhang et al., 1994). Injecting leptin into leptin-deficient mice reduces the animals' appetites, speeds up their metabolisms, and makes them more active; as a result, the animals shed weight (Friedman, 2003). Some extremely obese individuals who lack leptin for genetic reasons likewise benefit from injections of the hormone. A 200-pound 9-year-old girl, whose legs were so large she could hardly walk, dramatically reduced her food intake and weight to normal levels after treatment with leptin (Farooqi et al., 2002).

Studies of mice suggest that leptin plays its most crucial role early in life, by altering the brain chemistry that influences how much an animal or person later eats. More specifically, leptin helps regulate body weight by strengthening neural circuits in the hypothalamus that reduce appetite and by weakening circuits that stimulate it (Elmquist & Flier, 2004). During a critical period in infancy, leptin influences the formation of those neural connections, and the set point is, well, set (Bouret, Draper, & Simerly, 2004). Some researchers speculate that because of this early neural plasticity, overfeeding infants while the hypothalamus is developing may later produce childhood obesity.

Researchers have identified a number of other genes that are linked to being overweight (Farooqi & O'Rahilly, 2004; Friedman, 2003; Herbert et al., 2006). For example, they have discovered a gene that modulates production of a protein that apparently converts excess calories into heat rather than fat. Possession of this gene may be one reason that slim people stay slim even when they temporarily overeat (Arsenijevic et al., 2000).

Findings such as these often raise the public's hopes for a breakthrough drug that will help people lose weight easily and quickly. One pharmaceutical company thought leptin would be the answer: Take leptin, lose weight! Alas, for most obese people, and for people who are merely overweight, taking leptin does not produce much weight loss (Comuzzie & Allison, 1998). Just to make life more complicated, leptin is only one influence on body weight. Dozens of genes and body chemicals are involved in appetite, metabolism rates, and weight regulation. You have receptors in your nose and mouth that keep urging you to eat more ("The food is right there! It's good! Eat!"), receptors in your gut telling you to quit ("You've had enough already!"), and

GET INVOLVED!

➤ASSESS YOUR BODY: ARE YOU "OVERWEIGHT"?

One way of assessing the risks of being excessively overweight is based on *body mass index* (BMI). If you go to www.NHLBIsupport.com/BMI, you can get your BMI calculated instantly, or you can do it yourself: (1) Multiply your weight in pounds by 703. (2) Multiply your height in inches by your height in inches. (3) Divide the answer in Step 1 by the answer in Step 2. That is your body mass index. A BMI of 25 or more is considered overweight, and 30 or more is obese. However, the BMI does not account for degree of fitness. The BMI would identify Brad Pitt, George Clooney, and Michael Jordan as "overweight" and Sylvester Stallone and baseball star Sammy Sosa as "obese."

leptin and other chemicals telling you that you have stored enough fat or not enough. One hormone makes you hungry and eager to eat more, and another turns off your appetite after a meal, making you eat less. The complexity of the mechanisms governing appetite and weight explains why appetite suppressing drugs inevitably fail in the long run: They target only one of the many factors that conspire to keep you the weight you are.

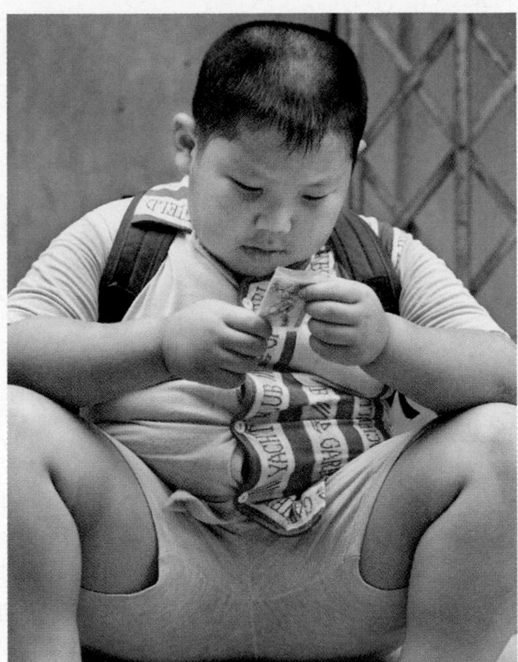

Obesity is a global problem. Children around the world are eating more like Americans—too much food, too much fast food.

The Overweight Debate. If genes are so strongly implicated in weight and body shape, and if most people have normal set points, why are so many people, all over the world, getting fatter? More than half of all American adults, and at least 25 percent of all children and teenagers, are now overweight or obese. The increase has been greatest among the very fat: The number of Americans who are at least 100 pounds overweight has quadrupled since the 1980s. Increases in obesity rates have occurred in both sexes, all social classes, and all age groups, and in many other countries (Taubes, 1998). The United Nations, so used to dealing with problems of starvation and malnutrition, has announced that "obesity is the dominant unmet global health issue," especially in the United States, Canada, Great Britain, Japan, and Australia, and even in coastal China and Southeast Asia.

Many health researchers are worried about this trend because obesity is considered a leading risk factor in diabetes, high blood pressure, heart disease, stroke, cancer, infertility, sleep apnea, and many other disorders. But are there comparable health risks to being overweight by, say, 20 to 30 pounds? What if a person is genetically predisposed to be fat, though not obese? Lately some scientists have been cautioning against the emotional reasoning that so often accompanies discussions of this subject in America, where "thin is in." They believe that for most people, the real health culprit is not overweight but lack of fitness. Fat people who are physically fit are healthier and have lower risk of illness, on average, than thin people who are sedentary (Campos, 2004). Because many overweight people have sedentary habits, few scientists have thought to separate these two factors.

Scientists are currently debating the extent of the problem and what can be done about it. One scientist, Jeffrey Friedman, the primary discoverer of the gene for leptin, said in an interview that the obesity epidemic is mainly a result of the fact that fat people are getting fatter; thin people have remained pretty much the same (Kolata, 2004). Thin people do not balloon into obesity, he observes—remember those hummingbird metabolisms that so many of them have—nor can fat people lose weight permanently through willpower, because body weight is genetically determined. Other scientists agree that genes play a powerful role, but they observe that changes in the environment and culture are the reason that so many people are putting on the pounds. After all, in between the extremes of thin and fat are the millions of people whose weights have risen 10 to 30 to 50 pounds, and that's not trivial. What has caused that increase?

Culture, Gender, and Weight

The leading environmental culprits causing the worldwide rise in weight have to do with sweeping cultural changes: (1) the increased abundance of fast food, which is inexpensive and very high in calories; (2) the habit of eating high-calorie food on the run rather than in leisurely meals; (3) the use of energy-saving devices, such as remote controls; (4) the speed and convenience of driving rather than walking or biking; (5) the growing sizes of typical servings of food and drink; and (6) the preference for watching television and videos rather than doing anything active (Critser, 2002; Robinson, 1999). The reason for the rising numbers of overweight people is simple: Calorie consumption is up and exercise is down.

The Culture of Consumption. Most human beings are genetically predisposed to gain weight when rich food is abundant because, in our species' evolutionary past, starvation was all too often a real possibility. Therefore, a tendency to store calories in the form of fat provided a definite survival advantage. Unfortunately, evolution did not design a comparable mechanism to prevent people who do not have hummingbird metabolisms from gaining weight when food is easily available, tasty, rich, varied, and cheap. That, of course, is precisely the situation today, surrounded as we are by $^{3}/_{4}$-pound burgers, fries, chips, tacos, candy bars, and pizzas. When diets are predictable, people habituate to what they are eating and eat less of it. (That is why all diets that restrict people to only a few kinds of foods work, at least at first.) As soon as food becomes more varied, however, people eat more and gain more weight (Raynor & Epstein, 2001). Moreover, in American culture, food and drink portions have become supersized, double or triple the size they were only one generation ago. Even babies and toddlers up to 2 years of age are being fed as much as 30 percent more calories than they need (Fox et al., 2004). In France, people eat rich food but much less of it than Americans do (Rozin et al., 2003). Their notions of what a proper portion is—for yogurt, soda, a salad, a sandwich, anything—are way lower than in the United States.

When people from other cultures move to the United States, they often put on pounds because of a change in dietary habits. For example, many Mexican-Americans born in the United States are fatter than those who were born in Mexico. In Mexico, poor people eat corn tortillas, which are cheap, and their diet overall is lower in fat and higher in fiber than that of their relatives to the north. But Mexican-Americans born in the United States tend to eat flour tortillas, which are made with lard and are thus much higher in calories, and they eat other high-fat foods because of acculturation to American ways. As a result, they have higher obesity rates than their kin in Mexico (Sundquist & Winkleby, 2000).

Another major influence on weight is exercise, which boosts the body's metabolic rate, even in people who are genetically susceptible to obesity (Esparza et al., 2000). When obese women are put on severely restricted diets, their metabolic rates drop sharply, as set-point theory would predict. But when they combine the diet with moderate physical activity—daily walking—they lose weight and their metabolic rates rise almost to previous levels (Wadden et al., 1990).

Eating habits and activity levels, in turn, are shaped by a culture's customs and standards of what the ideal body should look like: fat, thin, muscular, soft. In many places around the world, especially where famine and crop failures are common, fat is taken as a sign of health, affluence in men, and sexual desirability in women (Stearns, 1997). Among the Calabari of Nigeria, brides are put in special fattening huts where they do nothing but eat, so as to become fat enough to please their husbands.

Cultural influences on obesity can also be observed among white farm families. Farmers originally ate large amounts of food for *intrinsic* reasons: When you do hard,

labor-intensive work, you need a lot of calories. But today many farm families eat for *extrinsic* motives: to be sociable and conform to family tradition. In the Farm Belt states of the American Midwest, people are expected to eat huge, hearty meals and plenty of sweet desserts. If you don't join in, an anthropologist from Iowa told *The New York Times*, you are being antisocial, insulting your hosts and rejecting your kin (Angier, 2000).

Gender and the Ideal Body. Ironically, while people of all ethnicities and social classes have been getting fatter, the cultural ideal for women in the United States, Canada, and Europe has been getting thinner. The ideal of the voluptuously curvy woman, big-breasted and big-hipped, was popular before World War I and after World War II. But in the flapper era of the 1920s and again starting in the 1960s, big breasts and hips became unfashionable. Today the American female ideal is an odd one: big breasts but no hips!

Why have these changes in cultural norms occurred? One explanation is that white men and women are more likely than African-Americans or Latinos to associate overweight with softness, laziness, and weakness (Crandall & Martinez, 1996). In particular, the curvy, big-breasted female body is associated in people's minds with femininity, nurturance, and motherhood. Hence, big breasts are fashionable in eras that celebrate women's role as mothers, such as after World War II, when women were encouraged to give up their wartime jobs and have many children (Stearns, 1997). However, among many whites, femininity is often also associated, alas, with incompetence. Thus, whenever women have entered traditionally male spheres of education and work, as they did in the 1920s and again beginning in the 1970s, bright, ambitious women have tried to look boyishly thin and muscular in order to avoid appearing soft, feminine, and dumb (Silverstein & Perlick, 1995). Today's big-breasted but otherwise skinny female ideal may reflect cultural ambivalence about whether women's proper role is domestic or professional.

Should a woman be voluptuous and curvy or slim as a reed? Should a man be thin and smooth or strong and buff? What explains cultural changes in attitudes toward the ideal body? During the 1950s, actresses like Jayne Mansfield embodied the postwar ideal: curvy, buxom, and "womanly." In the 1980s and 1990s, many women struggled to be skinny and boyish; today, they want to be thin but also have prominent breasts, like Naomi Watts. Men, too, have been caught up in body-image changes. The 1960s' ideal was the soft and scrawny hippie; today's ideal man is tough and muscular.

bulimia An eating disorder characterized by episodes of excessive eating (bingeing) followed by forced vomiting or use of laxatives (purging).

anorexia (anorexia nervosa) An eating disorder characterized by fear of being fat, a distorted body image, radically reduced consumption of food, and emaciation.

The cultural ideal for American men has changed, too. Until relatively recently, most heavily muscled men were laborers and farmers, so being physically strong and muscular was considered unattractive, a sign of being working class. In the past decade, pressures have increased for middle-class men to be buff and strong (Bordo, 2000). Today, having a strong, muscular body is a sign of affluence rather than poverty. It means a man has the money and the time to join a gym and work out.

The Body as Battleground: Eating Disorders

Because the motivation to eat, or not eat, is so complicated, you can see why many people, especially women, find themselves caught in a battle between their biology and their culture. Evolution has designed women to store fat, which is necessary for the onset of menstruation, healthy childbearing, nursing, and, after menopause, the production and storage of estrogen. In cultures that think women should be very thin, therefore, many women become obsessed with weight and are continually dieting, forever fighting their bodies' need for a little healthy roundness.

Some people lose that battle, developing serious eating disorders that reflect an irrational terror of being fat. In **bulimia**, the person binges (eats vast quantities of rich food) and then purges by inducing vomiting or using laxatives. In **anorexia**, the person eats hardly anything and therefore becomes dangerously thin; anorexics have severely distorted body images, thinking they are fat even when they are emaciated. Although many people with these disorders recover, others damage their health permanently, or, in the case of anorexia, die of heart or kidney failure or complications of osteoporosis. Their weakened bones simply collapse.

Genes may play a role in the development of eating disorders, but so do psychological factors, including depression and anxiety, low self-esteem, perfectionism, a distorted body image, drug use, and perceived pressure from peers to lose weight (Presnell, Bearman, & Stice, 2004; Ricciardelli & McCabe, 2004). Cultural factors also are important. For example, bulimia is rare to nonexistent in non-Western cultures and has only become a significant problem in Western cultures with the rise of the thin ideal for women (Keel & Klump, 2003). Ballerinas, actresses, jockeys, some other athletes, and of course models are under enormous professional pressure to be thin. (In 2006, many fashion models had become so gaunt and emaciated that the Fashion Week organizers in Madrid, Spain, announced they would ban superthin models, women with a body mass index lower than 18.) In the United States, a recent meta-analysis found that women's levels of dissatisfaction with their bodies, once highest for Anglo women, now cross all ethnic lines; Asian-American, African-American, Hispanic, and Anglo women are virtually alike (Grabe & Hyde, 2006). Unhappiness with one's body, in turn, increases the likelihood of disordered eating. In a study of women students from Hong Kong, Taiwan, and Japan who were studying in the United States, those who had internalized Western notions of the ultrathin ideal were more likely to develop eating disorders (Stark-Wroblewski, Yanico, & Lupe, 2005).

THINKING CRITICALLY

ASK QUESTIONS

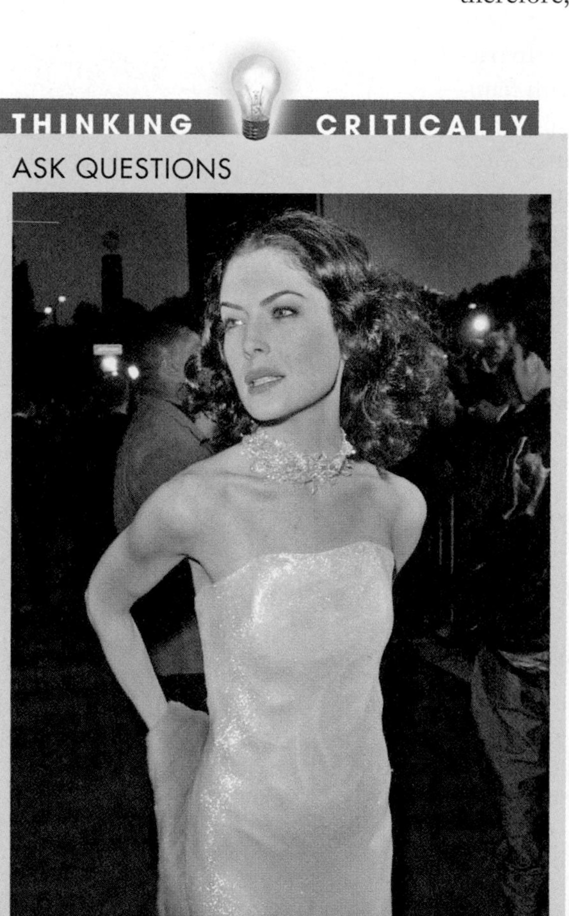

Lara Flynn Boyle has always denied that she has an eating disorder. Where is the line between being fashionably thin and being dangerously gaunt?

Eating disorders and body-image distortions among boys and men are increasing too, though they take different forms. Just as anorexic women see their gaunt bodies as being too fat, some men have the delusion that their muscular bodies are too puny. So they abuse steroids and exercise or pump iron compulsively (Pope, Phillips, & Olivardia, 2000). Many Amer-

ican men mistakenly think that most women prefer extremely muscular guys, partly because media images of muscular men in the United States often show them with bared pecs or abs. As a result, some men develop a distorted body image in which they think they are not muscular and strong enough. In contrast, Chinese men in Taiwan and pastoral nomads of northern Kenya do not think the heavily muscled male body is especially desirable or attractive, and these cultures do not promote media images of muscular males. Men in these cultures have fewer body-image disorders than American men do and virtually no interest in muscle-building drugs (Campbell, Pope, & Filiault, 2005; Yang, Gray, & Pope, 2005).

In sum, within a given environment, genetic predispositions for a certain body weight and metabolism interact with psychological needs, cultural norms, and individual habits to shape, in this case quite literally, who we are.

QUICK quiz

Is all this information about eating making you hungry for knowledge?

1. *True or false*: Most fat people are heavy because their emotional problems cause them to overeat.
2. What theory seems to explain why thin people rarely become fat and fat people have so much trouble losing weight?
3. Which hormone helps regulate appetite by telling the hypothalamus that the body has stored enough fat?
4. Rising rates of overweight and obesity can best be explained by (a) genetic changes over the past few decades, (b) a lack of willpower, (c) an abundance of high-calorie food and sedentary lifestyles, (d) the increase in eating disorders.

5. Bill, who is thin, reads in the newspaper that genes set the range of body weight and shape. "Oh, good," he exclaims, "now I can eat all the junk food I want; I was born to be skinny." What's wrong with Bill's conclusion?

Answers:

1. false **2.** set-point theory **3.** leptin **4.** c **5.** Bill is right to recognize that there may be limits to how heavy he can become. But he is oversimplifying and jumping to conclusions. Many people who have a set point for leanness will gain considerable weight on rich food and excess calories, especially if they don't exercise. Also, junk food is unhealthy for reasons that have nothing to do with becoming overweight.

WHAT'S AHEAD

- When someone says "I love you," can you be sure what the person means?
- Do men and women differ in the ability to love?
- How are your beliefs about love affected by your income?

Love is where you find it, and where you find it may be unexpected—as this orphaned baby hippo and 100-year-old tortoise discovered.

The Social Animal: Motives to Love

Do you have a favorite love story? Is it one where the couple falls madly in love at first sight and, after a couple of silly misunderstandings, lives happily ever after, without a single quarrel or miserable moment? Or is it more like the story of Annie Oakley and Frank Butler, one of lifelong mutual respect and companionship? What *is* love, anyway—the crazy, passionate, heart-palpitating feeling of falling for another person, or the steady, stable feeling of deep and abiding attachment and trust?

Adult romantic love, with its exchange of loving gazes and depth of passionate attachment, may have its origins in the biology of the baby–mother bond.

The Biology of Love

Psychologists who study love (a tough job, but someone has to do it) distinguish *passionate ("romantic") love*, characterized by a whirlwind of intense emotions and sexual passion, from *companionate love*, characterized by affection and trust (Hatfield & Rapson, 1996). Passionate love is the stuff of crushes, infatuations, "love at first sight," and the early stage of love affairs. It may burn out completely or evolve into companionate love.

In this era of PET scans and biotechnical advances, it was inevitable that researchers would seek to explain passionate love by rummaging around in the brain. Neuroscientists hope to find answers to the great mysteries of attraction: why people often are hopelessly smitten with someone who is "unsuitable," why the heart seems to overrule the head in matters of love ("He/she is perfectly nice, but I just didn't feel any *chemistry*"), and why many people feel obsessed with a new beloved and can barely sleep or eat when they are parted.

Many biologically oriented researchers believe that the neurological origins of passionate love begin in infancy, in the baby's attachment to the mother. In this view, maternal and romantic love, the deepest of human attachments, share a common evolutionary purpose—preserving the species—and so they share common neural mechanisms, the ones that make attachment and pair-bonding feel good. And, in fact, certain key neurotransmitters and hormones that are involved in pleasure and reward are activated in the mother–baby pair-bond and again later in the pair-bond of adult lovers and even of passionate friends (Bartels & Zeki, 2004; Diamond, 2004). The hormone *oxytocin* plays a crucial role in the attachment-caregiving system, influencing feelings and expressions of love, caring, and trust not only between mothers and babies but also between friends and between lovers (Taylor et al., 2000b). In one extraordinary study, researchers administered oxytocin in a nasal spray to volunteers, who were later more likely than control subjects to trust one another in various risky interactions (Kosfeld et al., 2005). In another study, couples given oxytocin increased their nonverbal expressions of love for one another—gazing, smiling, and fondling—in contrast to couples given a placebo (Gonzaga et al., 2006). We can just imagine what the pharmaceutical industry will try to do with this information!

Studies of animals also find that the characteristic feelings and actions that occur during attachment are mediated by reward circuits in the brain and involve the release of *endorphins*, the brain's natural opiates (see Chapter 4). When baby mice and other animals are separated from their mothers, they cry out in distress, and the mother's touch (or lick) releases endorphins that soothe the infant. But when puppies, guinea pigs, and chicks are injected with low doses of either morphine or endorphins, the animals show much less distress than usual when separated from their mothers; the chemicals seem to be a biological replacement for mom (Panksepp et al., 1980). And when mice are genetically engineered to lack certain opioid receptors, they become less attached to their mothers and do not show signs of distress when separated from them. This is the same kind of social aloofness that autistic children display (Moles, Kieffer, & D'Amato, 2004). These findings suggest that endorphin-stimulated euphoria may be a child's initial motive for seeking affection and cuddling—that, in effect, a child attached to a parent is a child addicted to love. The addictive quality of adult passionate love, including the physical and emotional distress that lovers feel when they are apart, may involve the same biochemistry (Diamond, 2004).

Using functional MRI, neuroscientists have found other neurological similarities between infant–mother love and adult romantic love. Two researchers, for example, have found that certain parts of the brain light up when people look at images of their sweethearts, in contrast to other parts that are activated when they see pictures of friends or

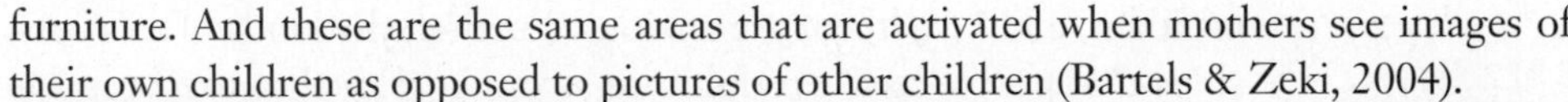

furniture. And these are the same areas that are activated when mothers see images of their own children as opposed to pictures of other children (Bartels & Zeki, 2004).

Clearly, then, the bonds of attachment are biologically based. Yet, as always, it is important to avoid biological reductionism and the conclusion that "love is all in our hormones" or "love occurs in this corner of the brain but not that one." Human love affairs involve many other factors that affect whom we choose, how we get along, and whether we stay with a partner over the years.

The Psychology of Love

Many romantics believe there is only one true love awaiting them. Considering that there are $6^1/_2$ billion people on the planet, the odds of finding said person are a bit daunting! What if you're in Omaha or Winnipeg and your True Love is in Dubrovnik or Kankakee? You could wander for years and never cross paths.

Fortunately, evolution has made it possible to form deep and lasting attachments without traveling the world. In fact, the first major predictor of whom we love is plain *proximity*: The people who are nearest to you are most likely to be dearest to you, too. We choose our friends and lovers from the set of people who live close by, or who study or work near us. Of course, today's love-seekers can use the Internet to find remote kindred spirits, but proximity remains a highly desirable attribute; dating sites can filter out anyone who is geographically undesirable. And *similarity*—in looks, attitudes, beliefs, values, personality, and interests—is the second key predictor of whom we love (Berscheid & Reis, 1998). Although it is commonly believed that opposites attract, the fact is that we tend to choose friends and loved ones who are most like us. Many students use Facebook to find romantic prospects who share their love of poker, the TV show *Smallville*, the hip-hop band Jurassic 5, or any other passion.

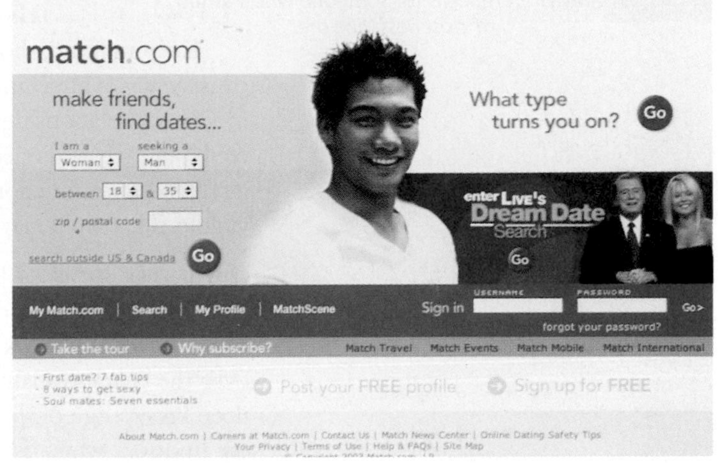

Internet services capitalize on the fact that like attracts like. "What type turns you on?" Usually, the type that is similar to you!

The Attachment Theory of Love. Once you find someone to love, *how* do you love? According to Phillip Shaver and Cindy Hazan (1993), adults, just like babies, can be *secure*, *anxious*, or *avoidant* in their attachments (see Chapter 14). Securely attached lovers are, well, secure: They are rarely jealous or worried about being abandoned. They are more compassionate and helpful than insecurely attached people and are quicker to understand and forgive their partners if the partner does something thoughtless or annoying (Mikulincer et al., 2005; Shaver & Mikulincer, 2006). Anxious lovers are always agitated about their relationships; they want to be close but worry that their partners will leave them. Other people often describe them as clingy, which may be why they are more likely than secure lovers to suffer from unrequited love (Aron, Aron, & Allen, 1998). Avoidant people distrust and avoid intimate attachments.

Where do these differences come from? According to the *attachment theory of love*, people's attachment styles as adults derive in large part from how their parents cared for them (Fraley & Shaver, 2000; Mikulincer & Goodman, 2006). Children form internal "working models" of relationships: Can I trust others? Am I worthy of being loved? Will my parents leave me? If a child's parents were cold and rejecting and provided little or no emotional and physical comfort, the child learns to expect other relationships to be the same. If children form secure attachments to trusted parents, they become more trusting of others, expecting to form other secure attachments with friends and lovers in adulthood (Feeney & Cassidy, 2003).

The distribution of the three basic styles of attachment among adults is in fact very similar to that found for infants: about 64 percent are secure, 25 percent are

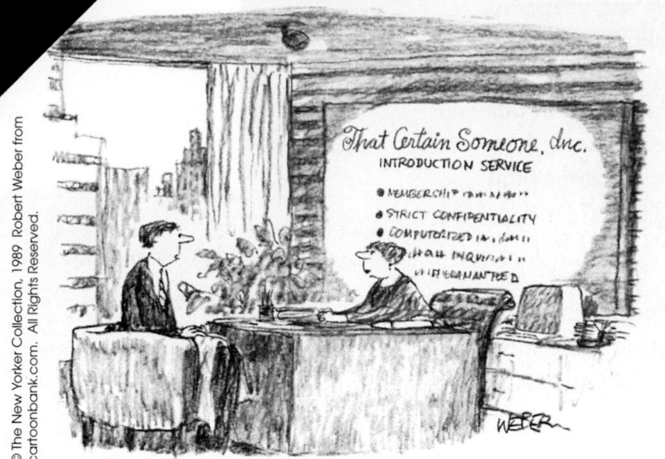

"My preference is for someone who's afraid of closeness, like me."

avoidant, and 11 percent are anxious. Further, the kinds of relationships that people have as adults are strongly related to their reports of how their parents treated them (Mickelson, Kessler, & Shaver, 1997). Securely attached adults report having had warm, close relationships with their parents. Although they recognize their parents' flaws, they describe their parents as having been more loving and kind than insecurely attached people do. Anxious people feel more ambivalence toward their parents, especially their mothers, and also describe their parents ambivalently, as having been both harsh and kind. And people with an avoidant attachment style describe their parents in almost entirely negative terms. These individuals are most likely to report having had cold, rejecting parents, extended periods of separation from their mothers, or childhood environments that prevented them from forging close ties with others (Hazan & Shaver, 1994; Klohnen & Bera, 1998).

Keep in mind, though, that a person's own temperament could also account for the consistency of attachment styles from childhood to adulthood, as well as for the working models of relationships that are formed during childhood. Certainly some parents are cold, punitive, and rejecting. But a child who is temperamentally fearful or whose reward circuits do not function normally may reject even a kind parent's efforts to console and cuddle. That child may therefore come to believe that all relationships are untrustworthy.

The Ingredients of Love. When people are asked to define the key ingredients of love, most agree that love is a mix of passion, intimacy, and commitment (Aron & Westbay, 1996; Lemieux & Hale, 2000; Sternberg, 1997). However, in most relationships, over the years, romantic passion subsides and intimacy increases. Intimacy is based on deep knowledge of the other person, which accumulates gradually, but passion is based on emotion, which is generated by novelty and change. That is why passion is usually highest at the beginning of a relationship, when two people begin to disclose things about themselves to each other, and lowest when knowledge of the other person's beliefs and habits is at its maximum, when it seems that there is nothing left to learn about the

GET INVOLVED!

➤WHAT IS YOUR LOVE ATTACHMENT STYLE?

Which of the following three statements, adapted from Hazan and Shaver (1994), best describes how you typically feel in your romantic relationships?

Secure style: I find it relatively easy to get close to others and am comfortable depending on them and having them depend on me. I don't often worry about being abandoned or about someone getting too close.

Avoidant style: I am somewhat uncomfortable being close; I find it difficult to trust others completely and difficult to allow myself to depend on them. I am nervous when anyone gets close, and often love partners want me to be more intimate than I feel comfortable being.

Anxious style: I find that others are reluctant to get as close as I would like. I often worry that my partner doesn't really love me or won't stay with me. I want to merge completely with another person, and this desire sometimes scares people away.

If you are currently in a dating relationship—and have the nerve!—ask your partner how he or she would reply. Are you well matched?

Passionate love starts relationships, but companionate love keeps them going

beloved. Biological factors such as the brain's opiate system may contribute to early passion, as we noted, but most psychologists believe that the factors that contribute to a long and intimate love relationship have more to do with the couple's attitudes, values, temperaments, power balance, and personalities than with hormones.

The critical-thinking guideline "define your terms" may never be more important than in matters of love. The way we define love deeply affects our satisfaction with relationships and even whether our relationships last. After all, if you believe that the only real love is romantic love, that love is defined by sexual passion and hot emotion, then you may decide you are out of love when the initial phase of attraction fades, as it eventually must—and you will be repeatedly disappointed. Robert Solomon (1994) argued that "We conceive of [love] falsely . . . We expect an explosion at the beginning powerful enough to fuel love through all of its ups and downs instead of viewing love as a process over which we have control, a process that tends to increase with time rather than wane."

THINKING CRITICALLY

DEFINE YOUR TERMS

Many people define love as an overwhelming romantic passion. What are the consequences of defining love that way? What other definitions might lead to greater satisfaction in a relationship over time?

Gender, Culture, and Love

Which sex is more romantic? Which sex truly understands true love? Which sex falls in love but won't commit? Pop-psych books are full of answers, along with advice for dealing with all those love-challenged heartbreakers who love you and leave you (fools that they are). But all stereotypes oversimplify. Neither sex loves more than the other in terms of love at first sight, passionate love, or companionate love over the long haul (Dion & Dion, 1993; Fehr, 1993; Hatfield & Rapson, 1996). Men and women are equally likely to suffer the heart-crushing torments of unrequited love. They are equally likely to be securely or insecurely attached (Feeney & Cassidy, 2003). Both sexes suffer mightily when a love relationship ends, assuming they did not want it to.

However, women and men do differ, on average, in how they *express* love. Males in many cultures learn early that revelations of emotion can be construed as evidence of vulnerability and weakness, which are considered unmasculine (see Chapter 11). Thus, men in such cultures often develop ways of revealing love that differ from the ways women do. In contemporary Western society, many women express feelings of love in words, whereas many men express these feelings in actions—doing things for the partner, supporting the family financially, or just sharing the same activity, such as watching TV or a football game together (Baumeister & Bratslavsky, 1999; Cancian, 1987; Swain, 1989). Similarly, many women tend to define intimacy as shared revelations of feelings, but many men define intimacy as just hanging out together.

These gender differences in ways of expressing the universal motives of love and intimacy do not just pop up out of nowhere; they reflect social, economic, and cultural forces. For example, for many years, Western men were more romantic than women in their choice of partner, and women in turn were far more pragmatic than men. One reason was that a woman did not just marry a man; she married a standard of living. Therefore, she could not afford to marry someone unsuitable or waste her time in a

Economic and social changes are transforming gender roles in all developed nations. But marriage for financial security is still the only option for many women from impoverished nations—like this bride, whose husband chose her from a mail-order catalogue.

relationship that was not going anywhere, even if she loved the guy. She married, in short, for extrinsic reasons rather than intrinsic ones. In contrast, a man could afford to be sentimental in his choice of partner. In the 1960s, two-thirds of a sample of college men said they would not marry someone they did not love, but only one-fourth of the women ruled out the possibility (Kephart, 1967).

As women entered the workforce and as two incomes became necessary in most families, however, the gender difference in romantic love faded, and so did economic motivations to marry, all over the world. Nowadays, in every developed nation, only tiny numbers of women and men would consider marrying someone they did not love, even if the person had all the right qualities. Pragmatic reasons for marriage, with romantic love being a remote luxury, persist only in countries where the extended family still controls female sexuality and the financial terms of marriage (Hatfield & Rapson, 1996). Yet even in these countries, such as India and Pakistan, the tight rules governing marriage choices are loosening. So are the rules forbidding divorce, even in extremely traditional nations such as Japan and South Korea.

As you can see, our motivations to love may start with biology and the workings of the brain, but they are shaped and directed by our early experiences with parents, the culture we live in, the historical era that shapes us, and something as utterly unromantic as economic dependency or self-sufficiency.

QUICK quiz

Are you passionately committed to quizzes yet?

1. How are adult passionate love and infant–mother love biologically similar?
2. The two major predictors of whom we love are _________ and _________.
3. Tiffany is wildly in love with Timothy, and he with her, but she can't stop worrying about his fidelity and doubting his love. She wants to be with him constantly, but when she feels jealous she pushes him away and finds it hard to forgive him. According to the attachment theory of love, which style of attachment does Tiffany have?
4. *True or false:* Until recently, men in Western societies were more likely than women to marry for love.

Answers:

1. Both involve the release of neurotransmitters, the hormone oxytocin, and endorphins that make attachment literally feel good, by activating the pleasure–reward circuits in the brain. **2.** proximity and similarity **3.** anxious **4.** true

WHAT'S**AHEAD**

- Is one kind of orgasm better or healthier for women than another?
- What part of the anatomy do psychologists think is the "sexiest sex organ"?
- Is the sexual kiss universal?
- Can psychological theories about smothering mothers or absent fathers explain why some men are gay?

The Erotic Animal: Motives for Sex

Most people believe that sex is a biological drive, merely a matter of doing what comes naturally. "What's there to discuss about sexual motivation?" they say. "Isn't it all intrinsic, inborn, inevitable, and inherently pleasurable?"

It is certainly true that in most other species, sexual behavior is genetically programmed. Without instruction, a male stickleback fish knows exactly what to do with a female stickleback, and a whooping crane knows when to whoop. But as sex researcher Leonore Tiefer (2004) has observed, for human beings "sex is not a natural act." For one thing, the activities that one culture considers natural—such as mouth-to-mouth kissing or oral sex—are often considered unnatural in another culture or historical time. Second, people have to learn from experience and culture what they are supposed to do with their sexual desires and how they are expected to behave. And third, people's motivations for sexual activity are by no means always and only for intrinsic pleasure. Human sexuality is influenced by a blend of biological, psychological, and cultural factors.

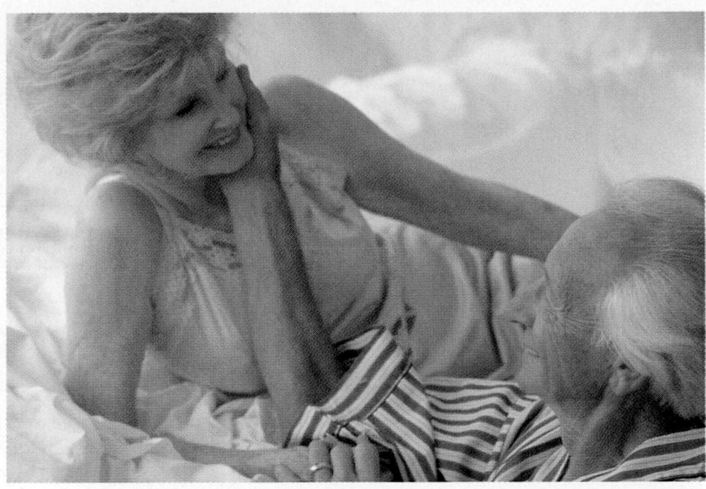

Desire and sensuality are lifelong pleasures.

The Biology of Desire

Biological researchers have contributed to our understanding of sexual motivation by sweeping away the cobwebs of superstition and ignorance about how the body works.

Hormones and Sexual Response. One biological factor that seems to promote sexual desire in both sexes is the hormone testosterone, an androgen (masculinizing hormone) that both sexes produce (see Chapter 4). Its role has been documented in studies of men who have been given synthetic hormones that suppress the production of testosterone; of men and women who have abnormally low testosterone levels; and of women who have kept diaries of their sexual activity while also having their hormone levels periodically measured (Bradford & Pawlak, 1993; Dabbs, 2000; Sherwin, 1998b).

This evidence has led drug companies and some physicians to promote testosterone treatments for women and men who complain of low sexual desire. But there are problems with this apparent solution. One is that there is still no consensus on how much sexual activity is "not enough" or on the difference between normally low and abnormally deficient levels of testosterone. Measures of testosterone taken at different intervals do not correlate strongly because the hormone fluctuates. The symptoms of androgen deficiency (low libido, fatigue, lack of well-being) are also those of depression and marital problems. And, in a significant number of cases, the side effects of androgen range from unpleasant to harmful (International Consensus Conference, 2002). Moreover, hormones and behavior travel a two-way street: Testosterone does contribute to sexual arousal, but sexual activity also produces higher levels of testosterone (Sapolsky, 1997).

Arousal and Orgasm. Physiological research has dispelled a lot of nonsense written about female sexuality, such as the once-common notions that "good" women don't have orgasms or that mature women should have the "right kind" of orgasm (Ehrenreich, 1978).

The first modern attack on these beliefs came from Alfred Kinsey and his associates (1948, 1953), in their pioneering books on male and female sexuality. Kinsey's team surveyed thousands of Americans about their sexual attitudes and behavior, and they also reviewed the existing research on sexual physiology. In *Sexual Behavior in the Human Female*, they observed that "males would be better prepared to understand females, and females to understand males, if they realized that they are alike in their basic anatomy and physiology." For example, the penis and the clitoris develop from the same embryonic tissues; they differ in size, of course, but not in sensitivity.

THINKING CRITICALLY
AVOID EMOTIONAL REASONING

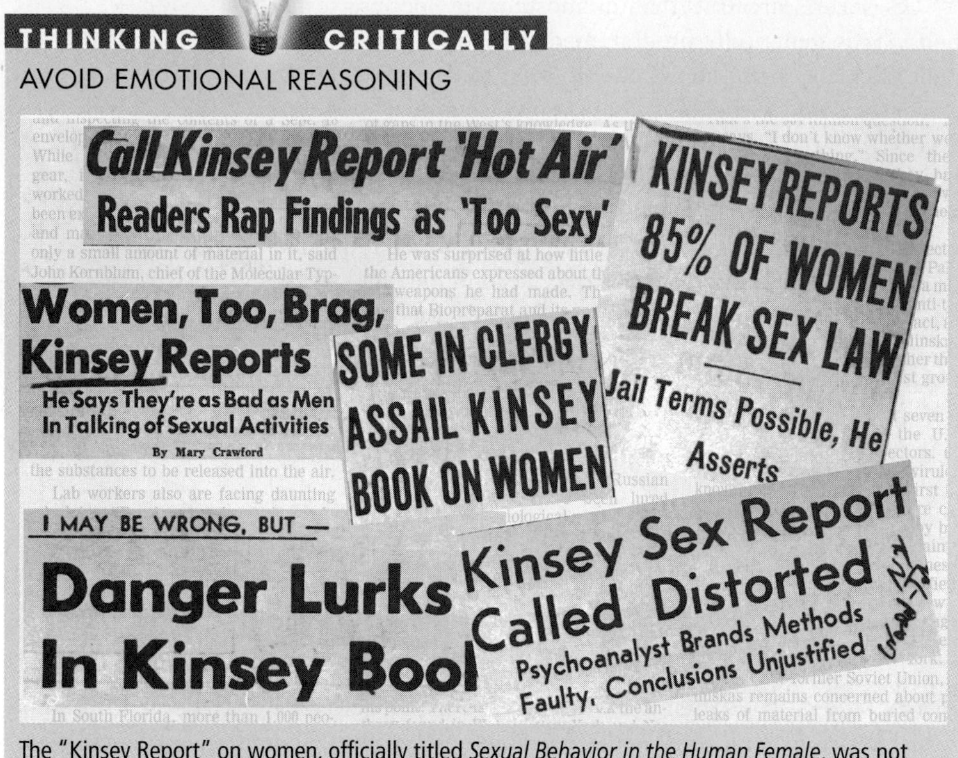

The "Kinsey Report" on women, officially titled *Sexual Behavior in the Human Female*, was not exactly greeted with praise and acceptance—or with clear thinking. Many people were so emotionally upset by the findings that many women enjoy sex and have had premarital sex that they chose to attack Kinsey instead of coolly appraising his research.

The idea that men and women are sexually similar in any way was extremely shocking in 1953. At that time many people believed that women were not as sexually motivated as men and that women cared more about affection than sexual satisfaction—notions soundly refuted by Kinsey's interviews. Kinsey did believe, however, that women overall have a "lesser sexual capacity" than men, reflected in women's lower frequency of masturbation and orgasm. Although he acknowledged that many women are taught to avoid, dislike, or feel ambivalent about sex, he tended to attribute this gender difference to biology.

The next wave of sex research began in the 1960s with the laboratory research of physician William Masters and his associate Virginia Johnson (1966). In studies of physiological changes during sexual arousal and orgasm, Masters and Johnson confirmed that male and female orgasms are indeed remarkably similar and that all orgasms are physiologically the same, regardless of the source of stimulation. But Masters and Johnson disagreed with Kinsey's assertion that women have a lesser sexual capacity than men. On the contrary, they argued, women's capacity for sexual response "infinitely surpasses that of men" because women, unlike most men, are able to have repeated orgasms until exhaustion or a ringing telephone makes them stop.

However, just as Kinsey might have underestimated women's sexual capacity, Masters and Johnson might have overestimated it. Their research was limited by the selection of a sample consisting only of men and women who were easily orgasmic, and they did not investigate how people's physiological responses might vary according to their age, experience, and culture (Tiefer, 2004). Thus, in their eagerness to show that the physiology of arousal and orgasm was the same in both sexes, Masters and Johnson tended to overlook individual differences. Since Masters and Johnson's

studies, sex researchers have learned much more about individual variation in sexual physiology and responsiveness (Ellison, 2000; Laumann et al., 1994).

"Go ahead. Press one for more options."

Sex and the "Sex Drive." The question of whether men and women are alike or different in some underlying, biologically based sex drive continues to provoke lively debate. Although women on average are certainly as capable as men of sexual pleasure, men have higher rates of almost every kind of sexual behavior, including masturbation, erotic fantasies, and orgasm (Oliver & Hyde, 1993; Peplau, 2003). These sex differences occur even when men are forbidden by cultural or religious rules to engage in sex at all; for example, Catholic priests have more of these sexual experiences than Catholic nuns do (Baumeister, Catanese, & Vohs, 2001).

Biological psychologists argue that these differences occur universally because the hormones and brain circuits involved in sexual behavior differ for men and women. They maintain that for men, the wiring for sex overlaps with that for dominance and aggression, which is why sex and aggression are more likely to be linked in men than women. For women, the circuits and hormones governing sexuality and nurturance seem to overlap, which is why sex and love are more likely to be linked in women than in men (Diamond, 2004).

Other psychologists, however, maintain that most gender differences in sexual behavior reflect women's and men's different roles and experiences in life and have little or nothing to do with biologically based drives or brain circuits (Eagly & Wood, 1999). Sex surveys generally find that men and women are, overall, more alike than different, for example in preferring sex with love (Laumann et al., 1994). In the sociocultural view, as long as large numbers of women learn to fear, dislike, or avoid sex, whether through cultural and familial messages or through coercive or otherwise unpleasant sexual experiences, it is impossible to know what women's sexual drive might really be like (Kaschak & Tiefer, 2002).

A middle view is that men's sexual behavior is more biologically influenced than is women's, whereas women's sexual desires and responsiveness are more affected by circumstances, the specific relationship, and cultural norms (Baumeister, 2000; Peplau et al., 2000).

The Psychology of Desire

Psychologists are fond of observing that the sexiest sex organ is the brain, where perceptions begin. People's values, fantasies, and beliefs profoundly affect their sexual desire and behavior. That is why a touch on the knee by an exciting new date feels terrifically sexy, but the same touch by a creepy stranger on a bus feels disgusting. It is why a worried thought can kill sexual arousal in a second, and why a fantasy can be more erotic than reality.

The Many Motives for Sex. To most people, the primary motives for sex are pretty obvious: to enjoy the pleasure of it, to express love and intimacy, or to make babies. But there are other motives too, not all of them so positive. Studies of several hundred college students and more than 1,500 older adults identified six factors underlying the many reasons that people give for having sex (Cooper, Shapiro, & Powers, 1998):

- ***Enhancement***—the emotional satisfaction or physical pleasure of sex
- ***Intimacy***—emotional closeness with your partner

The many motivations for sex range from sex for profit to sex for fun.

- ***Coping***—dealing with negative emotions and disappointments
- ***Self-affirmation***—reassurance that you are attractive or desirable
- ***Partner approval***—the desire to please or appease your partner, perhaps to avoid your partner's anger or rejection
- ***Peer approval***—the wish to impress your friends, be part of the group, and conform to what everyone else seems to be doing

In this research, men and women did not differ in their motives for intimacy, but men more strongly endorsed all the other motives, especially peer approval. The older people were, the more likely they were to have sex for intimacy and for self-enhancement (pleasure), and the less likely they were to have sex for peer or partner approval. White adolescents were more often motivated by a desire for intimacy than black adolescents were, and black teenagers were more often motivated by coping and peer pressure.

Perhaps you can think of other motives for sex, too: spiritual transcendence, money or perks, duty or feelings of obligation, power over the partner, submission to the partner in order to avoid his or her anger or rejection, rebellion. . . . People's motives for having sex affect many aspects of their sexual behavior, including whether they engage in sex in the first place, whether they enjoy it, whether they have unprotected or otherwise risky sex, and whether they have few or many partners (Browning et al., 2000). Extrinsic motives, such as having sex for purposes of coping and gaining approval, are most strongly associated with risky sexual behavior, including having many partners, not using birth control, and pressuring a partner into sex (Cooper, Shapiro, & Powers, 1998; Hamby & Koss, 2003; Impett, Peplau, & Gable, 2005).

Unfortunately, significant numbers of women and men are having sex for extrinsic rather than intrinsic motives. In one study, college students in dating relationships kept a daily diary of their sexual experiences. Fifty percent of the women and 26 percent of the men reported consenting to unwanted sexual activity during that time (O'Sullivan & Allgeier, 1998). Men typically do so because of peer pressure, inexperience, a desire for popularity, or a fear of seeming homosexual or unmasculine. Women typically do so because they do not want to lose the relationship; because they feel obligated, once the partner has spent time and money on them; because the partner makes them feel guilty; or because they want to satisfy the partner and avoid conflict (Impett, Gable, & Peplau, 2005).

People's motives for consenting to unwanted sex depend in part on their own feelings of security in the relationship. In a study of 125 college women, one-half to two-thirds of Asian-American, white, and Latina women had consented to having sex when they didn't really want to, and all of the African-American women said they had. Do you remember the attachment theory of love discussed earlier? Anxiously attached women were the most willing to consent to unwanted sex, especially if they feared their partners were less committed than they were. They reported that they often had sex out of feelings of obligation and to prevent the partner from leaving. Securely attached women also occasionally had unwanted sex, but their reasons were different: to gain sexual experience, to satisfy their curiosity, or to actively please their partners and further the intimacy between them (Impett, Gable, & Peplau, 2005).

Sexual Coercion and Rape. One of the most persistent differences in the sexual experiences of women and men has to do with their perceptions of, and experiences with, sexual coercion. In a nationally representative survey of more than 3,000 Americans ages 18 to 59, nearly one-fourth of the women said that a man, usually a husband or boyfriend, had forced them to do something sexually that they did not want to do

This ad, which is directed at men, emphasizes the importance of respect and communication in sexual relationships. Do you think it is effective? Why or why not?

(Laumann et al., 1994). But only about 3 percent of the men said they had ever forced a woman into a sexual act. Obviously, what many women regard as coercion is not always seen as coercive by men (Hamby & Koss, 2003). On the other hand, about half of all women who report a sexual assault that meets the legal definition of rape—being forced to engage in sexual acts against their will—do not label it as rape (McMullin & White, 2006). College women tend to define rape as being forced into intercourse by an acquaintance or stranger, or as having been molested as a child. They are least likely to call their experience rape if they were sexually assaulted by a boyfriend, were drunk or otherwise drugged, or were forced to have oral or digital sex (Kahn, 2004).

Although the public image of the rapist tends to be one of a menacing stranger, in most cases the rapist is known to the victim. They may have dated once or a few times; they may even be married (Koss, 1993; Russell, 1990). What causes some men to rape? There appear to be several different motivations:

- ***Peer approval.*** College men who have physically coerced their dates into having sex have often been pressured by male friends to prove their masculinity by scoring (Kanin, 1985).
- ***Anger, revenge, or a desire to dominate or humiliate the victim.*** This motive is apparent among soldiers who rape captive women during war and then often kill them (Olujic, 1998). Similarly, reports of the systematic rapes of female cadets at the U.S. Air Force Academy suggest that the rapists' motives were to humiliate the women and get women to leave the Academy. Aggressive motives also occur in the rape of men by other men, usually by anal penetration (King & Woollett, 1997). This form of rape typically occurs in youth gangs, where the intention is to humiliate rival gang members, and in prison, where again the motive is to conquer and degrade the victim.
- ***Narcissism and hostility toward women.*** Sexually aggressive males often are narcissistic, are unable to empathize with women, and feel entitled to have sexual relations with whatever woman they choose. They misperceive women's behavior in social situations, equate feelings of power with sexuality, and accuse women of provoking them (Bushman et al., 2003; Drieschner & Lange, 1999; Malamuth et al., 1995; Zurbriggen, 2000).
- ***Contempt for the victim and a sadistic pleasure in inflicting pain.*** A minority of rapists are men who are primarily motivated to injure or murder their victims.

You can see that the answer to the question "Why do people have sex?" is not at all obvious. It is not a simple matter of "doing what's natural." In addition to the intrinsic motives of intimacy, pleasure, procreation, and love, extrinsic motives include

intimidation, dominance, insecurity, appeasing the partner, approval from peers, and the wish to prove oneself a real man or a desirable woman.

THINKING CRITICALLY

EXAMINE THE EVIDENCE

Many people think that all sexual behavior, including kissing, is universal and caused by a simple physiological drive. What evidence disputes this common assumption?

The Culture of Desire

Think about kissing. Westerners like to think about kissing, and to do it, too. But if you think kissing is natural, try to remember your first serious kiss and all you had to learn about noses, breathing, and the position of teeth and tongue. The sexual kiss is so complicated that some cultures have never gotten around to it. They think that kissing another person's mouth—the very place that food enters!—is disgusting (Tiefer, 2004). Others have elevated the sexual kiss to high art; why do you suppose one version is called French kissing?

As the kiss illustrates, having the physical equipment to perform a sexual act is not all there is to sexual motivation. People have to learn what is supposed to turn them on (or off), which parts of the body and what activities are erotic (or repulsive), and even how to have pleasurable sexual relations (Laumann & Gagnon, 1995).

Thus, to men in cultures where women are required to cover up completely in public, the sight of a woman's ankle can be arousing; to Western men today, an ankle doesn't do it. In some cultures, oral sex is regarded as a bizarre sexual deviation; in others, it is considered not only normal but also supremely desirable. In many cultures, men believe that women who have experienced the sexual pleasure of kissing or being caressed, or who enjoy orgasms, will become unfaithful, so sexual relations are limited to quick intercourse; in others, men's satisfaction and pride depend on knowing the woman is sexually satisfied too. In some cultures, sex itself is seen as something joyful and beautiful, an art to be cultivated as one might cultivate the skill of gourmet cooking. In others, it is considered ugly and dirty, something to be gotten through as quickly as possible.

How do cultures transmit their rules and requirements about sex to their members? During childhood and adolescence, people learn their culture's *gender roles*, collections of rules that determine the proper attitudes and behavior for men and women. Just as an actor in the role of Hamlet needs a script to learn his part, a person following a gender role needs a **sexual script** that instructs men and women on how to behave in sexual situations (Gagnon & Simon, 1973; Laumann & Gagnon, 1995). If you are a teenage girl, are you supposed to be sexually adventurous and assertive or sexually modest and passive? What if you are a teenage boy? What if you are an older woman or man? The answers differ from culture to culture, as members act in accordance with the sexual scripts for their gender, age, religion, social status, and peer group.

In many parts of the world, boys acquire their attitudes about sex in a competitive atmosphere where the goal is to impress other males, and they talk and joke about masturbation and other sexual experiences with their friends. While their traditional sexual scripts are encouraging them to value physical sex, traditional scripts are teaching girls to value relationships and make themselves attractive. Many girls learn that their role is to be sexually desirable (which is good), but not to indulge in their own sexual pleasures (which would be bad). Modern scripts for women in many places are changing, however, as illustrated by the sexual scripts followed by the characters in *Grey's Anatomy* or *Sex and the City*.

sexual scripts Sets of implicit rules that specify proper sexual behavior for a person in a given situation, varying with the person's gender, age, religion, social status, and peer group.

These teenagers are following the sexual scripts for their gender and culture—the boys, by ogling and making sexual remarks about girls in order to impress their peers, and the girls, by preening and wearing makeup to look good for boys.

Gay men and lesbians follow sexual scripts, too. But theirs tend to be more flexible than heterosexual scripts in establishing rules for the relationship because most partners are not following a traditional gender role (Kurdek, 2005; Peplau & Spalding, 2000).

Scripts can be powerful determinants of behavior. Because African-American women now account for 58 percent of reported AIDS cases among women, researchers have sought to understand how sexual scripts might be reducing their likelihood of practicing safe sex. In interviews with 14 black women ages 22 to 39, researchers found that the women's behavior was governed by scripts fostering these beliefs: *Men control relationships; women sustain relationships; male infidelity is normal; men control sexual activity; women want to use condoms, but men control condom use* (Bowleg, Lucas, & Tschann, 2004). As one woman summarized, "The ball was always in his court." These scripts, the researchers noted, are rooted in African-American history and the recurring scarcity of men available for long-term commitments. The scripts originated to preserve the stability of the family, but today they encourage some women to establish and maintain sexual relationships at the expense of their own needs and safety.

Gender, Culture, and Sex

As we discuss in Chapter 3, evolutionary psychologists believe that gender roles and sexual scripts simply reflect hardwired biological sex differences that resulted from natural selection. In contrast, social and cultural psychologists believe that gender roles and sexual scripts reflect a culture's economic, demographic, and social

GET INVOLVED!

➤IS THE DOUBLE STANDARD STILL ALIVE?

Think of all the words you know to describe a sexually active woman and then think of words for a sexually active man. Is one list longer than the other? Are the two lists equally negative or positive in their connotations? What does this exercise tell you about the survival of the double standard and your culture's sexual scripts?

arrangements. As evidence for their point of view, they have found that when those arrangements change, so do women's and men's attitudes and behavior. A meta-analysis of 530 studies, involving nearly 270,000 individuals, showed that in America, young people's sexual attitudes and behavior changed dramatically between 1943 and 1999, with the largest changes occurring among girls and young women (Wells & Twenge, 2005). Approval of premarital sex leapt from 12 percent to 73 percent among young women, and from 40 percent to 79 percent among young men; feelings of sexual guilt decreased sharply for both sexes; and, for women, average age at first intercourse dropped from 19 to 15 over the five decades, with small fluctuations.

Most people choose sexual partners by using the same criteria they apply in the search for love partners: similarity and proximity (availability). What happens, then, when large-scale demographic changes result in a lopsided ratio of heterosexual men and women? In China and India, countries in which most parents value boys and disparage girls, the ratio of young men to women is now about 120 to 100, a result of decades of abortions of female fetuses. In contrast, among African-Americans there are more women than available men, because so many young black men are unemployed, are in prison, or die young.

More than 20 years ago, an important book assessed the social and sexual consequences of these uneven ratios (Guttentag & Secord, 1983). When men are scarce, the ball is always in their court: Men are more likely to have multiple sexual partners, divorce rates and single-parent families increase, and women become more independent. When women are scarce, men vie for wives, divorce rates drop, both sexes have fewer sexual partners, and women become less independent. Societies that have large numbers of young, unemployed, and unattached men, such as the Taliban in Afghanistan, are also more vulnerable to internal disruption and violence (Hudson & den Boer, 2004).

Sexual attitudes and motives likewise change along with women's economic status. Whenever women have needed marriage to ensure their social and financial security, they have regarded sex as a bargaining chip, an asset to be rationed rather than an activity to be enjoyed for its own sake (Hatfield & Rapson, 1996). A woman with no economic resources of her own cannot afford to casually seek sexual pleasure if that means risking an unwanted pregnancy, the security of marriage, her reputation in society, her physical safety, or, in some cultures, her very life. When women become self-supporting and able to control their own fertility, however, they are more likely to want sex for pleasure rather than as a means to another goal.

The TV series *Sex and the City* rewrote the traditional sexual script for women—literally. The four friends always felt free to shop for men in many of the "sex markets" of New York.

Lopsided sex ratios and other social factors also help account for the different sexual practices, values, and norms that occur within a nation. One research team, surveying a random sample of more than 2,000 people in Chicago, has used the term *sex market* to describe a geographical and cultural boundary within which people seek partners (Laumann et al., 2004). Big cities will have many different sex markets, formed by the ethnicity, age, status, and sexual orientation of their "shoppers." A bisexual African-American man, an immigrant Latina woman, a single young white woman, and an older gay man will seek out different sex markets that determine where and how they will find sexual partners: through work, church, bars, friends, social institutions, the Internet, and so on. Sex markets vary tremendously in the sexual behavior they

consider appropriate, the sexual scripts they endorse for their members, and the meanings they attribute to sex—which is why so many groups in America are quarreling about what is right or normal sexual behavior. Although big cities consist of many different sex markets, people rarely travel across them. They prefer the familiarity and proximity of the market they know best.

BIOLOGY and Sexual Orientation

Elusive Causes, Recent Clues

Why is it that most people become heterosexual, some homosexual, and others bisexual? Many psychological explanations for homosexuality have been proposed over the years, but none of them has been supported. Homosexuality is not a result of having a smothering mother, an absent father, or emotional problems. It is not caused by same-sex sexual play in childhood or adolescence, which is actually quite common (Lamb, 2002). It is not caused by seduction by an older adult (Rind, Tromovich, & Bauserman, 1998). It is not caused by parental practices or role models. Most gay men recall that they rejected the typical boy role and boys' toys and games from an early age, in spite of enormous pressures from their parents and peers to conform to the traditional male role (Bailey & Zucker, 1995). Conversely, the overwhelming majority of children of gay parents do not become gay, as a learning model would predict, although they are more likely than the children of straight parents to be open-minded about homosexuality and gender roles (Bailey et al., 1995; Patterson, 1992).

Many researchers, therefore, have been turning to biological explanations of sexual orientation. One line of supporting evidence is that homosexual behavior—including courtship displays, sexual activity, and rearing of young by two males or two females—has been documented in some 450 species, including bottlenose dolphins, penguins, and primates (Bagemihl, 1999). Sexual orientation also seems to be moderately heritable, particularly in men (Bailey, Dunn, & Martin, 2000; Rahman & Wilson, 2003). But the large majority of gay men and lesbians do not have a close gay relative, and their siblings, including twins, are overwhelmingly likely to be heterosexual (Peplau et al., 2000).

In the early 1990s, a few studies of gay men reported associations between sexual orientation and specific areas of the brain (Allen & Gorski, 1992; LeVay, 1991). These studies got lots of press, but they were not replicated (Byne, 1995). Researchers have also examined the role of prenatal exposure to androgens and how this might affect brain organization and partner preference (Rahman & Wilson, 2003). Female babies accidentally exposed in the womb to masculinizing hormones are more likely than other girls to become bisexual or lesbian and to prefer typical boys' toys and activities (Collaer & Hines, 1995; Meyer-Bahlburg et al., 1995). However, most androgenized girls do not become lesbians, and most lesbians were not exposed in the womb to atypical prenatal hormones (Peplau et al., 2000).

One new line of research is investigating the possibility that other prenatal events might predispose a child toward a same-sex orientation. For example, more than a dozen studies have found that the probability of a man's becoming gay rises significantly according to the number of older brothers he has—gay or not—when these brothers are born of the same mother. (Remember, though, that the percentage

THINKING CRITICALLY

EXAMINE THE EVIDENCE

Many people think that homosexuality is abnormal, unnatural, or a matter of preference, but there is ample evidence of same-sex sexual activity in more than 450 nonhuman species. These young male penguins, Squawk and Milou, entwine their necks, kiss, call to each other, and have sex—and they firmly reject females. Another male pair in the same zoo, Silo and Roy, seemed so desperate to incubate an egg together that they put a rock in their nest and sat on it. Their human keeper was so touched that he gave them a fertile egg to hatch. Silo and Roy sat on it for the necessary 34 days until their chick, Tango, was born, and then they raised Tango beautifully. "They did a great job," said the zookeeper.

Nicole Bengiveno/The New York Times

of males who become homosexual is very small.) A recent study of 944 homosexual and heterosexual men suggests that this "brother effect" has nothing to do with family environment, but rather with conditions within the womb before birth (Bogaert, 2006). In this study, the only factor that predicted sexual orientation was having older biological brothers; growing up with older stepbrothers or adoptive brothers (or sisters) had no influence at all. The increased chance of homosexuality occurred even when men had older brothers born to the same mother but raised in a different home. No one yet has any idea, however, what prenatal influence might account for these results.

Several other intriguing biological findings are also associated with sexual orientation. In two studies, a team of Swedish scientists exposed people to two odors: a testosterone derivative found in men's sweat and an estrogen-like compound found in women's urine. It appears that when a hormone is from the sex you are *not* turned on by, your olfactory system registers it, but not your hypothalamus and through that, your sexual arousal and response system. Thus, the brain activity of homosexual women in response to the odors was similar to that of heterosexual men, and the brain activity of gay men was similar to that of heterosexual women

(Berglund, Lindström, & Savic, 2006; Savic, Berglund, & Lindström, 2005). But the researchers wisely noted that their study could not answer questions of cause and effect. "We can't say whether the differences are because of pre-existing differences in their brains, or if past sexual experiences have conditioned their brains to respond differently," said the lead researcher.

The basic problem with trying to find a single origin of sexual orientation is that sexual identity and behavior take different forms, and they don't correlate strongly (Savin-Williams, 2006). Some people are heterosexual in behavior but have homosexual fantasies and even define themselves as gay or lesbian. Some men, such as prisoners, are homosexual in behavior because they lack opportunities for heterosexual sex, but they do not define themselves as gay and prefer women as sexual partners. In some cultures, teenage boys go through a homosexual phase that they do not define as homosexual and that does not affect their future relations with women (Herdt, 1984). Some gay men are feminine in interests and manner, but many are not; some lesbians are "butch" (i.e., masculine in interests and manner) but many other lesbians are not (Singh et al., 1999).

Moreover, although some lesbians have an exclusively same-sex orientation their whole lives, many have more fluid sexual orientations: They have sex with the person they fall in love with, male or female (Peplau et al., 2000). Some women are lesbian for a particular time in their lives, as reflected in the joking term LUG—lesbian until graduation (Diamond, 2003). In Lesotho, in South Africa, women have intimate relations with other women, including passionate kissing and oral sex, but they do not define these acts as sexual, as they do when a man is the partner (Kendall, 1999).

Biological factors cannot account for the diversity of such customs or for the diversity of experience among gay men and lesbians. At present, therefore, we must tolerate uncertainty about the origins of sexual orientation. Perhaps the origins will turn out to differ, on average, for males and females, and also differ among individuals, whatever their primary orientation.

Now, how are you reacting to these findings? Your responses are probably affected by your feelings about the subject. Many gay men and lesbians welcome biological research on the grounds that it supports what they have been saying all along: Sexual orientation is not a matter of choice but a fact of nature. Others fear that people who are prejudiced against homosexuals will use this research to argue that gay people have a biological defect that should be eradicated. But people who are hostile to homosexuals can use any theory, biological or psychological, to justify their wish to eliminate homosexuality. They have often used learning theories to argue, mistakenly, that "if it's learned, it can be unlearned," and thus to subject gay men, and even "unboyish" boys as young as 3 years old, to harsh and punitive forms of behavior modification (Burke, 1996).

Political storms about sex research are no less heated today than they were in Kinsey's time. Some conservative and evangelical Christians, including the Traditional Values Coalition, are trying to block research on sexual behavior they say the Bible disapproves of, such as masturbation, homosexuality, and any form of sexual behavior outside of marriage. Other conservative Christians, however, call on modern research to make the case that homosexuality is not a preference but a natural disposition. In their book *What God Has Joined Together: A Christian Case for Gay Marriage*, David Myers and Letha Scanzoni (2005) argue that the Bible's seven brief comments opposing same-sex behavior are really condemnations of the exploitation of children, promiscuity, idolatry, and acting against

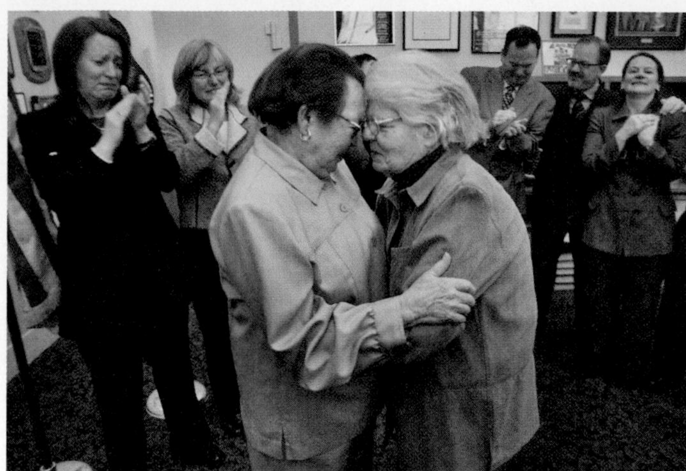

Stephanie Diani/The New York Times

Gay and lesbian couples have all the joys and problems of straight couples. On the left, Phyllis Lyon and Del Martin, who have been together for more than 50 years, embrace after their marriage at City Hall in San Francisco. On the right, Tom Howard is shown with the three children he is raising with his partner. Howard left his job as a professor in order to be a stay-at-home dad. Why does the issue of legalizing gay and lesbian marriage evoke so much emotion and controversy?

one's nature, and that these verses pale in importance beside the Bible's thousands of verses about love, compassion, and empathy.

As you see, research on sexuality can be used for many purposes and political goals, depending on the values and attitudes of the culture in which such findings emerge and people's own religious passions or personal beliefs. But as long as people are morally opposed to homosexuality, preconceptions and prejudice are likely to cloud their reactions to anything that psychologists learn about it.

QUICK quiz

Were you motivated to learn about sexual motivation?

1. Biological research finds that (a) male and female sexual responses are physiologically very different, (b) all women can have multiple orgasms, (c) testosterone promotes sexual desire in both sexes.
2. Research on the motives of rapists finds that rape is usually a result of (a) thwarted sexual desire, (b) hostility or a need for peer approval, (c) crossed signals, (d) female provocation.
3. When men are scarce, what are some consequences for the sexual behavior of both sexes?
4. Under what conditions are women most likely to use sex as a "bargaining chip"? (a) when they are employed and thus have their own money to bargain with, (b) when they don't know how to play poker, (c) when they are using birth control, (d) when they are financially dependent
5. *True or false:* Exclusively psychological theories of the origins of homosexuality have never been supported.

Answers:

1. c 2. b 3. Men are more likely to have multiple sexual partners, divorce rates and single-parent families increase, and women become more independent. 4. d 5 true

WHAT'S AHEAD

- Why is doing your best an ineffective goal to set for yourself?
- When you are learning a new skill, which should you concentrate on: mastering it or performing it well in front of others?
- Which aspects of a job are more important than money in increasing your work satisfaction and involvement?
- How is the *desire* to achieve affected by the *opportunity* to achieve?

The Competent Animal: Motives to Achieve

Almost every adult works. But work does not only mean paid employment. Students work at studying. Homemakers work, often more hours than salaried employees, at running a household. Artists, poets, and actors work, even if they are paid erratically (or not at all). Most people are motivated to work in order to meet the basic needs for food and shelter. Yet survival does not explain why some people want to do their work well and others want just to get it done. And it does not explain why some people work to make a basic living and then put their passions for achievement into unpaid activities—learning to become an accomplished trail rider or traveling to Madagascar to catch sight of a rare bird for their bird-watching list. What keeps everybody doing what they do?

Psychologists, particularly those in the field of *industrial/organizational* psychology, have measured the psychological qualities that spur achievement and success and also the environmental conditions that influence productivity and satisfaction. Their findings apply not only to understanding why people thrive or wilt at their jobs, but also to understanding people's aspirations and achievements in general.

"Finish it? Why would I want to finish it?"

The Effects of Motivation on Work

In the early 1950s, David McClelland and his associates (1953) speculated that some people have a **need for achievement** that motivates them as much as hunger motivates people to eat. To measure the strength of this motive, McClelland used a variation of the **Thematic Apperception Test (TAT)**, which requires the test-taker to make up a story about a set of ambiguous pictures, such as a young man sitting at a desk. (The TAT is one of many *projective tests*, which are based on the assumption that a person will project unconscious motives and feelings onto an ambiguous stimulus; see Chapter 16.) The strength of the achievement motive, said McClelland (1961), is captured in the fantasies the test-taker reveals. "In fantasy anything is at least symbolically possible," he explained. "A person may rise to great heights, sink to great depths, kill his grandmother, or take off for the South Sea Islands on a pogo stick."

The TAT is one of the few projective tests that has modest empirical support for the measurement of achievement motivation. But it does not have strong test–retest reliability, meaning that people's responses are easily influenced by what is going on at that moment in their lives rather than by some inner drive to succeed (Lilienfeld, Wood, & Garb, 2000). Some people might tell stories of achieving against all odds, not

need for achievement A learned motive to meet personal standards of success and excellence in a chosen area.

Thematic Apperception Test (TAT) A projective test that asks respondents to interpret a series of drawings showing scenes of people; usually scored for unconscious motives, such as the need for achievement, power, or affiliation.

because they are determined to do so, but because they are idly daydreaming about dazzling the world on *American Idol.* But the method launched many investigations into the question of why some people seem to have a drive to make it no matter what, and others drift along.

The Importance of Goals. Today the predominant approach to understanding achievement motivation emphasizes goals rather than inner drives: What you accomplish depends on the goals you set for yourself and the reasons you pursue them. Not just any old goals will promote achievement, though. A goal is most likely to improve your motivation and performance when three conditions are met (Higgins, 1998; Locke & Latham, 2002):

- ***The goal is specific.*** Defining a goal vaguely, such as "doing your best," is as ineffective as having no goal at all. You need to be specific about what you are going to do and when you are going to do it: "I will write four pages of this paper today."
- ***The goal is challenging but achievable.*** You are apt to work hardest for tough but realistic goals. The highest, most difficult goals produce the highest levels of

The Many Motives of Accomplishment

IMMORTALITY

William Faulkner
(1897–1962)
Novelist

"Really the writer doesn't want success . . . He wants to leave a scratch on that wall [of oblivion]—Kilroy was here—that somebody a hundred or a thousand years later will see."

KNOWLEDGE

Helen Keller
(1880–1968)
Blind/deaf author and lecturer

"Knowledge is happiness, because to have knowledge—broad, deep knowledge—is to know true ends from false, and lofty things from low."

JUSTICE

Martin Luther King, Jr.
(1929–1968)
Civil rights activist

"I have a dream . . . that my four little children will one day live in a nation where they will not be judged by the color of their skin but the content of their character."

AUTONOMY

Georgia O'Keeffe
(1887–1986)
Artist

"[I] found myself saying to myself—I can't live where I want to, go where I want to, do what I want to . . . I decided I was a very stupid fool not to at least paint as I wanted to."

motivation and performance, unless, of course, you choose impossible goals that you can never attain.

- ***The goal is framed in terms of getting what you want rather than avoiding what you do not want.*** **Approach goals** are positive experiences that you seek directly, such as getting a better grade or learning to scuba dive. **Avoidance goals** involve the effort to avoid unpleasant experiences, such as trying not to make a fool of yourself at parties or trying to avoid being dependent.

approach goals Goals framed in terms of desired outcomes or experiences, such as learning to scuba dive.

avoidance goals Goals framed in terms of avoiding unpleasant experiences, such as trying not to look foolish in public.

All of the motives discussed in this chapter are affected by approach versus avoidance goals. People who frame their goals in specific, achievable approach terms (e.g., "I'm going to lose weight by jogging three times a week") feel better about themselves, are happier, feel more competent, are more optimistic, and are less depressed than people who frame the same goals in avoidance terms (e.g., "I'm going to lose weight by cutting out rich foods") (Coats, Janoff-Bulman, & Alpert, 1996; Updegraff, Gable, & Taylor, 2004). Framing goals in terms of approach or avoidance can even affect the quality of close relationships. For example, people who have sex for *approach* motives—to enjoy their own physical pleasure, to promote a partner's happiness, or to seek enhanced intimacy—tend to have happier and less conflicted relationships than those who have sex to *avoid* a partner's loss of interest or quarrels with the partner (Impett, Peplau, & Gable, 2005).

Can you guess why approach goals produce better results than avoidance goals? Approach goals allow you to focus on what you can actively do to accomplish them and on the intrinsic pleasure of the activity. Avoidance goals make you focus on what you have to give up (Elliot & Sheldon, 1998).

POWER

Henry Kissinger
(b. 1923)
Former Secretary of State

"Power is the ultimate aphrodisiac."

DUTY

Eleanor Roosevelt
(1884–1962)
Humanitarian, lecturer, stateswoman

"As for accomplishments, I just did what I had to do as things came along."

EXCELLENCE

Florence Griffith Joyner
(1959–1998)
Olympic gold medallist

"When you've been second best for so long, you can either accept it, or try to become the best. I made the decision to try and be the best."

GREED

Ivan Boesky
(b. 1937)
Financier, convicted of insider trading violations

"Greed is all right . . . I think greed is healthy. You can be greedy and still feel good about yourself."

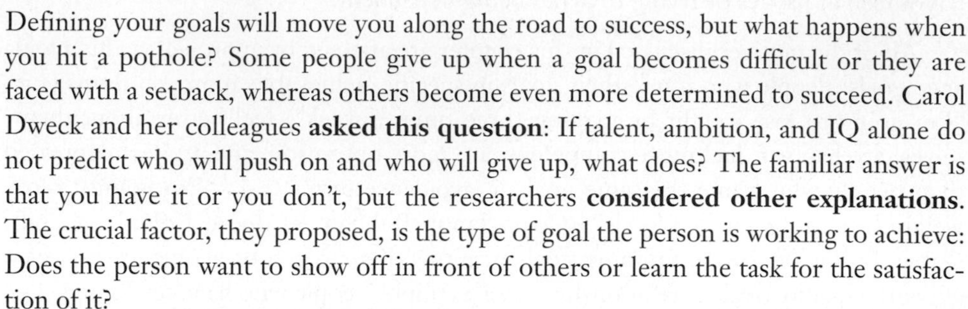

MOTIVATING CHILDREN (AND OURSELVES) TO LEARN

Why will some children become engrossed in a project and work on it for hours, whereas others give up in frustration if they can't get it just right?

Defining your goals will move you along the road to success, but what happens when you hit a pothole? Some people give up when a goal becomes difficult or they are faced with a setback, whereas others become even more determined to succeed. Carol Dweck and her colleagues **asked this question**: If talent, ambition, and IQ alone do not predict who will push on and who will give up, what does? The familiar answer is that you have it or you don't, but the researchers **considered other explanations**. The crucial factor, they proposed, is the type of goal the person is working to achieve: Does the person want to show off in front of others or learn the task for the satisfaction of it?

First, the researchers **defined their terms** by distinguishing performance goals from mastery goals. People who are motivated by **performance goals** are concerned primarily with being judged favorably and avoiding criticism. Those who are motivated by **mastery (learning) goals** are concerned with increasing their competence and skills and finding intrinsic pleasure in what they are learning (Dweck & Sorich, 1999; Grant & Dweck, 2003). Dweck hypothesized that when people who are motivated by performance goals do poorly, they will often decide the fault is theirs and stop trying to improve. Because their goal is to demonstrate their abilities, they set themselves up for grief when they temporarily fail, as all of us must if we are to learn anything new. In contrast, people who are motivated to master new skills will generally regard failure as a source of useful information that will help them improve. Failure and criticism are less likely to discourage them because they know that learning takes time.

But why do some children choose performance goals and others choose mastery goals? To find out, and to pinpoint the different consequences of having one type of goal or the other, Claudia Mueller and Dweck (1998) conducted a series of experiments with young children. Having **examined the previous evidence**, they suspected that a leading influence on children's goals was whether parents and teachers praised them for their "natural" intelligence or for their diligent efforts.

In one study, 128 Anglo, African-American, and Hispanic fifth graders were asked to work independently on sets of puzzle problems. After four minutes, the experimenter came in, told the children to stop, and scored their results. She then gave them one of two types of feedback that constituted the experimental manipulation. She told all of them that they had done well, but she praised some of them for their ability ("You must be smart at these problems!") and others for their effort ("You must have worked hard at these problems!"). (Children in the control condition received no additional feedback.) The children then got another four minutes to work on a more difficult set of problems, but this time the experimenter told them they had done a lot worse. Finally, the children described which goals they preferred to work for: performance (e.g., doing "problems that aren't too hard, so I don't get many wrong") or mastery (e.g., doing "problems that I'll learn a lot from, even if I won't look so smart"). They also rated their desire to persist on the problems and their enjoyment in doing them, and explained why they thought they had failed. At the end of the experiment, the researcher informed the children that the second set of problems was for older seventh graders, so that the children would not go home feeling defeated or unhappy with their scores.

performance goals Goals framed in terms of performing well in front of others, being judged favorably, and avoiding criticism.

mastery (learning) goals Goals framed in terms of increasing one's competence and skills.

The researchers found that children praised for being smart rather than for working hard tended to lose the pleasure of learning and focused instead on how well they were doing. After these children failed the second set of problems, they tended to give up on subsequent ones, enjoyed them less, and actually performed less well than children who had been praised for their efforts. As you can see in the accompanying figure, nearly 70 percent of fifth graders who were praised for their intelligence later chose performance goals rather than learning goals, compared to fewer than 10 percent of children who were praised for their efforts. The graph also reveals another unwelcome side effect of being praised for intelligence rather than effort: The children were much more likely to lie to other kids about how well they had done. After all, showing off was what mattered to them.

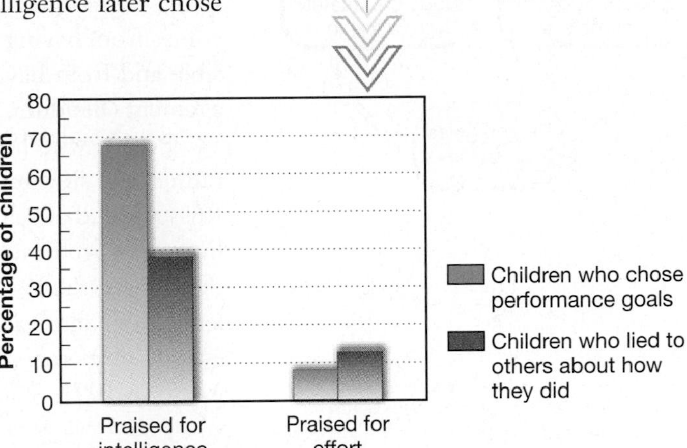

Mueller and Dweck **analyzed an assumption** that is widely held in American society: that intelligence and ability are fixed traits that you can't do anything about. This assumption often makes it difficult for people to **avoid emotional reasoning**: They decide that if they fail, they are stupid and they might as well give up. But Dweck and her colleagues showed that when children realize that all effort is subject to improvement, they realize that they can always try again. That is the key to mastery. As one learning-oriented child said to the experimenters, "Mistakes are our friends" (Dweck & Sorich, 1999).

Mastery goals are powerful intrinsic motivators at all levels of education and throughout life. Students who are in college primarily to master new areas of knowledge choose more challenging projects, persist in the face of difficulty, use deeper and more elaborate study strategies, are less likely than other students to cheat, and *enjoy* learning more than do students who are there only to get a degree and a meal ticket (Elliot & McGregor, 2001; Grant & Dweck, 2003). Researchers who study work motivation, however, are careful to **avoid oversimplification**. After all, people who are motivated by performance goals, as Olympic athletes and world-class musicians surely are, often do improve their performance. Ambitious individuals who are determined to become the best in their field are able to successfully blend performance and mastery goals (Barron & Harackiewicz, 2001).

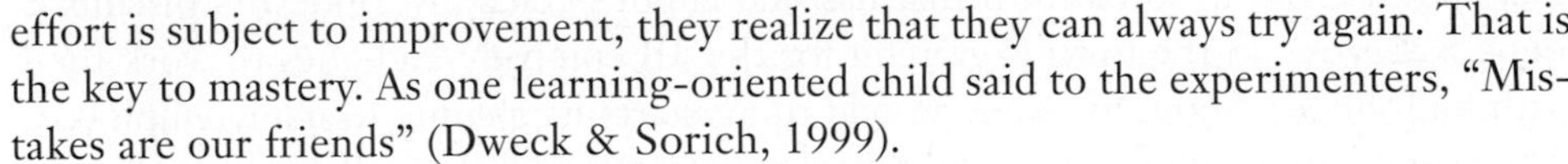

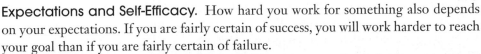

Expectations and Self-Efficacy. How hard you work for something also depends on your expectations. If you are fairly certain of success, you will work harder to reach your goal than if you are fairly certain of failure.

A classic experiment showed how quickly experience affects these expectations. Young women were asked to solve 15 anagram puzzles. Before working on each one, they had to estimate their chances of solving it. Half of the women started off with very easy anagrams, but half began with insoluble ones. Sure enough, those who started with the easy ones increased their estimates of success on later ones. Those who began with the impossible ones decided they would all be impossible. These expectations, in turn, affected the young women's ability to actually solve the last 10 anagrams, which were the same for everyone. The higher the expectation of success, the more anagrams the women solved (Feather, 1966). Once acquired, therefore, expectations can create a **self-fulfilling prophecy** (Merton, 1948): Your expectations make you behave in ways that make the expectation come true. You expect to succeed,

self-fulfilling prophecy An expectation that comes true because of the tendency of the person holding it to act in ways that bring it about.

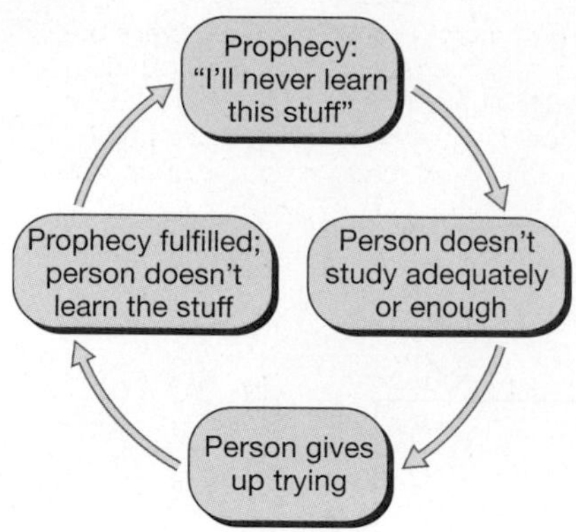

so you work hard—and succeed. Or you expect to fail, so you don't do much work—and do poorly.

Where do expectations come from? One source is your level of confidence in your abilities. Do you feel able to handle challenges? No one is born with a feeling of confidence, or **self-efficacy**. You acquire it through experience in mastering new skills, overcoming obstacles, and learning from occasional failures. Self-efficacy also comes from having successful role models who teach you that your ambitions are possible and from having people around to give you constructive feedback and encouragement (Bandura, 1997, 2001, 2006).

People who have a strong sense of self-efficacy are quick to cope with problems rather than stewing and brooding about them. Studies in North America, Europe, and Russia find that self-efficacy has a positive effect on just about every aspect of people's lives: how well they do on a task, the grades they earn, how persistently they pursue their goals, the kind of career choices they make, their ability to solve complex problems, their motivation to work for political and social goals, their health habits, and even their chances of recovery from heart attack (Bandura et al., 2001; Ewart, 1995; Maddux, 1995; Stajkovic & Luthans, 1998).

The Effects of Work on Motivation

Imagine that you live in a town that has one famous company, Boopsie's Biscuits & Buns. Everyone in the town is grateful for the 3B company and goes to work there with high hopes. Soon, however, an odd thing starts happening to many employees. They complain of fatigue and irritability. They are taking lots of sick leave. Productivity declines. What's going on at Boopsie's Biscuits & Buns? Is everybody suffering from sheer laziness?

Most observers would answer that something is wrong with those employees. But what if something is wrong with Boopsie's? Some people undoubtedly do lack motivation, but accomplishment does not depend on internal motives alone. Psychologists also want to know how the work we do, as well as the conditions under which we do it, nurture or crush our motivation to succeed.

THINKING CRITICALLY

ASK QUESTIONS

If a person isn't doing well at work, North Americans tend to ask, "What's the matter with that person's motivation? How come that person is a lazy slug?" What other questions would lead to different answers about why the employee seems so lazy?

Working Conditions. Several aspects of the work environment are likely to increase work motivation and satisfaction and reduce the chances of emotional burnout (Bond et al., 2004; Maslach et al., 2001; Rhoades & Eisenberger, 2002):

- The work feels meaningful and important to employees.
- Employees have control over many aspects of their work, such as setting their own hours and making decisions.
- Tasks are varied rather than repetitive.
- The company maintains clear and consistent rules.
- Employees have supportive relationships with their superiors and co-workers.
- Employees receive useful feedback about their work, so they know what they have accomplished and what they need to do to improve.
- The company offers opportunities for its employees to learn and advance.

Companies that foster these conditions tend to have more productive and satisfied employees. Workers tend to become more creative in their thinking and feel better about themselves and their work than they do if they feel stuck in routine jobs that give them no control or flexibility over their daily tasks. Conversely, when people are put in situations that frustrate their desire and ability to succeed, they become dissatisfied and stressed out, and their desire to succeed declines (Jenkins, 1994).

self-efficacy A person's belief that he or she is capable of producing desired results, such as mastering new skills and reaching goals.

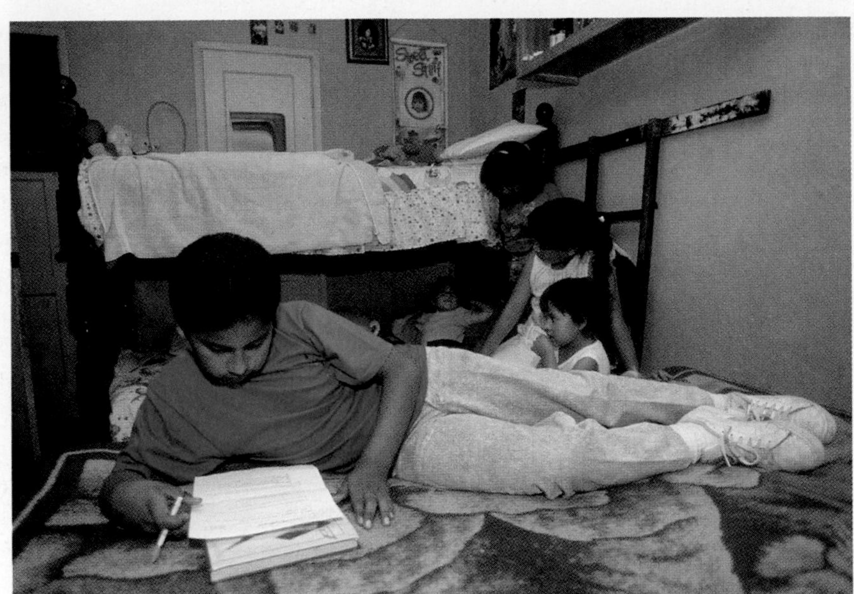

Like employees, students can have poor working conditions that affect their motivation. They may have to study in crowded quarters or may have small siblings who interrupt and distract them.

Did you notice anything missing from that list of beneficial working conditions? Where is money, supposedly the great motivator? Actually, work motivation is related not to the amount of money you get, but to how and when you get it. The strongest motivator is *incentive pay*, bonuses that are given upon completion of a goal rather than as an automatic raise (Locke et al., 1981). Incentive pay increases people's feelings of competence and accomplishment ("I got this raise because I deserved it"). This doesn't mean that people should accept low pay so they will like their jobs better or that they should never demand cost-of-living raises!

Opportunities to Achieve. Another important working condition that affects achievement is having the *opportunity* to achieve. When someone does not do well at work, others are apt to say it is the individual's own fault because he or she lacks the internal drive to make it. But what the person may really lack is a fair chance to make it, and this is especially true for those who have been subjected to systematic discrimination. At one time, for example, women were said to be less successful than men in the workplace because women had an internalized "fear of success." Yet this apparently internal motive vanished as opportunities for women improved and sex discrimination was made illegal. Once in a career, people may become more motivated to advance up the ladder or less so, depending on how many rungs they are permitted to climb. Men *and* women who work in jobs with no prospect of promotion tend to play down the importance of achievement, fantasize about quitting, and emphasize the social benefits of their jobs instead of the intellectual or financial benefits (Kanter, 1977/1993).

One external factor that affects many people's motivation to work in a particular field is the proportion of men and women in that occupation (Kanter, 1977/1993). When occupations are segregated by gender, many people form gender stereotypes about the requirements of such careers: Female jobs require kindness and nurturance; male jobs require strength and smarts. These stereotypes, in turn, stifle many people's aspirations to enter a nontraditional career and also create prejudices in employers (Agars, 2004; Cejka & Eagly, 1999). When law, veterinary medicine, and bartending were almost entirely male professions, and nursing, teaching, and child care were almost entirely female, few women aspired to enter the "male" professions and few men to enter the "female" ones. As job segregation began breaking down, however, people's career motivations changed. Today, it isn't at all unusual to see a female lawyer, vet, or bartender or a male nurse or even nanny.

And although women are still a minority in engineering, math, and science, their numbers are rising: In 1970–1971, women earned 0.6 percent of the doctorates in engineering, 7.6 percent of those in mathematics, and 16.3 percent of those in biological sciences. By 2001–2002, the percentages had jumped to 17.3 percent, 29 percent, and 44.3 percent, respectively (Cox & Alm, 2005). As these numbers have increased, the view that women are not suited to engineering, math, and science has been fading, though slowly.

In sum, work motivation and satisfaction depend on the right fit between qualities of the individual and conditions of the work:

QUICK quiz

Work on your understanding of work motivation.

1. Horatio wants to earn a black belt in karate. Which way(s) of thinking about this goal are most likely to help him reach it? (a) "I should do the best I can," (b) "I should be sure not to lose many matches," (c) "I will set specific goals that are tough but attainable," (d) "I will set specific goals that I know I can reach easily," (e) "I will strive to achieve key milestones on the way to my goal."
2. Ramón and Ramona are learning to ski. Every time she falls, Ramona says, "This is the most humiliating experience I've ever had! Everyone is watching me behave like a clumsy dolt!" When Ramón falls, he says, "&*!!@$@! I'll show these dratted skis who's boss!" Why is Ramona more likely than Ramón to give up? (a) She *is* a clumsy dolt, (b) she is less competent at skiing, (c) she is focused on learning, (d) she is focused on performance.
3. Which of these factors significantly increase work motivation? (a) specific goals, (b) regular pay, (c) feedback, (d) general goals, (e) being told what to do, (f) being able to make decisions, (g) the chance of promotion, (h) having routine, predictable work
4. An employer is annoyed by the behavior of an employee and is thinking of firing her. Her work is competent, but she rarely arrives on time, doesn't seem as motivated as others to do well, and has begun to take an unusual number of sick days. The boss has decided she is lazy and unmotivated. What guidelines of critical thinking is the boss overlooking, and what information should the boss consider before taking this step?

Answers:

1. c, e **2.** d **3.** a, c, f, g **4.** The boss is jumping to the conclusion that his employee has low work motivation. This may be true, but because her work is competent, the boss should *consider other explanations* and *examine the evidence*. Perhaps the work conditions are unsatisfactory: There may be few opportunities for promotion; she may have been getting no feedback that lets her know she is doing well or that could help her improve; perhaps the company does not provide child care, so she is arriving late because she has child-care obligations. What other possible explanations come to mind?

- Does more money produce more happiness?
- What kind of conflict do you have when you want to study for a big exam but you also want to go out partying?
- Do you have to satisfy basic needs for security and belonging before you can become "self-actualized"?

Motives, Values, and Well-Being

In all the domains of human motivation that we have examined, a key conclusion emerges: People who are motivated by the intrinsic satisfaction of an activity are happier and more satisfied than those motivated solely by extrinsic rewards (Deci & Ryan, 1985; Kasser & Ryan, 2001). We saw, too, how intrinsic motivation in any domain will rise or fall depending on the goals we choose and the way we think of them. Goals, in turn, are determined by our values about what is important in life: freedom, religion, equality, wealth, fame, wisdom, serenity, salvation, sexual passion, the desire to improve the world, or anything else. Psychological research cannot tell us which values to choose, but it does help illuminate the consequences of our choices.

For example, many Americans are more motivated to make money than to find activities they enjoy. Psychotherapist Allen Kanner began noticing that the children he was treating, who 10 years earlier said they wanted to be astronauts, baseball players, ballerinas, and doctors when they grew up, now tell him they just want to be rich. They don't want to play with conventional toys but only with better, newer toys (Kanner & Kasser, 2003). Yet research finds repeatedly that having positive, intrinsically enjoyable *experiences* makes most people happier than having *things*: Doing is more satisfying than buying (Van Boven & Gilovich, 2003). Although people imagine that greater wealth will bring greater happiness, once they are at a level that provides basic comfort and security, more isn't necessarily better. They adjust quickly to the greater wealth and then think they need even more of it to be happier (Gilbert, 2006).

In addition, according to studies conducted in both America (an affluent nation) and Russia (a struggling nation), people who are primarily motivated to get rich have poorer psychological adjustment and lower well-being than do people whose primary values are self-acceptance, affiliation with others, or wanting to make the world a better place (Ryan et al., 1999). This is especially true when the reasons for striving for money are, again, extrinsic (e.g., you do it to impress others) rather than intrinsic (e.g., you do it so you can afford to do the volunteer work you love) (Carver & Baird, 1998; Srivastava, Locke, & Bartol, 2001).

Whichever values and goals you choose, if they are in conflict, the discrepancy can produce emotional stress and unhappiness. Two motives conflict when the satisfaction of one leads to the inability to act on the other—when, that is, you want to have your cake and eat it, too. Researchers have identified three kinds of motivational conflicts (Lewin, 1948):

1 **Approach-approach conflicts** occur when you are equally attracted to two or more possible activities or goals. For example, you would like to be a veterinarian *and* a rock singer; you would like to go out Tuesday night with friends *and* study like mad for an exam Wednesday.

THE FAR SIDE® By GARY LARSON
© 1985 FarWorks, Inc. All Rights Reserved/Dist. by Creators Syndicate
DAMNED if you do
DAMNED if you don't
"C'mon, c'mon–it's either one or the other."
The Far Side® by Gary Larson © 1985 FarWorks, Inc. All Rights Reserved. The Far Side® and the Larson® signature are registered trademarks of FarWorks, Inc. Used with permission.

A classic avoidance–avoidance conflict.

2 **Avoidance-avoidance conflicts** require you to choose between the lesser of two evils because you dislike both alternatives. Novice parachute jumpers, for example, must choose between the fear of jumping and the fear of losing face if they don't jump.

3 **Approach-avoidance conflicts** occur when a single activity or goal has both a positive and a negative aspect. For example, you want to be a powerful executive but you worry about losing your friends if you succeed. In culturally diverse nations, differing cultural values produce many approach–avoidance conflicts, as our students have revealed. A Chicano student said he wants to become a lawyer, but his parents, valuing family closeness, worry that if he goes to graduate school, he will become independent and feel superior to his working-class family. A black student from a poor neighborhood, in college on scholarship, is torn between wanting to leave his background behind him forever and returning to help his home community. And a white student wants to be a marine biologist, but her friends tell her that only nerdy guys and dweebs go into science.

Conflicts like these are inevitable, part of the price and pleasure of living. But if conflicts remain unresolved, they can take an emotional toll. In students, high levels of conflict and ambivalence about goals and values are associated with anxiety, depression, headaches and other symptoms, and more visits to the health center (Emmons & King, 1988). In contrast, students who strive for goals that are consistent with the qualities they value are healthier and have a greater sense of meaning and purpose in life than do those who are pursuing goals discrepant with their core values (Sheldon & Houser-Marko, 2001).

Are some psychological goals more important to our well-being than others? The humanist psychologist Abraham Maslow (1970) thought so. Maslow envisioned people's motives as forming a pyramid, a *hierarchy of needs*. At the bottom level of the pyramid were basic survival needs for food, sleep, and water; at the next level were security needs, for shelter and safety; at the third level were social needs, for belonging and

affection; at the fourth level were esteem needs, for self-respect and the respect of others; and at the top were needs for self-actualization and self-transcendence. Maslow argued that your needs must be met at each level before you can even think of the matters posed by the level above it. You can't worry about achievement if you are hungry, cold, and poor. You can't become self-actualized if you haven't satisfied your needs for self-esteem and love. Human beings behave badly, he argued, only when their lower needs are frustrated.

This theory, which seemed so logical and optimistic about human progress, became immensely popular. Motivational speakers still often refer to it, using colorful pictures of Maslow's pyramid. But the theory, which was based mostly on Maslow's observations and intuitions, has had little empirical support (Sheldon et al., 2001; Smither, 1998). On the contrary, people may have *simultaneous* needs for comfort and safety and also for attachments, self-esteem, and competence. And individuals who have met their lower needs do not inevitably seek higher ones, nor is it the case that people behave badly only when their lower needs are frustrated. Higher needs may even supersede lower ones. History is full of examples of people who would rather die of torture or starvation than sacrifice their convictions, or who would rather explore, risk, or create new art than be safe and secure at home.

A different way of thinking about universal psychological needs has been developed by researchers who studied large samples of students in the United States and South Korea (Sheldon et al., 2001). Although students are not actually typical of all human beings, and two cultures do not represent all cultures on the planet, the findings are provocative and support many of the points of this chapter. The top four psychological needs turned out to be *autonomy* (feeling that you are making choices based on your "true interests and values"), *competence* (feeling able to master challenges), *relatedness* (feeling close to others who are important to you), and *self-esteem* (having self-respect). Other needs were of lesser importance, including pleasure, self-actualization (which was at the top of Maslow's list), popularity, and, at the bottom, once again . . . money and luxury.

QUICK quiz

Do you wish to approach or avoid this quiz?

1. A Pakistani student says she desperately wants an education and a career as a pharmacist, but she also does not want to be disobedient to her parents, who have arranged a marriage for her back home. Which kind of conflict does she have?
2. Maslow's popular hierarchy of needs has several flaws. What are they?
3. Letitia just got her law degree. She wants to work in environmental law, but a corporate firm specializing in real-estate contracts has offered her a job and an enormous salary that seem too good to refuse. Why should she think carefully and critically in making a decision?

Answers:

1. approach–avoidance **2.** It was not based on extensive empirical research; it has not been well supported by research; the needs he proposed can be simultaneous rather than hierarchical; higher needs often supersede lower ones. **3.** She should think critically because taking a job primarily for its extrinsic benefits might suppress her intrinsic satisfaction in the work. Also, people motivated solely to acquire money often have poorer psychological adjustment and lower well-being than people who are motivated by work they enjoy. And although while money provides material benefits, psychological needs such as autonomy, competence, self-esteem, and connection to others are also important.

In this chapter, we have seen that psychological well-being depends on finding activities and choosing goals that are intrinsically satisfying; on being able to resolve conflicts between competing goals; and on feeling that we have the freedom to choose which goals we want to pursue. The motives and goals that inspire us, and the choices we make in their pursuit, are what give our lives passion, color, and meaning.

In a commencement address some years ago, Mario Cuomo, the former governor of New York, had these words of wisdom for the graduating students: "When you've parked the second car in the garage, and installed the hot tub, and skied in Colorado, and wind-surfed in the Caribbean, when you've had your first love affair and your second and your third, the question will remain: Where does the dream end for me?"

Taking Psychology with You

Get Motivated!

At the end of the first chapter of this book, we discussed not only what psychology can do for you but also what it cannot. As we hope this chapter has shown, psychology can teach us a great deal about the many motives of human life: about the dilemmas we create for ourselves about eating and weight, the meanings of love, the mysteries of sex, and the conditions that enhance or suppress the pursuit of achievement. Psychology cannot tell us which motives, goals, and values to choose in the first place: beauty, love, wealth, security, passion, freedom, fame, the desire to improve the world, or anything else. However, it can tell us how to achieve the goals that are important to us and how to ensure that those goals are intrinsically satisfying.

Think for a moment about your own values and goals, for now and for the future. Would you like to improve your love life? Enjoy school more? Lose weight? Become a better tennis player? Let's apply some of the lessons of motivational research to your own life.

- **Seek activities that are intrinsically pleasurable, even if they don't pay off.** If you really, really want to study Swahili or Swedish even though these languages are not in your prelaw requirements, try to find a way to do it. If you are not enjoying your major or your job, consider finding a career that would be more intrinsically pleasurable, or at least make sure you have other projects and activities that you do enjoy for their own sake.
- **Focus on learning goals, not only on performance goals.** In general, you will be better able to cope with setbacks if your goal is to learn rather than to show how good you are. Regard failure as a chance to learn rather than as a sign of incompetence.
- **Assess your working conditions.** Everyone has working conditions. Whether you are a student, a self-employed writer, or a homemaker, if your motivation and well-being are starting to wilt, check out your environment. Are you getting support from others? Do you have opportunities to develop ideas and vary your routine, or are you expected to do the same thing day after day? Are there barriers that might limit your advancement in your chosen field?
- **Take steps to resolve motivational conflicts.** Are you torn between competing goals? For instance, are you unhappily stuck between the goal of achieving independence and a desire to be cared for by your parents? The reconciliation of conflicts like these is important for your well-being (Emmons & King, 1988).

Most important, think critically about the goals you have chosen for yourself: Are they what you want to do or what someone else wants you to do? Do they reflect your values? If you are not happy with your body, your relationships, or your work, why not? Think about it.

Summary

- *Motivation* refers to an inferred process within a person or animal that causes that organism to move toward a goal—to satisfy a biological need or achieve a psychological ambition—or away from an unpleasant situation. A few primary drives are based on physiological needs, but all human motives are affected by psychological, social, and cultural factors. Motivation may be *intrinsic*, for the inherent pleasure of an activity, or *extrinsic*, for external rewards.

The Hungry Animal: Motives to Eat

- Overweight and obesity are not simply a result of failed willpower, emotional disturbance, or overeating. Hunger, weight, and eating are regulated by a set of bodily mechanisms, such as *basal metabolism rate* and number of fat cells, that keep people close to their genetically influenced *set point*. Genes influence body shape, distribution of fat, and whether the body will convert excess calories into fat. Genes may also account for certain types of obesity; for example, the *ob* gene regulates *leptin*, which enables the hypothalamus to regulate appetite and metabolism.
- Genetics alone cannot explain why rates of overweight and obesity are rising all over the world among all social classes, ethnicities, and ages. The reasons reflect the interaction of an evolved genetic disposition to gain weight when rich food is plentiful and an environment that provides cheap, varied, high-calorie food and rewards sedentary lifestyles. Eating habits and activity levels are also affected by cultural standards of what the ideal body should look like—heavy or thin, soft or muscular.
- When genetic predispositions clash with culture, physical and mental problems can result. In cultures that foster overeating and regard overweight as a sign of attractiveness and health, obesity is acceptable, but obesity increases the risk of various physical problems. In cultures that foster unrealistically thin bodies, eating disorders increase, especially *bulimia* and *anorexia*. These disorders are far more common in women than in men, but as pressures on men to have muscular bodies have increased, rates of body-image problems and eating disorders among men are increasing too.

The Social Animal: Motives to Love

- All human beings have a need for connection, attachment, and love. Psychologists who study love distinguish *passionate ("romantic") love* from *companionate love*. Biologically oriented researchers believe that the neurological origins of passionate love begin in the baby's attachment to the mother. Attachment stimulates the release of various brain chemicals, including the hormone *oxytocin*, associated with bonding and trust, and endorphins, which create rushes of pleasure and reward.
- Two strong predictors of whom people will love are *proximity* and *similarity*. Once in love, people form different kinds of attachments. *Attachment theory* views adult love relationships, like those of infants, as being secure, avoidant, or anxious. People's attachment styles tend to be stable from childhood to adulthood and affect their close relationships.
- For most people, love consists of passion, intimacy, and commitment. Men and women are equally likely to feel love and need attachment, but they differ, on average, in how they express feelings of love and how they define intimacy. In Western societies, women often express love in words, whereas men express it in actions. But as women have entered the workforce in large numbers and pragmatic (extrinsic) reasons for marriage have faded, the two sexes have become more alike in endorsing romantic love as a requirement for marriage.

The Erotic Animal: Motives for Sex

- Biological research finds that testosterone influences sexual desire in both sexes, although hormones do not cause sexual behavior in a simple, direct way. The Kinsey surveys of male and female sexuality and the laboratory research of Masters and Johnson showed that physiologically, there is no right kind of orgasm for women to have, and that both sexes are capable of sexual arousal and response.
- Some researchers believe that men have a higher frequency of many sexual behaviors, on average, because they have a stronger sex drive than women do. Others believe that gender differences in sexual motivation and behavior are a result of differences in roles, cultural norms, and opportunity. A compromise view is that male sexuality is more biologically influenced than is women's, whereas female sexuality is more governed by circumstances, relationships, and cultural norms.
- Men and women have sex to satisfy many different psychological motives, including pleasure, intimacy, coping, self-affirmation, the partner's approval, or peer approval. Extrinsic motives for sex, such as the need for approval, are associated with riskier sexual behavior than intrinsic motives are. Both sexes may agree to intercourse for

nonsexual motives: Men sometimes feel obligated to make a move to prove their masculinity, and women sometimes feel obliged to give in to preserve the relationship. People's motives for consenting to unwanted sex vary, depending on their feelings of security and commitment in the relationship.

- A major gender difference in sexual experience has to do with rape and perceptions of sexual coercion: What many women regard as coercion is not always seen as such by men. Men who rape do so for diverse reasons, including peer pressure; anger, revenge, or a desire to humiliate the victim; narcissism and hostility toward women; and sometimes sadism.
- Cultures differ widely in determining what parts of the body people learn are erotic, which sexual acts are considered erotic or repulsive, and whether sex itself is good or bad. Cultures transmit these ideas through *gender roles* and *sexual scripts*, which specify appropriate behavior during courtship and sex, depending on a person's gender, age, and sexual orientation.
- As in the case of love, gender differences (and growing similarities) in sexuality are strongly affected by cultural and economic factors, such as the ratio of women to men and the resulting availability of partners. As gender roles have become more alike, so has the sexual behavior of men and women, with women wanting sex for pleasure rather than as a bargaining chip. Big cities have many different "sex markets," geographical and cultural areas in which people seek partners, and people tend not to cross them.
- As discussed in "Biology and Sexual Orientation," traditional psychological explanations for homosexuality have not been supported. Genetic and hormonal factors seem to be involved, although the evidence is stronger for gay men than for lesbians. The more older biological brothers a man has, the greater his likelihood of becoming homosexual, suggesting that prenatal events might be involved. In spite of the evidence of a biological contribution to sexual orientation, there is great variation in the expression of homosexuality around the world; women's sexual orientation seems more fluid than men's. Research on this issue is sensitive because people's reactions to scientific findings on the origins of homosexuality are affected by their emotional and religious feelings about the topic.

The Competent Animal: Motives to Achieve

- The study of achievement motivation began with research using the *Thematic Apperception Test (TAT)*. People who are motivated by a high *need for achievement* set high but realistic standards for success and excellence. The TAT has empirical problems, but it launched the study of the factors that motivate achievement.
- People achieve more when they have specific, focused goals; when they set high but achievable goals for themselves; and when they have *approach goals* (seeking a positive outcome) rather than *avoidance goals* (avoiding an unpleasant outcome). People who focus on approach goals have greater well-being, better health, and even better intimate and sexual relationships than those who focus on avoidance goals.
- As discussed in "Close-up on Research," the motivation to achieve depends not only on ability, but also on whether people set *mastery (learning) goals*, in which the focus is on learning the task well, or *performance goals*, in which the focus is on performing well for others. Mastery goals lead to persistence in the face of failures and setbacks; performance goals often lead to giving up after failure. High achievers find a balance between striving for mastery and maximum performance. People's expectations can create *self-fulfilling prophecies* of success or failure. These expectations stem from one's level of *self-efficacy*.
- Work motivation also depends on circumstances of the job itself. Working conditions that promote motivation and satisfaction are those that provide workers with a sense of meaningfulness, control, variation in tasks, clear rules, feedback, and social support. *Incentive pay* is more effective than predictable raises in elevating work motivation. Other conditions that affect people's work motivation are the gender ratio of members in an occupation and whether the job provides opportunities for promotion and success.

Motives, Values, and Well-Being

- Satisfaction and well-being increase when people enjoy the intrinsic satisfaction of an activity and when their goals and values are in harmony. Having positive, intrinsically enjoyable experiences makes most people happier than having things. In an *approach–approach conflict*, a person is equally attracted to two goals. In an *avoidance–avoidance conflict*, a person is equally repelled by two goals. An *approach–avoidance conflict* is the most difficult to resolve because the person is both attracted to and repelled by the same goal. Prolonged conflict can lead to physical symptoms and reduced well-being.
- Abraham Maslow believed that human motives could be ranked in a *hierarchy of needs*, from basic biological needs for survival to higher psychological needs for self-actualization. This popular theory has not been well supported empirically. A more recent approach suggests that people have four major psychological needs, for autonomy, relatedness, competence, and self-esteem.

KEY TERMS

- motivation 440
- drives 440
- intrinsic motivation 440
- extrinsic motivation 440
- set point 441
- basal metabolism rate 441
- leptin 442
- *ob* gene 442
- bulimia 446
- anorexia 446
- passionate and companionate love 448
- oxytocin 448
- endorphins 448
- proximity and similarity effects 449
- attachment theory of love 449
- gender roles 458
- sexual scripts 458
- industrial/organizational psychology 465
- need for achievement 465
- Thematic Apperception Test (TAT) 465
- approach and avoidance goals 467
- performance goals 468
- mastery (learning) goals 468
- self-fulfilling prophecy 469
- self-efficacy 470
- incentive pay 471
- approach and avoidance conflicts 473
- Maslow's hierarchy of needs 474

How Motivated Are You?

NOW YOU HAVE READ CHAPTER TWELVE — ARE YOU PREPARED FOR THE EXAM?

High achievers need feedback from others. True or False?

What are three types of needs?
(pages 465–470)

true

Sex refers to physical diffferences and gender refers to psychological and social differences. True or False?

What is gender
(pages 451–452)

true

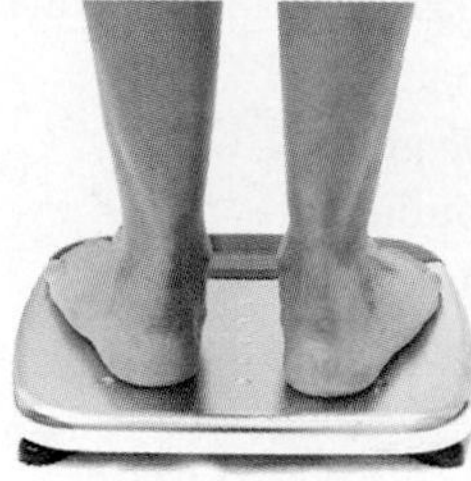

Samantha has weighed about 125 lbs most of her adult life. However, it seems like whenever Samantha gains weight it is easy to lose and get back to 125. But, when she wants to go below 125, it takes forever and even the slightest deviation from her diet gets her back to 125. Samantha's weight of 125 pounds is likely her _____, and she should stop trying to go below 125 pounds.

What happens in the body to cause hunger?
(pages 440–441)

set point

What incentive do you need to excel?
To help you prepare and excel, take the practice tests on **www.mypsychlab.com** and try out the activities, simulations and e-book exercises.

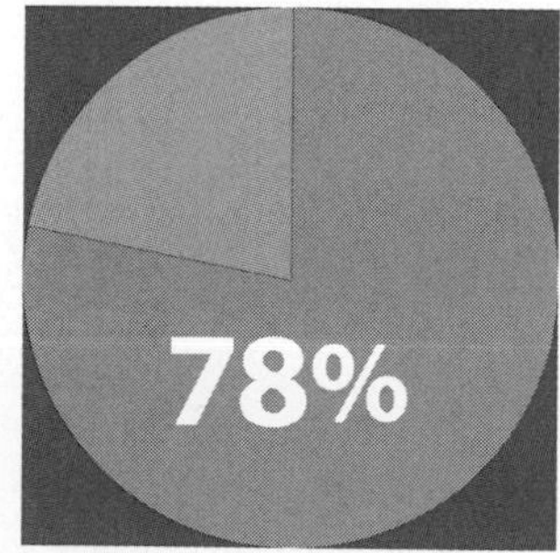

Seventy-eight percent of Montclair State University's Introduction to Psychology students surveyed replied that they would recommend MyPsychLab to other students.

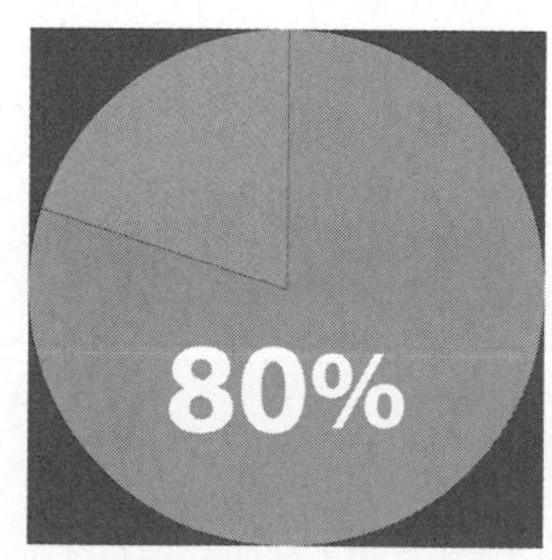

Eighty percent of Patrick Henry Community College's Introduction to Psychology students surveyed who took the course on-site replied that they found the MyPsychLab Apply It exercises useful.

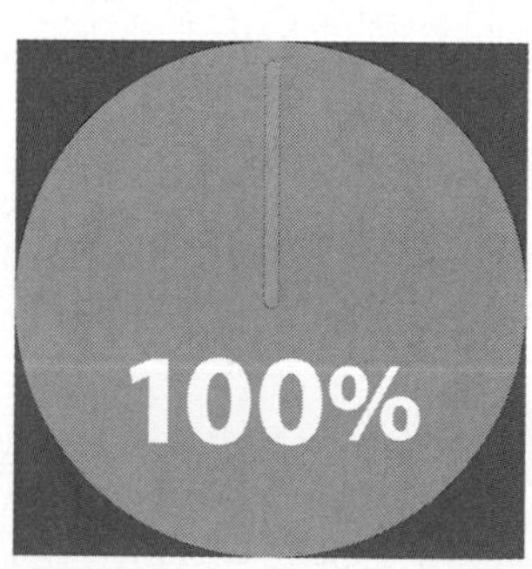

One hundred percent of Oklahoma City University's Introduction to Psychology students surveyed replied that MyPsychLab was effective in helping them understand the textbook, prepare for tests, and learn more about psychology.

APPLY IT

Masters and Johnson identified four stages of the human sexual response cycle. Although the stages are similar in men and women, there are some differences. Examine these two figures from your text.

Figure 1:

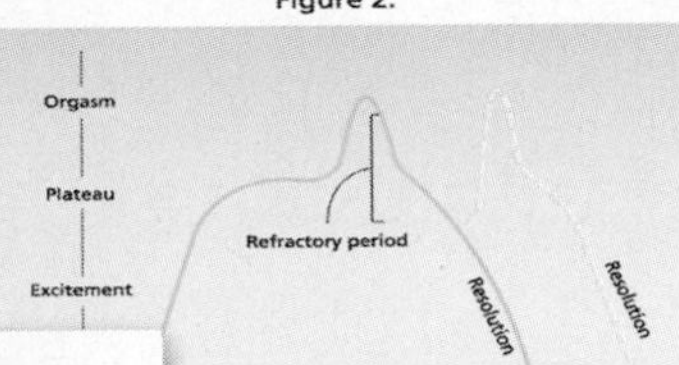

Figure 2:

Orgasm
Plateau
Excitement
Refractory period
Resolution
Resolution

ponse cycle and Figure 2 depicts the female

E-BOOK

Look at the following photograph from your text of Alfred Kinsey conducting an interview.

Kinsey gathered much of his data on human sexual behavior using personal interviews.

Answer the following question:

Kinsey's use of personal interviews ensured the validity of his findings.

True or False?
◯ True ◯ False

This chapter introduces important studies on human sexuality conducted to date. Use the resources in MyPsychLab to help you better understand these studies.

THEORIES OF PERSONALITY

CHAPTER THIRTEEN

People often say that this or that person has not yet found himself. But the self is not something that one finds. It is something that one creates.

THOMAS SZASZ

CHAPTER

OUTLINE

She was the eldest daughter of eight children in an Italian immigrant family. Only 6 years old when her mother died, she became the dutiful caretaker of her siblings. She faithfully attended Catholic school and, throughout childhood, was deeply religious. But her earliest passion was to dance, and when her reluctant father finally allowed her to take lessons, her instructors immediately recognized and encouraged her talent. As a young woman, driven to succeed, she dropped out of college and made her way to New York with a one-way ticket and $35 in her purse. She found part-time work, met some musicians, connected with some influential DJs . . . and became the superstar the world knows as Madonna.

Today, Madonna works tirelessly and demands total control over her shows: writing the songs, producing the music, choreographing her dances, creating her costumes, doing her own makeup. Her friends and associates have observed that she also obsessively controls her films, public appearances, and even her private life in the service of her public image. And that image is a continual work in progress. As reporter Jock McGregor (1997) observed, "She is always changing her image, whether it is from the good girl gone bad to the virgin in white; from Marilyn Monroe to the 1920s gangster moll; from androgynous, cold robot to naked sex symbol; from glamour queen to cosmic spirit and finally to doting mother." In 2004, on her "Re-invention World Tour," the Material Girl changed her name from the Christian Madonna to the Jewish Esther and began incorporating signs and symbols of the Kabbalah, a mystical wing of Judaism. In 2006, in her "Confessions" tour, Madonna said her goal would be to "turn the world into one big dance floor." The show would be "all out disco, with lots of disco balls." Esther was soooo 2004, part of the "older stuff I did on my Re-Invention tour." The "older stuff" she referred to was two years old.

Who is Madonna: the flamboyant performer who loves to shock or the "doting mother"? Was she born to be an exhibitionist, or did she create a persona to make herself famous? Which personality traits best describe her: extroverted, ambitious, outrageous, motherly, obsessive, funny, selfish, rebellious? Who is the "real" Madonna amid the changing public images? *Is* there a real one?

personality A distinctive and relatively stable pattern of behavior, thoughts, motives, and emotions that characterizes an individual.

trait A characteristic of an individual, describing a habitual way of behaving, thinking, or feeling.

psychoanalysis A theory of personality and a method of psychotherapy developed by Sigmund Freud; it emphasizes unconscious motives and conflicts.

psychodynamic theories Theories that explain behavior and personality in terms of unconscious energy dynamics within the individual.

In this chapter, we will see how psychologists answer such questions—how they define and study personality. **Personality** refers to a distinctive pattern of behavior, mannerisms, thoughts, motives, and emotions that characterizes an individual over time and across different situations. This pattern consists of many distinctive **traits**, habitual ways of behaving, thinking, and feeling: shy, outgoing, friendly, hostile, gloomy, confident, and so on.

For much of the twentieth century, Freudian psychoanalytic theory was the dominant approach to explaining personality differences. Its sweeping view held that a person's conflicts, guilts, defenses, and ways of dealing with others could be traced to unconscious dynamics originating in early childhood. By the end of the twentieth century, however, biological research was offering an entirely different view of personality: that about half of the variation in personality traits—the reason that Shawn is shy and Finella is outgoing—is due to genetic variations and has nothing to do with unconscious motives or how your parents treated you.

In this chapter, we will begin with the oldest theory of personality, the psychodynamic view, so that you will have a sense of how influential it was, why it still appeals to some, and why many of its ideas have become outdated. Next we will consider evidence for the newest theory, the genetic view. Few scientists think anymore that babies are tiny lumps of clay, shaped entirely by their experiences, or that parents alone determine whether their infant becomes an adventurer, a sourpuss, a worrywart, . . . or an extrovert like Madonna. On the other hand, if only half of the human variation in personality traits is due to genetics, what is responsible for the other half?

To answer that question, we will then examine three leading approaches to personality that are neither psychodynamic nor biological: the environmental view, which emphasizes the role of social learning, situations, parents, and peers; the cultural view, which emphasizes cultural influences on traits and behavior; and the humanist view, which emphasizes self-determination and free will.

WHAT'S**AHEAD**

- In Freud's theory of personality, why are the id and the superego always at war?
- When people say you're being "defensive," what defenses might they be thinking of?
- How do psychologists regard Freud today—as a genius or a fraud?
- What would Carl Jung have had to say about Harry Potter's arch-enemy, Lord Valdemort?
- What are the "objects" in the object-relations approach to personality?

Psychodynamic Theories of Personality

Sigmund Freud (1856–1939).

A man apologizes for "displacing" his frustrations at work onto his family. A woman suspects that she is "repressing" a childhood trauma. An alcoholic reveals that he is no longer "in denial" about his drinking. A teacher informs a divorcing couple that their 8-year-old child is "regressing" to immature behavior. All of this language—about displacing, repressing, denying, and regressing—can be traced to the first psychodynamic theory of personality, Sigmund Freud's theory of **psychoanalysis**.

Freud's theory is called **psychodynamic** because it emphasizes the movement of psychological energy within the person, in the form of attachments, conflicts, and motivations. Today's psychodynamic theories differ from Freudian theory and from one another, but they all share an emphasis on unconscious processes going on within the mind. They also share an assumption that adult personality and ongoing problems

are formed primarily by experiences in early childhood. These experiences produce unconscious thoughts and feelings, which later form characteristic habits, conflicts, and often self-defeating behavior.

No one disputes the profound influence that Sigmund Freud had on the twentieth century, but there is enormous dispute about the lasting value of his work. Freud saw himself as one of the great geniuses of history, and many people agree with that assessment. But many contemporary scientists think he was a flat-out fraud whose ideas have not stood the test of time; one Nobel Prize–winning scientist called his work a "dinosaur in the history of ideas" (Medawar, 1982). In this section, we will introduce you to Freud's ideas and to two modern psychodynamic approaches. We will try to show you why attitudes toward Freud today range from reverence to contempt, and why he evokes such controversy.

Freud and Psychoanalysis

To enter the world of Sigmund Freud is to enter a realm of unconscious motives, passions, guilty secrets, unspeakable yearnings, and conflicts between desire and duty. These unseen forces, Freud believed, have far more power over our personalities than our conscious intentions do. The unconscious reveals itself, said Freud, in art, dreams, jokes, apparent accidents, and slips of the tongue (which came to be called "Freudian slips"). According to Freud (1920/1960), the British member of Parliament who referred to the "honourable member from Hell" when he meant to say "from Hull" was revealing his actual, unconscious appraisal of his colleague.

"VERY WELL, I'LL INTRODUCE YOU. EGO, MEET ID. NOW GET BACK TO WORK."

The Structure of Personality. In Freud's theory, personality consists of three major systems: the id, the ego, and the superego. Any action we take or problem we have results from the interaction and degree of balance among these systems (Freud, 1905, 1920/1960, 1923/1962).

The **id**, which is present at birth, is the reservoir of unconscious psychological energies and the motives to avoid pain and obtain pleasure. The id contains two competing instincts: the life, or sexual, instinct (fueled by psychic energy called the **libido**) and the death, or aggressive, instinct. As energy builds up in the id, tension results. The id may discharge this tension in the form of reflex actions, physical symptoms, or uncensored mental images and unbidden thoughts.

The **ego**, the second system to emerge, is a referee between the needs of instinct and the demands of society. It bows to the realities of life, putting a rein on the id's desire for sex and aggression until a suitable, socially appropriate outlet for them can be found. The ego, said Freud, is both conscious and unconscious, and it represents "reason and good sense."

The **superego**, the last system of personality to develop, represents morality and parental authority; it includes the conscience, the inner voice that says you did something wrong. The superego, which is partly conscious but largely unconscious, judges the activities of the id, handing out good feelings of pride and satisfaction when you do something well and handing out miserable feelings of guilt and shame when you break the rules.

According to Freud, the healthy personality must keep all three systems in balance. Someone who is too controlled by the id is governed by impulse and selfish desires. Someone who is too controlled by the superego is rigid, moralistic, and bossy. Someone who has a weak ego is unable to balance personal needs and wishes with social duties and realistic limitations.

If a person feels anxious or threatened when the wishes of the id conflict with social rules, the ego has weapons at its command to relieve the tension. These unconscious strategies, called **defense mechanisms**, deny or distort reality, but

id In psychoanalysis, the part of personality containing inherited psychic energy, particularly sexual and aggressive instincts.

libido (li-BEE-do) In psychoanalysis, the psychic energy that fuels the life or sexual instincts of the id.

ego In psychoanalysis, the part of personality that represents reason, good sense, and rational self-control.

superego In psychoanalysis, the part of personality that represents conscience, morality, and social standards.

defense mechanisms Methods used by the ego to prevent unconscious anxiety or threatening thoughts from entering consciousness.

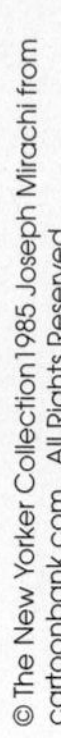

"I'm sorry, I'm not speaking to anyone tonight. My defense mechanisms seem to be out of order."

they also protect us from conflict and anxiety. They become unhealthy only when they cause self-defeating behavior and emotional problems. Here are some of the primary defenses identified by Freud and later analysts (A. Freud, 1967; Vaillant, 1992):

1 **Repression** occurs when a threatening idea, memory, or emotion is blocked from consciousness. A woman who had a frightening childhood experience that she cannot remember, for example, is said to be repressing her memory of it. Freud used the term *repression* to mean both unconscious expulsion of disturbing material from awareness and conscious suppression of such material (McNally, 2003). But modern analysts tend to think of it only as an unconscious defense mechanism.

2 **Projection** occurs when a person's own unacceptable or threatening feelings are repressed and then attributed to someone else. A person who is embarrassed about having sexual feelings toward members of a different ethnic group, for example, may project this discomfort onto them, saying, "Those people are dirty-minded and oversexed."

3 **Displacement** occurs when people direct their emotions (especially anger) toward things, animals, or other people that are not the real object of their feelings. A boy who is forbidden to express anger toward his father, for example, may "take it out" on his toys or his younger sister. When displacement serves a higher cultural or socially useful purpose, as in the creation of art or inventions, it is called *sublimation*. Freud argued that society has a duty to help people sublimate their unacceptable impulses for the sake of civilization. Sexual passion, for example, may be sublimated into the creation of art or literature.

4 **Reaction formation** occurs when a feeling that produces unconscious anxiety is transformed into its opposite in consciousness. A woman who is afraid to admit to herself that she fears her husband may instead cling to the belief that she loves him deeply. A person who is aroused by erotic images may angrily assert that pornography is disgusting. How does such a transformed emotion differ from a true emotion? In reaction formation the professed feeling is excessive, and the person is extravagant and compulsive about demonstrating it, as when a woman says of an abusive husband: "Of course I love him! I *never* have any bad thoughts about him! He's perfect!"

5 **Regression** occurs when a person reverts to a previous phase of psychological development. An 8-year-old boy who is anxious about his parents' divorce may regress to earlier habits of thumb sucking or clinging. Adults may regress to immature behavior when they are under pressure—for example, by having temper tantrums when they don't get their way.

6 **Denial** occurs when people refuse to admit that something unpleasant is happening, such as mistreatment by a partner; that they have a problem, such as drinking too much; or that they are feeling a forbidden emotion, such as anger. Denial protects a person's self-image and preserves the illusion of invulnerability: "It can't happen to me."

A Freudian would say that this woman's smoking and nail-biting are signs of an oral fixation.

The Development of Personality. Freud argued that personality develops in a series of *psychosexual stages*, in which sexual energy takes different forms as the child matures. Each new stage produces a certain amount of frustration, conflict, and anxiety. If these are not resolved properly, normal development may be interrupted, and the child may remain *fixated*, or stuck, at the current stage.

For example, said Freud, some people remain fixated at the *oral stage*, which occurs during the first year of life, when babies experience the world through their mouths. As adults, they will seek oral gratification in smoking, overeating, nail biting, or chewing on pencils; some may become clinging and dependent, like a nursing child. Others remain fixated at the *anal stage*, at ages 2 to 3, when toilet training and control of bodily wastes are the key issues. They may become "anal retentive," holding everything in, obsessive about neatness and cleanliness. Or they may become just the opposite, "anal expulsive"—messy and disorganized.

For Freud, however, the most crucial stage for the formation of personality was the *phallic (Oedipal) stage*, which lasts roughly from age 3 to age 5 or 6. During this stage, said Freud, the child unconsciously wishes to possess the parent of the other sex and to get rid of the parent of the same sex. Children often announce proudly that "I'm going to marry Daddy (or Mommy) when I grow up," and they reject the same-sex "rival." Freud labeled this phenomenon the **Oedipus complex**, after the Greek legend of King Oedipus, who unwittingly killed his father and married his mother.

Boys and girls, Freud believed, go through the Oedipal stage differently. Boys are discovering the pleasure and pride of having a penis, so when they see a naked girl for the first time, they are horrified. Their unconscious exclaims (in effect), "Her penis has been cut off! Who could have done such a thing to her? Why, it must have been her powerful father. And if he could do it to her, my father could do it to me!" This realization, said Freud, causes the boy to repress his desire for his mother and identify with his father. He accepts his father's authority and the father's standards of conscience and morality; the superego has emerged.

Freud admitted that he did not quite know what to make of girls, who, lacking the penis, could not go through the same steps. He speculated that a girl, upon discovering male anatomy, would panic that she had only a puny clitoris instead of a stately penis. She would conclude that she already had lost her penis. As a result, Freud said, girls do not have the powerful motivating fear that boys do to give up their Oedipal feelings and develop a strong superego; they have only a lingering sense of "penis envy."

Freud believed that when the Oedipus complex is resolved, at about age 5 or 6, the child's personality is fundamentally formed. Unconscious conflicts with parents, unresolved fixations and guilts, and attitudes toward the same and the other sex will continue to replay themselves throughout life. The child settles into a supposedly nonsexual *latency* stage, in preparation for the *genital stage*, which begins at puberty and leads to adult sexuality.

In Freud's view, then, your adult personality is shaped by how you progressed through the early psychosexual stages, which defense mechanisms you developed to reduce anxiety, and whether your ego is strong enough to balance the conflict between the id (what you would like to do) and the superego (your conscience).

Oedipus complex In psychoanalysis, a conflict occurring in the phallic (Oedipal) stage, in which a child desires the parent of the other sex and views the same-sex parent as a rival.

As you might imagine, Freud's ideas were not exactly received with yawns. Sexual feelings in 5-year-olds! Repressed longings in respectable adults! Unconscious meanings in dreams! Penis envy! This was strong stuff in the early years of the twentieth century, and before long psychoanalysis had captured the public imagination in Europe and America. But it also produced a sharp rift with the emerging schools of empirical psychology.

This rift continues to divide scholars today. Many believe that the overall framework of Freud's theory is timeless and brilliant, even if some specific ideas have proved faulty (Westen, 1998). Others think that psychoanalytic theory is nonsense, with little empirical support, and that Freud was not the brilliant theoretician, impartial scientist, or even successful clinician that he claimed to be. On the contrary, Freud often bullied his patients into accepting his explanations of their symptoms and ignored all evidence disconfirming his ideas (McNally, 2003; Powell & Boer, 1995; Sulloway, 1992; Webster, 1995). In one famous case, he pressured an 18-year-old patient, "Dora" (Ida Bauer), to accept the unwanted sexual advances of one of her father's friends, attributing her "hysterical" refusal to her own supposedly repressed sexual desires. Dora angrily left treatment after three months (Lakoff & Coyne, 1993).

On the positive side, Freud welcomed women into the profession of psychoanalysis, wrote eloquently about the devastating results to women of society's suppression of their sexuality, and argued, ahead of his time, that homosexuality was neither a sin nor a perversion but a "variation of the sexual function" and "nothing to be ashamed of" (Freud, 1961). Freud was thus a mixture of intellectual vision and blindness, sensitivity and arrogance. His provocative ideas left a powerful legacy to psychology—one that others began to tinker with immediately.

QUICK quiz

Have Freudian concepts registered in your unconscious?

Which Freudian concepts do the following events suggest?

1. A 4-year-old girl wants to snuggle on Daddy's lap but refuses to kiss her mother.
2. A celibate priest writes poetry about sexual passion.
3. A man who is angry at his boss shouts at his kids for making noise.
4. A woman whose father was cruel to her when she was little insists over and over that she loves him dearly.
5. A racist justifies segregation by saying that black men are only interested in sex with white women.
6. A 9-year-old boy who moves to a new city starts having tantrums.

Answers:

1. Oedipus complex **2.** sublimation **3.** displacement **4.** reaction formation **5.** projection **6.** regression

Other Psychodynamic Approaches

Some of Freud's followers stayed in the psychoanalytic tradition and modified Freud's theories from within. Women, as you might imagine, were not too pleased about "penis envy." Clara Thompson (1943/1973) and Karen Horney [HORN-eye] (1926/1973) argued that it was insulting philosophy and bad science to claim that half the human race is dissatisfied with its anatomy. When women feel inferior to men, they said, we should look for explanations in the disadvantages that women live with and their second-class status. In fact, Horney added, if anyone has an envy problem, it is men. Men have "womb envy": They envy women's ability to bear children.

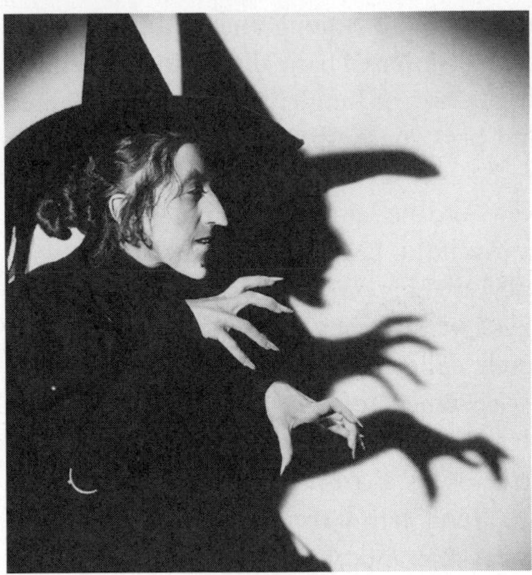

In *The Wizard of Oz*, the Wicked Witch of the West is a beloved example of the archetype of evil. *Star Wars'* Darth Vader turns out to be the dark shadow of his son Luke Skywalker.

Others broke away from Freud, or were actively rejected by him, and went off to start their own schools. Today, there are many psychodynamic approaches, but two are especially popular: those of Carl Jung and of the object-relations theorists.

Jungian Theory. Carl Jung (1875–1961) was originally one of Freud's closest friends and a member of his inner circle, but the friendship ended with a furious quarrel about the nature of the unconscious. In addition to the individual's own unconscious, said Jung (1967), all human beings share a vast **collective unconscious**, containing universal memories, symbols, images, and themes, which he called **archetypes**.

An archetype can be an image, such as the "magic circle," called a *mandala* in Eastern religions, which Jung thought symbolizes the unity of life and "the totality of the self." Or it can be a figure found in fairy tales, legends, and popular stories, such as the Hero, the nurturing Earth Mother, the Powerful Father, or the Wicked Witch. It can even be an aspect of the self. For example, the *shadow* archetype reflects the prehistoric fear of wild animals and represents the bestial, evil side of human nature. Scholars have found that some basic archetypes, such as the Hero and the Earth Mother, do appear in the stories and images of virtually every society (Campbell, 1949/1968; Neher, 1996). Jungians would consider Darth Vader, Dracula, the Dark Lord Sauron, and Harry Potter's tormentor Valdemort as expressions of the shadow archetype.

Two of the most important archetypes, in Jung's view, are those of maleness and femaleness. Jung (like Freud) recognized that "masculine" and "feminine" qualities exist in both sexes. The *anima* represents the feminine archetype in men; the *animus* represents the masculine archetype in women. Problems can arise, however, if a person tries to repress his or her internal, opposite archetype—that is, if a man denies his softer feminine side or if a woman denies her masculine side.

Although Jung shared with Freud a fascination with the darker aspects of the personality, he (along with other dissenters from Freudian orthodoxy) had confidence in the positive, forward-moving strengths of the ego. He believed that people are motivated not only by past conflicts but also by their future goals and their desire to fulfill

collective unconscious In Jungian theory, the universal memories and experiences of humankind, represented in the symbols, stories, and images (archetypes) that occur across all cultures.

archetypes [AR-ki-tipes] Universal, symbolic images that appear in myths, art, stories, and dreams; to Jungians, they reflect the collective unconscious.

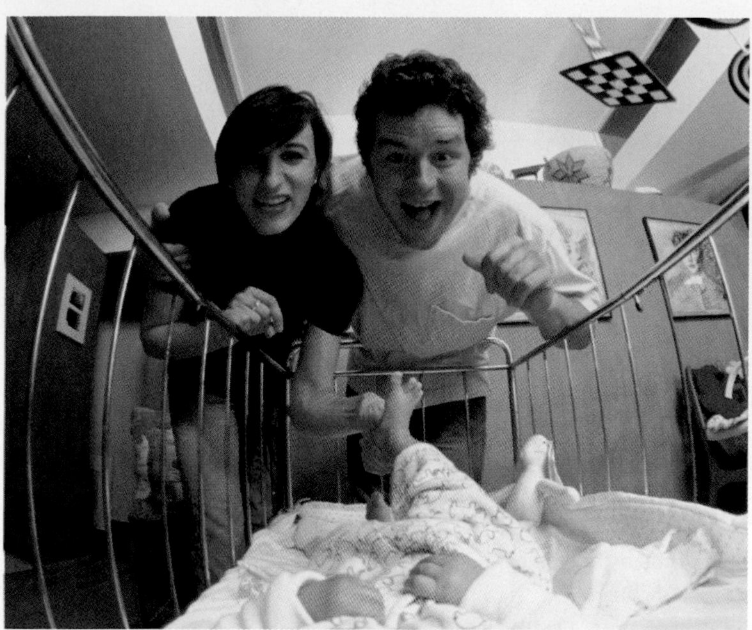

According to object-relations theory, a baby constructs unconscious representations of his or her parents that will influence the child's relations with others throughout life.

themselves. Jung was also among the first to identify extroversion/introversion as a basic dimension of personality. Nonetheless, many of Jung's ideas were more suited to mysticism and philosophy than to empirical psychology, which may be why so many Jungian ideas became popular with New Age movements.

Jung had a psychotic breakdown after his split with Freud. And he revealed his own "dark side" when he supported the Nazis, writing vicious attacks on Jews and claiming that their collective unconscious differed from that of gentiles (so much for its "universality"). But he continued to treat patients and attract many worshipful followers by virtue of his charisma (Hayman, 2001). Like Freud, therefore, Jung left a troubling personal legacy along with theories that appealed to legions of believers.

The Object-Relations School. Freud essentially regarded the baby as if it were an independent, greedy little organism ruled by its own instinctive desires; other people were relevant only insofar as they gratified the infant's drives or blocked them. But by the 1950s, increased awareness of the importance of human attachments led to a very different view of infancy, put forward by the **object-relations school**, developed in Great Britain by Melanie Klein, D. W. Winnicott, and others.

To object-relations theorists, the central problem in life is to find a balance between the need for independence and the need for others. This balance requires constant adjustment to separations and losses: small ones that occur during quarrels, moderate ones such as leaving home for the first time, and major ones such as divorce or death. The way we react to these separations, according to object-relations analysts, is largely determined by our experiences in the first year or two of life.

The reason for the clunky word "object" in object-relations, instead of the warmer words "human" or "parent," is that the infant's attachment is not only to a real person (usually the mother) but also to the infant's evolving perception of her. The child creates a *mental representation* of the mother—someone who is kind or fierce, protective or rejecting. The child's representations of important adults, whether realistic or distorted, unconsciously affect personality throughout life, influencing how the person relates to others—with trust or suspicion, acceptance or criticism. Object-relations theorists have applied this approach in many ways: for example, to predict whether a client will benefit from psychotherapy (Mallinckrodt, Porter, & Kivlighan, 2005), to help people deal with disability and other losses in life (Goldstein, 2002), and even to try to explain why some distrustful, cynical people harass others on the Internet (Whitty & Carr, 2006).

The object-relations school also departs from Freudian theory regarding the nature of male and female development (Sagan, 1988; Winnicott, 1957/1990). In the object-relations view, children of both sexes identify first with the mother. Girls, who are the same sex as the mother, do not need to separate from her; the mother treats a daughter as an extension of herself. But boys, to develop a masculine identity, must break away from the mother; the mother encourages a son to be independent and separate. Thus men, in this view, develop more rigid boundaries between themselves and other people than women do.

object-relations school A psychodynamic approach that emphasizes the importance of the infant's first two years of life and the baby's formative relationships, especially with the mother.

Evaluating Psychodynamic Theories

Although modern psychodynamic theorists differ in many ways, they share a general belief that to understand personality we must explore its unconscious dynamics and origins. Many psychologists in other fields, however, regard most psychodynamic ideas as literary metaphors rather than as scientific explanations (Cioffi, 1998; Crews, 1998). Critics argue that psychodynamic theories are guilty of three scientific failings:

THINKING CRITICALLY

ANALYZE ASSUMPTIONS

Freud and his followers assumed they could derive general principles of personality by studying patients in therapy, that childhood traumas inevitably have lifelong emotional consequences, and that memories are reliable guides to the past. What is wrong with these assumptions?

1 **Violating the principle of falsifiability.** As we saw in Chapter 2, a theory that is impossible to disconfirm in principle is not scientific. Many psychodynamic concepts about unconscious motivations are, in fact, impossible to confirm or disconfirm. Followers often accept an idea because it seems intuitively right or their experience seems to support it. Anyone who doubts the idea or offers disconfirming evidence is then accused of being "defensive" or "in denial." This way of dismissing criticism is neither scientific nor fair!

2 **Drawing universal principles from the experiences of a few atypical patients.** Freud and most of his followers generalized from a few individuals, often patients in therapy, to all human beings. Of course, the problem of overgeneralizing from small samples occurs in other areas of psychology too, and sometimes valid insights about human behavior can be obtained from case studies. The problem occurs when the observer fails to confirm these observations by studying other samples and incorrectly infers that what applies to a few individuals applies to all. For example, some psychodynamically oriented therapists, believing in Freud's notion of a childhood "latency" stage, have assumed that if a child masturbates or enjoys sex play, the child has probably been sexually molested. But masturbation and sexual curiosity are by no means typical only of abused children; these are normal and common behaviors among children in the general population (Friedrich et al., 1998; Lamb, 2002).

3 **Basing theories of personality development on retrospective accounts and the fallible memories of patients.** Most psychodynamic theorists have not observed random samples of children at different ages, as modern child psychologists do, to construct their theories of development. Instead they have worked backward, creating theories based on themes in adults' recollections of childhood. The analysis of memories can be an illuminating way to achieve insights about our lives; in fact, it is the only way we can think about our own lives! But, as we saw in Chapter 10, memory is often inaccurate, influenced as much by what is going on in our lives now as by what happened in the past. If you are currently not getting along with your mother, you may remember all the times when she was hard on you and forget the counterexamples of her kindness.

THINKING CRITICALLY

EXAMINE THE EVIDENCE

Freud claimed, without much evidence, that all little girls suffer from "penis envy." But studies of preschool girls and boys find that young children of *both* sexes are curious about, and often imagine having, the reproductive abilities of the other sex (Linday, 1994).

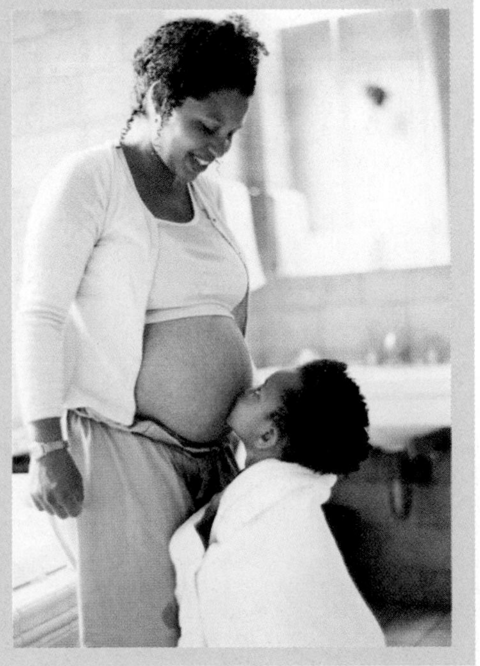

Retrospective analysis has another problem: It creates an *illusion of causality* between events. People often assume that if A came before B, then A must have caused B. For example, if your mother spent three months in the hospital when you were 5 years old and today you feel shy and insecure in college, an object-relations analyst would probably draw a connection between the two facts. But a lot of other things could be causing your shyness and insecurity, such as being away from home for the first time, at a large and impersonal college. When psychologists conduct longitudinal studies, following people from childhood to adulthood, they often get a very different picture of causality from the one that emerges by looking backward (see Chapter 14).

In recent years, some psychologists have been testing psychodynamic ideas empirically. They have identified nonconscious processes in thought, memory, and behavior; and they have found evidence for some of the major defense mechanisms, such as reaction formation, projection, denial, and displacement (Baumeister, Dale, & Sommer, 1998; Cramer, 2000; Marcus-Newhall et al., 2000). More generally, research confirms the psychodynamic idea that we are often unaware of the motives behind our own puzzling or self-defeating actions. However, the modern, empirical study of personality has taken quite a different turn from the all-embracing observations and intuitions of Freud and his descendants, as we are about to see.

QUICK quiz

Are you feeling defensive about answering this quiz?

1. An 8-year-old boy is behaving aggressively, hitting classmates and disobeying his teacher. Which of the following explanations of his behavior might come from a Freudian, Jungian, or object-relations analyst?
   a. The boy is expressing his *shadow* archetype.
   b. The boy is expressing the aggressive energy of the id and has not developed enough ego control.
   c. The boy has had unusual difficulty separating from his mother and is compensating by behaving aggressively.

2. What criticism of all three of the preceding explanations might be made by a psychological scientist?

3. In the 1950s and 1960s, many psychoanalysts, observing unhappy gay men who had sought therapy, concluded that homosexuality was a mental illness. What violation of the scientific method were they committing?

Answers:

1. a. Jung b. Freud c. object-relations analyst **2.** All three explanations are nonfalsifiable; that is, there is no way to disconfirm them or confirm them. They are just subjective interpretations. **3.** The analysts were drawing inappropriate conclusions from patients in therapy, failing to test these conclusions with gay men who were not in therapy or with heterosexuals. When such research was done, using appropriate control groups, it turned out that gay men were not more mentally disturbed or depressed than heterosexuals (Hooker, 1957).

WHAT'S AHEAD

- How reliable are those tests that tell you what "personality type" you are?
- How can psychologists tell which personality traits are more central or important than others?
- Which five dimensions of personality seem to describe people the world over?

The Modern Study of Personality

People love to fit themselves and their friends into "types." They have been doing it forever. Early Greek philosophers thought our personalities fell into four fundamental categories depending on mixes of body fluids. For example, if you were an angry, irritable sort of person, you supposedly had an excess of choler, and even now the word *choleric* describes a hothead. And if you were slow-moving and unemotional, you supposedly had an excess of phlegm, making you a "phlegmatic" type.

Popular Personality Tests

That particular theory is long gone, but other unscientific tests of personality types still exist, aimed at predicting how people will do at work, whether they will get along with others, or whether they will succeed as leaders. One such test, the Myers-Briggs Type Indicator, is hugely popular in business, at motivational seminars, and with matchmaking services; at least 2.5 million Americans a year take it (Gladwell, 2004). The test assigns people to one of 16 different types, depending on how the individual combines various tendencies, such as being introverted or extroverted, logical or intuitive. Unfortunately, the Myers-Briggs is not much more reliable than measuring body fluids; one study found that fewer than half of the respondents scored as the same type a mere five weeks later. And there is little evidence to support the test's key premise that knowledge of a person's type reliably predicts behavior on the job or in relationships (Barbuto, 1997; Paul, 2004; Pittenger, 1993).

THE FAR SIDE® BY GARY LARSON

The glass is half full!
The glass is half empty.
Half full... No! Wait! Half empty!.. No, half... What was the question?
Hey! I ordered a cheeseburger!
Larson

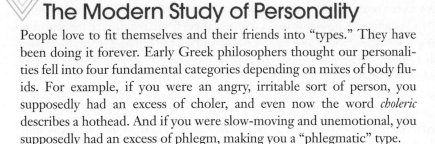

The four basic personality types

In addition, the personality-assessment industry has developed more than 2,500 personality tests to measure specific traits and tendencies that business and government would love to be able to identify: for example, the tendency to steal, take drugs, or be disloyal on the job (Ehrenreich, 2001). But it is important to think critically about these tests and examine the evidence for and against them, because many of them are nearly useless from a scientific point of view. (In "Taking Psychology with You," we discuss handwriting analysis, another popular but unreliable effort to measure personality.)

However, there are many measures of personality traits that are scientifically valid and useful in research. **Objective tests (inventories)** are standardized questionnaires that require written responses, typically to multiple-choice or true–false items. They provide information about literally hundreds of different aspects of personality, including needs, values, interests, self-esteem, emotional problems, and typical ways of responding to situations. For example, the Minnesota Multiphasic Personality Inventory (MMPI) is used to assess personality disorders (see Chapter 16). And the Multidimensional Personality Questionnaire (MPQ) is often used to identify key dimensions of personality and the traits that make up each one (Krueger, 2000).

Using well-constructed inventories, psychologists have identified hundreds of traits, ranging from sensation seeking (the enjoyment of risk) to "erotophobia" (the fear of sex). Are some of these traits more important or central than others? Do some of them overlap or cluster together?

Core Personality Traits

For Gordon Allport, one of the most influential psychologists in the empirical study of personality, the answer to both questions was yes. Allport (1937, 1961) recognized that not all traits have equal weight and significance in people's lives. Most of us, he

objective tests (inventories) Standardized questionnaires requiring written responses; they typically include scales on which people are asked to rate themselves.

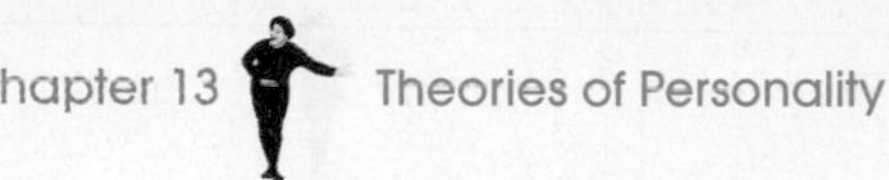

said, have five to ten *central traits* that reflect a characteristic way of behaving, dealing with others, and reacting to new situations. For instance, some people see the world as a hostile, dangerous place, whereas others see it as a place for fun and frolic. *Secondary traits*, in contrast, are more changeable aspects of personality, such as music preferences, habits, casual opinions, and the like.

Raymond B. Cattell advanced the study of this issue by applying a statistical method called **factor analysis**. Performing a factor analysis is like adding water to flour: It causes the material to clump up into little balls. When applied to traits, this procedure identifies clusters of correlated items that seem to be measuring some common, underlying factor. The traits of assertiveness, willingness to tell jokes in large groups, and taking pleasure in meeting new people might share the common factor of extroversion. Using questionnaires, life descriptions, and observations of thousands of people, Cattell (1965, 1973) measured dozens of personality traits, including humor, intelligence, creativity, dominance, and emotional disorders. Out of these he identified 16 factors, later noting that really only six of them had been repeatedly confirmed.

Today, hundreds of factor-analytic studies support the existence of a cluster of central personality traits. Although researchers are still debating exactly how many traits belong to this inner core—some say three, others say as many as nine—most personality researchers agree on the centrality of five "robust factors," known informally as the *Big Five* (Jang et al., 1998; McCrae et al., 2005, 2006; Paunonen, 2003):

Where do you think this man would score on extroversion?

1 **Extroversion versus introversion** describes the extent to which people are outgoing or shy. It includes such traits as being talkative or silent, sociable or reclusive, adventurous or cautious, eager to be in the limelight or inclined to stay in the shadows.

2 **Neuroticism (negative emotionality) versus emotional stability** describes the extent to which a person suffers from such traits as anxiety, an inability to control impulses, and a tendency to feel negative emotions such as anger, guilt, contempt, and resentment. Neurotic individuals are worriers, complainers, and defeatists, even when they have no major problems. They are always ready to see the sour side of life and none of its sweetness.

3 **Agreeableness versus antagonism** describes the extent to which people are good-natured or irritable, cooperative or abrasive, secure or suspicious and jealous. It reflects the tendency to have friendly relationships or hostile ones.

4 **Conscientiousness versus impulsiveness** describes the degree to which people are responsible or undependable, persevering or quick to give up, steadfast or fickle, tidy or careless, self-disciplined or impulsive.

5 **Openness to experience versus resistance to new experience** describes the extent to which people are curious, imaginative, questioning, and creative or conforming, unimaginative, predictable, and uncomfortable with novelty.

factor analysis A statistical method for analyzing the intercorrelations among various measures or test scores; clusters of measures or scores that are highly correlated are assumed to measure the same underlying trait or ability (factor).

People's personalities are often reflected in how they arrange their work spaces!

Culture can affect the prominence of these traits and how they are reflected in language (Toomela, 2003). Nonetheless, in spite of some semantic and cultural variations, the Big Five have emerged as distinct, central personality dimensions throughout the world, in countries as diverse as Britain, Canada, the Czech Republic, China, Ethiopia, Turkey, the Netherlands, Japan, Spain, the Philippines, Germany, Portugal, Israel, Korea, Russia, and Australia (Digman & Shmelyov, 1996; Katigbak et al., 2002; McCrae et al., 2005; Somer & Goldberg, 1999). One monumental research venture gathered data from thousands of people across 50 cultures. In this massive project as in many smaller ones, the five personality factors have emerged whether you ask people for self-reports or have people assessed by friends or independent observers (McCrae et al., 2005; Terracciano & McCrae, 2006; Watson, Hubbard, & Wiese, 2000).

Moreover, the Big Five are remarkably stable over a lifetime, especially once a person hits 30. There is some good news, however, for crabby neurotics, especially young ones. A survey of thousands of people in 10 countries, and a meta-analysis of 92 longitudinal studies, found that although young people, ages 16 to 21, are the most neurotic (emotionally negative) and the least agreeable and conscientious, people tend to become more agreeable and conscientious and less negative between ages 30 and 40 (Costa et al., 1999; Roberts, Walton, & Viechtbauer, 2006). In later adulthood people tend to become less extroverted and less open to new experiences (see Figure 13.1). Because these changes have been found in many different countries, they may reflect the universality of adult experiences—such as work and family responsibilities—or common maturational changes over the life span.

The Big Five do not provide a complete picture of personality, of course. Clinical psychologists note that important traits involved in mental disorders are missing, such as psychopathy (impulsivity and lack of remorse), self-absorption, and obsessionality

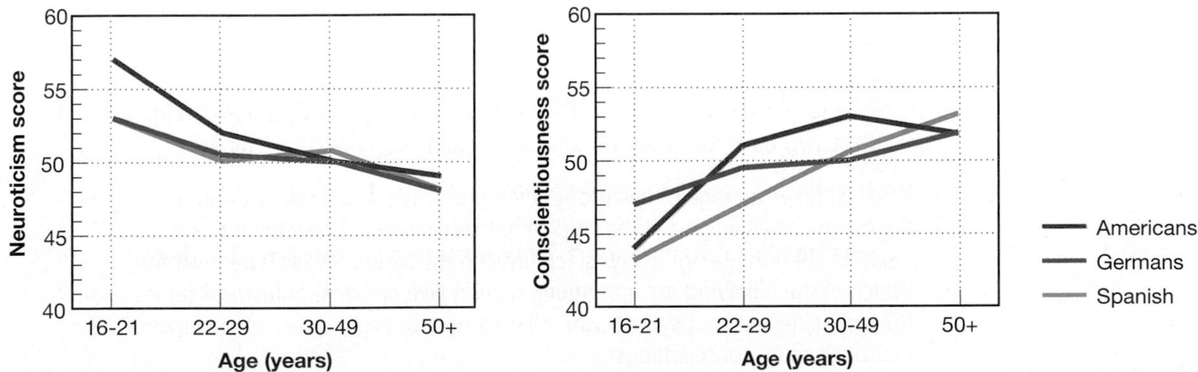

FIGURE 13.1 Consistency and Change in Personality over the Life Span

Although the Big Five traits are fairly stable, changes do occur over the life span. As you can see, neuroticism (negative emotionality) is highest among young adults and then declines, whereas conscientiousness is lowest among young adults and then steadily increases (Costa et al., 1999).

GET INVOLVED!

➤RATE YOUR TRAITS

For each of the ten items that follow, write a number from 1 to 7 indicating the extent to which you see that trait as being characteristic of you, where 1 = "I *disagree* strongly that this trait describes me" to 7 = "I *agree* strongly that this trait describes me." Use the midpoint, 4, if you neither agree nor disagree that the trait describes you. (This self-test was designed by Samuel D. Gosling.)

1. ____ Extroverted, enthusiastic
2. ____ Critical, quarrelsome
3. ____ Dependable, self-disciplined
4. ____ Anxious, easily upset
5. ___ Open to new experiences, complex
6. ___ Reserved, quiet
7. ___ Sympathetic, warm
8. ___ Disorganized, careless
9. ___ Calm, emotionally stable
10. ___ Conventional, uncreative

To score yourself on The Big Five traits, use this key:

Extroversion:	High on question 1, low on question 6
Neuroticism:	High on question 4, low on question 9
Agreeableness:	High on question 7, low on question 2
Conscientiousness:	High on question 3, low on question 8
Openness:	High on question 5, low on question 10

Now ask a friend or relative to rate you on each of the ten items. How closely does that rating match your own? If there is a discrepancy, what might be the reason for it?

(Westen & Shedler, 1999). Personality researchers note that other important traits are missing, such as religiosity, dishonesty, humorousness, independence, and conventionality (Abrahamson, Baker, & Caspi, 2002; Paunonen & Ashton, 2001). But most researchers today agree that the Big Five do lie at the core of key personality variations among healthy individuals.

QUICK quiz

Show that you have the trait of conscientiousness by taking this quiz.

1. What is the advantage of inventories over projective tests in measuring personality?
2. Raymond Cattell advanced the study of personality by (a) developing case-study analysis, (b) using factor analysis, (c) devising the Myers-Briggs Type Inventory.
3. Which of the following are *not* among the Big Five personality factors? (a) introversion, (b) agreeableness, (c) psychoticism, (d) openness to experience, (e) intelligence, (f) neuroticism, (g) conscientiousness
4. Which one of the Big Five typically decreases by age 30? (a) agreeableness, (b) extroversion, (c) openness to experience, (d) neuroticism

Answers:

1. In general, they have better reliability and validity 2. b 3. c, e 4. d

- Do puppies have personalities? What about octopuses?
- Is it possible to be born irritable or easygoing?
- To what extent are personality differences among people influenced by their genetic differences?
- Are people who have highly heritable personality traits stuck with them forever?

Genetic Influences on Personality

A mother we know was describing her two children: "My daughter has always been difficult, intense, and testy," she said, "but my son is the opposite, placid and good-natured. They came out of the womb that way." Was this mother right? Is it possible to be born touchy or good-natured? What aspects of personality might have an inherited component?

Researchers measure genetic contributions to personality in three ways: by studying personality traits in other species, by studying the temperaments of human infants and children, and by doing heritability studies of twins and adopted individuals. These methods, to date, permit us only to *infer* the existence of relevant genes; just as, if you find your toddler covered in chocolate, it's pretty safe to infer that candy is somewhere close by. Scientists hope that the actual genes underlying key traits will one day be discovered, and dozens of possible associations between specific genes and personality traits have already been reported (Fox et al., 2005b; Plomin et al., 2001). You will be hearing lots more about genetic discoveries in the coming years, so it is important to understand what they mean—and don't mean.

BIOLOGY and Animal Traits

Do Puppies Have Personalities?

A psychologist who was interviewed in the *Los Angeles Times* described Susie, one of his clients, as irritable, grumpy, and manipulative. Hardly a comment to make headlines, except that Susie is a bear (Gosling & John, 1999).

In recent years, scientists have been drawing on research in physiology, genetics, ecology, and ethology (the study of animals in their natural habitats) to investigate the nature of "personality" in our fellow animals, in order to better understand the evolutionary and biological underpinnings of human personality traits (Jones & Gosling, 2005). These investigators argue that just as it has been evolutionarily adaptive for human beings to vary in their ways of responding to the world and those around them (see Chapter 3), so it has been for animals. For example, it would be beneficial for a species if some, but not all, of its members were bold or impulsive enough to risk life and limb to confront a stranger or experiment with a new food and other members were more cautious.

When we think of an individual who has a "personality," we usually think of a human being. But bears, dogs, pigs, hyenas, goats, cats, and of course primates also have distinctive, characteristic ways of behaving that make them different from their fellows (Gosling, 2001). At one time, scientists were reluctant to refer to those distinctive patterns as "personality traits"; attributing human qualities to nonhuman creatures was a sign of anthropomorphism (see Chapter 9). Then, in 1993, scientists published the first academic article that referred to "personality" in a nonhuman species. Can you guess what species it was? Dogs? Horses? No—it

Family portraits of dogs, as of people, often reveal different personalities. Usually, someone is showing off, someone is grumpy, and someone isn't paying attention at all.

was the humble, squishy octopus! When the researchers dropped a crab into a tank of octopuses, some of them would aggressively grab that dinner right away; others seemed more "passive" and waited for the crab to swim near them; and some waited and attacked the crab when no one was watching (Mather & Anderson, 1993). In their later work, these researchers found that these personality dispositions among octopuses could be reliably identified by independent observers. Apparently, you don't have to be a person to have a personality. You don't even have to be a primate.

In another imaginative set of studies, Samuel D. Gosling and his colleagues (2003) recruited dog owners and their dogs in a local park. All the owners provided personality assessments of their dogs and filled out the same personality inventory for themselves. The owners then designated another person who knew them and their dogs and who could judge the personalities of both. In a second study, the owners brought their dogs to an enclosed section of the park where three independent observers rated the dogs, so the researchers could compare the owners' judgments of their dogs' personalities with the observers' ratings. And in a third study, the investigators took photos of the dogs at play in order to examine the effects of breed and appearance on the animals' personalities. The dog owners, their friends, and the neutral observers all agreed quite strongly in their ratings of the dogs' personalities along four of the Big Five traits: extroversion, agreeableness, emotional reactivity (neuroticism), and openness to experience. (Conscientiousness requires considerable cognitive ability and so far has turned up only in humans and chimpanzees.)

To date, Gosling and his colleagues have found evidence of most of the Big Five traits in 64 different species. So when you hear your dog-crazy friend say, "Barkley is such a shy and nervous little pup, whereas Barker is outgoing and sociable," she is probably right.

Heredity and Temperament

Let's turn now to human personalities. Even in the first weeks after birth, human babies differ in activity level, mood, responsiveness, heart rate, and attention span (Belsky, Hsieh, & Crnic, 1996; Fox et al., 2005a). Some are irritable and cranky; others are placid and sweet-natured. Some will cuddle up in an adult's arms and snuggle; others squirm and fidget, as if they cannot stand being held. Some smile easily; others

Extreme shyness and fear of new situations tend to be biologically based, stable aspects of temperament, both in human beings and in monkeys. On the right, a timid infant rhesus monkey cowers behind a friend in the presence of an outgoing stranger.

fuss and cry. These differences appear even when you control for possible prenatal influences, such as the mother's nutrition, drug use, or problems with the pregnancy. The reason is that babies are born with genetically determined **temperaments**, dispositions to respond to the environment in certain ways. Temperaments include *reactivity* (how excitable, arousable, or responsive a baby is), *soothability* (how easy it is to calm an upset baby), impulsivity, and positive and negative emotionality. Temperaments are quite stable over time and are the clay out of which later personality traits are molded (Else-Quest et al., 2006; Rothbart, Ahadi, & Evans, 2000).

For example, highly reactive infants, even at 4 months of age, are excitable, nervous, and fearful; they overreact to any little thing, even a colorful picture placed in front of them. As toddlers, they tend to be wary and fearful of new things—toys that make noise, odd-looking robots—even when their moms are right there with them. At 5 years, many of these children are still timid and uncomfortable in new situations. At 7 years, many still have symptoms of anxiety. They are afraid of being kidnapped, they need to sleep with the light on, and they are afraid of sleeping in an unfamiliar house—even if they have never experienced any sort of trauma. In contrast, nonreactive infants take things easy. They lie there without fussing; they rarely cry; they babble happily. As toddlers, they are outgoing and curious about new toys and events. They continue to be easygoing and extroverted throughout childhood (Fox et al., 2005a; Kagan, 1997). Children at these two extremes differ physiologically, too (Rothbart, Ahadi, & Evans, 2000). During mildly stressful tasks, reactive children are more likely than nonreactive children to have increased heart rates, heightened brain activity, and high levels of stress hormones.

You can see, then, how biologically based temperaments might form the basis of the later personality traits we call "diligence," "assertiveness," "shyness," or "negative emotionality."

Heredity and Traits

A third way to study genetic contributions to personality is to estimate the **heritability** of specific traits within groups of children or adults. As we saw in Chapter 3, heritability refers to the proportion of the total variation in a trait that is attributable to genetic variation within a group. Estimates of heritability come from *behavioral-genetic studies* of adopted children and of identical and fraternal twins reared apart and together. (If you need to review these methods and how they are used to estimate the role of genetics, see pages 91–93.)

temperaments Physiological dispositions to respond to the environment in certain ways; they are present in infancy and in many nonhuman species and are assumed to be innate.

heritability A statistical estimate of the proportion of the total variance in some trait that is attributable to genetic differences among individuals within a group.

THINKING CRITICALLY

TOLERATE UNCERTAINTY

Identical twins Gerald Levey (left) and Mark Newman were separated at birth and raised in different cities. When they were reunited at age 31, they discovered some astounding similarities. Both were volunteer firefighters, wore mustaches, and were unmarried. Both liked to hunt, watch old John Wayne movies, and eat Chinese food. They drank the same brand of beer, held the can with the little finger curled around it, and crushed the can when it was empty. It's tempting to conclude that all of these similarities are due to heredity, but we should also consider other explanations: Some could result from shared environmental factors such as social class and upbringing and some could be due merely to chance. For any given set of twins, we can never know for sure.

Findings from adoption and twin studies have provided compelling support for a genetic contribution to personality. Identical twins reared apart will often have unnerving similarities in gestures, mannerisms, and moods; indeed, their personalities often seem as similar as their physical features. If one twin tends to be optimistic, glum, or excitable, the other will probably be that way too (Braungert et al., 1992; Plomin et al., 2001).

Behavioral-genetic findings have produced remarkably consistent results on the heritability of traits. Whether the trait is one of the Big Five or one of many others from aggressiveness to overall happiness, heritability is typically around .50 (Bouchard, 1997a; Jang et al., 1998; Loehlin, 1992; Lykken & Tellegen, 1996; Waller et al., 1990). This means that within a group of people, about 50 percent of the variation in such traits is attributable to genetic differences among the individuals in the group. These findings have been replicated in many countries.

Some researchers have even reported high heritability for such specific activities as getting divorced (McGue & Lykken, 1992) and watching a lot of television in childhood (Plomin et al., 1990). How on earth can divorce and TV watching be heritable? Our prehistoric ancestors didn't get married, let alone divorced, and they certainly didn't watch TV! Perhaps, though, certain traits or temperaments that *are* heritable could predispose a person to do these things.

Evaluating Genetic Theories

We think you will agree that these behavioral-genetic findings are pretty amazing. Psychologists hope that one intelligent use of such findings will be to help people become more accepting of themselves and their children. Although we can all learn to make improvements and modifications to our personalities, most of us probably will never be able to *transform* our personalities completely because of our genetic dispositions and temperaments—a realization that might make people more realistic about what psychotherapy can do for them, and about what they can do for their children (Efran, Greene, & Gordon, 1998).

On the other hand, it is also important not to leap to conclusions or oversimplify by claiming that "It's all in our genes!" and overlooking the role of the environment and experience in modifying traits. A genetic *predisposition* does not necessarily imply genetic *inevitability*. A person might have a gene that, for example, predisposes him or her to depression, but without certain environmental stresses or circumstances, the person will never become depressed (see Chapter 16). When people oversimplify, they mistakenly assume that personality problems that have a genetic component are permanent—say, that someone is "born to be bad" or to be a miserable grump forever. That belief can affect their behavior and actually make matters worse. Oversimplification can also lead people to incorrectly assume that if a problem, such as depression

"THERE'S ANOTHER HEREDITARY DISEASE THAT RUNS IN THE ROYAL FAMILY. YOUR GRANDFATHER WAS A STUBBORN FOOL, YOUR FATHER WAS A STUBBORN FOOL, AND YOU ARE A STUBBORN FOOL."

or shyness, has a genetic contribution, it will respond only to medication so there is no point trying other interventions; we discuss this fallacy further in Chapter 17.

As Robert Plomin (1989), a leading behavioral geneticist, observed, "The wave of acceptance of genetic influence on behavior is growing into a tidal wave that threatens to engulf the second message of this research: These same data provide the best available evidence for the importance of environmental influences." Let us now see what some of those influences might be.

THINKING CRITICALLY

DON'T OVERSIMPLIFY

Some personality traits, such as shyness, are highly heritable. Some people think that means "genes are everything"—that a shy person can never learn to be comfortable in new situations, so there's no point trying to change. What is a more accurate way to think about the impact of heredity on personality?

QUICK quiz

We hope you have a few quiz-taking genes.

1. What three broad lines of research support the hypothesis that personality differences are due in part to genetic differences?
2. In behavioral-genetic studies, the heritability of personality traits, including the Big Five, is typically about (a) .50, (b) .90, (c) .10 to .20, (d) zero.
3. A newspaper headline announces "Couch Potatoes Born, Not Made: Kids' TV Habits May Be Hereditary." Why is this headline misleading? What other explanations of the finding are possible? What aspects of TV watching *could* have a hereditary component?

Answers:

1. Research on animal personalities, human temperaments, and the heritability of traits **2.** a **3.** The headline implies that there is a "TV-watching gene," but there obviously isn't any such gene. The writer is failing to consider other explanations. For example, perhaps some temperaments dispose people to be sedentary or passive, and this disposition leads to a tendency to watch a lot of television.

WHAT'S**AHEAD**

- If personality traits are stable, why don't people always behave consistently across situations?
- How would a social-cognitive theorist explain why Madonna is so different as a performer and as a mom?
- How much can parents shape their children's personalities?
- How do your peers influence your personality?

Environmental Influences on Personality

The "environment" may be half of the influence on personality, but what *is* the environment, exactly? In this section, we will consider the relative influence of three aspects of the environment: the particular situations you find yourself in, how your parents treat you, and who your peers are.

Situations and Social Learning

The very definition of a trait is that it is consistent across situations. But people often behave one way with their parents and a different way with their friends, one way at home and a different way in other situations. The reason for people's inconsistency, in

learning terms, is that different behaviors are rewarded, punished, or ignored in different contexts. For example, you are likely to be more extroverted in an audience of screaming, cheering "American Idol" fans than at home with relatives who would regard such noisy displays with alarm and condemnation. Because of such variations in our behavior across situations, strict behaviorists think it does not even make sense to talk about "personality." In their view, people don't have "traits"; they simply show certain behavior patterns in some situations and not others.

Social-cognitive learning theorists, on the other hand, argue that people do acquire central personality traits from their learning history and their resulting expectations and beliefs. (To refresh your memory of learning principles and of how strict behaviorists differ from social-cognitive learning theorists, see Chapter 7.) A child who studies hard and gets good grades, attention from teachers, admiration from friends, and praise from parents will come to expect that hard work in other situations will also pay off. That child will become, in terms of personality traits, "ambitious" and "industrious." A child who studies hard and gets poor grades, is ignored by teachers and parents, and is rejected by friends for being a grind will come to expect that working hard isn't worth it. That child will become (in the view of others) "unambitious" or "lazy."

DON'T OVERSIMPLIFY

ZUMA Press

Who is the "real" Madonna—doting mother or flamboyant performer? By understanding reciprocal determinism, we can avoid oversimplifying. Our genetic dispositions and personality traits cause us to choose some situations over others, but situations then influence which aspects of our personalities we express.

Today, most personality researchers recognize that people can have a core set of stable traits *and* that their behavior can vary across situations (Fleeson, 2004). There is a continual interaction between your particular qualities and the situation you are in. Your temperaments, habits, and beliefs influence how you respond to others, whom you hang out with, and the situations you seek (Bandura, 2001; Cervone & Shoda, 1999; Mischel & Shoda, 1995). In turn, the situation influences your behavior and beliefs, rewarding some behaviors and extinguishing others. In social-cognitive learning theory, this process is called **reciprocal determinism**.

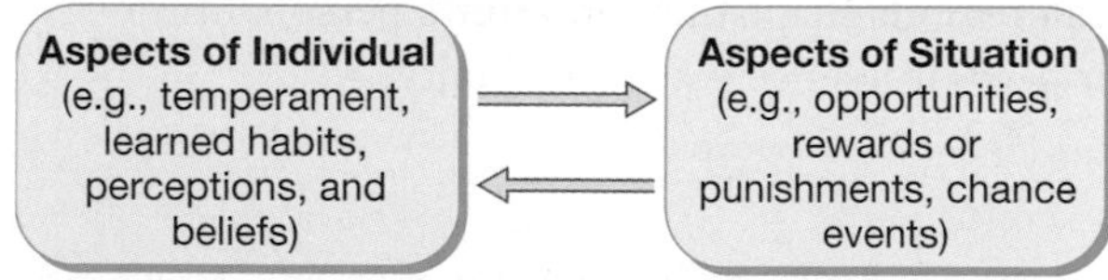

reciprocal determinism In social-cognitive theories, the two-way interaction between aspects of the environment and aspects of the individual in the shaping of personality traits.

nonshared environment Unique aspects of a person's environment and experience that are not shared with family members.

The two-way process of reciprocal determinism (as opposed, say, to the one-way determinism of "genes determine everything" or "everything is learned") helps answer a question asked by everyone who has a sibling: What makes children who grow up in the same family so different, apart from their genes? The answer seems to be: an assortment of experiences that affect each child differently, chance events that cannot be predicted, situations that children find themselves in, and peer groups that the children belong to (Harris, 2006; Plomin, Asbury, & Dunn, 2001; Rutter et al., 2001). Behavioral geneticists refer to these unique and chance experiences that are not shared with other family members as the **nonshared environment**: for example, being in Mrs. Miller's class in the fourth grade (which might inspire you to become a scientist),

winning the lead in the school play (which might push you toward an acting career), or being bullied at school (which might have caused you to see yourself as weak and powerless). All of these experiences work reciprocally with your own interpretation of them, your temperament, and your perceptions (did Mrs. Miller's class excite you or bore you?).

Keeping the concept of reciprocal determinism in mind, let us take a look at two of the most powerful environmental influences in people's lives: their parents and their friends.

Parental Influence—and Its Limits

In April 1999, Dylan Klebold and Eric Harris, teenagers enraged at the popularity of school jocks and resentful about their own inadequacies, killed 12 classmates and a teacher at Columbine High School in Littleton, Colorado, in a coldly premeditated plan. Then they committed suicide. In the ensuing atmosphere of panic and blame, many people tried to find reasons for the boys' rampage. They blamed the boys' genes, the media, violent video games, the availability of guns, and, above all, their parents. The parents should have known, people said. They should have done something to prevent the tragedy. Or they did something very wrong in raising their sons; maybe they were neglectful or abusive.

These claims reflect an entrenched Western belief that parental child-rearing practices are the strongest influence, maybe even the *sole* influence, on children's personality development. For many decades, few psychologists thought to question this assumption, and many still accept it. Yet the belief that personality is primarily determined by how parents treat their children has begun to crumble under the weight of three lines of evidence (Harris, 1998, 2006):

EXAMINE THE EVIDENCE

Most people assume that parents are almost entirely responsible for their children's personality and behavior. What evidence challenges this popular belief?

1 The shared environment of the home has little if any influence on personality. In behavioral-genetic research, the "shared environment" includes the family you grew up with and the experiences and background you shared with your siblings and parents. If these had as powerful an influence as commonly assumed, then studies should find a strong correlation between the personality traits of adopted children and those of their adoptive parents. In fact, the correlation is weak to nonexistent, indicating that the influence of child-rearing practices and family life is nil compared to the influence of genetics (Cohen, 1999; Plomin, Asbury, & Dunn, 2001). As we just saw, it is only the nonshared environment that has a strong impact.

2 Few parents have a single child-rearing style that is consistent over time and that they use with all their children. Developmental psychologists have tried for many years to identify the effects of specific child-rearing practices on children's personality traits. The problem is that parents are inconsistent from day to day and over the years. Their child-rearing practices vary, depending on their own stresses, moods, and marital satisfaction (Holden & Miller, 1999). As one child we know said to her exasperated mother, "Why are you so mean to me today, Mommy? I'm this naughty every day." Moreover, parents tend to adjust their methods of child rearing according to the temperament of the child; they are often more lenient with easygoing children and more punitive with difficult ones.

Parents may try to keep constant tabs on their children, but how much control do they really have over how their children turn out?

3 Even when parents try to be consistent in the way they treat their children, there may be little relation between what they do and how the children turn out. Some children of troubled and abusive parents are resilient and do not suffer lasting emotional damage, as we will see in Chapter 14; some children of the kindest and most nurturing parents succumb to drugs, mental illness, or gangs. By all accounts, the parents of Dylan Klebold were loving and involved with their son (Garbarino & Bedard, 2001).

Of course, parents do influence their children in lots of ways. They contribute to their children's religious beliefs, intellectual and occupational interests, feelings of self-esteem or inadequacy, adherence to traditional or modern notions of masculinity and femininity, helpfulness to others, skills, and values (Beer, Arnold, & Loehlin, 1998; Krueger, Hicks, & McGue, 2001; McCrae et al., 2000). Above all, what parents do profoundly affects the quality of their relationship with their children—whether their children feel loved, secure, and valued or humiliated, frightened, and worthless (Harris, 1998).

Parents also have some influence even on traits in their children that are highly heritable. In one longitudinal study that followed children from age 3 to age 21, kids who were impulsive, uncontrollable, and aggressive at age 3 were far more likely than calmer children to grow up to be impulsive, unreliable, and antisocial and more likely to commit crimes (Caspi, 2000). Early temperament was a strong and consistent predictor of these later personality traits. But not *every* child came out the same way. What protected some of those at risk, and helped them move in a healthier direction, was having parents who made sure they stayed in school, supervised them closely, and gave them consistent discipline. Another longitudinal study found that among children born with a genetic predisposition to extreme shyness and fearfulness, only those who had the gene *and* whose mothers had little social support (which increases stress) were still very shy at age 7 (Fox et al., 2005b). Perhaps the socially isolated mothers were extremely protective of their children, not exposing them to other people, and thus they were inadvertently rewarding their children's shyness rather than helping them modify it.

Nevertheless, it is clear that the parent–child relationship is not a one-way street in which parents determine everything about their kids. Because of reciprocal determinism, the relationship runs in both directions, with parents and children continually influencing one another. And yet, once children leave home, starting in preschool, parental influence on children's behavior *outside* the home begins to wane. The "nonshared environment"—peers, chance events, and circumstances—takes over.

The Power of Peers

Should the parents of Dylan Klebold and Eric Harris have known how angry and resentful their sons felt in their private souls, angry enough to inflict a bloody revenge on their classmates? When two psychologists surveyed 275 freshmen at Cornell Uni-

GET INVOLVED!

➤SITUATION AND SELF

Are you a different "person" when you are alone, with your parents, hanging out with friends, in class, or at a party? If so, in what ways? Do you have a "secret self" that you do not show to your family? Consider the Big Five factors (or any other personality traits that are important to you) as you answer these questions.

versity, they found that most of them had "secret lives" and private selves that they never revealed to their parents (Garbarino & Bedard, 2001). Most reported committing crimes, drinking, doing drugs, and having sex without their parents knowing anything about it. The researchers concluded that Dylan Klebold was just an extreme case of a common adolescent phenomenon: showing only one facet of your personality to your parents and an entirely different one to your peers.

Have you ever been in this situation, as the excluded student or the one doing the excluding? Being rejected by peers is one of the most painful experiences that adolescents report having.

Children, like adults, live in two environments: their homes and their world outside the home. At home children learn how their parents want them to behave and what they can get away with; as soon as they leave home, however, they conform to the dress, habits, language, and rules of their peers. Children who were law-abiding in the fifth grade may start breaking the law in high school, if that is what it takes—or what they think it takes—to win the respect of their peers (Harris, 1998).

Adolescent culture often consists of many different peer groups, organized by interests (jocks, Goths, nerds, musicians, artists), ethnicity, or status and popularity. Unfortunately, children and teenagers who are temperamentally fearful and shy, have few or no friends, or are physically unattractive or weak are more likely than other kids to be bullied, victimized, and rejected by their peers (Hodges & Perry, 1999).

It has been difficult to tease apart the effects of parents and peers because parents usually try to arrange things so that their children's environments duplicate their own values and customs. To see which has the stronger influence on personality and behavior, therefore, we must look at situations in which the peer group's values clash with the parents' values. For example, when parents value academic achievement and their child's peers do not, who wins? The answer, typically, is peers (Harris, 1998, 2006).

In a study of 15,000 students at nine different American high schools, researchers sought reasons for the average difference in school performance of Asian-Americans, African-Americans, Latinos, and whites (Steinberg, Dornbusch, & Brown, 1992). Asian-American students, who had the highest grades on the average, reported having the highest level of peer support for academic achievement. They studied together in groups, cheered one another on, and praised one another's success. But many African-American students regarded academic success as a sign of selling out to the white establishment. High-achieving black students often said they had few black friends for this reason; they felt they had to choose between doing well in school and being popular with their peers. Black educators believe that this dilemma still sharply affects some African-American students, contributing to the gap in academic performance between blacks and whites (Ogbu, 2003). But it also affects students of *any* ethnicity or gender whose peer group thinks that academic success is only for sellouts or geeks (Arroyo & Zigler, 1995).

Peers, like parents, shape the expression of personality traits, causing us to emphasize some attributes or abilities and downplay others. Of course, as the theory

of reciprocal determinism would predict, our temperaments and dispositions also cause us to select particular peer groups (if they are available) instead of others, and our temperaments also influence how we behave within the group. But once we are among peers, most of us go along with them, molding facets of our personalities to the pressures of the group.

In sum, core personality traits may stem from genetic dispositions, but they are profoundly shaped by learning, peers, situations, experience, and, as we will see next, the largest environment of all: the culture.

QUICK quiz

Do your peers take these quizzes? Does the answer determine whether you will?

1. What three lines of evidence have challenged the belief that parents are the major influence on their children's personalities?
2. Which contributes most to the variation among siblings in their personality traits: (a) the unique experiences they have that are not shared with their families, (b) the family environment that all of them share, or (c) the way their parents treat them?

Answers:

1. The shared family environment has little if any influence on personality; few parents have a consistent child-rearing style; and even when parents try to be consistent in the way they treat their children, there may be little relation between what they do and how the children turn out. 2. a

WHAT'S AHEAD

- How does culture influence your personality—and even whether you think you have a stable "self"?
- Why are punctuality and aggressiveness more than just individual personality traits?
- Why are men in the South and West more likely to get angry at personal insults than other American men are?

Cultural Influences on Personality

If you get an invitation to come to a party at 7 P.M., what time are you actually likely to get there? If someone gives you the finger or calls you a rude name, are you more likely to become furious or laugh it off? Most Western psychologists regard conscientiousness about time and quickness to anger as personality traits that result partly from genetic dispositions and partly from experience. But **culture** also has a profound effect on people's behavior, attitudes, and the traits they value or disdain. It provides countless rules that govern our actions and shape our beliefs (see Chapter 8).

Many people fail to appreciate the deep influence of culture on individuals. In contrast to biology, which they regard as real and tangible, they think of culture as merely a light veneer on human behavior, or perhaps as a source of useful information for tourist travel ("In Spain, people eat dinner after midnight"). For decades, psychologists assumed that they could generalize from studies of people in their own culture to people everywhere. Today many psychologists recognize that culture is just as pow-

culture A program of shared rules that governs the behavior of members of a community or society and a set of values, beliefs, and attitudes shared by most members of that community.

Individualistic Americans exercise by running, walking, bicycling, and skating, all in different directions and wearing different clothes. Collectivist Japanese employees at their hiring ceremony exercise in identical fashion.

erful an influence on personality and behavior as any biological process. For example, while "neuroticism" is a genetically influenced Big Five trait, it is also affected by events going on in the world around us. Two meta-analyses comparing young Americans in 1952 and 1993 found substantially higher levels of anxiety and other negative emotions (neuroticism) in the 1990s' generation. Why? Over the decades, young people have come to feel that their lives are less stable, safe, and secure (Twenge, 2000).

Culture, Values, and Traits

It is not always easy to see how cultural rules affect your own personality, but here's a demonstration. Take as much time as you like to answer this question: "Who are you?" "I am _____."

Your response to "Who are you?" will be influenced by your cultural background, particularly whether your culture emphasizes individualism or community (Hofstede & Bond, 1988; Markus & Kitayama, 1991; Triandis, 1996). In **individualist cultures**, the independence of the individual often takes precedence over the needs of the group, and the self is often defined as a collection of personality traits ("I am outgoing, agreeable, and ambitious") or in occupational terms ("I am a psychologist"). In **collectivist cultures**, group harmony often takes precedence over the wishes of the individual, and the self is defined in the context of relationships and the community ("I am the son of a farmer, descended from three generations of storytellers on my mother's side and five generations of farmers on my father's side . . .").

As Table 13.1 shows, individualist and collectivist ways of defining the self influence many aspects of life, including which personality traits we value, how we express emotions, and how much we value having relationships or maintaining freedom

individualist cultures Cultures in which the self is regarded as autonomous, and individual goals and wishes are prized above duty and relations with others.

collectivist cultures Cultures in which the self is regarded as embedded in relationships, and harmony with one's group is prized above individual goals and wishes.

TABLE 13.1

Some Average Differences Between Individualist and Collectivist Cultures

Members of Individualist Cultures	Members of Collectivist Cultures
Define the self as autonomous, independent of groups.	Define the self as an interdependent part of groups.
Give priority to individual, personal goals.	Give priority to the needs and goals of the group.
Value independence, leadership, achievement, self-fulfillment.	Value group harmony, duty, obligation, security.
Give more weight to an individual's attitudes and preferences than to group norms as explanations of behavior.	Give more weight to group norms than to individual attitudes as explanations of behavior.
Attend to the benefits and costs of relationships; if costs exceed advantages, a person is likely to drop a relationship.	Attend to the needs of group members; if a relationship is beneficial to the group but costly to the individual, the individual is likely to stay in the relationship.

Source: Triandis, 1996.

(Campbell et al., 1996; Kashima et al., 1995). Individualist and collectivist outlooks even affect whether we believe that personality is stable across situations. In a revealing study comparing Japanese and Americans, the Americans reported that their sense of self changes only 5 to 10 percent in different situations, whereas the Japanese said that 90 to 99 percent of their sense of self changes (de Rivera, 1989). For the group-oriented Japanese, it is important to enact *tachiba,* to perform your social roles correctly so that there will be harmony with others. Americans, in contrast, tend to value "being true to your self" and having a "core identity." You can see that even notions of what personality means and whether it is consistent across situations are deeply affected by culture.

Culture and Traits. When people fail to understand the influence of culture on behavior, they often attribute another person's mysterious or annoying actions to individual personality traits when they are really due to cultural norms. Take cleanliness. How often do you bathe—once a day, once a week? Do you regard baths as healthy and invigorating or as a disgusting wallow in dirty water? How often, and where, do you wash your hands—or feet? A person who would seem obsessively clean in one culture might seem an appalling slob in another (Fernea & Fernea, 1994).

Or consider helpfulness. Many years ago, in a classic cross-cultural study of children in Kenya, India, Mexico, the Philippines, Okinawa, the United States, and five other cultures, researchers measured how often children behaved altruistically (offering help, support, or unselfish suggestions) or egoistically (seeking help and attention or wanting to dominate others) (Whiting & Edwards, 1988; Whiting & Whiting, 1975). American children were the least altruistic on all measures and the most egoistic. The most altruistic children came from societies in which children are assigned many tasks, such as caring for younger children and gathering and preparing food. These children knew that their work made a genuine contribution to the well-being or economic survival of the family. In cultures that value individual achievement and self-advancement, taking care of others has less importance, and altruism as a personality trait is not cultivated to the same extent.

Or consider tardiness. Individuals differ in whether they try to be places "on time" or are always late, but cultural norms affect how individuals regard time in the first place. In northern Europe, Canada, and the

In many cultures, children are expected to contribute to the family income and to take care of their younger siblings. These experiences encourage helpfulness over independence.

United States, time is organized into linear segments in which people do one thing "at a time" (Hall, 1983; Hall & Hall, 1990). The day is divided into appointments, schedules, and routines, and because time is a precious commodity, people don't like to "waste" time or "spend" too much time on any one activity (hence the popularity of multitasking). In such cultures, being on time is taken as a sign of conscientiousness or thoughtfulness and being late as a sign of indifference or intentional disrespect. Therefore, it is considered the height of rudeness (or high status) to keep someone waiting. But in Mexico, southern Europe, the Middle East, South America, and Africa, time is organized along parallel lines. People do many things at once, and the needs of friends and family supersede mere appointments. Latinos and Middle Easterners think nothing of waiting for hours or days to see someone. The idea of having to be somewhere "on time," as if time were more important than a person, is unthinkable.

In culturally diverse North America, the two time systems keep bumping into each other. An Anglo judge in Miami got into hot water when he observed that "Cubans always show up two hours late for weddings"—late in his culture's terms, that is. The judge was accurate in his observation; the problem was his implication that something was wrong with Cubans for being "late." And "late" compared to what, by the way? The Cubans were perfectly on time for Cubans.

CLOSE-UP on Research

CULTURE AND TESTOSTERONE

A good example of how culture "gets into" personality comes from the study of culture and male aggression. Richard Nisbett (1993) **analyzed the common assumption** that male violence is an inevitable result of testosterone. He **asked some provocative questions**: Given that men everywhere have testosterone, why do rates of male aggressiveness vary enormously across cultures and throughout history? Why are rates of violence higher in some regions of the United States than others? How does culture get "under the skin" to influence male aggression? To answer these questions, Nisbett and his colleagues began a program of research that is a wonderful illustration of the many methods that psychologists can use to investigate an interesting problem—from gathering information from history and cross-cultural studies to doing controlled experiments in the lab to determine cause and effect.

By **examining the evidence** from historical records, Nisbett (1993) found that the American South, along with some western regions of the country originally settled by Southerners, have much higher rates of white homicide and other violence than the rest of the country has—but only particular kinds of violence: the use of fists or guns to protect a man's sense of honor, protect his property, or respond to perceived insults. Nisbett **considered various explanations**, such as poverty or racial tensions. But when he controlled for regional differences in poverty and the percentage of blacks in the population, by county, "Southernness" remained an independent predictor of homicide. Nisbett also ruled out a history of slavery as an explanation: Regions of the South that had the highest concentrations of slaves in the past have the lowest white homicide rates today.

Nisbett **avoided the trap of emotional reasoning**, which he might have fallen into by stereotyping people from the South and deciding that there was

THINKING CRITICALLY

ANALYZE ASSUMPTIONS AND BIASES

Many people assume that men can't help being violent because of their testosterone. Yet, on average, men in agricultural economies are far more cooperative and nonviolent than men in herding economies. Amish farmers have always had very low rates of violence, whereas in the Old West, the cattle-herding cowboy culture was a violent one. (Fortunately, the shootout here is just a reenactment.)

just something violent in the southern personality. Instead, he hypothesized that the higher rates of violence in the South must derive from economic causes—that the higher rates occur in cultures that were originally based on herding, in contrast to cultures based on agriculture. People who depend economically on agriculture tend to develop and promote cooperative strategies for survival. But people who depend on their herds are extremely vulnerable; their livelihoods can be lost in an instant by the theft of their animals. To reduce the likelihood of theft, Nisbett theorized, herders learn to be hyperalert to any possibly threatening act and respond to it immediately with force. This would explain why cattle rustling and horse thievery were capital crimes in the Old West, and why Mediterranean and Middle Eastern herding cultures even today place a high value on male aggressiveness. When Nisbett **examined the evidence** for this hypothesis, looking at agricultural practices within the South, he found that homicide rates were indeed more than twice as high in the hills and dry plains areas (where herding occurs) as in farming regions.

The emphasis on aggressiveness and vigilance in herding communities, in turn, fosters a *culture of honor*, in which even apparently small disputes and trivial insults (trivial to people from other cultures, that is) put a man's reputation for toughness on the line, requiring him to respond with violence to restore his status (Cohen, 1998). Although the herding economy has become much less important in the South and West, the legacy of its culture of honor remains. These regions have rates of honor-related homicides (such as murder to avenge a perceived insult to one's family) that are *five times higher* than in other regions of the country. Cultures of honor also have higher rates of domestic violence. Both sexes in

such cultures believe it is appropriate for a man to physically assault a woman if he believes she is threatening his honor and reputation—say, by being unfaithful or by leaving him (Vandello & Cohen, 2003).

Next, Nisbett and his colleagues actually brought Northern and Southern male students into their lab and conducted three experiments to measure how these students would respond psychologically and physiologically to being insulted (Cohen et al., 1996). The physiological measures were levels of cortisol, a hormone associated with high levels of stress (see Chapter 15), and testosterone, which is associated with dominance and aggression. Participants were 173 white male undergraduates, who were told that the experiment would assess their performance on various tasks and that the experimenter would be taking saliva samples to measure their blood sugar levels throughout the procedure. After the young men gave their baseline saliva sample, they had to walk down the hall to another room. As they did, a confederate of the experimenter—who seemed to be another student participant—bumped into them and called them an insulting name (a seven-letter word beginning with "a," if you want to know). In the final phase of the experiment, as the young men were filling out a questionnaire, the experimenter took a "post-bump" saliva sample from each of them.

As you can see in the figure, Northerners responded calmly to the insult; if anything, they thought it was funny. But many Southerners were immediately inflamed and their levels of cortisol and testosterone shot up.

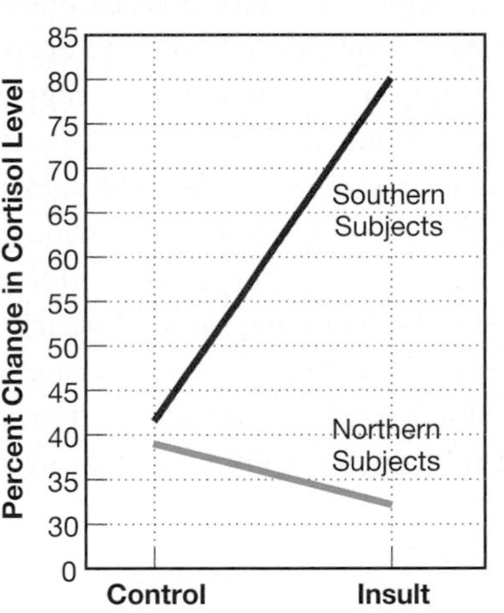

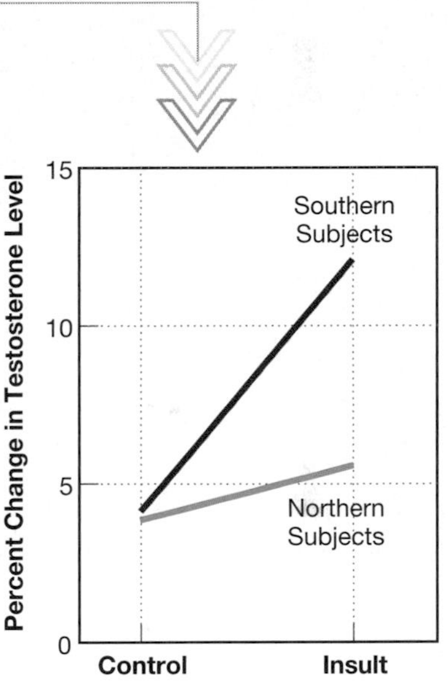

In subsequent versions of this experiment, Southerners were also more likely to feel that their masculinity had been threatened, and they were more likely to retaliate aggressively than Northerners were. Southerners and Northerners who were not insulted were alike on most measures, with the exception that young men from the South were actually more polite and deferential. It appears that Southerners have more obliging manners than Northerners—until they are insulted. Then, look out.

Nisbett and his colleagues have **considered other explanations** for variations in male aggressiveness across cultures. Their work identified only one particular contributing factor: being raised in a culture of honor. Another factor has to do with the dangers a culture faces. In cultures in which competition for resources is fierce and survival is difficult, men are "toughened up" and pushed to take risks, even with their lives (Gilmore, 1990). In contrast, in cultures in which resources are abundant and there are no serious hazards or enemies to worry about—such as the Ifaluk, the Tahitians, and the people of Sudest Island near New Guinea—men do not feel they have to prove themselves and they are not raised to be tough and aggressive (Lepowsky, 1994; Levy, 1984). When a society becomes more peaceful, so do its men.

Evaluating Cultural Approaches

A woman we know, originally from England, married a Lebanese man. They were happy together but had the usual number of marital misunderstandings and squabbles. After a few years, they visited his home town in Lebanon, where she had never been before. "I was stunned," she told us. "All the things I thought he did because of his *personality* turned out to be because he's *Lebanese!* Everyone there was just like him!"

Our friend's reaction illustrates both the contributions and the limitations of cultural studies of personality. She was right in recognizing that some of her husband's behavior was attributable to his culture; for example, his Lebanese notions of time were very different from her English notions. But she was wrong to infer that the Lebanese ‘like him": Individuals are affected by their culture, but they vary within it.

THINKING CRITICALLY

DON'T OVERSIMPLIFY

People often speak of "the" German personality or "the" British character. How can we think about the cultural factors that influence personality traits without stereotyping?

Cultural psychologists face the problem of how to describe cultural influences on personality without oversimplifying or stereotyping (Church & Lonner, 1998). As one student of ours put it, "How come when we students speak of 'the' Japanese or 'the' blacks or 'the' whites or 'the' Latinos, it's called stereotyping, and when you do it, it's called 'cross-cultural psychology'?" This question shows excellent critical thinking! The study of culture does not rest on the assumption that all members of a culture behave the same way or have the same personality traits. As we have seen in this chapter, people vary according to their temperaments, beliefs, and learning histories, and this variation occurs within every culture.

Moreover, regional variations occur in every society. America may be an "individualist" culture overall, but the deep South, with its history of strong regional identity, is more collectivist than the rugged, independent West (Vandello & Cohen, 1999). The Chinese and the Japanese both value group harmony, but the Chinese are more likely to promote individual achievement, whereas the Japanese are more likely to strive for group consensus (Dien, 1999).

Finally, in spite of their differences, cultures have many human concerns and needs in common—for love, attachment, family, work, and religious or communal tradition. Nonetheless, cultural rules are what, *on average*, make Swedes different from Bedouins and Cambodians different from Italians. The traits that we value, our sense of self versus community, and our notions of the right way to behave—all key aspects of personality—begin with the culture in which we are raised.

QUICK quiz

At the moment, you live in a culture that values the importance of quizzes.

1. Cultures whose members regard the "self" as a collection of stable personality traits are (individualist/collectivist).
2. Which cultural practice tends to foster the traits of helpfulness and altruism? (a) Every family member "does his or her own thing," (b) parents insist that children obey, (c) children contribute to the family welfare, (d) parents remind children often about the importance of being helpful.
3. Why, according to one theory, do men in the American South and West respond more aggressively to perceived insults than other American men do?

Answers:

1. individualist **2.** c **3.** These men come from regions in which economies based on herding gave rise to "cultures of honor," requiring males to be vigilant and aggressive toward potential threats.

WHAT'S**AHEAD**

- How does the humanist vision of personality differ from psychodynamic and genetic views?
- In the humanist view, what's wrong with saying to a child, "I love you because you've been good"?
- What is your life story—and how does it influence how you see your personality?

The Inner Experience

A final way to look at personality starts from each person's own point of view, from the inside out. Biology may hand us temperamental dispositions that benefit or limit us, the environment may deal us some tough or fortunate experiences, our parents may treat us as we would or would not have wished, but the sum total of our personality is how we, individually, weave all of these elements together.

humanist psychology A psychological approach that emphasizes personal growth, resilience, and the achievement of human potential.

unconditional positive regard To Carl Rogers, love or support given to another person with no conditions attached.

Humanist Approaches

One "inner" approach to personality comes from **humanist psychology,** which was launched as a movement in the early 1960s. The movement's chief leaders—Abraham Maslow (1908–1970), Carl Rogers (1902–1987), and Rollo May (1909–1994)—argued that it was time to replace psychoanalysis and behaviorism with a "third force" in psychology, one that would draw a fuller picture of human potential and personality. Psychologists who take a humanist approach to personality emphasize our uniquely human capacity to determine our own actions and futures.

Abraham Maslow. The trouble with psychology, said Maslow (1970, 1971), was that it had ignored many of the positive aspects of life, such as joy, laughter, love, happiness, and *peak experiences*, rare moments of rapture caused by the attainment of excellence or the experience of beauty. The traits that Maslow thought most important to personality were not the Big Five, but rather the qualities of the *self-actualized person*—the person who strives for a life that is meaningful, challenging, and satisfying.

For Maslow, personality development could be viewed as a gradual progression toward self-actualization. Most psychologists, he argued, had a lopsided view of human nature, a result of their emphasis on studying emotional problems and negative traits such as neuroticism or insecurity. As Maslow (1971) wrote, "When you select out for careful study very fine and healthy people, strong people, creative people . . . then you get a very different view of mankind. You are asking how tall can people grow, what can a human being become?"

You are never too old for self-actualization. Hulda Crooks, shown here at age 91 climbing Mt. Fuji, took up mountain climbing at 54. "It's been a great inspiration for me," she said. "When I come down from the mountain I feel like I can battle in the valley again." She died at the age of 101.

Carl Rogers. As a clinician, Carl Rogers (1951, 1961) was interested not only in why some people cannot function well but also in what he called the fully functioning individual. How you behave, he said, depends on your subjective reality, not on the external reality around you. Fully functioning people experience *congruence*, or harmony, between the image they project to others and their true feelings and wishes. They are trusting, warm, and open, rather than defensive or intolerant. Their beliefs about themselves are realistic.

To become fully functioning people, Rogers maintained, we all need **unconditional positive regard**, love and support for the people we are, without strings (conditions) attached. This doesn't mean that Winifred should be allowed to

kick her brother when she is angry with him or that Wilbur may throw his dinner out the window because he doesn't like pot roast. In these cases, a parent can correct the child's behavior without withdrawing love from the child. The child can learn that the behavior, not the child, is what is bad. "House rules are 'no violence,' children," is a very different message from "You are horrible children for behaving so badly."

Unfortunately, Rogers observed, many children are raised with *conditional* positive regard: "I will love you if you behave well, and I won't love you if you behave badly." Adults often treat each other this way, too. People treated with conditional regard begin to suppress or deny feelings or actions that they believe are unacceptable to those they love. The result, said Rogers, is incongruence, a sense of being out of touch with your feelings, of not being true to your "real self," which in turn produces low self-regard, defensiveness, and unhappiness. A person experiencing incongruence scores high on neuroticism, becoming bitter and negative.

Existential psychologists remind us of the inevitable struggles of human existence, such as the fight against loneliness and alienation.

Rollo May. May shared with the humanists a belief in free will. But he also emphasized some of the inherently difficult and tragic aspects of the human condition, including loneliness, anxiety, and alienation. In books such as *Love and Will* and *The Meaning of Anxiety*, May brought to American psychology elements of the European philosophy of **existentialism**. This doctrine emphasizes the inevitable challenges of human existence, such as the search for the meaning of life, the need to confront death, and living with the burden of responsibility for our actions.

Free will, wrote May, carries a price in anxiety and despair, which is why so many people try to escape from freedom into narrow certainties and blame others for their misfortunes. For May, our personalities reflect the ways we cope with the struggles to find meaning in existence, to use our freedom wisely, and to face suffering and death bravely. May popularized the humanist idea that we can choose to make the best of ourselves by drawing on inner resources such as love and courage, but he added that we can never escape the harsh realities of life and loss.

Narrative Approaches

In the past two decades, another "inner" approach has focused on the importance of the *life narrative*, the story that each of us develops over time to explain ourselves and make meaning of everything that has happened to us (Bruner, 1990; McAdams & Pals, 2006; Sarbin, 1997a, b). In the narrative view, your distinctive personality rests on the story you tell to answer the question "Who am I?"

Because the narrative approach to personality emphasizes how the stories we tell give us an identity, shape our behavior, and motivate us to pursue or abandon our goals, it integrates the many diverse influences on personality that we have discussed in this chapter. Do you believe you are a victim of bad childhood experiences or a survivor of them? Do you believe that your mood swings are caused by a biochemical imbalance or an imbalanced love affair? When you tell about your life to others, do you play the hero or the passive bystander?

The life narrative you create for yourself reflects your needs and justifies the actions you take, or fail to take, to solve your problems (Molden & Dweck, 2006). For example, therapist David Epston worked with an immigrant woman named Marisa, who had been abused and rejected all her life. "To tell a story about your life turns it into a history," he told her, "one that can be left behind, and makes it easier for you to create a future of your own design" (quoted in O'Hanlon, 1994). Marisa came to see that she could tell a new story about her experiences, one that did not emphasize the tragedies that had befallen her but rather her triumphs in overcoming them. "My life has a future now," she told Epston. "It will never be the same again."

existentialism A philosophical approach that emphasizes the inevitable dilemmas and challenges of human existence.

In the narrative view, your stories about how you see and explain yourself are the essence of your personality, capturing everything that has happened to you and all the factors that affect your biology, psychology, and relationships. They are what make you unique in all the world.

Evaluating Humanist and Narrative Approaches

As with psychodynamic theories, the major criticism of humanist psychology is that many of its assumptions are untestable. Freud looked at humanity and saw destructive drives, selfishness, and lust. Maslow and Rogers looked at humanity and saw cooperation, selflessness, and love. May looked at humanity and saw fear of freedom, loneliness, and the struggle for meaning. These differences, say critics, may tell us more about the observers than about the observed.

Many humanist concepts, although intuitively appealing, are hard to define operationally (see Chapter 2). How can we know whether a person is self-fulfilled or self-actualized? How can we tell whether a woman's decision to quit her job and become a professional rodeo rider represents an "escape from freedom" or a freely made choice? And what exactly is unconditional positive regard? If it is defined as unquestioned support of a child's efforts at mastering a new skill, or as assurance that the child is loved in spite of his or her mistakes, then it is clearly a good idea. But in the popular culture, it has often been interpreted as an unwillingness ever to say "no" to a child or to offer constructive criticism and set limits, which children need.

THINKING CRITICALLY

DEFINE YOUR TERMS

Unconditional positive regard sounds like a good thing, but what does it mean, exactly? Does it mean giving loved ones your total support and approval, no matter what they do? Does it permit setting limits and offering constructive criticism?

Despite such concerns, humanist psychologists have added balance to the study of personality. A contemporary specialty known as "positive psychology" (see Chapter 1) follows in the footsteps of humanism by focusing on the qualities that enable people to be optimistic and resilient in times of stress (Gable & Haidt, 2005; Seligman & Csikszentmihaly, 2000). Influenced in part by the humanists, psychologists are studying many positive human traits, such as courage, altruism, the motivation to excel, and self-confidence. Developmental psychologists are studying ways to foster children's empathy and creativity. And some researchers are studying the emotional and existential effects of the fear of death. When people are made aware of death, they resort not only to conscious efforts to suppress frightening thoughts but also to nonconscious defenses to make themselves feel better and safer and their lives more meaningful (Pyszczynski, Greenberg, & Solomon, 2000).

As for narrative approaches in psychology, research is flourishing, confirming the unifying role of the "stories we tell" about ourselves in shaping our distinctive personalities (McAdams & Pals, 2006). Cognitive psychologists emphasize how our stories shape and distort our memories. Psychotherapists are exploring the ways in which clients who tell self-defeating life stories might turn them around, creating more hopeful and positive ones. Social and cultural psychologists examine how a culture or society's

dominant myths and "shared stories" influence people's ambitions and expectations, political views, and beliefs that the world can be improved—or will never change.

The humanist, existential, and narrative views of personality share one central message: that we have the power to choose our own destinies, even when fate delivers us into tragedy. Across psychology, this message has fostered a new appreciation of human resilience in the face of adversity.

QUICK quiz

Exercise free will, as a humanist would advise you to, by choosing to take this quiz.

1. According to Carl Rogers, a man who loves his wife only when she is looking her best is giving her positive regard that is (a) conditional or (b) unconditional.
2. The humanist who described the importance of having peak experiences was (a) Abraham Maslow, (b) Rollo May, (c) Carl Rogers.
3. A humanist and a Freudian psychoanalyst are arguing about human nature. What underlying assumptions about psychology and human potential are they likely to bring to their discussion? How can they resolve their differences without either–or thinking?

Answers:

1. a **2.** a **3.** The Freudian assumes that human nature is basically selfish and destructive; the humanist assumes that it is basically loving and cooperative. They can resolve this either–or debate by recognizing that human beings have both capacities, and that the situation and culture often determine which capacity is expressed at a given time.

Now that you have read about the major influences on personality (see Review 13.1), how would you "explain" Madonna? Some aspects of her character and temperament, such as extroversion and conscientiousness, seem likely to have a genetic component. Her personality was perhaps also shaped, however, by unique experiences in her childhood and young adulthood that were not shared with her siblings: having the opportunity to take dance classes, later seizing the chance and running away to New York. Madonna's chameleon-like persona, which changes every couple of years, is further shaped and rewarded by today's postmodern culture, which values image over reality, transience over permanence, style over substance, celebrity over obscurity. Psychodynamic theorists might wonder whether Madonna's unconscious motivations for success and her constant changing of public personalities stem from the shock of losing her mother when she was only 6; Madonna was her mother's first name, too. Humanists might remind us that we do not know anything about the real Madonna, because the faces she presents to the public might reveal nothing at all about her inner, private self. And psychologists who study life narratives will have a full-time job keeping up with the stories that Madonna spins about herself!

For Madonna and for all the rest of us, genetic influences, learned habits, cultural norms, unconscious fears and conflicts, and visions of possibility, filtered through our interior sense of self and our life story, give each of us the stamp of our personality, the qualities that make us feel uniquely . . . us.

REVIEW 13.1

The Major Influences on Personality

Influence		Description
Psychodynamic		Unconscious dynamics shape human motives, guilts, conflicts, and defenses.
Genetic		Children are born with particular temperaments, and most traits are highly influenced by genes.
Environmental		Learning, situations, and unique experiences affect which traits are encouraged.
Experience	Parents	Modify and shape a child's temperament and genetic predispositions; affect gender roles, attitudes, self-concept; affect the quality of the relationship with the child.
	Peer group	Influences an individual's values, behavior, ambitions, goals, etc.
	Situation	Determines which behaviors are rewarded and which are punished or ignored, thereby shaping the expression or suppression of particular traits.
	Chance events	May influence a person's experiences and choices in unexpected ways, thus encouraging the development of some traits over others.
Cultural		Cultural norms specify which traits are valued, affect basic notions of the self and personality, and shape behaviors from aggressiveness to altruism.
Humanist		Despite genetic, environmental, cultural, and psychodynamic influences, people can exercise free will to become the kind of person they want to be.

Taking Psychology with You

How to Avoid the "Barnum Effect"

How well does the following paragraph describe you?

Some of your aspirations tend to be pretty unrealistic. At times you are extroverted, affable, and sociable, while at other times you are introverted, wary, and reserved. You pride yourself on being an independent thinker and do not accept others' opinions without satisfactory proof. You prefer a certain amount of change and variety, and you become dissatisfied when hemmed in by restrictions and limitations. At times you have serious doubts as to whether you have made the right decision or done the right thing.

When people believe that this description was written just for them, as the result of a personalized horoscope or handwriting analysis, they all say the same thing: "It describes me *exactly!*" Everyone thinks this description is accurate because it is vague enough to apply to almost everyone and it is flattering. Don't we all consider

ourselves to be "independent thinkers"?

This is why many psychologists worry about the "Barnum effect" (Snyder & Shenkel, 1975). P. T. Barnum was the great circus showman who said, "There's a sucker born every minute." He knew that the formula for success was to "have a little something for everybody"—and that is just what unscientific personality profiles, horoscopes, and handwriting analysis (graphology) have in common. They have "a little something for everyone" and are therefore nonfalsifiable.

For example, graphologists claim that they can identify your personality traits from the form and distribution of your handwritten letters. Wide spacing between words means you feel isolated and lonely. If your lines drift upward, you are an "uplifting" optimist, and if your lines droop downward, you are a pessimist who feels you are being "dragged down." If you make large capital *I*'s, you have a large ego.

Graphologists are not the same as handwriting experts, who are trained to determine, say, whether a document is a forgery. Graphologists, like astrologers, usually know little or nothing about the scientific method, how to correct for their biases, or how to empirically test their claims. That is why the many different graphological approaches usually conflict. For example, according to one system, a certain way of crossing *t*'s reveals someone who is vicious and sadistic; according to another, it reveals a practical joker (Beyerstein, 1996).

Whenever graphology *has* been tested empirically, it has failed. A meta-analysis of 200 published studies found no validity or reliability to graphology in predicting work performance, aptitudes, or personality. No school of graphology fared better than any other, and no graphologist was able to perform better than untrained amateurs making guesses from the same writing samples (Dean, 1992; Klimoski, 1992).

"Handwriting analysis has revealed that Spencer is not in fact my husband."

If graphology were just an amusing game, no one would worry about it, but unfortunately it can have harmful consequences. Graphologists have been hired by companies to predict a person's leadership ability, attention to detail, willingness to be a good team player, and more. They pass judgment on people's honesty, generosity, and even supposed criminal tendencies. How would you feel if you were turned down for a job because some graphologist branded you a potential thief on the basis of your alleged "desire-for-possession hooks" on your *S*'s?

If you do not want to be taken in by graphology or the many other methods that rely on the Barnum effect, research offers this advice:

- **Beware of all-purpose descriptions that could apply to anyone.** Sometimes you doubt your decisions; who among us has not? Sometimes you feel outgoing and sometimes shy; who does not? Do you "have sexual secrets that you are afraid of confessing"? Just about everybody does.

- **Beware of your own selective perceptions.** Most of us are so impressed when an astrologer, psychic, or graphologist gets something right that we overlook all the descriptions that are plain wrong. Be aware of the confirmation bias—the tendency to explain away all the descriptions that don't fit.

- **Resist flattery.** This is a hard one! It is easy to reject a profile that describes you as selfish or stupid. Watch out for the ones that tell you how wonderful and smart you are, what a great leader you will be, or how modest you are about your abilities.

If you keep your critical faculties with you, you won't end up paying hard cash for soft answers or taking a job you dislike because it fits your "personality type." In other words, you'll have proved Barnum wrong.

Summary

- Personality refers to an individual's distinctive and relatively stable pattern of behavior, motives, thoughts, and emotions. Personality is made up of many different *traits*, characteristics that describe a person across situations.

Psychodynamic Theories of Personality

- Sigmund Freud was the founder of *psychoanalysis*, which was the first *psychodynamic* theory. Modern psychodynamic theories share an emphasis on unconscious processes and a belief in the formative role of childhood experiences and early unconscious conflicts.
- To Freud, the personality consists of the *id* (the source of sexual energy, which he called the *libido*, and the aggressive instinct); the *ego* (the source of reason); and the *superego* (the source of conscience). *Defense mechanisms* protect the ego from unconscious anxiety. They include, among others, repression, projection, displacement (one form of which is sublimation), reaction formation, regression, and denial.
- Freud believed that personality develops in a series of *psychosexual stages*, with the *phallic (Oedipal) stage* most crucial. During this stage, Freud believed, the *Oedipus complex* occurs, in which the child desires the parent of the other sex and feels rivalry with the same-sex parent. When the Oedipus complex is resolved, the child identifies with the same-sex parent, but females retain a lingering sense of inferiority and "penis envy"—a notion later contested by female psychoanalysts like Clara Thompson and Karen Horney.
- Carl Jung believed that people share a *collective unconscious* that contains universal memories and images, or *archetypes*. Personality, in this view, includes many archetypes, such as the *shadow* (evil) and the *anima* and *animus*.
- The *object-relations school* emphasizes the importance of the first two years of life rather than the Oedipal phase; the infant's relationships to important figures, especially the mother, rather than sexual needs and drives; and the problem in male development of breaking away from the mother.
- Psychodynamic approaches have been criticized for violating the principle of falsifiability; for overgeneralizing from atypical patients to everyone; and for basing theories on the unreliable memories and retrospective accounts of patients, which can create an *illusion of causality*. However, some psychodynamic ideas have received empirical support, including the existence of nonconscious processes and defenses.

The Modern Study of Personality

- Most popular tests that divide personality into "types" are not valid or reliable. In research, psychologists typically rely on *objective tests (inventories)*, such as the Minnesota Multiphasic Personality Inventory or the Multidimensional Personality Questionnaire, to identify and study personality traits and disorders.
- Gordon Allport argued that people have a few *central traits* that are key to their personalities and a greater number of *secondary traits* that are less fundamental. Raymond Cattell used *factor analysis* to identify clusters of traits that he considered the basic components of personality. There is strong evidence, from studies around the world, for the *Big Five* dimensions of personality: extroversion versus introversion, neuroticism (negative emotionality) versus emotional stability, agreeableness versus antagonism, conscientiousness versus impulsiveness, and openness to experience versus resistance to new experience. Although these dimensions are quite stable over time and across circumstances, some of them do change over the life span, reflecting maturational development or common adult responsibilities.

Genetic Influences on Personality

- As discussed in "Biology and Animal Traits," members of many other species, including octopuses, pigs, hyenas, bears, horses, dogs, and all primates, vary in the same characteristic traits that humans do—such as shyness, aggressiveness, extroversion, agreeableness, and neuroticism. This evidence suggests that certain key personality traits have an evolutionary, biological basis.
- In human beings, individual differences in *temperaments*—ways of reacting to the environment—appear to be inborn, emerging early in life and influencing subsequent personality development. Temperamental differences in extremely reactive and nonreactive children may be due to variations in the responsiveness of the sympathetic nervous system to change and novelty.
- *Behavioral-genetic* data from twin and adoption studies suggest that the *heritability* of many adult personality traits is around .50. Genetic influences create dispositions and set limits on the expression of specific traits. But even traits that are highly heritable are often modified throughout life by circumstances, chance, and learning.

Environmental Influences on Personality

- People often behave inconsistently in different circumstances when behaviors that are rewarded in one situation are punished or ignored in another. According to *social-cognitive learning theory*, personality results from the interaction of the environment and aspects of the individual, in a pattern of *reciprocal determinism*.
- Behavioral geneticists have found that an important influence on personality is the *nonshared environment*, the unique experiences that each child in a family has.
- Three lines of evidence challenge the popular assumption that parents have the greatest impact on their children's personalities and behavior: (1) Behavioral-genetic studies find that shared family environment has little if any influence on variations in personality; (2) few parents have a consistent child-rearing style over time and with all their children; and (3) even when parents try to be consistent, there may be little relation between what they do and how the children turn out. However, parents can modify their children's temperaments, prevent children at risk of delinquency and crime from choosing a path of antisocial behavior, modify the extent of a child's shyness, influence many of their children's values and attitudes, and teach them to be kind and helpful. And, of course, parents profoundly affect the quality of their relationship with their children.
- One major environmental influence on personality comes from a person's peer groups, which can be more powerful than parents. Most children and teenagers behave differently with their parents than with their peers.

Cultural Influences on Personality

- Many qualities that Western psychologists treat as individual personality traits are heavily influenced by *culture*. People from *individualist cultures* define themselves in different terms than those from *collectivist cultures*, and they perceive their "selves" as more stable across situations. Cultures vary in their norms for many behaviors, such as cleanliness and tardiness. Altruistic children tend to come from cultures in which their families assign them many tasks that contribute to the family's well-being or economic survival.
- As described in the "Close-up on Research," male violence is not simply a result of male testosterone; it is also influenced by the economic requirements of the culture a man grows up in. Herding economies foster male aggressiveness more than agricultural economies do. Men in *cultures of honor*, including certain regions of the American South and West, are more likely to become angry when they feel insulted and to behave aggressively to restore their sense of honor than are men from other cultures; when they are insulted, their levels of cortisol and testosterone rise quickly, whereas men from other cultures generally do not show this reaction.
- Cultural theories of personality face the problem of describing broad cultural differences and their influences on personality without promoting stereotypes or overlooking universal human needs.

The Inner Experience

- *Humanist psychologists* focus on a person's subjective sense of self and the free will to change. They emphasize human potential and the strengths of human nature, as in Abraham Maslow's concepts of *peak experiences* and *self-actualization*. Carl Rogers stressed the importance of *unconditional positive regard* in creating a fully functioning person. Rollo May brought *existentialism* into psychology, emphasizing some of the inherent challenges of human existence that result from having free will, such as the search for meaning in life.
- As another way of understanding personality from the "inside," some personality psychologists today study *life narratives*, the stories people create to explain themselves and make sense of their lives.
- Some ideas from humanist psychology are subjective and difficult to measure, but others have fostered research on positive aspects of personality, such as optimism, hope, and resilience under adversity. Research on the importance of life narratives has influenced the study of personality, memory, psychotherapy, and other areas.
- Genetic influences, life experiences and learned habits, cultural norms, unconscious fears and conflicts, and our private, inner sense of self all combine in complex ways to create our distinctive personalities.

KEY TERMS

personality 482
trait 482
Sigmund Freud 482
psychoanalysis 482
psychodynamic theories 482
id 483
libido 483
ego 483
superego 483
defense mechanisms 483
repression 484
projection 484
displacement and sublimation 484
reaction formation 484
regression 484
denial 485
psychosexual stages (oral, anal, phallic, latency, genital) 485
Oedipus complex 485
Clara Thompson and Karen Horney 486
Carl Jung 487
collective unconscious 487
archetypes 487
shadow 487
anima, animus 487
object-relations school 488
mental representations 488
illusion of causality 490
objective tests (inventories) 491
Gordon Allport 491
central and secondary traits 492
Raymond Cattell 492
factor analysis 492
the "Big Five" personality traits 492
temperaments 497
heritability 497
social-cognitive learning theory 500
reciprocal determinism 500
nonshared environment 500
culture 504
individualist versus collectivist cultures 505
culture of honor 508
humanist psychology 511
Abraham Maslow 511
peak experiences 511
self-actualization 511
Carl Rogers 511
congruence 511
unconditional positive regard 511
Rollo May 512
existentialism 512
life narratives 512

What Type Are You?

NOW YOU HAVE READ CHAPTER THIRTEEN — ARE YOU PREPARED FOR THE EXAM?

Many have compared Freud's idea of the mind to an iceberg. If that were the case and you were standing on the deck of a ship in Alaska, what part of the mind would you see above the water?

How did Freud view the divisions of the conscious mind? (pages 483–484)

ego

Individualistic would describe the cultural personality of the United States according to Hofstede's dimensions of cultural personality. True or false?

What were Hofstede's dimensions of cultural personality? (pages 504–507)

true

In Chapter 13, you learned about a number of different ways to identify an individual's personality. One key ingredient to improve your study habits is to understand yourself and how you learn. Just like personality, learning styles can be described a lot of different ways. One description divides learning styles into three types: visual, auditory, and kinesthetic.

A **visual learning style** focuses on retaining and recalling information visually. An **auditory learning style** relies on receiving and recalling information verbally. The **kinesthetic learning style** focuses on actually doing something during the learning process.

The activities available to you at **www.mypsychlab.com** are designed to appeal to a variety of learning styles. Check out the practice tests, Flash Cards and simulations to help you determine what style of studying suits you best.

How did Freud view the divisions of the conscious mind?

Students often confuse the levels of awareness suggested by Freud with his three components of personality. Check out the definitions of the levels of awareness with your Flash Cards **(conscious, preconscious and unconscious).**

45	13	71
preconscious mind	conscious mind	unconscious mind
level of the mind in which information is available but not currently conscious	level of the mind that is aware of immediate surroundings and perceptions	level of the mind in which thoughts, feelings, memories, and other information are kept that are not easily or voluntarily brought into consciousness
45	13	71

What are the three parts of the personality and how do they interact?

Now think about the three components that Freud suggested make up an individual's personality; the **id,** the **ego,** and the **superego.** Look at these terms in your Flash Cards and try the quizzes and activities on Freud in this section of MyPsychLab.

APPLY IT

Early psychologists who agreed with Freud's basic idea that the unconscious plays an important role in human behavior, but disagreed with some of the specific aspects of Freud's theories have been called NeoFreudians.

From the menu below, match up the theory and the picture with the correct NeoFreudian:

The NeoFreudian psychoanalyst pictured above, ____________ believed that social relationships (not sexual urges) guided the development of personality.

✓
- Erik Erikson
- Carl Jung
- Alfred Adler
- Karen Horney

A national survey of students at five college campuses using MyPsychLab for at least one semester revealed extremely positive results.

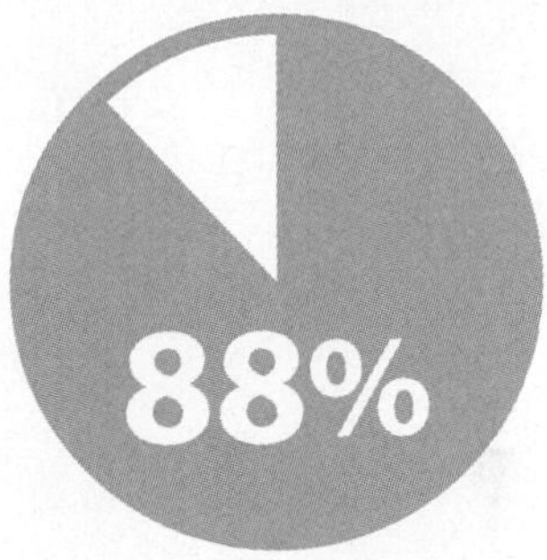

88% of students agreed: "The diagnostic tests helped me know what topics I needed to study further and helped me prepare for my tests."

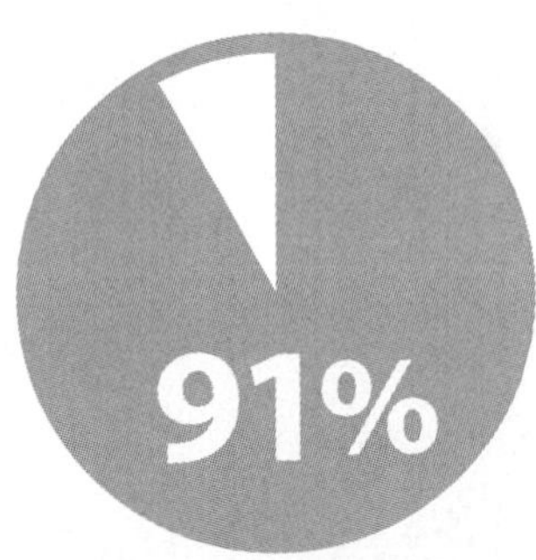

91% of students agreed: "The exit tests helped me know what topics I needed to focus on and helped me prepare for my class tests."

What can you find in MyPsychLab?

Self-Directed Tests • Videos • Simulations • eBook • Flash Cards • Web Links . . . and more — organized by chapter, section and learning objective.

DEVELOPMENT OVER THE LIFE SPAN

CHAPTER FOURTEEN

Time is a dressmaker specializing in alterations.

FAITH BALDWIN

CHAPTER 14

OUTLINE

A few years ago, a 63-year-old woman gave birth to a healthy baby girl. The child was conceived through in vitro fertilization, with sperm from the woman's 60-year-old husband and an egg donated by a younger woman. The woman and her family were delighted, but some fertility experts and ethicists had misgivings. Dr. Mark Sauer, who pioneered the use of donor eggs in older women, said, "I lose my comfort level after 55 because I have to believe that there are quality-of-life issues involved in raising a child at (the parent's) age. When (the baby) is 5, her mother will be 68. And I have to believe that a 78-year-old dealing with a teenager may have some problems."

How do *you* react to the idea of a 63-year-old woman having a baby? Would it make any difference if the mother were "only" 55 years old, or 50, or 45? How do you feel about a man fathering a baby when he is in his 70s or 80s? Do you feel the same about older fathers as you do about older mothers? Is there a right time to become a parent? For that matter, is there a right time to do anything in life—go to school, get married, retire, . . . die?

The universal human journey from birth to death was once far more predictable than it is today. Going to college, starting a family, choosing a job, and advancing up the ladder to retirement were all events that tended to happen in sequence. But because of demographic changes, an unpredictable economy, a high divorce rate, advances in reproductive technology, and many other forces, millions of people are now doing things out of order, if they do them at all. Today these events—going to college, having children, changing careers, starting new families—may occur in almost any decade of adulthood.

Developmental psychologists study physiological and cognitive changes across the life span and how these are affected by a person's genetic predispositions, culture, circumstances, and experiences. Some focus on children's mental and social development, including **socialization**, the process by which children learn the rules and behavior expected of them by society. Others specialize in the study of adolescents, adults, or the very old. In this chapter, we will explore some of their major findings, starting at the very beginning of human development, with the period before birth, and continuing through adulthood into old age.

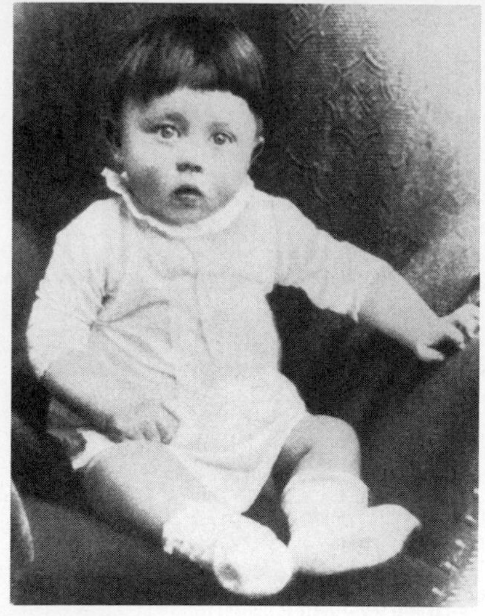

Development depends on the genetic hand you are dealt at birth, the resources and opportunities your parents provide for you, experiences that happen to you, and the unexpected events of history. What futures might you imagine for these three children? At the end of this chapter, you'll see who they are.

WHAT'S**AHEAD**

- How can a pregnant woman reduce the risk of damage to the embryo or fetus?
- How does culture affect how a baby physically matures?
- Why is cuddling so important for infants (not to mention adults)?
- If you have a 1-year-old, why shouldn't you worry if your baby cries when left with a new baby-sitter?
- Do the experiences of the first year of life affect a child's brain forever?

From Conception Through the First Year

A baby's development, before and after birth, is a marvel of *maturation*, the sequential unfolding of genetically influenced behavior and physical characteristics. In only 9 months of a mother's pregnancy, a cell grows from a dot this big (.) to a squalling bundle of energy who looks just like Aunt Sarah. In another 15 months, that bundle of energy grows into a babbling toddler who is curious about everything. No other time in human development brings so many changes, so fast.

Prenatal Development

Prenatal development is divided into three stages: the germinal, the embryonic, and the fetal. The *germinal stage* begins at fertilization, when the male sperm unites with the female ovum (egg); the fertilized single-celled egg is called a *zygote*. The zygote soon begins to divide, and in 10 to 14 days it has become a cluster of cells that attaches itself to the wall of the uterus. The outer portion of this cluster will form part of the placenta and umbilical cord, and the inner portion becomes the embryo. The placenta, connected to the embryo by the umbilical cord, serves as the growing embryo's link for food from the mother. It allows nutrients to enter and wastes to exit, and it screens out some, but not all, harmful substances.

socialization The processes by which children learn the behaviors, attitudes, and expectations required of them by their society or culture.

Once implantation is completed, about two weeks after fertilization, the *embryonic stage* begins, lasting until the eighth week after conception, at which point the embryo is

only $1\frac{1}{2}$ inches long (Moore & Persaud, 2003). During the fourth to eighth weeks, the hormone testosterone is secreted by the rudimentary testes in embryos that are genetically male; without this hormone, the embryo will develop to be anatomically female. After eight weeks, the *fetal stage* begins. The organism, now called a *fetus*, further develops the organs and systems that existed in rudimentary form in the embryonic stage. Although it used to be thought that the last trimester was the most important time for growth of the nervous system, we now know that important events in neural development occur throughout gestation (Nelson, Thomas, & de Haan, 2006).

Although the womb is a fairly sturdy protector of the growing embryo or fetus, some harmful influences can cross the placental barrier (O'Rahilly & Müller, 2001). These influences include the following:

1 **German measles** (rubella), especially early in the pregnancy, can affect the fetus's eyes, ears, and heart. The most common consequence is deafness. Rubella is preventable if the mother has been vaccinated, which can be done up to three months before pregnancy.

2 **X-rays or other radiation and toxic chemicals** can cause fetal deformities and cognitive abnormalities that can last throughout life. Exposure to lead is associated with attention problems and lower IQ scores (see Chapter 3), as is exposure to mercury, found most commonly in contaminated fish (Newland & Rasmussen, 2003).

3 **Sexually transmitted diseases** can cause mental retardation, blindness, and other physical disorders. Genital herpes affects the fetus only if the mother has an outbreak at the time of delivery, which exposes the newborn to the virus as the baby passes through the birth canal. (This risk can be avoided by having a cesarean section.) HIV, the virus that causes AIDS, can also be transmitted to the fetus, especially if the mother has developed AIDS and has not been treated.

4 **Cigarette smoking** during pregnancy increases the likelihood of miscarriage, premature birth, abnormal fetal heartbeat, and an underweight baby. The negative effects may last long after birth, showing up in increased rates of infant sickness, sudden infant death syndrome (SIDS), and, in later childhood, hyperactivity, learning difficulties, and even antisocial behavior (Button, Thapar, & McGuffin, 2005).

5 **Regular consumption of alcohol** can kill neurons throughout the fetus's developing brain and impair the child's later mental abilities, attention span, and academic achievement (Ikonomidou et al., 2000; Streissguth, 2001). Having more than two drinks

Many parents hope to have an influence on their offspring even before their babies are born.

a day significantly increases the risk of *fetal alcohol syndrome (FAS)*, which is associated with low birth weight, a smaller brain, facial deformities, lack of coordination, and mental retardation. FAS is the leading cause of nonhereditary mental retardation, but it is simply the extreme end of a spectrum of alcohol-related birth defects that range from mild to severe (Sampson et al., 2000). Because alcohol can affect many different aspects of fetal brain development, most specialists recommend that a pregnant woman abstain from drinking alcohol.

6 **Drugs other than alcohol** can be harmful to the fetus, whether they are illicit ones such as morphine, cocaine, and heroin, or commonly used legal substances such as antibiotics, antihistamines, tranquilizers, acne medication, and diet pills. Cocaine can cause subtle impairments in children's cognitive and language abilities and larger ones in the ability to manage impulses and frustrations (Lester, LaGasse, & Seifer, 1998; Stanwood & Levitt, 2001).

The lesson is clear. A pregnant woman does well to stop smoking and drinking alcohol, and to take no other drugs of any kind unless they are medically necessary—and then to accept the fact that her child will never be properly grateful for all that sacrifice!

The Infant's World

Newborn babies could never survive on their own, but they are far from being passive and inert. Many abilities, tendencies, and characteristics are universal in human beings and are present at birth or develop very early, given certain experiences.

Physical and Perceptual Abilities. Newborns begin life with several *motor reflexes*, automatic behaviors that are necessary for survival. They will suck on anything suckable, such as a nipple or finger. They will grasp tightly a finger pressed on their tiny palms. They will turn their heads toward a touch on the cheek or corner of the mouth and search for something to suck on, a handy rooting reflex that allows them to find the breast or bottle. Many of these reflexes eventually disappear, but others—such as the knee-jerk, eye-blink, and sneeze reflexes—remain. Pediatricians test infants for these reflexes to see whether the baby is developing properly.

Babies are also equipped with a set of inborn perceptual abilities. They can see, hear, touch, smell, and taste (bananas and sugar water are in, rotten eggs are out). A newborn's visual focus range is only about 8 inches, the average distance between the baby and the face of the person holding the baby, but visual ability develops rapidly. Newborns can distinguish contrasts, shadows, and edges. And they can discriminate their mother or other primary caregiver on the basis of smell, sight, or sound almost immediately.

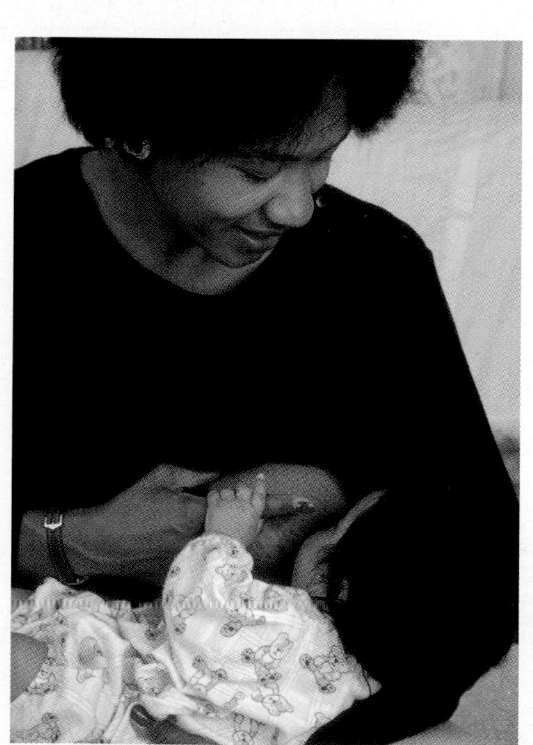

The grasping and sucking reflexes at work.

Culture and Maturation. Although infants everywhere develop according to the same maturational sequence, many aspects of their development depend on cultural customs that govern how their parents hold, touch, feed, and talk to them (Rogoff, 2003). For example, in the United States, Canada, and Germany and most other European countries, babies are expected to sleep for eight uninterrupted hours by the age of 4 or 5 months. This milestone is considered a sign of neurological maturity, although many babies wail when the parent puts them in the crib at night and leaves the room. But among Mayan Indians, rural Italians, African villagers, Indian Rajput villagers, and urban Japanese, this nightly clash of

wills rarely occurs because the infant sleeps with the mother for the first few years of life, waking and nursing about every four hours. These differences in babies' sleep arrangements reflect cultural and parental values. Mothers in close-knit agricultural communities believe it is important to sleep with the baby in order for both to forge a close bond; many urban North American and German parents believe it is important to foster the child's independence as soon as possible (Keller et al., 2005; Morelli et al., 1992).

Developmental milestones can change quickly when there is a cultural change in baby-care practices. For example, the milestone for crawling has traditionally been about 6 to 8 months. Nowadays, however, many babies do not begin crawling at that age, or even at all; they go directly from sitting to toddling. Why? When babies are put to sleep on their stomachs, from that position a little squirming and a push-up leads to crawling. But since the early 1990s, physicians have been advising parents to put babies on their backs to sleep, to avoid the risk of suffocation. In that position, it is more difficult for a baby to roll over and start crawling, and more and more babies never do. Yet they are perfectly normal by every other measure (Davis et al., 1998). And they all eventually get up and walk.

Most Navaho babies calmly accept being strapped to a cradle board (left), whereas white babies will often protest vigorously (right). Yet despite cultural differences in such practices, babies everywhere eventually sit up and walk.

Attachment

Emotional attachment is a universal capacity of all primates and is crucial for health and survival all through life. The mother is usually the first and primary object of attachment for an infant, but in many cultures (and other species), babies become just as attached to their fathers, siblings, and grandparents (Hrdy, 1999).

Interest in the importance of early attachment began with the work of British psychiatrist John Bowlby (1969, 1973), who observed the devastating effects on babies raised in orphanages without touches or cuddles, and on other children raised in conditions of severe deprivation or neglect. The babies were physically healthy but emotionally despairing, remote, and listless. By becoming attached to their caregivers, Bowlby said, children gain a secure base from which they can explore the environment and a haven of safety to return to when they are afraid. Ideally, infants will find a balance between feeling securely attached to the caregiver and feeling free to explore and learn in new environments. Adults, too, continuously balance the need for closeness and security with the need for independence and exploration (Elliot & Reis, 2003).

Contact Comfort. Attachment begins with physical touching and cuddling between infant and parent. **Contact comfort**, the pleasure of being touched and held, continues to be important throughout life, and as we discussed in Chapter 12, it releases a flood of pleasure-producing endorphins. In hospital settings, even the mildest touch by a nurse or physician on the patient's arm or forehead reassures and comforts (Field, 1998).

Margaret and Harry Harlow first demonstrated the importance of contact comfort by raising infant rhesus monkeys with two kinds of artificial mothers (Harlow, 1958; Harlow & Harlow, 1966). One, which they called the "wire mother," was a forbidding construction of wires and warming lights, with a milk bottle connected to it. The other, the "cloth mother," was constructed of wire but covered in foam rubber and cuddly terry cloth (see Figure 14.1). At the time, many psychologists thought that babies become attached to their mothers simply because mothers provide food (Blum, 2002). But the Harlows' baby monkeys ran to the terry-cloth "mother" when they were frightened or startled, and cuddling up to it calmed them down. Human children, too, often seek contact comfort when they are in an unfamiliar situation, are scared by a nightmare, or fall and hurt themselves.

contact comfort In primates, the innate pleasure derived from close physical contact; it is the basis of the infant's first attachment.

FIGURE 14.1 The Comfort of Contact

Infants need cuddling as much as they need food. In Margaret and Harry Harlow's studies, infant rhesus monkeys were reared with a cuddly terry-cloth "mother" and with a bare wire "mother" that provided milk (left). The infants would cling to the terry mother when they were not being fed, and when they were frightened (as the infant on the right was by a toy spider put in his enclosure), it was the terry mother they ran to.

separation anxiety The distress that most children develop, at about 6 to 8 months of age, when their primary caregivers temporarily leave them with strangers.

Separation and Security. Once babies are emotionally attached to the mother or other caregiver, separation can be a wrenching experience. Between 6 and 8 months of age, babies become wary or fearful of strangers. They wail if they are put in an unfamiliar setting or are left with an unfamiliar person. And they show **separation anxiety** if the primary caregiver temporarily leaves them. This reaction usually continues until the middle of the second year, but many children show signs of distress until they are about 3 years old (Hrdy, 1999). All children go through this phase, though cultural childrearing practices influence how strongly the anxiety is felt and how long it lasts (see Figure 14.2). In cultures where babies are raised with lots of adults and other children, separation anxiety is not as intense or as long-lasting as it can be in countries where babies form attachments primarily or exclusively with the mother (Rothbaum et al., 2000).

To study the nature of the attachment between mothers and babies, Mary Ainsworth (1973, 1979) devised an experimental method called the *Strange Situation*. A mother brings her baby into an unfamiliar room containing lots of toys. After a while a stranger comes in and attempts to play with the child. The mother leaves the baby with the stranger. She then returns and plays with the child, and the stranger leaves. Finally, the mother leaves the baby alone for three minutes and returns. In each case, observers carefully note how the baby behaves with the mother, with the stranger, and when the baby is alone.

STYLES OF ATTACHMENT

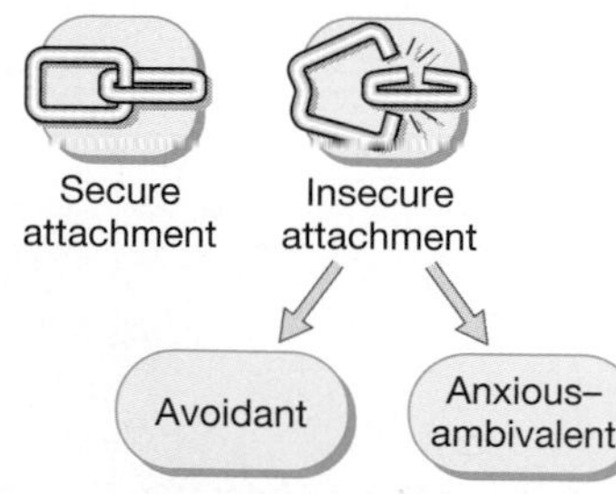

Ainsworth divided children into three categories on the basis of their reactions to the Strange Situation. Some babies are *securely attached*: They cry or protest if the parent leaves the room; they welcome her back and then play happily again; they are clearly more attached to the mother than to the stranger. Other babies are *insecurely attached*, and this insecurity can take two forms. The child may be *avoidant*, not caring if the mother leaves the room, making little effort to seek contact with her on her return, and treating the stranger about the same as the mother. Or the child may be *anxious* or *ambivalent*, resisting contact with the mother at reunion but protesting loudly if she leaves. Anxious-ambivalent babies may cry to be picked up and then demand to be put down, or they may behave as if they are angry with the mother and resist her efforts to comfort them. Insecure attachment is associated with later emotional and behavioral problems in children, such as

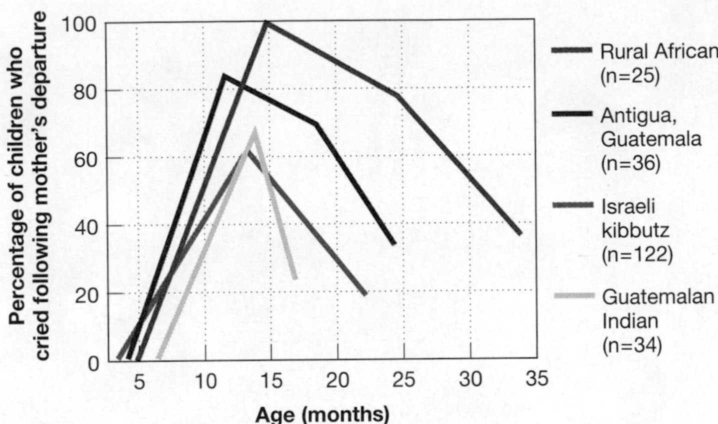

FIGURE 14.2 The Rise and Fall of Separation Anxiety
At around 6 months of age, many babies begin to show separation anxiety when the person who is their main source of attachment tries handing them over to someone else or leaves the room. This anxiety typically peaks at about a year of age and then steadily declines. But the proportion of children responding this way varies across cultures. It is high among rural African children and low among children raised in a communal Israeli kibbutz, where children become attached to many adults (Kagan, Kearsley, & Zelazo, 1978).

aggressiveness, poor social relationships, and acting out (Gauthier, 2003; Mickelson, Kessler, & Shaver, 1997; NICHD Early Child Care Research Network, 2006).

What Causes Insecure Attachment? Ainsworth believed that the difference between secure, avoidant, and anxious-ambivalent attachment lies primarily in the way mothers treat their babies during the first year. Mothers who are sensitive and responsive to their babies' needs, she said, create securely attached infants; mothers who are uncomfortable with or insensitive to their babies create insecurely attached infants. To many, the implication was that babies needed exactly the right kind of mothering from the very start in order to become securely attached, and that putting a child in day care would retard this important development—notions that have caused considerable insecurity among mothers!

"Please, Jason. Don't you want to grow up to be an autonomous person?"

Ainsworth's measure of attachment, however, did not take the baby's experience into account. Babies who become attached to many adults, because they live in large extended families or have spent a lot of time with adults in day care, may seem to be avoidant in the Strange Situation because they don't panic when their mothers leave. But perhaps they have simply learned to be comfortable with strangers. Moreover, although there is a modest correlation between a mother's sensitivity and a child's secure attachment, this doesn't tell us which causes what, or whether something else causes both sensitivity and attachment (De Wolff & van IJzendoorn, 1997). Programs designed to help new mothers become less anxious and more attuned to their babies do help some moms become more sensitive, but these programs only modestly affect the child's degree of secure attachment (Bakermans-Kranenburg, van IJzendoorn, & Juffer, 2003).

The emphasis on maternal sensitivity also overlooks the fact that most children, all over the world, form a secure attachment to their mothers in spite of wide variations in child-rearing practices (Mercer, 2006). For example, German babies are frequently left on their own for a few hours at a stretch by mothers who believe that even babies should become self-reliant. And among the Efe of Africa, babies spend about half their time away from their mothers in the care of older children and other adults (Tronick, Morelli, & Ivey, 1992). Yet German and Efe children are not insecure, and they develop as normally as children who spend more time with their mothers.

Likewise, time spent in day care has no effect on the security of a child's attachment. In a longitudinal study of more than 1,000 children, researchers compared

Longitudinal studies find that good day care does not affect the security of children's attachments and often produces many social and intellectual benefits.

infants who were in child care 30 hours or more a week, from age 3 months to age 15 months, with children who spent fewer than 10 hours a week in child care. The two groups did not differ on any measure of attachment, and children in high-quality day care did better on measures of social, language, and cognitive development than children at home (NICHD Early Child Care Research Network, 2002). (Unfortunately, according to a National Research Council report, most child-care facilities in the United States are mediocre or inadequate, which may be why some children in day care do have more behavioral problems than they would at home [Marshall, 2004].)

What factors, then, promote insecure attachment?

- *Abandonment and deprivation in the first two years of life.* For example, Romanian babies raised in orphanages for their first two years are less likely than babies adopted earlier to become securely attached to their eventual adoptive parents, although most ultimately do fine (Rutter et al., 2004).
- *Parenting that is abusive, neglectful, or erratic because the parent is chronically irresponsible or depressed.* A South African research team observed 147 mothers with their 2-month-old infants and followed up when the babies were 18 months old. Children whose mothers had suffered from postpartum depression, leading the women to be either too intrusive with their infants or too remote and insensitive, were more likely to be insecurely attached at 18 months (Tomlinson, Cooper, & Murray, 2005).
- *The child's own genetically influenced temperament.* Babies who are fearful and prone to crying from birth are more likely to show insecure behavior in the Strange Situation (Belsky et al., 1996; Seifer et al., 1996).
- *Changing, stressful circumstances in the child's family.* Infants and young children may temporarily shift from secure to insecure attachment, becoming clingy and fearful of being left alone, if their families are undergoing a period of stress, as during parental divorce or a parent's chronic illness (Belsky et al., 1996; Mercer, 2006).

The bottom line, however, is that infants are biologically disposed to become attached to their caregivers. Normal, healthy attachment will occur within a wide range of cultural, family, and individual variations in child-rearing customs.

How Critical Are the Early Years?

Many psychologists believe that the first one to three years of life are crucial to a child's mental development, largely because of the rapid growth of the brain during this time. During the baby's first 15 months, there is an explosion of new synapses, the connections among neurons in the brain (see Chapter 4). In fact, too many synapses are produced. As the brain integrates and consolidates early experience, unnecessary synapses are pruned away, leaving behind a more efficient neural network (Segalowitz & Schmidt, 2003).

Some psychologists and popular writers have interpreted these facts to mean that infants need maximum stimulation and crucial experiences in order to develop an optimum number of synapses. They fear that if a baby does not start out well or get enough mental stimulation, the baby's whole life will be influenced for the worse. Of course, brain development can indeed be impaired in infants who are completely deprived of contact comfort and attention, or whose developing brains are damaged in the womb (Rutter et al., 2004). But media accounts and ads for "baby genius" products that promise to stimulate and enhance early brain development have tended to exaggerate and oversimplify the research. The brain is not formed, once and for all, in the first year (see Chapter 4). The process of synapse formation and pruning in different parts of the brain continues all through childhood and again in adolescence, and synapses keep developing even into the later years (Greenough, Cohen, & Juraska, 1999; Kolb, Gibb, & Robinson, 2003).

Still, many questions about early brain development remain unanswered. We know that there are critical periods during the first year for the development of normal perceptual abilities (see Chapter 6), but we do not know the extent or impact of critical periods for intellectual development. We do not know which early experiences, if any, are essential in early brain development or when they must occur. In the absence of such information, the public would be wise to be wary of fads and exaggerated claims. The first year is important in brain development, but so is prenatal care and so is what happens in a child's later years. In "Taking Psychology with You," we consider other information that might alleviate the anxieties many parents feel about whether they are doing the right thing.

THINKING CRITICALLY

DON'T OVERSIMPLIFY

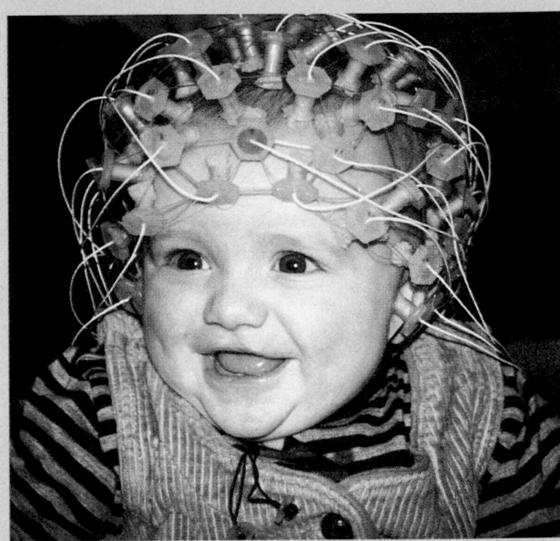

This baby is wearing a device that allows researchers to record the electrical activity of her brain as she learns. Such methods are yielding many discoveries about the developing brain. But some people are oversimplifying them, jumping to the conclusion that infants need constant mental stimulation to achieve maximum intelligence.

QUICK quiz

Are you feeling secure, anxious, or avoidant about quizzes?

1. Name as many potentially harmful influences on fetal development as you can.
2. Melanie is playing happily on a jungle gym at her day-care center when she falls off and badly scrapes her knee. She runs to her caregiver for a consoling cuddle. Melanie seeks ______.
3. *True or false*: To develop normally, infants must sleep in their own cribs, apart from their mothers.
4. A baby left in the Strange Situation does not protest when his mother leaves the room, and he seems to ignore her when she returns. What style of attachment does this behavior reflect?
5. In Item 4, what else besides the child's style of attachment could account for the child's reaction?

Answers:

1. German measles early in pregnancy; exposure to radiation or toxic chemicals such as lead or mercury; sexually transmitted diseases; the mother's use of cigarettes, alcohol, or other drugs **2.** contact comfort **3.** false **4.** insecure (avoidant) **5.** the child's own temperament and the child's familiarity with being temporarily left alone

WHAT'S**AHEAD**

- Why do so many parents speak baby talk?
- What important accomplishment are infants revealing when they learn to play peekaboo?
- Why will most 5-year-olds choose a tall, narrow glass of lemonade over a short, fat glass containing the same amount?

Cognitive Development

A friend of ours told us about a charming exchange he had with his 2-year-old grandson. "You're very old," the little boy said. "Yes, I am," said his grandfather. "I'm very new," said the child. Two years old, and already this little boy's mind is working away, making observations, trying to understand the differences he observes, and using language (creatively!) to describe them. The development of language and thought from infancy throughout childhood is a marvel to anyone who knows a child—or was one.

Language

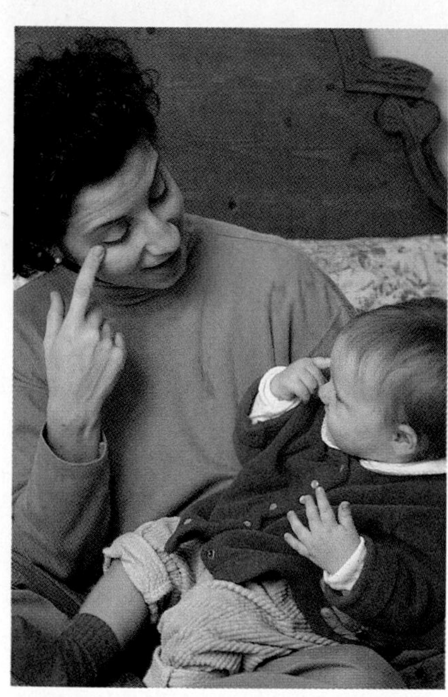

Say out loud, "Where is your eye?" Now repeat the question as if you were talking to this baby. Chances are your voice will shift to "parentese," becoming more singsong, rhythmic, and higher in pitch. The melodic rhythms of baby talk help babies learn language.

In Chapter 3 we saw that the ability to use language is an evolutionary adaptation of the human species. In only a few years, children are able to understand thousands of words, use rules of syntax to string them together in meaningful sentences, and produce and understand an endless number of new word combinations.

The acquisition of language begins in the first few months. Infants may only be able to cry and coo, but they are already responsive to the pitch, intensity, and sound of language, and they react to the emotions and rhythms in voices. When most people speak to babies, their pitch is higher and more varied than usual and their intonation and emphasis on vowels are exaggerated. Adult use of baby talk, which researchers call *parentese*, has been documented all over the world, from Sweden to Japan. Parentese helps babies learn the melody and rhythm of their native language (Burnham, Kitamura, & Vollmer-Conna, 2002; Fernald & Mazzie, 1991).

By 4 to 6 months of age, babies can often recognize their own names and other words that are regularly spoken with emotion, such as "mommy" and "daddy." They also know many of the key consonant and vowel sounds of their native language and can distinguish such sounds from those of other languages (Kuhl et al., 1992). Over time, exposure to the baby's native language reduces the child's ability to perceive speech sounds in other languages. Thus Japanese infants can hear the difference between the English sounds *la* and *ra*, but older Japanese children cannot. Because this contrast does not exist in their language, they become insensitive to it.

Between 6 months and 1 year, infants become increasingly familiar with the sound structure of their native language. They are able to distinguish words from the flow of speech. They will listen longer to words that violate their expectations of what words should sound like and even to sentences that violate their expectations of how sentences should be structured (Jusczyk, 2002; Jusczyk, Houston, & Newsome, 1999). They start to babble, making many ba-ba and goo-goo sounds, endlessly repeating sounds and syllables. At seven and a half months, they begin to remember words they have heard, but because they are also attending to the speaker's intonation, speaking rate, and volume, they can't always recognize the same word when it is spoken by different people (Houston & Jusczyk, 2003). Then, by $10^{1}/_{2}$ months, they can suddenly do it—a remarkable leap forward in only three months. And at about a year of age,

though the timing varies considerably, children take another giant step: They start to name things. They already have some concepts in their minds for familiar people and objects, and their first words represent these concepts ("mama," "doggie," "truck").

Also at the end of the first year, babies develop a repertoire of symbolic gestures, another important tool of communication. They gesture to refer to objects (e.g., sniffing to indicate "flower"), to request something (smacking the lips for "food"), to describe objects (raising the arms for "big"), and to reply to questions (opening the palms or shrugging the shoulders for "I don't know"). They clap in response to pictures of things they like, from Teletubbies to baseball games. Children whose parents encourage them to use gestures acquire larger vocabularies, have better comprehension, are better listeners, and are less frustrated in their efforts to communicate than babies who are not encouraged to use gestures (Goodwyn & Acredolo, 1998). When babies begin to speak, they continue to gesture along with their words (just as adults gesture when talking), suggesting that gestures are not a substitute for language but are deeply related to its development (Mayberry & Nicoladis, 2000).

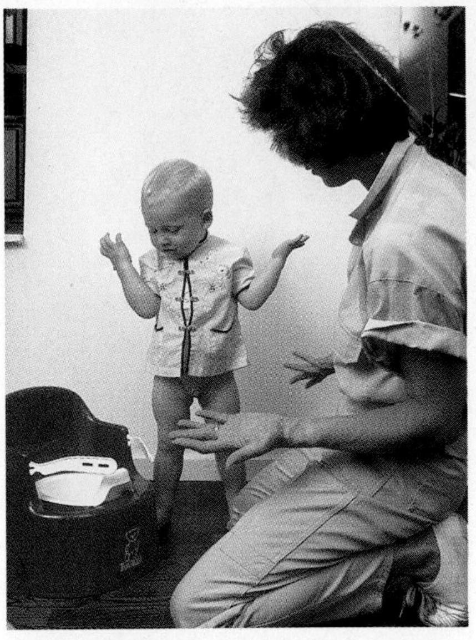

Symbolic gestures emerge early!

Between the ages of 18 months and 2 years, toddlers begin to produce words in two- or three-word combinations ("Mama here," "go 'way bug," "my toy"). The child's first combinations of words have been described as **telegraphic**. When people had to pay for every word in a telegram, they quickly learned to drop unnecessary articles (*a*, *an*, or *the*) and auxiliary verbs (*is* or *are*), but they still conveyed the message. Similarly, the two-word sentences of toddlers omit articles, word endings, auxiliary verbs, and other parts of speech, but these sentences are remarkably accurate in conveying meaning. Children use two-word sentences to locate things ("there toy"), make demands ("more milk"), negate actions ("no want," "all gone milk"), describe events ("Bambi go," "hit ball"), describe objects ("pretty dress"), show possession ("Mama dress"), and ask questions ("where Daddy?"). Pretty good for a little kid, don't you think?

By the age of 6, the average child has a vocabulary of between 8,000 and 14,000 words, meaning that children acquire about five to eight new words a day between the ages of 2 and 6. (When did you last learn and use eight new words in a day?) They absorb new words as they hear them. They form a quick impression of the likely meaning of the word by using their knowledge of grammatical contexts, and from the social context in which they hear the words used (Golinkoff & Hirsh-Pasek, 2006; Rice, 1990).

telegraphic speech A child's first word combinations, which omit (as a telegram did) unnecessary words.

Review 14.1 summarizes the early stages of language development.

REVIEW 14.1

The Early Development of Language

First few months	Babies cry and coo; they respond to emotions and rhythms in voices.
4–6 months	Babies begin to recognize key vowel and consonant sounds of their native language.
6 months–1 year	Infants' familiarity with the sound structure of their native language increases; they can distinguish words from the flow of speech; they eventually can recognize the same word when it is spoken by different people.
End of first year	Infants start to name things based on familiar concepts and use symbolic gestures to communicate.
18–24 months	Children begin to speak in two- and three-word phrases (telegraphic speech).
2–6 years	Children rapidly acquire new words in the context in which they hear them.

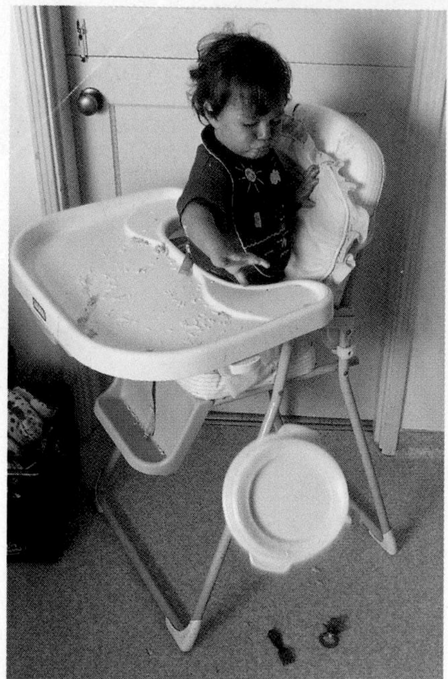

This young scientist is trying to figure out cause and effect: "If I throw this dish, what will happen?"

Thinking

Children do not think the way adults do. For most of the first year of life, if something is out of sight, it's out of mind: If you cover a baby's favorite rattle with a cloth, the baby thinks the rattle has vanished and stops looking for it. And a 4-year-old may protest that a sibling has more fruit juice when it is only the shapes of the glasses that differ, not the amount of juice.

Yet children are smart in their own way. Like good little scientists, children are always testing their child-sized theories about how things work (Gopnik, Meltzoff, & Kuhl, 1999). When your toddler throws her spoon on the floor for the sixth time as you try to feed her, and you say, "That's enough! I will *not* pick up your spoon again!" the child will immediately test your claim. Are you serious? Are you angry? What will happen if she throws the spoon again? She is not doing this to drive you crazy, though it might feel that way. Rather, she is learning that her desires and yours can differ, and that sometimes those differences are important and sometimes they are not.

How and why does children's thinking change? Do their cognitive abilities unfold naturally, like the blooming of a flower, almost independent of what else is happening in their lives? Or are children little information processors, striving to make sense of things and solve problems, coming up with right and wrong answers depending on the problem at hand and what they have been taught?

In the 1920s, Swiss psychologist Jean Piaget [Zhan Pee-ah-ZHAY] (1896–1980) proposed a theory of cognitive development to explain children's charming mistakes. Piaget was to child development what Freud was to psychoanalysis and Skinner to behaviorism. Piaget created the "flower-blooming" school of cognitive development, and although many of his specific conclusions have been rejected or modified over the years, his keen observations of children caused a revolution in thinking about how thinking develops and inspired thousands of studies by investigators all over the world.

Piaget's great insight was that children's errors are as interesting as their correct responses. Children will say things that seem cute or wildly illogical to adults. But the strategies that children use to think and solve problems, said Piaget, are not random or meaningless. They reflect a predictable interaction between the child's maturational stage and the child's experience in the world.

Piaget's Theory of Cognitive Stages. According to Piaget (1929/1960, 1952a, 1984), as children develop, their minds constantly adapt to new situations and experiences. Sometimes they *assimilate* new information into their existing mental categories; for example, a German shepherd and a terrier both fit the category *dogs*. At other times, however, children must change their mental categories to *accommodate* their new experiences; for example, a cat does not belong to the category *dogs* and a new category is required, one for *cats*. Both processes are constantly interacting, Piaget said, as children go through four stages of cognitive development:

1 **The sensorimotor stage (birth to age 2).** In this stage, the infant learns through concrete actions: looking, touching, putting things in the mouth, sucking, grasping. "Thinking" consists of coordinating sensory information with bodily movements. Gradually these movements become more purposeful as the child explores the environment and learns that specific movements will produce specific results. Pulling a cloth away will reveal a hidden toy; letting go of a fuzzy toy duck will cause it to drop out of reach; banging on the table with a spoon will produce dinner (or Mom, taking the spoon away).

A major accomplishment at this stage, said Piaget, is **object permanence**, the understanding that something continues to exist even when you can't see it or touch it. In the first few months, he observed, infants will look intently at a little toy, but if you hide it behind a piece of paper they will not look behind the paper or make an effort to get the

object permanence The understanding, which develops throughout the first year, that an object continues to exist even when you cannot see it or touch it.

toy. By about 6 months of age, however, infants begin to grasp the idea that the toy exists whether or not they can see it. If a baby of this age drops a toy from her playpen, she will look for it; she also will look under a cloth for a toy that is partially hidden. By 1 year of age, most babies have developed an awareness of the permanence of objects; even if a toy is covered by a cloth, it must be under there. This is when they love to play peekaboo.

Object permanence, said Piaget, represents the beginning of the child's capacity to use mental imagery and symbols. The child becomes able to hold a concept in mind, to learn that the word *fly* represents an annoying, buzzing creature and that *Daddy* represents a friendly, playful one.

egocentric thinking Seeing the world from only your own point of view; the inability to take another person's perspective.

conservation The understanding that the physical properties of objects—such as the number of items in a cluster or the amount of liquid in a glass—can remain the same even when their form or appearance changes.

2 **The preoperational stage (ages 2 to 7).** During this stage, the use of symbols and language accelerates. But Piaget described this stage largely in terms of what (he thought) children cannot do. For example, children lack the cognitive abilities necessary for understanding abstract principles and mental *operations*. An operation is a train of thought that can be run backward or forward. Multiplying 2 times 6 to get 12 is an operation; so is the reverse operation, dividing 12 by 6 to get 2. Thus a preoperational child knows that Jessie is his sister, but he may not get the reverse operation, the idea that he is Jessie's brother. Piaget also believed (mistakenly, as we will see) that preoperational children cannot take another person's point of view because their thinking is **egocentric**: They see the world only from their own frame of reference and cannot imagine that others see things differently.

Further, said Piaget, preoperational children cannot grasp the concept of **conservation**, the notion that physical properties do not change when their form or appearance changes. Children at this age do not understand that an amount of liquid or a number of blocks remains the same even if you pour the liquid from one glass to another of a different size or if you stack the blocks (see Figure 14.3). If you pour liquid from a short, fat glass into a tall, narrow glass, preoperational children will say there is more liquid in the second glass. They attend to the appearance of the liquid (its height in the glass) to judge its quantity, and so they are misled.

FIGURE 14.3 Piaget's Principle of Conservation

In a typical test for conservation of number (left), the number of blocks is the same in two sets, but those in one set are then spread out and the child must say whether one set has more blocks than another. Preoperational children think that the set that takes up more space has more blocks. In a test for conservation of quantity (right), the child is shown two short glasses with equal amounts of liquid. Then the contents of one glass are poured into a tall, narrower glass, and the child is asked whether one container now has more. Most preoperational children do not understand that pouring liquid from a short glass into a taller one leaves the amount of liquid unchanged. They judge only by the height of liquid in the glass.

GET INVOLVED!

➤A TEST OF CONSERVATION

If you know any young children, try one of Piaget's conservation experiments. A simple one is to make two rows of seven buttons or pennies, aligned identically. Ask the child whether one row has more. Now simply spread out the buttons in one row, and ask the child again whether one row has more. If the child says "Yes," ask which one, and why. Try to do this experiment with a 3-year-old and a 7- or 8-year-old. You will probably see a big difference in their answers.

3 The concrete operations stage (ages 7 to 12). By this stage, children have developed significantly and have overcome some of their earlier limitations. They are able to take other people's perspectives and they make fewer logical errors. However, Piaget observed, these newfound abilities are usually tied to information that is concrete, that is, to actual experiences that have happened or concepts that have a tangible meaning to them. So children at this stage still make errors of reasoning when they are asked to think about abstract ideas ("patriotism" or "future education") or things that are not physically at hand. During these years, nonetheless, children's cognitive abilities expand rapidly. They come to understand the principles of conservation, reversibility, and cause and effect. They learn mental operations, such as addition, subtraction, multiplication, and division. They are able to categorize things (e.g., oaks as trees) and to order things serially from smallest to largest, lightest to darkest, and shortest to tallest.

4 The formal operations stage (age 12 through adulthood). In this last stage, said Piaget, teenagers become capable of abstract reasoning. They understand that ideas can be compared and classified, just as objects can. They are able to reason about situations they have not experienced firsthand, and they can think about future possibilities. They are able to search systematically for answers to problems. They can formulate explicit hypotheses about how things work and why people do what they do (they are budding psychologists). They are able to draw logical conclusions from premises common to their culture and experience. (Review 14.2 summarizes Piaget's stages of cognitive development.)

REVIEW 14.2

Piaget's Stages of Cognitive Development

Stage		Major Accomplishments
Sensorimotor (ages 0–2)	"Ball"	Object permanence Beginning of representational thought
Preoperational (ages 2–7)		Accelerated use of symbols and language
Concrete operations (ages 7–12)		Understanding of conservation Understanding of identity Understanding of serial ordering
Formal operations (ages 12–adulthood)	"if x then y"	Abstract reasoning Ability to compare and classify ideas

Vygotsky's Theory of Sociocultural Influences. Americans were forever asking Piaget what they could do to speed up their children's mental development. Piaget was amused by what he called "the American question." Forget it, he would tell them. You can't rush the qualitative changes that occur as children go through each cognitive stage.

In contrast, the Russian psychologist Lev Vygotsky (1896–1934), who was born the same year as Piaget but died at the age of only 38, emphasized the *sociocultural* influences on children's cognitive development. Vygotsky (1962, 1978) believed that the child develops mental representations of the world through culture and language, and that adults do play a major role in their children's development by constantly guiding and teaching them. Once children acquire language and internalize the rules of their culture, said Vygotsky, they start using *private speech*, talking to themselves to direct their own behavior. At first, children's private speech is actually spoken aloud. You can often observe preschoolers talking to themselves when they have done something they know is naughty or when they are faced with a problem. Over time, private speech becomes internalized and truly private—that is, silent.

Vygotsky did not share Piaget's view that children go through invariant stages. Once children have language, he said, their cognitive development may proceed in any number of directions, depending on what adults teach them, what their culture makes possible for them, and the particular environment they live in.

Current Views of Cognitive Development. Piaget was a brilliant observer of children, and his major point has been well supported: New reasoning abilities depend on the emergence of previous ones. You cannot learn algebra before you can count, and you cannot learn philosophy before you understand logic. But since Piaget's original work, research has built on and expanded some of his ideas and revised others:

1 **Cognitive abilities develop in continuous, overlapping waves rather than discrete steps or stages.** If you observe children at different ages, as Piaget did, it will seem that they reason differently. But if you study the everyday learning of children at any given age, you will find that a child may use several different strategies to solve a problem, some more complex or accurate than others (Siegler, 2006). Learning occurs gradually, with retreats to former ways of thinking as well as advances to new ones. Children's reasoning ability also depends on the circumstances—who is asking them questions, the specific words used, the materials used, and what they are reasoning about—and not just on the stage they are in. In short, cognitive development is *continuous*; new abilities do not simply pop up when a child turns a certain age (Courage & Howe, 2002).

2 **Preschoolers are not as egocentric as Piaget thought.** Most 3- and 4-year-olds *can* take another person's perspective (Flavell, 1999). When 4-year-olds play with 2-year-olds, for example, they modify and simplify their speech so the younger children will understand (Shatz & Gelman, 1973). One preschooler we know showed her teacher a picture she had drawn of a cat and an unidentifiable blob. "The cat is lovely," said the teacher, "but what is this thing here?" "That has nothing to do with you," said the child. "That's what the *cat* is looking at."

By about ages 3 to 4, children also begin to understand that you cannot predict what a person will do just by observing a situation or knowing the facts. You also

theory of mind A system of beliefs about the way one's own mind and the minds of others work, and of how individuals are affected by their beliefs and feelings.

have to know what the person is feeling and thinking; the person might even be lying. They start asking why other people behave as they do ("Why is Johnny so mean?"). In short, they are developing a **theory of mind**, a system of beliefs about how their own and other people's minds work and how people are affected by their beliefs and emotions (see Chapter 9). They start using verbs like *think* and *know*, and by age 4 they understand that what another person thinks might not match their own beliefs (Flavell, 1999; Lillard, 1998; Wellman, Cross, & Watson, 2001). To cognitive psychologists, the ability to understand that people can have false beliefs is a major milestone, because it means the child is beginning to question how we know things. The ability to think this way is a foundation for later higher-order, scientific thinking.

Possible event

Impossible event

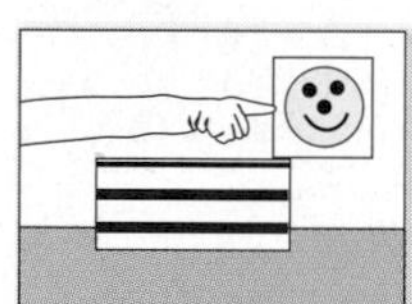

FIGURE 14.4 Testing Infants' Knowledge

In this clever procedure, a baby watches as a box is pushed from left to right along a striped platform. The box is pushed until it reaches the end of the platform (a possible event) or until only a bit of it rests on the platform (an impossible event). Babies look longer at the impossible event, suggesting that it surprises them. Somehow they know that an object needs physical support and can't just float on air (Baillargeon, 1994).

3 Children understand far more than Piaget gave them credit for—and some adults understand far less. Taking advantage of the fact that infants look longer at novel or surprising stimuli than at familiar ones, psychologists have designed delightfully imaginative methods of testing what babies know. As we discuss in Chapter 3, these methods reveal that babies may be born with mental modules or core knowledge systems for numbers and other features of the physical world (Quinn, 2002; Spelke, 2000). For example, at only 4 months of age, babies will look longer at a ball if it seems to roll through a solid barrier, leap between two platforms, or hang in midair than they do when the ball obeys the laws of physics. This suggests that the unusual event is surprising to them (see Figure 14.4). And infants as young as $2^1/_2$ to $3^1/_2$ months are aware that objects continue to exist even when masked by other objects, a form of object permanence that Piaget never imagined possible in babies so young (Baillargeon, 1999, 2004).

Conversely, not all adolescents and adults develop the ability for formal reasoning and reflective judgment (see Chapter 9). Some never develop the capacity for formal operations, and others think concretely unless a specific problem requires abstract thought.

4 Cognitive development is spurred by the growing speed and efficiency of information processing. Children reason just as Piaget said they do, with the tasks he gave them, but subsequent cognitive research has discovered why their thinking changes. As children mature, their working memory expands, they become better able to inhibit irrelevant and distracting thoughts and focus on a problem, and their general speed of processing increases. All of these changes help them reason more logically and efficiently (Luna et al., 2004).

5 Cognitive development is greatly affected by a child's culture. On this point, Vygotsky was correct and ahead of his time. Culture—the world of tools, language, rituals, beliefs, games, and social institutions—profoundly shapes and structures children's cognitive development, fostering some abilities and neglecting others (Tomasello, 2000). For example, traditional nomadic hunting peoples, such as the Inuit of Canada, the Pirahã of the Amazon jungle, and the Aborigines of Australia, do not quantify things and do not need to (Dasen, 1994; Gordon, 2004). The Aborigines have number words only up to five and the Pirahã count only one and two; after that, all quantities are described as "many." In such cultures, the conservation of quantity develops late, if at all. But nomadic hunters excel in spatial abilities, because spatial orientation is crucial for finding water holes and successful hunting routes. In contrast, children who live in settled agri-

cultural communities, such as the Baoulé of the Ivory Coast, develop rapidly in the ability to quantify and much more slowly in spatial reasoning.

As you see, our understanding of children's cognitive maturation has undergone significant modification since Piaget's time. Nonetheless, Piaget left an enduring legacy: the insight that children are not passive vessels into which education and experience are poured. Children actively interpret their worlds, using their developing abilities to assimilate new information and figure things out.

Experience and culture influence cognitive development. Children who work with clay, wood, and other materials, such as this young potter in India, tend to understand the concept of conservation sooner than children who have not had this kind of experience.

QUICK quiz

Please use language (and thought) to answer these questions.

1. "More cake!" and "Mommy come" are examples of __________ speech.
2. Understanding that two rows of six pennies are equal in number, even if one row is flat and the other is stacked up, is an example of __________.
3. Understanding that a toy exists even after Mom puts it in her purse is an example of __________, which develops during the __________ stage.
4. Three-year-old Tasha accidentally breaks a glass. "You bad girl!" she exclaims. Reprimanding herself is an example of Vygotsky's notion of __________.
5. A 5-year-old who tells his dad that "Sally said she saw a bunny but she was lying" has developed a __________.
6. List five findings from contemporary research on children's cognitive development that have expanded or modified Piaget's theory.

Answers:

1. telegraphic 2. conservation 3. object permanence, sensorimotor 4. private speech 5. theory of mind 6. The changes from one stage to another occur in continuous, overlapping waves rather than distinct stages. Children are less egocentric than Piaget thought. Children know more and know it earlier than he believed, whereas some adults understand less. Children's cognitive development is spurred by the growing expansion of working memory and speed of information processing. And cognitive development is affected by cultural practices and experiences.

- Are children born to be selfish little savages or do they have a "moral sense"?
- What is wrong with "because I say so" as a way of getting children to behave?
- Why are some children able to resist a forbidden treat whereas others gobble it up as soon as adults are out of sight?

Learning to Be Good

How do children learn to tell right from wrong, resist the temptation to behave selfishly, and obey the rules of social conduct? In the 1960s, Lawrence Kohlberg (1964), inspired by Piaget's work, argued that children's ability to understand right from wrong

evolved along with the rest of their cognitive abilities, progressing through three levels. In studies of how children reason about moral dilemmas, he found that very young children obey rules because they fear being punished if they disobey, and later because they think it is in their best interest to obey. At about age 10, their moral judgments shift to ones based on conformity and loyalty to others, and then to an understanding of the rule of law. In adulthood, a few individuals go on to develop a moral standard based on universal human rights. For example, Martin Luther King, Jr. fought against laws supporting segregation, Mohandas Gandhi advocated nonviolent solutions to injustice in India, and Susan B. Anthony fought for women's right to vote.

Kohlberg was right that moral reasoning ability increases during the school years. Unfortunately, so do cheating, lying, cruelty, and the cognitive ability to rationalize these actions. As Thomas Lickona (1983) wryly summarized, "We can reach high levels of moral reasoning, and still behave like scoundrels." Accordingly, developmental psychologists today place greater emphasis on how children learn to regulate their own emotions and behavior. Most children learn to inhibit their wishes to beat up their younger siblings, steal a classmate's toy, or scream at the top of their lungs if they don't get their way. The child's emerging ability to understand right from wrong, and to behave accordingly, depends on the emergence of conscience and moral emotions such as shame, guilt, and empathy (Kochanska et al., 2005).

Even very young children are capable of feeling empathy for others and taking another person's point of view. They do not obey rules only because they are afraid of what will happen to them if they disobey, but also because they understand right from wrong. By age 5, they know the difference between doing the right thing and obeying orders; for example, they know it is wrong to hurt someone even if a teacher tells them to (Turiel, 2002). Therefore, many psychologists conclude that the capacity for understanding right from wrong, like that for language, is inborn. As Jerome Kagan (1984) wrote, "Without this fundamental human capacity, which nineteenth-century observers called a *moral sense*, the child could not be socialized."

The moral sense and a desire to behave well with others can be nurtured or extinguished, however, by experiences in a child's life. For example, when you did something wrong as a child, did the adults in your family spank you, shout at you, threaten you, or explain the error of your ways? One of the most common methods used by parents to enforce moral standards and good behavior is **power assertion**, which includes threats, physical punishment, depriving the child of privileges, and generally taking advantage of being bigger, stronger, and more powerful. Of course, a parent may have no alternative other than "Do it because I say so!" if the child is too young to understand a rule or impishly keeps trying to break it. But when power assertion consists of sheer parental bullying and frequent physical punishment, it is associated with greater aggressiveness in children, reduced empathy, and poorer moral reasoning (Gershoff, 2002; Hoffman, 1994; Lopez, Bonenberger, & Schneider, 2001). When parents are verbally abusive, insulting and ridiculing the child ("You are so stupid, I wish you had never been born"), the results are especially devastating (Moore & Pepler, 2006).

This does not mean that power assertion has the same effects on all children, in all environments, and in all cultures (Collins et al., 2000). For one thing, cultures tend to differ in their preferred methods of discipline; Chinese and African-American families are often sterner than middle-class white families, but the children generally regard their parents' discipline as evidence of concern, not abusiveness. Thus, the context in which the discipline occurs makes an enormous difference. Is the parent–child relationship fundamentally loving and trusting or one full of hostility and fighting?

power assertion A method of child rearing in which the parent uses punishment and authority to correct the child's misbehavior.

Consider spanking. "My parents spanked me and I am fine," some people say, and they may well be right. The occasional, moderate use of spanking has no long-term detrimental outcomes for most middle-class children (Baumrind, Larzelere, & Cowan, 2002). The reason is that it typically occurs in an otherwise loving context, as a quick action of last resort when a child is misbehaving. Physical punishment backfires, however, when it is used inappropriately or harshly, causing the child to become angry and resentful. Many parents resort to spanking whenever they don't know what else to do. If the family atmosphere is one of anger, quarreling, and constant efforts to subdue the children, the use of physical punishment can easily spiral out of control (Gershoff, 2002). Morever, harsh but ineffective discipline methods are often transmitted to the next generation: Aggressive parents teach their children that the way to raise children is by behaving aggressively (Capaldi et al., 2003).

THINKING CRITICALLY
AVOID EMOTIONAL REASONING
Most people hold passionate feelings about spanking: either it is good for the child or devastating for the child. Could both views be wrong?

A strategy that is more successful than spanking and other forms of power assertion is **induction**, in which the parent appeals to the child's own abilities, empathy, helpful nature, affection for others, and sense of responsibility. A parent using induction might explain to a misbehaving child that the child's actions could harm or upset another person ("You made Doug cry; it's not nice to bite"; "You must never poke anyone's eyes because that could hurt them seriously"). Or the parent might appeal to the child's own helpful inclinations ("I know you're a person who likes to be good to others"), which is far more effective than citing external reasons to be good ("You'd better be nice or you won't get dessert"). Children whose parents use induction and emphasize the importance of empathy tend to feel guilty if they hurt others. They are more likely to internalize standards of right and wrong and be considerate of others (Berkowitz & Grych, 2000; Eisenberg et al., 2002; Hoffman, 1994).

Induction is not the same as being overly *permissive*—letting children do anything they want—or being uninvolved or unconcerned. Parents who use induction tend to be *authoritative* and democratic rather than arbitrarily *authoritarian* or permissive. That is, they give emotional support to the child and listen to the child's concerns and wishes, but they also require good behavior; they set high but reasonable expectations and teach their children how to meet them (Baumrind, 1989, 1991; Berkowitz &

induction A method of child rearing in which the parent appeals to the child's own abilities, sense of responsibility, and feelings for others in correcting the child's misbehavior.

POWER ASSERTION
The parent uses physical force, threats, insults, or other kinds of power to get the child to obey.

Example: "Do it because I say so"; "Stop that right now"; hitting
Result: The child obeys, but only when the parent is present; the child often feels resentful.

INDUCTION
The parent appeals to the child's good nature, empathy, love for the parent, and sense of responsibility to others and offers explanations of rules.

Example: "You're too grown up to behave like that"; "Fighting hurts your little brother. "
Result: The child tends to internalize reasons for good behavior.

Grych, 2000). They have high demands for maturity and self-control in their children, but they also express a lot of sensitivity and warmth and they are highly involved with their children's lives. Their children have greater skills in *self-regulation*, the ability to control and modify their impulses, thoughts, and feelings, than do children of parents who rely on power assertion.

CLOSE-UP on Research

SELF-CONTROL AND CONSCIENCE

How do children learn to resist temptation?

As we have just seen, parenting styles are linked with whether and how children learn to behave themselves. Yet some psychologists have **questioned the assumption** that styles of discipline are the primary ingredient in determining a child's moral behavior. They have wondered whether something might intervene between how the parent treats the child and the child's willingness to listen. As we saw in discussing maternal sensitivity and the child's attachment style, one possibility is the child's own temperament.

To explore the links between parental discipline, the child's self-regulation, and the emergence of conscience, Grazyna Kochanska and Amy Knaack (2003) conducted a longitudinal study of 106 children. They **asked three questions**: At what age does self-regulation emerge? Is it related to the later internalization of moral standards? Is it related to how a mother disciplines her child? The researchers studied young children at ages 22, 33, and 45 months, measuring the children's self-regulatory abilities and observing the mothers' methods of discipline as they interacted with their children. When the children were 56 and 73 months, the researchers measured the development of conscience and a moral self.

The researchers began by **defining their terms**. They defined self-regulation as "effortful control," the child's ability to suppress his or her initial wish to do something in favor of doing something else that is not as much fun. But how would you measure this ability in a little kid? Kochanska and Knaack designed a series of tests, all cleverly disguised as games. Some of the games required the child to whisper instead of shout, walk instead of run, ignore the dominant image in a picture and find a more subtle one, and delay gratification by not reaching immediately for an M&M under a cup or resisting the urge to open a bag to get a toy inside.

The researchers also measured the mothers' use of induction or power assertion in several ways. One was to observe what the mothers did when they were asked to get their child to clean up the play area or to prevent the child from playing with some appealing, easily accessible toys. Did the mother explain the reasons for her request to the child (induction) or did she issue strict orders (power assertion)? After interacting with her child, the mother left the room, and the child was free to obey or disobey, as the researchers observed what the child did in her absence.

When the children were 56 months old, the researchers assessed their moral development. They had the children play a game in which the experimenter held two large puppets that took opposite positions on nine moral actions. For example, one puppet would say, "When I'm by myself, I usually don't do things Mom says not

to do" and the other would say, "Sometimes, when I'm by myself, I do things Mom says not to do." The children had to say which puppet they were more like. The nine moral actions included being willing to apologize, feeling empathy, being concerned about others' wrongdoing, feeling guilty after doing something naughty or wrong, and being concerned about their parents' feelings. The researchers also measured the children's actual behavior—for example, whether they cheated on the rules in playing a ball-tossing game. Then the researchers devised a composite conscience score for each child. Finally, when the children were 73 months old, their mothers rated them on the frequency of antisocial problems such as being irritable and quick to fly off the handle, destroying their own or others' belongings, or fighting with other children.

The researchers, therefore, **amassed considerable evidence** to examine. First, as you can see in the top row of the table below, the correlations between effortful self-control, measured at 22, 33, and 45 months of age, and the children's later conscience score at 56 months were positive and very high (except for the very youngest children). Second, the correlations between effortful control and later antisocial problems were negative and also statistically significant, meaning that children who were most able to regulate their impulses early in life were *least* likely to get in trouble later by fighting or destroying things. Third, you can see that the child's ability to delay gratification and regulate feelings was also negatively associated with the mother's use of power assertion, meaning that mothers who ordered their children to "behave" tended to have children who were impulsive and aggressive.

	Child Effortful Control			
	22 Months	33 Months	45 Months	Overall
Conscience score at 56 months	.21	.59	.64	.58
Aggression problems at 73 months	−.28	−.33	−.32	−.37
Mother's use of power assertion	−.33	−.49	−.52	−.54

The researchers **considered another interpretation** of that last correlational finding: Perhaps some mothers relied on power assertion *because* their children were impulsive and aggressive and did not behave. Indeed, in this study, children who were defiant and rebellious were more likely to provoke power assertion by their mothers. Moreover, effortful control was highly stable and consistent over time and across all the tasks the children did, suggesting, as the researchers said, that it is a characteristic of children's personality.

Other longitudinal studies have replicated the stability of self-regulation (Raffaelli, Crockett, & Shen, 2005). (Self-regulation may underlie two of the Big Five personality traits discussed in Chapter 13, conscientiousness and agreeableness.) However, the mother's use of power assertion independently continued to predict the child's effortful control. This pattern of findings teaches us to **avoid oversimplification**, for example by concluding that "it's all in what the mother does" or that "it's all in the child's personality." Mothers and children, it seems, raise each other.

QUICK quiz

Exercise self-regulation by taking this quiz.

1. What is a major limitation of cognitive theories of moral reasoning in understanding how children develop a conscience?
2. Which method of disciplining an aggressive child is most likely to teach empathy? (a) induction, (b) authoritarian firmness, (c) power assertion, (d) spanking
3. What early ability predicts the development of conscience later on?

Answers:

1. Moral behavior is not necessarily related to the ability to reason morally. **2.** a **3.** self-regulation, the ability to control one's immediate impulses and wishes

WHAT'S AHEAD

- Why do some people fail to identify themselves as either male or female?
- How would a biologically oriented psychologist explain why most little boys and girls are "sexist" in their choice of toys?
- What happens to children's notions about gender once they are able to distinguish males from females?
- How do teachers unintentionally encourage boys to be aggressive?
- If a little girl "knows" that girls can't be doctors, does this mean she will never go to medical school?

Gender Development

No parent ever excitedly calls a relative to exclaim, "It's a baby! It's a $7^1/_2$-pound, black-haired baby!" The baby's sex is the first thing everyone notices and announces. How soon do children themselves notice that boys and girls are different sexes and understand which sex they themselves are? How do children learn the rules of masculinity and femininity, the things that boys do that are different from what girls do? Why, as one friend of ours observed, do most preschool children act like the "gender police," insisting, say, that boys can't be nurses and girls can't be doctors? And why do some children come to feel they don't belong to the sex everyone else thinks they do?

Gender Identity

Let's start by clarifying some terms. **Gender identity** refers to a child's sense of being male or female, of belonging to one sex and not the other. **Gender typing** is the process of socializing children into their gender roles, and thus reflects society's ideas about which abilities, interests, traits, and behaviors are appropriately masculine or feminine. A person can have a strong gender identity and not be gender typed: A man may be confident in his maleness and not feel threatened by doing "unmasculine" things such as needlepointing a pillow; a woman may be confident in her femaleness and not feel threatened by doing "unfeminine" things such as serving in combat.

gender identity The fundamental sense of being male or female; it is independent of whether the person conforms to the social and cultural rules of gender.

gender typing The process by which children learn the abilities, interests, and behaviors associated with being masculine or feminine in their culture.

In the past, psychologists tried to distinguish the terms *sex* and *gender*, reserving "sex" for the physiological or anatomical attributes of males and females and "gender" for differences that are learned. Thus they might speak of a sex difference in the frequency of baldness but a gender difference in fondness for romance novels. Today, these two terms are often used interchangeably because, as we have noted repeatedly in this book, nature and nurture are inextricably linked. It is not easy to separate physiological and anatomical traits from psychological ones (Golombok & Fivush, 1994; Roughgarden, 2004).

Ann Bonny and Mary Read convicted of Piracy Nov.r 28th 1720 at
a Court of Vice Admiralty held at St.Jago de la Vega in ye Island of Jamaica.

George Ruhe/The New York Times

Throughout history and across cultures, there have been people who were transgender. Some women have lived as men, as did the eighteenth-century pirates Ann Bonny and Mary Read (left). Some men have lived as women, as did We-Wha, a Zuni Indian man, shown in a photo taken about 1885. Today many transgender individuals are outspoken about their sexual and gender identities. Luke Woodward (right), who was born and raised female, has come out as a male, and is active in a campus movement to make life better for fellow transgender students.

The complexity of sex and gender development is especially apparent in the cases of people who do not fit the familiar categories of male and female. Every year, thousands of babies are born with **intersex conditions**, formerly known as hermaphroditism. In these conditions, which occur in about one of every 2,000 births, chromosomal or hormonal anomalies cause the child to be born with ambiguous genitals, or genitals that conflict with the infant's chromosomes. A child who is genetically female, for example, might be born with an enlarged clitoris that looks like a penis. A child who is genetically male might be born with androgen insensitivity, a condition that causes the external genitals to appear to be female (Roughgarden, 2004; Zucker, 1999).

As adults, many intersexed individuals call themselves *transgender*, a term describing a broad category of people who do not fit comfortably into the usual categories of male and female, masculine and feminine. Some are comfortable living with the physical and psychological attributes of both sexes, considering themselves to be "gender queer" and even refusing to be referred to as he or she. But many feel uncomfortable in their sex of rearing and wish to be considered a member of the other sex; their gender identity is at odds with their anatomical sex or appearance. They are *transsexual*, feeling that they are male in a female body or vice versa; they often try to make a full transition to the other sex through surgery or hormones, or by simply taking on the dress and attributes of the sex they wish to be. Intersexed people and transsexuals have been found in virtually all cultures throughout history (Denny, 1998; Roughgarden, 2004).

Influences on Gender Development

To understand the typical course of gender development, as well as the variations, developmental psychologists study the interacting influences of biology, cognition, and learning on gender identity and gender typing.

Biological Influences. Starting in the preschool years, boys and girls congregate primarily with other children of their sex, and most prefer the toys and games of their own sex (Maccoby, 1998). They will play together if required to, but given their druthers, they usually choose to play with same-sex friends. The kind of play that young boys and girls enjoy also differs, on average. Little boys, like young males in all primate species, are more likely than females to go in for physical roughhousing, risk taking, and aggressive displays. These sex differences occur all over the world, almost

intersex conditions (intersexuality) Conditions, occurring in about one of every 2,000 births, in which chromosomal or hormonal anomalies cause a child to be born with ambiguous genitals, or genitals that conflict with the infant's chromosomes (formerly called *hermaphroditism*).

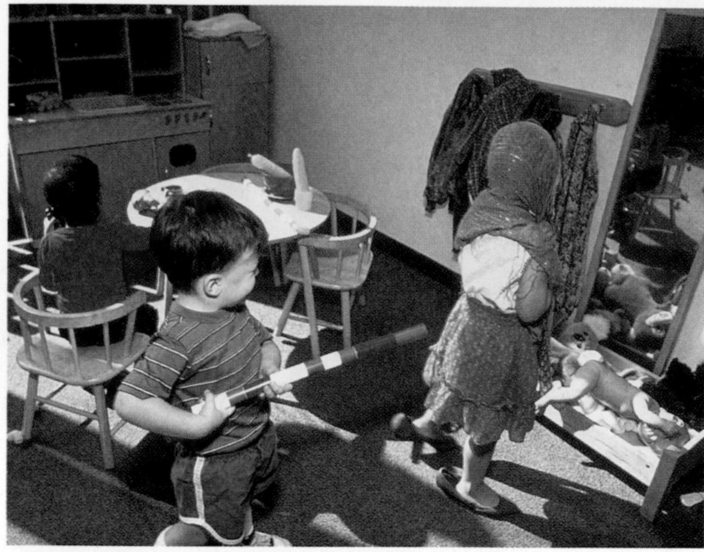

Look familiar? In a scene typical of many nursery schools and homes, the boy builds a gun out of anything he can, and the girl dresses up in any pretty thing she can find. Psychologists (and parents) debate whether such gender typing is biologically based or a result of the emergence of gender schemas.

regardless of how adults treat children—for example, whether they encourage boys and girls to play together or separate them (Lytton & Romney, 1991; Maccoby, 1998, 2002). Similarly, many parents lament that although they try to give their children the same toys, it makes no difference; their sons want trucks and guns and their daughters want dolls.

Biological researchers believe that these play and toy preferences have a basis in prenatal hormones, particularly the presence or absence of prenatal androgens (masculinizing hormones). Girls who were exposed to prenatal androgens in the womb are later more likely than nonexposed girls to prefer "boys' toys" such as cars and fire engines, and they are also more physically aggressive than other girls (Berenbaum & Bailey, 2003). Most androgenized girls, however, develop a female gender identity and do not see themselves as male in any way.

What, then, does create gender identity? In the past, gender identity was believed to be almost entirely learned, a result of the child's socialization and learning. Then, a few years ago, a widely publicized case study appeared to show that gender identity is hardwired in the brain. At the age of 7 months, a genetically and hormonally male child had lost his penis in a freak accident during a routine surgical procedure. When he was nearly 2 years old, his desperate parents, on the advice of a leading scientist in the field of gender identity, agreed to raise him as a girl, renaming him Brenda. But Brenda preferred boys' toys and by the age of 14 refused to keep living as a female. Her father told her the truth and, in relief, Brenda turned to a male identity (Diamond & Sigmundson, 1997). He changed his name to David, had reconstructive surgery to build a penis, and, in his 20s, got married. Tragically, the story did not end happily. After David's twin brother, who had schizophrenia, committed suicide, and after David lost his job and separated from his wife, he became deeply depressed. In 2004, at the age of 38, David killed himself.

Unfortunately, dramatic case studies such as this one cannot answer the question of whether gender identity is fixed in the brain prenatally and is thus unchangeable. Perhaps David's experience was atypical. Perhaps there is a critical period after birth during which gender identity develops. (David's parents did not decide to raise him as a girl until he was nearly two.) A similar case had a very different outcome: Another infant who lost his penis was assigned to become a female at the age of 7 months and ended up with a female gender identity (Bradley et al., 1998; Zucker, 2002).

When Kenneth Zucker (1999) did a major review of the hundreds of cases of children whose sex of rearing was discrepant with their anatomical or genetic sex, he found that the picture is enormously complex, depending on the interactions of genes, prenatal hormones, anatomical structures, and experiences in life. You can see this complexity in the results of a longitudinal follow-up study of 16 genetic males who had a rare condition that caused them to be born without a penis. The babies were otherwise normal males, with testicles and appropriate androgen levels. Fourteen of these babies had been socially and surgically assigned to the female sex, according to the custom when they were born. But the parents of two of the boys did not consent to the procedure and raised their sons as male. Those two developed a male gender identity. All 16 have interests and attitudes that are considered typical of males. But of the 14 who were surgically reassigned as females, eight have declared themselves male, five are living as females, and one has an unclear gender identity (Reiner & Gearheart, 2004).

THINKING CRITICALLY

TOLERATE UNCERTAINTY

Most people fall into one of two categories, male or female. This makes it difficult for parents and doctors to be certain about how best to treat infants who are born with intersex conditions. Should such infants be assigned surgically to one sex or the other, or should they be left alone until they are grown? In the absence of clear answers, how would you make this decision?

gender schema A cognitive schema (mental network) of knowledge, beliefs, metaphors, and expectations about what it means to be male or female.

Because of the many factors involved in gender identity, a fierce battle is currently raging among physicians, sex researchers, and intersexed people themselves about the best approach to take with intersexed babies (Zucker, 1999). Should physicians intervene surgically or hormonally, or do nothing and eventually let the child decide what sex he or she wishes to be? For the present, we will all have to live with uncertainty about what the best course of action is, until we know better how nature and nurture interact to produce a gender identity as male, female, or transgender.

Cognitive Influences. Cognitive psychologists explain the mystery of children's gender segregation and toy and play preferences by studying children's changing cognitive abilities. Even before babies can speak, they recognize that there are two sexes. By the age of 9 months, most babies can discriminate male from female faces (Fagot & Leinbach, 1993), and they can match female faces with female voices (Poulin-Dubois et al., 1994). By the age of 2 to 3, toddlers can label themselves as boys or girls, but it is not until the age of 4 or 5 that most children develop a stable gender identity, a sense of themselves as being male or female regardless of what they wear or how they behave. Only then do they understand that what boys and girls do does not necessarily indicate what sex they are: A girl remains a girl even if she can climb a tree, and a boy remains a boy even if he has long hair.

Cognitive processes are involved in the behavioral differences between boys and girls that emerge during the preschool years. Once children can label themselves and others consistently as being a boy or a girl, they change their behavior to conform to the category they belong to. They begin to prefer same-sex playmates and sex-traditional toys without being explicitly taught to do so (Martin, Ruble, & Szkrybalo, 2002). They become more gender typed in their toy play, games, aggressiveness, and verbal skills than children who still cannot consistently label males and females. Most notably, girls stop behaving aggressively (Fagot, 1993). It is as if they go along behaving like boys until they know they are girls. At that moment, but not until that moment, they seem to decide: "Girls don't do this; I'm a girl; I'd better not either."

It's great fun to watch 3- to 5-year-old children struggle to figure out what makes boys and girls different: "The ones with eyelashes are girls; boys don't have eyelashes," said one 4-year-old to her aunt in explaining her drawing. After dinner at an Italian restaurant, a 4-year-old told his parents that he'd got the answer: "Men eat pizza and women don't" (Bjorkland, 2000). By the age of 5, children consolidate their knowledge, with all of its mistakes and misconceptions, into a **gender schema**, a mental network of beliefs and expectations about what it means to be male or female and about what each sex is supposed to wear, do, feel, and think (Bem, 1993; Martin & Ruble, 2004). Gender schemas even include metaphors. For example, after age 4, children of both sexes will usually say that rough, spiky, black, or mechanical things are male and that soft, pink, fuzzy, or flowery things are female; that black bears are male and pink poodles are female (Leinbach, Hort, & Fagot, 1997). Gender schemas are most rigid between ages 5 and 7; at this age, it's really hard to dislodge a child's notion of what boys and girls can do (Martin, Ruble, & Szkrybalo, 2002). A little girl at this stage will tell you stoutly that "girls can't be doctors" even if her own mother is a doctor.

"Jason, I'd like to let you play, but soccer is a girls' game."

One puzzle of gender development is that virtually all over the world, boys' gender schemas are more rigid than girls' are. That is, boys express stronger preferences for masculine toys and activities

Not long ago, the idea of women serving in the military and men teaching preschoolers would have offended or at least startled many people. Today, as a result of changing economic conditions, gender schemas have become less rigid in Western countries, and these images have lost their power to shock.

than girls do for feminine ones, and boys are harsher on themselves and other boys who fail to behave in gender-typed ways (Bussey & Bandura, 1992; Maccoby, 1998). One reason may be that most societies value masculine occupations and traits more than feminine ones, and males have higher status. So when boys behave like (or play with) girls, they lose status, and when girls behave like boys, they gain status (Serbin, Powlishta, & Gulko, 1993).

Many people retain inflexible gender schemas throughout their lives, feeling uncomfortable or angry with men or women who break out of traditional roles—let alone with transgendered individuals who don't fit either category or want to change the one they grew up with. However, with increasing experience and cognitive sophistication, older children often become more flexible in their gender schemas, especially if they have friends of the other sex and if their families and cultures encourage such flexibility (Martin & Ruble, 2004). Children begin to modify their gender schemas, understanding, say, that women can be engineers and men can be cooks.

Cultures and religions, too, differ in their schemas for the roles of women and men. In all industrialized nations, for example, it is taken for granted that women and men alike should be educated; indeed, laws mandate a minimum education for both sexes. But in Afghanistan, even after the overthrow of the Taliban and its prohibition on female education, many girls who attend school continue to receive death threats. Gender schemas can be very powerful, and events that challenge their legitimacy can be enormously threatening. How flexible are your own gender schemas?

Learning Influences. A third influence on gender development is the environment, which is full of subtle and not-so-subtle messages about what girls and boys are supposed to do. Behavioral and social-cognitive learning theorists study how the process of gender socialization instills these messages in children (Bussey & Bandura, 1999). Although many adults say they treat boys and girls equally or that "my little girl was just naturally feminine but my boy was born to be a boxer," research disputes their claims.

Gender socialization begins at the moment of birth. Parents tend to portray their newborn girls as more feminine and delicate than boys, and boys as stronger and more

GET INVOLVED!

➤CAN YOU IMAGINE BEING THE OTHER SEX?

If you woke up tomorrow and found that you had been transformed into a member of the other sex, how would your life change, if at all? Would anything be different about your attitudes, behavior, habits, experiences, choices, preferences, and feelings? Write down your first reactions, and then ask a few of your male and female friends the same question. If possible, ask young children, too. Do their answers differ depending on their sex? If so, how? What does this exercise reveal about gender socialization and schemas?

athletic than girls, although it is hard to know how athletic a newborn boy could be and all newborns are pretty delicate (Karraker, Vogel, & Lake, 1995). Many parents are careful to dress their baby in outfits they consider to be the correct color and pattern for his or her sex. Clothes don't matter to the infant, of course, but they are signals to adults about how to treat the child. Adults often respond to the same baby differently, depending on whether the child is dressed as a boy or a girl (Stern & Karraker, 1989).

Adults respond to boys and girls differently even when the children are behaving in exactly the same way. In one observational study, 12- to 16-month-old boys and girls were equally assertive (as measured by the frequency of their efforts to get an adult's attention) and verbal (as measured by their attempts to communicate with others). But teachers responded far more often to assertive boys than to shy ones and to verbal girls than to nonverbal ones. Subtly, the teachers were reinforcing gender-typed behavior. When the researchers observed the same children a year later, a gender difference was now apparent, with boys behaving more assertively and girls talking more to teachers (Fagot et al., 1985). Social-learning theorists believe that the teachers' reinforcements created this gender difference, although it is also possible that the teachers were merely anticipating changes that would have occurred anyway because of genetic influences.

Parents, teachers, and other adults convey their beliefs and expectations about gender even when they are entirely unaware that they are doing so. For example, when parents believe that boys are naturally better at math or sports and that girls are naturally better at English, they unwittingly communicate those beliefs by how they respond to a child's success or failure. They may tell a son who did well in math, "You're a natural math whiz, Johnny!" But if a daughter gets good grades, they may say, "Wow, you really worked hard in math, Joanie, and it shows!" The implication is that girls have to try hard but boys have a natural gift. Messages like these are not lost on children. Both sexes tend to lose interest in activities that are supposedly not natural for them, even when they all start out with equal abilities (Dweck, 2006; Frome & Eccles, 1998).

cathy® by Cathy Guisewite

In today's fast-moving world, society's messages to men and women keep shifting. As a result, gender development has become a lifelong process, in which gender schemas, attitudes, and behavior evolve as people have new experiences and as society itself changes. Five-year-old children may behave like sexist piglets while they are trying to figure out what it means to be male or female. Their behavior is shaped by a combination of hormones, genetics, cognitive schemas, parental and social lessons, religious and cultural customs, and experiences. But their gender-typed behavior as 5-year-olds often has little to do with how they will behave at 25 or 45. Children can grow up in an extremely gender-typed family and yet, as adults, find themselves in careers or relationships they would never have imagined for themselves. If 5-year-olds are the gender police, many adults end up breaking the law.

QUICK quiz

Quiz-taking is appropriate behavior for all sexes and genders.

1. Three-year-old Paulo thinks that if he changed from wearing pants to wearing dresses he could become a girl. He still lacks a stable ________.
2. *True or false:* All intersexed people are transsexual.
3. A biological psychologist would say that a 3-year-old boy's love of going "vroom, vroom" with his truck collection is probably a result of ________.
4. Which statement about gender schemas is *false*? (a) They are present in early form by 1 year of age; (b) they are permanent conceptualizations of what it means to be masculine or feminine; (c) they eventually expand to include many meanings and associations to being male and female; (d) they probably reflect the status of women and men in society.

5. Herb hopes his 4-year-old daughter will become a doctor like him, but she refuses to play with the toy stethoscope he bought her and insists that she will be a princess when she grows up. What conclusions can Herb draw about his daughter's future career?

Answers:

1. gender identity **2.** false **3.** biological factors such as prenatal hormones, specifically androgens **4.** b **5.** Not many. His daughter's rigid gender-typed behavior is typical when children are acquiring gender schemas, but it does not predict much of anything about her adult interests or occupation.

WHAT'S AHEAD

- What are the pros and cons of going through puberty earlier than most of your classmates?
- During adolescence, are extreme turmoil and unhappiness the exception or the rule?
- Should teenage criminals be considered "not guilty by reason of adolescence"?

Adolescence

Adolescence refers to the period of development between **puberty**, the age at which a person becomes capable of sexual reproduction, and adulthood. In some cultures, the time span between puberty and adulthood is only a few months; a sexually mature boy or girl is expected to marry and assume adult tasks. In modern Western societies, however, teenagers are not considered emotionally mature enough to assume the full rights, responsibilities, and roles of adulthood.

puberty The age at which a person becomes capable of sexual reproduction.

The Physiology of Adolescence

menarche [men-ARR-kee] The onset of menstruation.

Until puberty, boys and girls produce roughly the same levels of male hormones (androgens) and female hormones (estrogens). At puberty, however, the brain's pituitary gland begins to stimulate hormone production in the adrenal and reproductive glands. From then on, boys have a higher level of androgens than girls do, and girls have a higher level of estrogens than boys do.

In boys, the reproductive glands are the testes (testicles), which produce sperm; in girls, the reproductive glands are the ovaries, which release eggs. During puberty, these organs mature and the individual becomes capable of reproduction. In girls, signs of sexual maturity are the development of breasts and **menarche**, the onset of menstruation. In boys, the signs are the onset of nocturnal emissions and the growth of the testes, scrotum, and penis. Hormones are also responsible for the emergence of *secondary sex characteristics*, such as a deepened voice and facial and chest hair in boys and pubic hair in both sexes. The onset of puberty depends on both biological and environmental factors. Menarche, for example, depends on a female's having a critical level of body fat, which is necessary to sustain a pregnancy. Body fat triggers the hormonal changes associated with puberty (Chehab et al., 1997). An increase in body fat among children in developed countries may help explain why the average age of puberty declined in Europe and North America until the mid-twentieth century. The average age of menarche now occurs at about 12 years and 8 months in white girls and a few months earlier in black girls.

Individuals vary enormously in the onset and length of puberty. Some girls go through menarche at 9 or 10 and some boys are still growing in height after age 19. If you entered puberty before most of your classmates, or if you matured much later than they did, you know that your experience of adolescence was different from that of the average teenager (whoever that is). Going through puberty out of synch with one's peers can produce feelings of alienation and depression, and body-image distortions that can lead to eating disorders (Ricciardelli & McCabe, 2004).

Early-maturing boys generally have a more positive view of their bodies than late-maturing boys do, and their relatively greater size and strength give them a boost in sports and the prestige that being a good athlete brings young men. But they are also more likely to smoke, drink alcohol, use other drugs, and break the law than later-maturing boys (Cota-Robles, Neiss, & Rowe, 2002; Duncan et al., 1985). Some early-maturing girls have the prestige of being socially popular, but, partly because others in their peer group regard them as being sexually precocious, they are also more likely to fight with their parents, drop out of school, have a negative body image, and be angry or depressed. Early menarche itself does not cause these problems; rather, it tends to accentuate existing behavioral problems and family conflicts. Girls who go through puberty relatively late, in contrast, have a more difficult time at first, but by the end of adolescence many are happier with their appearance and are more popular than their early-maturing classmates (Caspi & Moffitt, 1991; Stattin & Magnusson, 1990).

To their embarrassment, children typically reach puberty at different times. These girls are all the same age, but they differ considerably in physical maturity.

BIOLOGY and the Teen Brain

Less Guilty by Reason of Adolescence?

When does a teenager become capable of thinking like an adult? This is not just an academic question; it can be a matter of life or death. In many American states, teenaged criminals are tried and sentenced as adults and, until recently, 21 states allowed the execution of juveniles under the age of 18, or even 16. In 2005, however, the Supreme Court banned the death penalty for juveniles as cruel and unusual punishment. The Court based this decision in part on evidence showing that adolescents often get into trouble not because of their hormones but because of their brains—in particular, because their brains are still neurologically immature (Spear, 2000). "The decision acknowledges what we all know and what science has now confirmed: that the brains of adolescents function in fundamentally different ways than the brains of adults," said psychiatrist David Fassler, on behalf of the American Psychiatric Association. Indeed, developmental psychologists are finding that full neurological and cognitive maturity does not occur until about age 25, much later than commonly believed. For that reason, Laurence Steinberg and Elizabeth Scott (2003) have argued that many teenagers who commit crimes should be considered "less guilty by reason of adolescence."

When people think of physical changes in adolescence, they usually think of hormones and maturing bodies. But the adolescent brain undergoes significant developmental changes, notably a major pruning of synapses. This pruning occurs primarily in the prefrontal cortex, which is responsible for impulse control and planning, and the limbic system, which is involved in emotional processing (Spear, 2000). In an interview in *The New York Times* (November 25, 2003), Steinberg said the process is "like eliminating all the unpaved roads in the brain and replacing them with superhighways." In Chapter 16 we will see that errors in the pruning process during adolescence may be involved in the onset of schizophrenia in vulnerable individuals.

Another change involves myelinization, which provides insulation for the cells and improves the efficiency of neural transmission (see Chapter 4), strengthening the connections between the emotional limbic system and the reasoning prefrontal cortex. This process may continue through the late teens or early twenties, which would help explain why the strong emotions of the adolescent years often overwhelm rational decision making and cause some teenagers to behave more impulsively than adults. It would explain why adolescents are more vulnerable to peer pressure that encourages them to try risky, dumb, or dangerous things—why taunts of "I dare you!" and "You're chicken!" have more power over a 15-year-old than a 25-year-old. Even when teenagers know they are doing the wrong thing, many lack the reasoning ability to foresee the consequences of their actions down the line (Reyna & Farley, 2006).

THINKING CRITICALLY

ANALYZE ASSUMPTIONS AND BIASES

Lee Malvo, age 18, along with his older partner-in-crime John Mohammed, killed ten people in sniper attacks in the Washington, D.C., area. Was he fully responsible for these heartless crimes? Many people assume that by late adolescence, teenagers are legally, socially, and physically adult. But some researchers in neuroscience and developmental psychology disagree.

If adolescence is literally a state of diminished responsibility, how should the courts treat teenage offenders? To what extent should adolescents be held accountable for their actions? When are they fully responsible, and how should the courts determine whether they are? What do you think?

The Psychology of Adolescence

The media love sensational stories about teenagers who are angry, live in emotional turmoil and anguish, feel lonely, hate their parents, and lack self-esteem. How realistic is this portrait of adolescence? Not very. The rate of violent crimes committed by adolescents has actually been plummeting steadily since 1993; in 1999, teenage homicide rates were the lowest they had been since 1966. As for self-worth, two meta-analyses of studies of nearly 150,000 young people found no sudden adolescent drop in self-esteem for either sex. As you can see in Figure 14.5, although males on average had slightly higher self-esteem than females, the difference was very small (Kling et al., 1999).

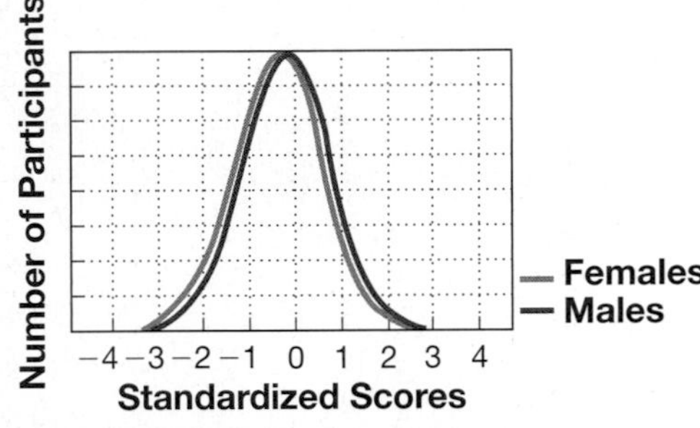

FIGURE 14.5 Gender (Non)differences in Self-Esteem
Popular books claim that girls and women have much lower self-esteem than boys and men, starting in adolescence. But studies of nearly 150,000 American adolescents find that the difference is very small (Kling et al., 1999).

Similarly, studies of representative samples of adolescents find that only a small minority are seriously troubled, angry, or unhappy. Most teenagers have supportive families, a sense of purpose and self-confidence, good friends, and the skill to cope with their problems. Extreme turmoil and unhappiness are the exception, not the rule. Adolescent rebellion is more a matter of generational attitudes and cultural norms than of anything inherent in adolescent development. The baby-boom generation protested the authority of their parents and even created the term "generation gap," but most teenage and college-age children today feel close to their parents, whom they typically see as allies rather than adversaries (Howe & Strauss, 2003).

Nevertheless, three kinds of problems are more common during adolescence than during childhood or adulthood: conflict with parents, mood swings and depression, and higher rates of reckless, rule-breaking, and risky behavior (Spear, 2000). In Western societies, these problems are the downside of growing up. Although quarrels with parents can be painful, they tend to signify a change from one-sided parental authority to a more reciprocal adult relationship. Rule-breaking often occurs because teenagers are developing their own standards and values, often by trying on the styles, actions, and attitudes of their peers, in contrast to those of their parents. Peers become especially important because they represent the values and style of the generation that teenagers identify with, the generation that they will share experiences with as adults (Bukowski, 2001; Harris, 1998; Hartup, 1999). As we saw in Chapter 13, many people report that rejection by peers during adolescence was more devastating than punitive treatment by parents.

Adolescents who are lonely, depressed, worried, or angry tend to express these concerns in ways characteristic of their sex. Boys are more likely than girls to externalize their emotional problems in acts of aggression and other antisocial behavior. Girls, in contrast, are more likely than boys to internalize their feelings and problems, for example by becoming withdrawn or developing eating disorders (Zahn-Waxler, 1996).

"So I blame you for everything—whose fault is that?"

If you are not in the midst of adolescent turmoil, try these questions.

1. What is the difference between *puberty* and *adolescence*?
2. The onset of menstruation is called __________.
3. Extreme turmoil and rebellion in adolescence are (a) nearly universal, (b) the exception rather than the rule, (c) rare.
4. *True or false*: Teenage boys have much higher self-esteem than teenage girls do.
5. What changes occur in the brain during adolescence?

Answers:

1. Puberty refers to the physiological process of sexual maturation; adolescence is a social category marking the years between puberty and adulthood. **2.** menarche **3.** b **4** false **5.** pruning of synapses, myelinization, and strengthening of connections between the limbic system and the prefrontal cortex

WHAT'S**AHEAD**

- What feelings are common during emerging adulthood, the years from 18 to 25?
- Does menopause make most women depressed and irrational?
- Do men go through a male version of menopause?
- Which mental abilities decline in old age, and which ones do not?

Adulthood

According to ancient Greek legend, the Sphinx was a monster—half lion, half woman—who terrorized passersby on the road to Thebes. The Sphinx would ask each traveler a question and then murder those who failed to answer correctly. (The Sphinx was a pretty tough grader.) The question was this: What animal walks on four feet in the morning, two feet at noon, and three feet in the evening? Only one traveler, Oedipus, knew the solution to the riddle. The animal, he said, is Man, who crawls on all fours as a baby, walks upright as an adult, and limps in old age with the aid of a staff.

The Sphinx was the first life-span theorist. Since then, many philosophers, writers, and scientists have speculated on the course of adult development. Are the changes of adulthood predictable, like those of childhood? What are the major psychological issues of adult life? Is mental and physical deterioration in old age inevitable?

Stages and Ages

One of the first modern theorists to propose a life-span approach to psychological development was psychoanalyst Erik H. Erikson (1902–1994). Just as children progress through stages, he said, so do adults. Erikson (1950/1963, 1982) wrote that all individuals go through eight stages in their lives. Each stage is characterized by a particular challenge, which he called a "crisis," that ideally should be resolved before the individual moves on.

1 **Trust versus mistrust** is the challenge that occurs during the baby's first year, when the baby depends on others to provide food, comfort, cuddling, and warmth. If these needs are not met, the child may never develop the essential trust of others necessary to get along in the world.

2 Autonomy (independence) versus shame and doubt is the challenge that occurs when the child is a toddler. The young child is learning to be independent and must do so without feeling too ashamed or uncertain about his or her actions.

3 Initiative versus guilt is the challenge that occurs as the preschooler develops. The child is acquiring new physical and mental skills, setting goals, and enjoying newfound talents, but must also learn to control impulses. The danger lies in developing too strong a sense of guilt over his or her wishes and fantasies.

4 Competence versus inferiority is the challenge for school-age children, who are learning to make things, use tools, and acquire the skills for adult life. Children who fail these lessons of mastery and competence may come out of this stage feeling inadequate and inferior.

5 Identity versus role confusion is the great challenge of adolescence, when teenagers must decide who they are, what they are going to do, and what they hope to make of their lives. Erikson used the term *identity crisis* to describe what he considered to be the primary conflict of this stage. Those who resolve it will come out of this stage with a strong identity, ready to plan for the future. Those who do not will sink into confusion, unable to make decisions.

6 Intimacy versus isolation is the challenge of young adulthood. Once you have decided who you are, said Erikson, you must share yourself with another and learn to make commitments. No matter how successful you are in work, you are not complete until you are capable of intimacy.

7 Generativity versus stagnation is the challenge of the middle years. Now that you know who you are and have an intimate relationship, will you sink into complacency and selfishness, or will you experience generativity—creativity and renewal? Parenthood is the most common route to generativity, but people can be productive, creative, and nurturant in other ways, in their work or their relationships with the younger generation.

8 Ego integrity versus despair is the final challenge of old age. As they age, people strive to reach the ultimate goals of wisdom, spiritual tranquility, and acceptance of their lives. Just as the healthy child will not fear life, said Erikson, the healthy adult will not fear death.

Erikson recognized that cultural and economic factors affect people's progression through these stages. Some societies, for example, make the passages relatively easy. If you know you are going to be a farmer like your parents and you have no alternative, you are unlikely to have an adolescent identity crisis (unless you hate farming). If you have many choices, however, as adolescents in urban societies often do, the transition can become prolonged (Schwartz, 2004). Similarly, cultures that place a high premium on independence and individualism will make it difficult for many of their members to resolve Erikson's sixth crisis, that of intimacy versus isolation.

Erikson's work reminds us that development is never finished; it is an ongoing process. His ideas were important because he placed adult development in the context of family, work, and society, and he specified many of the essential concerns of adulthood: trust, competence, identity, generativity, and the ability to enjoy life and accept death.

According to Erik Erikson, children must master the crisis of competence and older adults must resolve the challenge of generativity. This child and her grandmother are certainly helping each other with their life tasks. But are the needs for competence and generativity important at only one stage of life?

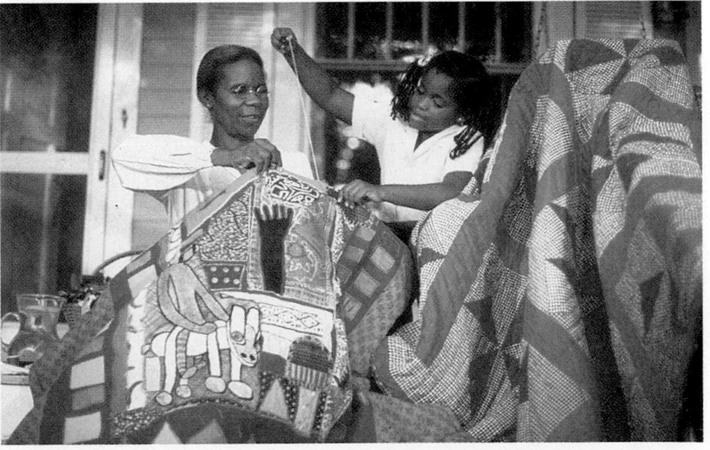

Erikson was aware that the psychological themes and crises of life can occur out of order, although that was not his emphasis. Later researchers, working at a time when people's lives had become less traditional and predictable, discovered just how out of order they can be. Although in Western societies adolescence is often a time of confusion about identity and aspirations, an identity crisis is not limited to the teen years. A man who has worked in one job all his life, and then is laid off and must find an entirely new career, may have an identity crisis too. Likewise, competence is not mastered once and for all in childhood. People learn new skills and lose old ones throughout their lives, and their sense of competence rises and falls accordingly. Moreover, people who are highly generative, in terms of being committed to helping their communities or the next generation, tend to do volunteer work or choose occupations that allow them to contribute to society throughout their lives (Mansfield & McAdams, 1996).

Stage theories, therefore, are not an adequate way of understanding how adults grow and change, or remain the same, across the life span. As one wise psychologist observed many years ago, "There is not one process of aging, but many; there is not one life course followed, but multiple courses. . . . The variety is as rich as the historic conditions people have faced and the current circumstances they experience" (Pearlin, 1982).

The Transitions of Life

Of course, certain events do tend to occur at particular times in life: going to school, learning to drive a car, having a baby, retiring from work. In all societies, people rely on a *social clock* to determine whether they are on time for these transitions or off time.

THINKING CRITICALLY

AVOID EMOTIONAL REASONING

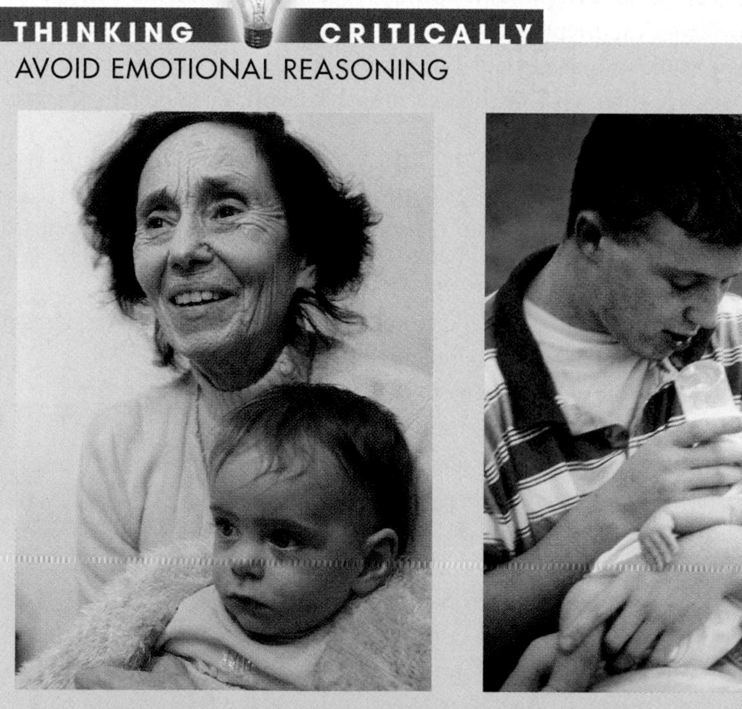

What is your reaction to these two first-time parents? Adriana Iliescu (left) gave birth at age 67. The young man on the right became a father at 15. Many people react negatively to individuals who they feel are "off time" for the transition to parenthood. How young is too young and how old is too old to become a parent?

The social clock consists of norms governing what people of the same age and historical generation are expected to do (Moen & Wethington, 1999; Neugarten, 1979).

Cultures have different social clocks. In some, young men and women are supposed to marry and start having children right after puberty, and work responsibilities come later. In others, a man may not marry until he has shown that he can support a family, which might not be until his 30s. Doing the right thing at the right time, compared to your friends, is reassuring. When nearly everyone your age goes through the same experience or enters a new role at the same time, adjusting to these transitions is relatively easy. Conversely, if you aren't doing these things and hardly anyone you know is doing them either, you will not feel out of step.

In modern societies, however, social clocks are not telling time the way they once did. Most people will face unanticipated transitions, events that happen without warning, such as being fired from a job because of downsizing. And many people have to deal with changes that they expect to happen that do not: for example, not getting married at the age they expected, not getting promoted, not being able to afford to retire, or realizing that they cannot have children (Schlossberg & Robinson, 1996). With this in mind, let's consider some of the major transitions of life.

Emerging Adulthood. In industrialized nations, major demographic changes have postponed the timing of career decisions, marriage or cohabitation, and parenthood until a person's late 20s or even 30s, on the average. Many young people between the ages of 18 and 25 (would that include anyone you know?) are in college and at least partly dependent financially on their parents. This phenomenon has created a phase of life that some call *emerging adulthood* (Arnett, 2000). When emerging adults are asked whether they feel they have reached adulthood, the majority answer: in some ways yes, in some ways no (see Figure 14.6).

In certain respects, emerging adults have moved beyond adolescence into maturity, becoming more emotionally controlled, more confident, less dependent, and less angry and alienated (Roberts, Caspi, & Moffitt, 2001). But they are also the group most likely to live unstable lives, feel unrooted, and take risks. Emerging adults move more often than people in other demographic groups do—back to their parents' homes and then out again, from one city to another, from living with roommates to living on their own. And their rates of risky behavior (such as binge drinking, having unprotected sex, and driving at high speeds or while drunk) are higher than those of any other age group, including adolescents.

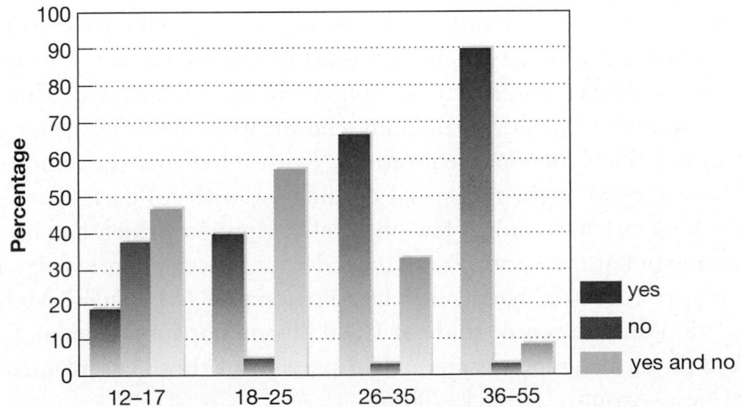

FIGURE 14.6 Are You an Adult Yet?
When people are asked, "Do you feel that you have reached adulthood?" the percentage that answers "yes" steadily increases over time. But as you can see, people between the ages of 18 and 25, emerging adults, are most likely to say "yes *and* no" (Arnett, 2000).

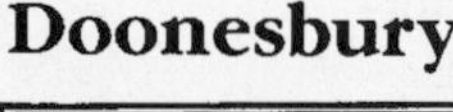

Of course, not all young people in this age group are alike. Some groups within the larger society, such as Mormons, promote early marriage and parenthood. And young people who are poor, who have dropped out of school, who had a child at 16, or who have few opportunities for good jobs will not have the income or leisure to explore many options. But the overall shift in all industrialized nations toward a global economy, increased education, and delayed career and family decisions means that emerging adulthood is likely to grow in importance as a distinct phase of prolonged exploration and freedom.

The Middle Years. For most women and men, the midlife years between 35 and 65 are the prime of life (MacArthur Foundation, 1999; Mroczek & Sprio, 2005). These years are typically a time of the greatest psychological well-being, good health, productivity, and community involvement. They are also often a time of reflection and reassessment. People look back on what they have accomplished, take stock of what they regret not having done, and think about what they want to do with their remaining years. When crises occur, it is for reasons not related to aging but to specific life-changing events, such as illness or the loss of a job or spouse (Wethington, 2000).

But doesn't menopause make most midlife women depressed, irritable, and irrational? **Menopause**, which usually occurs between ages 45 and 55, is the cessation of menstruation after the ovaries stop producing estrogen and progesterone. Menopause does produce physical symptoms in many women, notably hot flashes, as the vascular system adjusts to the decrease in estrogen. But only about 10 percent of all women have unusually severe physical symptoms.

The negative view of menopause as a syndrome that causes depression and other negative emotional reactions is based on women who have had an early menopause following a hysterectomy (removal of the uterus) or who have had a lifetime history of depression. But these women are not typical. According to many surveys of thousands of healthy, randomly chosen women in the general population, most women view menopause positively (with relief that they no longer have to worry about pregnancy or menstrual periods) or with no particular feelings at all. The vast majority have only a few physical symptoms (which can be annoying and bothersome but are temporary) and most do not become depressed; only 3 percent even report regret at having reached menopause (McKinlay, McKinlay, & Brambilla, 1987). In one recent study of 1,000 postmenopausal women, fewer than half reported physical symptoms and only 5 percent of those complained of mood symptoms (Ness, Aronow, & Beck, 2006).

menopause The cessation of menstruation and of the production of ova; it is usually a gradual process lasting up to several years.

GET INVOLVED!

➤"YOU'RE AS OLD AS YOU FEEL"

Ask five people, each about a decade apart in age and one of whom is at least 70, how old they feel. (You may include yourself.) What is the gap, if any, between their chronological age and their psychological age? Is the gap larger among the older individuals? Ask why they perceive an age gap between their actual years and how old they feel.

Although women lose their fertility after menopause and men theoretically remain fertile throughout their lives, men have a biological clock too. Testosterone diminishes, although it never drops as sharply in men as estrogen does in women. The sperm count may gradually drop, and the sperm that remain are more susceptible to genetic mutations that can increase the risk of certain diseases in children conceived by older fathers (Wyrobek et al., 2006). For example, fathers over 50 have three times the risk of conceiving a child who develops schizophrenia as fathers under age 25 (Malaspina, 2001) and being an older father increases the probability that a child will be autistic (Reichenberg et al., 2006).

The physical changes of midlife do not by themselves predict how people will feel about aging or how they will respond to it (Schaie & Willis, 2002). How a culture views aging, as something natural and inevitable or a process to be fought tooth and nail, is far more important to how people adjust.

Old Age

When does old age start? Not long ago you would have been considered old in your 60s. Today, the fastest-growing segment of the population in North America consists of people over the age of 85. There were 4 million Americans age 85 or older in 2000, and the Census Bureau projects that there may be as many as 31 million by 2050. Close to 1 million of them will be over the age of 100. How will these people do? *Gerontologists*, researchers who study aging and the old, have been providing some answers.

Various aspects of intelligence, memory, and other forms of mental functioning decline significantly with age. Older adults score lower on tests of reasoning, spatial

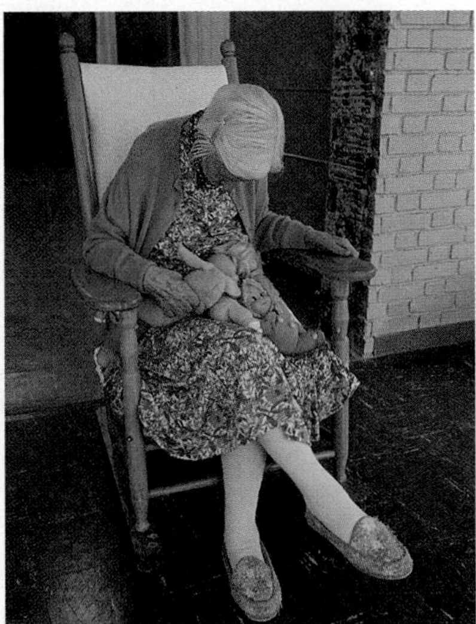

The two images of old age: More and more old people are living healthy, active, mentally stimulating lives. But with increasing longevity, many people are also falling victim to degenerative diseases such as Alzheimer's.

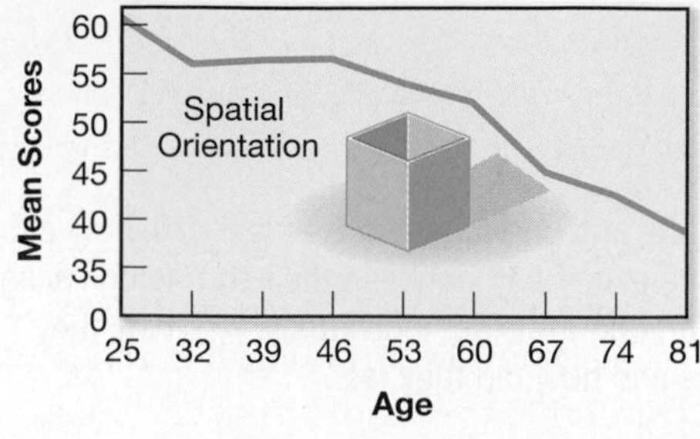

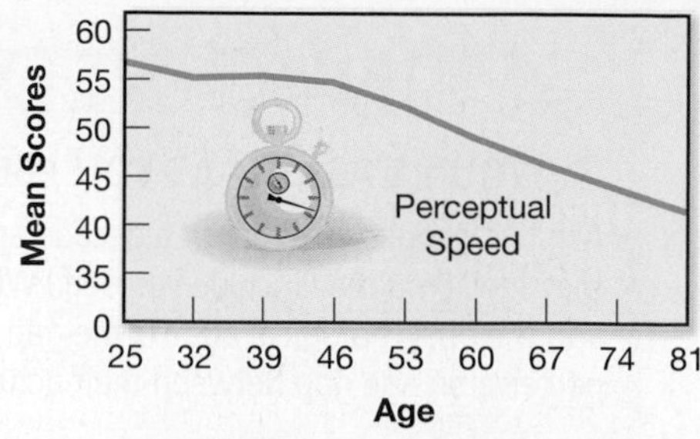

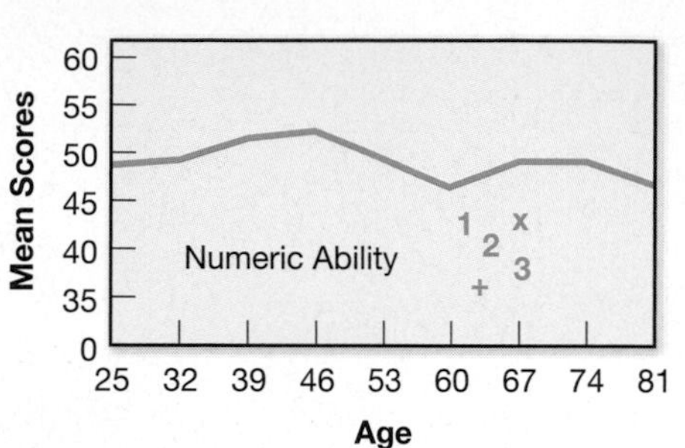

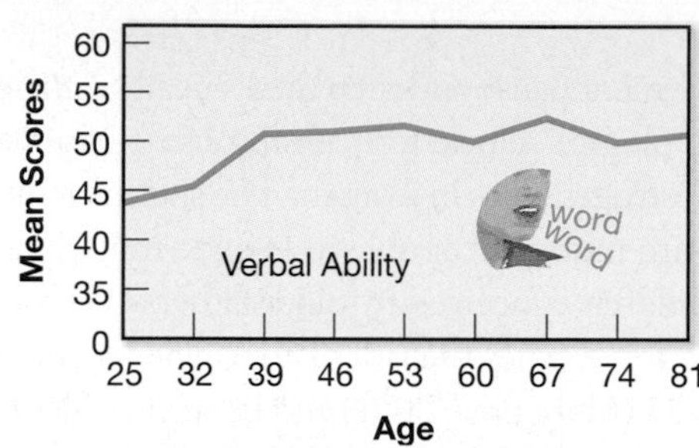

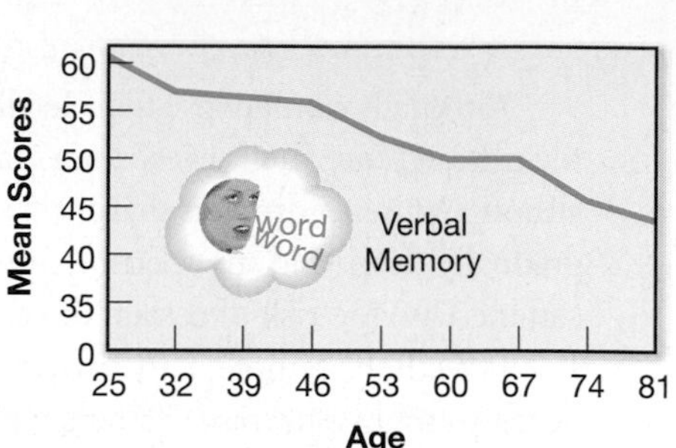

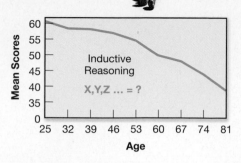

FIGURE 14.7 Changes in Mental Functioning over Time
As these graphs show, some intellectual abilities tend to dwindle with age, but numerical and verbal abilities remain relatively steady over the years.

fluid intelligence The capacity for deductive reasoning and the ability to use new information to solve problems; it is relatively independent of education and tends to decline in old age.

crystallized intelligence Cognitive skills and specific knowledge of information acquired over a lifetime; it is heavily dependent on education and tends to remain stable over the lifetime.

ability, and complex problem solving than do younger adults. The ability to produce and spell familiar words declines, a change that often causes great frustration and annoyance (Burke & Shafto, 2004). It takes older people longer to retrieve names, dates, and other information; in fact, the speed of cognitive processing in general slows down significantly. However, older people vary considerably, with some declining mentally and others remaining sharp (Salthouse, 2006).

Fortunately, not all cognitive abilities worsen with age. **Fluid intelligence** is the capacity for deductive reasoning and the ability to use new information to solve problems. It reflects an inherited predisposition, and it parallels other biological capacities in its growth and later decline (Bosworth & Schaie, 1999; Li et al., 2004). **Crystallized intelligence** consists of knowledge and skills built up over a lifetime, the kind of intelligence that gives us the ability to do arithmetic, define words, or take political positions. It depends heavily on education and experience, and it tends to remain stable or even improve over the life span (see Figure 14.7). This is why physicians, lawyers, teachers, farmers, musicians, insurance agents, politicians, psychologists, and people in many other occupations can continue working well into old age.

Psychologists have made great strides in separating conditions once thought to be an inevitable part of old age from those that are preventable or treatable:

- Apparent senility in the elderly is often caused by malnutrition, prescription medications, harmful combinations of medications, and even over-the-counter drugs (such as sleeping pills and antihistamines), all of which can be hazardous to old people.
- Depression, passivity, and memory problems may result from the loss of meaningful activity, intellectual stimulation, goals to pursue, and control over events (Hess, 2005; Langer, 1983; Schaie & Zuo, 2001).
- Weakness, frailty, and even diseases associated with old age are often caused by being inactive and sedentary (Booth & Neufer, 2005).

THINKING CRITICALLY

CONSIDER OTHER EXPLANATIONS

People assume that aging inevitably produces senility, depression, weakness, and a decline in mental abilities. What else could be causing these problems?

Many of the physical and mental losses of old age are genetically based and occur across cultures, but others have to do with behavioral and psychological factors (Park & Gutchess, 2006). A crucial protective factor is aerobic exercise and strength training, which maintain physical strength and flexibility, boost the brain's blood supply, promote the development of new cells, and can even suppress genetic predispositions for various infirmities (Booth & Neufer, 2005). The result is greatly improved cognitive functioning in skills such as planning, concentration, and scheduling (Colcombe & Kramer, 2004). Mental stimulation also promotes the growth of neural connections in the brain, even well into old age (Hultsch et al., 1999; Kleim et al., 1998). Older adults can sometimes do as well on memory tests as people in their 20s, when given instruction and training. In one longitudinal study, older people who had shown a decline in inductive reasoning and spatial orientation over a 14-year span were given five hours of training in these skills. This brief intervention produced significant improvements in two-thirds of the sample, and many performed at or above the level of skill they had had 14 years earlier. The effects were still apparent up to seven years later (Kramer & Willis, 2002).

Perhaps the best news is that as people get older, most become better able to regulate negative feelings and emphasize the positive. The frequency of intense negative emotions is highest among people aged 18 to 34, then drops sharply to age 65. After 65, it levels off, rising only slightly among old people facing crises of illness and bereavement (Charles & Carstensen, 2004; Charles, Reynolds, & Gatz, 2001). Apparently, many people do grow wiser, or at least more tranquil, with age.

Some researchers who study aging are therefore optimistic. In their view, people who have challenging occupations and interests, who remain active mentally, who exercise regularly, and who adapt flexibly to change and loss are likely to maintain their cognitive abilities and well-being. "Use it or lose it," they say. Other researchers, however, are less optimistic (Salthouse, 2006). "When you've lost it, you can't use it," they reply. They are worried about the growing numbers of people living into their 90s and beyond, when rates of cognitive impairment and dementia rise dramatically. The challenge for society is to make sure that the many people who will be living into advanced old age can keep using their brains instead of losing them.

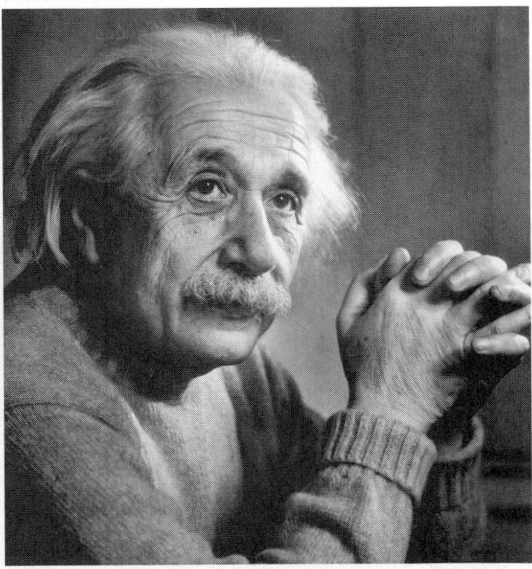

Remember the cute children pictured at the beginning of this chapter? They are Adolph Hitler, Queen Elizabeth II, and Albert Einstein. Now that you have read this chapter, what kinds of influences can you think of—genetic, familial, and historical—that might explain what made these three famous people so remarkably different?

QUICK quiz

People of any age can answer this quiz.

1. The key psychological issue during adolescence, said Erikson, is a(n) __________ crisis.
2. What new phase of life development has been created because of demographic changes, and what years does it include?
3. Most women react to menopause by (a) feeling depressed, (b) regretting the loss of femininity, (c) going a little crazy, (d) feeling relieved or neutral.
4. Which of these statements about the decline of mental abilities in old age is *false*? (a) It can often be lessened with training programs; (b) crystallized intelligence inevitably declines sharply; (c) it is sometimes a result of malnutrition, medication, or disease rather than aging; (d) it is slowed when people live in stimulating environments.
5. Suddenly, your 80-year-old grandmother has become confused and delusional. Before concluding that old age has made her senile, what other explanation should you rule out?

Answers:

1. identity **2.** emerging adulthood, ages 18 to 25 **3.** d **4.** b **5.** You should rule out the possibility that she is taking too many medications, even nonprescription drugs.

WHAT'S**AHEAD**

- Do terrible childhood experiences inevitably affect a person forever?
- What makes most children resilient in the face of adversity?

The Wellsprings of Resilience

Most people take it for granted that the path from childhood to adolescence to adulthood is a fairly straight one. We think of the lasting attitudes, habits, and values our parents taught us. We continue to have deep attachments to our families, even when we are fighting with them. And many people carry with them the scars of emotional wounds they suffered as children. Children who have been beaten, neglected, or constantly subjected to verbal or physical abuse by their parents are more likely than other children to have emotional problems, become delinquent and violent, commit crimes, have low IQs, drop out of school, develop mental disorders such as depression, and develop chronic stress-related illnesses (Emery & Laumann-Billings, 1998; Margolin & Gordis, 2004; Repetti, Taylor, & Seeman, 2002).

And yet, when research psychologists began to question the entrenched assumption that early trauma always has long-lasting negative effects and considered the evidence for alternative views, they got quite a different picture. Most children, they found, are resilient, eventually overcoming even the effects of war, childhood illness, having abusive or alcoholic parents, early deprivation, or being sexually molested (Cohen, 1999; Kaufman & Zigler, 1987; McNally, 2003; Rathbun, DiVirgilio, & Waldfogel, 1958; Rind, Tromovitch, & Bauserman, 1998; Rutter, 2004; Werner, 1989; West & Prinz, 1987). In Chapter 17, we report research showing that most adults eventually recover after disaster, too. For example, a study of thousands of Jewish immigrants to America who had survived the Holocaust found a picture of resiliency and successful integration into their new lives rather than persisting traumatic distress (Helmreich, 1992).

THINKING  **CRITICALLY**

ANALYZE ASSUMPTIONS AND BIASES

Many people are convinced that childhood traumas always cause emotional problems in adulthood. What is wrong with this assumption, and what evidence does it overlook?

Psychologist Ann Masten (2001) has observed that most people assume there is something special and rare about people who recover from adversity. But "the great surprise" of the research, she concluded, is how ordinary resilience is. Many of the children who outgrow early deprivation and trauma have easygoing temperaments or personality traits, such as self-efficacy and self-control, that help them roll with even severe punches. They have a secure attachment style, which helps them work through traumatic events in a way that heals their wounds and restores hope and emotional balance (Mikulincer, Shaver, & Horesh, 2006). If children lack secure attachments with their own parents, they may be rescued by love and attention from their siblings, extended family, peers, or other caring adults. And some have experiences outside the family—in schools, places of worship, or other organizations—that give them a sense of competence, moral support, solace, religious faith, and self-esteem (Cowen et al., 1990; Garmezy, 1991).

Perhaps the most powerful reason for the resilience of so many children, and for the changes that all of us make throughout our lives, is that we are all constantly interpreting our experiences. We can decide to repeat the mistakes our parents made or break free of them. We can decide to remain prisoners of childhood or to strike out in new directions at age 20, 50, or 70. In the next decades, as the world changes in unpredictable ways, the territory of adulthood will continue to expand, providing new frontiers as well as fewer signposts and road maps to guide us. Increasingly, age will be what we make of it.

Taking Psychology with You

Bringing Up Baby

Every year or so another best-selling book arrives to tell parents they've been doing it all wrong. Years ago the public was warned that a new mother must bond with her baby right away, right after birth, or dire things would happen to the baby's development. Then it turned out that although immediate bonding is certainly nice, adopted babies will bond to parents just fine even if the adoption took place several days, months, or years after the child's birth (Eyer, 1992).

Throughout the twentieth century and still today, countless books have advised parents to treat their children in very specific, if contradictory, ways: Pick them up, don't pick them up; respond when they cry, don't respond when they cry; let them sleep with you, never let them sleep with you; be affectionate, be stern; be highly sensitive to their every need so they will securely attach to you, don't overreact to their every mood or complaint or you will spoil them (Hulbert, 2003).

No need to panic. As we have seen in this chapter, babies and young children thrive under a wide variety of childrearing methods. They bring their own temperaments to the matter, too: Most respond readily to induction, but others require stricter discipline. And as children grow up, they are subject to the influences of their peers and generation and to particular experiences that shape their interests and motivation.

Well, then, how should you treat your children? Should you be strict or lenient, powerful or permissive? Should you require your child to stop having tantrums, to clean up his or her room, to be polite? Should you say, "Oh, nothing I do will matter, anyway"

or "Children need to express themselves in any way they please"? Child development research suggests certain overall guidelines to help parents teach children to be confident, considerate, and helpful:

- **Set high expectations that are appropriate to the child's age and temperament, and teach the child how to meet them.** Some parents make few demands on their children, either unintentionally or because they believe a parent should not impose standards. Others make many demands, such as requiring children to be polite, help with chores, control their anger, be thoughtful of others, and do well in school. The children of parents who make few demands tend to be aggressive, impulsive, and immature. The children of parents who have high expectations tend to be helpful and above average in competence and self-confidence (Damon, 1995). But the demands must be appropriate for the child's age. You can't expect 2-year-olds to dress themselves, and before you can expect children to get up on time, they have to know how to work an alarm clock.
- **Explain, explain, explain.** Induction—telling a child why you have applied a rule—teaches a child to be responsible. Punitive methods ("Do it or I'll spank you") may result in compliance, but the child will tend to disobey as soon as you are out of sight. Explanations also teach children how to reason and understand; they reward curiosity and open-mindedness. While setting standards for your children, you can also allow them to express disagreements and feelings. This does not mean you have to argue with a 4-year-old about the merits of table manners or permit antisocial and destructive behavior. Once you have explained a rule, you need to enforce it consistently.
- **Encourage empathy.** Call the child's attention to the effects of his or her actions on others, appeal to the child's sense of fair play and desire to be good, and teach the child to take another person's point of view. Even very young children are capable of empathy. Vague orders, such as "Don't fight," are less effective than showing the child how fighting disrupts and hurts others. For boys especially, aggression and empathy are strongly and negatively related: The higher the one, the lower the other (Eisenberg et al., 2002).
- **Notice, approve of, and reward good behavior.** Many parents punish the behavior they dislike, a form of attention that often is rewarding to the child. It is much more effective to praise the behavior you do want, which teaches the child how to behave.

Even with the best skills and intentions, you cannot control everything that happens to your child or your child's basic temperamental dispositions. "The idea that we can make our children turn out any way we want is an illusion. Give it up," advises Judith Harris (1998) in her book *The Nurture Assumption*. But, she adds, parents do have the power to make their children's lives miserable or secure. And they deeply affect the quality of the relationship they will have with their child throughout life: one filled with conflict and resentment, or one that is close and loving.

Summary

- *Developmental psychologists* study how people grow and change over the life span. Many study *socialization*, the process by which children learn the rules and behavior society expects of them.

From Conception Through the First Year

- *Maturation* is the unfolding of genetically influenced behavior and characteristics. Prenatal development consists of the *germinal*, *embryonic*, and *fetal* stages. Harmful influences that can adversely affect the fetus's development include German measles, toxic chemicals, some sexually transmitted diseases, cigarettes, alcohol (which can cause *fetal alcohol syndrome* and cognitive deficits), illegal drugs, and even over-the-counter medications.
- Babies are born with *motor reflexes* and a number of perceptual abilities. Cultural practices affect the timing of physical milestones.
- Babies' innate need for *contact comfort* gives rise to emotional attachment to their caregivers, and by the age of 6 to

8 months, infants begin to feel *separation anxiety*. Studies of the *Strange Situation* have distinguished *secure* from *insecure* attachment; insecurity can take one of two forms, *avoidant* or *anxious-ambivalent* attachment.

- Styles of attachment are relatively unaffected by the normal range of child-rearing practices, and also by whether or not babies spend time in day care. Insecure attachment is promoted by parents' rejection, mistreatment, or abandonment of their infants; by a mother's postpartum depression, which can affect her ability to care for the baby; by the child's own fearful, insecure temperament; or by stressful family situations.
- The brain develops all through childhood, adolescence, and adulthood. No one knows how much of the brain's synaptic growth in the first year or two is due to genetics or experiences, or what kinds of experience are important.

Cognitive Development

- Infants are responsive to the pitch, intensity, and sound of language, which may be why adults in many cultures speak to babies in *parentese*, using higher-pitched words and exaggerated intonation of vowels. At 4 to 6 months of age, babies begin to recognize the sounds of their own language. They go through a babbling phase from age 6 months to 1 year, and at about 1 year, they start saying single words and using symbolic gestures. At age 2, children speak in two- or three-word *telegraphic* sentences that convey a variety of messages.
- Jean Piaget argued that cognitive development depends on an interaction between maturation and a child's experiences in the world. Children's thinking changes and adapts through *assimilation* and *accommodation*. Piaget proposed four stages of cognitive development: *sensorimotor* (birth to age 2), during which the child learns *object permanence*; *preoperational* (ages 2 to 7), during which language and symbolic thought develop, although the child remains *egocentric* in reasoning and has difficulty with some mental *operations*; *concrete operations* (ages 7 to 12), during which the child comes to understand *conservation*, identity, and serial ordering; and *formal operations* (age 12 to adulthood), during which abstract reasoning develops.
- Lev Vygotsky, working at about the same time as Piaget, emphasized a sociocultural approach to children's cognitive development. He noted that once children develop language, they begin speaking to themselves, using *private speech* to direct their own behavior.
- Researchers have built on Piaget's work, expanding and modifying his findings. The changes from one stage to another are not as clear-cut as Piaget implied; development is more continuous and overlapping. Also, young children have more cognitive abilities, at earlier ages, than Piaget thought, and older people may never achieve the ability for formal operations. Young children are not always egocentric in their thinking. By the age of 4 or 5 they have developed a *theory of mind* to account for their own and other people's behavior. Cultural practices affect the pace and content of cognitive development.

Learning to Be Good

- Lawrence Kohlberg proposed that as children mature cognitively, they go through three levels of moral reasoning. But people can reason morally without behaving morally. Developmental psychologists study how children learn to internalize standards of right and wrong and behave accordingly. This ability depends on the emergence of conscience and the moral emotions of guilt, shame, and empathy, and on the ability of children to learn to regulate their impulses, wishes, and feelings.
- Parental methods of discipline have different consequences for a child's moral behavior. *Power assertion* is associated with children who are aggressive and fail to internalize moral standards. However, the effects of physical punishment, such as spanking, depend on the family context and on the severity and frequency of the punishment. *Induction* is associated with children who develop empathy, internalize moral standards, and can resist temptation. In general, *authoritative* parents, who use induction and set limits, have better results with their children than do *authoritarian* or permissive parents.
- As discussed in the "Close-up on Research," the ability of very young children to regulate and control their impulses and feelings is associated with the subsequent internalization of moral standards and conscience. This ability is enhanced by mothers who use induction as a primary form of discipline. It also may reflect a relatively stable personality trait, because it tends to emerge very early in life and to be consistent over time and across situations.

Gender Development

- Gender development includes the emerging awareness of *gender identity*, the understanding that a person is biologically male or female regardless of what he or she does or

wears, and *gender typing*, the process by which boys and girls learn what it means to be masculine or feminine. Some individuals are born with *intersex* physical conditions and may consider themselves to be *transgender*. Some live comfortably with the physical and psychological attributes of both sexes; others are *transsexual*, feeling that they are male in a female body or vice versa.

- Universally, young children tend to prefer same-sex toys and playing with other children of their own sex. Biological psychologists account for this phenomenon in terms of genes and prenatal androgens, which appear to be involved in gender-typed play. Cognitive psychologists study how children develop *gender schemas* for "male" and "female" categories and qualities, which in turn shape their gender-typed behavior. Gender schemas tend to be inflexible at first. Later they become more flexible as the child cognitively matures and assimilates new information, if the child's culture promotes flexible gender schemas. Learning theorists study the direct and subtle reinforcers and social messages that foster gender typing.
- Gender development changes over the life span, depending on people's experiences with work and family life and larger events in society. Gender differences in motivation and behavior tend to be greatest in childhood and adolescence, but often decline in adulthood.

Adolescence

- *Adolescence* begins with the physical changes of *puberty*. In girls, puberty is signaled by *menarche* and the development of breasts; in boys, it begins with the onset of nocturnal emissions and the development of the testes, scrotum, and penis. Boys and girls who enter puberty early tend to have a more difficult later adjustment than do those who enter puberty later than average.
- As discussed in "Biology and the Teen Brain," the adolescent brain undergoes a major pruning of synapses, primarily in the prefrontal cortex and the limbic system, and myelinization, which improves the efficiency of neural transmission and strengthens the connections between these two brain areas. These neurological changes may not be complete until the early 20s, which would help explain why the strong emotions of the adolescent years often overwhelm rational decision making and why teenagers behave more impulsively than adults. This evidence may have important implications for how teenagers should be treated by the law if they commit crimes.
- Most adolescents do not go through extreme emotional turmoil, anger, or rebellion, do not dislike their parents, and do not suffer from unusually low self-esteem. However, conflict with parents, mood swings and depression, and reckless behavior do increase in adolescence. The peer group becomes especially important. Boys tend to externalize their emotional problems in acts of aggression and other antisocial behavior; girls tend to internalize their problems by becoming depressed or developing eating disorders.

Adulthood

- Erik Erikson proposed that life consists of eight stages, each with a unique psychological challenge, or crisis, that must be resolved, such as an *identity crisis* in adolescence. Erikson identified many of the essential concerns of adulthood and showed that development is a lifelong process. However, psychological issues or crises are not confined to particular chronological periods or stages.
- Adults often evaluate their development according to a *social clock* that determines whether they are on time or off time for a particular event. When most people in an age group go through the same event at about the same time, transitions are easier than when people feel out of step.
- In industrialized nations, major demographic changes have postponed the timing of career decisions, marriage or commitment to a partner, and parenthood until a person's late 20s on the average. The result is that many young people between the ages of 18 and 25, especially if they are not financially independent, find themselves in a life phase often called *emerging adulthood*. For many, this phase is qualitatively different from both adolescence and adulthood.
- The middle years are generally not a time of turmoil or crisis but the prime of most people's lives. In women, *menopause* begins in the late 40s or early 50s. Many women have temporary physical symptoms, but most do not regret the end of fertility or become depressed and irritable. In middle-aged men, hormone production slows down but fertility continues, although mutations in sperm increase the risk of birth defects in offspring of older fathers.
- *Gerontologists* have revised our ideas about old age, now that people are living longer and healthier lives. The speed of cognitive processing slows down, and *fluid intelligence* parallels other biological capacities in its eventual decline. *Crystallized intelligence*, in contrast, depends heavily on cul-

ture, education, and experience, and it tends to remain stable over the life span.

- Many supposedly inevitable results of aging, such as senility, depression, and physical frailty, are often avoidable. They may result from disease, medication, or poor nutrition, and also from lack of stimulation, control of one's environment, and exercise. Exercise and mental stimulation promote the growth of synapses in the human brain, even well into old age, although some mental losses are inevitable.

The Wellsprings of Resilience

- Children who experience violence or neglect are at risk of many problems later in life. But the majority of children are resilient and are able to overcome early adversity. Psychologists now study not only the sad consequences of neglect, poverty, and violence but also the reasons for resilience under adversity, which they find more common and ordinary than was once believed.

KEY TERMS

developmental psychology 521
socialization 521
maturation 522
germinal, embryonic, fetal stages 522
zygote 522
fetus 523
fetal alcohol syndrome 524
motor reflexes 524
contact comfort 525
separation anxiety 526
Strange Situation 526
kinds of attachment (Ainsworth): secure, avoidant, anxious-ambivalent 526
"parentese" 530
telegraphic speech 531
Jean Piaget 532
assimilation 532
accommodation 532
sensorimotor stage 532
object permanence 532
preoperational stage 533
mental operations 533
egocentric thinking 533
conservation 533
concrete operations stage 534
formal operations stage 534
Lev Vygotsky 535
private speech 535
theory of mind 536
power assertion 538
induction 539
authoritarian versus authoritative parental styles 539
self-regulation 540
gender identity 542
gender typing 542
intersex conditions (hermaphroditism) 543
transgender 543
transsexual 543
gender schema 545
puberty 548
menarche 549
secondary sex characteristics 549
Erik Erikson 552
identity crisis 553
social clock 554
emerging adulthood 555
menopause 556
gerontology 557
fluid intelligence 558
crystallized intelligence 558

How Does This Apply to Me?

NOW YOU HAVE READ CHAPTER FOURTEEN — ARE YOU PREPARED FOR THE EXAM?

Your little brother picks up objects, feels every part of them, and then puts them in his mouth. What stage of Jean Piaget's model of cognitive development does this behavior suggest?

What are the different ways of looking at cognitive development? (pages 532–533)

sensorimotor stage

Jeremy is 17 years old. According to Erikson, his chief task will be acquiring a sense of ______.

How do adolescents develop formal operations and moral thinking? (pages 553–554)

identity

Which theory correctly explains why the aging process occurs?

How do adults deal with the issues of work, relationships, parenting, and death? (pages 557–560)

No theory to date has thoroughly explained the aging process.

Students often get mixed up on the relationship between DNA, genes, and chromosomes. Remember, chromosomes are the largest unit. Chromosomes can be made up of genes, and genes can be broken down into DNA. Go to the "Conception through First Year" section of **MyPsychLab** to better understand these concepts.

TELL ME **MORE** >>

"MyPsychLab used many everyday situations as examples to help me understand what I needed."

Student
Oklahoma State University

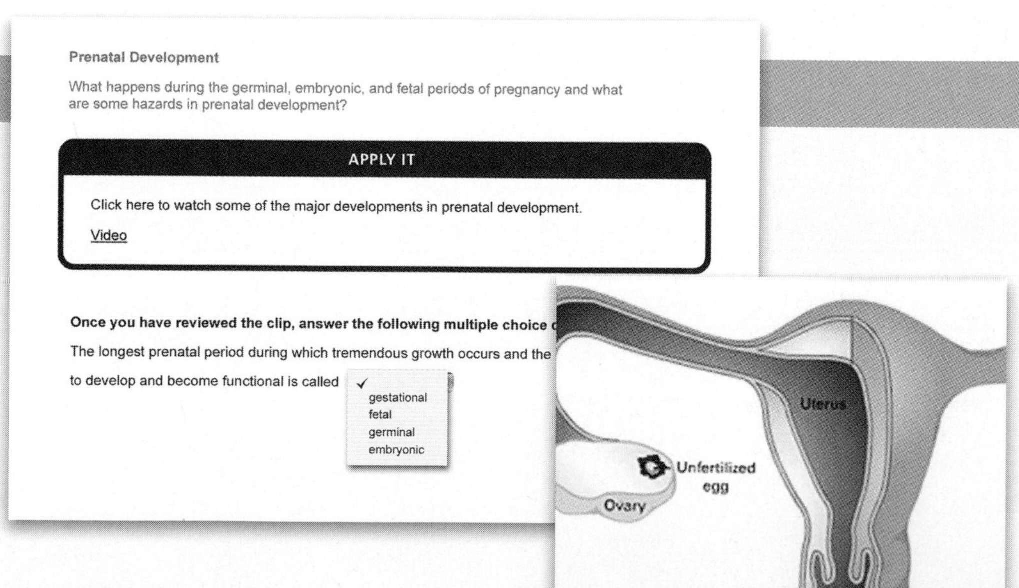

Prenatal Development
What happens during the germinal, embryonic, and fetal periods of pregnancy and what are some hazards in prenatal development?
APPLY IT
Click here to watch some of the major developments in prenatal development.
Video
Once you have reviewed the clip, answer the following multiple choice
The longest prenatal period during which tremendous growth occurs and the
to develop and become functional is called
gestational
fetal
germinal
embryonic
Uterus
Unfertilized egg
Ovary

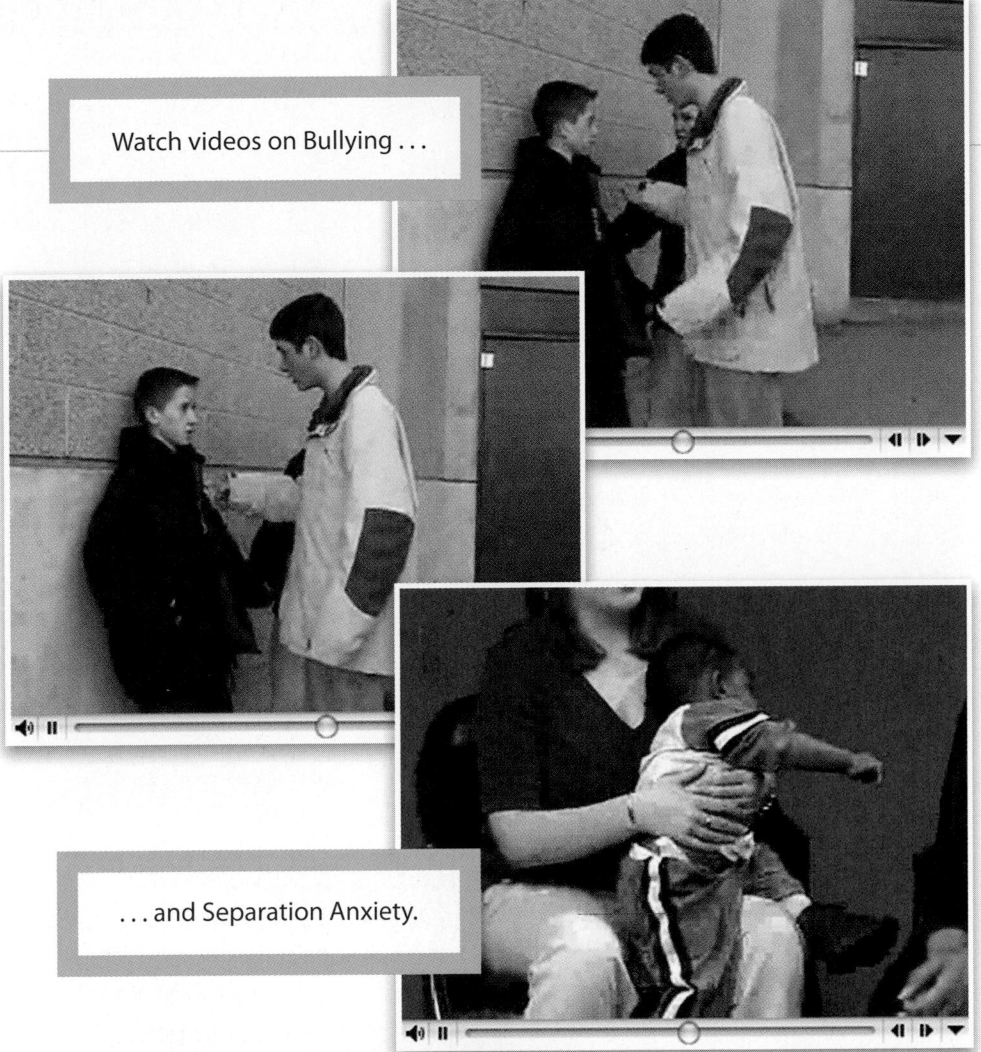

Watch videos on Bullying . . .

. . . and Separation Anxiety.

Stage	Age
Sensorimotor	0-2 years
Preoperational	2-7 years
Concrete Operational	7-12 years
Formal Operational	12 years and on

Perhaps the most influential theory on cognitive development is Jean Piaget's theory. He proposed four stages of cognitive development.

What are the different ways of looking at cognitive development?

Check out the videos in this chapter of MyPsychLab to get a better understanding of these stages.

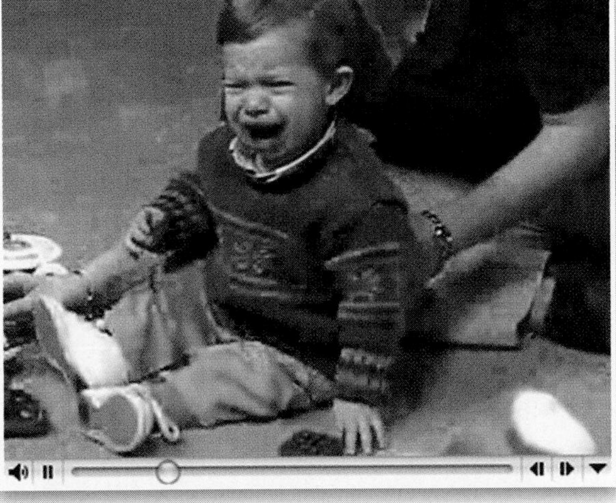

See more on the study card "Study Tips for the Most Difficult Topics in Introductory Psychology" found in the back of your book.

TELL ME **MORE** >>

"The program was a wonderful asset in test preparation."

Student
Clayton State University and College

CHAPTER FIFTEEN

The process of living is the process of reacting to stress.

STANLEY SARNOFF

CHAPTER 15

Sean and his father have been battling for years. Sean feels that his father is always ready to criticize him for the slightest flaw. No matter what he does, he can't seem to get his father's approval. Sean is now living on his own and doing well, but every time his father comes to visit, Sean gets a migraine.

OUTLINE

Vicente is working two jobs to make ends meet. His supervisor at one job is making his life miserable, but Vicente can't afford to offend him, so he says nothing. His blood pressure is high and lately he's been having awful stomachaches, but he can't see a way of improving his situation.

Valerie gets caught in a massive traffic jam and is late for class. That afternoon, rushing to get her notes together for an overdue assignment, Val spills coffee all over herself and the papers. When she gets home, she discovers that a pipe has burst and her kitchen is flooded.

All of these people are certainly under stress, but, as you see, their experiences are far from the same. The popular use of the word *stress* includes recurring conflicts (Sean and his father), continuing pressures that seem uncontrollable (Vicente), or small irritations that wear you down (Val). Everyone complains about stress; the big question is whether these events are linked to illness. Why does Sean get migraines during yet another miserable visit with his father? Are Vicente's stomachaches related to the pressures of his job or to a bad digestive system? Val may be having an annoying day, but will it increase her chances of getting the flu? And can any of them, by controlling their stress levels, prevent illness and maintain good health?

We will explore these questions by looking at findings from *health psychology*, which is concerned with the biological, psychological, social, and cultural factors that influence health and illness. We will see that although good health is not "all in your mind" and not entirely under your control, your thoughts, emotions, and actions do play a role in whether you fall ill—and how quickly you recover when you do.

WHAT'S **AHEAD**

- Which stressors pose the greatest hazard to your health?
- Are you more likely to get a cold when you are stressed out?

The Stress–Illness Mystery

First, some good news. Everyday hassles—such as traffic, lousy weather, broken plumbing, lost keys, or a computer that crashes when a deadline is near—are exasperating, but they do not pose a threat to health. But other stressful experiences or situations—*stressors*—do increase the risk of illness when they severely disrupt a person's life, when they

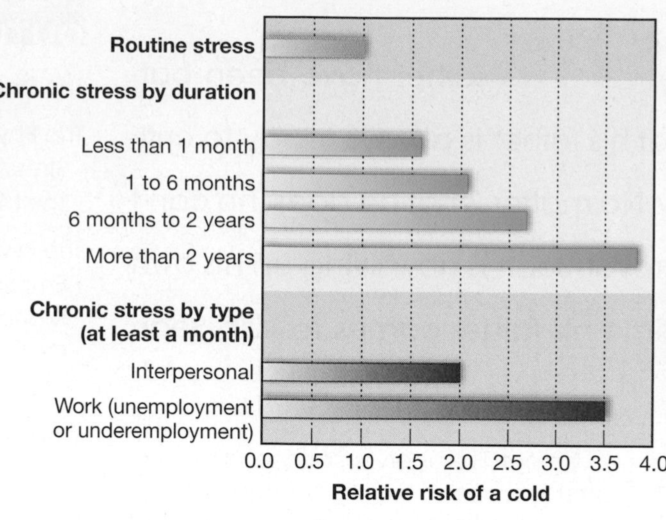

FIGURE 15.1 Stress and the Common Cold

Chronic stress lasting a month or more boosts the risk of catching a cold. The risk is increased among people undergoing problems with their friends or loved ones, and is highest among people who are out of work (Cohen et al., 1998).

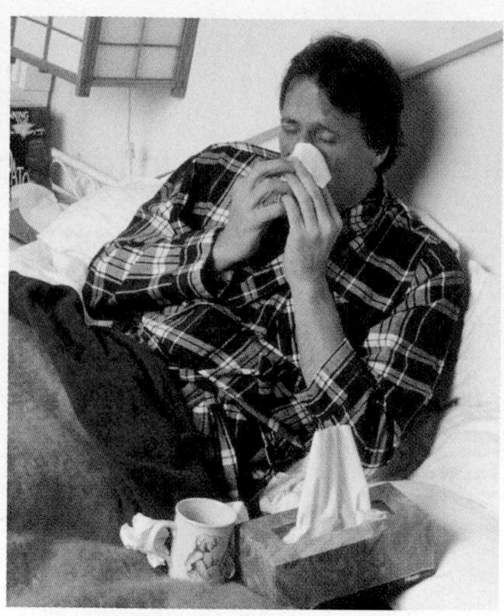

are uncontrollable, or when they are chronic, lasting at least six months. Here are some of them:

1 **Work-related problems.** Because work is central in most people's lives, the effects of unemployment or of a chronically stressful work environment can be especially severe. Work-related stress can even increase a person's vulnerability to the common cold. In one study, heroic volunteers were given either ordinary nose drops or nose drops containing a cold virus, and then were quarantined for five days. The people most likely to get a cold's miserable symptoms were those who had been underemployed or unemployed for at least a month (see Figure 15.1). The longer the work problems had lasted, the greater the likelihood of illness (Cohen et al., 1998).

2 **Noise.** Children who live or go to school near noisy airports have higher blood pressure and higher levels of stress hormones, are more distractible, and have more learning and attention difficulties than do children in quieter environments (Cohen et al., 1980; Evans, Bullinger, & Hygge, 1998). In adults, constant loud noise contributes to cardiovascular problems, irritability, fatigue, and aggressiveness (Staples, 1996).

Middle-class stress is a luxury to people whose health is chronically jeopardized by poverty, exposure to toxic materials, malnutrition, and lack of access to medical care.

3 **Bereavement and loss.** In the two years following bereavement, widowed people, especially men, are more susceptible to illness and physical ailments, and their mortality rate is higher than would otherwise be expected (Stroebe, Stroebe, & Schut, 2001).

4 **Poverty, powerlessness, and low status.** People at the lower rungs of the socioeconomic ladder have worse health and higher mortality rates for almost every disease and medical condition than do those at the top (Adler & Snibbe, 2003). In America, one obvious reason is that poor people cannot afford medical care. They are also more likely to eat high-calorie, fast-food diets that increase the chances of obesity and diabetes. Another reason for the poorer health of low-income people is that they often live with continuous environmental stressors—higher crime rates, discrimination, fewer community services, run-down

housing, and greater exposure to hazards such as chemical contamination—and the constant emotional stressors of fear, anxiety, and anger (Gallo & Matthews, 2003). These conditions affect urban blacks disproportionately and may help account for their high incidence of hypertension (high blood pressure), which can lead to kidney disease, strokes, and heart attacks (Clark et al., 1999).

However, before you try to persuade your instructors that the stress of chronic studying is bad for your health, consider this mystery: None of the chronic stressors we just discussed leads in a direct, simple way to illness or affects everyone in the same way. Although some people's health is affected by noise, bereavement, losing a job, poverty, or discrimination, *most* individuals living with these stressors do not get sick; indeed, the great majority are resilient (Bonanno, 2004; Taylor, Repetti, & Seeman, 1997). Some people exposed to a flu virus are sick all winter; others don't even get the sniffles. Some people in high-pressure careers wind up with heart disease; others work just as hard but remain healthy. Why?

THINKING CRITICALLY

ASK QUESTIONS; BE WILLING TO WONDER

Some people exposed to major stressors are sick for months; others don't even get the sniffles. Why? By asking this question, health psychologists have come up with a better understanding of stress, as this chapter will show.

To understand why prolonged stress makes trouble for some people but not others, health researchers focus on three factors that we will discuss in the rest of this chapter: (1) *individual physiological differences* in the cardiovascular, endocrine, immune, and other bodily systems; (2) *psychological factors*, such as attitudes, emotions, and perceptions of events; and (3) *people's behavior under stress*, which ranges from actions that increase the risk of illness to constructive coping that reduces the negative effects of stress.

- What happens to your body when you try to cross a busy street against the light?
- Why is being under stress not enough to make you ill?
- How do psychological factors affect the immune system?

The Physiology of Stress

The modern era of stress research began in 1956, when Canadian physician Hans Selye (1907–1982) published *The Stress of Life*. Selye was the first scientist to try to figure out how external stressors get "under the skin" to make us ill. Environmental stressors such as heat, cold, noise, pain, and danger, Selye wrote, disrupt the body's equilibrium. The body then mobilizes its resources to fight off these stressors and restore normal functioning.

Selye described the body's response to external stressors of all kinds as a **general adaptation syndrome,** a sequence of physiological reactions that occur in three phases:

1 The alarm phase, in which the body mobilizes the sympathetic nervous system to meet the immediate threat. The threat could be anything from taking a test you haven't studied for to running from an angry dog. As we saw in Chapter 11, the release of *adrenal hormones*, epinephrine and norepinephrine, occurs with any intense emotion. They produce a boost in energy, tense muscles, reduced sensitivity to pain, the shutting down of digestion (so that blood will flow more efficiently to the brain, muscles, and skin), and a rise in blood pressure. Decades before Selye, psychologist Walter Cannon (1929) described these changes as the "fight or flight" response, a phrase still in use.

general adaptation syndrome According to Hans Selye, a series of physiological responses to stressors that occur in three phases: alarm, resistance, and exhaustion.

2 **The resistance phase**, in which the body attempts to resist or cope with a stressor that cannot be avoided. During this phase, the physiological responses of the alarm phase continue, but these very responses make the body more vulnerable to *other* stressors. For example, when your body has mobilized to fight off the flu, you may find you are more easily annoyed by minor frustrations. In most cases, the body will eventually adapt to the stressor and return to normal.

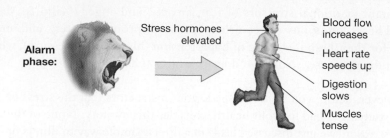

3 **The exhaustion phase**, in which persistent stress depletes the body of energy, increasing vulnerability to physical problems and eventually illness. The same reactions that allow the body to respond effectively in the alarm and resistance phases are unhealthy as long-range responses. Tense muscles can cause headache and neck pain. Increased blood pressure can become chronic hypertension. If normal digestive processes are interrupted or shut down for too long, digestive disorders may result.

Selye did not believe that people should aim for a stress-free life. Some stress is positive and productive, he said, even if it also requires the body to expend short-term energy: for example, competing in an athletic event, falling in love, or working hard on a project you enjoy. And some negative stress is simply unavoidable; it's called life!

Stress and the Body

Many of Selye's ideas proved to be particularly insightful, such as his observation that the same biological changes that are adaptive in the short run, because they permit the body to respond quickly to danger, can become hazardous in the long run (McEwen, 1998). Modern researchers are learning exactly how this happens, along with other details about the physiology of stress and its effects.

When you are under stress, your brain's hypothalamus sends messages to the endocrine glands along two major pathways. One, as Selye observed, activates the sympathetic division of the autonomic nervous system for "fight or flight," producing the release of epinephrine and norepinephrine from the inner part (medulla) of the adrenal glands. In addition, we now know, the hypothalamus initiates activity along the **HPA axis** (HPA stands for hypothalamus–pituitary–adrenal cortex): The hypothalamus releases chemical messengers that communicate with the pituitary gland, which in turn sends messages to the outer part (cortex) of the adrenal glands. The adrenal cortex secretes *cortisol* and other hormones that elevate blood sugar and protect the body's tissues from inflammation in case of injury (see Figure 15.2). Interestingly, not all stressors produce a rise in cortisol. Cortisol is most likely to be triggered by *psychological* stressors: when people's self-preservation is threatened, when they have no control over the task at hand, or when they feel that they are

HPA (hypothalamus–pituitary–adrenal cortex) axis A system activated to energize the body to respond to stressors. The hypothalamus sends chemical messengers to the pituitary, which in turn prompts the adrenal cortex to produce cortisol and other hormones.

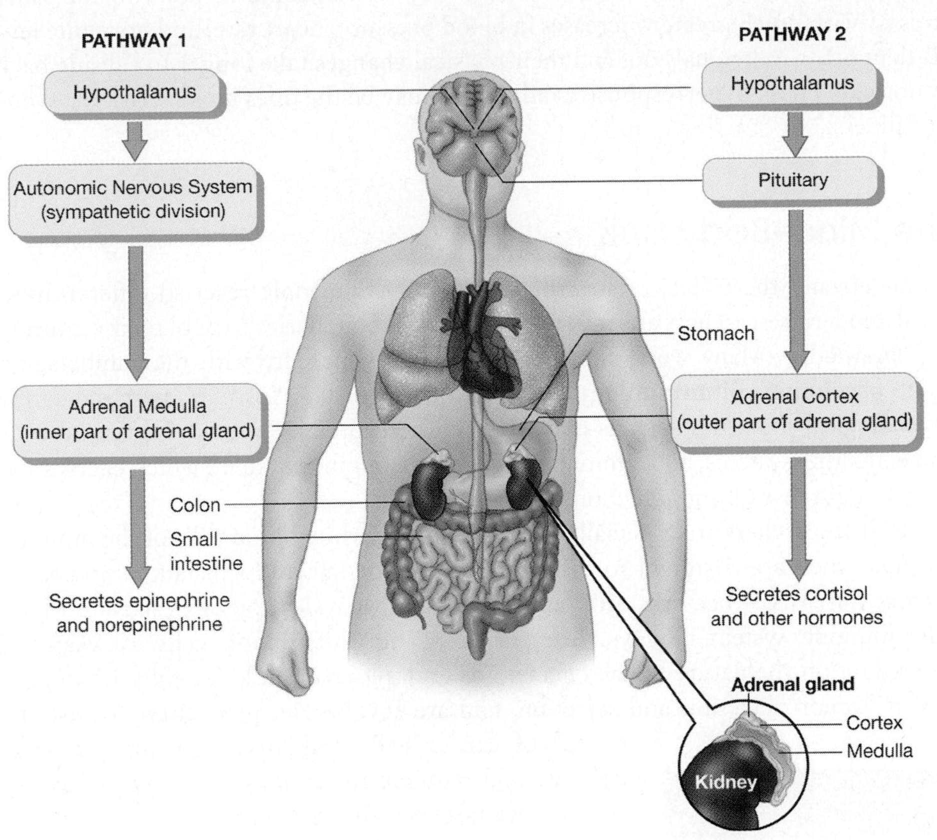

FIGURE 15.2 The Brain and Body Under Stress

When a person is in danger or under stress, the hypothalamus sends messages to the endocrine glands along two major pathways. In one, the hypothalamus activates the sympathetic division of the autonomic nervous system, which stimulates the adrenal medulla to produce epinephrine and norepinephrine. The result is the many bodily changes associated with "fight or flight." In the other pathway, messages travel along the HPA axis to the adrenal cortex, which produces cortisol and other hormones. The result is increased energy and protection from tissue inflammation in case of injury.

being judged negatively by others (Dickerson & Kemeny, 2004). You'll see why this matters shortly.

One result of HPA axis activation is increased energy, which is crucial for short-term responses to stress (Kemeny, 2003). But if cortisol and other stress hormones stay high too long, they can be harmful, contributing to hypertension, immune disorders, other physical ailments, and possibly emotional problems. And, most annoyingly for people worried about their weight, elevated levels of cortisol motivate animals (and presumably humans, too) to seek out rich comfort foods and store the extra calories as abdominal fat.

However, as we noted earlier, not all stressors affect everyone physiologically the same way. People's responses vary according to their learning history, gender, preexisting medical conditions, and genetic predisposition for high blood pressure, heart disease, obesity, diabetes, or other health problems (McEwen, 2000; Røysamb

Alas, the same stress hormones that help in the short run can have unwanted long-term consequences.

psychoneuroimmunology (PNI) The study of the relationships among psychology, the nervous and endocrine systems, and the immune system.

et al., 2003; Taylor et al., 2000b). This is why some people respond to the same stressor with much greater increases in blood pressure, heart rate, and hormone levels than other individuals do, and their physical changes take longer to subside back to normal. These hyperresponsive individuals may be the ones most at risk for eventual illness.

The Mind–Body Link

To understand the effects of stressors and learn why people react so differently to them, modern researchers are crossing professional boundaries to pool their resources and knowledge. Many work in an interdisciplinary specialty with the cumbersome name **psychoneuroimmunology,** or **PNI** for short. The "psycho" part stands for psychological processes such as emotions and perceptions; "neuro" for the nervous and endocrine systems; and "immunology" for the immune system, which enables the body to fight disease and infection.

PNI researchers are especially interested in the white blood cells of the immune system, which are designed to recognize foreign or harmful substances *(antigens)*, such as flu viruses, bacteria, and tumor cells, and then destroy or deactivate them. The immune system deploys different kinds of white blood cells as weapons, depending on the nature of the enemy. For example, natural killer cells are important in tumor detection and rejection, and are involved in protection against the spread of cancer cells and viruses. Helper T cells enhance and regulate the immune response; they are the primary target of the HIV virus that causes AIDS. Chemicals produced by the immune cells are sent to the brain, and the brain in turn sends chemical signals to stimulate or restrain the immune system. Anything that disrupts this communication loop—drugs, surgery, or chronic stress—can weaken or suppress the immune system (Segerstrom & Miller, 2004).

The immune system consists of fighter cells that look more fantastical than any alien creature Hollywood could think up. This one is about to engulf and destroy a cigarette-shaped parasite that causes a tropical disease.

Some PNI researchers have gotten right down to the level of cell damage to see how stress can lead to illness, aging, and even premature death. At the end of every chromosome is a protein complex that, in essence, tells the cell how long it has to live. Every time a cell divides, enzymes whittle away a tiny piece of this protein; when it is reduced to almost nothing, the cell stops dividing and dies. One team of researchers compared two groups of healthy women between the ages of 20 and 50: 19 who had healthy children and 39 who were primary caregivers of a child chronically ill with a serious disease, such as cerebral palsy. Of course, the mothers of the sick children felt that they were under stress, but they also had significantly greater cell damage than did the mothers of healthy children. In fact, the cells of the highly stressed women looked like those of women at least ten years older, and the part of the chromosome responsible for cell life was much shorter (Epel et al., 2004).

The puzzle, though, is that many human beings are not harmed by chronic stressors and environmental conditions. The reason has to do with the biggest difference between humans and other species: our perceptions of what is happening to us. Consider crowding. Mice get really nasty when they're crowded, but many people love crowds. Not many other species would voluntarily choose to get squashed in Times Square on New Year's Eve or in a mosh pit at a rock concert. Human beings show signs of stress not when they are actually crowded but when they *feel* crowded, trapped, or forced to endure unwanted interactions with others (Evans, Lepore, & Schroeder, 1996). Individuals and cultures differ in the amount of personal space and population density they consider normal and desirable; Asians and Latinos typically feel less crowded than Anglos do, given the same number of people. But regardless of culture, when people feel crowded, especially in their home living arrangements, they are more likely to develop emotional and physical symptoms (Evans, Lepore, & Allen, 2000). Similarly, feeling poor in relation to your surroundings is actually more detrimental to health than literally being poor, even controlling for all the health disadvantages of poor diet and poor medical care. In the United States, low socioeconomic status predicts poor health most strongly in communities with the greatest inequality between rich and poor (Sapolsky, 2005).

THINKING CRITICALLY

CONSIDER OTHER INTERPRETATIONS

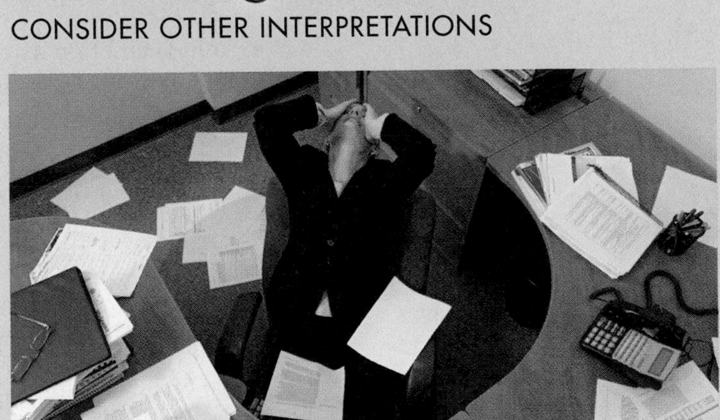

Most people think stress is something "out there" that just happens to them. But there is another way of looking at stress—as something in you, something that depends on your thoughts and emotions. For example, do you see your work as an endless set of assignments you will never complete, or as challenging tasks to master? The answer will affect how stressed you are.

As you can see, then, psychological factors play a big role in whether a person feels stressed. Selye himself once observed, "It's not what happens [to you] that counts; it is how you take it" (quoted in Ray, 2004). In the rest of this chapter, we will learn how right he was.

QUICK quiz

We hope these questions are not a source of stress for you.

1. Which of these statements is true? (a) Most people who suffer the death of a loved one become sick; (b) work problems and unemployment pose a greater health risk than conflicts in relationships; (c) people with high incomes often have more stressful lives than low-income people; (d) daily hassles are as hazardous to health as major stressors.
2. Steve is unexpectedly called on in class. He hasn't the faintest idea of the answer, and he feels his heart start to pound and his palms sweat. According to Selye, he is in the _______ phase of his stress response.
3. Key stress hormones released by the adrenal glands are epinephrine, norepinephrine, and _______.
4. *True or false?* Modern research confirms the folk belief that crowding is stressful and can make people sick.

Answers:

1. b **2.** alarm **3.** cortisol **4.** false; it depends on how people *feel* about being crowded.

WHAT'S**AHEAD**

- Which emotion may be most hazardous to your heart?
- Does chronic depression lead to physical illness?
- Is confession as healthy for the body as it is for the soul?
- Why do optimists tend to live longer than pessimists?
- Why does it matter whether you think you control your own destiny or your destiny controls you?

The Psychology of Stress

Pop-psych books often claim that people think themselves into bad health and therefore can also think themselves into good health. In this section, we will consider some myths and truths about the role of psychological factors in stress and health.

Emotions and Illness

Perhaps you have heard people say things like "She was so depressed, it's no wonder she got cancer," or "He's always so angry, he's going to give himself a heart attack one day." Can your emotions make you sick?

First of all, we can eliminate the popular belief that there is a "cancer-prone" personality. (This notion was actually first promoted by the tobacco industry to draw attention away from smoking as a leading cause of cancer.) Studies of thousands of people around the world, from Japan to Finland, have found no link between personality traits and risk of cancer (Nakaya et al., 2003).

Second, we need to distinguish between the effects of negative attitudes and emotions on healthy people and on people who are ill. Many studies find that once a person has a virus, disease, or medical condition, negative emotions can indeed affect the course of the illness and of recovery. Feeling anxious, depressed, and helpless, for example, can delay the healing of wounds after surgery, whereas feeling hopeful can significantly speed healing (Kiecolt-Glaser et al., 1998). Loneliness and worry can suppress the immune system and permit existing viruses, such as herpes, to erupt (Kiecolt-Glaser et al., 1985a). And people who become depressed after a heart attack are significantly more likely to die from cardiac causes in the succeeding year, even controlling for severity of the disease and other risk factors (Frasure-Smith et al., 1999). But can anger and depression be direct causes of illness all on their own?

A classic Type A personality.

Hostility and Depression. One of the first modern efforts to link emotions and illness occurred in the 1970s, with research on the "Type A" personality, a set of qualities thought to be associated with heart disease—ambitiousness, impatience, anger, working hard, and having high standards for oneself. Later work ruled out all of these factors except one: The toxic ingredient in the Type A personality turned out to be hostility.

By "hostility" we do not mean the irritability or anger that everyone feels on occasion, but *cynical* or *antagonistic hostility*, which characterizes people who are mistrustful of others and always ready to provoke mean, furious arguments

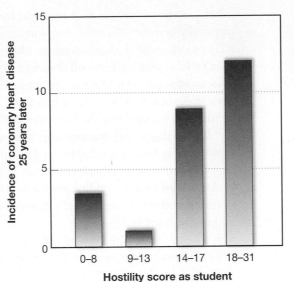

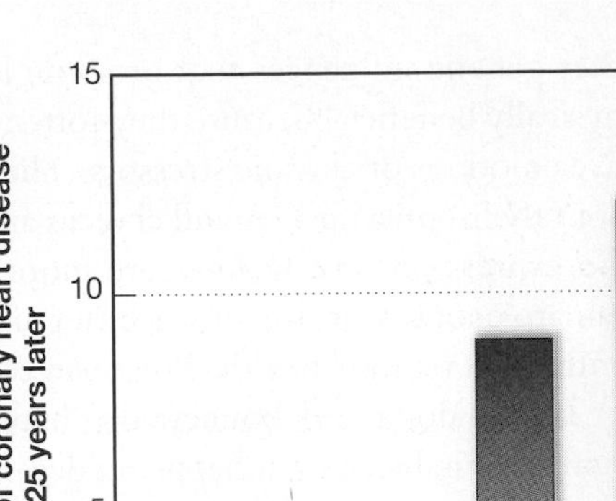

FIGURE 15.3 Hostility and Heart Disease

Anger is more hazardous to health than a heavy workload. Men who had the highest hostility scores as young medical students were the most likely to have coronary heart disease 25 years later (Williams, Barefoot, & Shekelle, 1985).

(Marshall et al., 1994; T. Miller et al., 1996). In a study of male physicians who had been interviewed as medical students 25 years earlier, those who were chronically angry and resentful were five times as likely as nonhostile men to get heart disease, even when other risk factors such as smoking and a poor diet were taken into account (Ewart & Kolodner, 1994; Williams, Barefoot, & Shekelle, 1985) (see Figure 15.3). These findings have been replicated in other large-scale studies, with African-Americans and whites, and with women as well as men (Williams et al., 2000). Proneness to anger is a significant risk factor, all on its own, for impairments of the immune system, elevated blood pressure, and heart disease (Suinn, 2001).

Clinical depression, too, is linked to at least a doubled risk of heart attack and cardiovascular disease, according to several large-scale longitudinal studies that found that chronic, severe depression precedes the development of heart disease by many years (Frasure-Smith & Lespérance, 2005; Schulz et al., 2000). A recent theory suggests that because depression, anxiety, and anger-hostility often occur together, like bunches of grapes, the real culprit in heart disease may be a general disposition toward negative emotions (Suls & Bunde, 2005). However, no connection has been found to date between depression and cancer or AIDS (Wulsin, Vaillant, & Wells, 1999).

Positive Emotions: Do They Help? Just as negative emotions can be unhealthful, positive emotions seem to be healthful. Consider the findings from a study of 180 Catholic nuns. Researchers examined autobiographies composed by the nuns when the women were about 22 years old, to see whether the quality of their writing predicted the onset of Alzheimer's disease later in life. (It did.) When other researchers scored the writings for their emotional content, they found a strong association between the frequency of positive emotions described—happiness, interest, love, hope, gratitude, contentment, amusement, relief—and longevity six decades later (Danner, Snowdon, & Friesen, 2001). The nuns whose life stories contained the most words describing positive emotions lived, on average, nine years longer than nuns who reported the fewest positive feelings! These differences in longevity could not have been due to, say, the stress of poverty, raising children, or particular experiences. The women all had the same experiences and standard of living, at least after they entered the convent.

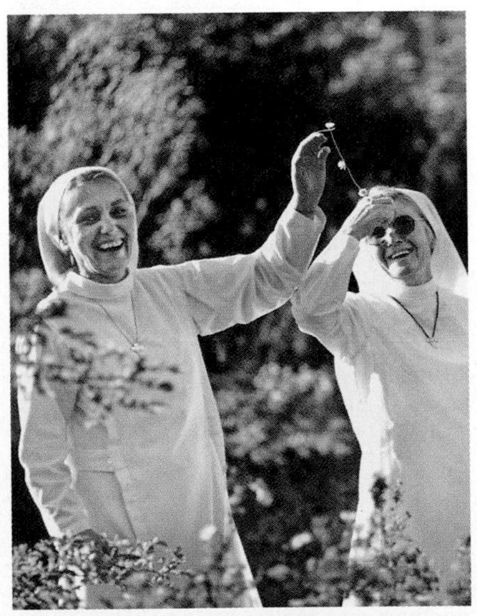

If hostility is hazardous, is humor healhful?

Psychologists are trying to find out just what it is about feeling happy, cheerful, and hopeful that could protect a person from getting sick. Of course, perhaps the cheerfulness of the long-lived nuns simply reflected an easygoing temperament or

other genetic influences that promote long life. But positive emotions could also be physically beneficial because they soften or counteract the high arousal caused by negative emotions or chronic stressors. They may dispose people to think more creatively about their opportunities and choices and to take action to achieve their goals. People who express positive feelings are more likely to attract friends and supporters, too, than are people who are always bitter and brooding, and, as we will see, social support contributes to good health (Pressman & Cohen, 2005).

If you don't feel bouncy and happy all the time, don't worry; everyone feels grumpy, irritable, and unhappy on occasion. But according to one study in which college students kept a daily diary of their positive and negative emotions for 28 days, the students who were really flourishing, who had the greatest emotional well-being, had a ratio of positive to negative emotions of at least 3 to 1 (Fredrickson & Losada, 2005). You might want to keep track of your own positive-to-negative emotion ratio for the next month to see where yours falls. Are positive emotions more typical of your emotional life than negative ones, or is it the other way around?

Managing Negative Emotions

If positive emotions are beneficial and negative emotions are risky, you might assume that the safest thing to do when you feel angry, depressed, or worried is to try to suppress the feeling. But anyone who has tried to banish an unwelcome thought, a bitter memory, or pangs of longing for an ex-lover knows how hard it can be to do this. When you are trying to avoid a thought, you are in fact processing the thought more frequently—rehearsing it. That is why, when you are obsessed with someone you were once romantically involved with, trying not to think of the person actually prolongs your emotional responsiveness to him or her (Wegner & Gold, 1995). Moreover, the continued inhibition of thoughts and emotions requires physical effort that can be stressful to the body. People who are able to express matters of great emotional importance to them show elevated levels of disease-fighting white blood cells, whereas people who suppress such feelings tend to have decreased levels (Petrie, Booth, & Pennebaker, 1998).

Given the findings on the harmful effects of feeling negative emotions and also of suppressing them, what is a person supposed to do with them? Occasional feelings of anger, anxiety, and sadness are, of course, inevitable. It is only when people hold on to them too long, rehearsing them and brooding about them, that they can create problems.

The Benefits of Confession. One way to get rid of negative emotions comes from research on the benefits of confession: divulging private thoughts and feelings that make you ashamed or depressed (Pennebaker, 2002). Such feelings can be created by holding on to painful secrets, but they can also be produced by normal but stressful transitions, such as starting college.

You might think there is little to confess about going to college, but it turns out that many freshmen feel scared that they won't do well and will disappoint their families, and they also feel anxious about being on their own. They think that they are the only ones feeling this way, so few reveal their worries. In one study, freshmen who wrote about these fears reported greater short-term homesickness and anxiety, compared to students who wrote about trivial topics. But by the end of the school year they had had fewer bouts of flu and fewer visits to the infirmary than the control group did (Pennebaker, Colder, & Sharp, 1990). This finding has been replicated in other studies, including among college students in Romania (Opre et al., 2005).

Everyone has secrets and private moments of sad reflection. But when you feel sad, anxious, or fearful for too long, keeping your feelings to yourself may increase your stress.

Confession is also beneficial for people who are carrying the burden of painful secrets. A group of college students was asked to write about either a personal trau-

GET INVOLVED!

➤TRUE CONFESSIONS

To see whether the research on the benefits of confession will be helpful to you, take a moment to jot down your deepest thoughts and feelings about being in college, your past, a secret, your future. . . anything you have never told anyone. Do this again tomorrow and then again for a few days in a row. Write down your feelings after writing, too. Are you upset? Troubled? Sad? Relieved? Does your account change over time? Research suggests that if you do this exercise now, you may have fewer colds, headaches, and trips to the doctor in the coming months.

matic experience or a neutral topic for 20 minutes a day for four days. Those who were asked to reveal their "deepest thoughts and feelings" about a traumatic event all had something to talk about. Many told stories of sexual coercion, physical beatings, humiliation, or parental abandonment. Yet most had never discussed these experiences with anyone. The researchers collected data on the students' physical symptoms, white blood cell counts, emotions, and visits to the health center. On every measure, the students who wrote about traumatic experiences were better off than those who did not (Pennebaker, Kiecolt-Glaser, & Glaser, 1988).

Of course, confession can make you feel worse if you reveal your secrets to someone who is judgmental, is unable to help, or betrays your confidence (Kelly, 1999). Moreover, confession's benefits occur only when it produces insight and understanding about the source or significance of the problem, thereby ending the stressful repetition of obsessive thoughts and unresolved feelings (Kennedy-Moore & Watson, 2001; Lepore, Ragan, & Jones, 2000). One young woman, who had been molested at the age of 9 by a boy a year older, at first wrote about her feelings of embarrassment and guilt. By the third day, she was writing about how angry she felt at the boy. By the last day, she had begun to see the whole event differently; he was a child too, after all. When the study was over, she said, "Before, when I thought about it, I'd lie to myself. . . . Now, I don't feel like I even have to think about it because I got it off my chest. I finally admitted that it happened."

The Benefits of Letting Grievances Go. Another important way of letting go of negative emotions is to give up the thoughts that produce grudges and replace them with a different perspective. In recent years, there has been a surge of research on anger's antidote: forgiveness. When people rehearse their grievances and hold grudges, their blood pressure, heart rate, and skin conductance rise (see Figure 15.4). Forgiving thoughts, as in the preceding example ("He was a child, too" or "What he did to me was horrible, but it's over now, and it's time for both of us to move on"), reduce these signs of physiological arousal and restore feelings of control (Witvliet, Ludwig, & Vander Laan, 2001). Forgiveness, like confession when it works, helps people see events in a new light. It promotes empathy, the ability to see the situation from another person's perspective. It strengthens and repairs relationships (Karremans et al., 2003).

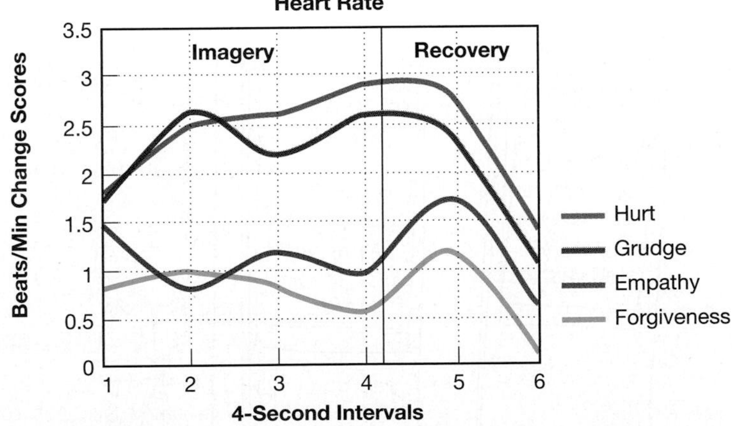

FIGURE 15.4 Heartfelt Forgiveness
Study participants were asked to think of someone whom they felt had offended or hurt them. Then they were asked to imagine unforgiving reactions (rehearsing the hurt and harboring a grudge) and forgiving reactions (feeling empathy, forgiving). People's heart rates increased much more sharply, and took longer to return to normal, when their thoughts were unforgiving (Witvliet, Ludwig, & Vander Laan, 2001).

Forgiveness does not mean that the offended person denies, ignores, or excuses the offense, which might be serious. It does mean that the victim is able, finally, to come to terms with the injustice and let go of obsessive feelings of hurt, rage, and vengefulness. As the Chinese proverb says, "He who pursues revenge should dig two graves."

In sum, health psychology suggests a middle path between keeping your cool and getting hot and bothered: learning to identify, express, and deal with negative emotions without ruminating on them and letting them erode your relationships or your own well-being.

Optimism and Pessimism

When something bad happens to you, what is your first reaction? Do you tell yourself not to panic, that you will somehow come through it okay, or do you gloomily mutter, "More proof that if something can go wrong for me, it will"?

In a fundamental way, optimism—the general expectation that things will go well in spite of occasional setbacks—makes life possible. If people are in a jam but believe things will get better eventually, they will keep striving to make that prediction come true. Even despondent fans of the Chicago Cubs, who have not won the World Series in living memory, maintain a lunatic optimism that "there's always next year." If the Boston Red Sox could do it in 2004, their first World Series win since 1918, surely there is hope.

Optimism is also a lot better for your health and well-being than pessimism is (Carver & Scheier, 1999; Peterson, 2000). This does not mean that an optimistic outlook will always prolong the life of a person who already has a serious illness: A team of Australian researchers who followed 179 patients with lung cancer over a period of eight years found that optimism made no difference at all in who lived or in how long they lived (Schofield et al., 2004). But optimism does seem to produce good health and even prolong life in people without life-threatening illnesses, whereas the "catastrophizing" style of pessimists is associated with untimely death (Maruta et al., 2000; Peterson et al., 1998).

Optimists do not deny their problems or avoid facing bad news; rather, they regard the problems and bad news as difficulties they can overcome. They may have better health than pessimists, therefore, partly because they take better care of themselves. They are more likely than pessimists to be active problem solvers, get support from friends, and seek information that can help them (Brissette, Scheier, & Carver, 2002). They do not give up at the first sign of a setback or escape into wishful thinking. They keep their sense of humor, plan for the future, and reinterpret the situation in a positive light (Aspinwall & Brunhart, 1996; Chang, 1998). Pessimists, in contrast, often do self-destructive things: They drink too much, smoke, fail to wear seat belts, drive too fast, and refuse to take medication for illness. This may be why pessimists, especially males, are more likely than optimists to die in accidents or as a result of violence (Peterson et al., 1998).

Pessimists, naturally, accuse optimists of being unrealistic, and often that is true! Yet health and well-being often depend on having some "positive illusions" about yourself, your abilities, and your circumstances (Taylor et al., 2000a). Positive illusions have both psychological benefits and physiological ones. Optimism is directly associated with better

immune function, such as a rise in the natural killer cells that fight infection (Räikkönen et al., 1999; Segerstrom et al., 1998). And people who see themselves in self-enhancing ways—thinking, for example, that they are smarter and healthier than average—also show immunological benefits. They have lower autonomic and HPA activation in the face of chronic difficulties, thereby reducing the wear and tear on their body's regulatory systems (Taylor et al., 2003).

Can pessimists be cured of their gloomy outlook? Optimists, naturally, think so. One way is by teaching pessimists to follow the oldest advice in the world: to count their blessings instead of their burdens. Even among people with serious illnesses, such as a neuromuscular disease, a focus on the positive aspects of life increases well-being and even reduces the number of physical symptoms they report (Emmons & McCullough, 2003).

QUICK quiz

Are you optimistic about your ability to answer these questions?

1. Which kind of anger seems most hazardous to health? (a) cynical hostility, (b) general grumpiness, (c) frequent irritability at small stressors, (d) occasional flat-out anger
2. Nguyen has many private worries about being in college that she is afraid to tell anyone. What might be the healthiest solution for her? (a) keeping her feeling to herself, (b) writing down her feelings in a diary, (c) talking frequently to strangers who won't judge her, (d) expressing her hostility whenever she feels it
3. Optimism is associated with (a) recovery from life-threatening illnesses, (b) denial of one's problems, (c) better immune function, (d) all of these.

Answers:

1. a 2. b 3. c

The Sense of Control

Optimism is related to another important ingredient of health: having a sense of control. **Locus of control** refers to your general expectation about whether you can control the things that happen to you (Rotter, 1990). People who have an *internal locus of control* ("internals") tend to believe that they are responsible for what happens to them. People who have an *external locus of control* ("externals") tend to believe that their lives are controlled by luck, fate, or other people. The Internal/External (I/E) Scale measures these dispositions. Respondents choose the statement in each pair of items with which they most strongly agree, as in these two items:

1. a. Many of the unhappy things in people's lives are partly due to bad luck.
   b. People's misfortunes result from mistakes they make.
2. a. Becoming a success is a matter of hard work; luck has little or nothing to do with it.
   b. Getting a good job depends mainly on being in the right place at the right time.

Over the years more than 2,000 studies based on the I/E Scale (including a version for children) have been published, with people of all ages and from many different ethnic groups. An internal locus of control emerges at an early age and is associated with good health, academic achievement, political activism, and emotional well-being (Lang & Heckhausen, 2001; Strickland, 1989). Where would you place your own locus of control, and do you think it affects your beliefs about the possibility of changing yourself or improving the world?

locus of control A general expectation about whether the results of your actions are under your own control (internal locus) or beyond your control (external locus).

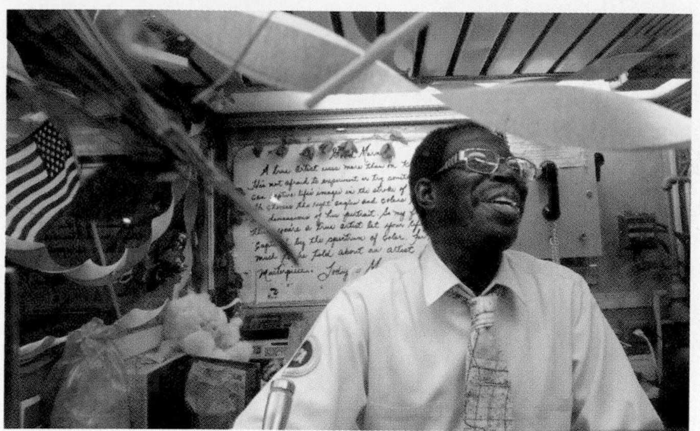

Robert James achieved an optimal balance between what he could not control in his job (working all day in a subway booth) and what he could control—how he decorated his small space, thought about his work, and dealt with people.

The Benefits of Control. Some time ago, we read a wonderful article about a New York man, Robert James, whom most people would think had one of the most miserable jobs imaginable: working all day long in a cramped booth in the New York City subway, protected by bulletproof glass (with a bullet hole in it). But Robert James was beloved by the subway passengers he met every day. He decorated his little space cheerfully for each season. He came to work wearing a subway-map tie and blue alligator boots. He made sure strangers got on the right trains. He passed messages, and sometimes a few bucks, between friends and family members. He wrote inspiring thoughts on his message board. Robert James could not do much to control the requirements of his job, but within those confines, he certainly controlled his environment. He turned a job that would seem dreary to most into an oasis of sunlight, for himself and all who came in contact with him.

People can tolerate all kinds of stressors if, like Robert James, they feel able to control them. The greatest threat to health and well-being occurs when people feel caught in a situation they cannot escape. Feelings of control can reduce or even eliminate the relationship between stressors and health that we described at the start of this chapter, as these examples illustrate:

- Among people exposed to cold viruses, those who feel in control of their lives are half as likely to actually develop colds as are people who feel that their lives are unpredictable, uncontrollable, and overwhelming (Cohen, Tyrrell, & Smith, 1993).
- Low-income people who have a strong sense of control and mastery over their lives are as healthy, and have equally high levels of well-being, as people from higher-income groups (Lachman & Weaver, 1998).
- People who have the greatest control over their work pace and activities—that is, executives and managers—have fewer illnesses and stress symptoms than do employees who have little opportunity to exercise initiative, who feel trapped doing repetitive tasks, and who have a low chance of promotion (Karasek & Theorell, 1990).

THINKING CRITICALLY

EXAMINE THE EVIDENCE

Who has more stress—corporate managers in highly competitive jobs or assembly-line workers in routine and predictable jobs? Research finds that people who are bossed suffer more from job stress than their bosses do, especially if the employees cannot control many aspects of their work (Karasek & Theorell, 1990).

- African-American professionals who have the resources and confidence to fight discrimination, and who feel in control of their work lives, are at lower risk of hypertension than are black workers who do not (Krieger & Sidney, 1996).
- When elderly residents of nursing homes are given more choices and control over their activities—even small activities such as tending plants—they become more alert and happier, and they live longer (Langer, 1983).

Feeling in control affects the immune system, which may be why it helps to speed up recovery from surgery and from some diseases (E. Skinner, 1996). As with optimism, feeling in control also makes people more likely to take action to improve their health when necessary. In a group of patients recovering from heart attacks, for example, those who thought the heart attack occurred because they smoked, didn't exercise, or had a stressful job were likely to change their bad habits and recover more quickly. In contrast, those who thought their illness was due to bad luck or fate—factors outside their control—were less likely to generate active plans for recovery and more likely to resume their old unhealthy habits (Affleck et al., 1987; Ewart, 1995).

Cultures differ in their degree of fatalism and in their beliefs about whether it is possible to take control of one's health. For example, in Germany, which has a highly structured social welfare system, people feel more psychological control over their health and work than Americans do (Staudinger, Fleeson, & Baltes, 1999). In some cultures, however, people feel they have almost no control over their health and lives. For example, in traditional Chinese astrology, certain birth years are considered unlucky, and people born in those years often fatalistically expect bad fortune. Sometimes this expectation can become a self-fulfilling prophecy, actually leading to earlier deaths among believers than among nontraditional Chinese or whites who have the same diseases (Phillips, Ruth, & Wagner, 1993).

The Limits of Control. Overall, then, a sense of control is a good thing. But the question must always be asked: Control over what? It is surely not beneficial for people to believe they can control absolutely every aspect of their lives; some things, such as death, taxes, or being a random victim of a crime, are out of anyone's control. Health and well-being are not enhanced by self-blame ("Whatever goes wrong with my health is my fault") or the belief that all disease can be prevented by doing the right thing ("If I take vitamins and hold the right positive attitude, I'll never get sick").

THINKING CRITICALLY

DEFINE YOUR TERMS

In general, it's good to feel in control of your life, but what does that mean exactly? Control over what? How much of your life? Can believing that you have total control ever be a bad thing?

Eastern and Western cultures tend to hold different attitudes toward the ability and desirability of controlling one's own life. In general, Western cultures celebrate **primary control**, in which people try to influence events by exerting direct control over them: If you are in a bad situation, you are supposed to change it, fix it, or fight it. The Eastern approach emphasizes **secondary control**, in which people try to accommodate to a bad situation by changing their own aspirations or desires: If you have a problem, you are supposed to live with it or act in spite of it (Rothbaum, Weisz, & Snyder, 1982).

A Japanese psychologist once offered some examples of Japanese proverbs that teach the benefits of yielding to the inevitable (Azuma, 1984): *To lose is to win* (giving in, to protect the harmony of a relationship, demonstrates the superior trait of generosity); *willow trees do not get broken by piled-up snow* (no matter how many problems pile up in your life, flexibility will help you survive them); and *the true tolerance is to tolerate the intolerable* (some "intolerable" situations are facts of life that no amount of protest will change). You can imagine how long "To lose is to win" would survive on an American football field, or how long most Americans would be prepared to tolerate the intolerable!

primary control An effort to modify reality by changing other people, the situation, or events; a "fighting back" philosophy.

secondary control An effort to accept reality by changing your own attitudes, goals, or emotions; a "learn to live with it" philosophy.

People who are ill or under stress can reap the benefits of both Western and Eastern forms of control by avoiding either–or thinking: for example, by taking

responsibility for future actions while not blaming themselves unduly for past ones. Among college freshmen who are doing poorly in their classes, future success depends on maintaining enough primary control to keep working hard and learning to study better, *and* on the ability to come to terms with the fact that success is not going to drop into their laps without effort (Hall et al., 2006). Among women who are recovering from sexual assault or coping with cancer, adjustment is related to a woman's belief that she is not to blame for being raped or for getting sick but that she *is* in charge of taking care of herself from now on (Frazier, 2003; Taylor, Lichtman, & Wood, 1984). "I felt that I had lost control of my body somehow," said a woman in one study, "and the way for me to get back some control was to find out as much as I could." This way of thinking allows a person to avoid guilt and self-blame while retaining self-efficacy, the belief that you are basically in charge of your own life and can take steps to get better.

Many problems require us to decide what we can change and to accept what we cannot; perhaps the secret of healthy control lies in knowing the difference.

QUICK quiz

You can increase your sense of control over the material in this section by answering these questions.

1. Maria has worked as a file clerk for 17 years. Which aspect of the job is likely to be most stressful for her? (a) the speed of the work, (b) the attention to many details, (c) the feeling of being trapped, (d) the daily demands from her boss
2. Anika usually takes credit for doing well on her work assignments and blames her failures on lack of effort. Benecia attributes her successes to luck and blames her failures on the fact that she is an indecisive Gemini. Anika has an ______ locus of control whereas Benecia has an ______ locus.
3. Adapting to the reality that you are getting older is an example of (primary/secondary) control; joining a protest to make a local company clean up its hazardous wastes is an example of (primary/secondary) control.

4. On television, a self-described health expert explains that "no one gets sick if they don't want to be sick, because all of us can learn to control our bodies." As a critical thinker, how should you assess this claim?

Answers:

1. c **2.** internal, external **3.** secondary, primary **4.** Skeptically. First, you should define your terms: What does "control" mean, and what kind of control is the supposed expert referring to? People can control some things, such as the decision to exercise and quit smoking, and they can control some aspects of treatment once they become ill; but they cannot control everything that happens to them. Second, you should examine the assumption that control is always a good thing. The belief that we have total control over our lives could lead to depression and unwarranted self-blame when illness strikes.

WHAT'S AHEAD

- When you are feeling overwhelmed, what are some good ways to calm down?
- Why is it important to move beyond the emotions caused by a problem and deal with the problem itself?
- Can tragedies and losses ever have beneficial outcomes?.
- When do friends reduce your stress, and when do they just make matters worse?

Coping with Stress

We have noted that most people who are under stress, even in continuing, difficult situations, do not become ill. In addition to feeling optimistic, maintaining some control, and not wallowing around in negative emotions, how do they manage to cope? The word *coping* implies that people are behaving in ways that barely help them keep their heads above water ("How are you doing?" "Oh, I'm coping"). But some people cope in ways that do more than help them *survive* adversity. They *thrive*, by learning from their experiences and coming out stronger because of them (Joseph & Linley, 2005; see Figure 15.5).

"Frankly, counselor, I don't care how stressful this is for your client—tell him to get out of that damn yoga position."

Cooling Off

The most immediate way to handle the physiological tension of stress is to calm down and reduce your body's physical arousal through meditation or relaxation. *Progressive relaxation* training—learning to alternately tense and relax the muscles, from toes to head—lowers blood pressure and stress hormones (Scheufele, 2000). So does the ancient Buddhist practice of "mindfulness meditation," which teaches, among other things, an ability to focus attention on a single object or idea and to cultivate emotional tranquility. An interdisciplinary team of researchers conducted a randomized, controlled study on the effects of an eight-week training program in mindfulness meditation. They measured brain electrical activity before and immediately after the program, and again four months later. At the end of the eight weeks, the researchers found that the meditators showed significant increases in parts of the brain associated with positive emotions and significant benefits in immune function (Davidson et al., 2003). A practice that calms the mind, apparently, also benefits the brain and the body.

Another effective way to calm down is through massage, which, along with meditation, is one of the oldest treatments for stress in the world. (The Chinese were recommending it in the second century B.C.) Meta-analyses of many dozens of studies have found that massage benefits human beings of every age, from premature infants to the very old. It benefits people with asthma and diabetes, adolescents with eating disorders, depressed elderly people, and hyperactive children (Field, 1998; Moyer, Rounds, & Hannum, 2004).

After you have scheduled meditation and massage into your busy week, go for a walk! A low level of physical activity is associated with decreased life expectancy for

Adverse event
Thriving
Recovering fully (resilience)
Surviving with Impairment
Succumbing
Level of functioning
Time

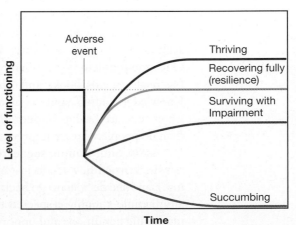

FIGURE 15.5 Responses to Adversity

People may respond to adversity by giving up, surviving with some impairment, recovering fully, or thriving—learning from the experience and coming out stronger because of it (Carver, 1998).

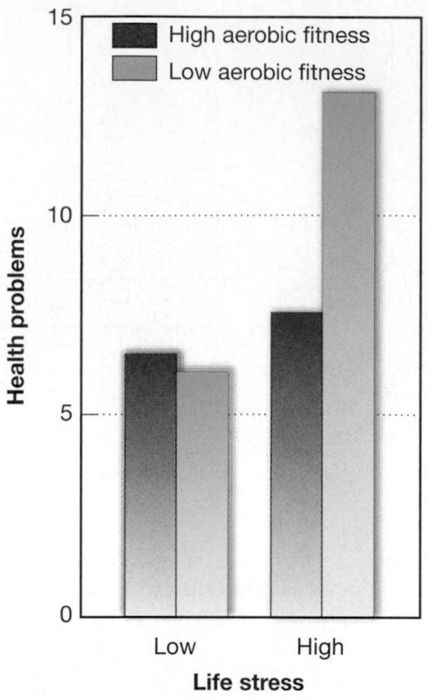

FIGURE 15.6 Fitness and Health

Among people under low stress, aerobically fit individuals had about the same number of health problems as those who were less fit. But among people under high stress, fit individuals had fewer health problems (Roth & Holmes, 1985).

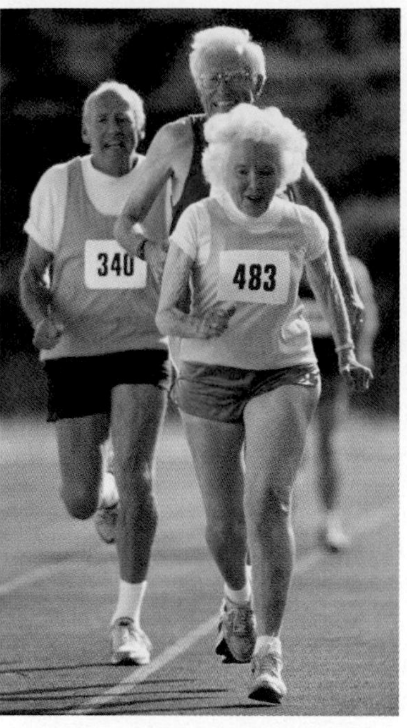

both sexes and contributes independently to the development of many chronic diseases (Vita et al., 1998). As you can see in Figure 15.6, when people are undergoing the same pressures, those who are physically fit have fewer health problems than people who are unfit. The more that people exercise, the less anxious, depressed, and irritable they are, and the fewer physical symptoms and colds they have (Hendrix et al., 1991).

Perhaps you can think of other ways to cool off when you are hot and bothered: listening to soothing music, writing in a journal, baking bread. Such activities give the body a chance to recover from the alarm phase of its stress response and from the intensity of negative emotions. But some problems call for more than cooling off. If your house has burned down or you need a serious operation, jogging and meditating will not be enough. Sometimes other coping strategies are necessary.

Solving the Problem

Years ago, at the age of 23, a friend of ours named Simi Linton was struck by tragedy. Linton, her new husband, and her best friend were in a horrific car accident. When she awoke in a hospital room, with only a vague memory of a crash and an ambulance, she learned that her husband and friend had been killed and that she herself had permanent spinal injury and would never walk again.

How in the world does anyone recover from such a devastating event? Some people advise survivors of disaster to "get it out of your system" or to "get in touch with your feelings." But survivors know they feel miserable. What should they *do*? This question gets to the heart of the difference between *emotion-focused* and *problem-focused coping* (Lazarus, 2000b; Lazarus & Folkman, 1984). Emotion-focused coping concentrates on the emotions the problem has caused, whether anger, anxiety, or grief. For a period of time after any tragedy or disaster, it is normal to give in to these emotions and even feel overwhelmed by them. In this stage, people often need to talk obsessively about the event in order to come to terms with it, make sense of it, and decide what to do about it (Lepore, Ragan, & Jones, 2000).

Eventually, though, most people become ready to concentrate on solving the problem itself. The specific steps in problem-focused coping depend on the nature of the problem: whether it is a pressing but one-time decision; a continuing difficulty, such as living with a disability; or an anticipated event, such as having an operation. Once the problem is identified, you can learn as much as possible about it from professionals, friends, books, and others in the same predicament (Clarke & Evans, 1998). Knowledge confers some control. For example, when people know what to expect when they are having surgery, they often get better more quickly and feel less pain than do people who are unprepared (Doering et al., 2000).

As for Simi Linton, she learned more about her medical condition and prognosis; she learned how to do just about everything in her wheelchair (including dancing!); and she decided to go back to school. She got a Ph.D. in psychology, remarried, and became a highly respected teacher, counselor, writer, and activist committed to improving conditions and opportunities for disabled people (Linton, 2006).

Rethinking the Problem

Sometimes things happen in life that you cannot change: You have a nasty neighbor who is not going to move; you lose a good job; you develop a chronic illness; you want to have children and learn that you can't have your own. Even when you cannot fix a problem, however, you can change the way you think about it. Here are three effective cognitive coping methods:

The ultimate example of reappraisal.

1 **Reappraising the situation.** Although you may not be able to get rid of the stressful problem, you can choose to think about it differently, a process called *reappraisal*. Problems can be turned into challenges and losses into unexpected gains. As we saw in Chapter 11 and in discussing the benefits of confession and forgiveness earlier, the way you think about a situation or provocation affects the emotions you feel about it. Reappraisal can turn anger into sympathy, worry into determination, and feelings of loss into feelings of opportunity (Folkman & Moskowitz, 2000). Maybe that job you lost was pretty dismal but you were too afraid to quit and look for another; now you can. Reappraisal improves well-being and reduces negative emotions, whereas just trying to suppress your negative emotions actually makes them worse (Gross & John, 2003).

2 **Learning from the experience.** Most victims of traumatic events and life-threatening illnesses report that the experience made them stronger, more resilient, and even better human beings because they grew and learned from the event (McFarland & Alvaro, 2000). A study of people with spinal-cord injuries found that fully two-thirds of them felt the disability had had positive aspects, such as helping them see the value in other people and gain a new appreciation of "brain, not brawn" (Schulz & Decker, 1985). The ability to find meaning and benefits even in the worst adversity seems crucial to psychological recovery. It even slows the course of serious diseases. In a longitudinal study of men with HIV who had been recently bereaved, those who "tried not to think about it" showed sharper declines in helper T cells (the cells that attack the virus) and were more likely to die during the follow-up period than were men who found meaning and purpose in the loss. The latter said they had acquired greater appreciation of the loved one, a perception of life as being fragile and precious, or other benefits. "I would say that his death lit up my faith," said one man (Taylor et al., 2000a).

Some people emerge from adversity with newfound or newly acquired skills, having been forced to learn something they had not known before—how to cope with the medical system, say, or how to manage a deceased parent's estate. Others discover sources of courage and strength they did not know they had. Those who draw lessons from the inescapable tragedies of life and find meaning in them are the ones who thrive as a result of adversity instead of simply surviving it (Davis, Nolen-Hoeksema, & Larson, 1998; Folkman & Moskowitz, 2000).

3 **Making social comparisons.** In a difficult situation, successful copers often compare themselves to others who are (they feel) less fortunate. No matter how bad off they are, even if they have fatal diseases, they find someone who is worse off (Taylor & Lobel, 1989; Wood, Michela, & Giordano, 2000). One AIDS sufferer said in an interview, "I made a list of all the other diseases I would rather not have than AIDS. Lou Gehrig's disease, being in a wheelchair; rheumatoid arthritis, when you are in knots and in terrible pain." Another said: "I really have an advantage in a sense over other people. I know there is a possibility that my life may not go on for as many years as other people's. I have the opportunity to look at my life, to make changes, and to deeply appreciate the time that I have" (Reed, 1990).

GET INVOLVED!

➤RETHINK YOUR STRESSES

The next time you feel stressed by a situation you can't control, observe your thoughts. What are you saying to yourself? Are your thoughts adding to your stress ("That stupid driver just tried to kill me!")? Try to apply the lessons on "rethinking the problem" to your own situation. For example, can you think of another explanation for a family member's annoying behavior? Can you think of something funny about your predicament, and will it make a good story later? Can you think of something good about the situation or a lesson it might offer you?

Sometimes successful copers also compare themselves to those who are doing better than they are (Collins, 1996). They might say, "Look at her—she's had such family troubles and survived that awful bout with cancer, and she's happier than ever with her life. How did she do it?" or "He and I have the same kinds of problems; how come he's doing so much better in school than I am? What does he know that I don't?" Such comparisons are beneficial when they provide a person with information about ways of coping, managing an illness, or improving a stressful situation (Suls, Martin, & Wheeler, 2002).

Drawing on Social Support

So far we have been discussing individual coping strategies, things you can do for yourself. But often these individual strategies are not enough, and it is necessary to draw on the help and *social support* of others in your network of family, friends, neighbors, and co-workers. Your health depends not only on what is going on in your body and mind but also on what is going on in your relationships: what you take from them and what you give to them.

When Friends Help You Cope. Think of all the ways in which family members, friends, neighbors, and co-workers can help you. They can offer concern and affection. They can help you evaluate problems and plan a course of action. They can offer resources and services by lending you money, going with you to the doctor, or taking notes in class for you when you are sick. Most of all, they are sources of attachment and connection, which everyone needs throughout life. Perhaps this is why old people who have dogs as companions visit medical clinics less often than their peers who have no pets—or who have cats! Dogs provide nonjudgmental companionship, the gift of a truly best friend (Siegel, 1990). Having a dog can lower the blood pressure of people in high-stress jobs, such as stockbrokers (Allen, 2003).

Friends are nice to have, and they even improve your health. Remember the study we described earlier, showing that stress increases your risk of getting a cold? Well, having a lot of friends and social contacts reduces that risk. In a group of more than 300 volunteers exposed to a flu virus, those with the most friends and social interactions were the least likely to get sick (Cohen et al., 2003). Social support is especially important for people who have extremely stressful jobs that require high cardiovascular responsiveness day after day, such as firefighters. The mere presence of a reassuring friend helps their heart rate and cortisol levels return to normal more quickly after a stressful episode (Roy, Steptoe, & Kirschbaum, 1998).

Friends don't have to be human. Kirby, dressed here in a sheep costume for Halloween, is a certified therapy dog who delights the hospital patients he visits.

People who live in a network of close connections actually live longer than those who do not. In two studies that followed thousands of adults for ten years, people who had many friends, connections, or memberships in religious and other groups lived longer, on average, than those who had few. The importance of having social networks was unrelated to physical health at the time the studies began, to socioeconomic status, and to risk factors like smoking (Berkman & Syme, 1979; House, Landis, & Umberson, 1988). And in another

study of older men and women who had had heart attacks, those who reported having no close contacts were twice as likely to die within the year as were those who said they had two or more people they could count on (Berkman, Leo-Summers, & Horwitz, 1992).

Social support enhances health in part because, like having an internal locus of control and feelings of optimism, it bolsters the immune system. Lonely people have poorer immune function than people who are not lonely; students in a network of friends have better immune function before, during, and after exam periods than students who are more solitary; and spouses of cancer patients, although under considerable stress themselves, do not show a drop in immune function if they have lots of social support (Hawkley et al., 2003; Uchino, Cacioppo, & Kiecolt-Glaser, 1996).

Sometimes, though, informal friendships and family relationships are not quite enough to get us through a rough patch. A more formal source of social support comes from joining with other people who have experienced the same illness, problem, or tragedy. People are particularly likely to benefit from such groups if they have an illness that is life-threatening or stigmatizing, disfigures them in any way, or causes embarrassment (Davison, Pennebaker, & Dickerson, 2000). Although being in a support group does not prolong the lives of people with terminal illnesses, it often lessens their suffering and pain (Goodwin et al., 2001).

CLOSE-UP on Research

HUGS AND HEALTH

Practical help, empathy, resources, and companionship are not all that other people can offer us when we are ill or stressed out by difficulties in our lives. One of the greatest benefits of social support is the physical affection and comfort it provides. Those close to us do not just touch us emotionally; they also touch us physically.

One research team discovered the power of touch when they **explored a question** that has long intrigued psychologists: Why do happily married couples enjoy better health, on average, than their single friends? One answer—that husbands and wives monitor one another's health, for example by limiting how much the other smokes or drinks—is partially true, but not enough to account for married people's better health in relation to singles.

The researchers—James Coan, Hillary Schaefer, and Richard Davidson (2006)—recruited 16 couples who filled out an in-depth questionnaire on their coping styles, degree of emotional intimacy, mutual interests, and happiness in their marriage. The wives then lay in an MRI machine, periodically receiving a mild electric shock on their ankle. The husbands were told to reach into the imaging machine at a particular time and hold their wife's hand. (For comparison, a stranger to the women also provided a comforting touch.) Naturally, the women felt pretty apprehensive about the whole experience, and their brain images showed activation in the hypothalamus and other regions involved with pain, physical arousal, and negative emotions. As we have seen earlier in this chapter, the activation of the brain's alarm system keeps us safe in the face of immediate danger, but if it is prolonged and unresolved, it can lead to physical symptoms that impair health.

When the researchers **examined the evidence**, they found that the moment the women felt their husband's reassuring hand, their brain activation subsided in all the regions that had been revved up to cope with threat and fear. The investigators **considered other explanations**: Perhaps it was touch alone that was important, regardless of who was providing it. But holding hands with a stranger, while comforting, did not produce as great a decrease in brain activation as did the husbands' touch. Moreover, as

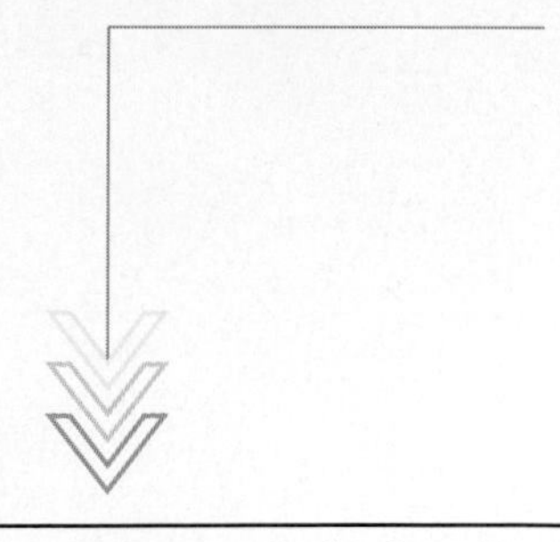

you can see in the accompanying figure, the women who showed the least activation were those in "super-couples," whose scores on the questionnaire showed an unusual degree of closeness and intimacy. For these women, the hypothamus and other area of the brain associated with the anticipation of pain were particularly soothed. Because physical pain is influenced so much by anticipation and fear, a supportive touch from a close partner literally blunted the sensation of pain. "The effect of this simple gesture of social support is that the brain and the body don't have to work as hard; they're less stressed in response to a threat," said James Coan, the study's lead investigator.

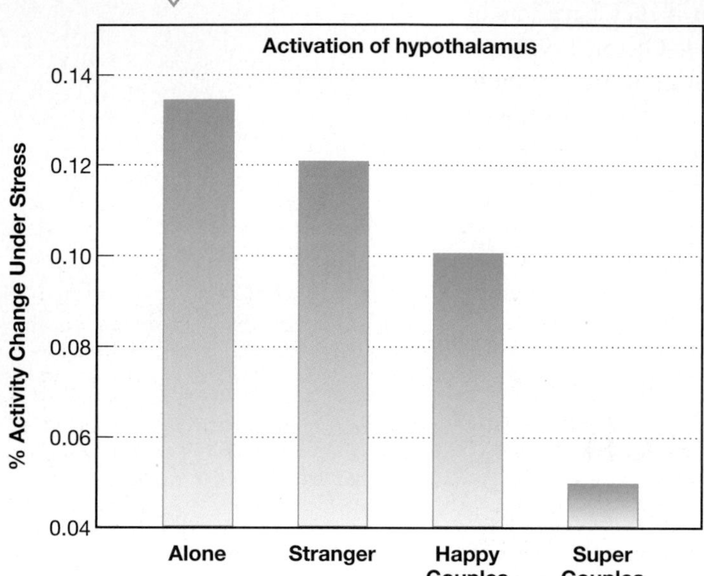

Of course, **we should not oversimplify**. The meaning of the touch—why it is offered and how it is interpreted by the person receiving it—is probably critical. But if the touch is an affectionate and welcome one, it can actually elevate some therapeutic hormones. Evidence for this idea comes from another study, in which 59 women ages 20 to 49, all in close relationships with a stable partner, reported how often they and their partners were physically affectionate in their everyday lives, for example by holding hands and hugging (Light, Grewen, & Amico, 2005). The researchers measured the women's heart rates, blood pressure, and levels of *oxytocin*, the hormone that induces relaxation and is associated with mothering and attachment (see Chapters 4 and 12). The women were then asked to sit and talk with their partners for a few minutes about a warm shared memory, watch a short romantic video, and give one another a hug. Finally the women were separated from their partners and asked to write and deliver a speech about a recent experience that was stressful or made them angry.

The researchers found that the women who had the highest oxytocin levels had lower blood pressure and heart rates throughout the experiment, including during the stressful phase, and the women who reported getting the most hugs from their partners had the highest oxytocin levels, also at all phases of the study. The researchers concluded that oxytocin might be a key link between hugging and lower blood pressure. And because high blood pressure is associated with heart disease, well, do the math . . . and do the hugging.

Attention, men: Feeling that your partner supports you is good for *your* heart and oxytocin levels, too (Grewen et al., 2005). Unfortunately, men often do not always let others know when they have physical or emotional problems, so they are less likely than women to seek and get the social support and practical help they need. Yet they could use it: Men in the United States die, on average, nearly seven years earlier than women do and have higher rates of the 15 leading causes of death. Why are men of all ages, nationalities, social classes, and ethnicities less likely than women to look for help for their problems? The familiar answer is that masculinity, for many men, means being tough, competitive, and emotionally inexpressive; "real men" go it alone. But two social psychologists have identified some conditions under which men who feel this way might ask for help (Addis & Mahalik, 2003):

- ***The man thinks the problem is normal and common rather than something he alone suffers from.*** For example, after the blizzard of ad campaigns for Viagra and its relatives, men have realized that problems with erectile dysfunction are not unusual but in fact quite common. Many men are therefore less reluctant than they once were to seek help for sexual difficulties.

- ***The problem is not central to the man's self-concept.*** When a man has problems that he feels are threatening to his core identity—for example, if a businessman is having trouble solving his company's problems, or if a man who is proud of his athletic ability becomes physically incapacitated—he is less likely to seek help than if the problem is less central or defining.
- ***The man feels able to reciprocate the help.*** For most men, masculinity involves the rule of reciprocity: If you help me repair my fence, I'll help you fix your lawn mower. Accordingly, men are more likely to accept support from others if they see a way to return the favor.
- ***Other men support the decision to seek help.*** If a depressed man socializes with friends who keep stressing the importance of being strong, being one's "own man," and so on, he is unlikely to seek help. But if he is in, say, a church group or other support group of men who are sharing their problems, he may feel more comfortable asking for help. This is the reason for the success of campaigns in which famous male athletes, celebrities, and politicians reveal their own battles with disease, emotional disorders, and sexual problems. Their honesty lets men know that help is at hand and that they aren't alone.

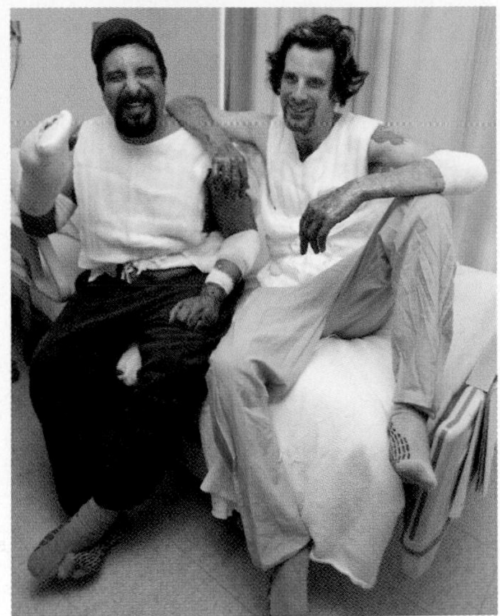

Men are more likely to seek social support when they feel they can reciprocate. William Long (left) and David Malagrino met in the hospital after surviving a terrible nightclub fire. "I'm there to cheer him up and take him out of his anger," said Long. "And when it's my turn for a bad moment, David takes me out of my sadness."

Coping with Friends. Of course, sometimes other people *aren't* helpful. Sometimes they themselves cause unhappiness, stress, and anger. Many people at midlife, particularly women, are stressed by the responsibilities of caring for their immediate families and also for their infirm and ailing parents, who may be suffering from dementia, chronic diseases, or other debilitating conditions (Vitaliano, Young, & Zhang, 2004). This extreme stress can increase the risks to the caregiver's own health, as we noted earlier in the study of cell damage in mothers of chronically sick children.

In close relationships, the same person who might be a source of support can instead become a source of stress, especially if the two parties are arguing all the time. Being in an unhappy, bitter, uncommunicative marriage can significantly impair health. It makes the partners depressed and angry, affects their health habits, and also directly influences their cardiovascular, endocrine, and immune systems. When married couples argue in a hostile fashion—criticizing, interrupting, or insulting the other person, and becoming angry and defensive—their stress hormones are significantly elevated and, afterward, their immune functions are impaired. In fact, any wounds or blisters a hostile couple has actually heal more slowly than they do in couples who do not argue in a hostile way (Kiecolt-Glaser et

Friends can be a source of support, and fun. . .

. . . and also sources of exasperation, anger, and misery.

al., 2005). Couples who argue in a positive fashion—trying to find common ground, compromising, listening to each other's concerns, and using humor to defuse tension—do not show these impairments (Kiecolt-Glaser et al., 1993). As one student of ours observed, "This study gives new meaning to the accusation 'You make me sick'!" It also suggests that learning to argue fairly and constructively has physical as well as psychological benefits.

In addition to being sources of conflict, friends and relatives may be unsupportive in times of disaster or illness simply out of ignorance or awkwardness. They may abandon you or say something stupid and hurtful. Sometimes they actively block your efforts to change bad health habits—say, to cut down on binge drinking or smoking—by making fun of you or pressuring you to conform to what "everyone" does. And sometimes, because they have never been in the same situation and do not know what to do to help, they offer the wrong kind of support. For example, they may try to cheer you up, saying "Everything will be fine," rather than let you talk about your fears or find solutions. That's when support groups are especially helpful, because everyone in the group has been there and understands.

Healing Through Helping

A final way to cope with stress, loss, and tragedy is by giving support to others, rather than always being on the receiving end. Julius Segal (1986), a psychologist who worked with Holocaust survivors, prisoners of war, hostages, refugees, and other survivors of catastrophe, wrote that a key element in their recovery was compassion, healing through helping. People gain strength, he said, by focusing less on their own woes and more on helping other people overcome theirs. People who frequently help their friends and family with practical and emotional support also live longer than self-oriented nonhelpers (Brown et al., 2003).

Why should this be so? The ability to look outside oneself, to be concerned with helping others, is related to virtually all of the successful coping mechanisms we have discussed (see Review 15.1). It stimulates optimism and restores feelings of control. It

REVIEW 15.1

Successful Ways of Coping with Stress

	Category	Examples
	Physical strategies	Relaxation Meditation Massage Exercise
	Problem-oriented strategies	Emotion-focused coping to reduce negative emotions Problem-focused coping
	Cognitive strategies	Reappraising the problem Learning from the problem Making social comparisons
	Social strategies	Relying on friends and family Finding a support group Helping others

encourages you to solve your problems instead of blaming others or venting your emotions. It helps you reappraise the situation by seeing it from another person's perspective, fosters forgiveness and empathy, and allows you to gain perspective on your own problems. Healing through helping thus helps you live with situations that are facts of life.

QUICK quiz

Can you cope with these refresher questions?

1. Finding out what your legal and financial resources are when you have been victimized by a crime is an example of (a) problem-focused coping, (b) emotion-focused coping, (c) distraction, (d) reappraisal.
2. Learning deep-breathing techniques to reduce anxiety about having been victimized by a crime is an example of (a) problem-focused coping, (b) emotion-focused coping, (c) avoidance, (d) reappraisal.
3. "This class drives me crazy, but I'm better off than my friends who aren't in college" is an example of (a) distraction, (b) social comparison, (c) denial, (d) empathy.
4. What hormone is elevated when happy couples hug one another?
5. Under what four conditions are men more likely to seek support from others instead of "going it alone"?
6. Your roommate has turned your room into a garbage dump, filled with rotten leftover food and unwashed clothes. Assuming that you don't like living with rotting food and dirty clothes, what coping strategies described in this section might help you?

Answers:

1. a **2.** b **3.** b **4.** oxytocin **5.** The man thinks the problem is common rather than something he alone suffers from; the problem is not central to the man's self-concept; the man feels able to reciprocate the help; other men support the decision to seek help. **6.** You might solve the problem by compromising (e.g., cleaning the room together). You might reappraise the seriousness of the problem ("I only have to live with this person until the end of the term") or compare your roommate to others who are worse ("At least mine is generous and friendly"). And you might mobilize some social support, perhaps by offering your friends a pizza if they help you clean up.

WHAT'S AHEAD

- What are three of the best things you can do to prolong your life?
- How can we think critically about mainstream and alternative approaches to health?

How Much Control Do We Have over Our Health?

It should be clear by now that the line between stress and illness is not straightforward and direct. Many factors are linked together in the long chain of cumulative events between stressors and illness or health, including genetic vulnerabilities to certain diseases, frequency and intensity of negative emotions, degree of optimism or pessimism, locus of control, coping strategies, and social networks (see Review 15.2).

Yet to hear some people talk, health is almost entirely a matter of "mind over matter." Even the worst diseases, they say, can be cured with laughter, vitamins, and positive thinking, and if you become sick, it's your own fault. This attitude is quite recent, a result of medical advances in the past 100 years. As industrialized societies conquered many of the environmental sources of infectious diseases, through innovations in water treatment, sewage disposal, and food storage, and through the

REVIEW 15.2

Factors that Increase the Risk of Illness

Factors	Examples
Environmental	Uncontrollable noise, poverty, lack of access to health care, discrimination
Experiential	Bereavement or divorce, traumatic events, chronic and severe job stress, unemployment
Biological	Viral or bacterial infections, disease, genetic vulnerability, toxins
Psychological	Hostility, possibly chronic depression, emotional inhibition, pessimism, external locus of control (fatalism), feeling powerless
Behavioral	Smoking, poor diet, lack of exercise, abuse of alcohol and other drugs, lack of sleep
Social	Lack of supportive friends and relatives, low involvement in groups

discovery of antibiotics and vaccines, public attention turned to diseases that are affected by what we eat and how we live. Accordingly, the focus of health professionals shifted from changing the environment to changing individuals (Taylor, Repetti, & Seeman, 1997).

THINKING CRITICALLY

DON'T OVERSIMPLIFY

Marlon and Maren are arguing about alternative versus traditional medicine. One thinks modern medicine is mechanical and too commercial. The other thinks alternative methods are silly and superstitious. How might they resolve their differences about the two approaches to health?

Many health psychologists fear that the public is oversimplifying the message of their research, by concluding that the factors that produce good health and long life are entirely psychological or entirely under our control, and that we need not worry about the environment. Clearly, as we saw in this chapter, people do have some control over the psychological and social factors involved in the onset and course of many illnesses, such as negative emotions, pessimism, and lack of supportive friends. And people do have control over three of the strongest predictors of longevity and health, which are not psychological at all: not smoking (or quitting), eating a healthful diet, and exercising regularly.

However, life is full of stressful experiences, chronic problems, and disastrous bolts out of the blue that we cannot predict or avoid. At such times, critical thinking becomes especially important, because the temptation is great to slide into oversimplified, either–or thinking: For example, *either* you get traditional medical procedures to treat a disease *or* you use alternative psychological ones, such as visual imagery, meditation, and support groups. These are not incompatible choices, of course. In fact, most physicians today, while endorsing traditional medical treatments, also appreciate the power of optimism and social support in their patients' recovery and well-being. They worry, however, that some people will put off crucial medical procedures in favor of relying exclusively on alternative treatments.

Successful coping does not mean eliminating all stress. It does not mean constant happiness or a life without pain. The healthy person faces problems, deals with them, and gets beyond them, but the problems are necessary if the person is to acquire coping skills that endure. To wish for a life without stress would be like wishing for a life without friends. The result might be calm, but it would be joyless. Daily hassles, chronic problems, and occasional tragedies are inescapable. How we handle them is the test of our humanity.

Taking Psychology with You

Health Habits You Can Live with

The marketplace is full of people who prey on the public's health worries by selling them worthless programs, pills, and devices. Many promoters of such products have impressive-looking but academically meaningless "credentials," often from unaccredited schools that offer mail-order degrees. At one of these places you can study "nutri-medical dentistry," for example, or "therapeutic nutri-medicine" (Raso, 1996).

Look out for unvalidated advice and watch your wallet. The findings from health psychology offer practical, free guidelines for maintaining good health and coping with stressors or illness when they occur:

- **Follow "good old-fashioned motherly advice" and practice good health habits.** You know them: Do not smoke; do not drink excessively or in binges; eat a healthful diet; wear seat belts; exercise regularly; and get enough sleep. These habits are important not only for prevention of illness but also for its treatment. When people become ill, they often stop taking care of themselves. They drink too much, stop exercising, and don't eat well, all of which can speed the course of the disease.
- **Learn how to regulate negative emotions.** Confessing your deepest thoughts and feelings—by writing them down, speaking into a recorder, or talking with a trusted friend or therapist—and finding the ability to forgive may help you let go of resentment, grudges, anger, and blame. The goal is to see the experience in a new light and think about it differently. But constant rehearsal and ventilation of your negative emotions is not therapeutic if you keep talking about them endlessly to anyone who will listen. The repeated expression of your feelings will not, by itself, help you achieve insight into the origins of your problems.
- **Take control of what you can, such as finding the best treatment for a medical problem or the best solution to a psychological one.** If you are under stress at school because you are not doing well, learning to relax or splurging on massages might help, but ultimately you will have to decide what you can do to improve your grades. If you are under stress at home because you are constantly quarreling with your partner or parents, talking with others about the problem might make you feel temporarily better, but ultimately you will have to figure out why you are fighting so much and learn how you can argue constructively.
- **Reappraise the situation or event to find meaning in it and see its positive aspects.** Many things happen that are out of your control: accidents, being born to particular parents, flu epidemics, natural disasters, and countless other events. But you do have control over how you cope with them. When you cannot change a fact of life, try to identify the challenges, opportunities, and learning experiences that it offers you.
- **Don't try to "go it alone"; get the social support you need.** Find individuals who understand your problems and who can offer practical as well as moral support. Whether your stress results from a one-time upsetting event or a chronic situation, try to find people who have "been there" and who can advise you on the best to cope.
- **Don't stay in a network that is not helpful; get rid of "social nonsupport."** Are your friends or colleagues encouraging you to maintain unhealthy practices that you would like to change? Are they preventing you from making improvements in your life? If so, you may need to think about finding new friends or new ways of sticking to your changed habits in spite of your old friends' efforts.

Health psychology offers many other practical applications of research that can improve your life. But if you find that you are not perfectly able to control every stressor that comes your way, don't get upset. After all, that will only add to your stress.

Summary

The Stress–Illness Mystery

- Several chronic *stressors* increase the risk of illness: constant, uncontrollable noise; bereavement and loss; unemployment and work-related problems; and poverty, low status, and powerlessness. However, most people who experience these stressors do not become ill. *Health psychologists* study the psychological, social, and biological factors that predict who gets sick and who stays healthy.

The Physiology of Stress

- Hans Selye argued that environmental stressors such as heat, pain, and danger produce a *general adaptation syndrome*, in which the body responds in three stages: *alarm*, which activates the "fight or flight" response of the autonomic nervous system; *resistance*; and *exhaustion*. If a stressor persists, it may overwhelm the body's ability to cope, and fatigue and illness may result.
- Modern research has modified and added to Selye's framework. When a person is under stress or in danger, the hypothalamus sends messages to the endocrine glands along two major pathways. One activates the sympathetic division of the autonomic nervous system, releasing *epinephrine* and *norepinephrine* from the inner part of the adrenal glands.
- The hypothalamus also initiates activity along the *HPA axis*. Chemical messengers travel from the hypothalamus to the pituitary and in turn to the outer part (cortex) of the adrenal glands. The adrenal cortex secretes *cortisol* and other hormones that elevate blood sugar and protect the body's tissues from inflammation. Excess levels of cortisol can become harmful in the long run. Responses to stress differ across individuals, depending on the type of stressor and the individual's own genetic predispositions.
- Researchers in the interdisciplinary field of *psychoneuroimmunology (PNI)* are studying the interaction among psychological factors, the nervous and endocrine systems, and the immune system (particularly the white blood cells that destroy foreign bodies, *antigens*, such as harmful bacteria, viruses, or tumor cells).

The Psychology of Stress

- Researchers have sought links between psychological factors and illness. Chronic anger, particularly in the form of *cynical (antagonistic) hostility*, is related to heart disease. Chronic depression seems to also be a risk factor in heart disease, but its link to other illnesses remains unclear. Positive emotions, such as happiness, joy, gratitude, hope, and love, are associated with better health and longevity.
- The effort to suppress thoughts, worries, secrets, and memories of upsetting experiences can paradoxically lead to obsessively ruminating on these thoughts and can be stressful to the body. Research finds that people benefit physiologically when they are able to let go of negative emotions through confession (expressing them on paper or to a trusted friend) or forgiveness.
- Other important psychological factors that affect health are being optimistic rather than pessimistic, even when optimism involves unrealistic but positive illusions, and having an *internal locus of control*. Optimism and control affect a person's ability to tolerate pain, live with ongoing illness and stress, and recover from disease. However, people can sometimes have too strong a sense of control; the healthiest balance is to take responsibility for getting well without blaming oneself for getting sick.
- Health and well-being may depend on the right combination of *primary control*, trying to change the stressful situation, and *secondary control*, learning to accept and accommodate to the stressful situation. Cultures differ in the kind of control they emphasize and value most.

Coping with Stress

- *Coping* involves active efforts to manage demands that feel stressful. One way to cope with stress is to reduce its physical effects, for example, through *progressive relaxation*, meditation, massage, and exercise. Another is to focus on solving the problem (*problem-focused coping*) rather than focusing solely on ventilating the emotions caused by the problem (*emotion-focused coping*). A third is to rethink the problem, through *reappraisal*, learning from and finding meaning in the experience, and *social comparison* with others who are less fortunate or who can provide inspiring examples of how to cope.
- *Social support* from friends, family, and other people is important in maintaining health and emotional well-being. People who have good friends, many social contacts, and a network of community relations have better health and actually live longer than those who do not. As the "Close-up on Research" shows, a touch or a hug from

a supportive partner calms the alarm circuits of the brain and raises levels of *oxytocin*, which may result in reduced heart rate and blood pressure.

- Men are, on average, less likely than women to seek social support and get help for physical and emotional problems. But several conditions increase men's likelihood of getting help, such as feeling that their problem is not unusual and feeling able to reciprocate any help they get.
- Family and friends can also be a source of stress. In close relationships, couples who fight in a hostile and negative way show impaired immune function.
- Giving support to others is also associated with health and hastens recovery from traumatic experiences.

How Much Control Do We Have over Our Health?

- Psychological factors and social networks are links in a long chain that connects stress and illness. Coping with stress does not mean trying to live without pain, problems, or losses. It means learning how to live with them.

KEY TERMS

health psychology 567
stressors 567
general adaptation syndrome 569
alarm/resistance/exhaustion phases of stress 569
adrenal hormones 569
epinephrine and norepinephrine 569
HPA axis (hypothalamus–pituitary–adrenal cortex) 570
cortisol 570
psychoneuroimmunology 572
antigens 572
cynical (antagonistic) hostility 574
locus of control (internal versus external) 579
primary control 581
secondary control 581
coping 583
progressive relaxation 583
emotion-focused coping 584
problem-focused coping 584
reappraisal 585
social comparison 585
social support 586
oxytocin 588

Are You Stressed? In Denial?

NOW YOU HAVE READ CHAPTER FIFTEEN — ARE YOU PREPARED FOR THE EXAM?

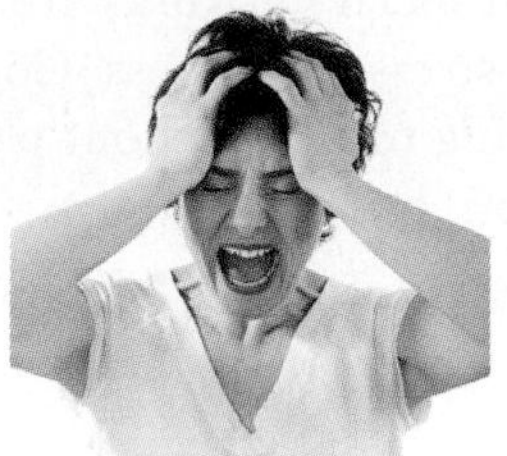

Maria is a tax accountant who is very busy from January to April 15, which is the tax return filing deadline. She feels that she must work very long hours during this time to meet the April 15 deadline for all of her clients. Maria is experiencing _______.

What are some sources of stress in everyday life? (pages 574–580)

pressure

A student who is failing but does not study because he refuses to believe that the instructor will really assign him an "F" at the end of the term is using the psychological defense mechanism of ______.

What are the psychological defense mechanisms? (pages 574–582)

denial

Eating a healthy breakfast has been shown to decrease the risk of obesity. True or False?

What are some ways to promote wellness in one's life? (pages 592–593)

true

One important component to understanding this chapter is to understand the difference between a stressor and stress. The **stressor** is the event that causes us to experience stress. The event can be external, such as getting stuck in traffic, or internal, such as worrying about an upcoming exam. Our reaction to the event is called **stress** and can be physical, emotional, mental, and behavioral.

Key Term

coping strategies

actions that people can take to master, tolerate, reduce, or minimize the effects of stressors.

Close

Key Term

problem-focused coping

coping strategies that try to eliminate the source of a stress or reduce its impact through direct actions.

Close

If you are feeling stressed about the next exam in your class, be sure to help yourself study by using the resources available to you at www.mypsychlab.com.

What are the different types of conflicts people must face?

Many students find the different types of conflicts confusing. Look over the Stress section in MyPsychLab. Try the pretests for the section and be sure to try the Apply It exercise.

TELL ME **MORE** >>

"The notecards and drills in MPL helped me learn what the chapter was about."

Student
Oklahoma State University

APPLY IT

The diagram below represents three possible types of conflict.

+ Approach —or— Approach + | − Avoid Avoid − | + − Avoid Approach

To better remember these three type of conflicts, think back to a time in your life when you experienced an approach-approach conflict (where you had to choose between two desirable alternatives), an avoidance-avoidance conflict (where you had to choose between two unpleasant alternatives), and an approach-avoidance conflict (where you had to choose between two alternatives that had both desirable and undesirable characteristics).

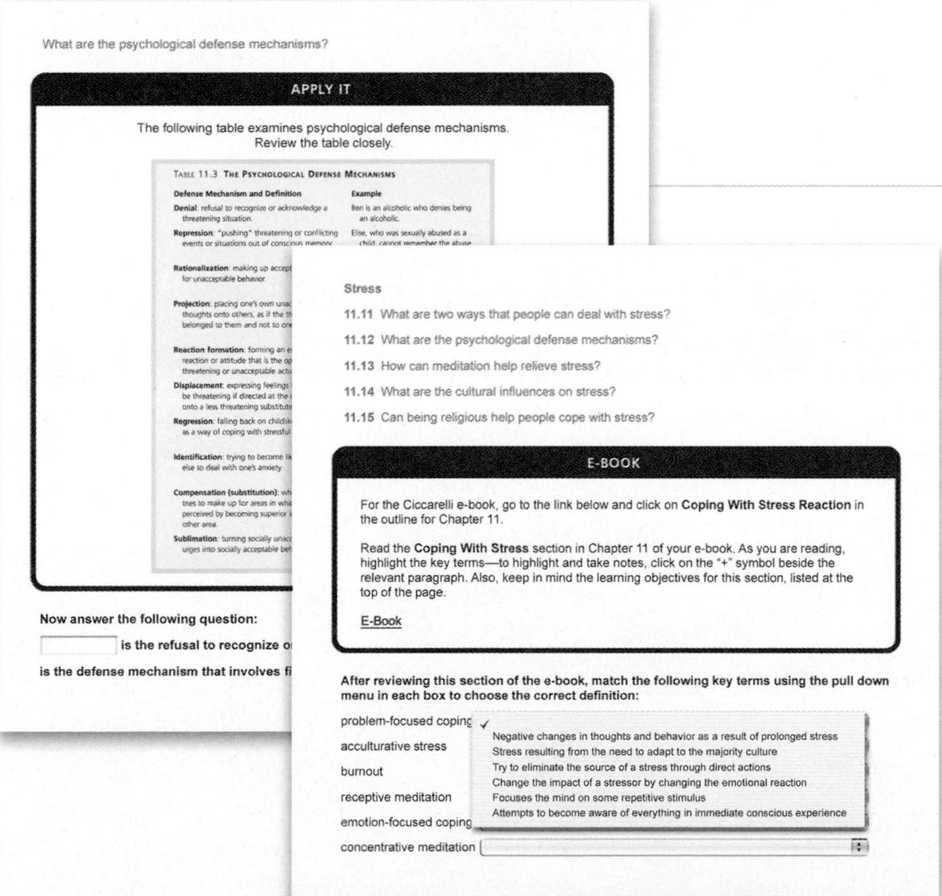

What are two ways that people can deal with stress?

Many coping strategies can be divided into those that deal with taking action (problem-focused) and those that deal with changing your own emotions or thoughts (emotion-focused).

Think about the types of coping strategies you use. Do you focus on emotions or actions? Take the quizzes in the Coping with Stress section of MyPsychLab and try out the eBook quiz to help you recognize your own coping strategies.

PSYCHOLOGICAL DISORDERS

CHAPTER SIXTEEN

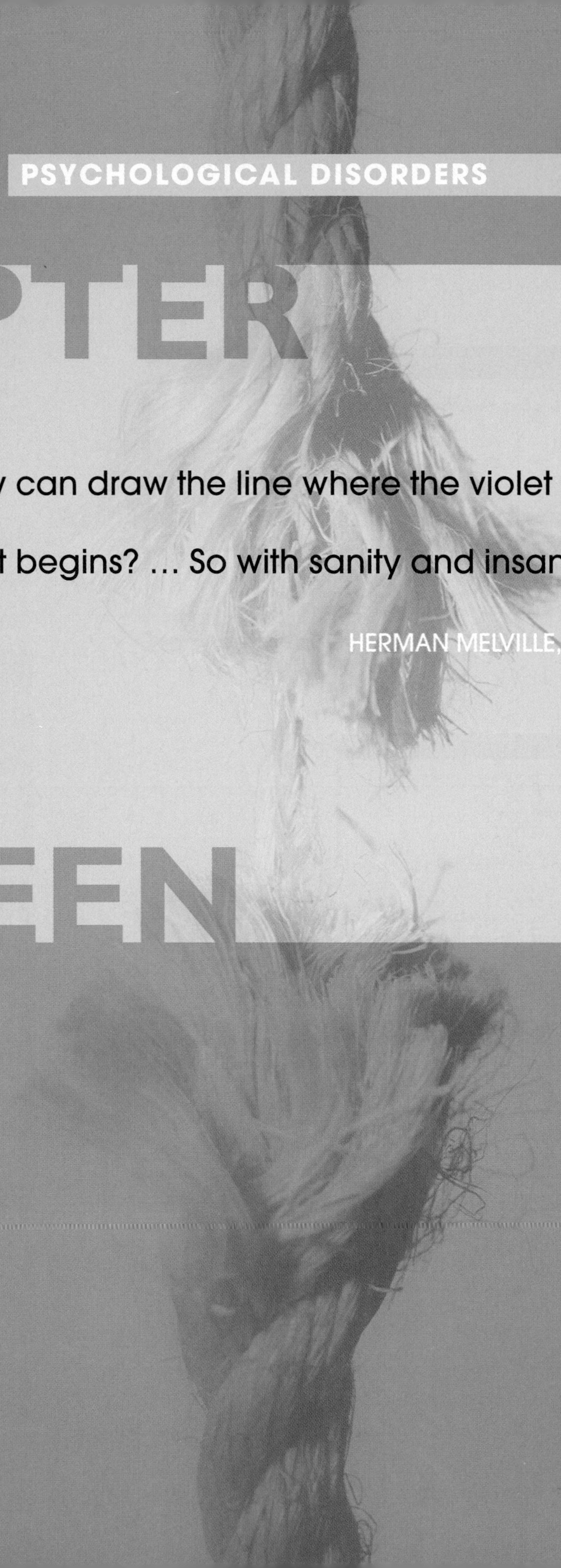

Who in the rainbow can draw the line where the violet tint ends and the orange tint begins? … So with sanity and insanity.

HERMAN MELVILLE, *BILLY BUDD*

CHAPTER 16

OUTLINE

Margaret Mary Ray believed with all her heart that late-night talk-show host David Letterman was in love with her. Caught up in this delusion, she stalked Letterman day and night for a decade, writing him letters and repeatedly breaking into his house. She camped out on his tennis court and once stole his car. The tabloids treated her delusions as a running joke. Finally, she gave up. She wrote to her mother, "I'm all traveled out," and put herself in front of a coal train. She was killed instantly.

Vincent Gigante, head of the Genovese crime family in New York, confessed that he had been pretending to be mentally ill for many years in order to avoid imprisonment. Gigante was known as the "Oddfather" because he would shuffle along the Manhattan streets in his bathrobe and slippers. He had convinced prominent psychiatrists that he was schizophrenic and suffering from dementia, which made him mentally incompetent to stand trial. He died in prison in 2005.

Matthew Small had a 4.0 average at his college in New Hampshire, until he entered the world of Azeroth. For seven months, he immersed himself in the virtual World of Warcraft, in which his character, a warrior-healer, accomplished glorious feats. He spent at least six hours a day collecting armor, swords, and other cybergear for his character, gloating to his friends about his "accomplishments" in the game. His work suffered. His close friends drifted away, and his grades slipped. Then, one day, he realized he had logged more than 1,000 hours playing the game in one semester and decided it was time to turn in his armor.

You don't have to be a psychologist to know that something was terribly wrong with Margaret Mary Ray. When people think of "mental illness," they usually think of individuals like her—people with delusions or people who behave in bizarre ways, such as walking the streets wearing layers of clothing on a hot summer day. Vincent Gigante took advantage of the public's awareness of the sad and dramatic examples of schizophrenic delusions. But what was Matthew Small's problem? Was he "addicted" to the Internet, or was he just a typical college student who wanted to enjoy himself and avoid studying?

Most psychological problems are far less dramatic than the public's impression of them and far more common. Some people go through episodes of complete inability to function, yet get along fine between those episodes. Many people function adequately every day, yet suffer constant melancholy, always feeling below par. And some people cannot control their worries or tempers. In this chapter, you will learn about the many psychological problems that cause people unhappiness and anguish. You will learn about the severe disorders that really do make people unable to control their behavior. But you will also learn why psychologists and psychiatrists often find it difficult to agree on a diagnosis, and why diagnosing mental problems is not the same as diagnosing medical problems such as diabetes or appendicitis.

One of the most common worries that people have is "Am I normal?" It is normal to fear being abnormal—especially when you are reading about psychological problems! But it is also normal to have problems. All of us on occasion have difficulties that seem too much to handle, and it is often unclear precisely when "normal" problems shade into "abnormal" ones.

WHAT'S **AHEAD**

- Is insanity the same thing as having a mental disorder?
- What are three approaches to defining "mental disorder"?
- Why is the standard guide to the diagnosis of mental disorders controversial?
- Why were slaves who tried to escape once considered to be mentally ill?
- How reliable are "projective" tests like the popular Rorschach Inkblot Test?

Defining and Diagnosing Disorder

Many people confuse unusual behavior—behavior that deviates from the norm—with mental disorder, but the two are not the same. A person may behave in ways that are statistically rare (collecting ceramic pigs, being a genius at math, committing murder) without having a mental illness. Conversely, some mental disorders, such as depression and anxiety, are extremely common.

People also confuse mental disorder and insanity. In the law, the definition of *insanity* rests primarily on whether a person is aware of the consequences of his or her actions and can control his or her behavior. But *insanity* is a legal term only; a person may have a mental illness and yet be considered sane by the court.

If frequency of the problem is not a guide, and insanity reflects only one extreme kind of mental illness, how then should we define a "mental disorder"?

Dilemmas of Definition

One problem is that the definition of a disorder depends on whether we are taking society's point of view, the view of people who are affected by the troubled individual, or the perspective of troubled individuals themselves.

1 Mental disorder as a violation of cultural standards. One definition emphasizes the roles and rules of the culture. Every society sets up standards for its members to follow, and those who break the most important rules governing appropriate behavior are usually considered deviant or disturbed. However, many of these rules are specific to a particular time or group. For example, it is not uncommon for bereaved people to have momentary visions of a deceased relative or to "hear" the loved one's voice. But in most of North America, these hallucinations are considered abnormal, and people who have them often fear they might be "crazy." In contrast, the Chinese, the Hopi, and members of many other cultures regard such visions as perfectly normal.

2 Mental disorder as emotional distress. A second approach identifies mental disorder in terms of a person's suffering—as from depression, anxiety, incapacitating fears, or problems with drugs. In this definition, a behavior that is unendurable or upsetting for one person, such as lack of interest in sex, may be acceptable and normal for another. But this definition does not cover the behavior of people who are clearly disturbed and dangerous to others, yet who are not troubled about their actions.

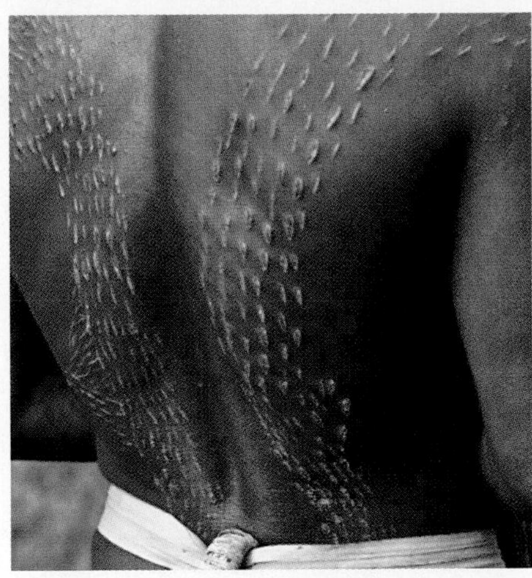

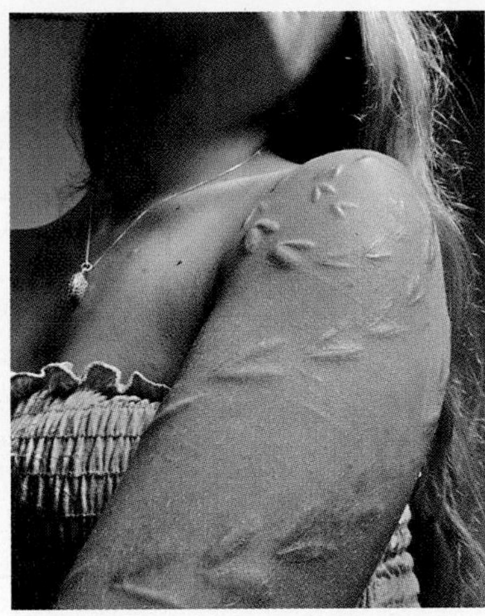

What's normal? In many places around the world, it is normal for women and men to create scars on their bodies for decoration or symbolic meaning. In Papua New Guinea, all young men to go through an initiation rite in which small, deep cuts are made on their backs to create permanent scars that signify a crocodile's scales (left). In contrast, in most places it is abnormal to mutilate oneself for the sole purpose of inflicting injury and pain, as the patient on the right has done. But what about the decorative scars on the arm of the 23-year-old woman from upstate New York (middle), who had them made by a "body artist"? She also has scars on her leg and her stomach, along with 29 piercings. Is her behavior "normal" or "abnormal"?

3 Mental disorder as behavior that is self-destructive or harmful to others. A third approach emphasizes the negative consequences of a person's behavior. Some behavior is harmful to the individual sufferer, such as the behavior of a woman who is so afraid of crowds that she cannot leave her house, a man who drinks so much that he cannot keep a job, or a student who is so anxious that she cannot take exams. In other cases, the individual may report feeling fine and deny that anything is wrong, yet will behave in ways that are disruptive, dangerous, or out of touch with reality—as when a child sets fires, a compulsive gambler loses the family savings, or a woman hears voices telling her to stalk a celebrity.

In this chapter, we define **mental disorder** broadly, as any behavior or emotional state that causes a person to suffer, is self-destructive, seriously impairs the person's ability to work or get along with others, or endangers others or the community. By this definition, many people will have some mental-health problem in the course of their lives, or their loved ones will. A nationwide survey of more than 9,000 randomly selected adults in the United States found that only about 7 percent of the population suffer from mental illnesses that are "seriously debilitating." But nearly half, at some time in their lives, temporarily fall prey to severe anxiety, depression, drug abuse, and other problems that can make their lives miserable (Kessler et al., 2005).

Dilemmas of Diagnosis

Even armed with a general definition of mental disorder, psychologists have found that classifying mental disorders into distinct categories is not an easy job. In this section we will see why this is so.

Classifying Disorders: The DSM. The standard reference manual used to diagnose mental disorders is the *Diagnostic and Statistical Manual of Mental Disorders* (DSM), published by the American Psychiatric Association (1994, 2000). The DSM's primary aim is *descriptive:* to provide clear diagnostic categories, so that clinicians and researchers can agree on which disorders they are talking about and then can study and treat these disorders. (For a list of the DSM's major categories, see Table 16.1.)

The DSM lists the symptoms of each disorder and, wherever possible, gives information about the typical age of onset, predisposing factors, course of the disorder, prevalence of the disorder, sex ratio of those affected, and cultural issues that might affect diagnosis.

mental disorder Any behavior or emotional state that causes an individual great suffering, is self-destructive, seriously impairs the person's ability to work or get along with others, or endangers others or the community.

TABLE 16.1

Major Diagnostic Categories in the DSM-IV

Disorders usually first diagnosed in infancy, childhood, or adolescence include mental retardation, attention deficit disorders (such as hyperactivity or an inability to concentrate), and developmental problems.
Delirium, dementia, amnesia, and other cognitive disorders are those resulting from brain damage, degenerative diseases such as syphilis or Alzheimer's, toxic substances, or drugs.
Substance-related disorders are problems associated with excessive use of or withdrawal from alcohol, amphetamines, caffeine, cocaine, hallucinogens, nicotine, opiates, or other drugs.
Schizophrenia and other psychotic disorders are disorders characterized by delusions, hallucinations, and severe disturbances in thinking and emotion.
Mood disorders include major depression, bipolar disorder (manic depression), and dysthymia (chronic depressed mood).
Anxiety disorders include generalized anxiety disorder, phobias, panic attacks with or without agoraphobia, posttraumatic stress disorder, and obsessive thoughts or compulsive rituals.
Eating disorders include anorexia nervosa (self-starvation because of an irrational fear of being or becoming fat) and bulimia nervosa (episodes of binge eating and vomiting).
Dissociative disorders include dissociative amnesia (in which important events cannot be remembered after a traumatic event) and dissociative identity disorder, characterized by the presence of two or more distinct identities or personalities.
Sexual and gender identity disorders include problems of sexual (gender) identity, such as transsexualism (wanting to be the other gender), problems of sexual performance (such as premature ejaculation or lack of orgasm), and paraphilias (needing unusual or bizarre imagery or acts for sexual arousal, as in sadomasochism or exhibitionism).
Impulse control disorders involve an inability to resist an impulse to perform some act that is harmful to the individual or to others, such as pathological gambling, stealing (kleptomania), setting fires (pyromania), or having violent rages.
Personality disorders are inflexible and maladaptive patterns that cause distress to the individual or impair the ability to function; they include paranoid, narcissistic, borderline, and antisocial personality disorders.
Additional conditions that may be a focus of clinical attention include "problems in living" such as bereavement, academic difficulties, spiritual problems, and acculturation problems.

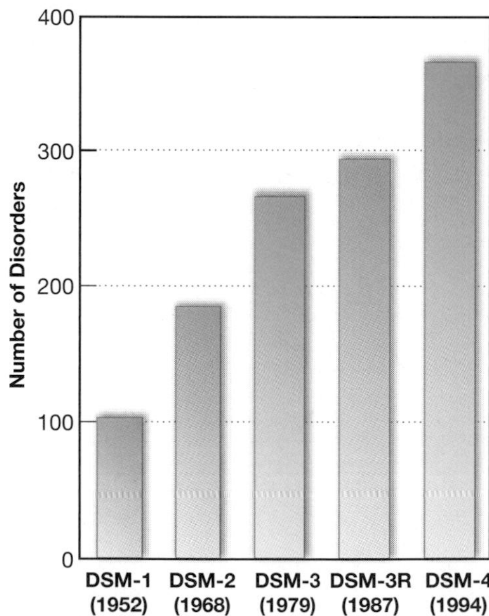

FIGURE 16.1 The Rising Number of Disorders in the DSM

Mental disorders in the DSM have increased nearly fourfold since the first edition (Houts, 2002).

In addition, clinicians are encouraged to evaluate each client according to five *axes*, or dimensions:

1. The primary clinical problem, such as depression.
2. Ingrained aspects of the client's personality that are likely to affect the person's ability to be treated, such as negative emotionality (neuroticism), a disposition to be pessimistic and bitter (see Chapter 13).
3. Medical conditions or medications that might contribute to the symptoms.
4. Social and environmental stressors that can make the disorder worse, such as job and housing troubles or having recently left a network of close friends.
5. A global assessment of the client's overall level of functioning in work, relationships, and leisure time, including whether the problem is of recent origin or of long duration and how incapacitating it is.

The DSM has had an extraordinary impact worldwide. Virtually all textbooks in psychiatry and psychology base their discussions of mental disorders on the DSM. Attorneys and judges often refer to the manual's list of mental disorders, even though the DSM warns that its categories "may not be wholly relevant to legal judgments." With each new edition of the manual, the number of mental disorders has grown (see Figure 16.1). The first edition, in 1952, was only 86 pages long and contained about 100 diagnoses. The DSM-IV, published in 1994 and slightly revised in 2000, is 900 pages long and contains nearly 400 diagnoses of mental disorder.

What is the reason for this explosion of mental disorders? Supporters of the new categories answer that it is important to distinguish disorders precisely in order to treat them properly. Critics point to an economic reason: Insurance companies require

clinicians to assign their clients an appropriate DSM code number for the diagnosed disorder, which puts pressure on compilers of the manual to add more diagnoses so that physicians and psychologists will be compensated.

THINKING CRITICALLY

ANALYZE ASSUMPTIONS AND BIASES

Many people assume that diagnosing mental disorders is as straightforward and objective as diagnosing appendicitis. Is this assumption correct?

Problems with the DSM. Because of the DSM's powerful influence, critics maintain that it is important to be aware of its limitations and some inherent problems in the very effort to classify and label mental disorders:

1 **The danger of overdiagnosis.** "If you give a small boy a hammer," wrote Abraham Kaplan (1967), "it will turn out that everything he runs into needs pounding." Likewise, say critics, if you give mental-health professionals a diagnostic label, it will turn out that everyone they run into has the symptoms of the new disorder.

Consider "attention deficit/hyperactivity disorder" (ADHD), a diagnostic label given to children and adults who are impulsive, messy, restless, and easily frustrated and who have trouble concentrating. Since ADHD was added to the DSM, it has become the fastest-growing disorder in America, where it is diagnosed at least ten times as often as it is in Europe. Critics therefore fear that parents, teachers, and mental-health professionals are overusing this diagnosis, especially on boys, who make up 80 to 90 percent of all ADHD cases. The critics argue that normal boyish behavior—being rambunctious, refusing to nap, being playful, not listening to teachers in school—is being turned into a psychological problem (Panksepp, 1998). A longitudinal study of more than a hundred 4- to 6-year-olds found that the number of children who met the criteria for ADHD declined over time (Lahey et al., 2005). Some remained highly impulsive and unable to concentrate, but others, it seems, simply matured!

2 **The power of diagnostic labels.** Being given a diagnosis reassures people who are seeking an explanation for their emotional symptoms or problems ("Whew! So *that's* what I've got!"). But once a person has been given a diagnosis, other people begin to see that person primarily in terms of the label; it sticks like lint. For example, when a rebellious, disobedient teenager is diagnosed as having "oppositional defiant disorder," people tend to see him as a person with a permanent, official condition; something is wrong with his personality. They then overlook other possible explanations of his actions: Maybe he is "defiant" because he has been mistreated or his parents don't listen to him. And once he is labeled, observers tend to ignore changes in his behavior and the times when he is not being defiant.

3 **The confusion of serious mental disorders with normal problems.** The DSM is not called "The Diagnostic and Statistical Manual of Mental Disorders and a Whole Bunch of Everyday Problems." Yet each edition of the DSM has added more everyday problems, including "disorder of written expression" (having trouble writing clearly), "mathematics disorder" (not doing well in math), "religious or spiritual problem," and "caffeine-induced sleep disorder" (which at least is easy to cure; just switch to decaf). Some critics fear that by lumping together such normal difficulties with true mental illnesses, such as schizophrenia, the DSM implies that everyday problems are comparable to disorders—and equally likely to require treatment (Houts, 2002).

4 **The illusion of objectivity and universality.** Finally, some psychologists argue that the whole enterprise of the DSM is a vain attempt to impose a veneer of science on an inherently subjective process (Houts, 2002; Kutchins & Kirk, 1997; Tiefer, 2004).

Harriet Tubman (on the left) poses with some of the people she helped to escape from slavery on her "underground railroad." Slaveholders welcomed the idea that Tubman and others who insisted on their freedom had a "mental disorder" called "drapetomania."

Many decisions about what to include as a disorder, say these critics, are based not on empirical evidence but on group consensus. The problem is that group consensus often reflects prevailing attitudes and prejudices rather than objective evidence.

It is easy to identify prejudices in *past* notions of mental problems. In the early years of the nineteenth century, a physician named Samuel Cartwright argued that many slaves were suffering from *drapetomania*, an urge to escape from slavery (Kutchins & Kirk, 1997; Landrine, 1988). (He made up the word from *drapetes*, the Latin word for "runaway slave," and *mania*, meaning "mad" or "crazy.") Thus, doctors could assure slave owners that a mental illness, not the intolerable condition of slavery, made slaves seek freedom. Today, of course, "drapetomania" seems foolish and cruel.

Over the years, psychiatrists have quite properly rejected many other "disorders" that reflected cultural prejudices and lacked empirical validation, such as lack of vaginal orgasm, childhood masturbation disorder, and homosexuality (Wakefield, 1992). But critics argue that many disorders still in the DSM are just as affected by contemporary prejudices and values. Today you don't have a disorder if you want to have sex "too often" (once called, in women, "nymphomania"), but you do if you do not want to have sex often "enough" (hypoactive sexual desire disorder) (Groneman, 2000). Emotional problems allegedly associated with menstruation remain in the DSM, but behavioral problems associated with testosterone have never even been considered for inclusion. In short, critics maintain, many diagnoses still depend on a cultural consensus, not on empirical evidence, about what constitutes normal behavior, as well as what constitutes a mental disorder.

Advantages of the DSM. Defenders of the DSM agree that the boundaries between "normal problems" and "mental disorders" are fuzzy and often difficult to determine (Kessler et al., 2005). They also recognize that many psychological symptoms fall along a continuum, ranging from mild to severe. But they believe that when the manual is used correctly and diagnoses are made with valid objective tests, the DSM improves the reliability of diagnosis (Beutler & Malik, 2002; Widiger & Clark, 2000). This is important, they maintain, because the DSM's categories help clinicians distinguish among disorders that share certain symptoms (such as anxiety, irritability, or delusions) in order to select the most appropriate treatment. The DSM's fifth edition, due out in 2010, will include findings from genetics, neuroscience, and behavioral science, which may further increase the reliability and validity of diagnoses.

The DSM-IV included, for the first time, a list of *culture-bound syndromes*, disorders that are specific to particular cultural contexts (see Table 16.2). For example, Latinos may respond to catastrophic stress with an *ataque de nervios*, a nervous attack of screaming, swooning, and agitation. (Students everywhere, however, will undoubtedly sympathize with the West African disorder of "brain fag," mental exhaustion due to excessive studying!) The DSM acknowledges that these syndromes rarely overlap with DSM diagnostic categories, yet they can cause great mental suffering in the cultures where they occur. At the same time, DSM defenders argue, some disorders are universal, although they might take different forms. In societies throughout the world, from the Inuit of Alaska to the Yoruba of Nigeria, some individuals have delusions, are severely depressed, suffer panic attacks, or cannot control their behavior (Butcher, Lim, & Nezami, 1998; Kleinman, 1988).

TABLE 16.2
From Amok to Zar: Some Culture-Bound Syndromes

Problem Name	Where Recognized	Description
Amok	Malaysia; similar patterns elsewhere	Brooding followed by a violent outburst; often precipitated by a slight or insult; seems to be prevalent only among men.
Ataque de nervios	Latin America and Mediterranean	An episode of uncontrollable shouting, crying, trembling, heat in chest rising to the head, verbal or physical aggression.
Brain fag	West Africa	"Brain tiredness," a mental and physical reaction to the challenges of schooling.
Ghost sickness	Native American tribes	Preoccupation with death and the dead, with bad dreams, fainting, appetite loss, fear, hallucinations, etc.
Pibloktoq	Arctic and subarctic Inuit communities	Episodes of extreme excitement of up to 30 minutes, during which the individual behaves irrationally or violently.
Qi-gong psychotic reaction	China	A short episode of mental symptoms after engaging in the Chinese folk practice of qi-gong, or "exercise of vital energy."
Taijin kyofusho	Japan	An intense fear that the body, its parts, or its functions displease, embarrass, or are offensive to others.
Zar	North Africa and Middle East	Belief in possession by a spirit, causing shouting, laughing, head banging, weeping, withdrawal, etc.

SOURCE: DSM-IV

Dilemmas of Measurement

Clinical psychologists and psychiatrists usually arrive at a diagnosis by interviewing a patient and observing the person's behavior when he or she arrives at the office, hospital, or clinic. But many also use psychological tests to help them decide on a diagnosis. Such tests are also commonly used in schools (e.g., to determine whether a child has a learning disorder or emotional problem) and in court settings (e.g., to try to determine which parent should have custody in a divorce case).

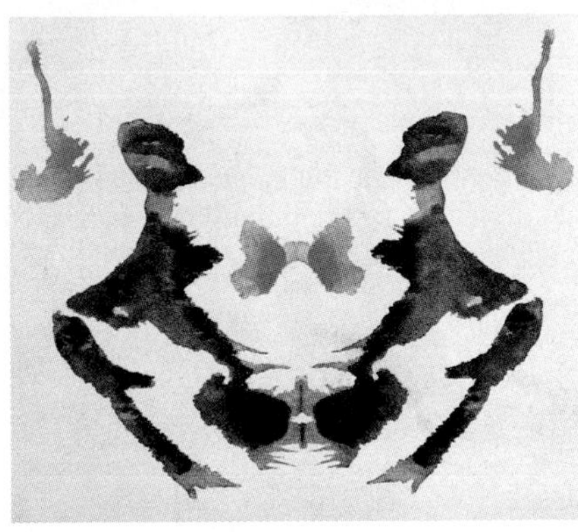
A Rorschach inkblot. What do you see in it?

Projective Tests. **Projective tests** consist of ambiguous pictures, sentences, or stories that the test taker interprets or completes. A child or adult may be asked to draw a person, a house, or some other object, or to finish a sentence (such as "My father . . ." or "Women are . . ."). The psychodynamic assumption behind all projective tests is that the person's unconscious thoughts and feelings will be "projected" onto the test and revealed in the person's responses. (See Chapter 13 for a discussion of psychodynamic theories and their emphasis on unconscious motives and conflicts.)

Projective tests can help clinicians establish rapport with their clients and can encourage clients to open up about anxieties and conflicts they might be ashamed to discuss. But the evidence is overwhelming that these tests lack reliability and validity, which makes them inappropriate for their most common uses—assessing personality traits or diagnosing mental disorders (Wood et al., 2003). They lack reliability because different clinicians often interpret the same person's scores differently, perhaps projecting their own beliefs and assumptions when they decide what a specific response means. The tests have low validity because they fail to measure what they are supposed to measure. One reason is that responses to a projective test are significantly affected by sleepiness, hunger, medication, worry, verbal ability, the clinician's instructions, the clinician's own personality (friendly and warm, or cool and remote), and other events occurring that day.

projective tests Psychological tests used to infer a person's motives, conflicts, and unconscious dynamics on the basis of the person's interpretations of ambiguous stimuli.

Rorschach Inkblot Test A projective personality test that requires respondents to interpret abstract, symmetrical inkblots.

One of the most popular projectives is the **Rorschach Inkblot Test**, which was devised by the Swiss psychiatrist Hermann Rorschach in 1921. It consists of ten cards with symmetrical abstract patterns, originally formed by spilling ink on paper and

folding the paper in half. The test taker reports what he or she sees in the inkblots, and the clinician interprets the answers according to the symbolic meanings emphasized by psychodynamic theories. One kind of response, for example, might be interpreted as evidence of a person's dependency.

Although the Rorschach is widely used among clinicians, efforts to confirm its reliability and validity have repeatedly failed. The Rorschach does not reliably diagnose depression, posttraumatic stress reactions, personality disorders, or serious mental disorders. Claims of the Rorschach's success often come from testimonials at workshops where clinicians are taught how to use the test, which is hardly an impartial way of assessing it (Wood et al., 2003).

THINKING CRITICALLY

EXAMINE THE EVIDENCE

For years, many therapists used anatomically detailed dolls as a projective test to determine whether a child had been sexually abused, but this practice has not been justified by empirical evidence.

Many psychotherapists use projective tests with young children to help them express feelings they cannot reveal verbally. But during the 1980s, some therapists began using projective methods for another purpose: to determine whether a child had been sexually abused. They claimed they could identify a child who had been abused by observing how the child played with "anatomically detailed" dolls (dolls with realistic genitals), and that is how many of them testified in hundreds of court cases (Ceci & Bruck, 1995).

Unfortunately, these therapists had not tested their beliefs by using a fundamental scientific procedure: comparison with a control group (see Chapter 2). They had not asked, "How do *nonabused* children play with these dolls?" When psychological scientists conducted controlled research to answer this question, they found that large percentages of nonabused children are also fascinated with the doll's genitals. They will poke at them, grab them, pound sticks into a female doll's vagina, and do other things that alarm adults! The crucial conclusion was that you cannot reliably diagnose sexual abuse on the basis of children's doll play (Bruck et al., 1995; Hunsley, Lee, & Wood, 2003; Koocher et al., 1995; Wood et al., 2003). You can see how someone who did not understand the problems with projective tests might end up making inferences about a child's behavior that were dangerously wrong.

Another situation in which projective tests are also used widely yet often inappropriately is in child-custody assessments. Understandably, when faced with divorcing partners who are bitterly quarreling, calling each other names, and accusing each other of being a terrible parent, the courts long for an objective way to determine which one is better suited to have custody. But when a panel of psychololgical scientists impartially examined the leading psychological assessment measures, most of which are projective tests, they found that "these measures assess ill-defined constructs, and they do so poorly, leaving no scientific justification for their use in child custody evaluations" (Emery, Otto, & O'Donohue, 2005).

Objective Tests. Many clinicians also use **objective tests (inventories)**, standardized questionnaires that ask about the test taker's behavior and feelings. Some inventories, such as the Beck Depression Inventory, the Spielberger State-Trait Anger Inventory, and the Taylor Manifest Anxiety Scale, assess specific emotional problems. The most widely used test for assessing personality and emotional disorders, the **Minnesota Multiphasic Personality Inventory (MMPI)**, is organized into ten categories, or *scales*, covering such problems as depression, paranoia, schizophrenia, and introversion. Four additional *validity scales* indicate whether a test taker is likely to be lying, defensive, or evasive while answering the items.

objective tests (inventories) Standardized objective questionnaires requiring written responses; they typically include scales on which people are asked to rate themselves.

Minnesota Multiphasic Personality Inventory (MMPI) A widely used objective personality test.

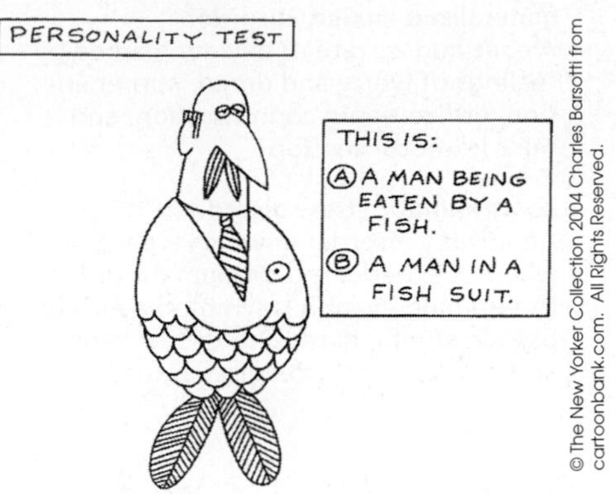

Inventories are generally more reliable and more valid than either projective methods or subjective clinical judgments (Dawes, 1994; Meyer et al., 2001). But inventories also have some limitations; one continuing problem is that they often fail to take into account differences among cultural, regional, and socioeconomic groups. In spite of recent revisions of the MMPI, for example, Mexican, Puerto Rican, and Argentine respondents score differently from non–Hispanic Americans, on average, on the Masculinity–Femininity Scale. This difference does not reflect emotional problems but traditional Latino attitudes toward sex roles (Cabiya et al., 2000). Also, the MMPI and other objective tests have a significant rate of false positives: That is, they sometimes label a person's responses as evidence of mental disorder when no serious problem actually exists (Guthrie & Mobley, 1994). And, finally, objective tests such as the MMPI are often inappropriately used in business, industry, legal settings, and schools by persons who are not well trained in testing.

We turn now to a closer examination of some of the disorders described in the DSM. Of course, we cannot cover all of them in one chapter, so we have singled out several that illustrate the range of psychological problems that afflict humanity, from the common to the very rare.

QUICK quiz

Your mental health will be enhanced if you can answer these questions.

1. Ruthie is afraid to leave her apartment unless she is with a close friend or relative, yet she says she feels fine and she angrily resists her friends' advice that she get help. What definition of mental disorder does Ruthie's behavior meet?
2. The primary purpose of the DSM is to (a) provide descriptive criteria for diagnosing mental disorders, (b) help psychologists assess normal as well as abnormal behavior, (c) describe the causes of common disorders, (d) keep the number of diagnostic categories of mental disorders to a minimum.
3. List four criticisms of the DSM.
4. What is the advantage of inventories, compared with clinical judgments and projective tests, in diagnosing mental disorders?

Answers:

1. Mental disorder as behavior that is self-destructive **2.** a **3.** It can foster overdiagnosis; it overlooks the power of diagnostic labels on the perceptions of clinicians and the behavior of clients; it confuses serious mental disorders with everyday problems in living; and it falsely implies that its diagnoses apply universally and are always based on objective evidence. **4.** Inventories have better reliability and validity.

WHAT'S**AHEAD** 

- What is the difference between ordinary anxiety and an anxiety disorder?
- Why is the most disabling of all phobias known as the "fear of fear"?
- When is checking the stove before leaving home a sign of caution, and when does it signal a disorder?

Anxiety Disorders

Anyone who is waiting for important news or living in an unpredictable situation quite sensibly feels *anxiety*, a general state of apprehension or psychological tension. And anyone who is in a dangerous and unfamiliar situation, such as making a first parachute

generalized anxiety disorder A continuous state of anxiety marked by feelings of worry and dread, apprehension, difficulties in concentration, and signs of motor tension.

posttraumatic stress disorder (PTSD) An anxiety disorder in which a person who has experienced a traumatic or life-threatening event has symptoms such as psychic numbing, reliving of the trauma, and increased physiological arousal.

jump or facing a peevish python, quite sensibly feels flat-out fear. In the short run, these emotions are adaptive because they energize us to cope with danger. They ensure that we don't make that first jump without knowing how to operate the parachute, and that we get away from that snake as fast as we can.

But sometimes fear and anxiety become detached from any actual danger, or these feelings continue even when danger and uncertainty are past. The result may be *chronic anxiety*, marked by long-lasting feelings of apprehension and doom; *panic attacks*, short-lived but intense feelings of anxiety; *phobias*, excessive fears of specific things or situations; or *obsessive-compulsive disorder*, in which repeated thoughts and rituals are used to ward off anxiety.

Anxiety and Panic

The chief characteristic of **generalized anxiety disorder** is continuous, uncontrollable anxiety or worry—a feeling of foreboding and dread—that occurs on a majority of days during a six-month period and that is not brought on by physical causes such as disease, drugs, or drinking too much coffee. Symptoms include restlessness or feeling keyed up, difficulty concentrating, irritability, jitteriness, sleep disturbance, and unwanted, intrusive worries.

Some people suffer from generalized anxiety disorder without having lived through any specific anxiety-producing event. They may have a physiological tendency to experience anxiety symptoms—sweaty palms, a racing heart, shortness of breath—when they are in challenging or uncontrollable situations. As we saw in Chapter 13, temperamentally shy children are already predisposed to react with anxiety in novel situations. Other chronically anxious people may have a history, starting in childhood, of being unable to control or predict their environments (Barlow, 2000; Mineka & Zinbarg, 2006). Whatever the origins of their anxiety, people with generalized anxiety disorder have mental habits that foster their worries and keep their anxiety bubbling along; they perceive everything as an opportunity for disaster (Riskind et al., 2000).

Posttraumatic Stress Disorder. Stress symptoms, including insomnia, agitation, and jumpiness, are entirely normal in the immediate aftermath of any crisis or trauma, such as war, rape, torture, natural disasters, sudden bereavement, or terrorist attacks. But if the symptoms persist for one month or longer and begin to impair a person's functioning, the sufferer may have **posttraumatic stress disorder (PTSD)**. Typical symptoms of PTSD include reliving the trauma in recurrent, intrusive thoughts; a sense of detachment from others and a loss of interest in familiar activities; and increased physiological arousal, reflected in insomnia, irritability, and impaired concentration.

Most people who live through a traumatic experience eventually recover without developing PTSD. One major national survey of Americans found that about 60 percent had experienced a traumatic event, but only 8 percent of the men and 20 percent of the women developed PTSD (Kessler et al., 1995). Some experts predicted an epidemic of PTSD after 9/11, but it never materialized (Bonanno et al., 2006). Why, then, if most people recover from a traumatic experience, do some continue to have PTSD symptoms for years, sometimes for decades?

One answer may involve a genetic predisposition. Behavioral–genetic studies of twins in the general population as well as among combat veterans have found that PTSD symptoms have a heritable component (Stein et al., 2002).

THINKING CRITICALLY

ASK QUESTIONS; BE WILLING TO WONDER

This grief-stricken soldier has just learned that the body bag on the flight with him contains the remains of a close friend who was killed in action. Understandably, many soldiers suffer posttraumatic stress symptoms. But why do most eventually recover, whereas others have PTSD for many years?

Another answer is that people who develop long-lasting PTSD often have a prior history of psychological problems and other traumatic experiences with poor emotional adjustment to them (Ozer et al., 2003). One reason for their poor adjustment is that they are more likely to have self-defeating, anxiety-producing ways of thinking in general—for example, they tend to "catastrophize" about every little thing that goes wrong, to believe they are inadequate, and to feel that no one can be trusted (Bryant & Guthrie, 2005). Many PTSD sufferers also lack the social, psychological, and neurological resources to deal with their difficult experiences. They are more likely than resilient people to have the personality trait of neuroticism and to have lower-than-average intelligence, which may impair their ability to cope cognitively with trauma (McNally, 2003).

Interestingly, in PTSD sufferers, the hippocampus is apt to be smaller than average (McNally, 2003). The hippocampus is crucially involved in autobiographical memory. An abnormally small one may figure in the difficulty of some trauma survivors to react to their memories as events from their past, which may be why they keep reliving them in the present. Originally, researchers thought that severe trauma caused neuron damage or loss of cells in the hippocampus, producing PTSD symptoms—impaired memory, recurrent fears, and so forth. But this hypothesis has been refuted. One team used MRIs to measure hippocampal size in identical twins, only one of whom in each pair had been in combat in Vietnam. If trauma shrinks the hippocampus, then the size of the hippocampus should have been different in the veterans who developed PTSD and their identical twins. But this was not what the researchers found. Two things were necessary for a vet to develop chronic PTSD: serving in combat *and* having a smaller hippocampus than normal (Gilbertson et al., 2002). Twins who had smaller hippocampi but no military service did not develop PTSD, and neither did the twins who *did* experience combat but who had normal-sized hippocampi.

In sum, many cases of PTSD seem to be a result of impaired cognitive and neurological functioning that existed *before* the trauma took place, triggered by the eventual traumatic experience.

panic disorder An anxiety disorder in which a person experiences recurring panic attacks, periods of intense fear, and feelings of impending doom or death, accompanied by physiological symptoms such as rapid heart rate and dizziness.

Panic Disorder. Another kind of anxiety disorder is **panic disorder**, in which a person has recurring attacks of intense fear or panic, often with feelings of impending doom or death. These panic attacks may last from a few minutes to (more rarely) several hours. Symptoms include trembling and shaking, dizziness, chest pain or discomfort, rapid heart rate, feelings of unreality, hot and cold flashes, sweating, and—as a result of all these scary physical reactions—a fear of dying, going crazy, or losing control. Many sufferers fear they are having a heart attack.

Although panic attacks seem to come out of nowhere, they in fact usually occur in the aftermath of stress, prolonged emotion, specific worries, or frightening experiences (McNally, 1998). For example, a friend of ours was on a plane that was a target of a bomb threat while airborne at 33,000 feet. He coped beautifully at the time, but two weeks later, seemingly out of nowhere, he had a panic attack.

Such delayed attacks after life-threatening scares are common. The essential difference between people who develop panic disorder and those who do not lies in *how they interpret their bodily reactions* (Barlow, 2000). Healthy people who have occasional panic attacks see them correctly as a result of a passing crisis or period of stress, comparable to another person's migraines. But people who develop panic disorder regard the attack as a sign of illness or impending death, and they begin to live their lives in restrictive ways, trying to avoid future attacks. This self-imposed restriction then makes this disorder particularly difficult for its sufferers (and their families).

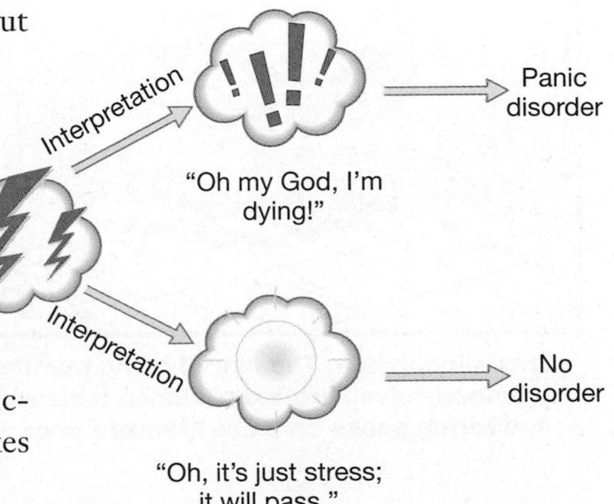

phobia An exaggerated, unrealistic fear of a specific situation, activity, or object.

agoraphobia A set of phobias, often set off by a panic attack, involving the basic fear of being away from a safe place or person.

People who have panic disorder are found throughout the world, although culture influences the particular symptoms they experience (Barlow, Chorpita, & Turovsky, 1996). Feelings of choking or being smothered, numbness, and fear of dying are most common in Latin America and southern Europe; fear of public places is most common in northern Europe and America; and fear of going crazy is more common in the Americas than in Europe. In Greenland, some fishermen suffer from "kayak-angst": a sudden attack of dizziness and fear that occurs while they are fishing in small, one-person kayaks (Amering & Katschnig, 1990).

Fears and Phobias

Are you afraid of bugs, snakes, or dogs? Are you vaguely uncomfortable with them or so afraid that you can't stand to be around one? A **phobia** is an exaggerated fear of a specific situation, activity, or thing. Some common phobias—such as fear of snakes, insects, heights (acrophobia), thunder (brontophobia), or being trapped in enclosed spaces (claustrophobia)—may have evolved to be easily acquired in human beings because these fears reflected real dangers for the species (Öhman & Mineka, 2003). Other phobias, such as a fear of cats or the color purple (porphyrophobia), may be acquired through classical conditioning or even through observation of a frightening event that is happening to someone else (Mineka & Zinbarg, 2006). Still other phobias, such as fear of dirt and germs (mysophobia) or of the number 13 (triskaidekaphobia), may reflect personality differences or cultural traditions. Whatever its source, a phobia is truly frightening and often incapacitating for its sufferer. It is not just a tendency to say "ugh" at tarantulas or skip the snake display at the zoo.

People who have a *social phobia* become extremely anxious in situations in which they will be observed by others—eating in a restaurant, speaking in front of a group or crowd, having to perform for others. They worry that they will do or say something that will be excruciatingly humiliating or embarrassing. These phobias are more severe forms of the occasional shyness and social anxiety that everyone experiences. For people with a social phobia, the mere thought of being in a new situation with unfamiliar people is scary enough to cause sweating, trembling, nausea, and an overwhelming feeling of inadequacy. So they don't go, increasing their isolation and imagined fears.

Luposlipaphobia: The fear of being pursued by timber wolves around a kitchen table while wearing socks on a newly waxed floor.

By far the most disabling fear disorder is **agoraphobia**. In ancient Greece, the *agora* was the social, political, business, and religious center of town, the public meeting place away from home. The fundamental fear in agoraphobia is of being trapped in a crowded public place, where escape might be difficult or where help might be unavailable if the person has a panic attack. Individuals with agoraphobia report many specific fears—of being in a crowded movie theater, driving in traffic or tunnels, or going to parties—but the underlying fear is of being away from a safe place, usually home, or a safe person, usually a parent or spouse.

Agoraphobia typically begins with a panic attack that seems to have no cause. The attack is so unexpected and scary that the agoraphobic-to-be begins to avoid situations that he or she thinks may provoke another one. A woman we know had a panic attack while driving on a freeway. This was a perfectly normal posttraumatic response to the suicide of her husband a few weeks earlier. But thereafter she avoided freeways—as if the freeway, and not the suicide, had caused the attack. Because so many of the actions associated with agoraphobia arise as a mistaken effort to avoid a panic attack, psychologists regard agoraphobia as a "fear of fear" rather than simply a fear of places.

GET INVOLVED!

➤WHAT SCARES YOU?

Everyone fears something. Stop for a moment to think about what you fear most. Is it heights? Snakes? Speaking in public? Ask yourself these questions: (1) How long have you feared this thing or situation? (2) How would you respond if you could not avoid this thing or situation? (3) How much would you be willing to rearrange your life to avoid this feared thing or situation? After considering these questions, would you regard your fear as a full-blown phobia or merely a normal source of apprehension?

Obsessions and Compulsions

Obsessive-compulsive disorder (OCD) is characterized by recurrent, persistent, unwished-for thoughts or images (*obsessions*) or by repetitive, ritualized, stereotyped behaviors that the person feels must be carried out to avoid disaster (*compulsions*). Of course, many people have trivial compulsions and practice superstitious rituals; baseball players are famous for them—one won't change his socks and another will eat chicken every day while he is on a hitting streak. Obsessions and compulsions become a disorder when they become uncontrollable and interfere with a person's life.

obsessive-compulsive disorder (OCD) An anxiety disorder in which a person feels trapped in repetitive, persistent thoughts (*obsessions*) and repetitive, ritualized behaviors (*compulsions*) designed to reduce anxiety.

People who have obsessive thoughts often find them frightening or repugnant: thoughts of killing a child, of becoming contaminated by a handshake, or of having unknowingly hurt someone in a traffic accident. Obsessive thoughts take many forms, but they are alike in reflecting impaired ways of reasoning and processing information.

People who suffer from compulsions likewise feel they have no control over them. The most common compulsions are hand washing, counting, touching, and checking. A woman *must* check the furnace, lights, locks, oven, and fireplace three times before she can sleep; or a man *must* wash his hands and face precisely eight times before he leaves the house. OCD sufferers usually realize that their behavior is senseless, and they are often tormented by their rituals. But if they try to forgo the ritual, they feel mounting anxiety that is relieved only by giving in to it. For one young man with OCD, stairs became a treadmill he could not get off: "At first I'd walk up and down the stairs only three or four times," he recalled. "Later I had to run up and down 63 times in 45 minutes. If I failed, I had to start all over again from the beginning" (quoted in King, 1989).

In many people with OCD, the prefrontal cortex is depleted of serotonin, which creates a kind of cognitive rigidity—an inability to let go of certain thoughts (Clarke et al., 2004). In addition, several parts of the brain are hyperactive in people with OCD. One area of the frontal lobes sends messages of impending danger to other areas involved in controlling the movement of the limbs and preparing the body to feel fear and respond to external threats. Normally, once danger is past or a person realizes that there is no cause for fear, the brain's alarm signal turns off. In people with OCD, however, false alarms keep clanging and the emotional networks keep sending out mistaken "fear!" messages (Schwartz et al., 1996). The sufferer feels in a constant state of danger and tries repeatedly to reduce the resulting anxiety.

Extreme hoarding is one form of obsessive-compulsive disorder. The person who lived here was unable to throw away any paper or magazine without feeling tremendous anxiety.

New biological research suggests, though, that OCD is not a single, unified disorder (Taylor, McKay, & Abramowitz, 2005). One subtype afflicts pathological hoarders who fill their homes with newspapers, bags of old clothing, used tissue boxes—all kinds of junk. They are tormented by fears of throwing out something they

QUICK quiz

We hope you don't feel anxious about matching each term on the left with its description on the right.

1. social phobia	**a.** need to perform a ritual
2. generalized anxiety disorder	**b.** fear of fear; of being trapped with no way of escape
3. posttraumatic stress disorder	**c.** continuing sense of doom
4. agoraphobia	**d.** repeated, unwanted thoughts
5. compulsion	**e.** fear of meeting new people
6. obsession	**f.** anxiety following severe shock

Answers:

1.e 2.c 3.f 4.b 5.a 6.d

will need later. A PET-scan study that compared obsessive hoarders with other people with obsessive symptoms found that hoarders had less activity in parts of the brain involved in decision making, problem solving, spatial orientation, and memory (Saxena et al., 2004). Perhaps these deficits explain why hoarders keep things (their inability to decide what to throw away creates a constant struggle) and why they often keep their papers and junk in the living room, kitchen, or even on the bed. They have trouble remembering where things are and thus feel the need to have them in sight.

WHAT'S**AHEAD**

- How can you tell whether you have major depression or just the blues?
- What are the "poles" in bipolar disorder?
- How do some people think themselves into depression?

Mood Disorders

In the DSM, *mood disorders* include disturbances in mood ranging from extreme depression to extreme mania. Of course, most people feel sad from time to time, and also joyful. And most people, at some time in their lives, will know the wild grief that accompanies tragedy and bereavement. These feelings, however, are a far cry from the clinical disorders described by the DSM.

Depression

Anxiety, painful though it is, is at least a sign that a person is engaged in the future: It reflects the belief that something bad will happen. But depressed people feel burned out about the future: They are sure that nothing good will ever happen. Some people go through life with constant but low-grade unhappiness; they can do what they need to but nearly always report their mood as sad or "down in the dumps." Others suffer from **major depression**, a serious mood disorder that involves emotional, behavioral, cognitive, and physical changes severe enough to disrupt a person's ordinary functioning. The writer William Styron, who fought and recovered from major depression, used the beginning of Dante's classic poem *The Divine Comedy* to convey his suffering:

In the middle of the journey of our life
I found myself in a dark wood.
For I had lost the right path.

major depression A mood disorder involving disturbances in emotion (excessive sadness), behavior (loss of interest in one's usual activities), cognition (thoughts of hopelessness), and body function (fatigue and loss of appetite).

"For those who have dwelt in depression's dark wood," wrote Styron in *Darkness Visible*, "and known its inexplicable agony, the return from the abyss is not unlike the ascent of the poet, trudging upward and upward out of hell's black depths and at last emerging into what he saw as 'the shining world.'"

People with major depression feel despairing and hopeless. They may think often of death or suicide. They feel unable to get up and do things; it takes an enormous effort even to get dressed. Their thinking patterns feed their bleak moods. They exaggerate minor failings, ignore or discount positive events, and interpret any little thing that goes wrong as evidence that nothing will ever go right. Emotionally healthy people who are sad or grieving do not see themselves as completely worthless and unlovable. Depressed people interpret losses as signs of failure and conclude that they will never be happy again.

Depression is accompanied by physical changes as well. The depressed person may overeat or stop eating, have difficulty falling asleep or sleeping through the night, have trouble concentrating, and feel tired all the time. Some sufferers have other physical reactions, such as headaches or inexplicable pain.

Major depression occurs at least twice as often among women as among men, all over the world. However, because women are more likely than men to talk about their feelings and more likely to seek help, depression in males is probably underdiagnosed. Men who are depressed often try to mask their feelings by withdrawing, abusing drugs, or behaving violently (Canetto, 1992; Kessler et al., 1995). As Susan Nolen-Hoeksema, a leading depression researcher, put it, "Women think and men drink."

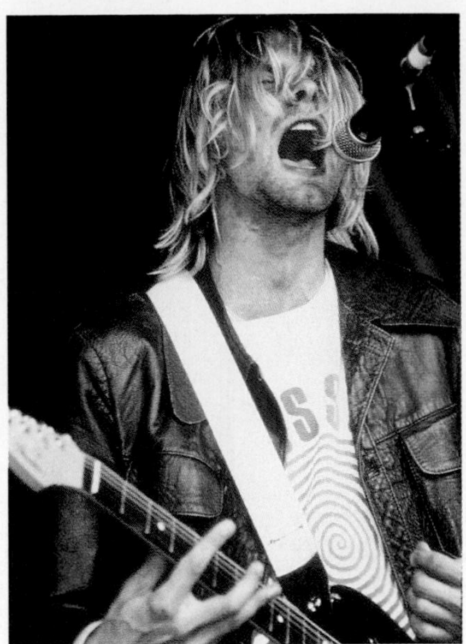

Even people who are rich, successful, and adored by millions can suffer from major depression. The suicide of Nirvana's lead singer, Kurt Cobain, shocked and saddened his many fans.

Bipolar Disorder

At the opposite pole from depression is *mania*, an abnormally high state of exhilaration. You might think it's impossible to feel too good, but mania is not the normal joy of being in love or winning the Pulitzer Prize. Instead of feeling fatigued and listless, the manic person is excessively wired and often irritable when thwarted. Instead of feeling hopeless and powerless, the person feels powerful and is full of plans; but these plans are usually based on delusional ideas, such as thinking that he or she has solved the world's problems. People in a state of mania often get into terrible trouble, going on extravagant spending sprees, making impulsive and bad decisions, or having risky sexual adventures.

When people experience at least one episode of mania alternating with episodes of depression, they are said to have **bipolar disorder** (formerly called *manic-depressive disorder*). This is a rarer problem than depression and distinctly different. Although more women than men suffer from depression, bipolar disorder occurs equally in both sexes. The great humorist Mark Twain had bipolar disorder, which he described as "periodical and sudden changes of mood . . . from deep melancholy to half-insane tempests and cyclones." Other writers, artists, musicians, and scientists have suffered from this disorder (Jamison, 1992). During the highs, many of these artists create their best work, but the price of the lows is disastrous relationships, bankruptcy, and sometimes suicide.

Origins of Depression

Psychologists have investigated many different contributing factors to major depression: genetic factors, life experiences, problems with close attachments, and cognitive habits. Few researchers think that any one of these factors alone produces chronic depression. Most researchers now emphasize a **vulnerability-stress model** of mental disorders, in which a person's vulnerabilities (in genetic predispositions, personality traits, or habits of thinking) interact with stressful events (such as sexual victimization, violence,

bipolar disorder A mood disorder in which episodes of both depression and mania (excessive euphoria) occur.

vulnerability-stress models Approaches that emphasize how individual vulnerabilities interact with external stresses or circumstances to produce mental disorders.

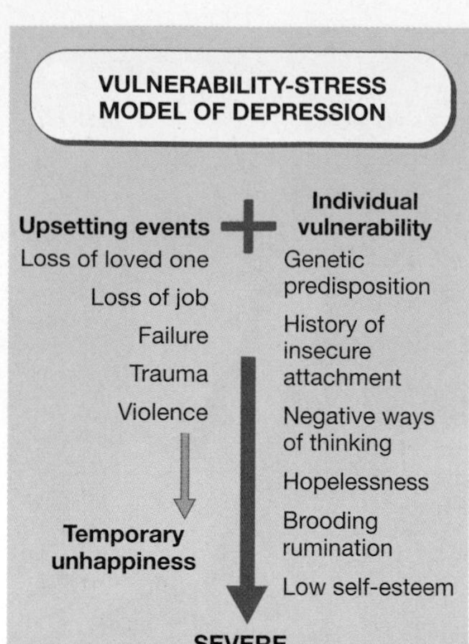

or loss of a close relationship) to produce any given case (Hankin & Abramson, 2001). Let's consider the evidence for each contributing factor in depression:

1 **Genetic factors.** Studies of adopted children and twins support the notion that major depression is a moderately heritable disorder (Bierut et al., 1999). Psychologists are hunting for the genes that might be involved, although it is unlikely that a single gene directly or inevitably "causes" severe depression. As in the case of posttraumatic stress disorder, a genetic predisposition must interact with stressful events to create the disorder.

Psychologists have identified one gene (called 5-HTT) that comes in two forms: a long form that apparently helps protect people from depression, and a short form that makes them more vulnerable to it (Caspi et al., 2003). In a study of 847 New Zealanders who were followed from birth to age 26, the researchers found that 43 percent of those who possessed two copies of the short form of this gene (one from each parent) became severely depressed in the aftermath of major stress (such as the loss of a job, disabling injuries, a death in the family, or abuse suffered in childhood). Yet only 17 percent of those with two copies of the long form of this gene became depressed, even when they suffered the same stresses. And people who inherited one long form of the gene from one parent and a short form from the other fell in between in their susceptibility to depression (33 percent).

Genes may exert their effects on depression by affecting levels of serotonin and other neurotransmitters in the brain. Genes may also affect production of the stress hormone cortisol, which, at high levels, can damage cells in the hippocampus and amygdala (Sapolsky, 2000; Sheline, 2000). In depressed patients, the system that regulates reactions to stress is in overdrive; it doesn't shut down when it should, and it keeps overproducing cortisol (Plotsky, Owens, & Nemeroff, 1998). Nonetheless, genes cannot account for all cases of depression; even among the New Zealanders with the greatest genetic vulnerability, more than half did not become depressed. Nor do genes seem to account for the sex difference in depression rates. In the New Zealand study, women were no more likely than men to have the short form of the 5-HTT gene.

2 **Life experiences and circumstances.** One powerful experience that often generates depression is violence. Inner-city adolescents of both sexes who are exposed to high rates of violence report higher levels of depression and more attempts to commit suicide than those who are not subjected to constant violence in their lives or communities (Mazza & Reynolds, 1999). Domestic violence also contributes to the higher rates of depression among women. One major longitudinal study followed men and women from ages 18 to 26, and compared those in physically abusive relationships with those in nonabusive ones. Although depressed women are more likely to enter abusive relationships to begin with, involvement in a violent relationship independently increased their rates of depression and anxiety—but, interestingly, not men's (Ehrensaft, Moffitt, & Caspi, 2006). Women are also more likely than men to be sexually abused as children and young adults, which creates a higher risk of depression in adulthood (Weiss, Longhurst, & Mazure, 1999).

In addition, the conditions of people's lives—the roles they occupy, their status, their satisfaction with work and family—can affect their likelihood of becoming depressed. Men are more likely than women to be both married and working full time, a combination of roles that is strongly associated with mental health and lower rates of depression (Brown, 1993). Women are more likely than men to live in poverty and suffer from discrimination, two additional sources of depression (Belle & Doucet, 2003).

3 Losses of important relationships. A third line of investigation emphasizes the loss of important relationships in setting off depression in vulnerable individuals. Many depressed people have a history of separations and losses, both past and present; insecure attachments; and rejection by parents or peers (Nolan, Flynn, & Garber, 2003; Weissman, Markowitz, & Klerman, 2000).

4 Cognitive habits. Finally, depression involves specific, negative ways of thinking about one's situation (Beck, 2005). Typically, depressed people believe that their situation is *permanent* ("Nothing good will ever happen to me") and *uncontrollable* ("I'm depressed because I'm ugly and horrible and I can't do anything about it"). Expecting nothing to get better, they do nothing to improve their lives and therefore remain unhappy. They feel hopeless and pessimistic, believing that nothing good will ever happen to them and that they are powerless to change the future (Abramson, Metalsky, & Alloy, 1989; Seligman, 1991).

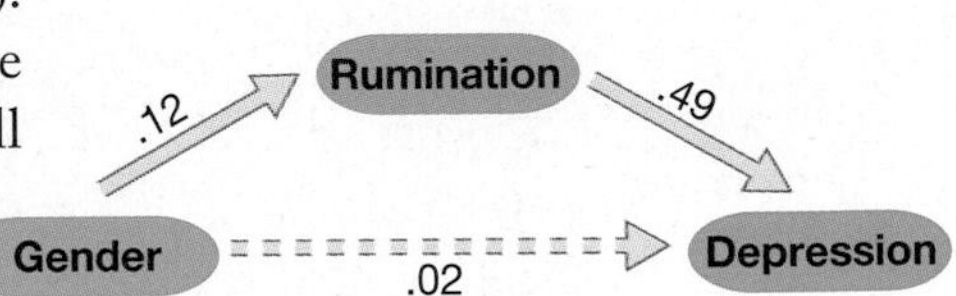

FIGURE 16.2 Gender and Depression

Women are far more likely than men to ruminate and brood when they are sad. This mental habit, however, can easily turn into depression. As the correlations show, the relationship between gender and depression is itself almost insignificant. But women are more likely to ruminate, and rumination, when combined with stressful experiences, is very highly correlated with depression (Nolen-Hoeksema, 2004).

One of the strongest bad cognitive habits associated with depression is *rumination*—brooding about everything that is wrong in your life, sitting alone thinking about how unmotivated you feel, and persuading yourself that no one loves you or ever will. People with ruminating cognitive styles that foster hopelessness are at greater risk of developing full-blown major depression than are people who are able to distract themselves, look outward, and seek solutions (Chorpita & Barlow, 1998). Beginning in adolescence, women are much more likely than men to develop a ruminating, introspective style, rehearsing the reasons for their unhappiness. This tendency contributes both to longer-lasting depressions in women and to the sex difference in reported rates, as you can see in Figure 16.2 (Nolen-Hoeksema, 2004).

CLOSE-UP on Research

RUMINATION VERSUS REFLECTION

The findings about rumination are pretty interesting, because just about all of us know what it feels like to think that everything is hopeless, to brood over hurt feelings, to rehearse real and imagined insults ("who does she thinks she is, anyway?"), and to wallow in our anxieties ("I'm never going to do well in this course—I can't possibly keep up"). When we think of examples like these, we can see why rumination might keep us stuck in an anxious, angry, or gloomy frame of mind. Three psychological scientists—Ethan Kross, Ozlem Ayduk, and Walter Mischel (2005)—decided to **ask questions** about this common mental habit, such as "How does rumination differ from thinking about a problem constructively?" and "How can we face our normal, negative emotions without becoming overwhelmed by them?" They **examined the widespread assumption** that often it is necessary to confront anxiety, anger, and depression in order to learn to regulate and manage them. They wanted to reconcile the findings on rumination with the finding, discussed in Chapter 15, that often the confession of negative feelings is directly beneficial to your health and well-being. When is it a good idea to think about what's wrong in your life, and when do such thoughts become self-defeating?

The researchers did an experiment that demonstrated why we should **not oversimplify** this question. Perhaps, they hypothesized, it's not rumination alone, but a kind of rumination, that prolongs depression and other negative emotions. As they **defined their terms**, they first distinguished "hot" thoughts from "cool" ones. Hot thoughts are reflexive, automatic, and emotionally arousing ("That rat! How dare he treat me that way!"). Cool thoughts are distanced, calmer, and more reflective ("It's very odd for him to be acting in that rat-like way. I wonder what's going on with him"). They next distinguished "self-immersed" thinking from taking a "self-distancing" perspective. When you are "self-immersed," you can't think beyond your own immediate feelings or what is happening to *you*. When you distance yourself, you can see yourself as another person might, more dispassionately, because your ego isn't as involved.

The investigators asked 155 students to think about an experience in which they felt overwhelming anger and hostility. Half of the students were instructed to recall this experience in a self-immersed way ("relive the situation as if it were happening to you all over again") and the other half, in a self-distancing way ("take a few steps back . . . watch the conflict unfold as if it were happening all over again to the distant you"). Each group was split in half again, with some asked to focus on *what* they were feeling and the others to focus on *why* they were feeling it. As you can see in the accompanying figure, the students who both distanced themselves from the experience and tried to explain the reasons for it (the "whys") felt less angry and upset overall than did any of the other groups.

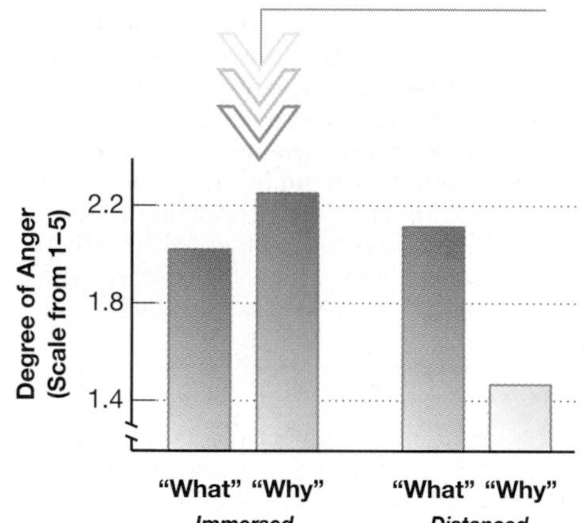

The researchers did not examine the particular kind of rumination that is involved in depression, and so we will have to **tolerate uncertainty** until the results are replicated to see if they will apply to that emotion, too. If they do, we may learn that one reason that rumination prolongs depression is that it tends to be "hot" and self-focused. Learning to take a cooler perspective, on our feelings and on our own behavior, can help us break out of negative emotions instead of feeding them and keeping them alive. This strategy is, in fact, the basis of cognitive therapy, which we will discuss in the next chapter.

The factors we have described, ranging from genetics to jobs, from what happens in people's lives to how they think about it, combine in different ways to produce any given case of depression. That is why the same precipitating event can affect two people entirely differently: why one is able to roll with the punches of life and another is knocked flat.

QUICK quiz

Don't let another quiz make you vulnerable to depression!

1. Biological researchers find that depressed people have unusually high levels of the stress hormone __________.
2. Depressed people tend to believe that the reasons for their unhappiness are (a) controllable, (b) temporary, (c) out of their hands, (d) caused by the situation.
3. A news headline announces that a gene has been identified as the cause of depression. Does this mean that everyone with the gene will become depressed? How should critical thinkers interpret this research?

Answers:

1. cortisol 2. c 3. No, it means that people with the gene are *more likely* to become depressed if they also undergo severely stressful experiences. Critical thinkers would also want to make sure the research is replicated, and they would realize that not all kinds of depression might be influenced by genetics.

WHAT'S**AHEAD**

- When does being self-centered become a disorder?
- What do a charming but heartless tycoon and a remorseless killer have in common?
- Why are some people seemingly incapable of feeling guilt and shame?

Personality Disorders

Personality disorders involve unchanging, maladaptive traits that cause great distress or an inability to get along with others. The DSM-IV describes such a disorder as "an enduring pattern of inner experience and behavior that deviates markedly from the expectations of the individual's culture [and] is pervasive and inflexible." Personality disorders are not caused by medical conditions, stress, or situations that temporarily induce a person to behave in ways that are out of character.

Narcissus fell in love with his own image, and now he has a personality disorder named after him—just what a narcissist would expect!

Problem Personalities

Personality disorders come in many varieties. **Paranoid personality disorder** involves pervasive, unfounded suspiciousness and mistrust of other people, irrational jealousy, secretiveness, and doubt about the loyalty of others. People with paranoid personalities have delusions of being persecuted by everyone from their closest relatives to government agencies, and their beliefs are immune to disconfirming evidence.

Narcissistic personality disorder involves an exaggerated sense of self-importance and self-absorption. The word *narcissism* gets its name from the Greek myth of Narcissus, a beautiful young man who fell in love with his own image. Narcissistic individuals are preoccupied with fantasies of their own importance, power, and brilliance. They demand constant attention and admiration and feel entitled to special favors, without, however, being willing to reciprocate.

Borderline personality disorder characterizes people who have a history of intense but unstable relationships in which they alternate between idealizing the partner and then devaluing the partner. They frantically try to avoid real or imagined abandonment by others, even if the "abandonment" is only a friend's brief vacation. They have profoundly unrealistic self-images. They are self-destructive and impulsive, often spending too much, abusing drugs, cutting themselves, and threatening to commit suicide. And they are emotionally volatile, careening from anger to euphoria to anxiety.

Notice that although these descriptions evoke flashes of recognition ("I know that type!"), it is hard to know where value judgments end (say, that someone is self-absorbed or suspicious) and a clear disorder begins (Maddux & Mundell, 1997). Cultures differ too in how they draw the line. American society often encourages people to pursue dreams of unlimited success, physical beauty, and ideal love, but such dreams might be considered signs of serious disturbance in a more group-oriented society. How would you distinguish between having a narcissistic personality disorder and being a normal member of a group or culture that encourages putting your own needs ahead of those of your family and friends and puts a premium on youth and beauty?

paranoid personality disorder A disorder characterized by unreasonable, excessive suspiciousness and mistrust, and irrational feelings of being persecuted by others.

narcissistic personality disorder A disorder characterized by an exaggerated sense of self-importance and self-absorption.

borderline personality disorder A disorder characterized by intense but unstable relationships, a fear of abandonment by others, an unrealistic self-image, and emotional volatility.

psychopathy A personality disorder characterized by a lack of remorse, empathy, anxiety, and other social emotions; the use of deceit and manipulation; and impulsive thrill seeking.

antisocial personality disorder (APD) A personality disorder characterized by a lifelong pattern of irresponsible, antisocial behavior such as lawbreaking, violence, and other impulsive, reckless acts.

Criminals and Psychopaths

Throughout history, people have been fascinated and horrified by the "bad seeds" among them—people who, even as children, are ready to break the rules and seem unable to be socialized. Societies have also recognized and feared the few members in their midst who lack all human connection to anyone else, people who can cheat, con, and kill without flinching. (In the 1800s these individuals were said to be afflicted with "moral insanity.")

In 1976, in his influential book *The Mask of Sanity*, Hervey Cleckley popularized and standardized the term *psychopath* to describe a person who lacks all conscience. A key characteristic of **psychopathy**, said Cleckley, is an inability to feel normal emotions. Psychopaths are incapable not only of remorse but also of fear of punishment and of shame, guilt, and empathy for the misery they cause others. Because they lack emotional connections to others, they often behave cruelly and irresponsibly—usually more for the thrill than for personal gain.

If caught in a lie or a crime, psychopaths may seem sincerely sorry and promise to make amends, but it is all an act. They can be utterly charming, but they use their charm to manipulate and deceive others (Cleckley, 1976; Hare, Hart, & Harpur, 1991). Some psychopaths are violent and sadistic, able to kill a pet, a child, or a random adult without a twinge of regret, but others direct their energies into con games or career advancement, abusing other people emotionally or economically rather than physically (Robins, Tipp, & Przybeck, 1991). A leading researcher in this field, Robert Hare, calls corporate psychopaths "snakes in suits."

In the 1990s, the clinicians who were revising the DSM decided to replace the term *psychopathy* with **antisocial personality disorder (APD)**, which applies to people who show "a pervasive pattern of disregard for, and violation of, the rights of others." People with APD repeatedly break the law; they are impulsive and seek quick thrills; they show reckless disregard for their own safety or that of others; they often get into physical fights or assault others; and they are irresponsible, failing to hold jobs or meet obligations (Widiger et al., 1996). Crucially for the diagnosis, they have had a history of these behavioral problems since childhood; they aren't just teenage delinquents who have been hanging out with a bad peer group. In people with APD, as one researcher found, rule breaking and irresponsibility start in early childhood and then take different forms at different ages: "biting and hitting at age 4, shoplifting and tru-

Some people with APD are sadistic and violent. Gary L. Ridgway (left), the deadliest convicted serial killer in U.S. history, strangled 48 women, placing their bodies in "clusters" around the country. He did this because, he said coolly, he wanted to keep track of them. "I killed so many women, I have a hard time keeping them straight," he told the court. But other people with APD use charm and elaborate scams to deceive and defraud. Babyfaced Christopher Rocancourt (right photo, wearing tie), shown with actor Mickey Rourke, conned celebrities and others into giving him money and doing him favors (some illegal) by adopting countless false identities, such as movie producer, cat burglar, diamond smuggler, or financier. After he was finally arrested on charges of passport counterfeiting, he persuaded authorities to free him on bond—and promptly jumped bail.

ancy at age 10, selling drugs and stealing cars at age 16, robbery and rape at age 22, and fraud and child abuse at age 30" (Moffitt, 1993). The DSM criteria for diagnosing APD also include "lack of remorse," the prime feature of psychopathy, but this entry is far down on the list and is not essential for the diagnosis.

The DSM made the change in labeling to emphasize the *behavioral* signs of antisocial personality disorder. But to many clinicians, the defining essence of psychopaths is their heartlessness and conniving charm. People who commit violent crimes may be antisocial, reckless, and irresponsible, these clinicians point out, yet differ greatly in their motivations for behaving this way. People with APD also vary widely in their capacity for empathy, remorse, guilt, anxiety, or loyalty (Hare, Hart, & Harpur, 1991). Thus, not all people with APD are psychopaths. Conversely, as we just noted, not all psychopaths are "antisocial" and aggressive in the typical ways that people with APD are. However, sometimes the two disorders converge, as in the case of sadistic, "cold-blooded" killers.

Researchers have identified a number of factors involved in these disorders.

1 **Abnormalities in the central nervous system.** Something certainly seems to be amiss in the emotional wiring of psychopaths, the wiring that allows all primates, not just human beings, to feel connected to others of their kind. When that wiring goes awry, even some chimpanzees will behave in ways that are comparable to the actions of human psychopaths. They, too, deceive and manipulate others to get their way and they are unmoved by the suffering of others of their kind (Lilienfeld et al., 1999a).

The psychopath's inability to feel emotional arousal—empathy, guilt, fear of punishment, and anxiety under stress—suggests some aberration in the central nervous system (Hare, 1965, 1996; Lykken, 1995; Raine et al., 2000). Indeed, psychopaths do not respond physiologically to the threat of punishment the way other people do; this may be why they can behave fearlessly in situations that would scare others to death. Normally, when a person is anticipating danger, pain, or punishment, the electrical conductance of the skin changes, a classically conditioned response that indicates anxiety or fear. But psychopaths are slow to develop such responses, which suggests that they are unable to feel the anxiety necessary for learning that their actions will have unpleasant consequences (see Figure 16.3). Their lack of empathy for others who are suffering also seems to have a physiological basis. When psychopaths are shown pictures of people crying and in distress, their skin conductance barely shifts, in contrast to that of nonpsychopaths, which shoots up (Blair et al., 1997).

This emotional flatness may help distinguish psychopaths from other aggressive people with antisocial personality disorder (Lorber, 2004). For example, antisocial, violent adolescents who have normal levels of physiological arousal in response to danger and threat, and whose responses can be classically conditioned, do not usually get involved in a life of crime as adults, suggesting that they "outgrow" the disorder with maturity (Raine & Liu, 1998). But those who are likely to become career criminals have the same unusually low levels of physiological arousal that psychopaths do.

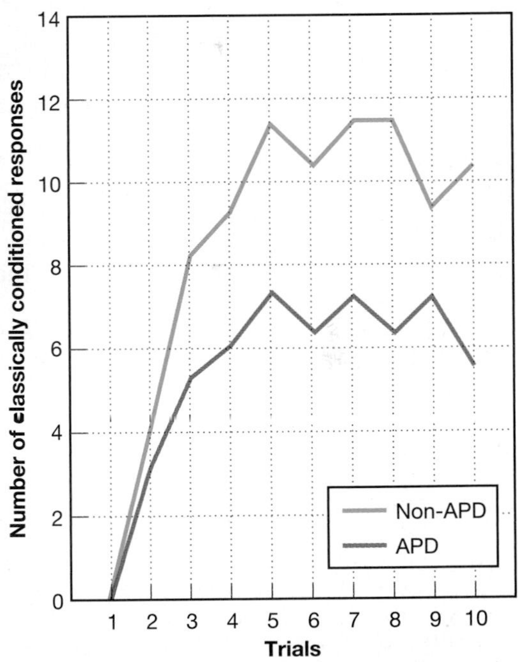

FIGURE 16.3 Emotions and Antisocial Personality Disorder

In several experiments, people with antisocial personality disorder (APD) were slow to develop classically conditioned responses to anticipated danger, pain, or shock—responses that indicate normal anxiety. This deficit may be related to the ability of psychopaths to behave in destructive ways without remorse or regard for the consequences (Hare, 1965, 1993).

2 **Impaired frontal-lobe functioning.** One trait shared by psychopaths and people with APD is impulsivity, an inability to control responses to frustration and provocation (Luengo et al., 1994; Raine, 1996). Such an inability, which often leads to breaking rules and laws, may have a biological basis. Many psychopaths have abnormalities in the prefrontal cortex, which, as we saw in Chapter 4, is responsible for planning and impulse control. They don't do as well as other individuals on neuropsychological tests of frontal-lobe functioning, and they have less gray matter in the frontal lobes than other

people do (Dinn & Harris, 2000). One PET-scan study found that cold-blooded "predatory" murderers had less brain activity in the frontal lobe than did men who murdered in the heat of passion or controls who had not murdered anybody (Raine et al., 1998).

One reason for these frontal-lobe abnormalities may be brain damage resulting from physical neglect, accidents, battering, or injury. Men convicted of violent crimes are more likely than nonviolent criminals and noncriminals to have been severely battered as children (Lewis, 1992; Milner & McCanne, 1991; Raine et al., 2001). And an in-depth analysis of two young adults whose prefrontal cortex was damaged in infancy—one was run over by a car when she was 15 months old and the other had a brain tumor removed—showed that both grew up to be compulsive liars, thieves, and heartless rule breakers. They could not hold jobs or plan for the future, could not distinguish right from wrong, and lacked empathy (Anderson et al., 1999).

3 **Genetic influences.** More than 100 studies have investigated the role of genetic influences, and meta-analyses find that genes account for 40 to 50 percent of the variation in antisocial behavior (Moffitt, 2005). In a longitudinal study of boys who had been physically abused in childhood, those who had a deficiency in a crucial gene later had far more arrests for violent crimes than did abused boys who had a normal gene (Caspi et al., 2002). Although only 12 percent of the abused boys had this genetic deficiency, they accounted for nearly half of all later convictions for violent crimes. However, boys who had the deficient gene but who were not maltreated did not grow up to be violent.

In short, as with depression and other disorders, the causes of psychopathy and APD reflect an interaction between an individual's own genetic or biological vulnerabilities and experiences or stressors, in this case physical abuse, parental neglect or rejection, or living in a subculture that rewards ruthlessness and hard-heartedness.

QUICK quiz

There is no such things as Test-Avoidance Personality Disorder, so take this quiz.

A. Can you diagnose each of the following disorders?

1. Ann can barely get out of bed in the morning. She feels that life is hopeless and despairs of ever feeling good about herself.

2. Connie constantly feels a sense of impending doom; for days her heart has been beating rapidly, and she can't relax.

3. Damon is totally absorbed in his own feelings and wishes.

4. Edna has a long history of unstable relationships, emotional ups and downs, and an intense fear of being abandoned.

5. Finn is the most charming of con artists; he can rob a widow of her life's savings without flinching.

B. What is the central difference in the diagnosis of psychopathy and antisocial personality disorder?

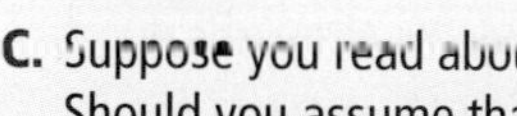

C. Suppose you read about a brutal assault committed by a gang member during a robbery. Should you assume that he has antisocial personality disorder? Why or why not?

Answers:

A. 1. major depression **2.** generalized anxiety disorder **3.** narcissistic personality disorder **4.** borderline personality disorder **5.** psychopathy **B.** Psychopathy is characterized by lack of remorse, guilt, shame, and empathy, whereas antisocial personality disorder is characterized by a lifelong history of reckless rule breaking, aggression, and irresponsibility. **C.** Committing a violent act does not necessarily mean a person has antisocial personality disorder. This gang member may have acted violently as a way of conforming to the norms of his fellow gang members or because he felt afraid of getting caught during the robbery.

- In what ways might genes contribute to alcoholism?
- Why is alcoholism more common in Ireland than in Italy?
- Why don't policies of abstinence from alcohol reduce problem drinking?
- If you take morphine to control chronic pain, does that mean you will become addicted to it?

Drug Abuse and Addiction

Most people who use drugs (legal, illegal, or prescription) use them in moderation; but some people depend too much on them, and others abuse drugs even at the cost of their own health. The DSM-IV defines *substance abuse* as "a maladaptive pattern of substance use leading to clinically significant impairment or distress." Symptoms of such impairment include failure to hold a job, care for children, or complete schoolwork; use of the drug in hazardous situations (e.g., while driving a car or operating machinery); and frequent conflicts with others about use of the drug or as a result of using the drug.

In Chapter 5, we described the major psychoactive drugs and their effects. In this section, focusing on the example of alcoholism, we will consider the two dominant approaches to understanding addiction and drug abuse—the biological model and the learning model—and then see how they might be reconciled.

Biology and Addiction

The *biological model* holds that addiction, whether to alcohol or any other drug, is due primarily to a person's biochemistry, metabolism, and genetic predisposition. Most of the genetic evidence comes from twin and family studies of alcoholism. These studies show that although genes are involved, it is too simple to say, as some people do, that "genes cause alcoholism." Evidence of an inherited vulnerability to alcohol is stronger for men than for women, but even this link depends on the *kind* of alcoholism (Cloninger, 1990; Goodwin et al., 1994; McGue, 1999; Schuckit & Smith, 1996). There is a heritable component in the kind of alcoholism that begins in adolescence and is linked to impulsivity, antisocial behavior, and criminality (Bohman et al., 1987; McGue, 1999). But for male alcoholics who begin drinking heavily in adulthood, genetic factors are only weakly involved, if at all.

For a while researchers thought they had found an "alcoholism gene" that affected brain receptors for dopamine, a neurotransmitter involved in the sensation of pleasure. This hypothesis has not been well supported (Plomin & McGuffin, 2003). Actually, the strongest evidence to date is not that genes are involved with alcoholism but with protection *against* alcoholism. There is a genetic factor that causes low activity of an enzyme that is important in the metabolism of alcohol. People who lack this enzyme respond to alcohol with unpleasant symptoms, such as flushing and nausea. This genetic protection is common among Asians but rare among Europeans, which may be one reason that rates of alcoholism are much lower in Asian than in Caucasian populations—the Asian sensitivity to alcohol discourages them from drinking a lot (Heath et al., 2003). On the other hand, Native Americans often have the same genetic protection that Asians do, yet they have much higher rates of alcoholism.

Within populations, genes might contribute to traits or temperaments (such as impulsivity) that predispose a person to become alcoholic. Genes may also affect how much a person needs to drink before feeling high. In an ongoing longitudinal study of

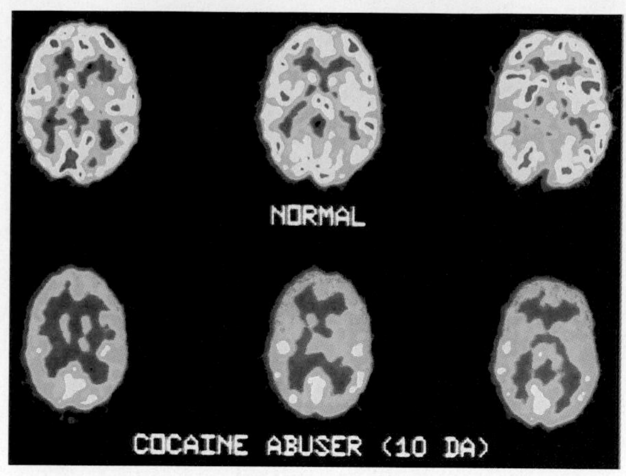

FIGURE 16.4 The Addicted Brain

PET studies show that the brains of cocaine addicts have fewer receptors for dopamine, a neurotransmitter involved in pleasurable sensations. (The more yellow and red in the brain image, the more receptors.) The brains of people addicted to methamphetamine, alcohol, and even food show a similar dopamine deficiency (Volkow et al., 2001).

450 young men, those who at age 20 had to drink more than others to feel any reaction were at increased risk of becoming alcoholic within the decade. This was true regardless of their initial drinking habits or family history of alcoholism (Schuckit, 1998; Schuckit & Smith, 1996). Some people may inherit not only a general susceptibility to substance abuse but also a vulnerability to specific drugs—such as nicotine (Tsuang et al., 2001). As with so many other disorders, however, tracking down the genes involved has been difficult.

The usual way of looking at the relationship between biological factors and addiction is to assume that the former cause the latter. However, there is strong evidence that the relationship also works the other way: *Addictions can result from the abuse of drugs* (Crombag & Robinson, 2004). Drugs change the brain. Heavy drinking alters brain function, reduces the level of painkilling endorphins, produces nerve damage, shrinks the cerebral cortex, and damages the liver. As you can see in Figure 16.4, heavy use of alcohol, cocaine, heroin, methamphetamine, or other drugs also reduces the number of receptors for dopamine (Volkow et al., 2001). These changes can then create addiction, a craving for more of the drug. Thus, drug abuse, which begins as a voluntary action, can turn into drug addiction, a compulsive behavior that the addict finds almost impossible to control.

Learning, Culture, and Addiction

The *learning model* examines the role of the environment, learning, and culture in encouraging or discouraging drug abuse and addiction. Four major findings underscore the importance of understanding these factors:

1 **Addiction patterns vary according to cultural practices and the social environment.** Alcoholism is much more likely to occur in societies that forbid children to drink but condone drunkenness in adults (as in Ireland) than in societies that teach children how to drink responsibly and moderately but condemn adult drunkenness (as in Italy, Greece, and France). In cultures with low rates of alcoholism (except for those committed to a religious rule that forbids use of all psychoactive drugs), adults demonstrate correct drinking habits to their children, gradually introducing them to alcohol in safe family settings. Alcohol is not used as a rite of passage into adulthood, nor is it associated with masculinity and power (Peele & Brodsky, 1991; Vaillant, 1983). Abstainers are not sneered at, and drunkenness is not considered charming, comical, or manly; it is considered stupid or obnoxious.

Within a particular country, addiction rates can rise or fall rapidly in response to cultural changes. In colonial America, the average person actually drank two to three times the amount of liquor consumed today, yet alcoholism was not a serious problem. Drinking was a universally accepted social activity; families drank and ate together. Alcohol was believed to produce pleasant feelings and relaxation, and Puritan ministers endorsed its use (Critchlow, 1986). Then, between 1790 and 1830, when the American frontier was expanding, drinking came to symbolize masculine independence and toughness. The saloon became the place for drinking away from home. As people stopped drinking in moderation, with their families, alcoholism rates shot up—as the learning model would predict.

Substance abuse and addiction problems also increase when people move from their culture of origin into another that has different drinking rules (Westermeyer, 1995). For example, in most Latino cultures, such as those of Mexico and Puerto Rico, drinking

THINKING CRITICALLY

ANALYZE ASSUMPTIONS AND BIASES

The disease model assumes that because the consequences of drug use are automatic, then if children are given any taste of a drink or a drug, they are more likely to become addicted. The learning model assumes that the cultural context is crucial in determining whether people will become addicted or learn to use drugs moderately. In fact, when children learn the rules of social drinking with their families, as at this Jewish family's seder (left), alcoholism rates are much lower than in cultures in which drinking occurs mainly in bars or in privacy. Likewise, when marijuana is used as part of a religious tradition, as it is by members of the Rastafarian church in Jamaica, use of the "wisdom weed" does not lead to addiction or harder drugs.

and drunkenness are considered male activities. Thus, Latina women tend to drink rarely, if at all, and they have few drinking problems—until they move into an Anglo environment, where their rates of alcoholism rise (Canino, 1994). Likewise, the cultural norm of moderate drinking among college women has been changing; college women are much more likely to drink in binges than they formerly were.

2 Policies of total abstinence tend to increase rates of addiction rather than reduce them. In the United States, the temperance movement of the early twentieth century held that drinking inevitably leads to drunkenness, and drunkenness to crime. The solution it won for the Prohibition years (1920 to 1933) was national abstinence. But this victory backfired: Again in accordance with the learning model, Prohibition reduced rates of drinking overall, but it *increased* rates of alcoholism among those who did drink. Because people were denied the opportunity to learn to drink moderately, they drank excessively when given the chance (McCord, 1989). And, of course, when a substance is forbidden, it becomes more attractive to some people. Most schools in America have zero-tolerance policies regarding marijuana and alcohol, but large numbers of students have tried them or use them regularly.

Historically, the United States has tried to eliminate drug abuse by promoting total abstinence. Here an 1880 woodcut shows a delegation from the women's temperance movement keeping records of men buying drinks, hoping to shame them into abstinence. Notice that in case that didn't work, a male ally has brought along a skunk to drive the men out of the bar!

3 Not all addicts have withdrawal symptoms when they stop taking a drug. When heavy users of a drug stop taking it, they often suffer such unpleasant symptoms as nausea, abdominal cramps, depression, and sleep problems, depending on the drug. But these symptoms are far from universal. During the Vietnam War, nearly 30 percent of American

soldiers were taking heroin in doses far stronger than those available on the streets of U.S. cities. These men believed themselves to be addicted, and experts predicted a drug-withdrawal disaster among the returning veterans. It never materialized; over 90 percent of the men simply gave up the drug, without significant withdrawal pain, when they came home to new circumstances (Robins, Davis, & Goodwin, 1974). Similarly, the majority of people who are addicted to cigarettes, tranquilizers, or painkillers are able to stop taking these drugs without outside help and without severe withdrawal symptoms (Prochaska, Norcross, & DiClemente, 1994). Many people find this information startling, even unbelievable. That is because people who can quit without help aren't entering programs to help them quit, so they are invisible to the general public and to the medical and therapeutic world! But they have been identified in random-sample community surveys.

One reason that many people are able, on their own, to quit abusing drugs is that the environment in which a drug is used (the setting) and a person's expectations (mental set) have a powerful influence on the drug's *physiological* effects as well as its psychological ones (see Chapter 5). For example, you might think a lethal dose of, say, amphetamines would be the same wherever the drug was taken. But studies of mice have found that the lethal dose varies depending on the mice's environment—whether they are in a large or small test cage, or whether they are alone or with other mice. Similarly, the physiological response of human addicts to certain drugs also changes, depending on whether the addicts are in a "druggy" environment, such as a crack house, or an unfamiliar one (Crombag & Robinson, 2004; Siegel, 2005). This is the primary reason that addicts need to change environments if they are going to kick their habits. It's not just to get away from a peer group that might be encouraging them, but also to literally change and "rewire" their brain's response to the drug.

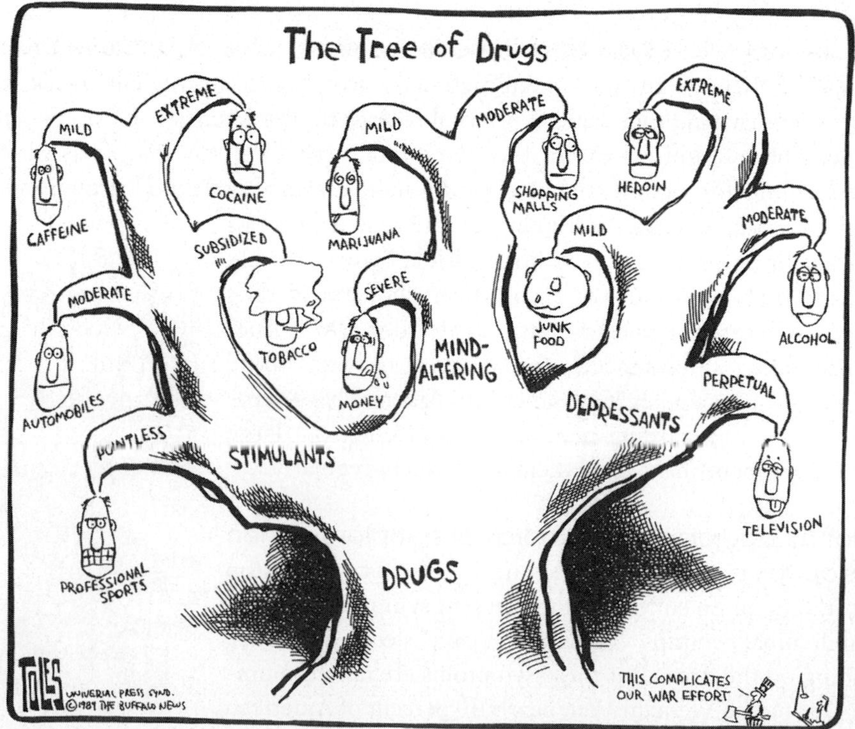

Most people assume that addictions are biochemical. This cartoon, by poking fun at the things people do to make themselves feel better, reminds us that a person can become dependent on many things besides alcohol or other drugs.

GET INVOLVED!

➤TEST YOUR MOTIVES FOR DRINKING

If you drink, why do you do so? Check all of the motives that apply to you:

_____ to relax
_____ to escape from worries
_____ to enhance a good meal
_____ to conform to peers
_____ to express anger
_____ to be sociable
_____ to cope with depression
_____ to get drunk and lose control
_____ to rebel against authority
_____ to relieve boredom
_____ other (specify)

Do your reasons promote abuse or responsible use? How do you respond physically to alcohol? What have you learned about drinking from your family, your friends, and cultural messages? What do your answers tell you about your own vulnerability to addiction?

4 Addiction does not depend on properties of the drug alone but also on the reasons for taking it. For decades, doctors were afraid to treat people with chronic pain by giving them narcotics, fearing they would become addicts. As a result of this belief, millions of people were condemned to live with chronic suffering from back pain, arthritis, nerve disorders, and other conditions. Then researchers found that the vast majority of pain sufferers—who use morphine and other opiates not to escape from the world, as addicts do, but to function in the world—do not become addicted (Portenoy, 1994). This was such good news that many researchers then went to the opposite extreme, optimistically believing that no one would become addicted to slow-release narcotic painkillers such as OxyContin. But again they underestimated the importance of the motives for taking the drugs. People who are searching for escape and euphoria will find a way to abuse *any* mood-altering drug, or, as many teenagers are now doing, to create drug "cocktails" to give them a high. That is why the abuse of narcotic painkillers and even the stimulants in flu medication has become a significant social problem.

In the case of alcohol, most people drink simply to be sociable, to conform to the group they are with, or to relax when they are stressed, and these people are unlikely to become addicted. *Problem* drinking occurs when people drink in order to disguise or suppress their anxiety or depression, or when they drink alone to drown their sorrows and forget their worries (Cooper et al., 1995; Mohr et al., 2001). College students who feel alienated and uninvolved with their studies are more likely than their happier peers to go binge drinking, with the conscious intention of getting drunk (Flacks & Thomas, 1998). In many cases, then, the decision to start abusing drugs depends more on your motives, and on the norms of your peer group, than on the chemical properties of the drug itself.

Debating the Causes of Addiction

The biological and learning models both contribute to our understanding of drug use and addiction. Yet, among many researchers and public-health professionals, these views are quite polarized, especially when it comes to thinking about treatment (see Review 16.1). The result is either–or thinking on a national scale: Either complete abstinence is the solution, or it is the problem. Those who advocate the disease model say that

alcoholics and problem drinkers must abstain completely. Those who champion the learning model argue that most problem drinkers can learn to drink moderately if they learn safe-drinking skills, acquire better ways of coping with stress, avoid situations that evoke conditioned responses to using drugs, and avoid friends who pressure them to drink excessively (Denning, Little, & Glickman, 2004; Marlatt et al., 1998; Sobell & Sobell, 1993).

How can we assess these two positions critically? Because alcoholism and problem drinking occur for many reasons, neither model offers the only solution. Many alcoholics cannot learn to drink moderately, especially if they have been drinking heavily for many years, by which time, as we saw earlier, physiological changes in their brains and bodies may have turned them from drug abusers into drug addicts. On the other hand, total-abstinence groups like Alcoholics Anonymous (AA) are ineffective for many people. According to its own surveys and those done independently, one-third to one-half of all people who join AA drop out. Many of these dropouts benefit from programs such as Harm Reduction, Rational Recovery, Moderation Management, and DrinkWise, which teach people how to drink moderately and keep their drinking under control (Denning, Little, & Glickman, 2004; Fletcher, 2001; Marlatt, 1996; Peele & Brodsky, 1991; Rosenberg, 1993).

AVOID EMOTIONAL REASONING

People disagree passionately about whether alcoholics can learn to drink moderately. How can we move beyond emotional reasoning on this contentious issue?

So instead of asking, "Can addicts and problem drinkers learn to drink moderately?" perhaps we should ask, "What are the factors that make it more or less likely that someone can learn to control problem drinking?" Problem drinkers who are most likely to become moderate drinkers have a history of less severe dependence on the drug. They lead more stable lives and have jobs and families. In contrast, those who are at greater risk of drug abuse or alcoholism have these risk factors: (1) They have a physiological vulnerability to a drug or have been using a drug long enough for it to damage or change their brain; (2) they believe that they have no control over the drug; (3) they live in a culture or a peer group that promotes and rewards binge drinking and discourages moderate drug use; and (4) they have come to rely on the drug as a way of avoiding problems, suppressing anger or fear, or coping with stress.

REVIEW 16.1

Biological and Learning Models of Addiction Contrasted

The biological and learning models of addiction differ in how they explain drug abuse and the solutions they propose:

The Biological Model	The Learning Model
Addiction is genetic, biological.	Addiction is a way of coping.
Once an addict, always an addict.	A person can grow beyond the need for alcohol or other drugs.
An addict must abstain from the drug forever.	Most problem drinkers can learn to drink in moderation.
A person is either addicted or not.	The degree of addiction will vary, depending on the situation.
The solution is medical treatment and membership in groups that reinforce one's permanent identity as a recovering addict.	The solution involves learning new coping skills and changing one's environment.
An addict needs the same treatment and group support forever.	Treatment lasts only until the person no longer abuses the drug.

SOURCE: Adapted from Peele & Brodsky, 1991.

If you are addicted to passing exams, answer these questions.

1. What is the most reasonable conclusion about the role of genes in alcoholism? (a) Without a key gene, a person cannot become alcoholic; (b) the presence of a key gene will almost always cause a person to become alcoholic; (c) genes may increase a person's vulnerability to some kinds of alcoholism.
2. Which cultural practice is associated with *low* rates of alcoholism? (a) gradual introduction to drinking in family settings, (b) infrequent binge drinking, (c) drinking as a rite of passage into adulthood, (d) policies of prohibition

3. In a national survey, 52 percent of American college students said they drink to get drunk and 42 percent said they usually binge when drinking. To reduce this problem, some schools and fraternities have instituted "zero-tolerance" programs. According to the research described in this section, are these programs likely to work? Why or why not?

Answers:

1. c 2. a 3. They are not likely to be successful because zero-tolerance programs do not address the *reasons* that students binge, do not affect the student culture that fosters binge drinking, and do not teach students how to drink moderately.

WHAT'S**AHEAD**

- Why are many clinicians and researchers skeptical about multiple personality disorder?
- Why did the number of "multiple personality" cases jump from a handful to many thousands in only a decade?

Dissociative Identity Disorder

In this section we will examine one of the most controversial diagnoses ever to arise in psychiatry and psychology: **dissociative identity disorder**, formerly and still popularly called *multiple personality disorder* (MPD). This label describes the apparent emergence, within one person, of two or more distinct identities, each with its own name, memories, and personality traits.

dissociative identity disorder A controversial disorder marked by the apparent appearance within one person of two or more distinct personalities, each with its own name and traits; formerly known as *multiple personality disorder (MPD).*

The MPD Controversy. Cases of multiple personality portrayed on TV, in popular books, and in films such as *The Three Faces of Eve* and *Sybil* have captivated the public for years, and they keep appearing. In 2005, Robert Oxnam wrote a book claiming that his alcoholism, bulimia, and rages were a result of having 11 competing "personalities," some old, some young, some male, some female. Among mental-health professionals, however, two competing views of MPD exist. On one side are those who think that MPD is common but often unrecognized or misdiagnosed. They believe the disorder originates in childhood as a means of coping with trauma, such as abuse (Gleaves, 1996). In this view, the trauma produces a mental "splitting" (*dissociation*): One personality emerges to handle everyday experiences, another personality (called an "alter") to cope with the bad ones. MPD patients are frequently described as having lived for years with several alters of which they were unaware until therapy.

On the other side are those who believe that most cases of MPD are unwittingly generated by clinicians themselves, during their interactions with vulnerable clients who have other psychological problems (Lilienfeld & Lohr, 2003). They point out that

"Would it be possible to speak with the personality that pays the bills?"

before 1980, only a handful of MPD cases had ever been diagnosed anywhere in the world; yet by the mid-1990s, *tens of thousands* of cases had been reported. (See Table 16.3.) MPD became a lucrative business, benefiting hospitals that opened MPD clinics, therapists who had a new disorder to treat, and psychiatrists and patients who wrote best-selling books. Skeptics think the sudden increase in cases was a sign that the disorder was being wildly overdiagnosed by its proponents. Clinicians who deeply believed in the prevalence of MPD may even have been creating the disorder in their clients through suggestive techniques, like hypnosis, and through the power of suggestion, sometimes bordering on coercion (Merskey, 1995; Rieber, 2006; Spanos, 1996).

You can see this pressure at work in the comments of psychiatrist Richard Kluft (1987), who wrote that efforts to determine the presence of MPD—that is, to get the person to reveal a "dissociated" personality—may require "between 2 1/2 and 4 hours of continuous interviewing. Interviewees must be prevented from taking breaks to regain composure . . . In one recent case of singular difficulty, the first sign of dissociation was noted in the 6th hour, and a definitive spontaneous switching of personalities occurred in the 8th hour." Mercy! After eight hours of "continuous interviewing" without a single break, how many of us wouldn't do what the interviewer wanted?

Clinicians who conducted such interrogations argued that they were merely *permitting* other personalities to reveal themselves. However, in numerous malpractice cases across the country, courts have ruled, on the basis of the testimony of scientific

TABLE 16.3
The Rise of Multiple Personality Disorder

1789	An early case is reported of a young German woman with several "personalities," including a French woman and a little boy.
1816	The first recorded case of "multiple personality" appears in the United States (Mary Reynolds).
1875	The condition is renamed "multiple personality" in France.
1886	Robert Louis Stevenson's *Dr. Jekyll and Mr. Hyde* popularizes the notion of two personalities in one body.
1957	*The Three Faces of Eve* is published and the film is released.
1960	**8 cases have been reported.**
1976	The movie *Sybil* is released.
1980	**The DSM includes the MPD diagnosis for the first time.**
1980	The book *Michelle Remembers* claims that "Satanic ritual abuse" is a leading cause of MPD.
1980–1991	Media coverage escalates in popular books and on talk shows that feature MPD "victims."
1985	Psychiatrist Richard Kluft claims to have treated 250 MPD patients.
1986	**6,000 cases have been reported in North America.**
1987	The first MPD inpatient treatment unit is established at Rush Presbyterian Hospital in Chicago; others follow across the country.
1995	**More than 40,000 cases have been reported in North America.**
1995	Diane Humenansky becomes the first psychiatrist found guilty of malpractice for inducing multiple personalities in a vulnerable patient.
1996–present	Other successful lawsuits are filed against major proponents of the MPD diagnosis and against treatment units in hospitals. Hospitals begin closing these units. Epidemic of cases subsides.

SOURCES: Acocella, 1999; Kenny, 1986; Loftus, 1996; Nathan, 1994; Pendergrast, 1995.

Why have the number of "alters" reported by people with MPD increased over the years? In the earliest cases, multiple personalities came only in pairs. In the 1886 story of *Dr. Jekyll and Mr. Hyde*, the kindly Dr. Jekyll turned into the murderous Mr. Hyde (shown in a scene from the movie, above, strangling his poor butler). At the height of the MPD epidemic in North America in the 1990s, people were claiming to have hundreds of alters, including cars and ducks.

experts in psychiatry and psychology, that it was more likely that these clinicians were actively *creating* personalities through suggestion and sometimes outright intimidation (Loftus, 1996). The MPD clinics in hospitals closed, psychiatrists became more wary, and the number of cases dropped sharply almost overnight.

The Sociocognitive Explanation. No one disputes that some troubled, highly imaginative individuals can produce many different "personalities" when asked. But the *sociocognitive explanation* of MPD holds that this phenomenon is simply an extreme form of the ability we all have to present different aspects of our personalities to others (Lilienfeld et al., 1999b). In this view, the diagnosis of MPD provides a culturally acceptable way for some troubled people to make sense of their problems (Hacking, 1995; Showalter, 1997). It allows them to account for sexual or criminal behavior that they now regret or find intolerably embarrassing; they can claim their "other personality did it." In turn, therapists who are looking for MPD reward such patients with attention and praise for revealing more and more personalities (Piper & Merskey, 2004).

THINKING CRITICALLY

CONSIDER OTHER INTERPRETATIONS

A man appeared on *60 Minutes* to talk about his new book, in which he described his 11 personalities—male and female, old and young. These emerged, he said, because he was sexually abused as a child. What else might explain how and why he developed "MPD"?

The story of the rise and fall of MPD offers an important lesson in critical thinking, because unskeptical media coverage of sensational MPD cases played a major role in fostering the rise of MPD diagnoses. When Canadian psychiatrist Harold Merskey (1992) reviewed the published cases of MPD, he was unable to find a single one in which a patient developed MPD without being influenced by the therapist's suggestions or reports about the disorder in books and the media. Even the famous case of "Sybil," a huge hit as a book, film, and television special, was a hoax. Sybil never had a traumatic childhood of sexual abuse, she did not have multiple personality disorder, and her "symptoms" were largely generated by her psychiatrist (Borch-Jacobson, 1997; Rieber, 2006).

Of course, there have been legitimate examples of this rare disorder. But even the authors of *The Three Faces of Eve* became alarmed by the media hype and proliferation of questionable cases. Thirty years later, they reported that of the hundreds of possible MPD cases that had been referred to them in the intervening years, they thought only one was a genuine multiple personality (Thigpen & Cleckley, 1984). Each case, therefore, must be examined on its own merits. But the story of MPD teaches us to think critically about disorders that become trendy: to consider other explanations, to examine assumptions and biases, and to demand good evidence.

QUICK quiz

Any one of your personalities may answer this question.

In August 2003, Donna Walker was arrested for trying to convince an Indiana couple that she was their long-missing daughter. She claimed that her "bad girl" personality (Allison) was responsible for this deception and also for her long history of perpetrating hoaxes on police, friends, and the media. Her "good girl" personality (Donna), she said, was a victim of childhood sexual abuse who spent years working as an FBI informant. The FBI verified that Walker had worked for them, although some of her reports were fabricated. One agent said that Walker has as many as seven personalities who come and go. As a critical thinker, what questions would you want to ask about Walker and her multiple-personality defense?

Answer:

Some possible questions to ask: Is there corroborating evidence for Walker's claims? (She said she was sexually abused from ages 4 to 13 by a family member and then by the minister of her church, and that she was sent to a psychiatric hospital at age 13.) How much of the rest of her life story can be independently corroborated? Did Walker only claim to have "other personalities" when she was in a jam with the law or was there evidence of MPD throughout her life? Could she have another mental disorder, such as schizophrenia or antisocial personality disorder?

WHAT'S**AHEAD**

- What's the difference between schizophrenia and a "split personality"?
- Is schizophrenia partly heritable?
- Could schizophrenia begin in the womb?

Schizophrenia

To be schizophrenic is best summed up in a repeating dream that I have had since childhood. In this dream I am lying on a beautiful sunlit beach but my body is in pieces. … I realize that the tide is coming in and that I am unable to gather the parts of my dismembered body together to run away. . . . This to me is what schizophrenia feels like; being fragmented in one's personality and constantly afraid that the tide of illness will completely cover me. (Quoted in Rollin, 1980)

In 1911, Swiss psychiatrist Eugen Bleuler coined the term **schizophrenia** to describe cases in which the personality loses its unity. Contrary to popular belief, people with schizophrenia do not have a "split" or "multiple" personality. As this haunting quotation illustrates, schizophrenia is a fragmented condition in which words are split from meaning, actions from motives, perceptions from reality. It is an example of a **psychosis**, a mental condition that involves distorted perceptions of reality and an inability to function in most aspects of life.

Symptoms of Schizophrenia

Schizophrenia is the cancer of mental illness: elusive, complex, and varying in form. The disorder involves the following symptoms:

1 **Bizarre delusions,** such as the belief that dogs are extraterrestrials disguised as pets. Some people with schizophrenia have delusions of identity, believing that they are Moses, Jesus, or another famous person. Some have paranoid delusions, taking innocent events—a stranger's cough, a helicopter overhead—as evidence that everyone is plotting against them. They often report that their thoughts have been inserted into their heads by someone controlling them or are being broadcast on television. Some, like Margaret Mary Ray, whose story opened this chapter, have delusions that a celebrity loves them.

2 **Hallucinations,** false sensory experiences that feel intensely real. By far the most common hallucination among people with schizophrenia is hearing voices; it is virtually a hallmark of the disease. Some sufferers of schizophrenia are so tormented by these voices that they commit suicide to escape them. One man described how he heard as many as 50 voices cursing him, urging him to steal other people's brain cells, or ordering him to kill himself. Once he picked up a ringing telephone and heard them screaming, "You're guilty!" over and over. They yelled "as loud as humans with megaphones," he told a reporter. "It was utter despair. I felt scared. They were always around" (Goode, 2003).

3 **Disorganized, incoherent speech,** consisting of an illogical jumble of ideas and symbols, linked by meaningless rhyming words or by remote associations called *word salads.* A patient of Bleuler's wrote, "Olive oil is an Arabian liquor-sauce which the Afghans, Moors and Moslems use in ostrich farming. The Indian plantain tree is

schizophrenia A psychotic disorder marked by delusions, hallucinations, disorganized and incoherent speech, inappropriate behavior, and cognitive impairments.

psychosis An extreme mental disturbance involving distorted perceptions and irrational behavior; it may have psychological or organic causes. (Plural: *psychoses.*)

the whiskey of the Parsees and Arabs. Barley, rice and sugar cane called artichoke, grow remarkably well in India. The Brahmins live as castes in Baluchistan. The Circassians occupy Manchuria and China. China is the Eldorado of the Pawnees" (Bleuler, 1911/1950).

4 Grossly disorganized and inappropriate behavior, which may range from childlike silliness to unpredictable and violent agitation. The person may wear three overcoats and gloves on a hot day, start collecting garbage, or hoard scraps of food.

5 Impaired cognitive abilities. People with schizophrenia do much worse than healthy people in almost every cognitive domain, especially verbal learning and recall of words and stories, language, perception, working memory, selective attention, and problem solving (Barch, 2003; Uhlhaas & Silverstein, 2005). Their speech is often impoverished; they make only brief, empty replies in conversation, because of diminished thought rather than an unwillingness to speak. Many of these cognitive impairments emerge in vulnerable children long before an actual schizophrenic breakdown occurs, and they last after the patient's psychotic symptoms subside as a result of medication (Heinrichs, 2005).

Other symptoms may appear months before hallucinations or delusions do, and they often persist even when more dramatic symptoms are in remission. For example, many people with schizophrenia lose the motivation to take care of themselves and interact with others; they may stop working or bathing, and become isolated and withdrawn. They seem emotionally "flat"; their facial expressions are unresponsive and they make poor eye contact. Some completely withdraw into a private world, sitting for hours without moving, a condition called *catatonic stupor.* (Catatonic states can also produce frenzied, purposeless behavior that goes on for hours.)

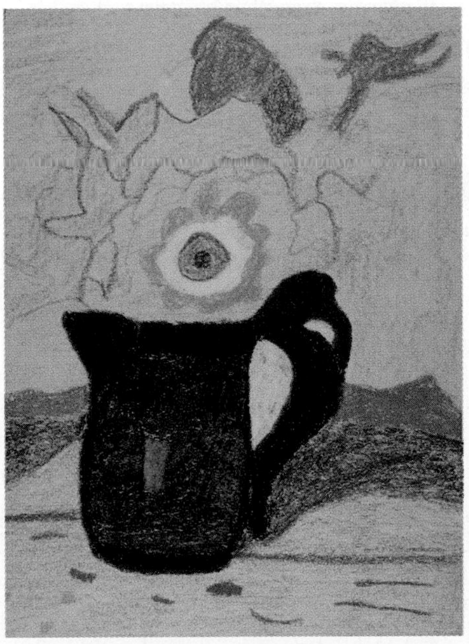

When people with schizophrenia are asked to draw pictures, their drawings are often distorted, lack color, include words, and reveal flat emotion. One patient was asked to copy a picture of flowers from a magazine (above). The initial result is shown below on the left. The drawing in the center shows improvement, and the drawing on the right shows how much the patient progressed after several months of treatment.

Although signs of schizophrenia may emerge early, the first full-blown psychotic episode typically occurs in late adolescence or early adulthood. In some individuals, the breakdown occurs suddenly; in others, it is more gradual, a slow change in personality. The more breakdowns and relapses the individual has had, the poorer the chances for complete recovery. Yet many people suffering from this illness learn to control the symptoms, often with the help of antipsychotic medication and community programs (see Chapter 17), and are able to work and have good family relationships (Harding, Zubin, & Strauss, 1992).

The mystery of this disease is that some people with schizophrenia are almost completely impaired in all spheres; others do well in certain areas. Still others have normal moments of lucidity in otherwise withdrawn lives. One adolescent crouched in a rigid catatonic posture in front of a television for the month of October; later, he was able to report on all the highlights of the World Series he had seen. A middle-aged man, hospitalized for 20 years, believing he was a prophet of God and that monsters were coming out of the walls, was able to interrupt his ranting to play a good game of chess (Wender & Klein, 1981).

Origins of Schizophrenia

Any disorder that has so many variations and symptoms will pose many problems for those trying to find its origins. Early psychodynamic and learning theories, which held that schizophrenia results from being raised by an erratic, cold, rejecting mother or from living in an unpredictable environment, have not been supported. Most researchers now believe that schizophrenia is caused by genetic problems that produce subtle abnormalities in the brain. As usual, however, genes must interact with certain stressors in the environment during prenatal development, birth, or adolescence. Here is some evidence on the contributing factors:

1 **Genetic predispositions.** A person has a much greater risk of developing schizophrenia if an identical twin develops the disorder, even if the twins are reared apart (Gottesman, 1991; Heinrichs, 2005). Children with one schizophrenic parent have a lifetime risk of 12 percent, and children with two schizophrenic parents have a lifetime risk of 35–46 percent, compared to a risk in the general population of only 1–2 percent (see Figure 16.5). In a Finnish study of identical twins, fully 83 percent of the variation in the risk of becoming schizophrenic was due to combined genetic factors and only 17 percent to unique environmental factors (Cannon et al., 1998). Researchers all over the world are trying to track down the genes that might be involved in specific symptoms, such as hallucinations, sensitivity to sounds, and cognitive impairments. One team has identified one such gene, called DISC1 or "disrupted-in-schizophrenia." Chromosomal aberrations on this gene are involved in schizophrenia and bipolar disorder, which share severe disturbances of emotion and cognition (Millar et al., 2005).

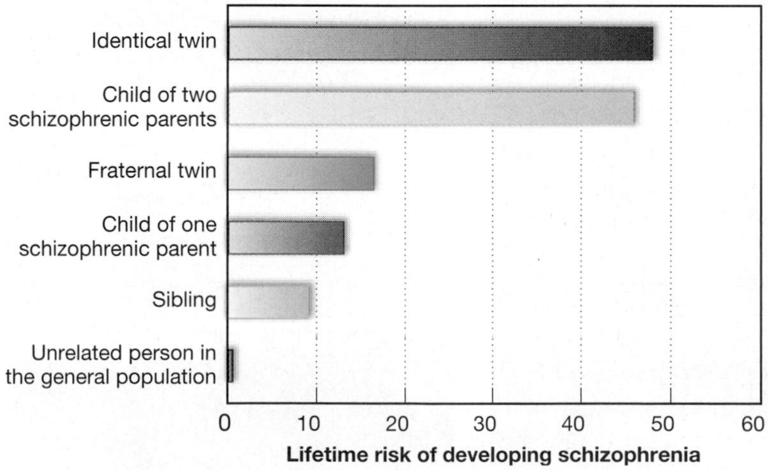

FIGURE 16.5 Genetic Vulnerability To Schizophrenia

This graph, based on combined data from 40 European twin and adoption studies conducted over seven decades, shows that the closer the genetic relationship to a person with schizophrenia, the higher the risk of developing the disorder. (Based on Gottesman, 1991.)

2 **Structural brain abnormalities.** Most individuals with schizophrenia have abnormalities in the brain,

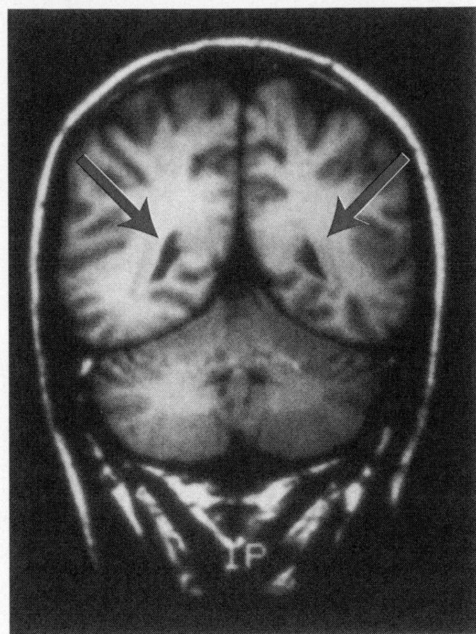

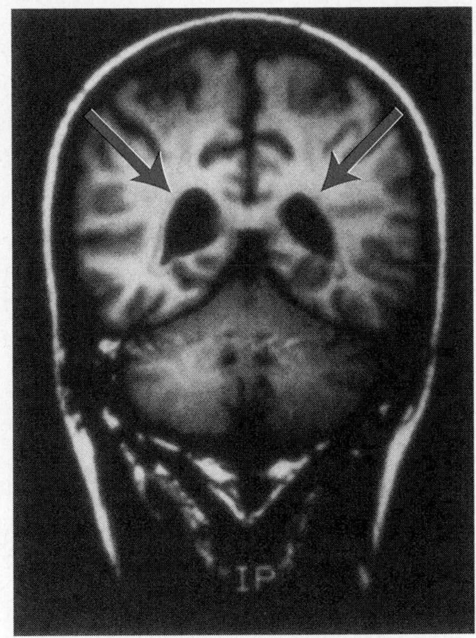

Healthy Schizophrenic

FIGURE 16.6 Schizophrenia and the Brain
People with schizophrenia are more likely to have enlarged ventricles (spaces) in the brain than healthy people are. These MRI scans of 28-year-old male identical twins show the difference in the size of ventricles between the healthy twin (left) and the one with schizophrenia (right).

including a decrease in the volume of the temporal lobe or hippocampus, reduced numbers of neurons in the prefrontal cortex, or enlargement of the *ventricles*, spaces in the brain that are filled with cerebrospinal fluid (see Figure 16.6) (Heinrichs, 2005; Zorrilla et al., 1997). Schizophrenics are also more likely than healthy individuals to have abnormalities in the thalamus, the traffic-control center that filters sensations and focuses attention (Andreasen et al., 1994; Gur et al., 1998). Schizophrenics also may have abnormalities in the auditory cortex and Broca's and Wernicke's areas, all involved in speech perception and processing. Such abnormalities might explain the nightmare of voice hallucinations.

3 **Neurotransmitter abnormalities.** Schizophrenia has been associated with abnormalities in several neurotransmitters, including serotonin, glutamate, and dopamine (Sawa & Snyder, 2002). However, similar neurotransmitter abnormalities are also found in many other mental disorders, such as depression, OCD, and alcoholism, making it difficult to know whether these abnormalities play a specific role in schizophrenia.

4 **Prenatal problems or birth complications.** Damage to the fetal brain significantly increases the likelihood of schizophrenia later in life. Such damage may occur if the mother suffers from malnutrition; schizophrenia rates rise during times of famine, as happened in China and elsewhere (St. Clair et al., 2005). Damage may also occur if the mother gets the flu virus during the first four months of prenatal development, which triples the risk of schizophrenia (Brown et al., 2004; Mednick, Huttunen, & Machón, 1994). And it may occur if there are complications during birth that injure the baby's brain or deprive it of oxygen (Cannon et al., 2000). However, prenatal stress—on the mother or the fetus—is a risk factor for the development of other psychological disorders later in life, too, not only schizophrenia (Huizink, Mulder, & Buitelaar, 2004).

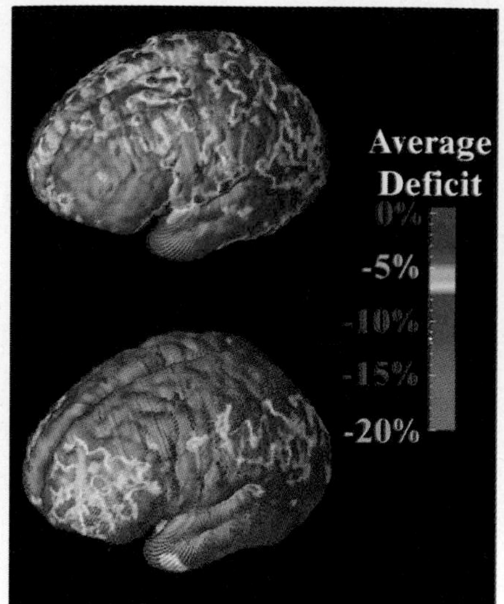

These dramatic images highlight areas of brain-tissue loss in adolescents with schizophrenia. Using a new method that detects fine changes, neuroscientists tracked the loss of gray matter over five years. The areas of greatest tissue loss (regions that control memory, hearing, motor functions, and attention) are shown in red and magenta; a healthy brain (top) looks almost entirely blue.

5 Adolescent abnormalities in brain development. The last factor contributing to schizophrenia occurs in adolescence, when the brain undergoes a natural pruning away of synapses. Normally, this pruning helps make the brain more efficient in handling the new challenges of adulthood. But it appears that schizophrenic brains aggressively prune away too many synapses, which may explain why the first full-blown schizophrenic episode typically occurs in adolescence or early adulthood. Healthy teenagers lose about 1 percent of the brain's gray matter between ages 13 and 18. But as you can see in the photo in the margin, in one study that tracked the loss of gray matter in the brain over five years, adolescents with schizophrenia showed much more extensive and rapid tissue loss, primarily in the sensory and motor regions (Thompson et al., 2001). "We were stunned to see a spreading wave of tissue loss that began in a small region of the brain," said Paul Thompson, who headed the study. "It moved across the brain like a forest fire, destroying more tissue as the disease progressed." The reason for the excessive pruning is not yet known, but it may involve genetic dispositions, fetal brain damage, or stressful life experiences (McGlashan & Hoffman, 2000).

Thus, the developmental pathway of schizophrenia is something of a relay. It starts with a genetic predisposition, which must combine with prenatal risk factors or birth complications that affect brain development. The resulting vulnerability then awaits events in adolescence—synaptic pruning within the brain or external stressors—that serve as a trigger for the disease (Conklin & Iacono, 2002). This model explains why one identical twin may develop schizophrenia but not the other: Both may have the genetic susceptibility, but only one may have been exposed to other risk factors in the womb, birth complications, or stressful life events. These factors may combine in different ways as well, explaining why some schizophrenics recover and others do not. The riddle of schizophrenia is likely to be several riddles, waiting to be solved.

QUICK quiz

The following quiz is not a hallucination.

1. What are the five major kinds of symptoms in schizophrenia?
2. What are the three likely stages in the "relay" that produces schizophrenia?

Answers:

1. delusions, hallucinations, disorganized speech, inappropriate behavior, and impaired cognitive abilities
2. genetic predispositions; prenatal risk factors or birth complications; events during adolescence, such as excessive pruning of synapses in the brain or external stressors

Mental Disorder and Personal Responsibility

We have come to the end of a long walk along the spectrum of psychological problems—from those that are normal conditions of life, such as occasional anxiety or "caffeine-induced sleep disorder," to mental disorders that can be severely disabling, such as major depression or schizophrenia.

One of the great debates generated by all diagnoses of mental disorder concerns the question of personal responsibility. In law and in everyday life, many people reach for a psychological reason to exonerate themselves of responsibility for their actions.

Romance writer Janet Dailey who, when caught, admitted she had plagiarized whole passages from another writer's work, said she was suffering from "a psychological problem that I never even suspected I had." Many people—as an excuse for some habit that is immoral, illegal, or fattening—claim they are "addicted" to the behavior, whether it is sex, shopping, eating chocolate, jogging, or spending hours on the Internet. These activities may be highly pleasurable, to be sure, but are they "addictions" in the customary meaning?

THINKING CRITICALLY

ASK QUESTIONS

The legal system is based on the assumption of personal responsibility, but it also recognizes that some people cannot control their behavior. When does a mental disorder become an excuse to "get away with murder," and when does it truly diminish a person's legal and moral responsibility?

Some psychologists think these activities are indeed comparable to drug addiction or to any other compulsive behavior: They can be maladaptive, disrupting the lives of those who spend thousands of hours shopping or having adventures in cyberspace instead of the real world; they can cause emotional distress to the individual or to his or her friends and family. Other psychologists, however, think that students who spend too much time on line are no different from previous generations who also found plenty of ways to distract themselves and avoid the common problems facing students everywhere—insecurity, worry about grades, a disappointing social life. This is not a "mental disorder," they say, it's a normal problem, called Learning To Pass Courses and Figure Out Life. Certainly, some students who use Internet addiction as an excuse for not studying are making an obvious effort to avoid responsibility for a bad grade. Others may be spending too much time on the Internet as a way of coping with depression, anxiety, or another emotional problem.

The difficulty of knowing where to draw the line of responsibility is apparent in the tragic story of Andrea Yates, a Texas woman who killed her five young children in a state of extreme despair. She had suffered from clinical depression and psychotic episodes for years and in her blackest depressions became mute and catatonic. She tried to kill herself twice. Her father, two brothers, and a sister had suffered varying degrees of mental illness, including depression. Yates was overwhelmed by raising and home schooling all of her children by herself, with no help from her reportedly domineering husband, who permitted her two hours a week of personal time. Although she suffered a postpartum psychotic episode after the birth of their fourth child and a clinical psychologist warned against her having another baby, her husband refused to consider birth control, although not for religious reasons. "We want as many as nature will allow," he said (Yardley, 2001). In 2002, Yates was convicted of murder and sentenced to life in prison after a jury rejected her claim that she was so psychotic that she thought she was saving the souls of her children by killing them. That conviction was overturned on appeal. In 2006, another jury found her not guilty by reason of insanity and she was sent to a mental institution. The defense saw this verdict as a triumph for the understanding of mental illness; the prosecution saw it as a failure of justice.

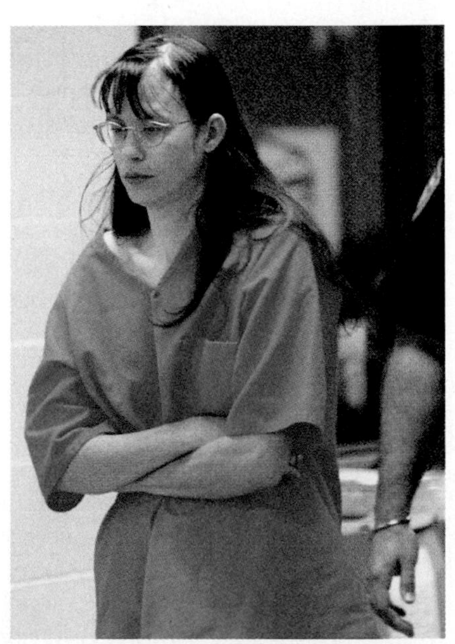

Andrea Yates was convicted of the murder of her children and sent to a mental institution. Do you agree that this was the appropriate punishment? Why or why not?

Does Andrea Yates deserve our condemnation for her horrible acts of murder or our pity? Was her punishment appropriate? Unquestionably, many people do suffer from mental disorders that make it difficult or even impossible for them to control their behavior. How can we distinguish impairments that legitimately reduce a person's responsibility for his or her actions from unjustified excuses? This issue becomes especially urgent in civil and criminal cases when defendants use psychological diagnoses to try to exonerate themselves or excuse their behavior—as Vincent Gigante, the "Oddfather," did so successfully for years.

We noted at the beginning of this chapter that "insanity" refers only to the defendant's ability to know right from wrong at the time the crime was committed. It is used in only a tiny percentage of all criminal cases. But in some jurisdictions, a defendant may claim to have "diminished responsibility" for a crime. This claim does not exonerate the defendant, but it may result in reduced charges, for example from premeditated first-degree murder to manslaughter. A diminished-capacity defense holds that the defendant

lacked the mental capacity to form a calculated and malicious plan but instead was impaired by mental illness or the great provocation of the situation. In some jurisdictions, diminished capacity and other mitigating factors are considered only at the sentencing phase, once the defendant has been found guilty.

When thinking about the relationship of mental disorder to personal responsibility, we face a dilemma. The law recognizes, rightly, that people who are mentally incompetent, delusional, or disturbed should not be judged by the same standards as mentally healthy individuals. At the same time, society has an obligation to protect its citizens from harm and to reject easy excuses for violations of the law. To balance these two positions, we need to find ways to ensure that people who commit crimes or behave reprehensibly face the consequences of their behavior. We must also ensure that people who are suffering from psychological problems have the compassionate support of society in their search for help. After all, psychological problems of one kind or another are challenges that all of us will face at some time in our lives.

Taking Psychology with You

When a Friend Is Suicidal

Suicide can be frightening to those who find themselves fantasizing about it, and it is devastating to the family and friends of those who go through with it. In the United States, it is the ninth leading cause of death, far surpassing homicide. The suicide rate is highest among white men over the age of 65, but suicide rates have nearly tripled in the past 40 years among adolescents and young adults, especially among college students and African-American teenagers. Every year about 1,300 college students commit suicide, and nearly 32,000 more make an unsuccessful attempt (Farrell, 2005).

Women are more likely than men to attempt suicide, primarily as a cry for help, whereas men are four times more likely than women to succeed. Moreover, men's efforts to commit suicide are not always obvious: Some men provoke confrontations with the police, hoping to be shot; some intentionally kill themselves in car accidents; and men are more likely than women to destroy themselves with drugs.

Because of the many widespread myths about suicide, it is important to become informed and know what to do in a crisis:

- **Take all suicide threats seriously.** Some people assume they can't do anything when a friend talks about committing suicide. "He'll just do it at another place, another time," they think. In fact, most suicides occur during an acute crisis. Once the person gets through the crisis, the desire to die fades. Others believe that if a friend is *talking* about committing suicide, he or she won't really *do* it. This belief also is false. Few people commit suicide without signaling their intentions. Most are ambivalent: "I want to kill myself, but I don't want to be dead—at least not forever." Most suicidal people want relief from the terrible pain of feeling that nobody cares and that life is not worth living. Getting these thoughts and fears out in the open is an important first step.
- **Know the danger signs.** A person is at risk of trying to commit suicide if he or she has tried to do it before; has become withdrawn and listless; has a history of depression; reveals specific plans for carrying out the suicide or gives away cherished possessions; expresses no concern about religious prohibitions or the impact on family members; and has access to a lethal method, such as a gun.

- **Get involved: Ask questions and get help.** If you believe a friend is suicidal, do not be afraid to ask, "Are you thinking of suicide?" This question does not "put the idea" in anyone's mind. If your friend is contemplating the action, he or she will probably be relieved to talk about it, which in turn will reduce feelings of isolation and despair. Don't try to talk your friend out of it by debating whether suicide is right or wrong, and don't put on phony cheerfulness. If your friend's words scare you, say so. By allowing your friend to unburden his or her grief, you help the person get through the immediate crisis.
- **Do not leave your friend alone.** If necessary, get the person to a clinic or a hospital emergency room, or call a local suicide hot line. Don't worry about doing the wrong thing. In an emergency, the worst thing you can do is nothing at all.
- **If you are the one who is contemplating suicide, remember that you are not alone and that help is a phone call or an e-mail away.** You can call the national hot-line number, 1-800-SUICIDE, or your school's counseling services. For more information, the Centers for Disease Control and Prevention have a Web site that provides facts about suicide (www.cdc.gov/safeusa/suicide.htm). Many students fear to get help because they think no one will understand, or they fear they will be made fun of by their friends, or they believe they cannot be helped. Wrong, wrong, wrong.

In her book *Night Falls Fast: Understanding Suicide,* Kay Jamison (1999), a psychologist who suffers from bipolar disorder, explored this difficult subject from the standpoint both of a mental-health professional and of a person who has "been there." In describing the aftermath of her own suicide attempt, she wrote: "I do know . . . that I should have been dead but was not—and that I was fortunate enough to be given another chance at life, which many others were not."

Summary

Defining and Diagnosing Disorder

- When defining *mental disorder*, mental-health professionals emphasize the violation of cultural standards, the emotional suffering caused by the behavior, and whether the behavior is harmful to others or society.
- *The Diagnostic and Statistical Manual of Mental Disorders* (DSM), which is used throughout the world, is designed to provide objective criteria and categories for diagnosing mental disorder. Critics argue that the diagnosis of mental disorders, unlike those of medical diseases, is inherently a subjective process that can never be entirely objective. They believe the DSM fosters overdiagnosis, overlooks the influence of diagnostic labels on clients and therapists, confuses serious mental disorders with everyday problems in living, and creates an illusion of objectivity and universality.
- Supporters of the DSM believe that when the DSM criteria are used correctly and when empirically validated objective tests are used, reliability in diagnosis improves. The DSM now lists many *culture-bound syndromes* in addition to disorders, such as depression and schizophrenia, that are found all over the world.
- In diagnosing psychological disorders, clinicians often use *projective tests* such as the Rorschach Inkblot Test or, with children, the use of anatomically detailed dolls. These methods have low reliability and validity, creating problems when they are used in the legal arena, as in custody disputes, or in diagnosing disorders. In general, *objective tests (inventories)*, such as the *MMPI*, are more reliable and valid than projective ones.

Anxiety Disorders

- *Generalized anxiety disorder* involves continuous, chronic anxiety, with signs of nervousness, worry, and irritability. When anxiety results from exposure to uncontrollable or unpredictable danger, it can lead to *posttraumatic stress disorder (PTSD)*, which involves mentally reliving the trauma, emotional detachment, and increased physiological arousal.
- Most people who live through a traumatic experience eventually recover without developing PTSD. But a minority do. The reasons for their increased vulnerability to posttraumatic symptoms include having a history of psychological problems and other traumatic experiences;

lacking social support and psychological resources; having lower-than-average intelligence; having a relatively smaller hippocampus than normal; and having a genetic vulnerability.

- *Panic disorder* involves sudden, intense attacks of profound fear. Panic attacks are common in the aftermath of stress or frightening experiences; those who go on to develop a disorder tend to interpret the attacks as a sign of impending disaster.
- *Phobias* are unrealistic fears of specific situations, activities, or things. Common *social phobias* include fears of speaking in public, going on a date, or being observed by others. *Agoraphobia*, the fear of being away from a safe place or person, is the most disabling phobia—a "fear of fear." It often begins with a panic attack, which the person tries to avoid in the future by staying close to "safe" places or people.
- *Obsessive-compulsive disorder (OCD)* involves recurrent, unwished-for thoughts or images (obsessions) and repetitive, ritualized behaviors (compulsions) that a person feels unable to control. Some people with OCD have depleted levels of serotonin in their prefontal cortex, which may contribute to their cognitive rigidity. Parts of the brain involved in fear and responses to threat are also more active than normal in people with OCD; the "alarm mechanism," once activated, does not turn off when danger is past. One kind of OCD creates pathological hoarding and may involve deficiencies in other parts of the brain.

Mood Disorders

- Symptoms of *major depression* include distorted thinking patterns, low self-esteem, physical ailments such as fatigue and loss of appetite, and prolonged grief and despair. Women are twice as likely as men to suffer from major depression, but depression in men may be underdiagnosed. In *bipolar disorder*, a person experiences episodes of both depression and *mania* (excessive euphoria). It is equally common in both sexes.
- *Vulnerability-stress models* of depression (or any other disorder) look at interactions between individual vulnerabilities and stressful experiences. Some people have a genetic predisposition to become depressed when they undergo severe stress, and others may be genetically protected. Genes may affect levels of serotonin and the stress hormone cortisol. For some vulnerable individuals, repeated losses of important people can set off episodes of major depression. Life experiences that increase the risk of depression include violence, problems with work and family, poverty, discrimination, and sexual abuse. Cognitive habits also play an important role: believing that the origin of one's unhappiness is permanent and uncontrollable; feeling hopeless and pessimistic; and brooding or ruminating about one's problems. "Close-up on Research" examines the differences between harmful or unproductive rumination and the kind of thoughts that can lead to solving problems.

Personality Disorders

- *Personality disorders* are characterized by rigid, self-destructive traits that cause distress or an inability to get along with others. They include, among others, *paranoid*, *narcissistic*, *borderline*, and *antisocial personality disorders*.
- The term *psychopath* describes people who lack conscience and emotional connection to others; they don't feel remorse, shame, guilt, or anxiety over wrongdoing, and they can charm and con others with ease. *Antisocial personality disorder (APD)* applies to people with a lifelong pattern of aggressive, reckless, impulsive, and criminal behavior. Not all psychopaths have APD, and not all people with APD are psychopaths, but in some individuals the two disorders converge. Researchers have identified abnormalities in the central nervous system and prefrontal cortex that are associated with lack of emotional responsiveness and with impulsivity. APD has a genetic component, but biological vulnerabilities must interact with stressful or violent environments to produce the disorder.

Drug Abuse and Addiction

- The effects of drugs depend on whether they are used moderately or are abused. Signs of *substance abuse* include impaired ability to work or get along with others, use of the drug in hazardous situations, recurrent arrests for drug use, and conflicts with others caused by drug use.
- According to the *biological model* of addiction, some people have a biological vulnerability to alcoholism and other addictions due to genetic factors that affect their metabolism, biochemistry, or personality traits. But heavy drug abuse also changes the brain in ways that make addiction more likely.
- Advocates of the *learning model* of addiction point out that addiction patterns vary according to culture, learning, and accepted practice; that many people can stop taking drugs without experiencing withdrawal symptoms; that drug abuse depends on the reasons for taking a drug; and that abuse increases when people are not taught moderate use.

- Although the biological and learning models are polarized on many issues, the evidence suggests that addiction and abuse result from an interaction between biological and psychological vulnerability and a person's culture, learning history, motives for taking a drug, and situation.

Dissociative Identity Disorder

- In *dissociative identity disorder* (formerly called *multiple personality disorder*, or *MPD*), two or more distinct personalities and identities appear to split off (*dissociate*) within one person. Considerable controversy surrounds the validity and nature of MPD. Some clinicians think it is common, often goes undiagnosed, and originates in childhood trauma. Others offer a *sociocognitive* explanation. They argue that most cases result from pressure and suggestion by clinicians who believe in the disorder, interacting with vulnerable patients who find MPD a plausible explanation for their problems. Media coverage of sensational alleged cases of MPD greatly contributed to the rise in the number of cases after 1980.

Schizophrenia

- *Schizophrenia* is a psychotic disorder involving delusions, hallucinations, disorganized speech (called *word salads*), inappropriate behavior, and severe cognitive impairments. Other symptoms, such as loss of motivation to take care of oneself and emotional flatness, may appear before a psychotic episode and persist even when the more dramatic symptoms are in remission. Some people with schizophrenia fall into a *catatonic stupor*. Cases of schizophrenia vary in their specific symptoms, severity, duration, and prognosis.
- Schizophrenia appears to involve genetic predispositions that lead to structural brain abnormalities, such as enlarged ventricles and neurotransmitter abnormalities. However, in the "relay" that produces the disorder, genetic predispositions must interact with certain stressors in the environment during prenatal development (such as the mother's malnutrition or a prenatal viral infection), birth complications, and excessive pruning of synapses during adolescence.

Mental Disorder and Personal Responsibility

- The diagnosis of mental disorder raises important questions for issues of personal responsibility in the law and everyday life. When people claim to have a mental disorder, psychologists and others struggle to decide whether the claim is an excuse for illegal or destructive behavior, or whether these individuals truly have a disorder that reduces their ability to control their behavior.

KEY TERMS

mental disorder 599
Diagnostic and Statistical Manual of Mental Disorders (DSM) 599
culture-bound syndromes 602
projective tests 603
Rorschach Inkblot Test 603
objective tests (inventories) 604
Minnesota Multiphasic Personality Inventory (MMPI) 604
generalized anxiety disorder 606
posttraumatic stress disorder (PTSD) 606
panic disorder (panic attack) 607
phobia 608
social phobia 608
agoraphobia 608
obsessive-compulsive disorder (OCD) 609
mood disorder 610
major depression 610
mania 611
bipolar disorder 611
vulnerability-stress model of depression 611
paranoid personality disorder 615
narcissistic personality disorder 615
borderline personality disorder 615
psychopathy 616
antisocial personality disorder (APD) 616
substance abuse 619
biological model of addiction 619
learning model of addiction 620
dissociative identity disorder (multiple personality disorder, MPD) 625
dissociation 625
sociocognitive explanation of MPD 627
schizophrenia 628
psychosis 628
"word salad" 628
catatonic stupor 629

What is the Diagnosis?

NOW YOU HAVE READ CHAPTER SIXTEEN — ARE YOU PREPARED FOR THE EXAM?

According to recent studies, approximately 22% of the U.S. adult population experiences a mental disorder in a given year. True or False?

What are the different types of psychological disorders, and how common are they? (pages 598–601)

true

Over the past few years, Sam has become extremely fearful of going to any public place such as a restaurant, concert, or even the grocery store. There are many days when Sam does not even leave his house for fear that he might be caught somewhere that would not be easy to escape from. Which anxiety disorder would Sam most likely be diagnosed with?

What are the different types of anxiety disorders and their symptoms? (pages 600–601)

agoraphobia

A person suffering from disordered thinking, bizarre behavior, and hallucinations, who is unable to distinguish between fantasy and reality, is likely suffering from_______.

What are the main symptoms of schizophrenia? (pages 628–632)

schizophrenia

Multiple categories of psychological disorders are presented in this chapter. In order to help yourself organize the new terms, in each of the sections describing the disorders within **MyPsychLab,** try the practice tests and the activities within your study plan.

TELL ME **MORE** >>

"I wish all classes had a site like MyPsychLab."

Student
Patrick Henry Community College

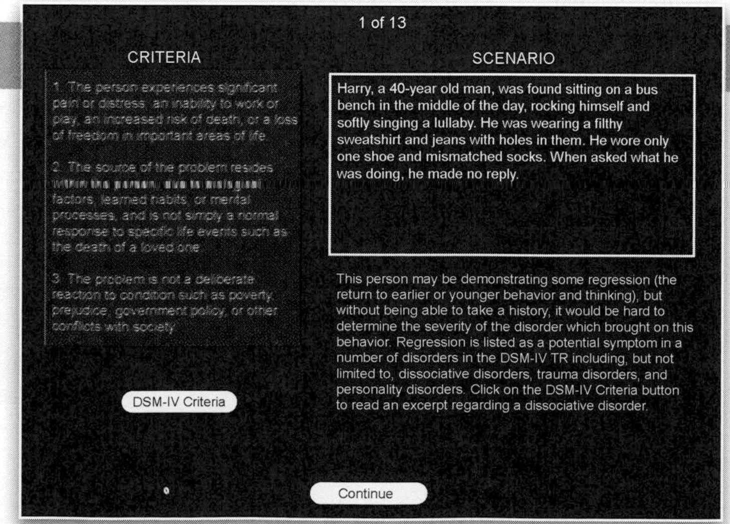

1 of 13
CRITERIA
1. The person experiences significant pain or distress, an inability to work or play, an increased risk of death, or a loss of freedom in important areas of life
2. The source of the problem resides
factors, learned habits, or mental processes, and is not simply a normal response to specific life events such as the death of a loved one
3. The problem is not a deliberate reaction to condition such as poverty, prejudice, government policy, or other conflicts with society
DSM-IV Criteria
SCENARIO
Harry, a 40-year old man, was found sitting on a bus bench in the middle of the day, rocking himself and softly singing a lullaby. He was wearing a filthy sweatshirt and jeans with holes in them. He wore only one shoe and mismatched socks. When asked what he was doing, he made no reply.
This person may be demonstrating some regression (the return to earlier or younger behavior and thinking), but without being able to take a history, it would be hard to determine the severity of the disorder which brought on this behavior. Regression is listed as a potential symptom in a number of disorders in the DSM-IV TR including, but not limited to, dissociative disorders, trauma disorders, and personality disorders. Click on the DSM-IV Criteria button to read an excerpt regarding a dissociative disorder.
Continue

50
psychological disorders

any pattern of behavior that causes people significant distress, causes them to harm others, or harms their ability to function in daily life

50

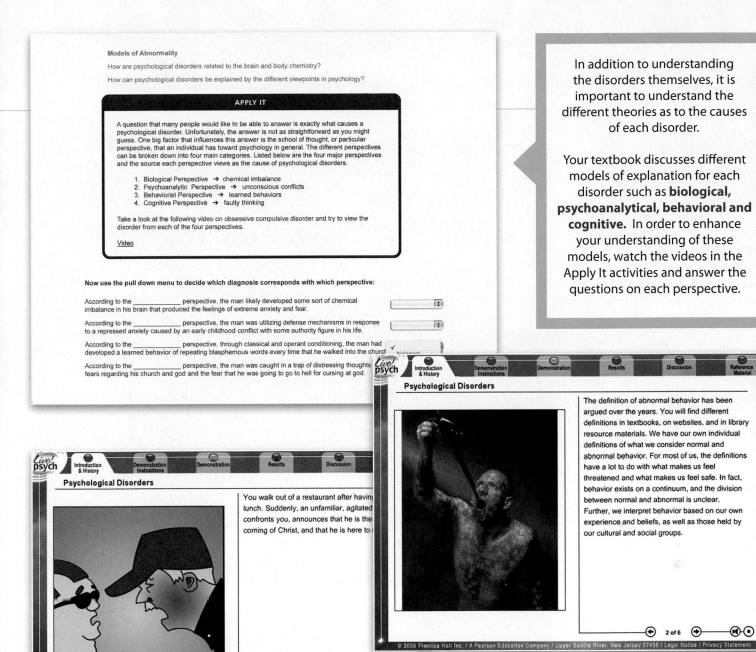

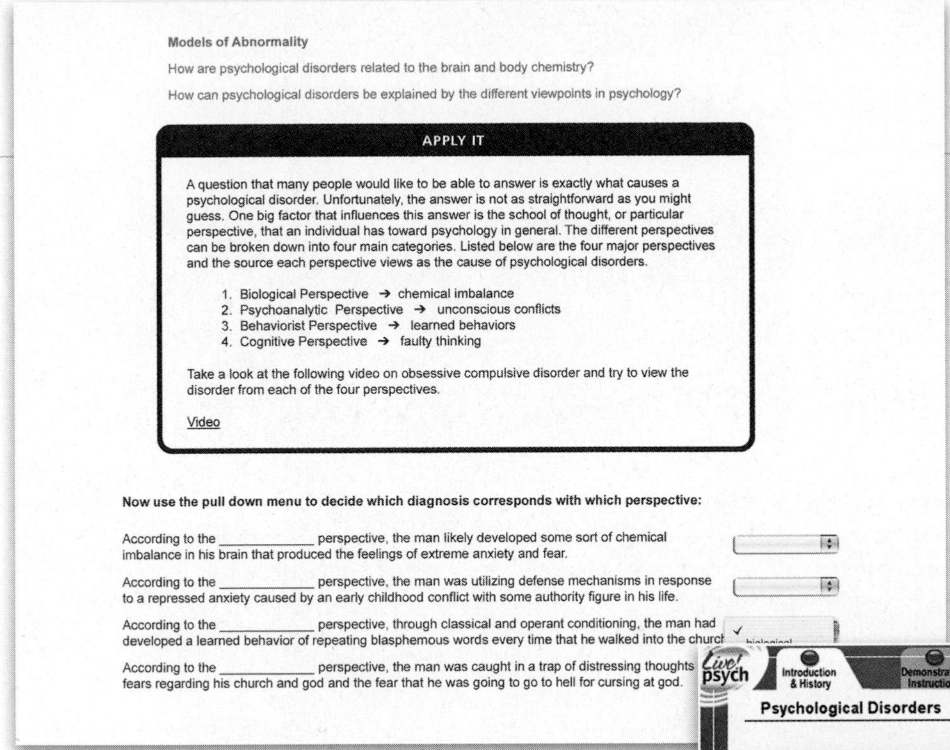

Models of Abnormality

How are psychological disorders related to the brain and body chemistry?

How can psychological disorders be explained by the different viewpoints in psychology?

APPLY IT

A question that many people would like to be able to answer is exactly what causes a psychological disorder. Unfortunately, the answer is not as straightforward as you might guess. One big factor that influences this answer is the school of thought, or particular perspective, that an individual has toward psychology in general. The different perspectives can be broken down into four main categories. Listed below are the four major perspectives and the source each perspective views as the cause of psychological disorders.

1. Biological Perspective → chemical imbalance
2. Psychoanalytic Perspective → unconscious conflicts
3. Behaviorist Perspective → learned behaviors
4. Cognitive Perspective → faulty thinking

Take a look at the following video on obsessive compulsive disorder and try to view the disorder from each of the four perspectives.

Video

Now use the pull down menu to decide which diagnosis corresponds with which perspective:

According to the ____________ perspective, the man likely developed some sort of chemical imbalance in his brain that produced the feelings of extreme anxiety and fear.

According to the ____________ perspective, the man was utilizing defense mechanisms in response to a repressed anxiety caused by an early childhood conflict with some authority figure in his life.

According to the ____________ perspective, through classical and operant conditioning, the man had developed a learned behavior of repeating blasphemous words every time that he walked into the churcl

According to the ____________ perspective, the man was caught in a trap of distressing thoughts fears regarding his church and god and the fear that he was going to go to hell for cursing at god.

In addition to understanding the disorders themselves, it is important to understand the different theories as to the causes of each disorder.

Your textbook discusses different models of explanation for each disorder such as **biological, psychoanalytical, behavioral and cognitive.** In order to enhance your understanding of these models, watch the videos in the Apply It activities and answer the questions on each perspective.

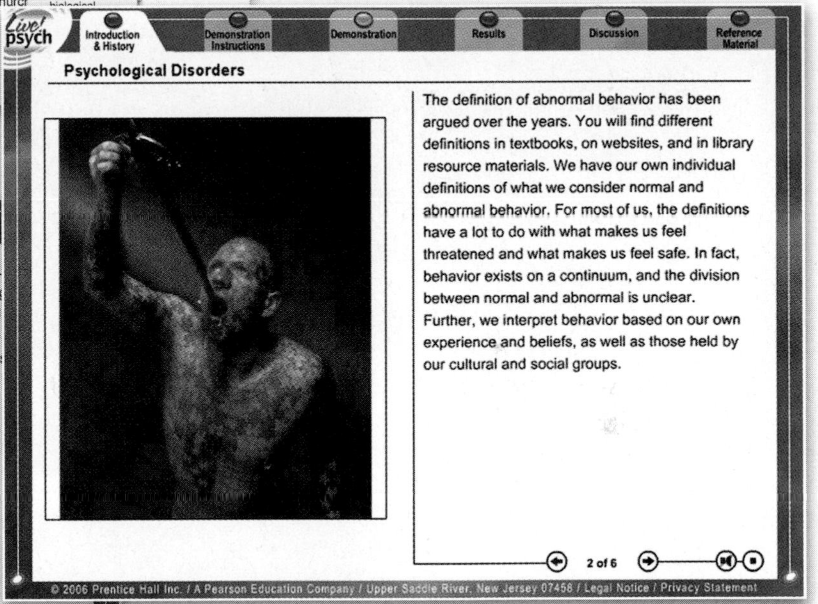

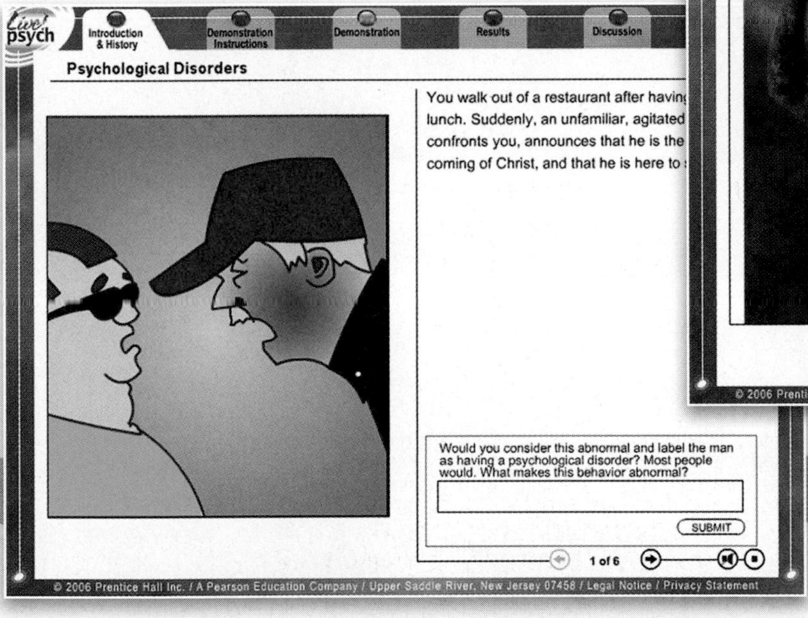

Live! psych | Introduction & History | Demonstration Instructions | Demonstration | Results | Discussion | Reference Material

Psychological Disorders

The definition of abnormal behavior has been argued over the years. You will find different definitions in textbooks, on websites, and in library resource materials. We have our own individual definitions of what we consider normal and abnormal behavior. For most of us, the definitions have a lot to do with what makes us feel threatened and what makes us feel safe. In fact, behavior exists on a continuum, and the division between normal and abnormal is unclear. Further, we interpret behavior based on our own experience and beliefs, as well as those held by our cultural and social groups.

2 of 6

© 2006 Prentice Hall Inc. / A Pearson Education Company / Upper Saddle River, New Jersey 07458 / Legal Notice / Privacy Statement

Live! psych | Introduction & History | Demonstration Instructions | Demonstration | Results | Discussion

Psychological Disorders

You walk out of a restaurant after havin lunch. Suddenly, an unfamiliar, agitated confronts you, announces that he is the coming of Christ, and that he is here to

Would you consider this abnormal and label the man as having a psychological disorder? Most people would. What makes this behavior abnormal?

SUBMIT

1 of 6

© 2006 Prentice Hall Inc. / A Pearson Education Company / Upper Saddle River, New Jersey 07458 / Legal Notice / Privacy Statement

TELL ME **MORE** >>

"There is not enough time in class to cover everything; using MyPsychLab helps me understand the material without the teacher."

Student
Georgia College and State University

What can you find in MyPsychLab?

Self-Directed Tests • Videos • Simulations • eBook • Flash Cards • Web Links . . . and more — organized by chapter, section and learning objective.

APPROACHES TO TREATMENT AND THERAPY

CHAPTER SEVENTEEN

> Your vision will become clear only when you can look into your own heart. . . . Who looks outside, dreams; who looks inside, awakes.
>
> CARL JUNG

IN THE aftermath of the attacks on the World Trade Center on September 11, 2001, many people across America developed emotional symptoms. Some were depressed and anxious. Some couldn't sleep. Many New Yorkers developed fears of leaving home, of riding in elevators, and, of course, of flying in planes. Firefighters, rescue workers, and families of the victims had recurring nightmares and flashbacks. The country had been through a shock, and if ever there was a time that people understood what it meant to have "posttraumatic stress disorder," this was it.

The vast majority of people who experience a traumatic event—including combat during war, the sudden death of a loved one, or a natural disaster such as an earthquake or hurricane—recover from their immediate postshock symptoms and go on to lead normal lives. The two greatest allies in helping them do this are time, which does heal, and the support of friends. For some people, however, time and friends are not enough, and they develop one or more of the disorders described in the previous chapter: depression, generalized anxiety disorder, specific phobias, or posttraumatic stress disorder. What kind of therapy might help them? People have many other problems too, ranging from normal life difficulties (such as marital conflict or fear of public speaking) to the delusions of schizophrenia. What kind of therapy might help them?

As we saw in Chapter 1, to become a licensed clinical psychologist, a person must have an advanced degree and a period of supervised training. However, the title *psychotherapist* is unregulated; anyone can set up any kind of program and call it "therapy"—and, by the thousands, they do! Increasingly in the United States and Canada, people can get credentialed as "experts" in various techniques and therapies—doing hypnotherapy, diagnosing child sexual abuse, becoming a practitioner of some pop-psych method—simply by attending a weekend seminar or a training program lasting a week or two. To protect themselves as well as to get the best possible help when it is necessary, consumers need to be informed and know how to choose that help wisely.

In this chapter, we will evaluate two major approaches to treatment. *Biological treatments,* primarily provided by psychiatrists or other physicians, include drugs or direct intervention in brain function. *Psychotherapy* covers an array of psychological interventions, including psychodynamic therapies, cognitive and behavior therapies, humanist therapies, and family or couples therapy. In addition to these major schools of psychotherapy, there are literally hundreds of offshoots and specialties. We will assess which kinds of therapy work best for which problems, which kinds of therapy are ineffective, and which ones carry a significant risk of harm to the client.

WHAT'S**AHEAD**

- What kinds of drugs are used to treat psychological disorders?
- Are antidepressants always the best treatment for depression?
- Can mental disorders be cured by brain surgery?
- Why is "shock therapy" hailed by some clinicians but condemned by others?

Biological Treatments for Mental Disorders

For hundreds of years, people have tried to identify the origins of mental illness, attributing the causes at various times to evil spirits, pressure in the skull, disease, or bad environments. The contemporary mental-health world continues to alternate between viewing mental disorders as diseases that can be treated medically and as emotional problems that must be treated psychologically (Luhrmann, 2000). Today, biological explanations and treatments are in the ascendance. This is partly because of evidence that some disorders have a genetic component or involve a biochemical or neurological abnormality (see Chapter 16), and partly, as we will see, because physicians and pharmaceutical companies are promoting biomedical solutions (Angell, 2004; Healy, 2002).

The Question of Drugs

The most commonly used biological treatment is medication that alters the production of or response to neurotransmitters in the brain (see Chapter 4). Because drugs are so widely prescribed these days, both for severe disorders such as schizophrenia and for more common problems such as anxiety and depression, consumers need to understand what these drugs are, how they can best be used, and their limitations.

Drugs Commonly Prescribed For Mental Disorders. The main classes of drugs used in the treatment of mental and emotional disorders are these:

1 **Antipsychotic drugs**, also called *neuroleptics*—older ones such as Thorazine and Haldol and second-generation ones such as Clozaril and the two market leaders Risperdal and Zyprexa—are used primarily in the treatment of schizophrenia and other psychoses. Increasingly, though, they are being prescribed for people with nonpsychotic disorders, such as severe depression, impulse control problems, dementia, and bipolar disorder. Because many psychoses are thought to be caused by an excess of the neurotransmitter dopamine, many antipsychotic drugs are designed to block or reduce the sensitivity of brain receptors that respond to dopamine. Some also increase levels of serotonin, a neurotransmitter that inhibits dopamine activity. Antipsychotic drugs can reduce agitation, delusions, and hallucinations, and they can shorten schizophrenic episodes. However, they offer little relief from other symptoms, such as jumbled thoughts, difficulty concentrating, apathy, emotional flatness, or inability to interact with others.

Although the newer drugs have been promoted as being safer and more effective, a large federally funded study found that the older medications often alleviate schizophrenia symptoms about as well as the newer, far more expensive ones do (Lieberman et al., 2005). The new drugs work but three-quarters of the people in the study stopped taking them. The reason is that the newer, atypical antipsychotics are as likely as the older ones to cause troubling negative side effects, especially muscle rigidity,

antipsychotic drugs Drugs used primarily in the treatment of schizophrenia and other psychotic disorders.

These photos show the effects of antipsychotic drugs on the symptoms of a young man with schizophrenia. In the photo on the left, he was unmedicated; in the photo on the right, he had taken medication. However, these drugs do not help all people with psychotic disorders.

hand tremors, and other involuntary muscle movements that can develop into a neurological disorder called *tardive* (late-appearing) *dyskinesia*. About one-fourth of all adults who take these drugs, and fully one-third of elderly patients who do so, develop this disorder (Saltz et al., 1991). Some of the newer drugs also have other risks, including weight gain that can lead to severe diabetes, which can cause medical complications and death (Masand, 2000). In 2003, the makers of Risperdal cautioned physicians to stop prescribing the drug to elderly patients with dementia, because it can cause strokes and is ineffective for this population. Although antipsychotic medication allows many people to be released from hospitals, these individuals cannot always care for themselves, and they often fail to keep taking their medication because of the unpleasant and sometimes dangerous side effects.

antidepressant drugs Drugs used primarily in the treatment of mood disorders, especially depression and anxiety.

2 **Antidepressant drugs** are used primarily in the treatment of depression, anxiety, phobias, and obsessive-compulsive disorder. *Monoamine oxidase inhibitors (MAOIs)*, such as Nardil, elevate the levels of norepinephrine and serotonin in the brain by blocking or inhibiting an enzyme that deactivates these neurotransmitters. *Tricyclic antidepressants*, such as Elavil, boost norepinephrine and serotonin levels by preventing the normal reabsorption, or "reuptake," of these substances by the cells that have released them. *Selective serotonin reuptake inhibitors (SSRIs)*, such as Prozac and Zoloft, work on the same principle as the tricyclics but specifically target serotonin. Cymbalta and Remeron target both serotonin and norepinephrine. Another drug, Wellbutrin, is chemically unrelated to the other antidepressants but is often prescribed for depression and, under the trade name Zyban, as an aid to quitting smoking.

All three classes of antidepressants are nonaddictive and about equally effective, but they all tend to produce some unpleasant physical reactions, including dry mouth, headaches, constipation, nausea, restlessness, gastrointestinal problems, weight gain, and, in as many as one-third of all patients, decreased sexual desire and blocked or delayed orgasm (Hollon, Thase, & Markowitz, 2002). The specific side effects may vary with the particular drug. MAOIs interact with certain foods (such as cheese) and have the most risks, such as

"Before Prozac, she loathed company."

tranquilizers Drugs commonly but often inappropriately prescribed for patients who complain of unhappiness, anxiety, or worry.

lithium carbonate A drug frequently given to people suffering from bipolar disorder.

dangerously high blood pressure in some individuals, so they are prescribed least often nowadays.

Some investigators are studying herbs like St. John's wort. A meta-analysis of clinical studies found that St. John's wort was more effective than a placebo for milder forms of depression (Kim, Streltzer, & Goebert, 1999), but the efficacy of this herb remains in dispute. Also, the herb is now known to affect metabolism and to interact with about half of all prescription medications, including birth-control pills, blood thinners, and some AIDS drugs (Markowitz et al., 2003). Anyone taking St. John's wort along with a prescription drug should inform his or her physician.

3 **Tranquilizers**, such as Valium and Xanax, increase the activity of the neurotransmitter gamma-aminobutyric acid (GABA). Although they were developed to treat people with mild anxiety, they are often overprescribed by general physicians for patients who complain of more serious mood disorders. Tranquilizers may help people with panic disorder and individuals who are having an acute anxiety attack, but they are not considered the treatment of choice over a long period of time. Symptoms almost always return if the medication is stopped, and a significant percentage of people who take tranquilizers overuse them and develop problems with withdrawal and tolerance (i.e., they need larger and larger doses).

4 A special category of drug, a salt called **lithium carbonate**, often helps people who suffer from bipolar disorder (depression alternating with euphoria). It may produce its effects by moderating levels of norepinephrine or by protecting brain cells from being overstimulated by another neurotransmitter, glutamate (Nonaka, Hough, & Chuang, 1998). Lithium must be given in exactly the right dose, and bloodstream levels of the drug must be carefully monitored, because too little will not help and too much is toxic—sometimes even fatal. Unfortunately, in some people, lithium produces short-term side effects (tremors) and long-term problems (kidney damage). Other drugs for people with bipolar disorder include Tegretol, Depakote, and some of the newer antipsychotics (McElroy & Keck, 2000).

For a review of these drugs and their uses, see Review 17.1.

REVIEW 17.1

Drugs Used in the Treatment of Psychological Disorders

	Antipsychotics (Neuroleptics)	Antidepressants	Tranquilizers	Lithium Carbonate
Examples	Thorazine Haldol Clozaril Risperdal	Prozac (SSRI) Nardil (MAOI) Elavil (tricyclic) Paxil (SSRI) Wellbutrin (other) Cymbalta (other)	Valium Xanax	
Primarily used for	Schizophrenia Other psychoses Impulsive anger Bipolar disorder	Depression Anxiety disorders Panic disorder Obsessive-compulsive disorder	Mood disorders Panic disorder	Bipolar disorder

Some Cautions About Drug Treatments. Without question, drugs have rescued some people from emotional despair, suicide, obsessive-compulsive disorder, and panic attacks. They have enabled severely depressed or mentally disturbed people to function and respond to psychotherapy. Yet many psychiatrists and drug companies are trumpeting the benefits of medication without informing the public of its limitations, so some words of caution are in order.

THINKING CRITICALLY

AVOID EMOTIONAL REASONING

A TV ad claims that a new drug is "a breakthrough drug for depression." A newspaper reports a "miracle cure" for people with schizophrenia. Such announcements always generate a lot of excitement. Why should people be cautious before concluding that a new drug is the miracle they are longing for it to be?

1 The placebo effect. New drugs, like new psychotherapies, often promise quick and effective cures. But the **placebo effect** ensures that many people will respond positively to a new drug just because of the enthusiasm surrounding it and because of their own expectations that the drug will make them feel better. After a while, when placebo effects decline, many drugs turn out to be neither as effective as promised nor as widely applicable. This has happened repeatedly with each new generation of tranquilizer and each new "miracle" antipsychotic drug and antidepressant, including Clozaril and Prozac (Healy, 2004; Moncrieff, 2001).

In fact, some investigators maintain that much of the effectiveness of antidepressants is due to a placebo effect (Khan et al., 2003; Kirsch & Saperstein, 1998). Even researchers who quarrel with that strong conclusion acknowledge that the drugs are less effective than commonly believed. Overall, only about half of all depressed patients respond positively to any given antidepressant medication, and of those, only about 40 percent are actually responding to the specific biological effects of the drugs (Hollon, Thase, & Markowitz, 2002). New research in neuroscience is illuminating the reason that placebos work for some people: The psychological expectation of improvement actually produces some of the same brain changes that medication does (Benedetti et al., 2005; see Chapter 6).

2 High relapse and dropout rates. A person may have short-term success with antipsychotic or antidepressant drugs. However, in part because of these drugs' unpleasant side effects, one-half to two-thirds of people stop taking them. When they do, they are quite likely to relapse, especially if they have not learned how to cope with their problems (Hollon, Thase, & Maskowitz, 2002).

3 Dosage problems. The challenge with drugs is to find the *therapeutic window*, the amount that is enough but not too much. This problem is compounded by the fact that the same dose of a drug may be metabolized differently in men and women, old people and young people, and different ethnic groups. When psychiatrist Keh-Ming Lin moved from Taiwan to the United States, he was amazed to learn that the dosage of antipsychotic drugs given to American patients with schizophrenia was often ten times higher than the dose for Chinese patients. In subsequent studies, Lin and his colleagues confirmed that Asian patients require significantly lower doses of the medication for optimal treatment (Lin, Poland, & Chien, 1990). Similarly, African-Americans suffering from depression or bipolar disorder seem to need lower dosages of tricyclic antidepressants and lithium than other ethnic groups do (Strickland et al., 1991, 1995). Groups may differ in the dosages they can tolerate because of variations in metabolic rates, amount of body fat, the number or type of drug receptors in the brain, or cultural practices such as smoking and eating certain foods.

4 Unknown long-term risks. We saw that antipsychotic drugs can have dangerous and even fatal consequences if taken for many years. Antidepressants have been assumed to be quite safe, but the effects of taking them indefinitely are still unknown.

placebo effect The apparent success of a medication or treatment due to the patient's expectations or hopes rather than to the drug or treatment itself.

One problem is that many of the studies that get no results, or that demonstrate a drug's hazards, go unpublished. In 2003, British drug authorities reported that nine unpublished studies of Paxil found that it tripled the risk of suicidal thoughts and suicide attempts in young people who were taking the drug compared to those given a placebo (Harris, 2003). Paxil and other SSRIs can cause a severe form of restlessness and agitation in the first few weeks they are taken, and this reaction might push vulnerable young people to a precipice. Today, the U.S. Food and Drug Administration (FDA) has cautioned against prescribing SSRIs to anyone under 18.

The general public and even many physicians do not realize that new drugs are often tested on only a few hundred people for only a few weeks or months, even when the drug is one that patients might take for years (Angell, 2004). (The cost of bringing most new drugs to market is very high, and manufacturers feel they cannot afford to wait years to determine whether there might be long-term hazards.) Many physicians and laypersons, feeling reassured if a drug is effective in the short run, overlook the possibility of long-term dangers, as well as the potential risks of drug interactions. Yet psychiatrists, understandably frustrated by the failure of existing antipsychotics and antidepressants to help all of their clients, are increasingly prescribing "cocktails" of medications—this one for anxiety, plus this one for depression, plus another to manage the side effects. They report anecdotal success in some cases, but as yet there has been virtually no research on the benefits and risks of these combination approaches.

Medications have saved lives and improved the lives of thousands of people suffering from severe mental illness as well as those suffering from milder forms of depression, anxiety, and other emotional problems. Yet the cautions we have listed are the reason that it is important to think critically about this issue. The popularity of drugs has been fueled by pressure from managed-care organizations, which prefer to pay for one patient visit for a prescription rather than ten visits for psychotherapy, and by drug company advertising. In 1997 the FDA permitted pharmaceutical companies to advertise directly to consumers, a practice still forbidden in Canada and Europe; sales of new drugs skyrocketed because of consumer demand.

Yet most consumers do not realize that once a drug is approved by the FDA, doctors are then permitted to prescribe it for other conditions and to populations other than those on which it was originally tested. That is why antidepressants are now being marketed for "social phobias"; why Prozac, when its patent expired, was renamed Sarafem and marketed to women for "premenstrual dysphoric disorder"; why Ritalin, widely given to school-aged children, is now being prescribed for 2- and 3-year-olds; why the number of antidepressants given to *preschoolers* has doubled; and why antipsychotics such as Risperdal are being used for nonpsychotic disorders such as impulsive aggression. Most worrisome for the future of impartial research is that most researchers who are studying the effectiveness of medication have strong financial ties to the pharmaceutical industry, in the form of lucrative consulting fees, funding for studies, stock investments, and patents. Studies that are independently funded often do not get the strong positive results that industry-funded drug trials do (Angell, 2004; Healy, 2002; Krimsky, 2003).

"I think the dosage needs adjusting. I'm not nearly as happy as the people in the ads."

As you can see from this discussion, consumers must critically weigh the benefits and limitations of medication for psychological problems—and resist the temptation to oversimplify. Drugs for mental disorders are neither totally miraculous, as some of their promoters say,

nor totally worthless, as some of their critics maintain. The effectiveness of antidepressants depends on why the individual is taking them, how severe the problem is, and whether the person learns how to function better and cope with the problem.

Direct Brain Intervention

For most of human history, a person suffering from mental illness often got a rather extreme form of "help." A well-meaning tribal healer or, in later centuries, a doctor would try to release the "psychic pressures" believed to be causing the symptoms by drilling holes in the victim's skull. It didn't work! However, the basic impulse—to try to cure mental illness by intervening directly in the brain—has continued.

One approach, **psychosurgery**, is designed to surgically destroy selected areas of the brain thought to be responsible for emotional disorders or disturbed behavior. The most famous form of modern psychosurgery was invented in 1935, when a Portuguese neurologist, Antonio Egas Moniz, drilled two holes into the skull of a mental patient and used a specially designed instrument to cut or crush nerve fibers running from the prefrontal lobes to other areas. This operation, called a *prefrontal lobotomy*, was supposed to reduce the patient's emotional symptoms without impairing intellectual ability. The procedure—which, incredibly, was never assessed or validated scientifically—was performed on tens of thousands of people. Tragically, lobotomies left many patients apathetic, withdrawn, and unable to care for themselves (Valenstein, 1986). Yet Moniz won a Nobel prize for his work.

Today, psychosurgery is rare, but some neurosurgeons have not given up on the effort to cure mental illness by operating on the brain. Some are burning holes in the frontal lobes of the brain as a last resort on people with intractable cases of obsessive-compulsive disorder and severe depression, people who have not responded to drugs or psychotherapy (Cosgrove & Rauch, 2003). Unfortunately, reports of success are largely anecdotal and no controlled studies have been conducted on any of the new forms of psychosurgery (Lopes et al., 2004).

Instead of operating on the brain, therefore, other psychiatrists and neurologists prefer to stimulate it electrically. The oldest method is **electroconvulsive therapy (ECT)**, or "shock therapy," which is used for the treatment of severe depression, although no one knows how or why it works. An electrode is placed on one side of the head (rarely on both), and a brief current is turned on. The current triggers a seizure that typically lasts one minute, causing the body to convulse. Today, unlike in the past, patients are given muscle relaxants and anesthesia, so they sleep through the procedure and their convulsions are minimized. ECT has helped some people who are suicidal and who have not responded to medication or any other treatments. However, the mood-improving effect of ECT is usually short-lived, and the depression almost always returns within a few weeks or months (Hollon, Thase, & Markowitz, 2002). And ECT is *ineffective* with other disorders, such as schizophrenia or alcoholism, though it is occasionally misused for these conditions. Critics of ECT have long argued that the method is often used improperly and that it can in fact damage the brain and impair memory. ECT's supporters respond that when ECT is used properly, it is safe and causes no long-term cognitive impairment, significant memory loss, or detectable brain damage (Abrams, 1997).

THINKING CRITICALLY

AVOID EMOTIONAL REASONING

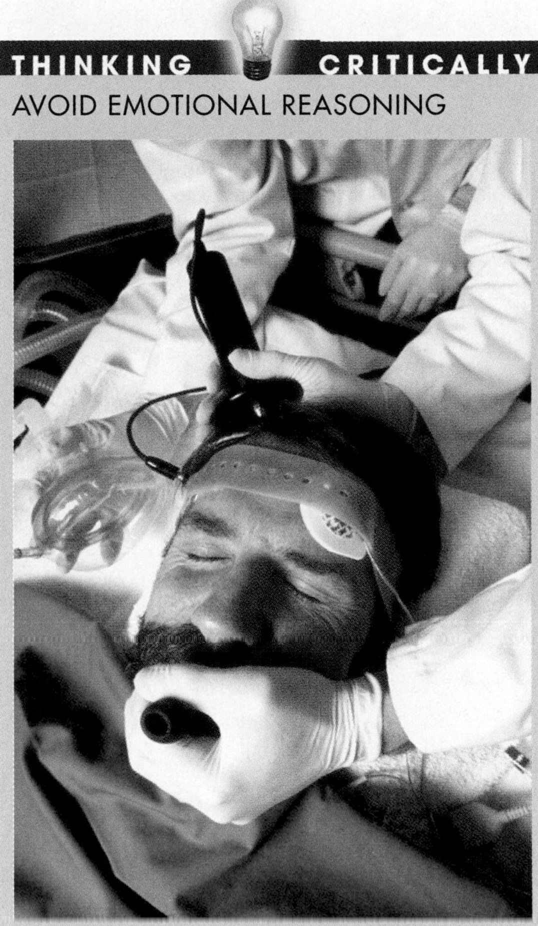

For decades ECT has been an emotionally contested issue with fervent supporters and critics. Today, most psychologists take a middle position: ECT can help some suicidally depressed people who have not responded to other treatments, but it must be used cautiously.

psychosurgery Any surgical procedure that destroys selected areas of the brain believed to be involved in emotional disorders or violent, impulsive behavior.

electroconvulsive therapy (ECT) A procedure used in cases of prolonged and severe major depression, in which a brief brain seizure is induced.

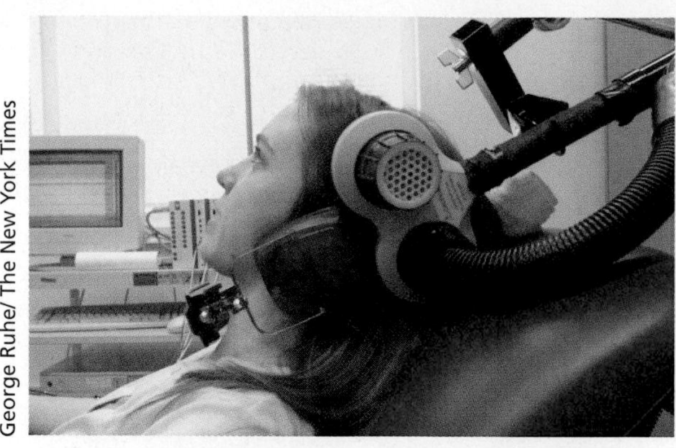

George Ruhe/ The New York Times

A researcher demonstrates transcranial magnetic stimulation (TMS), now being used to treat not only depression but also the auditory hallucinations of schizophrenia.

While this debate continues, researchers are looking for milder ways to electrically stimulate the brains of severely depressed individuals. One method, *transcranial magnetic stimulation (TMS)*, involves the use of a pulsing magnetic coil held to a person's skull over the left prefrontal cortex. This area of the brain is less active in people with depression, and repeated TMS seems to give it a boost. The patient stays awake, and the procedure does not cause memory loss or other side effects (Wasserman & Lisanby, 2001). In one well-controlled study of depressed patients who had not improved on medication, those who were given TMS treatments every day for four weeks were more likely to improve than those given a "sham" treatment with no stimulation (Fitzgerald et al., 2003). Nonetheless, as yet, no one knows why magnetic stimulation might ease a patient's emotional suffering.

QUICK quiz

No amount of electric shock will stimulate test-taking ability.

A. Match these treatments with the problems for which they are typically used.

1. antipsychotic drugs	**a.** suicidal depression
2. antidepressant drugs	**b.** bipolar disorder
3. lithium carbonate	**c.** schizophrenia
4. electroconvulsive therapy	**d.** depression and anxiety
	e. obsessive-compulsive disorder

B. Give four reasons to be cautious about claims that drugs for psychological disorders are miracle cures.

C. Tanya has had occasional episodes of depression that seem to be getting worse. Her physician prescribes an antidepressant. Before taking it, what questions should Tanya ask herself and the doctor?

Answers:

A. 1. c 2. d, e 3. b 4. a **B.** Placebo effects are common; dropout and relapse rates are high; appropriate dosages can be difficult to determine and can vary by sex, age, and ethnicity; and some drugs have unknown or long-term risks. **C.** Has the physician prescribed the drug without taking her full medical and psychological history? Has the physician considered other possible reasons for her depression? Would psychotherapy be appropriate, either with or without medication? Does the medication have any unpleasant side effects or long-term risks? Will the doctor continue to monitor her reactions to the drug on a regular basis?

WHAT'S AHEAD

- Why are psychodynamic therapies called "depth" therapies?
- How can therapies based on learning principles help you change your bad habits?
- How do cognitive therapists help people get rid of self-defeating thoughts?
- Why do humanist therapists focus on the "here and now" instead of the "why and how"?
- Why do family therapists prefer to treat families rather than individuals?

Kinds of Psychotherapy

All good psychotherapists want to help clients think about their lives in new ways and find solutions to the problems that plague them. In this section we will consider the major schools of psychotherapy. To illustrate the philosophy and methods of each one, we will focus on a fictional fellow named Murray. Murray is a smart guy whose problem is all too familiar to many students: He procrastinates. He just can't seem to settle down and write his term papers. He keeps getting incompletes, and before long the incompletes turn to F's. Why does Murray procrastinate, manufacturing his own misery? What kind of therapy might help him?

psychoanalysis A method of "depth" psychotherapy developed by Sigmund Freud, emphasizing the exploration of unconscious motives and conflicts.

free association In psychodynamic therapies, the process of saying freely whatever comes to mind in connection with dreams, memories, fantasies, or conflicts.

psychodynamic therapies Psychotherapies that share the psychoanalytic goal of exploring the unconscious dynamics of personality, although they differ from Freudian analysis in various ways.

transference In psychodynamic therapies, a critical process in which the client transfers unconscious emotions or reactions, such as emotional feelings about his or her parents, onto the therapist.

Psychodynamic Therapy

Sigmund Freud was the father of the "talking cure," as one of his patients called it. In his method of **psychoanalysis**, patients talk not about their immediate problems but about their dreams and their memories of childhood. Freud believed that intensive analysis of these dreams and memories would give patients insight into the unconscious reasons for their symptoms. With insight and emotional release, the person's symptoms would disappear.

In orthodox psychoanalysis, which is rarely practiced today, the client meets with the therapist as often as several times a week for a period of years. The client lies on a sofa, with the analyst sitting out of view, and says whatever comes to mind without censoring, a technique called **free association**. The analyst listens to the client's free associations and dreams, but rarely comments. There is no rush to solve the problem that brought the client into therapy. In fact, a person may come in complaining of a symptom, such as anxiety or headaches, and the therapist may not get around to that symptom for months or even years. The analyst views the symptom as only the tip of the mental iceberg.

Freud's psychoanalytic method has evolved into many different forms of **psychodynamic therapy**, which share the goal of exploring the unconscious dynamics of personality, such as defenses and conflicts (see Chapter 13). Proponents of these therapies often refer to them as "depth" therapies because the goal is to delve into the deep, unconscious processes believed to be the source of the patient's problems, rather than to concentrate on "superficial" symptoms and conscious beliefs. As we saw in Chapter 13, one modern psychodynamic approach is based on *object-relations theory*, which emphasizes the unconscious influence of people's earliest mental representations of their parents and how these affect reactions to separations and losses throughout life.

A major element of most psychodynamic therapies, from Freudian to present forms, is **transference**, the client's transfer (displacement) of emotional elements of his or her inner life—usually feelings about the client's parents—outward onto the analyst. Have you ever found yourself responding to a new acquaintance with unusually quick affection or dislike, and later realized it was because the person reminded you of a relative whom you loved or loathed? That experience is similar to transference. In therapy, a woman who has failed to resolve her Oedipal love for her father might believe she has fallen in love with the analyst. A man who is unconsciously angry at his mother for rejecting him might become furious with his analyst for going on vacation. Through analysis of transference in the therapy setting, psychodynamic therapists believe, clients can see their emotional conflicts in action and work through them (Schafer, 1992; Westen, 1998).

THINKING CRITICALLY

ANALYZE ASSUMPTIONS

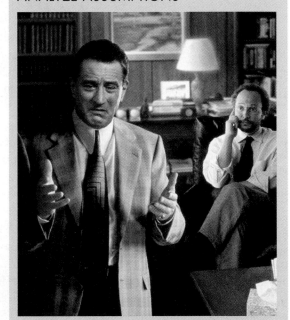

Why do so many people assume that all therapy is psychoanalytic? The answer: That's the image widely conveyed in the media. Many popular TV shows and movies, such as *The Sopranos* and *Analyze This* (with Robert DeNiro as a mobster patient and Billy Crystal as his psychoanalyst), feature psychodynamic therapists.

Today, most psychodynamic therapists reject the orthodox psychoanalytic approach of having the silent analyst listen to a client free associating. They face the client, they are more goal directed, and they limit therapy to a specific number of sessions, say, 10 or 20. Perhaps they might help our friend Murray gain the insight that he procrastinates as a way of expressing anger toward his parents. He might realize that he is angry because they insist that he study for a career he dislikes. Ideally, Murray will come to this insight by himself. If the analyst suggests it, Murray might feel too defensive to accept it.

Behavior and Cognitive Therapy

Unlike psychodynamic therapists, psychologists who practice behavior therapy or cognitive therapy would not worry much about Murray's past, his parents, or his unconscious anxieties. Psychologists who practice behavior therapy would get right to the problem: What are the reinforcers in Murray's environment that are maintaining his behavior? "Mur," they would say, "Forget about insight. You have lousy study habits." Psychologists who practice cognitive therapy would focus on helping Murray understand how his beliefs about studying, writing papers, and success are woefully unrealistic. Often these two approaches are combined.

Behavioral Techniques. **Behavior therapy** is based on *applied behavioral analysis*, the application of techniques derived from the behavioral principles of classical and operant conditioning that we discussed in Chapter 7. (You may want to review those principles before going on.) Here are some of these methods (Kazdin, 2001):

1 Exposure. The most widely used behavioral approach for treating fears and panic is **graduated exposure**. When people are afraid of some situation, object, or upsetting memory, they usually do everything they can to avoid confronting or thinking of it. Naturally, this only makes the fear worse. Exposure treatments, either in the client's imagination or in actual situations, are aimed at reversing this tendency. In graduated exposure, the client controls the degree of confrontation with the source of the fear. For example, someone who is trying to avoid thinking of a traumatic event might be asked to imagine the event over and over, until it no longer evokes the same degree of panic. A more dramatic form of exposure is **flooding**, in which the therapist takes the client directly into the feared situation and remains there until the client's panic and anxiety decline. Thus a person suffering from agoraphobia might be taken into a department store or a subway, an action that would normally be terrifying to contemplate. Notice how different this approach is from the psychodynamic one, in which the goal is to uncover the presumably unconscious reason that the agoraphobic feels afraid of going out.

2 Systematic desensitization. Systematic desensitization is an older behavioral method, a step-by-step process of breaking down a client's conditioned associations with a feared object or experience (Wolpe, 1958). It is based on the classical-conditioning procedure of *counterconditioning*, in which a stimulus (such as a dog) for an unwanted response (such as fear) is paired with some other stimulus or situation that elicits a response incompatible with the undesirable one (see Chapter 7). In this case, the incompatible response is usually relaxation. The client learns to relax deeply while imagining or looking at a sequence of feared stimuli, arranged in a hierarchy from the least frightening to the most frightening. The hierarchy itself is provided by the

behavior therapy A form of therapy that applies principles of classical and operant conditioning to help people change self-defeating or problematic behaviors.

graduated exposure In behavior therapy, a method in which a person suffering from a phobia or panic attacks is gradually taken into the feared situation or exposed to a traumatic memory until the anxiety subsides.

flooding In behavior therapy, a form of exposure treatment in which the client is taken directly into the feared situation until his or her panic subsides.

systematic desensitization In behavior therapy, a step-by-step process of desensitizing a client to a feared object or experience; it is based on the classical-conditioning procedure of counterconditioning.

client. The sequence for a person who is terrified of spiders might be to read the classic children's story *Charlotte's Web*, then look at pictures of small, cute spiders, then look at pictures of tarantulas, then move on to observing a real spider, and so on. At each step the person must become relaxed before going on. Eventually, the fear responses are extinguished.

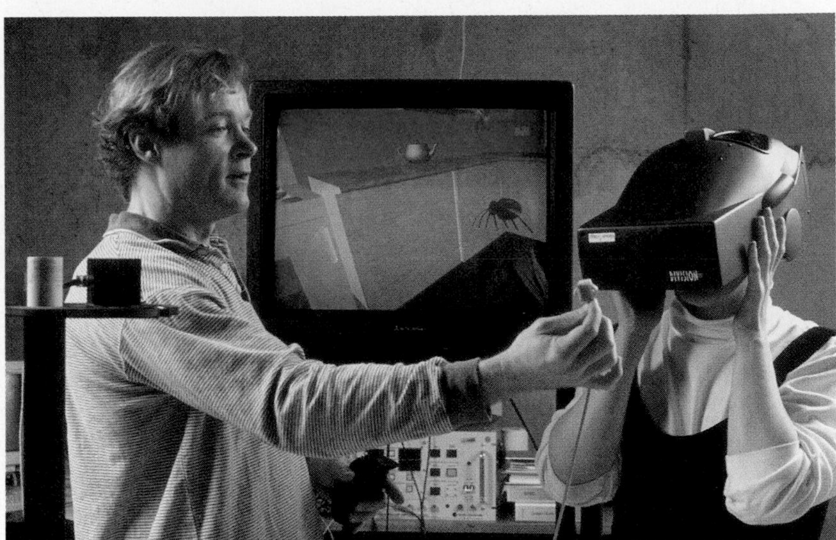

In this "virtual reality" version of systematic desensitization, people with spider phobias are gradually exposed to computerized but extremely lifelike images of spiders in a realistic, three-dimensional environment (Wiederhold & Wiederhold, 2000).

3 **Behavioral self-monitoring.** Before people can change their behavior, they have to identify the reinforcers that are supporting their unwanted habits: attention from others, temporary relief from tension or unhappiness, or tangible rewards such as money or a good meal. One way to do this is for the client to keep a record of the behavior that he or she wishes to change. A man who wants to curb his overeating may not be aware of how much he eats throughout the day to relieve tension; a behavioral record might show that he eats more junk food than he realized in the late afternoon. A mother might complain that her child "always" has temper tantrums; a behavioral record will show when, where, and with whom they occur. Once the unwanted behavior is identified, along with the reinforcers that have been maintaining it, a treatment program can be designed to change it. For instance, the man might find other ways to reduce stress and make sure that he is nowhere near junk food in the late afternoon. The mother can learn to respond to her child's tantrum not with her attention (or a cookie to buy silence) but with a time-out: banishing the child to a corner where no positive reinforcers are available.

4 **Skills training.** It is not enough to tell someone "Don't be shy" if the person does not know how to make small talk with others, or "Don't yell!" if the person does not know how to express feelings calmly. Therefore, some behavior therapists use operant-conditioning techniques, modeling, and role-playing to teach the skills a client might lack. For example, a shy person might learn how to converse in social settings by focusing on other people rather than on his or her own insecurity. Skills-training programs have been designed for all kinds of behavioral problems, such as teaching parents how to discipline their children, impulsive adults how to manage anger, and people with schizophrenia how to get along in the world. One widely used therapy for autistic children applies principles of operant conditioning to reduce the child's inappropriate or self-destructive behavior and help the child acquire specific social and linguistic skills (Green, 1996a, b).

A behaviorist would treat Murray's procrastination in several ways. Murray might not know how he actually spends his time when he is avoiding his studies. Afraid that he hasn't time to do everything, he does nothing. Monitoring his own behavior with a diary would let Murray know exactly how he spends his time, and how much time he should realistically allot to a project. Instead of having a vague, impossibly huge goal, such as "I'm going to reorganize my life," Murray would establish specific small goals, such as reading the two books necessary for an English paper and writing one page of an assignment. If Murray does not know how to write clearly, however, even writing one page might feel overwhelming; he might also need some skills training, such as a

behavioral self-monitoring In behavior therapy, a method of keeping careful data on the frequency and consequences of the behavior to be changed.

skills training In behavior therapy, an effort to teach the client skills that he or she may lack, as well as new constructive behaviors to replace self-defeating ones.

GET INVOLVED!

➤CURE YOUR FEARS

In Chapter 16, a Get Involved exercise asked you to identify your greatest fear. Now see whether systematic desensitization procedures will help you conquer it. Write down a list of situations that evoke your fear, starting with one that produces little anxiety (e.g., seeing a photo of a tiny brown spider) and ending with the most frightening one possible (e.g., looking at live tarantulas at the pet store). Then find a quiet room where you will have no distractions or interruptions, sit in a comfortable reclining chair, and relax all the muscles of your body. Breathe slowly and deeply. Imagine the first, easiest scene, remaining as relaxed as possible. Do this until you can confront the image without becoming the least bit anxious. When that happens, go on to the next scene in your hierarchy. Do not try this all at once; space out your sessions over time. Does it work?

Cognitive therapists encourage clients to emphasize the positive (the early sunny signs of spring) rather than always focusing on the negative (the lingering icy clutch of winter). Poet Michael Casey described the first daffodil that bravely rises through the snow as "a gleam of laughter in a sullen face."

basic composition class. Most important, the therapist would change the reinforcers that are maintaining Murray's "procrastination behavior"—perhaps the immediate gratification of partying with friends—and replace them with reinforcers for getting the work done.

Cognitive Techniques. As we saw in Chapter 11, gloomy thoughts can generate an array of negative emotions and self-defeating behavior. The underlying premise of **cognitive therapy** is that constructive thinking can do the opposite, reducing or dispelling anger, fear, and depression. This is not a new idea. It originated 2,000 years ago, with the Stoic philosophers, and was popularized in the United States in the "mind cure" movement of the nineteenth century (Caplan, 1998).

Today, cognitive therapists help clients identify the beliefs and expectations that might be unnecessarily prolonging their unhappiness, conflicts, and other problems (Persons, Davidson, & Tompkins, 2001). Clients examine the evidence for their beliefs—say, that everyone is mean and selfish, that ambition is hopeless, or that love is doomed. They learn to consider other explanations for the behavior of people who annoy them: For example, perhaps their father's strict discipline was intended not to control but to protect them. By requiring people to identify their assumptions and biases, examine the evidence, and consider other interpretations, cognitive therapy, as you can see, teaches critical thinking.

One of the best-known contemporary schools of cognitive therapy is Albert Ellis's **rational emotive behavior therapy (REBT)** (Ellis, 1993; Ellis & Blau, 1998). In this approach, which reflects Ellis's own no-nonsense, get-on-with-it attitude, the therapist uses rational arguments to directly challenge a client's unrealistic beliefs or expectations. Ellis has pointed out that people who are emotionally upset often *overgeneralize:* They decide that one annoying act by someone means that person is totally bad in every way, or that a normal mistake they made is evidence that they are rotten to the core. Many people also *catastrophize*, transforming a small problem into disaster: "I failed this test, and now I'll flunk out of school, and no one will ever like me, and even my cat will hate me, and I'll never get a job." Ellis also observed that many people drive themselves crazy with notions of what they "must" do. The therapist challenges these thoughts directly, showing the client why they are irrational and misguided.

Another leading form of cognitive therapy, devised by Aaron Beck (1976, 2005), avoids direct challenges to the client's beliefs. Beck pioneered in the application of cognitive therapy for depression. As we saw in Chapter 16, depression often arises from

cognitive therapy A form of therapy designed to identify and change irrational, unproductive ways of thinking and, hence, to reduce negative emotions.

rational emotive behavior therapy (REBT) A form of cognitive therapy devised by Albert Ellis, designed to challenge the client's unrealistic thoughts.

GET INVOLVED!

➤MIND OVER MOOD

See whether cognitive-therapy techniques can help you control your moods. Think of a time recently when you felt a particularly strong emotion, such as depression, anger, or anxiety. On a piece of paper, record (1) the situation—who was there, what happened, and when; (2) the intensity of your feeling at the time, from weak to strong; and (3) the thoughts that were going through your mind (e.g., "She never cares about what I want to do"; "I hate being angry"; "He's going to leave me").

Now examine your thoughts. What is the worst thing that could happen if those thoughts are true? Are your thoughts accurate or are you "mind-reading" the other person's intentions and motives? Is there another way to think about this situation or the other person's behavior? If you practice this exercise repeatedly, you may learn how your thoughts affect your moods—and find out that you have more control over your feelings than you realized (Greenberger & Padesky, 1995).

specific pessimistic thoughts—for example, that the sources of your misery are permanent and that nothing good will ever happen to you again. For Beck, these beliefs are not "irrational"; rather, they are unproductive or based on misinformation. A therapist using Beck's approach would ask you to test your beliefs against the evidence. If you say, "But I *know* no one likes me," the therapist might say, "Oh, yes? How do you know? Do you really not have a single friend? Has anyone in the past year been nice to you?"

A cognitive therapist might treat Murray's procrastination by having Murray write down his thoughts about work, read the thoughts as if someone else had said them, and then write a rational response to each one. This technique would encourage Murray to examine the validity of his assumptions and beliefs. Many procrastinators are perfectionists; if they cannot do something perfectly, they will not do it at all. Unable to accept their limitations, they set impossible standards and catastrophize:

Negative Thought	Rational Response
If I don't get an A+ on this paper, my life will be ruined.	My life will be a lot worse if I keep getting incompletes. It's better to get a B or even a C than to do nothing.
My professor is going to think I'm an idiot when he reads this. I'll feel humiliated by his criticism.	He hasn't accused me of being an idiot yet. If he makes some criticisms, I can learn from them and do better next time.

Strict behaviorists consider thoughts to be "behaviors" that are modifiable by learning principles; they do not regard thoughts themselves as causes of behavior. But most psychologists believe that thoughts and behavior influence each other, which is why *cognitive-behavior therapy* (CBT) is more common than either cognitive or behavior therapy alone.

Humanist and Existential Therapy

Humanist therapy, like its parent philosophy humanism, starts from the assumption that human nature is basically good and that people behave badly or develop problems when they are warped by self-imposed limits. Humanist therapists, therefore, want to know how clients subjectively see their own situations and how they construe the world around them. These therapists generally do not dig into the client's past but instead focus on helping the person to develop the will and confidence to change and achieve his or her goals. That is why these therapists explore what is going on "here and now," not past issues of "why and how."

humanist therapy A form of psychotherapy based on the philosophy of humanism, which emphasizes the client's free will to change rather than past conflicts.

client-centered (nondirective) therapy A humanist approach, devised by Carl Rogers, which emphasizes the therapist's empathy with the client and the use of unconditional positive regard.

existential therapy A form of therapy designed to help clients explore the meaning of existence and face the great questions of life, such as death, freedom, alienation, and loneliness.

In **client-centered (nondirective) therapy**, developed by Carl Rogers, the therapist's role is to listen to the client's needs in an accepting, nonjudgmental way and offer what Rogers called *unconditional positive regard* (see Chapter 13). Whatever the client's specific complaint is, the goal is to build the client's self-esteem and self-acceptance and help the client find a more productive way of seeing his or her problems. Thus a Rogerian might assume that Murray's procrastination masks his low self-regard and that Murray is out of touch with his real feelings and wishes. Perhaps he is not passing his courses because he is trying to please his parents by majoring in pre-law, when he would secretly rather become an artist.

Rogers (1951, 1961) believed that effective therapists must be warm and genuine. For Rogerians, *empathy*, the therapist's ability to understand and accept what the client says, is the crucial ingredient of successful therapy. The therapist shows a basic level of empathy by listening carefully and being able to restate accurately the client's remarks: "You tell me that you feel frustrated, Murray, because no matter how hard you try, you don't succeed." And the therapist shows advanced empathy by understanding the *meaning* of the client's remarks: "Working that hard without results must really make you unhappy and maybe make you feel a bit sorry for yourself." The client, according to humanist therapists, will eventually internalize the therapist's support and become more self-accepting.

Existential therapy helps clients explore the meaning of existence and face with courage the great questions of existence, such as death, freedom, alienation from oneself and others, loneliness, and meaninglessness. Existential therapists, like humanist therapists, believe that our lives are not inevitably determined by our pasts or our circumstances; we have the power and free will to choose our own destinies. As Irvin Yalom (1989) explained, "The crucial first step in therapy is the patient's assumption of responsibility for his or her life predicament. As long as one believes that one's problems are caused by some force or agency outside oneself, there is no leverage in therapy."

Yalom argues that the goal of therapy is to help clients cope with the inescapable realities of life and death and the struggle for meaning. However grim our experiences may be, he believes, "they contain the seeds of wisdom and redemption." Perhaps the most remarkable example of a man able to find seeds of wisdom in a barren landscape was Victor Frankl (1905–1997), who developed a form of existential therapy after surviving a Nazi concentration camp. In that pit of horror, Frankl (1955) observed, some people maintained their sanity because they were able to find meaning in the experience, shattering though it was.

Some observers believe that, ultimately, all therapies are existential. In different ways, therapy helps people determine what is important to them, what values guide them, and what changes they will have the courage to make. An existential therapist might help Murray think about the significance of his procrastination, what his ultimate goals in life are, and how he might find the strength to carry out his ambitions.

Some family therapists use photographs to help people identify themes and problems in their family histories. Does this picture convey a happy and cohesive family to you or a divided one? Shortly after it was taken, the couple divorced; the father took custody of the children. . . and the mother kept the dog (Entin, 1992).

Family and Couples Therapy

Murray's situation is getting worse. His father has begun to call him Tomorrow Man, which upsets his mother, and his younger brother, the math major, has been calculating how much tuition money Murray's incompletes are costing. His older sister, Isabel, the biochemist who never had an incomplete in her life, now proposes that all of them go to a family therapist. "Murray's not the only one in this family with complaints," she says.

Family therapists would maintain that Murray's problem developed in the context of his family, that it is sustained by the dynamics of his family, and that any change he makes will affect all members of his family (McDaniel, Lusterman, & Philpot, 2001). One of the most famous early

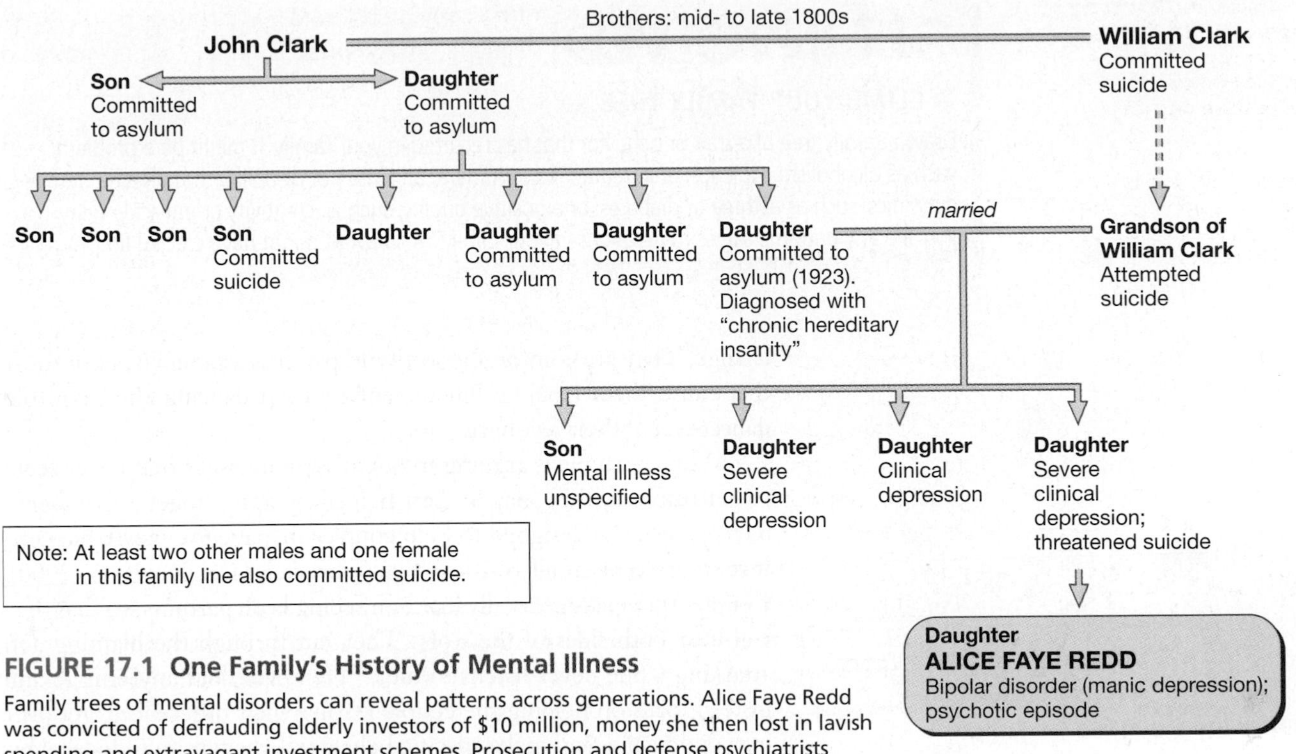

FIGURE 17.1 One Family's History of Mental Illness

Family trees of mental disorders can reveal patterns across generations. Alice Faye Redd was convicted of defrauding elderly investors of $10 million, money she then lost in lavish spending and extravagant investment schemes. Prosecution and defense psychiatrists agreed that she suffered from bipolar disorder. Alice Redd's daughter constructed this multigenerational family record of depression and suicide in an effort to have her mother committed for treatment, but the court sentenced Redd to 15 years in prison.

family therapists, Salvador Minuchin (1984), compared the family to a kaleidoscope, a changing pattern of mosaics in which the pattern is larger than any one piece. In this view, efforts to isolate and treat one member of the family without the others are doomed. Only if all family members reveal their differing perceptions of each other can mistakes and misperceptions be identified. A teenager, for instance, may see his mother as crabby and nagging when actually she is tired and worried. A parent may see a child as rebellious when in fact the child is lonely and desperate for attention.

Family members are usually unaware of how they influence one another. By observing the entire family, the family therapist hopes to discover tensions and imbalances in power and communication. For example, in some families a child may have a chronic illness or a psychological problem, such as anorexia, that affects the workings of the whole family. One parent may become overinvolved with the sick child while the other parent retreats, and each may start blaming the other. The child, in turn, may cling to the illness or disorder as a way of expressing anger, keeping the parents together, getting the parents' attention, or asserting control.

Some family therapists look for patterns of behavior across generations. The therapist and client may create a family tree showing psychologically significant events across as many generations as possible (McGoldrick, Gerson, & Shellenberger, 1999). This method may reveal historical patterns, as you can see in Figure 17.1.

Even when it is not possible to treat the whole family, some therapists will treat individuals in a **family-systems perspective**, which recognizes that people's behavior in a family is as interconnected as that of two dancers (Bowen, 1978; Cox & Paley, 2003). Clients learn that if they change in any way, even for the better, their families may protest noisily or may send subtle messages that read, "Change back!" Why? Because when one family member changes, each of the others must change too. As the saying goes, it takes two to tango, and if one dancer stops, so must the other. But most people do not like

family-systems perspective An approach to doing therapy with individuals or families by identifying how each family member forms part of a larger interacting system.

GET INVOLVED!

➤CLIMB YOUR FAMILY TREE

Draw a family tree of a trait or behavior that has recurred in your family. It might be a problem, such as alcoholism, violence, or parental abandonment; an illness or disability that affected family dynamics, such as asthma or diabetes; or a positive quality, such as creativity or musical ability. Do you see any patterns across generations in your family? If so, what might have caused them?

"I've been a cow all my life, honey. Don't ask me to change now.'

change. They are comfortable with old patterns and habits, even those that cause them trouble. They want to keep dancing the same old dance, even if their feet hurt.

When a couple is arguing frequently about issues that never seem to get resolved, they may be best helped by going together to *couples therapy*, which is designed to help couples manage the inevitable conflicts that occur in all relationships (Christensen & Jacobson, 2000). Couples therapists generally insist on seeing both partners, so that they will hear both sides of the story. They cut through the blaming and attacking ("She never listens to me!" "He never does anything!") and instead focus on helping the couple resolve their differences, get over hurt and blame, and make specific behavioral changes to reduce anger and conflict. Recently, however, many couples therapists have been moving away from the "fix all the differences" approach and are instead helping couples learn to accept and live with qualities in both partners that aren't going to change much (Hayes, 2004). For example, a wife can stop trying to turn her calm, steady husband into a spontaneous adventurer ("After all, that's what I originally loved about him—he's as steady as a rock") and a husband can stop trying to make his shy wife more assertive ("I have always loved her remarkable serenity").

Family and couples therapists may use psychodynamic, behavioral, cognitive, or humanist approaches in their work; they share only a focus on the family or the couple. In Murray's case, a family therapist would observe how Murray's procrastination fits his family dynamics. Perhaps it allows Murray to get his father's attention and his mother's sympathy. Perhaps it keeps Murray from facing his greatest fear: that if he does finish his work, it will not measure up to his father's impossibly high standards. The therapist will not only help Murray change his work habits but will also help his family deal with a changed Murray.

The kinds of psychotherapy that we have discussed are all quite different in theory, and so are their techniques (see Review 17.2). Yet in practice, many psychotherapists take an *integrative approach*, drawing on methods and ideas from various schools and avoiding strong allegiances to any one theory. This flexibility enables them to treat clients with whatever methods are most appropriate and effective. For example, some therapists may use behavioral methods to quickly help a client suffering from a phobia, but they may also apply principles from "depth" psychology to help the client explore the role the phobia has come to play in his or her life.

In discussing theories of personality in Chapter 13, we described the importance of the life narrative—the story that each of us develops to explain who we are and how we got that way (McAdams & Pals, 2006). In a fundamental way, all successful therapies, regardless of their approach, share a key element: They are able to motivate the client into wanting to change, and they replace a client's pessimistic or unrealistic life narrative with one that is more hopeful or attainable (Howard, 1991; Schafer, 1992).

REVIEW 17.2
The Major Schools of Therapy Compared

	Primary Goal	Methods
Psychodynamic		
Psychoanalytic	Insight into unconscious motives and feelings	Probing unconscious motives through dream analysis, free association, transference; several visits a week with little participation by analyst
Psychodynamic	Same	Analyst more active and directive; therapy briefer
Cognitive-Behavioral		
Behavioral	Modification of self-defeating behaviors	Graduated exposure (flooding), systematic desensitization, behavioral records, skills training
Cognitive	Modification of irrational or unvalidated beliefs	Challenging unwarranted beliefs (catastrophizing, mind-reading) or prompting client to test beliefs against evidence
Humanist and Existential		
Humanist	Insight; self-acceptance and self-fulfillment; new, optimistic perceptions of self and world	Providing a nonjudgmental setting in which to discuss issues; use of empathy and unconditional positive regard by therapist
Existential	Finding meaning in life and accepting inevitable losses	Varies with therapist; philosophic discussions about meaning of life, client's goals, finding courage
Family and Couples		
Family	Modification of family patterns	May use any of the preceding methods to change family patterns that perpetuate problems and conflicts
Couples	Resolution of conflicts, breaking out of destructive habits	May use any of the preceding methods to help the couple communicate better, resolve conflicts, or accept what cannot be changed

QUICK quiz

Don't be a procrastinator like our friend Murray; take this quiz now.

Match each method or concept with the therapy associated with it.

1. transference
2. systematic desensitization
3. facing the fear of death
4. reappraisal of thoughts
5. unconditional positive regard
6. exposure to feared situation
7. avoidance of "catastrophizing"
8. analysis of generational patterns

a. cognitive therapy
b. psychodynamic therapy
c. humanist therapy
d. behavior therapy
e. family therapy
f. existential therapy

Answers:

1.b 2.d 3.f 4.a 5.c 6.d 7.a 8.e

WHAT'S AHEAD

- What is the "therapeutic alliance," and why does it matter?
- What sorts of people make the best therapists and the best clients?
- What is the "scientist–practitioner gap" and why has it been widening?
- Which form of psychotherapy is most likely to help if you are anxious or depressed?
- Under what conditions can psychotherapy be harmful?

Evaluating Psychotherapy

Poor Murray! He is getting a little baffled by all these therapies. He wants to make a choice soon; no sense in procrastinating about that, too! Is there any scientific evidence, he wonders, that might help him decide which therapy—or therapist—will be best for him?

The Therapeutic Alliance

A therapeutic alliance begins with the therapist's warmth and empathy and the client's willingness to be helped.

Psychotherapy is, first and foremost, a relationship. As in all relationships, its success depends on the qualities that each person brings to the encounter. Successful therapy often also depends on the bond the therapist and client establish between them, called the **therapeutic alliance**. When both parties respect and understand one another and agree on the goals of treatment, the client is more likely to improve, regardless of the specific techniques the therapist uses (Klein et al., 2003).

Qualities of the Participants. Clients who are most likely to do well in therapy are, not surprisingly, motivated to improve and solve their problems (Orlinsky & Howard, 1994). They tend to have support from their families and a personal style of dealing actively with problems instead of avoiding them. Personality traits also influence whether a person will be able to change in therapy. As we saw in Chapter 13, some people are characteristically negative and bitter; others are more agreeable and positive, even in the midst of emotional crises. Hostile, negative individuals are more resistant to therapy and less likely to benefit from it; so are people with long-standing personality problems or psychotic disorders (Kopta et al., 1994). The personality of the therapist affects the outcome of therapy, too, particularly the qualities that Carl Rogers praised: empathy, warmth, and genuineness. The most successful therapists make their clients feel respected, accepted, and understood (Miller, 2000).

Culture and the Therapeutic Connection. Many therapists and clients establish successful therapeutic alliances in spite of coming from different backgrounds. But sometimes cultural differences cause misunderstandings that result from ignorance or prejudice (Comas-Dìaz & Greene, 1994). A lifetime of experience with racism and a general "cultural distrust" may keep some African-Americans from revealing feelings that they believe a white therapist would not understand or accept (Whaley, 2001). Misunderstandings and prejudice may be one reason that Asian-American, Latino, and African-American clients are more likely to stay in therapy when their therapists' ethnicity matches their own. But a cultural "match" is also important because it often makes it more likely that clients and therapists share perceptions of what the client's problem is, agree on the best way of coping, and have the same expectations about what therapy can accomplish (Zane et al., 2005).

In establishing a bond with clients, therapists must distinguish normal cultural patterns from individual psychological problems. An Irish-American family therapist, Monica McGoldrick (1996), described some problems that are typical of Irish-American families. These problems arise from Irish history and religious beliefs, and they are deeply ingrained. "In general, the therapist cannot expect the family to turn into a physically affectionate, emotionally intimate group, or to enjoy being in therapy very much," she observed. "The notion of Original Sin—that you are guilty before you are born—leaves them with a heavy sense of burden. Someone not sensitized to these

therapeutic alliance The bond of confidence and mutual understanding established between therapist and client, which allows them to work together to solve the client's problems.

Some psychotherapists fit their approach to the client's cultural background. For example, most Puerto Rican children know the tales of Juan Bobo (left), a foolish child ("bobo") who is always getting into trouble. The therapists on the right have adapted these stories for Puerto Rican children who are coping with new problems and temptations in America. The children and their mothers watch a videotape of the folktale, discuss it together, and role-play its major themes, such as controlling aggression and understanding right from wrong. This method has been more successful than traditional therapies in reducing the children's transitional anxieties and improving their attention spans and achievement motivation (Constantino & Malgady, 1996).

issues may see this as pathological. It is not. But it is also not likely to change and the therapist should help the family tolerate this inner guilt rather than try to get rid of it."

More and more psychotherapists are becoming "sensitized to the issues" caused by cultural differences (Arredondo et al., 2005). For example, many Latino and Asian clients are likely to react to a formal interview with a therapist with relative passivity and deference, leading some therapists to misdiagnose this cultural norm as a problem with shyness. In Latin American cultures, *susto,* or "loss of the soul," is a common response to extreme grief or fright; the person believes that his or her soul has departed along with that of the deceased relative. A psychotherapist unfamiliar with this culturally determined response might conclude that the sufferer was delusional or psychotic. Latino clients are also more likely than Anglos to value harmony in their relationships, which often translates into an unwillingness to express negative emotions or confront family members or friends directly, so therapists need to help such clients find ways to communicate better within that cultural context (Arredondo & Perez, 2003).

Being aware of cultural differences, however, does not mean that the therapist should stereotype clients. Some Asians, after all, do have problems with excessive shyness, some Latinos do have emotional disorders, and some Irish do not carry burdens of guilt! It does mean that therapists must ensure that their clients find them to be trustworthy and effective; and it means that clients must be aware of their own prejudices, too.

The Scientist–Practitioner Gap

Now suppose that Murray has found a nice psychotherapist who seems pretty smart and friendly. Is a good alliance enough? How important is the *kind* of therapy that an individual practices? Have some methods of psychotherapy been scientifically shown to be more effective than others, are some totally useless, and are some potentially harmful?

These questions have generated a huge debate among clinical practitioners and psychological scientists. Many psychotherapists believe that trying to evaluate psychotherapy using standard empirical methods is an exercise in futility: Numbers and graphs, they say, cannot possibly capture the complex exchange that takes place between a therapist and a client. What "works" in psychotherapy is usually not a good technique but a good *relationship.* Psychotherapy, they maintain, is an art that you acquire from clinical experience; it is not a science. You can't measure its effectiveness

the way you can measure, say, the effectiveness of a new drug, because so many diverse ingredients go into a good psychotherapeutic experience (Wampold, 2001). Other clinicians fear that efforts to measure the effectiveness of psychotherapy oversimplify the process, because, among other reasons, many patients have an assortment of emotional problems and need therapy for a longer time than research can reasonably allow (Westen, Novotny, & Thompson-Brenner, 2004).

THINKING CRITICALLY

ANALYZE ASSUMPTIONS AND BIASES

Most psychotherapists assume that therapy is an art, an exchange between therapist and client whose essence cannot be captured by research. How valid is this assumption? Given the many therapies that lack scientific support, should consumers assume they can rely on the testimonials of satisfied clients?

For their part, psychological scientists agree that therapy is often a complex process. But that is no reason it cannot be scientifically investigated, they argue, just like any other complex psychological process such as the development of language or personality (Crits-Christoph, Wilson, & Hollon, 2005). Moreover, they are concerned that when therapists fail to keep up with empirical findings in the field, their clients may suffer. It is crucial, scientists say, for therapists to be aware of research findings on the most beneficial methods for particular problems, on ineffective or potentially harmful techniques, and on topics relevant to their practice, such as memory, hypnosis, and child development (Lilienfeld, Lynn, & Lohr, 2003).

Over the years, the breach between scientists and therapists has widened, creating what is commonly called the *scientist–practitioner gap*. As we saw in Chapter 1, one reason for the growing split has been the rise of professional schools that are not connected to academic psychology departments and that train students solely to do therapy. Graduates of these schools sometimes know little about research methods or even about research assessing different therapy techniques.

The scientist–practitioner gap has also widened because of the proliferation of new therapies trying to gain a foothold in a crowded market. Some of these therapies are packaged and promoted without any scientific support at all (Beyerstein, 1999). One such therapy, Neurolinguistic Programming (NLP), claims to match people's learning styles with their "brain types" and thereby enhance their communication skills. The U.S. National Research Council concluded that there is no credible evidence for NLP's claims or methods (Druckman & Swets, 1988).

Other therapies repackage established techniques, using a new name and terminology. For example, Eye Movement Desensitization and Reprocessing (EMDR) is built on the tried-and-true behavioral techniques of desensitization and exposure for treating anxiety (Lohr, Tolin, & Lilienfeld, 1998). EMDR's founder, Francine Shapiro (1995), added eye-movement exercises: Clients move their eyes from side to side, following the therapist's moving finger, while concentrating on the memory to be desensitized. Shapiro's (1994) explanation for why such eye movements work is that "the system may become unbalanced due to a trauma or through stress engendered during a developmental window, but once appropriately catalyzed and maintained in a dynamic state by EMDR, it transmutes information to a state of therapeutically appropriate resolution." (If you do not understand that, don't worry; we don't either.)

Thousands of therapists have been trained to do EMDR, and they have claimed success in treating everything from post-traumatic stress disorder and panic attacks to eating disorders and sexual dysfunction. EMDR has even won endorsements from some prominent psychologists. Yet there is no evidence from controlled studies that it is any better than standard exposure treatments (Goldstein et al., 2000; Lohr et al., 1999; Taylor et al., 2003). One clinical researcher who reviewed the evidence concluded that the eye movements that are supposedly essential to this technique do not constitute "anything more than pseudoscientific window dressing" (Lilienfeld, 1996).

Problems in Assessing Therapy. Because of the proliferation of therapies, including many that are questionable at best, and because of economic pressures on insurers and rising health costs, clinical psychologists are increasingly being called on to provide empirical assessments of therapy. But you can't just ask people if the therapy helped them, because no matter what kind of therapy is involved, clients are motivated to tell you it worked. "Dr. Blitznik is a genius!" they will exclaim. "I would *never* have taken that job (or moved to Cincinnati, or found my true love) if it hadn't been for Dr. Blitznik!" Every kind of therapy ever devised produces enthusiastic testimonials from people who feel it saved their lives.

The problem with testimonials is that none of us can be our own control group. How do people know they wouldn't have taken the job, moved to Cincinnati, or found true love anyway—maybe even sooner, if Dr. Blitznik had not kept them in treatment? Second, Dr. Blitznik's success could be due to the placebo effect: The client's anticipation of success and the buzz about Dr. B.'s fabulous new method might be the active ingredients, rather than Dr. B.'s therapy itself. And third, notice that you never hear testimonials from the people who dropped out, who weren't helped, or who actually got worse. So researchers cannot be satisfied with testimonials, no matter how glowing. They know that thanks to the *justification of effort* effect (see Chapter 9), people who have put time, money, and effort into something will tell you it was worth it. No one wants to say, "Yeah, I saw Dr. Blitznik for five years, and boy, was it ever a waste of time." To guard against these problems, some clinical researchers conduct **randomized controlled trials**, in which people with a given problem or disorder are randomly assigned to one or more treatment groups or to a control group.

randomized controlled trials Research designed to determine the effectiveness of a new medication or form of therapy, in which people with a given problem or disorder are randomly assigned to one or more treatment groups or to a control group.

CLOSE-UP on Research

DOES CRISIS DEBRIEFING HELP?

Sometimes the results of randomized controlled trials have been surprising, even shocking. For example, in the aftermath of natural and human-made disasters, such as earthquakes or terrorist attacks, disaster therapists often arrive on the scene to treat survivors for symptoms of trauma, hoping to prevent survivors from later developing posttraumatic stress disorder (PTSD). In one of the most popular interventions, called Critical Incident Stress Debriefing (CISD), survivors gather in a group for "debriefing," which generally lasts from one to three hours. Participants are expected to disclose their thoughts and emotions about the traumatic experience, and the group leader warns members about possible trauma symptoms that might develop.

Several independent investigators have **analyzed the assumptions** that underlie CISD: that a traumatic experience almost invariably causes long-lasting posttraumatic stress disorder (as we saw in Chapter 16, it does not); that venting negative emotions is "cathartic" and helps you "get rid" of them (as we saw in Chapter 11, it often does just the opposite); and that early intervention—getting to survivors in the immediate aftermath of a disaster—is necessary to head off the development of serious PTSD. All of these assumptions seem to be perfectly reasonable, but when psychological scientists **avoided emotional reasoning** ("It feels reasonable, so it must be true") and **examined the evidence** for them, they were in for a surprise.

A woman comforts her sister after a devastating earthquake in which the sister lost her home. There is a widespread belief that most survivors of any disaster will need the help of therapists to avoid developing posttraumatic stress disorder. What do randomized controlled studies show?

Richard Gist, a community psychologist who works with firefighters and has witnessed many tragedies and disasters in that capacity, investigated the efficacy of

debriefing following a plane crash in Sioux City, Iowa, in which 112 of 296 passengers died. Rescue teams faced with the grisly job of recovering bodies were randomly assigned to either CISD or no treatment and were followed up two years later (Gist, Lubin, & Redburn, 1998). The researchers found no evidence that "debriefed" firefighters were doing any better than those who had not had the intervention; in fact, there was a slight but statistically significant trend toward the *worsening* of anxiety symptoms in those who had been in CISD. The rescuers who were doing the best had relied on informal souces of support and help—friends and co-workers who had shared the experience.

Researchers have **considered other explanations** for these findings. Perhaps the results were unique to the kind of disaster or to the kind of survivors, in this case professional firefighters who are used to dealing with traumatic events. But many other studies have replicated and extended these findings with a wide assortment of human tragedies and with all sorts of people, including victims of burns, accidents, miscarriages, violent crimes, and combat (van Emmerik et al., 2002; McNally, Bryant, & Ehlers, 2003).

For example, in one randomized controlled trial, people who were victims of serious car accidents were followed for three years; some had received the CISD intervention and some had not. As you can see in the accompanying figure, almost everyone had recovered in only four months and remained fine after three years; those who received the intervention actually fared worse on several measures. The researchers, however, **did not oversimplify** their results. They divided the survivors into two groups: those who had had a highly emotional reaction to the accident at the outset ("high scorers"), and those who had not. For the latter group, the intervention made no difference; they improved quickly. But look at what happened to the people who really were quite traumatized by the accident: If they did *not* get CISD, they were fine in four months, too, like everyone else. But for those who *did* get the intervention, CISD actually blocked their improvement, and they had higher stress symptoms than all the others in the study even after three years. The researchers concluded that "psychological debriefing is ineffective and has adverse long-term effects. It is not an appropriate treatment for trauma victims" (Mayou et al., 2000). In 2005, the World Health Organization, which deals with survivors of trauma around the world, agreed with this assessment (van Ommeren, Saxena, & Saraceno, 2005).

You can see, then, why the scientific assessment of psychotherapeutic claims and methods is so important.

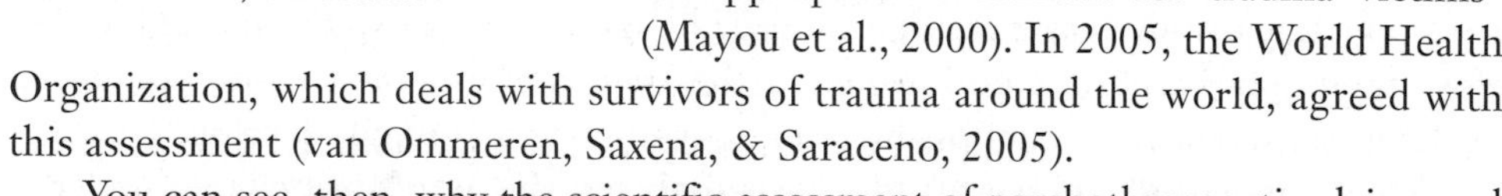

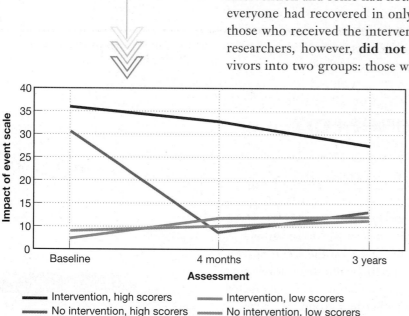

When Therapy Helps

We turn now to the evidence showing the benefits of psychotherapy and which therapies work best. There have been a number of important efforts to review the overall effectiveness of different therapeutic approaches for different disorders (e.g., Chambless et al., 1998; Chambless & Ollendick, 2001; Hollon, Thase, & Markowitz, 2002).

For many problems and most emotional disorders, cognitive and behavior therapies have emerged as the method of choice:

IN THE BLEACHERS By Steve Moore

THERE. SEE? IT'S JUST STITCHED ANIMAL HIDE... HERE. TOUCH IT. CARESS IT. CLUTCH IT TO YOUR BOSOM.
MOORE
© 1996 Universal Press Syndicate
6-12

Batters overcoming ***bonkinogginophobia*****, a fear of the ball.**

- ***Depression.*** Cognitive therapy's greatest success has been in the treatment of mood disorders, especially depression (Beck, 2005). As we saw earlier in this chapter, it is often as effective as antidepressants, and people in cognitive therapy are less likely than those on drugs to relapse when the treatment is over. The reason may be that the lessons learned in cognitive therapy last a long time after treatment, according to follow-ups done from 15 months to many years later (Antonuccio et al., 1999; Hollon, Thase, & Markowitz, 2002; McNally, 1994; Seligman et al., 1999).
- ***Prevention of suicide.*** In a randomized controlled study of 120 adults who had attempted suicide and had been sent to a hospital emergency room, those who were given ten sessions of cognitive therapy, in comparison to those who were simply given the usual follow-up care (being tracked and given referrals for help), were only about half as likely to attempt suicide again in the next 18 months. They also scored significantly lower on tests of depressive mood and hopelessness (Brown et al., 2005).
- ***Anxiety disorders.*** Exposure techniques are more effective than any other treatment for posttraumatic stress disorder, agoraphobia, and specific phobias such as fear of dogs or flying. Cognitive-behavior therapy is often more effective than medication for panic disorder, generalized anxiety disorder, and obsessive-compulsive disorder (Dalgleish, 2004; Mitte, 2005).
- ***Anger and impulsive violence.*** Cognitive therapy is often successful in reducing chronic anger, abusiveness, and hostility, and it also teaches people how to express anger more calmly and constructively (Deffenbacher et al., 2003; Kassinove, 1995).
- ***Health problems.*** Cognitive and behavior therapies are highly successful in helping people cope with pain, chronic fatigue syndrome, headaches, and irritable bowel syndrome; quit smoking or overcome other addictions; recover from eating disorders such as bulimia and binge eating; overcome insomnia and improve their sleeping patterns; and manage other health problems (Butler et al., 1991; Crits-Christoph, Wilson, & Hollon, 2005; Skinner et al., 1990; Stepanski & Perlis, 2000; Wilson & Fairburn, 1993).
- ***Childhood and adolescent behavior problems.*** Behavior therapy is the most effective treatment for behavior problems that range from bed-wetting to impulsive anger, and even for problems that have biological origins, such as autism, as we noted earlier. A meta-analysis of more than 100 studies of children and adolescents found that behavioral treatments worked better than others regardless of the child's age, the therapist's experience, or the specific problem (Weisz et al., 1995).
- ***Relapse prevention.*** Cognitive-behavioral approaches have also been highly effective in reducing the rate of relapse among people with problems such as substance abuse, depression, sexual offending, and even schizophrenia (Witkiewitz & Marlatt, 2004).

However, no single type of therapy can help everyone. Cognitive-behavior therapies are designed for specific, identifiable problems, but sometimes people seek therapy for less clearly defined reasons, such as wishing to introspect about their feelings or explore moral issues. Moreover, in spite of their many successes, behavior and cognitive therapies

have had failures, especially with people who are unmotivated to carry out a behavioral or cognitive program or who have ingrained personality disorders and psychoses.

Sometimes a single session of encouragement and practical advice is enough to bring improvement. A therapy for treating alcohol abuse, *motivational interviewing*, which focuses specifically on increasing a client's motivation to change problem drinking, has been shown to be effective in as few as one or two sessions (Burke et al., 2003; Miller & Rollnick, 2002). Some problems, however, are chronic or particularly difficult to treat and respond better to combined approaches rather than a single one. Young adults with schizophrenia are greatly helped by family intervention therapies that teach parents behavioral skills for dealing with their troubled children, and that educate the family about how to cope with the illness constructively (Chambless et al., 1998; Goldstein & Miklowitz, 1995). In studies over a two-year period, only 30 percent of the schizophrenic patients in such family interventions relapsed, compared to 65 percent of those whose families were not involved. In the treatment of sex offenders, combined methods are essential because of the complex causes of pedophilia, rape, and other sex crimes. One leading approach combines cognitive therapy, behavioral techniques, group therapy, and social-skills training (Abel et al., 1988; Kaplan, Morales, & Becker, 1993).

Thus far, then, we can see that the factors contributing to successful therapy are qualities of the participants, the therapeutic alliance, and the specific methods of the therapy:

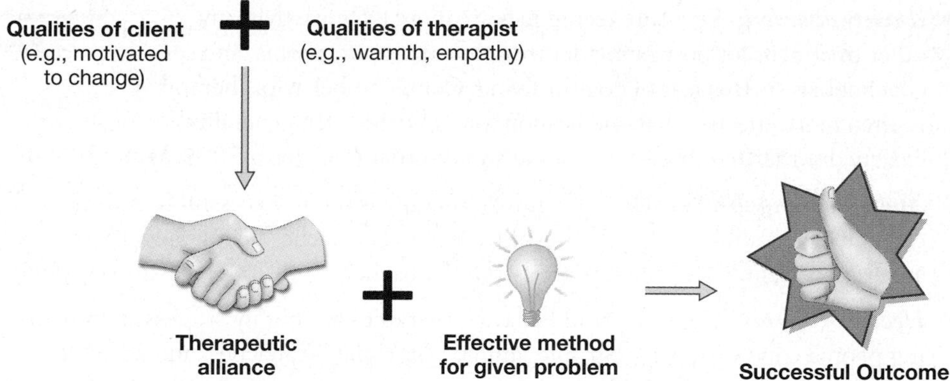

Special Problems and Populations. Some therapies are targeted for the problems of particular populations. For example, *rehabilitation psychologists* are concerned with the assessment and treatment of people who are physically disabled, temporarily or permanently, because of chronic pain, physical injuries, epilepsy, addictions, or other conditions. They conduct research to find the best ways to teach disabled people to live independently, improve their motivation, enjoy their sex lives, and follow healthy regimens. Because more people are surviving traumatic injuries and living long enough to develop chronic medical conditions, rehabilitation psychology is one of the fastest-growing areas of health care.

Other problems require more than one-on-one help from a psychotherapist. *Community psychologists* set up programs at a community level, often coordinating outpatient services at local clinics with support from family and friends. Some community programs help people who have severe mental disorders, such as schizophrenia, by setting up group homes where the mentally ill get counseling, job and skills training, and a support network. Without such community support, many mentally ill people are treated at hospitals, released to the streets, and stop taking their medications. Their psychotic symptoms return, they are rehospitalized, and a revolving-door cycle is established (Luhrmann, 2000).

Tribes in the American Northwest and British Columbia in Canada have been renewing their ancient cultural tradition of building ocean-going canoes and using them to visit other tribes. In Seattle, a community program designed to prevent drug abuse and other problems among urban Indian adolescents uses these canoe journeys as a metaphor for the journey of life. The youths learn the psychological and practical skills, along with the cultural values, that they would need to undertake a canoe journey—skills they will also need to navigate throughout life (Hawkins, Cummins, & Marlatt, 2004).

Community psychologists can prevent problems, too. In the Pacific Northwest, where substance abuse among Native Americans and Alaska Natives has widespread and devastating effects, successful prevention and intervention programs combine bicultural life-skills training and community involvement (Hawkins, Cummins, & Marlatt, 2004).

An important community intervention called *multisystemic therapy* (MST) has been highly successful in reducing teenage violence, criminal activity, drug abuse, and school problems in troubled inner-city communities. Its practitioners combine family systems techniques with behavioral methods, but apply them in the context of forming "neighborhood partnerships" with local leaders, residents, parents, and teachers to help prevent or reduce teenagers' problems (Henggeler et al., 1998; Swenson et al., 2005). The premise of multisystemic therapy is that because aggressiveness and drug abuse are often reinforced or caused by the adolescent's family, classroom, peers, and local culture, you can't successfully treat the adolescent without also "treating" his or her environment. Indeed, MST has been shown to be more effective than other methods on their own (Schaeffer & Borduin, 2005).

BIOLOGY and Psychotherapy

How Treating the Mind Changes the Brain

We noted at the beginning of this chapter that one of the longest debates in the history of treating mental disorders has been over which kind of treatment is better: medical or psychological. The pro-drug people often dismiss psychotherapy, which they regard as an unnecessary waste of time, and psychotherapists often disdain what they see as the temporary "quick fix" of medication.

One reason for this continuing quarrel about treatment is a common but mistaken assumption: that if a disorder appears to have biological origins or involve biochemical abnormalities, then biological treatments must be most appropriate. In fact, however, changing your behavior and thoughts through psychotherapy or other new experiences can also change the way your brain functions, just as the expectations associated with a placebo can.

This fascinating link between mind and brain was first illustrated dramatically in PET-scan studies of people with obsessive-compulsive disorder. Among those who were taking the SSRI Prozac, the metabolism of glucose in a critical part of the brain improved, suggesting that the drug was having a beneficial effect by "calming"

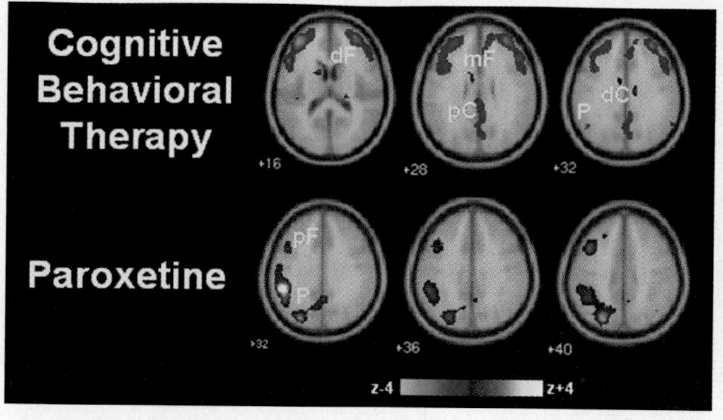

FIGURE 17.2 Psychotherapy and the Brain
These PET scans show changes in glucose metabolism in the brains of depressed people in cognitive-behavior therapy (CBT) and those on the antidepressant paroxetine (an SSRI). Metabolic increases are shown in orange and decreases in blue. Both treatments were helpful but affected some brain regions differently. For example, people in CBT showed increased activity in a part of the limbic system and reduced activity in parts of the frontal cortex. The pattern was the opposite for people taking the SSRI (Goldapple et al., 2004).

that area. But exactly the *same* brain changes occurred in patients who were getting cognitive-behavior therapy and no medication (Baxter et al., 1992; Schwartz et al., 1996). These findings may help explain why medication and therapy often have similar outcomes for certain disorders: They affect the brain in similar ways.

Other studies suggest that in the complex case of depression, medication and therapy may produce *different* but equally beneficial changes in the brain. One recent study used PET scans to record metabolic activity in the brains of clinically depressed patients at the beginning of treatment (cognitive-behavior therapy or an SSRI) and again at the end. People in cognitive-behavior therapy showed reduced activity in a part of the frontal cortex, an area of the brain involved in self-monitoring and reasoning. As you can see in Figure 17.2, people taking the SSRI showed no change in this brain area, but they *did* show decreased activity in an area of the limbic system associated with mood regulation (Goldapple et al., 2004). Both treatments were effective in reducing symptoms of depression, but apparently for different reasons: CBT helps people reduce the frequency of gloomy, negative thoughts, and SSRIs improve mood.

Recall that depression has different origins (see Chapter 16) and comes in different degrees of intensity. That may be why the same intervention—whether a medication or psychotherapy—does not benefit all sufferers and why some sufferers who are not helped by either one alone *do* benefit from their combination (Hollon, Thase, & Markowitz, 2002; Keller et al., 2000). Researchers today are therefore moving away from polarized positions on medication "versus" psychotherapy for mental and emotional disorders in hopes of helping practitioners target the best solution for individual patients.

The benefits of a combined approach are apparent even when medication is clearly necessary, as it is for most cases of bipolar disorder. A friend of a clinical psychologist we know said, "Lithium cuts out the highs as well as the lows. I don't miss the lows, but I gotta admit that there were some aspects of the highs that I do miss. It took me a while to accept that I had to give up those highs. Wanting to keep my job and my marriage helped!" (quoted in Davison, Neale, & Kring, 2004). The drug alone could not have helped this man learn to live with his illness.

When Therapy Harms

In May 2000, police arrested four people on charges of recklessly causing the death of 10-year-old Candace Newmaker during a session of "rebirthing" therapy. The procedure, which its proponents claim helps adopted children form attachments to their adoptive parents by "reliving" birth, was captured on closed-circuit television as the girl's mother watched in a nearby room.

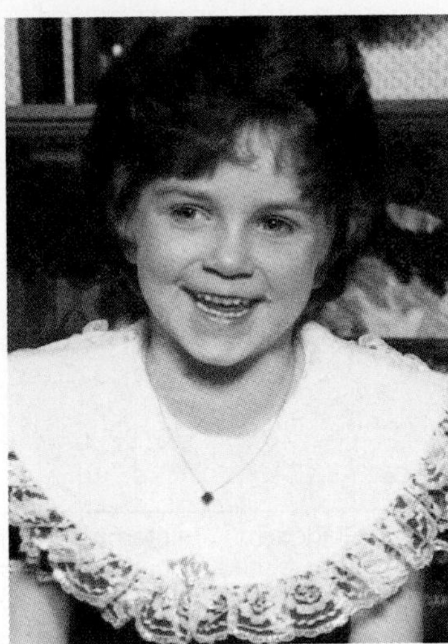

Candace Newmaker, age 10 (left), was smothered to death during a session of "rebirthing" therapy. The therapists, Julie Ponder and Connell Watkins (right), were convicted of reckless child abuse resulting in death and were sentenced to 16 years in prison.

The child was completely wrapped in a blanket that supposedly simulated the womb and was surrounded by large pillows. The therapists then pressed in on the pillows to simulate contractions and told the girl to push her way out of the blanket over her head. Candace repeatedly said that she could not breathe and felt she was going to die. But instead of unwrapping her, the therapists said, "You've got to push hard if you want to be born—or do you want to stay in there and die?"

Candace lost consciousness and was rushed to a local hospital, where she died the next day. Connell Watkins and Julie Ponder, unlicensed social workers who operated the counseling center, were sentenced to 16 years in prison for reckless child abuse resulting in death. Their two assistants, Brita St. Clair and Jack McDaniels, who used the age-old "we were only following orders" defense, were sentenced to ten years' probation for sitting on the struggling child as she smothered to death. To date, eight other children have died during this kind of therapy; one child committed suicide; and five were rescued in the nick of time.

Every treatment and intervention, including aspirin, carries risks, and so does psychotherapy. But the risks to clients increase when any of the following occurs:

1 The use of empirically unsupported, potentially dangerous techniques. The techniques used in "rebirthing" therapy are unsupported by scientific research. This therapy was born in the 1970s, when its founder claimed he had reexperienced his own birth while taking a bath. (Many psychological problems, he somehow decided, can be traced to a traumatic experience in the womb or during birth.) But the basic assumptions of this method—that people can recover from trauma, insecure attachment, or other psychological problems by "reliving" their births—are completely contradicted by the vast research on infancy, attachment, memory, and posttraumatic stress disorder and its treatment. For that matter, why should anyone assume that the experience of being born is traumatic? Isn't it pretty nice to be let out of cramped quarters and see daylight and beaming parental faces?

> **THINKING CRITICALLY**
>
> **ANALYZE ASSUMPTIONS AND BIASES**
>
> New therapies are often established on the basis of untested assumptions that someone thought sounded plausible—for example, that accurate memories can be "uprooted" through hypnosis or that emotional problems stem from the "trauma" of childbirth. What is wrong with basing a new form of therapy on an untested assumption?

Rebirthing is one of a variety of practices, collectively referred to as "attachment therapy," that are based on the use of harsh tactics that allegedly will help children "bond" with their parents. These techniques include withholding food, isolating the children for extended periods, humiliating them, wrapping them in sheets or blankets, pressing great weights upon them, and requiring them to exercise to exhaustion or, conversely, to spend hours sitting motionless. As we saw in Chapter 7, however, severe, abusive punishments are ineffective in treating behavior problems and often backfire, making the child angry,

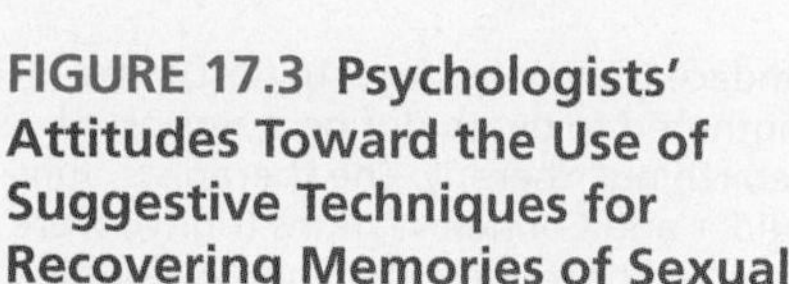

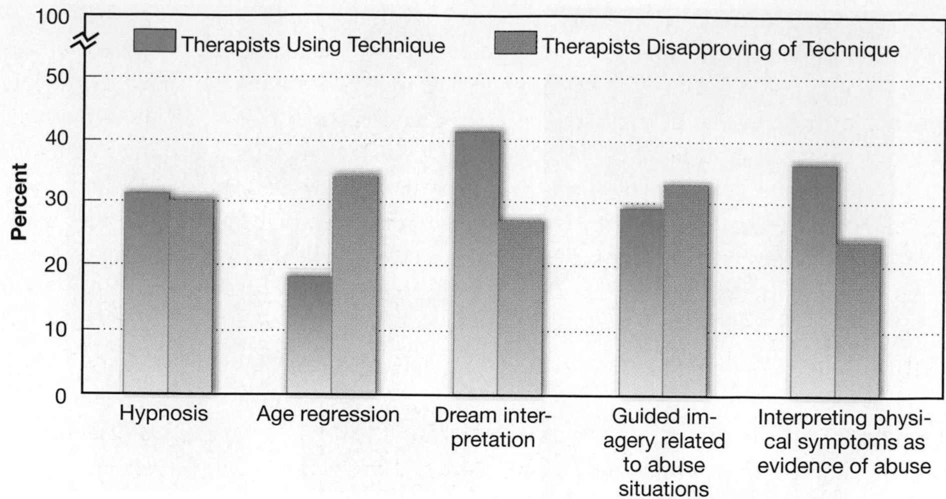

FIGURE 17.3 Psychologists' Attitudes Toward the Use of Suggestive Techniques for Recovering Memories of Sexual Abuse

Between one-fourth and one-third of licensed clinical psychologists have used suggestive methods regularly "to help clients recall memories of sexual abuse," although these techniques can produce confabulation and false memories. The percentages are from two combined samples of American clinical psychologists with Ph.D.s, randomly drawn from names listed in the National Register of Health Service Providers in Psychology (Poole et al., 1995). The numbers have not changed appreciably in recent years.

resentful, and withdrawn. They are hardly a way to help an adopted or emotionally troubled child feel more attached to his or her parents. The American Psychiatric Association officially opposes attachment therapies, noting that "there is *no* scientific evidence to support the effectiveness of such interventions." The American Professional Society on the Abuse of Children has also taken a strong stand condemning attachment therapies and the unvalidated assumptions on which they are based.

Other kinds of unsupported and potentially harmful therapy are aimed at helping clients retrieve painful memories. In Chapter 10 we saw that memory does not work like a video camera or tape recorder; memories are not "buried" in the brain, awaiting methods that will magically root them out. Yet many therapists still use unreliable methods such as hypnosis, sodium amytal (a barbiturate misleadingly called "truth serum"), guided imagery, and dream analysis—all of which are known to enhance a client's suggestibility (Mazzoni, Loftus, & Kirsch, 2001). When a therapist tells clients that their dreams are memories of something that really happened, many clients begin to confuse their dreams with reality (Mazzoni et al., 1999).

Many research psychologists are greatly concerned that a significant minority of registered, licensed psychotherapists—between one-fourth and one-third of them—have used one or more of these inappropriate techniques specifically to help clients "retrieve" memories of sexual abuse, as you can see in Figure 17.3 (Poole et al., 1995). Research in the United States and Canada finds that the percentages have not declined appreciably in recent years (Katz, 2001; Nunez, Poole, & Memon, 2002; Polusny & Follette, 1996).

2 **Inappropriate or coercive influence, which can create new problems for the client.** In a healthy therapeutic alliance, therapist and client come to agree on an explanation for the client's problems. Of course, the therapist will influence this explanation, according to his or her training and philosophy. Some therapists, however, cross the line. They so zealously believe in the prevalence of certain problems or disorders that they actually induce the client to produce the symptoms they are looking for (McHugh, 1993; McNally, 2003; Merskey, 1995; Watters & Ofshe, 1999). Therapist influence, and sometimes downright coercion, is a likely reason for the huge numbers of people who were diagnosed with multiple personality disorder in the 1980s and 1990s (see Chapter 16) and for an epidemic of recovered memories of sexual abuse during this period (see Chapter 10).

3 **Prejudice or cultural ignorance on the part of the therapist.** Some therapists may be prejudiced against some clients because of the client's gender, culture, religion, or sexual orientation. A therapist may try to induce a client to conform to the therapist's stan-

dards and values, even if they are not appropriate for the client or in the client's best interest. For example, for many years gay men and lesbians who entered therapy were told that homosexuality was a mental illness that could be cured. Some of the so-called treatments were harsh, such as electric shock for "inappropriate" arousal. Although these methods were discredited many years ago (Davison, 1976), other "reparative" therapies that supposedly turn gay men and lesbians into heterosexuals still surface from time to time. They are often promoted in campaigns by conservative Christians who believe that homosexuality is a sin, with testimonials from alleged converts. But there is no reliable empirical evidence from scientifically designed studies supporting these claims, and both the American Psychological Association and the American Psychiatric Association have gone on record opposing reparative therapies on ethical and scientific grounds.

4 Sexual intimacies or other unethical behavior on the part of the therapist. The APA's ethical guidelines prohibit therapists from having any sexual intimacies with their clients or violating other professional boundaries. Occasionally, some therapists behave like cult leaders, persuading their clients that their mental health depends on staying in therapy and severing their connections to their "toxic" families (Singer, 1995; Watters & Ofshe, 1999). Such "psychotherapy cults" are created by the therapist's use of techniques that foster the client's isolation, prevent the client from terminating therapy, and reduce the client's ability to think critically (see Chapter 8).

To avoid these risks and benefit from what good, effective psychotherapy has to offer, people looking for the right therapy must become educated consumers—able and willing to use the critical-thinking skills we have emphasized throughout this book.

QUICK quiz

Find out whether you are an educated consumer of quizzes.

1. Which of the following is the most important predictor of successful therapy? (a) how long it lasts, (b) the insight it provides the client, (c) the bond between therapist and client, (d) whether the therapist and client are matched according to gender
2. In general, which type of psychotherapy is most effective for anxiety and depression?
3. What kind of psychologist is trained to help people cope with chronic illness or disability or recover from injury?
4. What are four possible sources of harm in psychotherapy?
5. Ferdie is spending too much time playing softball and not enough time studying, so he signs up for "sportaholic therapy (ST)." The therapist tells him the cure for his "addiction" is to quit softball cold turkey and tap his temples three times whenever he feels the urge to play. After a few months, Ferdie announces that ST isn't helping and he's going to stop coming. The therapist gives him testimonials of other clients who swear by ST, explaining that Ferdie's doubts are actually a sign that the therapy is working. What are some problems with this argument? (Bonus: What kind of therapy might help Ferdie manage his time better?)

Answers:

1. c **2.** cognitive-behavior **3** rehabilitation psychologist **4.** the use of empirically unsupported techniques, prejudice or biased treatment, inappropriate or coercive influence, and unethical behavior **5.** The therapist has violated the principle of falsifiability (see Chapter 2). If Ferdie is helped by the treatment, that shows it works; if he is not helped, that still shows it works but Ferdie is "denying" its benefits. Also, Ferdie is not hearing testimonials from people who have dropped out of ST and were not helped by it. (Bonus: A good behavioral time-management program might help, so Ferdie can play softball *and* get other things done, too.)

The Value and Values of Psychotherapy

Modern psychotherapy has been of enormous value to many people. But psychotherapists themselves have raised some important questions about the values inherent in what they do (Cushman, 1995; Hillman & Ventura, 1992). How much personal change is possible, and do some therapists promise their clients too much? Does psychotherapy, by encouraging people to look inward to their feelings and woes, foster a preoccupation with the self over relationships and the importance of contributing to the larger world? Does it promise unrealistic notions of endless happiness and complete self-fulfillment?

THINKING CRITICALLY

ASK QUESTIONS

The benefits of psychotherapy are well documented, but we can ask questions about its implicit messages. Does psychotherapy foster unrealistic expectations of personal change? Does it promote individualism at the expense of community and relationships?

Many people in North America have an optimistic, can-do, let's-fix-this-fast attitude toward all problems, whether mental, physical, or social. In contrast, as discussed in Chapter 15, Eastern cultures have a less optimistic view of change, and they tend to be more tolerant of events they regard as being outside of human control. In the Japanese practice of Morita therapy, therefore, clients are taught to accept and live with their most troubling emotions, instead of trying to eradicate these psychological weeds from the lawn of life (Reynolds, 1987). Some Western psychotherapists also now teach techniques of mindful meditation and greater self-acceptance instead of constant self-improvement, and they have been successful with problems ranging from depression to borderline personality disorder (Hayes, 2004; Kabat-Zinn, 1994; Linehan, 1993; Segal, Williams, & Teasdale, 2001).

Most people get all the help they need from talking things over with good friends or with others who are in the same situation they are. But if you have a persistent problem that you do not know how to solve, one that causes you considerable unhappiness and that has lasted six months or more, it may be time to look for help. As the research in this chapter suggests, consumers who are thinking about psychotherapy should consider these important matters:

- ***Choosing a therapist.*** Make sure you are dealing with a reputable individual with appropriate credentials and training. Your school counseling center is a good place to start. You might also seek out a university psychology clinic, where you can get therapy with a graduate student in training; these students are closely supervised and the fees will be lower. If you know the kind of therapy you want, check your phone book; many therapists are listed according to the kind of therapy they do.
- ***Choosing a therapy.*** As we have seen, not all therapies are equally effective for all problems. You should not spend four years in psychodynamic therapy for panic attacks, which can generally be helped in a few sessions of cognitive-behavior therapy. Likewise, if you have a specific emotional problem, such as depression, anger, or anxiety, or if you are coping with chronic health problems, look for a cognitive or behavior therapist. Begin by talking to a competent psychotherapist or counselor about your problems and what intervention might help you, before you begin medication if that is possible. However, if you just want to discuss your life with a wise and empathic counselor, the kind of therapy may not matter so much.
- ***Deciding when to leave.*** For the common emotional problems of life, short-term treatment is usually sufficient. Some people are helped in only one or two sessions; about half improve within 8 to 11 sessions, and three-fourths improve within six months to a year. After a year, further change is usually minimal (Kopta et al., 1994). However, people with more severe mental disorders do often require and benefit from continued therapeutic care (Shadish et al., 2000).

If you begin a time-limited treatment, such as a seven-session airplane-phobia program, you ought to stick with it to the end. In unlimited therapy, however, you have the right to determine when enough is enough, especially if the therapist has been unable to help you with your problem after a considerable length of time. If you have made a real effort to work with a therapist and there has been no result after ample time and effort, the reason could have as much to do with the treatment or the therapist as with you.

In the hands of an empathic and knowledgeable practitioner, psychotherapy can help you make decisions and clarify your values and goals. It can teach you new skills and new ways of thinking. It can help you get along better with your family and break out of destructive family patterns. It can get you through bad times when no one seems to care or to understand what you are feeling. It can teach you how to manage depression, anxiety, and anger.

However, despite its many benefits, psychotherapy cannot transform you into someone you're not. It cannot turn an introvert into an extrovert. It cannot cure an emotional disorder overnight. It cannot provide a life without problems. And it is not intended to substitute for experience—for work that is satisfying, relationships that are sustaining, activities that are enjoyable. As Socrates knew, the unexamined life is not worth living. But as we would add, the unlived life is not worth examining.

Taking Psychology with You

How to Evaluate Self-Help Groups and Books

Not all psychological problems require the aid of a professional. Nowadays, thousands of programs and books are designed to help people help themselves. In the United States, more than 2,000 self-help books are published every year, and an estimated 7 to 15 million adults belong to self-help groups. Do these books and groups help?

Self-help groups are available (online and in person) for alcoholics and relatives of alcoholics; people suffering from depression, anorexia, or schizophrenia; women with breast cancer; parents of murdered children; diabetics; rape victims; stepparents; relatives of Alzheimer's patients; and people with just about any other concern you can think of (Davison, Pennebaker, & Dickerson, 2000). Members say that the primary benefits are the awareness that they are not alone, encouragement when they are feeling down, and help in feeling better about themselves.

Self-help groups offer understanding, empathy, and solutions to shared problems. Such groups can be reassuring and supportive in ways that family, friends, and psychotherapists sometimes may not be. For example, people with disabilities face unique challenges that involve coping not only with physical problems but also with the condescension, hostility, and prejudice of many nondisabled people (Linton, 1998). Other disabled people, who share these challenges, can offer the right kind of empathy and useful advice.

Self-help groups do not provide psychotherapy, and they are not designed to help people with serious psychological difficulties. They are not regulated by law or by professional standards, and they vary widely in their philosophies and methods. Some are accepting and tolerant, offering support and spiritual guidance. Others are confrontational and coercive, and members who disagree with the premises of the group may be made to feel deviant, crazy, or "in denial." If you choose to become part of a support group, be sure it falls in the first category.

As for self-help books, there is one for every problem, from how to toilet train your children to how to find happiness. When self-help books propose a specific, well-supported program for

the reader to follow, they can actually be as effective as treatment administered by a therapist—*if* the reader follows through with the program (Rosen, Glasgow, & Moore, 2003). Unfortunately, most books do not do this. After serving as chair of the APA's Task Force on Self-Help Therapies, Gerald Rosen (1981) concluded, "Psychologists have published untested materials, advanced exaggerated claims, and accepted the use of misleading titles that encourage unrealistic expectations regarding outcome." That was many years ago, and the situation is worse today. The information in this chapter suggests some guidelines for evaluating a self-help book:

- **The book's advice should be based on sound scientific theory and should propose a program that has been empirically supported.** It should not be based on the author's pseudoscientific theories, armchair observations, or political views. This criterion rules out, among other kinds of books, most of the love manuals in which the author's own tales of woe become the basis of an entire philosophy of love, marriage, and happiness. Personal accounts by people who have survived difficulties can be helpful and inspirational, of course, but an author's own experience is not grounds for generalizing to everyone.
- **The book should not promise the impossible.** This rules out books that promise perfect sex, total love, or high self-esteem in 30 days. It also rules out books or tapes that promote techniques whose effectiveness has been disconfirmed by research, such as dream analysis or "subliminal" messages.
- **The advice should be organized in a systematic program.** It should be given step by step, not as a vague pep talk to "take charge of your life" or "find love in your heart," and the reader should be told how to evaluate his or her progress.

Formal and informal support groups provide a setting for sharing concerns and exchanging constructive advice, as these men with AIDS are doing.

Some books do meet these criteria. One is *Changing for Good* (Prochaska, Norcross, & DiClemente, 1994), which describes the ingredients of effective change that apply to people in and out of therapy. But as long as people yearn for a magic bullet to cure their problems, quick-fix solutions will find a ready audience.

Summary

Biological Treatments for Mental Disorders

- Over the centuries, people trying to understand and treat psychological disorders have alternated between biological and psychological explanations. Today, biological treatments are in the ascendance because of research findings on the genetic and biological causes of some disorders and because of economic and social factors.
- The medications most commonly prescribed for mental disorders include *antipsychotic drugs*, used in treating schizophrenia and other psychotic disorders; *antidepressants*, used in treating depression, anxiety disorders, and obsessive-compulsive disorder; tranquilizers, often prescribed for emotional problems; and *lithium carbonate*, a salt used to treat bipolar disorder.
- Drawbacks of drug treatment include the *placebo effect*; high dropout and relapse rates among people who take medications without also learning how to cope with their problems; the difficulty of finding the correct dose (the *therapeutic window*) for each individual, compounded by the fact that a person's ethnicity, sex, and age can influence a drug's effectiveness; and the long-term risks of medication, known and unknown, and of possible drug interactions when several are being taken. Medication can be helpful and can even save lives, but in an age in which

commercial interests are heavily invested in promoting drugs for psychological problems, the public is largely unaware of drugs' limitations and potential risks. Medication should not be prescribed uncritically and routinely, especially when nondrug therapies can work as well as drugs for many mood and behavioral problems.

- When drugs and psychotherapy have failed to help seriously disturbed people, some psychiatrists have intervened directly in the brain. *Psychosurgery*, which destroys selected areas of the brain thought to be responsible for a psychological problem, is rarely done today. *Electroconvulsive therapy* (ECT), in which a brief current is sent through the brain, has been used successfully to treat suicidal depression. However, controversy exists about its effects on the brain and the appropriateness of its use. A newer method, *transcranial magnetic stimulation (TMS)*, in which a magnetic coil is applied over the left prefrontal cortex, is being studied as a way of treating severe depression.

Kinds of Psychotherapy

- *Psychodynamic ("depth") therapies* include Freudian *psychoanalysis* and its modern variations, such as approaches based on *object-relations theory*. These therapies explore unconscious dynamics by using *free association* and by focusing on the process of *transference* to break through the patient's defenses.
- *Behavior therapists* draw on classical and operant principles of learning, called *applied behavioral analysis*. Behavior therapists use such methods as *graduated exposure*, and sometimes immediate exposure, called *flooding*; *systematic desensitization*, based on *counterconditioning*; *behavioral self-monitoring*; and *skills training*.
- *Cognitive therapists* aim to change the irrational thoughts involved in negative emotions and self-defeating actions. Albert Ellis's *rational emotive behavior therapy (REBT)* and Aaron Beck's form of cognitive therapy are two leading approaches.
- *Humanist therapy* holds that human nature is essentially good and attempts to help people feel better about themselves by focusing on here-and-now issues and on their capacity for change. Carl Rogers's *client-centered (nondirective) therapy* emphasizes the importance of the therapist's empathy and ability to provide *unconditional positive regard*. *Existential therapy* helps people cope with the dilemmas of existence, such as the meaning of life and the fear of death.
- *Family therapies* share the view that individual problems develop in the context of the whole family network. They share a *family-systems perspective*, understanding that any one person's behavior in the family affects everyone else, sometimes across generations. In *couples therapy*, the therapist usually sees both partners in a relationship to help them resolve ongoing quarrels and disputes or to help them accept and live with qualities of both partners that are unlikely to change.
- In practice, most therapists are *integrative*, drawing on many methods and ideas. Whatever their approach, successful therapies help people form more adaptive "life stories."

Evaluating Psychotherapy

- Successful therapy requires a *therapeutic alliance* between the therapist and the client, so that they understand each other and can work together. The clients who benefit most from psychotherapy are motivated to solve their problems; hostile, negative individuals are more resistant to treatment. For their part, good therapists are empathic and constructive. When therapist and client are of different ethnicities, the therapist must be able to distinguish normal cultural patterns from signs of mental illness, and both parties must be aware of potential prejudice and misunderstandings.
- A *scientist–practitioner gap* has developed because of the different assumptions held by researchers and many clinicians regarding the value of empirical research for doing psychotherapy and for assessing its effectiveness. The gap has led to a proliferation of scientifically unsupported psychotherapies.
- In assessing the effectiveness of psychotherapy, researchers need to control for the placebo effect and the *justification of effort* effect. They rely on *randomized controlled trials* to determine which therapies are empirically supported. For example, as the "Close-up on Research" feature discusses, randomized controlled trials have shown that postcrisis debriefing programs are usually ineffective at best and can even slow recovery for some survivors.
- Some psychotherapies are better than others for specific problems. Behavior therapy and cognitive-behavior therapy are the most effective for depression, anxiety disorders, anger problems, certain health problems (such as pain, insomnia, and eating disorders), and childhood and adolescent behavior problems. Family systems therapies, especially when combined with behavioral techniques as in *multisystemic therapy*, are helpful for children and young adults with schizophrenia and for aggressive adolescents. Some problems and target populations, such as sex offenders, respond best to combined therapeutic approaches. Some methods, such as *motivational interviewing*, have been able to change a client's willingness to begin a program of change in only a session or two.

KEY TERMS

- antipsychotic drugs (neuroleptics) 640
- tardive dyskinesia 641
- antidepressant drugs 641
- monoamine oxidase inhibitors (MAOIs) 641
- tricyclic antidepressants 641
- selective serotonin reuptake inhibitors (SSRIs) 641
- tranquilizers 642
- lithium carbonate 642
- placebo effect 643
- therapeutic window 643
- psychosurgery 645
- prefrontal lobotomy 645
- electroconvulsive therapy (ECT) 645
- transcranial magnetic stimulation (TMS) 646
- psychoanalysis 647
- free association 647
- psychodynamic ("depth") therapies 647
- object-relations (psychodynamic) therapy 647
- transference 647
- behavior therapy 648
- applied behavior analysis 648
- graduated exposure 648
- flooding 648
- systematic desensitization 648
- counterconditioning 648
- behavioral self-monitoring 649
- skills training 649
- cognitive therapy 650
- rational emotive behavior therapy (REBT) 650
- humanist therapy 651
- client-centered (nondirective) therapy 652
- unconditional positive regard 652
- existential therapy 652
- family therapy 652
- family-systems perspective 653
- couples therapy 654
- integrative approach to psychotherapy 654
- therapeutic alliance 656
- scientist-practitioner gap 658
- randomized controlled trials 659
- motivational interviewing 662
- rehabilitation psychologists 662
- community psychologists 662
- multisystemic therapy 663

Are You Ready for the Final?

NOW YOU HAVE READ CHAPTER SEVENTEEN — ARE YOU PREPARED FOR THE EXAM?

The major goal of nondirective therapy is to help clients become more aware of their feelings. True or False?

What is Humanist therapy? (pages 651–653)

true

Group therapy provides social support for people who have similar problems. However, an extremely shy person is not likely to do as well in group therapy. True or False?

What are the advantages and disadvantages of group therapy?

true

In family therapy, the therapist would most likely focus on one individual who has been identified as the source of the problem. True or False?

What are the different types of group therapy? (pages 652–655)

false

As you near the end of the semester, you may be preparing for finals or other exams. Spend some time thinking about the test-taking techniques that you use and exploring some tips that you may not have tried. You have most likely developed some strategies for test-taking whether you realize it or not. Think about how you take a test. Now read through the following suggestions and select one or two to try for your next exam.

- ✔ Arrive to the test on time
- ✔ Before answering any questions, unload the information
- ✔ Read the directions carefully
- ✔ Budget your time wisely
- ✔ Look for clues
- ✔ Answer all the questions
- ✔ Use all of the class time

An important task in this chapter is to understand the differences between the multiple types of therapy. Use the practice tests and activities at **www.mypsychlab.com** to ensure you understand the differences.

TELL ME **MORE** >>

"Preparing for tests using MyPsychLab is amazing. It is a mini review covering an entire chapter using the vocabulary review and online questions."

Student
Oklahoma State University

Complete the table using the items below:

The Major Schools of Therapy Compared

	Primary Goal	Methods
Psychodynamic		
Cognitive-behavioral		
Humanist		
Family		

Behavioral techniques such as systematic desensitization, exposure, and flooding; cognitive exercises to identify and change faulty beliefs

Insight; self-acceptance and self-fulfillment

Providing a safe, nonjudgmental setting in which to discuss life issues

Working with couples, families, and sometimes individuals to identify and change patterns that perpetuate problems

Insight into unconscious motives and feelings

Modification of behavior and irrational beliefs

Probing the unconscious through dream analysis, free association, transference, other forms of "depth therapy"

Modification of individual habits and family patterns

9
behavior therapies
action therapies based on the principles of classical and operant conditioning and aimed at changing disordered behavior without concern for the original causes of such behavior
9

15
cognitive-behavioral therapy (CBT)
action therapy in which the goal is to help clients overcome problems by learning to think more rationally and logically
15

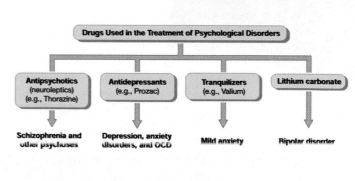

Drugs Used in the Treatment of Psychological Disorders

- Antipsychotics (neuroleptics) (e.g., Thorazine) → Schizophrenia and other psychoses
- Antidepressants (e.g., Prozac) → Depression, anxiety disorders, and OCD
- Tranquilizers (e.g., Valium) → Mild anxiety
- Lithium carbonate → Bipolar disorder

Epilogue

Taking Psychology with You

We (human beings) never stop investigating. We are never satisfied that we know enough to get by. Every question we answer leads on to another question. This has become the greatest survival trick of our species. DESMOND MORRIS

You have come a long way since the beginning of this book. It is now time to stand back and ask yourself where you've been and what you've learned from the many studies, topics, and controversies that you have read about. What fundamental principles emerge, and how can you take them with you into your own life?

The Five Strands of Human Experience

In Chapter 1, we described five general perspectives on human behavior that guide the assumptions and methods of psychologists. Each of these perspectives on human experience offers questions to ask when trying to understand or change a particular aspect of your own life:

1 ***Biological influences.*** As physical creatures, we are influenced by our bodies and our brains. Physiology affects the rhythms of our lives, our perceptions of reality, our ability to learn, the intensity of our emotions, our temperaments, and in some cases our vulnerability to emotional disorder.

Thus, when you are distressed, you might want to start by asking yourself what might be going on in your body. Do you have a physical condition that might be affecting your behavior? Do you have a temperamental tendency to be easily aroused or to be calm? Are alcohol or other drugs altering your ability to make decisions or behave as you would like? Might an irregular schedule be disrupting your physical functions and impairing your efficiency? Are you under unusual pressures that increase your physical stress?

2 ***Learning influences.*** From the moment of birth, we begin learning and are exquisitely sensitive to our environments. What we do and how we do it are often a result of our learning histories and the specific situations we are in. We respond to the environment, and, in turn, our acts have consequences that influence future behavior. The right environment and rewards can help us cope better with disabilities, get along better with others, and even become more creative and happy. The wrong kind can foster boredom, hostility, and discontent.

So, as you analyze a situation, you will want to examine the contingencies and consequences governing your behavior and that of others. What rewards are maintaining your behavior? Of the many messages being aimed at you by television, books, parents, and teachers, which have the greatest influence? Who are your role models, the people you most admire and wish to emulate?

3 ***Social and cultural influences.*** Although most Westerners think of themselves as independent creatures, everyone conforms to some extent to the expectations and demands of others. Spouses, lovers, friends, bosses, parents, and perfect strangers "pull our strings" in ways we may not recognize. We conform to group pressures, obey authorities, and blossom or wilt in close relationships. Throughout life, we need "contact comfort"—sometimes in the literal touch or embrace of others and sometimes in shared experience or conversation. Further, we are all strongly influenced by our culture's norms and society's roles, which specify countless verbal and nonverbal rules governing the behavior of employers and employees, husbands and wives, parents and children, strangers and friends, and men and women. Whenever you find yourself wondering irritably why "*those* people are behaving that way," chances are that a cultural difference or misunderstanding is at work.

So, in solving problems, you might think about the people in your life who are affecting you. Do your friends and relatives support you or hinder you in achieving your goals? How do your ethnicity and nationality affect you? What gender roles do they specify for you and your partners in close relationships, and what would happen if you ignored the norms of your role? Are your conflicts with others a result of cultural misunderstandings—due, for instance, to differing rules for expressing emotion?

4 ***Cognitive influences.*** Our species is, above all, the animal that explains things. These explanations may not always be realistic or sensible, but they continually influence our actions and choices. When you have a problem, ask yourself how you are framing the situation you are in. What biases might you bring to your assessment of the problem—e.g., the confirmation bias, the hindsight bias, the self-serving bias? Are your explanations of what is causing the problem reasonable? Have you checked them

out to see if they are right or wrong? Are you wallowing in negative thoughts? Do you attribute your successes to luck but take all the blame for your failures—or do you take credit for your successes and blame everyone else for your failures? Are you responding to other people's expectations in a mindless way?

5 ***Unconscious influences.*** People are often unaware of their implicit attitudes, unconscious perceptions, and the defense mechanisms they use to protect their self-esteem. If you find that you are repeating self-defeating patterns or having unreasonable emotional reactions to a person or situation, you might want to consider why. Do other people "push your buttons" for reasons you cannot explain? Are you displacing feelings about your parents onto your friends or intimates? Are you carrying around "unfinished business" from childhood losses and hurts?

Keep in mind that no single one of these factors operates in isolation from the others. The forces that govern our behavior are as intertwined as strands of ivy on a wall, and it can be hard to see where one strand begins and another ends. This message, if enough people believed it, would probably put an end to the pop-psych industry, which promotes single, simple answers to real-life complexities. Some simplifiers of psychology try to reduce human problems to biochemical imbalances or genetic defects. Others argue that anyone can "fulfill any potential," regardless of biology or environment, and that solving problems is merely a matter of having enough determination.

In this book, we have tried to show that the concerns and dilemmas of life do not divide up neatly according to the chapters of an introductory psychology text (even ours). For example, to understand shyness or loneliness, you might consider whether you have a temperamental disposition toward introversion and shyness; your personal learning history; childhood experiences and what you observed from adult role models; how stress, diet, drugs, and sleep patterns might be affecting your mood; and whether you come from a culture that encourages or prohibits assertiveness. It may seem daunting to keep so many factors in mind. But once you get into the habit of seeing a situation from many points of view, relying on single-answer approaches will feel like wearing blinders. And it's a habit that will inoculate you against appealing pop-psych ideas that are unsupported by evidence.

Psychology in Your Life

If the theories and findings in this book are to be of long-lasting personal value to you, they must jump off the printed page and into your daily life. To give you some practice in applying them, let's consider an all-too-common problem—what to do when love is dwindling in a close relationship—and some ideas about where to look in this book for principles and findings that may shed light on it. Our list is far from exhaustive; feel free to come up with additional ideas.

Let's say you have been romantically involved with someone for a year. When the relationship began, you felt very much in love, and you thought your feelings were returned. But for a long time now, your partner's treatment of you has been anything but loving. In fact, your partner makes fun of your faults in front of others and yells at you about the slightest annoyance. Sometimes your partner ignores you for days on end, as if to punish you for some imagined wrong. Your friends advise you to leave the relationship, yet you can't shake the feeling that your partner really loves you. You still occasionally have a great time together, and your partner appears distressed whenever you threaten to leave. You wish you could either improve the relationship or get out, and your inability to act leaves you feeling angry and depressed.

Consider just a few of the topics covered in this book that can contribute to understanding your problem and possibly resolving it:

- *Approach–avoidance conflicts* (Chapter 12) may help explain why you are both attracted to and repelled by this relationship, and why the closer you approach, the more you want to leave (and vice versa). When a goal is both attractive and painful, it is not unusual to feel uncertain and to vacillate about possible courses of action.
- *Intermittent reinforcement* (Chapter 7) may explain why you persist in apparently self-defeating behavior. If staying in the relationship brought *only* punishment or if your partner *always* ignored you, it would be easier to leave. But because your partner intermittently is kind and loving, your "staying around" behavior is rewarded, thereby becoming resistant to extinction.
- Past *observational learning* (Chapter 7) may help account for your present behavior. Perhaps your parents have a relationship like the one you are in, and their way of interacting is what you have learned to expect in your own relationships.
- If you have an *external locus of control* (Chapter 15), you feel that you cannot control what happens to you; you tend to feel that you are merely a victim of fate, chance, or the wishes of others. People with an internal locus of control feel more in charge of their lives and are less inclined to blame outside circumstances for their difficulties.
- *Cognitive-dissonance theory* (Chapter 9) suggests that you may be trying to keep your attitudes and behavior consistent. The cognition "I am in this relationship and choose to be with this person" is dissonant with "This person ignores and mistreats me." Because you are still unable to break up and alter the first cognition, you are working on the second cognition, hoping that your partner will change for the better.

- Research on *gender differences* finds that men and women often have different unstated rules about expressing emotion and different definitions of love (Chapters 11 and 12). Perhaps traditional gender roles are preventing you and your partner from communicating your true preferences and feelings.
- *Attribution theory* (Chapter 8) addresses the consequences of holding dispositional explanations of another person's behavior (it's due to something about the person) or situational explanations (it's due to something about the circumstances). Recall that unhappy couples tend to make dispositional attributions when the partner does something wrong or thoughtless ("My partner is mean"); happy couples look for situational attributions ("My partner is under a lot of pressure at work"). You might test possible reasons that your partner is treating you badly. Is the behavior characteristic of your partner in many situations—that is, is it typical of his or her personality—or might it be a temporary result of stress or something in the unique relationship with you?

Depending on the origins of your problem, you might choose to cope with the situation as it is; change your attributions about your partner; use learning principles to try to alter your own or your partner's behavior; consider how your perceptions and beliefs are affecting your emotions; seek psychotherapy, with or without your partner (Chapter 17); or leave the relationship.

Our example was an individual problem, but the applications of psychology extend beyond personal concerns to social ones, as we have seen throughout this book: disputes between neighbors and nations; prejudice and cross-cultural relations: ways of improving eyewitness testimony; better methods of interviewing children; the formulation of social policies, such as ways of improving school performance or reducing drug abuse; and countless other issues.

Of course, research findings often change as new questions are asked, new methods become available, and new theories evolve. That is why the one chapter that may ultimately be most useful to you is the one you may have assumed to be least useful: Chapter 2, "How Psychologists Do Research." The best way to take psychology with you is to understand its basic ways of approaching problems and questions—that is, its principles of critical and scientific thinking. Old theories give way to new ones, dated results yield to contemporary ones, dead-end investigations halt and new directions are taken. But the methods of psychology continue, and critical thinking is their hallmark.

Appendix

STATISTICAL METHODS

Nineteenth-century English statesman Benjamin Disraeli reportedly once named three forms of dishonesty: "lies, damned lies, and statistics." It is certainly true that people can lie with the help of statistics. It happens all the time: Advertisers, politicians, and others with some claim to make either use numbers inappropriately or ignore certain critical ones. (When hearing that "four out of five doctors surveyed" recommended some product, have you ever wondered just how many doctors were surveyed and whether they were representative of all doctors?) People also use numbers to convey a false impression of certainty and objectivity when the true state of affairs is uncertainty or ignorance. But it is people, not statistics, that lie. When statistics are used correctly, they neither confuse nor mislead. On the contrary, they expose unwarranted conclusions, promote clarity and precision, and protect us from our own biases and blind spots.

If statistics are useful anywhere, it is in the study of human behavior. If human beings were all alike, and psychologists could specify all the influences on behavior, there would be no need for statistics. But any time we measure human behavior, we are going to wind up with different observations or scores for different individuals. Statistics can help us spot trends amid the diversity.

This appendix will introduce you to some basic statistical calculations used in psychology. Reading the appendix will not make you into a statistician, but it will acquaint you with some ways of organizing and assessing research data. If you suffer from a "number phobia," relax: You do not need to know much math to understand this material. However, you should have read Chapter 2, which discussed the rationale for using statistics and described various research methods. You may want to review the basic terms and concepts covered in that chapter. Be sure that you can define *hypothesis*, *sample*, *correlation*, *independent variable*, *dependent variable*, *random assignment*, *experimental group*, *control group*, *descriptive statistics*, *inferential statistics*, and *test of statistical significance*. (Correlation coefficients, which are described in some detail in Chapter 2, will not be covered here.)

To read the tables in this appendix, you will also need to know the following symbols:

N = the total number of observations or scores in a set

X = an observation or score

Σ = the Greek capital letter sigma, read as "the sum of"

$\sqrt{\ }$ = the square root of

(*Note:* Boldfaced terms in this appendix are defined in the glossary at the end of the book.)

Organizing Data

Before we can discuss statistics, we need some numbers. Imagine that you are a psychologist and that you are interested in that most pleasing of human qualities, a sense of humor. You suspect that a well-developed funny bone can protect people from the negative emotional effects of stress. You already know that in the months following a stressful event, people who score high on sense-of-humor tests tend to feel less tense and moody than more sobersided individuals do. You realize, though, that this correlational evidence does not prove cause and effect. Perhaps people with a healthy sense of humor have other traits, such as flexibility or creativity, that act as the true stress buffers. To find out whether humor itself really softens the impact of stress, you do an experiment.

First, you randomly assign subjects to two groups, an experimental group and a control group. To keep our calculations simple, let's assume there are only 15 people per group. Each person individually views a silent film that most North Americans find fairly stressful, one showing Australian aboriginal boys undergoing a puberty rite involving genital mutilation. Subjects in the experimental group are instructed to make up a humorous monologue while watching the film. Those in the control group are told to make up a straightforward narrative. After the film, each person answers a mood questionnaire that measures current feelings of tension, depression, aggressiveness, and anxiety. A person's overall score on the questionnaire can range from 1 (no mood disturbance) to 7 (strong mood disturbance). This procedure provides you with 15 "mood disturbance" scores for each group. Have people who tried to be humorous reported less disturbance than those who did not?

Constructing a Frequency Distribution

Your first step might be to organize and condense the "raw data" (the obtained scores) by constructing a **frequency distribution** for each group. A frequency distribution shows how often each possible score actually occurred. To construct one, you first order all the possible scores from highest to lowest. (Our mood disturbance scores will be ordered from 7 to 1.) Then you tally how often each score was actually obtained. Table A.1 gives some hypothetical raw data for the two groups, and Table A.2 shows the two frequency distributions based on these data. From these distributions you can see that the two groups differed. In the experimental group, the extreme scores of 7 and 1 did not occur at all, and the most common score was the middle one, 4. In the control group, a score of 7 occurred four times, the most common score was 6, and no one obtained a score lower than 4.

TABLE A.1

Some Hypothetical Raw Data

These scores are for the hypothetical humor-and-stress study described in the text.

Experimental group	4,5,4,4,3,6,5,2,4,3,5,4,4,3,4
Control group	6,4,7,6,6,4,6,7,7,5,5,5,7,6,6

Because our mood scores have only seven possible values, our frequency distributions are quite manageable. Suppose, though, that your questionnaire had yielded scores that could range from 1 to 50. A frequency distribution with 50 entries would be cumbersome and might not reveal trends in the data clearly. A solution would be to construct a *grouped frequency distribution* by grouping adjacent scores into equal-sized *classes* or *intervals*. Each interval could cover, say, five scores (1–5, 6–10, 11–15, and so forth). Then you could tally the frequencies within each *interval*. This procedure would reduce the number of entries in each distribution from 50 to only 10, making the overall results much easier to grasp. However, information would be lost. For example, there would be no way of knowing how many people had a score of 43 versus 44.

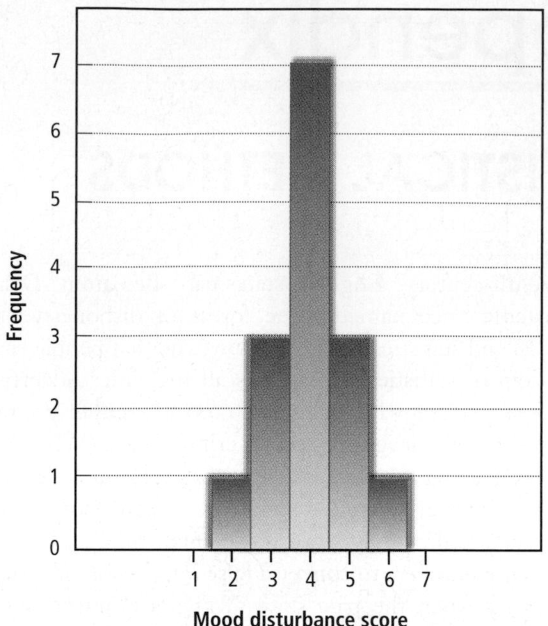

FIGURE A.1 A Histogram
This graph depicts the distribution of mood disturbance scores shown on the left side of Table A.2.

Graphing the Data

As everyone knows, a picture is worth a thousand words. The most common statistical picture is a **graph**, a drawing that depicts numerical relationships. Graphs appear at several points in this book, and are routinely used by psychologists to convey their findings to others. From graphs, we can get a general impression of what the data are like, note the relative frequencies of different scores, and see which score was most frequent.

In a graph constructed from a frequency distribution, the possible score values are shown along a horizontal line (the *x-axis* of the graph) and frequencies along a vertical line (the *y-axis*), or vice versa. To construct a **histogram**, or **bar graph**, from our mood scores, we draw rectangles (bars) above each score, indicating the number of times it occurred by the rectangle's height (Figure A.1).

A slightly different kind of "picture" is provided by a **frequency polygon**, or **line graph**. In a frequency polygon, the frequency of each score is indicated by a dot placed directly over the score on the horizontal axis, at the appropriate height on the vertical axis. The dots for the various scores are then joined together by straight lines, as in Figure A.2. When necessary an "extra" score, with a frequency of zero, can be added at each end of the horizontal axis, so that the polygon will rest on this axis instead of floating above it.

A word of caution about graphs: They may either exaggerate or mask differences in the data, depending on which units are used on the vertical axis. The two graphs in Figure A.3, although they look quite different, actually depict the same data. Always read the units on the axes of a graph; otherwise, the shape of a histogram or frequency polygon may be misleading.

TABLE A.2

Two Frequency Distributions

The scores are from Table A.1.

Experimental Group			Control Group		
Mood Disturbance Score	Tally	Frequency	Mood Disturbance Score	Tally	Frequency
7		0	7	////	4
6	/	1	6	~~////~~/	6
5	///	3	5	///	3
4	~~////~~//	7	4	//	2
3	///	3	3		0
2	/	1	2		0
1		0	1		0
		$N = 15$			$N = 15$

Describing Data

Having organized your data, you are now ready to summarize and describe them. As you will recall from Chapter 2, procedures for doing so are known as **descriptive statistics**. In the following discussion, the word *score* will stand for any numerical observation.

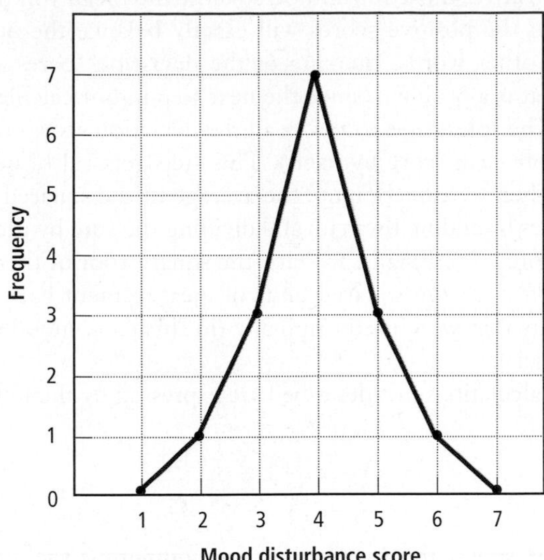

FIGURE A.2 A Frequency Polygon
This graph depicts the same data as Figure A.1.

Measuring Central Tendency

Your first step in describing your data might be to compute a **measure of central tendency** for each group. Measures of central tendency characterize an entire set of data in terms of a single representative number.

The Mean. The most popular measure of central tendency is the arithmetic mean, usually called simply the **mean**. It is often expressed by the symbol *M*. Most people are thinking of the mean when they say "average." We run across means all the time: in grade point averages, temperature averages, and batting averages. The mean is valuable to the psychologist because it takes all the data into account and it can be used in further statistical analyses. To compute the mean, you simply add up a set of scores and divide the total by the number of scores in the set. Recall that in mathematical notation, Σ means "the sum of," X stands for the individual scores, and N represents the total number of scores in a set. Thus the formula for calculating the mean is:

$$M = \frac{\Sigma X}{N}$$

Table A.3 shows how to compute the mean for our experimental group. Test your ability to perform this calculation by computing the mean for the control group yourself. (You can find the answer, along with other control group statistics, on page A-7.) Later, we will describe how a psychologist would compare the two means statistically to see if there is a significant difference between them.

The Median. Despite its usefulness, sometimes the mean can be misleading, as we noted in Chapter 2. Suppose you piled some children on a seesaw in such a way that it was perfectly balanced, and then a 200-pound adult came and sat on one end. The center of gravity would quickly shift toward the adult. In the same way, one extremely high score can dramatically raise the mean (and one extremely low score can dramatically lower it). In real life, this can be a serious problem. For example, in the calculation of a town's mean income, one millionaire would offset hundreds of poor people. The mean income would be a misleading indication of the town's actual wealth.

When extreme scores occur, a more representative measure of central tendency is the **median**, or midpoint in a set of scores or observations ordered from highest to lowest. In any set of scores, the same *number* of scores falls above the median as below it. The median is not affected by extreme scores. If you were calculating the median income of that same town, the one millionaire would offset only one poor person.

When the number of scores in the set is odd, calculating the median is a simple matter of counting in from the ends to the middle. However, if the number of scores is even, there will be two middle scores. The simplest solution is to find the mean of those two scores and use that number as the median. (When the data are from a grouped frequency distribution, a more complicated procedure is required, one beyond the scope of this appendix.) In our experimental group, the median score is 4 (see Table A.3 again). What is it for the control group?

The Mode. A third measure of central tendency is the **mode**, the score that occurs most often. In our experimental group, the modal score is 4. In our control group, it is 6. In some distributions, all scores occur with equal frequency, and there is no mode. In others, two or more scores "tie" for the distinction of

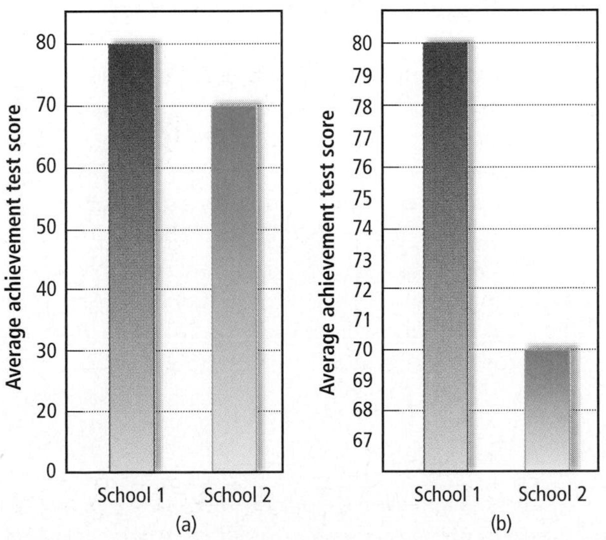

FIGURE A.3 Same Data, Different Impressions
These two graphs depict the same data, but have different units on the vertical axis.

TABLE A.3
Calculating a Mean and a Median

The scores are from the left side of Table A.1.

Mean (*M*)

$$M = \frac{4+5+4+4+3+6+5+2+4+3+5+4+4+3+4}{15} = \frac{60}{15} = 4$$

Median

Scores, in order: 2, 3, 3, 3, 4, 4, 4, [4], 4, 4, 4, 5, 5, 5, 6

↑

Median

being most frequent. Modes are used less often than other measures of central tendency. They do not tell us anything about the other scores in the distribution; they often are not very "central"; and they tend to fluctuate from one random sample of a population to another more than either the median or the mean.

Measuring Variability

A measure of central tendency may or may not be highly representative of other scores in a distribution. To understand our results, we also need a **measure of variability** that will tell us whether our scores are clustered closely around the mean or widely scattered.

The Range. The simplest measure of variability is the **range,** which is found by subtracting the lowest score from the highest one. For our hypothetical set of mood disturbance scores, the range in the experimental group is 4 and in the control group it is 3. Unfortunately, though, simplicity is not always a virtue. The range gives us some information about variability but ignores all scores other than the highest and lowest ones.

The Standard Deviation. A more sophisticated measure of variability is the **standard deviation (SD)**. This statistic takes every score in the distribution into account. Loosely speaking, it gives us an idea of how much, on the average, scores in a distribution differ from the mean. If the scores were all the same, the standard deviation would be zero. The higher the standard deviation, the more variability there is among scores.

To compute the standard deviation, we must find out how much each individual score deviates from the mean. To do so we simply subtract the mean from each score. This gives us a set of *deviation scores*. Deviation scores for numbers above the mean will be positive, those for numbers below the mean will be negative, and the positive scores will exactly balance the negative ones. In other words, the sum of the deviation scores will be zero. That is a problem, since the next step in our calculation is to add. The solution is to *square* all the deviation scores (that is, to multiply each score by itself). This step gets rid of negative values. Then we can compute the average of the squared deviation scores by adding them up and dividing the sum by the number of scores (*N*). Finally, we take the square root of the result, which takes us from squared units of measurement back to the same units that were used originally (in this case, mood disturbance levels).

The calculations just described are expressed by the following formula:

$$SD = \sqrt{\frac{\Sigma(X - M)^2}{N}}$$

Table A.4 shows the calculations for computing the standard deviation for our experimental group. Try your hand at computing the standard deviation for the control group.

TABLE A.4
Calculating a Standard Deviation

Scores (*X*)	Deviation scores (*X* - *M*)	Squared deviation scores $(X - M)^2$
6	2	4
5	1	1
5	1	1
5	1	1
4	0	0
4	0	0
4	0	0
4	0	0
4	0	0
4	0	0
4	0	0
3	−1	1
3	−1	1
3	−1	1
2	−2	4
	0	14

$$SD = \sqrt{\frac{\Sigma(X - M)^2}{N}} = \sqrt{\frac{14}{15}} = \sqrt{.93} = .97$$

Note: When data from a sample are used to estimate the standard deviation of the population from which the sample was drawn, division is by *N* - 1 instead of *N*, for reasons that will not concern us here.

Remember, a large standard deviation signifies that scores are widely scattered, and that therefore the mean is not terribly typical of the entire population. A small standard deviation tells us that most scores are clustered near the mean, and that therefore the mean is representative. Suppose two classes took a psychology exam, and both classes had the same mean score, 75 out of a possible 100. From the means alone, you might conclude that the classes were similar in performance. But if Class A had a standard deviation of 3 and Class B had a standard deviation of 9, you would know that there was much more variability in performance in Class B. This information could be useful to an instructor in planning lectures and making assignments.

Transforming Scores

Sometimes researchers do not wish to work directly with raw scores. They may prefer numbers that are more manageable, such as when the raw scores are tiny fractions. Or they may want to work with scores that reveal where a person stands relative to others. In such cases, raw scores can be transformed to other kinds of scores.

Percentile Scores. One common transformation converts each raw score to a **percentile score** (also called a *centile rank*). A percentile score gives the percentage of people who scored at or below a given raw score. Suppose you learn that you have scored 37 on a psychology exam. In the absence of any other information, you may not know whether to celebrate or cry. But if you are told that 37 is equivalent to a percentile score of 90, you know that you can be pretty proud of yourself; you have scored as well as, or higher than, 90 percent of those who have taken the test. On the other hand, if you are told that 37 is equivalent to a percentile score of 50, you have scored only at the median—only as well as, or higher than, half of the other students. The highest possible percentile rank is 99, or more precisely, 99.99, because you can never do better than 100 percent of a group when you are a member of the group. (Can you say what the lowest possible percentile score is? The answer is on page A-7.) Standardized tests such as those described in previous chapters often come with tables that allow for the easy conversion of any raw score to the appropriate percentile score, based on data from a larger number of people who have already taken the test.

Percentile scores are easy to understand and easy to calculate. However, they also have a drawback: They merely rank people and do not tell us how far apart people are in terms of raw scores. Suppose you scored in the 50th percentile on an exam, June scored in the 45th, Tricia scored in the 20th, and Sean scored in the 15th. The difference between you and June may seem identical to that between Tricia and Sean (five percentiles). But in terms of raw scores you and June are probably more alike than Tricia and Sean, because exam scores usually cluster closely together around the midpoint of the distribution and are farther apart at the extremes. Because percentile scores do not preserve the spatial relationships in the original distribution of scores, they are inappropriate for computing many kinds of statistics. For example, they cannot be used to calculate means.

Z-scores. Another common transformation of raw scores is to **z-scores**, or **standard scores**. A z-score tells you how far a given raw score is above or below the mean, using the standard deviation as the unit of measurement. To compute a z-score, you subtract the mean of the distribution from the raw score and divide by the standard deviation:

$$z = \frac{X - M}{SD}$$

Unlike percentile scores, z-scores preserve the relative spacing of the original raw scores. The mean itself always corresponds to a z-score of zero, since it cannot deviate from itself. All scores above the mean have positive z-scores and all scores below the mean have negative ones. When the raw scores form a certain pattern called a *normal distribution* (to be described shortly), a z-score tells you how high or low the corresponding raw score was, relative to the other scores. If your exam score of 37 is equivalent to a z-score of +1.0, you have scored 1 standard deviation above the mean. Assuming a roughly normal distribution, that's pretty good, because in a normal distribution only about 16 percent of all scores fall at or above 1 standard deviation above the mean. But if your 37 is equivalent to a z-score of –1.0, you have scored 1 standard deviation below the mean—a poor score.

Z-scores are sometimes used to compare people's performance on different tests or measures. Say that Elsa earns a score of 64 on her first psychology test and Manuel, who is taking psychology from a different instructor, earns a 62 on his first test. In Elsa's class, the mean score is 50 and the standard deviation is 7, so Elsa's z-score is (64 – 50)/7 = 2.0. In Manuel's class, the mean is also 50, but the standard deviation is 6. Therefore, his z-score is also 2.0 [(62 – 50)/6]. Compared to their respective classmates, Elsa and Manuel did equally well. But be careful: This does not imply that they are equally able students. Perhaps Elsa's instructor has a reputation for giving easy tests and Manuel's for giving hard ones, so Manuel's instructor has attracted a more industrious group of students. In that case, Manuel faces stiffer competition than Elsa does, and even though he and Elsa have the same z-score, Manuel's performance may be more impressive.

You can see that comparing z-scores from different people or different tests must be done with caution. Standardized tests, such as IQ tests and various personality tests, use z-scores derived from a large sample of people assumed to be representative of the general population taking the tests. When two tests are standardized for similar populations, it is safe to compare z-scores on them. But z-scores derived from special samples, such as students in different psychology classes, may not be comparable.

Curves

In addition to knowing how spread out our scores are, we need to know the pattern of their distribution. At this point we come to a rather curious phenomenon. When researchers make a very large number of observations, many of the physical and psychological variables they study have a distribution that approximates a pattern called a **normal distribution.** (We say "approximates" because a perfect normal distribution is a theoretical construct and is not actually found in nature.) Plotted in a frequency polygon, a normal distribution has a symmetrical, bell-shaped form known as a **normal curve** (see Figure A.4).

A normal curve has several interesting and convenient properties. The right side is the exact mirror image of the left. The mean, median, and mode all have the same value and are at the exact center of the curve, at the top of the "bell." Most observations or scores cluster around the center of the curve, with far fewer out at the ends, or "tails" of the curve. Most important, as Figure A.4 shows, when standard deviations (or z-scores) are used on the horizontal axis of the curve, the percentage of scores falling between the mean and any given point on the horizontal axis is always the same. For example, 68.26 percent of the scores will fall between plus and minus 1 standard deviation from the mean; 95.44 percent of the scores will fall between plus and minus 2 standard deviations from the mean; and 99.74 percent of the scores will fall between plus and minus 3 standard deviations from the mean. These percentages hold for any normal curve, no matter what the size of the standard deviation. Tables are available showing the percentages of scores in a normal distribution that lie between the mean and various points (as expressed by z-scores).

The normal curve makes life easier for psychologists when they want to compare individuals on some trait or performance. For example, since IQ scores from a population form a roughly normal curve, the mean and standard deviation of a test are all the information you need in order to know how many people score above or below a particular score. On a test with a mean of 100 and a standard deviation of 15, about 68.26 percent of the population scores between 85 and 115—1 standard deviation below and 1 standard deviation above the mean (see Chapter 9).

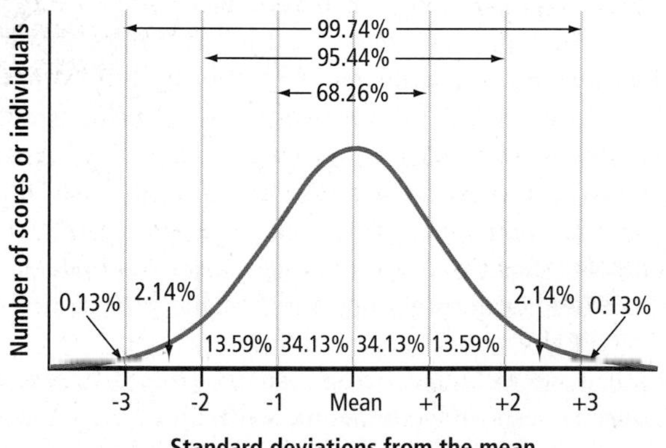

FIGURE A.4 A Normal Curve

When standard deviations (or z-scores) are used along the horizontal axis of a normal curve, certain fixed percentages of scores fall between the mean and any given point. As you can see, most scores fall in the middle range (between +1 and -1 standard deviations from the mean).

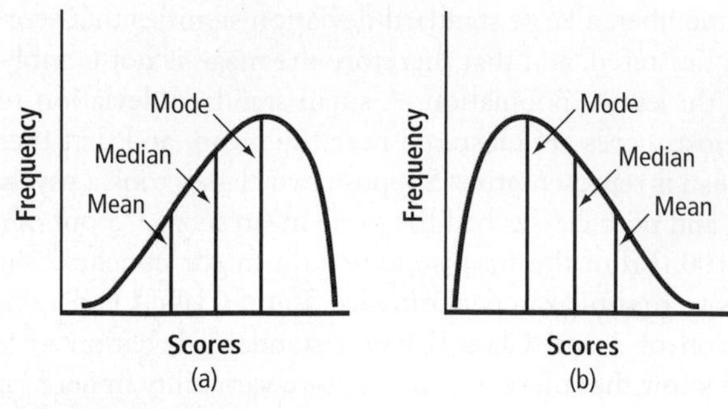

FIGURE A.5 Skewed Curves

Curve (a) is skewed negatively, to the left. Curve (b) is skewed positively, to the right. The direction of a curve's skewness is determined by the position of the long tail, not by the position of the bulge. In a skewed curve, the mean, median, and mode fall at different points.

Not all types of observations, however, are distributed normally. Some curves are lopsided, or *skewed,* with scores clustering at one end or the other of the horizontal axis (see Figure A.5). When the "tail" of the curve is longer on the right than on the left, the curve is said to be positively, or right, skewed. When the opposite is true, the curve is said to be negatively, or left, skewed. In experiments, reaction times typically form a right-skewed distribution. For example, if people must press a button whenever they hear some signal, most will react quite quickly; but a few will take an unusually long time, causing the right "tail" of the curve to be stretched out.

Knowing the shape of a distribution can be extremely valuable. Paleontologist Stephen Jay Gould (1985) once told how such information helped him cope with the news that he had a rare and serious form of cancer. Being a researcher, he immediately headed for the library to learn all he could about his disease. The first thing he found was that it was incurable, with a median mortality of only eight months after discovery. Most people might have assumed that a "median mortality of eight months" means "I will probably be dead in eight months." But Gould realized that although half of all patients died within eight months, the other half survived longer than that. Since his disease had been diagnosed in its early stages, he was getting top-notch medical treatment, and he had a strong will to live, Gould figured he could reasonably expect to be in the half of the distribution that survived beyond eight months. Even more cheering, the distribution of deaths from the disease was right-skewed: The cases to the left of the median of eight months could only extend to zero months, but those to the right could stretch out for years. Gould saw no reason why he should not expect to be in the tip of that right-hand tail.

ANSWERS TO QUESTIONS IN THIS CHAPTER:

Control group statistics:

$$\text{Mean} = \frac{\Sigma X}{N} = \frac{87}{15} = 5.8$$

Median = 6

$$\text{Standard Deviation} = \sqrt{\frac{\Sigma(X - M)^2}{N}} = \sqrt{\frac{14.4}{15}} = \sqrt{.96} = .98$$

Lowest possible percentile score: 1 (or, more precisely, .01)

For Stephen Jay Gould, statistics, properly interpreted, were "profoundly nurturant and life-giving." They offered him hope and inspired him to fight his disease. The initial diagnosis was made in July of 1982. Gould remained professionally active for 20 more years. When he died in 2002, it was from an unrelated type of cancer.

Drawing Inferences

Once data are organized and summarized, the next step is to ask whether they differ from what might have been expected purely by chance (see Chapter 2). A researcher needs to know whether it is safe to infer that the results from a particular sample of people are valid for the entire population from which the sample was drawn. **Inferential statistics** provide this information. They are used in both experimental and correlational studies.

The Null Versus the Alternative Hypothesis

In an experiment, the scientist must assess the possibility that his or her experimental manipulations will have no effect on the subjects' behavior. The statement expressing this possibility is called the **null hypothesis**. In our stress-and-humor study, the null hypothesis states that making up a funny commentary will not relieve stress any more than making up a straightforward narrative will. In other words, it predicts that the difference between the means of the two groups will not deviate significantly from zero. Any obtained difference will be due solely to chance fluctuations. In contrast, the **alternative hypothesis** (also called the *experimental* or *research hypothesis*) states that on the average the experimental group will have lower mood disturbance scores than the control group.

The null hypothesis and the alternative hypothesis cannot both be true. Our goal is to reject the null hypothesis. If our results turn out to be consistent with the null hypothesis, we will not be able to do so. If the data are inconsistent with the null hypothesis, we will be able to reject it with some degree of confidence. Unless we study the entire population, though, we will never be able to say that the alternative hypothesis has been proven. No matter how impressive our results are, there will always be some degree of uncertainty about the inferences we draw from them. Since we cannot prove the alternative hypothesis, we must be satisfied with showing that the null hypothesis is unreasonable.

Students are often surprised to learn that in traditional hypothesis testing it is the null hypothesis, not the alternative hypothesis, that is tested. After all, it is the alternative hypothesis that is actually of interest. But this procedure does make sense. The null hypothesis can be stated precisely and tested directly. In the case of our fictitious study, the null hypothesis predicts that the difference between the two means will be zero. The alternative hypothesis does not permit a precise prediction because we don't know how much the two means might differ (if, in fact, they do differ). Therefore, it cannot be tested directly.

Testing Hypotheses

Many computations are available for testing the null hypothesis. The choice depends on the design of the study, the size of the sample, and other factors. We will not cover any specific tests here. Our purpose is simply to introduce you to the kind of reasoning that underlies hypothesis testing. With that in mind, let us return once again to our data. For each of our two groups we have calculated a mean and a standard deviation. Now we want to compare the two sets of data to see if they differ enough for us to reject the null hypothesis. We wish to be reasonably certain that our observed differences did not occur entirely by chance.

What does it mean to be "reasonably certain"? How different from zero must our result be to be taken seriously? Imagine, for a moment, that we had infinite resources and could somehow repeat our experiment, each time using a new pair of groups, until we had "run" the entire population through the study. It can be shown mathematically that if only chance were operating, our various experimental results would form a normal distribution. This theoretical distribution is called "the sampling distribution of the difference between means," but since that is quite a mouthful, we will simply call it the *sampling distribution* for short. If the null hypothesis were true, the mean of the sampling distribution would be zero. That is, on the average, we would find no difference between the two groups. Often, though, because of chance influences or *random error*, we would get a result that deviated to one degree or another from zero. On rare occasions, the result would deviate a great deal from zero.

We cannot test the entire population, though. All we have are data from a single sample. We would like to know whether the difference between means that we actually obtained would be close to the mean of the theoretical sampling distribution (if we could test the entire population) or far away from it, out in one of the "tails" of the curve. Was our result highly likely to occur on the basis of chance alone or highly unlikely?

Before we can answer that question, we must have some precise way to measure distance from the mean of the sampling distribution. We must know exactly how far from the mean our

obtained result must be to be considered "far away." If only we knew the standard deviation of the sampling distribution, we could use it as our unit of measurement. We don't know it, but fortunately, we can use the standard deviation of our *sample* to estimate it. (We will not go into the reasons that this is so.)

Now we are in business. We can look at the mean difference between our two groups and figure out how far it is (in terms of standard deviations) from the mean of the sampling distribution. As mentioned earlier, one of the convenient things about a normal distribution is that a certain fixed percentage of all observations falls between the mean of the distribution and any given point above or below the mean. These percentages are available from tables. Therefore, if we know the "distance" of our obtained result from the mean of the theoretical sampling distribution, we automatically know how likely our result is to have occurred strictly by chance.

To give a specific example, if it turns out that our obtained result is 2 standard deviations above the mean of the theoretical sampling distribution, we know that the probability of its having occurred by chance is less than 2.3 percent. If our result is 3 standard deviations above the mean of the sampling distribution, the probability of its having occurred by chance is less than .13 percent—less than 1 in 800. In either case, we might well suspect that our result did not occur entirely by chance after all. We would call the result **statistically significant**. (Psychologists usually consider any highly unlikely result to be of interest, no matter which direction it takes. In other words, the result may be in either tail of the sampling distribution.)

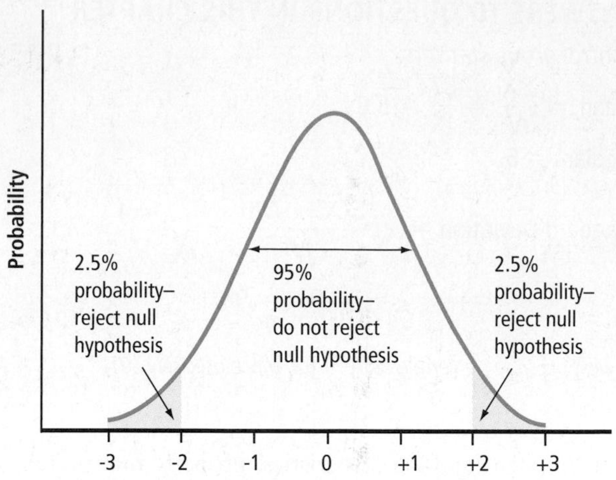

Figure A.6 Statistical Significance

This curve represents the theoretical sampling distribution discussed in the text. The curve is what we would expect by chance if we did our hypothetical stress-and-humor study many times, testing the entire population. If we used the conventional significance level of .05, we would regard our obtained result as significant only if the probability of getting a result that far from zero by chance (in either direction) totaled 5 percent or less. As shown, the result must fall far out in one of the tails of the sampling distribution. Otherwise, we cannot reject the null hypothesis.

To summarize: Statistical significance means that if only chance were operating, our result would be highly improbable, so we are fairly safe in concluding that more than chance was operating—namely, the influence of our independent variable. We can reject the null hypothesis, and open the champagne. As we noted in Chapter 2, psychologists usually accept a finding as statistically significant if the likelihood of its occurring by chance is 5 percent or less (see Figure A.6). This cutoff point gives the researcher a reasonable chance of confirming reliable results as well as reasonable protection against accepting unreliable ones.

Some cautions are in order, though. As noted in Chapter 2, conventional tests of statistical significance have drawn serious criticisms in recent years. Statistically significant results are not always psychologically interesting or important. Further, statistical significance is related to the size of the sample. A large sample increases the likelihood of reliable results. But there is a trade-off: The larger the sample, the more probable it is that a small result having no practical importance will reach statistical significance. On the other hand, with the sample sizes typically used in psychological research, there is a good chance of falsely concluding that an experimental effect has not occurred when one actually has (Hunter, 1997). For these reasons, it is always useful to know how much of the total variability in scores was accounted for by the independent variable (the **effect size**). (The computations are not discussed here.) If only 3 percent of the variance was accounted for, then 97 percent was due either to chance factors or to systematic influences of which the researcher was unaware. Because human behavior is affected by so many factors, the amount of variability accounted for by a single psychological variable is often modest. But sometimes the effect size is considerable even when the results don't quite reach significance.

Oh, by the way, the study of humor's effect on stress and health turns out to be pretty complicated. The results depend on how you define "sense of humor," how you do the study, and what aspects of humor you are investigating. Researchers are learning that humor probably doesn't help people live longer or hasten recovery from injury or illness. But it is certainly more emotionally beneficial than moping around. So, when gravity gets you down, try a little levity.

Summary

1. When used correctly, statistics expose unwarranted conclusions, promote precision, and help researchers spot trends amid diversity.
2. Often, the first step in data analysis is to organize and condense data in a *frequency distribution*, a tally showing how often each possible score (or interval of scores) occurred. Such information can also be depicted in a *histogram* (bar graph) or a *frequency polygon* (line graph).

3. Descriptive statistics summarize and describe the data. *Central tendency* is measured by the *mean*, *median*, or, less frequently, the *mode*. Since a measure of central tendency may or may not be highly representative of other scores in a distribution, it is also important to analyze variability. A large *standard deviation* means that scores are widely scattered about the mean; a small one means that most scores are clustered near the mean.
4. Raw scores can be transformed into other kinds of scores. *Percentile scores* indicate the percentage of people who scored at or below a given raw score. *Z-scores* (*standard scores*) indicate how far a given raw score is above or below the mean of the distribution.
5. Many variables have a distribution approximating a *normal distribution*, depicted as a *normal curve*. The normal curve has a convenient property: When standard deviations are used as the units on the horizontal axis, the percentage of scores falling between any two points on the horizontal axis is always the same. Not all types of observations are distributed normally, however. Some distributions are *skewed* to the left or right.
6. Inferential statistics can be used to test the *null hypothesis* and to tell a researcher whether a result differed significantly from what might have been expected purely by chance. Basically, hypothesis testing involves estimating where the obtained result would have fallen in a theoretical *sampling distribution* based on studies of the entire population in question. If the result would have been far out in one of the tails of the distribution, it is considered statistically significant. A statistically significant result may or may not be psychologically interesting or important, so many researchers also compute the *effect size*.

Key Terms

frequency distribution A-1
graph A-2
histogram/bar graph A-2
frequency polygon/line graph A-2
descriptive statistics A-2
measure of central tendency A-3
mean A-3
median A-3
mode A-3
measure of variability A-4
range A-4
standard deviation A-4
deviation score A-4
percentile score (centile rank) A-5
z-score (standard score) A-5
normal distribution A-6
normal curve A-6
right- and left-skewed distributions A-6
inferential statistics A-7
null hypothesis A-7
alternative hypothesis A-7
sampling distribution A-7
statistically significant A-8
effect size A-8

ANSWERS TO GET INVOLVED EXERCISES

Some solutions to the nine-dot problem in the Get Involved exercise on page 337, Chapter 9 (from Adams, 1986):

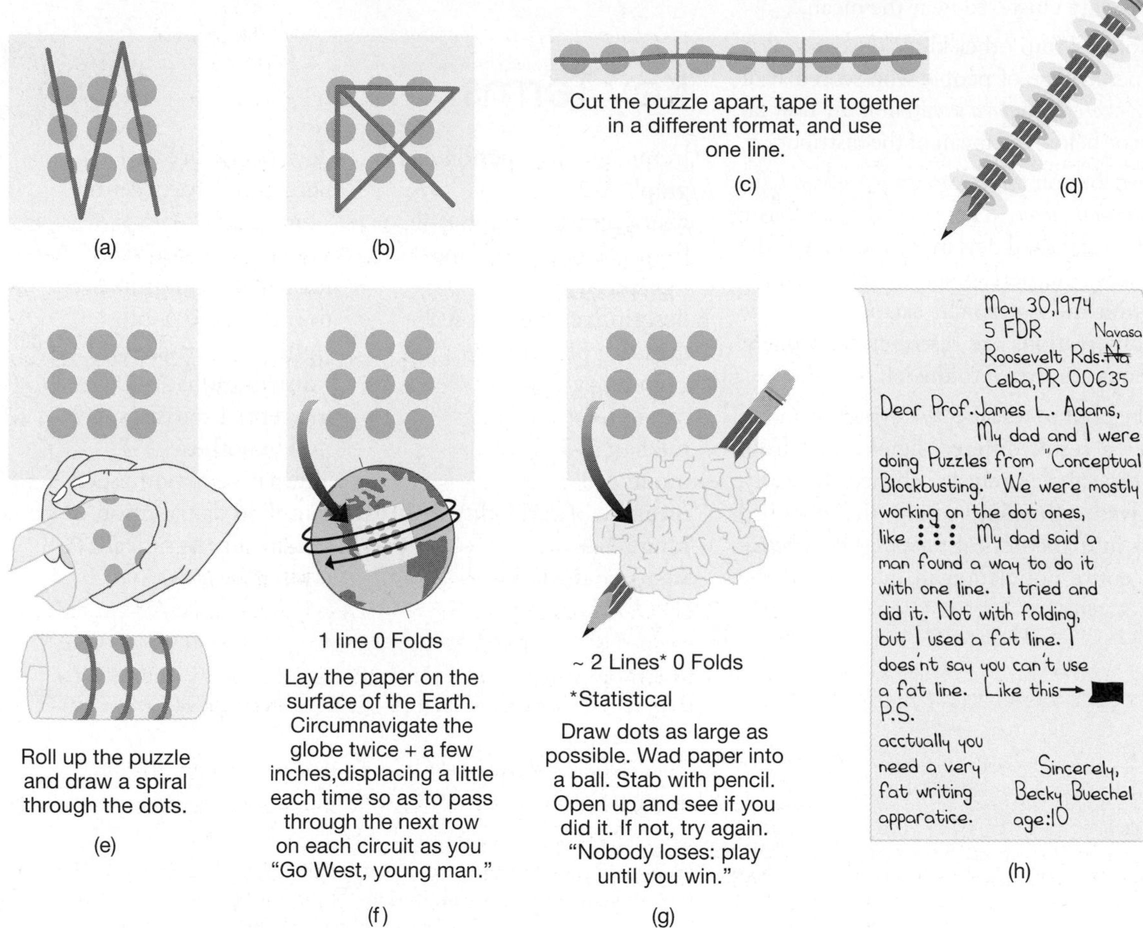

(a)
(b)
Cut the puzzle apart, tape it together in a different format, and use one line.
(c)
(d)
Roll up the puzzle and draw a spiral through the dots.
(e)
1 line 0 Folds
Lay the paper on the surface of the Earth. Circumnavigate the globe twice + a few inches,displacing a little each time so as to pass through the next row on each circuit as you "Go West, young man."
(f)
~ 2 Lines* 0 Folds
*Statistical
Draw dots as large as possible. Wad paper into a ball. Stab with pencil. Open up and see if you did it. If not, try again. "Nobody loses: play until you win."
(g)
May 30,1974
5 FDR
Roosevelt Rds. Navasa
Celba, PR 00635
Dear Prof. James L. Adams,
My dad and I were doing Puzzles from "Conceptual Blockbusting." We were mostly working on the dot ones, like ⁝⁝⁝ My dad said a man found a way to do it with one line. I tried and did it. Not with folding, but I used a fat line. I does'nt say you can't use a fat line. Like this→
P.S.
acctually you need a very fat writing apparatice.
Sincerely,
Becky Buechel
age:10
(h)

Answers to the creativity test on page 359, Chapter 9:

back, party, book, match, cheese

Answers to the Get Involved exercises on pages 374 and 376, Chapter 10:

Rudolph's eight friends were **Dasher, Dancer, Prancer, Vixen, Comet, Cupid, Donder**, and **Blitzen**.

Glossary

absolute threshold The smallest quantity of physical energy that can be reliably detected by an observer.

acculturation The process by which members of minority groups come to identify with and feel part of the mainstream culture.

action potential A brief change in electrical voltage that occurs between the inside and the outside of an axon when a neuron is stimulated; it serves to produce an electrical impulse.

activation–synthesis theory The theory that dreaming results from the cortical synthesis and interpretation of neural signals triggered by activity in the lower part of the brain.

adrenal hormones Hormones that are produced by the adrenal glands and that are involved in emotion and stress.

affect heuristic The tendency to consult one's emotions instead of estimating probabilities objectively.

agoraphobia A set of phobias, often set off by a panic attack, involving the basic fear of being away from a safe place or person.

algorithm A problem-solving strategy guaranteed to produce a solution even if the user does not know how it works.

alternative hypothesis An assertion that the independent variable in a study will have a certain predictable effect on the dependent variable; also called an *experimental* or *research hypothesis*.

amnesia The partial or complete loss of memory for important personal information.

amygdala [uh-MIG-dul-uh] A brain structure involved in the arousal and regulation of emotion and the initial emotional response to sensory information.

anorexia (anorexia nervosa) An eating disorder characterized by fear of being fat, a distorted body image, radically reduced consumption of food, and emaciation.

antidepressant drugs Drugs used primarily in the treatment of mood disorders, especially depression and anxiety.

antipsychotic drugs Drugs used primarily in the treatment of schizophrenia and other psychotic disorders.

antisocial personality disorder (APD) A personality disorder characterized by a lifelong pattern of irresponsible, antisocial behavior such as lawbreaking, violence, and other impulsive, reckless acts.

applied psychology The study of psychological issues that have direct practical significance; also, the application of psychological findings.

approach goals Goals framed in terms of desired outcomes or experiences, such as learning to scuba dive.

archetypes [AR-ki-tipes] Universal, symbolic images that appear in myths, art, stories, and dreams; to Jungians, they reflect the collective unconscious.

arithmetic mean An average that is calculated by adding up a set of quantities and dividing the sum by the total number of quantities in the set.

attribution theory The theory that people are motivated to explain their own and other people's behavior by attributing causes of that behavior to a situation or a disposition.

autonomic nervous system The subdivision of the peripheral nervous system that regulates the internal organs and glands.

availability heuristic The tendency to judge the probability of a type of event by how easy it is to think of examples or instances.

avoidance goals Goals framed in terms of avoiding unpleasant experiences, such as trying not to look foolish in public.

axon A neuron's extending fiber that conducts impulses away from the cell body and transmits them to other neurons.

basic concepts Concepts that have a moderate number of instances and that are easier to acquire than those having few or many instances.

basic psychology The study of psychological issues in order to seek knowledge for its own sake rather than for its practical application.

behavior modification The application of operant conditioning techniques to teach new responses or to reduce or eliminate maladaptive or problematic behavior; also called *applied behavior analysis*.

behavior therapy A form of therapy that applies principles of classical and operant conditioning to help people change self-defeating or problematic behaviors.

behavioral genetics An interdisciplinary field of study concerned with the genetic bases of individual differences in behavior and personality.

behavioral self-monitoring In behavior therapy, a method of keeping careful data on the frequency and consequences of the behavior to be changed.

behaviorism An approach to psychology that emphasizes the study of observable behavior and the role of the environment as a determinant of behavior.

binocular cues Visual cues to depth or distance requiring two eyes.

biological perspective A psychological approach that emphasizes bodily events and changes associated with actions, feelings, and thoughts.

biological rhythm A periodic, more or less regular fluctuation in a biological system; it may or may not have psychological implications.

bipolar disorder A mood disorder in which episodes of both depression and mania (excessive euphoria) occur.

borderline personality disorder A disorder characterized by intense but unstable relationships, a fear of abandonment by others, an unrealistic self-image, and emotional volatility.

brain stem The part of the brain at the top of the spinal cord, consisting of the medulla and the pons.

brightness Lightness or luminance; the dimension of visual experience related to the amount (intensity) of light emitted from or reflected by an object.

bulimia An eating disorder characterized by episodes of excessive eating (bingeing) followed by forced vomiting or use of laxatives (purging).

case study A detailed description of a particular individual being studied or treated.

cell body The part of the neuron that keeps it alive and determines whether it will fire.

central nervous system (CNS) The portion of the nervous system consisting of the brain and spinal cord.

cerebellum A brain structure that regulates movement and balance and is involved in the learning of certain kinds of simple responses.

cerebral cortex A collection of several thin layers of cells covering the cerebrum; it is largely responsible for higher mental functions. *Cortex* is Latin for "bark" or "rind."

cerebral hemispheres The two halves of the cerebrum.

cerebrum [suh-REE-brum] The largest brain structure, consisting of the upper part of the brain; divided into two hemispheres, it is in charge of most sensory, motor, and cognitive processes. From the Latin for "brain."

childhood (infantile) amnesia The inability to remember events and experiences that occurred during the first two or three years of life.

chromosomes Within every cell, rod-shaped structures that carry the genes.

chunk A meaningful unit of information; it may be composed of smaller units.

circadian [sur-CAY-dee-un] rhythm A biological rhythm with a period (from peak to peak or trough to trough) of about 24 hours; from the Latin *circa*, "about," and *dies*, "a day."

classical conditioning The process by which a previously neutral stimulus acquires the capacity to elicit a response through association with a stimulus that already elicits a similar or related response.

client-centered (nondirective) therapy A humanist approach, devised by Carl Rogers, which emphasizes the therapist's empathy with the client and the use of unconditional positive regard.

cochlea [KOCK-lee-uh] A snail-shaped, fluid-filled organ in the inner ear, containing the organ of Corti, where the receptors for hearing are located.

coefficient of correlation A measure of correlation that ranges in value from −1.00 to +1.00.

cognitive dissonance A state of tension that occurs when a person simultaneously holds two cognitions that are psychologically inconsistent or when a person's belief is incongruent with his or her behavior.

cognitive ethology The study of cognitive processes in nonhuman animals.

cognitive perspective A psychological approach that emphasizes mental processes in perception, memory, language, problem solving, and other areas of behavior.

cognitive schema An integrated mental network of knowledge, beliefs, and expectations concerning a particular topic or aspect of the world.

cognitive therapy A form of therapy designed to identify and change irrational, unproductive ways of thinking and, hence, to reduce negative emotions.

collective unconscious In Jungian theory, the universal memories and experiences of humankind, represented in the symbols, stories, and images (archetypes) that occur across all cultures.

collectivist cultures Cultures in which the self is regarded as embedded in relationships, and harmony with one's group is prized above individual goals and wishes.

computer neural networks Mathematical models of the brain that "learn" by adjusting the connections among hypothetical neurons in response to incoming data.

concept A mental category that groups objects, relations, activities, abstractions, or qualities having common properties.

conditioned response (CR) The classical-conditioning term for a response that is elicited by a conditioned stimulus; it occurs after the conditioned stimulus is associated with an unconditioned stimulus.

conditioned stimulus (CS) The classical-conditioning term for an initially neutral stimulus that comes to elicit a conditioned response after being associated with an unconditioned stimulus.

conditioning A basic kind of learning that involves associations between environmental stimuli and the organism's responses.

cones Visual receptors involved in color vision.

confabulation Confusion of an event that happened to someone else with one that happened to you, or a belief that you remember something when it never actually happened.

confirmation bias The tendency to look for or pay attention only to information that confirms one's own belief.

conservation The understanding that the physical properties of objects—such as the number of items in a cluster or the amount of liquid in a glass—can remain the same even when their form or appearance changes.

consolidation The process by which a long-term memory becomes durable and stable.

contact comfort In primates, the innate pleasure derived from close physical contact; it is the basis of the infant's first attachment.

continuous reinforcement A reinforcement schedule in which a particular response is always reinforced.

control condition In an experiment, a comparison condition in which subjects are not exposed to the same treatment as in the experimental condition.

convergence The turning inward of the eyes, which occurs when they focus on a nearby object.

corpus callosum [CORE-puhs cah-LOW-suhm] The bundle of nerve fibers connecting the two cerebral hemispheres.

correlation A measure of how strongly two variables are related to one another.

correlational study A descriptive study that looks for a consistent relationship between two phenomena.

counterconditioning In classical conditioning, the process of pairing a conditioned stimulus with a stimulus that elicits a response that is incompatible with an unwanted conditioned response.

critical thinking The ability and willingness to assess claims and make judgments on the basis of well-supported reasons and evidence rather than emotion or anecdote.

cross-sectional study A study in which subjects of different ages are compared at a given time.

crystallized intelligence Cognitive skills and specific knowledge of information acquired over a lifetime; it is heavily dependent on education and tends to remain stable over the lifetime.

cue-dependent forgetting The inability to retrieve information stored in memory because of insufficient cues for recall.

culture A program of shared rules that govern the behavior of people in a community or society, and a set of values, beliefs, and customs shared by most members of that community.

dark adaptation A process by which visual receptors become maximally sensitive to dim light.

decay theory The theory that information in memory eventually disappears if it is not accessed; it applies better to short-term than to long-term memory.

declarative memories Memories of facts, rules, concepts, and events ("knowing that"); they include semantic and episodic memories.

deductive reasoning A form of reasoning in which a conclusion follows necessarily from certain premises; if the premises are true, the conclusion must be true.

deep processing In the encoding of information, the processing of meaning rather than simply the physical or sensory features of a stimulus.

defense mechanisms Methods used by the ego to prevent unconscious anxiety or threatening thoughts from entering consciousness.

deindividuation In groups or crowds, the loss of awareness of one's own individuality.

dendrites A neuron's branches that receive information from other neurons and transmit it toward the cell body.

dependent variable A variable that an experimenter predicts will be affected by manipulations of the independent variable.

depressants Drugs that slow activity in the central nervous system.

descriptive methods Methods that yield descriptions of behavior but not necessarily causal explanations.

descriptive statistics Statistical procedures that organize and summarize research data.

dialectical reasoning A process in which opposing facts or ideas are weighed and compared, with a view to determining the best solution or resolving differences.

difference threshold The smallest difference in stimulation that can be reliably detected by an observer when two stimuli are compared; also called *just noticeable difference (jnd)*.

diffusion of responsibility In groups, the tendency of members to avoid taking action because they assume that others will.

discriminative stimulus A stimulus that signals when a particular response is likely to be followed by a certain type of consequence.

display rules Social and cultural rules that regulate when, how, and where a person may express (or must suppress) emotions.

dissociation A split in consciousness in which one part of the mind operates independently of others.

dissociative identity disorder A controversial disorder marked by the apparent appearance within one person of two or more distinct personalities, each with its own name and traits; formerly known as *multiple personality disorder (MPD)*.

DNA (deoxyribonucleic acid) The chromosomal molecule that transfers genetic characteristics by way of coded instructions for the structure of proteins.

doctrine of specific nerve energies The principle that different sensory modalities exist because signals received by the sense organs stimulate different nerve pathways leading to different areas of the brain.

double-blind study An experiment in which neither the subjects nor the individuals running the study know which subjects are in the control group and which are in the experimental group until after the results are tallied.

effect size In an experiment, the amount of variance in the data accounted for by the independent variable.

ego In psychoanalysis, the part of personality that represents reason, good sense, and rational self-control.

egocentric thinking Seeing the world from only your own point of view; the inability to take another person's perspective.

elaborative rehearsal Association of new information with already stored knowledge and analysis of the new information to make it memorable.

electroconvulsive therapy (ECT) A procedure used in cases of prolonged and severe major depression, in which a brief brain seizure is induced.

electroencephalogram (EEG) A recording of neural activity detected by electrodes.

emotion A state of arousal involving facial and bodily changes, brain activation, cognitive appraisals, subjective feelings, and tendencies toward action, all shaped by cultural rules.

emotion work Expression of an emotion that the person does not really feel, often because of a role requirement.

emotional intelligence The ability to identify your own and other people's emotions accurately, express your emotions clearly, and regulate emotions in yourself and others.

empirical Relying on or derived from observation, experimentation, or measurement.

endocrine glands Internal organs that produce hormones and release them into the bloodstream.

endogenous Generated from within rather than by external cues.

endorphins [en-DOR-fins] Chemical substances in the nervous system that are similar in structure and action to opiates; they are involved in pain reduction, pleasure, and memory and are known technically as *endogenous opioid peptides*.

entrainment The synchronization of biological rhythms with external cues, such as fluctuations in daylight.

entrapment A gradual process in which individuals escalate their commitment to a course of action to justify their investment of time, money, or effort.

episodic memories Memories of personally experienced events and the contexts in which they occurred.

equilibrium The sense of balance.

ethnic identity A person's identification with a racial or ethnic group.

ethnocentrism The belief that one's own ethnic group, nation, or religion is superior to all others.

evolution A change in gene frequencies within a population over many generations; a mechanism by which genetically influenced characteristics of a population may change.

evolutionary psychology A field of psychology emphasizing evolutionary mechanisms that may help explain human commonalities in cognition, development, emotion, social practices, and other areas of behavior.

existential therapy A form of therapy designed to help clients explore the meaning of existence and face the great questions of life, such as death, freedom, alienation, and loneliness.

existentialism A philosophical approach that emphasizes the inevitable dilemmas and challenges of human existence.

experiment A controlled test of a hypothesis in which the researcher manipulates one variable to discover its effect on another.

experimenter effects Unintended changes in subjects' behavior due to cues inadvertently given by the experimenter.

explicit memory Conscious, intentional recollection of an event or of an item of information.

extinction The weakening and eventual disappearance of a learned response. In classical conditioning, it occurs when the conditioned stimulus is no longer paired with the unconditioned stimulus; in operant conditioning, it occurs when a response is no longer followed by a reinforcer.

extrinsic motivation The pursuit of an activity for external rewards, such as money or fame.

extrinsic reinforcers Reinforcers that are not inherently related to the activity being reinforced.

facial feedback The process by which the facial muscles send messages to the brain about the basic emotion being expressed.

factor analysis A statistical method for analyzing the intercorrelations among various measures or test scores; clusters of measures or scores that are highly correlated are assumed to measure the same underlying trait, ability, or aptitude (factor).

familiarity effect The tendency of people to feel more positive toward a person, item, product, or other stimulus the more familiar they are with it.

family-systems perspective An approach to doing therapy with individuals or families by identifying how each family member forms part of a larger interacting system.

feature detectors Cells in the visual cortex that are sensitive to specific features of the environment.

feminist psychology A psychological approach that analyzes the influence of social inequities on gender relations and on the behavior of the two sexes.

field research Descriptive or experimental research conducted in a natural setting outside the laboratory.

flooding In behavior therapy, a form of exposure treatment in which the client is taken directly into the feared situation until his or her panic subsides.

fluid intelligence The capacity for deductive reasoning and the ability to use new information to solve problems; it is relatively independent of education and tends to decline in old age.

fraternal (dizygotic) twins Twins that develop from two separate eggs fertilized by different sperm; they are no more alike genetically than are any other pair of siblings.

free association In psychodynamic therapies, the process of saying freely whatever comes to mind in connection with dreams, memories, fantasies, or conflicts.

frequency distribution A summary of how frequently each score in a set occurred.

frequency polygon (line graph) A graph showing a set of points obtained by plotting score values against score frequencies; adjacent points are joined by straight lines.

frontal lobes Lobes at the front of the brain's cerebral cortex; they contain areas involved in short-term memory, higher-order thinking, initiative, social judgment, and (in the left lobe, typically) speech production.

functionalism An early psychological approach that emphasized the function or purpose of behavior and consciousness.

fundamental attribution error The tendency, in explaining other people's behavior, to overestimate personality factors and underestimate the influence of the situation.

g factor A general intellectual ability assumed by many theorists to underlie specific mental abilities and talents.

ganglion cells Neurons in the retina of the eye, which gather information from receptor cells (by way of intermediate bipolar cells); their axons make up the optic nerve.

gate-control theory The theory that the experience of pain depends in part on whether pain impulses get past a neurological "gate" in the spinal cord and thus reach the brain.

gender identity The fundamental sense of being male or female; it is independent of whether the person conforms to the social and cultural rules of gender.

gender schema A cognitive schema (mental network) of knowledge, beliefs, metaphors, and expectations about what it means to be male or female.

gender typing The process by which children learn the abilities, interests, and behaviors associated with being masculine or feminine in their culture.

general adaptation syndrome According to Hans Selye, a series of physiological responses to stressors that occur in three phases: alarm, resistance, and exhaustion.

generalized anxiety disorder A continuous state of anxiety marked by feelings of worry and dread, apprehension, difficulties in concentration, and signs of motor tension.

genes The functional units of heredity; they are composed of DNA and specify the structure of proteins.

genetic marker A segment of DNA that varies among individuals, has a known location on a chromosome, and can function as a genetic landmark for a gene involved in a physical or mental condition.

genome The full set of genes in each cell of an organism (with the exception of sperm and egg cells).

Gestalt principles Principles that describe the brain's organization of sensory information into meaningful units and patterns.

glia [GLY-uh or GLEE-uh] Cells that support, nurture, and insulate neurons, remove debris when neurons die, enhance the formation and maintenance of neural connections, and modify neuronal functioning.

graduated exposure In behavior therapy, a method in which a person suffering from a phobia or panic attacks is gradually taken into the feared situation or exposed to a traumatic memory until the anxiety subsides.

graph A drawing that depicts numerical relationships.

groupthink The tendency for all members of a group to think alike for the sake of harmony and to suppress disagreement.

heritability A statistical estimate of the proportion of the total variance in some trait that is attributable to genetic differences among individuals within a group.

heuristic A rule of thumb that suggests a course of action or guides problem solving but does not guarantee an optimal solution.

higher-order conditioning In classical conditioning, a procedure in which a neutral stimulus becomes a conditioned stimulus through association with an already established conditioned stimulus.

hindsight bias The tendency to overestimate one's ability to have predicted an event once the outcome is known; the "I knew it all along" phenomenon.

hippocampus A brain structure involved in the storage of new information in memory.

histogram (bar graph) A graph in which the heights (or lengths) of bars are proportional to the frequencies of individual scores or classes of scores in a distribution.

hormones Chemical substances, secreted by organs called *glands*, that affect the functioning of other organs.

HPA (hypothalamus–pituitary–adrenal cortex) axis A system activated to energize the body to respond to stressors. The hypothalamus sends chemical messengers to the pituitary, which in turn prompts the adrenal cortex to produce cortisol and other hormones.

hue The dimension of visual experience specified by color names and related to the wavelength of light.

humanist psychology A psychological approach that emphasizes free will, personal growth, resilience, and the achievement of human potential.

humanist therapy A form of psychotherapy based on the philosophy of humanism, which emphasizes the client's free will to change rather than past conflicts.

hypnosis A procedure in which the practitioner suggests changes in a subject's sensations, perceptions, thoughts, feelings, or behavior.

hypothalamus A brain structure involved in emotions and drives vital to survival, such as fear, hunger, thirst, and reproduction; it regulates the autonomic nervous system.

hypothesis A statement that attempts to predict or to account for a set of phenomena; scientific hypotheses specify relationships among events or variables and are empirically tested.

id In psychoanalysis, the part of personality containing inherited psychic energy, particularly sexual and aggressive instincts.

identical (monozygotic) twins Twins that develop when a fertilized egg divides into two parts that develop into separate embryos.

implicit learning Learning that occurs when you acquire knowledge about something without being aware of how you did so and without being able to state exactly what it is you have learned.

implicit memory Unconscious retention in memory, as evidenced by the effect of a previous experience or previously encountered information on current thoughts or actions.

inattentional blindness Failure to consciously perceive something you are looking at because you are not attending to it.

independent variable A variable that an experimenter manipulates.

individualist cultures Cultures in which the self is regarded as autonomous, and individual goals and wishes are prized above duty and relations with others.

induction A method of child rearing in which the parent appeals to the child's own abilities, sense of responsibility, and feelings for others in correcting the child's misbehavior.

inductive reasoning A form of reasoning in which the premises provide support for a conclusion, but it is still possible for the conclusion to be false.

inferential statistics Statistical procedures that allow researchers to draw inferences about how statistically meaningful a study's results are.

informed consent The doctrine that human research subjects must participate voluntarily and must know enough about the study to make an intelligent decision about whether to participate.

instinctive drift During operant learning, the tendency for an organism to revert to instinctive behavior.

intelligence An inferred characteristic of an individual, usually defined as the ability to profit from experience, acquire knowledge, think abstractly, act purposefully, or adapt to changes in the environment.

intelligence quotient (IQ) A measure of intelligence originally computed by dividing a person's mental age by his or her chronological age and multiplying the result by 100; it is now derived from norms provided for standardized intelligence tests.

intermittent (partial) schedule of reinforcement A reinforcement schedule in which a particular response is sometimes but not always reinforced.

internal desynchronization A state in which biological rhythms are not in phase (synchronized) with one another.

intersex conditions (intersexuality) Conditions, occurring in about one of every 2,000 births, in which chromosomal or hormonal anomalies cause a child to be born with ambiguous genitals, or genitals that conflict with the infant's chromosomes (formerly called *hermaphroditism*).

intrinsic motivation The pursuit of an activity for its own sake.

intrinsic reinforcers Reinforcers that are inherently related to the activity being reinforced.

justification of effort The tendency of individuals to increase their liking for something that they have worked hard or suffered to attain; a common form of dissonance reduction.

just-world hypothesis The notion that many people need to believe that the world is fair and that justice is served, that bad people are punished and good people rewarded.

kinesthesis [KIN-es-THEE-sís] The sense of body position and movement of body parts; also called *kinesthesia*.

language A system that combines meaningless elements such as sounds or gestures to form structured utterances that convey meaning.

language acquisition device According to many psycholinguists, an innate mental module that allows young children to develop language if they are exposed to an adequate sampling of conversation.

latent learning A form of learning that is not immediately expressed in an overt response; it occurs without obvious reinforcement.

lateralization Specialization of the two cerebral hemispheres for particular operations.

learning A relatively permanent change in behavior (or behavioral potential) due to experience.

learning perspective A psychological approach that emphasizes how the environment and experience affect a person's or animal's actions; it includes *behaviorism* and *social-cognitive learning theories*.

libido (li-BEE-do) In psychoanalysis, the psychic energy that fuels the life or sexual instincts of the id.

limbic system A group of brain areas involved in emotional reactions and motivated behavior.

linkage studies Studies that look for patterns of inheritance of genetic markers in large families in which a particular condition is common.

lithium carbonate A drug frequently given to people suffering from bipolar disorder.

localization of function Specialization of particular brain areas for particular functions.

locus of control A general expectation about whether the results of your actions are under your own control (internal locus) or beyond your control (external locus).

longitudinal study A study in which subjects are followed and periodically reassessed over a period of time.

long-term memory (LTM) In the three-box model of memory, the memory system involved in the long-term storage of information.

long-term potentiation A long-lasting increase in the strength of synaptic responsiveness, thought to be a biological mechanism of long-term memory.

loudness The dimension of auditory experience related to the intensity of a pressure wave.

lucid dream A dream in which the dreamer is aware of dreaming.

maintenance rehearsal Rote repetition of material in order to maintain its availability in memory.

major depression A mood disorder involving disturbances in emotion (excessive sadness), behavior (loss of interest in one's usual activities), cognition (thoughts of hopelessness), and body function (fatigue and loss of appetite).

mastery (learning) goals Goals framed in terms of increasing one's competence and skills.

mean *See* arithmetic mean.

measure of central tendency A number intended to characterize an entire set of data.

measure of variability A number that indicates how dispersed scores are around the mean of the distribution.

median A measure of central tendency; the value at the midpoint of a distribution of scores when the scores are ordered from highest to lowest.

medulla [muh-DUL-uh] A structure in the brain stem responsible for certain automatic functions, such as breathing and heart rate.

melatonin A hormone, secreted by the pineal gland, that is involved in the regulation of daily biological (circadian) rhythms.

menarche [men-ARR-kee] The onset of menstruation.

menopause The cessation of menstruation and of the production of ova; it is usually a gradual process lasting up to several years.

mental age (MA) A measure of mental development expressed in terms of the average mental ability at a given age.

mental disorder Any behavior or emotional state that causes an individual great suffering, is self-destructive, seriously impairs the person's ability to work or get along with others, or endangers others or the community.

mental image A mental representation that mirrors or resembles the thing it represents; mental images occur in many and perhaps all sensory modalities.

mental set A tendency to solve problems using procedures that worked before on similar problems.

meta-analysis A procedure for combining and analyzing data from many studies; it determines how much of the variance in scores across all studies can be explained by a particular variable.

metacognition The knowledge or awareness of one's own cognitive processes.

Minnesota Multiphasic Personality Inventory (MMPI) A widely used objective personality test.

mirror neurons A class of cells, distributed throughout various parts of the brain, that fire when an animal sees or hears an action *and* carries out the same

action on its own; these cells are far more evolved and varied in human beings than in other animals.

mnemonics Strategies and tricks for improving memory, such as the use of a verse or a formula.

mode A measure of central tendency; the most frequently occurring score in a distribution.

monocular cues Visual cues to depth or distance, which can be used by one eye alone.

mood-congruent memory The tendency to remember experiences that are consistent with one's current mood and overlook or forget experiences that are not.

motivation An inferred process within a person or animal that causes movement either toward a goal or away from an unpleasant situation.

MRI (magnetic resonance imaging) A method for studying body and brain tissue, using magnetic fields and special radio receivers.

myelin sheath A fatty insulation that may surround the axon of a neuron.

narcissistic personality disorder A disorder characterized by an exaggerated sense of self-importance and self-absorption.

narcolepsy A sleep disorder involving sudden and unpredictable daytime attacks of sleepiness or lapses into REM sleep.

natural selection The evolutionary process in which individuals with genetically influenced traits that are adaptive in a particular environment tend to survive and to reproduce in greater numbers than do other individuals; as a result, their traits become more common in the population.

need for achievement A learned motive to meet personal standards of success and excellence in a chosen area.

negative correlation An association between increases in one variable and decreases in another.

negative reinforcement A reinforcement procedure in which a response is followed by the removal, delay, or decrease in intensity of an unpleasant stimulus; as a result, the response becomes stronger or more likely to occur.

nerve A bundle of nerve fibers (axons and sometimes dendrites) in the peripheral nervous system.

neurogenesis The production of new neurons from immature stem cells.

neuron A cell that conducts electrochemical signals; the basic unit of the nervous system; also called a *nerve cell.*

neurotransmitter A chemical substance that is released by a transmitting neuron at the synapse and that alters the activity of a receiving neuron.

nonconscious processes Mental processes occurring outside of and not available to conscious awareness.

nonshared environment Unique aspects of a person's environment and experience that are not shared with family members.

normal curve A symmetrical, bell-shaped frequency polygon representing a normal distribution.

normal distribution A theoretical frequency distribution having certain special characteristics. For example, the distribution is symmetrical; the mean, mode, and median all have the same value; and the farther a score is from the mean, the less the likelihood of obtaining it.

norms In test construction, established standards of performance.

norms (social) Rules that regulate social life, including explicit laws and implicit cultural conventions.

null hypothesis An assertion that the independent variable in a study will have no effect on the dependent variable.

object permanence The understanding, which develops throughout the first year, that an object continues to exist even when you cannot see it or touch it.

objective tests (inventories) Standardized questionnaires requiring written responses; they typically include scales on which people are asked to rate themselves.

object-relations school A psychodynamic approach that emphasizes the importance of the infant's first two years of life and the baby's formative relationships, especially with the mother.

observational learning A process in which an individual learns new responses by observing the behavior of another (a model) rather than through direct experience; sometimes called *vicarious conditioning*.

observational study A study in which the researcher carefully and systematically observes and records behavior without interfering with the behavior; it may involve either naturalistic or laboratory observation.

obsessive-compulsive disorder (OCD) An anxiety disorder in which a person feels trapped in repetitive, persistent thoughts (*obsessions*) and repetitive, ritualized behaviors (*compulsions*) designed to reduce anxiety.

occipital [ahk-SIP-uh-tuhl] lobes Lobes at the lower back part of the brain's cerebral cortex; they contain areas that receive visual information.

Oedipus complex In psychoanalysis, a conflict occurring in the phallic (Oedipal) stage, in which a child desires the parent of the other sex and views the same-sex parent as a rival.

operant conditioning The process by which a response becomes more likely to occur or less so, depending on its consequences.

operational definition A precise definition of a term in a hypothesis, which specifies the operations for observing and measuring the process or phenomenon being defined.

opiates Drugs, derived from the opium poppy, that relieve pain and commonly produce euphoria.

opponent-process theory A theory of color perception that assumes that the visual system treats pairs of colors as opposing or antagonistic.

organ of Corti [CORE-tee] A structure in the cochlea containing hair cells that serve as the receptors for hearing.

oxytocin A hormone, secreted by the pituitary gland, that stimulates uterine contractions during childbirth, facilitates the ejection of milk during nursing, and seems to promote, in both sexes, attachment and trust in relationships.

panic disorder An anxiety disorder in which a person experiences recurring panic attacks, periods of intense fear, and feelings of impending doom or death, accompanied by physiological symptoms such as rapid heart rate and dizziness.

papillae [pa-PILL-ee] Knoblike elevations on the tongue, containing the taste buds. (Singular: *papilla.*)

parallel distributed processing (PDP) model A model of memory in which knowledge is represented as connections among thousands of interacting processing units, distributed in a vast network, and all operating in parallel.

paranoid personality disorder A disorder characterized by unreasonable, excessive suspiciousness and mistrust, and irrational feelings of being persecuted by others.

parasympathetic nervous system The subdivision of the autonomic nervous system that operates during relaxed states and that conserves energy.

parietal [puh-RYE-uh-tuhl] lobes Lobes at the top of the brain's cerebral cortex; they contain areas that receive information on pressure, pain, touch, and temperature.

percentile score A score that indicates the percentage of people who scored at or below a given raw score; also called *centile rank*.

perception The process by which the brain organizes and interprets sensory information.

perceptual constancy The accurate perception of objects as stable or unchanged despite changes in the sensory patterns they produce.

perceptual set A habitual way of perceiving, based on expectations.

performance goals Goals framed in terms of performing well in front of others, being judged favorably, and avoiding criticism.

peripheral nervous system (PNS) All portions of the nervous system outside the brain and spinal cord; it includes sensory and motor nerves.

personality A distinctive and relatively stable pattern of behavior, thoughts, motives, and emotions that characterizes an individual.

PET scan (positron-emission tomography) A method for analyzing biochemical activity in the brain, using injections of a glucoselike substance containing a radioactive element.

phantom pain The experience of pain in a missing limb or other body part.

phobia An exaggerated, unrealistic fear of a specific situation, activity, or object.

phrenology The now discredited theory that different brain areas account for specific character and personality traits, which can be "read" from bumps on the skull.

pitch The dimension of auditory experience related to the frequency of a pressure wave; the height or depth of a tone.

pituitary gland A small endocrine gland at the base of the brain, which releases many hormones and regulates other endocrine glands.

placebo An inactive substance or fake treatment used as a control in an experiment or given by a medical practitioner to a patient.

placebo effect The apparent success of a medication or treatment due to the patient's expectations or hopes rather than to the drug or treatment itself.

plasticity The brain's ability to change and adapt in response to experience—for example, by reorganizing or growing new neural connections.

pons A structure in the brain stem involved in, among other things, sleeping, waking, and dreaming.

positive correlation An association between increases in one variable and increases in another—or between decreases in one and in another.

positive reinforcement A reinforcement procedure in which a response is followed by the presentation of, or increase in intensity of, a reinforcing stimulus; as a result, the response becomes stronger or more likely to occur.

postdecision dissonance In the theory of cognitive dissonance, tension that occurs when you believe you may have made a bad decision.

posttraumatic stress disorder (PTSD) An anxiety disorder in which a person who has experienced a traumatic or life-threatening event has symptoms such as psychic numbing, reliving of the trauma, and increased physiological arousal.

power assertion A method of child rearing in which the parent uses punishment and authority to correct the child's misbehavior.

prejudice A strong, unreasonable dislike or hatred of a group, based on a negative stereotype.

primary control An effort to modify reality by changing other people, the situation, or events; a "fighting back" philosophy.

primary emotions Emotions considered to be universal and biologically based; they generally include fear, anger, sadness, joy, surprise, disgust, and contempt.

primary punisher A stimulus that is inherently punishing; an example is electric shock.

primary reinforcer A stimulus that is inherently reinforcing, typically satisfying a physiological need; an example is food.

priming A method used to measure unconscious cognitive processes, in which a person is exposed to information and is later tested to see whether the information affects behavior or performance on another task or in another situation.

principle of falsifiability The principle that a scientific theory must make predictions that are specific enough to expose the theory to the possibility of disconfirmation; that is, the theory must predict not only what will happen but also what will not happen.

proactive interference Forgetting that occurs when previously stored material interferes with the ability to remember similar, more recently learned material.

procedural memories Memories for the performance of actions or skills ("knowing how").

projective tests Psychological tests used to infer a person's motives, conflicts, and unconscious dynamics on the basis of the person's interpretations of ambiguous stimuli.

proposition A unit of meaning that is made up of concepts and expresses a single idea.

prototype An especially representative example of a concept.

psychedelic drugs Consciousness-altering drugs that produce hallucinations, change thought processes, or disrupt the normal perception of time and space.

psychoactive drug A drug capable of influencing perception, mood, cognition, or behavior.

psychoanalysis A theory of personality and a method of psychotherapy, originally formulated by Sigmund Freud, that emphasizes unconscious motives and conflicts.

psychodynamic perspective A psychological approach that emphasizes unconscious dynamics within the individual, such as inner forces, conflicts, or the movement of instinctual energy.

psychodynamic theories Theories that explain behavior and personality in terms of unconscious energy dynamics within the individual.

psychodynamic therapies Psychotherapies that share the psychoanalytic goal of exploring the unconscious dynamics of personality, although they differ from Freudian analysis in various ways.

psychological tests Procedures used to measure and evaluate personality traits, emotional states, aptitudes, interests, abilities, and values.

psychology The discipline concerned with behavior and mental processes and how they are affected by an organism's physical state, mental state, and external environment; the term is often represented by Ψ, the Greek letter psi (usually pronounced "sy").

psychometrics The measurement of mental abilities, traits, and processes.

psychoneuroimmunology (PNI) The study of the relationships among psychology, the nervous and endocrine systems, and the immune system.

psychopathy A personality disorder characterized by a lack of remorse, empathy, anxiety, and other social emotions; the use of deceit and manipulation; and impulsive thrill seeking.

psychosis An extreme mental disturbance involving distorted perceptions and irrational behavior; it may have psychological or organic causes. (Plural: *psychoses*.)

psychosurgery Any surgical procedure that destroys selected areas of the brain believed to be involved in emotional disorders or violent, impulsive behavior.

puberty The age at which a person becomes capable of sexual reproduction..

punishment The process by which a stimulus or event weakens or reduces the probability of the response that it follows.

random assignment A procedure for assigning people to experimental and control groups in which each individual has the same probability as any other of being assigned to a given group.

randomized controlled trials Research designed to determine the effectiveness of a new medication or form of therapy, in which people with a given problem or disorder are randomly assigned to one or more treatment groups or to a control group.

range A measure of the spread of scores, calculated by subtracting the lowest score from the highest score.

rapid eye movement (REM) sleep Sleep periods characterized by eye movement, loss of muscle tone, and vivid dreams.

rational emotive behavior therapy (REBT) A form of cognitive therapy devised by Albert Ellis, designed to challenge the client's unrealistic thoughts.

reasoning The drawing of conclusions or inferences from observations, facts, or assumptions.

recall The ability to retrieve and reproduce from memory previously encountered material.

reciprocal determinism In social-cognitive theories, the two-way interaction between aspects of the environment and aspects of the individual in the shaping of personality traits.

recognition The ability to identify previously encountered material.

reinforcement The process by which a stimulus or event strengthens or increases the probability of the response that it follows.

relearning method A method for measuring retention that compares the time required to relearn material with the time used in the initial learning of the material.

reliability In test construction, the consistency of scores derived from a test, from one time and place to another.

representative sample A group of subjects, selected from a population for study, which matches the population on important characteristics such as age and sex.

repression In psychoanalytic theory, the selective, involuntary pushing of threatening or upsetting information into the unconscious.

reticular activating system (RAS) A dense network of neurons found in the core of the brain stem; it arouses the cortex and screens incoming information.

retina Neural tissue lining the back of the eyeball's interior, which contains the receptors for vision.

retinal disparity The slight difference in lateral separation between two objects as seen by the left eye and the right eye.

retroactive interference Forgetting that occurs when recently learned material interferes with the ability to remember similar material stored previously.

rods Visual receptors that respond to dim light.

role A given social position that is governed by a set of norms for proper behavior.

Rorschach Inkblot Test A projective personality test that requires respondents to interpret abstract, symmetrical inkblots.

saturation Vividness or purity of color; the dimension of visual experience related to the complexity of light waves.

schizophrenia A psychotic disorder marked by delusions, hallucinations, disorganized and incoherent speech, inappropriate behavior, and cognitive impairments.

seasonal affective disorder (SAD) A controversial disorder in which a person experiences depression during the winter and an improvement of mood in the spring.

secondary control An effort to accept reality by changing your own attitudes, goals, or emotions; a "learn to live with it" philosophy.

secondary emotions Emotions that develop with cognitive maturity and vary across individuals and cultures.

secondary punisher A stimulus that has acquired punishing properties through association with other punishers.

secondary reinforcer A stimulus that has acquired reinforcing properties through association with other reinforcers.

selective attention The focusing of attention on selected aspects of the environment and the blocking out of others.

self-efficacy A person's belief that he or she is capable of producing desired results, such as mastering new skills and reaching goals.

self-fulfilling prophecy An expectation that comes true because of the tendency of the person holding it to act in ways that bring it about.

self-serving bias The tendency, in explaining one's own behavior, to take credit for one's good actions and rationalize one's mistakes.

semantic memories Memories of general knowledge, including facts, rules, concepts, and propositions.

semicircular canals Sense organs in the inner ear that contribute to equilibrium by responding to rotation of the head.

sensation The detection of physical energy emitted or reflected by physical objects; it occurs when energy in the external environment or the body stimulates receptors in the sense organs.

sense receptors Specialized cells that convert physical energy in the environment or the body to electrical energy that can be transmitted as nerve impulses to the brain.

sensory adaptation The reduction or disappearance of sensory responsiveness when stimulation is unchanging or repetitious.

sensory deprivation The absence of normal levels of sensory stimulation.

sensory register A memory system that momentarily preserves extremely accurate images of sensory information.

separation anxiety The distress that most children develop, at about 6 to 8 months of age, when their primary caregivers temporarily leave them with strangers.

serial-position effect The tendency for recall of the first and last items on a list to surpass recall of items in the middle of the list.

set point The genetically influenced weight range for an individual; it is maintained by biological mechanisms that regulate food intake, fat reserves, and metabolism.

sex hormones Hormones that regulate the development and functioning of reproductive organs and that stimulate the development of male and female sexual characteristics; they include androgens, estrogens, and progesterone.

sexual scripts Sets of implicit rules that specify proper sexual behavior for a person in a given situation, varying with the person's gender, age, religion, social status, and peer group.

shaping An operant-conditioning procedure in which successive approximations of a desired response are reinforced.

short-term memory (STM) In the three-box model of memory, a limited-capacity memory system involved in the retention of information for brief periods; it is also used to hold information retrieved from long-term memory for temporary use.

signal-detection theory A psychophysical theory that divides the detection of a sensory signal into a sensory process and a decision process.

significance tests Statistical tests that show how likely it is that a study's results occurred merely by chance.

single-blind study An experiment in which subjects do not know whether they are in an experimental or a control group.

skills training In behavior therapy, an effort to teach the client skills that he or she may lack, as well as new constructive behaviors to replace self-defeating ones.

sleep apnea A disorder in which breathing briefly stops during sleep, causing the person to choke and gasp and momentarily awaken.

social cognition An area in social psychology concerned with social influences on thought, memory, perception, and beliefs.

social identity The part of a person's self-concept that is based on his or her identification with a nation, religious or political group, occupation, or other social affiliation.

social-cognitive theories Theories that emphasize how behavior is learned and maintained through observation and imitation of others, positive consequences, and cognitive processes such as plans, expectations, and beliefs.

socialization The processes by which children learn the behaviors, attitudes, and expectations required of them by their society or culture.

sociobiology An interdisciplinary field that emphasizes evolutionary explanations of social behavior in animals, including human beings.

sociocultural perspective A psychological approach that emphasizes social and cultural influences on behavior.

somatic nervous system The subdivision of the peripheral nervous system that connects to sensory receptors and to skeletal muscles; sometimes called the *skeletal nervous system.*

source misattribution The inability to distinguish an actual memory of an event from information you learned about the event elsewhere.

spinal cord A collection of neurons and supportive tissue running from the base of the brain down the center of the back, protected by a column of bones (the spinal column).

spontaneous recovery The reappearance of a learned response after its apparent extinction.

standard deviation A commonly used measure of variability that indicates the average difference between scores in a distribution and their mean; more precisely, the square root of the average squared deviation from the mean.

standardize In test construction, to develop uniform procedures for giving and scoring a test.

state-dependent memory The tendency to remember something when the rememberer is in the same physical or mental state as during the original learning or experience.

statistically significant A term used to refer to a result that is extremely unlikely to have occurred by chance.

stem cells Immature cells that renew themselves and have the potential to develop into mature cells; given encouraging environments, stem cells from early embryos can develop into any cell type.

stereotype A summary impression of a group, in which a person believes that all members of the group share a common trait or traits (positive, negative, or neutral).

stereotype threat A burden of doubt a person feels about his or her performance, due to negative stereotypes about his or her group's abilities.

stimulants Drugs that speed up activity in the central nervous system.

stimulus discrimination The tendency to respond differently to two or more similar stimuli. In classical conditioning, it occurs when a stimulus similar to the conditioned stimulus fails to evoke the conditioned response; in operant conditioning, it occurs when an organism learns to make a response in the presence of other, similar stimuli that differ from it on some dimension.

stimulus generalization After conditioning, the tendency to respond to a stimulus that resembles one involved in the original conditioning. In classical conditioning, it occurs when a stimulus that resembles the conditioned stimulus elicits the conditioned response; in operant conditioning, it occurs when a response that has been reinforced (or punished) in the presence of one stimulus occurs (or is suppressed) in the presence of other, similar stimuli.

structuralism An early psychological approach that emphasized the analysis of immediate experience into basic elements.

subconscious processes Mental processes occurring outside of conscious awareness but accessible to consciousness when necessary.

successive approximations In the operant-conditioning procedure of shaping, behaviors that are ordered in terms of increasing similarity or closeness to the desired response.

superego In psychoanalysis, the part of personality that represents conscience, morality, and social standards.

suprachiasmatic [soo-pruh-kye-az-MAT-ick] nucleus (SCN) An area of the brain containing a biological clock that governs circadian rhythms.

surveys Questionnaires and interviews that ask people directly about their experiences, attitudes, or opinions.

sympathetic nervous system The subdivision of the autonomic nervous system that mobilizes bodily resources and increases the output of energy during emotion and stress.

synapse The site where transmission of a nerve impulse from one nerve cell to another occurs; it includes the axon terminal, the synaptic cleft, and receptor sites in the membrane of the receiving cell.

synesthesia A condition in which stimulation of one sense also evokes another.

systematic desensitization In behavior therapy, a step-by-step process of desensitizing a client to a feared object or experience; it is based on the classical-conditioning procedure of counterconditioning.

tacit knowledge Strategies for success that are not explicitly taught but that instead must be inferred.

taste buds Nests of taste-receptor cells.

telegraphic speech A child's first word combinations, which omit (as a telegram did) unnecessary words.

temperaments Physiological dispositions to respond to the environment in certain ways; they are present in infancy and in many nonhuman species and are assumed to be innate.

temporal lobes Lobes at the sides of the brain's cerebral cortex; they contain areas involved in hearing, memory, perception, emotion, and (in the left lobe, typically) language comprehension.

thalamus A brain structure that relays sensory messages to the cerebral cortex.

Thematic Apperception Test (TAT) A projective test that asks respondents to interpret a series of drawings showing scenes of people; usually scored for unconscious motives, such as the need for achievement, power, or affiliation.

theory An organized system of assumptions and principles that purports to explain a specified set of phenomena and their interrelationships.

theory of mind A system of beliefs about the way one's own mind and the minds of others work, and of how individuals are affected by their beliefs and feelings.

therapeutic alliance The bond of confidence and mutual understanding established between therapist and client, which allows them to work together to solve the client's problems.

timbre The distinguishing quality of a sound; the dimension of auditory experience related to the complexity of the pressure wave.

tolerance Increased resistance to a drug's effects accompanying continued use.

trait A characteristic of an individual, describing a habitual way of behaving, thinking, or feeling.

tranquilizers Drugs commonly but often inappropriately prescribed for patients who complain of unhappiness, anxiety, or worry.

transcranial magnetic stimulation (TMS) A method of stimulating brain cells, using a powerful magnetic field produced by a wire coil placed on a person's head; it can be used by researchers to temporarily inactivate neural circuits and is also being used therapeutically.

transference In psychodynamic therapies, a critical process in which the client transfers unconscious emotions or reactions, such as emotional feelings about his or her parents, onto the therapist.

triarchic [try-ARE-kick] theory of intelligence A theory of intelligence that emphasizes information-processing strategies, the ability to creatively transfer skills to new situations, and the practical application of intelligence.

trichromatic theory A theory of color perception that proposes three mechanisms in the visual system, each sensitive to a certain range of wavelengths; their interaction is assumed to produce all the different experiences of hue.

unconditional positive regard To Carl Rogers, love or support given to another person with no conditions attached.

unconditioned response (UR) The classical-conditioning term for a reflexive response elicited by a stimulus in the absence of learning.

unconditioned stimulus (US) The classical-conditioning term for a stimulus that elicits a reflexive response in the absence of learning.

validity The ability of a test to measure what it was designed to measure.

validity effect The tendency of people to believe that a statement is true or valid simply because it has been repeated many times.

variables Characteristics of behavior or experience that can be measured or described by a numeric scale.

volunteer bias A shortcoming of findings derived from a sample of volunteers instead of a representative sample; the volunteers may differ from those who did not volunteer.

vulnerability-stress models Approaches that emphasize how individual vulnerabilities interact with external stresses or circumstances to produce mental disorders.

withdrawal Physical and psychological symptoms that occur when someone addicted to a drug stops taking it.

working memory In many models of memory, a memory system comprising short-term memory plus the mental processes that control retrieval of information from long-term memory and interpret that information appropriately for a given task.

z-score (standard score) A number that indicates how far a given raw score is above or below the mean, using the standard deviation of the distribution as the unit of measurement.

References

Abel, Gene G.; Mittelman, Mary; Becker, Judith V.; et al. (1988). Predicting child molesters' response to treatment. *Annals of the New York Academy of Sciences, 528*, 223–234.

Abrahamson, Amy C.; Baker, Laura A.; & Caspi, Avshalom (2002). Rebellious teens? Genetic and environmental influences on the social attitudes of adolescents. *Journal of Personality and Social Psychology, 83*, 1392–1408.

Abrams, David B., & Wilson, G. Terence (1983). Alcohol, sexual arousal, and self-control. *Journal of Personality and Social Psychology, 45*, 188–198.

Abrams, R. (1997). *Electroconvulsive therapy* (3rd ed.). Oxford, England: Oxford University Press.

Abramson, Lyn Y.; Metalsky, Gerald I.; & Alloy, Lauren B. (1989). Hopelessness depression: A theory-based subtype of depression. *Psychological Review, 96*, 358–372.

Acocella, Joan (1999). *Creating hysteria: Women and multiple personality disorder.* San Francisco: Jossey-Bass.

Adair, John G., & Vohra, Neharika (2003). The explosion of knowledge, references, and citations: Psychology's unique response to a crisis. *American Psychologist, 58*, 15–23.

Adams, James L. (1986). *Conceptual blockbusting: A guide to better ideas* (3rd ed.). Boston: Addison-Wesley.

Addis, Michael E., & Mahalik, James R. (2003). Men, masculinity, and the contexts of help seeking. *American Psychologist, 58*, 5–14.

Ader, Robert (2000). True or false: The placebo effect as seen in drug studies is definitive proof that the mind can bring about clinically relevant changes in the body: The placebo effect: If it's all in your head, does that mean you only think you feel better? *Advances in Mind-Body Medicine, 16*, 7–11.

Adler, Nancy E., & Snibbe, Alana C. (2003). The role of psychosocial processes in explaining the gradient between socioeconomic status and health. *Current Directions in Psychological Science, 12*, 119–123.

Adolphs, Ralph (2001). Emotion, social cognition, and the human brain. Invited address presented at the annual meeting of the American Psychological Society, Toronto.

Affleck, Glenn; Tennen, Howard; Croog, Sydney; & Levine, Sol (1987). Causal attribution, perceived control, and recovery from a heart attack. *Journal of Social and Clinical Psychology, 5*, 339–355.

Agars, Mark D. (2004). Reconsidering the impact of gender stereotypes on the advancement of women in organizations. *Psychology of Women Quarterly, 28*, 103–111.

Ainsworth, Mary D. S. (1973). The development of infant–mother attachment. In B. M. Caldwell & H. N. Ricciuti (Eds.), *Review of child development research* (Vol. 3). Chicago: University of Chicago Press.

Ainsworth, Mary D. S. (1979). Infant–mother attachment. *American Psychologist, 34*, 932–937.

Air Force Research Laboratory (2000, Fall). *Lab study finds voice analysis detects stress.* Air Force Research Laboratory Web site, Information Directorate: News@afrl.

Alford, C. Fred (2001). *Whistleblowers: Broken lives and organizations.* Ithaca, NY: Cornell University Press.

Alford, John R.; Funk, Carolyn L.; & Hibbing, John R. (2005). Are political orientations genetically transmitted? *American Political Science Review, 99*, 153–167.

Alkon, Daniel L. (1989). Memory storage and neural systems. *Scientific American, 261*, 42–50.

Allen, Karen (2003). Are pets a healthy pleasure? The influence of pets on blood pressure. *Current Directions in Psychological Science, 12*, 236–239.

Allen, Laura S., & Gorski, Robert A. (1992). Sexual orientation and the size of the anterior commissure in the human brain. *Proceedings of the National Academy of Sciences, 89*, 7199–7202.

Allport, Gordon W. (1937). *Personality: A psychological interpretation.* New York: Holt, Rinehart and Winston.

Allport, Gordon W. (1954/1979). *The nature of prejudice.* Reading, MA: Addison-Wesley.

Allport, Gordon W. (1961). *Pattern and growth in personality.* New York: Holt, Rinehart and Winston.

Amabile, Teresa M. (1983). *The social psychology of creativity.* New York: Springer-Verlag.

Amedi, Amir; Merabet, Lotfi; Bermpohl, Felix; & Pascual-Leone, Alvaro (2005). The occipital cortex in the blind: Lessons about plasticity and vision. *Current Directions in Psychological Science, 14*, 306–311.

American Enterprise Institute (2004, July 6). *Attitudes about homosexuality and gay marriage.* Compiled by Karlyn Bowman and Bryan O'Keefe. Available at the AEI Web site, www.aei.org/news/newsID.20867,filter.all/news_ detail.asp.

American Psychiatric Association (1994). *The diagnostic and statistical manual of mental disorders* (4th ed.). Washington, DC: American Psychiatric Association.

American Psychiatric Association (2000). *The diagnostic and statistical manual of mental disorders, IV-TR.* Washington, DC: American Psychiatric Association.

Amering, Michaela, & Katschnig, Heinz (1990). Panic attacks and panic disorder in cross-cultural perspective. *Psychiatric Annals, 20*, 511–516.

Amodio, David M.; Harmon-Jones, Eddie; & Devine, Patricia G. (2003). Individual differences in the activation and control of affective race bias as assessed by startle eyeblink response and self-report. *Journal of Personality and Social Psychology, 84*, 738–753.

Anastasi, Anne, & Urbina, Susan (1997). *Psychological testing* (7th ed.). Upper Saddle River, NJ: Prentice-Hall.

Anderson, Adam K., & Phelps, Elizabeth A. (2000). Expression without recognition: Contributions of the human amygdala to emotional communication. *Psychological Science, 11*, 106–111.

Anderson, Amanda (2005). *The way we argue now: A study in the cultures of theory.* Princeton, NJ: Princeton University Press.

Anderson, Cameron; Keltner, Dacher; & John, Oliver P. (2003). Emotional convergence between people over time. *Journal of Personality and Social Psychology, 84*, 1054–1068.

Anderson, Craig A.; Berkowitz, Leonard; Donnerstein, Edward; et al. (2003). The influence of media violence on youth. *Psychological Science in the Public Interest, 4*(3) [whole issue].

Anderson, Craig A., & Bushman, Brad J. (2001). Effects of violent video games on aggressive behavior, aggressive cognition, aggressive affect, physiological arousal, and prosocial behavior: A meta-analytic review of the scientific literature. *Psychological Science, 12*, 353–359.

Anderson, John R. (1990). *The adaptive nature of thought.* Hillsdale, NJ: Erlbaum.

Anderson, Michael C.; Ochsner, Kevin N.; Kuhl, Brice; et al. (2004). Neural systems underlying the suppression of unwanted memories. *Science, 303*, 232–235.

Anderson, S. W.; Bechara, A.; Damasio, H.; Tranel, D.; & Damasio, A. R. (1999). Impairment of social and moral behavior related to early damage in human prefrontal cortex. *Nature Neuroscience, 2*, 1032–1037.

Andreasen, Nancy C.; Arndt, Stephan; Swayze, Victor, II; et al. (1994). Thalamic abnormalities in schizophrenia visualized through magnetic resonance image averaging. *Science, 266*, 294–298.

Angell, Marcia (2004). *The truth about the drug companies: How they deceive us and what to do about it.* New York: Random House.

Angier, Natalie (2000, November 7). Who is fat? It depends on culture. *The New York Times*, Science Times, D1–2.

Antonova, Irina; Arancio, Ottavio; Trillat, Anne-Cecile; et al. (2001). Rapid increase in clusters of presynaptic proteins at onset of long-lasting potentiation. *Science, 294*, 1547–1550.

Antonuccio, David O.; Danton, William G.; & DeNelsky, Garland Y.; et al. (1999). Raising questions about antidepressants. *Psychotherapy and Psychosomatics, 68*, 3–14.

Antonuccio, David O.; Danton, William G.; & McClanahan, Terry M. (2003). Psychology in the prescription era. *American Psychologist, 58*, 1028–1043.

Antrobus, John (1991). Dreaming: Cognitive processes during cortical activation and high afferent thresholds. *Psychological Review, 98*, 96–121.

Antrobus, John (2000). How does the dreaming brain explain the dreaming mind? *Behavioral and Brain Sciences, 23*, 904–907.

APA Commission on Violence and Youth (1993). *Violence and youth: Psychology's response.* Washington, DC: American Psychological Association.

Arbib, Michael A. (2005). From monkey-like action recognition to human language: An evolutionary framework for neurolinguistics. *Behavioral and Brain Sciences, 28*, 105–167.

Arbib, Michael A.; & Mundhenk, T. Nathan (2005). Schizophrenia and the mirror system: An essay. *Neuropsychologia, 43*, 268–280.

Archer, John (2004). Sex differences in aggression in real-world settings: A meta-analytic review. *Review of General Psychology, 8*, 291–322.

Archer, Simon N.; Robilliard, Donna L.; Skene, Debra J.; et al. (2003). A length polymorphism in the circadian clock gene Per3 is linked to delayed sleep phase syndrome and extreme diurnal preference. *Sleep, 26*, 413–415.

Arendt, Hannah (1963). *Eichmann in Jerusalem: A report on the banality of evil.* New York: Viking.

Arkes, Hal R. (1993). Some practical judgment and decision-making research. In N. J. Castellan, Jr., et al. (Eds.), *Individual and group decision making: Current issues.* Hillsdale, NJ: Erlbaum.

Arkes, Hal R.; Boehm, Lawrence E.; & Xu, Gang (1991). The determinants of judged validity. *Journal of Experimental Social Psychology, 27*, 576–605.

Arnett, Jeffrey J. (2000). Emerging adulthood: A theory of development from the late teens through the twenties. *American Psychologist, 55*, 469–480.

Aron, Arthur; Aron, Elaine N.; & Allen, Joselyn (1998). Motivations for unreciprocated love. *Personality and Social Psychology Bulletin, 24*, 787–796.

Aron, Arthur, & Westbay, Lori (1996). Dimensions of the prototype of love. *Journal of Personality and Social Psychology, 70*, 535–551.

Aronson, Elliot (2000). *Nobody left to hate.* New York: Freeman.

Aronson, Elliot (2004). *The social animal* (9th ed.). New York: Worth.

Aronson, Elliot, & Mills, Judson (1959). The effect of severity of initiation on liking for a group. *Journal of Abnormal and Social Psychology, 59*, 177–181.

Aronson, Elliot, & Patnoe, Shelley (1997). *Cooperation in the classroom: The jigsaw method.* New York: Longman.

Aronson, Joshua, & Salinas, Moises F. (1997). Stereotype threat, attribution ambiguity, and Latino underperformance. Unpublished manuscript, University of Texas, Austin.

Arredondo, Patricia, & Perez, Patricia (2003). Counseling paradigms and Latina/o Americans. In F. Harper & J. McFadden (Eds.), *Culture and counseling: New approaches.* Boston: Allyn & Bacon.

Arredondo, Patricia; Rosen, Daniel C.; Rice, Tiffany; Perez, Patricia; & Tovar-Gamero, Zoila G. (2005). Multicultural counseling: A 10-year content analysis of the *Journal of Counseling & Development. Journal of Counseling and Development, 83*, 155–161.

Arroyo, Carmen G., & Zigler, Edward (1995). Racial identity, academic achievement, and the psychological well-being of economically disadvantaged adolescents. *Journal of Personality and Social Psychology, 69*, 903–914.

Arsenijevic, D.; Onuma, H.; Pecqueur, C.; et al. (2000, December 26). Disruption of the uncoupling protein-2 gene in mice reveals a role in immunity and reactive oxygen species production. *Nature Genetics, 4*, 387–388.

Asch, Solomon E. (1952). *Social psychology.* Englewood Cliffs, NJ: Prentice-Hall.

Asch, Solomon E. (1965). Effects of group pressure upon the modification and distortion of judgments. In H. Proshansky & B. Seidenberg (Eds.), *Basic studies in social psychology.* New York: Holt, Rinehart and Winston.

Aserinsky, Eugene, & Kleitman, Nathaniel (1953). Regularly occurring periods of eye motility, and concomitant phenomena, during sleep. *Science, 118*, 273–274.

Aserinsky, Eugene, & Kleitman, Nathaniel (1955). Two types of ocular motility occurring in sleep. *Journal of Applied Physiology, 8*, 1–10.

Ashmore, Richard D.; Deaux, Kay; & McLaughlin-Volpe, Tracy (2004). An organizing framework for collective identity: Articulation and significance of multidimensionality. *Psychological Bulletin, 130*, 80–114.

Aspinwall, Lisa G., & Brunhart, Susanne M. (1996). Distinguishing optimism from denial: Optimistic beliefs predict attention to health threats. *Personality and Social Psychology Bulletin, 22*, 993–1003.

Atkinson, Richard C., & Shiffrin, Richard M. (1968). Human memory: A proposed system and its control processes. In K. W. Spence & J. T. Spence (Eds.), *The psychology of learning and motivation: Vol. 2. Advances in research and theory.* New York: Academic Press.

Atkinson, Richard C., & Shiffrin, Richard M. (1971, August). The control of short-term memory. *Scientific American, 225*(2), 82–90.

Atran, Scott (2003, March 7). Genesis of suicide terrorism. *Science, 299*, 1534–1539.

AuBuchon, Peter G., & Calhoun, Karen S. (1985). Menstrual cycle symptomatology: The role of social expectancy and experimental demand characteristics. *Psychosomatic Medicine, 47*, 35–45.

Axel, Richard (1995, October). The molecular logic of smell. *Scientific American*, 154–159.

Azrin, Nathan H., & Foxx, Richard M. (1974). *Toilet training in less than a day.* New York: Simon & Schuster.

Azuma, Hiroshi (1984). Secondary control as a heterogeneous category. *American Psychologist, 39*, 970–971.

Baddeley, Alan D. (1992). Working memory. *Science, 255*, 556–559.

Bagemihl, Bruce (1999). *Biological exuberance: Animal homosexuality and natural diversity.* New York: St. Martin's Press.

Bahill, A. Terry, & Karnavas, William J. (1993). The perceptual illusion of baseball's rising fastball and breaking curveball. *Journal of Experimental Psychology: Human Perception & Performance, 19*, 3–14.

Bahrick, Harry P. (1984). Semantic memory content in permastore: Fifty years of memory for Spanish learned in school. *Journal of Experimental Psychology: General, 113*, 1–29.

Bahrick, Harry P.; Bahrick, Phyllis O.; & Wittlinger, Roy P. (1975). Fifty years of memory for names and faces: A cross-sectional approach. *Journal of Experimental Psychology: General, 104,* 54–75.

Bailey, J. Michael; Bobrow, David; Wolfe, Marilyn; & Mikach, Sarah (1995). Sexual orientation of adult sons of gay fathers. *Developmental Psychology, 31,* 124–129.

Bailey, J. Michael; Dunne, Michael P.; & Martin, Nicholas G. (2000). Genetic and environmental influences on sexual orientation and its correlates in an Australian twin sample. *Journal of Personality and Social Psychology, 78,* 524–536.

Bailey, J. Michael; Gaulin, Steven; Agyei, Yvonne; & Gladue, Brian A. (1994). Effects of gender and sexual orientation on evolutionarily relevant aspects of human mating psychology. *Journal of Personality and Social Psychology, 66,* 1081–1093.

Bailey, J. Michael, & Zucker, Kenneth J. (1995). Childhood sex-typed behavior and sexual orientation: A conceptual analysis and quantitative review. *Developmental Psychology, 31,* 43–55.

Baillargeon, Renée (1994). How do infants learn about the physical world? *Current Directions in Psychological Science, 5,* 133–140.

Baillargeon, Renée (1999). Young infants' expectations about hidden objects: A reply to three challenges. *Developmental Science, 2,* 115–163.

Baillargeon, Renée (2004). Infants' physical world. *Current Directions in Psychological Science, 13,* 89–94.

Baker, Mark C. (2001). *The atoms of language: The mind's hidden rules of grammar.* New York: Basic Books.

Baker, Robin (1996). *The sperm wars: The science of sex.* New York: Basic Books.

Bakermans-Kranenburg, Marian J.; van IJzendoorn, Marinus H.; & Juffer, Femmie (2003). Less is more: Meta-analyses of sensitivity and attachment interventions in early childhood. *Psychological Bulletin, 129,* 195–215.

Ball, K.; Berch, D. B.; Helmers, K. F.; et al. (2002, November 13). Effects of cognitive training interventions with older adults: A randomized controlled trial. *Journal of the American Medical Association, 288,* 2271–2281.

Ballenger, James C.; Burrows, Graham D.; DuPont, Robert L.; et al. (1988). Alprazolam in panic disorder and agoraphobia: Results from a multicenter trial. *Archives of General Psychiatry, 45,* 413–421.

Bandura, Albert (1977). *Social learning theory.* Englewood Cliffs, NJ: Prentice-Hall.

Bandura, Albert (1986). *Social foundations of thought and action: A social cognitive theory.* Englewood Cliffs, NJ: Prentice-Hall.

Bandura, Albert (1997). *Self-efficacy: The exercise of control.* New York: Freeman.

Bandura, Albert (1999). Moral disengagement in the perpetration of inhumanities. *Personality and Social Psychology Review, 3,* 193–209.

Bandura, Albert (2001). Social cognitive theory: An agentic perspective. *Annual Review of Psychology, 52,* 1–26. Palo Alto, CA: Annual Reviews.

Bandura, Albert (2006). Toward a psychology of human agency. *Perspectives on Psychological Science, 1,* 164–180.

Bandura, Albert; Caprara, Gian Vittorio; Barbaranelli, Claudio; Pastorelli, Concetta; & Regalia, Camillo (2001). Sociocognitive self-regulatory mechanisms governing transgressive behavior. *Journal of Personality and Social Psychology, 80,* 125–135.

Bandura, Albert; Ross, Dorothea; & Ross, Sheila A. (1963). Vicarious reinforcement and imitative learning. *Journal of Abnormal and Social Psychology, 67,* 601–607.

Banks, Martin S. (with Philip Salapatek) (1984). Infant visual perception. In P. Mussen (Series Ed.), M. M. Haith & J. J. Campos (Vol. Eds.), *Handbook of child psychology: Vol. II. Infancy and developmental psychobiology* (4th ed.). New York: Wiley.

Barash, David P. (2001, April 20). Deflating the myth of monogamy. *The Chronicle of Higher Education,* B16–B17.

Barash, David P., & Lipton, Judith Eve (2001). *The myth of monogamy: Fidelity and infidelity in animals and people.* New York: W. H. Freeman.

Barbuto, J. E. (1997). A critique of the Myers-Briggs Type Indicator and its operationalization of Carl Jung's psychological types. *Psychological Reports, 80,* 611–625.

Barch, Deanna M. (2003). Cognition in schizophrenia: Does working memory work? *Current Directions in Psychological Science, 12,* 146–150.

Bargh, John A. (1999, January 29). The most powerful manipulative messages are hiding in plain sight. *The Chronicle of Higher Education,* B6.

Barinaga, Marcia (1992). Challenging the "no new neurons" dogma. *Science, 255,* 1646.

Barlow, David H. (2000). Unraveling the mysteries of anxiety and its disorders from the perspective of emotion theory. *American Psychologist, 55,* 1247–1263.

Barlow, David H.; Chorpita, Bruce F.; & Turovsky, Julia (1996). Fear, panic, anxiety, and disorders of emotion. In D. A. Hope et al. (Eds.), *Nebraska Symposium on Motivation, 1995: Perspectives on anxiety, panic, and fear.* Lincoln, NE: University of Nebraska Press.

Baron-Cohen, S., & Harrison, J. E. (Eds.) (1997). *Synaesthesia: Classic and contemporary readings.* Cambridge, MA: Blackwell.

Barone, David F.; Maddux, James E.; & Snyder, C. R. (1997). *Social cognitive psychology: History and current domains.* New York: Plenum Press.

Barrett, Deirdre (2001). *The committee of sleep.* New York: Crown/Random House.

Barrett, Lisa F. (2006). Are emotions natural kinds? *Perspectives on Psychological Science, 1,* 28–58.

Barrish, Barbara M. (1996). The relationship of remembered parental physical punishment to adolescent self-concept. *Dissertation Abstracts International, Section B, 57,* 2171.

Barron, Kenneth S., & Harackiewicz, Judith M. (2001). Achievement goals and optimal motivation: Testing multiple goal models. *Journal of Personality and Social Psychology, 80,* 706–722.

Barsky, S. H.; Roth, M. D.; Kleerup, E. C.; Simmons, M.; & Tashkin, D. P. (1998). Histopathologic and molecular alterations in bronchial epithelium in habitual smokers of marijuana, cocaine, and/or tobacco. *Journal of the National Cancer Institute, 90,* 1198–1205.

Bartels, Andreas, & Zeki, Semir (2004). The neural correlates of material and romantic love. *NeuroImage, 21,* 1155–1166.

Bartlett, Frederic C. (1932). *Remembering.* Cambridge, England: Cambridge University Press.

Bartlett, Monica Y., & DeSteno, David (2006). Gratitude and prosocial behavior: Helping when it costs you. *Psychological Science, 17,* 319–325.

Bartoshuk, Linda M. (1998). Born to burn: Genetic variation in taste. Paper presented at the annual meeting of the American Psychological Association, San Francisco.

Bartoshuk, Linda M.; Duffy, V. B.; Lucchina, L. A.; et al. (1998). PROP (6-n-propylthiouracil) supertasters and the saltiness of NaCl. *Annals of the New York Academy of Sciences, 855,* 793–796.

Bassetti, C.; Vella, S.; Donati, F.; et al. (2000). SPECT during sleepwalking. *Lancet, 356,* 484–485.

Basson, Rosemary; McInnis, Rosemary; Smith, Mike D.; Hodgson, Gemma; & Koppiker, Nandan (2002). Efficacy and safety of sidenafil citrate in women with sexual dysfunction associated with female sexual arousal disorder. *Journal of Women's Health and Gender-Based Medicine, 11,* 367–377.

Bateman, B.; Warner, J. O.; Hutchinson E.; et al. (2004). The effects of a double blind, placebo controlled, artificial food colourings and benzoate

preservative challenge on hyperactivity in a general population sample of preschool children. *Archives of Diseases in Childhood, 89*, 506–511.

Bauer, Patricia (2002). Long-term recall memory: Behavioral and neurodevelopmental changes in the first 2 years of life. *Current Directions in Psychological Science, 11*, 137–141.

Bauer, Patricia J., & Dow, Gina Annunziato (1994). Episodic memory in 16- and 20-month-old children: Specifics are generalized but not forgotten. *Developmental Psychology, 30*, 403–417.

Baumeister, Roy F. (2000). Gender differences in erotic plasticity: The female sex drive as socially flexible and responsive. *Psychological Bulletin, 126*, 347–374.

Baumeister, Roy F., & Bratslavsky, Ellen (1999). Passion, intimacy, and time: Passionate love as a function of change in intimacy. *Personality and Social Psychology Review, 3*, 49–67.

Baumeister, Roy F.; Campbell, Jennifer D.; Krueger, Joachim I.; & Vohs, Kathleen D. (2003). Does high self-esteem cause better performance, interpersonal success, happiness, or healthier lifestyles? *Psychological Science in the Public Interest, 4*(1)[whole issue].

Baumeister, Roy F.; Catanese, Kathleen R.; & Vohs, Kathleen D. (2001). Is there a gender difference in strength of sex drive? Theoretical views, conceptual distinctions, and a review of relevant evidence. *Personality and Social Psychology Review, 5*, 242–273.

Baumeister, Roy F.; Dale, Karen; & Sommer, Kristin L. (1998). Freudian defense mechanisms and empirical findings in modern social psychology: Reaction formation, projection, displacement, undoing, isolation, sublimation, and denial. *Journal of Personality, 66*, 1081–1124.

Baumeister, Roy F.; Stillwell, Arlene M.; & Heatherton, Todd F. (1994). Guilt: An interpersonal approach. *Psychological Bulletin, 115*, 243–267.

Baumrind, Diana (1989). Rearing competent children. In W. Damon (Ed.), *Child development today and tomorrow*. San Francisco: Jossey-Bass.

Baumrind, Diana (1991). Parenting styles and adolescent development. In R. Lerner, A. C. Petersen, & J. Brooks-Gunn (Eds.), *The encyclopedia of adolescence*. New York: Garland.

Baumrind, Diana; Larzelere, Robert E.; & Cowan, Philip (2002). Ordinary physical punishment—Is it harmful? Commentary on Gershoff's Review. *Psychological Bulletin, 128*, 580–589.

Baxter, Lewis R.; Schwartz, Jeffrey M.; Bergman, Kenneth S.; et al. (1992). Caudate glucose metabolic rate changes with both drug and behavior therapy for obsessive-compulsive disorder. *Archives of General Psychiatry, 49*, 681–689.

Bechara, Antoine; Dermas, Hanna; Tranel, Daniel; & Damasio, Antonio R. (1997). Deciding advantageously before knowing the advantageous strategy. *Science, 275*, 1293–1294.

Beck, Aaron T. (1976). *Cognitive therapy and the emotional disorders*. New York: International Universities Press.

Beck, Aaron T. (2005). The current state of cognitive therapy: A 40-year retrospective. *Archives of General Psychiatry, 62*, 953–959.

Becker, Selwyn W., & Eagly, Alice H. (2004). The heroism of women and men. *American Psychologist, 59*, 163–178.

Beer, Jennifer S.; Heerey, Erin A.; Keltner, Dacher; et al. (2003). The regulatory function of self-conscious emotion: Insights from patients with orbitofrontal damage. *Journal of Personality and Social Psychology, 85*, 594–604.

Beer, Jeremy M.; Arnold, Richard D.; & Loehlin, John C. (1998). Genetic and environmental influences on MMPI factor scales: Joint model fitting to twin and adoption data. *Journal of Personality and Social Psychology, 74*, 818–827.

Belle, Deborah, & Doucet, Joanne (2003). Poverty, inequality, and discrimination as sources of depression among U.S. women. *Psychology of Women Quarterly, 27*, 101–113.

Belsky, Jay; Hsieh, Kuang-Hua; & Crnic, Keith (1996). Infant positive and negative emotionality: One dimension or two? *Developmental Psychology, 32*, 289–298.

Bem, Daryl J., & Honorton, Charles (1994). Does psi exist? Replicable evidence for an anomalous process of information transfer. *Psychological Bulletin, 115*, 4–18.

Bem, Sandra L. (1993). *The lenses of gender.* New Haven, CT: Yale University Press.

Benedetti, Fabrizio, & Levi-Montalcini, Rita (2001). Opioid and non-opioid mechanisms of placebo analgesia. Paper presented at the annual meeting of the American Psychological Society, Toronto.

Benedetti, Fabrizio; Mayberg, Helen S.; Wager, Tor D. ; et al. (2005, November 9). Neurobiological mechanisms of the placebo effect. *The Journal of Neuroscience, 45*, 10390–10402.

Benjamin, Ludy T., Jr. (1998). Why Gorgeous George, and not Wilhelm Wundt, was the founder of psychology: A history of popular psychology in America. Invited address presented at the National Institute on the Teaching of Psychology, St. Petersburg Beach.

Benjamin, Ludy T., Jr. (2003). Why can't psychology get a stamp? *Journal of Applied Psychoanalytic Studies, 5*, 443–454.

Ben-Shachar, Michal; Hendler, Talma; Kahn, Itamar; et al. (2003). The neural reality of syntactic transformations: Evidence from functional magnetic resonance imaging. *Psychological Science, 14*, 433–440.

Ben-Shakhar, Gershon, & Elaad, Eitan (2003). The validity of psychophysiological detection of information with the Guilty Knowledge Test: A meta-analytic review. *Journal of Applied Psychology, 88*, 131–151.

Beran, Michael J., & Beran, Mary M. (2004). Chimpanzees remember the results of one-by-one addition of food items to sets over extended time periods. *Psychological Science, 15*, 94–99.

Bereiter, Carl, & Bird, Marlene (1985). Use of thinking aloud in identification and teaching of reading comprehension strategies. *Cognition and Instruction, 2*, 131–156.

Berenbaum, Sheri A., & Bailey, J. Michael (2003). Effects on gender identity of prenatal androgens and genital appearance: Evidence from girls with congenital adrenal hyperplasia. *Journal of Clinical Endocrinology and Metabolism, 88*, 1102–1106.

Berger, F.; Gage, F. H.; & Vijayaraghavan, S. (1998). Nicotinic receptor-induced apoptotic cell death of hippocampal progenitor cells. *Journal of Neuroscience, 18*, 6871–6881.

Berglund, Hans; Lindström, Per; & Savic, Ivanka (2006). Brain response to putative pheromones in lesbian women. *Proceedings of the National Academy of Sciences, 103*, 8269-8274.

Berkman, Lisa F.; Leo-Summers, L.; & Horwitz, R. I. (1992). Emotional support and survival after myocardial infarction: A prospective, population-based study of the elderly. *Annals of Internal Medicine, 117*, 1003–1009.

Berkman, Lisa F., & Syme, S. Leonard (1979). Social networks, host resistance, and mortality: A nine-year follow-up study of Alameda County residents. *American Journal of Epidemiology, 109*, 186–204.

Berko, Jean (1958). The child's learning of English morphology. *Word, 14*, 150–177.

Berkowitz, Marvin W., & Grych, John H. (2000). Early character development and education. *Early Education & Development, 11*, 55–72.

Bernieri, Frank J.; Gillis, John S.; Davis, Janet M.; & Grahe, Jon E. (1996). Dyad rapport and the accuracy of its judgment across situations: A lens model analysis. *Journal of Personality and Social Psychology, 71*, 110–129.

Berntsen, Dorthe, & Thomsen, Dorthe K. (2005). Personal memories for remote historical events: Accuracy and clarity of flashbulb memories related to World War II. *Journal of Experimental Psychology: General, 134*, 242–257.

Berry, John W. (1994). Acculturative stress. In W. J. Lonner & R. S. Malpass (Eds.), *Psychology and culture*. Needham Heights, MA: Allyn & Bacon.

Berscheid, Ellen, & Reis, Harry T. (1998). Attraction and close relationships. In D. T. Gilbert, S. T. Fiske, & G. Lindzey (Eds.), *The handbook of social psychology, Vol. 2* (4th ed.). New York: McGraw-Hill.

Best, Joel (2001). *Damned lies and statistics*. Berkeley: University of California Press.

Bettelheim, Bruno (1967). *The empty fortress*. New York: Free Press.

Beutler, Larry E. (2000). David and Goliath: When empirical and clinical standards of practice meet. *American Psychologist, 55*, 997–1007.

Beutler, Larry E., & Malik, Mary L. (Eds.) (2002). *Rethinking the DSM: A psychological perspective*. Washington, DC: American Psychological Association.

Beyerstein, Barry L. (1996). Graphology. In G. Stein (Ed.), *The encyclopedia of the paranormal*. Amherst, NY: Prometheus Books.

Beyerstein, Barry L. (1999). Fringe psychotherapies: The public at risk. In W. Sampson (Ed.), *A Guide to Alternative Medicine*. London: Gordon and Breech.

Bierut, Laura Jean; Heath, Andrew C.; Bucholz, Kathleen K.; et al. (1999). Major depressive disorder in a community-based twin sample: Are there different genetic contributions for men and women? *Archives of General Psychiatry, 56*, 557–563.

Birdwhistell, Ray L. (1970). *Kinesics and context: Essays on body motion communication*. Philadelphia: University of Pennsylvania Press.

Birkhead, Tim (2001). *Promiscuity: An evolutionary history of sperm competition*. Cambridge, MA: Harvard University Press.

Bischof, Matthias, & Bassetti, Claudio L. (2004). Total dream loss: A distinct neuropsychological dysfunction after bilateral PCA stroke. *Annals of Neurology*, published online Sept. 10, 2004. (DOI: 10.1002/ana.20246.)

Bjork, Daniel W. (1993). *B. F. Skinner: A life*. New York: Basic Books.

Bjork, Elizabeth L.; Bjork, Robert A.; & Anderson, M. C. (1998). Varieties of goal-directed forgetting. In J. M. Golding & C. M. MacLoed (Eds.), *Intentional forgetting*. Mahwah, NJ: Erlbaum.

Bjork, Robert A. (October, 2000). Human factors 101: How about just trying things out? *APS Observer, 13*, 3, 30.

Bjorkland, D. F. (2000). *Children's thinking: Developmental function and individual differences*. Belmont, CA: Wadsworth.

Blackmore, Susan (2001, March/April). Giving up the ghosts: End of a personal quest. *Skeptical Inquirer, 25*.

Blagrove, Mark (1996). Problems with the cognitive psychological modeling of dreaming. *Journal of Mind and Behavior, 17*, 99–134.

Blair, R. D. J.; Jones, L.; Clark, F.; & Smith, M. (1997). The psychopathic individual: A lack of responsiveness to distress cues? *Psychophysiology, 45*, 192–198.

Blakemore, Colin, & Cooper, Grahame F. (1970). Development of the brain depends on the visual environment. *Nature, 228*, 477–478.

Blanchette, Isabelle, & Richards, Anne (2004). Reasoning about emotional and neutral materials. *Psychological Science, 15*, 745–752.

Blass, Thomas (1993). What we know about obedience: Distillations from 30 years of research on the Milgram paradigm. Paper presented at the annual meeting of the American Psychological Association, Toronto.

Blass, Thomas (Ed.) (2000). *Obedience to authority: Current perspectives on the Milgram paradigm*. Mahwah, NJ: Erlbaum.

Blazer, Dan G.; Kessler, Ronald C.; & Swartz, Marvin S. (1998). Epidemiology of recurrent major and minor depression with a seasonal pattern: The National Comorbidity Survey. *British Journal of Psychiatry, 172*, 164–167.

Bleuler, Eugen (1911/1950). *Dementia praecox or the group of schizophrenias*. New York: International Universities Press.

Bliss, T. V., & Collingridge, G. L. (1993). A synaptic model of memory: Long-term potentiation in the hippocampus. *Nature, 361*(6407), 31–39.

Bloom, Mia (2005). *Dying to kill: The allure of suicide terror.* New York: Columbia University Press.

Bloom, Paul (2004). Can a dog learn a word? *Science, 304*, 1605–1606.

Blum, Deborah (2002). *Love at Goon Park: Harry Harlow and the science of affection*. Cambridge, MA: Perseus Books.

Boesch, Cristophe (1991). Teaching among wild chimpanzees. *Animal Behavior, 41*, 530–532.

Bogaert, Anthony F. (2006, June 28). Biological versus nonbiological older brothers and men's sexual orientation. *Proceedings of the National Academy of Sciences*, published online June 28, 2006, 10.1073/pnas.0511152103.

Bohannon, John N., & Stanowicz, Laura (1988). The issue of negative evidence: Adult responses to children's language errors. *Developmental Psychology, 24*, 684–689.

Bohannon, John N., & Symons, Victoria (1988). Conversational conditions of children's imitation. Paper presented at the biennial Conference on Human Development, Charleston, South Carolina.

Bohman, Michael; Cloninger, R.; Sigvardsson, S.; & von Knorring, Anne-Liis (1987). The genetics of alcoholism and related disorders. *Journal of Psychiatric Research, 21*, 447–452.

Bolshakov, Vadim Y., & Siegelbaum, Steven A. (1994). Postsynaptic induction and presynaptic expression of hippocampal long-term depression. *Science, 264*, 1148–1152.

Bonanno, George A. (2004). Loss, trauma, and human resilience. *American Psychologist, 59*, 20–28.

Bonanno, George A.; Galea, Sandro; Bucciarelli, Angela; & Vlahov, David (2006). Psychological resilience after disaster. *Psychological Science, 17*, 181–186.

Bond, Meg A.; Punnett, Laura; Pyle, Jean L.; et al. (2004). Gendered work conditions, health, and work outcomes. *Journal of Occupational Health Psychology, 91*, 28–45.

Bond, Rod, & Smith, Peter B. (1996). Culture and conformity: A meta-analysis of studies using Asch's (1952b, 1956) line judgment task. *Psychological Bulletin, 119*, 111–137.

Bonnet, Michael H. (1990). The perception of sleep onset in insomniacs and normal sleepers. In R. R. Bootzin, J. F. Kihlstrom, & D. L. Schacter (Eds.), *Sleep and cognition*. Washington, DC: American Psychological Association.

Booth, Frank W., & Neufer, P. Darrell (2005). Exercise controls gene expression. *American Scientist, 93*, 28–35.

Borch-Jacobsen, Mikkel (1997, April 24). Sybil—The making of a disease: An interview with Dr. Herbert Spiegel. *The New York Review of Books*, pp. 60–64.

Bordo, Susan (2000). *The male body*. New York: Farrar, Straus and Giroux.

Boring, Edwin G. (1953). A history of introspection. *Psychological Bulletin, 50*, 169–187.

Bornstein, Robert F.; Leone, Dean R.; & Galley, Donna J. (1987). The generalizability of subliminal mere exposure effects: Influence of stimuli perceived without awareness on social behavior. *Journal of Personality and Social Psychology, 53*, 1070–1079.

Boroditsky, Lera (2003). Linguistic relativity. In L. Nadel (Ed.), *Encyclopedia of cognitive science*. London: Nature Publishing Group.

Boroditsky, Lera; Schmidt, Lauren; & Phillips, Webb (2003). Sex, syntax, and semantics. In D. Gentner & S. Goldin-Meadow (Eds.), *Language in mind: Advances in the study of language and thought*. Cambridge: MIT Press.

Bosworth, Hayden B., & Schaie, K. Warner (1999). Survival effects in cognitive function, cognitive style, and sociodemographic variables in the Seattle Longitudinal Study. *Experimental Aging Research, 25*, 121–139.

Bouchard, Claude; Tremblay, A.; Despres, J. P.; et al. (1990, May 24). The response to long-term overfeeding in identical twins. *New England Journal of Medicine, 322*, 1477–1482.

Bouchard, Thomas J., Jr. (1995). Nature's twice-told tale: Identical twins reared apart—what they tell us about human individuality. Paper presented at the annual meeting of the Western Psychological Association, Los Angeles.

Bouchard, Thomas J., Jr. (1997a). The genetics of personality. In K. Blum & E. P. Noble (eds.), *Handbook of psychiatric genetics*. Boca Raton, FL: CRC Press.

Bouchard, Thomas J., Jr. (1997b). IQ similarity in twins reared apart: Findings and responses to critics. In R. J. Sternberg & E. Grigorenko (Eds.), *Intelligence: Heredity and environment*. New York: Cambridge University Press.

Bouchard, Thomas J., Jr. (2004). Genetic influence on human psychological traits: A survey. *Current Directions in Psychological Science, 13*, 148–151.

Bouchard, Thomas J., Jr., & McGue, Matthew (1981). Familial studies of intelligence: A review. *Science, 212*, 1055–1058.

Bouchard, Thomas J., Jr., & McGue, Matthew (2003). Genetic and environmental influences on human psychological differences. *Journal of Neurobiology, 54*, 4–45.

Bouret, Sebastien G.; Draper, Shin J.; & Simerly, Richard B. (2004). Trophic action of leptin on hypothalamic neurons that regulate feeding. *Science, 304*, 108–110.

Bousfield, W. A. (1953). The occurrence of clustering in the recall of randomly arranged associates. *Journal of General Psychology, 49*, 229–240.

Bowden, Charles L.; Calabrese, Joseph R.; McElroy, Susan L.; et al. (2000). A randomized, placebo-controlled 12-month trial or divalproex and lithium in treatment of outpatients with bipolar I disorder. *Archives of General Psychiatry, 57*, 481–489.

Bowen, Murray (1978). *Family therapy in clinical practice*. New York: Jason Aronson.

Bower, Bruce (1998, February 21). All fired up: Perception may dance to the beat of collective neuronal rhythms. *Science News, 153*, 120–121.

Bowers, Kenneth S.; Regehr, Glenn; Balthazard, Claude; & Parker, Kevin (1990). Intuition in the context of discovery. *Cognitive Psychology, 22*, 72–110.

Bowlby, John (1969). *Attachment and loss. Vol. 1. Attachment*. New York: Basic Books.

Bowlby, John (1973). *Attachment and loss: Vol. 2. Separation*. New York: Basic Books.

Bowlby, John (1982). *Attachment and loss. Vol. 1. Attachment* (Rev. ed.). New York: Basic Books.

Bowleg, Lisa; Lucas, Kenya J.; & Tschann, Jeanne M. (2004). "The ball was always in his court": An exploratory analysis of relationship scripts, sexual scripts, and condom use among African American women. *Psychology of Women Quarterly, 28*, 70–82.

Bradford, John M., & Pawlak, Anne (1993). Effects of cyproterone acetate on sexual arousal patterns of pedophiles. *Archives of Sexual Behavior, 22*, 629–641.

Bradley, Susan J., Oliver, Gillian D., Chernick, Avinoam B., & Zucker, Kenneth J. (1998). Experiment of nature: Ablatio penis at 2 months, sex reassignment at 7 months, and a psychosexual follow-up in young adulthood. *Pediatrics, 102*, E91. Available at http://www.pediatrics.org/cgi/content/full/101/1/e9.

Brainerd, C. J.; Reyna, V. F.; & Brandse, E. (1995). Are children's false memories more persistent than their true memories? *Psychological Science, 6*, 359–364.

Brauer, Markus; Wasel, Wolfgang; & Niedenthal, Paula (2000). Implicit and explicit components of prejudice. *Review of General Psychology, 4*, 79–101.

Braun, Kathryn A.; Ellis, Rhiannon; & Loftus, Elizabeth F. (2002). Make my memory: How advertising can change our memories of the past. *Psychology & Marketing, 19*, 1–23.

Braungert, J. M.; Plomin, Robert; DeFries, J. C.; & Fulker, D. W. (1992). Genetic influence on tester-rated infant temperament as assessed by Bayley's Infant Behavior Record: Nonadoptive and adoptive siblings and twins. *Developmental Psychology, 28*, 40–47.

Brazelton, Timony R.; Rossi, Fabio M.; Keshet, Gilmor I.; & Blau, Helen M. (2000). From marrow to brain: Expression of neuronal phenotypes in adult mice. *Science, 290*, 1775–1779.

Breland, Keller, & Breland, Marian (1961). The misbehavior of organisms. *American Psychologist, 16*, 681–684.

Brennan, Patricia A., & Mednick, Sarnoff A. (1994). Learning theory approach to the deterrence of criminal recidivism. *Journal of Abnormal Psychology, 103*, 430–440.

Brewer, James; Zhao, Zuo; Desmond, John E.; et al. (1998). Making memories: Brain activity that predicts how well visual experience will be remembered. *Science, 281*, 1185–1187.

Brewer, Marilynn B., & Gardner, Wendi (1996). Who is this "we"? Levels of collective identity and self representations. *Journal of Personality and Social Psychology, 71*, 83–93.

Briggs, John (1984, December). The genius mind. *Science Digest, 92*(12), 74–77, 102–103.

Brissette, Ian; Scheier, Michael F.; & Carver, Charles S. (2002). The role of optimism in social network development, coping, and psychological adjustment during a life transition. *Journal of Personality and Social Psychology, 82*, 102–111.

Brockner, Joel, & Rubin, Jeffrey Z. (1985). *Entrapment in escalating conflicts: A social psychological analysis*. New York: Springer-Verlag.

Broks, Paul (2004). *Into the silent land: Travels in neuropsychology*. New York: Grove Press.

Brooks-Gunn, J. (1986). Differentiating premenstrual symptoms and syndromes. *Psychosomatic Medicine, 48*, 385–387.

Brosnan, Sarah F., & de Waal, Frans B. M. (2003). Monkeys reject unequal pay. *Nature, 425*, 297–299.

Brown, Alan S. (2004). *The déjà vu experience: Essays in cognitive psychology*. New York: Psychology Press.

Brown, Alan S.; Begg, M. D.; Gravenstein, S.; et al. (2004). Serologic evidence of prenatal influenza in the etiology of schizophrenia. *Archives of General Psychiatry, 61*, 774–780.

Brown, D., Scheflin, A. W., & Whitfield, C. L. (1999). Recovered memories: The current weight of the evidence in science and in the courts. *Journal of Psychiatry and Law, 27*, 5–156.

Brown, George W. (1993). Life events and affective disorder: Replications and limitations. *Psychosomatic Medicine, 55*, 248–259.

Brown, Gregory K.; Ten Have, Thomas; Henriques, Gregg R.; et al. (2005, August 3). Cognitive therapy for the prevention of suicide attempts. *Journal of the American Medical Association, 294*, 563–570.

Brown, Robert, & Middlefell, Robert (1989). Fifty-five years of cocaine dependence [letter]. *British Journal of Addiction, 84*, 946.

Brown, Roger (1986). *Social psychology* (2nd ed.). New York: Free Press.

Brown, Roger; Cazden, Courtney; & Bellugi, Ursula (1969). The child's grammar from I to III. In J. P. Hill (Ed.), *Minnesota Symposium on Child Psychology* (Vol. 2). Minneapolis: University of Minnesota Press.

Brown, Roger, & Kulik, James (1977). Flashbulb memories. *Cognition, 5*, 73–99.

Brown, Roger, & McNeill, David (1966). The "tip of the tongue" phenomenon. *Journal of Verbal Learning and Verbal Behavior, 5*, 325–337.

Brown, Ryan P., & Josephs, Robert A. (1999). A burden of proof: Stereotype relevance and gender differences in math performance. *Journal of Personality and Social Psychology, 76,* 246–257.

Brown, Stephanie L.; Nesse, Randolph M.; Vinokur, Amiram D.; & Smith, Dylan M. (2003). Providing social support may be more beneficial than receiving it: Results from a prospective study of mortality. *Psychological Science, 14,* 320–327.

Brown Center on Education Policy (2003). *Do students have too much homework?* Washington, DC: Brookings Institution.

Browning, James R.; Hatfield, Elaine; Kessler, Debra; & Levine, Tim (2000). Sexual motives, gender, and sexual behavior. *Archives of Sexual Behavior, 29,* 135–153.

Bruck, Maggie (2003). Effects of suggestion on the reliability and credibility of children's reports. Invited address at the annual meeting of the American Psychological Society, Atlanta.

Bruck, Maggie; Ceci, Stephen J.; Francoeur, E.; & Renick, A. (1995). Anatomically detailed dolls do not facilitate preschoolers' reports of a pediatric examination involving genital touching. *Journal of Experimental Psychology: Applied, 1,* 95–109.

Bruinius, Harry (2006). *Better for all the world: The secret history of forced sterilization and America's quest for racial purity.* New York: Alfred A. Knopf.

Bruner, Jerome S. (1990). *Acts of meaning.* Cambridge, MA: Harvard University Press.

Bryant, Richard A., & Guthrie, Rachel M. (2005). Maladaptive appraisals as a risk factor for posttraumatic stress. *Psychological Science, 16,* 749–752.

Buchert, R.; Thomasius, R.; Nebeling, B.; et al. (2003). Long-term effects of "ecstasy" use on serotonin transporters of the brain investigated by PET. *Journal of Nuclear Medicine, 44,* 375–384.

Buck, Linda, & Axel, Richard (1991). A novel multigene family may encode odorant receptors: A molecular basis for odor recognition. *Cell, 65,* 175–187.

Budiansky, Stephen (1998). *If a lion could talk: Animal intelligence and the evolution of consciousness.* New York: Free Press.

Bukowski, William M. (2001). Friendship and the worlds of childhood. In D. W. Nangle & C. A. Erdley (Eds.), The role of friendship in psychological adjustment. *New directions for child and adolescent development, No. 91.* San Francisco, CA: Jossey-Bass.

Buller, David J. (2005). *Adapting minds: Evolutionary psychology and the persistent quest for human nature.* Cambridge MA: MIT Press.

Burke, Brian L.; Arkowitz, Hal; & Menchola, Marisa (2003). The efficacy of motivational interviewing: A meta-analysis of controlled clinical trials. *Journal of Consulting and Clinical Psycholology, 71,* 843–861.

Burke, Deborah M.; MacKay, Donald G.; Worthley, Joanna S.; & Wade, Elizabeth (1991). On the tip of the tongue: What causes word finding failures in young and older adults? *Journal of Memory and Language, 30,* 237–246.

Burke, Deborah M., & Shafto, Meredith A. (2004). Aging and language production. *Current Directions in Psychological Science, 13,* 21–24.

Burke, Phyllis (1996). *Gender shock.* New York: Basic Books.

Burnham, Denis; Kitamura, Christine; & Vollmer-Conna, Uté (2002, May 24). What's new, pussycat? On talking to babies and animals. *Science, 296,* 1435.

Bushman, Brad J. (1995). Moderating role of trait aggressiveness in the effects of violent media on aggression. *Journal of Personality and Social Psychology, 69,* 950–960.

Bushman, Brad J., & Anderson, Craig A. (2001). Media violence and the American public: Scientific facts versus media misinformation. *American Psychologist, 56,* 477–489.

Bushman, Brad J.; Bonacci, Angelica M.; Pedersen William C.; et al. (2005). Chewing on it can chew you up: Effects of rumination on triggered displaced aggression. *Journal of Personality and Social Psychology, 88,* 969–983.

Bushman, Brad; Bonacci, Angelica M.; van Dijk, Mirjam; & Baumeister, Roy F. (2003). Narcissism, sexual refusal, and aggression: Testing a narcissistic reactance model of sexual coercion. *Journal of Personality and Social Psychology, 84,* 1027–1040.

Buss, David M. (1994). *The evolution of desire: Strategies of human mating.* New York: Basic Books.

Buss, David M. (1995). Evolutionary psychology: A new paradigm for psychological science. *Psychological Inquiry, 6,* 1–30.

Buss, David M. (1996). Sexual conflict: Can evolutionary and feminist perspectives converge? In D. M. Buss & N. Malamuth (Eds.), *Sex, power, conflict: Evolutionary and feminist perspectives.* New York: Oxford University Press.

Buss, David M. (1999). *Evolutionary psychology: The new science of the mind.* Boston: Allyn and Bacon.

Buss, David M. (2000). *The dangerous passion: Why jealousy is as necessary as love or sex.* New York: The Free Press.

Bussey, Kay, & Bandura, Albert (1992). Self-regulatory mechanisms governing gender development. *Child Development, 63,* 1236–1250.

Bussey, Kay, & Bandura, Albert (1999). Social-cognitive theory of gender development and differentiation. *Psychological Review, 106,* 676–713.

Butcher, James N.; Lim, Jeeyoung; & Nezami, Elahe (1998). Objective study of abnormal personality in cross-cultural settings: The MMPI-2. *Journal of Cross-Cultural Psychology, 29,* 189–211.

Butler, S.; Chalder, T.; Ron, M.; et al. (1991). Cognitive behaviour therapy in chronic fatigue syndrome. *Journal of Neurology, Neurosurgery & Psychiatry, 54,* 153–158.

Button, T. M. M.; Thapar, A.; & McGuffin, P. (2005). Relationship between antisocial behaviour, attention-deficit hyperactivity disorder and maternal prenatal smoking. *British Journal of Psychiatry, 187,* 155–160.

Buunk, Bram; Angleitner, Alois; Oubaid, Viktor; & Buss, David M. (1996). Sex differences in jealousy in evolutionary and cultural perspective: Tests from the Netherlands, Germany, and the United States. *Psychological Science, 7,* 359–363.

Buxbaum, Laurel J.; Kyle, Kathleen M.; & Menon, Rukmini (2005). On beyond mirror neurons: Internal representations subserving imitation and recognition of skilled object-related actions in humans. *Cognitive Brain Research, 25,* 226–239.

Byne, William (1995). Science and belief: Psychobiological research on sexual orientation. *Journal of Homosexuality, 28,* 303–344.

Cabiya, Jose J.; Lucio, Emilia; Chavira, Denise A.; et al. (2000). MMPI-2 scores of Puerto Rican, Mexican, and U.S. Latino college students: A research note. *Psychological Reports, 87,* 266–268.

Cacioppo, John T.; Berntson, Gary G.; Lorig, Tyler S.; et al. (2003). Just because you're imaging the brain doesn't mean you can stop using your head: A primer and set of first principles. *Journal of Personality and Social Psychology, 85,* 650–661.

Cadinu, Mara; Maass, Anne; Rosabianca, Alessandra; & Kiesner, Jeff (2005). Why do women underperform under stereotype threat? Evidence for the role of negative thinking. *Psychological Science, 16,* 472–578.

Cahill, Larry (2005, May). His brain, her brain. *Scientific American, 292,* 40–47.

Cahill, Larry; Prins, Bruce; Weber, Michael; & McGaugh, James L. (1994). ß-adrenergic activation and memory for emotional events. *Nature, 371,* 702–704.

Calder, A. J.; Keane, J.; Manes, F.; Antoun, N.; & Young, A. W. (2000). Impaired recognition and experience of disgust following brain injury. *Nature Neuroscience, 3,* 1077–1078.

Camerer, Colin F. (2003). Strategizing in the brain. *Science, 300,* 1673–1675.

Cameron, Judy; Banko, Katherine M.; & Pierce, W. David (2001). *Pervasive negative effects of rewards on intrinsic motivation : The myth continues.* Behavior Analyst, 24, 1–44.

Campbell, Benjamin C.; Pope, Harrison G.; & Filiault, Shaun (2005). Body image among Ariaal men from Northern Kenya. *Journal of Cross-Cultural Psychology, 36*, 371–379.

Campbell, Frances A., & Ramey, Craig T. (1995). Cognitive and school outcomes for high risk students at middle adolescence: Positive effects of early intervention. *American Educational Research Journal, 32*, 743–772.

Campbell, Jennifer; Trapnell, Paul D.; Heine, Steven J.; et al. (1996). Self-concept clarity: Measurement, personality correlates, and cultural boundaries. *Journal of Personality and Social Psychology, 70*, 141–156.

Campbell, Joseph (1949/1968). *The hero with 1,000 faces* (2nd ed.). Princeton, NJ: Princeton University Press.

Campbell, W. Keith, & Sedikides, Constantine (1999). Self-threat magnifies the self-serving bias: A meta-analytic integration. *Review of General Psychology, 3*, 23–43.

Campos, Paul (2004). *The obesity myth: Why America's obsession with weight is hazardous to your health.* New York: Gotham Books.

Cancian, Francesca M. (1987). *Love in America: Gender and self-development.* Cambridge, England: Cambridge University Press.

Canetto, Silvia S. (1992). Suicide attempts and substance abuse: Similarities and differences. *Journal of Psychology, 125*, 605–620.

Canino, Glorisa (1994). Alcohol use and misuse among Hispanic women: Selected factors, processes, and studies. *International Journal of the Addictions, 29*, 1083–1100.

Canli, Turhan; Desmond, John E.; Zhao, Zuo; & Gabrieli, John D. E. (2002). Sex differences in the neural basis of emotional memories. *Proceedings of the National Academy of Sciences, 99*, 10789–10794.

Cannon, Tyrone D.; Huttunen, Matti O.; Loennqvist, Jouko; et al. (2000). The inheritance of neuropsychological dysfunction in twins discordant for schizophrenia. *American Journal of Human Genetics, 67*, 369–382.

Cannon, Tyrone D.; Kaprio, Jaakko; Loennqvist, Jouko; Huttunen, Matti O.; & Koskenvuo, Markku (1998). The genetic epidemiology of schizophrenia in a Finnish twin cohort: A population-based modeling study. *Archives of General Psychiatry, 55*, 67–74.

Cannon, Walter B. (1929). *Bodily changes in pain, hunger, fear and rage* (2nd ed.). New York: Appleton.

Capaldi, Deborah M.; Pears, Katherine C.; Patterson, Gerald R.; & Owen, Lee D. (2003). Continuity of parenting practices across generations in an at-risk sample: A prospective comparison of direct and mediated associations. *Journal of Abnormal Child Psychology, 31*, 127–142.

Caplan, Eric (1998). *Mind games: American culture and the birth of psychotherapy.* (See Chapter 4: Inventing psychotherapy: The American Mind Cure movement, 1830–1900.) Berkeley: University of California Press.

Carnagey, Nicholas L., & Anderson, Craig A. (2005). The effects of reward and punishment in violent video games on aggressive affect, cognition, and behavior. *Psychological Science, 16*, 882–889.

Carroll, James M., & Russell, James A. (1996). Do facial expressions signal specific emotions? Judging emotion from the face in context. *Journal of Personality and Social Psychology, 70*, 203–218.

Carskadon, Mary A.; Mitler, Merrill M.; & Dement, William C. (1974). A comparison of insomniacs and normals: Total sleep time and sleep latency. *Sleep Research, 3*, 130 [Abstract].

Carter, Betty, & McGoldrick, Monica (Eds.) (1988). *The changing family life cycle: A framework for family therapy* (2nd ed.). New York: Gardner Press.

Cartwright, Rosalind (1977). *Night life: Explorations in dreaming.* Englewood Cliffs, NJ: Prentice-Hall.

Cartwright, Rosalind D. (1996). Dreams and adaptations to divorce. In D. Barrett (Ed.), *Trauma and dreams.* Cambridge: Harvard University Press.

Cartwright, Rosalind D.; Young, Michael A.; Mercer, Patricia; & Bears, Michael (1998). Role of REM sleep and dream variables in the prediction of remission from depression. *Psychiatry Research, 80*, 249–255.

Carver, Charles S. (1998). Resilience and thriving: Issues, models, and linkages. *Journal of Social Issues, 54*, 245–266.

Carver, Charles S., & Baird, Eryn (1998). The American dream revisited: Is it what you want or why you want it that matters? *Psychological Science, 9*, 289–292.

Carver, Charles S., & Scheier, Michael F. (1999). Optimism. In C. R. Snyder (Ed.), *Coping: The psychology of what works.* New York: Oxford University Press.

Caspi, Avshalom (2000). The child is father of the man: Personality continuities from childhood to adulthood. *Journal of Personality and Social Psychology, 78*, 158–172.

Caspi, Avshalom; McClay, Joseph; Moffitt, Terrie E.; et al. (2002, August 2). Role of genotype in the cycle of violence in maltreated children. *Science, 297*, 851–857.

Caspi, Avshalom, & Moffitt, Terrie E. (1991). Individual differences are accentuated during periods of social change: The sample case of girls at puberty. *Journal of Personality and Social Psychology, 61*, 157–168.

Caspi, Avshalom; Sugden, Karen; Moffitt, Terrie E.; et al. (2003). Influence of life stress on depression: Moderation by a polymorphism in the 5-HTT gene. *Science, 301*, 386–389.

Cattell, Raymond B. (1965). *The scientific analysis of personality.* Baltimore, MD: Penguin.

Cattell, Raymond B. (1973). *Personality and mood by questionnaire.* San Francisco: Jossey-Bass.

Ceci, Stephen J. (1996). *On intelligence: A bioecological treatise on intellectual development.* Cambridge, MA: Harvard University Press.

Ceci, Stephen J., & Bruck, Maggie (1995). *Jeopardy in the courtroom: A scientific analysis of children's testimony.* Washington, DC: American Psychological Association.

Cejka, Mary Ann, & Eagly, Alice H. (1999). Gender-stereotypic images of occupations correspond to the sex segregation of employment. *Personality and Social Psychology Bulletin, 25*, 413–423.

Cermak, Laird S., & Craik, Fergus I. M. (Eds.) (1979). *Levels of processing in human memory.* Hillsdale, NJ: Erlbaum.

Cervone, Daniel, & Shoda, Yuichi (1999). Beyond traits in the study of personality coherence. *Current Directions in Psychological Science, 8*, 27–32.

Chambless, Dianne L., & Ollendick, T. H. (2001). Empirically supported psychological interventions: Controversies and evidence. *Annual Review of Psychology, 52*, 685–716.

Chambless, Dianne L.; & the Task Force on Psychological Interventions (1998). Update on empirically validated therapies II. *The Clinical Psychologist, 51*, 3–16.

Chance, Paul (1999). *Learning and behavior* (4th ed.). Pacific Grove: Brooks/Cole.

Chang, Edward C. (1998). Dispositional optimism and primary and secondary appraisal of a stressor. *Journal of Personality and Social Psychology, 74*, 1109–1120.

Chang, Kenneth (2000, September 12). Can robots rule the world? Not yet. *New York Times*, Science section, B1.

Charles, S. T., & Carstensen, Laura L. (2004). A life-span view of emotional functioning in adulthood and old age. In P. Costa (Ed.), *Recent advances in psychology and aging* (Vol. 15). Amsterdam: Elsevier.

Charles, Susan T.; Reynolds, Chandra A.; & Gatz, Margaret (2001). Age-related differences and change in positive and negative affect over 23 years. *Journal of Personality and Social Psychology, 80*, 136–151.

Chaudhari, Nirupa; Landin, A. M.; & Roper, S. D. (2000). A metabotropic glutamate receptor variant functions as a taste receptor. *Nature Neuroscience, 3,* 113–119

Chaves, J. F. (1989). Hypnotic control of clinical pain. In N. P. Spanos & J. F. Chaves (Eds.), *Hypnosis: The cognitive-behavioral perspective.* Buffalo, NY: Prometheus Books.

Chehab, Farid F.; Mounzih, K.; Lu, R.; & Lim, M. E. (1997, January 3). Early onset of reproductive function in normal female mice treated with leptin. *Science, 275,* 88–90.

Cheney, Dorothy L., & Seyfarth, Robert M. (1985). Vervet monkey alarm calls: Manipulation through shared information? *Behavior, 94,* 150–166.

Chipuer, Heather M.; Rovine, Michael J.; & Plomin, Robert (1990). LISREL modeling: Genetic and environmental influences on IQ revisited. *Intelligence, 14,* 11–29.

Choi, Incheol; Dalal, Reeshad; Kim-Prieto, Chu; & Park, Hyekyung (2003). Culture and judgment of causal relevance. *Journal of Personality and Social Psychology, 84,* 46–59.

Choi, Incheol, & Nisbett, Richard (2000). Cultural psychology of surprise: Holistic theories and recognition of contradiction. *Journal of Personality and Social Psychology, 79,* 890–905.

Chomsky, Noam (1957). *Syntactic structures.* The Hague, Netherlands: Mouton.

Chomsky, Noam (1980). Initial states and steady states. In M. Piatelli-Palmerini (Ed.), *Language and learning: The debate between Jean Piaget and Noam Chomsky.* Cambridge, MA: Harvard University Press.

Chorpita, Bruce F., & Barlow, David H. (1998). The development of anxiety: The role of control in the early environment. *Psychological Bulletin, 124,* 3–21.

Chrisler, Joan C. (2000). PMS as a culture-bound syndrome. In J. C. Chrisler, C. Golden, & P. D. Rozee (Eds.), *Lectures on the psychology of women* (2nd ed.). New York: McGraw-Hill.

Christakis, Dimitri A.; Zimmerman, Frederick J.; DiGiuseppe, David L.; & McCarty, Carolyn A. (2004). Early television exposure and subsequent attentional problems in children. *Pediatrics, 113,* 708–713.

Christensen, Andrew, & Jacobson, Neil S. (2000). *Reconcilable differences.* New York: Guilford.

Christensen, Larry, & Burrows, Ross (1990). Dietary treatment of depression. *Behavior Therapy, 21,* 183–194.

Chun, Kevin M.; Organista, Pamela B.; & Marin, Gerardo (Eds.) (2002).*Acculturation: Advances in theory, measurement, and applied research.* Washington, DC: American Psychological Association.

Chung, Young; Klimanskaya, Irina; Becker, Sandy; et al. (2005). Embryonic and extraembryonic stem cell lines derived from single mouse blastomeres. *Nature, 439,* 216–219.

Church, A. Timothy, & Lonner, Walter J. (1998). The cross-cultural perspective in the study of personality: Rationale and current research. *Journal of Cross-Cultural Psychology, 29,* 32–62.

Cialdini, Robert B. (2001). *Influence: Science and practice* (4th ed.). Boston: Allyn & Bacon.

Cialdini, Robert B.; Trost, Melanie R.; & Newsom, Jason T. (1995). Preference for consistency: The development of a valid measure and the discovery of surprising behavioral implications. *Journal of Personality and Social Psychology, 69,* 318–328.

Cinque, Guglielmo (1999). *Adverbs and functional heads: A cross-linguistic approach.* New York: Oxford University Press.

Cioffi, Delia, & Holloway, James (1993). Delayed costs of suppressed pain. *Journal of Personality and Social Psychology, 64,* 274–282.

Cioffi, Frank (1998). *Freud and the question of pseudoscience.* Chicago, IL: Open Court.

Clancy, Susan A. (2005). *Abducted: How people come to believe they were kidnapped by aliens.* Cambridge, MA: Harvard University Press.

Clark, Margaret S.; Milberg, Sandra; & Erber, Ralph (1987). Arousal state dependent memory: Evidence and some implications for understanding social judgments and social behavior. In K. Fiedler & J. P. Forgas (Eds.), *Affect, cognition and social behavior.* Toronto, Canada: Hogrefe.

Clark, Rodney; Anderson, Norman B.; Clark, Vernessa R.; & Williams, David R. (1999). Racism as a stressor for African Americans: A biopsychosocial model. *American Psychologist, 54,* 805–816.

Clarke, H. F.; Dalley, J. W.; Crofts, H. S.; et al. (2004, May 7). Cognitive inflexibility after prefrontal serotonin depletion. *Science, 304,* 878–880.

Clarke, Peter, & Evans, Susan H. (1998). *Surviving modern medicine.* Rutgers, NJ: Rutgers University Press.

Clarke-Stewart, Allison; Malloy, Lindsay C.; & Allhusen, Virginia D. (2004). Verbal ability, self-control, and close relationships with parents protect children against misleading suggestions. *Applied Cognitive Psychology, 18,* 1037–1058.

Cleckley, Hervey (1976). *The mask of sanity* (5th ed.). St. Louis, MO: Mosby.

Cloninger, C. Robert (1990). *The genetics and biology of alcoholism.* Cold Springs Harbor, ME: Cold Springs Harbor Press.

Coan, James A.; Schaefer, Hillary; & Davidson, Richard J. (2006). Lending a hand: Social regulation of the neural response to threat. *Psychological Science, 17.*

Coats, Erik J.; Janoff-Bulman, Ronnie; & Alpert, Nancy (1996). Approach versus avoidance goals: Differences in self-evaluation and well-being. *Personality and Social Psychology Bulletin, 22,* 1057–1067.

Cohen, David B. (1999). *Stranger in the nest: Do parents really shape their child's personality, intelligence, or character?* New York: Wiley.

Cohen, Dov (1998). Culture, social organization, and patterns of violence. *Journal of Personality and Social Psychology, 75,* 408–419.

Cohen, Dov; Nisbett, Richard E.; Bowdle, Brian F.; & Schwarz, Norbert (1996). Insult, aggression, and the Southern culture of honor: An "experimental ethnography." *Journal of Personality and Social Psychology, 70,* 945–960.

Cohen, Sheldon; Doyle, William J.; Skoner, D. P.; et al. (1997). Social ties and susceptibility to the common cold. *Journal of the American Medical Association, 277,* 1940–1944.

Cohen, Sheldon; Doyle, William J.; Turner, Ronald; et al. (2003). Sociability and susceptibility to the common cold. *Psychological Science, 14,* 389–395.

Cohen, Sheldon; Evans, Gary W.; Krantz, David S.; & Stokols, Daniel (1980). Physiological, motivational, and cognitive effects of aircraft noise on children. *American Psychologist, 35,* 231–243.

Cohen, Sheldon; Frank, Ellen; Doyle, William J.; et al. (1998). Types of stressors that increase susceptibility to the common cold in healthy adults. *Health Psychology, 17,* 214–223.

Cohen, Sheldon; Tyrrell, David A.; & Smith, Andrew P. (1993). Negative life events, perceived stress, negative affect, and susceptibility to the common cold. *Journal of Personality and Social Psychology, 64,* 131–140.

Colcombe, Stanley, & Kramer, Arthur F. (2003). Fitness effects on the cognitive function of older adults: A meta-analytic study. *Psychological Science, 14,* 125–130.

Cole, Michael, & Scribner, Sylvia (1974). *Culture and thought.* New York: Wiley.

Collaer, Marcia L., & Hines, Melissa (1995). Human behavioral sex differences: A role for gonadal hormones during early development? *Psychological Bulletin, 118,* 55–107.

Collins, Allan M., & Loftus, Elizabeth F. (1975). A spreading-activation theory of semantic processing. *Psychological Review, 82,* 407–428.

Collins, Barry E., & Brief, Diana E. (1995). Using person-perception vignette methodologies to uncover the symbolic meanings of teacher behaviors in the Milgram paradigm. *Journal of Social Issues, 51,* 89–106.

Collins, Rebecca L. (1996). For better or worse: The impact of upward social comparison on self-evaluations. *Psychological Bulletin, 119,* 51–69.

Collins, W. Andrew; Maccoby, Eleanor E.; Steinberg, Laurence; Hetherington, E. Mavis; & Bornstein, Marc H. (2000). Contemporary research on parenting: The case of nature and nurture. *American Psychologist, 55,* 218–232.

Colman, Andrew (1991). Crowd psychology in South African murder trials. *American Psychologist, 46,* 1071–1079.

Comas-Díaz, Lillian, & Greene, Beverly (1994). *Women of color: Integrating ethnic and gender identities in psychotherapy.* New York: Guilford.

Comuzzie, Anthony G., & Allison, David B. (1998). The search for human obesity genes. *Science, 280,* 1374–1377.

Conklin, Heather M., & Iacono, William G. (2002). Schizophrenia: A neurodevelopmental perspective. *Current Directions in Psychological Science, 11,* 33–37.

Conroy, John (2000). *Unspeakable acts, ordinary people: The dynamics of torture.* New York: Knopf.

Cooper, M. Lynne; Frone, Michael R.; Russell, Marcia; & Mudar, Pamela (1995). Drinking to regulate positive and negative emotions: A motivational model of alcohol use. *Journal of Personality and Social Psychology, 69,* 990–1005.

Cooper, M. Lynne; Shapiro, Cheryl M.; & Powers, Anne M. (1998). Motivations for sex and risky sexual behavior among adolescents and young adults: A functional perspective. *Journal of Personality and Social Psychology, 75,* 1528–1558.

Copi, Irving M., & Burgess-Jackson, Keith (1992). *Informal logic* (2nd ed.). New York: Macmillan.

Corkin, Suzanne (1984). Lasting consequences of bilateral medial temporal lobectomy: Clinical course and experimental findings in H. M. *Seminars in Neurology, 4,* 249–259.

Corkin, Suzanne; Amaral, David G.; Gonzalez, R. Gilberto; et al. (1997). H. M.'s medial temporal lobe lesion: Findings from magnetic resonance imaging. *Journal of Neuroscience, 17,* 3964–3979.

Cosgrove, G. R., & Rauch, S. L. (2003). Stereotactic cingulotomy. *Neurosurg Clin North America, 14,* 225–235.

Cosmides, Leda; Tooby, John; & Barkow, Jerome H. (1992). Introduction: Evolutionary psychology and conceptual integration. In J. H. Barkow, L. Cosmides, & J. Tooby (Eds.), *The adapted mind: Evolutionary psychology and the generation of culture.* New York: Oxford University Press.

Costa, Paul T., Jr.; McCrae, Robert R.; Martin, Thomas A.; et al. (1999). Personality development from adolescence through adulthood: Further cross-cultural comparisons of age differences. In V. J. Molfese & D. Molfese (Eds.), *Temperament and personality development across the life span.* Hillsdale, NJ: Erlbaum.

Costantino, Giuseppe, & Malgady, Robert G. (1996). Culturally sensitive treatment: Cuento and hero/heroine modeling therapies for Hispanic children and adolescents. In E. D. Hibbs & P. S. Jensen (Eds.), *Psychosocial treatments for child and adolescent disorders: Empirically based strategies for clinical practice.* Washington, DC: American Psychological Association.

Cota-Robles, S.; Neiss, M.; & Rowe, D. C. (2002). The role of puberty in violent and nonviolent delinquency among Anglo American, Mexican American, and African American boys. *Journal of Adolescent Research, 17,* 364–376.

Council, J. R.; Kirsch, Irving; & Grant, D. L. (1996). Imagination, expectancy and hypnotic responding. In R. G. Kunzendorf, N. K. Spanos, & B. J. Wallace (Eds.), *Hypnosis and imagination.* Amityville, NY: Baywood.

Courage, Mary L., & Howe, Mark L. (2002). From infant to child: The dynamics of cognitive change in the second year of life. *Psychological Bulletin, 128,* 250–277.

Cowan, Nelson (2001). The magical number 4 in short-term memory: A reconsideration of mental storage capacity. *Behavioral and Brain Sciences, 24,* 87–185.

Cowen, Emory L.; Wyman, Peter A.; Work, William C.; & Parker, Gayle R. (1990). The Rochester Child Resilience Project (RCRP): Overview and summary of first year findings. *Development and Psychopathology, 2,* 193–212.

Cox, Martha J., & Paley, Blair (2003). Understanding families as systems. *Current Directions in Psychological Science, 12,* 193–196.

Cox, W. Michael, & Alm, Richard (2005, February 28). Scientists are made, not born. *The New York Times* op-ed page (online).

Craik, Fergus I. M., & Lockhart, Robert (1972). Levels of processing: A framework for memory research. *Journal of Verbal Learning and Verbal Behavior, 11,* 671–684.

Craik, Fergus I. M., & Tulving, Endel (1975). Depth of processing and the retention of words in episodic memory. *Journal of Experimental Psychology: General, 104,* 268–294.

Crair, Michael C.; Gillespie, Deda C.; & Stryker, Michael P. (1998). The role of visual experience in the development of columns in cat visual cortex. *Science, 279,* 566–570.

Cramer, Phebe (2000). Defense mechanisms in psychology today: Further processes for adaptation. *American Psychologist, 55,* 637–646.

Crandall, Christian S., & Eshelman, Amy (2003). A justification-suppression model of the expression and experience of prejudice. *Psychological Bulletin, 129,* 414–446.

Crandall, Christian S., & Martinez, Rebecca (1996). Culture, ideology, and antifat attitudes. *Personality and Social Psychology Bulletin, 22,* 1165–1176.

Crawford, Mary, & Marecek, Jeanne (1989). Psychology constructs the female: 1968–1988. *Psychology of Women Quarterly, 13,* 147–165.

Crews, Frederick (Ed.) (1998). *Unauthorized Freud: Doubters confront a legend.* New York: Viking.

Critchlow, Barbara (1986). The powers of John Barleycorn: Beliefs about the effects of alcohol on social behavior. *American Psychologist, 41,* 751–764.

Crits-Christoph, Paul; Wilson, G. Terence; & Hollon, Steven D. (2005). Empirically supported psychotherapies: Comment on Westen, Novotny, and Thompson-Brenner (2004). *Psychological Bulletin, 131,* 412–417.

Critser, Greg (2002). *Supersize.* New York: Houghton-Mifflin.

Croizen, Jean-Claude, & Claire, Theresa (1998). Extending the concept of stereotype threat to social class: The intellectual underperformance of students from low socioeconomic backgrounds. *Personality and Social Psychology Bulletin, 24,* 588–594.

Crombag, Hans S., & Robinson, Terry E. (2004). Drugs, environment, brain, and behavior. *Current Directions in Psychological Science, 13,* 107–111.

Cronbach, Lee (1990). *Essentials of psychological testing* (5th ed.). New York: Harper & Row.

Cummings, Brian J.; Uchida, Nobuko; Tamaki, Stanley J.; et al. (2005). Human neural stem cells differentiate and promote locomotor recovery in spinal cord-injured mice. *Proceedings of the National Academy of Science, 102,* 14069–14074.

Cunningham, William A.; Preacher, Kristopher J.; & Banaji, Mahzarin R. (2001). Implicit attitude measures: Consistency, stability, and convergent validity. *Psychological Science, 12,* 163–170.

Currie, Elliot (1998). *Crime and punishment in America.* New York: Henry Holt.

Curtiss, Susan (1977). *Genie: A psycholinguistic study of a modern-day "wild child."* New York: Academic Press.

Curtiss, Susan (1982). Developmental dissociations of language and cognition. In L. Obler & D. Fein (Eds.), *Exceptional language and linguistics.* New York: Academic Press.

Cvetkovich, George T., & Earle, Timothy C. (1994). Risk and culture. In W. J. Lonner & R. Malpass (Eds.), *Psychology and culture.* Boston: Allyn & Bacon.

Cytowic, Richard E. (2002). *Synethesia: A union of the senses* (2nd ed.). Cambridge, MA: MIT Press.

Czeisler, Charles A.; Duffy, Jeanne F.; Shanahan, Theresa L.; et al. (1999). Stability, precision, and near-24-hour period of the human circadian pacemaker. *Science, 284,* 2177–2181.

D'Antonio, Michael (2004, May 2). How we think. *Los Angeles Times Magazine,* 18–20, 30–32.

Dabbs, James M., Jr. (2000). *Heroes, rogues, and lovers: Testosterone and behavior.* New York: McGraw-Hill.

Dadds, Mark R.; Bovbjerg, Dana H.; Redd, William H.; & Cutmore, Tim R. H. (1997). Imagery in human classical conditioning. *Psychological Bulletin, 122,* 89–103.

Daley, Tamara C.; Whaley, Shannon E.; Sigman, Marian D.; et al. (2003). IQ on the rise: The Flynn Effect in rural Kenyan children. *Psychological Science, 14,* 215–219.

Dalgleish, Tim (2004). Cognitive approaches to posttraumatic stress disorder: The evolution of multirepresentational theorizing. *Psychological Bulletin, 130,* 228–260.

Dalton, K. S.; Morris, D. L.; Delanoy, D. I.; et al. (1996). Security measures in an automated ganzfeld system. *Journal of Parapsychology, 60,* 129–147.

Daly, Martin, & Wilson, Margo (1983). *Sex, evolution, and behavior* (2nd ed.). Belmont, CA: Wadsworth.

Damak, Sami; Rong, Minqing; Yasumatsu, Keiko; et al. (2003). Detection of sweet and umami taste in the absence of taste receptor T1r3. *Science, 301,* 850–853.

Damasio, Antonio R. (1994). *Descartes' error: Emotion, reason, and the human brain.* New York: Grosset/Putnam.

Damasio, Antonio R. (2003). *Looking for Spinoza: Joy, sorrow, and the feeling brain.* San Diego: Harcourt.

Damasio, A. R.; Grabowski, T. J.; Bechara, A.; et al. (2000). Subcortical and cortical brain activity during the feeling of self-generated emotions. *Nature Neuroscience, 3,* 1049–1056.

Damasio, Hanna; Grabowski, Thomas J.; Frank, Randall; et al. (1994). The return of Phineas Gage: Clues about the brain from the skull of a famous patient. *Science, 264,* 1102–1105.

Damasio, Hanna; Grabowski, Thomas J.; Tranel, Daniel; et al. (1996). A neural basis for lexical retrieval. *Nature, 380,* 499–505.

Damon, William (1995). *Greater expectations.* New York: Free Press.

Danner, Deborah D.; Snowdon, David A.; & Friesen, Wallace V. (2001). Positive emotions in early life and longevity: Findings from the nun study. *Journal of Personality and Social Psychology, 80,* 804–813.

Darley, John M. (1995). Constructive and destructive obedience: A taxonomy of principal agent relationships. In A. G. Miller, B. E. Collins, & D. E. Brief (Eds.), Perspectives on obedience to authority: The legacy of the Milgram experiments. *Journal of Social Issues, 51*(3), 125–154.

Darley, John M., & Latane, Bibb (1968). Bystander intervention in emergencies: Diffusion of responsibility. *Journal of Personality and Social Psychology, 8,* 377–383.

Darwin, Charles (1859). *On the origin of species.* [A facsimile of the first edition, edited by Ernst Mayer, 1964.] Cambridge, MA: Harvard University Press.

Darwin, Charles (1872/1965). *The expression of the emotions in man and animals.* Chicago: The University of Chicago Press.

Darwin, Charles (1874). *The descent of man and selection in relation to sex* (2nd ed.). New York: Hurst.

Dasen, Pierre R. (1994). Culture and cognitive development from a Piagetian perspective. In W. J. Lonner & R. S. Malpass (Eds.), *Psychology and culture.* Needham Heights, MA: Allyn & Bacon.

Daum, Irene, & Schugens, Markus M. (1996). On the cerebellum and classical conditioning. *Psychological Science, 5,* 58–61.

Davelaar, Eddy J.; Goshen-Gottstein, Yonatan; Ashkenazi, Amir; et al. (2004). The demise of short-term memory revisited: Empirical and computational investigations of recency effects. *Psychological Review, 112,* 3–42.

Davey, Graham C. (1992). Classical conditioning and the acquisition of human fears and phobias: A review and synthesis of the literature. *Advances in Behaviour Research and Therapy, 14,* 29–66.

Davidson, Richard J.; Abercrombie, H.; Nitschke, J. B.; & Putnam, K. (1999). Regional brain function, emotion, and disorders of emotion. *Current Opinion in Neurobiology, 9,* 228–234.

Davidson, Richard J.; Kabat-Zinn, J.; Schumacher, J.; et al. (2003). Alterations in brain and immune function produced by mindfulness meditation. *Psychosomatic Medicine, 65,* 564–570.

Davidson, Richard J.; Pizzagalli, Diego A.; Nitschke, Jack B., & Putnam, Katherine (2002). Depression: Perspectives from affective neuroscience. *Annual Review of Psychology, 53,* 545–574.

Davies, Michael J.; Baer, David J.; Judd, Joseph T; et al. (2002). Effects of moderate alcohol intake on fasting insulin and glucose concentrations and insulin sensitivity in postmenopausal women: A randomized controlled trial. *Journal of the American Medical Association, 287,* 2559–2562.

Davies, Michaela; Stankov, Lazar; & Roberts, Richard D. (1998). Emotional intelligence: In search of an elusive construct. *Journal of Personality and Social Psychology, 75,* 989–1015.

Davis, B. E.; Moon, R. Y.; Sachs, H. C.; & Ottolini, M. C. (1998). Effects of sleep position on infant motor development. *Pediatrics, 102,* 1135–1140.

Davis, Christopher G.; Nolen-Hoeksema, Susan; & Larson, Judith (1998). Making sense of loss and benefiting from the experience: Two construals of meaning. *Journal of Personality and Social Psychology, 75,* 561–574.

Davis, Karen D.; Kiss, Z. H.; Luo, L.; et al. (1998). Phantom sensations generated by thalamic microstimulation. *Nature, 391,* 385–387.

Davis, Michael; Myers, Karyn M.; Ressler, Kerry J.; & Rothbaum, Barbara O. (2005). Facilitation of extinction of conditioning fear by D-cycloserine. *Current Directions in Psychological Science, 14,* 214–219.

Davis, Penelope J. (1999). Gender differences in autobiographical memory for childhood emotional experiences. *Journal of Personality and Social Psychology, 76,* 498–510.

Davis, T. L. (1995). Gender differences in masking negative emotions: Ability or motivation? *Developmental Psychology, 31,* 660–667.

Davison, Gerald C. (1976). Homosexuality: The ethical challenge. *Journal of Consulting and Clinical Psychology, 44,* 157–162.

Davison, Gerald C.; Neale, John M.; & Kring, Ann M. (2004). *Abnormal psychology* (9th ed.). New York: Wiley.

Davison, Kathryn P.; Pennebaker, James W.; & Dickerson, Sally S. (2000). Who talks? The social psychology of illness support groups. *American Psychologist, 55,* 205–217.

Dawson, Neal V.; Arkes, Hal R.; Siciliano, C.; et al. (1988). Hindsight bias: An impediment to accurate probability estimation in clinicopathologic conferences. *Medical Decision Making, 8*(4), 259–264.

Dean, Geoffrey (1992). The bottom line: Effect size. In B. Beyerstein & D. Beyerstein (Eds.), *The write stuff: Evaluations of graphology—The study of handwriting analysis.* Buffalo, NY: Prometheus Books.

de Bono, Edward (1985). *De Bono's thinking course.* New York: Facts on File.

Deci, Edward L.; Koestner, Richard; & Ryan, Richard M. (1999). A meta-analytic review of experiments examining the effects of extrinsic rewards on intrinsic motivation. *Psychological Bulletin, 125,* 627–668.

Deci, Edward L., & Ryan, Richard M. (1985). *Intrinsic motivation and self-determination of human behavior.* New York: Plenum.

Deffenbacher, Jerry L.; Deffenbacher, David M.; Lynch, Rebekah S.; & Richards, Tracy L. (2003). Anger, aggression, and risky behavior: A comparison of high and low anger drives. *Behaviour Research and Therapy, 41,* 701–718.

Dehaene, S.; Spelke, E.; Pinel, P.; et al. (1999). Sources of mathematical thinking: Behavioral and brain-imaging evidence. *Science, 284,* 970–974.

Dement, William (1978). *Some must watch while some must sleep.* New York: Norton.

Dement, William (1992). *The sleepwatchers.* Stanford, CA: Stanford Alumni Association.

Dennett, Daniel C. (1991). *Consciousness explained.* Boston: Little, Brown.

Denning, Patt; Little, Jeannie; & Glickman, Adina (2004). *Over the influence: The harm reduction guide for managing drugs and alcohol.* New York: Guilford.

Denny, Dallas (Ed.) (1998). *Current concepts in transgender identity.* New York: Garland Press.

DePaulo, Bella M. (1992). Nonverbal behavior and self-presentation. *Psychological Bulletin, 111,* 203–243.

DePaulo, Bella M.; Lindsay, James J.; Malone, Brian E.; et al. (2003). Cues to deception. *Psychological Bulletin, 129,* 74–118.

de Rivera, Joseph (1989). Comparing experiences across cultures: Shame and guilt in America and Japan. *Hiroshima Forum for Psychology, 14,* 13–20.

De Robertis, Michael M., & Delaney, Paul A. (2000). A second survey of the attitudes of university students to astrology and astronomy. *Journal of the Royal Astronomical Society of Canada, 94,* 112–122.

DeValois, Russell L., & DeValois, Karen K. (1975). Neural coding of color. In E. C. Carterette & M. P. Friedman (Eds.), *Handbook of perception* (Vol. 5). New York: Academic Press.

Devlin, B.; Daniels, Michael; & Roeder, Kathryn (1997). The heritability of IQ. *Nature, 388,* 468–471.

de Waal, Frans (1997, July). Are we in anthropodenial? *Discover,* 50–53.

de Waal, Frans (2001). *The ape and the sushi master: Cultural reflections by a primatologist.* New York: Basic Books.

de Waal, Frans B. M. (2002). Evolutionary psychology: The wheat and the chaff. *Current Directions in Psychological Science, 11,* 187–191.

De Wolff, Marianne, & van IJzendoorn, Marinus H. (1997). Sensitivity and attachment: A meta-analysis on parental antecedents of infant attachment. *Child Development, 68,* 571–591.

Diamond, Lisa M. (2003). Was it a phase? Young women's relinquishment of lesbian/bisexual identities over a 5-year period. *Journal of Personality and Social Psychology, 84,* 352–364.

Diamond, Lisa M. (2004). Emerging perspectives on distinctions between romantic love and sexual desire. *Current Directions in Psychological Science, 13,* 116–119.

Diamond, M., & Sigmundson, H. K. (1997). Sex reassignment at birth: Long-term review and clinical implications. *Archives of Pediatrics and Adolescent Medicine, 151,* 298–304.

Diamond, Marian C. (1993, Winter–Spring). An optimistic view of the aging brain. *Generations, 17,* 31–33.

Dickerson, Sally S., & Kemeny, Margaret E. (2004). Acute stressors and cortisol responses: A theoretical integration and synthesis of laboratory research. *Psychological Bulletin, 130,* 355–391.

Dickinson, Alyce M. (1989). The detrimental effects of extrinsic reinforcement on "intrinsic motivation." *The Behavior Analyst, 12,* 1–15.

Dien, Dora S. (1999). Chinese authority-directed orientation and Japanese peer-group orientation: Questioning the notion of collectivism. *Review of General Psychology, 3,* 372–385.

Digman, John M., & Shmelyov, Alexander G. (1996). The structure of temperament and personality in Russian children. *Journal of Personality and Social Psychology, 71,* 341–351.

Dijksterhuis, Ap; Bos, Maarten W.; Nordgren, Loran F.; & van Baaren, Rick B. (2006). On making the right choice: The deliberation-without-attention effect. *Science, 311,* 1005–1007.

Dimberg, Ulf; Thunberg, Monika; & Elmehed, Kurt (2000). Unconscious facial reactions to emotional facial expressions. *Psychological Science, 11,* 86–89.

Dinges, David F.; Whitehouse, Wayne G.; Orne, Emily C.; Powell, John W.; Orne, Martin T.; & Erdelyi, Matthew H. (1992). Evaluating hypnotic memory enhancement (hypermnesia and reminiscence) using multitrial forced recall. *Journal of Experimental Psychology: Learning, Memory, and Cognition, 18,* 1139–1147.

Dinn, W. M., & Harris, C. L. (2000). Neurocognitive function in antisocial personality disorder. *Psychiatry Research, 97,* 173–190.

Dion, Kenneth L., & Dion, Karen K. (1993). Gender and ethnocultural comparisons in styles of love. *Psychology of Women Quarterly, 17,* 463–474.

Doering, Stephan; Katzlberger, Florian; Rumpold, Gerhard; et al. (2000). Videotape preparation of patients before hip replacement surgery reduces stress. *Psychosomatic Medicine, 62,* 365–373.

Dollard, John, & Miller, Neal E. (1950). *Personality and psychotherapy: An analysis in terms of learning, thinking, and culture.* New York: McGraw-Hill.

Dolnick, Edward (1990, July). What dreams are (really) made of. *The Atlantic Monthly, 226,* 41–45, 48–53, 56–58, 60–61.

Domhoff, G. William (1996). *Finding meaning in dreams: A quantitative approach.* New York: Plenum.

Domhoff, G. William (2003). *The scientific study of dreams: Neural networks, cognitive development, and content analysis.* Washington, DC: American Psychological Association.

Doty, Richard M.; Peterson, Bill E.; & Winter, David G. (1991). Threat and authoritarianism in the United States, 1978–1987. *Journal of Personality and Social Psychology, 61,* 629–640.

Dovidio, John F. (2001). On the nature of contemporary prejudice: The third wave. *Journal of Social Issues,* 57 (Winter), 829–849.

Dovidio, John F., & Gaertner, Samuel L. (2000). Aversive racism and selection decisions: 1989 and 1999. *Psychological Science, 11,* 315–319.

Dovidio, John F.; Gaertner, Samuel L.; & Validzic, Ana (1998). Intergroup bias: Status, differentiation, and a common in-group identity. *Journal of Personality and Social Psychology, 75,* 109–120.

Drayna, Dennis; Manichaikul, Ani; de Lange, Marlies; et al. (2001). Genetic correlates of musical pitch recognition in humans. *Science, 291,* 1969–1972.

Drevets, W. C. (2000). Neuroimaging studies of mood disorders. *Biological Psychiatry, 48,* 813–829.

Drieschner, K., & Lange, A. (1999). A review of cognitive factors in the etiology of rape: Theories, empirical studies, and implications. *Clinical Psychology Review, 19*, 57–77.

Druckman, Daniel, & Swets, John A. (Eds.) (1988). *Enhancing human performance: Issues, theories, and techniques.* Washington, DC: National Academy Press.

Dumit, Joseph (2004). *Picturing personhood: Brain scans and biomedical identity.* Princeton, NJ: Princeton University Press.

Dunbar, R. I. M. (2004). Gossip in evolutionary perspective. *Review of General Psychology, 8*, 100–110.

Duncan, Paula D.; Ritter, Philip L.; Dornbusch, Sanford M.; et al. (1985). The effects of pubertal timing on body image, school behavior, and deviance. *Journal of Youth and Adolescence, 14*, 227–235.

Dunn, Elizabeth W.; Wilson, Timothy D.; & Gilbert, Daniel T. (2003). Location, location, location: The misprediction of satisfaction in housing lotteries. *Personality and Social Psychology Bulletin, 29*, 1421–1432.

Dunning, David (2005). *Self-insight: Roadblocks and detours on the path to knowing thyself.* New York: Psychology Press.

Dunning, David; Heath, Chip; & Suls, Jerry M. (2004). Flawed self-assessment: Implications for health, education, and the workplace. *Psychological Science in the Public Interest, 5*, 69–106.

Dunning, David; Johnson, Kerri; Ehrlinger, Joyce; & Kruger, Justin (2003). Why people fail to recognize their own incompetence. *Current Directions in Psychological Science, 12*, 83–87.

Durga, Jane; van Boxtel, M. P.; Schouten, E. G.; et al. (2006). Folate and the methylenetetrahydrofolate reductase 667→T mutation correlate with cognitive performance. *Neurobiology of Aging, 27*, 334–343.

Dweck, Carol S. (2006). *Mindset: The new psychology of success.* New York: Random House.

Dweck, Carol S., & Sorich, Lisa A. (1999). Mastery-oriented thinking. In C. R. Snyder (Ed.), *Coping: The psychology of what works.* New York: Oxford University Press.

Dym, Barry, & Glenn, Michael L. (1993). *Couples: Exploring and understanding the cycles of intimate relationships.* New York: HarperCollins.

Eagly, Alice H., & Wood, Wendy (1999). The origins of sex differences in human behavior: Evolved dispositions versus social roles. *American Psychologist, 54*, 408–423.

Earl-Novell, Sarah L., & Jessup, Donna C. (2005). The relationship between perceptions of premenstrual syndrome and degree performance. *Assessment & Evaluation in Higher Education, 30*, 343–352.

Ebbinghaus, Hermann M. (1885/1913). *Memory: A contribution to experimental psychology* (H. A. Ruger & C. E. Bussenius, trans.). New York: Teachers College Press, Columbia University.

Edwards, Kari, & Smith, Edward E. (1996). A disconfirmation bias in the evaluation of arguments. *Journal of Personality and Social Psychology, 71*, 5–24.

Efran, Jay S.; Greene, Mitchell A.; & Gordon, Don E. (1998, March/April). Lessons of the new genetics: Finding the right fit for our clients. *Family Therapy Networker, 22*, 26–41.

Ehrenreich, Barbara (1978). *For her own good: 150 years of the experts' advice to women.* New York: Doubleday.

Ehrenreich, Barbara (2001, June 4). What are they probing for? [Essay.] *Time*, 86.

Ehrensaft, Miriam K.; Moffitt, Terrie E.; & Caspi, Avshalom (2006). Is domestic violence followed by an increased risk of psychiatric disorders among women but not among men? A longitudinal cohort study. *American Journal of Psychiatry, 163*, 885–892.

Eich, E., & Hyman, R. (1992). Subliminal self-help. In D. Druckman & R. A. Bjork (Eds.), *In the mind's eye: Enhancing human performance.* Washington, DC: National Academy Press.

Eisenberg, Nancy; Guthrie, Ivanna K.; Cumberland, Amanda; et al. (2002). Prosocial development in early adulthood: A longitudinal study. *Journal of Personality and Social Psychology, 82*, 993–1006.

Ekman, Paul (1994). Strong evidence for universals in facial expressions: A reply to Russell's mistaken critique. *Psychological Bulletin, 115*, 268–287.

Ekman, Paul (1997). What we have learned by measuring facial behavior. In P. Ekman & E. L. Rosenberg (Eds.), *What the face reveals.* Oxford, England: Oxford University Press.

Ekman, Paul (2003). *Emotions revealed.* New York: Times Books.

Ekman, Paul; Friesen, Wallace V.; & O'Sullivan, Maureen (1988). Smiles when lying. *Journal of Personality and Social Psychology, 54*, 414–420.

Ekman, Paul; Friesen, Wallace V.; O'Sullivan, Maureen; et al. (1987). Universals and cultural differences in the judgments of facial expression of emotion. *Journal of Personality and Social Psychology, 53*, 712–717.

Elfenbein, Hillary A., & Ambady, Nalini (2002). On the universality and cultural specificity of emotion recognition: A meta-analysis. *Psychological Bulletin, 128*, 203–235.

Elfenbein, Hillary A., & Ambady, Nalini (2003). When familiarity breeds accuracy: Cultural exposure and facial emotion recognition. *Journal of Personality and Social Psychology, 85*, 276–290.

Elliot, Andrew J., & McGregor, Holly A. (2001). A 2 x 2 achievement goal framework. *Journal of Personality and Social Psychology, 80*, 501–519.

Elliot, Andrew J., & Reis, Harry T. (2003). Attachment and exploration in adulthood. *Journal of Personality and Social Psychology, 85*, 317–331.

Elliot, Andrew J., & Sheldon, Kennon M. (1998). Avoidance personal goals and the personality-illness relationship. *Journal of Personality and Social Psychology, 75*, 1282–1299.

Ellis, Albert (1993). Changing rational-emotive therapy (RET) to rational emotive behavior therapy (REBT). *Behavior Therapist, 16*, 257–258.

Ellis, Albert, & Blau, S. (1998). Rational emotive behavior therapy. *Directions in Clinical and Counseling Psychology, 8*, 41–56.

Ellison, Carol R. (2000). *Women's sexualities.* Oakland, CA: New Harbinger.

Elmquist, Joel K., & Flier, Jeffrey S. (2004, April 2). The fat-brain axis enters a new dimension. *Science, 304*, 63–64.

Else-Quest, Nicole M.; Hyde, Janet S.; Goldsmith, H. Hill; & Can Hulle, Carol A. (2006). Gender differences in temperament: A meta-analysis. *Psychological Bulletin, 132*, **33-72.**

Emery, Robert E., & Laumann-Billings, Lisa (1998). An overview of the nature, causes, and consequences of abusive family relationships. *American Psychologist, 53*, 121–135.

Emery, Robert E.; Otto, Randy K.; & O'Donohue, William T. (2005). A critical assessment of child custody evaluations: Limited science and a flawed system. *Psychological Science in the Public Interest, 6*, 1–29.

Emmons, Robert A., & King, Laura A. (1988). Conflict among personal strivings: Immediate and long-term implications for psychological and physical well-being. *Journal of Personality and Social Psychology, 54*, 1040–1048.

Emmons, Robert A., & McCullough, Michael E. (2003). Counting blessings versus burdens: An experimental investigation of gratitude and subjective well-being in daily life. *Journal of Personality and Social Psychology, 84*, 377–389.

Englander-Golden, Paula; Whitmore, Mary R.; & Dienstbier, Richard A. (1978). Menstrual cycle as focus of study and self-reports of moods and behavior. *Motivation and Emotion, 2*, 75–86.

Engle, Randall W. (2002). Working memory capacity as executive attention. *Current Directions in Psychological Science, 11*, 19–23.

Entin, Alan D. (1992). Family photographs: Visual icons and emotional history. Paper presented at the annual meeting of the American Psychological Association, Washington, DC.

Epel, E. S.; Blackburn, E. H.; Lin, J.; et al. (2004, December 7). Accelerated telomere shortening in response to life stress. *Proceedings of the National Academy of Science*, 101, 17312–17315.

Ericksen, Julia A., & Steffen, Sally A. (1999). *Kiss and tell: Surveying sex in the twentieth century.* Cambridge, MA: Harvard University Press.

Erikson, Erik H. (1950/1963). *Childhood and society* (2nd ed.). New York: Norton.

Erikson, Erik H. (1982). *The life cycle completed.* New York: Norton.

Eriksson, P. S.; Perfilieva, E; Bjork-Eriksson, T.; et al. (1998). Neurogenesis in the adult human hippocampus. *Nature Medicine, 4*, 1313–1317.

Eron, Leonard D. (1995). Media violence: How it affects kids and what can be done about it. Invited address presented at the annual meeting of the American Psychological Association, New York.

Ervin-Tripp, Susan (1964). Imitation and structural change in children's language. In E. H. Lenneberg (Ed.), *New directions in the study of language.* Cambridge, MA: MIT Press.

Escera, Carles; Cilveti, Robert; & Grau, Carles (1992). Ultradian rhythms in cognitive operations: Evidence from the P300 component of the event-related potentials. *Medical Science Research, 20*, 137–138.

Esparza, J.; Fox, C.; Harper, I. T.; et al. (2000, January 24). Daily energy expenditure in Mexican and USA Pima Indians: Low physical activity as a possible cause of obesity. *International Journal of Obesity and Related Metabolic Disorders, 1*, 55–59.

Evans, Christopher (1984). *Landscapes of the night* (edited and completed by Peter Evans). New York: Viking.

Evans, Gary W.; Bullinger, Monika; & Hygge, Staffan (1998). Chronic noise exposure and physiological response: A prospective study of children living under environmental stress. *Psychological Science, 9*, 75–77.

Evans, Gary W.; Lepore, Stephen J.; & Allen, Karen Mata (2000). Cross-cultural differences in tolerance for crowding: Fact or fiction? *Journal of Personality and Social Psychology, 79*, 204–210.

Evans, Gary W.; Lepore, Stephen J.; & Schroeder, Alex (1996). The role of interior design elements in human responses to crowding. *Journal of Personality and Social Psychology, 70*, 41–46.

Ewart, Craig K. (1995). Self-efficacy and recovery from heart attack. In J. E. Maddux (Ed.), *Self-efficacy, adaptation, and adjustment: Theory, research, and application.* New York: Plenum.

Ewart, Craig K., & Kolodner, Kenneth B. (1994). Negative affect, gender, and expressive style predict elevated ambulatory blood pressure in adolescents. *Journal of Personality and Social Psychology, 66*, 596–605.

Eyer, Diane E. (1992). *Mother-infant bonding: A scientific fiction.* New Haven, CT: Yale University Press.

Eyferth, Klaus (1961). [The performance of different groups of the children of occupation forces on the Hamburg-Wechsler Intelligence Test for Children.] *Archiv für die Gesamte Psychologie, 113*, 222–241.

Fagan, Joseph F., III (1992). Intelligence: A theoretical viewpoint. *Current Directions in Psychological Science, 1*, 82–86.

Fagot, Beverly I. (1993, June). Gender role development in early childhood: Environmental input, internal construction. Invited address presented at the annual meeting of the International Academy of Sex Research, Monterey, CA.

Fagot, Beverly I.; Hagan, R.; Leinbach, Mary D.; & Kronsberg, S. (1985). Differential reactions to assertive and communicative acts of toddler boys and girls. *Child Development, 56*, 1499–1505.

Fagot, Beverly I., & Leinbach, Mary D. (1993). Gender-role development in young children: From discrimination to labeling. *Developmental Review, 13*, 205–224.

Falk, Ruma, & Greenbaum, Charles W. (1995). Significance tests die hard: The amazing persistence of a probabilistic misconception. *Theory & Psychology, 5*(1), 75–98.

Fallon, James H.; Keator, David B.; Mbogori, James; et al. (2004). Hostility differentiates the brain metabolic effects of nicotine. *Cognitive Brain Research, 18*, 142–148.

Fallone, Gahan; Acebo, Christine; Seifer, Ronald; & Carskadon, Mary A. (2005). Experimental restriction of sleep opportunity in children: Effects on teacher ratings. *Sleep, 28*, 1280–1286.

Farha, Bryan, & Steward, Gary Jr. (2006, January/February). Paranormal beliefs: An analysis of college students. *Skeptical Inquirer,* pp. 37–40.

Farooqi, I. Sadaf; Matarese, Giuseppe; Lord, Graham M.; et al. (2002). Beneficial effects of leptin on obesity, T cell hyporesponsiveness, and neuroendocrine/metabolic dysfunction of human congenital leptin deficiency. *Journal of Clinical Investigation, 110*, 1093–1103.

Farooqi, I. Sadaf, & O'Rahilly, Stephen (2004). Monogenic human obesity syndromes. *Recent Progress in Hormone Research, 59*, 409–424.

Farrell, Elizabeth F. (2005, December 16). Need therapy? Check your in box. *Chronicle of Higher Education*, A35.

Fausto-Sterling, Anne (1997). Beyond difference: A biologist's perspective. *Journal of Social Issues, 53*, 233–258.

FDA Drug Bulletin (1990, April). *Two new psychiatric drugs. 20*(1), 9.

Feather, N. T. (1966). Effects of prior success and failure on expectations of success and subsequent performance. *Journal of Personality and Social Psychology, 3*, 287–298.

Feeney, Brooke C., & Cassidy, Jude (2003). Reconstructive memory related to adolescent-parent conflict interactions. *Journal of Personality and Social Psychology, 85*, 945–955.

Fehr, Beverley (1993). How do I love thee . . . Let me consult my prototype. In S. Duck (Ed.), *Individuals in relationships* (Vol. 1). Newbury Park, CA: Sage.

Fehr, Beverley; Baldwin, Mark; Collins, Lois; et al. (1999). Anger in close relationships: An interpersonal script analysis. *Personality and Social Psychology Bulletin, 25*, 299–312.

Fehr, Ernest & Fischbacher, Urs (2003). The nature of human altruism. *Nature, 425*, 785–791.

Fein, Steven, & Spencer, Steven J. (1997). Prejudice as self-image maintenance: Affirming the self through derogating others. *Journal of Personality and Social Psychology, 73*, 31–44.

Fellows J. L.; Trosclair, A.; Adams, E. K.; & Rivera, C. C. (2002). Annual smoking attributable mortality, years of potential life lost and economic costs: United States 1995-1999. *Morbidity and Mortality Weekly Report, 51*, 300–303.

Fernald, Anne, & Mazzie, Claudia (1991). Prosody and focus in speech to infants and adults. *Developmental Psychology, 27*, 209–221.

Fernandez, Ephrem, & Turk, Dennis C. (1992). Sensory and affective components of pain: Separation and synthesis. *Psychological Bulletin, 112*, 205–217.

Fernea, Elizabeth, & Fernea, Robert (1994). Cleanliness and culture. In W. J. Lonner & Malpass (Eds.), *Psychology and culture.* Boston: Allyn & Bacon.

Ferrari, Pier Francesco; Rozzi, Stefano; & Fogassi, Leonardo (2005). Mirror neurons responding to observation of actions made with tools in monkey ventral premotor cortex. *Journal of Cognitive Neuroscience, 17*, 212–226.

Festinger, Leon (1957). *A theory of cognitive dissonance.* Evanston, IL: Row, Peterson.

Festinger, Leon, & Carlsmith, J. Merrill (1959). Cognitive consequences of forced compliance. *Journal of Abnormal and Social Psychology, 58*, 203–210.

Festinger, Leon; Pepitone, Albert; & Newcomb, Theodore (1952). Some consequences of deindividuation in a group. *Journal of Abnormal and Social Psychology, 47,* 382–389.

Festinger, Leon; Riecken, Henry W.; & Schachter, Stanley (1956). *When prophecy fails.* Minneapolis: University of Minnesota Press.

Fiedler, K.; Nickel, S.; Muehlfriedel, T.; & Unkelbach, C. (2001). Is mood congruency an effect of genuine memory or response bias? *Journal of Experimental Social Psychology, 37,* 201–214.

Field, Tiffany M. (1998). Massage therapy effects. *American Psychologist, 53,* 1270–1281.

Fields, Howard (1991). Depression and pain: A neurobiological model. *Neuropsychiatry, Neuropsychology, and Behavioral Neurology, 4,* 83–92.

Fields, R. Douglas (2004, April). The other half of the brain. *Scientific American,* 54–61.

Fiez, J. A. (1996). Cerebellar contributions to cognition. *Neuron, 16,* 13–15.

Fine, Ione; Wade, A. R.; Brewer, A. A.; et al. (2003). Long-term deprivation affects visual perception and cortex. *Nature Neuroscience, 6,* 915–916.

Fink, Max (1999). *Electroshock: Restoring the mind.* New York: Oxford University Press.

Fischer, Ann R.; Tokar, David M.; Good, Glenn E.; & Snell, Andrea F. (1998). More on the structure of male role norms. *Psychology of Women Quarterly, 22,* 135–155.

Fischer, Pamela C.; Smith, Randy J.; Leonard, Elizabeth; et al. (1993). Sex differences on affective dimensions: Continuing examination. *Journal of Counseling and Development, 71,* 440–443.

Fischhoff, Baruch (1975). Hindsight is not equal to foresight: The effect of outcome knowledge on judgment under uncertainty. *Journal of Experimental Psychology: Human Perception and Performance, 1,* 288–299.

Fishbein, Harold D. (1996). *Peer prejudice and discimination.* Boulder, CO: Westview Press.

Fisher, S., & Greenberg, R. (1996). *Freud scientifically appraised.* New York: John Wiley.

Fitzgerald, P. B.; Brown, T. L.; Marston, N. A.; et al. (2003). Transcranial magnetic stimulation in the treatment of depression: a double-blind, placebo-controlled trial. *Archives of General Psychiatry, 60,* 1002–1008.

Fivush, Robyn, & Hamond, Nina R. (1991). Autobiographical memory across the school years: Toward reconceptualizing childhood amnesia. In Flacks, Richard, & Thomas, Scott L. (1998, November 27). Among affluent students, a culture of disengagement. *Chronicle of Higher Education,* A48.

Flacks, Richard, & Thomas, Scott L. (1998, November 27). Among affluent students, a culture of disengagement. *Chronicle of Higher Education,* A48.

Flavell, John H. (1999). Cognitive development: Children's knowledge about the mind. *Annual Review of Psychology, 50,* 21–45.

Fleeson, William (2004). Moving personality beyond the person-situation debate. *Current Directions in Psychological Science, 13,* 83–87.

Fletcher, Anne M. (2001). *Sober for good.* New York: Houghton-Mifflin.

Flett, Gordon L.; Hewitt, Paul L.; Blankstein, Kirk R.; & Gray, Lisa (1998). Psychological distress and the frequency of perfectionistic thinking. *Journal of Personality and Social Psychology, 75,* 1363–1381.

Flor, Herta; Kerns, Robert D.; & Turk, Dennis C. (1987). The role of spouse reinforcement, perceived pain, and activity levels of chronic pain patients. *Journal of Psychosomatic Research, 31,* 251–259.

Flynn, James R. (1987). Massive IQ gains in 14 nations: What IQ tests really measure. *Psychological Bulletin, 95,* 29–51.

Flynn, James R. (1999). Searching for justice: the discovery of IQ gains over time. *American Psychologist, 54,* 5–20.

Folkman, Susan, & Moskowitz, Judith T. (2000). Positive affect and the other side of coping. *American Psychologist, 55,* 647 654.

Forgas, Joseph P. (1998). On being happy and mistaken: Mood effects on the fundamental attribution error. *Journal of Personality and Social Psychology, 75,* 318–331.

Forgas, Joseph P., & Bond, Michael H. (1985). Cultural influences on the perception of interaction episodes. *Personality and Social Psychology Bulletin, 11,* 75–88.

Foulkes, D. (1962). Dream reports from different states of sleep. *Journal of Abnormal and Social Psychology, 65,* 14–25.

Foulkes, David (1999). *Children's dreaming and the development of consciousness.* Cambridge, MA: Harvard University Press.

Fouts, Roger S. (with Stephen T. Mills) (1997). *Next of kin: What chimpanzees have taught me about who we are.* New York: Morrow.

Fouts, Roger S., & Rigby, Randall L. (1977). Man–chimpanzee communication. In T. A. Seboek (Ed.), *How animals communicate.* Bloomington: University of Indiana Press.

Fox, Mary Kay; Pac, Susan; Devaney, Barbara; & Jankowski, Linda (2004). Feeding Infants and Toddlers Study: what foods are infants and toddlers eating? *Journal of the American Dietetic Association, 104,* 22–30.

Fox, Nathan A., & Davidson, Richard J. (1988). Patterns of brain electrical activity during facial signs of emotion in 10-month-old infants. *Developmental Psychology, 24,* 230–236.

Fox, Nathan A.; Henderson, Heather A.; Marshall, Peter J.; et al. (2005a). Behavioral inhibition: Linking biology and behavior within a developmental framework. *Annual Review of Psychology, 56,* 235–262.

Fox, Nathan A.; Nichols, Kate E.; Henderson, Heather A.; et al. (2005b). Evidence for a gene-environment interaction in predicting behavioral inhibition in middle childhood. *Psychological Science, 16,* 921–926.

Fraga, Mario F.; Ballestar, Esteban; Paz, Maria F.; et al. (2005). Epigenetic differences arise during the lifetime of monozygotic twins. *Proceedings of the National Academy of Sciences, 102,* 10604–10609.

Fraley, R. Chris, & Shaver, Phillip R. (2000). Adult romantic attachment: Theoretical developments, emerging controversies, and unanswered questions. *Review of General Psychology, 4,* 132–154.

Frank, Mark G., & Stennett, Janine (2001). The forced-choice paradigm and the perception of facial expressions of emotion. *Journal of Personality and Social Psychology, 80,* 75–85.

Frankl, Victor E. (1955). *The doctor and the soul: An introduction to logotherapy.* New York: Knopf.

Frasure-Smith, Nancy, & Lespèrance, Francois (2005). Depression and coronary heart disease: Complex synergism of mind, body, and environment. *Current Directions in Psychological Science, 14,* 39–43.

Frasure-Smith, Nancy; Lesperance, F.; Juneau, M.; Talajic, M.; & Bourassa, M. G. (1999). Gender, depression, and one-year prognosis after myocardial infarction. *Psychosomatic Medicine, 61,* 26–37.

Frazier, Patricia A. (2003). Perceived control and distress following sexual assault: A longitudinal test of a new model. *Journal of Personality and Social Psychology, 84,* 1257–1269.

Fredrickson, Barbara L., & Losada, Marcial F. (2005). Positive affect and the complex dynamics of human flourishing. *American Psychologist, 60,* 678–686.

Freedman, Hill, & Combs, Gene (1996). *Narrative therapy.* New York: Norton.

Freedman, Jonathan (2002). *Media violence and its effect on aggression.* Toronto, Ontario, Canada: University of Toronto Press.

Frensch, Peter A., & Rünger, Dennis (2003). Implicit learning. *Current Directions in Psychological Science, 12,* 13–18.

Freud, Anna (1967). *Ego and the mechanisms of defense* (The writings of Anna Freud, Vol. 2) (Rev. ed.). New York: International Universities Press.

Freud, Sigmund (1900/1953). The interpretation of dreams. In J. Strachey (Ed.), *The standard edition of the complete psychological works of Sigmund Freud* (Vols. 4 and 5). London: Hogarth Press.

Freud, Sigmund (1905). Three essays on the theory of sexuality. In J. Strachey (Ed.), *Standard edition* (Vol. 7).

Freud, Sigmund (1905a). Fragment of an analysis of a case of hysteria. In J. Strachey (Ed. and Trans.), *Standard edition of the complete psychological works of Sigmund Freud* (Vol. 7).

Freud, Sigmund (1920/1960). *A general introduction to psychoanalysis* (Joan Riviere, Trans.). New York: Washington Square Press.

Freud, Sigmund (1923/1962). *The ego and the id* (Joan Riviere, Trans.). New York: Norton.

Freud, Sigmund (1924a). The dissolution of the Oedipus complex. In J. Strachey (Ed.), *Standard edition* (Vol. 19).

Freud, Sigmund (1924b). Some psychical consequences of the anatomical distinction between the sexes. In J. Strachey (Ed.), *Standard edition* (Vol. 19).

Freud, Sigmund (1961). *Letters of Sigmund Freud, 1873–1939.* Edited by Ernst L. Freud. London: Hogarth Press.

Fridlund, Alan J. (1994). *Human facial expression: An evolutionary view.* San Diego: Academic Press.

Friedman, Jeffrey M. (2003). A war on obesity, not the obese. *Science, 299,* 856–858.

Friedrich, William; Fisher, Jennifer; Broughton, Daniel; et al. (1998). Normative sexual behavior in children: A contemporary sample. *Pediatrics, 101,* 1–8. See also http://www.pediatrics.org/cgi/content/ full/101/4/e9.

Frome, Pamela M., & Eccles, Jacquelynne S. (1998). Parents' influence on children's achievement-related perceptions. *Journal of Personality and Social Psychology, 74,* 435–452.

Frye, Richard E.; Schwartz, B. S.; & Doty, Richard L. (1990). Dose-related effects of cigarette smoking on olfactory function. *Journal of the American Medical Association, 263,* 1233–1236.

Fuchs, C. S.; Stampfer, M. J.; Colditz, G. A.; et al. (1995, May 11). Alcohol consumption and mortality among women. *New England Journal of Medicine, 332,* 1245–1250.

Furedy, John J. (1996). The North American polygraph and psychophysiology: Disinterested, uninterested, and interested perspectives. *International Journal of Psychophysiology, 21,* 97–105.

Gable, Shelly L., & Haidt, Jonathan (2005). What (and why) is positive psychology? *Review of General Psychology, 9,* 103–110.

Gaertner, Samuel L.; Mann, Jeffrey A.; Dovidio, John F.; et al. (1990). How does cooperation reduce intergroup bias? *Journal of Personality and Social Psychology, 59,* 692–704.

Gage, Fred H.; Kempermann, G.; Palmer, T. D.; et al. (1998). Multipotent progenitor cells in the adult dentate gyrus. *Journal of Neurobiology, 36,* 249–266.

Gagnon, John, & Simon, William (1973). *Sexual conduct: The social sources of human sexuality.* Chicago: Aldine.

Galanter, Eugene (1962). Contemporary psychophysics. In R. Brown, E. Galanter, H. Hess, & G. Mandler (Eds.), *New directions in psychology.* New York: Holt, Rinehart and Winston.

Gallant, Jack L.; Braun, Jochen; & Van Essen, David C. (1993). Selectivity for polar, hyperbolic, and Cartesian gratings in macaque visual cortex. *Science, 259,* 100–103.

Gallant, Sheryle J.; Hamilton, Jean A.; Popiel, Debra A.; et al. (1991). Daily moods and symptoms: Effects of awareness of study focus, gender, menstrual-cycle phase, and day of the week. *Health Psychology, 10,* 180–189.

Gallo, Linda C., & Matthews, Karen A. (2003). Understanding the association between socioeconomic status and physical health: Do negative emotions play a role? *Psychological Bulletin, 129,* 10–51.

Galotti, Kathleen (1989). Approaches to studying formal and everyday reasoning. *Psychological Bulletin, 105,* 331–351.

Gao, Jia-Hong; Parsons, Lawrence M.; Bower, James M.; et al. (1996). Cerebellum implicated in sensory acquisition and discrimination rather than motor control. *Science, 272,* 545–547.

Garbarino, James, & Bedard, Claire (2001). *Parents under siege.* New York: The Free Press.

Garcia, John, & Gustavson, Carl R. (1997, January). Carl R. Gustavson (1946–1996): Pioneering wildlife psychologist. *APS Observer,* 34–35.

Garcia, John, & Koelling, Robert A. (1966). Relation of cue to consequence in avoidance learning. *Psychonomic Science, 4,* 23–124.

Gardner, Howard (1983). *Frames of mind: The theory of multiple intelligences.* New York: Basic Books.

Gardner, Howard (1995). Perennial antinomies and perpetual redrawings: Is there progress in the study of mind? In R. L. Solso & D. W. Massar (Eds.), *The science of the mind: 2001 and beyond.* New York: Oxford University Press.

Gardner, Martin (2006, January/February). The memory wars: Part I. *Skeptical Inquirer, 30,* 28–31.

Gardner, R. Allen, & Gardner, Beatrice T. (1969). Teaching sign language to a chimpanzee. *Science, 165,* 664–672.

Garmezy, Norman (1991). Resilience and vulnerability to adverse developmental outcomes associated with poverty. *American Behavioral Scientist, 34,* 416–430.

Garry, Maryanne, & Loftus, Elizabeth F. (2000). Imagination inflation is not a statistical artifact. Paper presented at the annual meeting of the American Psychological & Law Society, New Orleans.

Garry, Maryanne, & Loftus, Elizabeth F. (May/June, 2004). I am Freud's brain. *Skeptical Inquirer,* 16–18.

Garry, Maryanne; Manning, Charles G.; Loftus, Elizabeth F.; & Sherman, Steven J. (1996). Imagination inflation: Imagining a childhood event inflates confidence that it occurred. *Psychonomic Bulletin & Review, 3,* 208–214.

Garry, Maryanne, & Polaschek, Devon L. L. (2000). Imagination and memory. *Current Directions in Psychological Science, 9,* 6–10.

Garven, Sena; Wood, James M.; Malpass, Roy S.; & Shaw, John S., III (1998). More than suggestion: The effect of interviewing techniques from the McMartin Preschool case. *Journal of Applied Psychology, 83,* 347–359.

Gauthier, Irene; Skudlarksi, P.; Gore, J. C.; & Anderson, A. W. (2000). Expertise for cars and birds recruits brain areas involved in face recognition. *Nature Neuroscience, 3,* 191–197.

Gauthier, Irene; Tarr, M. J.; Anderson, A. W.; et al. (1999). Activation of the middle fusiform "face area" increases with expertise in recognizing novel objects. *Nature Neuroscience, 2,* 568–573.

Gauthier, Yvon (2003, May-June). Infant mental health as we enter the third millennium: Can we prevent aggression? *Infant Mental Health Journal, 243,* 296–308.

Gawande, Atul (1998, September 21). The pain perplex. *The New Yorker,* 86, 88, 90, 92–94.

Gazzaniga, Michael S. (1967). The split brain in man. *Scientific American, 217*(2), 24–29.

Gazzaniga, Michael S. (1983). Right hemisphere language following brain bisection: A 20-year perspective. *American Psychologist, 38,* 525–537.

Gazzaniga, Michael S. (1985). *The social brain: Discovering the networks of the mind.* New York: Basic Books.

Gazzaniga, Michael S. (1988). *Mind matters.* Boston: Houghton-Mifflin.

Gazzaniga, Michael S. (1998). *The mind's past.* Berkeley, CA: University of California Press.

Gazzaniga, Michael S. (2005). *The ethical brain.* Washington, DC: Dana Press.

Geary, David C. (1995). Reflections of evolution and culture in children's cognition: Implications for mathematical development and instruction. *American Psychologist, 50,* 24–37.

Geary, David C., & Huffman, Kelly J. (2002). Brain and cognitive evolution: Forms of modularity and the functions of mind. *Psychological Bulletin, 128,* 667–698.

Gelernter, David (1997, May 19). How hard is chess? *Time,* 72–73.

Gentner, Dedre, & Goldin-Meadow, Susan (Eds.) (2003). *Language in mind: Advances in the study of language and thought.* Cambridge: MIT Press.

Gershoff, Elizabeth T. (2002). Parental corporal punishment and associated child behaviors and experiences: A meta-analytic and theoretical review. *Psychological Bulletin, 128,* 539–579.

Gibson, Eleanor, & Walk, Richard (1960). The "visual cliff." *Scientific American, 202,* 80–92.

Gigerenzer, Gerd (2004). Dread risk, September 11, and fatal traffic accidents. *Psychological Science, 15,* 286–287.

Gilbert, Daniel (2006). *Stumbling on happiness.* New York: Knopf.

Gilbert, Daniel (2006, July 2). If only gay sex caused global warming. *Los Angeles Times,* Comment section, M1, M6.

Gilbert, Daniel T.; Lieberman, Matthew D.; Morewedge, Carey K.; & Wilson, Timothy D. (2004). The peculiar longevity of things not so bad. *Psychological Science, 15,* 14–19.

Gilbertson, Mark W.; Shenton, Martha E.; Ciszewski, Aleksandra; et al. (2002). Hippocampal volume predicts pathologic vulnerability to psychological trauma. *Nature Neuroscience, 5,* 1242–1247.

Gilmore, David D. (1990). *Manhood in the making: Cultural concepts of masculinity.* New Haven, CT: Yale University Press.

Gist, Richard, & Lubin, Bernard (Eds.) (1999). *Response to disaster: Psychosocial, community, and ecological approaches.* Philadelphia, PA: Brunner/Mazel (Taylor & Francis).

Gist, Richard; Lubin, Bernard; & Redburn, Bradley G. (1998). Psychosocial, ecological, and community perspectives on disaster response. *Journal of Personal and Interpersonal Loss, 3,* 25–51.

Gladue, Brian A. (1994). The biopsychology of sexual orientation. *Current Directions in Psychological Science, 3,* 150–154.

Gladwell, Malcolm (2004, September 20). Personality plus. *The New Yorker,* 42–48.

Glanzer, Murray, & Cunitz, Anita R. (1966). Two storage mechanisms in free recall. *Journal of Verbal Learning and Verbal Behavior, 5,* 351–360.

Gleaves, David H. (1996). The sociocognitive model of dissociative identity disorder: A reexamination of the evidence. *Psychological Bulletin, 120,* 42–59.

Glick, Peter; Fiske, Susan T.; Mladinic, Antonio; et al. (2000). Beyond prejudice as simple antipathy: Hostile and benevolent sexism across cultures. *Journal of Personality and Social Psychology, 79,* 763–775.

Glick, Peter; Lameiras, Maria; Fiske, Susan T.; et al. (2004). Bad but bold: Ambivalent attitudes toward men pedict gender inequality in 16 nations. *Journal of Personality and Social Psychology, 86,* 713–728.

Glick, Peter; Sakalli-Ugurlu, Nuray; Ferreira, Maria Cristina; & de Souza, Marcos Aguiar (2002). Ambivalent sexism and attitudes toward wife abuse in Turkey and Brazil. *Psychology of Women Quarterly, 26,* 292–297.

Gobodo-Madikizela, Pumla (1994). The notion of the "collective" in South African "political" murder cases: The "deindividuation" argument revisited. Paper presented to the biennial conference of the American Psychology and Law Society, Santa Fe, NM.

Gold, Paul E. (1987). Sweet memories. *American Scientist, 75,* 151–155.

Goldapple, Kimberly; Segal, Zindel; Garson Carol; et al. (2004). Modulation of cortical-limbic pathways in major depression: Treatment-specific effects of cognitive behavior therapy. *Archives of General Psychiatry, 61,* 34–41.

Golden, Robert M.; Gaynes, Bradley N.; Ekstrom, R. David; et al. (2005). The efficacy of light therapy in the treatment of mood disorders: A review and meta-analysis of the evidence. *American Journal of Psychiatry, 162,* 656–662.

Goldin-Meadow, Susan (2003). *The resilience of language.* New York: Psychology Press.

Goldman-Rakic, Patricia S. (1996). Opening the mind through neurobiology. Invited address at the annual meeting of the American Psychological Association, Toronto, Canada.

Goldstein, Alan J.; de Beurs, Edwin; Chambless, Dianne L.; & Wilson, Kimberly A. (2000). EMDR for panic disorder with agoraphobia: Comparison with waiting list and credible attention-placebo control conditions. *Journal of Consulting and Clinical Psychology, 68,* 947–956.

Goldstein, Eda G. (2002). *Object relations theory and self psychology in social work practice.* New York: Free Press.

Goldstein, Jill M.; Seidman, Larry J.; Horton, Nicholas J.; et al. (2001). Normal sexual dimorphism of the adult human brain assessed by in vivo magnetic resonance imaging. *Cerebral Cortex, 11,* 490–497.

Goldstein, Michael J. (1987). Psychosocial issues. *Schizophrenia Bulletin, 13*(1), 157–171.

Goldstein, Michael, & Miklowitz, David (1995). The effectiveness of psychoeducational family therapy in the treatment of schizophrenic disorders. *Journal of Marital and Family Therapy, 21,* 361–376.

Golinkoff, Roberta M., & Hirsh-Pasek, Kathy (2006). Baby wordsmith: From associationist to social sophisticate. *Current Directions in Psychological Science, 15,* 30–33.

Golombok, Susan, & Fivush, Robyn (1994). *Gender development.* New York: Cambridge University Press.

Golub, Sharon (1992). *Periods: From menarche to menopause.* Newbury Park, CA: Sage.

Gonzaga, Gian C.; Turner, Rebecca A.; Keltner, Dacher; et al. (2006). Romantic love and sexual desire in close relationships. *Emotion, 6,* 163-179.

Goode, Erica (2003, May 6). Experts see mind's voices in new light. *The New York Times,* Science Times, D1, D4.

Goode, Erica (2003, August 26). Studying modern-day Pavlov's dogs, of the human variety. *The New York Times,* F5.

Goodwin, Donald W.; Knop, Joachim; Jensen, Per; et al. (1994). Thirty-year follow-up of men at high risk for alcoholism. In T. F. Babor & V. M. Hesselbrock (Eds.), *Types of alcoholics: Evidence from clinical, experimental, and genetic research.* New York: New York Academy of Sciences.

Goodwin, Doris Kearns (2005). *Team of rivals: The political genius of Abraham Lincoln.* New York: Simon & Schuster.

Goodwin, P. J.; Leszcz, M.; Ennis, M.; et al. (2001, December 13). The effect of group psychosocial support on survival in metastatic breast cancer. *New England Journal of Medicine, 345,* 1719–1726.

Goodwyn, Susan, & Acredolo, Linda (1998). Encouraging symbolic gestures: A new perspective on the relationship between gesture and speech. In J. Iverson & S. Goldin-Meadow (Eds.), *The nature and functions of gesture in children's communication.* San Francisco: Jossey-Bass.

Gopnik, Alison; Meltzoff, Andrew N.; & Kuhl, Patricia K. (1999). *The scientist in the crib.* New York: Morrow.

Gopnik, Myrna, & Goad, Heather (1997). What underlies inflectional error patterns in genetic dysphasia? *Journal of Neurolinguistics, 10,* 109–137.

Gordon, Peter (2004). Numerical cognition without words: Evidence from Amazonia. *Science*, published online August 19, 2004; 10.1126/science.1094492.

Gorn, Gerald J. (1982). The effects of music in advertising on choice behavior: A classical conditioning approach. *Journal of Marketing, 46*, 94–101.

Gosling, Samuel D. (2001). From mice to men: What can we learn about personality from animal research? *Psychological Bulletin, 127*, 45–86.

Gosling, Samuel D., & John, Oliver P. (1999). Personality dimensions in nonhuman animals: A cross-species review. *Current Directions in Psychological Science, 8*, 69–75.

Gosling, Samuel D.; Kwan, Virginia S. Y.; & John, Oliver P. (2003). A dog's got personality: A cross-species comparative approach to personality judgments in dogs and humans. *Journal of Personality and Social Psychology, 85*, 1161–1169.

Gosling, Samual D.; Vazire, Simine; Srivatava, Sanjay; & John, Oliver P. (2004). Should we trust web-based studies? A comparative analysis of six preconceptions about Internet questionnaires. *American Psychologist, 59*, 93–104.

Gottesman, Irving I. (1991). *Schizophrenia genesis: The origins of madness.* New York: Freeman.

Gottfredson, Linda S. (2002). g: Highly general and highly practical. In R. J. Sternberg & E. L. Grigorenko (Eds.), *The general intelligence factor: How general is it?* Mahwah, NJ: Erlbaum.

Gottfried, Jay A.; O'Doherty, John; & Dolan, Raymond J. (2003). Encoding predictive reward value in human amygdala and orbitofrontal cortex. *Science, 301*, 1104–1107.

Gougoux, Frederic; Zatorre, Robert J.; Lassonde, Maryse; et al. (2005). A functional neuroimaging study of sound localization: Visual cortex activity predicts performance in early-blind individuals. *PloS Biology, 3*, 324–333.

Gould, Elizabeth; Beylin, A; Tanapat, Patima; et al. (1999). Learning enhances adult neurogenesis in the hippocampal formation. *Nature Neuroscience, 2*, 260–265.

Gould, Elizabeth; Reeves, Alison J.; Graziano, Michael S. A.; & Gross, Charles G. (1999). Neurogenesis in the neocortex of adult primates. *Science, 286*, 548–552.

Gould, Elizabeth; Tanapat, Patima; McEwen, Bruce S.; et al. (1998). Proliferation of granule cell precursors in the dentate gyrus of adult monkeys is diminished by stress. *Proceedings of the National Academy of Science, 95*, 3168–3171.

Gould, Stephen Jay (1987). *An urchin in the storm.* New York: W. W. Norton.

Gould, Stephen Jay (1994, November 28). Curveball. [Review of *The Bell Curve*, by Richard J. Herrnstein and Charles Murray.] *New Yorker*, 139–149.

Gould, Stephen Jay (1996). *The mismeasure of man* (Rev. ed.). New York: Norton.

Gourevich, Philip (1998). *We wish to inform you that tomorrow we will be killed with our families: Stories from Rwanda.* New York: Farrar, Straus & Giroux.

Grabe, Shelly, & Hyde, Janet S. (2006). Ethnicity and body dissatisfaction among women in the United States: A meta-analysis. *Psychological Bulletin, 132*, 622–640.

Graf, Peter, & Schacter, Daniel A. (1985). Implicit and explicit memory for new associations in normal and amnesic subjects. *Journal of Experimental Psychology: Learning, Memory, and Cognition, 11*, 501–518.

Graham, Jill W. (1986). Principled organizational dissent: A theoretical essay. *Research in Organizational Behavior, 8*, 1–52.

Grahe, Jon E., & Bernieri, Frank J. (1999). The importance of nonverbal cues in judging rapport. *Journal of Nonverbal Behavior, 23*, 253–269.

Grant, Heidi, & Dweck, Carol S. (2003). Clarifying achievement goals and their impact. *Journal of Personality and Social Psychology, 85*, 541–553.

Grant, Igor; Gonzalez, Raul; Carey, Catherine L.; et al. (2003). Non-acute (residual) neurocognitive effects of cannabis use: A meta-analytic study. *Journal of the International Neuropsychological Society, 9*, 679–689.

Gray, Jeremy R. (2004). Integration of emotion and cognitive control. *Current Directions in Psychological Science, 13*, 46–49.

Green, Gina (1996a). Behavioral treatment of autistic persons: A review of research from 1980 to the present. *Research in Developmental Disabilities, 17*, 433–465.

Green, Gina (1996b). Early behavioral intervention for autism: What does research tell us? In C. Maurice, G. Green, & S. C. Luce (Eds.), *Behavioral Intervention for Young Children with Autism.* Austin, TX: PRO-ED.

Greenberger, Dennis, & Padesky, Christine A. (1995). *Mind over mood: A cognitive therapy treatment manual for clients.* New York: Guilford.

Greenough, William T. (1984). Structural correlates of information storage in the mammalian brain: A review and hypothesis. *Trends in Neurosciences, 7*, 229–233.

Greenough, William T., & Anderson, Brenda J. (1991). Cerebellar synaptic plasticity: Relation to learning vs. neural activity. *Annals of the New York Academy of Sciences, 627*, 231–247.

Greenough, William T., & Black, James E. (1992). Induction of brain structure by experience: Substrates for cognitive development. In M. Gunnar & C. A. Nelson (Eds.), *Behavioral developmental neuroscience: Vol. 24. Minnesota Symposia on Child Psychology.* Hillsdale, NJ: Erlbaum.

Greenwald, Anthony G.; McGhee, Debbie E.; & Schwartz, Jordan L. K. (1998). Measuring individual differences in implicit cognition: The Implicit Association Test. *Journal of Personality and Social Psychology, 74*, 1464–1480.

Greenwald, Anthony G.; Spangenberg, Eric R.; Pratkanis, Anthony R.; & Eskenazi, Jay (1991). Double-blind tests of subliminal self-help audiotapes. *Psychological Science, 2*, 119–122.

Gregory, Richard L. (1963). Distortion of visual space as inappropriate constancy scaling. *Nature, 199*, 678–679.

Grewen, Karen M.; Girdler, Susan S.; Amico, Janet; & Light, Kathleen C. (2005). Effects of partner support on resting oxytocin, cortisol, norepinephrine, and blood pressure before and after warm partner contact. *Psychosomatic Medicine, 67*, 531–538.

Griffin, Donald R. (1992). *Animal minds.* Chicago: University of Chicago Press.

Griffin, Donald R. (2001). *Animal minds: Beyond cognition to consciousness.* Chicago: University of Chicago Press.

Grinspoon, Lester, & Bakalar, James B. (1993). *Marihuana, the forbidden medicine.* New Haven, CT: Yale University Press.

Groneman, Carol (2000). *Nymphomania: A history.* New York: Norton.

Gross, James J. (1998). The emerging field of emotion regulation: An integrative review. *Review of General Psychology, 2*, 271–299.

Gross, James J. (2001). Emotion regulation in adulthood: Timing is everything. *Current Directions in Psychological Science, 10*, 214–219.

Gross, James J., & John, Oliver, P. (2003). Individual differences in two emotion regulation processes: Implications for affect, relationships, and well-being. *Journal of Personality and Social Psychology, 85*, 348–362.

Grossman, Michele, & Wood, Wendy (1993). Sex differences in intensity of emotional experience: A social role interpretation. *Journal of Personality and Social Psychology, 65*, 1010–1022.

Groves, James E. (Ed.) (1996). *Essential papers on short-term dynamic therapy.* New York: New York University Press.

Guan, Kaomei; Nayernia, Karim; Maier, Lars S.; et al. (2006). Pluripotency of spermatogonial stem cells from adult mice testes. *Nature, 440*, 1199–1203. [Letter]

Guilford, J. P. (1988). Some changes in the structure-of-intellect model. *Educational and Psychological Measurement, 48,* 1–4.

Gur, Ruben C.; Gunning-Dixon, Faith; Bilker, Wareen B.; & Gur, Raquel E. (2002). Sex differences in temporo-limbic and frontal brain volumes of healthy adults. *Cerebral Cortex, 12,* 998–1003.

Gur, R. E.; Maany, V.; Mozley, P. D.; et al. (1998). Subcortical MRI volumes in neuroleptic-naive and treated patients with schizophrenia. *American Journal of Psychiatry, 155,* 1711–1717.

Guralnick, M. J. (Ed.) (1997). *The effectiveness of early intervention.* Baltimore: Brookes.

Gustavson, Carl R.; Garcia, John; Hankins, Walter G.; & Rusiniak, Kenneth W. (1974). Coyote predation control by aversive conditioning. *Science, 184,* 581–583.

Gustavson, Carl R.; Kelly, Daniel J.; Sweeney, Michael; & Garcia, John (1976). Pre-lithium aversions I: Coyotes and wolves. *Behavioral Biology, 17,* 61–72.

Guterman, Lila (2004, June 25). Gray matters. *The Chronicle of Higher Education,* A22–A24.

Guthrie, Paul C., & Mobley, Brenda D. (1994). A comparison of the differential diagnostic efficiency of three personality disorder inventories. *Journal of Clinical Psychology, 50,* 656–665.

Guthrie, Robert (1976). *Even the rat was white: A historical view of psychology.* New York: Harper & Row.

Guttentag, Marcia, & Secord, Paul (1983). *Too many women?* Beverly Hills, CA: Sage.

Guzman-Marin, Ruben; Suntsova, Natalia; Methippara, Melvi; et al. (2005). Sleep deprivation suppresses neurogenesis in the adult hippocampus of rats. *European Journal of Neuroscience, 22,* 2111–2116.

Haber, Ralph N. (1970, May). How we remember what we see. *Scientific American, 222,* 104–112.

Hacking, Ian (1995). *Rewriting the soul: Multiple personality and the sciences of memory.* Princeton: Princeton University Press.

Haimov, I., & Lavie, P. (1996). Melatonin—A soporific hormone. *Current Directions in Psychological Science, 5,* 106–111.

Hall, Calvin (1953a). A cognitive theory of dreams. *Journal of General Psychology, 49,* 273–282.

Hall, Calvin (1953b). *The meaning of dreams.* New York: McGraw-Hill.

Hall, Edward T. (1959). *The silent language.* Garden City, NY: Doubleday.

Hall, Edward T. (1976). *Beyond culture.* New York: Anchor.

Hall, Edward T. (1983). *The dance of life: The other dimension of time.* Garden City, NY: Anchor Press/Doubleday.

Hall, Edward T., & Hall, Mildred R. (1987). *Hidden differences: Doing business with the Japanese.* Garden City, NY: Anchor Press/Doubleday.

Hall, Edward T., & Hall, Mildred R. (1990). *Understanding cultural differences.* Yarmouth, ME: Intercultural Press.

Hall, G. Stanley (1899). A study of anger. *American Journal of Psychology, 10,* 516–591.

Hall, Nathan C.; Perry, Raymond P.; Ruthig, Joelle C.; et al. (2006). Primary and secondary control in achievement settings: A longitudinal field study of academic motivation, emotions, and performance. *Journal of Applied Social Psychology, 36,* 1430–1470.

Halliday, G. (1993). Examination dreams. *Perceptual and Motor Skills, 77,* 489–490.

Halpern, Diane (2002). *Thought and knowledge: An introduction to critical thinking* (4th ed.). Hillsdale, NJ: Erlbaum.

Hamby, Sherry L., & Koss, Mary P. (2003). Shades of gray: A qualitative study of terms used in the measurement of sexual victimization. *Psychology of Women Quarterly, 27,* 243–255.

Hancox, Robert J.; Milne, Barry J.; & Poulton, Richie (2005). Association of television viewing during childhood with poor educational achievement. *Archives of Pediatric and Adolescent Medicine, 259,* 614–618.

Haney, Craig; Banks, Curtis; & Zimbardo, Philip (1973). Interpersonal dynamics in a simulated prison. *International Journal of Criminology and Penology, 1,* 69–97.

Haney, Craig, & Zimbardo, Philip (1998). The past and future of U.S. prison policy: Twenty-five years after the Stanford Prison Experiment. *American Psychologist, 53,* 709–727.

Hankin, Benjamin L., & Abramson, Lyn Y. (2001). Development of gender differences in depression. An elaborated cognitive vulnerability-transactional stress theory. *Psychological Bulletin, 127,* 773–796.

Hardie, Elizabeth A. (1997). PMS in the workplace: Dispelling the myth of cyclic function. *Journal of Occupational and Organizational Psychology, 70,* 97–102.

Harding, Courtenay M.; Zubin, Joseph; & Strauss, John S. (1992). Chronicity in schizophrenia: Revisited. *British Journal of Psychiatry, 161*(Suppl. 18), 27–37.

Hare, Robert D. (1965). Temporal gradient of fear arousal in psychopaths. *Journal of Abnormal Psychology, 70,* 442–445.

Hare, Robert D. (1993). *Without conscience: The disturbing world of the psychopaths among us.* New York: Pocket Books.

Hare, Robert D. (1996). Psychopathy: A clinical construct whose time has come. *Criminal Justice and Behavior, 23,* 24–54.

Hare, Robert D.; Hart, Stephen D.; & Harpur, Timothy J. (1991). Psychopathy and the DSM-IV criteria for antisocial personality disorder. *Journal of Abnormal Psychology, 100,* 391–398.

Haritos-Fatouros, Mika (1988). The official torturer: A learning model for obedience to the authority of violence. *Journal of Applied Social Psychology, 18,* 1107–1120.

Harkins, Stephen G., & Szymanski, Kate (1989). Social loafing and group evaluation. *Journal of Personality and Social Psychology, 56,* 934–941.

Harlow, Harry F. (1958). The nature of love. *American Psychologist, 13,* 673–685.

Harlow, Harry F., & Harlow, Margaret K. (1966). Learning to love. *American Scientist, 54,* 244–272.

Harlow, Harry F.; Harlow, Margaret K.; & Meyer, D. R. (1950). Learning motivated by a manipulation drive. *Journal of Experimental Psychology, 40,* 228–234.

Harmon-Jones, Eddie, & Sigelman, Jonathan (2001). State anger and prefrontal brain activity: Evidence that insult-related relative left-prefrontal activation is associated with experienced anger and aggression. *Journal of Personality and Social Psychology, 80,* 797–803.

Harmon-Jones, Eddie; Abramson, Lyn Y.; Sigelman, Jonathan; et al. (2002). Proneness to hypomania/mania symptoms or depression symptoms and asymmetrical frontal cortical responses to an anger-evoking event. *Journal of Personality and Social Psychology, 82,* 610–618.

Harris, Christine (2003). Factors associated with jealousy over real and imagined infidelity: An examination of the social-cognitive and evolutionary psychology perspectives. *Psychology of Women Quarterly, 27,* 319–329.

Harris, Gardiner (2003, August 7). Debate resumes on the safety of depression's wonder drugs. *The New York Times,* A1, C4.

Harris, Judith R. (1998). *The nurture assumption.* New York: The Free Press.

Harris, Judith R. (2006). *No two alike: Human nature and human individuality.* New York: Norton.

Harris, Lasana T., & Fiske, Susan T. (2006). Dehumanizing the lowest of the low: Neuro-imaging responses to extreme outgroups. *Psychological Science,* in press.

Harris, Lasana T.; Todorov, Alexander; & Fiske, Susan T. (2005). Attributions on the brain: Neuro-imaging dispositional inferences, beyond theory of mind. *NeuroImage, 28*, 763–769.

Hart, A. J.; Whalen, P. J.; Shin, L. M.; et al. (2000). Differential response in the human amygdala to racial outgroup vs. ingroup face stimuli. *NeuroReport, 11*, 2351–2355.

Hart, Jason W.; Bridgett, David J.; Karau, Steven J. (2001). Coworker ability and effort as determinants of individual effort on a collective task. *Group Dynamics, 5*, 181–190.

Hart, John, Jr.; Berndt, Rita S.; & Caramazza, Alfonso (1985, August 1). Category-specific naming deficit following cerebral infarction. *Nature, 316*, 339–340.

Hartup, William (1999). Peer experience and its developmental significance. In M. Bennett (Ed.), *Developmental Psychology: Achievements and prospects.* Philadelphia, PA: Psychology Press.

Haslam, S. Alexander, & Reicher, Stephen (2003, Spring). Beyond Stanford: Questioning a role-based explanation of tyranny. *Society for Experimental Social Psychology Dialogue, 18*, 22–25.

Hatfield, Elaine, & Rapson, Richard L. (1996). *Love and sex: Cross-cultural perspectives.* Boston: Allyn & Bacon.

Hauser, Marc (2000). *Wild minds: What animals really think.* New York: Holt.

Haut, Jennifer S.; Beckwith, Bill E.; Petros, Thomas V.; & Russell, Sue (1989). Gender differences in retrieval from long-term memory following acute intoxication with ethanol. *Physiology and Behavior, 45*, 1161–1165.

Hawkins, Elizabeth H.; Cummins, Lillian H.; & Marlatt, G. Alan (2004). Preventing substance abuse in American Indian and Alaska Native Youth: Promising strategies for healthier communities. *Psychological Bulletin, 130*, 304–323.

Hawkins, Scott A., & Hastie, Reid (1990). Hindsight: Biased judgments of past events after the outcomes are known. *Psychological Bulletin, 107*, 311–327.

Hawkley, Louise C.; Burleson, Mary H.; Berntson, Gary G.; & Cacioppo, John T. (2003). Loneliness in everyday life: Cardiovascular activity, psychosocial context, and health behaviors. *Journal of Personality and Social Psychology, 85*, 105–120.

Hayes, Steven C. (2004). Acceptance and commitment therapy and the new behavior therapies: Mindfulness, acceptance, and relaitonship. In S. C. Hayes, V. M. Follette, & M. M. Linehan (2004). *Mindfulness and acceptance: Expanding the cognitive-behavioral tradition.* New York: Guilford.

Hayman, Ronald (2001). *A life of Jung.* New York: W. W. Norton.

Hazan, Cindy, & Diamond, Lisa M. (2000). The place of attachment in human mating. *Review of General Psychology, 4*, 186–204.

Hazan, Cindy, & Shaver, Phillip R. (1994). Attachment as an organizational framework for research on close relationships. *Psychological Inquiry, 5*, 1–22.

Healy, David (2002). *The creation of psychopharmacology.* Cambridge, MA: Harvard University Press.

Healy, David (2004). *Let them eat Prozac.* New York: New York University Press.

Heath, A. C.; Madden, P. A. F.; Bucholz, K. K.; et al. (2003). Genetic and genotype x environment interaction effects on risk of dependence on alcohol, tobacco, and other drugs: new research. In R. Plomin et al. (Eds.), *Behavioral genetics in the postgenomic era.* Washington, DC: APA Books.

Hébert, Richard (September, 2001). Code overload: Doing a number on memory. *APS Observer, 14*, 1, 7–11.

Heinrichs, R. Walter (2005). The primacy of cognition in schizophrenia. *American Psychologist, 60*, 229–242.

Heller, Wendy; Nitschke, Jack B.; Miller, Gregory A. (1998). Lateralization in emotion and emotional disorders. *Current Directions in Psychological Science, 7*, 26–32.

Helmreich, William (1992). *Against all odds: Holocaust survivors and the successful lives they led.* New York: Simon & Schuster.

Helson, Ravenna; Roberts, Brent; & Agronick, Gail (1995). Enduringness and change in creative personality and the prediction of occupational creativity. *Journal of Personality and Social Psychology, 6*, 1173–1183.

Henderlong, Jennifer, & Lepper, Mark (2002). The effects of praise on children's intrinsic motivation: A review and synthesis. *Psychological Bulletin, 128*, 774–795.

Hendrix, William H.; Steel, Robert P.; Leap, Terry L.; & Summers, Timothy P. (1991). Development of a stress-related health promotion model: Antecedents and organizational effectiveness outcomes. *Journal of Social Behavior and Personality, 6*, 141–162.

Henggeler, Scott W.; Schoenwald, Sonya K.; Borduin, Charles M.; et al. (1998). *Multisystemic treatment of antisocial behavior in children and adolescents.* New York: Guilford Press.

Henrich, Joseph; Boyd, Robert; Bowles, Samuel; et al. (2001). In search of Homo Economicus: Behavioral experiments in 15 small scale societies. *American Economics Review, 91*, 73–78.

Herbert, Alan; Gerry, Norman P.; McQueen, Matthew B.; et al. (2006, April 14). A common genetic variant is associated with adult and childhood obesity. *Science, 312*, 279–283.

Herdt, Gilbert (1984). *Ritualized homosexuality in Melanesia.* Berkeley: University of California Press.

Herek, Gregory M., & Capitanio, J. P. (1996). "Some of my best friends": Intergroup contact, concealable stigma, and heterosexuals' attitudes toward gay men and lesbians. *Personality and Social Psychology Bulletin, 22*, 412–424.

Herman, John H. (1992). Transmutative and reproductive properties of dreams: Evidence for cortical modulation of brainstem generators. In J. Antrobus & M. Bertini (Eds.), *The neuropsychology of dreaming.* Hillsdale, NJ: Erlbaum.

Herman, Judith (1992). *Trauma and recovery.* New York: Basic Books.

Herman, Louis M. (1987). Receptive competencies of language-trained animals. In J. S. Rosenblatt, C. Beer, M. C. Busnel, & P. J. B. Slater (Eds.), *Advances in the study of behavior* (Vol. 17). Petaluma, CA: Academic Press.

Herman, Louis M.; Kuczaj, Stan A.; & Holder, Mark D. (1993). Responses to anomalous gestural sequences by a language-trained dolphin: Evidence for processing of semantic relations and syntactic information. *Journal of Experimental Psychology: General, 122*, 184–194.

Herman, Louis M., & Morrel-Samuels, Palmer (1996). Knowledge acquisition and asymmetry between language comprehension and production: Dolphins and apes as general models for animals. In M. Bekoff & D. Jamieson et al. (Eds.), *Readings in animal cognition.* Cambridge, MA: MIT Press.

Heron, Woodburn (1957). The pathology of boredom. *Scientific American, 196*(1), 52–56.

Herrnstein, Richard J., & Murray, Charles (1994). *The bell curve: Intelligence and class structure in American life.* New York: Free Press.

Herz, Rachel S., & Cupchik, Gerald C. (1995). The emotional distinctiveness of odor-evoked memories. *Chemical Senses, 20*, 517–528.

Hess, Thomas M. (2005). Memory and aging in context. *Psychological Bulletin, 131*, 383–406

Hess, Ursula; Adams, Reginald B., Jr.; & Kleck, Robert (2004). Facial appearance, gender, and emotion expression. *Emotion, 4*, 378–388.

Hess, Ursula; Adams, Reginald B., Jr.; & Kleck, Robert (2005). Who may frown and who should smile? Dominance, affiliation, and the display of happiness and anger. *Cognition and Emotion, 19*, 515–536.

Higgins, E. Tory (1998). Promotion and prevention: Regulatory focus as a motivational principle. *Advances in Experimental Social Psychology, 30*, 1–46.

Hilgard, Ernest R. (1977). *Divided consciousness: Multiple controls in human thought and action.* New York: Wiley-Interscience.

Hilgard, Ernest R. (1986). *Divided consciousness: Multiple controls in human thought and action* (2nd ed.). New York: Wiley.

Hilts, Philip J. (1995). *Memory's ghost: The strange tale of Mr. M. and the nature of memory.* New York: Simon & Schuster.

Hines, Terence M. (1998). Comprehensive review of biorhythm theory. *Psychological Reports, 83*, 19–64.

Hirsch, Helmut V. B., & Spinelli, D. N. (1970). Visual experience modifies distribution of horizontally and vertically oriented receptive fields in cats. *Science, 168*, 869–871.

Hirst, William; Neisser, Ulric; & Spelke, Elizabeth (1978, January). Divided attention. *Human Nature, 1*, 54–61.

Hobson, J. Allan (1988). *The dreaming brain.* New York: Basic Books.

Hobson, J. Allan (1990). Activation, input source, and modulation: A neurocognitive model of the state of the brain mind. In R. R. Bootzin, J. F. Kihlstrom, & D. L. Schacter (Eds.), *Sleep and cognition.* Washington, DC: American Psychological Association.

Hobson, J. Allan (2002). *Dreaming: An introduction to the science of sleep.* New York: Oxford University Press.

Hobson, J. Allan; Pace-Schott, Edward F.; & Stickgold, Robert (2000). Dreaming and the brain: Toward a cognitive neuroscience of consicous states. *Behavioral and Brain Sciences, 23*, 793–842, 904–1018, 1083–1121.

Hochschild, Arlie (1983). *The managed heart.* Berkeley: University of California Press.

Hodges, Ernest V. E., & Perry, David G. (1999). Personal and interpersonal antecedents and consequences of victimization by peers. *Journal of Personality and Social Psychology, 76*, 677–685.

Hoekstra, Hopi E.; Hirschmann, Rachel J.; & Bundey, Richard A.; et al. (2006). A single amino acid mutation contributes to adaptive color pattern in beach mice. *Science 313*, 101-104.

Hofferth, Sandra L., & Sandberg, John F. (2000). *Changes in America's children's time, 1981–1987.* Report No. 00-456, Population Studies Center at the Institute for Social Research. Ann Arbor: University of Michigan.

Hoffmann, Diane E., & Rothenberg, Karen H. (2005). When should judges admit or compel genetic tests? *Science, 310*, 241–242.

Hoffman, Martin L. (1994). Discipline and internalization. *Developmental Psychology, 30*, 26–28.

Hoffrage, Ulrich; Hertwig, Ralph; & Gigerenzer, Gerd (2000). Hindsight bias: A by-product of knowledge updating? *Journal of Experimental Psychology: Learning, Memory, & Cognition, 26*, 566–581.

Hofstede, Geert, & Bond, Michael H. (1988). The Confucius connection: From cultural roots to economic growth. *Organizational Dynamics*, 5–21.

Holden, Constance (1997). Thumbs up for acupuncture. [News report.] *Science, 278*, 1231.

Holden, George W., & Miller, Pamela C. (1999). Enduring and different: A meta-analysis of the similarity in parents' child rearing. *Psychological Bulletin, 125*, 223–254.

Holland, Rob W.; Hendriks, Merel; & Aarts, Henk (2005). Smells like clean spirit: Nonconscious effects of scent on cognition and behavior. *Psychological Science, 16*, 689–693.

Hollon, Steven D.; Thase, Michael E.; & Markowitz, John C. (2002). Treatment and prevention of depression. *Psychological Science in the Public Interest, 3*, 39–77.

Hooker, Evelyn (1957). The adjustment of the male overt homosexual. *Journal of Projective Techniques, 21*, 18–31.

Horgan, John (1995, November). Get smart, take a test: A long-term rise in IQ scores baffles intelligence experts. *Scientific American, 273*, 12,14.

Horney, Karen (1926/1973). The flight from womanhood. *The International Journal of Psycho-Analysis*, 7, 324–339. Reprinted in J. B. Miller (Ed.), *Psychoanalysis and women.* New York: Brunner/Mazel, 1973.

Hotz, Robert Lee (2000, November 29). Women use more of brain when listening, study says. *Los Angeles Times*, A1, A18–19.

House, James S.; Landis, Karl R.; & Umberson, Debra (1988, July 19). Social relationships and health. *Science, 241*, 540–545.

Houston, Derek M., & Jusczyk, Peter W. (2003). Infants' long-term memory for the sound patterns of words and voices. *Journal of Experimental Psychology: Human Perception & Performance, 29*, 1143–1154.

Houts, Arthur C. (2002). Discovery, invention, and the expansion of the modern Diagnostic and Statistical Manuals of Mental Disorders. In L. E. Beutler & M. L. Malik (Eds.), *Rethinking the DSM: A psychological perspective.* Washington, DC: American Psychological Association.

Howard, George S. (1991). Culture tales: A narrative approach to thinking, cross-cultural psychology, and psychotherapy. *American Psychologist, 46*, 187–197.

Howe, Mark L., & Courage, Mary L. (1993). On resolving the enigma of infantile amnesia. *Psychological Bulletin, 113*, 305–326.

Howe, Mark L.; Courage, Mary L.; & Peterson, Carole (1994). How can I remember when "I" wasn't there? Long-term retention of traumatic experiences and emergence of the cognitive self. *Consciousness and Cognition, 3*, 327–355.

Howe, Neil, & Strauss, William (2003). *Millennials go to college.* American Association of Collegiate Registrars and Admissions Officers, and LifeCourse Associates, available at http://www.aacrao.org.

Hrdy, Sarah B. (1988). Empathy, polyandry, and the myth of the coy female. In R. Bleier (Ed.), *Feminist approaches to science.* New York: Pergamon.

Hrdy, Sarah B. (1994). What do women want? In T. A. Bass (Ed.), *Reinventing the future: Conversations with the world's leading scientists.* Reading, MA: Addison-Wesley.

Hrdy, Sarah B. (1999). *Mother nature.* New York: Pantheon.

Huang, L.; Shanker, Y. G.; Dubauskaite, J.; et al. (1999). Ggamma13 colocalizes with gustducin in taste receptor cells and mediates IP3 responses to bitter denatonium. *Nature Neuroscience, 2*, 1055–1062.

Hubel, David H., & Wiesel, Torsten N. (1962). Receptive fields, binocular interaction and functional architecture in the cat's visual cortex. *Journal of Physiology (London), 160*, 106–154.

Hubel, David H., & Wiesel, Torsten N. (1968). Receptive fields and functional architecture of monkey striate cortex. *Journal of Physiology (London), 195*, 215–243.

Hudson, Valerie M., & den Boer, Andrea M. (2004). *Bare branches: The security implications of Asia's surplus male population.* Cambridge, MA: MIT Press.

Huggins, Martha K.; Haritos-Fatouros, Mika; & Zimbardo, Philip G. (2003). *Violence workers: Police torturers and murderers reconstruct Brazilian atrocities.* Berkeley, CA: University of California Press.

Huizink, Anja C.; Mulder, Edu J. H.; & Buitelaar, Jan K. (2004). Prenatal stress and risk for psychopathology: Specific effects or induction of general susceptibility. *Psychological Bulletin, 130*, 115–142.

Hulbert, Ann (2003). *Raising America: Experts, parents and a century of advice about children.* New York: Knopf.

Hultsch, David F.; Hertzog, Christopher; Small, Brent J.; & Dixon, Roger A. (1999). Use it or lose it: Engaged lifestyle as a buffer of cognitive decline in aging? *Psychology and Aging, 14*, 245–263.

Hunsley, John; Lee, Catherine M.; & Wood, James (2003). Controversial and questionable assessment techniques. In S. O. Lilienfeld, S. J. Lynn, & J. M. Lohn (Eds.), *Science and pseudoscience in clinical psychology.* New York: Guilford.

Hunt, Morton M. (1959/1967). *The natural history of love.* New York: Minerva Press.

Hunter, John E. (1997). Needed: A ban on the significance test. *Psychological Science, 8,* 3–7.

Hupka, Ralph B. (1981). Cultural determinants of jealousy. *Alternative Lifestyles, 4,* 310–356.

Hupka, Ralph B. (1991). The motive for the arousal of romantic jealousy. In P. Salovey (Ed.), *The psychology of jealousy and envy.* New York: Guilford Press.

Hupka, Ralph B.; Lenton, Alison P.; & Hutchison, Keith A. (1999). Universal development of emotion categories in natural language. *Journal of Personality and Social Psychology, 77,* 247–278.

Hur, Yoon-Mi; Bouchard, Thomas J., Jr.; & Lykken, David T. (1998). Genetic and environmental influence on morningness-eveningness. *Personality and Individual Differences, 25,* 917–925.

Hyde, Janet S. (2005). The gender similarities hypothesis. *American Psychologist, 60,* 581–592.

Hyman, Ira E., Jr., & Pentland, Joel (1996). The role of mental imagery in the creation of false childhood memories. *Journal of Memory and Language, 35,* 101–117.

Iacoboni, Marco; Molnar-Szakacs, Istvan; Gallese, Vittorio; et al. (2005). Grasping the intentions of others with one's own mirror neuron system. *Public Library of Science: Biology 3*(3): e79. DOI: 10.1371/journal.pbio.003079.

Ikonomidou, Chrysanthy; Bittigau, Petra; Ishimaru, Masahiko J.; et al. (2000, February 11). Ethanol-induced apoptotic neurodegeneration and fetal alcohol syndrome. *Science, 287,* 1056–1060.

Illes, Judy; Kirschen, Matthew P.; & Gabrieli, John D. E. (2003) From neuroimaging to neuroethics. *Nature Neuroscience 6*(3):250.

Impett, Emily A.; Gable, Shelly; & Peplau, Letitia A. (2005). Giving up and giving in: The costs and benefits of daily sacrifice in intimate relationships. *Journal of Personality and Social Psychology, 89,* 327–344.

Impett, Emily A.; Peplau, Letitia A.; & Gable, Shelly (2005). Approach and avoidance sexual motives: Implications for personal and interpersonal well-being. *Personal Relationships, 12,* 465–482.

Inglehart, Ronald (1990). *Culture shift in advanced industrial society.* Princeton, NJ: Princeton University Press.

International Consensus Conference (2002, June). *Female Androgen Deficiency Syndrome: Definition, Diagnosis, and Classification: International Consensus Conference, Princeton, NY.* http://www.medscape.com/ viewprogram/302

Inzlicht, Michael, & Ben-Zeev, Talia (2000). A threatening intellectual environment: Why females are susceptible to experiencing problem-solving deficits in the presence of males. *Psychological Science, 11,* 365–371.

Irvine, Janice M. (1990). *Disorders of desire: Sex and gender in modern American sexology.* Philadelphia: Temple University Press.

Islam, Mir Rabiul, & Hewstone, Miles (1993). Intergroup attributions and affective consequences in majority and minority groups. *Journal of Personality and Social Psychology, 64,* 936–950.

Ito, Tiffany A., & Urland, Geoffrey R. (2003). Race and gender on the brain: Electrocortical measures of attention to the race and gender of multiply categorizable individuals. *Journal of Personality and Social Psychology, 85,* 616–626.

Izard, Carroll E. (1990). Facial expressions and the regulation of emotions. *Journal of Personality and Social Psychology, 58,* 487–498.

Izard, Carroll E. (1994a). Four systems for emotion activation: Cognitive and noncognitive processes. *Psychological Review, 100,* 68–90.

Izard, Carroll E. (1994b). Innate and universal facial expressions: Evidence from developmental and cross-cultural research. *Psychological Bulletin, 115,* 288–299.

Izumikawa, Masahiko; Minoda, Ryosei; Kawamoto, Karen A.; et al. (2005). Auditory hair cell replacement and hearing improvement by *Atoh1* gene therapy in deaf mammals. *Nature Medicine, 11,* 271–276.

Jackson, Daren C.; Mueller, Corrina J.; Dolski, Isa; Dalton, Kim M.; Nitschke, Jack B.; et al. (2003). Now you feel it, now you don't: Frontal brain electrical asymmetry and individual differences in emotion regulation. *Psychological Science, 14,* 612–617.

Jacobs, Gregg D.; Pace-Schott, Edward F.; Stickgold, Robert; & Otto, Michael W. (2004). Cognitive behavior therapy and pharmacotherapy for chronic insomnia: A randomized controlled trial and direct comparison. *Archives of Internal Medicine, 164,* 1888–1896.

Jacobsen, Paul B; Bovbjerg, Dana H.; Schwartz, Marc D.; et al. (1995). Conditioned emotional distress in women receiving chemotherapy for breast cancer. *Journal of Consulting & Clinical Psychology, 63,* 108–114.

Jaffe, Eric (2005). How random is that? Students are convenient research subjects but they're not a simple sample. *APS Observer, 18,* 19–30.

James, William (1890/1950). *Principles of psychology* (Vol. 1). New York: Dover.

James, William (1902/1936). *The varieties of religious experience.* New York: Modern Library.

Jamison, Kay (1992). *Touched with fire: Manic depressive illness and the artistic temperament.* New York: Free Press.

Jamison, Kay (1999). *Night falls fast: Understanding suicide.* New York: Knopf.

Jancke, Lutz; Schlaug, Gottfried; & Steinmetz, Helmuth (1997). Hand skill asymmetry in professional musicians. *Brain and Cognition, 34,* 424–432.

Jang, Kerry L.; McCrae, Robert R.; Angleitner, Alois; et al. (1998). Heritability of facet-level traits in a cross-cultural twin sample: Support for a hierarchical model of personality. *Journal of Personality and Social Psychology, 74,* 1556–1565.

Janis, Irving L. (1982). *Groupthink: Psychological studies of policy decisions and fiascoes* (2nd ed.). Boston: Houghton-Mifflin.

Janis, Irving L. (1989). *Crucial decisions: Leadership in policymaking and crisis management.* New York: Free Press.

Janis, Irving L.; Kaye, Donald; & Kirschner, Paul (1965). Facilitating effects of "eating-while-reading" on responsiveness to persuasive communications. *Journal of Personality and Social Psychology, 1,* 181–186.

Jenkins, John G., & Dallenbach, Karl M. (1924). Obliviscence during sleep and waking. *American Journal of Psychology, 35,* 605–612.

Jenkins, Sharon Rae (1994). Need for power and women's careers over 14 years: Structural power, job satisfaction, and motive change. *Journal of Personality and Social Psychology, 66,* 155–165.

Jensen, Arthur R. (1969). How much can we boost IQ and scholastic achievement? *Harvard Educational Review, 39,* 1–123.

Jensen, Arthur R. (1981). *Straight talk about mental tests.* New York: Free Press.

Jensen, Arthur R. (1998). *The g factor: The science of mental ability.* Westport, CT: Praeger/Greenwood.

Jiang, Yuhong; Saxe, Rebecca; & Kanwisher, Nancy (2004). Functional magnetic resonance imaging provides new constraints on theories of the psychological refractory period. *Psychological Science, 15,* 390–396.

Johns, Michael; Schmader, Toni; & Martens, Andy (2005). Knowing is half the battle: Teaching stereotype threat as a means of improving women's math performance. *Psychological Science, 16,* 175–179.

Johnson, Marcia K. (1995). The relation between memory and reality. Paper presented at the annual meeting of the American Psychological Association, New York.

Johnson, Marcia K.; Hashtroudi, Shahin; & Lindsay, D. Stephen (1993). Source monitoring. *Psychological Bulletin, 114,* 3–28.

Johnson, Robert, & Downing, Leslie (1979). Deindividuation and valence of cues: Effects of prosocial and antisocial behavior. *Journal of Personality and Social Psychology, 37,* 1532–1538.

Joiner, Thomas E. (1994). Contagious depression: Existence, specificity to depressed symptoms, and the role of reassurance seeking. *Journal of Personality and Social Psychology, 67,* 287–296.

Jones, Amanda C., & Gosling, Samuel D. (2005). Temperament and personality in dogs (Canis familiaris): A review and evaluation of past research. *Applied Animal Behaviour Science, 95,* 1–53.

Jones, Edward E. (1990). *Interpersonal perception.* New York: Macmillan.

Jones, James M. (1991). Psychological models of race: What have they been and what should they be? In J. D. Goodchilds (Ed.), *Psychological perspectives on human diversity in America.* Washington, DC: American Psychological Association.

Jones, Mary Cover (1924). A laboratory study of fear: The case of Peter. *Pedagogical Seminary, 31,* 308–315.

Jones, Steve (1994). *The language of genes.* New York: Anchor/Doubleday.

Jordan, Kerry E.; & Brannon, Elizabeth M. (2006). The multisensory representation of number in infancy. *Proceedings of the National Academy of Sciences, 103,* 3486–3489.

Joseph, Stephen, & Linley, P. Alex (2005). Positive adjustment to threatening events: An organismic valuing theory of growth through adversity. *Review of General Psychology, 9,* 262–280.

Jost, John T.; Glaser, Jack; Kruglanski, Arie W.; & Sulloway, Frank J. (2003). Political conservatism as motivated social cognition. *Psychological Bulletin, 129,* 339–375.

Judd, Charles M.; Park, Bernadette; Ryan, Carey S.; et al. (1995). Stereotypes and ethnocentrism: Diverging interethnic perceptions of African American and white American youth. *Journal of Personality and Social Psychology, 69,* 460–481.

Jung, Carl (1967). *Collected works.* Princeton, NJ: Princeton University Press.

Jusczyk, Peter W. (2002). How infants adapt speech-processing capacities to native-language structure. *Current Directions in Psychological Science, 11,* 15–18.

Jusczyk, Peter W.; Houston, D.; & Newsome, M. (1999). The beginnings of word segmentation in English-learning infants. *Cognitive Psychology, 39,* 159–207.

Just, Marcel A.; Carpenter, Patricia A.; Keller, T. A.; et al. (2001). Interdependence of nonoverlapping cortical systems in dual cognitive tasks. *NeuroImage, 14,* 417–426.

Kagan, Jerome (1984). *The nature of the child.* New York: Basic Books.

Kagan, Jerome (1989). *Unstable ideas: Temperament, cognition, and self.* Cambridge, MA: Harvard University Press.

Kagan, Jerome (1997). Temperament and the reactions to unfamiliarity. *Child Development, 68,* 139–143.

Kagan, Jerome; Kearsley, Richard B.; & Zelazo, Philip R. (1978). *Infancy: Its place in human development.* Cambridge, MA: Harvard University Press.

Kahn, Arnold S. (2004). 2003 Carolyn Sherif Award Address: What college women do and do not experience as rape. *Psychology of Women Quarterly, 28,* 9–15.

Kahneman, Daniel (2003). A perspective on judgment and choice: Mapping bounded rationality. *American Psychologist, 58,* 697–720.

Kahneman, Daniel, & Treisman, Anne (1984). Changing views of attention and automaticity. In R. Parasuraman, D. R. Davies, & J. Beatty (Eds.), *Varieties of attention.* New York: Academic Press.

Kaiser, Cheryl R.; Vick, S. Brooke; & Major, Brenda (2004). A prospective investigation of the relationship between just-world beliefs and the desire for revenge after September 11, 2001. *Psychological Science, 15,* 503–506.

Kameda, Tatsuya, & Sugimori, Shinkichi (1993). Psychological entrapment in group decision making: An assigned decision rule and a groupthink phenomenon. *Journal of Personality and Social Psychology, 65,* 282–292.

Kaminski, Juliane; Call, Josep; & Fisher, Julia (2004). Word learning in a domestic dog: Evidence for "fast mapping." *Science, 304,* 1682–1683.

Kandel, Eric R., & Schwartz, James H. (1982). Molecular biology of learning: Modulation of transmitter release. *Science, 218,* 433–443.

Kanin, Eugene J. (1985). Date rapists: Differential sexual socialization and relative deprivation. *Archives of Sexual Behavior, 14,* 219–231.

Kanner, Allen, & Kasser, Tim (2003). *Psychology and consumer culture: The struggle for a good life in a materialistic society.* Washington DC: American Psychological Association.

Kanter, Rosabeth M. (1977/1993). *Men and women of the corporation.* New York: Basic Books.

Kanwisher, Nancy (2000). Domain specificity in face perception. *Nature Neuroscience, 3,* 759.

Kaplan, Abraham (1967). A philosophical discussion of normality. *Archives of General Psychiatry, 17,* 325–330.

Kaplan, Meg S.; Morales, Miguel; & Becker, Judith V. (1993). The impact of verbal satiation of adolescent sex offenders: A preliminary report. *Journal of Child Sexual Abuse, 2,* 81–88.

Karasek, Robert, & Theorell, Tores (1990). *Healthy work: Stress, productivity, and the reconstruction of working life.* New York: Basic Books.

Karau, Steven J., & Williams, Kipling D. (1993). Social loafing: A meta-analytic review and theoretical integration. *Journal of Personality and Social Psychology, 65,* 681–706.

Karney, Benjamin, & Bradbury, Thomas N. (2000). Attributions in marriage: State or trait? A growth curve analysis. *Journal of Personality and Social Psychology, 78,* 295–309.

Karni, Avi; Tanne, David; Rubenstein, Barton S.; Askenasy, Jean J. M.; & Sagi, Dov (1994). Dependence on REM sleep of overnight improvement of a perceptual skill. *Science, 265,* 679–682.

Karraker, Katherine H.; Vogel, Dena A.; & Lake, Margaret A. (1995). Parents' gender-stereotyped perceptions of newborns: The eye of the beholder revisited. *Sex Roles, 33,* 687–701.

Karremans, Johan C.; Van Lange, Paul A. M.; Ouwerkerk, Jaap W.; & Kluwer, Esther S. (2003). When forgiving enhances psychological well-being: The role of interpersonal commitment. *Journal of Personality and Social Psychology, 84,* 1011–1026.

Kaschak, Ellyn, & Tiefer, Leonore (Eds.) (2002). *A new view of women's sexual problems.* Binghamton, NY: Haworth Press.

Kashima, Yoshihisa; Yamaguchi, Susumu; Kim, Uichol; et al. (1995). Culture, gender, and self: A perspective from individualism–collectivism research. *Journal of Personality and Social Psychology, 69,* 925–937.

Kasser, Tim, & Ryan, Richard M. (1996). Further examining the American dream: Correlates of financial success as a central life aspiration. *Personality and Social Psychology Bulletin, 22,* 280–287.

Kasser, Tim, & Ryan, Richard M. (2001). Be careful what you wish for: Optimal functioning and the relative attainment of intrinsic and extrinsic goals. In P. Schmuck & K. M. Sheldon (Eds.), *Life goals and well-being.* Lengerich, Germany: Pabst Science Publishers.

Kassinove, Howard (Ed.) (1995). *Anger disorders: Definition, diagnosis, treatment.* Washington, DC: Taylor & Francis.

Katigbak, Marcia S.; Church, A. Timothy; & Akamine, Toshio X. (1996). Cross-cultural generalizability of personality dimensions: Relating indigenous and imported dimensions in two cultures. *Journal of Personality and Social Psychology, 70,* 99–114.

Katigbak, Marcia S.; Church, A. Timothy; Guanzon-Lapeña, Ma. Angeles; et al. (2002). Are indigenous personality dimensions culture specific?

Philippine inventories and the Five-Factor model. *Journal of Personality and Social Psychology, 82*, 89-101.

Katz, Zender (2001). Canadian psychologists' education, trauma history, and the recovery of memories of childhood sexual abuse. (Doctoral Dissertation, Simon Fraser University, 2001.) *Dissertations Abstracts International, 61*, 3848.

Kaufman, Joan, & Zigler, Edward (1987). Do abused children become abusive parents? *American Journal of Orthopsychiatry, 57*, 186–192.

Kazdin, Alan E. (2001). *Behavior modification in applied settings* (6th ed.). Belmont, CA: Wadsworth.

Keating, Caroline F. (1994). World without words: Messages from face and body. In W. J. Lonner & R. Malpass (Eds.), *Psychology and culture*. Needham Heights, MA: Allyn & Bacon.

Keck, Paul E., Jr., & McElroy, Susan L. (1998). Pharmacological treatment of bipolar disorders. In P. E. Nathan & J. M. Gorman (Eds.), *A guide to treatments that work*. New York: Oxford University Press.

Keel, Pamela K., & Klump, Kelly L. (2003). Are eating disorders culture-bound syndromes? Implications for conceptualizing their etiology. *Psychological Bulletin, 129*, 747–769.

Keen, Sam (1986). *Faces of the enemy: Reflections of the hostile imagination*. San Francisco: Harper & Row.

Keller, Heidi; Abels, Monika; Lamm, Bettina; et al. (2005). Ecocultural effects on early infant care: A study in Cameroon, India, and Germany. *Ethos*, 33, 512–541.

Keller, Martin B.; McCullough, James P.; Klein, Daniel N.; et al. (2000, May 18). A comparison of nefazodone, the cognitive behavioral-analysis system of psychotherapy, and their combination for the treatment of chronic depression. *New England Journal of Medicine, 342*, 1462–1470.

Kelly, Anita E. (1999). Revealing personal secrets. *Current Directions in Psychological Science, 8*, 105–109.

Kelly, Dennis (1981). Disorders of sleep and consciousness. In E. Kandel & J. Schwartz (Eds.), *Principles of neural science*. New York: Elsevier-North Holland.

Kelman, Herbert C., & Hamilton, V. Lee (1989). *Crimes of obedience: Toward a social psychology of authority and responsibility*. New Haven, CT: Yale University Press.

Keltner, Dacher, & Anderson, Cameron (2000). Saving face for Darwin: The functions and uses of embarrassment. *Current Directions in Psychological Science, 9*, 187–192.

Kemeny, Margaret E. (2003). The psychobiology of stress. *Current Directions in Psychological Science, 12*, 124–129.

Kempermann, G.; Brandon, E. P., & Gage, F. H. (1998). Environmental stimulation of 120/SvJ mice causes increased cell proliferation and neurogenesis in the adult dentate gyrus. *Current Biology, 8*, 939–942.

Kendall [no first name] (1999). Women in Lesotho and the (Western) construction of homophobia. In E. Blackwood & S. E. Wieringa (Eds.), *Female desires: Same-sex relations and transgender practices across cultures*. New York: Columbia University Press.

Kendler, Kenneth S.; Pedersen, Nancy; Johnson, Lars; Neale, Michael C.; & Mathie, A. (1993). A Swedish pilot twin study of affective illness, including hospital and population ascertained subsamples. *Archives of General Psychiatry, 50*, 699–706.

Kennedy, Donald, & Norman, Colin (2005). Introduction to special issue: What don't we know? *Science, 309*, 75.

Kennedy-Moore, Eileen, & Watson, Jeanne C. (2001). How and when does emotional expression help? *Review of General Psychology, 5*, 187–212.

Kenny, Michael G. (1986). *The passion of Ansel Bourne: Multiple personality in American culture*. Washington, DC: Smithsonian Press.

Kenrick, Douglas T.; Sundie, Jill M.; Nicastle, Lionel D.; & Stone, Gregory O. (2001). Can one ever be too wealthy or too chaste? Searching for nonlinearities in mate judgment. *Journal of Personality and Social Psychology, 80*, 462–471.

Kenrick, Douglas T., & Trost, Melanie R. (1993). The evolutionary perspective. In A. E. Beall & R. J. Sternberg (Eds.), *The psychology of gender*. New York: Guilford Press.

Kephart, William M. (1967). Some correlates of romantic love. *Journal of Marriage and the Family, 29*, 470–474.

Kerr, Michael E., & Bowen, Murray (1988). *Family evaluation: An approach based on Bowen theory*. New York: Norton.

Kessler, Ronald C.; Chiu, W. T.; Demler, O.; Merikangas, K. R.; & Walters, E. E. (2005). Prevalence, severity, and comorbidity of 12-month DSM-IV disorders in the National Comorbidity Survey Replication. *Archives of General Psychiatry, 62*, 590–592.

Kessler, Ronald C.; Sonnega, A.; Bromet, E.; et al. (1995). Posttraumatic stress disorder in the National Comorbidity Survey. *Archives of General Psychiatry, 52*, 1048–1060.

Khan, A.; Detke, M.; Khan, S. R.; & Mallinckrodt, C. (2003). Placebo response and antidepressant clinical trial outcome. *Journal of Nervous and Mental Diseases, 191*, 211–218.

Kida, Thomas (2006). *Don't believe everything you think: The 6 basic mistakes we make in thinking*. Amherst, NY: Prometheus Books.

Kiecolt-Glaser, Janice K.; Garner, Warren; Speicher, Carl; et al. (1985). Psychosocial modifiers of immunocompetence in medical students. *Psychosomatic Medicine, 46*, 7–14.

Kiecolt-Glaser, Janice K.; Loving, T. J.; Stowell, J. R.; et al. (2005). Hostile marital interactions, proinflammatory cytokine production, and wound healing. *Archives of General Psychiatry, 62*, 1377–1384.

Kiecolt-Glaser, Janice K.; Malarkey, William B.; Chee, MaryAnn; et al. (1993). Negative behavior during marital conflict is associated with immunological down-regulation. *Psychosomatic Medicine, 55*, 395–409.

Kiecolt-Glaser, Janice K.; Page, Gayle G.; Marucha, Phillip T.; et al. (1998). Psychological influences on surgical recovery: Perspectives from psychoneuroimmunology. *American Psychologist, 53*, 1209–1218.

Kihlstrom, John F. (1994). Hypnosis, delayed recall, and the principles of memory. *International Journal of Clinical and Experimental Hypnosis, 40*, 337–345.

Kihlstrom, John F. (1995). From a subject's point of view: The experiment as conversation and collaboration between investigator and subject. Invited address presented at the annual meeting of the American Psychological Society, New York.

Killeen, Peter R. (2005). An alternative to null-hypothesis significance. *Psychological Science, 16*, 345–353.

Kim, Hannah L.; Streltzer, Jon; & Goebert, Deborah (1999). St. John's wort for depression: A meta-analysis of well-defined clinical trials. *Journal of Nervous and Mental Diseases, 187*, 532–538.

Kim, Heejung, & Markus, Hazel Rose (1999). Deviance or uniqueness, harmony or conformity? A cultural analysis. *Journal of Personality and Social Psychology, 77*, 785–800.

Kim, Karl H. S.; Relkin, Norman R.; Lee, Kyoung-Min; & Hirsch, Joy (1997). Distinct cortical areas associated with native and second languages. *Nature, 388*, 171–174.

Kimmel, Michael (1995). *Manhood in America: A cultural history*. New York: Free Press.

King, M., & Woollett, E. (1997). Sexually assaulted males: 115 men consulting a counseling service. *Archives of Sexual Behavior, 26*, 579–588.

King, Pamela (1989, October). The chemistry of doubt. *Psychology Today, 58*, 60.

King, Patricia M., & Kitchener, Karen S. (1994). *Developing reflective judgment: Understanding and promoting intellectual growth and critical thinking in adolescents and adults*. San Francisco: Jossey Bass.

Kinoshita, Sachiko, & Peek-O'Leary, Marie (2005). Does the compatibility effect in the race Implicit Association Test reflect familiarity or affect? *Psychonomic Bulletin & Review, 12*, 442–452.

Kinsey, Alfred C.; Pomeroy, Wardell B.; & Martin, Clyde E. (1948). *Sexual behavior in the human male.* Philadelphia: Saunders.

Kinsey, Alfred C.; Pomeroy, Wardell B.; Martin, Clyde E.; & Gebhard, Paul H. (1953). *Sexual behavior in the human female.* Philadelphia: Saunders.

Kirsch, Irving (1997). Response expectancy theory and application: A decennial review. *Applied and Preventive Psychology, 6*, 69–70.

Kirsch, Irving (2004). Conditioning, expectancy, and the placebo effect: Comment on Stewart-Williams and Podd (2004). *Psychological Bulletin, 130*, 341–343.

Kirsch, Irving, & Lynn, Steven J. (1995). The altered state of hypnosis: Changes in the theoretical landscape. *American Psychologist, 50*, 846–858.

Kirsch, Irving, & Lynn, Steven J. (1998). Dissociation theories of hypnosis. *Psychological Bulletin, 123*, 100–113.

Kirsch, Irving; Montgomery, G.; & Sapirstein, G. (1995). Hypnosis as an adjunct to cognitive behavioral psychotherapy: A meta-analysis. *Journal of Consulting and Clinical Psychology, 63*, 214–220.

Kirsch, Irving, & Sapirstein, Guy (1998). Listening to Prozac but hearing placebo: A meta-analysis of antidepressant medication. *Prevention & Treatment, 1*, Article 0002a, posted electronically June 26, 1998 on the Web site of the American Psychological Association.

Kirsch, Irving; Silva, Christopher E.; Carone, James E.; Johnston, J. Dennis; & Simon, B. (1989). The surreptitious observation design: An experimental paradigm for distinguishing artifact from essence in hypnosis. *Journal of Abnormal Psychology, 98*, 132–136.

Kish, Stephen J. (2003) What is the evidence that Ecstasy (MDMA) can cause Parkinson's disease? *Movement Disorders 18*, 1219–1223.

Kitayama, Shinobu, & Markus, Hazel R. (1994). Introduction to cultural psychology and emotion research. In S. Kitayama & H. R. Markus (Eds.), *Emotion and culture: Empirical studies of mutual influence.* Washington, DC: American Psychological Association.

Kitchener, Karen S.; Lynch, Cindy L.; Fischer, Kurt W.; & Wood, Phillip K. (1993). Developmental range of reflective judgment: The effect of contextual support and practice on developmental stage. *Developmental Psychology, 29*, 893–906.

Klauer, Sheila G.; Dingus, Thomas A.; Neale, Vicki L.; et al. (2006). *The impact of driver inattention on near-crash/crash risk: An analysis using the 100-car naturalistic driving study data* [pdf]. Performed by Virginia Tech Transportation Institute, Blacksburg, VA, sponsored by National Highway Traffic Safety Administration, Washington, DC DOT HS 810 594.

Kleim, J. A.; Swain, R. A.; Armstrong, K. A.; et al. (1998). Selective synaptic plasticity within the cerebellar cortex following complex motor skill learning. *Neurobiology of Learning and Memory, 69*, 274–289.

Klein, Daniel N.; Schwartz, Joseph E.; Santiago, Neil J.; et al. (2003). Therapeutic alliance in depression treatment: Controlling for prior change and patient characteristics. *Journal of Consulting & Clinical Psychology, 71*, 997–1006.

Klein, Raymond, & Armitage, Roseanne (1979). Rhythms in human performance: 1 1/2-hour oscillations in cognitive style. *Science, 204*, 1326–1328.

Klein, Stanley B.; Cosmides, Leda; Costabile, Kristi A.; & Mei, Lisa (2002). Is there something special about the self? A neuropsychological case study. *Journal of Research in Personality, 36*, 490–506.

Kleinke, Chris L.; Peterson, Thomas R.; & Rutledge, Thomas R. (1998). Effects of self-generated facial expressions on mood. *Journal of Personality and Social Psychology, 74*, 272–279.

Kleinman, Arthur (1988). *Rethinking psychiatry: From cultural category to personal experience.* New York: Free Press.

Klima, Edward S., & Bellugi, Ursula (1966). Syntactic regularities in the speech of children. In J. Lyons & R. J. Wales (Eds.), *Psycholinguistics papers.* Edinburgh, Scotland: Edinburgh University Press.

Klimanskaya, Irina; Chung, Young; Becker, Sandy; et al. (2006). Human embryonic stem cell lines derived from single blastomeres. Published online 23 August 2006 [doi:10.1038/nature05142].

Klimoski, R. (1992). Graphology and personnel selection. In B. Beyerstein & D. Beyerstein (Eds.), *The write stuff: Evaluations of graphology—The Study of handwriting analysis.* Buffalo, NY: Prometheus Books.

Kling, Kristen C.; Hyde, Janet S.; Showers, Carolin J.; & Buswell, Brenda N. (1999). Gender differences in self-esteem: A meta-analysis. *Psychological Bulletin, 125*, 470–500.

Klohnen, Eva C., & Bera, Stephan (1998). Behavioral and experiential patterns of avoidantly and securely attached women across adulthood: A 31-year longitudinal perspective. *Journal of Personality and Social Psychology, 74*, 211–223.

Kluft, Richard P. (1987). The simulation and dissimulation of multiple personality disorder. *American Journal of Clinical Hypnosis, 30*, 104–118.

Kochanska, Grazyna; Forman, David R.; Aksan, Nazan; & Dunbar, Stephen B. (2005). Pathways to conscience: Early mother-child mutually responsive orientation and children's moral emotion, conduct, and cognition. *Journal of Child Psychology and Psychiatry*, 46, 19–34.

Kochanska, Grazyna, & Knaack, Amy (2003). Effortful control as a personality characteristic of young children: Antecedents, correlates, and consequences. *Journal of Personality, 71*, 1087–1112.

Kohlberg, Lawrence (1964). Development of moral character and moral ideology. In M. Hoffman & L. W. Hoffman (Eds.), *Review of child development research.* New York: Russell Sage Foundation.

Köhler, Wolfgang (1925). *The mentality of apes.* New York: Harcourt, Brace.

Köhler, Wolfgang (1929). *Gestalt psychology.* New York: Horace Liveright.

Köhler, Wolfgang (1959). Gestalt psychology today. Presidential address to the American Psychological Association, Cincinnati. [Reprinted in E. R. Hilgard (Ed.), *American psychology in historical perspective: Addresses of the presidents of the American Psychological Association, 1892–1977.* Washington, DC: American Psychological Association, 1978.]

Kolata, Gina (2004, June 8). The fat epidemic: He says it's an illusion. *The New York Times*, Science section, D5.

Kolb, Bryan; Gibb, Robbin; & Robinson, Terry E. (2003). Brain plasticity and behavior. *Current Directions in Psychological Science, 12*, 1–5.

Koocher, Gerald P.; Goodman, Gail S.; White, C. Sue; et al. (1995). Psychological science and the use of anatomically detailed dolls in child sexual-abuse assessments. *Psychological Bulletin, 118*, 199–222.

Koppelstaetter, Florian; Siedentopf, Christian; Poeppel, Thorsten; et al. (2005). Influence of caffeine excess on activation patterns in verbal working memory. Paper presented at the annual meeting of the Radiological Society of America, Chicago.

Korol, Donna L., & Gold, Paul E. (1998). Glucose, memory, and aging. *American Journal of Clinical Nutrition, 67*, 764S–771S.

Kosfeld, Michael; Heinrichs, Markus; Zak, Paul J.; et al. (2005). Oxytocin increases trust in humans. *Nature, 435*, 673–676.

Koss, Mary P. (1993). Rape: Scope, impact, interventions, and public policy responses. *American Psychologist, 48*, 1062–1069.

Kosslyn, Stephen M. (1980). *Image and mind.* Cambridge, MA: Harvard University Press.

Kosslyn, Stephen M.; Pascual-Leone, A.; Felician, O.; et al. (1999). The role of area 17 in visual imagery: Convergent evidence from PET and rTMS. *Science, 284*, 167–170.

Kosslyn, Stephen M.; Thompson, William L.; Costantini-Ferrando, Maria F.; et al. (2000). Hypnotic visual illusion alters color processing in the brain. *American Journal of Psychiatry, 157,* 1279–1284.

Koyama, Tetsua; McHaffie, John G.; Laurienti, Paul J.; & Coghill, Robert C. (2005). The subjective experience of pain: Where expectations become reality. *Proceedings of the National Academy of Sciences, 102,* 12950–12955.

Kraft, Ulrich (2005, October). Mending the spinal cord. *Scientific American Mind,* pp. 68–73.

Kramer, Arthur F., & Willis, Sherry L. (2002). Enhancing the cognitive vitality of older adults. *Current Directions in Psychological Science, 11,* 173–177.

Kraut, Robert; Olson, Judith; Banaji, Mahzarin; et al. (2004). Psychological research online: Report of Board of Scientific Affairs Advisory Group on the conduct of research on the Internet. *American Psychologist, 59,* 105–117.

Kreps, Bonnie (1990). *Subversive thoughts, authentic passions.* San Francisco: Harper & Row.

Krieger, Nancy, & Sidney, S. (1996). Racial discrimination and blood pressure: The CARDIA study of young black and white adults. *American Journal of Public Health, 86,* 1370–1378.

Krimsky, Sheldon (2003). *Science in the private interest.* Lanham, MD: Rowman & Littlefield.

Kring, Ann M., & Gordon, Albert H. (1998). Sex differences in emotion: Expression, experience, and physiology. *Journal of Personality and Social Psychology, 74,* 686–703.

Kripke, Daniel F. (1974). Ultradian rhythms in sleep and wakefulness. In E. D. Weitzman (Ed.), *Advances in sleep research* (Vol. 1). Flushing, NY: Spectrum.

Kroll, Barry M. (1992). *Teaching hearts and minds: College students reflect on the Vietnam War in literature.* Carbondale: Southern Illinois University Press.

Kross, Ethan; Ayduk, Ozlem; & Mischel, Walter (2005). When asking "why" does not hurt: Distinguishing rumination from reflective processing of negative emotions. *Psychological Science, 16,* 709–715.

Krueger, Robert F. (2000). Phenotypic, genetic, and nonshared environmental parallels in the structure of personality: A view from the Multidimensional Personality Questionnaire. *Journal of Personality and Social Psychology, 79,* 1057–1067.

Krueger, Robert F.; Hicks, Brian M.; & McGue, Matt (2001). Altruism and antisocial behavior: Independent tendencies, unique personality correlates, distinct etiologies. *Psychological Science, 12,* 397–402.

Krupa, David J.; Thompson, Judith K.; & Thompson, Richard F. (1993). Localization of a memory trace in the mammalian brain. *Science, 260,* 989–991.

Krützen, Michael; Mann, Janet; Heithaus, Michael R.; et al. (2005). Cultural transmission of tool use in bottlenose dolphins. *Proceedings of the National Academy of Sciences, 102:* 8939–8943; published online before print as 10.1073/pnas.0500232102.

Kuhl, Patricia K.; Williams, Karen A.; Lacerda, Francisco; et al. (1992, January 31). Linguistic experience alters phonetic perception in infants by 6 months of age. *Science, 255,* 606–608.

Kuhn, Deanna; Weinstock, Michael; & Flaton, Robin (1994). How well do jurors reason? Competence dimensions of individual variation in a juror reasoning task. *Psychological Science, 5,* 289–296.

Kuncel, Nathan R.; Hezlett, Sarah A.; & Ones, Deniz S. (2004). Academic performance, career potential, creativity, and job performance: Can one construct predict them all? *Journal of Personality and Social Psychology, 86,* 148–161.

Kunda, Ziva (1990). The case for motivated reasoning. *Psychological Bulletin, 108,* 480–498.

Kurdek, Lawrence A. (2005). What do we know about gay and lesbian couples? *Current Directions in Psychological Science, 14,* 251–254.

Kutchins, Herb, & Kirk, Stuart A. (1997). *Making us crazy: DSM. The psychiatric bible and the creation of mental disorders.* New York: Free Press.

LaBerge, Stephen, & Levitan, Lynne (1995). Validity established of DreamLight cues for eliciting lucid dreaming. *Dreaming: Journal of the Association for the Study of Dreams, 5,* 159–168.

Lachman, Margie E., & Weaver, Suzanne L. (1998). The sense of control as a moderator of social class differences in health and well-being. *Journal of Personality and Social Psychology, 74,* 763–773.

Lachman, Sheldon J. (1996). Processes in perception: Psychological transformations of highly structured stimulus material. *Perceptual and Motor Skills, 83,* 411–418.

LaFrance, Marianne; Hecht, Marvin A.; & Paluck, Elizabeth L. (2003). The contingent smile: A meta-analysis of sex differences in smiling. *Psychological Bulletin, 129,* 305–334.

Lahey, B. B.; Pelham, W. E.; Loney, J.; et al. (2005). Instability of the DSM-IV Subtypes of ADHD from preschool through elementary school. *Archives of General Psychiatry,* 62, 896–902.

Lai, Cecilia S. L.; Fisher, Simon E.; Hurst, Jane A.; et al. (2001). A forkhead-domain gene is mutated in a severe speech and language disorder. *Nature, 413,* 519–523.

Lai, Hui-Ling, & Good, Marion (2005). Music improves sleep quality in older adults. *Journal of Advanced Nursing, 49,* 234–244.

Laird, James D. (1974). Self-attribution of emotion: The effects of expressive behavior on the quality of emotional experience. *Journal of Personality and Social Psychology, 29,* 475–486.

Lakin, Jessica L., & Chartrand, Tanya L. (2003). Using nonconscious behavioral mimicry to create affiliation and rapport. *Psychological Science, 14,* 334–339.

Lakoff, Robin T., & Coyne, James C. (1993). *Father knows best: The use and abuse of power in Freud's case of "Dora."* New York: Teachers College Press.

Lamb, Sharon (2002). *The secret lives of girls.* New York: The Free Press.

Landrine, Hope (1988). Revising the framework of abnormal psychology. In P. Bronstein & K. Quina (Eds.), *Teaching a psychology of people.* Washington, DC: American Psychological Association.

Lang, Ariel J.; Craske, Michelle G.; Brown, Matt; & Ghaneian, Atousa (2001). Fear-related state dependent memory. *Cognition & Emotion, 15,* 695–703.

Lang, Frieder R., & Heckhausen, Jutta (2001). Perceived control over development and subjective well-being: Differential benefits across adulthood. *Journal of Personality and Social Psychology, 81,* 509–523.

Langer, Ellen J. (1983). *The psychology of control.* Beverly Hills, CA: Sage.

Langer, Ellen J. (1989). *Mindfulness.* Reading, MA: Addison-Wesley.

Langer, Ellen J. (1997). *The power of mindful learning.* Reading, MA: Addison-Wesley.

Langer, Ellen J.; Blank, Arthur; & Chanowitz, Benzion (1978). The mindlessness of ostensibly thoughtful action: The role of placebic information in interpersonal interaction. *Journal of Personality and Social Psychology, 36,* 635–642.

Lanphear, B. P.; Hornung, R.; Ho, M.; et al. (2002). Environmental lead exposure during early childhood. *Journal of Pediatrics, 140,* 49–47.

Lanphear, B. P.; Hornung, R.; Khoury, J.; et al. (2005). Low-level environmental lead exposure and children's intellectual function: An international pooled analysis. *Environmental Health Perspectives, 113,* 894–899.

Larsen, Jeff T.; McGraw, A. Peter; Mellers, Barbara A.; & Cacioppo, John T. (2004). The agony of victory and the thrill of defeat. *Psychological Science, 15,* 325–330.

Latané, Bibb; Williams, Kipling; & Harkins, Stephen (1979). Many hands make light the work: The causes and consequences of social loafing. *Journal of Personality and Social Psychology, 37,* 822–832.

Laumann, Edward O.; Ellingson, Stephen; Mahay, Jenna; Paik, Anthony; & Youm, Yoosik (Eds.) (2004). *The sexual organization of the city.* Chicago: University of Chicago Press.

Laumann, Edward O., & Gagnon John H. (1995). A sociological perspective on sexual action. In R. G. Parker & J. H. Gagnon (Eds.), *Conceiving sexuality: Approaches to sex research in a postmodern world.* New York: Routledge.

Laumann, Edward O.; Gagnon, John H.; Michael, Robert T.; & Michaels, Stuart (1994). *The social organization of sexuality.* Chicago: University of Chicago Press.

Laurence, J. R., & Perry, C. (1988). *Hypnosis, will, and memory: A psycho-legal history.* New York: Guilford Press.

Lavie, Peretz (1976). Ultradian rhythms in the perception of two apparent motions. *Chronobiologia, 3,* 21–218.

Lazarus, Richard S. (2000a, Spring). Reason and our emotions: A hard sell. *The General Psychologist, 35,* 16–20.

Lazarus, Richard S. (2000b). Toward better research on stress and coping. *American Psychologist, 55,* 665–673.

Lazarus, Richard S., & Folkman, Susan (1984). *Stress, appraisal, and coping.* New York: Springer.

Leach, Colin W.; Spears, Russell; Branscombe, Nyla R.; & Doosje, Bertjan (2003). Malicious pleasure: Schadenfreude at the suffering of another group. *Journal of Personality and Social Psychology, 84,* 932–943.

LeDoux, Joseph E. (1996). *The emotional brain.* New York: Simon & Schuster.

Leinbach, Mary D.; Hort, Barbara E.; & Fagot, Beverly I. (1997). Bears are for boys: Metaphorical associations in young children's gender stereotypes. *Cognitive Development, 12,* 107–130.

Lemieux, Robert, & Hale, Jerold L. (2000). Intimacy, passion, and commitment among married individuals: Further testing of the Triangular Theory of Love. *Psychological Reports, 87,* 941–948.

Lenneberg, Eric H. (1967). *Biological foundations of language.* New York: Wiley.

Lent, James R. (1968, June). Mimosa cottage: Experiment in hope. *Psychology Today,* 51–58.

Lepore, Stephen J.; Ragan, Jennifer D.; & Jones, Scott (2000). Talking facilitates cognitive-emotional processes of adaptation to an acute stressor. *Journal of Personality and Social Psychology, 78,* 499–508.

Lepowsky, Maria (1994). *Fruit of the motherland: Gender in an egalitarian society.* New York: Columbia University Press.

Lepper, Mark R.; Greene, David; & Nisbett, Richard E. (1973). Undermining children's intrinsic interest with extrinsic rewards. *Journal of Personality and Social Psychology, 28,* 129–137.

Leproult, Rachel; Copinschi, Georges; Buxton, Orfeu; & Van Cauter, Eve (1997). Sleep loss results in an elevation of cortisol levels the next evening. *Sleep, 20,* 865–870.

Leproult, Rachel; Van Reeth, Olivier; Byrne, Maria M.; et al. (1997). Sleepiness, performance, and neuroendocrine function during sleep deprivation: Effects of exposure to bright light or exercise. *Journal of Biological Rhythms, 12,* 245–258.

Lerner, Harriet G. (1989). *The dance of intimacy.* New York: Harper & Row.

Lerner, Melvin J. (1980). *The belief in a just world: A fundamental delusion.* New York: Plenum.

Lester, Barry M.; LaGasse, Linda L.; & Seifer, Ronald (1998, October 23). Cocaine exposure and children: The meaning of subtle effects. *Science, 282,* 633–634.

LeVay, Simon (1991). A difference in hypothalamic structure between heterosexual and homosexual men. *Science, 253,* 1034–1037.

Levenson, Robert W. (1992). Autonomic nervous system differences among emotions. *Psychological Science, 3,* 23–27.

Levenson, Robert W.; Carstensen, Laura L.; & Gottman, John M. (1994). Influence of age and gender on affect, physiology, and their interrelations: A study of long-term marriages. *Journal of Personality & Social Psychology, 67,* 56–68.

Levenson, Robert W.; Ekman, Paul; & Friesen, Wallace V. (1990). Voluntary facial action generates emotion-specific autonomic nervous system activity. *Psychophysiology, 27,* 363–384.

Levin, Daniel T. (2000). Race as a visual feature: Using visual search and perceptual discrimination tasks to understand face categories and the cross-race recognition deficit. *Journal of Experimental Psychology: General, 129,* 559–574.

Levine, James A.; Eberhardt, Norman L.; & Jensen, Michael D. (1999, January 8). Role of nonexercise activity thermogenesis in resistance to fat gain in humans. *Science, 283,* 212–214.

Levine, Joseph, & Suzuki, David (1993). *The secret of life: Redesigning the living world.* Boston: WGBH Educational Foundation.

Levine, Judith (2002). *Harmful to minors.* Minneapolis: University of Minnesota Press.

Levine, Robert V. (2003, May-June). The kindness of strangers. *American Scientist, 91,* 227–233.

Levine, Robert V.; Martinez, Todd S.; Brase, Gary; & Sorenson, Kerry (1994). Helping in 36 U.S. cities. *Journal of Personality and Social Psychology, 67,* 69–82.

Levy, Becca. (1996). Improving memory in old age through implicit self-stereotyping. *Journal of Personality and Social Psychology, 71,* 1092–1107.

Levy, David A. (1997). *Tools of critical thinking: Metathoughts for psychology.* Boston: Allyn & Bacon.

Levy, Jerre; Trevarthen, Colwyn; & Sperry, Roger W. (1972). Perception of bilateral chimeric figures following hemispheric deconnection. *Brain, 95,* 61–78.

Levy, Robert I. (1984). The emotions in comparative perspective. In K. R. Scherer & P. Ekman (Eds.), *Approaches to emotion.* Hillsdale, NJ: Erlbaum.

Lewin, Kurt (1948). *Resolving social conflicts.* New York: Harper.

Lewis, Dorothy O. (1992). From abuse to violence: Psychophysiological consequences of maltreatment. *Journal of the American Academy of Child and Adolescent Psychiatry, 31,* 383–391.

Lewontin, Richard C. (1970). Race and intelligence. *Bulletin of the Atomic Scientists, 26*(3), 2–8.

Lewontin, Richard C. (2001, March 5). Genomania: A disorder of modern biology and medicine. Invited address at the University of California, Los Angeles.

Lewontin, Richard C.; Rose, Steven; & Kamin, Leon J. (1984). *Not in our genes: Biology, ideology, and human nature.* New York: Pantheon.

Lewy, Alfred J.; Ahmed, Saeeduddin; Jackson, Jeanne L.; & Sack, Robert L. (1992). Melatonin shifts human circadian rhythms according to a phase response curve. *Chronobiology International, 9,* 380–392.

Li, Shu-Chen; Lindenberger, Ulman; Hommel, Bernhard; et al. (2004). Transformations in the couplings among intellectual abilities and constituent cognitive processes across the life span. *Psychological Science, 15,* 155–163.

Lichtenstein, Sarah; Slovic, Paul; Fischhoff, Baruch; et al. (1978). Judged frequency of lethal events. *Journal of Experimental Psychology: Human Learning and Memory, 4,* 551–578.

Lickona, Thomas (1983). *Raising good children.* New York: Bantam.

Lieberman, J. A.; Stroup, T. S.; McEvoy, J. P.; et al. (2005, September 22). Effectiveness of antipsychotic drugs in patients with chronic schizophrenia. *New England Journal of Medicine, 353,* 1209–1223.

Lieberman, Matthew (2000). Intuition: A social cognitive neuroscience approach. *Psychological Bulletin, 126,* 109–137.

Lien, Mei-Ching; Ruthruff, Eric; & Johnston, James C. (2006). Attentional limitations in doing two tasks at once: The search for exceptions. *Current Directions in Psychological Science, 16,* 89–93.

Liepert, J.; Bauder, H.; Miltner, W. H.; et al. (2000). Treatment-induced cortical reorganization after stroke in humans. *Stroke, 31,* 1210–1216.

Light, Kathleen C.; Grewen, Karen M.; & Amico, Janet A. (2005). More frequent partner hugs and higher oxytocin levels are linked to lower blood pressure and heart rate in premenopausal women. *Biological Psychology, 69,* 5–21.

Lilienfeld, Scott O. (1993, Fall). Do "honesty" tests really measure honesty? *Skeptical Inquirer, 18,* 32–41.

Lilienfeld, Scott O. (1996, January/February). EMDR treatment: Less than meets the eye? *Skeptical Inquirer,* 25–31.

Lilienfeld, Scott O.; Gershon, Jonathan; Duke, Marshall; Marino, Lori; & De Waal, Frans B. M. (1999a). A preliminary investigation of the construct of psychopathic personality (psychopathy) in chimpanzees (Pan troglodytes). *Journal of Comparative Psychology, 113,* 365–375.

Lilienfeld, Scott O., & Lohr, Jeffrey (2003). Dissociative identity disorder: Multiple personalities, multiple controversies. In S.O. Lilienfeld, S. J. Lynn, & J. M. Lohr (Eds.), *Science and pseudoscience in clinical psychology.* New York: Guilford.

Lilienfeld, Scott O.; Lynn, Steven Jay; Kirsch, Irving; et al. (1999b). Dissociative identity disorder and the sociocognitive model: Recalling the lessons of the past. *Psychological Bulletin, 125,* 507–523.

Lilienfeld, Scott O.; Lynn, Steven Jay; & Lohr, Jeffrey M. (Eds.) (2003). *Science and pseudoscience in clinical psychology.* New York: Guilford.

Lillard, Angeline S. (1998). Ethnopsychologies: Cultural variations in theories of mind. *Psychological Bulletin, 123,* 3–32.

Lin, Keh-Ming; Poland, Russell E.; & Chien, C. P. (1990). Ethnicity and psychopharmacology: Recent findings and future research directions. In E. Sorel (Ed.), *Family, culture, and psychobiology.* New York: Legas.

Lin, L.; Hungs, M.; & Mignot, E. (2001). Narcolepsy and the HLA region. *Journal of Neuroimmunology, 117,* 9–20.

Linday, Linda A. (1994). Maternal reports of pregnancy, genital, and related fantasies in preschool and kindergarten children. *Journal of the American Academy of Child and Adolescent Psychiatry, 33,* 416–423.

Lindsay, D. Stephen; Hagen, Lisa; Read, J. Don; et al. (2004). True photographs and false memories. *Psychological Science, 15,* 149–154.

Lindsay, D. Stephen, & Read, J. D. (1994). Psychotherapy and memories of childhood sexual abuse: A cognitive perspective. *Applied Cognitive Psychology, 8,* 281–338.

Linehan, Marsha, M. (1993). *Cognitive-behavioral treatment of borderline personality disorder.* New York: Guidford Press.

Linton, Marigold (1978). Real-world memory after six years. An in vivo study of very long-term memory. In M. M. Gruneberg, P. E. Morris, & R. N. Sykes (Eds.), *Practical aspects of memory.* London: Academic Press.

Linton, Simi (1998). *Claiming disability: Knowledge and identity.* New York: New York University Press.

Linton, Simi (2006). *My body politic.* Ann Arbor, MI: University of Michigan Press.

Linville, P. W.; Fischer, G. W.; & Fischhoff, B. (1992). AIDS risk perceptions and decision biases. In J. B. Pryor & G. D. Reeder (Eds.), *The social psychology of HIV infection.* Hillsdale, NJ: Erlbaum.

Lipps, Jere H. (2004, January/February). Judging authority. *Skeptical Inquirer,* 35–37.

Lissner, L.; Odell, P. M.; D'Agostino, R. B.; et al. (1991, June 27). Variability of body weight and health outcomes in the Framingham population. *New England Journal of Medicine, 324,* 1839–1844.

Locke, Edwin A., & Latham, Gary P. (1990). Work motivation and satisfaction: Light at the end of the tunnel. *Psychological Science, 1,* 240–246.

Locke, Edwin A., & Latham, Gary P. (2002). Building a practically useful theory of goal setting and task motivation. *American Psychologist, 57,* 705–717.

Locke, Edwin A.; Shaw, Karyll; Saari, Lise; & Latham, Gary (1981). Goal-setting and task performance: 1969–1980. *Psychological Bulletin, 90,* 125–152.

Loehlin, John C. (1992). *Genes and environment in personality development.* Newbury Park CA: Sage.

Loehlin, John C.; Horn, J. M.; & Willerman, L. (1996). Heredity, environment, and IQ in the Texas adoption study. In R. J. Sternberg & E. Grigorenko (Eds.), *Intelligence: Heredity and environment.* New York: Cambridge University Press.

Loftus, Elizabeth F. (1996). Memory distortion and false memory creation. *Bulletin of the American Academy of Psychiatry and the Law, 24,* 281–295.

Loftus, Elizabeth F., & Greene, Edith (1980). Warning: Even memory for faces may be contagious. *Law and Human Behavior, 4,* 323–334.

Loftus, Elizabeth F., & Ketcham, Katherine (1994). *The myth of repressed memory.* New York: St. Martin's Press.

Loftus, Elizabeth F.; Miller, David G.; & Burns, Helen J. (1978). Semantic integration of verbal information into a visual memory. *Journal of Experimental Psychology: Human Learning and Memory, 4,* 19–31.

Loftus, Elizabeth F., & Palmer, John C. (1974). Reconstruction of automobile destruction: An example of the interaction between language and memory. *Journal of Verbal Learning and Verbal Behavior, 13,* 585–589.

Loftus, Elizabeth F., & Pickrell, Jacqueline E. (1995). The formation of false memories. *Psychiatric Annals, 25,* 720–725.

Loftus, Elizabeth F., & Zanni, Guido (1975). Eyewitness testimony: The influence of the wording of a question. *Bulletin of the Psychonomic Society, 5,* 86–88.

Lohr, Jeffrey M.; Montgomery, Robert W.; Lilienfeld, Scott O.; & Tolin, David F. (1999). Pseudoscience and the commercial promotion of trauma treatments. In R. Gist & B. Lubin (Eds.), *Response to disaster: Psychosocial, community, and ecological approaches.* Philadelphia, PA: Brunner/Mazel (Taylor & Francis).

Lohr, Jeffrey M.; Tolin, D. F.; & Lilienfeld, Scott O. (1998). Efficacy of Eye Movement Desensitization and Reprocessing: Implications for behavior therapy. *Behavior Therapy, 29,* 123–156.

Lonner, Walter J. (1995). Culture and human diversity. In E. Trickett, R. Watts, & D. Birman (Eds.), *Human diversity: Perspectives on people in context.* San Francisco: Jossey-Bass.

Lopes, A. C.; de Mathis, M. E.; Canteras, M. M.; et al. (2004). Update on neurosurgical treatment for obsessive compulsive disorder [original article in Portuguese]. *Rev bras Psiquiatr, 26,* 62–66.

Lopez, N. L, Bonenberger, J. L, & Schneider, H. G. (2001). Parental disciplinary history, current levels of empathy, and moral reasoning in young adults. *North American Journal of Psychology, 3,* 193–204.

López, Steven R. (1995). Testing ethnic minority children. In B. B. Wolman (Ed.), *The encyclopedia of psychology, psychiatry, and psychoanalysis.* New York: Holt.

Lorber, Michael F. (2004). Psychophysiology of aggression, psychopathy, and conduct problems: A meat-analysis. *Psychological Bulletin, 130,* 531–552.

Lubinski, David (2004). Introduction to the special section on cognitive abilities: 100 years after Spearman's (1904) "'General intelligence,' objectively

determined and measured." *Journal of Personality and Social Psychology, 86,* 96–111.

Lucchina, L. A.; Curtis, O. F.; Putnam, P.; et al. (1998). Psychophysical measurement of 6-n-propylthiouracil (PROP) taste perception. *Annals of the New York Academy of Sciences, 855,* 816–819.

Luders, Eileen; Narr, Katherine L.; Thompson, Paul M.; et al. (2004). Gender differences in cortical complexity. *Nature Neuroscience,* 7, 799–800.

Luengo, M. A.; Carrillo-de-la-Peña, M. T.; Otero, J. M.; & Romero, E. (1994). A short-term longitudinal study of impulsivity and antisocial behavior. *Journal of Personality and Social Psychology, 66,* 542–548.

Luepnitz, Deborah A. (1988). *The family interpreted: Feminist theory in clinical practice.* New York: Basic Books.

Lugaresi, Elio; Medori, R.; Montagna, P.; et al. (1986, October 16). Fatal familial insomnia and dysautonomia with selective degeneration of thalamic nuclei. *New England Journal of Medicine, 315,* 997–1003.

Luhrmann, T. M. (2000). *Of two minds: the growing disorder in American psychiatry.* New York: Knopf.

Luna, Beatriz; Garver, Krista E.; Urban, Trinity A.; et al. (2004). Maturation of cognitive processes from late childhood to adulthood. *Child Development, 75,* 1357–1372.

Luria, Alexander R. (1968). *The mind of a mnemonist* (L. Soltaroff, Trans.). New York: Basic Books.

Luria, Alexander R. (1980). *Higher cortical functions in man* (2nd Rev. ed.). New York: Basic Books.

Lutz, Catherine (1988). *Unnatural emotions.* Chicago: University of Chicago Press.

Lykken, David T. (1995). *The antisocial personalities.* Hillsdale, NJ: Erlbaum.

Lykken, David T. (1998). *A tremor in the blood: Uses and abuses of the lie detector.* New York: Plenum Press.

Lykken, David T., & Tellegen, Auke (1996). Happiness is a stochastic phenomenon. *Psychological Science,* 7, 186–189.

Lynn, Steven J.; Kirsch, Irving; Barabasz, Arreed; et al. (2000). Hypnosis as an empirically supported clinical intervention: The state of the evidence and a look to the future. *International Journal of Clinical and Experimental Hypnosis, 48,* 239–259.

Lynn, Steven Jay; Rhue, Judith W.; & Weekes, John R. (1990). Hypnotic involuntariness: A social cognitive analysis. *Psychological Review, 97,* 69–184.

Lytton, Hugh, & Romney, David M. (1991). Parents' differential socialization of boys and girls: A meta-analysis. *Psychological Bulletin, 109,* 267–296.

Lyubomirsky, Sonja; Caldwell, Nicole D.; & Nolen-Hoeksema, Susan (1998). Effects of ruminative and distracting responses to depressed mood on retrieval of autobiographical memories. *Journal of Personality and Social Psychology, 75,* 166–177.

Maas, James B. (1998). *Power sleep.* New York: Villard.

Maass, Anne; Cadinu, Mara; Guarnieri, Gaia; & Grasselli, Annalisa (2003). Sexual harassment under social identity threat: The computer harassment paradigm. *Journal of Personality and Social Psychology, 85,* 853–870.

MacArthur Foundation Research Network on Successful Midlife Development (1999). Report of latest findings (Orville G. Brim, director; 2145 14th Avenue, Vero Beach, FL 32960).

Maccoby, Eleanor E. (1998). *The two sexes: Growing up apart, coming together.* Cambridge, MA: Belknap Press/Harvard University Press.

Maccoby, Eleanor E. (2002). Gender and group process: A developmental perspective. *Current Directions in Psychological Science, 11,* 54–58.

Mack, Arien (2003). Inattentional blindness: Looking without seeing. *Current Directions in Psychological Science, 12,* 180–184.

MacKinnon, Donald W. (1968). Selecting students with creative potential. In P. Heist (Ed.), *The creative college student: An unmet challenge.* San Francisco: Jossey-Bass.

MacLean, Paul (1993). Cerebral evolution of emotion. In M. Lewis & J. M. Haviland (Eds.), *Handbook of emotions.* New York: Guilford Press.

Macleod John; Oakes Rachel; Copello, Alex; et al. (2004). Psychological and social sequelae of cannabis and other illicit drug use by young people: a systematic review of longitudinal, general population studies. *The Lancet, 363,* 1568–1569.

Macmillan, Malcolm (2000). *An odd kind of fame: Stories of Phineas Gage.* Cambridge: MIT Press, 2000.

Macrae, C. Neil, & Bodenhausen, Galen V. (2000). Social cognition: Thinking categorically about others. *Annual Review of Psychology, 51,* 93–120.

Macrae, C. Neil; Kelley, William M.; & Heatherton, Todd F. (2004). A self less ordinary: The medial prefrontal cortex and you. In M. S. Gazzaniga (Ed.), *Cognitive Neurosciences III.* Cambridge, MA: MIT Press.

Macrae, C. Neil; Milne, Alan B.; & Bodenhausen, Galen V. (1994). Stereotypes as energy-saving devices: A peek inside the cognitive toolbox. *Journal of Personality and Social Psychology, 66,* 37–47.

Maddux, James E. (Ed.) (1995). *Self-efficacy, adaptation, and adjustment: Theory, research, and application.* New York: Plenum.

Maddux, James E., & Mundell, Clare E. (1997). Disorders of personality. In V. Derlega, B. Winstead, & W. Jones (Eds.), *Personality: Contemporary theory and research* (2nd ed.). Chicago: Nelson-Hall.

Madsen, Kreesten M.; Hviid, Anders; Vestergaard, Mogens; et al. (2002). A population-based study of measles, mumps, and rubella vaccination and autism. *New England Journal of Medicine, 347,* 1477–1482.

Madsen, Kreesten M.; Lauritsen, M. B.; Pedersen, C. B.; et al. (2003). Thimerserol and the occurrence of autism. Negative ecological evidence from Danish population-based data. *Pediatrics, 112,* 604–606.

Maguire, Eleanor A.; Gadian, David G.; Johnsrude, Ingrid S.; et al. (2000). Navigation-related structural change in the hippocampi of taxi drivers. *Proceedings of the National Academy of Sciences, 97,* 4398–4403.

Major, Brenda; Spencer, Steven; Schmader, Toni; et al. (1998). Coping with negative stereotypes about intellectual performance: The role of psychological disengagement. *Personality and Social Psychology Bulletin, 24,* 34–50.

Maki, Pauline M.; & Resnick, Susan M. (2000). Longitudinal effects of estrogen replacement therapy on PET cerebral blood flow and cognition. *Neurobiology of Aging, 21,* 373–383.

Malamuth, Neil M.; Linz, Daniel; Heavey, Christopher L.; et al. (1995). Using the confluence model of sexual aggression to predict men's conflict with women: A 10-year follow-up study. *Journal of Personality and Social Psychology, 69,* 353–369.

Malaspina, Dolores (2001). Paternal factors and schizophrenia risk: De novo mutations and imprinting. *Schizophrenia Bulletin, 27,* 379–393.

Mallinckrodt, Brent; Porter, Mary Jo; & Kivlighan, Dennis M. (2005). Client attachment to therapist, depth of in-session exploration, and object relations in brief psychotherapy. *Psychotherapy: Theory, Research, Practice, Training, 42,* 85–100.

Manning, Carol A.; Hall, J. L.; & Gold, Paul E. (1990). Glucose effects on memory and other neuropsychological tests in elderly humans. *Psychological Science, 1,* 307–311.

Mansfield, Elizabeth D., & McAdams, Dan P. (1996). Generativity and themes of agency and community in adult autobiography. *Personality and Social Psychology Bulletin, 22,* 721–731.

Maquet, Pierre; Laereys, S.; Peigneux, P.; et al. (2000). Experience-dependent changes in cerebral activation during human REM sleep. *Nature Neuroscience, 8,* 831–836.

Marcus, Gary (2004). *The birth of the mind: How a tiny number of genes creates the complexities of human thought.* New York: Basic Books.

Marcus, Gary F. (1999). *The algebraic mind.* Cambridge, MA: MIT Press.

Marcus, Gary F.; Pinker, Steven; Ullman, Michael; et al. (1992). Overregularization in language acquisition. *Monographs of the Society for Research in Child Development, 57* (Serial No. 228), 1–182.

Marcus, Gary F.; Vijayan, S.; Rao, S. Bandi; & Vishton, P. M. (1999). Rule learning by seven-month-old infants. *Science, 283,* 77–80.

Marcus-Newhall, Amy; Pedersen, William C.; Carlson, Mike; & Miller, Norman (2000). Displaced aggression is alive and well: A meta-analytic review. *Journal of Personality and Social Psychology, 78,* 670–689.

Margolin, Gayla, & Gordis, Elana B. (2004). Children's exposure to violence in the family and community. *Current Directions in Psychological Science, 13,* 152–155.

Markowitz, J. S.; Donovan, J. L.; DeVane, C. L.; et al. (2003, September 17). Effect of St John's wort on drug metabolism by induction of cytochrome P450 3A4 enzyme. *Journal of the American Medical Association, 290,* 1519–1520.

Markus, Hazel R., & Kitayama, Shinobu (1991). Culture and the self: Implications for cognition, emotion, and motivation. *Psychological Review, 98,* 224–253.

Markus, Rob; Panhuysen, Geert; Tuiten, Adriaan; & Koppeschaar, Hans (2000). Effects of food on cortisol and mood in vulnerable subjects under controllable and uncontrollable stress. *Physiology and Behavior, 70,* 333–342.

Marlatt, G. Alan (1996). Models of relapse and relapse prevention: A commentary. *Experimental and Clinical Psychopharmacology, 4,* 55–60.

Marlatt, G. Alan; Baer, John S.; Kivlahan, Daniel R.; et al. (1998). Screening and brief intervention for high-risk college student drinkers. *Journal of Consulting and Clinical Psychology, 66,* 604–615.

Marlatt, G. Alan, & Rohsenow, Damaris J. (1980). Cognitive processes in alcohol use: Expectancy and the balanced placebo design. In N. K. Mello (Ed.), *Advances in substance abuse* (Vol. 1). Greenwich, CT: JAI Press.

Marsh, Elizabeth J., & Tversky, Barbara (2004). Spinning the stories of our lives. *Applied Cognitive Psychology, 18,* 491–503.

Marshall, Grant N.; Wortman, Camille B.; Vickers, Ross R., Jr.; et al. (1994). The five-factor model of personality as a framework for personality health research. *Journal of Personality and Social Psychology, 67,* 278–286.

Marshall, Nancy L. (2004). The quality of early child care and children's development. *Current Directions in Psychological Science, 13,* 165-168.

Martin, Carol Lynn, & Ruble, Diane (2004). Children's search for gender cues. *Current Directions in Psychological Science, 13,* 67–70.

Martin, Carol Lynn; Ruble, Diane N.; & Szkrybalo, Joel (2002). Cognitive theories of early gender development. *Psychological Bulletin, 128,* 903–933.

Martin, Garry, & Pear, Joseph (1999). *Behavior modification: What it is and how to do it* (6th ed.). Upper Saddle River, NJ: Prentice-Hall.

Martin, Stacia K., & Eastman, Charmane I. (1998). Medium-intensity light produces circadian rhythm adaption to simulated night-shift work. *Sleep, 21,* 154–165.

Martinez, Gladys M.; Chandra, Anjani; Abma, Joyce C.; et al. (2006). Fertility, contraception, and fatherhood: Data on men and women from Cycle 6 of the 2002 National Survey of Family Growth. DHHS Publication No. (PHS) 2006-1978. Washington, DC: Centers for Disease Control.

Martino, Gail, & Marks, Lawrence E. (2001). Synesthesia: Strong and weak. *Current Directions in Psychological Science, 10,* 61–69.

Martinson, Brian C.; Anderson, Melissa S.; & de Vries, Raymond (2005). Scientists behaving badly. *Nature, 435,* 737–738.

Maruta, T.; Colligan R. C.; Malinchoc, M.; & Offord, K. P. (2000). Optimists vs. pessimists: Survival rate among medical patients over a 30-year period. *Mayo Clinic Proceedings, 75,* 140–143.

Masand, P. S. (2000). Side effects of antipsychotics in the elderly. *Journal of Clinical Psychiatry, 61*(suppl. 8), 43–49.

Maslach, Christina; Schaufeli, Wilmar B.; & Leiter, Michael P. (2001). Job burnout. *Annual Review of Psychology, 52,* 397–422.

Maslow, Abraham H. (1970). *Motivation and personality* (2nd ed.). New York: Harper & Row.

Maslow, Abraham H. (1971). *The farther reaches of human nature.* New York: Viking.

Masten, Ann S. (2001). Ordinary magic: Resilience processes in development. *American Psychologist, 56,* 227–238.

Masters, William H., & Johnson, Virginia E. (1966). *Human sexual response.* Boston: Little, Brown.

Masuda, Takahiko, & Nisbett, Richard E. (2001). Attending holistically versus analystically: Comparing the context sensitivity of Japanese and Americans. *Journal of Personality and Social Psychology, 81,* 922–934.

Mather, Jennifer A., & Anderson, Roland C. (1993). Personalities of octopuses (Octopus rubescens). *Journal of Comparative Psychology, 197,* 336–340.

Mather, Mara; Shafir, Eldar; & Johnson, Marcia K. (2000). Misremembrance of options past: Source monitoring and choice. *Psychological Science, 11,* 132–138.

Matthews, Gerald; Zeidner, Moshe; & Roberts, Richard D. (2003) *Emotional intelligence: Science and myth.* Cambridge, MA: MIT Press/ Bradford Books.

Matthews, John (Ed.) (1994). *McGill working papers in linguistics* (Vol. 10 [1 & 2]). [Special Issue: Linguistic aspects of familial language impairment.] Montreal, Quebec: McGill University.

Maurer, Daphne; Lewis, Terri L.; Brent, Henry P.; & Levin, Alex V. (1999). Rapid improvement in the acuity of infants after visual input. *Science, 286,* 108–110.

Maviel, Thibault; Durkin, Thomas P.; Menzaghi, Frédérique; & Bontempi, Bruno (2004). Sites of neocortical reorganization critical for remote spatial memory. *Science, 305,* 96–99.

Max, M.; Shanker, Y. G.; Huang, L.; et al. (2001). Tas1r3, encoding a new candidate taste receptor, is allelic to the sweet responsiveness locus Sac. *Nature Genetics, 28,* 58–63.

Maxfield, Michael, & Widom, Cathy S. (1996). The cycle of violence. Revisited 6 years later. *Archives of Pediatric and Adolescent Medicine, 150,* 390–395.

Mayberry, Rachel I., & Nicoladis, Elena (2000). Gesture reflects language development: Evidence from bilingual children. *Current Directions in Psychological Science, 9,* 192–196.

Mayer, John D.; McCormick, Laura J.; & Strong, Sara E. (1995). Mood-congruent memory and natural mood: New evidence. *Personality and Social Psychology Bulletin, 21,* 736–746.

Mayer, John D., & Salovey, Peter (1997). What is emotional intelligence? In P. Salovey & D. Sluyter (Eds.), *Emotional development and emotional intelligence: Implications for educators.* New York: Basic Books.

Mayou, R. A.; Ehlers, A.; & Hobbs, M. (2000). Psychological debriefing for road traffic accident victims. *British Journal of Psychiatry, 176,* 589–593.

Mazza, James J., & Reynolds, William M. (1999). Exposure to violence in young inner-city adolescents: Relationships with suicidal ideation, depression, and PTSD symptomatology. *Journal of Abnormal Child Psychology, 27,* 203–213.

Mazzoni, Giuliana A.; Loftus, Elizabeth F.; & Kirsch, Irving (2001). Changing beliefs about implausible autobiographical events: A little plausibility goes a long way. *Journal of Experimental Psychology: Applied, 7,* 51–59.

Mazzoni, Giuliana A.; Loftus, Elizabeth F.; Seitz, Aaron; & Lynn, Steven J. (1999). Changing beliefs and memories through dream interpretation. *Applied Cognitive Psychology, 13,* 125–144.

McAdams, Dan P., & Pals, Jennifer L. (2006). A new Big Five: Fundamental principles for an integrative science of personality. *American Psychologist, 61,* 204–217.

McCarthy, John (1997). AI as sport [Review of Kasparov versus Deep Blue: Computer chess comes of age, by Monty Newborn]. *Science, 276,* 1518–1519.

McClearn, Gerald E.; Johanson, Boo; Berg, Stig; et al. (1997). Substantial genetic influence on cognitive abilities in twins 80 or more years old. *Science, 176,* 1560–1563.

McClelland, David C. (1961). *The achieving society.* New York: Free Press.

McClelland, David C.; Atkinson, John W.; Clark, Russell A.; & Lowell, Edgar L. (1953). *The achievement motive.* New York: Appleton-Century-Crofts.

McClelland, James L. (1994). The organization of memory: A parallel distributed processing perspective. *Revue Neurologique, 150,* 570–579.

McCord, Joan (1989). Another time, another drug. Paper presented at conference on Vulnerability to the Transition from Drug Use to Abuse and Dependence, Rockville, MD.

McCrae, Robert R. (1987). Creativity, divergent thinking, and openness to experience. *Journal of Personality and Social Psychology, 52,* 1258–1265.

McCrae, Robert R.; Terracciano, Antonio; & members of the Personality Profiles of Cultures Project (2005). Universal features of personality traits from the observer's perspective: Data from 50 cultures. *Journal of Personality and Social Psychology, 88,* 547–561.

McCrae, Robert R.; Terracciano, Antonio; Costa, Paul T. Jr.; & Ozer, Daniel J. (2006). Person-factors in the California adult Q-set: Closing the door on personality trait types? *European Journal of Personality, 20,* 29–44.

McDaniel, Susan H.; Lusterman, Don-David; & Philpot, Carol L. (Eds.) (2001). *Casebook for integrating family therapy: An ecosystemic approach.* Washington, DC: American Psychological Association.

McDonough, Laraine, & Mandler, Jean M. (1994). Very long-term recall in infancy. *Memory, 2,* 339–352.

McElroy, Susan L., & Keck, Paul E., Jr. (2000). Pharmacologic agents for the treatment of acute bipolar mania. *Biological Psychiatry, 48,* 539–557.

McEwen, Bruce S. (1998). Protective and damaging effects of stress mediators. *New England Journal of Medicine, 338,* 171–179.

McEwen, Bruce S. (2000). Allostasis and allostatic load: Implications for neuropsychopharmacology. *Neuropsychopharmacology 22,* 108–124.

McFarland, Cathy, & Alvaro, Celeste (2000). The impact of motivation on temporal comparisons: Coping with traumatic events by perceiving personal growth. *Journal of Personality and Social Psychology, 79,* 327–343.

McFarlane, Jessica; Martin, Carol L.; & Williams, Tannis M. (1988). Mood fluctuations: Women versus men and menstrual versus other cycles. *Psychology of Women Quarterly, 12,* 201–223.

McFarlane, Jessica M., & Williams, Tannis M. (1994). Placing premenstrual syndrome in perspective. *Psychology of Women Quarterly, 18,* 339–373.

McGaugh, James L. (1990). Significance and remembrance: The role of neuromodulatory systems. *Psychological Science, 1,* 15–25.

McGinnis, Michael, & Foege, William (1993, November 10). Actual causes of death in the United States. *Journal of the American Medical Association, 270,* 2207–2212.

McGlashan, Thomas H., & Hoffman, Ralph E. (2000). Schizophrenia as a disorder of developmentally reduced synaptic connectivity. *Archives of General Psychiatry, 57,* 637–648.

McGlynn, Susan M. (1990). Behavioral approaches to neuropsychological rehabilitation. *Psychological Bulletin, 108,* 420–441.

McGoldrick, Monica (1996). Irish families. In M. McGoldrick, J. Giordano, & J. K. Pearce (Eds.), *Ethnicity and family therapy* (2nd ed.). New York: Guilford.

McGoldrick, Monica; Gerson, Randy; & Shellenberger, Sylvia (1999). *Genograms: Assessment and intervention* (2nd ed.). New York: W. W. Norton.

McGregor, Ian, & Holmes, John G. (1999). How storytelling shapes memory and impressions of relationship events over time. *Journal of Personality and Social Psychology, 76,* 403–419.

McGregor, Ian, & Little, Brian R. (1998). Personal projects, happiness, and meaning: On doing well and being yourself. *Journal of Personality and Social Psychology, 74,* 494–512.

McGregor, Jock (1997). *The icon of postmodernity.* Retrieved 9/3/01 from www.studyofmadonna.com/articles.htm.

McGue, Matt (1999). The behavioral genetics of alcoholism. *Current Directions in Psychological Science, 8,* 109–115.

McGue, Matt; Bouchard, Thomas J., Jr.; Iacono, William G.; & Lykken, David T. (1993). Behavioral genetics of cognitive ability: A life-span perspective. In R. Plomin & G. E. McClearn (Eds.), *Nature, nurture, and psychology.* Washington, DC: American Psychological Association.

McGue, Matt, & Lykken, David T. (1992). Genetic influence on risk of divorce. *Psychological Science, 3,* 368–373.

McHugh, Paul R.; Lief, Harold I.; Freyd, Pamela P.; & Fetkewicz, Janet M. (2004). From refusal to reconciliation: Family relationships after an accusation based on recovered memories. *Journal of Nervous and Mental Disease, 192,* 525–531.

McKee, Richard D., & Squire, Larry R. (1992). Equivalent forgetting rates in long-term memory for diencephalic and medial temporal lobe amnesia. *Journal of Neuroscience, 12,* 3765–3772.

McKee, Richard D., & Squire, Larry R. (1993). On the development of declarative memory. *Journal of Experimental Psychology: Learning, Memory, and Cognition, 19,* 397–404.

McKemy, D. D.; Neuhausser, W. M.; Julius, D. (2002). Identification of a cold receptor reveals a general role for TRP channels in thermosensation. *Nature, 416,* 52–58.

McKinlay, John B.; McKinlay, Sonja M.; & Brambilla, Donald (1987). The relative contributions of endocrine changes and social circumstances to depression in mid-aged women. *Journal of Health and Social Behavior, 28,* 345–363.

McLeod, Beverly (1985, March). Real work for real pay. *Psychology Today,* 42–44, 46, 48–50.

McMullin, Darcy, & White, Jacqueline W. (2006). Long-term effects of labeling a rape experience. *Psychology of Women Quarterly, 30,* 96–105.

McNally, Richard J. (1994). *Panic disorder: A critical analysis.* New York: Guilford.

McNally, Richard J. (1998). Panic attacks. In *Encyclopedia of mental health* (Vol. 3). New York: Academic Press.

McNally, Richard J. (2003). *Remembering trauma.* Cambridge, MA: Harvard University Press.

McNally, Richard J.; Bryant, Richard A.; & Ehlers, Anke (2003). Does early psychological intervention promote recovery from posttraumatic stress? *Psychological Science in the Public Interest, 4,* 45–79.

McNaughton, B. L., & Morris, R. G. M. (1987). Hippocampal synaptic enhancement and information storage within a distributed memory system. *Trends in Neuroscience, 10,* 408–415.

McNay, Ewan C.; Canal, Clinton E.; Sherwi, Robert S.; & Gold, Paul E. (2006). Modulation of memory with septal injections of morphine and glucose: Effects on extracellular glucose levels in the hippocampus. *Physiology & Behavior, 87,* 298–303.

McNeill, David (1966). Developmental psycholinguistics. In F. L. Smith & G. A. Miller (Eds.), *The genesis of language: A psycholinguistic approach.* Cambridge, MA: MIT Press.

Mealey, Linda (1996). Evolutionary psychology: The search for evolved mental mechanisms underlying complex human behavior. In J. P. Hurd (Ed.),

Investigating the biological foundations of human morality (Vol. 37). Lewiston, NY: Edwin Mellen Press.

Mealey, Linda (2000). *Sex differences: Developmental and evolutionary strategies.* San Diego: Academic Press.

Medawar, Peter B. (1979). *Advice to a young scientist.* New York: Harper & Row.

Medawar, Peter B. (1982). *Pluto's republic.* Oxford, England: Oxford University Press.

Mednick, Sara C.; Nakayama, Ken; Cantero, Jose L,; et al. (2002). The restorative effect of naps on perceptual deterioration. *Nature Neuroscience, 5,* 677–681.

Mednick, Sarnoff A. (1962). The associative basis of the creative process. *Psychological Review, 69,* 220–232.

Mednick, Sarnoff A.; Huttunen, Matti O.; & Machón, Ricardo (1994). Prenatal influenza infections and adult schizophrenia. *Schizophrenia Bulletin, 20,* 263–267.

Medvec, Victoria H.; Madey, Scott F.; & Gilovich, Thomas (1995). When less is more: Counterfactual thinking and satisfaction among Olympic medalists. *Journal of Personality and Social Psychology, 69,* 603–610.

Meeus, Wim H. J., & Raaijmakers, Quinten A. W. (1995). Obedience in modern society: The Utrecht studies. In A. G. Miller, B. E. Collins, & D. E. Brief (Eds.), Perspectives on obedience to authority: The legacy of the Milgram experiments. *Journal of Social Issues, 51*(3), 155–175.

Meindl, James R., & Lerner, Melvin J. (1985). Exacerbation of extreme responses to an out-group. *Journal of Personality and Social Psychology, 47,* 71–84.

Meissner, Christian A. & Brigham, John C. (2001). Thirty years of investigating the own-race bias in memory for faces: A meta-analytic review. *Psychology, Public Policy, & Law, 7,* 3–35.

Meltzoff, Andrew N., & Gopnik, Alison (1993). The role of imitation in understanding persons and developing a theory of mind. In S. Baron-Cohen, H. Tager-Flusberg, & D. Cohen (Eds.), *Understanding other minds.* New York: Oxford University Press.

Melzack, Ronald (1992, April). Phantom limbs. *Scientific American, 266,* 120–126. [Reprinted in the special issue Mysteries of the Mind, 1997.]

Melzack, Ronald (1993). Pain: Past, present and future. *Canadian Journal of Experimental Psychology, 47,* 615–629.

Melzack, Ronald, & Wall, Patrick D. (1965). Pain mechanisms: A new theory. *Science, 13,* 971–979.

Mennella, Julie A.; Jagnow, C. P.; & Beauchamp, Gary K. (2001). Prenatal and postnatal flavor learning by human infants. *Pediatrics, 107,* E88.

Menon, Tanya; Morris, Michael W.; Chiu, Chi-yue; & Hong, Ying-yi (1999). Culture and the construal of agency: Attribution to individual versus group dispositions. *Journal of Personality and Social Psychology, 76,* 701–717.

Mercer, Jean (2006). *Understanding attachment.* Westport, CT: Praeger.

Merikle, Philip M., & Skanes, Heather E. (1992). Subliminal self-help audiotapes: A search for placebo effects. *Journal of Applied Psychology, 77,* 772–776.

Merskey, Harold (1992). The manufacture of personalities: The production of MPD. *British Journal of Psychiatry, 160,* 327–340.

Merskey, Harold (1995). The manufacture of personalities: The production of multiple personality disorder. In L. M. Cohen, J. N. Berzoff, & M. R. Elin (Eds.), *Dissociative identity disorder: Theoretical and treatment controversies.* Northvale, NJ: Aronson.

Merton, Robert K. (1948). The self-fulfilling prophecy. *Antioch Review, 8,* 193–210.

Mesquita, Batja, & Frijda, Nico H. (1992). Cultural variations in emotions: A review. *Psychological Bulletin, 112,* 179–204.

Mesquita, Batja; Masuda, Taka; Leu, Janxin; Ellsworth, Phoebe; & Karasawa, Mayumi (2004). A cultural lens on facial behavior in emotions. Paper presented at the annual meeting of the American Psychological Society, Chicago.

Meyer, Gregory J.; Finn, Stephen E.; Eyde, Lorraine D.; et al. (2001). Psychological testing and psychological assessment. *American Psychologist, 56,* 128–165.

Meyer-Bahlburg, Heino F. L.; Ehrhardt, Anke A.; Rosen, Laura R.; et al. (1995). Prenatal estrogens and the development of homosexual orientation. *Developmental Psychology, 31,* 12–21.

Mezulis, Amy H.; Abramson, Lyn Y.; Hyde, Janet S.; & Hankin, Benjamin L. (2004). Is there a positivity bias in attributions? *Psychological Bulletin, 130,* 711–747.

Mickelson, Kristin D.; Kessler, Ronald C.; & Shaver, Phillip R. (1997). Adult attachment in a nationally representative sample. *Journal of Personality and Social Psychology, 73,* 1092–1106.

Mieda, Michihiro; Willie, Jon T.; Hara, Junko; et al. (2004). Orexin peptides prevent cataplexy and improve wakefulness in an orexin neuron-ablated model of narcolepsy in mice. *Proceedings of the National Academy of Science, 101,* 4649–4654.

Mikulincer, Mario, & Goodman, Gail (Eds.) (2006). *Dynamics of romantic love: Attachment, caregiving, and sex.* New York: Guilford.

Mikulincer, Mario; Shaver, Phillip R.; Gillath, Omri; & Nitzberg, R. E. (2005). Attachment, caregiving, and altruism: Boosting attachment security increases compassion and helping. *Journal of Personality and Social Psychology, 89,* 817–839.

Mikulincer, Mario; Shaver, Phillip R.; & Horesh, Nita (2006). Attachment bases of emotion regulation and posttraumatic adjustment. In D. K. Snyder, J. A. Simpson, & J. N. Hughes (Eds.), *Emotion regulation in couples and families: Pathways to dysfunction and health.* Washington, DC: American Psychological Association.

Milgram, Stanley (1963). Behavioral study of obedience. *Journal of Abnormal and Social Psychology, 67,* 371–378.

Milgram, Stanley (1974). *Obedience to authority: An experimental view.* New York: Harper & Row.

Millar, J. Kirsty; Pickard, Benjamin S.; Mackie, Shaun; et al. (2005, November 18). DISC1 and PDE4B are interacting genetic factors in schizophrenia that regulate cAMP signaling. *Science, 310,* 1187–1191.

Miller, Bruce L.; Seeley, William W.; Mychack, Paula; et al. (2001). Neuroanatomy of the self: Evidence from patients with frontotemporal dementia. *Neurology, 57,* 817–821.

Miller, George A. (1956). The magical number seven, plus or minus two: Some limits on our capacity for processing information. *Psychological Review, 63,* 81–97.

Miller, Gregory E., & Cohen, Sheldon (2001). Psychological interventions and the immune system: A meta-analytic review and critique. *Health Psychology, 20,* 47–63.

Miller, Inglis J., & Reedy, Frank E. (1990). Variations in human taste bud density and taste intensity perception. *Physiology and Behavior, 47,* 1213–1219.

Miller, Joan G.; Bersoff, David M.; & Harwood, Robin L. (1990). Perceptions of social responsibilities in India and in the United States: Moral imperatives or personal decisions? *Journal of Personality and Social Psychology, 58,* 33–47.

Miller, Neal E. (1978). Biofeedback and visceral learning. *Annual Review of Psychology, 29,* 421–452.

Miller, Todd Q.; Smith, Timothy W.; Turner, Charles W.; et al. (1996). A meta-analytic review of research on hostility and physical health. *Psychological Bulletin, 119,* 322–348.

Miller, William R. (2000). Rediscovering fire: Small interventions, large effects. *Psychology of Addictive Behaviors, 14,* 6–18.

Miller, William R., & Rollnick, Stephen (2002). *Motivational interviewing: Preparing people for change,* 2nd ed. New York: Guilford Press.

Miller-Jones, Dalton (1989). Culture and testing. *American Psychologist, 44,* 360–366.

Milner, Brenda (1970). Memory and the temporal regions of the brain. In K. H. Pribram & D. E. Broadbent (Eds.), *Biology of memory.* New York: Academic Press.

Milner, J. S., & McCanne, T. R. (1991). Neuropsychological correlates of physical child abuse. In J. S. Milner (Ed.), *Neuropsychology of aggression.* Norwell, MA: Kluwer Academic.

Milton, Julie, & Wiseman, Richard (1999). Does Psi exist? Lack of replication of an anomalous process of information transfer. *Psychological Bulletin, 125,* 387–391.

Milton, Julie, & Wiseman, Richard (2001). Does psi exist? Reply to Storm and Ertel (2001). *Psychological Bulletin, 127,* 434–438.

Mineka, Susan, & Zinbarg, Richard (2006). A contemporary learning theory perspective on the etiology of anxiety disorders: It's not what you thought it was. *American Psychologist, 61,* 10–26.

Minuchin, Salvador (1984). *Family kaleidoscope.* Cambridge, MA: Harvard University Press.

Mischel, Walter (1973). Toward a cognitive social learning reconceptualization of personality. *Psychological Review, 80,* 252–253.

Mischel, Walter, & Shoda, Yuichi (1995). A cognitive affective system theory of personality: Reconceptualizing situations, dispositions, dynamics, and invariance in personality structures. *Psychological Review, 102,* 246–268.

Mishkin, Mortimer, & Appenzeller, Tim (1987). The anatomy of memory. *Scientific American, 256,* 80–89.

Mistry, Jayanthi, & Rogoff, Barbara (1994). Remembering in cultural context. In W. J. Lonner & R. Malpass (Eds.), *Psychology and culture.* Needham Heights, MA: Allyn & Bacon.

Mitte, Kristin (2005). Meta-analysis of cognitive-behavioral treatments for generalized anxiety disorder: A comparison with pharmacotherapy. *Psychological Bulletin, 131,* 785–795.

Miyamoto, Yuri, & Kitayama, Shinobu (2002). Cultural variation in correspondence bias: The critical role of attitude diagnosticity of socially constrained behavior. *Journal of Personality and Social Psychology, 83,* 1239–1248.

Miyamoto, Yuri; Nisbett, Richard E.; & Masuda, Takahiko (2006). Culture and the physical environment: Holistic versus analytic perceptual affordances. *Psychological Science, 17,* 113–119.

Modigliani, Andre, & Rochat, François (1995). The role of interaction sequences and the timing of resistance in shaping obedience and defiance to authority. In A. G. Miller, B. E. Collins, & D. E. Brief (Eds.), Perspectives on obedience to authority: The legacy of the Milgram experiments. *Journal of Social Issues, 51*(3), 107–125.

Moen, Phyllis, & Wethington, Elaine (1999). Midlife development in a life course context. In S. L. Willis & J. E. Reid (Eds.), *Life in the middle: Psychological and social development in middle age.* San Diego, CA: Academic Press.

Moffitt, Terrie E. (1993). Adolescence-limited and life-course-persistent antisocial behavior: A developmental taxonomy. *Psychological Review, 100,* 674–701.

Moffitt, Terrie E. (2005). The new look of behavioral genetics in developmental psychopathology: Gene–environment interplay in antisocial behaviors. *Psychological Bulletin, 131,* 533–554.

Moghaddam, Fathali M. (2005). The staircase to terrorism: A psychological exploration. *American Psychologist, 60,* 161–169.

Mohr, Cynthia; Armeli, Stephen; Tennen, Howard; et al. (2001). Daily interpersonal experiences, context, and alcohol consumption: Crying in your beer and toasting good times. *Journal of Personality and Social Psychology, 80,* 489–500.

Molden, Daniel C., & Dweck, Carol S. (2006). Finding "meaning" in psychology: A lay theories approach to self-regulation, social perception, and social development. *American Psychologist, 61,* 192–203.

Moles, Anna; Kieffer, Brigitte; & D'Amato, Francesca (2004). Deficit in attachment behavior in mice lacking the µ-opioid receptor gene. *Science, 304,* 1983–1986.

Molnar-Szakacs, Istvan; Iacoboni, Marco; Koski, Lida; & Mazziotta, John C. (2005). Functional segregation with pars opercularis of the inferior frontal gyrus: Evidence from fMRI studies of imitation and action observation. *Cerebral Cortex, 15,* 986–994.

Molteni, Raffaella; Barnard, R. J.; Ying, Zhe; et al. (2002). A high-fat, refined sugar diet reduces hippocampal brain-derived neurotrophic factor, neuronal plasticity, and learning. *Neuroscience 112,* 803–814.

Monahan, Jennifer L.; Murphy, Sheila T.; & Zajonc, R. B. (2000). Subliminal mere exposure: Specific, general, and diffuse effects. *Psychological Science, 11,* 462–466.

Moncrieff, Joanna (2001). Are antidepressants overrated? A review of methodological problems in antidepressant trials. *Journal of Nervous and Mental Disease, 189,* 288–295.

Montmayeur, J. P.; Liberies, S. D.; Matsunami, H.; & Buck, L. B. (2001). A candidate taste receptor gene near a sweet taste locus. *Nature Neuroscience, 4,* 492–498.

Moore, K. L., & Persaid, T. V. N. (2003). *The developing human: Clinically oriented embryology.* New York: W. B. Saunders.

Moore, Robert Y. (1997). Circadian rhythms: Basic neurobiology and climical applications. *Annual Review of Medicine, 48,* 253–266.

Moore, Timothy E. (1992, Spring). Subliminal perception: Facts and fallacies. *Skeptical Inquirer, 16,* 273–281.

Moore, Timothy E. (1995). Subliminal self-help auditory tapes: An empirical test of perceptual consequences. *Canadian Journal of Behavioural Science, 27,* 9–20.

Moore, Timothy E., & Pepler, Debra J. (2006). Wounding words: Maternal verbal aggression and children's adjustment., *Journal of Family Violence 21,* 89–93.

Morelli, Gilda A.; Rogoff, Barbara; Oppenheim, David; & Goldsmith, Denise (1992). Cultural variation in infants' sleeping arrangements: Questions of independence. *Developmental Psychology, 28,* 604–613.

Morin, Charles M. (2004). Cognitive-behavioral approaches to the treatment of insomnia. *Journal of Clinical Psychiatry, 65[suppl. 16],* 33–40.

Morley, Katherine I., & Montgomery, Grant W. (2001). The genetics of cognitive processes: Candidate genes in humans and animals. *Behavior Genetics, 31,* 511–531.

Morris, Martha C.; Evans, Denis A.; Bienias, Julia L. et al. (2004). Dietary niacin and the risk of Alzheimer's disease and cognitive decline. *Journal of Neurology, Neurosurgery, and Psychiatry, 75,* 1039–1093.

Moscovici, Serge (1985). Social influence and conformity. In G. Lindzey & E. Aronson (Eds.), *Handbook of social psychology* (Vol. 2, 3rd ed.). New York: Random House.

Moscovitch, Morris; Winocur, Gordon; & Behrmann, Marlene (1997). What is special about face recognition? Nineteen experiments on a person with visual object agnosia and dyslexia but normal face recognition. *Journal of Cognitive Neuroscience, 9,* 555–604.

Mostert, Mark P. (2001). Facilitated communication since 1995: A review of published studies. *Journal of Autism and Developmental Disorders, 31,* 287–313.

Moyer, Christopher A.; Rounds, James; & Hannum, James W. (2004). A meta-analysis of massage therapy research. *Psychological Bulletin, 130,* 3–18.

Mozell, Maxwell M.; Smith, Bruce P., Smith, Paul E.; Sullivan, Richard L.; & Swender, Philip (1969). Nasal chemoreception in flavor identification. *Archives of Otolaryngology, 90,* 367–373.

Mroczek, D. K., & Sprio, A., III (2005). Changes in life satisfaction during adulthood: Findings from the veterans affairs normative aging study. *Journal of Personality and Social Psychology, 88,* 189–202.

Mueller, Claudia M., & Dweck, Carol S. (1998). Praise for intelligence can undermine children's motivation and performance. *Journal of Personality and Social Psychology, 75,* 33–52.

Mukamal, Kenneth J.; Conigrove, Katherine M; Mittleman, Murray A.; et al. (2003). Roles of drinking pattern and type of alcohol consumed in coronary heart disease in men. *New England Journal of Medicine, 348,* 109–118.

Müller, Ralph-Axel; Courchesne, Eric; & Allen, Greg (1998). The cerebellum: So much more. [Letter.] *Science, 282,* 879–880.

Mumme, Donna L., & Fernald, Anne (2003). The infant as onlooker: Learning from emotional reactions observed in a television scenario. *Child Development, 74,* 221–237.

Murphy, Sheila T.; Monahan, Jennifer L.; & Zajonc, R. B. (1995). Additivity of nonconscious affect: Combined effects of priming and exposure. *Journal of Personality and Social Psychology, 69,* 589–602.

Murray, Charles (1998). *Income, inequality, and IQ.* Washington, DC: American Enterprise Institute.

Myers, David G., & Scanzoni, Letha D. (2005). *What God has joined together: The Christian case for gay marriage.* San Francisco: HarperSanFrancisco.

Myers, Ronald E., & Sperry, R. W. (1953). Interocular transfer of a visual form discrimination habit in cats after section of the optic chiasm and corpus callosum. *Anatomical Record, 115,* 351–352.

Nachman, Michael W.; Hoekstra, Hopi E., and D'Agostino, Susan L. (2003). The genetic basis of adaptive melanism in pocket mice. *Proceedings of the National Academy of Science, 100,* 5268–5273.

Nakaya, Naoki; Tsubono, Yoshitaka; Hosokawa, Toru; et al. (2003). Personality and the risk of cancer. *Journal of the National Cancer Institute, 95,* 799–805.

Nash, Michael R. (1987). What, if anything, is regressed about hypnotic age regression? A review of the empirical literature. *Psychological Bulletin, 102,* 42–52.

Nash, Michael R. (2001, July). The truth and the hype of hypnosis. *Scientific American, 285,* 46–49, 52–55.

Nash, Michael R., & Barnier, Amanda J., (2007). *The Oxford Handbook of Hypnosis.* Oxford, UK: Oxford University Press.

Nash, Michael R., & Nadon, Robert (1997). Hypnosis. In D. L. Faigman, D. Kaye, M. J. Saks, & J. Sanders (Eds.), *Modern scientific evidence: The law and science of expert testimony.* St. Paul, MN: West.

Nathan, Debbie. (1994, fall). Dividing to conquer? Women, men, and the making of multiple personality disorder. *Social Text, 40,* 77–114.

National Science Board (2000). *Science & engineering indicators 2000.* Chapter 8: Science and technology: Attitudes and public understanding. Arlington, VA: National Science Foundation. [A reprint of the relevant section of this chapter can be found in the January/February 2001 issue of *Skeptical Inquirer,* pp. 12–15.]

Needleman, Herbert L.; Riess, Julie A.; Tobin, Michael J.; et al. (1996). Bone lead levels and delinquent behavior. *Journal of the American Medical Association, 275,* 363–369.

Neher, Andrew (1996). Jung's theory of archetypes: A critique. *Journal of Humanistic Psychology, 36,* 61–91.

Neisser, Ulric (Ed.) (1998). *The rising curve: Long-term gains in IQ and related measures.* Washington, DC: American Psychological Association.

Neisser, Ulric, & Harsch, Nicole (1992). Phantom flashbulbs: False recollections of hearing the news about Challenger. In E. Winograd & U. Neisser (Eds.), *Affect and accuracy in recall: Studies of "flashbulb memories."* New York: Cambridge University Press.

Nelson, C. A.; Thomas, K.; & de Haan, M. (2006). Neural bases of cognitive development. In D. Kuhn & R. S. Siegler (Eds.), *Handbook of child psychology: Vol. 2. Cognition, perception, and language* (6th ed.). Hoboken, NJ: Wiley.

Nelson, Geoffrey; Westhues, Anne; & MacLeod, Jennifer (2003). A meta-analysis of longitudinal research on preschool prevention programs for children. *Prevention & Treatment, 6,* article 31. [Posted online, December 18, 2003.]

Nelson, Thomas O., & Dunlosky, John (1991). When people's judgments of learning (JOLs) are extremely accurate at predicting subsequent recall: The "delayed JOL effect." *Psychological Science, 2,* 267–270.

Nelson, Thomas O., & Leonesio, R. Jacob (1988). Allocation of self-paced study time and the "labor in vain effect." *Journal of Experimental Psychology: Learning, Memory, and Cognition, 14,* 676–686.

Ness, Jose; Aronow, Wilbert S.; & Beck, Gwen (2006). Menopausal symptoms after cessation of hormone replacement therapy. *Maturitas,* 53, 356–361.

Neugarten, Bernice (1979). Time, age, and the life cycle. *American Journal of Psychiatry, 136,* 887–894.

Newcombe, Nora S.; Drummey, Anna B.; Fox, Nathan A.; et al. (2000). Remembering early childhood: How much, how, and why (or why not). *Current Directions in Psychological Science, 9,* 55–58.

Newland, M. Christopher, & Rasmussen, Erin B. (2003). Behavior in adulthood and during aging is affected by contaminant exposure in utero. *Current Directions in Psychological Science, 12,* 212–217.

Newman, Leonard S., & Baumeister, Roy F. (1996). Toward an explanation of the UFO abduction phenomenon: Hypnotic elaboration, extraterrestrial sadomasochism, and spurious memories. *Psychological Inquiry, 7,* 99–126.

NICHD Early Child Care Research Network (2002). Child-care structure-process-outcome: Direct and indirect effects of child-care quality on young children's development. *Psychological Science, 13,* 199–206.

NICHD Early Child Care Research Network (2006). Infant-mother attachment classification: Risk and protection in relation to changing maternal caregiving quality. *Developmental Psychology, 42,* 38–58.

Nickerson, Raymond S. (1998). Confirmation bias: A ubiquitous phenomenon in many guises. *Review of General Psychology, 2,* 175–220.

Nickerson, Raymond A., & Adams, Marilyn Jager (1979). Long-term memory for a common object. *Cognitive Psychology, 11,* 287–307.

NIH Technology Assessment Panel on Integration of Behavioral and Relaxation Approaches into the Treatment of Chronic Pain and Insomnia (1996). *Journal of the American Medical Association, 276,* 313–318.

Nisbett, Richard E. (1993). Violence and U.S. regional culture. *American Psychologist, 48,* 441–449.

Nisbett, Richard E., & Ross, Lee (1980). *Human inference: Strategies and shortcomings of social judgment.* Englewood Cliffs, NJ: Prentice-Hall.

Nolan, Susan A.; Flynn, Cynthia; & Garber, Judy (2003). Prospective relations between rejection and depression in young adolescents. *Journal of Personality and Social Psychology, 85,* 745–755.

Nolen-Hoeksema, Susan (2004). Lost in thought: Rumination and depression. Paper presented at the National Institute on the Teaching of Psychology, St. Petersburg, Florida.

Nonaka, S.; Hough, C. J.; & Chuang, De-Maw (1998, March 3). Chronic lithium treatment robustly protects neurons in the central nervous system

against excitotoxicity by inhibiting N-methyl-D-aspartate receptor-mediated calcium influx. *Proceedings of the National Academy of Sciences, 95*, 2642–2647.

Norcross, John C., Kohout, Jessica L., & Wicherski, Marlene (2005). Graduate study in psychology: 1971 to 2004. *American Psychologist, 60*, 959–975.

Norman, Donald A. (1988). *The psychology of everyday things*. New York: Basic Books.

Nunez, Narina; Poole, Debra A.; & Memon, Amina (2002). Psychology's two cultures revisited: Implications for the integration of science with practice. *Scientific Review of Mental Health Practice, 1*.

Nunn, J. A.; Gregory, L. J.; Brammer, M.; et al. (2002). Functional magnetic resonance imaging of synesthesia: Activation of V4/V8 by spoken words. *Nature neuroscience, 5*, 371–375.

Nyberg, Lars; Habib, Reza; McIntosh, Anthony R.; & Tulving, Endel. (2000). Reactivation of encoding-related brain activity during memory retrieval. *Proceedings of the National Academy of Sciences, 97*, 11120–11124.

Ó Scalaidhe, Séamas P.; Wilson, Fraser A. W.; & Goldman-Rakic, Patricia S. (1997). A real segregation of face-processing neurons in prefrontal cortex. *Science, 278*, 1135–1138.

Oatley, Keith, & Jenkins, Jennifer M. (1996). *Understanding emotions*. Cambridge, MA: Blackwell.

Ogbu, John U. (2003). *Black American students in an affluent suburb: A study of academic disengagement*. Mahwah, NJ: Erlbaum.

Ogden, Jenni A., & Corkin, Suzanne (1991). Memories of H. M. In W. C. Abraham, M. C. Corballis, & K. G. White (Eds.), *Memory mechanisms: A tribute to G. V. Goddard*. Hillsdale, NJ: Erlbaum.

O'Hanlon, Bill (1994, November/December). The third wave. *Family Therapy Networker*, 18–29.

Öhman, Arne, & Mineka, Susan (2001). Fears, phobias, and preparedness: Toward an evolved module of fear and fear learning. *Psychological Review, 108*, 483–522.

Öhman, Arne, & Mineka, Susan (2003). The malicious serpent: Snakes as a prototypical stimulus for an evolved module of fear. *Current Directions in Psychological Science, 12*, 5–9.

Olds, James (1975). Mapping the mind onto the brain. In F. G. Worden, J. P. Swazy, & G. Adelman (Eds.), *The neurosciences: Paths of discovery*. Cambridge, MA: Colonial Press.

Olds, James, & Milner, Peter (1954). Positive reinforcement produced by electrical stimulation of septal area and other regions of the rat brain. *Journal of Comparative and Physiological Psychology, 47*, 419–429.

Oliver, Mary Beth, & Hyde, Janet S. (1993). Gender differences in sexuality: A meta-analysis. *Psychological Bulletin, 114*, 29–51.

Olson, James M.; Vernon, Philip A.; Harris, Julie Aitken; & Jang, Kerry L. (2001). The heritability of attitudes: A study of twins. *Journal of Personality and Social Psychology, 80*, 845–850.

Olsson, Andreas; Ebert, Jeffrey; Banaji, Mahzarin; & Phelps, Elizabeth A. (2005). The role of social groups in the persistence of learned fear. *Science, 309*, 785–787.

Olsson, Andreas, & Phelps, Elizabeth (2004). Learned fear of "unseen" faces after Pavlovian, observational, and instructed fear. *Psychological Science, 15*, 822–828.

Olujic, M. B. (1998). Embodiment of terror: Gendered violence in peacetime and wartime in Croatia and Bosnia-Herzegovina. *Medical Anthropology Quarterly, 12*, 31–50.

Opre, Adrian; Coman, Alin; Kallay, Eva; et al. (2005). Reducing distress in college students by expressive writing. A pilot study on a Romanian sample. *Cognitie Creier Comportament, 9*, 53–64. Romanian Association for Cognitive Science, Romania, www.cognitrom.ro.

O'Rahilly, Ronan, & Müller, Fabiola (2001). *Human embryology and teratology*. New York: Wiley.

Orlinsky, David E., & Howard, Kenneth I. (1994). Unity and diversity among psychotherapies: A comparative perspective. In B. Bongar & L. E. Beutler (Eds.), *Foundations of psychotherapy: Theory, research, and practice*. New York: Oxford University Press.

O'Sullivan, L. F., & Allgeier, Elizabeth R. (1998). Feigning sexual desire: Consenting to unwanted sexual activity in heterosexual dating relationships. *Journal of Sex Research, 35*, 234–243.

Ozer, Emily J.; Best, Suzanne R.; Lipsey, Tami L.; & Weiss, Daniel S. (2003). Predictors of posttraumatic stress disorder and symptoms in adults: A meta-analysis. *Psychological Bulletin, 129*, 52–73.

Özgen, Emre (2004). Language, learning, and color perception. *Current Directions in Psychological Science*, 13, 95-98.

Page, Gayle G.; Ben-Eliyahu, Shamgar; Yirmiya, Raz; & Liebeskind, John C. (1993). Morphine attenuates surgery-induced enhancement of metastatic colonization in rats. *Pain, 54*, 21–28.

Pagel, James F. (2003). Non-dreamers. *Sleep Medicine, 4*, 235–241.

Panksepp, Jaak (1998). Attention deficit hyperactivity disorders, psychostimulants, and intolerance of childhood playfulness: A tragedy in the making? *Current Directions in Psychological Science, 7*, 91–98.

Panksepp, Jaak; Herman, B. H.; Vilberg, T.; et al. (1980). Endogenous opioids and social behavior. *Neuroscience and Biobehavioral Reviews, 4*, 473–487.

Park, Denise, & Gutchess, Angela (2006). The cognitive neuroscience of aging and culture. *Current Directions in Psychological Science, 15*, 105–108.

Park, Robert L. (2000). *Voodoo science: The road from foolishness to fraud*. New York: Oxford University Press.

Parker, Elizabeth S.; Birnbaum, Isabel M.; & Noble, Ernest P. (1976). Alcohol and memory: Storage and state dependency. *Journal of Verbal Learning and Verbal Behavior, 15*, 691–702.

Parker, Elizabeth S.; Cahill, Larry; & McGaugh, James L. (2006). A case of unusual autobiographical remembering. *Neurocase, 12*, 35–49.

Parker, Gordon; Parker, Kay; & Eyers, Kerrie (2003). Cognitive behavior therapy for depression: Choose horses for courses. *American Journal of Psychiatry, 160*, 825–834.

Parlee, Mary B. (1982). Changes in moods and activation levels during the menstrual cycle in experimentally naive subjects. *Psychology of Women Quarterly, 7*, 119–131.

Parlee, Mary B. (1994). The social construction of premenstrual syndrome: A case study of scientific discourse as cultural contestation. In M. G. Winkler & L. B. Cole (Eds.), *The good body: Asceticism in contemporary culture*. New Haven, CT: Yale University Press.

Pascual-Leone, Alvaro; Amedi, Amir; Fregni, Felipe; & Merabet, Lofte B. (2005). The plastic human brain cortex. *Annual Review of Neuroscience, 28*, 377–401.

Patterson, Charlotte J. (1992). Children of lesbian and gay parents. *Child Development, 63*, 1025–1042.

Patterson, Charlotte J. (1995). Sexual orientation and human development: An overview. *Developmental Psychology, 31*, 3–11.

Patterson, David R. (2004). Treating pain with hypnosis. *Current Directions in Psychological Science, 13*, 252–255.

Patterson, David R., & Jensen, Mark P. (2003). Hypnosis and clinical pain. *Psychological Bulletin, 129*, 495–521.

Patterson, Francine, & Linden, Eugene (1981). *The education of Koko*. New York: Holt, Rinehart and Winston.

Paul, Annie M. (2004). *The cult of personality*. New York: The Free Press.

Paul, Richard W. (1984, September). Critical thinking: Fundamental to education for a free society. *Educational Leadership*, 4–14.

Paunonen, Sampo V. (2003). Big Five factors or personality and replicated predictions of behavior. *Journal of Personality & Social Psychology, 84*, 411–422.

Paunonen, Sampo V., & Ashton, Michael C. (2001). Big Five factors and facets and the prediction of behavior. *Journal of Personality and Social Psychology, 81*, 524–539.

Pavlov, Ivan P. (1927). *Conditioned reflexes* (G. V. Anrep, Trans.). London: Oxford University Press.

Pearlin, Leonard (1982). Discontinuities in the study of aging. In T. K. Hareven & K. J. Adams (Eds.), *Aging and life course transitions: An interdisciplinary perspective*. New York: Guilford.

Peele, Stanton, & Brodsky, Archie, with Mary Arnold (1991). *The truth about addiction and recovery*. New York: Simon & Schuster.

Peier, A. M.; Moqrich, A.; Hergarden, A. C.; et al. (2002). A TRP channel that senses cold stimuli and menthol. *Cell, 108*, 705–715.

Pellegrini, Anthony D., & Galda, Lee (1993). Ten years after: A reexamination of symbolic play and literacy research. *Reading Research Quarterly, 28*, 163–175.

Pendergrast, Mark (1995). *Victims of memory* (2nd ed.). Hinesburg, VT: Upper Access Press.

Peng, Kaiping, & Nisbett, Richard E. (1999). Culture, dialectics, and reasoning about contradiction. *American Psychologist, 54*, 741–754.

Pennebaker, James W. (2002). Writing, social processes, and psychotherapy: From past to future. In S. J. Lepore & J. M. Smyth (Eds.), *The writing cure: How expressive writing promotes health and emotional well-being*. Washington, DC: American Psychological Association.

Pennebaker, James W.; Colder, Michelle; & Sharp, Lisa K. (1990). Accelerating the coping process. *Journal of Personality and Social Psychology, 58*, 528–527.

Pennebaker, James W.; Kiecolt-Glaser, Janice; & Glaser, Ronald (1988). Disclosure of traumas and immune function: Health implications for psychotherapy. *Journal of Consulting and Clinical Psychology, 56*, 239–245.

Pennisi, Elizabeth (2005). Why do humans have so few genes? *Science, 309*, 80.

Peplau, Letita Anne (2003). Human sexuality: How do men and women differ? *Current Directions in Psychological Science, 12*, 37–40.

Peplau, Letitia Anne, & Spalding, Leah R. (2000). The close relationships of lesbians, gay men and bisexuals. In C. Hendrick & S. Hendrick (Eds.), *Close relationships: A sourcebook*. Thousand Oaks, CA: Sage.

Peplau, Letitia Anne; Spalding, Leah R.; Conley, Terri D.; & Veniegas, Rosemary C. (2000). The development of sexual orientation in women. *Annual Review of Sex Research, 10*, 70–99.

Pepperberg, Irene (2000). *The Alex studies: Cognitive and communicative abilities of grey parrots*. Cambridge, MA: Harvard University Press.

Pepperberg, Irene M. (2002). Cognitive and communicative abilities of grey parrots. *Current Directions in Psychological Science, 11*, 83–87.

Pepperberg, Irene M. (2006). Grey parrot (*Psittacus erithacus*) numerical abilities: Addition and further experiments on a zero-like concept. *Journal of Comparative Psychology, 120*, 1–11.

Perera, Frederica P.; Rauh, Virginia; Whyatt, Robin M.; et al. (2006). Effect of prenatal exposure to airborne polycyclic aromatic hydrocarbons on neurodevelopment in the first three years of life among inner-city children. *Environ Health Perspectives*, doi:10.1289/ehp.9084. Available via http://dx.doi.org/ [Online 24 April].

Perloff, Robert (1992, Summer). "Where ignorance is bliss, 'tis folly to be wise." *The General Psychologist Newsletter, 28*, 34.

Persons, Jacqueline; Davidson, Joan; & Tompkins, Michael A. (2001). *Essential components of cognitive-behavior therapy for depression*. Washington, DC: American Psychological Association.

Pert, Candace B., & Snyder, Solomon H. (1973). Opiate receptor: Demonstration in nervous tissue. *Science, 179*, 1011–1014.

Pesetsky, David (1999). Introduction to symposium: "Grammar: What's innate?" Paper presented at the annual meeting of the American Association for the Advancement of Science, Anaheim.

Peterson, Christopher (2000). The future of optimism. *American Psychologist, 55*, 44–55.

Peterson, Christopher; Seligman, Martin E. P.; Yurko, Karen H.; et al. (1998). Catastrophizing and untimely death. *Psychological Science, 9*, 127–130.

Peterson, Donald R. (2003). Unintended consequences: Ventures and misadventures in the education of professional psychologists. *American Psychologist, 58*, 791–800.

Peterson, Lloyd R., & Peterson, Margaret J. (1959). Short-term retention of individual verbal items. *Journal of Experimental Psychology, 58*, 193–198.

Peterson, Robert A. (2001). On the use of college students in social science research: Insights from a second-order meta-analysis. *Journal of Consumer Research, 28*, 450–461.

Petrie, Keith J.; Booth, Roger J.; & Pennebaker, James W. (1998). The immunological effects of thought suppression. *Journal of Personality and Social Psychology, 75*, 1264–1272.

Pettigrew, Thomas T., & Tropp, Linda R. (2006). A meta-analytic test of intergroup contact theory. *Journal of Personality and Social Psychology, 90*, 751–783.

Pfungst, Oskar (1911/1965). *Clever Hans (The horse of Mr. von Osten): A contribution to experimental animal and human psychology*. New York: Holt, Rinehart and Winston.

Phillips, D. P.; Ruth, T. E.; & Wagner, L. M. (1993, November 6). Psychology and survival. *Lancet, 342*(8880), 1142–1145.

Phillips, Micheal D.; Lowe, M. J.; Lurito, J. T.; et al. (2001). Temporal lobe activation demonstrates sex-based differences during passive listening. *Radiology, 220*, 202–207.

Phinney, Jean S. (1990). Ethnic identity in adolescents and adults: Review of research. *Psychological Bulletin, 108*, 499–514.

Phinney, Jean S. (1996). When we talk about American ethnic groups, what do we mean? *American Psychologist, 51*, 918–927.

Piaget, Jean (1929/1960). *The child's conception of the world*. Paterson, NJ: Littlefield, Adams.

Piaget, Jean (1952a). *The origins of intelligence in children*. New York: International Universities Press.

Piaget, Jean (1952b). *Play, dreams, and imitation in childhood*. New York: W. W. Norton.

Piaget, Jean (1984). Piaget's theory. In P. Mussen (Series Ed.) & W. Kessen (Vol. Ed.), *Handbook of child psychology: Vol. 1. History, theory, and methods* (4th ed.). New York: Wiley.

Pierce, W. David; Cameron, Judy; Banko, Katherine M.; & So, Sylvia (2003). Positive effects of rewards and performance standards on intrinsic motivation. *Psychological Record, 53*, 561–579.

Pika, Simone, & Mitani, John (2006). Referential gesture communication in wild chimpanzees (*Pan troglodytes*). *Current Biology, 16*, 191–192.

Pincus, Tamar, & Morley, Stephen (2001). Cognitive-processing bias in chronic pain: A review and integration. *Psychological Bulletin, 127*, 599–617.

Pinker, Steven (1994). *The language instinct: How the mind creates language*. New York: Morrow.

Pinker, Steven (1997). *How the mind works*. New York: Norton.

Pinker, Steven (1999). *Words and rules: The ingredients of language*. New York: Basic Books.

Pinker, Steven (2002). *The blank slate: The modern denial of human nature*. New York: Viking.

Piper, August, & Merskey, Harold (2004). The persistence of folly: A critical examination of dissociative identity disorder. Part I: The excesses of an improbable concept. *Canadian Journal of Psychiatry, 49,* 592–600. [Note: Part II (The defence and decline of multiple personality or dissociative identity disorder) appeared in the following issue of the *Canadian Journal of Psychiatry, 49,* 678–683.]

Pittenger, David J. (1993). The utility of the Myers-Briggs Type Indicator. *Review of Educational Research, 63,* 467–488.

Pizzagalli, Diego A.; Sherwood, Rebecca A.; Henriques, Jeffrey B.; & Davidson, Richard J. (2005). Frontal brain asymmetry and reward responsiveness: A source-localization study. *Psychological Science, 16,* 805–813.

Plant, E. Ashby, & Devine, Patricia G. (1998). Internal and external motivation to respond without prejudice. *Journal of Personality and Social Psychology, 75,* 811–832.

Plant, E. Ashby; Hyde, Janet S.; Keltner, Dacher; & Devine, Patricia G. (2000). The gender stereotyping of emotions. *Psychology of Women Quarterly, 24,* 81–92.

Plomin, Robert (1989). Environment and genes: Determinants of behavior. *American Psychologist, 44,* 105–111.

Plomin, Robert; Asbury, Kathryn; & Dunn, Judith F. (2001). Why are children in the same family so different? Nonshared environment a decade later. *Canadian Journal of Psychiatry, 46,* 225–233

Plomin, Robert; Corley, Robin; DeFries, J. C.; & Fulker, D. W. (1990). Individual differences in television viewing in early childhood: Nature as well as nurture. *Psychological Science, 1,* 371–377.

Plomin, Robert, & Crabbe, John (2000). DNA. *Psychological Bulletin, 126,* 806–828.

Plomin, Robert, & DeFries, John C. (1985). *Origins of individual differences in infancy: The Colorado Adoption Project.* New York: Academic Press.

Plomin, Robert; DeFries, John C.; Craig, Ian W.; & McGuffin, Peter (2003). *Behavioral genetics in the postgenomic era.* Washington, DC: American Psychological Association.

Plomin, Robert; DeFries, John C.; McClearn, Gerald E.; & McGuffin, Peter (2001). *Behavioral genetics* (4th ed.). New York: Worth.

Plomin, Robert, & McGuffin, Peter (2003). Psychopathology in the postgenomic era. *Annual Review of Psychology, 54,* 205–228.

Plotsky, Paul M.; Owens, Michael J.; & Nemeroff, Charles B. (1998). Psychoneuroendocrinology of depression: Hypothalamic-pituitary-adrenal axis. *Psychoneuroendocrinology, 21,* 293–307.

Pollak, Richard (1997). *The creation of Dr. B: A biography of Bruno Bettelheim.* New York: Simon & Schuster.

Polusny, Melissa A., & Follette, Victoria M. (1996). Remembering childhood sexual abuse: A national survey of psychologists' clinical practices, beliefs, and personal experiences. Professional Psychology: *Research and Practice, 27,* 41–52.

Poole, Debra A., & Lamb, Michael E. (1998). *Investigative interviews of children.* Washington, DC: American Psychological Association.

Pope, Harrison G., Jr.; Phillips, Katharine A.; & Olivardia, Roberto (2000). *The Adonis complex: The secret crisis of male body obsession.* New York: Free Press.

Portenoy, Russell K. (1994). Opioid therapy for chronic nonmalignant pain: Current status. In H. L. Fields & J. C. Liebeskind (Eds.), *Progress in pain research and management. Pharmacological approaches to the treatment of chronic pain: Vol. 1.* Seattle: International Association for the Study of Pain.

Posthuma, D.; De Gues, E. J.; Baare, W. F.; et al. (2002). The association between brain volume and intelligence is of genetic origin. *Nature Neuroscience, 5,* 83–84.

Posthuma, Danielle, & de Geus, Eco J. C. (2006). Progress in the molecular-genetic study of intelligence. *Current Directions in Psychological Science,* 15, 151–155.

Postmes, Tom, & Spears, Russell (1998). Deindividuation and antinormative behavior: A meta-analysis. *Psychological Bulletin, 123,* 238–259.

Potter, W. James (1987). Does television viewing hinder academic achievement among adolescents? *Human Communication Research, 14,* 27–46.

Poulin-Dubois, Diane; Serbin, Lisa A.; Kenyon, Brenda; & Derbyshire, Alison (1994). Infants' intermodal knowledge about gender. *Developmental Psychology, 30,* 436–442.

Powell, Russell A., & Boer, Douglas P. (1995). Did Freud misinterpret reported memories of sexual abuse as fantasies? *Psychological Reports,* 77, 563–570.

Pratkanis, Anthony, & Aronson, Elliot (2001). *The age of propaganda.* (Rev. ed.). New York: W. H. Freeman.

Premack, David, & Premack, Ann James (1983). *The mind of an ape.* New York: Norton.

Presnell, Katherine; Bearman, Sarah Kate; & Stice, Eric (2004). Risk factors for body dissatisfaction in adolescent boys and girls: A prospective study. *International Journal of Eating Disorders, 36,* 389–401.

Press, Gary A.; Amaral, David G.; & Squire, Larry R. (1989, September 7). Hippocampal abnormalities in amnesic patients revealed by high-resolution magnetic resonance imaging. *Nature, 341,* 54–57.

Pressman, Sarah D., & Cohen, Sheldon (2005). Does positive affect influence health? *Psychological Bulletin, 131,* 925–971.

Preston, Jesse, & Epley, Nicholas (2005). Explanations versus applications: The explanatory power of valuable beliefs. *Psychological Science,* 16, 826–832.

Principe, Gabrielle; Kanaya, Tamoe; Ceci, Stephen J.; & Singh, Mona (2006). Believing is seeing: How rumors can engender false memories in preschoolers. *American Psychologist, 17,* 243–248.

Probst, Paul (2005). "Communication unbound—or unfound"?—Ein integratives Literatur-Review zur Wirksamkeit der "Gestützten Kommunikation" ("Facilitated Communication/FC") bei nichtsprechenden autistischen und intelligenzgeminderten Personen. *Zeitschrift für Klinische Psychologie, Psychiatrie und Psychotherapie. 53,* 93–128.

Prochaska, James O.; Norcross, John C.; & DiClemente, Carlo C. (1994). *Changing for good.* New York: Morrow.

Pronin, Emily; Gilovich, Thomas; & Ross, Lee (2004). Objectivity in the eye of the beholder: Divergent perceptions of bias in self versus others. *Psychological Review, 111,* 781–799.

Pryor, Karen (1999). *Don't shoot the dog: The new art of teaching and training.* New York: Bantam Books.

Ptito, Maurice; Moesgaard, Solvej M.; Gjedde, Albert; & Kupers, Ron (2005). Cross-modal plasticity revealed by electrotactile stimulation of the tongue in the congenitally blind. *Brain, 128,* 606–614.

Punamaeki, Raija-Leena, & Joustie, Marja (1998). The role of culture, violence, and personal factors affecting dream content. *Journal of Cross-Cultural Psychology, 29,* 320–342.

Pynoos, R. S., & Nader, K. (1989). Children's memory and proximity to violence. *Journal of the American Academy of Child and Adolescent Psychiatry, 28,* 236–241.

Pyszczynski, Tom; Greenberg, Jeff; & Solomon, Sheldon (2000). Proximal and distal defense: A new perspective on unconscious motivation. *Current Directions in Psychological Science, 9,* 156–160.

Quinn, Diane M., & Spencer, Steven J. (2001). The interference of stereotype threat with women's generation of mathematical problem-solving strategies. *Journal of Social Issues, 57,* 55–71.

Quinn, Paul (2002). Category representation in young infants. *Current Directions in Psychological Science, 11,* 66–70.

Quinn, Paul, & Bhatt, Ramesh (2005). Learning perceptual organization in infancy. *Psychological Science, 16,* 511–515.

Radetsky, Peter (1991, April). The brainiest cells alive. *Discover, 12,* 82–85, 88, 90.

Radford, Benjamin (June, 2005). Psychic predictions (and rationalizations) fail again. *Skeptical Briefs,* 15, 529.

Raffaelli, Marcela; Crockett, Lisa J.; & Shen, Yuh-ling (2005). Developmental stability and change in self-regulation from childhood to adolescence. *The Journal of Genetic Psychology, 166,* 54–75.

Rahman, Qazi, & Wilson, Glenn D. (2003). Born gay? The psychobiology of human sexual orientation. *Personality and Individual Differences, 34,* 1337–1382.

Räikkönen, Katri; Matthews, Karen A.; Flory, Janine D.; et al. (1999). Effects of optimism, pessimism, and trait anxiety on ambulatory blood pressure and mood during everyday life. *Journal of Personality and Social Psychology, 76,* 104–113.

Raine, Adrian (1996). Autonomic nervous system factors underlying disinhibited, antisocial, and violent behavior. Biosocial perspectives and treatment implications. *Annals of the New York Academy of Sciences, 794,* 46–59.

Raine, Adrian; Lencz, Todd; Bihrle, Susan; LaCasse, Lori; & Colletti, Patrick (2000). Reduced prefrontal gray matter volume and reduced autonomic activity in antisocial personality disorder. *Archives of General Psychiatry, 57,* 119–127.

Raine, Adrian, & Liu, Jiang-Hong (1998). Biological predispositions to violence and their implications for biosocial treatment and prevention. *Psychology, Crime & Law, 4,* 107–125.

Raine, Adrian; Meloy, J. R.; Bihrle, S.; et al. (1998). Reduced prefrontal and increased subcortical brain functioning assessed using positron emission tomography in predatory and affective murderers. *Behavioral Science and Law, 16,* 319–332.

Raine, Adrian; Park, Sohee; Lencz, Todd; et al. (2001). Reduced right hemisphere activation in severely abused violent offenders during a working memory task: An fMRI study. *Aggressive Behavior, 27,* 111–129.

Ramey, Craig T., & Ramey, Sharon Landesman (1998). Early intervention and early experience. *American Psychologist, 53,* 109–120.

Rapkin, Andrea J.; Chang, Li C.; & Reading, Anthony E. (1988). Comparison of retrospective and prospective assessment of premenstrual symptoms. *Psychological Reports, 62,* 55–60.

Raser, Jonathan M., & O'Shea, Erin K. (2005). Noise in gene expression: Origins, consequences, and control. *Science, 309,* 2010–2013.

Raso, Jack (1996, July/August). Alternative health education and pseudocredentialing. *Skeptical Inquirer,* 39–45.

Ratcliffe, Heather (2000, January 28). Midwest UFO sightings get once-over from scientists. *Detroit News,* Religion section [online version].

Rathbun, Constance; DiVirgilio, Letitia; & Waldfogel, Samuel (1958). A restitutive process in children following radical separation from family and culture. *American Journal of Orthopsychiatry, 28,* 408–415.

Rauschecker, Josef P. (1999). Making brain circuits listen. *Science, 285,* 1686–1687.

Ravussin, Eric; Lillioja, Stephen; Knowler, William; et al. (1988). Reduced rate of energy expenditure as a risk factor for body-weight gain. *New England Journal of Medicine, 318,* 467–472.

Ray, Oakley (2004). How the mind hurts and heals the body. *American Psychologist, 59,* 29–40.

Raynor, Hollie A., & Epstein, Leonard H. (2001). Dietary variety, energy regulation, and obesity. *Psychological Bulletin, 127,* 325–341.

Raz, Amir; Fan, Jin; & Posner, Michael I. (2005). Hypnotic suggestion reduces conflict in the human brain. *Proceedings of the National Academy of Science, 102,* 9978–9983.

Raz, Amir; Kirsch, Irving; Pollard, Jessica; & Nitkin-Kamer, Yael (2006). Suggestion reduces the Stroop effect. *Psychological Science,* 17, 91–95.

Reber, Paul J.; Stark, Craig E. L.; & Squire, Larry R. (1998). Contrasting cortical activity associated with category memory and recognition memory. *Learning & Memory, 5,* 420–428.

Redd, W. H.; Dadds, M. R.; Futterman, A. D.; Taylor, K.; & Bovbjerg, D. (1993). Nausea induced by mental images of chemotherapy. *Cancer, 72,* 629–636.

Redelmeier, Donald A., & Tversky, Amos (1996). On the belief that arthritis pain is related to the weather. *Proceedings of the National Academy of Sciences, 93,* 2895–2896.

Reed, Geoffrey M. (1990). Stress, coping, and psychological adaptation in a sample of gay and bisexual men with AIDS. Unpublished doctoral dissertation, University of California, Los Angeles.

Reedy, F. E.; Bartoshuk, L. M.; Miller, I. J.; Duffy, V. B.; Lucchina, L.; & Yanagisawa, K. (1993). Relationships among papillae, taste pores, and 6-n-propylthiouracil (PROP) suprathreshold taste sensitivity. *Chemical Senses, 18,* 618–619.

Regard, Marianne, & Landis, Theodor (1997). "Gourmand syndrome": Eating passion associated with right anterior lesions. *Neurology, 48,* 1185–1190.

Reichenberg, Abraham; Gross, Raz; Weiser, Mark; Bresnahan, Michealine; et al. (2006). Advancing paternal age and autism. *Archives of General Psychiatry, 63,* 1026–1032.

Reid, R. L. (1991). Premenstrual syndrome. *New England Journal of Medicine, 324,* 1208–1210.

Reiner, William G., & Gearhart, John P. (2004, January 22). Discordant sexual identity in some genetic males with cloacal exstrophy assigned to female sex at birth. *New England Journal of Medicine, 350,* 333–341.

Reiss, Diana, & Marino, Lori (2001). Mirror self-recognition in the bottlenose dolphin: A case of cognitive convergence. *Proceedings of the National Academy of Science, 98,* 5937–5942.

Rensink, Ronald (2004). Visual sensing without seeing. *Psychological Science, 15,* 27–32.

Repetti, Rena L.; Taylor, Shelley E.; & Seeman, Teresa E. (2002). Risky families: Family social environments and the mental and physical health of offspring. *Psychological Bulletin, 128,* 330–366.

Rescorla, Robert A. (1988). Pavlovian conditioning: It's not what you think it is. *American Psychologist, 43,* 151–160.

Restak, Richard (1983, October). Is free will a fraud? *Science Digest, 91*(10), 52–55.

Restak, Richard M. (1994). *The modular brain.* New York: Macmillan.

Revell, Victoria L., & Eastman, Charmane I. (2005). How to fool Mother Nature into letting you fly around or stay up all night. *Journal of Biological Rhythms, 20,* 353–365.

Reyna, Valerie, & Farley, Frank (2006). Risk and rationality in adolescent decision making. *Psychological Science in the Public Interest,* 7, 1–44.

Reynolds, Brent A., & Weiss, Samuel (1992). Generation of neurons and astrocytes from isolated cells of the adult mammalian central nervous system. *Science, 255,* 1707–1710.

Reynolds, Kristi; Lewis, L. Brian; Nolen, John David L.; et al. (2003). Alcohol consumption and risk of stroke: A meta-analysis. *Journal of the American Medical Association, 289,* 579–588.

Rhoades, Linda, & Eisenberger, Robert (2002). Perceived organizational support: A review of the literature. *Journal of Applied Psychology, 87,* 698–714.

Ricciardelli, Lina A., & McCabe, Marita P. (2004). A biopsychosocial model of disordered eating and the pursuit of muscularity in adolescent boys. *Psychological Bulletin, 130,* 179–205.

Rice, Mabel L. (1990). Preschoolers' QUIL: Quick incidental learning of words. In G. Conti-Ramsden & C. E. Snow (Eds.), *Children's language* (Vol. 7). Hillsdale, NJ: Erlbaum.

Richards, Ruth L. (1991). Everyday creativity and the arts. Paper presented at the annual meeting of the American Psychological Association, San Francisco.

Richardson, John T. E. (Ed.) (1992). *Cognition and the menstrual cycle.* New York: Springer-Verlag.

Richardson-Klavehn, Alan, & Bjork, Robert A. (1988). Measures of memory. *Annual Review of Psychology, 39*, 475–543.

Ridley-Johnson, Robyn; Cooper, Harris; & Chance, June (1983). The relation of children's television viewing to school achievement and I.Q. *Journal of Educational Research, 76*, 294–297.

Rieber, Robert W. (2006). *The bifurcation of the self.* New York: Springer.

Riessman, Catherine K. (1990). *Divorce talk.* New Brunswick, NJ: Rutgers University Press.

Rind, Bruce; Tromovitch, Philip; & Bauserman, Robert (1998). A meta-analytic examination of assumed properties of child sexual abuse using college samples. *Psychological Bulletin, 124*, 22–53.

Riskind, John H.; Williams, Nathan L.; Gessner, Theodore L.; et al. (2000). The looming maladaptive style: Anxiety, danger, and schematic processing. *Journal of Personality and Social Psychology, 79*, 837–852.

Roan, Shari (2002, April 29). Late-late motherhood. *The Los Angeles Times*, S1, S6.

Roberson, Debi; Davies, Ian; & Davidoff, Jules (2000). Color categories are not universal: Replications and new evidence in favor of linguistic relativity. *Journal of Experimental Psychology: General, 129*, 369–398.

Roberts, Brent W.; Caspi, Avshalom; & Moffitt, Terrie E. (2001). The kids are alright: Growth and stability in personality development from adolescence to adulthood. *Journal of Personality and Social Psychology, 81*, 670–683.

Roberts, Brent W.; Walton, Kate E.; & Viechtbauer, Wolfgang (2006). Patterns of mean-level change in personality traits across the life course: A meta-analysis of longitudinal studies. *Psychological Bulletin, 132*, 1–25.

Robins, Lee N.; Davis, Darlene H.; & Goodwin, Donald W. (1974). Drug use by U.S. Army enlisted men in Vietnam: A follow-up on their return home. *American Journal of Epidemiology, 99*, 235–249.

Robins, Lee N.; Tipp, Jayson; & Przybeck, Thomas R. (1991). Antisocial personality. In L. N. Robins & D. A. Regier (Eds.), *Psychiatric disorders in America.* New York: Free Press.

Robins, Richard W.; Gosling, Samuel D.; & Craik, Kenneth H. (1999). An empirical analysis of trends in psychology. *American Psychologist, 54*, 117–128.

Robinson, Thomas N. (1999, October 27). Reducing children's television viewing to prevent obesity: A randomized controlled trial. *Journal of the American Medical Association, 282*, 1561–1567.

Robinson, Thomas; Wilde, M. L.; Navracruz, L. C.; et al. (2001). Effects of reducing children's television and video game use on aggressive behavior: a randomized controlled trial. *Archives of Pediatric and Adolescent Medicine, 155*, 13–14.

Rocha, Beatriz A.; Scearce-Levie, Kimberly; Lucas, Jose J.; et al. (1998). Increased vulnerability to cocaine in mice lacking the serotonin-1B receptor. *Nature, 393*, 175–178.

Roediger, Henry L. (1990). Implicit memory: Retention without remembering. *American Psychologist, 45*, 1043–1056.

Roediger, Henry L., & McDermott, Kathleen B. (1995). Creating false memories: Remembering words not presented in lists. *Journal of Experimental Psychology; Learning, Memory, & Cognition, 21*, 803–814.

Rogers, Carl (1951). *Client-centered therapy: Its current practice, implications, and theory.* Boston: Houghton-Mifflin.

Rogers, Carl (1961). *On becoming a person.* Boston: Houghton-Mifflin.

Rogers, Ronald W., & Prentice-Dunn, Steven (1981). Deindividuation and anger-mediated interracial aggression: Unmasking regressive racism. *Journal of Personality and Social Psychology, 41*, 63–73.

Rogoff, Barbara (2003). *The cultural nature of human development.* New York: Oxford University Press.

Rollin, Henry (Ed.) (1980). *Coping with schizophrenia.* London: Burnett.

Romanczyk, Raymond G.; Arnstein, Laura; Soorya, Latha V.; & Gillis, Jennifer (2003). The myriad of controversial treatments for autism: A critical evaluation of efficacy. In S.O. Lilienfeld, S. J. Lynn, & J. M. Lohr (Eds.), *Science and pseudoscience in clinical psychology.* New York: Guilford.

Rosch, Eleanor H. (1973). Natural categories. *Cognitive Psychology, 4*, 328–350.

Rosen, Gerald M. (1981). Guidelines for the review of do-it-yourself treatment books. *Contemporary Psychology, 26*, 189–191.

Rosen, Gerald M.; Glasgow, Russell E.; & Moore, Timothy E. (2003). Self-help therapy: The science and business of giving psychology away. In S.O. Lilienfeld, S. J. Lynn, & J. M. Lohr (Eds.), *Science and pseudoscience in clinical psychology.* New York: Guilford.

Rosenberg, Harold (1993). Prediction of controlled drinking by alcoholics and problem drinkers. *Psychological Bulletin, 113*, 129–139.

Rosenblum, Erica B. (2005). The genetics of reptile color evolution at the community level. Invited symposium address, meeting of Evolution 2005, Fairbanks, Alaska.

Rosenthal, Jack (2006, August 27). Precisely false vs. approximately right: A reader's guide to pools. *The New York Times.* [Published online at www.nytimes.com.]

Rosenthal, Norman E. (1998). *Winter blues: Seasonal affective disorder: What it is and how to overcome it.* New York: Guilford Press.

Rosenthal, Robert (1966). *Experimenter effects in behavioral research.* New York: Appleton-Century-Crofts.

Rosenthal, Robert (1994). Interpersonal expectancy effects: A 30-year perspective. *Current Directions in Psychological Science, 3*, 176–179.

Rosenzweig, Mark R. (1984). Experience, memory, and the brain. *American Psychologist, 39*, 365–376.

Roser, Matt E., & Gazzaniga, Michael S. (2004). Automatic brains: Interpretive minds. *Current Directions in Psychological Science, 13*, 56–59.

Roth, David L.; & Holmes, David S. (1985). Influence of physical fitness in determining the impact of stressful life events on physical and psychologic health. *Psychosomatic Medicine, 47*, 164–173.

Rothbart, Mary K.; Ahadi, Stephan A.; & Evans, David E. (2000). Temperament and personality: Origins and outcomes. *Journal of Personality and Social Psychology, 78*, 122–135.

Rothbaum, Fred; Weisz, John; Pott, Martha; et al. (2000). Attachment and culture: Security in the United States and Japan. *American Psychologist, 55*, 1093–1104.

Rothbaum, Fred M.; Weisz, John R.; & Snyder, Samuel S. (1982). Changing the world and changing the self: A two-process model of perceived control. *Journal of Personality and Social Psychology, 42*, 5–37.

Rothenberg, Karen H., & Terry, Sharon F. (2002). Before it's too late—addressing fear of genetic information. *Science, 297*, 196–197.

Rothermund, Klaus, & Wentura, Dirk (2004). Underlying processes in the Implicit Association Test: Dissociating salience from associations. *Journal of Experimental Psychology: General, 133*, 139–165.

Rotter, Julian B. (1990). Internal versus external control of reinforcement: A case history of a variable. *American Psychologist, 45*, 489–493.

Roughgarden, Joan (2004). *Evolution's rainbow: Diversity, gender, and sexuality in nature and people.* Berkeley: University of California Press

Rovee-Collier, Carolyn (1993). The capacity for long-term memory in infancy. *Current Directions in Psychological Science, 2,* 130–135.

Roy, Mark P.; Steptoe, Andrew; & Kirschbaum, Clemens (1998). Life events and social support as moderators of individual differences in cardiovascular and cortisol reactivity. *Journal of Personality and Social Psychology, 75,* 1273–1281.

Røysamb, Espen; Tambs, Kristian; Reichborn-Kjennerud, Ted; et al. (2003). Happiness and health: Environmental and genetic contributions to the relationship between subjective well-being, perceived health, and somatic illness. *Journal of Personality and Social Psychology, 85,* 1136–1146.

Rozin, Paul; Kabnick, Kimberly; Pete, Erin; et al. (2003). The ecology of eating: Smaller portion sizes in France than in the United States help explain the French paradox. *Psychological Science, 14,* 450–454.

Rozin, Paul; Lowery, Laura; & Ebert, Rhonda (1994). Varieties of disgust faces and the structure of disgust. *Journal of Personality and Social Psychology, 66,* 870–881.

Rubinstein, Joshua S.; Meyer, David E.; & Evans, Jeffrey E. (2001). Executive control of cognitive processes in task switching. *Journal of Experimental Psychology: Human Perception and Performance, 27,* 763–797.

Rudman, Laurie A. (2004). Sources of implicit attitudes. *Current Directions in Psychological Science,* 79–82.

Ruggiero, Vincent R. (1988). *Teaching thinking across the curriculum.* New York: Harper & Row.

Ruggiero, Vincent R. (2004). *The art of thinking: A guide to critical and creative thought* (7th ed.). Pearson/Longman.

Rumbaugh, Duane M. (1977). *Language learning by a chimpanzee: The Lana project.* New York: Academic Press.

Rumbaugh, Duane M.; Savage-Rumbaugh, E. Sue; & Pate, James L. (1988). Addendum to "Summation in the chimpanzee (Pan troglodytes)." *Journal of Experimental Psychology: Animal Behavior Processes, 14,* 118–120.

Rumelhart, David E., & McClelland, James L. (1987). Learning the past tenses of English verbs: Implicit rules or parallel distributed processing. In B. MacWhinney (Ed.), *Mechanisms of language acquisition.* Hillsdale, NJ: Erlbaum.

Rumelhart, David E.; McClelland, James L.; & the PDP Research Group (1986). *Parallel distributed processing: Explorations in the microstructure of cognition* (Vols. 1 and 2). Cambridge, MA: MIT Press.

Rushton, J. Philippe (1988). Race differences in behavior: A review and evolutionary analysis. *Personality and Individual Differences, 9,* 1009–1024.

Russell, Diana E. H. (1990). *Rape in marriage* (Rev. ed.). Bloomington: Indiana University Press.

Russell, James A., & Fehr, Beverley (1994). Fuzzy concepts in a fuzzy hierarchy: Varieties of anger. *Journal of Personality and Social Psychology, 67,* 186–205.

Rusting, Cheryl L., & Nolen-Hoeksema, Susan (1998). Regulating responses of anger: Effects of rumination and distraction on angry mood. *Journal of Personality and Social Psychology, 74,* 790–803.

Rutherford, S. (2001). Any differences? An analysis of gender and divisional management styles in a large airline. *Gender, Work and Organization, 8,* 326–345.

Rutter, Michael; O'Connor, Thomas G.; & the English and Romanian Adoptees (ERA) Study Team (2004). Are there biological programming effects for psychological development? Findings from a study of Romanian adoptees. *Developmental Psychology, 40,* 81–94.

Rutter, Michael; Pickles, Andrew; Murray, Robin; & Eaves, Lindon (2001). Testing hypotheses on specific environmental causal effects on behavior. *Psychological Bulletin, 127,* 291–324.

Ryan, Richard M.; Chirkov, Valery I.; Little, Todd D.; et al. (1999). The American dream in Russia: Extrinsic aspirations and well-being in two cultures. *Personality and Social Psychology Bulletin, 25,* 1509–1524.

Rymer, Russ (1993). *Genie: An abused child's flight from silence.* New York: HarperCollins.

Saarni, Carolyn (1989). Children's understanding of strategic control of emotional expression in social transactions. In C. Saarni & P. L. Harris (Eds.), *Children's understanding of emotion.* Cambridge, England: Cambridge University Press.

Sack, Robert L., & Lewy, Alfred J. (1997). Melatonin as a chronobiotic: Treatment of circadian desynchrony in night workers and the blind. *Journal of Biological Rhythms, 12,* 595–603.

Sackett, Paul R.; Hardison, Chaitra M.; & Cullen, Michael J. (2004). On interpreting stereotype threat as accounting for African American-White differences on cognitive tests. *American Psychologist, 59,* 7–13.

Sacks, Oliver (1985). *The man who mistook his wife for a hat and other clinical tales.* New York: Simon & Schuster.

Saffran, J. R.; Aslin, R. N.; & Newport, E. L. (1996). Statistical learning by 8-month-old infants. *Science, 274,* 1926–1928.

Sagan, Eli (1988). *Freud, women, and morality: The psychology of good and evil.* New York: Basic Books.

Sage, Cyrille; Huang, Mingqian; Karimi, Kambiz; et al. (2005). Proliferation of functional hair cells in vivo in the absence of the retinoblastoma protein. *Science, 307,* 114–118.

Sahley, Christie L.; Rudy, Jerry W.; & Gelperin, Alan (1981). An analysis of associative learning in a terrestrial mollusk: 1. Higher-order conditioning, blocking, and a transient US preexposure effect. *Journal of Comparative Physiology, 144,* 1–8.

Salovey, Peter, & Grewal, Daisy (2005). The science of emotional intelligence. *Current Directions in Psychological Science, 14,* 281–285.

Salthouse, Timothy A. (1998). The what and where of cognitive aging. Address presented at the annual meeting of the American Psychological Association, San Francisco.

Salthouse, Timothy A. (2006). Mental exercise and mental aging: Evaluating the validity of the "use it or lose it" hypothesis. *Perspectives on Psychological Science, 1,* 68–87.

Saltz, Bruce L.; Woerner, M. G.; Kane, J. M.; et al. (1991, November 6). Prospective study of tardive dyskinesia incidence in the elderly. *Journal of the American Medical Association, 266*(17), 2402–2406.

Sameroff, Arnold J.; Seifer, Ronald; Barocas, Ralph; et al. (1987). Intelligence quotient scores of 4-year-old children: Social-environmental risk factors. *Pediatrics, 79,* 343–350.

Sampson, Paul D.; Streissguth, Ann P.; Bookstein, Fred L.; & Barr, Helen M. (2000). On categorizations in analyses of alcohol teratogenesis. *Environmental Health Perspectives, 108,* 421–428.

Sanfey, Alan G.; Rilling, James K.; Aronson, Jessica K. (2003). The neural basis of economic decision-making in the Ultimatum Game. *Science, 300,* 1755–1758.

Sapolsky, Robert M. (1997). *The trouble with testosterone.* New York: Touchstone.

Sapolsky, Robert M. (2000). The possibility of neurotoxicity in the hippocampus in major depression: A primer on neuron death. *Biological Psychiatry, 48,* 755–765.

Sapolsky, Robert M. (2005). The influence of social hierarchy on primate health. *Science, 308,* 648–652.

Sarbin, Theodore R. (1991). Hypnosis: A fifty year perspective. *Contemporary Hypnosis, 8,* 1–15.

Sarbin, Theodore R. (1997a). The poetics of identity. *Theory & Psychology, 7,* 67–82.

Sarbin, Theodore R. (1997b). The power of believed-in imaginings. *Psychological Inquiry, 8,* 322–325.

Saucier, Deborah M., & Kimura, Doreen (1998). Intrapersonal motor but not extrapersonal targeting skill is enhanced during the midluteal phase of the menstrual cycle. *Developmental Neuropsychology, 14*, 385–398.

Saucier, Gerard (2000). Isms and the structure of social attitudes. *Journal of Personality and Social Psychology, 78*, 366–385.

Savage-Rumbaugh, Sue, & Lewin, Roger (1994). *Kanzi: The ape at the brink of the human mind.* New York: Wiley.

Savage-Rumbaugh, Sue; Shanker, Stuart; & Taylor, Talbot (1998). *Apes, language and the human mind.* New York: Oxford University Press.

Savic, Ivanka; Berglund, Hans; & Lindström, Per (2005, May 17). Brain response to putative pheromones in homosexual men. *Proceedings of the National Academy of Sciences, 102*, 7356–7361.

Savin-Williams, Ritch C. (2006). Who's gay? Does it matter? *Current Directions in Psychological Science, 15*, 40–44.

Sawa, Akira, & Snyder, Solomon H. (2002, April 26). Schizophrenia: Diverse approaches to a complex disease. *Science, 296*, 692–694.

Sax, Linda; Lindholm, Jennifer; Astin, Alexander; et al. (2002). T*he American freshman: National norms for fall* 2002. Higher Education Research Institute. Los Angeles: University of California, Los Angeles.

Saxe, Leonard (1994). Detection of deception: Polygraph and integrity tests. *Current Directions in Psychological Science, 3*, 69–73.

Saxena, S.; Brody, A. L.; Maidment, K. M.; et al. (2004). Cerebral glucose metabolism in obsessive-compulsive hoarding. *American Journal of Psychiatry*, 161, 1038–1048.

Scarmeas, Nikolaos; Stern, Yaakov, Tang, Ming-Xin; et al. (2006). Mediterranean diet and risk of Alzheimer's disease. *Annals of Neurology, 59*, 6.

Scarr, Sandra (1993). Biological and cultural diversity: The legacy of Darwin for development. *Child Development, 64*, 1333–1353.

Scarr, Sandra; Pakstis, Andrew J.; Katz, Soloman H.; & Barker, William B. (1977). Absence of a relationship between degree of white ancestry and intellectual skill in a black population. *Human Genetics, 39*, 69–86.

Scarr, Sandra, & Weinberg, Robert A. (1994). Educational and occupational achievement of brothers and sisters in adoptive and biologically related families. *Behavioral Genetics, 24*, 301–325.

Schachter, Stanley, & Singer, Jerome E. (1962). Cognitive, social, and physiological determinants of emotional state. *Psychological Review, 69*, 379–399.

Schacter, Daniel L. (1999). The seven sins of memory: Insights from psychology and cognitive neuroscience. *American Psychologist, 54*, 182–203.

Schacter, Daniel L. (2001). *The seven sins of memory: How the mind forgets and remembers.* Boston: Houghton-Mifflin.

Schacter, Daniel L.; Chiu, Chi-yue; & Ochsner, Kevin N. (1993). Implicit memory: A selective review. *Annual Review of Neuroscience, 16*, 159–182.

Schaeffer, Cindy M., & Borduin, Charles M. (2005). Long-term follow-up to a randomized clinical trial of multisystemic therapy with serious and violent juvenile offenders. *Journal of Consulting and Clinical Psychology, 73*, 445–453.

Schafer, Roy (1992). *Retelling a life: Narration and dialogue in psychoanalysis.* New York: Basic Books.

Schaie, K. Warner (1993). The Seattle longitudinal studies of adult intelligence. *Current Directions in Psychological Science, 2*, 171–175.

Schaie, K. Warner, & Zuo, Yan-Ling (2001). Family environments and cognitive functioning. In R. J. Sternberg & E. Grigorenko (Eds.), *Cognitive development in context.* Hillsdale, NJ: Erlbaum.

Schank, Roger, with Peter Childers (1988). *The creative attitude.* New York: Macmillan.

Schellenberg, E. Glenn (2004). Music lessons enhance IQ. *Psychological Science 15*, 511–514.

Scherer, Klaus R. (1997). The role of culture in emotion-antecedent appraisal. *Journal of Personality and Social Psychology, 73*, 902–922.

Scheufele, Peter M. (2000). Effects of progressive relaxation and classical music on measurements of attention, relaxation, and stress responses. *Journal of Behavioral Medicine, 23*, 207–228.

Schlossberg, Nancy K., & Robinson, Susan P. (1996). *Going to plan B.* New York: Simon & Schuster/Fireside.

Schlosser, Eric (2003). *Reefer madness: Sex, drugs, and cheap labor in the American black market.* Boston: Houghton-Mifflin.

Schmelz, M.; Schmidt, R.; Bickel, A.; et al. (1997). Specific C-receptors for itch in human skin. *Journal of Neuroscience, 17*, 8003–8008.

Schmidt, Frank L., & Hunter, John (2004). General mental ability in the world of work: Occupational attainment and job performance. *Journal of Personality and Social Psychology, 86*, 162–173.

Schmitt, David P. (2003). Universal sex differences in the desire for sexual variety: Tests from 52 nations, 6 continents, and 13 islands. *Journal of Personality and Social Psychology, 85*, 85–104.

Schnell, Lisa, & Schwab, Martin E. (1990, January 18). Axonal regeneration in the rat spinal cord produced by an antibody against myelin-associated neurite growth inhibitors. *Nature, 343*, 269–272.

Schofield, P.; Ball, D.; Smith, J. G.; et al.(2004). Optimism and survival in lung carcinoma patients. *Cancer, 100*, 1276–1282.

Schuckit, Marc A. (1998). Relationship among genetic, environmental, and psychological variables in predicting alcoholism. Invited address presented at the annual meeting of the American Psychological Association, San Francisco.

Schuckit, Marc A., & Smith, T. L. (1996). An 8-year follow-up of 450 sons of alcoholic and control subjects. *Archives of General Psychiatry, 53*, 202–210.

Schulz, Richard; Beach, S. R.; Ives, D. G.; et al. (2000). Association between depression and mortality in older adults: The Cardiovascular Health Study. *Archives of Internal Medicine, 160*, 1761–1768.

Schulz, Richard, & Decker, Susan (1985). Long-term adjustment to physical disability: The role of social support, perceived control, and self-blame. *Journal of Personality and Social Psychology, 48*, 1162–1172.

Schuman, Howard, & Scott, Jacqueline (1989). Generations and collective memories. *American Journal of Sociology, 54*, 359–381.

Schwartz, Barry (2004). *The paradox of choice: Why more is less.* New York: Ecco Press.

Schwartz, Jeffrey; Stoessel, Paula W.; Baxter, Lewis R.; et al. (1996). Systematic changes in cerebral glucose metabolic rate after successful behavior modification treatment of obsessive–compulsive disorder. *Archives of General Psychiatry, 53*, 109–113.

Sears, Pauline, & Barbee, Ann H. (1977). Career and life satisfactions among Terman's gifted women. In J. C. Stanley, W. C. George, & C. H. Solano (Eds.), *The gifted and the creative: A fifty-year perspective.* Baltimore, MD: Johns Hopkins University Press.

Segal, Julius (1986). *Winning life's toughest battles.* New York: McGraw-Hill.

Segal, Zindel V.; Williams, J. Mark G.; & Teasdale, John D. (2001). *Mindfulness-based cognitive therapy for depression*: A new approach to preventing relapse. New York: Guilford Press.

Segall, Marshall H.; Campbell, Donald T.; & Herskovits, Melville J. (1966). *The influence of culture on visual perception.* Indianapolis: Bobbs-Merrill.

Segall, Marshall H.; Dasen, Pierre P.; Berry, John W.; & Poortinga, Ype H. (1999). *Human behavior in global perspective.* (2nd ed.). Boston: Allyn & Bacon.

Segalowitz, Sidney J., & Schmidt, Louis A. (2003). Developmental psychology and the neurosciences. In J. Valsiner & K. Connolly (Eds.), *Handbook of Developmental Psychology.* London: Sage Publishers.

Segerstrom, Suzanne C., & Miller, Gregory E. (2004). Psychological stress and the human immune system: A meta-analytic study of 30 years of inquiry. *Psychological Bulletin, 130,* 601–630.

Segerstrom, Suzanne C.; Taylor, Shelley E.; Kemeny, Margaret E.; & Fahey, John L. (1998). Optimism is associated with mood, coping, and immune change in response to stress. *Journal of Personality and Social Psychology, 74,* 1646–1655.

Seidenberg, Mark S. (1997). Language acquisition and use: Learning and applying probabilistic constraints. *Science, 275,* 1599–1603.

Seidenberg, Mark S.; MacDonald, Maryellen C.; & Saffran, Jenny R. (2002). Does grammar start where statistics stop? *Science, 298,* 553–554.

Seidlitz, Larry, & Diener, Edward (1998). Sex differences in the recall of affective experiences. *Journal of Personality and Social Psychology, 74,* 262–271.

Seifer, Ronald; Schiller, Masha; Sameroff, Arnold; et al. (1996). Attachment, maternal sensitivity, and infant temperament during the first year of life. *Developmental Psychology, 32,* 12–25.

Sekuler, Robert, & Blake, Randolph (1994). *Perception* (3rd ed.). New York: Knopf.

Seligman, Martin E. P. (1991). *Learned optimism.* New York: Knopf.

Seligman, Martin E. P., & Csikszentmihaly, Mihaly (2000). Positive psychology: An introduction. *American Psychologist, 55,* 5–14.

Seligman, Martin E. P., & Hager, Joanne L. (1972, August). Biological boundaries of learning: The sauce-béarnaise syndrome. *Psychology Today,* 59–61, 84–87.

Seligman, Martin E. P.; Schulman, Peter; DeRubeis, Robert J.; & Hollon, Steven D. (1999). The prevention of depression and anxiety. *Prevention & Treatment, 2,* electronic posting December 21, 1999 on the Web site of the American Psychological Association.

Selye, Hans (1956). *The stress of life.* New York: McGraw-Hill.

Senghas, Ann, & Coppola, Marie (2001). Children creating language: How Nicaraguan Sign Language acquired a spatial grammar. *Psychological Science, 12,* 323–328.

Serbin, Lisa A.; Powlishta, Kimberly K.; & Gulko, Judith (1993). The development of sex typing in middle childhood. *Monographs of the Society for Research in Child Development, 58*(2), Serial No. 232, v-74.

Serpell, Robert (1994). The cultural construction of intelligence. In W. J. Lonner & R. S. Malpass (Eds.), *Psychology and culture.* Needham Heights, MA: Allyn & Bacon.

Shapiro, Francine (1994). EMDR: In the eye of a paradigm shift. *Behavior Therapist, 17,* 153–156.

Shapiro, Francine (1995). *Eye movement desensitization and reprocessing: Basic principles, protocols, and procedures.* New York: Guilford.

Sharman, Stephanie J.; Manning, Charles G.; & Garry, Maryanne (2005). Explain this: Explaining childhood events inflates confidence for those events. *Applied Cognitive Psychology, 19,* 16–74.

Shatz, Marilyn, & Gelman, Rochel (1973). The development of communication skills: Modifications in the speech of young children as a function of the listener. *Monographs of the Society for Research in Child Development, 38.*

Shaver, Phillip R., & Hazan, Cindy (1993). Adult romantic attachment: Theory and evidence. In D. Perlman & W. H. Jones (Eds.), *Advances in personal relationships* (Vol. 4). London: Kingsley.

Shaver, Phillip R., & Mikulincer, Mario (2006). Attachment and forgiveness in romantic relationships. Paper presented at the annual meeting of the Society for Personality and Social Psychology, Palm Springs, CA.

Shaver, Phillip R.; Wu, Shelley; & Schwartz, Judith C. (1992). Cross-cultural similarities and differences in emotion and its representation: A prototype approach. In M. S. Clark (Ed.), *Review of Personality and Social Psychology* (Vol. 13). Newbury Park, CA: Sage.

Shaw, Philip; Greenstein, Dede; Lerch, Jason; et al. (2006). Intellectual ability and cortical development in children and adolescents. *Nature, 440,* 676–679.

Shaywitz, Bennett A.; Shaywitz, Sally E.; Pugh, Kenneth R.; et al. (1995). Sex differences in the functional organization of the brain for language. *Nature, 373,* 607–609.

Shea, Chrisopher (2001, September). White man can't contextualize. *Lingua Franca,* 44–47, 49–51.

Sheldon, Kennon M.; Elliot, Andrew J.; Kim, Youngmee; & Kasser, Tim (2001). What is satisfying about satisfying events? Testing 10 candidate psychological needs. *Journal of Personality and Social Psychology, 80,* 325–339.

Sheldon, Kennon M., & Houser-Marko, Linda (2001). Self-concordance, goal attainment, and the pursuit of happiness: Can there be an upward spiral? *Journal of Personality and Social Psychology, 80,* 152–165.

Sheline, Yvette I. (2000). 3D MRI studies of neuroanatomic changes in unipolar major depression: The role of stress and medical comorbidity. *Biological Psychiatry, 48,* 791–800.

Shepard, Roger N., & Metzler, Jacqueline (1971). Mental rotation of three-dimensional objects. *Science, 171,* 701–703.

Shepperd, James A. (1995). Remedying motivation and productivity loss in collective settings. *Current Directions in Psychological Science, 4,* 131–140.

Sherif, Muzafer (1958). Superordinate goals in the reduction of intergroup conflicts. *American Journal of Sociology, 63,* 349–356.

Sherif, Muzafer; Harvey, O. J.; White, B. J.; Hood, William; & Sherif, Carolyn (1961). *Intergroup conflict and cooperation: The Robbers Cave experiment.* Norman: University of Oklahoma Institute of Intergroup Relations.

Sherman, Bonnie R., & Kunda, Ziva (1989). Motivated evaluation of scientific evidence. Paper presented at the annual meeting of the American Psychological Society, Arlington, VA.

Shermer, Michael (1997). *Why people believe weird things: Pseudoscience, superstition, and other confusions of our time.* New York: Freeman.

Sherwin, Barbara B. (1998a). Estrogen and cognitive functioning in women. *Proceedings of the Society for Experimental Biological Medicine, 217,* 17–22.

Sherwin, Barbara B. (1998b). Use of combined estrogen-androgen preparations in the postmenopause: Evidence from clinical studies. *International Journal of Fertility & Women's Medicine, 43,* 98–103.

Shields, Stephanie A. (2005). The politics of emotion in everyday life: "Appropriate" emotion and claims on identity. *Review of General Psychology, 9,* 3–15.

Showalter, Elaine (1997). *Hystories: Hysterical epidemics and modern culture.* New York: Columbia University Press.

Sidanius, Jim; Pratto, Felicia; & Bobo, Lawrence (1996). Racism, conservatism, affirmative action, and intellectual sophistication: A matter of principled conservatism or group dominance? *Journal of Personality and Social Psychology, 70,* 476–490.

Siegel, Judith M. (1990). Stressful life events and use of physician services among the elderly: The moderating role of pet ownership. *Journal of Personality and Social Psychology, 58,* 1081–1086.

Siegel, Ronald K. (1989). *Intoxication: Life in pursuit of artificial paradise.* New York: Dutton.

Siegel, Shepard (2005). Drug tolerance, drug addiction, and drug anticipation. *Current Directions in Psychological Science, 14,* 296–300.

Siegler, Robert S. (2006). Microgenetic analyses of learning. In D. Kuhn & R. S. Siegler (Eds.), *Handbook of child psychology: Vol. 2. Cognition, perception, and language* (6th ed.). New York: Wiley.

Silke, Andrew (Ed.) (2003). *Terrorists, victims, and society: Psychological perspectives on terrorism and its consequences.* New York: Wiley.

Silverstein, Brett, & Perlick, Deborah (1995). *The cost of competence: Why inequality causes depression, eating disorders, and illness in women.* New York: Oxford University Press.

Simcock, Gabrielle, & Hayne, Harlene (2002). Breaking the barrier: Children fail to translate their preverbal memories into language. *Psychological Science, 13,* 225–231.

Simon, Herbert A. (1955). A behavioral model of rational choice. *Quarterly Journal of Economics, 69,* 99–118.

Simon, Taryn (January 26, 2003). Freedom row. *The New York Times Magazine,* 32, 37.

Simons, Daniel J., & Chabris, Christopher F. (1999). Gorillas in our midst: Sustained inattentional blindness for dynamic events. *Perception, 28,* 1059–1974.

Sims, Ethan A. (1974). Studies in human hyperphagia. In G. Bray & J. Bethune (Eds.), *Treatment and management of obesity.* New York: Harper & Row.

Sinaceur, Marwan; Heath, Chip; & Cole, Steve (2005). Emotional and deliberative reactions to a public crisis: Mad cow disease in France. *Psychological Science, 16,* 247–254.

Sinclair, Lisa, & Kunda, Ziva (1999). Reactions to a Black professional: Motivated inhibition and activation of conflicting stereotypes. *Journal of Personality and Social Psychology,* 77, 885–904.

Singer, Margaret T. (2003). *Cults in our midst* (Rev. ed.). New York: Wiley.

Singer, Margaret T. (with Janja Lalich) (1995). *Cults in our midst.* San Francisco: Jossey-Bass.

Singh, Devendra; Vidaurri, Melody; Zambarano, Robert J.; & Dabbs, James M., Jr. (1999). Lesbian erotic role identification: Behavioral, morphological, and hormonal correlates. *Journal of Personality and Social Psychology, 76,* 1035–1049.

Sininger, Y. S., & Cone-Wesson, B. (2004). Asymmetric cochlear processing mimics hemispheric specialization. *Science, 305,* 1581.

Sivak, Michael, & Flannagan, Michael J. (2003). Flying and driving after the September 11 attacks. *American Scientist, 91,* 6–8.

Skinner, B. F. (1938). *The behavior of organisms: An experimental analysis.* New York: Appleton-Century-Crofts.

Skinner, B. F. (1948/1976). *Walden Two.* New York: Macmillan.

Skinner, B. F. (1956). A case history in the scientific method. *American Psychologist, 11,* 221–233.

Skinner, B. F. (1972). The operational analysis of psychological terms. In *B. F. Skinner, Cumulative record* (3rd ed.). New York: Appleton-Century-Crofts.

Skinner, B. F. (1990). Can psychology be a science of mind? *American Psychologist, 45,* 1206–1210.

Skinner, B. F., & Vaughan, Margaret (1984). *Enjoy old age.* New York: W. W. Norton.

Skinner, Ellen A. (1996). A guide to constructs of control. *Journal of Personality and Social Psychology,* 71, 549–570.

Skinner, J. B.; Erskine, A.; Pearce, S. A.; et al. (1990). The evaluation of a cognitive behavioural treatment programme in outpatients with chronic pain. *Journal of Psychosomatic Research, 34,* 13–19.

Skreslet, Paula (1987, November 30). The prizes of first grade. *Newsweek,* 8.

Slade, Pauline (1984). Premenstrual emotional changes in normal women: Fact or fiction? *Journal of Psychosomatic Research, 28,* 1–7.

Slavin, Robert E., & Cooper, Robert (1999). Improving intergroup relations: Lessons learned from cooperative learning programs. *Journal of Social Issues, 55,* 647–663.

Slobin, Daniel I. (Ed.) (1985). *The cross-linguistic study of language acquisition* (Vols. 1 and 2). Hillsdale, NJ: Erlbaum.

Slobin, Daniel I. (Ed.) (1991). *The cross-linguistic study of language acquisition* (Vol. 3). Hillsdale, NJ: Erlbaum.

Slovic, Paul; Finucane, Melissa L.; Peters, Ellen.; & MacGregor, Donald G. (2002). The affect heuristic. In T. Gilovich, D. Griffin, & D. Kahneman (Eds.), *Heuristics and biases: The psychology of intuitive judgment.* New York: Cambridge University Press.

Smilek, Daniel; Dixon, Mike J.; Cudahy, Certa; & Merikle, Philip (2002). Synesthetic color experiences influence memory. *Psychological Science, 13,* 548–552.

Smith, David N. (1998). The psychocultural roots of genocide: Legitimacy and crisis in Rwanda. *American Psychologist, 53,* 743–753.

Smith, James F., & Kida, Thomas (1991). Heuristics and biases: Expertise and task realism in auditing. *Psychological Bulletin, 109,* 472–489.

Smith, Larissa L., & Reise, Steven P. (1998). Gender differences on negative affectivity: An IRT study of differential item functioning on the Multidimensional Personality Questionnaire Stress Reaction Scale. *Journal of Personality and Social Psychology, 75,* 1350–1362.

Smith, Peter B., & Bond, Michael H. (1994). *Social psychology across cultures: Analysis and perspectives.* Boston: Allyn & Bacon.

Smither, Robert D. (1998). *The psychology of work and human performance* (3rd ed.). New York: Longman.

Snow, Barry R; Pinter, Isaac; Gusmorino, Paul; et al. (1986). Sex differences in chronic pain: Incidence and causal mechanisms. Paper presented at the annual meeting of the American Psychological Association, Washington, DC.

Snowdon, Charles T. (1997). The "nature" of sex differences: Myths of male and female. In P.A. Gowaty (Ed.), *Feminism and evolutionary biology.* New York: Chapman and Hall.

Snyder, C. R., & Shenkel, Randee J. (1975, March). The P. T. Barnum effect. *Psychology Today,* 52–54.

Sobell, Mark B., & Sobell, Linda C. (1993). *Problem drinkers: Guided self-change treatment.* New York: Guilford.

Solomon, Paul R. (1979). Science and television commercials: Adding relevance to the research methodology course. *Teaching of Psychology, 6,* 26–30.

Solomon, Robert C. (1994). *About love.* Lanham, MD: Littlefield Adams.

Somer, Oya, & Goldberg, Lewis R. (1999). The structure of Turkish trait-descriptive adjectives. *Journal of Personality and Social Psychology, 76,* 431–450.

Sommer, Robert (1969). *Personal space: The behavioral basis of design.* Englewood Cliffs, NJ: Prentice-Hall.

Sommer, Robert (1977, January). Toward a psychology of natural behavior. *APA Monitor.* (Reprinted in *Readings in psychology* 78/79. Guilford, CT: Dushkin, 1978.)

Sorce, James F.; Emde, Robert N.; Campos, Joseph; & Klinnert, Mary D. (1985). Maternal emotional signaling: Its effect on the visual cliff behavior of 1-year-olds. *Developmental Psychology, 21,* 195–200.

Spanos, Nicholas P. (1991). A sociocognitive approach to hypnosis. In S. J. Lynn & J. W. Rhue (Eds.), *Theories of hypnosis: Current models and perspectives.* New York: Guilford Press.

Spanos, Nicholas P. (1996). *Multiple identities and false memories: A sociocognitive perspective.* Washington, DC: American Psychological Association.

Spanos, Nicholas P.; Burgess, Cheryl A.; Roncon, Vera; et al. (1993). Surreptitiously observed hypnotic responding in simulators and in skill-trained and untrained high hypnotizables. *Journal of Personality and Social Psychology, 65,* 391–398.

Spanos, Nicholas P.; Menary, Evelyn; Gabora, Natalie J.; et al. (1991). Secondary identity enactments during hypnotic past-life regression: A sociocognitive perspective. *Journal of Personality and Social Psychology, 61,* 308–320.

Spanos, Nicholas P.; Stenstrom, Robert J.; & Johnson, Joseph C. (1988). Hypnosis, placebo, and suggestion in the treatment of warts. *Psychosomatic Medicine, 50,* 245–260.

Spear, Linda P. (2000a). Neurobiological changes in adolescence. *Current Directions in Psychological Science, 9,* 111–114.

Spear, Linda P. (2000b). The adolescent brain and age-related behavioral manifestations. *Neuroscience and Biobehavioral Review, 24,* 417–463.

Spearman, Charles (1927). *The abilities of man.* London: Macmillan.

Spelke, Elizabeth S. (2000). Core knowledge. *American Psychologist, 55,* 1233–1243.

Spencer, M. B., & Dornbusch, Sanford M. (1990). Ethnicity. In S. S. Feldman & G. R. Elliott (Eds.), *At the threshold: The developing adolescent.* Cambridge, MA: Harvard University Press.

Sperling, George (1960). The information available in brief visual presentations. *Psychological Monographs, 74*(498).

Sperry, Roger W. (1964). The great cerebral commissure. *Scientific American, 210*(1), 42–52.

Sperry, Roger W. (1982). Some effects of disconnecting the cerebral hemispheres. *Science, 217,* 1223–1226.

Spilich, George J.; June, Lorraine; & Renner, Judith (1992). Cigarette smoking and cognitive performance. *British Journal of Addiction, 87,* 113–126.

Spitz, Herman H. (1997). *Nonconscious movements: From mystical messages to facilitated communication.* Mahwah, NJ: Erlbaum.

Sprecher, Susan; Sullivan, Quintin; & Hatfield, Elaine (1994). Mate selection preferences: Gender differences examined in a national sample. *Journal of Personality and Social Psychology, 66,* 1074–1080.

Spring, Bonnie; Chiodo, June; & Bowen, Deborah J. (1987). Carbohydrates, tryptophan, and behavior: A methodological review. *Psychological Bulletin, 102,* 234–256.

Springer, Sally P., & Deutsch, Georg (1998). *Left brain, right brain: Perspectives from cognitive neuroscience.* New York: Freeman.

Squier, Leslie H., & Domhoff, G. William (1998). The presentation of dreaming and dreams in introductory psychology textbooks: A critical examination with suggestions for textbook authors and course instructors. *Dreaming, 8,* 149–168.

Squire, Larry R. (1987). *Memory and the brain.* New York: Oxford University Press.

Squire, Larry R.; Ojemann, Jeffrey G.; Miezin, Francis M.; et al. (1992). Activation of the hippocampus in normal humans: A functional anatomical study of memory. *Proceedings of the National Academy of Science, 89,* 1837–1841.

Squire, Larry R., & Zola-Morgan, Stuart (1991). The medial temporal lobe memory system. *Science, 253,* 1380–1386.

Srivastava, Abhishek; Locke, Edwin A.; & Bartol, Kathryn M. (2001). Money and subjective well-being: It's not the money, it's the motives. *Journal of Personality and Social Psychology, 80,* 959–971.

Staats, Carolyn K., & Staats, Arthur W. (1957). Meaning established by classical conditioning. *Journal of Experimental Psychology, 54,* 74–80.

Stadler, Michael A., & Frensch, Peter A. (1998). *Handbook of implicit learning.* Thousand Oaks, CA: Sage.

Stajkovic, Alexander D., & Luthans, Fred (1998). Self-efficacy and work-related performance: A meta-analysis. *Psychological Bulletin, 124,* 240–261.

Stanovich, Keith (1996). *How to think straight about psychology* (4th ed.). New York: HarperCollins.

Stanwood, Gregg D., & Levitt, Pat (2001). *The effects of cocaine on the developing nervous system.* In C. A. Nelson & M. Luciana (Eds.), *Handbook of developmental cognitive neuroscience.* Cambridge, MA: The MIT Press.

Staples, Susan L. (1996). Human response to environmental noise: Psychological research and public policy. *American Psychologist, 51,* 143–150.

Stapley, Janice C., & Haviland, Jeannette M. (1989). Beyond depression: Gender differences in normal adolescents' emotional experiences. *Sex Roles, 20,* 295–308.

Stark-Wroblewski, Kim; Yanico, Barbara J.; & Lupe, Steven (2005). Acculturation, internalization of Western appearance norms, and eating pathology among Japanese and Chinese international student women. *Psychology of Women Quarterly, 29,* 38–46.

Stattin, Haken, & Magnusson, David (1990). *Pubertal maturation in female development.* Hillsdale, NJ: Erlbaum.

Staub, Ervin (1996). Cultural-social roots of violence. *American Psychologist, 51,* 117–132.

Staub, Ervin (1999). The roots of evil: Social conditions, culture, personality, and basic human needs. *Personality and Social Psychology Review, 3,* 179–192.

Staudinger, Ursula M.; Fleeson, William; & Baltes, Paul B. (1999). Predictors of subjective physical health and global well-being: Similarities and differences between the United States and Germany. *Journal of Personality and Social Psychology, 76,* 305–319.

St. Clair, D.; Xu, M.; Wang, P.; et al. (2005, August 3). Rates of adult schizophrenia following prenatal exposure to the Chinese famine of 1959–1961. *Journal of the American Medical Association, 294,* 557–562.

Stearns, Peter N. (1997). *Fat history: Bodies and beauty in the modern West.* New York: New York University Press.

Steele, Claude M. (1992, April). Race and the schooling of Black Americans. *Atlantic Monthly,* 68–78.

Steele, Claude M. (1997). A threat in the air: How stereotypes shape intellectual identity and performance. *American Psychologist, 52,* 613–629.

Steele, Claude M., & Aronson, Joshua (1995). Stereotype threat and the intellectual test performance of African-Americans. *Journal of Personality and Social Psychology, 69,* 797–811.

Stein, M. B.; Jang, K. L.; Taylor, S.; Vernon, P. A.; & Livesley, W. J. (2002). Genetic and environmental influences on trauma exposure and post-traumatic stress disorder symptoms: A general population twin study. *American Journal of Psychiatry, 159,* 1675–1681.

Steinberg, Laurence, & Scott, Elizabeth S. (2003). Less guilty by reason of adolescence. *American Psychologist, 58,* 1009–1018.

Steinberg, Laurence D.; Dornbusch, Sanford M.; & Brown, B. Bradford (1992). Ethnic differences in adolescent achievement: An ecological perspective. *American Psychologist, 47,* 723–729.

Steiner, Robert A. (1989). *Don't get taken!* El Cerrito, CA: Wide-Awake Books.

Stenberg, Craig R., & Campos, Joseph (1990). The development of anger expressions in infancy. In N. Stein, B. Leventhal, & T. Trabasso (Eds.), *Psychological and biological approaches to emotion.* Hillsdale, NJ: Erlbaum.

Stepanski, Edward, & Perlis, Michael (2000). Behavioral sleep medicine: An emerging subspecialty in health psychology. *Journal of Psychosomatic Research, 49,* 343–347.

Stephan, Walter G. (1999). *Reducing prejudice and stereotyping in schools.* New York: Teachers College Press.

Stephan, Walter G.; Ageyev, Vladimir; Coates-Shrider, Lisa; et al. (1994). On the relationship between stereotypes and prejudice: An international study. *Personality and Social Psychology Bulletin, 20,* 277–284.

Stern, Marilyn, & Karraker, Katherine H. (1989). Sex stereotyping of infants: A review of gender labeling studies. *Sex Roles, 20,* 501–522.

Sternberg, Robert J. (1988). *The triarchic mind: A new theory of human intelligence.* New York: Viking.

Sternberg, Robert J. (1995). *In search of the human mind.* Orlando, FL: Harcourt Brace.

Sternberg, Robert J. (1997). Construct validation of a triangular love scale. *European Journal of Social Psychology, 27,* 313–335.

Sternberg, Robert J. (2004). Culture and intelligence. *American Psychologist, 59,* 325–338.

Sternberg, Robert J.; Forsythe, George B.; Hedlund, Jennifer; et al. (2000). *Practical intelligence in everyday life.* New York: Cambridge University Press.

Sternberg, Robert J., & Wagner, Richard K. (1989). Individual differences in practical knowledge and its acquisition. In P. Ackerman, R. J. Sternberg, & R. Glaser (Eds.), *Individual differences.* New York: Freeman.

Sternberg, Robert J.; Wagner, Richard K.; Williams, Wendy M.; & Horvath, Joseph A. (1995). Testing common sense. *American Psychologist, 50,* 912–927.

Stevenson, Harold W.; Chen, Chuansheng; & Lee, Shin-ying (1993, January 1). Mathematics achievement of Chinese, Japanese, and American children: Ten years later. *Science, 259,* 53–58.

Stevenson, Harold W., & Stigler, James W. (1992). *The learning gap.* New York: Summit.

Stewart-Williams, Steve, & Podd, John (2004). The placebo effect: Dissolving the expectancy versus conditioning debate. *Psychological Bulletin, 130,* 324–340.

Stickgold, Robert (2005). Sleep-dependent memory consolidation. *Nature, 437,* 1272–1278.

Stoch, M. B., & Smythe, P. M. (1963). Does undernutrition during infancy inhibit brain growth and subsequent intellectual development? *Archives of Diseases in Childhood, 38,* 546–552.

Strack, Fritz; Martin, Leonard L.; & Stepper, Sabine (1988). Inhibiting and facilitating conditions of the human smile: A nonobtrusive test of the facial-feedback hypothesis. *Journal of Social and Personality Psychology, 54,* 768–777.

Strahan, Erin J.; Spencer, Steven J.; & Zanna, Mark P. (2002). Subliminal priming and persuasion: Striking while the iron is hot. *Journal of Experimental Social Psychology.*

Strange, Deryn; Garry, Maryanne; & Sutherland, Rachel (2003). Drawing out children's false memories. *Applied Cognitive Psychology, 17,* 607–619.

Straus, Murray A., & Kantor, Glenda Kaufman (1994). Corporal punishment of adolescents by parents: A risk factor in the epidemiology of depression, suicide, alcohol abuse, child abuse, and wife beating. *Adolescence, 29,* 543–561.

Streissguth, Ann P. (2001). Recent advances in fetal alcohol syndrome and alcohol use in pregnancy. In D. P. Agarwal & H. K. Seitz (Eds.), *Alcohol in health and disease.* New York: Marcel Dekker.

Streyffeler, Lisa L., & McNally, Richard J. (1998). Fundamentalists and liberals: personality characteristics of Protestant Christians. *Personality and Individual Differences, 24,* 579–580.

Strickland, Bonnie R. (1989). Internal–external control expectancies: From contingency to creativity. *American Psychologist, 44,* 1–12.

Strickland, Tony L.; Lin, Keh-Ming; Fu, Paul; et al. (1995). Comparison of lithium ratio between African-American and Caucasian bipolar patients. *Biological Psychiatry, 37,* 325–330.

Strickland, Tony L.; Ranganath, Vijay; Lin, Keh-Ming; et al. (1991). Psychopharmacological considerations in the treatment of black American populations. *Psychopharmacology Bulletin, 27,* 441–448.

Stroebe, Margaret; Strobe, Wolfgang; & Schut, Henk (2001). Gender differences in adjustment to bereavement: An empirical and theoretical review. *Review of General Psychology, 5,* 62–83.

Stunkard, Albert J. (Ed.) (1980). *Obesity.* Philadelphia: Saunders.

Suddendorf, Thomas, & Whiten, Andrew (2001). Mental evolution and development: Evidence for secondary representation in children, great apes, and other animals. *Psychological Bulletin, 127,* 629–650.

Suedfeld, Peter (1975). The benefits of boredom: Sensory deprivation reconsidered. *American Scientist, 63*(1), 60–69.

Suinn, Richard M. (2001). The terrible twos—Anger and anxiety. *American Psychologist, 56,* 27–36.

Sullivan, Michael J. L.; Tripp, Dean A.; & Santor, Darcy (1998). Gender differences in pain and pain behaviour: The role of catastrophizing. Paper presented at the annual meeting of the American Psychological Association, San Francisco.

Sulloway, Frank J. (1992). *Freud, biologist of the mind: Beyond the psychoanalytic legend* (Rev. ed.). Cambridge, MA: Harvard University Press.

Suls, Jerry, & Bunde, James (2005). Anger, anxiety, and depression as risk factors for cardiovascular disease: The problems and implications of overlapping affective dispositions. *Psychological Bulletin, 131,* 260–300.

Suls, Jerry; Martin, René; & Wheeler, Ladd (2002). Social comparison: Why, with whom, and with what effect? *Current Directions in Psychological Science, 11,* 159–163.

Sundquist, J., & Winkleby, M. (2000, June). Country of birth, acculturation status and abdominal obesity in a national sample of Mexican-American women and men. *International Journal of Epidemiology, 29,* 470–477.

Suomi, Stephen J. (1991). Uptight and laid-back monkeys: Individual differences in the response to social challenges. In S. Branch, W. Hall, & J. E. Dooling (Eds.), *Plasticity of development.* Cambridge, MA: MIT Press.

Swain, Scott (1989). Covert intimacy: Closeness in men's friendships. In B. J. Risman & P. Schwartz (Eds.), *Gender in intimate relationships.* Belmont, CA: Wadsworth.

Swenson, Cynthia C.; Henggeler, Scott W.; Taylor, Ida S.; & Addison, Oliver W. (2005). *Multisystemic therapy and neighborhood partnerships: Reducing adolescent violence and substance abuse.* New York: Guilford Press.

Symons, Donald (1979). *The evolution of human sexuality.* New York: Oxford University Press.

Tajfel, Henri; Billig, M. G.; Bundy, R. P.; & Flament, C. (1971). Social categorization and intergroup behavior. *European Journal of Social Psychology, 1,* 149–178.

Tajfel, Henri, & Turner, John C. (1986). The social identity theory of intergroup behavior. In S. Worchel & W. G. Austin (Eds.), *Psychology of intergroup relations.* Chicago: Nelson-Hall.

Talarico, Jennifer M., & Rubin, David C. (2003). Confidence, not consistency, characterizes flashbulb memories. *Psychological Science, 14,* 455–461.

Talmi, Deborah; Grady, Cheryl L.; Goshen-Gottstein, Yonatan; & Moscovitch, Morris (2005). Neuroimaging the serial position curve: A test of single-store versus dual-store models. *Psychological Science, 16,* 716–723.

Tangney, June P.; Wagner, Patricia E.; Hill-Barlow, Deborah; et al. (1996). Relation of shame and guilt to constructive versus destructive responses to anger across the lifespan. *Journal of Personality and Social Psychology, 70,* 797–809.

Taubes, Gary (1998). As obesity rates rise, experts struggle to explain why. *Science, 280,* 1367–1368.

Tavris, Carol (1989). *Anger: The misunderstood emotion* (Rev. ed.). New York: Simon & Schuster/Touchstone.

Taylor, Annette Kujawski, & Kowalski, Patricia (2004). Naïve psychological science: The prevalence, strength, and sources of misconceptions. *Psychological Record, 54,* 15–25.

Taylor, Donald M., & Porter, Lana E. (1994). A multicultural view of stereotyping. In W. J. Lonner & R. Malpass (Eds.), *Psychology and culture.* Needham Heights, MA: Allyn & Bacon.

Taylor, Shelley E.; Kemeny, Margaret E.; Reed, Geoffrey M.; Bower, Julienne E.; & Gruenewald, Tara L. (2000a). Psychological resources, positive illusions, and health. *American Psychologist, 55,* 99–109.

Taylor, Shelley E.; Klein, Laura C.; Lewis, Brian P.; et al. (2000b). Biobehavioral responses to stress in females: Tend-and-befriend, not fight-or-flight. *Psychological Review, 107,* 411–429.

Taylor, Shelley E.; Lerner, Jennifer S.; Sherman, David K.; et al. (2003). Are self-enhancing cognitions associated with healthy or unhealthy biological profiles? *Journal of Personality and Social Psychology, 85,* 605–615.

Taylor, Shelley E.; Lichtman, Rosemary R.; & Wood, Joanne V. (1984). Attributions, beliefs about control, and adjustment to breast cancer. *Journal of Personality and Social Psychology, 46,* 489–502.

Taylor, Shelley E., & Lobel, Marci (1989). Social comparison activity under threat: Downward evaluation and upward contacts. *Psychological Review, 96,* 569–575.

Taylor, Shelley E.; Repetti, Rena; & Seeman, Teresa (1997). Health psychology: What is an unhealthy environment and how does it get under the skin? *Annual Review of Psychology* (Vol. 48). Palo Alto, CA: Annual Reviews.

Taylor, Steven; McKay, Dean; & Abramowitz, Jonathan S. (2005). Is obsessive-compulsive disorder a disturbance of security motivation? *Psychological Review, 112,* 650–657.

Taylor, Steven; Thordarson, Dana S.; Maxfield, Louise; et al. (2003). Comparative efficacy, speed, and adverse effects of three PTSD treatments: Exposure therapy, EMDR, and relaxation training. *Journal of Consulting and Clinical Psychology,* 71, 330–338.

Terman, Lewis M., & Oden, Melita H. (1959). *Genetic studies of genius: Vol. 5. The gifted group at mid-life.* Stanford, CA: Stanford University Press.

Terracciano, Antonio, & McCrae, Robert R. (2006, February). "National character does not reflect mean personality traits levels in 49 cultures": Reply. *Science, 311,* 777–779.

Thase, Michael E.; Fasiczka, Amy L.; Berman, Susan R.; et al. (1998). Electroencephalographic sleep profiles before and after cognitive behavior therapy of depression. *Archives of General Psychiatry, 55,* 138–144.

Thigpen, Corbett H., & Cleckley, Hervey M. (1984). On the incidence of multiple personality disorder: A brief communication. *International Journal of Clinical and Experimental Hypnosis, 32,* 63–66.

Thompson, Clara (1943/1973). Penis envy in women. *Psychiatry, 6,* 123–125. Reprinted in J. B. Miller (Ed.), *Psychoanalysis and women.* New York: Brunner/Mazel, 1973.

Thompson, P. M.; Cannon, T. D.; Narr, K. L.; et al. (2001). Genetic influences on brain structure. *Nature Neuroscience, 4,* 1253–1258.

Thompson, Paul M.; Vidal, Christine N.; Giedd, Jay N.; et al. (2001). Mapping adolescent brain change reveals dynamic wave of accelerated gray matter loss in very early-onset schizophrenia. *Proceedings of the National Academy of Sciences of the USA, 98,* 11650–11655.

Thompson, Richard F. (1983). Neuronal substrates of simple associative learning: Classical conditioning. *Trends in Neurosciences, 6,* 270–275.

Thompson, Richard F. (1986). The neurobiology of learning and memory. *Science, 233,* 941–947.

Thompson, Richard F., & Kosslyn, Stephen M. (2000). Neural systems activated during visual mental imagery: A review and meta-analyses. In A. W. Toga & J. C. Mazziotta (Eds.), *Brain mapping: The systems.* San Diego, CA: Academic Press.

Thompson, Robin; Emmorey, Karen; & Gollan, Tamar H. (2005). "Tip of the fingers" experiences by deaf signers. *Psychological Science, 16,* 856–860.

Thorndike, Edward L. (1898). Animal intelligence: An experimental study of the associative processes in animals. *Psychological Review Monograph Supplement, 2* (Whole No. 8).

Thorndike, Edward L. (1903). *Educational psychology.* New York: Columbia University Teachers College.

Thornhill, Randy, & Palmer, Craig T. (2000). *A natural history of rape: Biological bases of sexual coercion.* Cambridge, MA: MIT Press.

Tiefer, Leonore (2004). *Sex is not a natural act, and other essays* (Rev. ed.). Boulder, CO: Westview.

Timmers, Monique; Fischer, Agneta H.; & Manstead, Antony S. R. (1998). Gender differences in motives for regulating emotions. *Personality and Social Psychology Bulletin, 24,* 974–985.

Tolman, Edward C. (1938). The determiners of behavior at a choice point. *Psychological Review, 45,* 1–35.

Tolman, Edward C., & Honzik, Chase H. (1930). Introduction and removal of reward and maze performance in rats. *University of California Publications in Psychology, 4,* 257–275.

Toma, J. G.; Akhavan, M.; Frenandes, K. J.; et al. (2001). Isolation of multipotent adult stem cells from the dermis of mammalian skin. *Nature Cell Biology, 3,* 778–784.

Tomasello, Michael (2000). Culture and cognitive development. *Current Directions in Psychological Science, 9,* 37–40.

Tomlinson, Mark; Cooper, Peter; & Murray, Lynne (2005). The mother–infant relationship and infant attachment in a South African periurban settlement. *Child Development, 76,* 1044–1054.

Toomela, Aaro (2003). Relationships between personality structure, structure of word meaning, and cognitive ability: A study of cultural mechanisms of personality. *Journal of Personality and Social Psychology, 85,* 723–735.

Tormala, Zakary L., & Petty, Richard E. (2002). What doesn't kill me makes me stronger: The effects of resisting persuasion on attitude certainty. *Journal of Personality and Social Psychology, 83,* 1298–1313.

Torrey, E. Fuller (2001). *Surviving schizophrenia* (4th ed.). New York: HarperCollins.

Tracy, Jessica L., & Robins, Richard W. (2004). Show your pride: Evidence for a discrete emotion expression. *Psychological Science, 15,* 194-197.

Tracy, Jessica L., Robins, Richard W.; & Lagattuta, Kristin H. (2005). Can children recognize pride? *Emotion, 5,* 251–257.

Travis, John (2000, September 23). Snap, crackle, and feel good? Magnetic fields that map the brain may also treat its disorders. *Science News 158,* 204.

Triandis, Harry C. (1996). The psychological measurement of cultural syndromes. *American Psychologist, 51,* 407–415.

Trivers, Robert (1972). Parental investment and sexual selection. In B. Campbell (Ed.), *Sexual selection and the descent of man.* New York: Aldine de Gruyter.

Trivers, Robert (2004). Mutual benefits at all levels of life. [Book review.] *Science, 304,* 965.

Tronick, Edward Z.; Morelli, Gilda A.; & Ivey, Paula K. (1992). The Efe forager infant and toddler's pattern of social relationships: Multiple and simultaneous. *Developmental Psychology, 28,* 568–577.

Tropp, Linda R., & Pettigrew, Thomas F. (2005). Relationships between intergroup contact and prejudice among minority and majority status groups. *Psychological Science,* 16, 951–957.

Tsuang, Ming T.; Bar, Jessica L.; Harley, Rebecca M.; Lyons, Michael J. (2001). The Harvard Twin Study of Substance Abuse: What we have learned. *Harvard Review of Psychiatry, 9,* 267–279.

Tulving, Endel (1985). How many memory systems are there? *American Psychologist, 40,* 385–398.

Turati, Chiara (2004). Why faces are not special to newborns: An alternative account of the face preference. *Current Directions in Psychological Science, 13,* 5–8.

Turiel, Elliot (2002). *The culture of morality.* Cambridge, England: Cambridge University Press.

Turkheimer, Eric (2000). Three laws of behavior genetics and what they mean. *Current Directions in Psychological Science, 9,* 160–164.

Turkheimer, Eric; Haley, Andreana; Waldron, Mary; D'Onofrio, Brian; & Gottesman, Irving I. (2003). Socioeconomic status modifies heritability of IQ in young children. *Psychological Science, 14,* 623–628.

Turner, C. F.; Ku, L.; Rogers, S. M.; et al. (1998). Adolescent sexual behavior, drug use, and violence: Increased reporting with computer survey technology. *Science, 280,* 867–873.

Turner, Marlene E.; Pratkanis, Anthony R.; & Samuels, Tara (2003). Identity metamorphosis and groupthink prevention: Examining Intel's departure from the DRAM industry. In A. Haslam, D. van Knippenberg, M. Platow, & N. Ellemers (Eds.), *Social identity at work: Developing theory for organizational practice.* Philadelphia, PA: Psychology Press.

Tustin, Karen, & Hayne, Harlene (2005). A new method to measure childhood amnesia in children, adolescents, and adults. Poster presented at the annual meeting of the International Society for the Study of Behavioural Development, Melbourne, Australia.

Tversky, Amos, & Kahneman, Daniel (1973). Availability: A heuristic for judging frequency and probability. *Cognitive Psychology, 5,* 207–232.

Tversky, Amos, & Kahneman, Daniel (1981). The framing of decisions and the psychology of choice. *Science, 211,* 453–458.

Twachtman-Cullen, Diane (1998). *A passion to believe: Autism and the facilitated communication phenomenon.* Boulder, CO: Westview Press.

Twenge, Jean (2000). The age of anxiety? Birth cohort change in anxiety and neuroticism, 1952–1993. *Journal of Personality and Social Psychology, 79,* 1007–1021.

Uchino, Bert N.; Cacioppo, John T.; & Kiecolt-Glaser, Janice K. (1996). The relationship between social support and physiological processes: A review with emphasis on underlying mechanisms and implications for health. *Psychological Bulletin, 119,* 488–531.

Uhlhaas, Peter J., & Silverstein, Steven M. (2005). Perceptual organization in schizophrenia spectrum disorders: Empirical research and theoretical implications. *Psychological Bulletin, 131,* 618–632.

Ullian, E. M.; Chrisopherson, K. S.; & Barres, B. A. (2004). Role for glia in synaptogenesis. *Glia, 47,* 209–216.

Updegraff, John A.; Gable, Shelly L.; & Taylor, Shelley E. (2004). What makes experiences satisfying? The interaction of approach-avoidance motivations and emotions in well-being. *Journal of Personality and Social Psychology, 86,* 496–504.

Urry, Heather L.; Nitschke, Jack B.; Dolski, Isa; et al. (2004). Making a life worth living: Neural correlates of well-being. *Psychological Science, 15,* 367–372.

Usher, JoNell A., & Neisser, Ulric (1993). Childhood amnesia and the beginnings of memory for four early life events. *Journal of Experimental Psychology: General, 122,* 155–165.

Uttall, William R. (2001). *The new phrenology: The limits of localizing cognitive processes in the brain.* Cambridge, MA: MIT Press/Bradford Books.

Vaillant, George E. (1983). *The natural history of alcoholism: Causes, patterns, and paths to recovery.* Cambridge, MA: Harvard University Press.

Vaillant, George E. (Ed.) (1992). *Ego mechanisms of defense.* Washington, DC: American Psychiatric Press.

Valenstein, Elliot (1986). *Great and desperate cures: The rise and decline of psychosurgery and other radical treatments for mental illness.* New York: Basic Books.

Van Baaren, Rick B.; Holland, Rob W.; Kawakami, Kerry; & van Knippenberg, Ad (2004). Mimicry and prosocial behavior. *Psychological Science, 15,* 71–74.

Van Boven, Leaf, & Gilovich, Thomas (2003). To do or to have? That is the question. *Journal of Personality and Social Psychology, 85,* 1193–1202.

Van Boven, Leaf; Kamada, Akiko; & Gilovich, Thomas (1999). The perceiver as perceived: Everyday intuitions about the correspondence bias. *Journal of Personality and Social Psychology, 77,* 1188–1199.

Van Cantfort, Thomas E., & Rimpau, James B. (1982). Sign language studies with children and chimpanzees. *Sign Language Studies, 34,* 15–72.

Van de Castle, Robert (1994). *Our dreaming mind.* New York: Ballantine Books.

Vandello, Joseph A., & Cohen, Dov (1999). Patterns of individualism and collectivism across the United States. *Journal of Personality and Social Psychology, 77,* 279–292.

Vandello, Joseph A., & Cohen, Dov (2003). Male honor and female fidelity: Implicit cultural scripts that perpetuate domestic violence. *Journal of Personality & Social Psychology, 84,* 997–1010.

Vandenberg, Brian (1985). Beyond the ethology of play. In A. Gottfried & C. C. Brown (Eds.), *Play interactions.* Lexington, MA: Lexington Books

Van Emmerik, Arnold A.; Kamphuis, Jan H.; Hulsbosch, Alexander M.; & Emmelkamp, Paul M. G. (2002, September 7). Single session debriefing after psychological trauma: A meta-analysis. *The Lancet, 360,* 766–771.

van Ijzendoorn, Marinus H.; Juffer, Femmie; & Klein Poelhuis, Caroline W. (2005). Adoption and cognitive development: A meta-analytic comparison of adopted and nonadopted children's IQ and school performance. *Psychological Bulletin, 131,* 301–316.

Van Ommeren, Mark; Saxena, Shekhar; & Saraceno, Benedetto (2005, January). Mental and social health during and after acute emergencies: Emerging consensus? *Bulletin of the World Health Organization, 83,* 71–76.

van Praag, H.; Kempermann, G.; & Gage, F. H. (1999). Running increases cell proliferation and neurogenesis in the adult mouse dentate gyrus. *Nature Neuroscience, 2,* 266–270.

van Schaik, Carel (2006, April). Why are some animals so smart? *Scientific American,* 64–71.

van Tilburg, Miranda A. L.; Becht, Marleen C.; & Vingerhoets, Ad J. J. M. (2003). Self-reported crying during the menstrual cycle: Sign of discomfort and emotional turmoil or erroneous beliefs? *Journal of Psychosomatic Obstetrics & Gynecology, 24,* 247–255.

Vecera, Shaun P.; Vogel, Edward, K.; & Woodman, Geoffrey F. (2002). Lower region: A new cue for figure-ground assignment. *Journal of Experimental Psychology: General, 131,* 194–205.

Vila, J., & Beech, H. R. (1980). Premenstrual symptomatology: An interaction hypothesis. *British Journal of Social and Clinical Psychology, 19,* 73–80.

Vingerhoets, Guy; Berckmoes, Celine; & Stroobant, Nathalie (2003). Cerebral hemodynamics during discrimination of prosodic and semantic emotion in speech studied by transcranial Doppler ultrasonography. *Neuropsychology, 1,* 93–99.

Vita, A. J.; Terry, R. B.; Hubert, H. B.; & Fries, J. F. (1998). Aging, health risks, and cumulative disability. *New England Journal of Medicine, 338,* 1035–1041.

Vitaliano, Peter P.; Young, Heather M.; & Zhang, Jianping (2004). Is caregiving a risk factor for illness? *Current Directions in Psychological Science, 13,* 13–16.

Vogel, Gretchen (2004). More data but not answers on powers of adult stem cells. *Science, 305,* 27.

Voigt, Benjamin F.; Kudaravalli, Sridhar; Wen, Xiaoquan; & Pritchard, Jonathan K. (2006). A map of recent positive selection in the human genome. *PLoS Biology, 4,* e72.

Volkow, Nora D.; Chang, Linda; Wang, Gene-Jack; et al. (2001). Association of dopamine transporter reduction with psychomotor impairment in methamphetamine abusers. *American Journal of Psychiatry, 158,* 377–382.

Voyer, Daniel; Voyer, Susan; & Bryden, M. P. (1995). Magnitude of sex differences in spatial abilities: A meta-analysis and consideration of critical variables. *Psychological Bulletin, 117,* 250–270.

Vroon, Piet (1997). *Smell: The secret seducer.* [Trans. by Paul Vincent.] New York: Farrar, Straus & Giroux.

Vygotsky, Lev (1962). *Thought and language.* Cambridge, MA: MIT Press.

Vygotsky, Lev (1978). *Mind in society: The development of higher psychological processes.* Cambridge, MA: Harvard University Press. (Originals published in 1930, 1933, and 1935.)

Wadden, Thomas A.; Foster, G. D.; Letizia, K. A.; & Mullen, J. L. (1990, August 8). Long-term effects of dieting on resting metabolic rate in obese outpatients. *Journal of the American Medical Association, 264,* 707–711.

Wade, Carole (2006). Some cautions about jumping on the brain-scan bandwagon. *APS Observer,* 19, 23–24

Wagenaar, Willem A. (1986). My memory: A study of autobiographical memory over six years. *Cognitive Psychology, 18,* 225–252.

Wager, Tor D.; Rilling, James K.; Smith, Edward E.; et al. (2004). Placebo-induced changes in fMRI in the anticipation and experience of pain. *Science, 303,* 1162–1167.

Wagner, Anthony D.; Schacter, Daniel L.; Rotte, Michael; et al. (1998). Building memories: Remembrance and forgetting of verbal experiences as predicted by brain activity. *Science, 281,* 1188–1191.

Wagner, Ullrich; Gais, Steffen; Haider, Hilde; et al. (2004). Sleep inspires insight. *Nature, 427,* 352–355.

Wakefield, Jerome C. (1992). Disorder as harmful dysfunction: A conceptual critique of DSM-III-R's definition of mental disorder. *Psychological Review, 99,* 232–247.

Walker, Anne (1994). Mood and well-being in consecutive menstrual cycles: Methodological and theoretical implications. *Psychology of Women Quarterly, 18,* 271–290.

Walker, David L.; Ressler, Kerry J.; Lu, Kwok-Tung; & Davis, Michael (2002). Facilitation of conditioned fear extinction by systemic administration or intra-amygdala infusions of D-cycloserine as assessed with fear-potentiated startle in rats. *The Journal of Neuroscience, 22,* 2343–2351.

Walker, Elaine F. (2002). Adolescent neurodevelopment and psychopathology. *Current Directions in Psychological Science, 11,* 24–28.

Walker-Andrews, Arlene S. (1997). Infants' perception of expressive behaviors: Differentiation of multimodal information. *Psychological Bulletin, 121,* 437–456.

Wallbott, Harald G.; Ricci-Bitti, Pio; & Bänninger-Huber, Eva (1986). Non-verbal reactions to emotional experiences. In K. R. Scherer, H. G. Wallbott, & A. B. Summerfield (Eds.), *Experiencing emotion: A cross-cultural study.* Cambridge, England: Cambridge University Press.

Waller, Niels G.; Kojetin, Brian A.; Bouchard, Thomas J., Jr.; et al. (1990). Genetic and environmental influences on religious interests, attitudes, and values: A study of twins reared apart and together. *Psychological Science, 1,* 138–142.

Wampold, Bruce (2001). *The great psychotherapy debate: Models, methods, and findings.* Mahwah, NJ: Erlbaum.

Wang, Alvin Y.; Thomas, Margaret H.; & Ouellette, Judith A. (1992). The keyword mnemonic and retention of second-language vocabulary words. *Journal of Educational Psychology, 84,* 520–528.

Wang, Qi (2001). Culture effects on adults' earliest childhood recollection and self-description: Implications for the relation between memory and the self. *Journal of Personality and Social Psychology, 81,* 220–233.

Warren, Gayle H., & Raynes, Anthony E. (1972). Mood changes during three conditions of alcohol intake. *Quarterly Journal of Studies on Alcohol, 33,* 979–989.

Wasserman, Eric W., & Lisanby, Sarah H. (2001). Therapeutic application of repetitive transcranial magnetic stimulation: A review. *Clinical Neurophysiology, 112,* 1367–1377.

Watkins, Linda R., & Maier, Steven F. (2003). When good pain turns bad. *Current Directions in Psychological Science, 12,* 232–236.

Watson, David; Hubbard, Brock; & Wiese, David (2000). Self-other agreement in personality and affectivity: The role of acquaintanceship, trait visibility, and assumed similarity. *Journal of Personality and Social Psychology, 78,* 546–558.

Watson, John B. (1925). *Behaviorism.* New York: Norton.

Watson, John B., & Rayner, Rosalie (1920). Conditioned emotional reactions. *Journal of Experimental Psychology, 3,* 1–14. (Reprinted in *American Psychologist, 55,* May 2000, 313–317.)

Watters, Ethan, & Ofshe, Richard (1999). *Therapy's delusions.* New York: Scribner.

Webster, Richard (1995). *Why Freud was wrong.* New York: Basic Books.

Wechsler, David (1955). *Manual for the Wechsler Adult Intelligence Scale.* New York: Psychological Corporation.

Wegner, Daniel M.; Fuller, Valeria A.; & Sparrlow, Betsy (2003). Clever hands: Uncontrolled intelligence in facilitated communication. *Journal of Personality and Social Psychology, 85,* 5–19.

Wegner, Daniel M., & Gold, Daniel B. (1995). Fanning old flames: Emotional and cognitive effects of suppressing thoughts of a past relationship. *Journal of Personality and Social Psychology, 68,* 782–792.

Wehr, Thomas A.; Duncan, Wallace C.; Sher, Leo; et al. (2001). A circadian signal of change of season in patients with seasonal affective disorder. *Archives of General Psychiatry, 58,* 1108–1114.

Weil, Andrew T. (1972/1986). *The natural mind: A new way of looking at drugs and the higher consciousness.* Boston: Houghton-Mifflin.

Weil, Andrew T. (1974a, June). Parapsychology: Andrew Weil's search for the true Geller. *Psychology Today,* 45–50.

Weil, Andrew T. (1974b, July). Parapsychology: Andrew Weil's search for the true Geller: Part II. The letdown. *Psychology Today,* 74–78, 82.

Weiner, Bernard (1986). *An attributional theory of motivation and emotion.* New York: Springer-Verlag.

Weiss, Erica; Longhurst, James G.; & Mazure, Carolyn M. (1999). Childhood sexual abuse as a risk factor for depression in women: Psychological and neurological correlates. *American Journal of Psychiatry, 156,* 816–828.

Weissman, Myrna M.; Markowitz, John C.; & Klerman, Gerald L. (2000). *Comprehensive guide to interpersonal psychotherapy.* New York: Basic Books.

Weisz, John R.; Weiss, Bahr; Han, Susan S.; et al. (1995). Effects of psychotherapy with children and adolescents revisited: A meta-analysis of treatment outcome studies. *Psychological Bulletin, 117,* 450–468.

Wellman, H. M.; Cross, D.; & Watson, J. (2001). Meta-analysis of theory-of-mind development: The truth about false belief. *Child Development, 72,* 655–684.

Wells, Brooke E., & Twenge, Jean (2005). Changes in young people's sexual behavior and attitudes, 1943–1999: A cross-temporal meta-analysis. *Review of General Psychology, 9,* 249–261.

Wells, Gary L., & Olson, Elisabeth A. (2003). Eyewitness testimony. *Annual Review of Psychology, 54,* 277–295.

Wells, Gary L.; Small, Mark; Penrod, Steven; et al. (1998). Eyewitness identification procedures: Recommendations for lineups and photospreads. *Law and Human Behavior, 22,* 602–647.

Wender, Paul H., & Klein, Donald F. (1981). *Mind, mood, and medicine: A guide to the new biopsychiatry.* New York: Farrar, Straus and Giroux.

Wenzel, Amy (2005). Autobiographical memory tasks in clinical research. In A. Wenzel and D. C. Rubin, *Cognitive methods and their application to clinical research.* Washington, DC: American Psychological Association.

Werner, Emmy E. (1989). High-risk children in young adulthood: A longitudinal study from birth to 32 years. *American Journal of Orthopsychiatry, 59,* 72–81.

Wertheimer, Michael (1958). Principles of perceptual organization. In D. C. Beardslee & M. Wertheimer (Eds.), *Readings in perception.* Princeton, NJ: Van Nostrand. [Original work published 1923.]

West, Melissa O., & Prinz, Ronald J. (1987). Parental alcoholism and childhood psychopathology. *Psychological Bulletin, 102,* 204–218.

Westen, Drew (1998). The scientific legacy of Sigmund Freud: Toward a psychodynamically informed psychological science. *Psychological Bulletin, 124,* 333–371.

Westen, Drew; Novotny, Catherine M.; & Thompson-Brenner, Heather (2004). The empirical status of empirically supported psychotherapies: Assumptions, findings, and reporting in controlled clinical trials. *Psychological Bulletin, 130,* 631–663.

Westen, Drew, & Shedler, Jonathan (1999). Revising and assessing axis II, Part II: Toward an empirically based and clinically useful classification of personality disorders. *American Journal of Psychiatry, 156,* 273–285.

Westermeyer, Joseph (1995). Cultural aspects of substance abuse and alcoholism: Assessment and management. *Psychiatric Clinics of North America, 18,* 589–605.

Wethington, Elaine (2000). Expecting stress: Americans and the "midlife crisis." *Motivation & Emotion, 24,* 85–103.

Whaley, Arthur L. (2001). Cultural mistrust: An important psychological construct for diagnosis and treatment of African Americans. *Professional Psychology: Research & Practice, 32,* 555–562.

Wheeler, David L. (1998, September 11). Neuroscientists take stock of brain-imaging studies. *Chronicle of Higher Education,* A20–A21.

Wheeler, Mark E.; Petersen, Steven E.; & Buckner, Randy L. (2000). Memory's echo: Vivid remembering reactivates sensory-specific cortex. *Proceedings of the National Academy of Sciences, 97*(20), 11125–11129.

Wheeler, Mary E., & Fiske, Susan T. (2005). Controlling racial prejudice: Social-cognitive goals affect amygdala and stereotype activation. *Psychological Science, 16,* 56–63.

Whiting, Beatrice B., & Edwards, Carolyn P. (1988). *Children of different worlds: The formation of social behavior.* Cambridge, MA: Harvard University Press.

Whiting, Beatrice, & Whiting, John (1975). *Children of six cultures.* Cambridge, MA: Harvard University Press.

Whitty, Monica T., & Carr, Adrian N. (2006). New rules in the workplace: Applying object-relations theory to explain problem Internet and email behaviour in the workplace. *Computers in Human Behavior, 22,* 235–250.

Whorf, Benjamin L. (1956). *Language, thought and reality.* Cambridge, MA: MIT Press. [Original work published 1940.]

Wickelgren, Ingrid (1997). Estrogen stakes claim to cognition. *Science, 276,* 675–678.

Widiger, Thomas, & Clark, Lee Anna (2000). Toward DSM-V and the classification of psychopathology. *Psychological Bulletin, 126,* 946–963.

Widiger, Thomas A.; Cadoret, Remi; Hare, Robert; et al. (1996). DSM-IV antisocial personality disorder field trial. *Journal of Abnormal Psychology, 105,* 3–16.

Wiederhold, Brenda K., & Wiederhold, Mark D. (2000). Lessons learned from 600 virtual reality sessions. *CyberPsychology & Behavior, 3,* 393–400.

Williams, Janice E.; Paton, Catherine C.; Siegler, Ilene C.; et al. (2000). Anger proneness predicts coronary heart disease risk. *Circulation, 101,* 2034–2039.

Williams, Justin H. G.; Waiter, Gordon D.; Gilchrist, Anne; et al. (2006). Neural mechanisms of imitation and "mirror neuron" functioning in autistic spectrum disorder. *Neuropsychologia, 44,* 610–621.

Williams, Kipling D., & Karau, Steven J. (1991). Social loafing and social compensation: The effects of expectations of co-worker performance. *Journal of Personality and Social Psychology, 61,* 570–581.

Williams, Redford B., Jr.; Barefoot, John C.; & Shekelle, Richard B. (1985). The health consequences of hostility. In M. A. Chesney & R. H. Rosenman (eds.), *Anger and hostility in cardiovascular and behavioral disorders.* New York: Hemisphere.

Wilner, Daniel; Walkley, Rosabelle; & Cook, Stuart (1955). *Human relations in interracial housing.* Minneapolis: University of Minnesota Press.

Wilson, Edward O. (1975). *Sociobiology: The new synthesis.* Cambridge, MA: Belknap/Harvard University Press.

Wilson, Edward O. (1978). *On human nature.* Cambridge, MA: Harvard University Press.

Wilson, G. Terence, & Fairburn, Christopher G. (1993). Cognitive treatments for eating disorders. *Journal of Consulting and Clinical Psychology, 61,* 261–269.

Wilson, Timothy D.; & Gilbert, Daniel T. (2005). Affective forecasting: Knowing what to want. *Current Directions in Psychological Science, 14,* 131–134.

Wilson, Timothy D.; Lindsey, S.; & Schooler, T. Y. (2000). A model of dual attitudes. *Psychological Review, 107,* 101–126.

Winick, Myron; Meyer, Knarig Katchadurian; & Harris, Ruth C. (1975). Malnutrition and environmental enrichment by early adoption. *Science, 190,* 1173–1175.

Winkielman, Piotr, & Berridge, Kent C. (2004). Unconscious emotion. *Current Directions in Psychological Science, 13,* 120–126.

Winnicott, D. W. (1957/1990). *Home is where we start from.* New York: Norton.

Wirz-Justice, Anna; Benedetti, Francesco; Berger, Mathias; et al. (2005). Chronotherapeutics (light and wake therapy) in affective disorders. *Psychological Medicine, 35,* 939–944.

Wispé, Lauren G., & Drambarean, Nicholas C. (1953). Physiological need, word frequency, and visual duration thresholds. *Journal of Experimental Psychology, 46,* 25–31.

Witelson, Sandra F.; Glazer, I. I.; & Kigar, D. L. (1994). Sex differences in numerical density of neurons in human auditory association cortex. *Society for Neuroscience Abstracts, 30* (Abstr. No. 582.12).

Witkiewitz, Katie, & Marlatt, G. Alan (2004). Relapse prevention for alcohol and drug problems: That was Zen, this is Tao. *American Psychologist, 59,* 224–235.

Wittchen, Hans-Ulrich; Kessler, Ronald C.; Zhao, Shanyang; & Abelson, Jamie (1995). Reliability and clinical validity of UM-CIDI DSM-III-R generalized anxiety disorder. *Journal of Psychiatric Research, 29,* 95–110.

Witvliet, Charlotte vanOyen; Ludwig, Thomas E.; & Vander Laan, Kelly L. (2001). Granting forgiveness or harboring grudges: Implications for emotion, physiology, and health. *Psychological Science, 12,* 117–123.

Wolfson, Amy R., and Carskadon, Mary A. (1998). Sleep schedules and daytime functioning in adolescents. *Child Development, 69,* 875–887.

Wolpe, Joseph (1958). *Psychotherapy by reciprocal inhibition.* Palo Alto, CA: Stanford University Press.

Wood, James M.; Nezworski, M. Teresa; Lilienfeld, Scott O.; & Garb, Howard N. (2003). *What's wrong with the Rorschach?* San Francisco: Jossey-Bass.

Wood, Joanne V.; Michela, John L.; & Giordano, Caterina (2000). Downward comparison in everyday life: Reconciling self-enhancement models with the mood-cognition priming model. *Journal of Personality and Social Psychology, 79,* 563–579.

Wood, Wendy; Lundgren, Sharon; Ouellette, Judith A.; et al. (1994). Minority influence: A meta-analytic review of social influence processes. *Psychological Bulletin, 115,* 323–345.

Woody, Erik Z., & Bowers, Kenneth S. (1994). A frontal assault on dissociated control. In S. J. Lynn & J. W. Rhue (Eds.), *Dissociation: Clinical, theoretical and research perspectives.* New York: Guilford.

Wu, Aiguo; Ying, Zhe; & Gómez-Pinilla, Fernando (2004). Dietary omega-3 fatty acids normalize BDNF levels, reduce oxidative damage, and counteract learning disability after traumatic brain injury in rats. *Journal of Neurotrauma, 21,* 1457–1467.

Wulsin, L. R.; Vaillant, G. E.; & Wells, V. E. (1999). A systematic review of the mortality of depression. *Psychosomatic Medicine, 61,* 6–17.

Wynne, Clive D. L. (2004). *Do animals think?* Princeton, NJ: Princeton University Press.

Wyrobek, A. J.; Eskenazi, B.; Young, S.; et al. (2006, June 9). Advancing age has differential effects on DNA damage, chromatin integrity, gene mutations, and aneuploidies in sperm. *Proceedings of the National Academy of Sciences, 103,* 9601–9606.

Yalom, Irvin D. (1989). *Love's executioner and other tales of psychotherapy.* New York: Basic Books.

Yang, Chi-Fu Jeffrey; Gray, Peter; & Pope, Harrison G. Jr. (2005). Male body image in Taiwan versus the West: Yanggang Zhiqi meets the Adonis Complex. *American Journal of Psychiatry, 162,* 263–269.

Yapko, Michael (1994). *Suggestions of abuse: True and false memories of childhood sexual trauma.* New York: Simon & Schuster.

Yardley, Jim (2001, September 8). Despair plagued mother held in children's deaths. *The New York Times,* A16.

Young, Malcolm P., & Yamane, Shigeru (1992). Sparse population coding of faces in the inferotemporal cortex. *Science, 256,* 1327–1331.

Yzerbyt, Vincent Y.; Corneille, Olivier; Dumont, Muriel; & Hahn, Kirstin (2001). The dispositional inference strikes back: Situational focus and dispositional suppression in causal attribution. *Journal of Personality and Social Psychology, 81,* 365–376.

Zajonc, R. B. (1968). Attitudinal effects of mere exposure. *Journal of Personality and Social Psychology, 9,* Monograph Supplement 2, 1–27.

Zajonc, R. B. (2003). The power of words. Invited address presented to the American Psychological Society, Atlanta.

Zelicoff, Alan P. (2001, July/August). Polygraphs and the national labs: Dangerous ruse undermines national security. *Skeptical Inquirer,* 21–23.

Zhang, Yiying; Hoon, M. A.; Chandrashekar, J.; et al. (2003). Coding of sweet, bitter, and umami tastes: different receptor cells sharing similar signaling pathways. *Cell, 112,* 293–301.

Zhang, Yiying; Proenca, Ricardo; Maffei, Margherita; et al. (1994). Positional cloning of the mouse obese gene and its human homologue. *Nature, 372*(6505), 425–432.

Zhu, L. X.; Sharma, S.; Stolina, M.; et al. (2000). Delta-9-tetrahydrocannabinol inhibits antitumor immunity by a CB2 receptor-mediated, cytokine-dependent pathway. *Journal of Immunology, 165,* 373–380.

Zimbardo, Philip G. (1970). The human choice: Individuation, reason, and order versus deindividuation, impulse, and chaos. In W. J. Arnold & D. Levine (Eds.), *Nebraska Symposium on Motivation,* 1969. Lincoln, NE: University of Nebraska Press.

Zimbardo, Philip G., & Leippe, Michael R. (1991). *The psychology of attitude change and social influence.* New York: McGraw-Hill.

Zimmer, Lynn, & Morgan, John P. (1997). *Marijuana myths, marijuana fact: A review of the scientific evidence.* New York: Lindesmith Center.

Zone, Nolon; Sue, Stanley; Chang, Janer; et al. (2005). Beyond ethnic match: Effects of client–therapist cognitive match in problem perception, coping orientation, and therapy goals on treatment outcomes. *Journal of Community Psychology, 33,* 569–585.

Zorrilla, L. T.; Cannon, T. D.; Kronenberg, S.; et al. (1997, December 15). Structural brain abnormalities in schizophrenia: A family study. *Biological Psychiatry, 42,* 1080–1086.

Zou, Dong-Jing; Feinstein, Paul; Rivers, Aimée L.; et al. (2004). Postnatal refinement of peripheral olfactory projections. *Science, 304,* 1976–1979.

Zou, Zhihua, & Buck, Linda (2006). Combinatorial effects of odorant mixes in olfactory cortex. *Science, 311,* 1477–1481.

Zubieta, Jon-Kar; Bueller, Joshua A.; Jackson, Lisa R.; et al. (2005). Placebo effects mediated by endogenous opioid activity on μ-opioid receptors. Journal of Neuroscience, 25, 7754–7762.

Zubieta, Jon-Kar; Heitzeg, M. M.; Smith, Y. R.; et al. (2003). COMT val158met genotype affects mu-opioid neurotransmitter responses to a pain stressor. *Science, 299,* 1240–1243.

Zucker, Kenneth J. (1999). Intersexuality and gender identity differentiation. *Annual Review of Sex Research, 10,* 1–69.

Zucker, Kenneth J. (2002). Intersexuality and gender identity differentiation. *Journal of Pediatric and Adolescent Gynecology, 15,* 3–13.

Zurbriggen, Eileen L. (2000). Social motives and cognitive power-sex associations: Predictors of aggressive sexual behavior. *Journal of Personality and Social Psychology, 78,* 559–581.

Credits

Table, Text, and Figure Credits

Chapter 2 *Page 41:* From p. 952 in "Insult, Aggression, and the Southern Culture of Honor" by Cohen, et al. in *Journal of Personality and Social Psychology, 70*. Copyright © 1996 by the American Psychological Association. Reprinted in accordance with APA guidelines; *p. 49:* Figure 2.2 (a & b) From UNDERSTANDING STATISTICS, An Informal Introduction for the Behavioral Sciences 1st edition by Wright. Copyright © 1976. Reprinted with permission of Wadsworth, a division of Thomson Learning: www.thomsonrights.com. Fax 800 730-2215; (c): From INTRODUCTION TO THE PRACTICE OF STATISTICS by David S. Moore and George P. McCabe. Copyright © 1989, 1993, 1999 by W. H. Freeman and Company. Reprinted with permission of W. H. Freeman and Company.

Chapter 3 *Page 86:* Figure 3.2 Adapted from "Evolutionary Psychology: A New Paradigm for Psychological Science" by David M. Buss, *Psychological Inquiry, 6*, (1995). Copyright © 1995 by Lawrence Erlbuam Associates, Inc. Reprinted by permission; *p. 87:* Figure 3.3 Adapted from "Evolutionary Psychology: A New Paradigm for Psychological Science" by David M. Buss, *Psychological Inquiry, 6*, (1995). Copyright © 1995 by Lawrence Erlbuam Associates, Inc. Reprinted by permission; *p. 95:* Figure 3.4 Bouchard & McGue, 1981; *p. 100:* Figure 3.6 Adapted from p. 14 in "Get Smart: Take a Test. A Long-Term Rise in IQ Scores Baffles Intelligence Experts" by J. Horgan, *Scientific American*, November 1995. Copyright © 1995. Reprinted by permission of Dimitry Schildlovsky.

Chapter 4 *Page 116:* Adapted from Gougoux, Zatorre, Lassonde, Maryse et al. (2005).

Chapter 5 *Page 154:* McFarlane, Martin & Williams, 1988; *p. 159:* Figure 5.2 Figure from "Physiology of Sleeping and Dreaming" in PRINCIPLES OF NEURAL SCIENCE by Dennis Kelly. Copyright © 1981. Reprinted by permission of The McGraw-Hill Companies.

Chapter 6 *Page 201:* Figure 6.5 Greebles created by Isabel Gauthier (Vanderbilt University), Scott Yu and Michael J. Tarr; *p. 215:* Figure 6.12 From "Taste Test" by Mozell, et al., *Archives of Otolarynology, 90*, (1969). Copyright © 1969 by American Medical Association. Reprinted by permission; *p. 217:* Figure 1, p. 690 from "Smells Like Clean Spirit: Nonconscious Effects of Scent on Cognition and Behavior" by R. W. Holland, M. Hendriks, & H. Aarts, *Psychological Science, 16*, (9). Copyright © 2005. Reprinted by permission of Blackwell Publishing Ltd.; *p. 220:* Figure 6.14 From Fig. 2 in "The Subjective Experience of Pain: Where Expectations Become Reality" by T. Koyama et al., *Proceedings of the National Academy of Sciences*, 102, (36), September 6, 2005. Copyright © 2005 by the National Academies of Sciences, USA. Reprinted by permission; *p. 223:* Figure 6.16 Blakemore & Cooper, 1970.

Chapter 7 *Page 238:* Figure 7.2 From "Acquisition and Extinction of a Salivary Response" by Ivan P. Pavlov in CONDITIONED RESPONSES translated by G. V. Anrep. Copyright 1927. Reprinted by permission of Oxford University Press, UK; *p. 246:* Figure 2 from "Cognitive Enhancers as Adjuncts to Psychotherapy: Use of D-Cycloserine in Phobic Individuals to Facilitate Extinction of Fear" by Kerry J. Ressler, et al., *Archives of General Psychiatry*, 61: (2004). Copyright © 2004 by American Medical Association. Reprinted by permission of the publisher; *p. 251:* Figure 7.5 From p. 96 in "Teaching Machines" by B. F. Skinner, *Scientific American*, November 1961. Copyright © 1961. Reprinted by permission; *p. 261:* From "Turning Play into Work" by David Green and Mark R. Lepper, *Psychology Today*, September 1974. Copyright © 1974 by Sussex Publishers, Inc. Reprinted by permission of *Psychology Today* Magazine; *p. 264:* Figure 7.6 From "Introduction and Removal of Reward and Maze Performance in Rate" by E. C. Tolman and C. H. Honzik, *Psychology, 4* (1930). Reprinted by permission.

Chapter 8 *Page 288:* Figure 8.2 Abridged Table 1, p. 159 from "Are Political Orientations Genetically Transmitted?" by Alford, Funk & Hibbing, *American Political Science Review, 99*, (2), May 2005. Copyright © 2005. Reprinted by permission of Cambridge University Press and the author; *p. 302:* Figure 8.3 From "The Robbers Cave Experiment" by Muzafer Sherif. Copyright © 1988 University Press of New England. Reprinted by permission; *p. 309:* Figure 8.4 American Enterprise Institute, 2004; *p. 310:* From "Deindividuation and Anger-Mediated Interracial Agression: Unmasking Regressive Racism" by R. W. Rogers & S. Prentice-Dunn, *Journal of Personality and Social Psychology, 41* (1981. Copyright © 1981 by the American Psychological Association.

Chapter 9 *Page 337:* From CONCEPTUAL BLOCKBUSTING by James Adams. Copyright © 1986 by James L. Adams. Reprinted by permission of Da Capo Press, a member of Perseus Books Group; *p. 340:* Figure 9.2 Aronson & Mills, 1959; *p. 344:* Figure 9.4 From p. 208 in ESSENTIALS OF PSYCHOLOGICAL TESTING 4th edition by Lee J. Cronbach. Copyright © 1984 by HarperCollins Publishers. Reprinted by permission; *p. 347:* Figure 9.5 Dunning, et al., 2003; *p. 351:* From p. 943 in "Self-Discipline Outdoes IQ in Predicting Academic Performance of Adolescents" by Duckworth and Seligman, *Psychological Science, 16*, (12). Copyright © 2005 by Blackwell Publishing Ltd. Reprinted by permission of the publisher.

Chapter 10 *Page 372:* Garven et al., 1998.

Chapter 11 *Page 414:* Figure from p. 146 in UNDERSTANDING EMOTIONS by Oatley & Jenkins. Copyright © 1996 by Blackwell Publishing Ltd. Reprinted by permission of the publisher; *p. 419:* Figure 11.3 Iacono & Lykken, 1997.

Chapter 12 *Page 469:* Adapted from pp. 42–43 in "Praise for Intelligence can Undermine Children's Motivation and Performance" by C. M. Mueller & C. W. Dweck, *Journal of Personality and Social Psychology, 75*, (1998). Copyright © 1998 by the American Psychological Association. Adapted with permission.

Chapter 13 *Page 493:* Figure 13.1 Costa et al., 1999; *p. 494:* Get Involved Reprinted from Appendix A, p. 525 in "A Very Brief Measure of the Big Five Personality Domains" by S. D. Gosling, P. J. Rentfrow & W. B. Swann, Jr., *Journal of Research in Personality, 37,* (2003), 504–528. Copyright © 2003 by Elsevier. Reprinted by permission of the publisher; *p. 509:* From "Insult, Aggression, and the Southern Culture of Honor" from Cohen et al., *Journal of Personality and Social Psychology, 70* (1996). Copyright © 1996 by the American Psychological Association. Reprinted in accordance with APA guidelines.
Chapter 14 *Page 527:* Figure 14.2 Kagan, Kearsley & Zelazo, 1978; *p. 536:* Figure 14.4 From "How Do Infants Learn About the Physical World?" by Rene Baillargeon, *Current Directions in Psychology, 5,* 1994. Copyright © 1994 by Blackwell Publishing Ltd. Reprinted by permission; *p. 551:* Figure 14.5 Figure 2 from "Gender Differences in Self-Esteem" by K. C. Kling, J. S. Hyde, C. J. Showers & B. N. Buswell, *Psychological Bulletin, 125,* (1999). Copyright © 1999 by the American Psychological Association. Reprinted by permission; *p. 555:* Figure 14.6 From "Conceptions of the Transition to Adulthood From Adolescence Through Mid-Life" by Jeffrey Arnett, *Journal of Adult Development, 8*(2), April 2001. Copyright © 2001 by Kluwer Academic/Plenum Publishers. By permission of Springer Science and Business Media.
Chapter 15 *Page 568:* Figure 15.1 From "Stress and the Common Cold" by Cohen et al. in *The New York Times*, May 12, 1998. Copyright © 1998 by The New York Times Co. Reprinted with permission; *p. 575:* Figure 15.3 Williams, Barefoot, & Shekelle, 1985; *p. 577:* Figure 15.4 From p. 165, "Granting Forgiveness" by Witvliet, Ludwig & Vander Laan, *Psychological Science*, *12* (2001). Copyright © 2001 by Blackwell Publishing. Reprinted by permission of the publisher; *p. 583:* Figure 15.5 From p. 127 in "Resilience and Thriving in Response to Challenge: An Opportunity for a Paradigm Shift in Women's Health" by V. E. O'Leary & J. R. Ickovics in *Women's Health: Research on Gender, Behavior and Policy, 1* (1994). Copyright © 1994. Reprinted by permission of Lawrence Erlbaum Associates; *p. 584:* Figure 15.6 From "Fitness and Health" in ABNORMAL PSYCHOLOGY by David Holmes. Copyright © 1991 by Addison Wesley Longman Publishers. Reprinted by permission of Addison Wesley Longman Publishers.
Chapter 16 *Page 600:* Figure 16.1 Houts, 2002; *p. 600:* Table 16.1 Reprinted with permission from the *Diagnostic and Statistical Manual of Mental Disorders*, Fourth Edition. Copyright © 1994 by the American Psychiatric Association; *p. 603:* Table 16.2 Reprinted with permission from the *Diagnostic and Statistical Manual of Mental Disorders*, Fourth Edition. Copyright © 1994 by the American Psychiatric Association; *p. 613:* Figure 16.2 Courtesy of Susan Nolen-Hoeksema, 2004; *p. 614:* Adapted figure, p. 712, from "When Asking 'Why' Does Not Hurt: Distinguishing Rumination from Reflective Processing of Negative Emotions" by E. Kross, O. Ayduk, & W. Mischel, *Psychological Science*, (2005), 16, pp. 709–715. (Blackwell Publishers, UK); *p. 617:* Figure 16.3 Hare, 1985; *p. 624:* Review 16.1 Adapted from Peele & Brodsky, 1991; *p. 630:* Figure 16.5 Based on Gottesman, 1991; *p. 631:* Figure 16.6 Andreasen et al., 1994.
Chapter 17 *Page 660:* Figure 1 from "Psychological Debriefing for Road Traffic Accident Victims" by R. A. Mayou, A. Ehlers, and M. Hobbs, *British Journal of Psychiatry, 176* (2000). Copyright © 2000. Reprinted by permission of The Royal College of Psychiatrists.
Appendix *Page A–10:* From CONCEPTUAL BLOCKBUSTING by James Adams. Copyright © 1986 by James L. Adams. Reprinted by permission of Da Capo Press, a member of Perseus Books Group.

Photographs and Cartoons

Chapter 1 *Page 2:* Getty Images—Photodisc; *p. 3:* www.photos.com/Jupiter Images; *p. 4:* (left) Woodfin Camp & Associates; *p. 4:* (center top) David Young-Wolff/PhotoEdit Inc.; *p. 4:* (center bottom) Robert Stolarik/Gamma Press USA, Inc.; *p. 4:* (right) William Thompson/Index Stock Imagery, Inc.; *p. 5:* (top) Stock Boston; *p. 6:* Bertolucci Leonello/Corbis/Sygma; *p. 7:* Universal Press Syndicate; *p. 8:* © The New Yorker Collection 1989 Lee Lorenz from cartoonbank.com. All Rights Reserved; *p. 9:* © The New Yorker Collection 2000 Edward Koren from cartoonbank.com. All Rights Reserved; *p. 10:* (left) James Nielsen/ZUMA Press; *p. 10:* (right) Gil Gilbert/Gil Gilbert Productions, Inc.; *p. 11:* (left) Andre Kole; *p. 11:* (right) © Daniel Laine/CORBIS All Rights Reserved; *p. 12:* (left) AP Wide World Photos; *p. 12:* (right) Fred Prouser/Corbis/Reuters America LLC; *p. 13:* (left) Getty Images, Inc.; *p. 13:* (right) AP Wide World Photos; *p. 17:* (top) Archives of the History of American Psychology—The University of Akron; *p. 17:* (bottom) German Information Center; *p. 18:* Library of Congress; *p. 19:* The Image Works; *p. 22:* Jupiter Images—Comstock Images; *p. 25:* © The New Yorker Collection 1994 Sam Gross from cartoonbank.com. All Rights Reserved; *p. 26:* (left) George Ruhe Photography; *p. 26:* (right) Michael Newman/PhotoEdit Inc.; *p. 28:* ScienceCartoonsPlus.com; *p. 29:* (left) Sean McCann/United States Olympic Committee; *p. 29:* (right) Kashi Photography.
Chapter 2 *Page 34:* © J.A. Kraulis/Masterfile Corporation; *p. 35:* © Dorling Kindersley; *p. 36:* (left and right) Courtesy of FRONTLINE/WGBH Educational Foundation; *p. 38:* (top) Jose L. Pelaez, Inc./Corbis/Stock Market; *p. 38:* (bottom) Unicorn Stock Photos; *p. 42:* Figure from Genie: A Psycholinguistic Study of a Modern Day "Wild Child" by Susan Curtiss, © 1977, Elsevier Science (USA), reproduced by permission of the publisher; *p. 44:* (left) Redux Pictures; *p. 44:* (right) Grant V. Faint/Getty Images Inc.—Image Bank; *p. 45:* (top) © The New Yorker Collection 1998 Roz Chast from cartoonbank.com All Rights Reserved; *p. 47:* © The New Yorker Collection 1970 Henry Martin from cartoonbank.com. All Rights Reserved; *p. 50:* (left) Tom Prettyman/PhotoEdit Inc.; *p. 50:* (right) Jose Azel/Aurora & Quanta Productions Inc.; *p. 53:* (bottom right) © 2004 Peter Mueller from cartoonbank.com. All Rights Reserved; *p. 58:* © 1990 Creators Syndicate Inc. By permission of Mell Lazarus and Creators Syndicate, Inc.; *p. 63:* ©The New Yorker Collection 2003 Mick Stevens from cartoonbank.com. All Rights Reserved; *p. 64:* (left) James Marshall/The Image Works; *p. 64:* (right) "Courtesy Living Links Center of the Yerkes National Primate Research Center, Emory University".

Chapter 3 *Page 70:* Michael Dunning's Choice/Getty Images; *p. 71:* www.photos.com/Jupiter Images; *p. 72:* (top) Richard Hutchings/Photo Researchers, Inc.; *p. 73:* (left) Biophoto Associates/ Photo Researchers, Inc.; *p. 73:* (right) Macmillan Publishers; *p. 75:* National History Museum, London, UK/Bridgeman Art Library; *p. 76:* "Copyright 2003 National Academy of Sciences, U.S.A."; *p. 77:* AP Wide World Photos; *p. 78:* (left) Laura Dwight Photography; *p. 78:* (right) Gerry Ellis/Minden Pictures; *p. 80:* (top left) Stock Boston; *p. 81:* (bottom) © "Baby Blues Partnership. Reprinted with special permission of King Features Syndicate"; *p. 82:* Ann Senghas/Ann Senghas; *p. 84:* Dan Bosler/Getty Images Inc.—Stone Allstock; *p. 85:* © The New Yorker Collection 1995 Donald Reilly from cartoonbank.com. All Rights Reserved; *p. 86:* (right) Getty Images, Inc.; *p. 87:* (top) Art Wolfe/Getty Images Inc.—Stone Allstock; *p. 89:* © CORBIS All Rights Reserved; *p. 90:* Jennifer K. Berman; *p. 95:* (right) ©Tee and Charles Addams Foundation; *p. 99:* (left) Shelley Katz/Shelley Katz Photographer; *p. 99:* (right) Lawrence Migdale/Photo Researchers, Inc.; *p. 101:* (left and right) Texas A & M University College of Veterinary Medicine; *p. 102:* © Tribune Media Services, Inc. All Rights Reserved. Reprinted with permission.

Chapter 4 *Page 106:* Getty Images—Photodisc; *p. 107:* www.photos.com/Jupiter Images; *p. 108:* Dan McCoy/Rainbow; *p. 111:* CNRI/Science Photo Library/Photo Researchers, Inc.; *p. 113:* Marc Lieberman/Salk Institute; *p. 114:* Dennis Kunkel/Phototake NYC; *p. 118:* Ron Sachs/Corbis/Sygma; *p. 119:* ScienceCartoons Plus.com; *p. 122:* (top) Keith Brofsky/Getty Images, Inc.—Photodisc; *p. 122:* (bottom) Photo Lennart Nilsson/Albert Bonniers Forlag AB; *p. 123:* (left) Michael E. Phelps/Mazziotta UCLA School of Medicine; *p. 123:* (right) Howard Sochurek, Inc.; *p. 124:* Brian Murphy/Brian Murphy; *p. 130:* (top left) Mike Baldwin/CartoonStock Ltd. CSL; *p. 130:* (bottom left) The Warren Anatomical Museum, Francis A. Countway Library of Medicine, Harvard Medical School; *p. 130:* (bottom right) from: Damasio H, Grabowski T, Frank R, Galaburda AM, Damasio AR: "The Return of Phineas Gage: Clues about the brain from a famous patient." "Science," 264:1102–1105, 1994. Department of Neurology and Image Analysis Facility, University of Iowa; *p. 132:* Garry Watson/Science Photo Library/Photo Researchers, Inc.; *p. 135:* Harley Schwadron/ CartoonStock Ltd. CSL; *p. 137:* ScienceCartoonsPlus.com; *p. 138:* Jennifer Berman/Jennifer K. Berman; *p. 139:* Radiological Society of North America, Radiology 2001; 220: 202–207, Figure 3; *p. 140:* Betsy Streeter/CartoonStock Ltd. CSL.

Chapter 5 *Page 146:* Getty Images—Photodisc; *p. 147:* www.photos.com/Jupiter Images; *p. 149:* (left and right) Tom Ives/Corbis/Sygma; *p. 150:* Jeff Greenberg/PhotoEdit Inc.; *p. 151:* ScienceCartoonsPlus.com; *p. 152:* Bryan and Cherry Alexander; *p. 153:* Amy Etra/PhotoEdit Inc.; *p. 155:* © The New Yorker Collection 1999 William Haefeli from cartoonbank.com. All Rights Reserved; *p. 158:* (left and right) Chandoha Photography; *p. 159:* (bottom left) Jessica T. Offir; *p. 159:* (bottom right) Earl Roberge/Photo Researchers, Inc.; *p. 160:* Jupiter Images—Nonstock; *p. 161:* R. Hutchings/PhotoEdit Inc.; *p. 163:* © The New Yorker Collection 1973 Dana Fradon from cartoonbank.com. All Rights Reserved; *p. 165:* J. Hobson/Photo Researchers, Inc.; *p. 169:* Bookstaver/AP Wide World Photos; *p. 170:* (top) ScienceCartoonsPlus.com; *p. 170:* (bottom) Ernest R. Hilgard; *p. 175:* (left) Woodfin Camp & Associates; *p. 175:* (center) Tibor Hirsch/Photo Researchers, Inc.; *p. 175:* (right) Kal Muller/Woodfin Camp & Associates; *p. 177:* Triangle, "The Sandoz Journal of Medical Science," 1955–56, Vol. 2, pp.117–124. © Novartis Pharma AG, Basel, Switzerland; *p. 180:* (left) Index Stock Imagery, Inc.; *p. 180:* (right) Jim Commentucci/The Image Works; *p. 181:* (top right) ©The New Yorker Collection 1975 Dana Fradon from cartoonbank.com. All Rights Reserved; *p. 181:* (bottom left) The Granger Collection; *p. 181:* (bottom right) The Granger Collection; *p. 182:* CORBIS-NY.

Chapter 6 *Page 188:* © J.A. Kraulis/Masterfile Corporation; *p. 189:* Private Collection/The Bridgeman Art Library; *p. 191:* Andy Manis/Andy Manis Photo; *p. 192:* (left and right) Gary Retherford/Gary Retherford; *p. 193:* (top) ©The New Yorker Collection 1998 Charles Barsotti from cartoonbank.com. All Rights Reserved; *p. 195:* (top, left and right) National Library of Medicine; *p. 195:* (bottom right) Beth Ava/Getty Images, Inc.—Taxi; *p. 196:* Picture Desk, Inc./Kobal Collection; *p. 200:* (bottom left) Giuseppe Arcimboldo (1527–93), "Vertumnus (Emperor Rudolf II)," 1590. Oil on wood, 70.5 × 57.5 cm. Stocklosters Slott, Sweden. Erich Lessing/Art Resource, NY; *p. 201:* Greebles created by Isabel Gauthier (Vanderbilt University), Scott Yu and Michael J. Tarr; *p. 203:* M.C. Escher's "Symmetry Drawing E69" © 2006 The M.C. Escher Company-Holland. All rights reserved; *p. 206:* (top left) © Dan Piraro. Reprinted with special permission of King Features Syndicate; *p. 206:* (bottom left) Roy Schneider/Roy Schneider; *p. 206:* (bottom right top) James Randklev/Getty Images Inc.—Stone Allstock; *p. 206:* (bottom right bottom) John Williamson/Photo Researchers, Inc.; *p. 207:* (left top) Nicholas Desciose/Photo Researchers, Inc.; *p. 207:* (left bottom) Cameramann International, LTD; *p. 207:* (right top) Topham/The Image Works; *p. 207:* (right bottom) Copyright Barrie Rokeach 2002. All Rights Reserved; *p. 211:* (left) Corbis/Stock Market; *p. 211:* (right) Ron Karten/Omni-Photo Communications, Inc.; *p. 212:* (bottom left) Scanning electron micrographs by Dr. Robert S. Preston and Prof. Joseph E. Hawkins, Kresge Hearing Research Institute, University of Michigan Medical School; *p. 216:* (bottom left) Chris Lisle/Corbis/Bettmann; *p. 219:* AP Wide World Photos; *p. 221:* © Atsuko Tanaka/CORBIS All Rights Reserved; *p. 222:* Professor Joseph Campos, University of California, Berkeley; *p. 224:* (top and bottom) Bill Steber/Nashville Tennessean; *p. 225:* (left) Yuri Miyamoto, Ph.D.; *p. 225:* (right) Yuri Miyamoto/Yuri Miyamoto, Ph.D.; *p. 227:* © Zits Partnership " Reprinted with special permission of King Features Syndicate"; *p. 228:* www.CartoonStock.com; *p. 229:* Culver Pictures, Inc.

Chapter 7 *Page 234:* Masterfile Royalty Free Division; *p. 235:* www.photos.com/Jupiter Images; *p. 236:* (left) The Granger Collection; *p. 240:* www.CartoonStock.com; *p. 241:* Hulton Archive/Getty Images Inc.—Hulton Archive Photos; *p. 242:* Brian Lowe/ZUMA Press; *p. 244:* Cameramann/The Image Works; *p. 245:* Steven Needham/Envision Stock Photography, Inc.; *p. 246:* (top) M. Davis/Virtually Better, Inc.; *p. 247:* © Reprinted with

special permission of King Features Syndicate; *p. 249:* ©The New Yorker Collection 1993 Tom Cheney from cartoonbank.com. All Rights Reserved; *p. 251:* (left) Joe McNally Photography; *p. 253:* © 2001 Charles Barsotti from cartoonbank.com. All Rights Reserved; *p. 254:* (left) Stephen Ferry/Getty Images, Inc—Liaison; *p. 254:* (right) Lesser Erik S. *p. 255:* ©The New Yorker Collection 1988 Bernard Schoenbaum from cartoonbank.com. All Rights Reserved; *p. 256:* Courtesy of The Dominion Post; *p. 257:* (left) Jim Gensheimer/San Jose Mercury News; *p. 257:* (right) Chris Maynard/ The New York Times; *p. 258:* Peter Glass/Peter Glass Photography; *p. 259:* Patrick Olear/PhotoEdit Inc.; *p. 263:* © The New Yorker Collection 1986 Lee Lorenz from cartoonbank.com. All Rights Reserved; *p. 265:* (top right) Ellen Senisi/Ellen Senisi; *p. 265:* (bottom) © The New Yorker Collection 1991 Jack Zeigler from cartoonbank.com. All Rights Reserved; *p. 267:* Albert Bandura, D. Ross & S.A. Ross, Imitation of film-mediated aggressive models. "Journal of Abnormal and Social Psychology", 1963, 66. P. 8; *p. 268:* Lon C. Diehl/PhotoEdit. Inc.

Chapter 8 *Page 274:* © R. Ian Lloyd/Masterfile Corporation; *p. 275:* Image Source/Royalty Free; *p. 276:* (top left) AP Wide World Photos; *p. 276:* (top right) Yves Herman/Corbis/Reuters America LLC; *p. 276:* (bottom left) Chuck Liddy/CORBIS- NY; *p. 276:* (bottom right) Corbis/Sygma; *p. 277:* Giuliano Colliva/Getty Images, Inc—Liaison; *p. 278:* (top left) Robert Azzi/Woodfin Camp & Associates; *p. 278:* (bottom left) Archives of the History of American Psychology—The University of Akron; *p. 278:* (bottom right) Copyright 1965 by Stanley Milgram. From the film OBEDIENCE, distributed by Penn State Media Sales; *p. 279:* Stanley Milgram/Alexandra Milgram; *p. 280:* AP Wide World Photos; *p. 281:* © Bettman/CORBIS; *p. 282:* David Alan Harvey/National Geographic Image Collection; *p. 283:* AP Wide World Photos; *p. 284:* Picture Desk, Inc./Kobal Collection; *p. 286:* CALVIN AND HOBBES © Watterson. Reprinted with permission of UNIVERSAL PRESS SYNDICATE. All rights reserved; *p. 287:* AP Wide World Photos; *p. 289:* Amy C. Etra/PhotoEdit Inc.; *p. 290:* A. Ramey/PhotoEdit Inc.; *p. 291:* The Yomiuri Shimbun; *p. 293:* (left) Alex Webb/Magnum Photos, Inc.; *p. 293:* (right) AP Wide World Photos; *p. 294:* ©The New Yorker Collection 1994 Mick Stevens from cartoonbank.com. All Rights Reserved; *p. 295:* ©The New Yorker Collection 1979 Henry Martin from cartoonbank.com. All Rights Reserved; *p. 296:* (top) Syndicated Features Limited/The Image Works; *p. 296:* (bottom) Philip G. Zimbardo, Inc.; *p. 297:* U.S. Navy/Getty Images, Inc—Liaison; *p. 298:* Time Inc. Magazine; *p. 300:* ©The New Yorker Collection 1997 Leo Cullum from cartoonbank.com. All Rights Reserved; *p. 301:* (top left) Monica Almeida/The New York Times; *p. 301:* (top right) Joel Gordon/Joel Gordon Photography; *p. 301:* (center right) David Young-Wolff/PhotoEdit Inc.; *p. 301:* (bottom, left to right) Tony Freeman/PhotoEdit Inc.; *p. 303:* Woodfin Camp & Associates; *p. 305:* (left) AP Wide World Photos; *p. 305:* (right) Copley News Service; *p. 306:* (left) National Archives and Records Administration; *p. 306:* (center) Getty Images, Inc.; *p. 306:* (top right) Julie Marcotte/fotografia/Stock Boston; *p. 306:* (bottom right) Photo by Matthew Trana, courtesy of Houston Community Newspapers; *p. 307:* (left) Corbis/Bettmann; *p. 307:* (center top) Courtesy of the Library of Congress; *p. 307:* (center bottom) National Archives and Records Administration; *p. 307:* (right) Mike Slocombe/IPNstock.com; *p. 311:* Courtesy of William A. Cunningham; *p. 312:* Tom Watson/Merrill Education; *p. 313:* A. Ramey/PhotoEdit Inc.; *p. 314:* (left and right) © UNICEF/HQ92-0602/I DREAM OF PEACE.

Chapter 9 *Page 320:* Simon Borns/Getty Images Inc.—Illustration Works, Inc.; *p. 321:* Laura Gardner; *p. 322:* Stock Boston; *p. 323:* (top left) Ralph Nelson/Picture Desk, Inc./Kobal Collection; *p. 323:* (top center) AP Wide World Photos; *p. 323:* (top right) Lefterus Pitarakis/AP Wide World Photos; *p. 323:* (bottom right) Visuals Unlimited; *p. 325:* Spencer Grant/PhotoEdit Inc.; *p. 326:* Jennifer K. Berman; *p. 328:* "© 201-785-Zits Partnership. Reprinted with special permission of King Features"; *p. 329:* PALLADIUM HOUSE; *p. 330:* Jennifer K. Berman; *p. 331:* Joel Gordon/Joel Gordon Photography; *p. 333:* James Watt/Animals Animals/Earth Scenes; *p. 334:* (bottom left) www.CartoonStock.com; *p. 338:* © The New Yorker Collection, 1995. Mick Stevens from cartoonbank.com. All Rights Reserved; *p. 340:* (right) ©CORBIS; *p. 342:* Laura Dwight/PhotoEdit Inc.; *p. 345:* (right) Gary Conner/PhotoEdit Inc.; *p. 348:* ©The New Yorker Collection 1988 Donald Reilly from cartoonbank.com. All Rights Reserved; *p. 349:* (top right) Eric R. Berndt/Unicorn Stock Photos; *p. 349:* (bottom left) Dima Gavrysh/AP Wide World Photos; *p. 349:* (bottom center) Bruce Roberts/Photo Researchers, Inc.; *p. 349:* (bottom right) Donn Smetzer/PhotoEdit Inc.; *p. 353:* Jeff Foott Productions; *p. 354:* SuperStock, Inc.; *p. 355:* (top) Janet Mann; *p. 355:* (bottom) © The New Yorker Collection 1990 Peter Steiner from cartoonbank.com. All Rights Reserved; *p. 356:* Georgia State University/LRC; *p. 357:* Michael Goldman Photography; *p. 358:* The Granger Collection, New York.

Chapter 10 *Page 362:* © Ron Stroud/Masterfile Corporation; *p. 363:* www.photos.com/Jupiter Images; *p. 364:* Ozier Muhammad/The New York Times; *p. 365:* (top) Picture Desk, Inc./Kobal Collection; *p. 365:* (bottom) Frank Siteman/Stock Boston; *p. 366:* AP Wide World Photos; *p. 367:* ScienceCartoonsPlus.com; *p. 368:* Wilson and Neff, Inc. Reprinted by permission of Harper Collins Publishers; *p. 369:* © CORBIS All Rights Reserved; *p. 370:* (left and right) Dr. Elizabeth Loftus; *p. 371:* Jim Pickerell/The Image Works; *p. 374:* From "Rudolph the Red-Nosed Reindeer" by Robert L. May. © 1939, 1967 by Robert L. May Company. Published Modern Curriculum Press, an imprint of Pearson Learning Group. Used by permission of Pearson Education, Inc.; *p. 377:* Bruce Brander/Photo Researchers, Inc.; *p. 378:* Travis Gering; *p. 379:* Jupiter Images Picturequest—Royalty Free; *p. 381:* Jacka Photography; *p. 384:* Jennifer K. Berman; *p. 385:* Fig. 3, from Reber, PJ, Stark, CEL & Squire, LR (1998). Contrasting cortical activity associated with category memory and recognition memory. Learning & Memory, 5, p. 420–428; *p. 386:* Jupiter Images—FoodPix—Creatas—Brand X—Banana Stock—PictureQuest; *p. 387:* Wasyl Szrodzinski/Photo Researchers, Inc.; *p. 388:* Tom Stewart/Corbis/Bettmann; *p. 389:* ScienceCartoonsPlus.com; *p. 390:* ©The New Yorker Collection 1987 Warren Miller from cartoonbank.com. All Rights Reserved;

p. 391: (bottom right) Karen Preuss/The Image Works; *p. 392:* (top, left and right) Loftus EF, Miller DG, Burns HJ, (1978). Semantic integration of verbal information into a visual memory. "Journal of Experimental Psychology"; Human Learning and Memory, 4, 19–31; *p. 394:* Picture Desk, Inc./Kobal Collection; *p. 395:* Strand Releasing; *p. 396:* © 2004 David Sipress from cartoonbank.com. All Rights Reserved; *p. 398:* Courtesy of Carolyn Rovee-Collier; *p. 399:* © The New Yorker Collection 1990 Jack Ziegler from cartoonbank.com. All Right Reserved; *p. 401:* Chuck Burton/AP Wide World Photos.

Chapter 11 *Page 406:* Masterfile Corporation; *p. 407:* istockphoto.com; *p. 408:* Howard Schatz/Schatz/Ornstein Studio; *p. 409:* (top, left to right) Michael Newman/PhotoEdit Inc.; Erika Stone; Laura Dwight Photography; Eric Gay/AP Wide World Photos; *p. 409:* (bottom, left to right) Fred Prouser/Corbis/Reuters America LLC; Jessica Tracy, University of British Columbia, Tracy, J.L., & Robins, R.W. (2004). Show your pride: Evidence for a discrete emotion expression. Psychological Science, 15, 194–197; Michael Philip Manheim/ImageState/International Stock Photography Ltd.; Itar-Tass/Sovfoto; *p. 410:* Heidi S. Mario; *p. 411:* (left and right) Frank J. Bernieri, PhD; *p. 412:* (left) Corbis/Sygma; *p. 412:* (right) Michael Mulvey/Dallas Morning News/CORBIS-NY; *p. 413:* David Matsumoto and Paul Ekman, www.PaulEkman.com; *p. 416:* Michael Nichols/National Geographic Society; *p. 417:* (left) Tony Freeman/PhotoEdit Inc.; *p. 417:* (right) CartoonStock Ltd. CSL; *p. 419:* (bottom) ScienceCartoonsPlus.com; *p. 421:* Hiep Vu/Masterfile Stock Image Library; *p. 422:* PCN Photography; *p. 424:* Darama/Corbis/Bettmann; *p. 427:* (top) Bryan and Cherry Alexander; *p. 427:* (bottom) Universitatsbibliothek Heidelberg; *p. 428:* Magnum Photos, Inc.; *p. 429:* (top) Index Stock Imagery, Inc.; *p. 429:* (bottom) Paul Brown/Rex Features USA Ltd.; *p. 431:* (top) © Charles Barsotti from cartoonbank.com. All Rights Reserved; *p. 431:* (bottom left) Janice Rubin; *p. 431:* (bottom right) Robb Kendrick/Aurora & Quanta Productions Inc; *p. 432:* (left) William Karel/Corbis/Sygma; *p. 432:* (right) AP Wide World Photos; *p. 434:* © Dan Piraro. Reprinted with special permisison of King Features Syndicate.

Chapter 12 *Page 438:* © Gary Rhijnsburger/Masterfile Corporation; *p. 439:* Steve Gorton © Dorling Kindersley; *p. 441:* (left) Dennis Stock/Magnum Photos, Inc.; *p. 441:* (right) Victor Englebert/Photo Researchers, Inc.; *p. 442:* Remi Banali/Gamma Press USA, Inc.; *p. 443:* Guang Niu/Corbis/Reuters America LLC; *p. 444:* Frazz reprinted by permission of United Feature Syndicate, Inc.; *p. 445:* (left) CinemaPhoto/Corbis/Bettmann; *p. 445:* (center left) CORBIS- NY; *p. 445:* (center right) Frank Siteman/Stock Boston; *p. 445:* (right) Phil McCarten/PhotoEdit Inc.; *p. 446:* AP Wide World Photos; *p. 447:* AP Wide World Photos; *p. 448:* Picture Press Bild- und Textagentur GmbH, Munich, Germany; *p. 449:* David Young-Wolff/PhotoEdit Inc.; *p. 450:* © The New Yorker Collection, 1989 Robert Weber from cartoonbank.com. All Rights Reserved; *p. 451:* JUMP START reprinted by permission of United Feature Syndicate, Inc.; *p. 452:* Magnum Photos, Inc.; *p. 453:* Bruce Ayres/Getty Images Inc.—Stone Allstock; *p. 454:* Reprinted by permission of The Kinsey Institute for Research in Sex, Gender, and Reproduction, Inc.; *p. 455:* © The New Yorker Collection Edward Koren from cartoonbank.com. All Rights Reserved; *p. 456:* (top) Getty Images, Inc—Liaison; *p. 456:* (bottom) Carol Ford/Getty Images Inc.—Stone Allstock; *p. 457:* Rachel Epstein/PhotoEdit Inc.; *p. 458:* Unicorn Stock Photos; *p. 459:* (left) Jupiter Images—FoodPix—Creatas—Brand X—Banana Stock—PictureQuest; *p. 459:* (right) Cassy Cohen/PhotoEdit Inc.; *p. 460:* Steve Sands/Corbis/Bettmann; *p. 462:* Nicole Bengiveno/The New York Times; *p. 464:* (left) CORBIS- NY; *p. 464:* (right) Stephanie Diani/The New York Times; *p. 465:* © The New Yorker Collection1985 W.B. Park from cartoonbank.com. All Rights Reserved; *p. 466:* (left) Courtesy of the Library of Congress; *p. 466:* (center left) Corbis/Bettmann; *p. 466:* (center right) Flip Schulke/Black Star; *p. 466:* (right) Corbis/Bettmann; *p. 467:* (left) Corbis/Sygma; *p. 467:* (center left) Marvin Koner/Black Star; *p. 467:* (center right) Corbis/Sygma; *p. 467:* (right) Carol Halebian/Getty Images, Inc—Liaison; *p. 468:* Daniel Bosler/Getty Images Inc.—Stone Allstock; *p. 471:* Spencer Grant/Index Stock Imagery, Inc.; *p. 474:* The Far Side® by Gary Larson © 1985 FarWorks, Inc. All Rights Reserved. Used with Permission.

Chapter 13 *Page 480:* © David Muir/Masterfile Corporation; *p. 481:* www.photos.com/Jupiter Images; *p. 482:* Courtesy of A.W. Freud et al./Collection of the Library of Congress; *p. 483:* ScienceCartoonsPlus.com; *p. 484:* © The New Yorker Collection 1985 Joseph Mirachi from cartoonbank.com. All Rights Reserved; *p. 485:* Innervisions; *p. 486:* ScienceCartoonsPlus.com; *p. 487:* (left) MGM/THE KOBAL COLLECTION/Picture Desk, Inc./Kobal Collection; *p. 487:* (right) Everett Collection; *p. 488:* Donna Day/Getty Images Inc.—Stone Allstock; *p. 489:* Ericka McConnell/Getty Images, Inc.—Taxi; *p. 491:* The Far Side® by Gary Larson © 1990 FarWorks, Inc. All Rights Reserved. Used with Permission; *p. 492:* Catherine Karnow/Woodfin Camp & Associates; *p. 493:* (top) Getty Images, Inc.; *p. 496:* Henry Horenstein/CORBIS- NY; *p. 497:* (left) Ellen Senisi/Ellen Senisi; *p. 497:* (right) Dr. Stephen J. Suomi; *p. 498:* (top) Peter Byron/PhotoEdit Inc.; *p. 498:* (bottom) ScienceCartoonsPlus.com; *p. 500:* (left) Marcel Thomas/ Cashew1digitalfotos.com; *p. 500:* (right) ZUMA Press; *p. 502:* JUMP START reprinted by permission of United Feature Syndicate, Inc.; *p. 503:* (top) Richard Hutchings/PhotoEdit Inc.; *p. 503:* (bottom) COMMITTED reprinted by permission of United Feature Syndicate, Inc.; *p. 505:* (left) Timothy Eagan/Woodfin Camp & Associates; *p. 505:* (right) Fujifotos/The Image Works; *p. 506:* (left) Betsy Lee; *p. 506:* (right) Alison Wright/Stock Boston; *p. 508:* (left) Peter Finger/CORBIS/CORBIS- NY; *p. 508:* (right) Alan Keohane © Dorling Kindersley; *p. 511:* AP Wide World Photos; *p. 512:* © Mark L. Stephenson/CORBIS All Rights Reserved; *p. 513:* ScienceCartoonsPlus.com; *p. 516:* © The New Yorker Collection 1998 George Booth from cartoonbank.com. All Rights Reserved.

Chapter 14 *Page 520:* © Andrew Judd/Masterfile Corporation; *p. 521:* John Knill/Getty Images/Digital Vision; *p. 522:* (left) UPI/Corbis/Bettmann; *p. 522:* (center) Popperfoto/Getty Images Inc.—Hulton Archive Photos; *p. 522:* (right) ALBERT EINSTEIN and related rights TM/© of The Hebrew University of Jerusalem, used

under license. Represented exclusively by Corbis Corporation. *p. 523:* ©Baby Blues Partnership. Reprinted with special permission of King Features Syndicate; *p. 524:* Laura Dwight/Corbis/Bettmann; *p. 525:* Doris Pinney Brenner; *p. 526:* (left and right) Martin Rogers/Woodfin Camp & Associates; *p. 527:* ©The New Yorker Collection 1985 Lee Lorenz from cartoonbank.com. All Rights Reserved; *p. 528:* Lawrence Migdale/Pix; *p. 529:* Mark H. Johnson/Department of Psychology, Birkbeck College, London; *p. 530:* Laura Dwight Photography; *p. 531:* Erika Stone; *p. 532:* Michael Newman/PhotoEdit Inc.; *p. 533:* (left and right) Laura Dwight/Laura Dwight Photography; *p. 537:* Mandal Ranjit/Photo Researchers, Inc.; *p. 539:* (left) Tony Freeman/PhotoEdit Inc.; *p. 539:* (right) PhotoEdit Inc.; *p. 540:* Nancy Richmond/The Image Works; *p. 543:* (left) The Granger Collection, New York; *p. 543:* (center) National Museum of Natural History, © 2004 Smithsonian Institution; *p. 543:* (right) George Ruhe/The New York Times; *p. 544:* Laura Dwight Photography; *p. 545:* ©The New Yorker Collection 1999 Christopher Weyant from cartoonbank.com. All Rights Reserved; *p. 546:* (left) Getty Images, Inc—Liaison; *p. 546:* (right) Brenda Black and Louis Toby/Black/Toby Photography; *p. 547:* CATHY © Cathy Guisewite. Reprinted with permission of UNIVERSAL PRESS SYNDICATE. All rights reserved; *p. 549:* Richard Hutchings/Photo Researchers, Inc.; *p. 550:* © Davis Turner/Corbis; *p. 551:* ©The New Yorker Collection 2001 Barbara Smaller from cartoonbank.com. All Rights Reserved; *p. 553:* Tom McCarthy/Index Stock Imagery, Inc.; *p. 554:* (left) © Bogdan Cristel/CORBIS All Rights Reserved; *p. 554:* (right) Michael Newman/PhotoEdit Inc.; *p. 556:* DOONESBURY © G. B. Trudeau. Reprinted with permission of UNIVERSAL PRESS SYNDICATE. All rights reserved; *p. 557:* (left) Charles Gupton/Charles Gupton Photography; *p. 557:* (right) Abigail Heyman; *p. 559:* (left) AP Wide World Photos; *p. 559:* (center) AP/Wide World Photos; *p. 559:* (right) Yousuf Karsh/Woodfin Camp & Associates.

Chapter 15 *Page 566:* © Zoran Milich/Masterfile Corporation; *p. 567:* www.photos.com/Jupiter Images; *p. 568:* (top right) Dion Ogust/The Image Works; *p. 568:* (bottom left) Marc Asnin/CORBIS-NY; *p. 571:* CATHY '2000 Cathy Guisewite. Reprinted with permission of UNIVERSAL PRESS SYNDICATE. All rights reserved; *p. 572:* Juergen Berger, Max-Planck Institute/Science Photo Library/Photo Researchers, Inc.; *p. 573:* Getty Images, Inc.; *p. 574:* © The New Yorker Collection 1995 Warren Miller from cartoonbank.com. All Rights Reserved; *p. 575:* (top left) Bill Varie/Corbis/Bettmann; *p. 575:* (bottom right) Barry Lewis/Barry Lewis; *p. 576:* Barbara Singer/Getty Images—Photonica Amana America, Inc.; *p. 578:* CartoonStock Ltd. CSL; *p. 580:* (top left) Angel Franco/The New York Times/New York Times Agency; *p. 580:* (bottom left) Stephen Agricola Photography/The Image Works; *p. 580:* (bottom right) Michael Greenlar/The Image Works; *p. 583:* (top right) ©The New Yorker Collection 2001 Robert Mankoff from cartoonbank.com. All Rights Reserved; *p. 583:* (bottom left) Los Angeles Times Photo By Gina Ferazzi; *p. 584:* Ken Fisher/Getty Images Inc.—Stone Allstock; *p. 585:* Mary Hancock; *p. 586:* Getty Images, Inc.; *p. 589:* (top) AP Wide World Photos; *p. 589:* (bottom left) Chris Haston/Picture Desk, Inc./Kobal Collection; *p. 589:* (bottom right) NBC Universal, Inc.

Chapter 16 *Page 596:* © Dave Robertson/Masterfile Corporation; *p. 597:* Getty Images, Inc—Stockbyte; *p. 599:* (left) © Bojan Brecelj/CORBIS All Rights Reserved; *p. 599:* (center) Al Campanie/The Image Works; *p. 599:* (right) Elena Dorfman/Redux Pictures; *p. 602:* Sophia Smith Collection, Smith College; *p. 603:* Yoav Levy/Phototake NYC; *p. 604:* Corbis/Bettmann; *p. 605:* ©The New Yorker Collection 2004 Charles Barsotti from cartoonbank.com. All Rights Reserved; *p. 606:* David Turnley/Corbis/Bettmann; *p. 608:* The Far Side® by Gary Larson © 1985 FarWorks, Inc. All Rights Reserved. Used with Permission; *p. 609:* Chet Gordon/The Image Works; *p. 611:* Mick Hutson/Retna Ltd.; *p. 615:* Corbis/Bettmann; *p. 616:* (left) AP Wide World Photos; *p. 616:* (right) Don Camp/Don Camp Photography; *p. 620:* Brookhaven National Laboratory; *p. 621:* (top left) Leland Bobbe/Getty Images Inc.—Stone Allstock; *p. 621:* (top right) © Daniel Laine/CORBIS All Rights Reserved; *p. 621:* (bottom right) Corbis/Bettmann; *p. 622:* Universal Press Syndicate; *p. 626:* (top) ©The New Yorker Collection 2001 Leo Cullum from cartoonbank.com. All Rights Reserved; *p. 626:* (bottom) CORBIS-NY; *p. 629:* (all) Al Vercoutere; *p. 631:* Dr. E. Fuller Torrey and Dr. Weinberger/National Institute of Mental Health; *p. 632:* "Courtesy, Dr. Arthur W. Toga, Laboratory of Neuro Imaging"; *p. 633:* AP Wide World Photos.

Chapter 17 *Page 638:* © Bill Frymire/Masterfile Corporation; *p. 639:* www.photos.com/Jupiter Images; *p. 641:* (top, left and right) Alvin H. Perlmutter Inc.; *p. 641:* (bottom) © The New Yorker Collection 1993 Lee Lorenz from cartoonbank.com. All Rights Reserved; *p. 644:* © The New Yorker Collection 2001 Barbara Smaller from cartoonbank.com. All Rights Reserved; *p. 645:* W McIntyre/Photo Researchers, Inc.; *p. 646:* George Ruhe/ The New York Times; *p. 647:* Photofest; *p. 648:* ScienceCartoonsPlus.com; *p. 649:* University of Washington HIT Lab/Mary Levin; *p. 650:* Getty Images/Retrofile; *p. 652:* Courtesy of Alan Entin, Ph. D., family psychologist; *p. 654:* ©The New Yorker Collection 2005. Jack Ziegler from cartoonbank.com. All Rights Reserved; *p. 656:* Jim Varney/Photo Researchers, Inc.; *p. 657:* (left) Giuseppe Costantino, Ph.D., Director; *p. 657:* (right) Government of Puerto Rico Economic Development Administration; *p. 658:* ScienceCartoonsPlus.com; *p. 659:* Jim Sugar/CORBIS-NY; *p. 661:* IN THE BLEACHERS © Steve Moore. Reprinted with permission of UNIVERSAL PRESS SYNDICATE. All rights reserved; *p. 663:* G. Alan Marlatt, Ph. D.; *p. 664:* Courtesy JAMA and Helen S. Mayberg, MD Professor, Psychiatry and Neurology, Emory University School of Medicine. ARCH GEN PSYCHIATRY/VOL 61, Page 37, JAN 2004. Copyright © 2006, American Medical Association. All rights reserved; *p. 665:* (left and right) AP Wide World Photos; *p. 670:* Michael Schumann/Corbis/SABA Press Photos, Inc.

Name Index

Subject Index

The names included in this Subject Index are subjects of the text presentation (e.g., Sigmund Freud). All names in the text, including those bibliographically cited, are in the Name Index.